# HANDBOOK OF PRIVATE PRACTICE

# HANDBOOK OF PRIVATE PRACTICE

## KEYS TO SUCCESS FOR MENTAL HEALTH PRACTITIONERS

*Edited by*

*Steven Walfish*

*Jeffrey E. Barnett*

AND

*Jeffrey Zimmerman*

OXFORD
UNIVERSITY PRESS

# OXFORD
UNIVERSITY PRESS

Oxford University Press is a department of the University of Oxford. It furthers
the University's objective of excellence in research, scholarship, and education
by publishing worldwide. Oxford is a registered trade mark of Oxford University
Press in the UK and certain other countries.

Published in the United States of America by Oxford University Press
198 Madison Avenue, New York, NY 10016, United States of America.

Library of Congress Cataloging-in-Publication Data
Walfish, Steven, editor. | Barnett, Jeffrey E., editor. | Zimmerman, Jeffrey, editor.
Title: Handbook of private practice : keys to success for mental health practitioners /
edited by Steven Walfish, Jeffrey E. Barnett, Jeffrey Zimmerman.
Description: Oxford ; New York : Oxford University Press, [2017] | Includes bibliographical references and index.
Identifiers: LCCN 2016048089 (print) | LCCN 2016049041 (ebook) | ISBN 9780190272166 |
ISBN 9780190272173 (ebook) | ISBN 9780190671884 (ebook)
Subjects: | MESH: Psychiatry—organization & administration | Practice Management—organization & administration |
Psychology—organization & administration | Private Practice—organization & administration
Classification: LCC RC467.95 (print) | LCC RC467.95 (ebook) | NLM WM 21 | DDC 616.890068—dc23
LC record available at https://lccn.loc.gov/2016048089

9 8 7 6 5 4 3 2 1
Printed by Webcom, Inc., Canada

This book is dedicated to the memory of our dear friend, colleague, and collaborator, Steve Walfish. The original idea for this book was Steve's. We (JB and JZ) each have a long and productive history of working with Steve on other book projects, as well as many other professional endeavors over the years. When given the opportunity to work with Steve on another book project, we immediately said "yes." Steve was an amazing colleague and friend. Working with him as a co-author or co-editor on book projects was always an easy collaboration. Steve was generous with his time and wisdom, he was supportive and encouraging, and his keen intellect always helped to make our ideas and written work better.

After beginning our work together on the Handbook of Private Practice it became evident that Steve was experiencing health difficulties. While seeking medical consultation to understand his symptoms and the needed treatment, Steve worked diligently on this book. Tragically, very shortly after Steve's underlying illness was diagnosed, he died. This has been a tremendous loss for each of us as well as for all those whose lives Steve touched—and this is a large number of individuals. It will come as no surprise to anyone who knew Steve that he had a very large network of close friends, and he was a very active and engaged friend. When we began contacting authors who had committed to writing chapters for this book, in addition to reactions of shock and loss, the prevailing response was to comment on how kind, thoughtful, and generous Steve had been in every interaction with them. For Steve it was all about relationships.

Steve Walfish was a deeply caring and compassionate individual, and an amazing friend and colleague to so many. Steve was that rare individual who was a full-time private practitioner and successful businessperson and entrepreneur who also was a productive scholar who actively advanced our profession and field through his writing, editing, workshops, and mentoring. Steve will be greatly missed. We dedicate this book to Steve's memory. It represents much of what he valued and believed in; sharing timely and relevant, cutting-edge information with private practitioners to assist them to be successful in their practices.

We also dedicate this book to our wives, Stephanie Barnett and Lauren Behrman, PhD, and to Steve's wife, Mary O'Horo. Mary was devoted to Steve and was his protector in his final days. The love and support of our partners, Stephanie and Lauren, has been invaluable to us as we have edited the authors' writings herein to bring this final work of Steve's to fruition. With the support of strong love relationships the challenges of practice and the challenges of life can be faced with the same courage and grace that Steve showed throughout his life and especially during the rapid course of his illness.

Jeffrey E. Barnett, PsyD, ABPP

Jeffrey Zimmerman, PhD, ABPP

# CONTENTS

## SECTION 1    PRIVATE PRACTICE ESSENTIALS

### BEGINNING IN PRACTICE

## MANAGING YOUR PRACTICE

## PRACTICE MANAGEMENT CONSULTANTS

## THE BUSINESS OF PRACTICE

## GROWING A PRACTICE

## COLLABORATION

## ETHICS AND LEGAL ISSUES

## SPECIAL ISSUES

## SECTION 2    NICHE CHAPTERS

## ASSESSMENT AND EVALUATION SERVICES

## PSYCHOTHERAPY SERVICES

## OTHER SERVICES

# ACKNOWLEDGMENTS

We want to explicitly acknowledge and thank all the contributors to this book. They worked hard presenting their knowledge and experience in a way that is accessible to mental health professionals with different backgrounds and experiences. Many of them made it clear that their chapter was their way of offering a tribute to Steve Walfish. This book also could not have been completed without the support, encouragement, and flexibility of our friends at Oxford University Press. When Steve passed they reached out to Steve's wife and assured us that even though our contracted date to deliver the manuscript was literally around the corner, we had as much time as we needed to grieve, adjust, and deliver the manuscript. We know of few major publishers who would offer that flexibility when they have a publication schedule to honor and a business to run. Thank you.

In particular, we express our deep thanks to our publisher at Oxford University Press, Sarah Harrington. Sarah has been with us since the beginning of this project and was our publisher for several other book projects. Sarah has been the consummate professional and has assisted us to consistently do our best work. We also express our appreciation to the editorial team at Oxford University Press, who each contributed to this book being published in its best possible form. This includes Devasena Vedamurthi at Newgen Knowledge Works, who handled the production and Wendy Walker, who handled the copyediting.

Lastly, we want to acknowledge the professionals, patients, and clients who have shaped the work you will read about. Their contributions, while often seeming to be invisible, need to be recognized as they have done the hard work of together creating an environment to foster growth, healing, and change.

Jeffrey E. Barnett, PsyD, ABPP
Jeffrey Zimmerman, PhD, ABPP

*Postscript:* While it is highly unusual to have a postscript to an acknowledgments section, I wanted to take a moment to also dedicate this book to Jeff Barnett for the incredible job he did reaching out to authors and pulling this book together after Steve died. Jeff jumped in with both feet, immediately taking on the complicated task of picking up where Steve left off so that we could get this book to production. Nothing interfered with Jeff's relentless drive to do whatever needed to be done as he reached out to authors, rapidly turned around the revisions of chapter manuscripts, and submitted the complete manuscript to Oxford University Press, only slightly behind our original schedule. Steve and I could not have asked for a better co-editor or colleague.

Jeffrey Zimmerman, PhD, ABPP

# ABOUT THE EDITORS

**Steven Walfish, PhD**, was a licensed psychologist and had been in independent practice in Atlanta since 2002. He was also a founding partner of the Practice Institute, LLC. He received his PhD in clinical/community psychology from the University of South Florida in 1981. He had previously been in independent practice in Tampa, Florida, and Edmonds and Everett, Washington. He had been the editor of the *Independent Practitioner* and served on the editorial boards of several journals. He was the first editor of the journal *Practice Innovations*. He published in the areas of substance abuse, weight loss surgery, and professional training and practice. He was a clinical assistant professor in the Department of Psychiatry and Behavioral Sciences, Emory University School of Medicine, where he supervised postdoctoral fellows.

Dr. Walfish was the recipient of the American Psychological Association (APA)'s Division of Consulting Psychology Award for Outstanding Research in Consulting Psychology, the Walter Barton Award for Outstanding Research in Mental Health Administration from the American College of Mental Health Administration, and the APA Division of Independent Practice Award for Mentoring. He was a Fellow of the American Psychological Association (Division 42) and the Georgia Psychological Association. He was past president of the APA Division of Psychologists in Independent Practice.

His first book (co-edited with Allen Hess) was *Succeeding in Graduate School: The Career Guide for Psychology Students*. His recent books include *Financial Success in Mental Health Practice: Essential Tools and Strategies for Practitioners* (with Jeff Barnett), *Earning a Living Outside of Managed Mental Health Care: 50 Ways to Expand Your Practice*, *Billing and Collecting for Your Mental Health Practice: Effective Strategies and Ethical Practice* (with Jeff Barnett), and *Translating Psychological Research into Practice* (co-edited with Lisa Grossman).

In 2016 Dr. Walfish posthumously received presidential citations from the APA and from the APA's Division of Independent Practice.

**Jeffrey E. Barnett, PsyD, ABPP,** is a licensed psychologist as well as a professor of psychology and associate dean at Loyola University Maryland. For over 30 years he has been actively engaged in contributing to and advancing the mental health professions. He has served as president of the Maryland Psychological Association and of three APA divisions, he has been chair of three APA boards or committees, and he has served in numerous volunteer governance and leadership positions on the state and national level. As a scholar in ethics, legal, and professional practice issues, he has published nine books and more than 200 articles and chapters, has given over 300 conference presentations and workshops, and has mentored hundreds of students and junior colleagues in the business of private practice. Recent books by Dr. Barnett include *The Ethics of Private Practice* (2014, with Jeff Zimmerman and Steve Walfish), *Billing and Collecting for Your Mental Health Practice* (2011, with Steve Walfish), and *Financial Success in Mental Health Practice* (2008, with Steve Walfish). He is a past journal editor and currently serves on the editorial boards of 10 peer-reviewed journals. In recognition of his many contributions to the mental health professions, Dr. Barnett has received numerous awards. These include the APA's Award for Distinguished Professional Contributions to Independent Practice, its Award for Outstanding Leaders in Psychology, and its Outstanding Ethics Educator Award.

**Jeffrey Zimmerman, PhD, ABPP,** is a licensed psychologist in Connecticut and New York and has been in independent practice for approximately 35 years. He returned to solo practice in 2007 after serving as founding and managing partner of a group practice for 22 years. He has a niche specialty practices in alternative dispute resolution for divorce, in addition to a general practice where he specializes in the treatment of anxiety, depression, and couples issues. He has also co-authored *The Ethics of Private Practice: A Practical Guide for Mental Health Clinicians, Financial Management for Your Mental Health Practice: Key Concepts Made Simple,* and two books on divorce. Dr. Zimmerman is also a founding partner of the Practice Institute, LLC. Since 1988 he has been an assistant clinical professor in the Department of Psychiatry, School of Medicine, University of Connecticut, Farmington, Connecticut.

Dr. Zimmerman received his doctorate in clinical psychology from the University of Mississippi (1980). Dr. Zimmerman is a past president of the Connecticut Psychological Association (1993–1994). In 1997 he became a fellow of the Connecticut Psychological Association. In 2004 he received the award for Distinguished Contributions to the Practice of Psychology from the Connecticut Psychological Association. In 2009 Dr. Zimmerman received American Board of Professional Psychology specialty board certification in clinical psychology. In 2010 Dr. Zimmerman was made a fellow of the APA in recognition of outstanding contributions to the profession of psychology. In 2016 he was awarded distinguished fellowship in the National Academies of Practice and the Psychology Academy as a distinguished practitioner and fellow. He was also elected to serve as president (2017) of the Society for the Advancement of Psychotherapy, Division 29 of the APA.

# CONTRIBUTORS

**Mary Karapetian Alvord, PhD**
Alvord, Baker & Associates, LLC
Silver Spring and Rockville, Maryland

**James A. Armontrout, MD**
University of California, San Francisco
San Francisco, California

**Sally Augustin, PhD**
Design With Science
La Grange Park, Illinois

**Laurie K. Baedke, MHA, FACHE, FACMPE**
Creighton University and
Private Consultancy
Omaha, Nebraska

**Ellen K. Baker, PhD**
Independent Practice
Washington, District of Columbia

**Jeffrey E. Barnett, PsyD, ABPP**
Loyola University Maryland and
Private Practice
Towson, Maryland

**Sara Smucker Barnwell, PhD**
University of Washington and
Independent Practice
Seattle, Washington

**Lauren Behrman, PhD**
Private Practice
The Practice Institute
New York, New York

**Ellen Belluomini, PhD, LCSW**
Dominican University
River Forest, Illinois

**Lisa H. Berghorst, PhD**
Alvord, Baker & Associates, LLC
Rockville, Maryland

**Caroljean Bongo, PsyD**
Private Practice
Cheyenne, Wyoming

**Linda Paulk Buchanan, PhD**
Atlanta Center for Eating Disorders
Atlanta, Georgia

**Linda F. Campbell, PhD**
University of Georgia
Athens, Georgia

**Patrick H. DeLeon, PhD, JD, MPH**
Uniformed Services University
Bethesda, Maryland

**Eric Y. Drogin, JD, PhD, ABPP**
Harvard Medical School
Boston, Massachusetts

**Elaine Ducharme, PhD**
Independent Practice
Glastonbury, Connecticut

**Lauren Moffitt Edwards, PhD**
Emory University and
Private Practice
Atlanta, Georgia

**Jessica Engle, MA, MFT**
Private Practice
Emeryville, California

**Jesse Fairchild, MS, LCPC**
Private Practice
North East, Maryland

**Carol A. Falender, PhD**
Pepperdine University and
University of California, Los Angeles
Los Angeles, California

**William E. Foote, PhD, ABPP**
University of New Mexico and
Independent Practice in Forensic Psychology
Albuquerque, New Mexico

**A. Steven Frankel, PhD, JD, ABPP**
University of Southern California and
Private Practice
Occidental, California

**Lisa Gabardi, PhD**
Independent Practice
Beaverton, Oregon

**Tiffany A. Garner, PsyD**
Private Practice
Towson, Maryland
Trellis Services
Sparks, Maryland

**Frank W. Gaskill, PhD**
Southeast Psych
Charlotte, North Carolina

**Rodney K. Goodyear, PhD**
University of Redlands and
University of Southern California
Los Angeles, California

**Lev Gottlieb, PhD**
UCLA School of Medicine and
Private Practice
Los Angeles, California

**Mary Gresham, PhD**
Independent Practice
Atlanta, Georgia

**Sandra Haber, PhD**
Independent Practice
New York, New York

**Kate F. Hays, PhD**
Independent Practice
Toronto, Ontario, Canada

**Lorna Hecker, PhD, LMFT, CHPS**
Purdue University Northwest
Hammond, Indiana

**Gordon I. Herz, PhD**
Independent Practice
Forward Psychology Group
Madison, Wisconsin

**Allison B. Hill, JD, PhD**
Independent Practice
Atlanta, Georgia

**Sarah Huffman, MSN**
Uniformed Services University
Bethesda, Maryland

**Helen G. Jenne, PsyD, FAACP**
Independent Practice
Atlanta, Georgia

David A. Jobes, PhD, ABPP
The Catholic University of America
Washington, District of Columbia

W. Brad Johnson, PhD
United States Naval Academy
Annapolis, Maryland
Johns Hopkins University
Baltimore, Maryland

Eileen Kennedy-Moore, PhD
Independent Practice
Princeton, New Jersey

Kyle D. Killian, PhD, LMFT
Capella University and
Private Practice
Belmont, Massachusetts

Aaron J. Kivisto, PhD
University of Indianapolis
Indianapolis, Indiana

Gerald P. Koocher, PhD, ABPP
DePaul University
Chicago, Illinois

Thomas M. Kozak, PhD
Private Practice
The Woodlands, Texas

Michael J. Lambert, PhD
Brigham Young University
Provo, Utah

Daniel Lennen, PsyD
Private Practice
Portland, Oregon

Diane V. Libby, CPA
Adams Samartino and Company
Bristol, Connecticut

Bernard J. Liebowitz, PhD, CMC
Liebowitz & Associates, LLC
Atlanta, Georgia

Catherine Gaines Ling, PhD,
FNP-BC, FAANP
University of South Florida
Tampa, Florida

Catherine C. Loomis, PhD, CBSM
Restorative Sleep, LLC
Milwaukee, Wisconsin

Shirley A. Maides-Keane, PhD
Maides-Keane Associates
Oak Brook, Illinois

Robert L. Mapou, PhD, ABPP
The Stixrud Group
Silver Spring, Maryland

Eric G. Mart, PhD, ABPP
Independent Practice
Portsmouth, New Hampshire

Jana N. Martin, PhD
American Insurance Trust
Rockville, Maryland

Nancy A. McGarrah, PhD
Private Practice
Atlanta, Georgia

Stephanie T. Mihalas, PhD, ABPP
UCLA School of Medicine and
Private Practice
Los Angeles, California

Andrea Kozak Miller, PhD
Capella University
Atlanta, Georgia

Agneta Morelli, MSc, MHP
Independent Consultancy
Gävle, Sweden

Barrie Morganstein, PhD
Private Practice
Southeast Psych
Charlotte, North Carolina

Susan S. Needles, LCSW
Private Practice
New York, New York

Greg J. Neimeyer, PhD
University of Florida
Gainesville, Florida

Hannah M. Paul, MJ
University of Indianapolis
Indianapolis, Indiana

Craig Pohlman, PhD, CEO
Southeast Psych
Charlotte, North Carolina

Adam J. Rodríguez, PsyD
Notre Dame de Namur University and
Private Practice
Portland, Oregon

Amy S. Rosett, PhD
Independent Practice
Encino, California

Annette Rotter, PhD
Independent Practice
White Plains, New York

Tony Rousmaniere, PsyD
University of Washington and
Private Practice
Seattle, Washington

Patricia A. Rupert, PhD
Loyola University of Chicago
Chicago, Illinois

Noelle Santorelli, PhD
Emory University and
Private Practice
Atlanta, Georgia

Joe Scroppo, PhD, JD
American Insurance Trust
Rockville, Maryland
Private Practice
Woodmere, New York

David L. Shapiro, PhD, ABPP
Nova Southeastern University
Fort Lauderdale, Florida

Steven Shearer, PhD
Anxiety and Stress Disorders Institute
  of Maryland
Baltimore, Maryland

Rachel G. Smook, PsyD
Independent Practice
Northborough, Massachusetts

Katherine S. Spencer, PsyD
Group Private Practice
Atlanta, Georgia

Chris E. Stout, PsyD
ATI Holdings, LLC, and
University of Illinois at Chicago
Chicago, Illinois

Rachael L. Suffrin, MA
DePaul University
Chicago, Illinois

Jeffrey C. Sung, MD
University of Washington and
Private Practice
Seattle, Washington

Jennifer M. Taylor, PhD
University of Utah
Salt Lake City, Utah

Janet T. Thomas, PsyD
Independent Practice
Saint Paul, Minnesota

Michael A. Tompkins, PhD
San Francisco Bay Area Center for
  Cognitive Therapy and
Independent Practice
Oakland, California

**Steven M. Tovian, PhD, ABPP**
Independent Practice
Highland Park, Illinois
Feinberg School of Medicine
Northwestern University
Chicago, Illinois

**Martin G. Tracy, JD**
American Insurance Trust
Rockville, Maryland

**Dave Verhaagen, PhD, ABPP**
Southeast Psych
Nashville, Tennessee

**Steven Walfish, PhD**
Independent Practice
Atlanta, Georgia

**Pauline Wallin, PhD**
Private Practice
The Practice Institute, LLC
Camp Hill, Pennsylvania

**Grace Wang, BA**
ATI Holdings, LLC
Bolingbrook, Illinois

**Geri D. Weitzman, PhD**
Private Practice
Palo Alto, California

**Donald E. Wiger, PhD**
Wiger & Associates
Saint Paul, Minnesota

**Sally Winston, PsyD**
Anxiety and Stress Disorders Institute
  of Maryland
Baltimore, Maryland

**Edward A. Wise, PhD**
Mental Health Resources, PLLC
Memphis, Tennessee

**Heather Wittenberg, PsyD**
Independent Practice
Maui, Hawaii

**Jeffrey N. Younggren, PhD**
University of Missouri
Columbia, Missouri

**Jeffrey Zimmerman, PhD, ABPP**
Independent Practice
New York, New York

# INTRODUCTION

Running a professional practice is an exciting, daunting, and at times frustrating endeavor. Deciding whether to go it alone or join with colleagues, how to deal with the healthcare system, how to structure your practice, and the myriad business decisions one faces in private practice can be overwhelming, especially if you have not had any business courses in graduate school or related experience or training. We conceived of this book to give you a chance to hear from experts about how they did it, the challenges they faced, and what you need to consider as you build, or perhaps reshape, your private practice. The goal of this book is to provide you with the practical information and guidance you will need to be successful in private practice.

The first part of this book addresses essential concepts related to beginning in practice, managing the practice, and the use of practice management consultants. It goes on to discuss the business of practice, growing a practice, building collaborative relationships to aid in growing your practice, and addressing common ethical and legal issues relevant to starting, running, and closing a private practice. This section concludes with a discussion of a range of special issues related to private practice that should help you to develop, maintain, and grow a successful private practice. There are 47 chapters in this section and plenty of opportunities for learning a great deal about how to take the concept of being in practice and turn it into a business that can go through its own developmental trajectory. The experts who have written these chapters shared their experience in the hope of assisting you to achieve success in your private practice.

The second section of this book includes 26 chapters, each dedicated to describing a niche area of practice and written by a private practitioner who actually is doing it. Each of these short chapters provides brief, readable descriptions of assessment practices, psychotherapy practices, and other unique uses of mental health professionals' skillsets that are applied outside of the more traditional medical model. We hope you will be inspired by the range of professional services these authors provide, each of which is built upon their general training and competence as a mental health clinician, augmented by their interests, experiences, creativity, and entrepreneurial spirit.

Each chapter follows the same format. The authors begin by discussing the niche practice itself. They then go on to address how their interest in the area developed and they describe the training they obtained to competently provide these services. They then address the joys and challenges associated with the niche area of practice for them as well as relevant business aspects of successfully running this niche area of practice. They conclude by making practical suggestions for developing the niche and by sharing a list of resources so you have some ideas of where to begin getting more detailed information should you be interested in learning more about or even pursuing this niche area of practice.

You can read this book cover to cover or use it as a reference, checking out the chapters that are most pertinent to you at a given time. We hope you keep this book close at hand, relying on it as you develop a practice environment that allows you to support yourself and your loved ones while you provide the best care possible to those you serve.

Steven Walfish, PhD
Jeffrey Barnett, PsyD, ABPP
Jeffrey Zimmerman, PhD, ABPP

# SECTION 1

# PRIVATE PRACTICE ESSENTIALS

# BEGINNING IN PRACTICE

# CHAPTER 1

# IS PRIVATE PRACTICE FOR YOU?

## Key Information and Considerations for Success

*Jeffrey E. Barnett and Jeffrey Zimmerman*

Working as a mental health professional in private (or independent) practice can be an exciting and rewarding career path. It is a unique career path with a number of features that make it different than practicing in other settings. Rather than being employed by an agency, government, hospital or medical center, clinic, or other entity, private practitioners either own their own business or provide professional services in someone else's practice. Most mental health clinicians are attracted to and enter this profession because of their desire to be psychotherapists or to provide other mental health assessment, treatment, and related services to help clients and impact their lives in a meaningful way. They do not tend to enter this field because of a great desire to own a business and to immerse themselves in the day-to-day details of running a business.

It can come as a surprise upon graduation and becoming licensed to practice independently that there are so many possible practice settings in which one may provide mental health services. While most graduate programs provide their students with an excellent foundation in the knowledge and skills needed to provide competent and effective clinical services, many recent graduates are unlikely to feel well prepared regarding the business aspects of practice. In fact, it appears that very few graduate programs in the mental health fields offer students courses in the business of practice. Thus, many mental health professionals may feel ill prepared to enter into and invest in owning the business of a private practice. Or, at a minimum, they likely have many questions about whether private practice is for them and, if so, just what knowledge and skills they need to be successful in private practice. This chapter provides a detailed review of the key issues relevant to selecting private practice as a career path and for being successful in the business of private practice.

Private practice has many unique features that separate it from other practice settings. Understanding and giving consideration to the nature, demands, challenges, and rewards of private practice can greatly assist the neophyte clinician to make an informed decision when answering the question "Is private practice for me?"

In this chapter we will relate each of the many settings and types of independent practice to the key features and considerations, giving you the opportunity to do a side-by-side comparison. We will look at options for being in solo practice or group practice (whether you start one or join an already established group) and being affiliated with other clinicians in a cost-sharing arrangement where you each own your own practice but share overhead expenses.

# ESSENTIAL FEATURES OF PRIVATE PRACTICE

Each practice environment has its own unique benefits and risks. Determining what is right for you requires having a thorough understanding of what you need at different points in your professional and personal lives and then fitting that with your practice environment. Key issues to consider include the following:

- Startup investment: The different private practice options to be reviewed come with different initial financial requirements to get started. Even if you do not have the needed cash on hand and can obtain a small business loan, you need to consider your comfort with this and willingness to accept the risk involved (as well as the potential for greater success!).
- Independent decision making: The need to make the important decisions relevant to running a successful practice can influence your preference to be in practice alone or work in a group practice setting where decision making may be shared. Knowing how much control you need to have over business decisions and clinical practice decisions that will impact your income and professional reputation is relevant to making this decision.
- Risk taking: Private practice options bring with them a range of risk. Depending on your current life circumstances and your personality (e.g., where you fit on a continuum of being risk averse to entrepreneurial), you may be influenced to select one practice setting over another. Your need for guaranteed income, your ability to tolerate dips in referrals and workload, your comfort investing for possible payoffs in the future, and your ability to tolerate unpredictability will each impact this decision.
- Referrals and business development: These are essential issues that are fundamental to the success of every private practice. If you prefer focusing your energies on clinical work with clients and would rather that others generate referrals for you and develop the business, this will impact your decision about the right practice setting for you.
- Administrative activities: There exists a range of administrative activities and tasks that are essential to running a successful private practice (e.g., scheduling, billing, collections, managing correspondence, filing). It is important to consider your comfort with doing or

overseeing these activities yourself or if you prefer to have others in the practice who will perform these tasks.

- Providing clinical and administrative management: Support staff employed in your practice must receive training, oversight, and ongoing administrative supervision. Clinical staff may need direction in working with their clients. They also will need to follow administrative policies and procedures to ensure office security, effective billing and collections, and accessibility to clinical services. Deciding if this is an activity you are comfortable performing and willing to do is an important consideration.
- Dealing with personnel issues: Those who supervise clinical and support staff need to be comfortable providing adequate oversight, needed feedback, and opportunities for remediation, and if necessary must be willing to terminate the employment of those who do not meet expectations. Those who would be uncomfortable doing so may not want to take on these responsibilities.
- Collegiality and clinical support: The need for and ability to easily interact with colleagues socially and interpersonally to help combat the possible isolation of clinical practice and professionally to have ready access for case consultation (both to receive it and to give it) will vary based on practice setting (e.g., solo private practice vs. group practice).
- Compensation: Predictability of compensation and the potential for earnings may each vary based on practice setting and contractual arrangement. Typically, the more stable and predictable your income, the less the potential for your earnings. Thus, there is greater potential for earnings but less predictability of earnings and less of a guarantee of earnings in different practice settings.
- Equity ownership: You may own your own practice, either alone or shared with others; be a part owner in a group practice, or work for others. Each brings with it certain rights, responsibilities, and obligations. Practice owners have increased responsibility and decision-making authority, along with both increased risk and potential financial rewards. Those who share ownership will need to share decision making with their partners.

Evaluating practice opportunities by considering these 10 factors can help you make sure you select the right type of private practice to best fit your personal and professional needs, both now and in the future. In applying these factors to determine the best private practice setting for you, there are a number of possible paths to choose. You may work in a salaried position in an organization and begin a private practice part time. This arrangement can continue over time, or can shift if you decide to grow the private practice to the point where you can leave the salaried position and work in the private practice full time. You also may start a full-time private practice from the outset, either on your own or in shared office space with other mental health (where each of you own your own separate practice but share expenses for space and services) and health professionals (such as in a pediatric or family practice clinic). Alternatively, you may decide to join a group practice, either by working for the practice owner(s) or with the intention of becoming an equity owner of the practice. Regardless of the decision made, thoughtful consideration of these 10 factors, and how they relate to the different practice environments described below, can assist you in making your best decision.

## STARTING YOUR OWN SOLO PRACTICE

- Startup investment: You have full responsibility for your startup costs. However, these can be reasonable if you rent office space part time and are thoughtful about what is needed (in terms of equipment and technology) at the outset.
- Independent decision making: You have complete independence.
- Risk taking: You are in complete control over how much risk you take, from slowly building a part-time practice while subletting office space part time to purchasing your own suite of offices and building a full-time private practice.
- Referrals and business development: You are completely responsible for developing referrals, for marketing your practice, and for planning and managing the growth of your practice.
- Administrative activities: They are your complete responsibility and you will need to decide how much to do yourself, when and how to hire others to do this work, and how much to invest in automating these activities.
- Providing clinical and administrative management: There is no management except as it relates to your own caseload.
- Dealing with personnel issues: None, unless you decide to hire administrative support staff as your practice grows over time.
- Collegiality and clinical support: This is not present unless you seek it from outside mentoring and peer support relationships or rent space in another practice where you will have the opportunity to interact with colleagues.
- Compensation: All the profits (income minus expenses) of the practice are yours.
- Equity ownership: You own the practice 100%. However, it may be difficult to sell as the equity is based on your personal contributions and reputation.

## STARTING YOUR OWN GROUP PRACTICE

- Startup investment: Shared with your partners in an equal or otherwise agreed-upon amount.
- Independent decision making: Shared with your partners. Sometimes this is done equally (one person, one vote) or by a ratio based on capitalization or equity brought into the venture (e.g., cash contributed or caseload being brought into the new entity).
- Risk taking: This is negotiated with your partners. Collectively, you decide on the amount of risk you will take; however, as one business entity, legally you and your partners may be held responsible for the actions of each other.
- Referrals and business development: This is shared, although sometimes some partners are more active in this activity (or others) based upon interests, skills, and agreed-upon responsibilities.
- Administrative activities: There are more required, as there are generally more units of service being provided. There can be an economy of scale achieved with shared administrative resources and support. For example, a group practice may be able to more

easily hire a competent full-time office manager compared to someone in solo practice, who might find the cost prohibitive.

- Providing clinical and administrative management: As staff members are hired, provisions need to be in place to train and oversee their functions.
- Dealing with personnel issues: Personnel issues are salient in a group practice, both in terms of hired staff and also relationship issues that can emerge among the partners. Addressing them in a timely and effective manner is essential for the success of the group practice.
- Collegiality and clinical support: This can be a major asset of a group practice, as colleagues can more easily be "buttonholed" to discuss difficult cases and ethical dilemmas. Additionally, interactions with practice colleagues can help reduce professional isolation and increase emotional support for coping with the stresses of private practice.
- Compensation: There is usually an interdependence (depending on the nuances of the practice structure) among the owners' compensation such that the income and expenses generated by each partner (and clinical staff) impact each individual partner's compensation.
- Equity ownership: The practice as an entity can develop its own "brand" and value, which can be sold to others (new partners) and possibly purchased in full at some point (e.g., by a local hospital, another practice, or someone wanting to own his or her own practice).

## STARTING OR JOINING AN EXPENSE-SHARING PRACTICE ARRANGEMENT

- Startup investment: Shared among the professionals entering into this arrangement. If you join a preexisting expense-sharing group of colleagues you may have to commit to a rental agreement and may have to buy your own furniture, equipment, and supplies.
- Independent decision making: Generally, the decision making is shared for office (but not clinically) related matters.
- Risk taking: From a practice development standpoint this is up to each individual, but it is shared when it comes to office decisions such as equipment, administrative staff, office space, and at times marketing.
- Referrals and business development: If they have different areas of clinical expertise, expense-sharing practitioners may be good referral sources for each other. However, at times the professionals associated with the practice can be competing for referrals. Generally, each practitioner is responsible for her or his own practice development decisions and actions.
- Administrative activities: Each member is responsible for her or his own administrative activities. However, if agreed to, these can be handled by shared staff or purchased from the administrative management arm of the practice on an as-needed basis.
- Providing clinical and administrative management: Generally, each clinician is her or his own solo practice, linked by a collective administrative management organization.

- Dealing with personnel issues: Administrative staff needs to be managed. There may also be a need to deal with issues among the expense-sharing colleagues if difficulties or concerns arise. Since it is not a formal group practice, procedures have to be developed by the clinicians to oversee the work done by support staff.
- Collegiality and clinical support: This can be a strength of an expense-sharing practice because, like a group practice, there is generally far less isolation compared to a solo practice.
- Compensation: Based on the net of the income generated less your share of the expenses associated with participating in the expense-sharing arrangement (e.g., your portion of rent, utilities, administrative support staff salary).
- Equity ownership: The expense-sharing practice may have some branding and name recognition (e.g., "ABC Mental Health Associates"); however, generally the equity is similar to that of each clinician being in solo practice.

## JOINING A GROUP PRACTICE

- Startup investment: There is no startup investment if you join as clinical staff and have your "practice" under the auspices of the group. If you join as a shareholder in the group you may have to negotiate a purchase of your share of ownership.
- Independent decision making: Decision making is shared and may vary based on percentage of ownership. If you are an employee and not a practice owner, there may be important decisions made by the practice owners that directly impact you clinically and financially.
- Risk taking: The group, not the individual shareholder, determines how much risk the practice is willing to take. However, being part of a group may result in less financial risk to you individually since the entire group generally shares risk.
- Referrals and business development: This can be a major asset of the group. It should have well-established referral partners and business initiatives in the communities served and thus may provide you with referrals immediately upon joining the group, as well as helping to connect you with potential referral partners in the community.
- Administrative activities: These are provided by the group. Generally, there are minimal activities for clinicians who are working for a group practice. Nevertheless, it is important to make sure the administrative activities are being handled accurately and in a timely fashion.
- Providing clinical and administrative management: These are provided by the group; however, as above, it is important to make sure the group functions well in this regard.
- Dealing with personnel issues: The owners of the group determine the policies and procedures followed by the clinical and administrative staff, and they deal with personnel issues. If you work for the group you are obligated to follow these policies.
- Collegiality and clinical support: Whether you join or start a group practice, this feature is often far stronger in a group practice compared to a solo practice. But selecting colleagues carefully is important to help ensure a good work environment.

- Compensation: Since the group covers most expenses (e.g., space, furniture, matching payroll taxes, administrative services, and equipment and supplies), provides you with referrals, and markets the practice, and since the owners seek some profit from the services you provide, the group may take a rather significant percentage of the collected fees you bring into the practice. In evaluating different opportunities, make sure you are aware of what your income potential is as well as what costs the practice is covering. Do not just simply look at the percentage kept by the practice. Consider your opportunities for increased income over time and address these issues during initial contract negotiations. Remember, the contract that you sign to join the practice may also be in effect 5, 10, 15, or 20 years later. Negotiate keeping this in mind and not just focusing on the present.
- Equity ownership: Unless you eventually join the practice as an owner you do not have equity ownership. Opportunities for equity ownership should be explored at the time you consider joining a group practice.

## PRIVATE PRACTICE PROS AND CONS

It is important to understand that private practice is not for everyone. First, many mental health professionals do not even enter clinical practice: they may be researchers, educators, consultants, administrators, and so on. For those who enter clinical practice, there are numerous practice settings in which to work. Some types of clinical practice are best suited for employment in an agency or organization. For example, social workers who conduct suspicion of child abuse investigations would typically need to be employed by the government agencies under whose auspices these investigations are conducted. Similarly, mental health clinicians who treat inpatients or work in a group home will typically be employed by the inpatient facility or the agency that manages the group home where the clients reside. Yet a wide range of outpatient mental health services are provided in the private practice setting, and the vast majority of individuals who seek out and receive these services do so in private practices.

In short, key issues to consider include your need for independence and decision-making authority, your need for control over your practice and your career, your need for predictability and financial certainty during your employment, your tolerance of risk, your comfort with and willingness to run a business, and whether you have an entrepreneurial spirit. Working as an employee for an organization, whether a private practice or other setting, usually brings with it more certainty and predictability, whereas working in your own solo practice is often more unpredictable and brings with it more risk. However, in the latter environment you have much more control over your future and the direction your career takes, you are the one who makes all decisions about the day-to-day management of your practice, and your efforts can potentially have a much larger impact on your earnings potential (which is typically much higher than working for an organization). Additionally, as a private practitioner, you get to decide how many hours you work each week, which days and hours you work, and even when you want to work or take off. While this level of autonomous decision making and flexibility comes with some risk with regard to security and earnings potential, it may fit your needs and life circumstances perfectly.

Clearly, this is a lot to consider. It is also important to give careful consideration to your particular life circumstances and your life plans. There is no one-size-fits-all approach to deciding if private practice is right for you. You need to consider your personal circumstances, such as being single or in a committed relationship, having children or other family members you are financially responsible for, and your other financial obligations, such as student loans and other debt. Each may impact your comfort with entering private practice and how much risk you feel comfortable taking on at a given point in time. People's situations and needs change over time, so the decision to enter private practice is not a one-time-only decision upon graduation and licensure.

As was highlighted earlier, there are a number of different practice setting arrangements you may pursue. It is certainly possible to shift from one to another at different times during your career. Private practice may be pursued either full time or part time in combination with other employment options depending on your needs, preferences, and comfort. It is also important to keep in mind that *risk* is a relative term. What one individual considers risky and to be avoided another individual may see as a wonderful opportunity, and what may seem risky at one point in your life may not be as circumstances change for you over time. These points highlight how the decision-making process you go through and how you view each relevant factor under consideration will be unique to you personally; you may revisit the process on multiple occasions during your career.

# HOW TO PREPARE FOR PRIVATE PRACTICE

## THINGS TO DO WHILE IN GRADUATE SCHOOL

Seek out pertinent coursework, such as private practice externships or practica. Enroll in any business-of-practice courses your graduate school offers. If your graduate school does not offer such a course, do some research and see if there may be relevant courses at other local institutions and if you may obtain authorization to enroll in one or more of them. If not, begin educating yourself on the essentials of the business of private practice by reading books or attending workshops on the topic. See the resources list at the end of this chapter for suggestions.

Talk to people in private practice, build relationships in areas you might want to work, learn who is doing the work you want to do and get to know them, build relationships with group practices, and consider taking a private practice internship or post-doc. In these discussions, topics to be covered should include areas where training is needed (e.g., developing a business plan, developing a practice marketing plan, understanding insurance and contracts, understanding the roles of various consultants who will help you be successful in practice).

It is also important to join your state or local professional association as well as your profession's national organization. These professional associations offer numerous resources and opportunities for the nascent private practitioner. Most professional associations offer email listservs for communication among members, mentoring programs for those new to the profession, and publications relevant to private practice and clinical practice in general. These professional organizations also often hold conferences or conventions at which the latest developments in your field are shared through presentations and workshops and at which there are numerous networking opportunities.

## THINGS TO DO AFTER GRADUATE SCHOOL

Many of the suggestions above remain relevant after graduate school. It is essential to be an active member of your profession's professional associations and to take advantage of all the resources and opportunities they offer. This can include private practice mentoring programs, ongoing continuing education activities relevant to private practice, publications, email listservs, conferences, and the like. Additionally, professional associations offer numerous networking opportunities that can help generate referrals from colleagues and can help reduce the isolation that can come with being in private practice.

Additional resources exist that may prove very helpful for the neophyte private practitioner. One such resource is The Practice Institute (TPI) (Disclosure: Jeffrey Zimmerman is a partner in  this organization). TPI offers a variety of practice consultation services, resources, and live programs designed to help mental health clinicians build thriving practices.

# RESOURCES

The following books or chapters on the business of practice provide a wealth of information on various aspects of private practice. They may be helpful in providing you with important information needed to make an informed decision about entering private practice. Additionally, they can provide you with essential information that may help you to be successful in private practice.

## PRIVATE PRACTICE DEVELOPMENT, ORGANIZATION, AND MANAGEMENT

- *Financial Success in Mental Health Practice* (by Walfish & Barnett; APA Books, 2009; 266 pages)
- *Getting Started in Private Practice* (by Stout & Grand; Wiley, 2004; 353 pages)
- *Getting Better at Private Practice* (by Stout; Wiley, 2012; 450 pages)
- *The Successful Therapist* (by Kase; Wiley, 2005; 353 pages)
- *Essentials of Private Practice* (by Hunt; Norton, 2004; 256 pages)
- *Building Your Ideal Private Practice, Second Edition* (by Grodzki; Norton, 2015; 384 pages)
- *How We Built Our Dream Practice: Innovative Ideas for How to Build Yours* (by Verhaagen & Gaskill; TPI Press, 2014; 160 pages)
- *Financial Management for Your Mental Health Practice: Key Concepts Made Simple* (by Zimmerman & Libby; TPI Press, 2015)

## MARKETING

- *Marketing for the Mental Health Professional: An Innovative Guide for Practitioners* (by Diana; Wiley, 2010; 208 pages)
- *Practice Building 2.0 for Mental Health Professionals: Strategies for Success in the Electronic Age* (by Todd; Norton, 2009; 248 pages)
- *Clients, Clients and More Clients: Create an Endless Stream of New Clients with the Power of Psychology* (by Kase; McGraw-Hill, 2011; 256 pages)

## NICHE PRACTICES OUTSIDE OF INSURANCE AND MANAGED CARE

- *How to Build a Thriving Fee-for-Service Practice: Integrating the Healing Side with the Business Side of Psychotherapy* (by Kolt; Academic Press, 1999; 258 pages)
- *Earning a Living Outside of Managed Care: 50 Ways to Expand Your Practice* (by Walfish; APA Books, 2010; 243 pages)
- *Rewarding Specialties for Mental Health Clinicians: Developing Your Practice Niche* (by LoPresti & Zuckerman; Guilford, 2003; 358 pages)
- *Breaking Free of Managed Care* (by Ackley; Guilford, 1999; 317 pages)
- *Saying Goodbye to Managed Care* (by Haber, Rodino, & Lipner; BookSurge, 2008; 230 pages)

## ETHICAL ISSUES AND CHALLENGES

- *Billing and Collecting for Your Mental Health Practice: Ethical and Effective Strategies* (by Barnett & Walfish; APA Books, 2011; 130 pages)
- *The Ethics of Private Practice: A Practical Guide for Clinicians* (by Barnett, Zimmerman, & Walfish; Oxford, 2014; 216 pages)

## PRACTICE DOCUMENTS AND FORMS

- *The Paper Office for the Digital Age* (Fifth Edition), (by Zuckerman & Kolmes, 2017, Guilford, 502 pages)
- *The Clinical Documentation Sourcebook* (by Wiger; Wiley, 2010; 336 pages)

## EARLY CAREER ISSUES

- *The Portable Mentor: Strategies for Early Career Psychologists, Second Edition* (by Prinstein, Springer 2013)

CHAPTER 2

# MODELS OF PRIVATE PRACTICE

## Which Practice is Best?

*Jeffrey Zimmerman*

The term "private practice" means different things to different people. It can be hard to decipher, especially if you are first starting out, and more so if you are interviewing for jobs in different private practices. How do you evaluate them? How do you compare them? How do you come to understand the value of joining a group as opposed to starting out on your own, or sharing office space with a colleague? In this chapter you will learn about some common forms of private practice, ways of looking at income streams, and some of the key elements that can be used to differentiate one practice from another.

## TYPES OF PRACTICE

Practices in their simplest form can best be differentiated by whether, as a legal entity, you are in practice by yourself or with others. These are hence termed solo or group practices, respectively. However, within each category there are different subtypes, as described below.

### SOLO PRACTICES

As the name implies, in a solo practice, you are the sole owner. You may have staff (administrative or clinical) but you are essentially fully responsible for all business and clinical decisions and ultimately the income generated. Solo practices take the following forms.

## SOLO OFFICE

The clinician has an office for which he or she is responsible (or is a subtenant renting space from another clinician). The clinician has complete autonomy both clinically and from a business perspective for all decisions made. This is perhaps the simplest and, if you are very social, perhaps the most isolating way to practice.

## OFFICE SHARING

As the name implies, someone in solo practice can share an office with another clinician. While legally and clinically the practices are separate entities, the clinicians in the space may all be co-tenants on a lease and may also share in other office overhead (e.g., furniture, hiring a billing clerk). Each clinician makes his or her own business decisions beyond the common decisions made by the office-mates. Having suite-mates can give you the opportunity for casual conversation and also for occasional clinical input.

## INTEGRATED SOLO PRACTICE

This heading may seem like an oxymoron, but an integrated practice is a solo practice that "lives" within another practice. For example, you may have a relationship with a group practice (see below) where you are not an owner of the group, but they provide space and administrative resources for you so that you can see your clients. Of course, you pay for those services in your agreement with the practice based on how your overhead is computed and paid for (i.e., via rent or perhaps paying a percentage of your collections). For example, if you are an assessment specialist, you might work in a group practice that specializes in psychotherapy. The practice could benefit from having you there and offering your skills to its clientele. You could benefit from having clients who need your services being able to access them in the location where they are already used to receiving services. A modification of this model also occurs when a mental health clinician integrates his or her practice with a non–mental health practice. For example, a mental health professional who specializes in working with children can integrate into a pediatric medical practice. The mental health clinician's office can be in the pediatric suite, but the practices would be separate entities even if they share many common clients/patients.

## GROUP PRACTICES

There are essentially four types of group practices that will be discussed below. They differ in how they are structured, more from a process standpoint than necessarily a legal or corporate standpoint (please see Chapter 16, "The Role of a CPA in Planning, Structuring, and Running a Private Practice," for a discussion of different corporate structures). There may be modifications of these four models as you think about starting your own group practice or evaluate other practices. However, these represent the genres that might form the core of the specific model or practice you are considering.

## CO-OP

This is in some ways similar to the office-sharing model above. However, the clinicians all operate under one legal entity or they are "doing business as" (DBA) such. In a co-op model each clinician usually has his or her own legal entity but the "group" develops its own brand in the community. Many co-op practices include the word "Associates" in their title as they represent that they have a loose affiliation with one another. In these practices each clinician works as he or she sees fit, and the clinicians actually might in some cases be competing with their other "associates" for the same work. Yet, they see a benefit of being represented as a group to the professional and lay communities.

## ALL PARTNERS

This group has a stronger affiliation in many ways than a co-op. For example, the compensation of one partner may be dependent on the others. The partners may make joint decisions about the overall well-being of the group (e.g., what services they are going to offer, what their policy is for being on call for one another). In a group such as this everyone is an owner of the practice (even if at different levels) and may consequently also be liable as a shareholder for debts accrued by the practice. The practice may have policies that it expects all owners to follow.

## PARTNERS AND ASSOCIATES

Many group practices are not exclusively composed of partners. In fact, if you are interviewing to affiliate with an established group practice there is a good chance that the practice has both partners (owners) and associates (non-owners). The partners have the financial responsibility for the practice and share in the risks and the profits. The associates have the benefit of the structure, financial assets, and reputation of the practice but do not have a legal say in the decision making. However, some of these groups are very inclusive and involve associates in planning and decision making.

## MULTIDISCIPLINARY PRACTICE

While most group practices are owned by like professionals (due to legal restrictions in many jurisdictions), they may have many different types of professionals working for the practice (as associates or employees). This can add to the diversity of services being provided and intra-practice referrals, rather than a competitive atmosphere where like professionals are all seeking the same work.

# KEY ELEMENTS OF PRACTICES

If you are evaluating what type of practice is going to be best for you, it is important to look beyond the general structure of the practice. Walfish and Barnett (2009) present a comprehensive list of considerations for joining a practice. These can also be viewed from the perspective of a practice owner as you prepare to interview candidates. Two similar practices might be quite different types of places to work or affiliate with. Consequently, it is important to compare practice environments across a number of different elements.

## AUTONOMY

How much autonomy do you need or want? Even two large group practices or, conversely, two small co-op practices can vary greatly in the amount of autonomy offered to the professionals who are involved. Carefully assess both your need for autonomy and its relationship to that of the others in the practice before deciding on whether a practice is a good fit for you.

## DECISION MAKING AND GOVERNANCE

While different practices vary in the amount of autonomy, there are nevertheless times when decisions need to be made related to the administration, services rendered, and business aspects of the practice and the physical space of the office itself. It is important to understand what the process is for making a decision or setting a policy when one or more of the people making the decision disagree (i.e., there is a lack of consensus). Are decisions made autocratically? Is there an executive committee of a few owners who make the decisions? For some people this would be absolutely fine, as they may not want to be "bothered" by those issues and view their ownership as one might if owning shares in a publicly traded company. For others, this would be intolerable if they wanted to have control over the business in which they were part owner. If being involved in the decision making is important, then you should assess whether there is a more democratic basis for decision making with one person getting one vote, or perhaps partners voting by their percentage of ownership. It is also important to assess if you want to be part of the decision-making mechanism or would rather do your clinical work and leave those decisions (or headaches) to others.

## CULTURE

In the business world there is a viewpoint that hiring employees is a decision made not just by virtue of the employee's skillset, but by addressing the question of "who do we want on the bus with us?" In other words, skills can be learned, but approach and fit with the culture or way of doing business is much more difficult to learn. If you are an organization that values an element of play and creativity and you hire someone who is serious, takes offense at humor, and wants to operate in a routine mechanistic way, how will that likely work out in the long run? Do you want to be part of a practice that values quality or one that prioritizes income generation at the expense of excellence? However, cultural considerations relate to both joining a practice and to building your own practice. Who do you want on the bus with you? The journey may be long (e.g., your entire career or a large part thereof ). Who do you want to travel with? The destinations may change over time and so may the colleagues with whom you most closely affiliate.

## 1099 VERSUS W-2

This is one of the more frequently asked questions that I get from people thinking of joining a practice or from those who are hiring people. It is often given a great deal of weight, but the answer is less complicated than you might expect. The primary distinction here is one set by the Internal Revenue Service (IRS) and ultimately relates to the payment of required payroll (or self-employment) taxes. Anecdotally, at the time of this writing, the IRS has for many years been more stringent in whether a (clinical or administrative) staff person is classified as an independent contractor (1099) or a regular employee (W-2). According to the IRS (n.d.) there are standards that need to be met in order to be classified as an independent contractor. The IRS states that it looks at the relationship between the employee and the employer in order to make this assessment. It evaluates the relationship across the following three major categories: behavioral (who controls what the worker does and how the job is done), financial (who controls the business aspects of the job, such as how the worker is paid, whether supplies are provided, and whether there is reimbursement of expenses), and the type of the relationship (whether there are contracts and employee benefits, and whether the work performed is a key aspect of the business). They go on to say that specific factors in each of these three categories collectively are weighed in making the determination. Your accountant can also help you better determine whether you or your employee could likely qualify as an independent contractor if you were audited by the IRS, and what the penalties would be if the 1099 status were overturned.

## INCOME POTENTIAL

A key element for any practice (whatever the form) is the potential for the owners and professional staff to earn income. What are the sources of income generated by the practice, and what are their relative impacts on cash flow, profit, and compensation? It is important to understand the practice's intentions and actions around the relative mix of insurance and private-pay clients and or other contracted services and how they relate to the bottom line. It also relates to how the practice is positioned in its market. Are there niches that this practice fills? Does the practice have unique value or branding in its community, or is it solely reliant on its commercial insurance contractors, which more than likely are paying for services at what could be considered "wholesale prices"? Often, people think compensation simply relates to the overall percentage that you are paid relative to your collections. However, they neglect to estimate and compare the anticipated collections (e.g., the difference in collections from a full caseload of managed care clients vs. an even lesser caseload of private-pay clients) and how the percentage then impacts their compensation. There are many times when a lower percentage applied to a higher collections amount actually yields more take-home compensation. Zimmerman and Libby (2015) provide a description of compensation models. Additionally, compensation is based not just on this percentage, but the cumulative amount of employee benefits and incentives that are available, as described below.

## EMPLOYEE BENEFITS

Looking at two practice options would not be complete without also carefully considering and assessing the employee benefits provided by each. Does the practice provide for some of your professional expenses (e.g., clinical consultation or mentorship, malpractice insurance, licensure renewals, furniture, phone, web presence)? What other employee benefits are also provided (e.g., some or all of your health insurance premiums, free parking, meals, retirement savings opportunities)? These can add up over the course of a year and are not trivial. They should be figured into the overall compensation, beyond straight salary and certainly beyond simply looking at the percentage of collections that go toward compensation.

## INCENTIVES

If you own or are joining a group practice, the issue of incentives is another important element worth considering. That is, beyond the routine clinical work and the compensation that is paid, what are the other incentives that are available for helping build the practice? For example, if you bring in more than the budgeted amount per year, is there some sort of incremental increase in compensation? Similarly, are successful marketing efforts compensated in some way? What occurs if a clinician is generating more referrals than he or she can handle or has built a program that enhances the practice's market share? Is there a chance to get equity in the practice at some point and become a partial owner for making long-term sustained significant contributions to the well-being of the practice, beyond providing quality clinical care? Incentives can go a long way to rewarding excellence and to promoting longevity. They also show that the practice values those behaviors (e.g., building a successful niche within the overall practice) that are "above and beyond" and help it grow. Some incentives can be outlined in the employment contract. Others can be offered on a discretionary basis (e.g., if the practice had a profitable year).

## EQUITY OWNERSHIP

If you have a solo practice your equity ownership is 100%. However, in any other practice there can be opportunities to actually become a "partner" in the practice. This may technically be titled something such as "shareholder," "member," or "owner" depending on the corporate status of the practice, but it relates to your ability to own a portion of the equity of the business. Equity ownership does not necessarily mean you have the ability to influence the day-to-day decision making of the business, as this is different from how (as discussed above) the governance of the practice occurs.

## POTENTIAL FOR THE FUTURE

This is often a less tangible element of the practice but is important to consider whether you own or are joining a practice. What is the trajectory of the practice? What is your ability to grow over time? Does the employment contract offer the ability to renegotiate compensation over time? Are the incentives (discussed above) specified in the contract? Is there language that speaks to the possibility of an equity share (partnership) in the future and the conditions under which such a discussion will take place? How will the practice adapt to changes that may occur in your clinical interests, lifestyle (e.g., becoming a parent), and needs? Will you have room and time to pursue writing, leadership positions in professional organizations, teaching, and other activities that might not yield revenue for the practice? These are all questions that need to be assessed when considering different practices and your long-term commitment to that practice, even if it is your own. Additionally, if you are looking to join a practice or have someone join yours, it is important to have a formal employment contract that you have reviewed by your attorney (see Chapter 17, "The Role of the Attorney in a Private Practice").

## CONCLUDING THOUGHTS

Overall, the key elements described in this chapter can all be applied to the different practice structures and to different practice opportunities you evaluate. You could, for example, create a grid of each element that is important to you and even apply a weighting to each element so that elements that are more important to you are weighed more heavily. You then could evaluate not only the different practice structures against one another from a theoretical perspective, but also specific practice opportunities so that you could better assess the "fit" of actual professional options. This gives you a chance to design or choose what "bus" you want to be on, and not just get on the first one that stops. It is important to reassess your own needs, especially as they change over the course of your career. Being in a practice environment that fits with your needs can lead to great professional and personal satisfaction as you do this most important and difficult work to make a positive difference in the lives of those you touch.

## REFERENCES

Independent Contractor (Self-Employed) or Employee? (n.d.). Retrieved from https://www.irs.gov/businesses/small-businesses-self-employed/independent-contractor-self-employed-or-employee.

Walfish, S., & Barnett, J. E. (2009). *Financial success in mental health practice: Essential tools and strategies for practitioners.* Washington, DC: American Psychological Association.

Zimmerman, J., & Libby, D. (2015). *Financial management for your mental health practice: Key concepts made simple.* Camp Hill, PA: TPI Press, The Practice Institute.

# CHAPTER 3

# STARTUP FINANCES

*Chris E. Stout and Grace Wang*

This chapter will examine the costs and approaches to meeting the expenses that are involved in starting a private practice. Readers may be surprised in realizing what should be considered in calculating the cost of doing business when opening and running a private practice. They may be surprised with the options available to them for paying off these expenses as well.

## WELCOME TO BEING AN ENTREPRENEUR!

Many clinicians may not consider themselves entrepreneurs or small (or large) business owners, but they are when they are in private practice. Many healthcare providers may not have academic training or any prior experience in business operations, management, budgeting, marketing, contracting, or the other myriad associated aspects of running a practice; however, to be successful and sustainable in their work of helping others, they will need to learn about these nonclinical issues. Indeed, arguably the most important aspects of establishing and running a practice are financial ones.

Maintaining a practice is predicated on being able to earn as much as it costs to provide the services and maintaining a livelihood by being able to make a profit. The clinician who cannot break even in terms of the costs of operation and fees collected will go out of business at best, and bankrupt at worst. The clinician who cannot make a profit will need another form of income for financial support (e.g., a spouse or partner, a trust fund, a "day job").

## WHAT IS IT GOING TO COST?

We will assume that you have already passed your licensing exam to practice. When calculating your monthly costs, consider including any student loan indebtedness as part of the expense of doing business. You can take advantage of certain economies when starting out, such as subletting office space rather than getting locked into a full-time annual lease or buying an office. Some psychologists with academic appointments may be able to use their offices after hours, with appropriate administrative approval. One author (CES) was able to use an administrative office in the evenings to see patients in a hospital setting. It is helpful to be creative, but also be sure to stay within ethical boundaries.

## STARTUP VERSUS ONGOING COSTS

Some costs may be one-time events (at least for a while), such as buying furniture if you are not subletting a furnished space, buying a work-only computer or printer, or getting your website up and running. Other costs may be both startup and ongoing expenses (e.g., rent, utilities, liability insurance). Others may be episodic (e.g., license renewals, professional conferences). While this chapter focuses on starting up primarily, it is nevertheless important to keep these costs in mind as well for ongoing viability.

## WHAT WILL YOUR PRACTICE BE LIKE?

Deepening on the nature of your practice, your needs (and thus costs) will vary. For example, some psychologists who do testing will have higher upfront costs in terms of purchasing equipment and materials, as well as ongoing scoring fees, but they may have no overhead if they are testing patients in other people's offices or in inpatient or school settings. This could be the opposite for analysts setting up shop. Sport psychologists may work on the field and in locker rooms and at training facilities of professional teams and need little in the way of rental space or furnishings. Forensic consultants generally work in courtrooms, prison facilities, or secure hospital settings and have higher travel costs. So, the nascent practitioner will need to consider the nature of how the practice will function. That will inform what aspects to consider in the startup's development.

## A LIST TO START WITH

What follows is a list of items to consider (Stout, 1996; Stout & Grand, 2004). The list is not necessarily exhaustive, and not every reader will want or need every item on the list. Again, consider what will be needed based on what your practice's function will be. These items are simply here to help you get started. Create a list of costs based on the goals and needs of your practice. List your monthly costs as in Figure 3.1.

| | |
|---|---|
| Office Establishment (consider security deposit, construction and moving costs)*: | $_____ |
| Utilities: | $_____ |
| Furnishings (maintain on ledger until paid in full. If you choose not to purchase furnishings, they can also be rented.):* | $_____ |
| Telephone equipment: | $_____ |
| Business stationery: | $_____ |
| Office supplies (monthly average): | $_____ |
| Marketing costs*: | $_____ |
| Computer*: | $_____ |
| Software*: | $_____ |
| Website domain*: | $_____ |
| Web site design*: | $_____ |
| *Divide by 12 months to calculate monthly amount | $_____ |

### ONGOING OPERATIONS

| | |
|---|---|
| Answering Service: | $_____ |
| Rent: | $_____ |
| Internet /Wi-Fi: | $_____ |
| Telephone service: | $_____ |
| Wireless phone service: | $_____ |
| Web site hosting and maintenance: | $_____ |

### INSURANCES

| | |
|---|---|
| Liability insurance*: | $_____ |
| Other insurance(s) (General liability, Fire, Disability, Health, Life, Renters, etc.)*: *Divide by 12 months to calculate monthly amount | $_____ |

### OUTSIDE FEES

| | |
|---|---|
| Attorney fees (contract review, for incorporation renewal, etc.)*: | $_____ |
| Annual incorporation fees*: | $_____ |
| Consultant fees (coaching, marketing plans, etc.)  *: | $_____ |
| Accountant fees*: | $_____ |
| Office expenses (photocopier lease, cleaning service, etc.): | $_____ |
| Secretarial services: | $_____ |
| Billing services, if desired: | $_____ |
| *Divide by 12 months to calculate monthly amount | |

(Continued)

(Continued)

| FEES OF THE PROFESSION | |
|---|---|
| Professional dues*: | $_____ |
| Books*: | $_____ |
| License renewal costs (divide by 24 if you pay this every other year): | $_____ |
| Subscriptions*: | $_____ |
| Continuing education (include parking, tuition/fees, travel expenses): | $_____ |
| Networking and business entertainment costs (estimate): | $_____ |
| *Add all and divide by 12 months to calculate monthly amount | |
| | |
| **TAXES AND RETIREMENT** | |
| State taxes (divide by 12 months to calculate monthly amount): | $_____ |
| Local taxes (divide by 12 months to calculate monthly amount): | $_____ |
| Federal taxes (divide by 12 months to calculate monthly amount): | $_____ |
| Retirement funds (SEP, Roth IRA, etc.) (estimate and divide by 12 months to calculate monthly amount): | $_____ |
| | |
| **MISCELLANEOUS** | |
| Supervision: | $_____ |
| Commuting costs (Train, Parking, Tolls, Gas, Car payment, servicing, insurance): | $_____ |
| Student Loan(s): | $_____ |
| | |
| **TOTAL:** | $_____ |

FIGURE 3.1: Initial office setup.

Note: This list does not include any expenses for political contributions, clinical materials (such a test kits, forms, etc.), wireless phone handset cost, business application fees (such as "Doing Business As" (DBA) notice, service marks, incorporation costs, etc.), or any other specialty equipment/materials (neuropsychological test equipment, biofeedback equipment, etc.).

# HOW DO I COMPARE...?

We thought it might be interesting to see how your expenses compare to a small, unscientific poll of practitioners from around the United States. We sent out a quick survey to the listservs of the American Psychological Association's Division 42 (Independent Practice), the Illinois Psychological Association, and some practitioners one of the authors (CES) knew. Twenty individuals responded.

We found that expenses varied dramatically from practice to practice. For instance, a suburban home practice or an urban practice that shares a building with other businesses can significantly cut down on rent costs. On the other hand, a practitioner in the city may choose to pay more for rent so long as amenities like quality library access, Internet access, secretarial services, mail service, a lounge, or office machinery are included in the cost. Some practitioners strike up creative rent agreements—for instance, one respondent pays $15/hour for rent, only pays for the sessions that take place, and agrees to pay $50/month if no sessions are scheduled.

Over half of the respondents said that utilities such as heat, electric, and water are included in the rent. Phone costs varied considerably. Some practitioners use their personal cellphone and attribute half of its cost to the business. Others use a free Google voice number and have calls forwarded to their personal cellphone. More costly options include a combination of separate phone lines, multiple landlines (up to four or five), private voicemail, and answering services.

While over half of respondents did not have employees or contractors to factor into their budget (as they are not usually essential expenses for a startup), some practitioners choose to hire bookkeepers, technicians, secretaries, or additional clinicians. Although not specifically mentioned by the respondents, some mental health professionals also prefer to hire a billing service. The annual cost of these workers could be as low as $2,400 or as high as $30,000. Other costs include software, office supplies, marketing, parking or transit, training, testing materials, subscriptions, website maintenance, and donations.

Any surprises? Those responding were primarily from the Midwest and in suburban and/ or urban locations, so rent and the like will certainly co-vary as a function of that. The average number of years in private practice was about 19, ranging from less than 1 year to 35 years. We will have more to say on this group's experiences below, but let's return to your costs of practice.

# DO THE MATH: IS YOUR BUSINESS VIABLE?

Next, calculate the sum of the above applicable items. This total will be your Practice Costs. Use these formulas to calculate your Hourly Cost. Note that this is the cost of doing business, not what your fee or cost to your patients is:

($X$ clinical service hours) × ($Y$ number of weeks worked annually, with time off for vacations, holidays, and weather taken into consideration) = Total Annual Hours Worked

For example, (30 hours worked per week) × (48 weeks) = 1,440
Next,

(Total Annual Hours Worked) × (80% [based on − 20% for bad debt, missed sessions, etc.]) = Total Billable Annual Hours

For example, 1,440 × 80% = 1,152
So,

(Practice Costs)/(Total Billable Annual Hours) = Hourly Cost

Hypothetically, if Practice Costs = $95,000, then $95,000/1,152 = $82.47/hour. Thus, in this case, it costs $82.47 to deliver that hour of therapy. In other words, assume you have annual practice costs of $95,000 and you plan to work 30 clinical hours per week for 48 weeks per year (figuring 4 total weeks of vacation). In this hypothetical that would be 1,440 billable hours worked, minus 20% for bad debt, missed sessions, and so forth. This equals 1,152 revenue-generating hours annually. To roughly to cover your annual costs, you need to generate at least $82.47/hour. If you add a modest 5% profit margin, it becomes $86.59/hour, or $90.74/hour for a 10% profit margin.

Of course, adding more hours worked (either more hours per week or more weeks per year) can reduce the Hourly Cost figure, or could perhaps allow for a greater margin of profit. Also, for those who are starting up, it may be a more conservative approach to further diminish these numbers in consideration of "ramping up" to what may be more likely after 12 to 24 months of practice. By better understanding the relationship of cost and productivity, you can more clearly understand how those with busy practices, low practice costs, and sufficient fees can do very well, versus those with high overhead costs, few service hours, or anemic payments.

It is also important to consider various other important factors of life when establishing your fee structure and practice schedule. Private practitioners need to budget (and pay for) quarterly taxes, social security, and other such obligations. It is important to have financial goals that would include retirement planning and possibly college savings plans, or a mortgage for a home. Soberly consider what would be realistic expectations for covering your living expenses as well as luxuries in the context of the number of income-producing hours you will actually need to work and the fees that are usual and customary.

## SO HOW DO YOU FINANCE YOUR STARTUP PRACTICE?

A number of options are available, but perhaps not all are a good fit and, frankly, not all may be available, as one colleague noted regarding her experience in the early 1990s:

> I tried to get a small business loan but was told that I didn't have established credit as a business, although . . . I had an LLC, a license, a registered name, colleagues that I shared an office with who could vouch for me, and established income. My understanding at the time was that I couldn't get the loan because I was a "woman" just starting out in practice. That's what the loan officer told me.

Our sample of respondents initially financed their practice's startup by personal savings (78%), a combination of personal savings and a credit card (11%), a loan from a family member (5.5%), and "equity from a whole life insurance policy that had been given to me when I got married, that I repaid within a year (5.5%).

We also asked if there were any expenses that were a surprise. We found that a few unexpected costs were licensing and credentialing (if you hire a company to do it for you), continuing education, computers and software, toys and books, accounting services and tax preparation, higher prices for commercial enterprises (as opposed to residences) for software licenses, rent, and so forth, and furniture costs.

# WHERE TO GET MONEY TO START YOUR PRACTICE

Many sources of capital are available, ranging from banks to life insurance companies to even crowdfunding. Each source has its advantages, and some are better suited to specific financing needs than others. You should assess your options to choose the most appropriate financing source that you can qualify for and feel most comfortable with. What follows are some avenues to consider.

## LOANS (DEBT FINANCING)

Several types of institutions provide debt financing (i.e., they loan you money and you are obliged to repay, with interest). These include the following:

1. Commercial banks
2. Leasing companies
3. Thrift institutions and credit unions
4. Life insurance companies
5. Commercial finance companies
6. Other sources (e.g., loans from relatives, Small Business Administration, crowdfunding)

## COMMERCIAL BANKS

Short-term credit from commercial banks is an extremely popular source of financing for all types of businesses, including mental health practices. In recent years, some banks have set up professional divisions with personal bankers who are experienced in meeting the needs of healthcare providers.

Bank borrowing may be the least expensive source of debt financing for secured loans (in which lenders recover property or assets in case of default), unsecured loans (in which lenders do not recover property or assets in case of default), working capital loans, equipment loans, and real estate loans. A practice may develop a relationship with a local commercial bank that assists in the practice's financial planning process. Larger, group practices may fare better with qualifying for such a loan.

Short-term loans offered by commercial banks have several unique characteristics:

- They are usually extended for a period of 90 days or less and may be secured or unsecured, depending on the amount of risk the bank faces.
- When a bank loan is secured, the lender normally executes a security agreement in which the practice pledges a certain business asset as collateral.

- A practice may pledge its accounts receivable (billings to clients and third-party payers for services rendered but not yet collected) as an asset. The amount in accounts receivable is an asset that represents money owed to the practice. However, this option is rare because banks do not often value mere potential assets. Furthermore, startups typically do not have accounts receivable until after the loan application process, so this option may not work for you.
- A commercial bank may also require your personal guarantee based on your personal assets.
- If the practice does not pledge any collateral against the loan, the bank may extend the loan on the practice's full faith and credit.

## LEASING COMPANIES

Leasing has become an increasingly popular source of debt financing. Almost any type of property can be leased, such as computer systems, equipment, furniture, and office space. As an alternative to normal debt financing, leasing offers you greater flexibility and convenience because the lessor (the institution, usually the bank, holding the lease) takes on some of the responsibilities of ownership, including maintenance and disposal. If you are reluctant to borrow, leasing can be an attractive alternative. The interest rate on the lease will most likely be somewhat higher than a loan extended by a commercial bank because the lessor assumes greater responsibility. Commercial banks and financial services companies are among the institutions that offer lease arrangements.

## THRIFT INSTITUTIONS

Thrift institutions include savings and loan associations, mutual savings banks, and credit unions. These institutions have traditionally been a source of debt financing for borrowers purchasing homes or durable goods. These organizations were deregulated in 1982 and have become an alternative way to finance professional practices, office buildings, and equipment. Practices seeking debt financing from thrift institutions can expect terms similar to those of commercial banks. Thrift institutions offer a wide range of services, such as leasing, credit cards, electronic funds transfer, and commercial lending.

## LIFE INSURANCE COMPANIES

Life insurance companies offer limited financing to healthcare practices in the form of secured real estate loans. Some healthcare buildings are financed by mortgage loans granted by insurance companies. Low-cost loans are also available from life insurers based on the cash value of a provider's life insurance policies.

## COMMERCIAL FINANCE COMPANIES

These are an alternative source for borrowers with high-risk credit ratings. These companies generally finance credit sales as well as provide funds for short-term purposes. They borrow large sums from investors and bankers and then lend them directly to businesses. As a result, their interest rates will almost always be higher than banks, thrift institutions, and life insurance companies, and the terms of the loan reflect the borrower's risky credit rating. Examples of these terms would be minimum cash balance requirements; collateral requirements, including personal assets; and remedies for the finance company in the event of default.

Commercial finance companies also provide other services, such as financing and factoring accounts receivable. As long as your accounts receivable can be fairly accurately valued and are usually easily converted to cash, they are suitable assets to pledge. As accounts receivable are collected, the indebtedness is reduced. When the full value of the receivable is not pledged, collections made in excess of the borrowed amount are returned to the practice. However, as stated above, this option may not be available to you, depending on both the value the bank places on potential assets (as opposed to realized assets) and the status of your accounts receivable at the point of your loan application.

Receivables may actually be sold to a financial institution. Commercial finance institutions prefer the sale be made "with recourse," meaning the risk of the account remains with the practice. If the accounts receivable are purchased from the practice without recourse, the process is called factoring. When a lending institution factors receivables, it assumes the credit risk and the service is more expensive to the practice. Usually, a factor charges a performance commission on invoice amounts and interest at a 3% to 4% increase over the prime lending rate.

Once you have selected a bank, consider consolidating all your accounts, including personal, business, savings, and pension accounts. By increasing the volume of business you offer the bank, you will increase in importance from the bank's perspective. This may result in preferential treatment for services or more favorable loan terms. Establishing a strong relationship and staying with a bank that provides superior service may be a valuable resource for you and your practice.

## OTHER SOURCES

### CREDIT CARDS

Some of those in our survey noted running up a tab on their credit cards. This involves high risk and high interest cost and is not recommended.

### LOAN FROM FAMILY OR FRIENDS

Borrowing money from family or friends can be risky; important relationships can be damaged if your payments are late or unexpected difficulties arise. If you choose this route, it may be a wise idea to have a clearly articulated contract drawn up and to make sure that both parties understand and agree to the terms before executing it.

## HOME EQUITY LINE OF CREDIT

If you own a home with sufficient equity, it may be possible to secure a line of credit on that amount of equity, up to a certain amount (often $250,000). Terms and rates vary, but those funds can be used to pay for almost any item, and at an interest rate much more favorable than that of credit cards and other loans. If it is not used, or is paid off, there are generally no carrying fees. In many instances the interest may be tax deductible.

## LINE OF CREDIT

Similar to a home equity line of credit, if your creditworthiness is established enough, a bank may be willing to provide a line of credit to be used for practice operations and expenses. The application may be similar to that of a commercial loan (see below). Again, terms may be more favorable, but the amount available may be less than with a home equity line. Similarly, if it is not used or is paid off, there are generally no carrying fees. Interest fees are deductible as a business expense.

## SMALL BUSINESS ADMINISTRATION LOAN

An often overlooked route for finding a loan is to go through the U.S. Small Business Administration (SBA). The SBA offers a variety of loans, including a general loan and an equipment/real estate loan, both of which are available to medical facilities like hospitals and clinics. For example, Dr. Steven Solomon of La Jolla, California, provides intimacy therapy services to couples. He applied for an SBA 7(a) loan and was approved for $100,000. He used the funds for computers, equipment, and training (U.S. Department of Commerce, n.d.).

## CROWDFUNDING

Some mental health providers who want to start their own private practice have turned to modern routes to obtain financial assistance. Within the past decade, crowdfunding has increased in popularity. While a private practice is not the typical crowdfunding benefactor, we found that individual providers have raised as much as $4,000 using crowdsourcing websites. It seems mental health providers tend to use gofundme.com as their crowdfunding website as opposed to others, such as indiegogo.com or kickstarter.com.

For example, a marriage and family therapist in California set a goal of $6,842 and raised $950 in six months to go toward her private practice that would aim to serve veterans and their families. She specified that donations would go to rent, a computer and a printer, and telephone service for six months. A mental health therapist in Bellevue, Washington, raised $1,299 of $7,000 in 14 months. She wants to help members of the LGBTQ community and indicated that donations will go to licensing costs, business cards, office space, professional organization fees, a website, insurance, and a business license. She wants to raise enough funds to cover expenses for six months as she builds her client base. A professional counselor in Brainerd, Montana, raised $1,230 of $2,700 in 16 months. Her goal is to start a private practice to help people experiencing anger, anxiety, and depression, among other things. Although perhaps ethically questionable, she also offered counseling sessions to donors as a "perk" or a "thank you" for their assistance. A psychotherapist in Portland, Oregon, who had already begun her private practice, raised $675 of $2,000 in 14 months. Her goal was to pay off expenses like overhead costs and student loans as she continues to build a client base. Finally, a counselor in Guaynabo, Puerto Rico, raised $4,300 of $5,000 in eight months. Her goal was twofold: to help people recover from trauma and to mentor students, graduates, and professionals in order to raise the standards in that geographic area for the profession.

## HOW LENDERS EVALUATE BORROWERS

Lenders make decisions about loans based on their knowledge of the borrower and the business. You will make a positive impression on the lending officer by submitting a well-prepared and complete set of informational documents. The principal document used to indicate your creditworthiness is the business plan (websites such as BizHumm offer free templates: http://bizhumm.com/dashboard/library/).

Another key factor in the loan process is the lender's impression of your credibility. The lender gains this perception from face-to-face contact with you (and your associates if you have them) and with the information provided to support the loan request. If you are borrowing funds for the first time, you can expect to provide more information to the loan officer than if you have a credit history with the bank.

Once you have established credibility, you must work to maintain it. You must continue to produce results that are consistent with your business plan objectives and financial projections. If you repeatedly return to the lender for expenses that were not properly considered in the business plan, you will decrease your chances of getting favorable terms.

When one of the authors (GW) investigated Bank of America's small business healthcare loans, she found that doctoral-level psychologists, licensed clinical social workers, and licensed clinical professional counselors are not eligible for this loan, only medical doctors. Furthermore, CitiBank has a loan for healthcare professionals starting their own practice, but it is currently geared toward physicians. Of course, if you are a medical doctor, this would not be a problem. If you are not, the bank might still consider you if you can legally partner with a medical doctor. But such an approach must be considered in a context of other practice aspects, not solely for access to debt financing.

## KEY INFORMATION FOR LOAN APPLICATIONS

Lenders consider three essential items when deciding whether to lend money.

First, how will the funds be used? You may want to borrow funds to finance startup. When you are starting or expanding a practice, you may need money for working capital, to purchase equipment, and to pay for improvements to the office. The lender needs to know how the funds will be used so the bank can obtain a security interest if property and equipment are being acquired. If the funds are to be used for working capital, the bank will require some other form of payment assurance. Knowing how the funds will be used also helps determine the interest rate and term of the loan. For example, the term of a loan to purchase a computer system would probably equal the useful life of the equipment.

Second, how much money is needed? The size of the loan depends on several factors:

1.  Determine the total planned expenditures and the amount that will be financed. This relates to the planning process as discussed earlier. You may invest some of your own funds and borrow only a portion of the total.
2.  Include the expenditures in the business plan developed to support the loan application. This pro forma business plan shows your future needs as well as the level of debt you can repay.
3.  The bank must understand how the loan relates to your strategic plan and will expect you to provide a written, polished document outlining such. For example, if you are adding providers and need $100,000 to expand, will that amount be used for working capital and improvements? Will another loan be required for related issues? You may find it easier to repay excess funds than to obtain additional funding if the size of the first loan is insufficient.

Finally, how will the money be repaid? You will be expected to demonstrate to the bank your ability to repay the loan. The main evidence is your business plan, which illustrates the ability to repay the debt from projected income in excess of expenses. You may also need a contingency plan showing what steps you would take if the financial projections proved incorrect. The contingency plan may indicate a source of repayment other than practice income, such as a guarantee based on your personal assets.

The data needed to answer these three questions will depend on several things:

1.  Your previous relationship with the bank
2.  The purpose of the loan
3.  The amount of the loan
4.  Your credit rating and demonstration of cash flow/profits (often considered when banks determine how the loan will be repaid)
5.  The percentage of total expenditure being sought (e.g., a practice borrowing $5,000 to purchase office furniture valued at $15,000 is borrowing only 33% of the total expenditure, which will be more favorably considered than a loan request of $12,000 for the same purpose)

Different banks require different levels of detail. For example, if a sole practitioner or a group with fewer than three providers applies for a loan at a local bank, the lender may rely more on personal financial information than on the practice's operating information.

# CONCLUSION

Healthcare providers who want to start a private practice are not just clinicians; they are also entre-preneurs. As such, they must consider the details of business management. They can no longer merely be occupied with the question, "Will my patient recover?" Rather, they must also consider, "Will my business succeed so that I can have a patient to help recover?" As you mull over the beginnings of your private practice, calculate your expenses, and explore your options for paying them off. Remember that this chapter is only the beginning of the resources available to you.

# NOTE

Portions of the last section of this chapter have been adapted from Stout and Grand (2004).

# REFERENCES

Stout, C. E. (1996, Spring). What should psychotherapy cost? *Illinois Psychologist*, 24–26.

Stout, C. E., & Grand, L. (2004). *Getting started in private practice*. New York: John Wiley & Sons.

U.S. Department of Commerce. Small Business Administration. (n.d.). *SBA loan keeps couples together*. Retrieved from https://www.sba.gov/offices/district/ca/san-diego/success-stories/sba-loan-keeps-couples-together.

# CHAPTER 4

# INSURANCE NEEDS OF THE PRIVATE PRACTITIONER

*Martin G. Tracy and Jana N. Martin*

Establishing and maintaining a successful private practice includes ensuring it provides the best protection for both mental health professionals and clients. Proper insurance coverage is necessary and important to provide such protection. This chapter focuses on essential insurance coverage clinicians should have before beginning to practice and as their practice grows. Most of the chapter focuses on professional liability insurance, followed by a discussion of the other coverage that anyone, regardless of profession, should carry.

Specifically, we will discuss (a) professional liability insurance (also known as malpractice or "errors and omissions" insurance), including administrative or licensure defense coverage; (b) business owner's insurance; and (c) life, disability, and business overhead insurance.

## WHAT IS INSURANCE?

Insurance is at its simplest a way to spread the risk of loss among the many to benefit those few who actually suffer a loss. The concept of insurance developed among merchants in antiquity as a way of spreading risk. If a Roman merchant knew he could profitably sell his goods in Greece, he ran the risk of bankruptcy if the ship transporting his goods was lost on the voyage. However, if a collective of 20 merchants pledged to reimburse one another for 5% of the goods any of them lost at sea, each could assume the risk of shipping his goods to distant markets.

Risk sharing became more inclusive over time. Common to all are the risks of death, disability, illness, fire, flood, and accidents. Life, disability, health, fire, homeowner's, and auto insurance were developed in recognition of these risks. Today an individual can pay an insurance company a fixed amount, called a premium, which is relatively small compared to the potential loss, in exchange for a promise to compensate the individual or the beneficiary per the terms of the insurance policy should the loss occur.

# PROFESSIONAL LIABILITY INSURANCE

An important element of the social contract in the United States is the concept of "duty." Generally, an adult is expected to behave as a "reasonable person" would in similar circumstances. When one negligently breaches this duty, causing harm to others, the legal system can force the negligent party to compensate them. This is the basis of American tort law. A lay definition of "tort" (Merriam-Webster, 2016) is an act that wrongly causes harm to someone but that is not a crime; it is dealt with in civil, rather than criminal, court.

Today, many tort lawsuits arise from automobile accidents due to driver negligence. For example, if a driver strikes a stopped school bus that then topples a utility pole, the driver's negligence clearly caused damages. The parents of the injured schoolchildren, the owner of the bus, and the utility company will all seek compensation from the negligent driver.

## THE ROLE OF LIABILITY INSURANCE

The driver's auto insurance company will retain an attorney to represent him or her, and it will pay damages for which the driver is liable, up to the coverage limits of his policy. If the driver has no auto liability coverage, he or she is still responsible for the damages. If he or she is unable to pay the compensation immediately, his or her wages can be garnished, any funds he or she may be entitled to (e.g., inheritances) can be seized, and property he or she owns can be burdened by liens filed by the accident victims. Thus, auto liability insurance enables individuals to assume the risk of driving every day.

Professionals (here, mental health professionals) incur special risks by holding themselves out to the community as possessors of special knowledge and skill. Society expects them to practice in accord with professional standards and to be accountable when they do not. Professional liability insurance frees individuals to assume the risk of professional practice by paying for their defense against allegations of negligence and by compensating those who are harmed by negligent practice.

Clinicians owe duties to their clients. In the healthcare professions, the duty is usually referred to as the "duty of care," defined as the obligation to employ "the knowledge and skill ordinarily possessed by members of the profession in good standing" (Knapp, Younggren, VandeCreek, Harris, & Martin, 2013, p. 19). Failure to meet the standard of care is commonly referred to as professional malpractice, and if the failure causes harm, the mental health professional can expect to be sued for malpractice. The person bringing the lawsuit is the "plaintiff" and the clinician is the "defendant."

Every mental health professional should carry professional liability insurance. Under the terms of such policies, the insurance company agrees to retain and pay counsel to defend the clinician against claims alleging negligence and to indemnify the professional—that is, pay the monetary damages that may be assessed by a judge or a jury against the professional—up to the policy limits, for negligent acts covered by the policy. Adequate liability insurance from a financially strong company, covering the clinician's scope of practice, allows the clinician to take on the risk of treating clients, even seriously ill ones, to alleviate their suffering.

Up to 75% of the lawsuits alleging malpractice filed against healthcare providers, including mental health professionals, are dismissed by the court, are dropped by the plaintiff, or result in a verdict in favor of the defendant. Still, the costs of even a single lawsuit are great (Forbes, 2013): Defending a simple malpractice claim can exceed $30,000, and more complex cases can generate defense costs exceeding $100,000, even if the mental health professional did nothing wrong and is exonerated by the court.

U.S. courts are open to everyone. While most lawsuits against mental health professionals are filed by plaintiffs' lawyers, anyone who believes he or she has been wronged, no matter how unreasonable this belief may be, can file even a handwritten complaint with the court clerk. The court clerk makes no decision regarding the merits of a complaint but must process it and enter it in the court's docket. Once the mental health professional is officially notified of the complaint, prompt notice to the liability insurance company is essential.

## PROFESSIONAL LIABILITY INSURANCE DETAILS

Once clinicians appreciate their need for professional liability insurance, they face a series of decisions. Liability policies vary widely from one company to another in the coverage they provide and the cost of that coverage.

## WHAT KIND OF POLICY IS BEST?

There are two types of professional liability insurance policies: occurrence and claims made. Deciding which to purchase is the first decision to be made. An occurrence policy provides coverage for claims arising from professional practice that *occurred while the policy was in force, regardless of when the claim is actually filed* (of course the claim itself must fall under the coverage of a professional liability policy). As long as the occurrence policy was in force when the professional practice giving rise to the claim occurred, it makes no difference whether the clinician is still covered by the occurrence policy (Knapp et al., 2013).

Claims-made policies are mechanically different. Under a claims-made policy, there is coverage for a claim arising from professional services rendered while the policy was in force *so long as that policy is still in force when the claim is made*. When a claims-made policy terminates, all coverage ends for any professional services provided while the policy was in force, unless the clinician, or his or her estate, takes action, as described below.

The following points should be considered when deciding between an occurrence policy and a claims-made policy.

First, occurrence policy premiums are significantly higher than claims-made policy premiums, especially in the early years of the claims-made policy. Because of the "infinite" extent of an occurrence policy, the company must collect all the money it will need for the rest of time to cover the claims arising from the coverage it issued in a particular policy year. First-year claims-made premiums are 25% to 35% of occurrence policy premiums, and rise each year until by the fifth year or so (the progression varies by company), premiums approximate the cost of an occurrence policy, all other variables being equal.

The logic to claims-made pricing is that during the first year, the insurance company must collect enough premium from its policyholders to cover all the claims that both are based on practice in that one year AND are reported in that same year. Malpractice claims are rarely asserted immediately after the alleged professional negligence took place, so few claims are reported by first-year policyholders. With each successive year, the likelihood of claims being filed increases, so premiums must increase. The claims-made coverage is continuous so long as the policy is renewed each year, and the period of coverage is uninterrupted. The claims-made policy's "retro-active date" is the earliest date on which the clinician's professional services are covered by the policy.

Second, to prevent a complete loss of coverage after the termination of a claims-made policy, further action must be taken by the insured clinician who wishes to switch from one carrier to another, or who is retiring or leaving private practice, or by the professional's estate. One option is to purchase an "extended reporting period" endorsement (ERP), also known as a "tail policy." Any insurance company that sells claims-made coverage must offer its policyholders the opportunity to purchase an ERP at the termination of the claims-made policy. The policyholder must make this decision to purchase within a limited period of time, usually no more than 90 days after the termination date. Purchasing the ERP is a one-time action, and the effect is to extend the coverage that existed under the claims-made policy into the future (note that an ERP does not cover any future practice—it only extends the right to report claims arising on or after the retroactive date and have them covered per the terms of the policy). The best course of action is to purchase an "unlimited ERP," which extends the right to report claims indefinitely into the future. The unlimited ERP can be seen as a means of converting a claims-made policy into an occurrence policy. Sometimes shorter-term ERPs (e.g., three-year ERPs) are available, but there will be no coverage for any new claims arising from past practice at the end of three years.

As a rule, the one-time premium for an unlimited ERP is two times the last annual premium the insured paid the carrier. Thus, if the third-year premium for a claims-made policy was $500, a clinician terminating the policy at the end of the third year should expect to pay approximately $1,000 for an unlimited ERP. Effectively, the carrier is collecting the premiums at the end of the claims-made policy that it would have collected over three years of occurrence coverage.

Many companies provide ERPs at no charge if the insured dies, retires after a certain number of years of practice, or becomes disabled. Each company, however, is free to set its own conditions for free tail coverage, and clinicians purchasing claims-made coverage should be aware of these conditions.

A second option is to purchase "prior acts coverage," also known as "nose coverage," from the new professional liability insurance company. Clinicians can ask their new carriers to provide coverage for their previous years of practice. In this way, they keep all coverage with a single company rather than having coverage with two different carriers. The new carrier adopts the previous insurance company's retroactive date and assumes liability for any new claims that the mental health professional reports based on practice after the retroactive date. This is an option only for those who are continuing to practice. Those retiring or entering employment where they do not need liability insurance, as well as the executors of the insured's estates, must purchase ERP coverage as described above if there is no provision for free tail coverage. There is no separate premium for prior acts coverage if the new carrier agrees to accept liability for prior acts. The premium is calculated as if the clinician had been insured by the new company since the prior policy's retroactive date.

There is no right or wrong answer on the occurrence versus claims-made decision. It is similar to the question of leasing versus buying a car or purchasing a smartphone from one manufacturer as opposed to one made by another. Professionals who are in the early phase of their careers may find the significantly lower cost of the first-year claims-made policy to be attractive. They must be aware, however, that premiums will increase each year for the first several years of coverage. They must also remember that terminating the claims-made policy may require them to purchase an ERP, unless free tail coverage is available under the company's rules as described above. Other clinicians like the simplicity of the occurrence form, knowing that they, and their estates, have coverage for all time for claims arising from each policy year.

## HOW MUCH COVERAGE SHOULD ONE PURCHASE?

Professional liability policies, both occurrence and claims-made, are priced and sold in units called "limits," and each policy has two limits—the "per claim limit" and the "policy aggregate limit." Decisions about limits to purchase are often influenced by their contracts with managed care companies, hospitals, group practices, governmental and nonprofit agencies, and others. Most of these agreements specify the minimum limits that the clinician must carry.

A $1 million/$3 million policy provides up to $1 million coverage for any one claim, and up to $3 million in aggregate for all claims that arise under that policy. Thus, a professional covered by such a policy and found liable for $1.1 million in damages in a single malpractice lawsuit would have $100,000 in uncovered liability. If a mental health professional is involved in three malpractice claims in a single policy period, in each of which the jury awarded $1 million in damages, the entire $3 million in damages is covered because the policy aggregate limit is $3 million and no claim exceeded $1 million.

Clinicians should ask any carrier they are considering whether the defense costs reduce the limit (in insurance jargon, "is defense inside the limit?") or are separate from or "outside" the limit. With defense costs "inside the limit," every dollar spent on defense reduces the amount available to pay damages. These policies can be less expensive, but many clinicians are reluctant to purchase a policy that, despite the premium savings, may discourage a vigorous defense. With costs outside the limit, the full limit is available to pay damages or settle the claim.

Finally, as detailed below, some companies subject certain kinds of claims, such as those alleging boundary violations or those for defense of a professional license, to a "sublimit," which is a much lower limit of coverage.

# READING THE POLICY

The coverage provided by professional liability policies varies from one company to another. There is no "standard" professional liability policy. Due diligence is essential. Clinicians must read the policies they purchase to ensure they are issued the coverage they need and want. Insurance companies today make this obligation easier by using "plain English" rather than the legalese that was previously the norm. While every section of the policy is important, understanding certain sections is critical.

The first is the *declarations page*. Most of the information on this page is a recitation of information provided by the mental health professional on the application, including name, address, specialty, the effective date, the per-claim and policy-aggregate limits, the retroactive date for claims-made policies, and other details of coverage applied for. If any information is incorrect or incomplete, the clinician should advise the company of this immediately.

The *conditions* section is often styled as "your obligations to the company." It consists of the following:

> *Payment of premium*: One of the key conditions is timely premium payment. The best coverage is worthless if the policy has lapsed for nonpayment of premium. Getting an insurance company to reinstate a lapsed policy is cumbersome and can be all but impossible if reinstatement would create coverage for a claim that would otherwise be uncovered due to the lapse.
>
> *Licensed practice*: Coverage may be limited to claims arising from professional practice only in the state where the professional is licensed, raising issues for those treating "snow birds" or students attending school in another state, or for those who treat clients by phone, email, or other Internet-enabled communication. Clinicians may wish to consult with personal counsel or the carrier's risk management staff to discuss such situations to make sure they are covered for all services they provide.
>
> *Cooperation*: The mental health professional must cooperate with the insurance company in the defense of any claims. "Cooperation" includes promptly reporting all claims and meeting with or speaking to in-house claims staff and outside defense counsel as requested. Clinicians cannot attempt to settle claims on their own and they cannot prejudice the company's position by altering or destroying relevant records. Clinicians contacting the plaintiff or plaintiff's counsel directly after a suit has been filed risk nullifying their coverage for breaching the duty to cooperate.

To avoid misunderstandings about the scope of coverage granted by a policy, insurance companies try to eliminate any ambiguous language by detailing what is NOT covered by the policy. The *exclusions* section of the policy may be its lengthiest and most detailed. Typically excluded from coverage are suits arising from intentional wrongdoing, the sale of certain products (e.g., dietary supplements, Seasonal Affective Disorder lights), unlicensed practice, and boundary violations. Depending on the company and the policy language, there may be no coverage at all (neither defense nor indemnification), or defense-only coverage (often seen in boundary violation exclusionary language) or defense plus a sublimit for the exclusion (some companies will limit the indemnification for boundary violations to a small amount—$25,000 or $50,000). Some companies will eliminate certain exclusions at the clinician's request in exchange for additional premium through the use of an "endorsement" as described below.

The *consent to settlement* section of the policy refers to the fact that most claims against professionals, including mental health professionals, are resolved not by judges or by juries, but by the parties themselves in a process of negotiation called a "settlement." In fact, there is an aphorism in liability insurance that "a good settlement is better than a perfect verdict." Why? Taking a case to court can be expensive, not just for the insurance company but for the clinician as well, who must take time away from practice to attend depositions, review records, meet with defense counsel, and speak with the company's claims staff. Further, the clinician's professional reputation is harmed, especially in smaller communities, when the existence of the suit becomes public knowledge and the focus of the local media. Even if the verdict or judgment favors the professional, the plaintiff may appeal, and depending on the findings of the appellate court, the case may need to be retried, requiring yet another round of time away from practice, more embarrassment, and more media attention. On the contrary, when a case is settled, the defendant does not admit liability but agrees to end the claim with the cooperation of the insurance company. There is no appeal, and the plaintiff is usually obligated to keep the terms of the settlement private.

The real issue for the mental health professional is who controls the settlement process. There are four typical kinds of consent-to-settlement language:

1. The insured clinician has a right to consent to or veto any proposed settlement. These policies, all other variables being the same, will be more expensive than the others.

2. The company has complete authority to settle claims. These policies are usually the least expensive policies.

3. The company and the insured submit settlement disagreements to binding arbitration. The cost of this kind of policy, as well as #4 described below, falls between the extremes of #1 and #2 above. Professionals have many reasons for resisting settlements: Fear of reputational damage, concern about future premium increases, and the belief that they did not deviate from the standard of care are the most common. The defense lawyer and the company's claims staff should be able to address these issues.

4. The professional has the absolute right to agree to or to reject any settlement offer that the company is amenable to, but if the professional rejects a settlement that was acceptable to the company, the professional becomes personally responsible for the excess of a later settlement or verdict over the rejected settlement offer. In insurance jargon, this is referred to as a "hammer clause" because it can be a formidable weapon for the company to force a settlement. Some companies may delete this provision by endorsement in exchange for a higher premium.

Clinicians who need to have coverage tailored to their individual needs will be issued a policy with *endorsements*. Here are three examples of common endorsements:

1. A professional covered by his employer's group practice policy needs individual coverage for six hours of private practice each week. The company will endorse the policy to limit coverage to the private practice.

2. A clinician wants a higher limit of licensure defense coverage. The company will accomplish this by adding an endorsement to the policy.
3. The policy contains a "hammer clause" (see above) for when the clinician objects to a settlement. The company may, at the clinician's request, replace that language with more favorable settlement language.

Some professional liability insurance policies offer ancillary coverage and benefits such as the following:

*General liability*: Some professional liability insurance covers claims arising from general negligence in the mental health professional's office. Examples include a client being injured in a fall in the waiting room, or the theft of a client's briefcase and laptop from the office coat closet. Depending on the carrier, coverage may be limited to claims brought by clients rather than extending coverage to claims brought by non-clients as well.

*Licensure defense or administrative defense*: The number of complaints filed with state licensure authorities is growing, and many insurance companies now include coverage for the costs of licensure defense (Knapp et al., 2013). Such coverage is essential. The limit for this coverage included in the policy is usually quite small— $5,000 or $10,000—but the clinician often has the option of purchasing higher limits for additional premium by endorsement, which typically is recommended due to the increasing number of board complaints filed, regardless of whether a malpractice claim is filed.

*Risk management education and consultation*: Many professional liability insurance companies provide some risk management education to their insureds. It may be as simple as a newsletter with articles about avoiding boundary violations or reminding insureds about their state's child abuse reporting requirement. Others go further, offering extensive online or in-person continuing education courses. Still others offer brief, one-on-one consultation with a consultant well versed in both mental health practice and law. The benefit of these services to the insured clinician can be immense. If insurance company staff provide these consultation services, the clinician should ask whether they disclose the substance of the conversation to the underwriting staff or keep it confidential. Even if the company uses independent outsiders to provide the services, clinicians should enquire about their confidentiality.

## GROUP PRACTICE CONSIDERATIONS

A common inducement for joining a group practice is automatic coverage under the group's professional liability policy, but any clinician in a group, especially a non-owner, should ask questions. Is it an occurrence or a claims-made policy? If it is a claims-made policy, will the group have the money to pay for an ERP if the group dissolves? Are all professional activities covered, or just those conducted under the auspices of the group? (If the clinician is considering an ancillary private practice, separate individual coverage, limited to the private practice, is recommended.) Does the group policy cover licensure defense for the individuals, and if so, how much coverage is provided? Who decides whether a claim should be contested or settled? (Even the most employee-friendly institution or group practice is predisposed to protect its own interests first, sometimes at the expense of the individuals implicated in a suit. A clinician with a separate, full-time, individual policy has the same rights any policyholder has, even where the group policy is the primary coverage.)

## THE PROCESS OF PURCHASING COVERAGE

At the time of publication, many insurance companies offer professional liability insurance to mental health professionals. For some of these companies, this coverage is a sideline; for others, it is one of their specialties. For example, the American Insurance Trust (The Trust), the sole preferred provider of liability insurance to members of the American Psychological Association, represents the largest block of psychologists' professional liability coverage in the United States. Its governing board is controlled by psychologists. No association membership is required for coverage through The Trust. Trust Risk Management Services, which offers professional liability coverage to other mental health professionals, also has a board and parent company board that consists largely of mental health professionals.

Clinicians should talk to their colleagues and their mentors for recommendations about liability insurance coverage and ask professional associations to which they belong for recommendations.

# BUSINESS OWNER'S INSURANCE POLICIES

Another important type of insurance policy that must be mentioned is the business owner's insurance policy, commonly referred to as BOP, covering claims alleging that the owner of a business (including a professional office) was negligent in the management of the office.

Two simple examples illustrate the importance of this kind of coverage:

1. A postal employee (a non-client) coming into the clinician's office to deliver a package trips over a carpet and suffers bodily injury.
2. A coffee maker in the office, left on over the weekend, overheats and starts a fire that damages several other offices in the building.

These claims do not arise from clinical practice and are thus not covered by the professional liability policy, but they can create significant business liability exposure and need to be covered by insurance.

# OTHER IMPORTANT PROTECTIONS FOR CLINICIANS IN INDEPENDENT PRACTICE

While most professionals understand the importance of purchasing a professional liability policy to cover expenses and protect their assets if they are the subject of a malpractice claim or licensing board complaint, they often do not place the same value on protecting their income in other ways. The income of independent practitioners and their ability to provide for their families and future is vulnerable to many other events such as illness, injury, or sudden death. In fact, most clinicians are more likely to be vulnerable to illness, injury, or disability resulting in time away from work than they are to having a malpractice claim filed against them. The Social Security Administration estimates that one in four 20-year-olds will become disabled and unable to work before they reach the age of 67. Over 37 million Americans are classified as disabled, and more than 50% of those are in their working years (18–64). The data also suggest that fewer than one in four Americans has enough money in savings to cover at least six months of expenses (Social Security Administration, 2015). Those who are self-employed or working part time with no protection in place are the most vulnerable (Young, 2015a). Despite all of these vulnerabilities, many mental health professionals do not have disability policies or office overhead policies.

An illness or injury can have a devastating effect upon independent practitioners' ability to earn a living and serve their patients' needs. When they become disabled, insurance policies such as disability insurance and office overhead insurance are designed to keep the income flowing and pay the bills.

## DISABILITY OR INCOME PROTECTION PLANS

Disability or income protection insurance keeps income coming in when clinicians become disabled and cannot work for a period of time. When people think of their assets, which might include their savings, home, car, and so on, they often neglect to include their job and the income it produces. This type of insurance provides income until the practitioner is able to return to work.

While Social Security benefits may pay for some living expenses, they likely will not be sufficient to cover all living and business expenses. Without an income protection plan or substantial savings or retirement funds, individuals' needs are not likely to be covered if they are unable to work. Additionally, around 70% of applicants are initially denied Social Security disability benefits. Those who do qualify might only receive around 40% of their income during their disability. Also, to qualify, individuals often need to be disabled to the extent that they would not be expected to return to the workforce (Young, 2015a).

Most disability insurance plans offer similar benefits and a choice about the amount of coverage, ranging from 50% to 67% of an individual's current income. Importantly, if insurance premiums are paid with after-tax dollars, the benefits individuals receive while disabled are generally not subject to federal income tax. Thus, benefits are actually closer to pre-disability earnings.

Income protection policies do have waiting periods—typically 28 days, 90 days, and 180 days. The shorter the waiting period, the higher the insurance premium. When choosing a waiting period, clinicians should determine how much cash they have in reserve and how long they could wait until the disability cash benefit starts coming in. The most commonly selected waiting period is 90 days (Young, 2015a).

One area of distinction among policies to consider is how the policy defines when (1) a disability qualifies and (2) benefits become payable. Many policies require individuals to be disabled such that they cannot perform the duties of their own occupation for a fixed period of time (e.g., one or two years). After that, the definition may change to an individual's inability to perform the duties of ANY occupation (e.g., a job for which they may not be trained or may not enjoy). This is referred to as an "own occupation any occupation" definition. Clinicians are encouraged to consider purchasing a policy that does not limit the definition after a period of time and to look for policies that define disability as the inability to perform the duties of their own occupation for the *entire* period of disability (The Trust, 2016a).

Disability premium rates vary widely, depending on features such as how broad the coverage is, but rates generally depend on the waiting period chosen, the amount of benefit per month, and the maximum period chosen to receive benefits (e.g., 5 years, 10 years, or to age 65).

Applying for disability insurance includes providing a medical history and possibly completing a physical examination. Practitioners are encouraged to obtain income protection coverage earlier in their work lives, when they are healthy, to improve the odds that they will be approved for coverage. Coverage through a group policy typically offers lower rates and it is especially advantageous when the group policy is based solely on favorable claims experience of mental health professionals.

## OFFICE OVERHEAD INSURANCE

Office overhead insurance helps to cover office expenses if clinicians become disabled. It is advantageous to have both an office overhead and an income protection policy. Office overhead insurance pays regularly occurring business expenses such as rent or mortgage interest payments; employee's salaries and payroll taxes; automobile leasing costs; office telephone charges and telephone answering service charges; office utility charges, including electricity, heating, air conditioning, and water expenses; office cleaning services; building maintenance expenses; interest on office equipment loans; outside billing services; accountants' services; property, state, and local business taxes; premiums for professional liability insurance and other coverage; interest charges on a business loan; dues for national, regional, or state professional associations; and many other miscellaneous expenses that are usual and fixed and needed for the conduct and operations of one's office (The Trust, 2016b).

Office overhead policies vary, but when purchasing a policy, clinicians might consider what the policy does and does not cover, the monthly benefits, the time period before benefits actually are paid, the time period during which benefits are paid, the definition of disability, coverage of expenses like dues, and what becomes of unused benefits (Young, 2015b).

Office overhead policies cover similar basic expenses, but some may tailor eligible expenses to the profession, so it is important to note what specifically is covered and what is not and make comparisons. When applying for this insurance, individuals may have to provide information on their health, medical history, and preexisting conditions that may affect insurability.

## LIFE INSURANCE

There are various forms of life insurance, but the least costly and most commonly purchased form is term life insurance. It is an affordable way to protect assets and family members for a specific period of time (5, 10, 15, or 20-plus years) and pay periodic premiums. If death occurs during the time period, the insurer pays a lump sum to beneficiaries. Term life is most commonly purchased as a safety net for a spouse, children, and other loved ones—with goals to include keeping the family functioning, paying burial expenses and debts, and financing a child's education. Because the benefit is paid all at once, it is important to have a plan to invest the funds to help meet specific goals (Young, 2015c).

Term life policies differ in what they cover, and some include extra features, while others require individuals to pay for riders to get those extra features. For example, policies may include an accelerated death benefit, which enables terminally ill policyholders to collect a large portion of the payout while they are still alive. Another is disability waiver of premium, which grants a waiver on paying premiums due to disability that has lasted more than six months. Some policies come with accidental death and dismemberment (AD&D), which offers double or triple the payout if death or loss of limbs is by accident.

Standard formulas recommend coverage that would provide between 6 and 10 times individuals' annual income, but the real number depends on the specific circumstances of those seeking coverage. Two households may earn equal incomes, but an individual with four young children may need more robust coverage than empty nesters with no mortgage and a substantial retirement fund. It is generally more economical to purchase larger death benefits, and it is also better to purchase earlier in life when applicants are healthy and premium rates are lower (The Trust, 2016c).

Insurers use rate classes, or risk-related categories, to determine premiums. Each individual's rate class is determined by a number of factors, including their overall health, family medical history, and lifestyle. Premium rates may increase periodically, generally every 5 years, up to an attained age, which is usually a maximum of 75 (Young, 2015c).

A medical/paramedical exam may be required when applying and is often arranged and subsidized by the insurance company. The exam will likely include blood and urine tests. Test results can affect approval or increase rates.

For those who have life insurance, it is important to ensure that benefits have kept up with inflation as well as any changes in life circumstances, such as marriage, children, mortgages, and jobs. As individuals' lives change, coverage should change to keep up (Young, 2015c).

Purchasing life insurance through a group often results in lower premiums and better features. Those who are insured through an employer's group plan may lose their coverage when they leave or switch jobs, so it is important for independent practitioners to have their own policy that spans various periods of employment.

Many people may minimize the need for life insurance, citing it as an "excessive expense," and find it uncomfortable to think about their own death. Disease rates, however, have been increasing along with everyday accidents. Life insurance helps mitigate the financial uncertainty resulting from the early death of a loved one. Purchasing life insurance is a sound financial security investment (The Trust, 2016c).

## CONCLUDING THOUGHTS

There are so many elements that are critical to building and maintaining a successful clinical practice, and, certainly, the cost of doing business, especially in the beginning, can be daunting. When practice budgets are considered, several cost-saving measures may be taken, and mental health professionals may be tempted to delay spending money on insurance coverage, taking their chances on avoiding claims, licensing board complaints, disability, office damage, and premature death or believing naively that they will be safe because they are good practitioners and take care of themselves. Some even look for the best "bargain" rates on professional liability insurance, not fully understanding that cheaper rates often reflect less breadth of coverage. These are dangerous risks that can be mitigated by clinicians thoroughly reviewing and comparing policies to ensure they are purchasing the kind of coverage they need and are making decisions not based solely on price. Even the best practitioners, including those who do not do anything wrong, are still susceptible to claims, complaints, and accidents. The worst time to discover you have inadequate coverage is when something goes terribly wrong and your net worth is in jeopardy. Protect your hard work and investment in your professional career so that your investment protects you.

## REFERENCES

Forbes. (May 5, 2013). Ten things you want to know about medical malpractice. Retrieved from http://www.forbes.com/sites/learnvest/2013/05/16/10-things-you-want-to-know-about-medical-malpractice/#40edc1b02323.

Knapp, S., Younggren, J., VandeCreek, L., Harris, E., & Martin, J. (2013). *Assessing and managing risk in psychological practice: An individualized approach* (2nd Edition). Rockville, MD: The Trust.

Merriam Webster Dictionary Online. (2016). [Definition of tort]. Retrieved from http://www.merriam-webster.com/dictionary/tort.

Social Security Administration. (May 2015). SSA Publication No. 05-10029.

The Trust. (2016a). Trust group income protection (disability) insurance [Product description page]. Retrieved from http://www.trustinsurance.com/products-services/income-protection.

The Trust. (2016b). Office overhead insurance [Product description page]. Retrieved from http://www.trust-insurance.com/products-services/office-overhead.

The Trust. (2016c). Trust group term life [Product description page]. Retrieved from http://www.trustinsurance.com/products-services/group-term-life.

Young, S. (2015a). What you need to know about income protection (disability) insurance [Video blog post]. Retrieved from https://www.youtube.com/watch?v=6wMDgzH9Igw.

Young, S. (2015b). What you need to know about office overhead insurance [Video blog post]. Retrieved from https://www.youtube.com/watch?v=Kd5mlqJ_xVs.

Young, S. (2015c). What you need to know about life insurance [Video blog post]. Retrieved from https://www.youtube.com/watch?v=AdAINQOM8mU.

CHAPTER 5

# TYPICAL FORMS USED IN A PRIVATE PRACTICE

*Donald E. Wiger*

Filling out forms in the practice of mental health treatment can lead to a variety of reactions ranging from complaints about the time and effort required to much relief after a successful audit. If writing the information requested on forms is viewed as being for the sake of nothing else but "more paperwork," indeed it can seem like a waste of time and effort. Forms must have a purpose that is clearly conveyed to both the practitioner and client as a positive tool in providing efficient treatment. A combination of proper training in documentation and an understanding of how forms can be extremely helpful tools in several aspects of mental health treatment often leads to treatment that is more on target.

Forms, in themselves, are not an end product; rather, they are a means of collecting information for documentation and can be of great help to clinicians in gathering and recording needed information for providing high-quality clinical services. Further, the specific information and data collected on forms is the evidence needed for adequate documentation, which is the result of integrating the information collected on mental health forms. For example, an auditor will examine the information collected on the forms to verify the documentation in areas such as the diagnosis, impairments, content of sessions, and medical necessity. Attempting to gather and record all relevant information from and about clients without the benefit of the types of forms described in this chapter can be a much less efficient and effective process, possibly leading to oversights and having consequences for the quality of the clinician's documentation and for the quality of the services provided to clients.

Too many practitioners put off filling out forms, and by the end of the week, they spend the good part of a day trying to remember what took place in previous sessions for their progress notes. Filling out forms is not meant to be a punishment or lead to resentment for the time it takes to fill them out. Many experienced practitioners have learned that when forms are filled out entirely during the session with a client, very little or no out-of-session time in needed. What is better, filling out forms between sessions, or relaxing to prepare for the next client? This answer is not difficult. This process holds true for completing intake notes, progress notes, treatment plans, and even testing. However, many experienced clinicians do not fill out client information during the sessions and are able to keep up with their documentation. The choice is a matter of circumstances, preference, and time management.

One of the yearly goals I have for interns every year is that when they conduct a psychological evaluation, they have the bulk of the tests scored by the time the client is finished with the interview and testing. The report is then dictated immediately, before the next client shows up. The transcriptionist then has no more than three days to type the report. Referral sources love to receive a full psychological or neuropsychological report in less than one week. One of the biggest reasons for a practice's growth is public relations and great customer service (see Chapter 24, "Optimizing Customer Service in Private Practice"). The proper use of forms clearly accelerates the process.

There are pros and cons for filling out forms during the session. The process works quite well primarily in areas of assessment and individual psychotherapy, which have been the focus of my experience. However, there are other areas of mental health treatment in which it may not be feasible or possible. For example, for clients who are in extremely hostile or highly affective situations, writing notes for much of the session could seem rather impersonal. There is certainly no "one size fits all" in any aspect of life, especially in the mental health field. In addition, the clinician's personality, training, cognitive style, and time availability are important factors in deciding when to fill out forms.

Although I write notes such as client quotes, observations, endorsements of symptoms, and other clinical data during a session with a client, most of the time is not spent in writing. That would seem fairly impersonal. I make as much eye contact as possible, but when I make notations I make sure that the client knows that everything he or she says to me is important. This can be accomplished both verbally and/or nonverbally. For example, when a client says something that is important or clinically relevant, I often nod my head, while making eye contact, and then write it down. I cannot remember every important thing that was said or observed during the session. My notes, the evidence of symptoms, impairments, progresses, setbacks, and need for services, then become much more clearly documented. Nonverbally, I am trying to get the message across as, "What you are saying is very important, so I need to write it down." In a sense, it can translate to a form of empathy and understanding. I have never had a client object to my taking notes during a session.

Forms do not control any aspect of the diagnostic or therapeutic process; doing an efficient job of filling out forms, and subsequent documentation, has little or nothing to do with being a successful practitioner. However, forms can be very helpful to even the most experienced practitioner in arriving at a documentable diagnosis, following the treatment plan, demonstrating the effects of treatment, and ensuring that ethics and legal requirements have been meet.

This chapter is not filled with sample forms, but rather it provides a framework as to what forms—or information contained in forms—are necessary for building and maintaining a productive and ethical mental health practice. Developing forms can be quite time-consuming, yet many practitioners make their own to best suit their practice. This chapter focuses on the forms necessary to cover the financial, legal, ethical, and clinical needs of a mental health practice. Clinics with specialized services, such as substance abuse, eating disorders, couples counseling, and much more, must simply incorporate additional intake and progress note information to fit the criteria for their specialty. In addition, the various regulatory agencies typically require several forms that are not typically used in a small to moderate-size private practice.

There are plenty of sources for purchasing established forms (e.g., Wiger, 2009; Zuckerman, & Kolmes, 2017). There is not room in one chapter to go over every possible form and handout that could be used in mental health clinical practice, but the main forms typically used in treatment are discussed in this chapter. In a book of mental health forms, Wiger (2009) provides over 60 forms for possible use by practitioners. Clearly, no clinic would use that many forms, but due to the size, specialty areas, accreditation requirements, and other factors, many forms that are not needed by most clinics would be helpful in others.

Five categories of forms, necessary for a practice to run smoothly, will be discussed: (1) pretreatment forms, (2) required HIPAA compliance forms, (3) assessment forms, (4) progress notes during treatment sessions, and (5) posttreatment forms. Other forms, such as those for practice management, are not the subject of this chapter.

# PRETREATMENT FORMS

It is necessary to collect client information prior to initiating mental health services for several reasons. It is a risky practice to begin treatment without collecting payment information, the reason for referral, and the severity of the client's impairments; matching the client with an appropriate clinician; choosing appropriate assessment procedures; and informing clients of their rights. The information contained on three forms listed below can be very helpful in preventing both financial loss and a mismatch between the practitioner and client.

It is crucial to inform the client or whoever is responsible for services about the practice's financial policies. This information can be discussed on the phone but should also be covered in a Financial or Payment Policy Form and signed by the client before services begin.

Several years ago, in the beginning stages of private practice, I did not have a contract for payment of services. I had no signed agreement that if insurance or another third party did not pay, the client would be responsible for the cost of services. Most of the time, when insurance did not pay for all or a portion of the services, I would bill the client and receive payment. However, about one out of four or five clients refused to pay, stating that we should have checked their insurance. A few clients, in fact, stated that since there was no contract, they were not responsible for those fees. Since we had no signed agreement related to those fees, we lost. I learned the lesson the hard way. Now, each client signs a Financial Policy Form and a Payment Contract for Services. The financial aspect of mental health is no different than any other business. Too many private practices have gone out of business due to lack of business acumen. It is important not to forget the following:

If you want to help people, the practice doors must stay open.
If you want your doors to stay open, you must pay your bills.
If you want to pay your bills, you have to collect money for the services you perform.
If you want to collect money, you need sound financial policies.

# FORM 1: CLIENT INFORMATION FORM

The Client Information Form is designed to collect information about how services will be paid for and the reasons for requesting treatment. Often, clients will contact a practice to schedule an appointment, yet they may know little about the services provided and whether the practitioner is a provider for their insurance company. This information can be provided in a brief screening by phone. Many clients are unaware that not every practitioner is a provider for every insurance company. Although it is ultimately the client's responsibility to check this information with his or her insurance provider, the client might not be aware of the process. If they are participating providers, practitioners must decide whether they will contact the client's insurance provider to verify coverage. The Client Information Form should indicate that the client explicitly authorized the clinician or office staff to verify benefits. Insurance companies typically provide information such as whether the client is current in his or her coverage, the deductible and co-pay amounts, covered services, and which services will need a prior authorization. However, providing a summary of coverage is not a guarantee of payment. For example, providing psychotherapy to a client who does not have a psychiatric diagnosis is not likely to be reimbursed. Most insurance companies initially pay for a diagnostic assessment, a certain number of counseling sessions, and perhaps some testing procedures. However, assuming that these services are covered can be a costly mistake.

Besides providing information to verify insurance benefits, the information collected from the client on this form also helps the practitioner decide if she or he, or at least one of the psychotherapists in the practice, has the professional training and experience to treat the client (referred to as "professional competencies" or "clinical competencies"). For example, if no one in the practice has a professional competency in treating individuals with substance abuse, it is suggested that a potential client with this need be referred elsewhere. It is clearly unethical to provide services without the previous training and supervision needed to provide competent professional service. Thus, determining this before treatment is provided to a new client is essential.

I recall a recent incident in which a client phoned and made an appointment with a psychotherapist. They spent over one hour in a diagnostic interview. By the end of the interview, the clinician told the client that he was not experienced in this client's issues. He then referred the client to another psychotherapist at a different clinic specializing in the client's area of concern. The problem that developed was that the original psychotherapist and the second psychotherapist each billed the insurance company for the diagnostic interview; since the deductible amount was not yet met, each bill went to the client. The client then filed a complaint stating that the first psychotherapist "ripped me off." This could have been avoided by collecting the appropriate information before services began, or at least offering an initial free consultation. The point is that if appropriate information had been collected prior to seeing the psychotherapist, it would have been known that there would have been a mismatch.

A Client Information Form, completed prior to providing any services, should contain the following types of information. It is often collected from one of two sources, the client (or responsible party) or the referral source. The following is an outline that should be tailored for the psychotherapist's specific practice. A primary goal is to obtain enough information to be sure that there is a match between the client's needs and the psychotherapist's professional competencies.

1. Client's full legal name
2. Current address
3. Phone number(s)
4. Date of birth
5. Type of service(s) requested
   a. Assessment (specific type)
   b. Treatment (specific type)
6. Specific purpose of seeking services. List specific areas of concern under headings such as:
   a. Mental health
   b. Behavioral issues
   c. Cognitive issues
   d. Relationships
   e. Other
7. Questions or concerns to be addressed
8. Payment information
   a. Cash
   b. Insurance
   c. Third party, not insurance
   d. Other
9. Special requests
   a. Practitioner's gender, age, experience, mode of treatment
   b. Appointment day, time
10. Emergency contacts

If the intended payment is by insurance, after this information has been collected, the insurance company or third-party payer should be contacted to verify coverage if you are a provider. Expiration of insurance coverage, lack of payment of premiums, changing jobs, or a number of other factors can lead to cancellation of benefits. Never assume that a client has insurance that is in effect simply because an insurance card was produced or the policy number was given on the phone. Verification of insurance coverage does not verify that the service provided will be covered; for example, the diagnosis may not reach medical necessity or be covered. Some clients do not even know that their insurance coverage has lapsed.

## FORM 2: FINANCIAL POLICY FORM, WITH PAYMENT CONTRACT

Just as practitioners should expect to be paid, consumers have the right to know the practitioner's financial policies. Typically, these are contained on two separate forms (Financial Policy Form, Payment Contract), but they can be combined.

Financial policies must be written in clearly understood terms that are not ambiguous or difficult for the client to understand. Important topics include, but are not limited to, who is ultimately responsible for payment of services such as if a third party denies payment, when payments are due, and methods of payment. The policies should include statements noting that having insurance does not guarantee that benefits will be paid for some or all of the services provided. Never guarantee anything from an insurance company or any third-party payer. The client's policy is between the policyholder and the insurance company, not your practice. Thus, make it clear that simply because the practitioner is a provider for an insurance company, it is not a guarantee of payment. In addition, make it clear to the client in the Payment Contract that any services provided that are not covered by the insurance company or third-party payer are the client's responsibility.

Without a payment contract the practitioner might not get paid. Because requirements differ by state, the contract should is reviewed by a business attorney before using it with clients.

True Informed Consent for Professional Services in the contract also includes the following information:

1. The hourly rate of pay for listed services (e.g., intake, testing, individual psychotherapy, group psychotherapy, report writing time, plus other services provided)
2. Missed appointment and late cancellation policy and fee
3. Separate listing of fees for services not covered by the third-party payer (e.g., insurance payment covers less testing time than that which was required, report writing time, extra counseling sessions beyond the scope of the insurance coverage, specific types of treatment or evaluation not covered by insurance)

Include the estimated insurance benefits with a clear notation that these benefits are not guaranteed by the practice, but they are what was quoted by the client's insurance company, and are not a guarantee of payment.

## FORM 3: RECIPIENT'S RIGHTS NOTIFICATION

This notice informs client of their rights as patients. It contains a fairly lengthy listing of rights as a patient, rights to receive information, the clinic's ethical obligations, and the patient's responsibilities.

# REQUIRED HEALTH INSURANCE PORTABILITY AND ACCOUNTABILITY ACT (HIPAA) COMPLIANCE FORMS

The Health Insurance Portability and Accountability Act (HIPAA) of 1996 is designed to protect consumers' health information and sets standards regarding the sharing of information. See http://www.hhs.gov/ocr/privacy/ for a full set of rules established by HIPAA (U.S. Department of Health and Human Services, 2003). Practitioners who do any electronic communication of Protected Health Information must use the following forms to be HIPAA compliant.

## FORM 4: PRIVACY OF INFORMATION POLICIES (HIPAA REQUIRED)

This notice can be posted and handed out to clients. It describes the clinic's legal duties to the client, how information is legally shared, and when confidentiality can be broken, such as in cases of duty to warn and protect, public safety, abuse, prenatal exposure to substances, in case of a client's death, professional misconduct, judicial proceedings, minors/guardianship, collection agencies, professional consultations, typing/dictation services, couple/family/relationship counseling, telephone calls/answering machines/voicemail, and other provisions. The form also covers the client's rights to receive, review, restrict access, and other means of reviewing and disseminating the records. Additionally, instructions are provided as to how to lodge a complaint toward a service provider. Some practitioners have separate forms for each of these procedures.

## FORM 5: REQUEST TO AMEND HEALTH RECORDS (HIPAA REQUIRED)

Clients have the right to request an amendment in their records if they believe it to be inaccurate. The form includes information as to what amendments to a client's records are to be made and to whom the amendments will be sent.

## FORM 6: REQUEST FOR RESTRICTED USE/ DISCLOSURE OF RECORDS (HIPAA REQUIRED)

The client or the representatives of the client may request a restricted use of disclosure of her or his records. For example, the client may request that only certain portions of the record be shared or that the records can be used for only certain purposes. The form includes the reasons for requesting the restrictions. The service provider reviews the request and notifies the client of the decision.

## FORM 7: REQUEST FOR ALTERNATIVE MEANS OF CONFIDENTIAL INFORMATION (HIPAA REQUIRED)

This brief form, signed by either the client or his or her representative, is a request for the practice to communicate information to a different address or phone number than the typical residence of the client.

## FORM 8: RELEASE OF INFORMATION CONSENT FORM (HIPAA REQUIRED)

Except for HIPAA exceptions, a written release of information is necessary to disseminate client information. When using a Release of Information form, the client requests that information is sent from one source to another, but not back and forth.

A Release of Information form minimally contains the name of the client, who will send and/or receive the information, and what information will be disclosed. HIPAA regulations require that a separate authorization is needed for the release of psychotherapy notes—that is, one cannot release psychotherapy notes if a release form states, "send entire record." However, HIPAA discourages requesting the entire record of clients. Rather, it is good practice to request the minimum amount of information necessary for the stated purpose of the release. Consents expire in one year unless the client authorizes the release for a shorter period of time. The form also includes the purpose for which the material will be disclosed, statements regarding the client's rights, and legal guidelines. If the client is a child or has a guardian, the guardian must sign. Obtaining proof of guardianship is suggested.

## FORM 9: RECORD OF REQUESTS FOR CLIENT INFORMATION (HIPAA REQUIRED)

This brief form, generally kept in the client's file, is a record of any requests that have been made for information about the client. Requests from both inside and outside the practice are recorded.

## FORM 10: REQUESTS FOR LISTING OF DISCLOSURES OF CLIENT'S RECORDS (HIPAA REQUIRED)

This request form, filled out by the client or representative, is a request to view who has requested his or her records. In addition, there should be an acknowledgment that these forms were signed by the client.

# ASSESSMENT FORMS

Assessment forms are intended to assist in gathering information in the initial interview sessions that identifies the client's diagnosis and medical necessity for psychotherapy or other services. Now that background information and legal requirements have been followed, it is time to see the client.

Unless the nature of the visit is a one-time crisis intervention, usually one to three sessions are spent in collecting information to assess the client's need for treatment, diagnosis, and type of treatment and to develop a treatment plan. A well-conducted diagnostic assessment session with the client can be quite therapeutic because the nature of the questions asked, coupled with empathy and understanding, often lead to the client feeling understood and trusting the practitioner. The same relationship and therapeutic skills employed in psychotherapy are necessary when conducting the initial interview. Thus, assessment is not simply a series of questions and information gathering. Clinical observations and the client's level of cooperation and insight are crucial to arriving at a proper diagnosis. For this reason, I am not a fan of primarily using checklists filled out by the client for the initial assessment. Never assign a diagnosis primarily based on checklists filled out by the client or others.

Although the diagnostic assessment is not intended to be psychotherapy, it is often an excellent time to build rapport and prepare the client for psychotherapy. I recall several incidents in which clients have been referred solely for a diagnostic assessment. As the interview progressed, and the questions became more personal, clients have often stated that the assessment, in itself, was therapeutic because the flow of information gathering increased their level of insight about their behaviors and mental health.

Assessment forms vary significantly depending on the specialties of the clinic. Various specializations (e.g., children, teens, adults, eating disorders, attention-deficit/hyperactivity disorder, behavioral issues, sexual concerns, chemical dependency, neuropsychological evaluations, learning disabilities, and any of the scores of possible specialties) each have an assessment form that is tailored to their area of focus. The following description of a Diagnostic Assessment Form is generic. Thus, a practice would add items pertaining to its specialty.

## FORM 11: DIAGNOSTIC ASSESSMENT FORM

The information contained on this form is what determines the diagnosis, medical necessity for services, and treatment plan. This is one of the first pieces of information requested by an auditor or clinical supervisor. It contains all of the information necessary to begin treatment. The information is collected on the first session, usually taking one to two hours.

During this first session, the clinician initially goes over the material written on Form 1, the Client Information Form, to be sure that the practitioner and client agree as to the purpose of the services being rendered. Then, much more specific information is collected to further validate the need for services and what specific treatment will take place.

All humans have some level of mental health concerns, such as feeling depressed or anxious some of the time. These are normal human emotions. It is expected that sometimes a person will have a change in appetite, become irritable, feel angry, not follow through with a task, or experience decreased self-esteem. A collection of "symptoms" is necessary but not sufficient to validate a "diagnosis." A mental health diagnosis may be given when it is documented that the mental health symptoms of a diagnosis are at least at a level of discomfort, for mild levels of diagnosis, or functionally impairing, for more severe levels of diagnosis. The most important information to be collected is a clear documentation of the medical necessity for services, especially if the payment is from an insurance company. The concept of "medical necessity" refers to the diagnosis and treatment of an illness or symptoms that meets the prevailing standards of care. Thus, the documentation needs to clearly describe personal distress or functional impairments that are due to a mental health disorder.

Insurance companies typically do not pay for services without a mental health diagnosis. It must be noted that a mental health diagnosis is not simply an endorsement of symptoms. This is the first of two parts needed to validate a diagnosis. As per the *Diagnostic and Statistical Manual of Mental Disorders*, Fifth Edition (American Psychiatric Association, 2013), and its predecessors, and the ICD-10 (CDC, 2016), for a diagnosis to be clinically significant, there must be a threshold of acuity in which the effects of the mental health disorder must result in clinically significant impairments in social, occupational, or other areas of functioning. The level of treatment is determined by the severity of the impairment. Thus, mental health forms must include space for (a) information that validates the symptoms of a diagnosis and (b) examples of the resulting distress or impairments due to the mental health disorder.

Some practitioners provide a different amount of documentation for clients depending on the requirements of the third-party payer. For example, third-party payers such as insurance companies, the VA, Social Security, state and county agencies, schools, or any other entity paying for services could require varying types of documentation material. Private-pay clients do not typically have any requirements for the forms used or for subsequent documentation, unless they want to submit for reimbursement on their own. While it can be tempting to "loosen up" on documentation, good documentation and the use of forms are part of providing quality care. I can recall several incidents over the years in which clients paid cash and never mentioned that the results of their assessment or treatment would eventually be used for purposes such as a court hearing, applying for disability, to obtain services, or a variety of other reasons. At times, the request for records occurred a few years after services were conducted. However, because the same set of forms and documentation principles were used for the private-pay client, the information in the file was clear rather than a vague memory.

The following are essential areas where information is gathered from clients using the Diagnostic Assessment Form. This form provides a useful format for the preparation of written reports.

## DEMOGRAPHIC INFORMATION

Demographic information includes primarily identification information such as name, address, phone number, and any other client information requested if there is a referral source.

## PHYSICAL DESCRIPTION

The physical description information is provided mainly for identification purposes. There are rare times in which a different person will attend the appointment. This could be due to someone using someone else's insurance benefits, or perhaps for monetary gain. I often conduct disability evaluations for various agencies and have on more than one occasion discovered that the person being interviewed was not the true client. There are actually fraudulent businesses in which people pay others a portion of their financial settlement if they pretend to be the client at the interview. These people "know how to answer the questions" correctly to obtain financial benefits. Therefore, checking the client's identification can be necessary in some situations.

## HISTORY OF PRESENT ILLNESS

Many mental health diagnoses require symptoms to be prevalent for a specific time period to arrive at the diagnosis—for instance, major depressive disorder (two weeks), persistent depressive disorder (one year), and generalized anxiety disorder (six months). Besides the time period, a detailed history of events, circumstances, examples, and consequences of mental health and behavioral concerns are helpful in establishing both a pattern of symptoms and mitigating factors.

Beside listing current mental health concerns, include a history of mental health and behavioral concerns such as how they have affected the client's functioning over time. Descriptors such as the "OFAID procedure" (Wiger, 2012)—(O) Onset, (F) Frequency, (A) Antecedents, (I) Intensity, and (D) Duration of symptoms and impairments—are very helpful in determining the degree and chronic effects of the client's mental health concerns.

## EDUCATION

Collecting a history of the client's education is much more than just demographics. Information such as highest grade or degree attained, grades, attendance, behavioral concerns, reasons for leaving school, functioning level, and future plans provide helpful information about the client's level of motivation, cognitive functioning, and behavioral history. An educational history can be very helping in estimating the client's premorbid level of functioning in cases such as head injuries, various illnesses, and declines in mental health functioning.

## EMPLOYMENT HISTORY

It is important to obtain information about employment because it is an excellent indicator of the client's historical level of persistence, ability, and employment stability and provides a fairly accurate estimate of his or her level of premorbid functioning, similar to educational functioning, noted above. For example, if a client has a master's degree and successfully held an executive position for over 20 years but suffered a head injury and current testing noted a full-scale IQ of 80, it would be reasonable to deduce that his current testing suggests significant cognitive declines. However, if the client previously left school in the ninth grade, due to poor academic performances, and had never held a job for more than a few months, a full-scale IQ of 80 would fall within an expected range. Without obtaining an accurate history, it is very difficult to know the client's level of premorbid functioning in many areas of functioning.

For clients coming in for counseling, evaluating the employment history is quite important. Assessing factors such as the average length of employment, typical reasons for leaving a job, attendance history, ability to relate to co-workers and authority figures, and any other aspects of employment that have been affected by mental health concerns is important for getting a more complete understanding of the client.

## CURRENT SIGNS AND SYMPTOMS

Although the terms "signs" and "symptoms" are similar and often used synonymously, they are different. The DSM-5 (American Psychiatric Association, 2013) defines "signs" as an objective description of mental health pathology as reported by the examiner, not the client, whereas "symptoms" are described as a subjective manifestation of mental health pathology as reported by the client, not the examiner.

This section is a continuation of the history, but the concerns are discussed in present terms. The information collected is not designed to formulate a diagnosis but rather to connect the buildup of previous concerns to how they remain problematic. Specific information is collected, including examples of the functional impairments currently impacting the client's mental health.

## PAST MENTAL HEALTH TREATMENT

A history of mental health treatment helps determine what has been helpful and what has not been helpful in the past. Factors such as why treatment was sought, frequency of treatment, type of treatment (e.g., individual, group, inpatient, outpatient), how long the client stayed in treatment, and why services were terminated are each important to assess.

## PAST MEDICAL TREATMENT

A medical history can help determine the relationship between the client's physical concerns and his or her mental health functioning. This information can be helpful in evaluating a possible somatization disorder, conversion symptoms, or exaggeration of symptoms.

## MEDICATIONS

Information about a client's medications is very helpful for several reasons. On a basic level, a list of medications informs the clinician about the current medications the client is receiving. In addition, it is beneficial to inquire about onset of taking mental health medications, their helpfulness, the client's compliance, any side effects, and any other factors related to treatment. Mental health professionals who are not psychiatrists or others who legally prescribe medications must be careful about making comments or recommendations about medications due to potential malpractice issues.

## LEGAL ISSUES

A client's history and current legal problems may provide some insight into his or her behavioral issues, levels of responsibility, and personality issues. The main information needed is the nature and chronicity of the legal problems. For example, there is a significant difference between the legal matters of someone who had a drunken-driving charge 30 years ago versus someone charged with several recent assaults. The emotional and behavioral effects of the clients' legal circumstance will be certainly different.

## CURRENT INTERESTS

A client's current interests can be a good measure of his or her mental health functioning, motivation, socialization, and any changes in functioning. In addition, incorporating the client's interests into the treatment plan can lead to more motivation to increase functioning levels.

## RELATIONSHIPS

Many mental health concerns (e.g., agoraphobia, social anxiety, depression, many personality disorders, autism, paranoia) include impairments in social functioning. The client's relationships with family, friends, coworkers, and authority figures and any changes in them provide much information that is useful for diagnosis and treatment planning. Information about the client's social supports can be quite helpful in treatment planning.

## SUBSTANCE USE AND ABUSE

There is a high correlation between mental health and substance abuse. Without evaluating each of these areas, treatment could easily be incomplete. Include information such as both past and current usage, reasons for using, effects of usage, treatment history, relapse history, current craving, and future treatment plans. A description of substance use can be quite helpful in describing how it affects the individual's ability to cope with stressors, relax, or escape. A decision will have to be made as to whether the chemical dependency or mental health issue will be treated first, or if treatment will take place simultaneously.

## MENTAL STATUS EXAM

The Mental Status Exam (MSE) is one of the most important parts of the initial intake. It consists of clinical observation in areas of the client's appearance, activity level, speech, attitude toward the examiner, affect/mood, stream of consciousness, and thought content. Typically, the information collected matches the symptoms of the diagnosis.

## AFFECT/MOOD

Affective observations refer to what was observed during the interview. Descriptions of the client's level of affect include the range, appropriateness, mobility, motor activity, predominant mood, and intensity. "Mood" refers to the client's subjective experience and descriptions of her or his current or usual mental health state. Collecting information about mood refers to asking the client several questions regarding the intensity, frequency, and duration of her or his affective disturbance. This information is used to validate the symptoms in formulating a diagnosis. There is a significant difference in two clients who claim to have the same level of depression, but one has been suicidal and treated for years while the other is experiencing a first bout of less acute depression. The diagnosis, treatment, and prognosis are all different between these two individuals.

## PERSONALITY DISORDERS

All too often personality disorders are overlooked in a diagnostic interview. Concerns in these areas will clearly affect the course of treatment. Personality disorders can be difficult to evaluate, especially when the client is in denial, has a low level of insight, or is not cooperative. However, the same procedures of endorsement of symptoms, observations, collateral information, and related impairments as in other clinical diagnoses are used to formulate a diagnosis.

## SENSORIUM/COGNITION

This section of the interview is a brief evaluation of the client's level of concentration, orientation, persistency, and academic level. This information can be part of the MSE, but I prefer to list the information separately because of its importance.

## TESTING

Depending on the nature of services, tests are available in areas such as cognition, memory, concentration, development, substance abuse, or the many other reasons that people receive mental health treatment. The information collected is designed to be integrated with the diagnostic interview. If services are being paid for by an insurance company, check the client's benefits prior to conducting psychological tests, because often a prior authorization for services is required.

## ASSESSMENT/DIAGNOSIS

The assessment section integrates all the information collected, including previous records, the clinical interview, observations, and testing. It is used to formulate the diagnosis and treatment plan.

# FORM 12: TREATMENT PLAN

The treatment plan is the blueprint for psychotherapy. It integrates the information collected in the diagnostic assessment and can be revised as more information is collected and as changes take place. The more specific the treatment plan, the more specific the treatment.

There are several formats for writing treatment plans. Many forms have three common elements, which are basically the problem area, goals and objectives, and treatment strategies.

## THE PROBLEM AREA

This section lists specific areas of impairment that will be addressed in mental health treatment. These impairments are to be clearly validated in the diagnostic assessment. Each of these should be treatable within the competencies of the mental health professional or referral sources. Vague terms such as "anxiety" or "depression" should be avoided because they do not clearly define specific functional impairments. Thus, more specific problem areas, which can be attributed to impairments in the client's life, are appropriate. Listing specific problem areas is clearer than stating vague terms such as "anxiety." Quantifying specific impairments gives a clear baseline. For example:

*Problem Area*: Missing three days of work per week due to panic attacks.

## GOALS AND OBJECTIVES

Each problem area should have treatment goals and objectives. It is common for treatment plans to have at least three goals. Goals are the overall desired behavioral or emotional effect of treatment objectives that are specific, quantifiable steps to reach the goals. Objectives are often increased to come closer to reach the goal as psychotherapy progresses. For example:

*Goal 1*: Increase social interactions.
*Objectives*: By June 10 initiate at least two new social interactions per week; by July 19 initiate at least four new social interactions per week.

## TREATMENT STRATEGIES

Treatment strategies are those that are within the competencies of the practitioner and have been demonstrated as effective for others with similar concerns. Typically, treatment strategies are listed for each goal/objective The type and frequency of treatment is listed. The estimated length of treatment depends on the severity of impairment, the client's effort and motivation, and clinical judgment. Any of these strategies can be revised. For example:

*Treatment Strategies*: Cognitive-behavioral therapy, individual, 1/week for 20 weeks

Progress notes are the only evidence of what takes place in a session. They are much more than a brief summary of the session. Just as the treatment plan is the result of the diagnostic assessment, the progress notes (or case notes) are the result of the treatment plan. The most common outlines for progress notes are SOAP (Subjective, Objective, Assessment, Plan) and DAP (Data, Assessment, Plan). The only difference between SOAP and DAP is that the "Subjective" and "Objective" sections in SOAP notes are combined into the "Data" section on the DAP format.

Much helpful information is collected in the *data* section, including what took place in the session, interventions, observations, test results, documentation of the diagnosis, current impairments, and stressors. Such observations validate the diagnosis but also provide information for treatment strategies for the session. It should be a reflection of the treatment plan.

In the *assessment* section, once the session is finished the practitioner evaluates the effects of treatment, treatment strategies, and the client's progress and setbacks. Overall, the section provides information to evaluate regarding outcomes of treatment.

Based on the assessment, a *plan* is made for future sessions. Perhaps treatment plan strategies, such as mode of therapy, level of objectives, number of session, or intensity of therapy will be revised.

# POSTTREATMENT FORMS

When treatment is no longer taking place, either because the treatment plan goals have been met or for other reasons, there should be a formal discharge from the practice. The following forms are designed to formally discharge the client.

## FORM 14: DISCHARGE SUMMARY

A discharge summary provides a summary of the effects of therapy. It provides evidence that at the time of termination either services were no longer medically necessary or specific referrals were given, or it provides a notation that the client ended services prematurely. Outcomes measures can be included.

## FORM 15: TERMINATION LETTER

A termination letter is sent to the client when services are no long being used. It is intended to free the practitioner of any further responsibility to the client or for the client's actions. Such a letter should at a minimum include a statement that the client is no longer a patient of the practice as well as pertinent referrals if appropriate. Additionally, it can serve as a marker of sorts of the transition point out of psychotherapy.

## SUMMARY

Clinical forms in the practice of mental health can be viewed as either an act of futility or an important part of clinical documentation. Forms provide a structure to organize clinical information in a manner that allows anyone reviewing a client's records to quickly access information about the client and the course of therapy. The information contained on clinical forms can be especially helpful for the practitioner in reviewing a client's progress and planning strategies for upcoming sessions. Files with vague documentation make too many demands on the practitioner's memory from session to session. Plus, when a client changes practitioners, often the only information available is what is contained in the records. Although forms, in themselves, do not serve as documentation, they provide the infrastructure and data necessary for clearly demonstrating the need for services, diagnosis, treatment planning, progress notes, and reason for termination of services.

## REFERENCES

American Psychiatric Association. (2013). *Diagnostic and statistical manual of mental disorders* (5th edition). Washington, DC: American Psychiatric Association.

Centers for Disease Control. (2016). *International Classification of Diseases, Tenth Revision, Clinical Modification*. Retrieved from http://www.cdc.gov/nchs/icd/icd10cm.htm.

U.S. Department of Health and Human Services, Office of Civil Rights. (2003). *Summary of the HIPAA privacy rule*. Retrieved from http://www.hhs.gov/ocr/privacy/.

Wiger, D. E. (2009). *The clinical documentation sourcebook: A comprehensive collection of mental health practice forms, handouts, and records* (4th ed.). Hoboken, NJ: John Wiley & Sons, Inc.

Wiger, D. E. (2012). *The psychotherapy documentation primer* (3rd ed.). Hoboken, NJ: John Wiley & Sons, Inc.

Zuckerman, E. L., & Kolmes, K. (2017). *The paper office for the digital age* (5th ed.). New York, NY: Guilford Press.

CHAPTER 6

# RECORDKEEPING IN PRIVATE PRACTICE

*Eric Y. Drogin and James A. Armontrout*

For private practitioners, there is a duality to the implications of recordkeeping that persists throughout our professional careers. Records inform, guide, and reinforce the client's evolving journey toward health and stability. When at various points we predictably stumble, outpace ourselves, and pause to reflect on progress and persisting obstacles alike, properly tended records represent an increasingly rich source of inspiration and reassurance that under the best of circumstances can mimic the most benign and desirable supportive functions of the co-therapist. Records can secure legal benefits and employment opportunities for clients, inform research that buttresses innovative new treatment techniques, and pave the way for effective multidisciplinary interventions that integrate psychotherapeutic, counseling, medical, and other sources of assistance.

Records are also a self-generated log of every misstep, lapse, and failure of judgment we commit or experience in our attempts to fulfill the therapeutic mission. Clients, colleagues, and courts clamor for the description, disclosure, or destruction of records in ways that can work against a cure, consume valuable clinical and administrative time, and ultimately lead to the loss of our ability to practice at all. The longer we practice, the larger, more unwieldy, and more expensive these archives may become, unless we delete records periodically in accordance with relevant laws in our own practice jurisdictions. Professional guidance for addressing these issues is often indistinct and ever-changing.

Lest the preceding paragraph seem to project too negative a perspective on this process, it should be acknowledged here that timely, relevant, and thoughtfully prepared records constitute tangible evidence of our reasonable, good-faith efforts to meet the standards of care of our professions. Records document our plans, decision making, and actions along with the client's level of cooperation and participation in the agreed-upon treatment plan. This chapter will address—in a chronologically logical order, and in a fashion geared to the identified needs of the private practitioner—the most prominent clinical, ethical, and legal issues in contemporary recordkeeping.

# CREATING RECORDS

Just when recordkeeping has actually begun can be the subject of considerable debate. An email message arrives from a colleague inquiring if we accept certain forms of third-party reimbursement, if we offer a certain form of treatment, or if we have experience in addressing a certain type of syndrome or disorder. If it is subsequently alleged that we overstepped our limitations concerning any of these notions, our initial responses could be the focus of increasingly sophisticated and enforceable "electronic discovery" methods designed to hold us legally accountable, perhaps years in the future. Information exchanged in the context of scheduling and rescheduling initial or follow-up appointments can appear in various formats. Given how important it may be to explain what occurred at the very inception of treatment, private practitioners are best advised to preserve and organize such contacts with the same care afforded any other exercise in clinical data gathering.

Standard 6.01 (Documentation of Professional and Scientific Work and Maintenance of Records) of the Ethical Principles of Psychologists and Code of Conduct of the American Psychological Association (2010; hereinafter the APA Ethics Code) specifies that private practitioners "create" records for a number of reasons, including to "facilitate provision of services later by them or by other professionals," to "ensure accuracy of billing and payments," and to "ensure compliance with law" (p. 8). This Standard makes it clear that generating records is potentially as impactful and ethically relevant a process as subsequently managing them in any other fashion.

The American Counseling Association's (2014) code of ethics (hereinafter the ACA Code of Ethics) advises that "counselors create, safeguard, and maintain documentation necessary for rending professional services" in order to "facilitate the delivery and continuity of services" (p. 4). The code of ethics of the American Association of Marriage and Family Therapists (2015; hereinafter the AAMFT Code of Ethics) refers more generally in this regard to "an enduring dedication to professional and ethical excellence" (p. 1), while the National Association of Social Workers (2008), in its code of ethics (hereinafter the NASW Code of Ethics), specifies a need to "facilitate the delivery of services and to ensure continuity of services provided to clients in the future" (p. 11).

Our charted documentation should reflect three distinct but overlapping qualities: legibility, clarity, and comprehensiveness. At the most basic level of concern, will anyone be able to figure out what a certain inscription actually says some weeks, months, or years in the future? If records are handwritten, then hastily scrawled words may be the problem in need of correction. If records are dictated, then periodic proofreading will be necessary to ensure that intended words and phrases are not garbled and that unintended substitution has not occurred. We recall one case, for example, in which the dictation program mistook "incompetent" for "incontinent."

The notion of clarity addresses not only vagueness but also a potentially excessive reliance upon acronyms and other symbolic representations. Subsequent treatment providers may or may not recognize that "GWNL" stood for "grossly within normal limits" and that "speech norm ×6" referred to unremarkable tone, volume, pressure, content, pace, and articulation of spoken words. Related concerns where such shorthand techniques are employed are blaming and flippancy. There is no room for humor—morbid or otherwise—in recordkeeping, as one psychiatric resident learned to his chagrin during a personal injury lawsuit that exploited his offhanded use of the hoary acronym "PBBB," meaning "Pine Box by Bedside."

Excessive detail can be problematic in considerations of efficiency and privacy alike, such that comprehensiveness is a "slippery slope" consideration in recordkeeping. Private practitioners are not expected to transcribe a psychotherapy session word for word in order to display diligent note taking, but by the same token we must avoid dismissing 50 minutes of mutually demanding work with such summary observations as "progress continues" or "prior issues resolved." Nonphysician mental health professionals may not be called upon to identify every single prescription medication currently taken by a client upon intake—psychiatrists, of course, may—but such unembellished notations as "on meds per referral" or "already medicated" may prove little more than puzzling if not clarified further at some point in the course of treatment.

Accuracy of billing and payments is a particular concern for private practitioners, who by definition cannot typically avail themselves of the same invoice filing, fee collection, and other financial support services as those used by colleagues who are employed in institutional settings. Billing irregularities can create friction between psychotherapists and clients and in extreme cases can incur allegations of insurance fraud. Inadvertent errors are by definition not fraudulent ones, but they may result in a temporary freezing of payments pending the conclusion of an investigation. Timeliness is rarely addressed but is a relevant factor here; private practitioners who get behind in their fee documentation and who must rely upon stray bits of scrap paper and months-old self-directed voice mail messages are all the more likely to make mistakes under time pressure when struggling to reconstruct billing records for submission to third-party payment sources and others.

Compliance with the law refers not only to how properly designed documentation contributes globally to the private practitioner's complex and evolving legal obligations, but also to the fashion in which a given jurisdiction's statutes, regulations, and case law may dictate the contents and process of recordkeeping per se. Whether venturing out into private practice for the first time, opening a private practice in a new state, or just seeking periodically to ensure that our grasp of legal dictates is sufficiently thorough and up to date, we need to remain aware of what such requirements are and develop strategies to accommodate them. Chapters in this *Handbook* on "Collaborating with Legal Professionals" (Chapter 31) and "The Role of an Attorney in a Private Practice" (Chapter 17) offer some additional guidance in this regard.

The APA (2007) has also promulgated "Record Keeping Guidelines" that—while "aspirational in intent" (p. 993)—offer at least some practical assistance in adhering to the mandatory rules expressed in the APA Ethics Code. With respect to Standard 6.01 of the APA Ethics Code, the APA guidelines provide a somewhat more detailed list of considerations in creating records, including the intent to "provide good care," "assist collaborating professionals in delivery of care," "ensure continuity of professional services in case of the psychologist's injury, disability, or death or with a change or provider," "provide for supervision or training if relevant," "provide documentation required for reimbursement or required administratively under contracts or laws," "effectively document any decision making, especially in high-risk situations," and "allow the psychologist to effectively answer a legal or regulatory complaint" (p. 995).

The APA guidelines also contain examples—too detailed for complete recounting in this chapter—of the sorts of content that may ensue from the private practitioner's attempts to arrive at "choices about the level of detail in which the case is documented" (APA, 2007, p. 995). Noting that "the records of psychological services may include information of three kinds," the guidelines offer a distinction between what would generally be "in the client's file" (including such material as "identifying data," "fees and billing information," and "health and developmental history"), "for each substantial contact" (including such material as "dates of service and duration of session," "types of services," and " formal or informal assessment of client status"), and "other specific information" (including such material as "plans for future interventions," "prognosis," and "relevant cultural and sociopolitical factors") (p. 996).

An overt focus on requirements and associated perils runs the risk of ignoring the many positive benefits of documentation. Properly guided documentation steadies the mental professional's orientation toward ultimate treatment goals. It decreases any tendencies toward excessive—and thus potentially stigmatizing—detail. Streamlined depictions of what transpires during service provision enable fellow mental health professionals to orient their own contributions toward what the patient or client is truly seeking as opposed to what stray or speculative observations may misleadingly suggest.

# MAINTAINING RECORDS

Once records have been created, they must then be properly maintained. This exercise does not merely consist of adding to and augmenting the initial content previously addressed in this chapter; rather, maintaining records involves a discrete, transformational level of documentation. A primary concern here—and at every other stage in the evolution of clinical records—is confidentiality. According to Standard 6.02, Maintenance, Dissemination, and Disposal of Confidential Records of Professional and Scientific Work, of the APA Ethics Code (APA, 2010), psychologists are required to "maintain confidentiality" with respect to "records under their control," including the use of "coding or other techniques to avoid the inclusion of personal identifiers" when records may be "available to persons whose access has not been consented to" by the client in question (p. 8).

The ACA Code of Ethics (2014) advises counselors to "maintain records and documentation necessary for rendering professional services" and to "ensure that records and documentation kept in any medium are secure and that only authorized persons have access to them" (pp. 7–8). According to the AAMFT Code of Ethics (2015), a marriage and family therapist "does not provide access to records without a written authorization from each individual competent to execute a waiver" (p. 3). The NASW Code of Ethics (2008) establishes that social workers should "protect the confidentiality of clients' written and electronic records and other sensitive information" (p. 6) by means of proper maintenance procedures.

Fisher (2012) afforded considerable attention to how "confidentiality and record keeping" are managed in the specific context of "independent clinical practice," acknowledging that for better or worse private practitioners are "completely responsible for developing, on their own, clear confidentiality policies" and for "preparing to explain it to clients in a simple and un-defensive manner" (p. 367). This recognition certainly comports with requirement described in Standard 10.01, Informed Consent to Therapy, of the APA Ethics Code (APA, 2010) that "psychologists inform clients/patients as early as is feasible in the therapeutic relationship" regarding "limits of confidentiality" (p. 13). Fisher (2012) plausibly recommended that private practitioners compose a "client handout" that "must be personalized to reflect each psychologist's actual intentions about confidentiality and disclosure, which means that no canned information form will suffice" (p. 347). Appropriately targeted composition of such handouts would be a critical concern; as Pope (2015) asserted, "a form filled with dense prose and multisyllabic legalese" could feature prominently in what he characterized as "a wonderful opportunity to sabotage the therapist-patient alliance, provide the patient with a Kafkaesque experience, and neglect the therapist's actual responsibilities" (p. 250).

As one can easily divine from Chapter 37 in this *Handbook*, "HIPAA 101 for the Private Practitioner," a particularly difficult notion for many of us to grasp and implement has been that of the separate maintenance in our records of psychotherapy notes if these notes involve electronic submissions. This is illustrated as clearly as it troublingly by a survey of 464 doctoral-level psychologists, conducted by DeLettre and Sobell (2010), who reported that

> Although 79% of those surveyed said that they were aware of the HIPAA Privacy Rule allowing for a separate set of notes, slightly less than half (46%) reported currently using such notes even though half (49%) felt that patients benefit most from the use of a separate set of psychotherapy notes. Surprisingly, 21% said they had never heard of the HIPAA provision allowing for a separate set of notes. (p. 160)

The APA's recordkeeping guidelines (APA, 2007) generally assert that "the usefulness of psychological service records often depends on the records being systematically updated and logically organized," which would help to ensure "thoroughness and accuracy of records, as well as efficient retrieval," in a fashion that "permits the psychologist to monitor ongoing care and interventions" (pp. 997–998). Additionally, these guidelines confirm that at times "the manner in which records are maintained may potentially affect the client in ways that may be unanticipated by the client" (p. 997), underscoring the importance of informed consent procedures mandated by each mental health profession's code of ethics.

Younggren (2010), citing what he was moved to characterize in the title of his article as "Rampant Record Keeping Chaos," characterized the APA's recordkeeping guidelines with respect to maintenance issues as "a document that provides significant theoretical and philosophical guidance to psychologists without much specificity" (p. 5). In an article co-authored by each person who had chaired the committee that promulgated the current version of these guidelines, Drogin, Connell, Foote, and Sturm (2010) similarly asserted that with respect to "maintenance of records" the guidelines left some notions either "unarticulated" or confusing "at first blush" (p. 238), and provided the following recommendation:

We now suggest adding another measure: the purchase or development of an overall electronic tracking system that is searchable by client name, date of initiation of services, and physical file location. This could be as simple and easy as compiling a word processing document—with appropriate password protection—to which the clinician adds an accounting of each file as it is either opened or sent away to long-term storage. (p. 239)

# STORING RECORDS

Records that were skillfully created and are expertly maintained will benefit no one and may harm many if they are inadvertently destroyed or illicitly procured. Although thematically related to the confidentiality concerns that form so much of the scholarly and practical discourse concerning the notion of record maintenance, matters of record storage and protection address additional elements of physical deterioration and outright theft. They are also evolving more quickly than most other recordkeeping considerations due to the ongoing enhancement of electronic data management options and increasingly sophisticated methods of hacking such data.

An essential aspect of protecting records is ensuring that arrangements have made in this regard in the event that private practitioners are temporarily—and perhaps permanently—incapable of overseeing this directly. Standard 6.01 of the APA Ethics Code directs psychologists to "make plans in advance to facilitate the appropriate transfer and to protect the confidentiality of records and data in the event of psychologists' withdrawal from positions or practice" (APA, 2010, p. 8). Such "withdrawal" may not, of course, be wholly or even partially voluntary. It is increasingly common to see various state jurisdictions—including, of course, those with regulations that incorporate the APA Ethics Code by reference—to direct private practitioners to construct and in some cases to file "professional wills" that specify to whom the responsibility for record protection will fall in the event of the therapist's death or disability.

According to the ACA Code of Ethics (2014), counselors store records in a fashion designed to "ensure reasonable future access" (p. 8) and identify a "colleague or records custodian" to manage records "in the case of the counselor's incapacitation, death, retirement, or termination of practice" (p. 9). The AAMFT Code of Ethics (2015) encourages marriage and family therapists to anticipate "moving a practice, closing a practice, or death" by means that "maintain confidentiality and safeguard the welfare of clients" (p. 3). Social workers are advised by the NASW Code of Ethics (2008) to "take reasonable precautions to protect client confidentiality in the event of the social worker's termination of practice, incapacitation, or death" (p. 6).

According to the APA's recordkeeping guidelines (APA, 2007):

> In anticipation of unexpected events, such as disability, death, or involuntary withdrawal from practice, the psychologist may wish to develop a disposition plan in which provisions are made for the control and management of the records by a trained individual or agency. In other circumstances, when the psychologist plans to leave employment, close a practice, or retire, similar arrangements may be made or the psychologist may wish to retain custody and control of client records. (p. 1002)

Devereaux and Gottlieb (2012) addressed from ethical and practical perspectives the now almost ubiquitous phenomenon of "cloud storage," drawing distinctions between the implications of such options as "on-demand self-service," "broad network access," "resource pooling," "rapid elasticity capabilities," and "measured service" (pp. 628–629). A detailed review of these paradigms is beyond the scope of this chapter, but it suffices to point out at this juncture that the difference lies in the service provider's contractually acknowledged obligations to provide (and block) access with varying levels and forms of accessibility and security. The APA's recordkeeping guidelines (APA, 2007) further underscore the need to "limit access of records to appropriately trained individuals and others with legitimate need to see the records" (p. 998). According to Devereaux and Gottlieb (2012), the following questions may be useful in choosing among cloud storage providers and packages:

1. How are employees monitored for access to consumer files?
2. Who will have access to these records and under what circumstances?
3. How robust are the firewalls and other security features compared to similar companies?
4. Have any breaches occurred in the past?
5. How are breaches handled? For example, are consumers notified?
6. What is the provider's experience working with protected data such as mental health records?
7. How are records deleted upon service termination? (p. 631)

A useful addition would be consideration of the use of offsite backups. If, for example, there is an equipment failure, fire, or earthquake in one's office, there would still exist a "mirror" file elsewhere that can be retrieved. Overall, such questions would be particularly useful bases for the construction of a Health Insurance Portability and Accountability Act (HIPAA)-compliant Business Associates Agreement when contracting with such companies.

When records are directly stored and protected by the private practitioner as opposed to a carefully chosen and monitored service provider, the APA's recordkeeping guidelines (APA, 2007) encourage psychologists to "keep paper records in a secure manner in safe locations where they may be protected from damage and destruction (e.g., fire, water, mold, insects)," to store "condensed records" as a backup resource "in separate locations so as to preserve a copy from natural or other disasters," and to offer "electronic records stored on magnetic and other electronic media" protection from "electric fields or mechanical insult, power surges or outage, and attack from viruses, worms, or other destructive programs" (p. 998). Locking file cabinets and other storage areas for various media is a paramount consideration.

# DISCLOSING RECORDS

Having created, maintained, and stored data in an ethical and legally consistent fashion, private practitioners are then subjected to what is probably the most stressful aspect of recordkeeping—requests (including outright demands) for the disclosure of this material. What can be provided?

To whom? How? When? It sometimes seems to be the case that clients, colleagues, and the courts clamor for records in the vaguest way ("my files"), with the most potentially complex of justifications ("I'm her mother"), with the tightest of deadlines ("the trial starts Tuesday").

In full recognition that many of these issues are addressed elsewhere in this *Handbook*—for example, in Chapter 39, "Dealing with Third Parties: Legal and Ethical Considerations," and Chapter 34, "Common Ethical Transgressions by Private Practitioners," to identify but two—it may be helpful to share here a few notions in particular with relevance to disclosing records. First, absent a very specifically worded court order, private practitioners need not bow to pressures to provide information "immediately," "instantly," "right away," "now," or "at once." Time must be afforded for due diligence, and it is when unnecessarily internalizing the requesting party's expressed sense of urgency that we tend to make the most—and worst—mistakes. Second, it is not advisable to acknowledge having had any contact with a client in the context of a third party's attempt to obtain records. An appropriate response to "I'm seeking records for so-and-so" is not, for example, "yes, he is my client, but I cannot release anything until I can get in touch with him and obtain the necessary permissions." A better reply would be something along the lines of "I can't confirm that I have or have not seen anyone, but if you can send your request in writing—as an electronic mail attachment, should you prefer—then I will respond on that basis." Third, the client's request or the court's order must be obtained *in writing*. Verbal instructions or assurances will never suffice for a transaction of this magnitude and importance.

For better or worse—and the debate on how to characterize the benefits or pitfalls of this development has raged back and forth now for nearly a decade and a half—the current version of the APA Ethics Code (2010) no longer requires psychologists to struggle as gamely as in the past when fielding requests for records that contain what Standard 9.04, Release of Test Data, defines as "test data" ("raw and scaled scores, client/patient responses to test questions or stimuli, and psychologists' notes and recordings concerning client/patient behavior during an examination"), such that now private practitioners "may" elect not to release this information "to protect a client/patient or others from substantial harm or misuse or misrepresentation of the data or the test" (pp. 12–13).

The most relevant and practical implication of the further instruction in Standard 9.01 that "in the absence of a client/patient release, psychologists provide test data only as required by law or court order" (APA, 2010, p. 12) is that releases, regulations, statutory mandates, and court orders *will* suffice for effectuating a release of records that contain test data. With respect to test materials—defined by Standard 9.11, Maintaining Test Security, as "manuals, instruments, protocols, and test questions or stimuli," private practitioners need only "make reasonable efforts to maintain the integrity and security of test materials and other assessment techniques consistent with law and contractual obligations, and in a manner that permits adherence to this Ethics Code" (APA, 2010, p. 13).

The APA's Committee on Legal Issues recently offered an updated version of Strategies for Private Practitioners Coping with Subpoenas or Compelled Testimony for Client/Patient Records or Test Data or Test Materials (APA, 2016). According to this particular source of guidance, we may ultimately decide to "determine whether the request for information carries the force of law," "contact the client/patient," "negotiate with the requester," and "file a motion to quash the subpoena or file a protective order" (pp. 2–4). Bases for "opposing or limiting production of client/

patient records or data" may include the court's lack of "jurisdiction," the private practitioner's lack of "custody or control of the records," the existence of some legal "privilege" that "insulates the records" from being disclosed, and a determination that "the information sought is not relevant to the issues before the court" (pp. 4–5). Private practitioners will instantly realize with these lists of options that consultation with legal counsel may be necessary to advance such arguments effectively.

The APA Ethics Code makes it clear in Standard 6.03, Withholding Records for Nonpayment, that private practitioners "may not withhold records under their control that are requested and needed for a client's/patient's emergency treatment solely because payment has not been received" (APA, 2010, p. 9). This is not, perhaps, the most effective language for achieving what was presumably the drafter's intent. On its face, this provision could be construed as calling for us to determine what sort of treatment is being contemplated, whether such treatment truly reflects "emergency" circumstances, and whether the records are truly "needed" to support such treatment—not to mention that the inclusion of any additional basis for withholding records would presumably enable nonpayment as a relevant justification. A simpler, safer approach is simply to provide records in response to any appropriate request and treat fee collections as a wholly separate issue.

The ACA Code of Ethics (2014) stresses the importance of informing clients about "procedures for nonpayment of fees" (p. 4) but does not address the issue of potential withholding of records in this context. By contrast, the AAMFT Code of Ethics (2015) directly states that "marriage and family therapists may not withhold records under their immediate control that are requested and needed for a client's treatment solely because payment has not been received for past services, except as otherwise provided by law" (p. 6). The NASW Code of Ethics (2008) asserts that "social workers should limit their clients' access to their records, or portions of their records, only in exceptional circumstances when there is compelling evidence that such access would cause serious harm to the client" (p. 7).

If records are going to be disclosed electronically or by means of what is now colloquially termed "snail mail," private practitioners should take pains to verify physical mailing addresses, email addresses, and fax numbers. Packages and messages should be labeled as confidential (with the latter being encrypted when feasible), and email signature blocks are best embellished with language warning that, for example, "the contents of this electronic message are or may be protected by the psychotherapist-client privilege, work product doctrine, and/or other applicable protections from disclosure. If the reader of this message is not the intended recipient, you are hereby notified that any use, dissemination, distribution or reproduction of this communication is strictly prohibited." It may also be prudent to recommend that the recipient notify the sender as well, so that the latter is made aware of the problem and can take action accordingly.

## DESTROYING RECORDS

What options do we have for trimming or simply discarding decades' worth of accumulated records? How long do we have to wait to do so? One option, of course, would be to have this material "digitized" and to bid the accumulated mountain of paper goodbye once and for all.

Scanning records into a computer and transforming them into electronic files is both time-consuming and costly—two notions that can intersect dramatically in the professional life of the private practitioner. There are also perhaps certain documents, including those that bear signatures or that are only temporarily in our custody, that must still be tended in their original "hard copy" form. As a general matter, one way to reduce the accumulation of paper records is to digitize prospectively, so that at least future rows of manila folders are leaner and thus less expensive and cumbersome to store.

According to Standard 6.02, Maintenance, Dissemination, and Disposal of Confidential Records of Professional and Scientific Work, of the APA Ethics Code (2010), the private practitioner's obligation to "maintain confidentiality" remains critical when "disposing of records," whether such records are "written, automated, or in any other medium" (pp. 8–9). More finesse is required, of course, than tossing files into the office dumpster or pressing "delete" on the office computer. Physically stored records must be shredded or incinerated by the private practitioner or by a disposal service that acknowledges in writing its adherence to established legal obligations. Many clinicians pay a surcharge to have the disposal service destroy records on site at the same time as these are removed from storage. A computer that has housed electronic records cannot be converted to other, less secured uses or handed over to another individual—professional or otherwise—without being subjected to the most up-to-date and thorough of data cleansing procedures.

"Spoliation" is the legal term for disposing of records when retaining them is required by case law, statutes, regulations, or a judge's order in a particular ongoing matter. For private practitioners conducting forensic evaluations, the APA's Specialty Guidelines for Forensic Psychology (APA, 2013) reflect a sensitivity to this issue when calling not only for a "reasonable level of knowledge and understanding of the legal and professional standards, laws, rules, and precedents that govern their participation in legal proceedings" (p. 9), but also for consideration of preserving records "until notified that all appeals in the matter have been exhausted, or sending a copy of any unique components/aspects of the record in their care and control to the retaining party before destruction of the record" (p. 16).

The APA's recordkeeping guidelines (APA, 2007) recommend that

> In the absence of a superseding requirement, psychologists may consider retaining full records until 7 years after the last date of service delivery for adults or until 3 years after a minor reaches the age of majority, whichever is later. In some circumstances, the psychologist may wish to keep records for a longer period, weighing the risks associated with obsolete or outdate information, or privacy loss, versus the potential benefits associated with preserving the records. (p. 999)

These collisions of potential interests tap directly into the "duality" of concerns that was identified at the beginning of this chapter. Whereas historically the primary focus of professional guidance in this regard was on making sure that records were kept for a sufficient period of time, there is now a "striking contrast" (Drogin, Connell, Foote, & Sturm, 2010, p. 239) to be found in the focus of the current version of the recordkeeping guidelines (APA, 2007), buttressed, for example, by suggestions that "the client may be served by the disposal of the record as soon as allowed," as some material may, for example, eventually prove "demeaning or embarrassing" (p. 999).

As an example, consider a client's descriptions of extensive childhood physical and sexual abuse by a named individual. In clinical practice this is unlikely to be required viewing for most clinicians who may ultimately access the medical record (e.g., internists, hospital nurses, or specialist physicians). It is unlikely that the author of the note will later need a detailed written narrative to recall the patient's story, and if this is needed that goal could be better accomplished with individual "psychotherapy notes" or "process notes." Insurance reviewers do not need access to said details, nor would a reviewing attorney or forensic evaluator in the event of a malpractice suit. Finally, the client, who supplied these details, might find it objectionable if copies ended up in the hands of friends, family members, or other important people in his or her life.

Overall, we must take into account the above-noted possibility of a superseding requirement. Virtually every jurisdiction now dictates how long certain types of mental health records must be retained, often based upon such factors as the context in which data were obtained, the age of the patient or client at the time that clinical services were rendered, and the extent to which the requisite retention may be tolled by various forms of subsequent use or access. Records do not *need* to be destroyed at a particular point in time; rather, regulations specify the earliest time when records *may* be destroyed.

In support of what the APA Ethics Code (2010) specifies in Standard 2.01, Boundaries of Competence, as a need for forensic evaluators to remain "reasonably familiar with the judicial or administrative rules governing their roles" (pp. 4–5) and in Standard 1.02, Conflicts between Ethics and Law, Regulations, or Other Governing Legal Authority, as a need for all private practitioners to consider how under certain circumstances we might "adhere to the requirements of the law, regulations, or other governing legal authority" (p. 4), we need to maintain a tracking system that enables us to determine the vintage of particular patient or client files, and in some cases that also documents when we might have accessed them for various purposes, so that a well-reasoned process for data disposition can be supported. That tracking system—including passwords for coded access—will itself need to be stored securely.

The ACA Code of Ethics (2014) advises counselors to "dispose of client records and other sensitive materials in a manner that protects client confidentiality" and to "apply careful discretion and deliberation before destroying records that may be needed by a court of law" (p. 8). According to the AAMFT Code of Ethics (2015), "disposal of records" by marriage and family therapists should only occur "in ways that maintain confidentiality and in accord with applicable laws and professional standards" (p. 3). Similarly, the NASW Code of Ethics (2008) indicates that social workers should "dispose of clients' records in a manner that protects confidentiality and is consistent with state statutes governing records and social work licensure" (p. 6).

Recordkeeping is, for the private practitioner, an exercise both supportive of the effective provision of clinical services and fraught with professional danger for those of us who could so easily lose track of an evolving array of physical, communicative, temporal, and financially demanding considerations. Periodic consultation with legal and ethical sources of guidance and faithful adherence to a properly developed, fully articulated, and periodically revised plan for creating, maintaining, storing, disclosing, and storing records is the most responsible way to ensure success in this regard.

# REFERENCES

American Association for Marriage and Family Therapy. (2015). *Code of Ethics.* Retrieved from http://www. aamft.org/iMIS15/AAMFT/Content/Legal_Ethics/Code_of_Ethics.aspx.

American Counseling Association. (2014). *ACA code of ethics.* Retrieved from https://www.counseling.org/ resources/aca-code-of-ethics.pdf.

American Psychological Association. (2007). Record keeping guidelines. *American Psychologist, 62,* 933–1004.

American Psychological Association. (2010). *Ethical principles of psychologists and code of conduct.* Retrieved from http://www.apa.org/ethics.

American Psychological Association. (2013). Specialty guidelines for forensic psychology. *American Psychologist, 68,* 7–19.

Committee on Legal Issues, American Psychological Association. (2016). Strategies for private practitioners coping with subpoenas or compelled testimony for client/patient records or test date or test materials. *Professional Psychology: Research and Practice, 47,* 1–11.

DeLettre, J. L., & Sobell, L. C. (2012). Keeping psychotherapy notes separate from the patient record. *Clinical Psychology and Psychotherapy, 17,* 160–163.

Devereaux, R. L., & Gottlieb, M. C. (2012). Record keeping in the cloud: Ethical considerations. *Professional Psychology: Research and Practice, 43,* 627–632.

Drogin, E. Y., Connell, M., Foote, W. E., & Sturm, C. A. (2010). The American Psychological Association's "Record Keeping Guidelines": Implications for the practitioner. *Professional Psychology: Research and Practice, 41,* 236–243.

Fisher, M. A. (2012). Confidentiality and record keeping. In S. J. Knapp, M. C. Gottlieb, M. M. Handelsman, & L. D. VandeCreek (Eds.), *APA handbook of ethics in psychology* (Vol. 1, pp. 333–375). Washington, DC: American Psychological Association.

National Association of Marriage and Family Therapists. (2015). *Code of ethics.* Retrieved from http://www. aamft.org/iMIS15/AAMFT/Content/Legal_Ethics/Code_of_Ethics.aspx.

National Association of Social Workers. (2008). *Code of ethics of the National Association of Social Workers.* Retrieved from https://www.socialworkers.org/pubs/code.

Pope, K. S. (2015). Record-keeping controversies: Ethical, legal, and clinical challenges. *Canadian Psychology, 56,* 348–356.

Younggren, J. N. (2010). Rampant record keeping chaos. *The Clinical Psychologist, 64*(3), 5–6.

# CHAPTER 7

# MEASURING CLINICAL PROGRESS WITH THE OQ-45 IN A PRIVATE PRACTICE SETTING

*Michael J. Lambert*

## HOW SUCCESSFUL ARE CLINICIANS AT PREDICTING IMPROVEMENT?

Since the inception of psychotherapy to the present day, clinicians' estimates of how many of their clients derive a benefit from their services has hovered around 85%, with most clinicians regarding the outcomes found in their own practice surpassing those obtained by other clinicians (Walfish et al., 2012). This is a rather high estimate compared with that derived from formal research estimates coming from randomized clinical trials quantifying benefits based mainly on measured change using client reports: Such estimates generally hover around two-thirds of clients either recovering or reliably improving (Hansen, Lambert, & Forman, 2003). The 85% figure is much higher than estimates of measured outcome based on outcomes in routine care, which are typically closer to one-third recovered or improved (Hansen, Lambert, & Forman, 2003). In such studies clients complete self-report questionnaires before they enter treatment and after they complete treatment. The posttherapy questionnaire score is subtracted from the pretherapy score, resulting in a difference score that represents amount of change and eventually the percentage of individuals who improve, recover, are unchanged, or get worse.

For example, in studies of depression a client self-report scale such as the Beck Depression Inventory (Beck, Ward, Mendelson, Mock, & Erbaugh, 1961) is completed by the client before and after treatment. It presumably measures degree of depressive symptomatic distress borne by the client at each point in time. Normative data are available to benchmark normal functioning and dysfunction as well as error of measurement, permitting a rather precise (or at least replicable) estimate of improvement in depressive symptomology.

In addition, it would be typical to have a trained expert interview the client before treatment and an independent expert interview the client after treatment, both rating the client's depressive symptoms using a scale like the Hamilton Depression Rating Scale. In clinical trials it would be highly unusual to get input from the treating clinician about his or her view of client benefit. Just what criteria clinicians use to make estimates of clients' success are unknown (and possibly too vague), and the clinician is assumed to have an overly favorable bias when it comes to evaluating the consequences of his or her own work. These methodological differences may explain why clinical trials often estimate that about two-thirds of clients (not 85%) benefit from treatment, while around 8% deteriorate (Hansen, Lambert, & Forman, 2003). Measured estimates of positive outcome in routine care are closer to 40%, less than half the number informally estimated by clinicians (Lambert, 2013). Perhaps because psychotherapists spend hours listening to their clients and know them intimately (while researchers do not), they have a more accurate view of actual benefits, including those that may not be precisely measured by researchers.

However, there appears to be a particular problem with psychotherapists' recognizing client deterioration in psychotherapy. To examine psychotherapists' accuracy in predicting poor treatment outcome, Hannan et al. (2005) asked 40 psychotherapists (20 trainees and 20 experienced professionals) at the end of each session with each of their clients if they believed the client would leave treatment in a deteriorated state, and, in addition, if the client was worse off at this particular session than when he or she entered treatment. We expected that experienced clinicians, given their extensive contact with clients over the years, would be more accurate in their judgments than trainees (who ranged from first-year graduate students to intern-level providers).

The psychotherapists were aware of the purpose of the study, understanding it to be a contest between experienced and less experienced providers, compared with statistical methods. They also understood that there was no consequence to the client for making any prediction, as the research was aimed at understanding how well clinicians could forecast negative final treatment outcome. They were aware that the dependent measure used to categorize client change was the Outcome Questionnaire-45 (OQ-45; to be described shortly), which was administered on a weekly basis, and understood the cutoff scores for judging deterioration, but they did not have access to the client's OQ-45 scores. They were reminded that the base rate for deterioration was likely to be 8%, so the phenomenon they were to predict was relatively rare, occurring in perhaps 1 in 10 of their clients. Thus, the experiment was a straightforward contest between licensed providers (with an average of 10 years postdoctoral experience), novice providers (mostly psychology trainees), and empirical algorithms.

During a three-week period predictions were made for 550 clients who participated in psychotherapy sessions. In every other way treatment continued as usual and clients' progress was followed until they terminated treatment, at which time their intake OQ-45 score could be compared with their end-of-treatment OQ-45 score. While 40 clients were deteriorated at termination of treatment, only 3 of 550 clients (0.01%) were predicted by their psychotherapist to leave treatment worse off than when they began treatment. In general, clients' eventual deterioration was not forecast by clinicians who were attempting to do so. Rather than experienced clinicians being better able to predict the phenomenon, they *did not identify a single client who deteriorated*—the only accurate prediction out of the three that were made was made by a trainee. In contrast, 36 of the 40 (90%) clients who deteriorated were predicted to do so based on applying actuarial predictive methods to data. This study provides evidence that psychotherapists not only cannot/ do not predict end-of-treatment deterioration, but they also see nearly 40% of clients as being in an improved state (based on the question "How is your client doing today compared to when they started treatment?") even though they were reporting more symptoms (on the OQ-45) than they had when they started treatment.

The ability of statistical methods based on the OQ-45 to predict treatment failure is well documented through five published studies (e.g., Lambert et al., 2002) suggesting that between 85% and 100% of clients who deteriorate can be identified well before treatment termination. It is no wonder that psychotherapists have a hard time preventing treatment failure; their perception of progress and outcome is at odds with measured mental health functioning. Just as we do not expect physicians to manage illness without measuring and monitoring lab test data, we cannot expect psychotherapists to manage treatment of clients well without psychological lab tests.

The tendency to ignore the warning signs of treatment failure probably has several causes:

1.  Self-assessment bias (the tendency to overvalue one's work) is common across professions and trades where individuals do not receive performance feedback.
2.  This bias is likely to be especially strong in complex situations such as psychotherapy, where practitioners have little control over client decision making, as well as social, biological, and contextual factors that affect mental health functioning.
3.  The work of Hill, Thompson, Cogar, and Denman (1993) based on video-assisted client recall of sessions suggests that clients intentionally hide or mask negative reactions within sessions, thus misleading psychotherapists.
4.  Since it would take considerable time for psychotherapists to assess a client's life functioning at each session without the use of a self-report measure, it is impossible for clinicians to gather the necessary data to judge progress.
5.  Prediction of treatment failure is too complex for the human mind, while a computer algorithm can quickly weigh the predictive factors such as "exact" degree of initial disturbance, and functioning later in treatment, and then compare change in a particular case against that made by hundreds of similar cases.

There is good reason to believe that psychotherapists are overly optimistic about the effects they have on clients' mental health functioning and that this tendency probably hinders positive treatment response for a substantial number of cases. This is because psychotherapists consistently fail to identify those individuals who go on to have a negative outcome. The obvious solution is to rely on science to identify potential treatment failures, a job it is better suited to than clinical intuition.

## MONITORING CLINICAL PROGRESS

There is one central reason for measuring clinical progress in a private practice setting: It has been shown to maximize client outcomes compared to practicing in the absence of measuring progress. In addition, the information can be used as a part of other sound professional practices such as estimating treatment length. This chapter describes the necessary characteristics of effective progress monitoring practices, the characteristics of one monitoring system, the degree to which progress monitoring can be expected to improve client treatment response, and how to implement monitoring.

Progress monitoring and feedback have roots in behaviorism, particularly operant conditioning, with its focus on targeting behavior for modification through the use of monitoring and reinforcement. Behavior therapies in this context typically monitored and modified specific behaviors (e.g., treatment of the behavior problems of an autistic child through the use of operant conditioning). The current use of monitoring and feedback under discussion bears little resemblance to behaviorism and the experimental analysis of behavior except for a similar devotion to tracking the "consequences" of treatment in the form of creating progress graphs and feeding back this information to psychotherapists (and clients). Rather than focusing on specific behaviors, the client's overall mental health functioning is the target of interest, and there is no particular focus on learning theories and human conditioning.

With regards to improving the treatment response of clients in psychotherapy, our work in this area began in 1992 with (1) development of a self-report measure (the Outcome Questionnaire-45 [OQ-45]) of psychological disturbance/functioning, (2) prediction of treatment failure, and (3) eventually the development of software (OQ-Analyst) aimed at scoring the measure, applying predictive algorithms, and delivering the feedback instantaneously to psychotherapists (www.OQMeasures.com). While there are thousands of self-report measures that could have been selected for use, and many other measures based on expert judge ratings, psychotherapist ratings, and naturalistic data such as arrest records, our aim was to develop a single measure that would capture four broad areas of adult mental health—symptomatic distress (mostly depression and anxiety), interpersonal problems, social role disturbance (work, school, homemaking), and well-being (positive functioning). Thus, instead of counting specific behaviors as a behaviorist might, monitoring of internal pain, interpersonal pain, and functioning in daily roles were the outcomes of interest. But more important than the specific measure chosen for use was its ability to predict treatment failure. Thus, many measures can accurately assess mental health functioning, but few have the proven capacity to identify potential treatment failures. It is not sufficient to select any measure for the purpose of progress monitoring since identification of clients at risk for treatment failure is such an important characteristic of suitable measures. Drapeau (2012) has reviewed 10 measures made specifically for monitoring, and the interested reader may want to review these alternative approaches. Because much of the discussion that follows is based on specific measures we developed for monitoring, before proceeding with general topics it is important to highlight a couple of measures that have been used extensively in our work.

# THE OQ-45

## MEASURE AND PSYCHOMETRICS

OQ-45 respondents estimate frequencies of occurrence of 45 symptoms, emotional states, interpersonal relationships, and social role functioning over the past week. Thirty-six negatively worded items (e.g., item 5, "I feel blue") are scored *Never* = 0, *Rarely* = 1, *Sometimes* = 2, *Frequently* = 3, and *Almost Always* = 4. Scoring is reversed (*Never* = 4, *Rarely* = 3, *Frequently* = 1, *Almost Always* = 0) for 9 positively worded items (e.g., item 13, "I am a happy person"). This yields a total score ranging from 0 to 180. Higher scores reveal more frequent symptoms, distress, interpersonal problems, and social dysfunction and less frequent positive emotional states, pleasant experiences, successful social relationships, and adaptive role functioning.

The Administration and Scoring Manual (Lambert et al., 2013) reports information on population norms, reliability, concurrent and construct validity, factor structure, and cross-cultural data. These data suggest that the OQ-45 provides an index of mental health/dysfunction and reflects the degree of disturbance a person is currently experiencing or willing to report. Evidence supporting the factor structure of the OQ-45 has been reported across a variety of client samples, and the findings have been replicated across settings and countries (e.g., Germany, Norway, Netherlands, Italy, Portugal, Israel, Poland, Canada). The studies vary in their findings but generally suggest a bi-factor model with a general psychological distress factor at one level and three subordinate factors similar to the subscales.

Normative data were collected nationally and internationally from samples gathered from community phone books, individuals attending colleges, and individuals working for a variety of business organizations. Such samples were combined to establish the level of functioning of non-clients (those taking psychoactive medications or participating in psychotherapy were screened out) and provide a benchmark for mental health. In contrast, client samples were gathered from inpatient samples, community mental health centers, outpatient clinics, private practice, university counseling centers, and employee assistance programs across the United States.

Using the preceding samples, normal functioning, dysfunction, and meaningful change could be empirically defined. A critical characteristic of outcome measures is defining clinically meaningful change. Clinically meaningful change refers to change in client functioning that is large enough to conclude that an individual client has been impacted by his or her participation in psychotherapy in meaningful ways. It provides markers for classifying a person's outcome as recovered, improved, unchanged, or deteriorated. In psychotherapy research meaningful change is commonly referred to as "clinically significant change" based on two criterion described by Jacobson and Truax (1991): that a client's score on an outcome measure changes enough that it is unlikely due to error of measurement (the Reliable Change Index) and that the client's score moves from one characterizing dysfunction to one that characterizes healthy functioning. Just as clinically significant change has been central in judging the relative value of empirically supported therapies as examined in clinical trials, it can help clinicians ground their clinical judgments about treatment success on empirically standardized defined criteria. Validity data for reliable change and clinically significant change as demarcations for meaningful client change have been published and suggest reasonable validity across instruments and measures. Results offer preliminary support for the use of the OQ-45 alone (instead of a battery of measures) to classify clients as functional or dysfunctional and to detect reliable change.

Lunnen and Ogles (1998) also reported a study that simultaneously used the OQ-45 and other measures of outcome to validate clinical significance cutoffs. The purpose of their study was to explore the practical meaning of cutoff scores and criteria for the Reliable Change Index. These authors compared the perceived level of change as subjectively reported from three distinct perspectives (client, psychotherapist, and significant other). They also compared reports of the therapeutic alliance and satisfaction across outcome groups. The results suggested that those clients who were classified as improved also were rated as most improved on psychotherapist and client ratings of perceived change. Improved clients also tended to have higher therapeutic alliance scores. Although more work needs to be done to validate the current cutoff scores, they appear to have important practical value and to be a central aspect of effectively using the OQ-45 and other measures.

According to a survey conducted by Hatfield and Ogles (2004), the OQ-45 is the third most frequently used self-report instrument for measuring adult client outcomes in the United States. Unlike most psychological tests, it was developed specifically for use in monitoring clients' mental health on a weekly basis during routine care. The measure is taken prior to each treatment session, requires about five minutes of client time, and comprises items that reflect the consequences of receiving care, while remaining stable in untreated controls.

## RELATED MEASURES

The OQ-Analyst software also contains a shorter version of the OQ-45, the OQ-30, also for adults, and a version, the Severe Outcome Questionnaire, for clients who have severe psychopathology such as bipolar disorder, schizophrenia, and other psychotic illnesses. In addition, the OQ-Analyst includes two measures for children, the 64-item Youth-Outcome Questionnaire and the 30-item Youth-Outcome Questionnaire, both in forms suitable for caregiver and youth self-report. The child measures include a problem-solving measure equivalent to the one used with adults.

## ASSESSMENT FOR SIGNAL CLIENTS (ASC)

When and if clients are at risk for a negative treatment outcome (about 18–40% of clients, depending on the treatment setting and clinician) they are asked to take the Assessment for Signal Clients (ASC; Lambert, 2010; Lambert, Bailey, White, Tingey, & Stevens, 2015). This 40-item self-report measure is designed to assess the kind and severity of problems that may be impeding treatment progress—specifically, problems with the therapeutic alliance, motivation, social support, and stressful life events. The items correspond to subscales that are then associated with specifically tailored interventions aimed at enhancing positive psychotherapy outcomes in clients predicted to be treatment failures. The ASC does not sum to a total score but provides a separate score and cutoff for each domain, along with a cutoff score for each item, that indicates a possible problem to be explored. The rationale for providing individual item feedback based on a cutoff score is that it enhances clinician problem solving more than a total subscale score.

For example, if the ASC alliance item "My therapist seems glad to see me" is rated below the cutoff, this suggests the psychotherapist may need to consider ways of greeting the client with more enthusiasm—feedback that is more actionable than just broadly indicating that there is a problem with the alliance. We find that clients who go off track for a positive outcome cluster into three types on the ASC: A third have problems internal to psychotherapy (i.e., alliance and

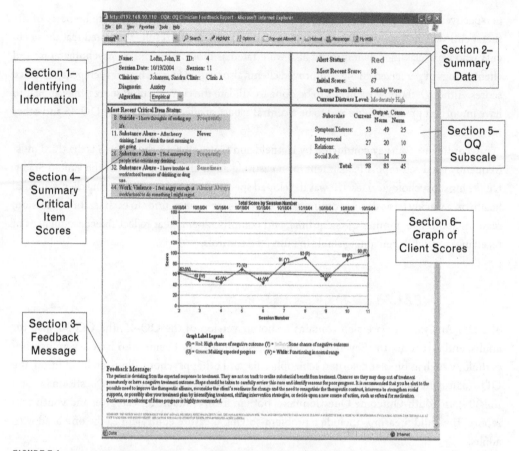

**FIGURE 7.1:** OQ-45 feedback graph displaying across 10 sessions of psychotherapy.

motivation); a third have problems external to psychotherapy (i.e., social support and negative life events); and a third have problems across all four areas (White et al., 2015).

The ASC is presented within the context of what we refer to as a Clinical Support Tool (CST). The CST contains a decision tree to organize psychotherapist problem solving, as well as a list of possible interventions that clinicians can consider in order to increase their responsiveness to the client. General suggestions, derived from the research literature, about ways to improve treatment are delineated in the CST. Given the importance of the therapeutic alliance as a predictor of outcome, it is suggested that the clinician consider the strength of the alliance before considering other variables that may be triggering negative effects.

Examples of psychotherapist feedback reports for the OQ-45 and ASC are provided in Figures 7.1 and 7.2. Clinicians enjoy seeing the graph of client progress over the course of psychotherapy, but the most important aspect of the report is in the upper right-hand corner indicating the client is a Not on Track case at the most recent session. The ASC report in Figure 7.2 indicates that "George" met the cutoff for having significantly poor ratings on the alliance and motivation subscales. Problem items within these subscales are listed, as well as significant items within the Social Support and Life Events categories, even though these latter two categories were not, on the whole, problematic. Clinicians can press the "display Intervention Handout" button for suggested actions to resolve problems that are hindering progress.

| | C-OQ45, GEORGE, | | | Subscales | Current Scores | Alerts |
|---|---|---|---|---|---|---|
| **Name:** | R | **ID:** | MRN0101 | | | |
| **Session Date:** | 12/25/2006 | **Session:** | 1 | Theraputic Alliance: | 39 | RED |
| **Clinician:** | Clinician, Bob | **Clinic:** | TX Dallas Clinic | Social Support: | 36 | |
| | | | | Motivation: | 30 | RED |
| **Diagnosis:** | Unknown Diagnosis | | | Life Events: | 29 | |
| **Instrument:** | ASC | | | | | |

Display Interventions Handout

| **Theraputic Alliance:**   RED | | **Social Support:** | |
|---|---|---|---|
| It is advisable that you address your relationship with the client. Please click 'Display Interventions Handout' button for more information. | | 15. I got the emotional help, and support I needed from someone in my family. | Strongly Disagree |
| 1. I felt cared for and respected as a person. | Neutral | | |
| 2. I felt my therapist understood me. | Neutral | 16. There was a special person who was around when I was in need. | Neutral |
| 3. I thought the suggestions my therapist made were useful. | Neutral | | |
| 4. I felt like I could trust my therapist completely. | Slightly Agree | 21. I felt connected to a higher power. | Strongly Disagree |
| 9. My therapist seemed to be glad to see me. | Neutral | | |
| 10. My therapist and I seemed to work well together to accomplish what I want. | Slightly Disagree | | |
| 11. My therapist and I had a similar understanding of my problems. | Slightly Disagree | | |

| **Motivation:**   RED | | **Life Events:** | |
|---|---|---|---|
| It is advisable that you address your client's motivation in therapy. Please click 'Display Interventions Handout' button for more information. | | 32. I had an interaction with another person that I found upsetting. | Strongly Agree |
| 23. I wonder what I am doing in therapy; actually I find it boring. | Slightly Agree | 38. I had health problems (such as physical pain). | Strongly Agree |
| 26. I had thoughts about quitting therapy; it's just not for me. | Slightly Agree | | |
| 27. I don't think therapy will help me feel any better. | Neutral | | |
| 28. I have no desire to work out my problems. | Strongly Agree | | |
| 31. I am in therapy because someone is requiring it of me. | Neutral | | |

FIGURE 7.2: Feedback report based on George's completion of the Assessment for Signal Client indication problem area for problem-solving.

To this point it is suggested that progress monitoring be based on defining outcome by using a five-minute client self-report measure aimed at quantifying depressive and anxiety-based symptoms, interpersonal problems, and societal role functioning as well as well-being/quality of life. These markers of mental health can be repeatedly measured over the course of treatment and compared with normative data as well as expected treatment response in other clients undergoing treatment. It is proposed that making monitoring a part of routine care will improve client outcomes. Is there evidence for this assertion?

# DO MEASURING, MONITORING, AND FEEDBACK ENHANCE PSYCHOTHERAPY OUTCOMES?

Table 7.1 lists 12 published clinical trials testing the effects of feedback on client well-being. The first six studies came out of our lab, with the raw data from these studies combined in a mega/meta-analysis published by Shimokawa, Lambert, and Smart (2010). The six studies have many similarities:

Each included consecutive cases seen in routine care regardless of client diagnosis or comorbid conditions (rather than being disorder specific).

Random assignment of client to experimental conditions (various feedback interventions) and treatment-as-usual conditions (no feedback) was made in four of the six studies, while reasonable measures were taken in two studies to ensure equivalence in experimental and control conditions at pretreatment.

Psychotherapists provided a variety of theoretically guided treatments, with most adhering to cognitive-behavioral and eclectic orientations and fewer representing psychodynamic and experiential orientations.

A variety of clinicians were involved—postgraduate psychotherapists and graduate students each accounted for about 50% of clients seen.

Psychotherapists saw both feedback and no-feedback cases, thus limiting the likelihood that outcome differences between conditions could be due to clinician effects.

The outcome measure as well as the methodology (rules/standards) for identifying not-on-track clients (failing cases) remained constant.

The length of treatment (dosage) was determined by client and therapist rather than by research design or arbitrary insurance limits.

Client characteristics such as gender, age, and ethnicity were generally similar across studies and came from the same university counseling center, with the exception of the Hawkins et al. study (2004), which was conducted in a hospital-based outpatient clinic.

The first discovery in this line of research was that progress monitoring and feedback was not helpful to all clients. Clients who make relatively steady progress continue to make steady progress

TABLE 7.1: Published Clinical Trials Examining the Effects of Progress Monitoring with Alarm Signals and Clinical Support Tool Feedback Using the OQ-45

| Study | NTotal/NOT[a] | Setting/Sample[b] | Significant Effect | CST | Effect Size (d) |
|---|---|---|---|---|---|
| Lambert et al. 2001 | 609/66 | CC | Yes | No | 0.44 |
| Lambert et al. 2002 | 1,422/240 | CC | Yes | No | 0.40 |
| Whipple et al. 2003 | 1,339/278 | CC | Yes | Yes | 0.70 |
| Hawkins et al. 2004 | 306/101 | OP | Yes | No | 0.28 |
| Harmon et al. 2007 | 1374/369 | CC | Yes | Yes | 0.73 |
| Slade et al. 2008 | 1101/328 | CC | Yes | Yes | 0.75 |
| Crits-Christoph et al. 2012 | 304/116 | SA | Yes | Yes | 0.48 |
| Simon et al. 2012 | 370/207 | OP | Yes | Yes | 0.12/0.34 |
| Simon et al. 2013 | 133/59 | ED/IP | Yes | Yes | 0.36 |
| De Jong et al. 2012[c] | 413/67 | OP | No/Yes | No | ? |
| Amble et al. 2014[d] | 259/? | OP | Yes | No | 0.32 |
| Propst et al. 2014[e] | 252/66 | IP/Som | Yes | Yes | 0.54 |

[a]The study N = the total sample; NOT = Not-on-Track cases (predicted treatment failure)
[b]CC = college counseling center clients; OP = outpatient clinics; SA = substance abuse clinics; ED = eating disorder patients; IP = inpatient treatment setting; Som = psychosomatic clients
[c]Study conducted in the Netherlands
[d]Study conducted in Norway
[e]Study conducted in Germany

even when their psychotherapist is notified that the progress from week to week is positive. This represents the majority of clients and reflects the fact that psychotherapy as it is routinely practiced is helping many individuals. The feedback did make a marked difference for clients who went significantly off track (about 18–40% of treated individuals, depending on the client population). The N's listed in Table 7.1 indicate the total number of individuals recruited into the study and the total number of Not-On-Track clients studied. The d statistic (effect size) presented is based on Not-On-Track clients. In the case of the Not-on-Track clients, notifying psychotherapists that the client was in trouble allowed clinicians and clients to change the future course of treatment. That is, psychotherapists and clients found a way to turn the course around, as can be seen in the small to large effect sizes.

Apparently this is achieved in many cases not with direct discussions with the client about OQ-45 or ASC scores, but rather via psychotherapist reflection and modifications of behaviors—for instance, becoming more responsive to client needs when the therapist becomes aware that progress is problematic. For example, an older male clinician was working with a college student who was approaching her wedding date and wanted his opinion about wedding gowns. He initially interpreted this topic as a matter of resistance to getting closer to her fears of marriage. Reflecting on the fact that she recently was identified as Not-on-Track on the OQ-45 and that her ASC showed definite problems with Social Support, he realized that as her wedding date approached she was beginning to have serious problems with her parents, who disapproved of her choice of partner. Each time she sought her mother's advice on the wedding, the mother used the opportunity to try to create doubt as to the wisdom of her choice. Her relationship with her parents was deteriorating. This gave the psychotherapist more insight into the meaning of his client seeking his opinion about dresses: She didn't have anyone else to turn to. He suggested that a conjoint session be scheduled with her parents to change the pattern that had emerged.

In other instances the psychotherapist initiated a discussion about progress: "Looks like you are feeling quite badly this week, and even worse than when we started. Most people are feeling more relief at this stage of treatment than you are, and I am hoping we can talk a bit about your progress." If the client has completed the ASC the discussion can be more specific: "I notice from the test I gave you that you don't really have anyone that you are close to that you can confide in right now. Has something changed?" Attention to lack of social support emerged as a therapeutic focus with a greater sense of immediacy. There are many things that psychotherapists might do with clients as a result of feedback and because they have the skills. These skills can be put to use once they are alerted to the existence of problems they have overlooked. It is often a matter of the psychotherapist being open and flexible.

The Shimokawa et al. (2010) summary found that feedback to psychotherapists with at-risk individuals reduced deterioration from 20.1% when no alarm signals are provided to 5.5% in feedback conditions that included the CST. The percentage of individuals who had a positive outcome more than doubled when feedback was offered, from 22.3% to 55.5%. These are rather dramatic effects when we consider that it takes a client about five minutes to take the OQ-45 and five minutes to take the ASC, the OQ-Analyst about one second to deliver a report through a wireless network to the clinician's computer, and the psychotherapist about 18 seconds to access the report—with graphs of progress and warning messages.

Since the Shimokawa et al. (2010) mega/meta-analysis, six additional studies have been published. These studies have expanded the evidence base showing the positive effects of feedback across treatment settings, client samples, and countries (Amble et al., 2014; Crits-Christoph et al., 2012; de Jong et al., 2012; Probst et al., 2013; Simon et al., 2012, 2013). The 12 studies published to date suggest that progress feedback with alarm signals enhances outcomes in both inpatient and outpatient settings, across a variety of client diagnoses ranging from the mildly disturbed to highly disturbed individuals who meet criteria for multiple Axis I as well as Axis II disorders. In addition, positive effects have been reported for clients as varied as those who are somaticizing, are abusing substances, or are severely depressed, as well as across four different languages and countries.

The effect sizes ($d$) presented in the last column of Table 7.1 need some explanation. They represent the difference between psychotherapists practicing a wide variety of single-school treatments ranging from cognitive-behavioral therapy to psychodynamic to humanistic and eclectic interventions according to their preferences. In both treatment-as-usual and feedback-assisted treatment, the same psychotherapists and treatments were used because randomization to treatment condition was typically done within psychotherapist—differences in client outcome contrasted client success with and without feedback. Typical $d$ values in psychotherapy research studies compare the posttreatment difference between an active treatment and a waitlist control (untreated individuals) and hover around an effect size of 0.60 (0.40–0.80), meaning that about 65% of treated clients will have a positive outcome compared to 35% of clients who are on a waitlist for the same time period (Lambert, 2013).

Re-analyses of older reviews as well as newer meta-analytic reviews have tended to produce smaller effect sizes than the original estimates. Nevertheless, the broad finding of psychotherapy benefit across a range of treatments for a variety of disorders remains, since even the smaller effects show treatments are working. Indeed, psychotherapy is more effective than many "evidence-based" medical practices, some of which are costly and produce significant side effects, including almost all interventions in cardiology (e.g., beta-blockers, angioplasty, statins), geriatric medicine (e.g., calcium and alendronate sodium for osteoporosis), and asthma (e.g., budesonide); influenza vaccine; and cataract surgery, among other treatments (Wampold, 2013). Considering the high burden of illness manifest in psychological disorders, and the fact that the psychotherapies studied last only weeks, the consequences of entering treatment versus having no formal treatment are dramatic.

In contrast, in studies examining one active treatment versus another active treatment (this is the most similar comparison to feedback-assisted treatment vs. treatment as usual), $d$ values typically hover around 0.0 to 0.20. For example, Elliott et al. (2013) identified 76 studies that compared humanistic psychotherapy to cognitive-behavioral therapy and found a mean difference of $d = 0.13$ in favor of the latter. However, this small difference disappeared when researcher allegiance effects were accounted for. Using the above information as a context, it is easy to see that the size of feedback effects for Not-on-Track clients summarized in Table 7.1 easily surpasses those found in comparisons of different psychotherapies (empirically supported psychotherapies), especially when the feedback includes the CST intervention. Relatively little training is needed to use the system, which received very high marks for training material and readiness for implementation by the Substance Abuse and Mental Health Services Administration's National Registry of Evidence-Based Programs and Practices (2014) when they rated the system as an evidence-based practice.

# THE USE OF MONITORING DATA FOR "MARKETING BY THE PRIVATE PRACTITIONER"

In addition to benefiting clients, measuring outcomes in private practice can be used to provide consumers of services with this information on outcomes. For example, Gordon I. Herz (2009) provided a sample letter with outcome data he routinely sends referring physicians following the treatment of his clients. Not only did physicians appreciate hearing back from this psychologist, but they were impressed that mental health functioning was measured and quantified against benchmarks provided by Dr. Herz from the test manual. Several suggestions for using data in this way can be made:

1. Provide physicians with pretest information (including degree of disturbance referenced against the normal population). Remember, more disturbed individuals change more during their participation in psychotherapy than less disturbed individuals, but it takes them longer to enter the ranks of normal functioning.
2. Improvement for these high-scoring individuals should therefore take advantage of classification of reliable change (pretreatment to posttreatment) as 14 or more points on the OQ-45. Individuals who start treatment in the normal range of functioning (for whom

the measured benefits of psychotherapy are hard to demonstrate) can be reported as functioning in the normal range even if they do not show improvement.

3. Try to obtain test score data from individuals who attend only a single session under your care. There is a good chance many of these clients will be satisfied with treatment and show a benefit.

4. Try to collect outcome data at every session of care, especially the first five sessions, as many clients (around 40%) will show a dramatic treatment response and experience much of the total gains they will experience during psychotherapy within this short time period. Missing measurement points during this time means you may miss capturing important improvements.

5. Frequently scheduled sessions (at least once a week) will produce more and faster change than sessions held less often (e.g., every other week) so that your clients will show (and have) less benefit if you stretch sessions out over time.

6. It is possible that simply communicating that you tracked client treatment response in relation to the typical client and in relation to normal functioning (in lieu of providing specific scores) will be sufficient to give referring parties confidence in your work (Lambert, 2010).

## IMPLEMENTATION

Presuming that psychotherapists are convinced by the data and arguments put forth in this chapter, a major consideration for implementation is time and money. From a practical perspective, the logistics of maintaining an ongoing treatment-monitoring system are easier to manage when assessment becomes a routine part of practice. A central question in such systems is who is responsible for data collection, with the related questions of when assessments are administered and who keeps track of this. Thus, if psychotherapists administer questionnaires, do they do this before or after the session? If assessment is intermittent, how does the psychotherapist know when to administer an assessment to client A, but not to client B? Is the psychotherapist expected to keep track of this along with the client case file, or is this handled on the management side and clinicians are informed as needed?

We have found that the most efficient system has been to simply make administration of assessments routine, with clients completing a questionnaire prior to each appointment either via the Internet or in the clinic/office. Clients need to come 10 minutes early for their appointment if administration takes place prior to a session. It is also feasible for clients to complete the assessment after the session. Originally we were concerned that after-session assessments might unduly affect the scores that are produced, but this does not appear to be the case. However, if the scores are gathered after the session, then feedback is delayed by the time between appointments.

The process of administration has become increasingly automated and can easily be handled as part of the routine administrative tasks of keeping client records using OQ-Analyst software. The National Registry of Evidence-Based Programs and Practices recently rated the OQ-Analyst a 3.9 (out of 4) as meeting their criteria for "readiness for dissemination" based on user guides and step-by-step instructions for implementation (www.nrepp.samhsa.gov/).

The OQ system was designed to be a tool to aid clinical decision making rather than to dictate or prescribe to clinicians. We are well aware that decisions regarding the continued provision of treatment, the modification of ongoing treatment, obtaining case consultation or supervision, or the application of clinical support tools or other techniques cannot be made on the basis of a single questionnaire or independent from clinical judgment. Thus, we envision the OQ system as analogous to a "lab test" in medical treatment, which can supplement and inform clinical decision making rather than replacing the clinician's judgment.

# REFERENCES

Amble, I., Grude, T., Stubdal, S. Andersen, B. J., & Wampold, B. E. (2014). The effect of implementing the Outcome Questionnaire-45.2 feedback system in Norway: A multisite randomized clinical trial in a naturalistic setting. *Psychotherapy Research, 25,* 1–9. doi: 10.1080/10503307.2014.92875

Beck, A. T., Ward, C. H., Mendelson, M., Mock, J., & Erbaugh, J. (1961). An inventory for measuring depression. *Archives of General Psychiatry, 4,* 53–63.

Crits-Christoph, P., Ring-Kurtz, S., Hamilton, J. L., Lambert, M. J., Gallop, R., McClure, B., Kulaga, A., & Rotrosen, J. (2012). A preliminary study of the effects of individual patient -level feedback in outpatient substance abuse treatment programs. *Journal of Substance Abuse Treatment, 42*(3), 301–309. doi: 10.1016/j.jsat.2011.09.003

De Jong, K., van Sluis, Nugter, M.A., Heiser, W. J., & Spinhoven, P. (2012). Understanding the differential impact of outcome monitoring: Therapist variables that moderate feedback effects in a randomized clinical trial. *Psychotherapy Research, 22,* 464–474. doi: 10.1080/10503307.2012.673023

Drapeau, M. (Ed.) (2012). Ten tools for progress monitoring in psychotherapy. *Integrating Science & Practice,* 2(2), 2–45.

Elliott, R., Greenberg, L. S., Watson, J., Timulak, L., & Freire, E. (2013). Research on Humanistic-Experiential psychotherapies. In M. J. Lambert (Ed.), *Bergin and Garfield's handbook of psychotherapy and behavior change.* New York: Wiley.

Hannan, C., Lambert, M. J., Harmon, C., Nielsen, S., Smart, D. W., Shimokawa, K., & Sutton, S. W. (2005). A lab test and algorithms for identifying clients at risk for treatment failure. *Journal of Clinical Psychology,* 61(2), 155–163. doi: 10.1002/jclp.20108

Hansen, N. B., Lambert, M. J., & Forman, E. M. (2003). An evaluation of the dose-response relationship in naturalistic treatment settings using survival analysis. *Mental Health Services Research, 5*(1), 1–12.

Harmon, C., Lambert, M. J., Slade, K. L., & Smart, D. W. (2007). Enhancing outcome for potential treatment failures: Therapist/client feedback and clinical support tools. *Psychotherapy Research, 17*(4), 379–392. doi: 10.1080/10503300600702331

Hatfield, D., & Ogles, B. M. (2004). The use of outcome measures by psychologists in clinical practice. *Professional Psychology: Research & Practice, 35*(5), 485–491. doi: 10/1037/0735-7028.35.5.485

Hawkins, E. J., Lambert, M. J., Vermeersch, D. A., Slade, K. L., & Tuttle, K. C. (2004). The therapeutic effects of providing patient progress information to therapists and patients. *Psychotherapy Research, 14*(3), 308–327. doi: 10.1093/ptr/kph027

Herz, G. (2009). Measuring progress and outcomes. *The Independent Practitioner, 29,* 179.

Hill, C. E., Thompson, B. J., Cogar, M. & Denman, D. W. (1993). Beneath the surface of long-term therapy: Therapist and client report of their own and each other's covert processes. *Journal of Counseling Psychology, 40,* 278–287.

Jacobson, N. S., & Truax, P. (1991). Clinical significance: A statistical approach to defining meaningful change in psychotherapy research. *Journal of Consulting and Clinical Psychology, 59*(1), 12–19. doi: 10.1037/0022-006x.59.1.12

Lambert, M. J. (2010). *Prevention of treatment failure: The use of measuring, monitoring, & feedback in clinical practice.* Washington, DC: APA Press.

Lambert, M. J. (2013). The efficacy and effectiveness of psychotherapy. In M. J. Lambert (Ed.), *Bergin & Garfield's handbook of psychotherapy and behavior change* (6th Ed., pp. 169–218). New York: Wiley.

Lambert, M. J., Bailey, R. J., White, M., Tingey, K. M., & Stevens, E. (2015). *Clinical Support Tool Manual—brief version-40.* Salt Lake City: OQMeasures.

Lambert, M. J., Kahler, M., Harmon, C., Burlingame, G. M., Shimokawa, K., & White, M. M. (2013). *Administration and scoring manual: Outcome Questionnaire OQ-45.2.* Salt Lake City: OQMeasures.

Lambert, M. J., Whipple, J. L., Bishop, M. J., Vermeersch, D. A., Gray, G. V., & Finch, A. E. (2002). Comparison of empirically derived and rationally derived methods for identifying clients at risk for treatment failure. *Clinical Psychology and Psychotherapy, 9,* 149–164.

Lambert, M. J., Whipple, J. L., Smart, D. W., Vermeersch, D. A., Nielsen S. L., & Hawkins E. J. (2001). The effects of providing therapists with feedback on patient progress during psychotherapy: Are outcomes enhanced? *Psychotherapy Research, 11*(1), 49–68. doi: 10.1080/713663852

Lambert, M. J., Whipple, J. L., Vermeersch, D. A., Smart, D. W., Hawkins E. J., Nielsen S. L., & Goates, M. K. (2002). Enhancing psychotherapy outcomes via providing feedback on client progress: A replication. *Clinical Psychology and Psychotherapy, 9*(2), 91–103. doi: 10.1002/cpp.324

Lunnen, K. M., & Ogles, B. M. (1998). A multiperspective, multivariable evaluation of reliable change. *Journal of Consulting and Clinical Psychology, 66*(2), 400–410. doi: 10.1080/10503300902849483

National Registry of Evidence-Based Practices & Programs. (2014). OQ-Analyst. Retrieved from www.nrepp.samhsa.gov/.

Probst, T., Lambert M. J., Loew, T., Dahlbender, R., Göllner, R., & Tritt, K. (2013). Feedback on patient progress and clinical support tools for therapists: Improved outcome for patients at risk of treatment failure in in-patient therapy under the conditions of routine practice. *Journal of Psychosomatic Research, 75,* 255–261.

Shimokawa, K., Lambert, M. J., & Smart, D. W. (2010). Enhancing treatment outcome of patients at risk of treatment failure: Meta-analytic and mega-analytic review of psychotherapy quality assurance system. *Journal of Consulting and Clinical Psychology, 78*(3), 298–311. doi: 10.1037/a0019247.

Simon, W., Lambert, M. J., Busath, G., Vazquez, A., Berkeljon, A., Hyer, K., Granley, M., & Berrett, M. (2013). Effects of providing patient progress feedback and clinical support tools to psychotherapists in an inpatient eating disorders treatment program: A randomized controlled study. *Psychotherapy Research, 23*(3), 287–300. doi: 10.1080/10503307.2013.787497.

Simon, W., Lambert, M. J., Harris, M. W., Busath, G., & Vazquez, A. (2012). Providing patient progress information and clinical support tools to therapists: Effects on patients at risk for treatment failure. *Psychotherapy Research, 22*(6), 638–647. doi: 10.1080/10503307.2012.698918.

Slade, K. L., Lambert, M. J., Harmon, S. C., Smart, D. W., & Bailey, R. (2008). Improving psychotherapy outcome: The use of immediate electronic feedback and revised clinical support tools. *Clinical Psychology & Psychotherapy, 15*(5), 287–303. doi: 10.1002/cpp.594.

Walfish, S., McAlister, B., O'Donnell, P., & Lambert, M. J. (2012). An investigation of self-assessment bias in mental health providers. *Psychological Reports, 110*(2), 639–644. doi: 10.2466/02.07.17.

Wampold, B. E. (2013). *The great psychotherapy debate: Models, methods, and findings.* New York: Routledge

Whipple, J. L., Lambert, M. J., Vermeersch, D. A., Smart D. W., Neilsen, S. L., & Hawkins, E. J. (2003). Improving the effects of psychotherapy: The use of early identification of treatment and problem-solving strategies in routine practice. *Journal of Counseling Psychology, 50*(1), 59–68. doi: 10.1037/0022-0167.50.1.59

White, M., Lambert, M. J., Bailey, R. J., McLaughlin, S. B., & Ogles, B. M. (2015). Understanding the Assessment for Signal Clients as a feedback tool for reducing treatment failure. *Psychotherapy Research, 25*, 724–734.

... ... ... ... ... ... Psychotherapy ... ... ... ... ...

# CHAPTER 8

# ENTREPRENEURSHIP BASICS FOR PRACTITIONERS

*Laurie K. Baedke*

To achieve success in professional practice, clinical competency is critical—but insufficient. Mental health professionals, psychiatrists, psychologists, psychotherapists, counselors, and other highly trained clinicians have years of advanced academic training under their belts, but sadly this rigorous schooling is almost always lacking in content about finance, marketing, law, human resources, and other cornerstones of business.

## DEMYSTIFYING THE CLINICIAN ENTREPRENEUR

*Merriam-Webster* defines the entrepreneur as "a person who starts a business and is willing to risk loss in order to make money" ("Entrepreneur," n.d., para. 1). The world often views entrepreneurs as mavericks, dreamers, innovators, and problem solvers.

Clinicians are driven to dedicate their lives to helping patients to achieve or maintain health by a sense of service, an acute perceptiveness of others' plights and needs, and a passion to apply strong listening, critical thinking, and communication skills for the betterment of clients facing crises and other challenges. Many clinicians are drawn to entrepreneurship by a passion to deliver patient care in a personalized format. They may desire to have autonomy or to build investment and passive income streams. Mental health professionals may be attracted to entrepreneurship as a channel to build new and innovative approaches to care, which result in stronger relationships and better outcomes for clients.

Historically, those in the mental health professions have not been immune from the constraints other types of healthcare practitioners have faced within the inflexible professional services model. Similar to an attorney or accountant, this approach directly links compensation to billable hours worked. Clinicians can avail themselves of entrepreneurship to scale efforts through others; for example, when larger group practices team up with employed practitioners, they provide profit to an owner based off others' work. This arrangement further affords the ability to retain the profit margin from one's own services instead of paying for the corporate overhead associated with a larger entity.

Alternatively, visionary and innovative clinicians may introduce completely new models of service delivery to their client population, such as group, membership, and premium services, or content and product sales. Flexibility may make entrepreneurship or self-employment an appealing proposition for those in the mental health professions at various stages of their lives or careers. For instance, a father may opt to work from home to rear his young children. Likewise, a later-stage careerist may retain her clients but, within this entrepreneurial model, she has the flexibility to scale back and balance travel, early retirement pursuits, and other fulfilling interests that might otherwise be competing with a fixed work schedule. In addition to tailoring one's practice style to meet personal life circumstances or to best meet client needs, the built-in flexibility associated with private practice also allows clinicians to leverage or develop new practice models and advanced technologies.

# TELEPRACTICE: A NEW MARKET

Telepractice represents the convergence of direct patient care and innovative technology. An emerging trend in healthcare, telepractice has the potential to expand the marketspace *substantially* for mental health clinicians. In fact, Transparency Market Research estimates the global telehealth market could reach $36.3 billion by 2020 (Sudip, 2015).

The telepractice model presents many opportunities to address longstanding challenges in mental health practice, such as the following:

- Access to quality care
- High costs of care
- Stigma associated with office visits
- Significant time commitment, travel, and scheduling considerations
- Clinician shortages in rural and other geographic areas or certain specialties

The June 2013 issue of *Telemedicine Journal and E-Health* explored how telehealth is being used to provide mental health assessment and treatment at distance. The 2013 review notes that "telemental health" has "increased access to care, and patients and providers are very satisfied with it for a wide variety of services." Technology presents a number of opportunities for telemental health providers, which have been extensively examined. Some of these models of care include the following:

- Integrated mental health screening, onsite therapy, and telepsychiatric consultation via phone, email, or video

- Phone and email consultation system for developmentally disabled adults and children
- Randomized controlled trial for depression in adults with disease management and telepsychiatric consultation
- Collaboration with telepsychiatrists and rural primary care physicians on antidepressant medications (Hilty et al., 2013, pp. 444–454)

Technology may be advancing rapidly, but reimbursement, regulations, and licensure are slower to respond to meet this new demand. The American Psychological Association (APA)'s Executive Director for Professional Practice, Katherine Nordal, PhD (2015), writes: "A growing number of states have instituted telepractice policies — either through statutes that govern the delivery of healthcare services or through state laws that include remote services within the scope of practice" (p. 64). Nordal continues: "Psychology licensing boards have issued advisory opinions on telepractice, indicating that those who provide services via electronic means to consumers within the state must be licensed in that state" (p. 64). Nordal also notes the APA has been actively involved in leading efforts to develop guidelines, establish policies, and facilitate technology-driven change in the mental health profession.

The size of the market for these services is undeniable; according to the U.S. Human Services Health Resources and Services Administration, there are 99 million Americans living in "mental health shortage areas" (Health Resources and Services Administration, 2016). The employment of mental health professionals is projected to grow significantly faster than the average for all occupations—at 23%—from 2012 to 2022 (U.S. Bureau of Labor Statistics, 2014). These and other promising models of care within the telemental health arena illustrate how entrepreneurial solutions are being introduced to advance the practice of mental health and better meet patient needs.

# CUTTING THROUGH ENTREPRENEURIAL MYTHS

Societal stereotypes tend to pair "entrepreneurship" alongside "success" and "autonomy." Entrepreneurship can certainly afford both of those things to the clinician, but "being your own boss" is also inextricably linked to struggle and failure. Mental health clinician entrepreneurs must learn to wear two hats: the trusted professional the client sees during his or her encounter, and the business owner persona tasked with myriad roles. Simultaneously, the clinician must be willing and able to oversee patient care, office management and staff oversight, billing, sales, customer service, facilities maintenance, operations, and a multitude of other functions. Are you unable or unwilling to take on all these diverse roles? To be successful, a business owner must either delegate or build a great, supportive team. As a clinician, it's helpful to envision a pie: What part of that whole will be invested toward direct patient care, and what part will be directed toward running the business?

Hospitals and healthcare organizations value on-staff practitioners as a means of growing or maintaining market share. Having a greater number of employed clinicians ensures that the organization is equipped to serve a steady stream of patients, gain leverage in negotiations with insurers, and enhance savings via larger economies of scale. Many of today's clinicians seek out salaried employment due to the pressures of staggering professional school debt, lack of business training, and the lifestyle perks—partly, a convenient schedule that more closely resembles a standard workweek. Since many young clinicians are saddled with substantial student loans, the idea of taking on additional financial obligations to start a private practice may be unthinkable. Accordingly, more entry-level clinicians are attracted to the relatively low risks of a salaried arrangement with a hospital or a large group practice.

Heightened government regulation, reimbursement uncertainties, and insurance contracting complexities add to the difficulties clinicians encounter when choosing between private small business and salaried employment. And while the cost of information technology infrastructure to support the private clinical practice is considerable and ever-increasing, healthcare providers arguably have fewer roadblocks to business investment than do many other entrepreneurs due to their traditionally strong salaries, good credit ratings, and proven market demand (Robeznieks, 2013).

Opportunities abound for mental health clinicians who are entering private practice. While the gulf between the demand for clinical specialties and the available clinicians to meet such demand is well publicized, the need for mental health professionals is particularly pronounced, as psychiatry was ranked among the top 10 most in-demand medical specialties by a recent *Merritt Hawkins' Review* (Merritt Hawkins, 2014). Further, *U.S. News* (2016) recently included psychologist, social worker, and marriage and family therapist in its listing of 100 best careers, and the Bureau of Labor Statistics (U.S. Department of Labor, 2016) predicts that the need for healthcare practitioners will increase by over 21% between 2012 and 2022.

# ATTRIBUTES OF SUCCESSFUL ENTREPRENEURS

Successful entrepreneurs and clinicians share many of the same characteristics—be it drive, a track record of high performance, or independence. In all likelihood, clinicians have unknowingly adopted an "entrepreneurial alter ego" as part of their professional identity.

Shiv Gaglani (2013) reflected on the qualities that prepared him for a leave of absence from Johns Hopkins University to start an education technology company, Osmosis. He honed in on three essential characteristics: *sustained effort, focus,* and *purpose.* Acknowledging "generalized differences," Gaglani writes in *Entrepreneur*:

> it appears that medical students are increasingly transforming into entrepreneurs to fix the broken parts of the healthcare system. They bring with them a relentless effort and focus, informed view, open mind and genuine sense of purpose. That's a good sign for healthcare, and a great one for business. (para. 10)

Research suggests that entrepreneurs are less risk averse than employed people, and the decision to go down this path is positively related to an increased willingness to take on risks. Carol

Dweck, the Lewis and Virginia Eaton Professor of Psychology at Stanford University and author of the bestselling book *Mindset: The New Psychology of Success* (2006), describes the "fixed mindset" as

> when people believe their basic qualities, their intelligence, their talents, their abilities, are just fixed traits. They have a certain amount, and that's that. But other people have a growth mindset. They believe that even basic talents and abilities can be developed over time through experience, mentorship, and so on. And these are the people who go for it. They're not always worried about how smart they are, how they'll look, what a mistake will mean. They challenge themselves and grow. (*Harvard Business Review*, 2015, para. 4)

Aspiring clinician entrepreneurs can glean a few lessons from Dweck's research:

1.  *Be a learner.* Simply defined, "mindset" is how information is uploaded and processed. There are "non-learners" with a fixed mindset, and there are "learners" with a flexible outlook. The former see talents and abilities as something one has or doesn't have to be successful. The latter perceive the ability to develop talents. They don't sweat skills that are lacking; they learn how to acquire them. They don't worry about making mistakes, but instead focus on learning from them to keep pushing forward.
2.  *Build a team.* Channel the African proverb, "If you want to go fast, go alone. If you want to go far, go together." To build something of substance that is scalable and sustainable always requires more than one individual can accomplish. Even the most adept solo practitioner, at some point, will need to enlist a receptionist, bookkeeper or accountant, and other key support staff. He or she can't be everything to everyone all the time.
3.  *Seek feedback.* Successful individuals consistently and relentlessly acquire objective input about their performance and strengths. They must get comfortable with the discomfort of hearing the honest, naked truth about their weaknesses, opportunities, and blind spots. They apply those truths to grow and improve. Don't be afraid to hire a business or executive coach to acquire this insight. Or, seek out those individuals who are in a position to observe. Ask them for feedback with the *genuine intent to learn.*
4.  *Surround yourself with mentors.* The most successful individuals in any field or pursuit sit under the wisdom of those who have gone before them, to observe their path and benefit from their lessons learned. Mentors come in many forms. Network with peers outside of the competitive marketspace, connect with accomplished entrepreneurs in the community from other industries, and keep company with colleagues who are retired from practice.
5.  *Execute.* While plans and strategies are great, execution is priceless. Even the most sophisticated or costly business plans, websites, or marketing brochures are worthless if you fail to put them in motion. The best education in entrepreneurship is often *failure.* There is value in learning from hardship, and in trying again from a better vantage point to achieve success than the first go-around.

# ENTREPRENEURIAL MODELS

The "Lean Startup" model has gained significant attention and respect in the entrepreneurial world. The philosophy is based on "lean manufacturing," the streamlined production method pioneered by Taiichi Ohno. The approach combines flow principles used by Henry Ford at the dawn of the 20th century with Training Within Industry (TWI) programs introduced in Japan in 1951. The idea that companies can shorten their business development cycles through iterative learning, trial and error, and continuous feedback lies at the heart of "lean" models and methods. As it relates to the startup world, there is no "perfect" business plan or silver bullet that guarantees entrepreneurial success and staves off failure. Instead, the Lean Startup philosophy values:

- Informed decision making
- Trimming the fat or reducing waste
- Willingness to pivot, and change and relaunch as needed

Eric Ries popularized this approach in *The New York Times* bestseller *The Lean Startup*. Since its publication in 2011, this take on business development has branched out worldwide from its Silicon Valley roots. Individuals, teams, and organizations of all types have found this method applicable, just as high-tech startups did before them. Ries continues to spread the merits of this movement globally on his website, TheLeanStartup.com, which extols other basic principles; namely, that "entrepreneurs are everywhere" and "entrepreneurship is learning," as well as notions of "validated learning," "innovation accounting," and "build-measure-learn." His charge to entrepreneurs is to work *smarter*, not *harder*—and not within the confines of a glossy, inflexible, and extensive business plan.

Clinician entrepreneurs, take note: There is value in studying models from outside of mental health. Learn from other industries to inform your journey toward professional and personal success and fulfillment. Adopt the practice of iterative learning and informed decision making to navigate startup or growth processes effectively and efficiently (Sprouter, 2011).

# THE ENTREPRENEURIAL LIFE CYCLE

Bill Carmody (2015), founder and chief executive officer of Trepoint, a digital marketing agency, has identified seven stages of business, similar to the life stages that a person may experience. Each stage has unique characteristics and challenges that must be addressed before progressing to the next stage and before "growing up" or maturing, in this case, as a clinical private practice.

*Stage 1* is the "birth of the company." Think of this as the prelaunch and startup phase all the way up to the first year of operations as a new business. Your vision may not be crystal clear, but the natural drive exists to create anew.

*Stage 2* (the "toddlers seek to survive and grow") is really about maintaining independence. Not unlike parenting toddlers, this phase revolves around survival. The "newness" hasn't worn off yet. Growth vacillates between rapid and nonexistent, because the practice isn't stabilized and standing on its own legs. While the bumps of the startup phase may be in the rearview mirror, the road remains uncertain; you can't go on cruise control just yet.

*Stage 3* of the practice is the "young adult" period. Volatility reigns. "It's at this stage," Carmody writes, "that many companies run into trouble as entrepreneurs, having tasted the success they were seeking and suddenly think they can do no wrong" (para. 4). It's not uncommon for organizations to cycle between the toddler and young adult phases for years, treading water because they haven't yet achieved the *stability* needed to move on to the next stage.

*Stage 4* ("adults in their prime") is when the company transitions from survival and volatility to predictable growth—the phase a company should remain at for as long as possible. Carmody notes this is when entrepreneurs seek interdependence. Practices that have reached this point are proactive, prudent, mature, and strong. With a forward-looking approach to cultivating continued growth, they are equally focused on internal and external factors to maintain their long-term success.

*Stages 5, 6, and 7* are defined by Carmody as "aging and early decline," "illness and rapid decline," and "death." Occasionally, partnerships become strained, the best members of the team strike out on their own, or the marketplace, a business, or an entire industry is disrupted. Should proactive and prudent planning fail to stave off the impact of these external changes, practices sometimes come to an end.

Awareness of these stages can be the gateway to viable planning, which positions the clinician entrepreneur for sustainable, long-term success. Take a page from the playbook of established corporate entities. Organizations of various sizes and industries have informed their decision making with intentional and consistent investments in strategic planning, self-assessment, and professional development.

Clinician entrepreneurs are already in an advantageous position. Survival rates vary dramatically by type of business and industry space. While it is estimated more than half of ventures will not make it to year number 7, healthcare and social assistance consistently rank among those industries with the highest survival rates. More than 40% of these organizations were still going strong 11 years on, compared to a quarter of 11-year-old construction firms still operating in 2015 (U.S. Bureau of Labor Statistics, 2016).

# PURPOSE

While "why" one starts a business often takes a backseat to "what" the business does, do not overlook this critical motivating factor. The challenges of entrepreneurship will at some point make even the most confident business owners question their "why." It is critical to achieve distinct clarity in your purpose, vision, and all-important "why" to position the business for success. Such awareness affords an additional benefit: the ability to leverage others' connections to that defined purpose and vision during the team buildout phase. Their buy-in and contributions build momentum and allow for the business to be scaled. Alignment is the key.

Speaker and author Simon Sinek has written an entire book on the subject, *Start With Why*. During a notable TED Talk in 2010, Sinek spoke about the discovery that the world's inspiring leaders and organizations thought, acted, and communicated in a codified way—what he dubbed the "golden circle." Put simply, "people don't buy what you do; they buy why you do it" (para. 14). Sinek continued: "The goal is not to do business with everybody who needs what you have. The goal is to do business with people who believe what you believe" (para. 6). The same sentiment applies to hiring. Sinek notes the goal is not only to hire people who need a job, but also to hire talent with beliefs similar to one's own.

There is power in clearly understanding one's own purpose. After all, how can a team align around a vision, mission, or passion if the entrepreneurial "lead" does not have a clear understanding of his or her own personal motivations? Synergy comes from alignment around a unified vision. The clinician entrepreneur should lead with a keen self-awareness; an acute understanding of yourself can help to foster a culture whereby each individual is encouraged to understand and appreciate and contribute his or her unique, individual purpose.

Each team member's attributes represent a unique contribution to the whole. True engagement occurs when the entire team—from entrepreneur-leader down—feels invested in the practice, like they have a place at the table. When each team member is empowered to thrive professionally and personally, the entire organization is better for it. A large body of research exists to support the notion that a highly engaged workforce is a productive workforce, and engagement starts with a clear purpose. Long gone are the days when someone can cruise by without an intentional focus on his or her culture and how he or she interfaces with employees. These considerations transcend the "soft," "touchy-feely" side of business; they have bottom-line implications and are critical to the business's return on investment.

Understanding your purpose offers a secondary advantage: the ability to withstand inevitable adversity. Bumps in the road are all the more likely for those who choose to chart their own path of business ownership. Overcoming adversity may be one of life's harshest realities, but after the dark storm of difficulty has passed, character and resilience remain—the silver lining of surviving such challenges. Understanding and reflecting on purpose is power. And, armed with awareness, you will be better equipped to navigate the trials and tribulations of entrepreneurship.

## CONCLUDING THOUGHTS

There are three key categories of considerations related to opting to be your own boss:

- Functions of the entrepreneur
- Advantages of entrepreneurship
- Disadvantages of entrepreneurship

Entrepreneurs must be willing to take on the following functions, develop the following characteristics, or find a collaborator who possesses them:

- Visionary thinking
- Ability to execute on strategy
- Tenacity
- Adaptability
- Willingness to delegate
- Shrewd decision making
- Risk taking
- Creditworthiness to obtain financing
- Business development; the ability to market and sell the services you provide
- Ability to identify teammates, support staff, and partners who align with your own passions and values
- Clear vision and diligence associated with the long-term picture; entrepreneurship as a marathon and not a sprint
- Commitment to lifelong learning
- Ability to receive feedback

There are many advantages to taking a road that remains less traveled among mental health professionals, including the following:

- Autonomy
- Flexibility
- Ability to build a practice to suit your style
- Ability to engage patients in practice design planning
- A return to "patient-centric"/relationship-based care
- Competitive opportunities for independent practices to compete with cost-effective, high-quality services
- Demand; healthcare as an industry has consistently out-survived and outperformed other industries, which heightens your odds of success
- Opportunity to deliver innovative solutions to significant, broad industry challenges

Any exploration of entrepreneurial opportunities must also consider the potential disadvantages, which include the following:

- Uncertainty
- Operational burdens
- Lack of resources when compared to larger healthcare organizations
- Financial risk; entrepreneurs put "skin in the game," placing personal capital on the line
- Lack of formal training in skills needed to launch a business in areas such as human resources, finance, and marketing
- Need to wear multiple hats; balancing the role of clinician and business owner

Any aspiring business owner should assess personal characteristics and traits that may be developed, with potential opportunities and pitfalls to determine the "why," vision, and pathway toward a rewarding new chapter in the life of a clinician: the clinician entrepreneur.

# RECOMMENDED READING

## BOOKS

Dweck, C. (2006). *Mindset: The new psychology of success.* New York: Random House.

Ramsey, D. (2011). *Entreleadership: 20 years of practical business wisdom from the trenches.* New York: Howard Books.

Gerber, M. E. (2004). *The E-Myth revisited: Why most small businesses don't work and what to do about it.* New York: HarperCollins.

Ries, E. (2011). *The lean startup: How today's entrepreneurs use continual innovation to create radically successful businesses.* New York: Crown Business.

Bossidy, L., & Charan, R. (2011). *Execution: The discipline of getting things done.* New York: Crown Business.

## PODCASTS (AVAILABLE THROUGH IPHONE AND ANDROID APPS)

- *Start a Therapy Practice,* Scott Harmon
- *Entreleadership,* Dave Ramsey
- *StartupCamp,* Dale Partridge
- *Entrepreneur On Fire (EO Fire),* John Lee Dumas
- *Building a Story Brand,* Donald Miller
- *This is Your Life,* Michael Hyatt

# REFERENCES

Carmody, B. (2015, July 4). *7 stages of the entrepreneur's life cycle: From independence to interdependence.* Retrieved from http://www.inc.com/bill-carmody/7-stages-of-the-entrepreneur-s-life-cycle-from-independence-to-interdependence.html.

Dweck, C. (2006). *Mindset: The new psychology of success.* New York: Random House.

Gaglani, S. (2013, October 30). Why medical schools are pumping out entrepreneurs. *Entrepreneur.* Retrieved from https://www.entrepreneur.com/article/229672.

*Harvard Business Review.* (2015). The right mindset for success. Retrieved from https://hbr.org/2012/01/the-right-mindset-for-success/.

Health Resources and Services Administration, U.S. Department of Health and Human Services. (2016). *Shortage designation: health professional shortage areas & medically underserved areas/populations.*

Hilty, D. M., Ferrer, D. C., Parish, M. B., Johnston, B., Callahan, E. J., & Yellowlees, P. M. (2013). The effectiveness of telemental health. *Telemedicine Journal and E-Health, 19*(6), 444–454.

*Merriam-Webster's Online Learner's Dictionary.* (n.d.). "Entrepreneur." Retrieved from http://www.merriam-webster.com/dictionary/entrepreneur.

Merritt Hawkins. (2014). *Merritt Hawkins 2014 review of physician and advanced practitioner recruiting incentives*. Retrieved from http://www.merritthawkins.com/uploadedFiles/MerrittHawkins/Surveys/2014_Merritt_Hawkins_Physician_Recruiting_Report_Infographic.pdf.

Nordal, K. C. (2015). Embracing telepsychology. *Monitor on Psychology, 46*(11), 64. Retrieved from http://www.apa.org/monitor/2015/12/perspectives.asp.

Ries, E. (2011). *The lean startup: How today's entrepreneurs use continual innovation to create radically successful businesses*. New York: Crown Business. Retrieved from http://www.startuplessonslearned.com/2008/09/lean-startup.html.

Robeznieks, A. (2013, September 17). Not all doctors giving up private practice. *Vital Signs Blog*. http://www.modernhealthcare.com/article/20130917/BLOG/309179996

Sinek, S. (2010). *How great leaders inspire action*. TED Talk. Retrieved from https://www.ted.com/talks/simon_sinek_how_great_leaders_inspire_action/transcript?language=en.

Sprouter. (2011). *How Eric Ries changed the framework for startup success*. Retrieved from http://www.startuplessonslearned.com/2008/09/lean-startup.html.

Sudip, S. (2015, November 4). *Global telemedicine market to be worth US$36.3 bn by 2020*. Retrieved from http://www.transparencymarketresearch.com/pressrelease/telemedicine-market.htm.

U.S. Bureau of Labor Statistics. (2014). *Occupational outlook handbook*. Retrieved from http://www.bls.gov/ooh/.

U.S. Bureau of Labor Statistics. (2016). *Business employment dynamics*. Retrieved from http://www.bls.gov/bdm/entrepreneurship/entrepreneurship.htm.

U.S. Department of Labor, Bureau of Labor Statistics. (2016). Occupational labor projections to 2022. Retrieved from http://www.bls.gov/opub/mlr/2013/article/occupational-employment-projections-to-2022.htm.

*U.S. News & World Report*. (2016). *U.S. News* career rankings. The 100 best jobs. Retrieved from http://money.usnews.com/careers/best-jobs/rankings.

# CHAPTER 9

# ENVISIONING YOUR IDEAL PRACTICE

*Dave Verhaagen*

Dreams sometimes begin in the most unlikely of places. For me, my ideal practice began in a Chinese restaurant many years ago. Frank Gaskill and I were in a group practice that was a sinking ship. We knew we had to get out, but we had no idea what to do. We met for lunch to talk over our options. During that conversation, we decided to take the risk and start our own practice. For two guys without one minute of business experience, this was a gut-check moment. Now Southeast Psych has dozens of therapists in four office locations across two states (North Carolina and Tennessee) and two continents (North America and New Zealand). It is regarded as one of the most innovative mental health practices anywhere, but at the time, it was just a germ of an idea—and a risky one at that. We made lots of mistakes along the way, but one of the things we did well was to start with a vision of what we wanted it to be. We weren't content simply to start a practice just to make a living. Instead, we wanted to create something special, something we could be proud of, and something that would do things other practices were not doing (Verhaagen & Gaskill, 2014).

I'll discuss those specifics, but the point isn't to model yourself after what we have done but to create your own ideal practice, a vibrant extension of you. I want you to think big and be bold. I want you to surprise yourself with how great your vision can become. First, though, we must start with the ugly truths.

## HARSH REALITY

I hope this chapter energizes and inspires you about starting your ideal mental health practice, but before I put your head up in the clouds, I need to bring you back down to earth. We have to eat our Brussels sprouts before we get our ice cream.

Let's begin with the harshest reality of starting a practice: *The odds are against you.* I know that short phrase probably made you gulp a little, but it's true. According to the Small Business Administration (2011), nearly 70% of businesses like yours make it to their second anniversary, but by five years, it's a coin toss, with only about 50% making it. By 10 years, it's only a third, and by 15 years, it's about a quarter. Those are frightening odds.

Here's another harsh reality: Running a business is much harder than you think. Billing, hiring, complaints, taxes, technology, and all the rest are part of the experience. It's demanding and draining. Much of it isn't fun or inspiring.

Before you bail out and retreat to that safe and secure agency position, let me give you a little hope with an analogy. Maybe you are a parent or would like to be a parent someday. Imagine an older, more experienced parent comes to sit with you one day when your first child is still a newborn.

"Are you still excited?" she asks.

"Yes, but I'm already a little worn out," you say.

"Well, I've got news for you," she begins. "It doesn't get any easier. When this little guy gets to be two or three, he'll give you more trouble than you can imagine a little person could cause a big person. Tantrums. Defiance. The works."

"That's what I've heard," you reply, thinking that you've probably got this covered, but feeling a little twinge of worry about what is to come.

"And when he gets older, you have all kinds of new worries and challenges. School, friends, sports, behavior, attitude, stress, work ethic, and a host of other things. It's a lot," she says.

"I'm sure it's a challenge," you say with a forced smile. "*Why is my friend being such a downer?*" you think to yourself.

"And then when he hits those teenage years, he'll act like you are the worst mom in the world, that you are crazy, that you are the most annoying human who's ever lived," she adds. "You might not like each other for a few years. Maybe he starts experimenting with alcohol or drugs. He might get an unhealthy obsession with a girlfriend. He may make some awful choices."

"That's going to be tough," you say, still wondering why she feels the need to tell you all this, especially since you've heard most of it before. There's also part of you that thinks your great parenting skills will probably spare you all of these problems, but you worry they may not.

"And then when they get to be young adults, there are issues you never even imagined," she continues, followed by her litany of troubles that young adults face. "It's more challenging than you ever thought."

By this point, you are really starting to worry. A fleeting thought runs through your head: "*Why did I want to have children? This sounds awful!*"

Just as the smile leaves your face, your friend chimes in one last time.

"But it's worth it," she says. "It's all worth it."

This conversation may be made up, but the reality isn't. Childrearing has challenges and frustrations and heartache, yet, at the end of the day, most people would say it was worth it, that it brought them more joy than they could have imagined, even as it brought them more hardship. You could live a life without children and be completely happy. Many people do. Those who choose to have kids, though, know there are joys in that journey you can't experience any other way. For most of us who choose to be parents, it's better to know the harsh realities up front and either be ready to face them or pleasantly surprised when it's not as bad as it might have been, than it is to be naive and get blindsided.

Starting a practice is a lot like birthing a baby. There is undoubtedly trouble ahead, but there is also great pleasure and happiness. It's good to know what you are up against from the outset.

Years ago, I wrote a parenting book based on my surveys of really great parents. I found the best parents had a sense of vision for their children from an early age. However, the vision wasn't focused on achievement ("She's going to be a doctor," "He'll be a great athlete") but on the *character* of the child. Visionary parents knew what character traits they wanted to instill in their child, and they worked from early in the child's life to develop that quality. They would say, "I want her to be a compassionate person," or "I want him to be someone who values hard work and honesty." They were not always successful in seeing these traits fully realized in their child, but the vision for it increased the likelihood of the outcome they desired.

The same is true of starting a practice. There is absolutely no guarantee you will be successful, but if you begin with a vision for your new baby, your chances are much higher.

# VISION

In his book *Start with Why*, Simon Sinek (2009) advises us to begin the process of starting a business or developing a product with why we are doing it, not what we are doing, and not how we will do it. Most businesses, especially the ones that fail, start with the *what*: "We offer great psychotherapy and assessment services. We have the best psychotherapists in town. Give us a call to set up an appointment today." Sounds good. Sort of. But it leaves you feeling weirdly uninspired.

Instead, the best businesses begin, as Sinek (2009) says, with the *why*. Let me give you an example from Southeast Psych. Our mission is "to put psychology into the hands of as many people as possible *to enhance their lives*." The *why* is embedded in the mission. We believe psychology can make people's lives better. So what do we do as a result? We try to get it to as many people as possible. Notice there is nothing in that statement that says anything about psychotherapy or assessment or consultation. We exist to get psychology to the masses, whatever form that may take. The *what* (psychotherapy, assessment, consultation, and so on) takes a back seat to the *why*.

Your *why* cannot be to make money. That is a result of passionately pursuing your purpose. Instead, your *why* must be deeper. Sinek (2009) argues that the reason for Apple's success is that they communicate the reason why they exist in their messages, which boils down to essentially this: Apple exists to challenge the status quo and think differently. They do this by making products that are different, innovative, beautifully designed, and easy to use. They just happen to make computers and phones. Would you care to buy one?

For Southeast Psych, we might say, "We believe psychology can make people's lives better, so we want to get it to as many people as possible through psychotherapy, assessment, and consulting, as well as through media like websites, podcasts, webinars, books, and videos. We hope you'll check us out."

Sinek (2009) concludes, "People don't buy *what* you do; they buy *why* you do it." So before you get lost in the tangle of computer networks and leasing agreements and employment contracts, begin with the *why*. Why do you do what you do? It's a deceptively difficult question.

Perhaps the answer is close to you. Perhaps you can answer it without hesitation. Most of us, however, will need time to reflect on this for ourselves. Let me suggest a strategy for getting to this important answer. Consider taking a morning and going to a quiet place. Maybe it's a park or a library or a chapel. Once there, spend a good 30 minutes practicing mindfulness, focusing only on your breathing and on the here and now. After you're in a mindful state, begin to answer—in writing—some or all of these five questions:

- Why did I want to go into this profession in the first place?
- What do I care about most, both personally and professionally?
- What talents and gifts do I want to use in my work?
- What theme consistently runs through my life?
- What legacy do I want to leave for others?

This exercise may take you two to three hours to complete, but once you are finished, you are likely to be much closer to answering the question of why you are embarking on this challenging journey. You will need that sense of purpose and direction to be successful, but you will also need it to sustain you through the tough times. When those discouraging days come and your thoughts run to, "There has got to be an easier way to make a living," the tendency will be to bail out, unless you feel a clear sense of purpose and calling to do all these hard things.

Once you have answered these questions, begin to craft a purpose statement. A good purpose statement should not be a paragraph long. It should be a sentence or even a phrase. Think like this: "We exist to _____." Or "Our purpose is to _____." It might look something like these:

- *Watson Psychotherapy* exists to restore and strengthen relationships.
- *Linda's Loft* helps children become more successful and more confident learners.
- *The Maverick* gives men and boys skills for effective living.
- *Inner Circle* promotes healthy mind, body, and spirit for women of all ages.
- *The Bradley Center* helps those who struggle with addiction live healthy and more fulfilling lives.

This is the seed that will then become your mission statement. Ideally your statement should include the *why* and the *what* of your ideal practice. The language should inspire you as you hope to inspire others.

Consider Starbucks' mission statement: *To inspire and nurture the human spirit—one person, one cup, and one neighborhood at a time.* It's an elegant, truly beautiful statement that tells you why they exist (to inspire and nurture the human spirit) and includes their focus on individuals and community. Coffee is almost incidental to the mission. It is what they make, but their mission is to inspire and nurture the human spirit. As a result, they focus on community service, a place conducive to conversation and deep thought, and engagement with their local neighborhood.

Imagine how different—and how less successful—Starbucks would be if its mission was something like, "Starbucks strives to make the best coffee in the world." On the surface, it sounds good, but there is nothing there about the reason they exist in that statement. No, Starbucks has become wildly successful because they have a higher purpose that is captured in their mission statement. In essence, they are not just selling coffee; they are hoping to inspire and nurture the human spirit. Coffee is just a tool to facilitate that goal.

If anything, you should err on the side of "more why" and "less what" in your mission. Consider Nike's mission statement: *to bring inspiration and innovation to every athlete in the world.* It's similar to Starbucks' mission with its focus on inspiration, but in this case, it mentions nothing about what they do. It says literally nothing about shoes or athletic gear. It only says they exist to bring inspiration and innovation to every athlete. (By the way, Nike co-founder Bill Bowerman said, "If you have a body, you are an athlete.")

Nike, Starbucks, and like-minded companies start with the *why*, and out of that clarity they craft mission statements that keep them pointed toward their higher purpose. You can do the same in your practice regardless of the size of the venture. Identify why you really want to start this practice, craft a short phrase of purpose, then create a true mission statement that lets you know both the *why* and the *what*. The clarity of this mission and purpose is one of the most important things you can ever do to have a successful practice that truly makes a difference.

# VALUES

At this point, you are on a roll, but there is still an important piece you must do up front. It's a step that will affect everything about your business for years to come. And while it may seem almost like an academic exercise at first, it is highly practical and immensely important: *You must clearly define your values.*

At Southeast Psych, we began with four values that created the acronym "FIRE": fun, innovation, relationships, and excellence. There has been nothing that has shaped our practice development more than these four governing values. Invariably when someone comes to our office for the first time, whether it is a client, another professional, or a journalist, he or she will say something like, "This place is really fun!" That's not something you hear people say about many other psychology practices, and it has become our calling card. The physical office promotes fun. We have life-size Darth Vader and Storm Trooper figures at the front. We have a studio with glass walls for everyone to look into to see what is happening. We have superhero art in the waiting room and movie posters down the hallways. In our newest expansion, we continued the *Star Wars* theme by having light sabers mounted on the walls of the hallway for illumination and Death Star lights overhead. We have gaming areas in all of our locations. The place feels fun. But it doesn't stop there. We hire people who are friendly and have great senses of humor and a tremendous sense of fun (see Chapter 14, "Issues in Hiring and Supervising Professional Staff and Support Personnel," for information on how we do this at Southeast Psych). You only have to be at our place for a few minutes to get the vibe that this is a place that values fun. We don't need to tell visitors that fun is a core value; they can feel it.

Our next core value is innovation, which is also readily apparent. We have a psychology-in-pop-culture website (shrinktank.com) that attracts thousands of visitors a month. We produce weekly podcasts and webinars. We create videos. We publish books. On the clinical side, we offer groups no one has ever thought of before ("Aspie Rock Band") and create clinical tools and instruments. We provide American Psychological Association–approved continuing education credits. The place is an incubator for innovation.

We also value honest, authentic relationships with each other, clients, and referral sources that feel like true partnerships. Excellence is also of paramount importance and is reflected in whom we hire and the quality of services we provide.

In other words, our values guide us every day. They inform our decision making. They serve as broad benchmarks for progress. They let us know whether we are staying true to ourselves.

The same must be true for you. You must start with a clear vision that gets crafted into a mission statement. You must also have clear values that guide everything you do. Take a look at this incomplete list and consider what values are most important to you:

Adventure

Balance

Beauty

Challenge

Collaboration

Compassion

Courage

Creativity

Diversity

Equality

Excellence

Forgiveness

Fun

Generosity

Gratitude

Growth

Harmony

Health

Impact

Innovation

Justice

Learning

Optimism

Peace

Relationships

Simplicity

Spirituality

Wisdom

Is there any value not represented on this list that you would add? Maybe words like "peace" or "kindness" or "strength" or "bravery" or "authenticity" should be considered. All of these values, as well as the new ones you contributed, are important, but they can't *all* be your core values. If everything good is a core value, then, in essence, nothing is actually a core value because there is not enough focus or prioritization. Narrow your list down to three to five. Ask yourself whether this short list of values accurately captures what is most important to you in your new business. If not, keep working on it. If so, you have made a huge step toward building your ideal practice.

I'll say it again: *There is not one thing we have done that has been more important than define our core values and remain true to them.* But don't try to copy what we have done. Let it flow out of your own core values and the values you want to inculcate in your ideal practice.

When you do this, your practice will embody what is important to you. These values begin to shape your culture. All organizations have a culture, whether intentionally created or not. Cultures that are shaped by clear, compelling values are intentionally created. It is no mistake that Southeast Psych has a culture of fun and innovation that is apparent from the time you walk in the door. That culture is driven by our values, not the other way around. We are constantly asking, "Are we having fun here? Are we being innovative? Are our relationships healthy? Are we doing everything with excellence?" The culture is intentionally created and must be constantly nurtured and guarded.

What will separate a practice that is merely a successful business from your ideal practice is whether or not you have clearly identified your mission and values—and whether you are intent on fulfilling that higher purpose and living out those principles that are so important to you.

# BOLDNESS

When I was in training, I had no money, like most grad students, so I would buy a cheap car for no more than $450, drive it until it exploded, abandon it on the side of the road, then go get myself another $450 car. I did this at least three times over four years. These cars were sort of like disposable razors, except they were actual cars. My friends used to make fun of me for this, but, to be honest, it worked for me. I spent less than $1,500 on car payments during those years, which, if I have my math right, is about $31.25 per month, nearly one-tenth of an expensive car payment. It was a cheap way to go, but it got the job done.

Some clinicians approach their practice development in the same way: Get the job done as cheaply as possible. They find a place with low rent and low overhead costs. They hire few, if any, support staff. They have no budget for marketing or materials. They offer nothing special that will cost them anything extra.

Early in my career, I went to work at a practice that operated this way. Everything was done on the cheap. The copier was small and ineffective. The waiting room was cramped and sparse. The scheduling was done by hand. You could argue that this was cost-effective: It saved money, kept costs low, and guaranteed more profit for the owners. However, in doing this, they also guaranteed there would be nothing special about the practice. The experience would not be special for either the clients or the staff. The business would never do anything surprising or innovative. It would never grow beyond its already small structure.

I would argue that while this strategy may work for buying cars when you are a poor grad student, it's a terrible way to operate if you want to build your ideal practice. In graduate school, living on corn dogs and buying cheap cars is a necessity, but in professional life, it is nearly always the product of fear.

## WHY FEAR?

To do any business right, you have to take risks and jump in wholeheartedly. But the prevailing sentiment among many practitioners is that they must play it safe. They rent a cheap, no-obligation professional suite or share space with a couple of other clinicians. They invest little in their physical facility and even less in the staff and the other enhancements that could make it a special experience.

The counter-argument is almost always that you don't have that kind of money. To be honest, I'm sure you don't. That's where the risk comes into play. That's where you need to consider taking out a loan, borrowing money, getting outside funding. If you want this thing you are creating to be special, you have to be all in with the experience. You have to be committed.

In this regard, I put my money where my mouth is. When Frank and I started Southeast Psych, we spent about six months in the planning stages. As a result, my income dropped about $50,000 from the year before, which is not an insubstantial drop for a person supporting a family with two kids on one income. We both put our houses up as collateral and took out a low-six-figure loan. We invested heavily in our place. One experienced psychotherapist in town visited us in the early days and said, "This is the nicest-looking practice I have ever seen." Since then, we have moved twice to bigger locations and opened up three other offices, all of which are nicer than the one before. In our central office, we have a full production studio for podcasting, webinars, video production, website management, and publishing. Across the hall, we have a social gathering area that serves food and has a full game room with several large-screen TVs. We continue to take the risk and continue to pour funds into our offices. But it's not just the offices where we take the risks. We hire a lot of staff, including positions that other practices would never even consider. We have a full-time hostess in our waiting area who serves people lemonade and coffee. We have a dedicated support staff member just for group therapy who handles registration, scheduling, and space coordination. We have two full-time intake coordinators. We have two checkout staff to ease congestion at the end of each hour.

We are proud of what we have developed, but my point is not to brag about ourselves, but to emphasize that you should invest heavily in your business. If you want to be the best in town and offer something truly special, then you must invest in your business.

Some might argue that successful entrepreneurs are actually more risk averse than other business people, and there is some support for that in the literature (Kim, 2013). But the consensus seems to be that entrepreneurs who do well have a high tolerance for *calculated risk*. They aren't reckless; they aren't impulsive. Instead, they weigh all the options, examine all the possibilities, but at the end of the day, they step out boldly. They go "all in" with their time and money. They don't do half-measures.

# DEVELOP A STRATEGIC PLAN

It is not just an investment of money and time that you need to make to have your ideal practice; you must also have an active and ongoing investment in strategic thinking. You need a strategic plan to be great. It will not happen by accident.

To develop a strategic plan, consider how you would answer all of these questions:

- Which individuals and organizations need to know what we do here? Make it a long list!
- How will I build authentic, mutually beneficial relationships with these people? The key here is for them to be real relationships.
- How will I build greater awareness of my brand in the larger community (e.g., social media, community talks, media marketing, events)?
- What kind of influence do I want both myself and the practice to have in this local community? In what specialty area? In what specific manner?
- How do I want to serve my local community, beyond our office walls?

Answer these questions, then step out boldly and reach your community. Be clear about what you are about and how you are distinctive, and the boldness will follow.

# BLESSING

We once had an intern who told us he was "philosophically opposed to marketing," which we took to mean "philosophically opposed to making a living." But upon deeper reflection, I understand his concern is that he didn't want to be exploitative or use relationships for personal gain. While I understand that, it also misses the point that if you are truly running a mission- and values-driven organization, you are not just taking from people. You are giving something to them that you honestly and deeply believe is valuable. That isn't some hokum to soothe a guilty conscience. It's true. We've learned that if you are truly passionate about what you do, letting people know about it only makes sense. You can truly be a blessing to others.

A blessing is something that brings well-being to someone. While the word is often used in a spiritual context, it has great relevance to you, regardless of your religious stance. One of our psychotherapists recalled a story of a client who, after two years of work, was moving to another city to accept a job promotion. During their final session, the client got tearful and was full of gratitude.

"You have been such a blessing to me," she said. "This place has been a blessing."

Hearing that story made me reflect upon why we do what we do. There are a lot of other ways to make money. There are many jobs that might be more fun. But we offer things like hope and healing and new ways of relating that are, unquestionably, a blessing to others. We can provide blessings to our clients, to our staff, and to our community.

There are many ways to do this, besides being an awesome, authentic, highly skilled clinician. Here are a few.

I've already discussed the importance of making your physical space a great experience for your clients. Imagine going even beyond that and making every interaction a special experience.

Imagine you're having dinner with a friend at a nice restaurant. At the end of the meal, the waiter thanks you for dining with them and gives you the check. He did a nice job, you think to yourself, before giving him your customary 15% tip.

But what would happen if he also gave you a couple of mints with the check? One study (Strohmetz, Rind, Fisher, & Lynn, 2002) suggests you would tip him about 3% more, on average. Not bad for a couple of mints!

But what if he brought you a couple of mints with the check by hand, separate from the check, and asked, "Would either of you care for a mint before you leave?"

Now, according to the study, you are likely to give him a 14% bigger tip.

But wait! What if he came back a second time with a second set of mints and offered more mints. "A couple more mints for the road?" he inquires.

Whether you say yes or no, you are now more likely to give him 21% more than you were originally going to give him.

What accounts for such a huge increase? After all, the only difference, it seems, was the offer of mints. According to the study, though, it wasn't about mints at all. It was about genuine concern for the customers. The waiter seemed interested enough to offer them something extra, and in the final condition, to come back around and offer again. In other words, he went the extra mile and seemed focused on making sure they had a good experience and were taken care of well. This personalization of experience makes a world of difference. The tip was just an expression of how they felt about it.

In your ideal practice, little things mean a lot, not because they are small but because they signify a desire to give the client a special, personalized experience. Walfish and Barnett (2009) refer to this as "customer delight." This means what customers' first phone contact is like, how they are greeted when they walk in the door, what they experience in the waiting area, and how it feels to check out are all important.

Give your clients not only the best therapeutic and assessment services you can, but also a special experience that exceeds all of their expectations. When you do, they'll leave thinking, "Wow, that was a great experience! Not only will I come back here, but I'm going to recommend this place to all my friends and family."

## BLESSING YOUR STAFF

Whether you have one support staff member or over a dozen, you want your people to feel like they work in the best place in the world. Fortunately, the business literature provides us with a lot of data to help with making this happen. While some surveys indicate that salary is the biggest factor in employee satisfaction, others don't put that near the top. A large survey of 200,000 people around the globe by Boston Consulting Group uncovered 26 factors in employee happiness and well-being (Strack, Von der Linden, Booker, & Strohmayr, 2014). Here are the top 10:

1. *Being shown appreciation for their work*—According to the survey, the number-one factor in employee happiness is being told that you really appreciate what they do. It ranked higher than job security, paycheck, and career development. Think about that!
2. *Good relationships with colleagues*—We spend so much of our day at work that it only makes sense that one of the biggest factors in employee satisfaction is the quality of relationships with co-workers. These relationships are key.
3. *Healthy work–life balance*—Companies that promote a good work–life balance by emphasizing the importance of family and leisure time, giving reasonable breaks and time off, and making this a priority that must be balanced against other important aspects of life tend to have happier staff.
4. *Good relationships with superiors*—The ability to have open, honest, and trusting relationships with supervisors is critical to a healthy work environment. Access to supervisors and key decision makers who really listen is essential.
5. *Company's financial stability*—A sense that the company is stable and secure and is likely to be around in 5 or 10 years creates a sense of safety for employees and makes them more emotionally invested and satisfied.
6. *Learning and career development*—Most employees want some sort of challenge and a prospect that if they work hard and do well, they can move up. This is vital because it keeps them mentally stimulated and fresh, while also providing them a chance for career and income mobility.
7. *Job security*—The belief that their job is secure is important to gaining employees' loyalty, trust, and satisfaction.
8. *Attractive salary*—Not all positions can pay that well, but even among those positions, you would be wise to offer salaries that start above the median for that type of work.
9. *Interesting job content*—Nearly everyone wants to do something that is interesting and that makes a difference. The more you can infuse your staff positions with a sense of meaning and higher purpose, the better. The more you can give employees interesting tasks as part of the more mundane parts of their work, the better.
10. *Company values*—You need clear values that shape the company culture, create clarity of purpose, and give employees a sense that they are part of something bigger than themselves.

You can be a blessing to your employees and make your practice—big or small—the best place in town to work.

## BLESSING YOUR COMMUNITY

I've consulted with practices in New York City and in little Southern towns. Regardless of the size, what's clear is that those businesses are part of a local community. You are serving your town—or maybe even your little part of town. I know a psychotherapist who has her office among the shops that line the streets to an entrance to a neighborhood. She sees herself as serving that particular neighborhood, and she does it by offering free trainings, sponsoring a table at a 5K race and other events, and providing materials for anyone to pick up. She makes a good living, but she sees her mission as being a blessing to that highly specific neighborhood.

When you build your ideal practice, imagine how you can benefit your clients beyond what they have come to expect. Imagine how you can encourage, support, and equip your local community. Imagine being actively in your local community by being part of local boards, participating in volunteer organizations, and contributing to building a better quality of life for everyone. Imagine how you can be a blessing to all of them.

## CONCLUDING THOUGHTS

Creating your ideal practice has something to do with how good you are with the mechanics of starting a business. You have to be able to hire well, set up technology, and have some business acumen for contracts and leases and all the rest. It also has to do with providing high-quality professional services that are needed by members of your community and that solve their problems and enhance their lives. But it has more to do with whether you can connect your new business with a mission and values that are important to you. From there, you have to step out boldly, fully committed to what you are doing, and be passionate about your vision. In doing so, you can be a blessing to all those whose lives you touch.

## REFERENCES

Kim, K. (2013, November 19). Risk-takers? Not most entrepreneurs. Retrieved from http://www.inc.com/kathleen-kim/entrepreneurs-more-cautious-not-risk-takers.html.

Sinek, S. (2009). *Start with why: How great leaders inspire everyone to take action*. New York: Portfolio.

Small Business Administration Office of Advocacy. (2011). Frequently asked questions. Retrieved from https://www.sba.gov/sites/default/files/sbfaq.pdf.

Strack, R., Von der Linden, C., Booker, M., & Strohmayr, A. (2014, October 6). Decoding global talent. Retrieved from https://www.bcgperspectives.com/content/articles/human_resources_leadership_decoding_global_talent.

Strohmetz, D. B., Rind, B., Fisher, R., & Lynn, M. (2002). Sweetening the till: The use of candy to increase restaurant tipping. *Journal of Applied Social Psychology. 32*(2), 200–309.

Verhaagen, D., & Gaskill, F. (2014). *How we built our dream practice*. Camp Hill, PA: TPI Press.

Walfish, S., & Barnett, J. (2009). *Financial success in mental health practice*. Washington, DC: APA Books.

CHAPTER 10

# DEVELOPING A BUSINESS PLAN

*Jesse Fairchild*

> *He who fails to plan is planning to fail.*
>
> Winston Churchill

A well-formulated business plan can be the skeleton upon which the body of your business is built. It provides structure and focus to which you can return as the business grows. Often, mental health practitioners skip this important step in favor of just jumping in and getting started with providing services, doing so at the potential expense of their business.

Business planning helps to clarify goals and objectives, provides a road map for future growth, and can be used to raise funds for a new business. It can also keep you on track over time to ensure that you are making decisions consistent with the goals you have set for your business. When making business decisions along the way (e.g., adding clinicians or employees, redefining your niche), you can always refer back to your original plan (and updates) for a reminder of your original goals and objectives.

Good business planning should involve a lot of thinking time and brainstorming. You will want to visit potential office locations, meet with local partners and competitors to determine areas of need or possible collaboration, and just generally dream about the future success of your business. Preliminary brainstorming and thinking about your business sets the stage for setting goals and envisioning an actual practice. From here details can be quantified, qualified, and fleshed out in a written business plan that honors your creative ideas. However, the initial conceptualizing of your business will not get you far if you cannot get it down on paper in a way that others can understand. Business plans will be used for many things, including funding, hiring, and marketing; therefore, if they are not clear and consistent in their message, they will be of limited use.

A good business plan should lay out the basics of your business, including its purpose, its design, and a plan for growth. It must also be flexible and revisited on a fairly regular basis. As your business grows, goals may need to be revisited or revised, and your plan will evolve along the way. While having a tangible document that you can share with potential investors, employees, or partners is important, the greatest value in business planning comes from the time you invest in this process to think about the details of how your business will function. Setting clear goals and direction for your business in your business plan will help to determine necessary steps to move forward.

From the time I established my solo practice in 2011 until now, when the practice sustains myself, five clinicians, interns, and administrative staff, the business plan has been a work in progress. In just four years of seeing clients we have served over 800 people. Returning to the original business plan and revising various aspects of it as the business has grown has been an important component in the success of the practice.

Many clinicians in the field of mental health are looking to establish themselves in a one-person private practice. While that is not the path I took, creating and writing an effective business plan follows the same general process regardless of the size of the envisioned practice. I had an intention to create a thriving practice that would provide work for multiple clinicians while meeting the needs of an underserved rural community, but the process of business planning would be the same had I wanted to be in practice just by myself.

It's easy enough to find an example of a business plan online by looking at the resources available at www.score.org or www.sba.gov. I will walk through the specifics of what should be included and how to develop each section. The basic sections of a business plan are an executive summary, a general company description, products and services, a marketing plan, an operational plan, and a financial plan.

## EXECUTIVE SUMMARY

The executive summary should be concise but compelling. It will be the last thing you write, even though it comes first in the business plan. This is where you sum up everything that will follow in the document. If you choose to use your business plan to obtain funding such as a small business loan or grant, this may be all a potential investor reads. This makes it an important section for funding or marketing purposes but less important for your own process of developing the business.

## GENERAL COMPANY DESCRIPTION

Begin with a general introduction to the business you aspire to build. By the time you are sitting down to write your plan, you will have spent a great deal of time brainstorming and creating ideas for your business. Taking these ideas and boiling them down to the specifics is what you are going for here. This is where you take the big-picture dream and start breaking it down into achievable steps.

First, consider your guiding principles or the values that make your business your own and are specific to how you see your role and that of your business. They often arise from things that have worked well or have not fit well for you in previous practices. My guiding principles were compassion, knowledge, and efficiency. These principles evolved for me during my work in other practices. They were core principles that guided my own work in private practice and they were specific principles that I felt were missing in my past workplaces. Compassion, for me, extended from beyond the compassion a clinician holds for a client; it extended to the ways in which clinicians treat each other and themselves. I knew that foundationally I wanted to create a practice that offered compassionate care to anyone it touched. I noticed that many practices felt cold and unwelcoming as they become more aligned with the medical model for provision of services, and I wanted to create a space that was filled with the warmth of compassionate connection. I also noticed that many clinicians left little time for continued knowledge building outside of the required continuing education units. It was my opinion that this made their work stagnant and limited. I wanted to create a work environment that honored a sharing of knowledge and continued learning for clinicians and clients. In my work under other business owners, I discovered that there was rarely an efficient provision of services, which made it more difficult for me to do the work of counseling. Most administrative employees had little understanding of what actually occurs in the counseling room, and many clinicians had never held an administrative position. All of these things had not only been on my mind but had been pointed out to me by clients. Every time a client had a complaint or suggestion about the practice, I listened and made note of it for my future practice. This gave me a starting point in terms of what I could offer that did not already exist in my area.

I paid attention to colleagues to see what was working and not working for them in terms of building caseloads and providing services. I talked with my colleagues to learn about their successes and frustrations in working for a private practice. I met regularly with my employer to discuss what was and was not effective as I built my caseload. I found other clinicians had little understanding of administrative processes that affect their bottom line, and our employer was typically not forthcoming with information that would be helpful to them, so an integral part of my practice became transparency and knowledge about business for my clinicians in order to create a compassionate, knowledgeable, and efficient environment in which to provide services.

The guiding principles you establish will be applied to your clients' experience and to the way in which the business runs. I have returned to my guiding principles time and time again as my business has grown. In this way they have truly guided both my growth and the growth of the business.

Craft a vision statement. The vision statement is your dream in words. This is what you are working toward, striving for, and building. It is a statement of where you see your company going and is the overarching goal of your business. Your vision statement should not be longer than one sentence and can be as short as just a few words. While the vision statement can be reworked over the life of a business, it should express your core values and intent and will remain fairly consistent over time. A strong vision statement is concise, inspiring, and easy to understand. A great example of this was Microsoft's initial vision statement by Bill Gates, "A PC in every household and home."

Initially the vision statement for my practice, Bodhi, was "To provide supportive mental health services within a holistic environment to children, adolescents, and adults in Cecil County." As the business plan came together, it was evident that this would not fully express what I envisioned. The process for creating a vision statement takes time and patience. If you feel you have come up with the perfect vision statement, sleep on it. Let it spend some time in your brain becoming comfortable. You will often come up with a second, more dynamic and expressive statement. Eventually

I realized the statement for my vision was "Empowering people on their journey of self-discovery and mental wellness."

Once you establish guiding principles and a vision statement, you can develop a mission statement. The mission statement speaks to how you will implement your vision. It is more specific than your vision statement and it operationalizes your vision. Essentially the vision statement projects a future state of your business, and the mission statement states what you will do now to get there. A well-crafted mission statement helps to define what the company offers to its stakeholders (clients, employees, owners, and the community). The mission statement can change over time and should be revisited frequently to determine its appropriateness to the current state of your business. It should always answer what the business does, how it does it, and for whom. Our mission statement at Bodhi is "To provide mental health counseling with compassion, knowledge, and efficiency in Cecil County, MD, and surrounding areas." For further discussion of mission statements and some examples, see Chapter 9, "Envisioning Your Ideal Practice."

Also in the general company description section it makes sense to flesh out what you know about the industry and the area in which you will be locating your business. Important points to mention are your understanding of the local competition, what services they provide, what services might be missing, and opportunities for growth. Some questions to answer in paragraph form may include the likelihood of growth in your field in the coming future, potential changes to the field in the immediate and long-term future, and how you plan to meet these shifts. If you are aware of any potential changes to the marketplace, you can position your practice as a solution to the upcoming changes. For instance, if you know a practice will be going out of business in the next few years, you can discuss the need to absorb their clients. If you know a new employer is coming to town, you can make some predictive assumptions about an increased need for employee assistance services. When I was planning for my practice, I knew that there would be an influx of people to our area due to the closing of an army base in New Jersey and the relocation of their staff to our area. In addition, I was aware that the potential (at that time) Affordable Care Act would increase the number of people with insurance to cover mental health services. Both of these potential changes were addressed in my business plan in terms of the increased need for services and my ability to meet that need.

Share some information on the strengths and core competencies of your business. What about your business model or structure might lend itself to potential success of the business? What makes you competitive? And finally, what experience, skills, or knowledge do you have that will lead to success? Be sure to describe any relevant experience you (or other partners) have.

Also in the general business description you can lay out what type of business structure you have chosen. The basic options are sole proprietorship, limited liability corporation (LLC), or incorporation. Discussing your options based on your particular situation with a qualified business adviser is recommended.

## PRODUCTS AND SERVICES

In this section of your plan you can describe the products and/or services your business will offer. Generally speaking, a private practice won't have products, although some practices might offer books, videos, or other products for sale depending on your niche. This is where you will describe your specific approach to providing services in the psychotherapy field. Services should be described in depth. This could include specific modalities and techniques as well as how you will provide services differently from another private practice. In my business plan I shared my experience in both a previous private practice and a substance abuse treatment facility and my successes in both positions. I also included information on my psychodynamic theoretical orientation and how I would bring on clinicians from different orientations to offer a wide variety of services. Finally, I included my educational background and specific trainings that supported my areas of specialty.

Consider the advantages and disadvantages you may have in providing services. Compare this with an overview of the industry as a whole and trends that may be happening in your area or in the field. Include discussion on what might give you a competitive advantage over others providing services in the area. Include pricing for all services. Be thorough and explanatory about what you are offering.

When describing your services, it is important to start considering a branding strategy. Branding bridges the gap between your services and the marketing of those services. It defines who you are as a "product" in contrast to others providing the same service. It is an often subtle way of expressing who you are as a business entity. Think of branding as a simple and effective way to get what you do into clients' minds so that it is easily recalled. Branding focuses on simply and elegantly presenting who you are as a business, your underlying values, and the essence of what you bring to the market. Branding will often be most noticeable in your business name, logo, and tagline but extends to every bit of marketing material you will eventually produce (e.g., forms, website, advertising material).

The process for establishing your brand can be tedious but is also inspiring as you bring to life your vision of the practice you are building. I spent a great deal of time throwing around ideas with a friend who was a branding consultant when I first envisioned my practice. I was able to boil down the essence of what I wanted to portray and with her help develop a business name, logo, and tagline. I began with some simple concepts. The original text I sent to develop a logo was:

> "I would like something with a white lotus . . . if there's any way to incorporate three lotuses (one in seed, one in bloom, and one ready to bloom) I'd really like that. I like pretty simple designs and limited color . . . maybe just white and green. The idea being that the white lotus represents White Tara. She represents that development of inner qualities, compassion, purity, wisdom, truth. She's vigilant and able to see all the suffering in the world, helping followers to overcome obstacles. She's known for long life, healing, and serenity. As I think about it I guess what I'm going for is something representing compassionate healing in the feminine form. Simple is better . . . delicate even if that's possible. My goal is to bring together mental health and more holistic healing (acupuncture, yoga, meditation, hypnosis, etc.) and I want to incorporate Buddhist accents (so to speak) throughout it all without feeling like you've walked into a temple."

From this description we landed on the name "Bodhi" for my practice, and a logo emerged (Figure 10.1). We went back and forth multiple times with different variations of text font and

FIGURE 10.1: Bodhi logo.

images until I found something that felt right. I also shared the designs with small groups of people to see what their reactions might be. A great concern in my situation was that I would be opening my practice in a rural county that had a history of being fairly conservative and unwelcoming of unfamiliar cultures. Eventually I decided that if my logo and business name couldn't exist in this county, then neither could I as a business owner, so I committed to the branding concept.

In establishing a business name, you can explore your way of working in addition to the area in which you will practice. Many practices are simply named for the clinician who is offering services. My official business name is Jesse Fairchild LLC, but I chose to do business as Bodhi. Using the name "Bodhi" meant explaining to people what exactly the word means. Bodhi is a Sanskrit word that most closely equates to the term "awakening" in English. My sense of psychotherapy is that every client walks in with a "problem," the answer to that problem, and the tools to get to the answer. My role is to help uncover what is already there and to accompany clients on a journey of self-discovery—an awakening to what already exists within. As I explain the meaning of Bodhi to each new client (and in all marketing materials), I am simultaneously explaining my worldview and the way in which I practice.

In addition to the business name and logo, a tagline is often helpful in branding your practice. The tagline for Bodhi evolved into "Awaken to your best self" as a direct reflection of the branding work I had done on the business name and logo.

Once you have established a brand, including a business name, logo, and tagline, it is time to move forward with a marketing strategy and plan.

## MARKETING PLAN

Marketing may be the area that most clinicians fail to truly accept as a vital part of a growing practice. For some reason, we forget that the basic building blocks of marketing are psychological principles, in which we are well versed. Effective marketing involves the basics of human behavior and why we do what we do. Creating a flexible and dynamic marketing plan is crucial to the success of your business. It does not need to be overly fancy with brochures, web presence, and advertising galore, but it does need to get news about your services out to potential clients and people who may refer clients to you in the most efficient and cost-effective way possible. Flying by the seat of your pants in marketing is never a good idea. Creating a basic plan for how you will promote your services and to whom will serve you well in the long run.

## MARKET RESEARCH

A valuable resource for collecting market information for your area is the local library. Most areas have someone at the local library who is focused on small business support; at the very least the reference librarian should have access to information that would be helpful. Information you might seek out would include demographic data on where people live in a given area so you can most effectively situate your business, locations of local transit points for ease of access to your site, or local funding sources. In addition, chambers of commerce, Small Business Association chapters, and trade journals can provide information on local businesses.

Use your own observations. If you are currently working at a practice you can potentially get information on current clients. What you are looking for is demographic information, not medical information. Keep track of where your own clients come from (ZIP code or town address information) and notice any trends that might inform a choice of location for your potential practice. Be careful of any potential violation of the Health Insurance Portability and Accountability Act (HIPAA) in terms of what you collect and or use in written business planning. Familiarize yourself with HIPAA at http://www.hhs.gov/hipaa/for-professionals. One of the observations I made in my previous practice was that clients were driving from another county to obtain services as there were limited mental health resources in their home area. Luckily, their home county happened to be my own home county, and that spurred the idea of starting a practice closer to home. Just knowing that I had a base of clients who were already driving a distance to see me seemed like a good place to start.

Consider visiting practices in the area where you hope to open your business. While many business enterprises are geared toward competition, the provision of mental health services can exist in a more collaborative and supportive atmosphere. Prior to opening my practice I visited the few clinicians in the area to get a sense of their services, clientele, and niche in the community. My initial goal was to fill gaps where I could and to see what differentiated me from them. We were able to be supportive of each other and in the end, when several of the other clinicians closed their practices for various reasons, they referred their clients to me because we had established a collaborative working relationship.

## FEES

There are several ways to set prices for your services. If you go through the process for paneling with insurance companies, they will indicate an allowable fee for services. Generally, this will be below most clinicians' usual and customary fees. When you did your market research on the competition you conceivably collected information on their fees, and you can set yours with consideration to your market. Another way to set prices is to determine what you want to earn. If you determine an annual salary you'd like to target, added to the annual cost of doing business, you can divide that by the number of hours you'd like to work to determine an hourly rate.

Some other things to consider for prices are whether you will have a fixed hourly fee for all services or differing rates for various services. Consider all potential services. I include rates for individual sessions (which vary by the length of time of the session), couples sessions, family sessions, specific services (e.g., hypnosis, evaluation, testing, translation), court fees, late cancels, and no-shows.

## ECONOMICS

Include whatever facts you can determine about your industry. What is the size of the market? What percentage of this market can you serve? What is the current demand? What trends are occurring in the market? Can the market sustain another practice? What obstacles exist to you entering the market, and how do you plan to overcome those obstacles? Consider how your practice can meet the unmet needs in the community. The research you have done on the local area should help you to determine if adequate general psychotherapy practices already exist and if a more specific need is going unmet.

Include a sales forecast. It is important to determine if you will be paneling with managed care organizations (MCOs), as this will determine what you will actually collect. Generally MCOs will be reimbursing at an allowable charge below where you set your fees. In addition, you should consider whether or not you will offer a sliding fee scale, which will also affect collections. Discuss how many clients you expect to serve and the ebb and flow of actual sessions. Create a spreadsheet (or table) that shows 12 months in the columns followed by two more columns for years. In the rows list your services, which may be simply one row of you seeing clients. Project numbers of potential clients multiplied by your hourly rate. Table 10.1 assumes that the goal is 25 clients a week at $100 per hour. The table is simplified to show the concept. In reality you will not necessarily be collecting exactly what you charge for a session; there may be reductions in fees due to MCOs and there may be clients who fail to pay for their sessions. Be sure to include these assumptions in an actual projected income. It assumes that there will be an initial 10 clients who will move from an established practice and that each month the client caseload will increase by 2 clients. It also assumes that in November and December there will be a dip in sessions due to the holidays. Years two and three assume an overall 10% increase in revenue. This is oversimplified for the purpose of providing an example. You should spend significant time determining what an actual flow of clients might be in your practice. Be sure to account for holidays, vacations, snow closings (if you live in a colder climate), and other things that could affect the number of sessions or number of clients in a given month.

TABLE 10.1: **Sample Sales Forecast**

| | 1/15 | 2/15 | 3/15 | 4/15 | 5/15 | 6/15 | 7/15 | 8/15 | 9/15 | 10/15 | 11/15 | 12/15 | Total 2015 | 2016 | 2017 |
|---|---|---|---|---|---|---|---|---|---|---|---|---|---|---|---|
| Ind. Session Revenue | 4000 | 4800 | 5600 | 6400 | 7200 | 8000 | 8800 | 9600 | 10000 | 10000 | 7500 | 7500 | 89400 | 98430 | 108273 |

In addition to income, the economics section should include a quick review of potential expenses associated with the business. Some basic expenses would include rent, liability and general insurance, utilities, office supplies, marketing expenses, training, business licenses, and professional fees (e.g., accountant, attorney).

## CUSTOMERS

Describe the group you plan to target for services. As you grow this may become a varied group of people, especially if you grow into a practice with multiple clinicians providing services to different groups of clients. However, if you, like most of us, are beginning with yourself as the sole provider of services, then it should be a fairly targeted and specific group.

I feel one of the best predictors of success is how well you define this target customer population in terms of your own strengths and weaknesses and practice goals. If one area of the business planning process deserves primary attention, this is it. Defining your ideal clients and how you will work with them is the pearl at the center of your practice oyster. It is the most central and centering aspect of your plan. If you have a good sense of your own strengths and weaknesses, along with your specific training and experience, you can define a niche in which you will flourish. Keep in mind that you can always engage in further education or training to build upon current strengths or to shore up any areas of weakness. Take the time to really look at what you bring to the table that is different from other clinicians; we all have something. Think of the clients with whom you've worked who fired you up clinically, the clients for whom you have a passion about their issues, their lifestyle, or their diagnosis. Consider which clients have stayed committed to working with you therapeutically. These are your ideal clients. They will be the end goal of your marketing plans. Everything you do should lead to them in terms of marketing.

One caveat: Some ideal client groups are too small to build a practice upon. It is worthwhile to define two potential target niches and also to be aware you may have to work outside of your niche to build a strong practice at first. You will probably have to work with other groups to build your practice effectively and to meet the needs of your community. However, never lose sight of those clients with whom you work most effectively and most passionately.

Over time your niche(s) may evolve. When I began my practice the niche I focused on was those dually diagnosed with substance abuse and mental health issues. It was a specialty I had years of experience in and was an area of great need, as many psychotherapists avoid working with substance abuse clients. I knew that I did not want to have a focus on dual diagnosis for long, but it would afford me the opportunity to build a client base and reputation in the area. I also wanted to focus on women in transition (graduating, marrying, having children, divorcing, grieving), and I included that in my descriptions of services and all marketing efforts. I simultaneously built these niches. Over the time I have been in my practice, my niche has evolved to working with women in transition, business owners, and grief counseling, specifically with those bereaved by suicide. Because I built my practice on a strong foundation of my experience and strengths, continued in training to build other areas of specialty, and hired other clinicians to take on areas in which I am not focused, I am now able to focus in areas that nourish my own professional growth.

## COMPETITION

Know your competitors. Even if you are planning to work collaboratively, you should learn all that you can about anyone providing mental health services in your area. Know their strengths and weaknesses. Know their clientele. Know their location. Know their marketing strategies as best you can. If you can meet with them and work collaboratively, do so. Learn what they've already tried. Learn how they'd like to partner. Consider how your potential business will compare with these established businesses. Choose several other practices in your area and consider their strengths and weaknesses. Use this information to create a competitive analysis that compares your potential business side by side with your major competitors. A simple competitive analysis might look like Table 10.2.

The data in this table can be helpful in that you begin to see gaps in services or ways in which your practice can provide services that are not available currently. For instance, in this table we see that only one other practice offers Saturday hours, which tend to be sought-after times of service. In addition, the other practice that offers Saturday hours does not begin until 10 a.m., leaving a gap in the early morning when you might be able to serve kids before their Saturday sports begin. Also, the table can be used to define important considerations for your practice, such as needing to have clear directions on your website and/or voicemail and to provide directions to new clients due to the difficulty in finding your office the first time. You can also see information valuable for referrals in that one practice offers medication management and another in-home services.

## STRATEGY

Now that you've looked at all of the pieces, you can bring it all together in an action plan. Consider how you will find your clients and get the word out to them. List organizations you plan to contact to introduce your services. Discuss what advertising you will use and in what ways. Advertising is a part of a marketing plan in that it is how you communicate about your services to potential clients and referral sources. Consider the image you hope to project and the ways in which your marketing plan can be in line with this. Include a budget for promotion by determining the actual costs of the marketing you've decided to do.

## PROPOSED LOCATION

Consider your needs for a location. Do you need just enough space for yourself? Do you want to share costs? Do you want to provide services out of your home? Consider locations that are available for rent such as doctor's offices in the evenings, churches, and other clinicians' offices. In addition, consider Americans with Disabilities Act accessibility requirements, parking needs, and lighting for evening hours. Consider the branding you have determined for your practice as well and how the potential location builds upon your brand.

In the lifetime of my practice I have had three locations. The first was a very small office space in a strip-mall type of building. It was located next to a pawnshop, a pet shop, a tattoo shop, and

TABLE 10.2: Sample Competitive Analysis

| | My Business | Competitor A | Competitor B | Competitor C | Competitor D | Competitor E |
|---|---|---|---|---|---|---|
| Hours | M–F 8–8 Sat 8–4 | M–F 9–7 | M–F 12–9 | M, W, F 8–6 T, Th 3–9 Sat 10–4 | Variable | M–F 8–2 |
| Location | On a major road but difficult to find first time | On a major road; well known | In a professional building | Multiple offices | Doctor's office and church office | In their home |
| Services Offered | Individual, couples, family sessions, employee assistance programs, workshops, hypnosis, eye movement desensitization and reprocessing (EMDR) | Medication management; in-school services; partial hospitalization; intensive outpatient program | Individual | Individual, couples, family, group | Individual, couples | Individual |
| Fees | $100–$150 | Unavailable | $125 | $100 | $75–$100 | $70 |
| Specialty Areas | Trauma, grief, infertility, geriatric, substance abuse | Dual diagnosis; childhood; family; chronic psychiatric care | Anxiety, depression | | Pastoral counseling | |

a hair salon. It was on a major thoroughfare and was easy to see from the road. It was big enough to accommodate a small waiting room, a clinical office, and a larger space for groups and administrative needs (filing, copier, desk). When the hair salon and pet shop left the building and a bail bondsman moved in, I knew it was time to move into another space. At this point I also knew I had maxed out my ability to meet the needs of clientele and needed a larger space to bring on new clinicians. The pawnshop was looking to expand at that time, so I negotiated a deal to have him buy out my lease and fund my moving expenses.

I found an office space in the center of town that could accommodate three clinical offices and a waiting room. It was in a Victorian house, and I was able to rent out the upstairs myself so that I could control who was living above our offices. It had ample street parking and was close to the post office and local shops so that parents could drop their children off for an appointment and go walking around town. It was also quite close to a private school to whom I was marketing our services.

After about a year in this office space we had a need for administrative support, but the building space would not support this effectively. I found a larger office space that I was able to build out in a way that effectively expressed the image and brand we had been developing. The newest office space holds four clinical offices, a waiting room, a meditation room, and administrative space. After one year in the office we were able to expand within the same building to offer another clinical office, two large group rooms, and a second bathroom. The colors and artwork are all consistent with the Bodhi brand. Also, the office is located in an unassuming dark-brown building. Clients often comment about the visual experience of walking into such a bland building and finding an oasis of calm and serenity. This was our goal in decorating the space, and it has been well received. A typical comment from new client's is that the space feels "calm and relaxing" allowing for a feeling of peacefulness from which their healing and inner work can begin. This is an example of how your brand can permeate all aspects of your practice.

# OPERATIONAL PLAN

The operational plan portion of your business plan will lay out the day-to-day operations of your practice. This is what will eventually become your standard operating procedures; therefore, you will return to it often to update and reflect the changes in your practice as it grows. Many of those procedures will develop as your business grows, but some very basic aspects can be addressed in your business plan. Basically you are describing how your business will run. Important aspects of a service-oriented business plan such as psychotherapy private practice are provision of services, personnel requirements, licensing information, credit policies, and managing accounts receivable and accounts payable.

What will the client's experience be from the moment of learning about your services to coming into your practice? Keep in mind your decisions about branding when describing this experience. Explain the ways in which client calls will be handled and by whom. Indicate how you will schedule clients, determine insurance benefits (if you are paneled with managed care), provide services, and accept payment. Be as specific as you can. Consider everything from the client's perspective and your ability to meet his or her needs. Walk through the experience in your mind, both from your perspective as the provider of services and from the client's perspective. Include information on how mental health emergencies will be handled as well as vacation or other time away from the practice.

What will you offer in terms of staffing? Will you be providing services as a sole provider? Will you bring on additional independent contractors or clinical staff? Will you need administrative support, either in house or an external professional hired to handle billing, scheduling, or collections?

Consider how your location will affect provision of services. Is there handicapped accessibility? Is there a waiting room, or do sessions need to be scheduled so they won't overlap? Does the location reflect your values, mission, and brand? In what ways can you use interior design and decoration to reinforce the physical representation of the work you are doing?

Consider the legal environment for running your business. What licenses do you need both to provide mental health services and to open a business? Check with all levels of government from state to local. After signing a lease on a second office I found out that the particular area in which I was located required specific permission from the town board to run a private practice. Luckily the town was welcoming and fast-tracked my application, but this could have been a costly mistake.

Consider how you will accept payments. Will you accept only cash or checks? Will you accept insurance? How will you accept credit card payments? How will you track accounts receivable and accounts payable? How will you collect payments if clients avoid payment at the time of service? These are important aspects of running a business and can often be complicated in a mental health private practice (please see other chapters for more in-depth discussion of some of these important business practices). Know the ethics of your licensure and how these impact collection of payments or termination of services for nonpayment.

I have discovered that many clinicians are uncomfortable asking for payment for services. Knowing ahead of time what your comfort level might be with payment is important in terms of determining staffing needs as well. When I started my practice I was handling all administrative aspects; given that I had training in various administrative tasks, including accounting, it was a good fit. I began with a ledger book for accounting and a weekly calendar for scheduling and used officeally.com for billing insurance companies. As I gained clientele I moved to using QuickBooks for accounting and continued with the paper calendar. When I brought on additional independent contractors I researched and found an online practice management system that could effectively handle scheduling and billing for multiple clinicians. I found that while I was fairly comfortable discussing issues of payment for services with my clients, some of my clinicians were far less comfortable with this. In addition to providing some supervision in this matter, I decided it was worth the cost to bring on an administrative person to handle this function. Many colleagues of mine who are in private practice just for themselves use billing agencies to deal with the insurance billing and collection portion of services. There is no wrong way to deal with these necessary aspects of running a private practice. Knowing your own strengths and interests will help to determine what aspects of the business you may need additional staff to handle.

# FINANCIAL PLAN

Attempting to get a sense of the potential financial picture for your business is important. If you are using your business plan to obtain funds, banks will require financial documents to determine if you are a good risk for their funds. If you are using your business plan to direct the path of your business, the financial plan can help you make decisions based on various potential financial outcomes. The basic financial documentation is fairly simple to pull together, but that doesn't mean it's easy. If you're in the business of providing mental health services, you conceivably had only one or two math classes while obtaining your degree, and those centered on statistics and not accounting. Your options are to do a little research on preparing financial documents or to hire an accountant or financial planner to help with the process. Neither is a better or worse choice. If you know this will hold you up in the business planning process, then it's important to understand your limits and to find appropriate support.

## FINANCIAL ASSUMPTIONS

The financial plan must begin with a brief list of financial assumptions upon which your numbers are based. This is where you explain how you got the numbers that will appear in the financial documents. After having thoroughly gone through the process to create a marketing plan, operational plan, and products and services descriptions you should have some idea of the costs inherent in running your potential business. If you recall, in the section on sales forecasting we looked at some assumptions for potential sales. This is what you will continue to do for the items you'll include in the financial section. Much like the executive summary, it is often easier to write the financial assumptions after you've worked through the other financial documents.

## PROFIT AND LOSS (P&L) STATEMENT

A P&L statement basically lays out income and expenses. In this case you will be forecasting potential income and expense over the next three to five years. I have found that using an Excel spreadsheet is the best option for a P&L statement as you can easily change numbers and see the overall effect. You can create a P&L statement that shows income and expense for each month for the total number of years or create a simple document that lays out income and expenses for several years in total side by side.

Income for a P&L statement at this stage of the game will likely be fairly simple—it will be the projected fees you will collect as a sole clinician. Consider the number of clients you believe you will see in a week, multiply by the number of weeks you want to work each year to obtain an annual total number of clients, and multiply that by the hourly fee you expect to collect. If you are planning on being paneled with insurance companies you will have to take into consideration the allowable amount you can bill rather than the actual fee you've set. If you are putting your own money into the business, be sure to include that in the initial month of the P&L. If you plan on taking loans, include those too, and be sure to include the payment schedule (including interest) in the expenses.

Expenses should include such things as rent, utilities, marketing, supplies, printing, licensure fees, insurance (malpractice and general liability), continuing education, equipment, furniture, taxes, and any other items you need to run your practice. Be aware that many of these costs change over time. Initial costs for equipment, furniture, supplies, and marketing may be much higher at the outset of the business than later on, though some may be one-time purchases and not an ongoing cost. Other costs, such as insurance or licensure fees, may be intermittent or even annual. If you plan to hire staff be sure to include payroll costs, including taxes and benefits.

Overall, on the P&L statement you should be conservative in your projections for income and on the higher side for expenses. Be sure to investigate actual costs rather than just guessing what a cost might be for something. Check with utility companies, insurance companies, and landlords to determine those expenses. Go to the office supply store and price out what you think you'll need to run your business. Check into costs for developing and maintaining a website, for leased equipment, and for your phone, answering service, and so forth.

## CASH FLOW

A statement of cash flow generally goes a little farther than a P&L to show cash on hand at any given time. Whereas a P&L shows basic income and expenditures, cash flow includes inflow from operations, investing, and financing. In this way a cash flow statement will show what money is coming in and going out from basic business functions (income for services and outgo for business operations expenses), what money is tied up in equipment or buildings (depreciation) or actual investments, and what money is available or owed from a loan or debt payment.

## BALANCE SHEET

A balance sheet takes into account all assets, liabilities, and equity to determine the financial health of the business. Whereas P&L and cash flow statements are over time (for your purposes a period of three years for each is appropriate, comprising the individual first 12 months and yearly totals for the last two years), a balance sheet is more of a picture of a moment in time.

Assets will include cash on hand (bank accounts), accounts receivable (outstanding payments due from clients or insurance), and fixed or long-term assets (e.g., equipment, depreciation, buildings). Keep in mind that accounts receivable may not always be considered assets given the likelihood that a portion may be written off or adjusted. The farther out your accounts receivable are, the less likely they will be recovered. Liabilities include accounts payable (any bills due in a given time period) and long-term liabilities (loans). Finally, equity includes anything contributed by you or other business partners.

Both the Small Business Administration (www.sba.gov) and SCORE (www.score.org) have resources for building a small business and specifically to help you understand financial planning and documents.

# A WORD OF ADVICE

Business planning may be the most important aspect of starting your own business. Give yourself the time and space to dream big things for your practice, and let your business plan be the firm ground in which you plant those dreams. Recognizing the importance of planning at the outset of your private practice venture will create a fertile environment for future goal setting and growth along the way.

# RESOURCES

Grodzki, L. (2000). *Building your ideal private practice*. New York: W.W. Norton & Co.

Grodzki, L. (2003). *Twelve months to your ideal private practice: A workbook*. New York: W.W. Norton & Co.

KU Work Group for Community Health and Development. (2015). Chapter 8, Section 2: Proclaiming Your Dream: Developing Vision and Mission Statements. Lawrence: University of Kansas. Retrieved from http://ctb.ku.edu/en/table-of-contents/structure/strategic-planning/vision-mission-statements/main

Shelton, H. (2014). *The secrets to writing a successful business plan: A pro shares a step-by-step guide to creating a plan that gets results*. Rockville, MD: Summit Valley Press.

Stout, C., & Grand, L. C. (2005). *Getting started in private practice: The complete guide to building your mental health practice*. Hoboken, NJ: John Wiley & Sons.

# MANAGING YOUR PRACTICE

# CHAPTER 11

# CONSIDERATIONS IN ACQUIRING OFFICE SPACE

*Jeffrey Zimmerman and Steven Walfish*

Perhaps the largest expenditure that you will make in the course of running your practice will be renting office space. If you are in a full-time practice and rent space for yourself, this can easily cost $700/month or $8,400/year. Depending on the location of your practice (e.g., large city) and the type of office that you rent (e.g., "Class A" office building), it can go much higher. Many leases are for more than one year, and while the costs are spread out monthly, a three-year lease for a modest office can easily be an obligation that exceeds $30,000 (as the rent, utilities, and other expenses are likely to increase from year to year). If you rent space with a colleague, the obligation (though not the cost, if both parties live up to their respective financial obligations) is likely to be close to double, as most leases require each of you to be fully responsible to the landlord for the total lease amount, regardless of your arrangements with each other. If you are in practice part time you may rent space less expensively or on an hourly basis, but the principles in this chapter will still be pertinent for you.

The decision about leasing office space is also important from many other perspectives. Your office is a visual and experiential statement of you and your practice. It is part of your branding. Where it is located, what the furnishings and décor are, who the other tenants in the building are, and even whether it is wheelchair accessible, all say something about you and your practice and contribute to the comfort your clients and referral partners have or do not have about your practice (at times regardless of your professional skills).

In this chapter we will discuss general considerations for leasing an office. We are going to assume that you do not have experience in the real estate field and that you do not have a close relative with that experience who can guide you. In fact, we are going to assume that you are at a distinct disadvantage making this business decision. You are entering a competitive process of business negotiations for which you are not trained and will be negotiating with experts in their field (real estate agents and commercial property owners). While you are providing mental health services all day, they are negotiating the leasing of commercial office space all day. They know the space you are considering, know the market, and know the lease agreement they will ask you to sign. They have negotiated perhaps hundreds of times before and know what is wrong with the space and the ambiguous clauses in the contract that they can take advantage of (although they likely will not point these out to you).

What you have going for you is that building owners likely look at empty space as quite undesirable. It seriously can cut into their profits. Their fixed expenses (e.g., mortgage, taxes, maintenance) still need to be paid even though there is no income coming in from the space that is empty (or soon to be empty). However, owners are likely to appear quite confident and not as desperate as we might expect. They have likely learned that appearing confident and secure can bring them higher rents than appearing desperate. You need to also gauge your appearance, as the more desperate you appear, the greater the likelihood that you will pay more in rent than you might otherwise.

## PREPARING TO BEGIN THE PROCESS

We believe the best way go through the process and to know that you are paying a reasonable rent for the space is to do your homework and prepare for the transaction that is about to occur. Zimmerman (2015) discusses the importance of carefully estimating how much space you will need and for how long (e.g., before you might expand). He suggests learning the market by looking at potentially desirable locations from the street, taking pictures of buildings that have "for rent" signs, and keeping detailed notes about each location. Zimmerman suggests creating a list of initial questions to ask when you call to get information about the space, such as the rent, size and configuration of the suite, what is included in the lease, occupancy dates, and so forth. This will allow you to compute some initial estimated costs of the space, taking into account the possibility of having to reconfigure the space.

## VISITING RENTAL OPTIONS

Visit the space at least once, but do not go on a "tour" of many spaces with a real estate agent. Drive yourself without the agent. Real estate agents know the most attractive streets to bring you to the space. They speak with you and distract you. This can keep you from approaching a building from many different directions so that you can learn the area surrounding the building. Assess how easy it is to enter and exit the property coming and going in all directions at different times of day. Noticing what it is like around "rush hour" is vital if you want to see clients in the early morning or late afternoon. Getting to your office should not be a noxious experience for you or your clients, and heavy traffic may dissuade them from continuing to see you. Is the property on a bus route? Real estate agents may also bring you right into the building and not give you a lot of time to get to look in the lobby and see who the other tenants are or check out the cleanliness of the public restrooms. It is important even to look at the shrubs and parking lot. All of these give you important clues about how the landlord cares for the property and in what kind of environment you will be spending the next number of years and the environment your clients will be visiting to see you. Think of the difference between a building that has a beauty salon, a fast-food restaurant, and a music store on the first floor, with you on the second floor, compared to one that has mostly lawyers and accountants, or mostly physicians, or mostly mental health clinicians. One may be a better fit for you and your practice than another. Looking closely at the directory in the lobby or the signs out front can provide a lot of important information.

Try not to look at the space as it is, but instead try to envision the space as it could be. Walls can be moved. Closets can be constructed. Sound attenuation can be added. Visiting the space is a time to pay close attention to details such as the following:

- What is the noise level in the suite and from outside the suite?
- What is the natural lighting during different times of the day? Will sun be shining in the eyes of those present?
- Are there smells coming from other suites?
- Is there enough closet space?
- What kind of control do you have over the thermostats (heating and cooling), especially after normal working hours?
- Do the windows open?
- Does carpeting and wallpapering or painting need to be done?

The site visit is a time to get a sense of whether the suite has potential. It is a time to ask questions. Be sure to take pictures and notes, as things easily get confusing over time when you see more than one space. Also, real estate agents and landlords may say one thing when you speak with them and not put it in writing. What is told to you needs to show up in the lease, as the lease is the binding legal agreement, not your assertions of what you remember being told.

# NARROWING DOWN YOUR OPTIONS

The next step is to compare the options based on your subjective experience (i.e., what it felt like being in the building and space) as well as the financial components of each deal. Some landlords may offer incentives for signing a longer lease (e.g., a number of months without having to pay rent, the landlord paying for some refurbishing of the space, or limits on increases for Common Area Maintenance [CAM] charges). You also can call some of the current tenants and ask them about their experience of being in the building. How is the landlord to work with? What problems are the tenants having in their space? What might they do differently if they were renting space now?

As you look at your options, remember that sometimes the property with the lowest rent is not necessarily the best fit for you and your clients. It may not even ultimately be best from a financial perspective, as there may be costs and increases over the term of the lease that make it more expensive in the long run.

# BEGINNING YOUR NEGOTIATIONS

Many potential tenants do not prepare for this critical phase of the process. We believe it is crucial to do your homework here, in advance of any discussions with the landlord or real estate agent. It can be helpful to do the following:

- Write down the verbal terms as you understand them.
- List your questions.
- Compare the rent per square foot and other terms with other properties you have seen and researched.
- Are there considerations that the landlord can provide that would make the lease more attractive (e.g., reserved parking spaces, extended hours of access, signage, some rent abatement for a period of time, lower annual increases, options to renew at a predetermined rent)?

If your questions are satisfactorily addressed, it is now time to ask for a draft copy of the lease. We recommend reading the lease before you show it to your attorney. Even though there may be clauses that are difficult to comprehend with their run-on sentences and legalese, it is important to make sure you see the terms that you have agreed to being clearly represented. Be sure if the lease refers to appendices that they are indeed included in the draft you are reviewing. Ask any questions you have after looking at the lease and write down any wording changes or changes in terms (as well as who you were speaking to and when). You can also say that you have not yet shown the lease to your attorney but wanted to make sure you first obtained answers to your initial questions.

If the answers make sense and the lease looks reasonable as best you can tell, it is then time to have it reviewed by your real estate attorney. This may not be the same person who helps you with malpractice or employment or tax questions. Real estate law is a specialty unto itself. There are nuances in many lease agreements and even clauses in the lease agreement that may not be legal. Your real estate attorney can help point these out to you as well as interpret the clauses that you were not able to understand on your own so you will understand what you may be agreeing to if you sign the lease.

# FINALIZING THE LEASE

Ask your attorney about worst-case scenarios, and get a list of additional talking points, questions, and wording changes. Negotiations can fall apart even at this late point in the process as there may be terms that are "deal breakers" for either you or the landlord. Landlords will also, even at this point, be trying to judge how likely you are to sign a lease and "close the deal," so it can be helpful to reiterate your interest in coming to agreement as you address your final concerns. Not only will this communicate your seriousness, it may help deal with what could be called "negotiating fatigue" if the process has been rather exhausting.

It is crucial then to reread the final draft of the lease in its entirety. You need to make sure all terms and agreed-on changes have been incorporated into the last draft. Attorneys can make mistakes, changes that have been agreed on can be omitted, and there can even be mathematical errors. "What you see [in the lease] is what you get," so be sure you understand and agree with what is in the final draft *before* you sign it. It is very difficult and costly, if not impossible, to make modifications after the lease is signed.

# OTHER CONSIDERATIONS AND IDEAS

### TAKE YOUR TIME

Landlords and real estate agents have lots of strategies to "close" a deal. One is to create a sense of urgency in the potential tenant. They may speak about other potential tenants who are expressing "great interest" in the space. They may give you deadlines that they claim have to be met in order to be able to rent the space. However, responding with a sense of urgency increases your risk that you will make a serious error as you make this decision.

### BE WILLING TO WALK AWAY

Landlords and real estate agents count on you getting emotionally "hooked" on the space. They seek to get small commitments or "yes" statements from you as they build to the ultimate, "Yes, I will take the space." The more desperate you appear, the more likely it will be that you will get worse terms than you might otherwise. One of the greatest strengths you have is the ability to end the negotiation at any time if it is not suiting you. One important concept, though, is the importance of balancing enough interest in order to show you are a serious prospect for the space with the lack of being "hooked" on the space. If you are arrogant or appear uninterested, the agent and the landlord will not want to spend their time on a deal they do not believe they can actually close. They will likely want to look for a potential tenant who has more interest and whom they predict will be more likely to ultimately sign a lease.

### ASK IF THERE ARE AUTOMATIC INCREASES
### IN THE FINANCIAL TERMS

Most Class A office buildings and medical office spaces operate on a concept called "triple net," and this is usually built into the lease. This is related to CAM fees (e.g., utilities, maintenance, landscaping) and the fees charged to each office based on a pro rata amount of square footage of the space you are renting. We are aware of one situation where one of the tenants was a large restaurant with tremendous utility usage. The mental health professionals had "sticker shock" when they saw they had to pay a large surcharge for their portion. We are aware of other situations where an increase in real estate taxes and the cost of landscaping improvements were passed on to the tenants in a pro-rated manner. Ask for a history of any such charges for the past three to five years.

## USE OTHER ADVISORS TO LOOK AT THE SPACE

Friends, adult family members, and colleagues can all help with questions you may have. They can give you a reason to return to the space and see if you feel the same way and hear the same terms on the second visit. Do not hesitate to include them after your first visit to the site.

# CONSIDERATIONS IN SUBLETTING SPACE

For a variety of reasons a private practitioner may not want to take responsibility for renting space from a landlord but would rather sublet space from someone who is taking responsibility for the lease. One reason might be that the clinician is just starting out in practice and may want a part-time office or may not want to sign a lease that requires a two- or three-year financial commitment. A second reason might be that the clinician wants to "test the waters" before making a longer and more significant financial commitment. The clinician also may want to affiliate or rent one room in an office suite of an existing practice but not have responsibility for a full lease, such as subletting space in a medical specialty office.

When subletting it is important to distinguish yourself both practically and professionally from the group where you are subletting. For example, if you are renting space from a group of mental health professionals, it may appear from a public perspective that you are part of a group practice. Signage in the lobby or outside the door can make it clear that there are separate providers in the space, and your informed consent paperwork should make this distinction for the client. Here are some other considerations and suggestions:

- Where will your records be stored? Will they be in a locked cabinet that only you have access to (preferred) or will they be integrated with all of the medical records of everyone in the space?
- Have your colleagues and support staff sign Health Insurance Portability and Accountability Act (HIPAA) business associate agreements. This binds them to maintaining confidentiality as they may inadvertently come in contact with the confidential information of your clients (e.g., faxes, files mistakenly left on your desk).
- Will you be using a common electronic billing system with the other clinicians in the practice? If so, make sure that others do not have access to your client billing records.
- What services will you have access to, and which expenses will you be responsible for, while in the practice (e.g., telephone landline, voicemail or answering service, fax machine, Wi-Fi/Internet, photocopier)? Will you be limited to copying a certain number of sheets per month?
- Will you be responsible only for your clients or will there be a shared call schedule? What type of coverage, if any, will be available to you if you are on vacation or ill?

- Will support staff for the practice also be your support staff? Will they answer the phones, take messages for you, and greet clients?
- Will you have access to the same office to see clients each day you are there or will you have to rotate to use other people's offices on their days off?
- If you rent for two or three days per week and you want to expand your practice, is there space to do so? What will the terms of this expansion look like?

As you can see from this list of questions, subletting is not as simple as wanting to practice and having a colleague who has some space who says, "Come and rent from me." It is even more complicated if you choose to rent space from a medical practice.

## CONSIDERATIONS IN INTEGRATED HEALTH

Significant opportunities are available for mental health clinicians with an interest in behavioral medicine to participate in integrated care. Coons and Gablis (2010) point out several factors that need to be considered in such an arrangement as it relates to leasing space, such as the following:

What are the terms of the agreement? Under what conditions and what timeframe may they ask you to leave the practice?

What will be the cost and availability of space? Readily available space to see clients may not be available, especially in a traditional type of psychotherapy office with perhaps two chairs and a couch. Often clinicians have to be flexible and make do with the space that is available.

Will a certain number of client referrals be required with the rental of space? Make sure this is not required, as all referrals have to be individualized and in the best interest of the client.

Will the clinician have access to the electronic health records of the clinic? If so, what privacy protections are available so that clients' mental health records cannot be accessed?

If the electronic health records are not accessible, what systems are in place to keep records from being accessed?

Will separate premises liability insurance need to be purchased?

What support staff will be available (e.g., receptionist) to the clinician?

## AN ALTERNATIVE TO LEASING: PURCHASING SPACE

As we noted above, the largest expenditure you are likely to have in your practice is in renting office space. For some clinicians, especially those who have a long-term vision, a better choice might be to purchase office space instead of leasing.

Of course, purchasing office space involves capital outlay and usually acquiring the debt of a loan or mortgage at the start and then a continued commitment to assume responsibility for all ongoing costs (e.g., continued maintenance, insurances, real estate taxes). Some of these costs are predictable (e.g., if it is a house you will need a new roof every 10 to 15 years), but some may not be (e.g., a natural disaster such as a fire or lightning striking the building and causing damage, significant changes in maintenance costs and taxes).

However, owning the space also is an investment. As such, while the value of real estate tends to rise, you never know what the value will be when you want to sell the property. As with the residential real estate market, an economic downturn (or other issue, such as environmental pollution on the land) might make the property worth less than you paid for it, or even unsalable, for a time. Tax incentives for owning space may also be pertinent; check them in advance of a purchase with your accountant.

If the investment is financed, you can fix the long-term cost that you will pay for space through the mortgage. This may vary depending on the financing you obtain. Conversely, when renting, each lease has an end point (usually one, three, or five years), at which time the new rental fees tend to increase.

If you also own a home, then a significant amount of your cash flow and debt will be focused on real estate. For many clinicians whose practices are not yet well established or who may not have a second income from a spouse or significant other, owning office space may be cost prohibitive. On the other hand, if you own space that has offices for additional clinicians, you might be able to rent that space and use this income to help pay the mortgage. If you successfully maintain your tenants over the long term, then in essence they will pay for the property and in the end you will own it outright. Of course, there is substantial risk that at least some of the space will go unrented for a period, and thus you will have to assume a greater financial responsibility.

Owning also means that you are responsible for maintaining the property. If you are renting and something breaks (e.g., the plumbing), you can simply call the landlord and ask him or her to come fix it. No extra costs are incurred and the annoyance of having to fix something is turned over to someone else. However, if you own the property you are the landlord and the maintenance crew (or you may contract out for these services), and there is no turning over responsibility to someone else. If you have tenants, you are also their maintenance department. If you have no patience or tolerance for this responsibility, then renting may suit you better than owning.

It is also important to know your long-term plans for practice. If you are not sure you want to remain in private practice or not sure you want to remain in the same geographic location, it is likely better to rent than to purchase. In this situation owning the space may serve as a weight and an impediment to making changes because it can reduce the ease of mobility and further expansion. Walfish and Barnett (2009) describe the rationale of the decision to own rather than rent by psychologists Nancy McGarrah and Barrie Alexander of Cliff Valley Psychologists. They knew they wanted to be in the same city and raise their families, so they thought purchasing would be a better long-term financial investment than renting.

Walfish and Barnett (2009) also present an interview with psychologist Tammy Martin-Causey, who decided to build her own building. She describes how she chose the location, chose a commercial real estate agent, and financed the project and discusses some of the challenges she faced in completing the project (e.g., a significant amount of paperwork, unexpected costs in building, requirements set forth by the lender). She advises those considering building to have adequate cash flow available in case of unexpected costs (not unlike building a home). She views the positives of building and owning office space as being able to design it exactly as you would like and owning an appreciating asset.

## CONCLUDING THOUGHTS

As stated in the beginning of this chapter, renting space is likely the largest expenditure that the private practitioner will encounter. If you are in practice for 20 years, the amount you will pay in rent will easily exceed $100,000. Whether you rent, sublet, or purchase space, it is important to consider the issues discussed in this chapter, as making mistakes related to space can be costly and annoying and distract you from doing fine clinical work.

## REFERENCES

Coons, H., & Gablis, J. (2010). Contractual issues for independent psychologists practicing in health care settings: Practical tips for establishing an agreement. *Independent Practitioner, 30,* 181–183.

Walfish, S., & Barnett, J. E. (2009) *Financial success in mental health practice: Essential tools and strategies for practitioners.* Washington, DC: APA Books.

Zimmerman, J. (2015). Leasing office space. *Independent Practitioner, 35,* 135–138.

# CHAPTER 12

# PSYCHOTHERAPY OFFICE DESIGNS THAT SUPPORT TREATMENT OBJECTIVES

*Sally Augustin and Agneta Morelli*

The field of environmental psychology is concerned with the interplay between people and their surroundings. It aims to provide a better understanding of how the environment as a whole affects individuals as well as how people change their environment. The term "environment" is defined broadly, encompassing, for example, natural spaces, social settings, and built environments (e.g., schools/universities, restaurants, stores, and offices of various sorts). The relationship between humans and the physical environment is complex, and explanatory models drawn from perceptual, cognitive, emotional, health, social, and neuro-psychology are used extensively by environmental psychologists.

As the design of psychotherapy office spaces influences behavior, emotion, and mental processes, it is wise to think of the design dimension as a part of the overall healing philosophy. Ideally the design should support the psychotherapeutic process that is used in the practice of healing, rehabilitation, recovery, and so forth. The office must support the psychotherapist and the clients as well as the different types of activities that may take place there.

When designing a psychotherapy office, it is important to be sensitive to individual differences and users' potentially conflicting needs. The ultimate design objective is to support the psychological well-being of everyone who will use a space. Psychotherapists are not a homogenous group and neither are clients. Individuals are affected differently by the physical environment because of their memories and past experiences. People interpret a setting in different ways depending on, for example, their cultural background, gender, age, and personal expectations. Therefore it is a good idea to offer options and choices in office design.

The physical environments of psychotherapy offices make particular sorts of experiences more or less likely to occur but do not determine them. For example, if a space has been designed to be calming, generally individuals will be calmer there than in a space that has not been designed to be relaxing, but there is no guarantee they will be tension free. The diverse sensory experiences in an environment are integrated cognitively, resulting in a coordinated psychological response to a space. For example, the color of walls does not alone determine the way the physical environment will influence a person's psychological state. Scents, sounds, textures, and sights all combine to generate a single effect.

## SENSORY EXPERIENCES

A sensory channel collects information, and those data serve as the basis of perception. Although sight, hearing, taste, smell, and touch are the five traditionally recognized senses, people can detect other stimuli beyond these. Our senses usually work together to provide us with a clear impression of the conditions and things around us. They allow us to learn, to protect ourselves, and to experience our world. Not all sensory experiences have the same degree of influence on experience. For example, the implications of seeing walls painted in a relaxing color are greater than those of viewing a single throw pillow in a more energizing shade.

In psychotherapy, a range of emotions are recognized and examined, and emotions are not judged or valued as positive or negative. However, it's best if psychotherapy offices make positive, calm moods more likely. People who are in a positive mood are likely to do a better job solving problems and making decisions, getting along with others, and thinking creatively. Even our immune systems function more effectively when we're in a positive mood. Having preferred sensory experiences has been linked to being in a positive mood.

The information given here focuses on ways to make positive, calm moods more probable but also supplies insights that can be used to make other mental states more likely, as desired. Cognitive sciences researchers have linked specific sensory experiences to particular moods, and people who are designing treatment rooms and waiting areas can apply these research findings to create desired client experiences.

## VISUAL ELEMENTS

About 80% of what we learn from the world around us is due to perception, learning, cognition, and activities mediated through vision. The ultimate purpose of the vision system is to supply information needed to act on, and respond to, our physical environment (in conjunction with other sensory channels) either with our muscles or through cognitive processes. Therefore, the visual qualities of the psychotherapy office such as light conditions, surface colors, shapes, patterns, views, and artwork are important aspects of the setting.

### LIGHT

Light can be labeled as being one color or another. Colors of light are measured in degrees Kelvin. Warm-colored light is around 2700 to 3000 Kelvin, while cool light is 4500 to 6000 Kelvin. Light bulbs are generally labeled with their degrees Kelvin or simply as "warm" or "cool." Lights that are warm make it more likely that people will be in a positive mood. Researchers recommend using cool lights in spaces where people should be alert and warm ones in areas where relaxation is desirable. People's mood and cognitive performance improve when they are in a space with daylight, so, when privacy concerns allow, it's great to let daylight into a waiting room or treatment area.

Room design generally includes several types of lighting, such as overall lighting, work or task lighting, and mood lighting. These categories of lighting will be required in the psychotherapy office as the space serves several functions: overall lighting for orientation, work lighting for the psychotherapist while reading or documenting, and mood light to promote for a comfortable therapeutic dialogue.

Researchers have studied the implications of psychotherapy office design on client behavior, focusing on the light levels in a space. The researchers found that during simulated counseling sessions in more dimly lit rooms (150 lux on the surface of the table between the mock counselor and counselee), study participants felt more pleasant and relaxed, had more positive impressions of the person playing the role of counselor, and provided more information about themselves than participants in a more brightly lit room (750 lux on the same table surface).

## SURFACE COLOR

Surface colors have an important influence on the user's experience of a space. Color saturation and brightness determine emotional response to shades seen, and cultures have associations to particular hues. A "hue" is the name given to a set of shades, such as green or blue or red. Saturation is how pure a color is, with maroon being less pure, and therefore less saturated, than candy apple red. A khaki green is less saturated than a Kelly green. Brightness refers to how much white is in a color, with baby blue being brighter than royal blue and pink being brighter than fire engine red. Colors that are not very saturated but relatively bright have been linked to positive relaxed mental states, while colors that are saturated and not very bright are generally energizing. We will use the colors shown at the Wikipedia webpage on shades of green (https://en.wikipedia.org/wiki/Category:Shades_of_green) to illustrate this point: Seeing the color Celadon (not Celadon Green) is relatively relaxing, while looking at a color such as Forest Green is relatively energizing.

Research has identified particular responses to seeing reds and greens, so these reactions should be considered when designing a psychotherapy office. Looking at reds, even briefly, similar to those in pens and pencils used by teachers to mark papers, has been found to impair performance on analytical tasks. Avoid these reds in spaces where people will be doing things such as taking intelligence tests. People identify angry faces more quickly against a red background than backdrops of other colors (Young, Elliot, Feltman, & Ambady, 2013), so this can be handy at the entrances to treatment facilities or offices. Viewing greens, in general, has been tied to enhanced creative thinking. Blues are most likely to be people's favorite color, and not many people identify yellow as their preferred color; when trying to pick colors for waiting and treatment rooms, select accordingly.

Color affects the perceived size of a space. Light colors can be used on the walls of a space to make it seem larger and dark colors can be used to make the walls seem closer to the viewer. Avoid making spaces seem unpleasantly big or too small.

Perceptions of wait times are influenced by the predominant colors in a space: Time seems to pass more slowly in warm-colored spaces than cool-colored ones.

We feel warmer in a space when it features warmer colors than we do when it showcases cooler ones. This has implications for social behavior, as described in the section on air temperature below.

How powerful someone seems to be is influenced by the color behind him or her. People in front of cool colors seem more powerful than those in front of warm ones; psychotherapists, depending on their therapeutic orientation, can use this finding to affect how clients perceive them, for example.

Humans are more comfortable in a space when the color of the floor is the darkest one in the room and the ceiling is the lightest, with walls being darker than the ceiling but not as dark as the floor.

Colors are rarely used alone, but monochromatic environments are restful as long as the colors used aren't whites, grays, or beiges. When a space is monochromatically white, gray, or beige, people, particularly those without design training, become quite stressed. When colors that are near each other on the color wheel are used together, the combinations are more relaxing, while combinations of those across from each other on the color wheel are more energizing.

A pattern that contains relatively few but some variety in shapes and colors has moderate visual complexity. Moderate levels of visual complexity are most comfortable for humans to view, so their use makes a space more comfortable as well. The interior spaces at Willson House Hospice (http://perkinswill.com/work/willson-hospice-house.html) have moderate visual complexity.

Liu and his research team spoke with psychotherapy clients about their preferred colors for the walls in psychotherapy offices, and the colors selected were relaxing (Liu, Ji, Chen, & Ye, 2014). Colors such as a not very saturated but relatively bright blue were preferred by psychotherapy clients for psychotherapy offices, for example.

## SHAPES AND PATTERNS

All people are comforted by looking at curved shapes, so more welcoming spaces have relatively more curved than straight design elements. What is important is the relative number of curved and straight lines in wallpapers and so forth. The same goes for furniture: Furniture that has gentle curves, for example on its arms or at its top, looks more comfortable than pieces with arms or backs featuring right angles.

Seeing wood grain destresses us, the same way seeing nature does, so using wood in furniture, flooring, and so forth in the psychotherapy office has clear benefits. People prefer to see natural finishes, so they are also good options for flooring and furniture.

## VIEWS

The psychotherapy session requires intellectual energy and cognitive effort and can be emotionally demanding for both client and clinician. When we do focused work for extended periods of time we become cognitively exhausted and feel stressed. Looking out a window at nature helps to restore our levels of mental energy, particularly if there is water in view, even a smallish fountain.

A growing amount of scientific evidence suggests that nature elements or nature views can be effective as stress-reducing, positive distractions that promote wellness in environments used for healing purposes. The ability of nature views to refresh and destress is well established. A number of studies of healthcare environments have presented strong evidence that even three to five minutes of contact with nature can significantly decrease stress, reduce anger and fear, and increase pleasant feelings. This calming effect can be achieved by providing views to the outside, interior gardens or aquariums, or artwork with a nature theme.

Diversions (which temporarily shift mental focus) that have a calming effect include not just artwork depicting scenes of nature but also fountains, green leafy plants, fireplaces, videos of nature, and aquariums. Adding a fountain that's six feet tall or so is possible in many outside areas viewed, which is convenient because plants can't be added to numerous exterior environments. Green leafy plants have been shown to reduce tension and have been linked to more creative thinking as well as improved cognitive performance and mood. The best options have flowers. If artificial plants truly look like live ones, they are a good substitute for the real thing, particularly if paired with a floral or other "plant-y" smell (see below for more research findings related to scent and design). Artificial plants are a good choice if clients suffer from allergies or asthma.

Seeing aquariums makes people feel calmer ("New study finds aquariums deliver health benefits," 2015). Cracknell, Pahl, and White, who completed this research, determined that "viewing aquarium displays led to noticeable reductions in blood pressure and heart rate, and that higher numbers of fish helped to hold people's attention for longer and improve their moods." (para. 3)

## ARTWORK

Artwork in any room, including the psychotherapy office, tends to be a focal point. In placing artwork, consider location and how it can contribute to the healing space. Art is often a place to rest the eyes and supports shifting our mind's focus to restore energy. Therefore, art at eye level while seated is preferable in the psychotherapy office. Art is also very personal, so it may be a good idea to consider the ethnic groups, gender, and age of the clients when choosing art.

Research has clearly identified the optimal sorts of art to use in healthcare environments to lower stress levels and to act as positive distractors, particularly in situations in which clients may be distressed or confused. Ulrich and Gilpin (2003), who have written the classic work on this topic, recommend the following types of art:

Landscapes or gardens with an open foreground into which the viewer could step.
Visual depth is important. Low hills and mountains in the distance are desirable.
Scenes viewed must be green (not arid) savanna-like spaces with clusters of broad
    canopy trees.
Foliage should be lush and flowers in bloom.
Calm, nonthreatening water scenes are optimal.
Artifacts with positive cultural associations (e.g., a barn) are advantageous.

Other appropriate images are familiar, healthy, fresh flowers; depictions of positive (e.g., friendly or caring) relationships among people; people at leisure in nature; and people with emotionally upbeat expressions on their faces. Abstract art can be confusing and upsetting to clients.

## OLFACTORY ELEMENTS

Particular scents have been found to produce particular responses in humans, whether people are aware they have smelled a particular odor or not. Our mood improves when we smell pleasant scents, and we feel less stressed when smelling pleasant scents and more tension when unpleasant ones are present. If there's a pleasant odor in a space we feel we've spent less time there than we do when that smell is absent.

Scenting must always be done with care, however. Lwin, Morrin, and Rong (2013) scented a room with peppermint and found that fright-based efforts to convince people to make dramatic life changes may be less successful when people are smelling pleasant odors.

Rigorous research links particular smells to more likely psychological outcomes. The scent of oranges has been tied to reduced tension levels. Floral odors are considered pleasant, regardless of culture, and have been associated with lower anxiety levels in general, although the odors of jasmine and hyacinth seem particularly likely to create this effect. The scent of vanilla has also been tied to lower anxiety levels. Lavender is a relaxing scent due to its influence on the immune system and blood chemistry. The scent of lemon improves mood and has been linked to improved performance on cognitive/mental tasks.

In a large cross-cultural study, the odors linked to feeling energized were grapefruit, tangerine, peppermint, and eucalyptus. Happiness/well-being has been linked to smelling sweet smells (particularly strawberry).

Sellaro (2015) and her colleagues probed links between scents and trust and found that study participants smelling lavender trusted others more than subjects who had smelled peppermint or had been in a control condition not exposed to any odor. The scent of peppermint did not decrease trust relative to the control condition.

Again, the factors of asthma or allergies must be considered, and artificial scents can be good choices for therapy offices.

## ACOUSTIC ELEMENTS

Verbal communication is most often at the heart of the therapeutic process and requires a supportive acoustic environment. In other words, a space where no unwanted sound and noise is experienced that would interfere with the therapeutic conversation is desirable.

Recent studies have shown that excessive noise can create stress, as evidenced by increased heart rate and blood pressure and reduced oxygen blood levels, in both adults and children. Good design—for example, the use of fabric wall hangings that can regulate noise—make the psychotherapy session less stressful for both clinician and client. Comfort levels and learning capacity are affected by negative acoustic conditions such as noise and disturbing sounds. Noise in office spaces may lower the levels of alertness; impede communication; obstruct working memory, speech intelligibility, and learning ability; and degrade self-assessed health and stress (Ljung, Israelsson, & Hygge 2013).

Our stress levels are lower when we're listening to nature sounds, including the sound of the ocean. Nature sounds also improve our mood ("Natural Sounds Improve Mood and Productivity, Study Finds," 2015).

If you are thinking of adding music to a waiting area or similar space and you do not have a particular reason to feature one sort of music or another, such as the age of clients, go classical. Research indicates that of all music genres, classical is most generally preferred (Ercegovac, Dobrata, & Kuscevic, 2015). This type of music might be suitable in the waiting room or if relaxation exercises are used in treatment.

Music can also be used to camouflage unwanted sounds such as air ventilation or fans. Adding white noise to a space makes people feel less self-conscious as they speak and enhances the perceived privacy in a space. White noise can be played in an area, similar to music. It is a random set of calm sounds, sounding much like a gentle wind.

## HAPTIC ELEMENTS

Haptic elements (those relating to the sense of touch), especially textures and how they are felt, are not often considered when a space is being designed. In general, softer textures are preferred to those that are harder/stiffer. Scientists have researched links between tactile experiences and social judgments/behaviors. Study participants negotiating with others while sitting in softer chairs (these had some padding on the seat; deep cushions are not required for this effect) did not drive as hard a bargain as ones sitting on harder chairs without the cushions.

Some materials retain warmth better than others, and researchers have identified links between physical warmth and interpersonal warmth. For example, researchers compared the opinions of people who had just held warm drinks with people who had just held cold drinks and found that individuals whose hands had just been warmed judged others to be more generous and caring than people who had just held cold drinks. Opinions were solicited after participants were no longer holding the warm or cool drinks.

Shiny surfaces are preferred (Meert, Pandelaere, & Patrick, 2014), but it is important to eliminate glare from spaces, because that makes us tense.

## INDOOR CLIMATE

Indoor climate is a combination of temperature, humidity, air movement, and air quality. Our mood and mental performance are best in spaces that are approximately 70 degrees Fahrenheit.

The quality of air in office buildings is a growing concern as it can have a drastic effect on health and can even affect social behavior; cigarette smoke and bad odors are particularly problematic. Lack of control over air that is noticeably bad may even foster negative feelings and aggression.

Having a sense of control of the indoor environment is often more important than the actual climate situation; there are many coping strategies for temperature comfort such as adjusting clothing, using blankets, opening windows, and regulating air conditioning. A psychotherapy office that provides clients with the option of regulating indoor climate would be preferable. More information on environmental control follows.

# SPATIAL CONCERNS

Several spatial conditions, such as having some control of the physical environment, influence client well-being. Human emotion and social behavior are also affected by the furniture's form and arrangement, and whether a client has an in-office "territory," for example.

## ENVIRONMENTAL CONTROL

Environmental control enhances well-being (Gifford, 2014). We can maintain control over our environment in many different ways, from establishing a territory, to chosing which chair to sit in, to setting lighting and temperature levels, to not getting lost in the building where an office is located. Devlin (2015) reports that healthcare clients need to feel in control of their physical experiences. Researchers have found that people do better on cognitive tasks when they work in areas with higher levels of control.

## TERRITORIALITY

When clients feel that they have a personal territory, even a temporary one, in a healthcare setting their well-being improves, which has positive implications for treatment outcomes (Devlin, 2015). A psychotherapy office can provide clients with opportunities to establish a temporary territory if clients can place objects that they've brought into the space near their seat, if they can make slight adjustments to the space, such as shifting a chair, and if the "owned" area is clearly demarcated, by, for example, the arms on a chair.

## PERSONAL SPACE

Interpersonal distances and physical contact are important to humans (Anderson, Gannon, & Kalchik, 2013). Anderson et al. report that important information is communicated through touch and the distances that people maintain from one another. Although there are some individual differences that influence these exchanges, shared culture results in consistencies within groups of people. The messages sent and received via touch and personal spacing have a significant influence on interactions between people and their resulting relationships. Among the information communicated via touch and spacing are relative status, affection, and the sort of relationship individuals may have (e.g., intimate, hostile).

When people are closer to each other than desired, they experience stress, which compromises their emotional state as well as their cognitive performance (Gifford, 2014). Preferred interpersonal distances vary between cultures. People from the United States and other Anglo-Saxon countries generally prefer larger personal spaces, Asians and Europeans prefer intermediate ones, and Latinos have, comparatively, the smallest personal space requirements. People from China tend to prefer smaller personal spaces than Japanese individuals (Kimura & Mao, 2013). Even within a culture there are slight variations in preferred personal spaces, with extraverts maintaining smaller ones than introverts.

When seats are easy to move slightly, or are wide enough so that people can chose to sit either closer or farther away from the person they are talking to, it is easier to create a space where people are at their desired distance from those with whom they are speaking.

## FAMILIARITY

People prefer to be in familiar sorts of places (i.e., ones similar to those experienced as pleasant in the past). Familiarity does not require that these spaces be identical, however, and some slight variations can prevent understimulation and undesirable mental ruminations. Situation-typical art and furniture are also generally preferred.

Familiarity is clearly important in medical facilities. For example, research has shown that although high-tech healthcare architecture is desirable, people are comforted by being in facilities that seem familiar. Studies have also determined that healthcare waiting rooms do not generate confidence in services to be rendered if they don't look like the waiting rooms that are anticipated. Art that is similar to pieces that the viewer has seen frequently in the past in similar situations is also best in healthcare settings. For example, art in healthcare facilities often features pastoral scenes.

## SEATING ARRANGEMENTS

People are most likely to participate in a meeting if they can make eye contact with the other people present. Circular tables de-emphasize leadership, which makes it more likely that the people present will interact more. The presence of a table has clear implications for how people act. Having some sort of table between people at a meeting, for example, increases the psychological distance, reducing the emotional connection between participants.

Research has shown that people prefer to talk, and are more likely to do so and form relationships with others, when they are speaking across the corner of a table (i.e., when their chairs are at 90-degree angles from each other). In this sort of arrangement, it is easy for people to make eye contact or not, as desired. People are more likely to cooperate with someone they are meeting with when they're sitting across from them as opposed to beside them, so during marriage counseling sessions, this arrangement of furniture can be useful (Gifford, 2014).

Purvis (2013) integrated information from environmental design and conflict mediation practice to determine how design can be used to support the mediation process. He found that parity was particularly important for conflict resolution. To ensure that the information provided by all participants is equally respected, everyone present should feel that they can sit on any of the seats in the area of the office used for discussions. In addition, all chairs should be of similar design and placed at equal distance from the mediator. Office amenities, such as views outside the space, must also be available to all participants. Mediators also felt that flexibility (e.g., the ability to adjust temperature or reposition furniture) was important in mediation spaces so that they remain physically comfortable and can support any foreseeable meeting contingency.

## FORM

Posture influences the way we think. Researchers have found out that when people are sitting in more open postures, their behavior and even their neuroendocrine levels change. An open posture is the one in which the trunk of our body is unprotected, because we are reclining, for example. A closed position is one in which we're sitting so that it seems like we're protecting our stomach—for example, with our shoulders hunched even a little bit. People sitting in more open positions feel more powerful and have a higher tolerance for risk, while people in more closed postures have the opposite perception.

When we're lying prone (e.g., stretched out on our backs on a couch), we seem to become less angry when provoked than people in similar situations who aren't in the same posture. Research indicates when we're lying down we think more creatively.

Researchers found that people sitting up straighter seem to have a more positive view of themselves than people who are slouching while sitting.

## PROSPECT AND REFUGE

Clients must feel safe in the office space during therapy to ensure a healing process. People are more comfortable and relaxed in spaces with prospect and refuge; these places give them the feeling of surveying the nearby area from a protected spot. Classic examples of prospect and refuge design options are inglenooks (i.e., a space recessed into a wall or chimney, for example, where people can sit) and window seats, but womb-type chairs, which shield the person sitting from view from the left or right and whose back often extends slightly over the seated person's head, can also be used to create this effect.

We also feel comfortable and secure when our backs are protected. Research has shown that seats that are placed directly in front of walls (tall or short), columns, or bushy plants or in booths are most popular at restaurants. Meeting rooms where most of the walls are solid make "protected back seating" more probable.

# RESEARCH ON DESIGN OF PSYCHOTHERAPY OFFICES

## SYMBOLIC COMMUNICATION

Devlin and Nasar, and teams of researchers they have coordinated, have made many important contributions to research on optimal psychotherapy office design.

Diplomas and certificates and family photographs have a silent conversation with everyone who views them. Research has shown that when more credentials are visible, psychotherapists are perceived to be more qualified and energetic. Researchers testing responses to four and nine credentials found no difference in how qualified the psychotherapist was perceived to be when either number was visible, but when nine credentials were on view, psychotherapists were seen as more energetic.

Using color photos of actual psychotherapy offices, researchers have found that the anticipated quality of care, the qualifications of the clinician, and the likelihood of choosing a particular psychotherapist were higher when offices seemed softer, were more personalized, and also were more orderly. Softer offices had soft materials on surfaces, as well as plants, table lamps, and furniture that could be moved; harder ones had smooth surfaces and bright lighting. A space was categorized as personalized when it included mementos and photographs, for example.

Devlin, Nasar, and Cubukcu (2014) learned that clients apparently have similar responses to psychotherapists' offices regardless of their national culture. They collected information in the United States, Turkey, and Vietnam and found that in each location there was a strong correlation between higher perceived quality of care and office softness/personalization and orderliness. Perceptions of comfort also increased with greater office softness/personalization and order.

Psychotherapy clients may be interested in working with counselors who recognize multicultural issues. Devlin, Borenstein, Finch, Hassan, Ianotti, and Koufopoulos (2013) found a perceived link between the cultural diversity of the office art/decorative elements on display (less diverse sets had more Western pieces) and a therapist's openness to multiculturalism; more diversity resulted in judgments of more openness to multiculturalism. In addition, greater numbers of culturally diverse pieces resulted in stronger perceptions of multiculturalism.

# CONCLUSION

Psychotherapy office design plays a role in the treatment process but is often overlooked by clinicians because they're simply not aware of the impact the setting has on clients' mental state and behavior. The primary goals for the psychotherapy office are to support clients as they heal at a fundamental level and to sustain the psychotherapist in his or her professional tasks. A healing physical environment for clients provides a framework and a foundation for psychotherapy. One of the most important objectives in creating a healing space is that it encourages clients to feel welcome, at ease, comfortable, in control, and, most importantly, safe. Design factors such as lighting, furniture, colors, images and their arrangement, and so forth may have a positive or negative impact on the psychotherapeutic process. If the environment is not in alignment with the goal of psychotherapy, it will be more challenging for the client to feel comfortable and ultimately do the important work necessary for healing and change to take place. To have a positive impact, consider the following tips when designing your office:

Use not very saturated but relatively bright green or blue hues.

Select furniture with round forms rather than straight.

Place the furniture to optimize posture and personal space.

Introduce nature elements to reduce stress levels. Try using nature sounds and scents in moderation in the waiting area to increase relaxation, for example.

## AUTHOR NOTE

The information presented in this chapter is based on rigorous, peer-reviewed studies. Space restrictions prevented all of those studies from being referenced here. A full list of citations is available from the first author at sallyaugustin@yahoo.com.

## REFERENCES AND RESOURCES

Anderson, P., Gannon, J., & Kalchik, J. (2013). Proxemic and haptic interaction: The closeness continuum. In J. Hall & M. Knapp (eds.), *Nonverbal communication: Handbooks of communication science* (pp. 295–329). Boston, MA: De Gruyter.

"Aquariums Deliver Health and Wellbeing Benefits." (2015). Press release, University of Exeter. Retrieved from www.ecehh.org/news/wellbeing-aquariums/.

Devlin, A. (2015). *Transforming the doctor's office.* New York: Routledge.

Devlin, A., Borenstein, B., Finch, C., Hassan, M., Iannotti, E., & Koufopoulos, J. (2013). Multicultural art in the therapy office: Community and student perceptions of the therapist. *Professional Psychology: Research and Practice, 44*(3), 168–176.

Devlin, A., Nasar, J., & Cubukcu, E. (2014). Students' impressions of psychotherapists' offices: Cross-cultural comparisons. *Environment and Behavior, 46*(8), 946–971.

Ercegovac, I., Dobrota, S., & Kuscevic, D. (2015). Relationship between music and visual art preferences and some personality traits. *Empirical Studies of the Arts, 33*(2), 207–227.

Gifford, R. (2014). *Environmental psychology* (5th ed.). Colville, WA: Optimal Books.

Kimura, M., & Mao, X. (2013, August). What are the differences of interpersonal communication with strangers between Japanese and Chinese people? Presentation at the 10th Asian Association of Social Psychology Biennial Conference, Yogyakarta, Indonesia.

Liu, W., Ji, J., Chen, H., & Ye, C. (2014). Optimal color design of psychological counseling room by design of experiments and response surface methodology. *PLoS ONE, 9*(3). Retrieved from http://www.plosone.org.

Ljung, R., Israelsson, K., & Hygge, S. (2013). Speech intelligibility and recall of spoken material heard at different signal-to-noise ratios and the role played by working memory capacity. *Applied Cognitive Psychology, 27*(2), 198–203.

Lwin, M., Morrin, M., & Rong, J. (2013). It can't be that bad if it smells this good: Do pleasant ambient odors diminish the persuasiveness of fear appeals? (pp. 295–297). Proceedings, Annual Winter Conference, Society for Consumer Psychology, February 28–March 2, San Antonio, TX.

Meert, K., Pandelaere, M., & Patrick, V. (2014). Taking a shine to it: How the preference for glossy stems from an innate need for water. *Journal of Consumer Psychology, 24*(2), 195–206.

"Natural Sounds Improve Mood and Productivity, Study Finds." (2015). Press release, Acoustical Society of America. Retrieved from http://www.newswise.com/articles/natural-sounds-improves-mood-and-productivity-study-finds.

Purvis, A. (2013). Eight characteristics of built space supportive to conflict mediation processes (pp. 139–145). In J. Wells & E. Pavlides (eds.), Proceedings of the 44th Annual Conference of the Environmental Design Research Association, McLean, VA.

Sellaro, R., van Dijk, W., Paccani, C., Hommel, B., & Colzato, L. (2015, January 13). A question of scent: Lavender aroma promotes interpersonal trust. *Frontiers in Psychology.* Retrieved from http://journal.frontiersin.org/article/10.3389/fpsyg.2014.01486/full.

Ulrich, R. S., & Gilpin, L. (2003). Healing arts: Nutrition for the soul. In S. B. Frampton, L. Gilpin, & P. A. Charmel (Eds.). *Putting patients first: Designing and practicing patient-centered care* (pp. 117–146). San Francisco, CA: John Wiley and sons.

Young, S., Elliot, A., Feltman, R., & Ambady, N. (2013). Red enhances the processing of facial expressions of anger. *Emotion, 13*(3), 380–384.

# CHAPTER 13

# TECHNOLOGY CONSIDERATIONS IN RUNNING A PRIVATE PRACTICE

*Ellen Belluomini*

Technology can offer challenges and opportunities for the private practitioner. This chapter first explores how psychotherapists of different ages experience boundaries and the Internet. The discussion progresses to methods of integrating technology assessment and digital testing and the impact of technology on the management of a private practice. Digital options per se are not unethical or inappropriate. Each area is viewed through a risk management and strengths lens. The intent is to guide the psychotherapist through the potential complications of digital options while emphasizing the ways in which technology can ease the management of a private practice.

## DIFFERENT GENERATIONS OF TECHNOLOGY USERS

Two concerned parents brought their 14-year-old son, Jason, to psychotherapy for symptoms of depression. They identified isolation from family, sleeping after school, and a lack of interest in prior friendships as behavioral indicators. His A average at school dropped to all C's during his freshman year. Jason presented as a precocious and outgoing adolescent who did not appreciate his parents' concern. The initial family intake provided dichotomous evidence of depression.

Jason shared his side of the story the next week. He said he had many friendships, but they existed primarily online in forums and chat groups, by instant messaging, and on social media sites. He became friends with "a man" in his 40s through an online forum on computer programming. This camaraderie boosted Jason's self-esteem as this online friend worked with him to develop new programs. They spent hours online late at night talking and hacking into various systems, including maneuvering through his parents' security firewall. He felt like an adult, not a teenager.

Jason spoke with ease while he proudly exhibited his aptitude with the computer in sessions. I asked about the most interesting computer trick "the man" he was working with showed him. Jason demonstrated a hack at the same time discussing his intent to purchase a bus ticket to New York during the long weekend ahead to meet him. The plan developed without the consent of his parents. Besides the goal of keeping this adolescent safe, I realized technology was going to be an integral part of assessment, relationship building, and treatment with Jason. This family's situation marked the beginning of practicing digital awareness in my sessions.

This scenario transpired over 12 years ago. Since then society has seen a rapid increase in technological innovation. Circuit speeds double every two years, bringing upgrades and new digital applications with this progress. The time involved to produce an information generation gap of technological progress continues to shorten. This gap is evident when we compare each generation's use of technology. Pew Research Center Internet, Science, and Tech researchers provide ongoing analysis about each generation's adaptation to a technologically advancing society.

Prensky (2001) coined the terms "digital immigrant" and "digital native" to describe those using the "language" of technology. Digital immigrants learned this new language of technology but did not grow up with technology. In contrast, digital natives grew up fluent in the thinking patterns of technological use. Digital immigrants notice these innovations and must work harder at decoding the uses for digital tools. And even digital natives, who grew up in a digital world, may struggle as innovation accelerates the learning curve.

## BOUNDARIES IN A DIGITAL AGE

Digital immigrants grew up with boundaries that consisted of well-defined ethical constraints. Only 20 years ago, psychology programs offered strict guidance against giving personal information to clients. Personal information consisted of a home phone number, address, and many personal details of the psychotherapist's life; even having pictures of family members in an office might have carried disapproval from colleagues. Following these guidelines created a sense of security and privacy for the practitioner and a safe, therapeutic environment for the client. Solutions to ethical dilemmas used a distinct formula of right and wrong scenarios, but then technology blossomed and these formerly sharp lines of ethics became imprecise.

Personal data are now in the public arena thanks to the Internet and search engines. Tech-savvy clients are now just a Google search away from learning details of their therapist's private life. The reaction of many practitioners is to avoid using social media, but there are plenty of other entities that post private details (e.g., real estate purchases, websites reviewing psychotherapists).

Many psychotherapists have difficulty understanding the risks involved with online behavior (McMinn, Bearse, Heyne, Smithberger, & Erb, 2011). Personal and professional boundaries have become blurred due to the multiple ways that social media and the Internet provide for connection. Dual relationships, both sexual and nonsexual, are the most common complaint to the American Psychological Association (APA Ethics Committee, 2014). However, the ability to access personal information online does not support an increase in complaints for psychotherapists: Dual relationship complaints have been steadily decreasing since 2006 (APA Ethics Committee, 2014). The meaning of this statistic is unclear. As a society we are experiencing a shift in how we view personal privacy: Reality television, smartphones, and social media give us full access to the private lives of people. How does this shape a client's experience with a professional? Actions that may previously have seemed "over the line" for a client may no longer be so in the information age. Psychotherapists need training and guidance about the new standards for dual relationships.

The mental health profession has been lax in addressing digital challenges other than telepsychology. Many therapists feared crossing unfamiliar ethical boundaries or were reluctant to investigate digital options without guidelines. The first formal ethical guidelines for technology in general therapeutic practice appeared in 2005 from the National Association of Social Work. Although they were vague and quickly became obsolete, these ethical standards guided practitioners who were willing to try using digital options in practice. The APA's 1997 code of ethics briefly mentioned the need for ethics dealing with technology. The current revision of the code, while describing the need for due diligence when using digital solutions, does not set an explicit standard for technological boundaries or integration throughout practice situations. The most comprehensive ethics code to date is that of the American Counseling Association (ACA, 2014), which devotes an entire section to distance counseling, technology, and social media. This code can provide education for all psychotherapists.

APA psychologists developed 18 practice-specific guidelines for practitioners addressing a common area of digital practice, telepsychology. Telepsychology is the only guideline focused specifically on technology practices, however (APA, 2013). Guidelines for practice neglect current issues such as social media guidelines and the impact of the "digital divide" on practice populations (the digital divide is the gulf between those who have access to computers and the Internet and those who do not). Many digital immigrant clinicians are reluctant to explore digital options for themselves or their clients. This may be because they hold fast to their prior ethical standards, they lack interest, or they are anxious about the introduction of technology. However, without the guidance of the profession, psychotherapists may be at risk for committing Health Insurance Portability and Accountability Act (HIPAA) violations, facing dual relationship issues, or continuing to be reluctant to use technological tools.

Digital natives, on the other hand, grew up with 24/7 technology access. They make little distinction between online and face-to-face connections. These natives frequently rush to buy the latest gadget or app. The history of a digital native's life is available online, sometimes from before birth if their parents were tech savvy. Privacy concerns of digital natives do not surface before young adulthood. New psychologists may worry about evidence of high school or college parties, extreme opinions, or other youthful behavior that exists online, whereas most digital immigrants do not worry about an inappropriate picture from college appearing in a Google search.

Older supervisors may be concerned about how they can serve as effective mentors for digital natives who are entering the field of psychology. But in reality the differences between the two age groups can benefit both. Younger clinicians can educate their supervisors on technological advances, and digital immigrants can provide a balance to the digital natives' exuberance in using digital platforms. Together, these two generations can create the right balance of ethical technology use.

# TECHNOLOGY ASSESSMENT OF FAMILIES

Combining structural family therapy assessment with technology assessment provides a unique view of the functionality with clients. Technology is a thread of communication, or lack thereof, in families leading to enmeshment, engagement, disengagement, or a combination of the three (Minuchin, 1974). As technological practices are weaving their way into society's attitudes and behaviors, a technology assessment is crucial for an accurate treatment plan.

Understanding digital behaviors can offer insight into the strengths and weaknesses affecting the client or family system. The time family members spend on their digital devices provides data about family engagement. Just as questions about chores or curfews reveal parenting styles, the boundaries on technology use need to be evaluated. Asking about the types of games played and programs used can offer a unique view into the client's perceptions of violence or relationships. Inquire about social media outlets and numbers of followers or "friends." What does the client's online behavior say about him or her? Even cultural and generational perceptions of technology can cause underlying conflict within a family system.

---

Here are some questions to ask children and adolescents about their online activity:

1. How do you communicate with friends?
2. What types of social media (e.g., Facebook) do you use? Is your profile private?
3. How do your parents communicate with you through technology?
4. Describe a time you wrote something online to a person you regret.
5. Describe a time you sent something you later regretted sending.
6. Has someone written you something online that hurt your feelings?
7. How do you respond if you see a friend post something bad on another friend's wall?
8. Have you ever felt bullied by someone through technology?
9. Have you ever blocked or deleted someone from an account online?
10. What is your favorite topic to explore online?
11. Identify any online sexual behavior you have participated in (e.g., sexy pictures on smartphone/email/social media, role-playing game, pornography, dating).
12. How do you meet friends online? (Children do not view people as strangers online.)
13. How many online friends do you have? (Ask for context.)
14. Describe some of the reactions of your family members to your use of (specific technology)—for example, "I never see you," "Get out of your room and off the computer!" or "Stop texting during dinner."
15. How do your parents monitor your use of technology? Can you get around it?

# CASE VIGNETTE

Sixteen-year-old Jane frequently used social media as a way to connect with friends and meet new people. She started having conversations with Ted on a new dating app. They decided to meet at the mall after a few weeks of texting. Jane felt she knew Ted very well. She considered him a friend and hoped it would lead to more. Ted brought two male friends with him to the "date." As the group walked around the mall, Ted said he had left his wallet in the car and asked if Jane could lend him $100, promising to return the money at the end of their date. Jane, excited because he said the word "date," took the group to an ATM and withdrew the money. Later, in the parking lot, the group of men pushed Jane down, stole her purse, and drove quickly away.

Jane was distraught but did not share the incident with her parents. She felt ashamed at being assaulted and robbed. She knew her parents would not approve of her meeting someone from the dating app. Jane's mother approached her after dinner and said she had received an email that Jane's bank account had reached the $500 spending limit. Jane had no choice but to share the traumatic incident.

Jane's parents took her to file a police report, starting an investigation into the robbery. Jane needed to disclose every text with the detectives. Due to the trauma and embarrassment of the incident, Jane turned inward. The investigators found the responsible party, a group of 20-year-olds who were assaulting vulnerable adolescents. As the court date drew near, Jane would not go out with friends or her parents. School and work became her only outside outlets.

Jane's parents insisted she attend a family birthday party at a skating rink in the mall where the attack took place. Jane became angry and unusually explosive trying to get out of going to the party. Her parents forced her to attend. Jane experienced her first panic attack at the party. Jane's parents, while supportive of their daughter, did not understand her behavior or subsequent panic attacks. They decided to bring Jane in for psychotherapy.

Unemployed and seeking disability, the father spent most of the day participating in a popular role-playing game (RPG). If he was not on the RPG, he was playing Internet games with his 12-year-old daughter. The father spent most of his waking hours on the computer with his online friends. The amount of time he spent gaming caused a significant strain on the marriage.

Jane's brother spent most of her time in the basement with their father playing video games or online playing a game creating environments out of cubes. There was no supervision regarding who contacted him. Many of the video games held adult ratings and centered around war or killing.

Jane used all the latest social media apps. Her followers numbered in the thousands. If not on social media, Jane would take part in her own RPG game. This online game catered to the adolescent fantasies of the popular genre of vampires, fairies, and other supernatural characters. Jane often ate meals in her room while she communicated online with friends.

In contrast, Jane's mother did not like technology. She used the Internet only to pay bills and access her work email. She resisted smartphone technology and showed her five-year-old flip phone with pride. She became frustrated when discussing any technology, deferring to her husband as the expert. She tried to set up boundaries on technology use, but the father would undermine the limits and consequences.

# LESSONS LEARNED

A technology-integrated assessment led to an understanding of this family's structure, subsystems, boundaries, and alignments (Minuchin, 1974). The family structure provided insights into the communication pattern with the help of a technology ecomap as a guide. Using a visual ecomap of tech behavior helped the family members understand the assets and deficits in communication and their relationships. A rigid boundary existed between the mother and the rest of the family. The father and his son were enmeshed, with no clear parental boundaries between them. They aligned their relationship to thwart the mother's household rules. Jane had disengaged from the family. She created a different support system online, at school, and at work. Neither parent had any idea how Jane spent her time online or her activities outside of the home.

The therapist's technology assessment identified many high-risk situations and communication problems within the family system. Dysfunctional behaviors may be intensified by technology, but technology is not the root problem. For a family that already has dysfunctional behaviors, an increase in stress can lead family members to use technology as an unhealthy distraction or addiction. The psychotherapist can make the family members aware of these ineffective communication patterns. Using qualitative and quantitative data about the family's technology patterns offers a path to address the underlying issues of disharmony. This family brainstormed new boundaries with technology and how technology could be used to increase their family bonds.Not all families will present with upfront technology issues. The technology assessment does not take the place of a social history or clinical assessments. However, assessing digital behaviors can provide another level of understanding the complex communication within the family system.

# PSYCHOLOGICAL TESTING

Using the computer for personality testing is not new to the field of psychology. MMPI results were first interpreted using a computer system in 1962, when computers filled large rooms. Extensive research exists on the MMPI's assessment and interpretation validity over the past 60 years. The use of technology for MMPI scoring meant a significant decrease in the amount of time spent by the psychotherapist doing calculations, time that can now be used to interpret the scores using clinician observations and client history. The MMPI can now be given online, prompting research into how technology can further benefit psychological testing methods.

The results from researchers' studies of the reliability and validity of other online psychological tests hold promise. Study results show both an increase in dependable responses due to the anonymity the Internet provides and no difference in disclosure rates between online and in-person administration (Brock et al., 2015). The caveat with online psychometric testing is the lack of qualitative equivalence with online participation versus in-person delivery. Online assessment options used in private practice need vetting to determine if they are congruent with the nondigital ones. The therapist who chooses to use an online test that has not been not researched should be aware that there may be discrepancies in the results.

The Q-global web-based administration, scoring, and reporting site by Pearson offers 27 common used assessment tools, including the BASC-3 and the MMPI-2 and MMPI-2 R/F. Other test companies, such as Psychological Assessment Resources (www.parinc.com), also offer web-based administration of some of their tests. Recommendations for operating systems and browser requirements are standard with software usage. These tests can be administered in the office with ease on a tablet. Computer tabulating software has dramatically reduced the amount of time needed for results to be available to the clinician.

# TECHNOLOGICAL INTERVENTIONS

Digital tools can increase adherence to treatment for clients who are comfortable with technology. Multiple studies support the efficacy of computer and Internet-based approaches to training or practicing therapeutic skills. The capacity for long-term change using technological interventions is evident in self-monitoring and self-awareness, self-efficacy and motivation, and environmental awareness research (Runyan & Steinke, 2015).

Apps that have been developed for smartphones and other mobile devices carry promise for interventions across the clinical spectrum. Ecological momentary intervention (EMI) techniques represent an area fertile for research and development. These tools allow clients to record their thoughts, feelings, and behaviors and to be present in the moment for a clinical intervention without a psychotherapist being present. Using notifications, banners, and other types of reminders enhances the technique.

While there is research on the overall efficacy of the Internet and computer-based software, there may not be evidence supporting the efficacy of a particular app. Practitioners can evaluate EMI apps through their awareness of clinical guidelines. Self-monitoring apps designed to increase motivation may offer prompts for goal setting, affirmative self-talk, or self-reflective questions. An app addressing environmental resources may involve in-app chat rooms with other people working on similar issues or computer-generated role plays of situational triggers (Runyan & Steinke, 2015). Apps providing tracking mechanisms and goal reinforcement for positive behaviors may provide longer-term results, like their computer counterparts exhibit.

Many apps for personal or professional use are available from the U.S. government. The Department of Health and Human Services, Department of Veterans Affairs, the National Center for Telehealth and Technology, and the National Institutes of Health offer a variety of well-designed mobile programs that clients can access for free. They include telehealth tracking tools, educational forums, tools addressing psychological health, and videos on a wide range of health and mental health issues. Many government mental health apps provide empirical results proving the efficacy for the method, if not necessarily the app.

Apple or Android apps provide a range of resources, some free and others expensive; cost does not equate with quality. Before recommending an app as a digital tool, assess whether it will be suitable for a particular client and familiarize yourself with how it functions. Displaying confidence and providing clear instructions that build on the client's technology knowledge will increase the client's adherence to use of the app (Runyan & Steinke, 2015).

# HIPAA RISKS AND COMPLIANCE

Use of electronic health records (EHR) can transform a private practice because psychotherapists can maintain client records in the office, at home, or on their smartphone. However, the availability of EHR systems across platforms increases the risk of HIPAA noncompliance. HIPAA standards represent one area of practice in which technology guidelines are up to date. The new expectations for HIPAA compliance fall not just on the vendor but on the practitioner as well (APA Practice Organization, 2013). EHR systems and HIPAA regulations may not be congruent with each other, especially if the EHR system is a few years old. Even if your EHR system states it is HIPAA compliant, this may not be the case: Compliance is merely a claim of the vendor and not a governmental certification.

The security of EHR has increased with the 2013 HIPAA revisions. EHR vendors must continually evaluate the security of their systems based upon 75 security controls. Not only is your practice's EHR system under scrutiny, but each device you use to access the program needs a yearly security risk analysis. There is not one EHR system that is completely secure from a privacy threat. EHR vendors may state their system is 100% secure, but providers beware: Any technology is vulnerable to a person with the appropriate knowledge and an Internet connection. HIPAA regulators require evidence of due diligence for security, not an expectation of perfection. Maintaining physical evidence through updated policy and procedure manuals is considered best practice for documenting HIPAA compliance.

Each technological device used by providers comes under HIPAA regulations. Many smartphones and tablets offer a fingerprint scan for access, allowing an added measure of security. A stolen digital device is any therapist's nightmare, but there are programs available that can purge the data on the device or disable it if it is lost. As long as the encryption on the phone meets the HIPAA security rules, clients do not need to be notified of a records breach. If the stolen device did not enable security protocols, however, all clients need to be notified of the violation. The HIPAA security protocol used to safeguard protected health information includes a password or fingerprint user authentication, a remote data wiping feature, disabling file share applications, use of up-to-date security software, deleting all data when exchanging devices, and not using public Wi-Fi networks unless the device has encryption apps for sending texts and emails.

One HIPAA threat that is often overlooked is the provider's printer, copy machine, or fax machine. Every client record that is faxed or copied has a file on the machine's drive. Disposal or repurposing of these machines requires special care to wipe the hard drive clean of records.

Some companies buy old copy machines and faxes exclusively for their data. Add this precaution to your disposal policies to increase security and client protection.

Using apps in a private practice requires diligence. The confidentiality risk for psychotherapists using mental health apps in their practice is unknown. HIPAA regulations state that apps should be evaluated for HIPAA compliance only if they store personal health information or offer a method of communication between the provider and the client (APA Practice Organization, 2013). These guidelines provide clinicians with a wide opportunity to use apps.

# ELECTRONIC HEALTH RECORDS

Client software has come a long way from the initial Access or Excel database programs. Software programs that track protected health information not only minimize your risk for HIPAA violations but can also offer benefits that can cut your time as a practice manager. Basic features include scheduling, simultaneous backup, DSM5 and ICD-10 connections in treatment notes, and electronic billing for insurance companies, providing a seamless connection between psychotherapist, client, and financial matters. Mobile apps offer clinicians a connection to their client and practice content anywhere and anytime. Some software includes an app for client use in scheduling and communication. These apps offer a way to communicate with a client within a HIPAA-compliant, encrypted system, and the communication automatically becomes part of the client record. Pregenerated voicemail calls, emails, or texts can be sent to clients as a reminder of upcoming appointments, minimizing no-shows.

Psychotherapists can choose from a number of private practice enhancements. EHR software can provide a dictation method for writing progress notes as well as tracking client outcomes for research or insurance companies. Some programs allow for personalization of online forms so they can be consistent with the system already in use. A single system can allow for alternative methods of marketing your practice and tracking your referral base.

EHRs vary in their offerings and efficiency. Free trials can expose therapists to different EHR elements. Defining needs versus wants can help you decide how much money you want to spend. A hidden cost is customer service help, so ask how much free help the company provides in implementing and maintaining the EHR.

The American Recovery and Reinvestment Act of 2009 offered a medical records stimulus, but it was not available to psychotherapists in private practice. Psychology and social work organizations have been working on adding these professions to the list of eligible providers. A bill, introduced in 2015 and still awaiting action, would include psychologists as eligible professionals who could apply for compensation for using EHR in their practice (H.R. 2646, 2015). Only psychologists billing under Medicare would be eligible. This bill would not only offer financial perks for EHR development but would also introduce a mandate with consequences if EHRs were not adapted.

# INFORMED CONSENT

Using EHRs or any other technology in your practice requires a change in your informed consent forms. A consent form should contain specific details. Areas to include on the form (and in discussion with clients) include the following:

1. Appropriate boundaries for texting or cellphone use
2. Explanation of how technology will be used in and out of sessions
3. The risks associated with use
4. Cost of technology for the client
5. Safety considerations
6. Security and confidentiality
7. Risks of using different types of technology
8. A list of all parties who will have access to the client's EHR (Jones & Moffitt, 2016)

This information can be integrated into your current consent form or can be given on an additional technology-specific consent form. A separate form can highlight the importance of each area in the digital consent. Specifying the boundaries of social media requests can clarify "friending" on Facebook, connecting through LinkedIn, or possible conflicts of interest in other online behavior. An upfront explanation of these social media limits will decrease confusion before, during, and after the clinical relationship. An example of a social media policy that clinicians may adapt to their own practice may be found at http://drkkolmes.com/social-media-policy/.

One critical element in confidentiality practices is the understanding that education on app safety and risk should not end when the client signs the consent form. Each type of technology used in sessions needs a benefit and risk review. An example of this would be how a "widget" appears on the screen. If a client is in a domestic violence situation, there are apps offering emergency services to victims. People often share phones with family members, so these apps increase the user's safety by using an innocuous-appearing widget likely to be of no interest to the perpetrator.

Client and psychotherapist alike should evaluate the security of all devices they use to prevent confidentiality gaps. Many clients do not know as much about privacy and security as the psychotherapist. If clients record vulnerable data on an app, the results of such disclosures need to be explored. Children or spouses may inadvertently open the app, exposing them to confidential material. A worse situation is if the phone is lost or stolen. Clients can make informed decisions about what they record once they understand the consequences. Many options exist to encrypt and protect data, minimizing the accessibility of apps holding sensitive information. Apps with these security measures add a necessary level of reassurance.

# MARKETING OPTIONS

A diverse online marketing strategy can save time and money in soliciting opportunities for a private practice. Websites are common tools that psychotherapists use for promotion. A website serves as an introduction to the therapeutic process; what does your website say about your practice? Well-developed website content helps readers understand why they should come to your practice. When developing your own practice website, view the websites of different private practices similar to yours in terms of size, population, and services offered. Identify which features draw you in or make you want to leave the page (but keep in mind the content is directed toward clients, not other professionals). Ask advice from different people and evaluate their opinions about your content. Websites can act as a focal point for referrals. Presentation materials, email signatures, promotional items, blog posts, and business cards all should carry the website link. Add downloadable links of consent and intake forms to begin the development of a client–psychotherapist relationship.

The use of social media sites for networking can create challenges for psychotherapists. Some private practices use Facebook to advertise their services. Facebook is a free and easy alternative to developing your own website. A "page" describes your services and provides a way for people to "like" and follow your content. But if a client chooses to respond to a post on the page, what does this mean for his or her privacy? How many of his or her friends now know the client is seeking services at the place described on the page? What if a person posts a suicidal or homicidal thought on the page? Consider these issues before you use unregulated social media options for advertising.

A practice thrives from a strong referral network. If you write a blog addressing ways to present information about mental health, you can market it to online psychology magazines, it can serve as subject matter for groups such as LinkedIn or Google plus, and it can earn you a reputation as a content expert. If writing is not an interest, you can use a blog to share other people's articles on a specific topic. Decide on a blog that fits your professional interests and passions, because if you become bored with the content the blog will quickly meet its end.

As a new clinician in practice, I joined a private online community in my area that provides resources, education, referrals, and problem solving. Many referrals are generated in this manner. If this type of community is not available, develop and become the moderator of one in your area. Professionals will remember those psychotherapists who offer advice to a problem or a referral outside their area.

# ONLINE RISK MANAGEMENT

Being aware of online privacy and security is critical to maintaining professionalism with clients. Using your name online can allow you to be found by anyone with a search engine. Years ago I wrote a book review on Amazon, not understanding the implication of my post at the time. It appeared whenever I Googled my name. I could not delete it. As a professional, I did not want this judgment to be accessible for clients to view. The review didn't contain any negative information, just my opinion, but I was still uncomfortable knowing any client could see the content. The ability to make comments "private" this past year allowed me to erase the comment from search engines, much to my relief.

Ignoring social media and its impact is no longer an option. Clients actively participate online, often with negative results, and understanding the impact of your behavior online is fundamental in balancing private versus professional information. It seems every week there is an article about an inappropriate tweet, picture, or comment that went viral, ruining someone's personal or professional life. Reputation is not easily earned and can be tarnished with a single misstep.

One recommendation for risk reduction is for psychotherapists to Google themselves regularly, both on the web and through images, to find out what information is public knowledge. You want to know what a client will find.

Social media allows for the documentation of every developmental stage. Tech-savvy parents now establish Facebook pages as virtual photo albums for their infants. Every detail of life is recorded, including possibly unsavory high school and college behaviors. Diligent digging can unearth Twitter conversations with friends or Pinterest boards displaying your hobbies and dietary preferences. Searchers can locate every place you visit with your smartphone, including every stop you make on your way home from work.

As a psychotherapist, an unprotected personal social media account is an ethics issue waiting to happen. Boundary issues may occur with no notice. Facebook updates the types of searches it performs to increase choices for users. One new feature recommended a line of faces you might want to "friend." After a few weeks of use, I found three client pictures on my page waiting to be "friended." I realized that Facebook accessed my contacts through the email account I was using. Since I check my business Gmail most often, I tied them together. And I realized that if I was seeing clients on Facebook, they were seeing not only me, but any picture I chose to use as a profile. I scrutinize the privacy settings on all my accounts, but with the advent of new ways to use data, privacy breaches are inevitable. I cannot predict the next way privacy can be an issue, but I can respond with ethical behavior (if I am fortunate enough to become aware of the problem). My response included changing the email address associated with all my social media accounts and carefully choosing my profile photos. A technology upgrade is a signal for psychotherapists to search for risks in new developments.

You can safely assume that your clients will Google your name. They may just be looking for your address, but all the information under your name will appear, ranging from your address and phone number to how much you paid for your house. A colleague of mine searched for her unusual name only to find it also belonged to a famous porn star. Awkward Internet items found on your name search fall into the category of "it's good to know in case it comes up." On one Internet search I discovered a link to my professional license, and the brief description stated my lack of license renewal. I immediately called the department of professional regulation. While I was on hold, I began clicking on each link to identify the issue. I discovered the site referred to my LSW, not my current LCSW license. If a client viewed my inactive license, I would now have an explanation. Googling yourself on a regular basis will let you know when your personal information becomes a professional liability.

## CONCLUSION

Technological advances will continue, and therapists can no longer ignore the impact of technology on personal and professional behaviors. While some professional mental health organizations provide technology protocols, the level of detail for a psychotherapist's protection is scant, so the responsibility for maintaining boundaries within a private practice falls upon the therapist. Be open to participating in conversations and trainings about technology and practice that provide evidence-based interventions and protections for you and your clients.

# REFERENCES

American Counseling Association. (2014). 2014 ACA code of ethics. Retrieved from https://www.counseling.org/resources/aca-code-of-ethics.pdf.

American Psychological Association. (2013). Guidelines for the practice of telepsychology. Retrieved from http://www.apa.org/practice/guidelines/telepsychology.aspx.

American Psychological Association Practice Organization. (2013). The privacy rule: A primer for psychologists. HIPAA: What you need to know now. Retrieved from http://www.apapracticecentral.org/business/hipaa/hippa-privacy-primer.pdf.

American Psychological Association Report of the Ethics Committee, 2013. (2014). *American Psychologist, 69*(5), 520–529 10p. doi: 10.1037/a0036642

Brock, R. L., Barry, R. A., Lawrence, E., Rolffs, J., Cerretani, J., & Zarling, A. (2015). Online administration of questionnaires assessing psychological, physical, and sexual aggression: Establishing psychometric equivalence. *Psychology of Violence, 5*(3), 294–304. doi: 10.1037/a0037835

Helping Families in Mental Health Crisis Act of 2015, H.R. 2646, 114th Congress. (2015-2016). Retrieved from https://www.congress.gov/bill/114th-congress/house-bill/2646.

Jones, N., & Moffitt, M. (2016). Ethical guidelines for mobile app development within health and mental health fields. *Professional Psychology: Research and Practice, 47*(2), 155–162. doi: http://dx.doi.org/10/1037/pro0000069

McMinn, M. R., Bearse, J., Heyne, L. K., Smithberger, A., & Erb, A. L. (2011). Technology and independent practice: Survey findings and implications. *Professional Psychology: Research and Practice, 42*(2), 176–184. doi: 10.1037/a0022719

Minuchin, S. (1974). *Families and family therapy.* Cambridge, MA: Harvard University Press.

Prensky, M. (2001, September/October). Digital natives, digital immigrants. *On the Horizon, 9*(5), 1–6.

Runyan, J. D., & Steinke, E. G. (2015). Virtues, ecological momentary assessment/intervention and smartphone technology. *Frontiers in Psychology, 481*(6), 1–24. doi: 10.3389/fpsyg.2015.00481

# CHAPTER 14

# ISSUES IN HIRING AND SUPERVISING PROFESSIONAL STAFF AND SUPPORT PERSONNEL

*Craig Pohlman*

Southeast Psych was founded in 2000 by Drs. Dave Verhaagen and Frank Gaskill. From the get-go, they set out to build a practice that was unique. They wanted to provide high-quality mental health services, but in their own mold. That meant a healthy dose of creativity, fun, *Star Wars*, and superheroes (check southeastpsych.com for evidence thereof). With the help of others who subsequently joined the practice, they authored a mission: to make psychology accessible to as many people as possible so that it can enhance their lives ("Psychology for All"). They also established four values that define our practice's culture: fun, innovation, relationship, and excellence (F-I-R-E). Culture is king at Southeast Psych, and our decision making is guided by those four values. For an in-depth look at how Southeast Psych was developed and how we function see Verhaagen and Gaskill (2014).

I was fortunate to join Southeast Psych in 2009. I became a member of the leadership team in 2012 and took the reins as chief executive officer (CEO) in 2013. We strongly believe that our most important assets at Southeast Psych are our people. We take pride in the talent, skill, knowledge, and dedication of our excellent clinicians and support staff. But as a culture-driven organization, we are even more proud of how our people embody fun, innovation, and strong relationships (within and beyond the practice). So we invest a great deal in hiring and supervising. We want the right people here for our culture and mission, and we want to support them so that they can continually advance the practice. In this chapter I will share some of what we have learned about recruiting, on-boarding, managing, and mentoring.

# GETTING THE RIGHT PEOPLE

The success of a hire is determined largely by the quality of the match between the person and the organization. Consequently, the recruiting process needs to start with clearly knowing your organizational identity. What is your mission? What are your values? Is your business more mission-driven or culture-driven? How would you describe your culture? I just described the mission, values, and culture of Southeast Psych. I could do that succinctly, but that should not belie the work that went into brainstorming, pondering, crafting, and then honing the mission statement and set of values. If you have not done so already, invest the time to make that happen. This process can be aided by any number of books on the topic and possibly with the aid of an outside facilitator.

With a clear sense of identity established, recruiting can begin. The skillsets and/or clinical specialties you're seeking need to be delineated, but just as important is describing what kind of fit you're looking for in terms of the mission, values, and culture. If your practice values a fast pace and efficiency, let applicants know that. If you're cutting edge and continually take on new therapies and technology, convey that. If you value calm and serenity, communicate that.

In our job searches at Southeast Psych (where we have over 40 providers and more than a dozen staff across two Charlotte, NC, offices, as well as one in Nashville, TN) we have advertised for position openings both in print and online, but we have had the most success with "word of mouth" advertising. Through various channels, professional and personal, we put out the message that we are looking to expand. We have brought in numerous outstanding clinicians and staff in this way. Although sometimes we have had to navigate around nepotism with relatives and friends, word of mouth generally is helpful as a prescreening mechanism. Those who talk about open positions usually describe our culture and mission, helping would-be applicants decide if they would be a good match with us.

At Southeast Psych, we have very little interest in job seekers who do not make the case for how they would mesh with our culture. Applicants who just send us a CV or résumé without a cover letter seldom get any consideration at all. Those who do include a letter but who don't reference our culture and how they would contribute to it seldom get considered either. If nothing else, it is a bad sign when an applicant has not done adequate research to know what we are all about.

When an applicant looks good on paper, we conduct an informal pre-interview. This usually involves one member of our leadership team or a veteran member of the practice meeting with the person offsite, perhaps over coffee. This interaction is primarily about establishing level of fit with our culture. This meeting is an added step to most organizations' recruiting processes, but it has worked for us by screening out nonviable applicants before entering what is a fairly rigorous formal interview.

We like to devote half a day to formal interviewing. If we are looking to fill multiple positions, we invite several candidates to the same morning. We start the day with a coffee hour and unstructured conversation. Members of our practice stop by for introductions, but we always assign one or two people to be there for the duration. We have learned a lot by observing how candidates introduce themselves and engage in conversation with each other; it has also been informative to see how they interact with our front desk staff upon arrival (e.g., are they warm or aloof?). Then I present for about 30 minutes on the history, mission, culture, and structure of the practice. For levity, I intersperse some trivia questions about our clinicians, such as who once broke a finger by tucking in a shirt, and then broke a different finger when making a bed (that would be Dave Verhaagen).

The bulk of our interview morning is devoted to tandem interviews. We assign each candidate to a pair of interviewers for an hour-long discussion and then to a second interviewing pair for another hour. In this way, we get the impressions of four interviewers based on fairly lengthy interactions. We make sure no interviewers who conducted pre-interviews or already know the candidate are involved in this process. Interviewers are given questions beforehand, but veering off-script is allowed and happens all of the time; the main reason for assigning questions is to minimize redundancy. Some of our questions are standard fare, such as asking about clinical specialty or describing a challenging experience at a previous position. We also have candidates respond to vignettes to get a sense of their clinical acumen. But being who we are, we have to throw in some unconventional questions like, "If you were a superhero, what would your power be and why?" We ask about things like how they decompress when work is stressful. We want to know about the last book they read and what movie character they would most like to meet. While conventional questions get at our value of excellence, unconventional questions help us assess the other values of fun, innovation, and relationships. Creative, amusing responses that forge a connection work well in our interviews. To be clear, we want clinicians and staff who have the skills and experience to provide mental health services of the highest quality, but fit with our culture is a prerequisite.

We wrap up the experience with a lunch. We like to cater here at our office and invite everyone at the practice to join. This meal is a great way to show the candidates our culture in action as we do not hold back with our humor and zaniness. We have been known to send in clinicians in costumes to crash the party. Around a large table with candidates interspersed, small and large conversations ensue on a variety of topics. Not only do candidates learn more about us, but we can see them in our milieu. If we observe someone getting along well with our folks and contributing to the fun, that's a good sign. On the other hand, when a candidate seems withdrawn or overwhelmed, that is a red flag. Not everyone at Southeast Psych is an extrovert, but even our more introverted people are confident enough to handle the high energy without getting lost in the shuffle; in fact, they provide a nice counterweight to many of our boisterous personalities.

Our interview process for support staff follows the same formula but is usually more streamlined. It is driven by our office managers, who provide orientation to the practice. Tandem interviews are used, but we might not have a full-practice lunch. The office manager collects input from interviewers (who could include clinicians), convenes a discussion if necessary, and ultimately makes the decision from this input.

For clinician candidates we gather our current clinicians for a group discussion. Between the coffee hour, tandem interviews, and lunch, each candidate will have interacted with numerous clinicians and staff, but even those who did not interact with a given candidate can contribute to this discussion by posing questions and serving as devil's advocates. We consider our sense of candidates' clinical skills (based on training, experience, and how they answered interview questions about clinical cases), including how they complement the expertise and specialties we already have. We ponder how well candidates could build their own practice. Could they forge relationships with referral partners? Could they give good presentations (a great way to self-market)? Could they hit the pavement with initiative and imagination to develop a client base? We think about their potential for innovation, for thinking outside the box. Southeast Psych is not only a private practice but also a media company. So when a candidate shows promise, say, in terms of writing or developing podcasts, videos, or webinars, our interest is piqued. Finally, we reflect on the fun and relationships values. Did they get our jokes? Did they make us laugh? Could we see them as a member of the Southeast Psych family?

This group discussion can go in all sorts of directions. As bright, well-educated professionals who read people for a living, clinicians often form strong opinions and relish in elaborating on them! My job is to herd the cats so that the discussion distills the myriad impressions to a recommendation. But the decision about whether or not to offer a clinical position is made by me and the leadership team. Input from the practice is vital, but decisions about clinicians joining the practice need to be made at the top.

## SUPPORTING SUPPORT STAFF

Clinicians at Southeast Psych sometimes joke that we work for our support staff. This is out of affection and reverence for the folks who keep the operation running and who make our lives go so smoothly: reception, checkout, intake, finance, and client relationships (we even have hostesses who attend to clients' needs in our waiting areas). Because of the importance of our support staff, Southeast Psych invests a lot in supporting them.

This starts with our office managers, whose job, simply, is to make sure our offices run well. One aspect of this is ensuring continuous coverage of key roles. They oversee training of new staff, but they delegate the actual training activities to staff veterans. Delegating like this allows new hires to learn from those in the front lines and to jumpstart personal relationships with colleagues. Having veterans conduct training also solidifies their own skills and knowledge. New hires are cross-trained; for instance, someone brought on board for reception also learns checkout and intake procedures. This provides a deeper understanding of office systems, as well as redundancy and flexibility when coverage issues arise (such as for illness or vacation).

Office managers provide new staff hires with orientation to our mission and culture. We have a handbook that describes the nuts and bolts of our operation, including roles and responsibilities. The handbook is a useful tool, and staff will refer back to it as needed, but even the most comprehensive, diligently prepared handbook will never be as effective as face-to-face training. The sequence of training typically starts with an explanation, then the new hire observing the skill or procedure, followed by the new hire performing the skill or procedure under gradually reduced supervision.

We place a lot of emphasis on communication at Southeast Psych and have built numerous mechanisms to keep everyone connected. As CEO, I meet with the office manager at my location on a monthly basis (other members of our leadership team meet with office managers at our other locations). During these meetings the office managers keep leadership informed about concerns and solutions that have been implemented. When needed, brainstorming and problem solving occurs regarding operations and staff. These meetings are an important way for leadership to keep staff informed about decisions and the direction of the practice. At our larger location the office manager has two "deputies" (senior intake coordinator and client relations), and the three of them meet monthly. Office managers meet briefly (about 15 minutes, unless more time is needed) with each staff person every month. Each manager also meets with the support staff team for the particular office at least monthly.

All of our Charlotte-based support staff convene for a two-hour, offsite lunch meeting every month. A clinician attends every month as a guest, and I attend quarterly. A good portion of these meetings is devoted to shooting the breeze, laughing, and maybe even playing a game. These gatherings are opportunities for people to get know one another (especially since the Charlotte offices are 30 minutes apart) and for team building. The guest clinician gets to know the staff and vice versa. That guest often gives a low-key presentation within his or her area of expertise that would benefit the staff. One such topic is healthy sleep habits; another might be team dynamics. When I attend I talk about the direction of the practice, reinforce the wonderful work they do, and listen to their concerns; we may engage in some valuable brainstorming and problem solving.

With all of these meetings, our staff members have numerous opportunities to interact with one another, their office manager, clinicians, and me. We find that this addresses the emotional needs of the people who keep our ship afloat in terms of hearing concerns and answering questions. In authentic ways, our support staff collaborate with clinicians to solve problems. These scheduled meetings are in addition to ad hoc interactions with office managers and members of the leadership team. Practice leaders have to be accessible.

In the pursuit of excellence, our staff takes part in professional development, such as webinars and book studies (shared reading and discussion). Many of the topics for professional development relate to customer service. One recent webinar topic was handling challenging client situations. Ethics-based training is critical. An example of a specific topic in this area would be how to comport oneself when a subpoena is delivered. Effective staff training on ethics starts with developing written policies in line with the American Psychological Association (APA)'s ethical standards. Ethics training activities may be applicable to support staff and clinicians alike, with topics such as informed consent and client confidentiality (Fisher, 2009). We are developing our own standards for the quantity of professional development hours for our staff, akin to what clinicians have for licensure renewal.

## CULTIVATING CLINICIANS

If you have not guessed by now, Southeast Psych is nothing like an office-sharing business. We really are an organization. Even though our clinicians have autonomy to develop their own practices, we want them to be part of our family and immersed in our culture. With that in mind, we do a lot with new clinicians to get them off to strong starts here. Then we do things to make sure they do well over the long term.

First, some of our new clinicians are fresh out of graduate school or an internship. These people have specific supervision requirements for licensure that we make sure are met. But beyond that we provide orientation and mentoring just as we do to all of our new clinicians. This starts with assigning each a mentor (this is a different person than a supervisor of record, if needed). Mentors make sure clinicians get oriented to our mission and culture, usually with individual meetings and setting up meetings with others in the practice. Orientation includes time with our support staff, learning about each phase of our operations and starting to form interpersonal relationships. To solidify understanding of systems, roles, and responsibilities, clinicians receive portions of the same handbook that staff members receive for their orientation.

Mentors meet with new-to-the-practice clinicians weekly (often over a meal) for a year. Thereafter they meet quarterly for a couple of years and then annually. This mentoring relationship provides support in a number of ways. First, even though we have a fun, vibrant practice with a lot of friendships, starting a new job is a big change, and big changes are usually stressful. Mentors help mentees deal with that stress. Several of our new clinicians moved to Charlotte to join us, some with families. We've had clinicians who were experienced but new to the world of private practice and all that entails, including having to build their own client base.

An important topic of mentoring meetings is establishing the mentee's clinical niche and identity. We want all of our clinicians to be known experts with a specific population (like children with anxiety) or treatment modality (such as dialectical behavior therapy [DBT]). Ideally, each also would have a unique philosophy or approach to his or her work. For example, my colleague Dr. Kelley Bolton works with girls on the autism spectrum or who have social cognition problems; she refers to her clients as "Supergirls" and uses a great deal of play therapy and arts and crafts. Kelley has a well-delineated personal brand that helps build her referral base and communicates to prospective clients what she is all about. Kelley also sees clients with other issues, including adults, so while having a niche and identity is great for linking a prospective client with a clinician, it does not necessarily need to limit the scope of what one does in a practice.

With that clinical identity as the cornerstone, the mentor and mentee can collaborate on a marketing plan. I actually hesitate to use that term, "marketing plan," because at Southeast Psych we emphasize relationships (one of our F-I-R-E values). So the plan they create starts with listing all of the people, at Southeast Psych and in the community, with whom they need to cultivate relationships. Depending on identity and niche, connections may be made with physicians, dieticians, educators, coaches, tutors, and other mental health providers. The mentor helps with making introductions, or finding others to make introductions. But sometimes the mentee needs to reach out directly and the mentor can help with how to do that, especially if self-marketing is new to the mentee.

Mentoring is an opportunity to develop ideas for projects, perhaps for the media division of Southeast Psych (see http://www.southeastpsych.com/southeast-psych-presents/). Projects could include blogs, books or chapters, presentations, or videos. These ideas could be part of the marketing plan for the new clinician or more about the long-term trajectory of his or her career. Some clinicians want their careers to be exclusively about their practices—and that is fine. But mentoring helps those who want to use their practices as foundations for a career that has a broader reach, such as developing a book series on parenting or creating a program for healthy eating and body image.

Mentoring has two other important benefits. First, it helps new additions to our family to assimilate into our culture. Mentors help them have fun, innovate, relate, and attain excellence.

Mentors are, in a sense, our cultural ambassadors. Second, mentoring also benefits mentors. Frank Gaskill, who has mentored many clinicians here over the years, has said that he derives a great deal of energy from mentoring. As a member of the leadership team, his strong and ongoing relationships with his mentees have helped us to manage Southeast Psych.

I meet with individual clinicians every few months over breakfast or lunch. There certainly is a mentoring aspect to these meetings as well. I ask the person how his or her practice is going. This question has a financial component, but we rarely specifically discuss dollars or client hours. More important to me is learning how the clinician feels in terms of quality of work, connections made, and professional identity. We may brainstorm directions to take with projects or career. These meetings also help me get feedback about my performance and about Southeast Psych as a whole.

Southeast Psych has several programs devoted to specific clinical issues, populations, or treatment approaches. Right now we have eight programs:

- Mind Matters: learning success, including assessments and advocacy
- Mind Over Body: sports psychology and performance coaching
- Food Wise: healthy eating and body image
- Wise Minds: DBT
- Rest Assured: sleep quality
- Aspire: autism spectrum disorders
- Purposeful Parenting: advancing positive parenting approaches
- Quarterlife: young adult males experiencing failure to launch

While it is not a requirement for our clinicians to be members of a program, most are and many participate in more than one. Programs promote collaboration on projects, such as a documentary film on father–daughter relationships ("A Voice That Carries"). Programs are a way for clinicians to support one another; this is especially true for Wise Minds and the extremely challenging DBT work they undertake with clients who have borderline personality disorder. Also, programs facilitate sharing of resources for marketing.

Finally, we have lunch meetings for clinicians every Wednesday. On the first and third Wednesdays of every month we start with announcements, which is a great way to share information about new initiatives (like a book) and services (such as a group). It is also a time for sharing significant personal information (recently one of my colleagues announced that she is pregnant!). We use the bulk of the remaining time staffing cases. We feel this is important not only for collegial support and provision of excellent client care but also for professional development and to learn about each other's areas of expertise; this can lead to internal referrals. We also use this time for activities such as sharing clinical success stories and for honoring recent accomplishments.

On the second Wednesday of each month we have an hour-long professional development presentation. Southeast Psych is an approved provider of continuing education credit with the APA, so a perk we provide our clinicians is that most, if not all, of their continuing education needs are met in house. Some of our presenters are guests, but many presenters are Southeast Psych clinicians, who deepen their knowledge and skills by developing and delivering these talks. An added advantage is that we learn more about what a presenter does with his or her practice (collectively we cover just about every clinical issue and population), and this creates a greater sense of community within the practice.

The fourth and fifth Wednesdays are "fun days." We close the practice for two hours, cater lunch, and watch movies or play games. When the weather is agreeable we might take food and fun outdoors. One Wednesday we set up a sort of carnival in the courtyard outside our building with croquet, corn hole, four-square, Frisbee golf, and so forth. We really enjoy these fun Wednesdays and we have formed a lot of great memories from these experiences.

# COMMUNICATION

We work hard on communication at Southeast Psych. One thing I have learned as a member of various organizations is that communication is *never* perfect. People will always miss key messages or announcements. Information will be miscommunicated or misremembered. But an organization can and should take steps to communicate as effectively as possible, to minimize miscommunication and memory lapses.

Our approach is to communicate repeatedly and in multiple ways. For example, I may announce a leadership decision during a weekly meeting, which is then sent out via email after, and then repeated by me in my CEO meetings and during small group meetings. We have actually created a communications grid that lists communication methods and whether they have a broad reach (to the whole practice) or a narrow reach (to individuals or small groups), as well as whether it is one-way communication (like an announcement) or two-way communication that allows for dialog. We are looking for ways to leverage technology for improved communication, such as videoconferencing between our offices and a cloud-based events calendar. As you can see in Table 14.1, we have a diverse portfolio of communication methods.

The advisory team is a collection of six people at Southeast Psych, clinicians and support staff, who meet with me every other month for lunch. These meetings help everyone get to know each other socially, especially across our two Charlotte offices. As CEO I have found these meetings valuable for several reasons. This group is an "ear to the ground," helping me to learn about issues and concerns around the practice. It is a forum for me to communicate to a smaller group in two-way fashion. These meetings have been great for brainstorming solutions to problems; major decisions need to be made by the leadership team, but having the input of this advisory team helps the leaders make better decisions. Every 12 months we rotate three members, who serve a 24-month term; this way we have both continuity and fresh perspectives on the advisory team.

In the previous section I mentioned programs at Southeast Psych. I meet with the program leaders as a group every other month over lunch. We always start these meetings with announcements from each program. Learning what other programs are doing is extremely valuable and routinely inspires new ideas and creates opportunities for collaboration. Then we discuss topics such as developing a leadership style and marketing strategy. These meetings are great communication venues, as I can take time to carefully explain decisions and initiatives to colleagues, who can then pass along information and thinking to members of the programs they lead.

TABLE 14.1 Communication Methods at Southeast Psych

| Method | Broad reach | Narrow reach | One-way | Two-way |
|---|---|---|---|---|
| Wednesday meeting announcements (at both offices) | ● | | ● | |
| Email follow-up on Wednesday meeting announcements | ● | | ● | |
| Advisory team | | ● | | ● |
| Program leaders meeting | | ● | | ● |
| E-newsletter | ● | | ● | |
| Breakfasts/lunches with CEO | ● | | | ● |
| CEO attending combined support staff meeting (quarterly) | | ● | | ● |
| Item-specific emails (like for professional development offerings) | ● | | ● | |
| CEO/leadership team member meeting monthly with office managers (who then share information with staff) | | ● | | ● |
| Town halls | ● | | | ● |
| Focus groups (smaller meetings on specific topics, like marketing) | | ● | | ● |
| Finance team meetings | | ● | | ● |

Every year or so we stage what we refer to as "town halls." We convene everyone who works at Southeast Psych at both Charlotte offices (clinicians, staff, personnel in our media company) offsite for two hours (we can use technology to include our Nashville office). Each town hall is devoted to a specific question or problem. Our advisory team has helped generate topics, which have included how we can enhance the client experience. Upon arrival at the meeting we randomly assign individuals to small groups so that each group has a mix of voices. I provide some background to the whole group and then get the small groups started with brainstorming. We alternate between brainstorming and whole-group discussion of ideas. Some wonderful thinking has taken place in our town halls. They are a great forum for clinicians and staff to collaborate. People leave feeling energized and that their input was heard. The leadership team then is tasked with putting action plans into motion and reporting back to the group.

## CLOSING THOUGHTS

The first of our four values at Southeast Psych is *fun*. One way in which we have fun is through social events like happy hours and parties. We have a secret gift exchange every holiday season. We stage lip-syncing battles. We have had paintball excursions and teams compete in road races and mud runs. We have had many baby and wedding showers. We are constantly pulling "wicked" practical jokes on each other. And in December 2015 we rented an entire movie theater so that all of our staff, clinicians, and families could watch the new *Star Wars* movie on opening night.

Fun sets us apart from other practices. Fun also lays the groundwork for the rest of our values. A fun atmosphere encourages innovation by stimulating creativity and making it safe to think outside the box. A sense of fun paves the way for deep and meaningful relationships, even when interactions have to do with serious issues. Fun promotes excellence by relieving stress from what can be daunting work in the mental health field. Plus, people tend to do their best work when they are enjoying what they are doing (just take a look at Google).

We feel strongly about fun, as well as innovation, relationships, and excellence. These values define our culture and guide our decision making and problem solving. They are the cornerstones for how we on-board and supervise clinicians and staff. We know who we are, which helps us know who we need to bring on board and how to support them once they are part of our family. Be sure you know who you are as a practice, and then let your identity be your guide.

# REFERENCES

Fisher, M. A. (2009). Ethics-based training for nonclinical staff in mental health settings. *Professional Psychology: Research and Practice*, 40(5), 459–466.

Verhaagen, D., & Gaskill, F. (2014). *How we built our dream practice: Innovative ways for you to build yours.* Camp Hill, PA: TPI Press.

CHAPTER 15

# BASIC BOOKKEEPING AND ACCOUNTING FOR THE PRIVATE PRACTITIONER

*Jeffrey Zimmerman and Diane V. Libby*

Many mental health professionals say "Oh no" when they think about bookkeeping and accounting. If they took a finance or accounting course in college they may have found it dreadful. The thought of doing complex computations and understanding debits, credits, assets, liabilities, and so forth is something that seems foreign and perhaps incomprehensible. In our experience it does not have to be so aversive. In fact, having a basic understanding of bookkeeping and accounting principles is crucial to running the business of your private practice. These principles apply to both solo and group practices across the various corporate structures associated with professional practice (e.g., sole proprietorship, professional corporation, limited liability company). You do not need a master's degree in business administration, finance, or accounting to manage the significant investment (of finances, time, and effort) you made in starting your practice. However, you do need some basic tools and knowledge so that you can manage your business, rather than have it manage you. When the business manages you, it is as if you are sitting on a horse, galloping through the woods—backwards (as a colleague of ours once said). We think it is far preferable to be holding the reins, facing forward, going at a safe and comfortable speed, and having a plan about which trails to take.

In this chapter, we will focus on some key concepts related to the financial management of your practice from bookkeeping and accounting perspectives. We will begin by discussing the importance of paying attention and knowing what is happening in your practice from a financial perspective. We will explain why it is important to keep it basic and not overcomplicate these important business processes. We will differentiate basic bookkeeping strategies from accounting strategies. We will also share ideas about how you can use your bookkeeping and accounting methodologies to inform your business decision making and how to use the standard reports that most billing and accounting systems generate to provide important data about the pulse of your business so that you are facing forward. Lastly, we will focus on building safeguards around your office finances into your practice and how you can choose and use an accountant, rather than the do-it-yourself method. Overall, the key, as it often is clinically, is to be able to follow sound assessment practices where you collect data and then use the data to make the needed financial decisions to manage your practice and your investment therein.

## PAYING ATTENTION

You have invested considerable assets of time, money, and emotional commitment into your practice. It deserves at least the attention you would give it if you were a venture capitalist having invested in such a practice. As stated in Walfish and Barnett (2009), in order to be successful you need to provide a quality service and have a quality approach to running your practice. At minimum this means being attentive to what is happening in your business from both a clinical and a financial perspective. If you don't attend to the business aspect of your practice, you might not be able to support the environment in which you have chosen to practice.

However, this does not have to be terribly time-consuming, labor-intensive, or onerous. It is more akin to doing modest exercise and getting regular medical checkups than training for the Olympics. The "modest exercise" relates to bookkeeping, accounting, and office procedures. The "regular medical checkups" relate to taking the pulse of your business by having metrics that you can easily track and understand. We will describe this below in more detail. However, the key is that the policies, procedures, and metrics must be relatively easy to implement. They do not have to require laborious data entry on an ongoing basis, and you do not have to purchase expensive software or hire staff to manage them. In fact, we (Zimmerman & Libby, 2015) believe that if your data-collection and office procedures are not difficult and laborious, you will actually have a much better chance of using them and benefiting from the information they yield. This information will help you make key business decisions such as:

- Do I hire an associate?
- Do I bring on a part-time office manager?
- Should I open another office?
- Do I purchase or lease the equipment I need?
- Do I market this special service I can provide?
- How can I earn more income?
- How can I provide services to a more diverse population of clients?
- Should I join another practice or healthcare provider group?
- Do I need to change my collections processes?
- Do I sign a contract to provide consulting services?
- Do I agree to work for a particular managed care company or discontinue a contract that is already in place?

Many people make these and other decisions based on their "gut feeling," but if they were investing in someone else's business they would expect to see a proposal, figures, and a rationale for the decision that made sense. You deserve the same thoughtful data-based decision making with regard to your own practice. Your bookkeeping and accounting methodologies and procedures can help provide the information that can guide you in these decisions. For example, if you know that Managed Care Company A pays $5 per visit more than Managed Care Company B, you might reactively determine that it is well worth renewing your contract with Managed Care Company A, especially if you see 50% more clients compared to Managed Care Company B. In fact, you might decide to discontinue the contract with the lower-paying company. However, if you have a bit more data, you may determine that the average turnaround time on your billing is much longer for Managed Care Company A, requiring significantly more staff time to dispute denials and resubmit "lost" claims. Looking at the decreased overall (or net) revenue associated with work from that company, you might actually completely reverse your initial inclination and instead decide to continue with Managed Care Company B rather than Managed Care Company A. All you needed to help make the decision was to know, for each company (in addition to the fee differential), the amount of overall claims and resubmittals and to have a rough understanding of how much time is spent following up on claims that are not paid in a timely manner when first submitted. Much of this information is easy to obtain from most standard patient accounts programs.

The key is actually implementing and using these programs and not just "winging it." We believe it is important to look at the data as you would do if you were consulting your physician trying to decide what to do about those occasional headaches you have. Should the decision about medicine, surgery, biofeedback, or meditation be made on the hunch of your doctor or on the data? We believe the data should be used not simply for the exercise of tracking information, but actually to help you make well-informed decisions about your practice that can impact its overall viability as well as your bottom line or take-home compensation.

## BASIC BOOKKEEPING AND ACCOUNTING

You must have a good accounting system for your practice. Most practices use accounting software packages to record their transactions (i.e., deposits and expenses). The process of recording the transactions or the financial activity of a practice is considered *bookkeeping*; the practice of reviewing the data recorded and using technical and analytic skills to review these data is *accounting*. In today's environment, almost all of the bookkeeping and accounting is done with a software package. Many practices use QuickBooks or a similar product for their accounting systems. They may also use another program or billing service to record their patient account information. Although a few holdouts are still using paper and pencil, that is not the most efficient or practical way to record your financial data.

Let's discuss some basic bookkeeping terms and their definitions.

A *chart of accounts* is the listing of the names of the accounts that your company has identified and made available for recording transactions. Examples would be patient fee income, rent expense, and payroll expense. These accounts are further classified into categories called assets, liabilities, equity, income, and expenses. These categories will be used in creating your financial reports, which we will define below.

*Accounts receivable* is the money owed to your practice from patients, insurance carriers, and other sources such as consulting contracts.

*Accounts payable* is the money your practice owes to others for products purchased or services performed. These are your outstanding bills (e.g., charge cards, leased equipment, rent, loans, health insurance and employee benefits).

*Payroll* is the cost of the wages that you pay to your employees. Managing the task of payroll is important. Payroll involves many different regulations from the U.S. Department of Labor, the Internal Revenue Service, and state tax departments; all must be adhered to. These regulations specify when to pay the taxes you withhold from employee wages, how you pay your employees, when overtime must be paid, and so forth. Your practice needs to either use a payroll service or have a bookkeeper who has the knowledge in payroll to meet all of these requirements. The penalties are steep for not complying with the rules, so be sure you have the proper resources lined up.

Your basic bookkeeping recording of transactions will be the start of how you measure your practice's financial well-being. Therefore, it is important to have a good bookkeeper to complete the initial recording (especially if you are not well organized or compulsive in these kinds of tasks). If the information is not entered correctly, the reports you view will be incorrect and may not make sense—or, worse yet, they will steer you in the wrong direction. You need to have correct data before using the reports generated by your billing and accounting software to help you make good practice management decisions.

Now let's look at some basic accounting terms and how they relate to your practice.

There are two primary methods of accounting for a healthcare practice, the *cash method* and the *accrual method*. Most healthcare practices use the cash basis of accounting for tax purposes. This accounting method allows you to report income as you collect it and deduct expenses as you pay them. In contrast, the accrual basis of accounting requires you to record income when it is earned—that is, at the time of service, even though you may not receive payment for this service for days or months (e.g., payment from an insurance company; monthly payments from a contract to provide evaluations). On the expense side you can take a deduction for an expense that you have incurred but not paid for as long as you are obligated for the purchase of the service or the product (e.g., legal services that have been rendered but you have 30 days to pay the invoice; office supplies that are purchased on account but you do not have to pay for them until you receive the invoice).

From an accounting standpoint, the reason that most healthcare practices use the cash basis of accounting is due to the uncertainty over what you will collect for your services. In many cases, you accept less than your actual billing under payer contracts with insurance companies. At times (we hope not often) a client will not pay for the services you provided. You would not want to pay income tax on the full amount of your billings or an estimated amount of billings when you will not likely collect that full amount.

The *balance sheet* is the financial report that summarizes your practice's financial position. The balance sheet is broken down into three sections: assets, liabilities, and equity. Your assets are the financial holdings of your practice, which includes your cash in the bank, accounts receivable, equipment, and furniture. Your liabilities are amounts owed to a third party, such as vendors, credit card companies, bank loans, and so forth. Your equity is the difference between your assets and your liabilities. You always want your assets to be greater than your liabilities to maintain a positive equity or, to put it another way, your investment in your practice.

The *profit and loss statement* provides information regarding the current-year profitability of the practice. This statement starts with your income collected (assuming you are running a cash-basis practice), such as patient fees, employee assistance program (EAP) fees, royalties, and rental income. The next section is a list of your practice expenses, such as rent, utilities, insurance, cost of administrative staff, cost of clinician employees, and office supplies. The current expenses would not include the payment of principal on outstanding loans for purposes of this statement. For example, if debt is incurred to cover a cash shortfall, the expenses you paid with the debt were deducted in the year they were paid. Since you already deducted the expenses, you cannot deduct the loan payments to repay the debt. The net of your income less your expenses will be your net income for the fiscal period. This net income is the funds available to you as the owner for compensation for your work in the practice, whether clinical or administrative. In a sole proprietorship or partnership entity structure, this is also the amount of income you would be using to figure your taxes, regardless of whether you actually take the income and move it from the business account to your personal account.

## BUDGETS

A *budget* is a projection of your profit and loss statement for your next fiscal year. Your practice's budget is a tool to help you reach your financial goals and objectives. Think of your budget as your road map to the next year. It will not be perfect, and there will be detours along the way, but during the year it will allow you to analyze where the detours are and how to fix or go around them or to reassess spending decisions. Your budget report is the tool you use each month to determine if you are on track to meet your financial goals. Most accounting software products can generate a budget report showing what your actual income and expenses were compared to what you budgeted them to be. The budget should be created using productivity goals for yourself and your clinicians if you are in a group practice.

All of these basic reports will help you determine the health of your business and will give you the information you need to make good management decisions. Analyzing comparative reports will point out some trends in your business. In other words, you will be able to view income and expenses across years to make note of any inconsistencies, and you can respond accordingly.

## DASHBOARDS

We have discussed how tracking key elements or variables related to your business is crucial to understanding it and to making needed decisions. One relatively easy way of understanding the business is to put some key elements on one or two pages (i.e., the "dashboard") and track them on

|               | Clinician 1 |          |           | Clinician 2 |          |           |
|---------------|-------------|----------|-----------|-------------|----------|-----------|
|               | Year 1      | Year 2*  | Total     | Year 1      | Year 2*  | Total     |
| Billed        | $200,000    | $230,000 | $430,000  | $180,000    | $240,000 | $420,000  |
| Income        | $120,000    | $140,000 | $260,000  | $135,000    | $160,000 | $295,000  |
| Billable hours| 1500        | 1650     | 3150      | 1400        | 1600     | 3000      |
| Amount billed/hr | $133     | $139     | $137      | $129        | $150     | $140      |
| Amount collect/hr | $80     | $85      | $83       | $96         | $100     | $98       |
| Uncollected   | $80,000     | $90,000  | $170,000  | $45,000     | $80,000  | $125,000  |
| % Uncollected | 40%         | 39%      | 40%       | 25%         | 33%      | 30%       |
| New cases     | 120         | 144      | 264       | 110         | 130      | 240       |
| Avg hrs/case  | 13          | 11       | 12        | 13          | 12       | 13        |
| Avg income/case | $1,000    | $972     | $985      | $1,227      | $1,231   | $1,229    |

*Year 2 is the most recent year

FIGURE 15.1: Sample Dashboard.

a quarterly basis, while also looking at annual trends (Walfish, Zimmerman, & Nordal, 2016). This is not something you have to do every week or month, although you certainly could.

Figure 15.1 is an example of such a dashboard that contains some basic information related to a two-person practice. For simplicity we are showing the data across two years, not across each quarter. We also are showing only what might be termed "productivity data" rather than other elements, such as referral origination or outstanding accounts receivable. The basic data (amount billed, income, billable hours, amount uncollected) would typically be generated from your billing software or by your outside billing agency. Easy computations provide the rest of the information.

Looking at the total billed amounts you can see that each clinician billed more in year 2 than in year 1. You can also see that Clinician 1 billed more in the two years compared to Clinician 2. However, Clinician 2 billed more the second year than Clinician 1. On the other hand, if you consider that productivity is really based on the income actually brought into the practice, then Clinician 2 actually brought more income into the practice over the two years, working 150 fewer clinical hours! We can see that Clinician 2 is billing and collecting more per hour (perhaps as a function of doing more work that is outside of managed care or more fee-intensive). Additionally, Clinician 2 is collecting better and, although on a per-case basis is seeing clients for roughly the same amount of hours, is actually generating more income per case. Clearly, just looking at the billing amounts would not give an accurate picture of the clinicians' relative productivity across the two years.

Generating more income per case may not be the vision or goal of this practice, nor does it need to be. Using the dashboard does not set the vision or values of the practice, but it does provide insights that can help you make needed business choices and assess your progress toward your overall goals. It can also raise important questions such as why collections are lower than anticipated and what new procedures can be put in place in an effort to increase the overall collection rate. This could be preferable to working more hours seeing clients, yet both could result in increased revenues and earnings. It also could stimulate a closer examination at the contracts you have, as well as even the types of services you offer, and possibly stimulate offering new services that fall outside of managed care.

Using your billing and accounting programs can offer you the following insights without requiring too much work:

- Productivity analyses (as above)
- Examining which referral partners or managed care contracts are best for the practice
- Looking at shifts in spending patterns or your expenses
- Understanding where there are gaps in your collections processes and where you might want to focus to improve collections and reduce your lost billing dollars
- Understanding what portion of income generated goes to your expenses and how that changes over time
- Understanding seasonal changes in revenue and hence the best times to take your vacations

You can easily track these figures and have a greater sense of what your practice is actually doing from a financial standpoint. And if you make changes based on the above data, you can then see what impact these changes have as you continue collecting these data over time.

## SAFEGUARDS

In addition to creating the metrics and reports for your analysis, it is also important to keep track of what is happening in your practice to reduce errors and to avoid employee theft. Remember, this is your practice and you are ultimately responsible for its well-being. You must be observant. Sometimes we get so wrapped up in providing professional services that we have blinders on as to what is happening in the rest of the office. We may be marketing and providing services but are not fully aware of what is happening in the business. "Minding the store" is as important as finding and doing the work. Sometimes listening (or overhearing) is critical to knowing what is going on in your office. Was your office manager's spouse recently laid off, leading to real personal cash-flow pressures? Does a staff person have a sick parent or child who distracts them from the boring task of posting transactions? In addition to listening, you should always be looking around the office as you go from point A to point B. Occasionally sit at an office manager's desk or a billing person's desk. Take a quick view of the work that is lying around uncompleted. Are there insurance denials sitting in a desk drawer that have not been addressed? Are there multiple unreturned phone messages sitting on the desk? These "finds" are important to the front desk operations, the collections activities, and the smooth and efficient running of the practice. They can have a direct impact on profitability.

It is also important to have checks and balances in place to be sure that the money that comes in for payment of fees is accounted for each day. There needs to be a reconciliation of the funds deposited into the bank account with the payments that are posted to your practice management system. This reconciliation should be done at least weekly, if not daily. Occasionally ask to see the reconciliation to let the staff members know that someone is looking at and holding the staff accountable for this report. If they think no one is watching, it opens the practice up to potential theft. Both authors are acutely aware of practices that have experienced substantial losses because of a lack of oversight and simply trusting that staff members will always do the right thing.

At least monthly, review your current and especially new vendors that are being paid. Be sure you know who the vendors are and what you are paying them for. This is to eliminate the possibility of a bookkeeper setting up a fictitious vendor and cutting checks to the vendor when in fact the bookkeeper is cashing those checks himself or herself. It also helps you confirm that you are not paying for goods and services that you are not receiving and that the prices charged are correct and what you have agreed to.

If you don't pay close attention to how the practice is running, you may have to personally make a financial contribution to the practice (or work for reduced compensation or for free) to cover routine business expenses. On the other hand, viewing your practice as a business entity and investment that needs your attention can help you make thoughtful decisions and feel in control over the practice and the financial implications of the difficult and important clinical services you are providing.

# CONSULTING WITH AN ACCOUNTANT

We believe that managing your practice is not a "do it yourself" (DIY) venture. The financial and tax-compliance aspects of running your practice can be considerable and can easily involve tens of thousands of dollars (if not more) of your earnings. This is not something about which mental health professionals receive training. Consequently, getting professional input is essential. Chapter 16 provides detailed information on how to most effectively consult with and utilize an accountant.

Your accountant and your bookkeeping and accounting procedures are essential resources and tools for running your practice business. Just as you attend to your clinical excellence, you should attend to the health of your practice—you, your family, and your practice deserve it.

# REFERENCES

Walfish, S., & Barnett, J. E. (2009). *Financial success in mental health practice: Essential tools and strategies for practitioners.* Washington, DC: American Psychological Association.

Walfish, S., Zimmerman, J., & Nordal, K. C. (2016). Building and managing a private practice. In J. C. Norcross, G. R. VandenBos, & D. K. Freedheim (Eds.), *APA handbook of clinical psychology* (5 vols.). Washington, DC: APA Books.

Zimmerman, J., & Libby, D. (2015). *Financial management for your mental health practice: Key concepts made simple.* Camp Hill, PA: TPI Press, The Practice Institute, LLC.

# PRACTICE MANAGEMENT CONSULTANTS

# CHAPTER 16

# THE ROLE OF A CERTIFIED PUBLIC ACCOUNTANT IN PLANNING, STRUCTURING, AND RUNNING A PRIVATE PRACTICE

*Diane V. Libby*

Managing your practice is not a "do it yourself" (DIY) venture. The financial and tax-compliance aspects of running your practice can be considerable and can easily involve tens of thousands of dollars (if not more) of your earnings. This is not something about which mental health professionals receive training. Consequently, getting professional input is essential. This chapter will explain the role a certified public accountant (CPA) can have in your practice and why it is important to the overall strength of your practice.

Your CPA is one of your most important advisors. A CPA is an accountant who has met education requirements and passed a certification examination. CPAs are licensed each year by their State Licensing Board and must meet education criteria each year to maintain that license; this ensures that they remain current with new accounting and tax laws. Your CPA will provide guidance in many areas of your practice, such as ensuring tax compliance, maintaining an accurate set of accounting books and records, and general business consulting.

As you establish your practice, you should assess a potential accountant using a number of different criteria (noted below). You will need to develop an effective working relationship that may last for years, if not decades, so finding the right professional partner is key. When choosing a CPA to work with, interview at least two professionals. The best way to find a good CPA is to ask your friends or colleagues about their CPA and their working relationship with them. The following is a list of the knowledge criteria and personal characteristics that you should use when choosing a CPA. These criteria are not only important now but will remain the critical areas you will use to assess your long-term relationship with your CPA. Although all of the criteria are important, the knowledge of current tax and accounting laws is extremely important as these change frequently and your CPA is the trusted advisor who will keep you in compliance.

- Good working knowledge of tax and accounting law
- Ability to respect your risk tolerance
- Relationship skills
- Ability to explain things in a concise and understandable fashion
- Reasonable fees and billing policies
- Understanding of the unique needs of a mental health clinician
- Ability to guide and train you in what elements of bookkeeping you can do yourself
- Ability to provide guidance in major financial decisions
- Knowledge of payroll systems
- Willingness to work with your attorney and other trusted advisors

These are all important points to ask in an initial consultation or interview with an accountant. If the CPA you are interviewing was a referral from a colleague, it may be helpful to take the information that you learned at the interview with the CPA and ask the colleague if his or her experience with the CPA mirrors what you were promised in the interview.

Once you complete your interviews, most likely you will have a sense about which person will add value to your practice. As a final check before you hire a CPA you can check the website hhtps://www.cpaverify.org to confirm that the CPA holds a current license and to check to see if any complaints have been filed against him or her with the State Licensing Board.

## ESTABLISHING THE ROLE YOUR ACCOUNTANT WILL TAKE IN YOUR PRACTICE

Once you have chosen your CPA, you need to define the role he or she will take in your practice. How often will you meet with your accountant? How often would you like the accountant to review your financials as you go through the year? Your CPA will bring to your practice all of the benefits listed in the section above on choosing a CPA. In addition, he or she can help you develop your practice's yearly budget. Your accountant should be asking you what role he or she should take. Do not be afraid to speak up if you would like something different from your accountant.

Your accountant should be available to meet with you or be available by phone for quick consultations. Most accountants would rather get a phone call for a quick question than have you make a decision on your own that may cost you more in tax dollars.

As your practice grows and your needs change, your CPA should be able to grow with you. Occasionally I hear that over time practices believe their CPA has become less responsive to their needs and questions; perhaps the accountant's focus has also changed. If this occurs, first discuss the issue with the accountant. Perhaps there has been a communication issue that can be easily resolved. If not, it may be time to find a new accountant. Remember, you control the relationship with each of your advisors and certainly need to have an accountant who adequately addresses your needs.

# HOW AN ACCOUNTANT CAN HELP SET UP YOUR PRACTICE

The initial setup of your practice will be filled with important decisions. Many of these decisions will be made with the advice of your accountant. Some of these decisions will be the following:

- Choice of entity, or the form in which you will operate—Examples of widely used entity choices are a limited liability company, a corporation, a sole proprietorship, and a partnership. These will be discussed in more detail later in the chapter.
- Accounting software—You will need computer software to record your transaction activity. Finding the right software to effectively manage your practice is important.
- Office staffing needs—What will your office staffing model look like and when should your staff be hired? Do you need a bookkeeper?
- Cash flow or budget projections—Properly planning your cash flow is critical for a new business.
- Financing options—Do I need financing? How do I find the financing I need?
- Payroll systems—How will I pay my employees and make sure that I am meeting all government requirements in doing so?
- Practice management software—Practice management software is your billing, scheduling, and management information system.
- Tax regulations for your type of entity and registering for appropriate taxes and tax identification numbers

These items are all important as you try to ensure that your practice has a strong start. Be sure you understand all of the rules, procedures, and internal systems in your practice. The more prepared you are prior to opening, the greater your ability to be available for clinical hours from day one instead of trying to take care of administrative tasks. If you simply open the practice without doing the initial setup work, you will be spending all of your time completing these administrative tasks and will not have time to have clinical, chargeable hours during the first month. If your decisions are driven by short-run considerations to fix a problem, they may not be the best long-term solution for the practice.

# ENTITY CHOICES FOR YOUR PRACTICE

When you are starting out in private practice, you must determine which entity choice will be most advantageous for your practice. You must consider a number of tax (both federal and state) and accounting factors in making the decision about entity choice. Your accountant will have a good working knowledge of entity choices for your practice and should be a key player in helping you make the right decision. There are many choices, depending on whether you are a group or solo practice. We will review some of the widely used entity choices available to your practice. However, whether you are in a single-member practice or a group practice, this is a key decision for you. There are many variables and possibly state requirements that you must review. You must consult with your CPA and/or your attorney to give you guidance. These trusted professionals will be able to review with you the pros and cons of the entity choices, taking into account your personal situation.

## SINGLE-MEMBER PRACTICES

First we will look at the entity choices for a single member practice.

## SCHEDULE C—SOLE PROPRIETOR

This type of business entity is one that is owned by a single person, and there is no legal distinction between the owner and the business. You can still have employees under this model of business, but there can be only one owner. The drawback to this type of ownership is that because there is no legal distinction between yourself personally and the business, your personal assets are at risk if the business were to be sued. Of course, there are ways to protect yourself through insurance, but you would need to determine with your advisor if the insurance is adequate or if you should look to another form of business entity for protection. This entity does not file a separate tax return but completes a Schedule C form with the business income and expenses that is part of the owner's individual tax return. Because there is no separate tax return with this type of entity, the accounting costs may be slightly less than a different structure where a separate filing exists. However, cost should not necessarily be the driving factor in entity choice; protection of assets should be of greater importance.

## SINGLE-MEMBER LIMITED LIABILITY COMPANY (LLC)

This type of entity is still owned by a single person or other entity, but it does have a separate legal distinction and therefore provides a degree of protection of personal assets from a business obligation. This entity does not file a separate tax return but completes a Schedule C form with the business income and expenses that is part of the owner's individual tax return. Because there is no separate tax return with this type of entity, the accounting costs may be slightly less than a different structure where a separate filing exists. However, cost should not necessarily be the driving factor in entity choice; protection of assets should be of greater importance. Depending on what state your practice is located in, there also may be some additional state filings with an LLC as compared to the sole proprietorship. An LLC entity will have some simplicity as compared to a corporation but should provide you with the same protection of your personal assets.

## PROFESSIONAL CORPORATION

This is an entity that is a corporation formed in the state your practice resides. A corporation is an entity that has a separate legal identity. The separate identity protects the owners from being sued or obligated individually for business debts or obligations. In many states a professional corporation has a unique set of regulations for those who provide professional personal services. The professional corporation files a separate tax form each year. The owner can take a salary from the business. There are special tax rules for a professional corporation that you will need to be aware of, so working with your accountant will be very important. Because this entity requires a separate return and has some specific tax requirements, the cost for the accounting and tax for this entity would be more than a single-member LLC.

## GROUP OR MULTI-OWNER PRACTICES

Now we will review the entity choices for a group practice.

## PROFESSIONAL CORPORATION

The group practice can also choose the professional corporation entity as noted above. This type of entity can work well for a group practice. The entity provides personal asset protection for the owners and allows the owners to take a salary from the corporation. The complication of a professional corporation is its tax structure. Any profits left in this type of corporation are taxed at the highest corporate rate. This creates the need for precise tax planning at year end to control any profits and possibly distribute profits if individual owners are in a lower tax bracket.

## PARTNERSHIP

This entity choice is also available to group practices. A partnership is an entity where two or more owners share the profits and liabilities of a business enterprise. There are all types of combinations of ownership and profit and loss sharing arrangements that can be defined in a partnership agreement. General partners can still be held personally liable for business debts and obligations. Income allocated to the partners as defined in the partnership agreement is passed through and taxed to the individuals as part of their personal return.

## LLC

An LLC is a separate and distinct legal entity and provides for personal asset protection for the LLC members. Most LLCs choose to be taxed as a partnership but can elect to be taxed as a corporation. LLCs will have operating agreements similar to partnership agreements. The agreement will speak to the allocation of ownership, profit and loss sharing percentages, withdrawal and buyout provisions for members, and many other provisions, such as death or disability of a partner and the dissolution of the LLC. The operating agreement is a critical document that should be completed and agreed upon among all members prior to starting business wherever possible.

No matter which group practice entity choice you make, it is important to have agreement regarding potential significant changes in the ownership such as death, disability, or withdrawal from the practice. These documents can be in the form of a buy/sell agreement, shareholder agreement, or LLC operating agreement. It is important to be clear and concise on these issues to prevent disagreements in the future.

Your CPA can help you work through the pros and cons of each entity type to reach a decision about entity choice that is right for you and your practice. The CPA will also make sure that you have all the appropriate documents in place to create a successful practice.

## PRACTICE EXPENSES

One of the first questions an accountant typically gets from a professional going into private practice is "What expenses will I be able to deduct?" The answer depends somewhat on the type of practice. Below are some common expenses:

- Rent and occupancy costs—These are the costs of your physical office space. They include your rent, utilities, and any common area building costs that you may be obligated to pay through your lease. All of these costs are fully deductible to your practice.
- Insurance costs—These will include your general liability insurance, malpractice insurance, and workers' compensation insurance. All of these insurance costs are fully deductible.
- Telephone and answering service costs—Costs for your main business telephone lines and answering service costs are fully deductible. If you provide mobile devices for the owners and employees, you can deduct the business portion of the devices and services. You will need to determine the business versus personal use of these costs.
- Continuing professional education—Expenses to attend seminars or courses to enhance your current practice will be deductible, including any travel expenses for you or the employee to attend. The deduction for meals is limited to 50% of the total cost.
- Payroll costs—Payroll costs, including payroll, payroll taxes, and fringe benefits for employees, are deductible. This would include the payroll cost of both office administrative staff and professional associates you may hire to work in the practice.
- Furniture, fixtures, and computers—The equipment needed to run your business is deductible. For tax purposes, the original cost of these items will determine the ability to deduct these costs as you purchase them versus having to depreciate or write them off over a period of years.
- Office supplies—Supplies needed to run the office, from paper to paper towels, are deductible when used in the office.

- Interest—Interest charges to the business on loans or credit cards where the proceeds were used to fund the business or purchase assets are deductible.
- Automobile expenses—Expenses for the business use of your vehicle are deductible. There are a number of ways to document the business use of your vehicle, and documentation is critical in sustaining this deduction if you are audited.
- Retirement plans—The costs incurred to set up and administer a retirement plan for the practice are deductible. Contributions made to the retirement plan of the practice for the benefit of the employees and the owners are also a deduction against income reported. Retirement plans are subject to their own set of tax and labor department rules to be sure that employees are fairly treated when entities are funding retirement plans. You will need to get the right advice and will possibly need a pension consultant to be sure that your contributions are proper and deductible.
- Billing costs—Costs incurred to complete your billing to insurance companies and patients are deductible as business expenses.
- Professional dues and licenses—Professional association dues and fees for obtaining licenses to practice are deductible to the practice. You do need to review the billing statements from the professional organizations as they may deem a portion of your dues to be nondeductible. This is typical where the professional organization is providing some lobbying activity; the portion of your dues that funds lobbying costs is not deductible.
- Bank and credit card charges—Bank service fees and fees assessed for patients paying by credit card are fully deductible.
- Computer services—The costs for services provided to maintain and update your computers and your network are fully deductible.
- Professional fees—Fees paid for accountants, attorneys, pension administrators, and other professionals are deductible if the fees were incurred for the benefit of the practice.
- Disability/life insurance—These costs may or may not be deductible. When purchasing these policies, seek the advice of your CPA to discuss the tax implications of these policies, the deductibility of the premiums, and how the policies should be titled.
- Advertising and marketing costs—The costs associated with marketing and advertising your business are deductible.
- Materials and supplies—Materials and supplies used in your business are deductible.
- Taxes—Real estate taxes, local property taxes on equipment, payroll taxes, and miscellaneous registration fees are deductible. State income taxes assessed to the entity would also be deductible for federal income tax purposes. The type of entity will determine if you pay income taxes at the entity level or at the individual level.
- Travel and entertainment expenses—If they are business related, travel and entertainment costs are deductible. Only 50% of the cost of meals and entertainment is deductible. To be deductible the expense must have a business purpose, so you should document who you were with and what was discussed.

You should review your common expenses with your CPA to determine if any specific recordkeeping may be required to comply with Internal Revenue Service regulations.

# OTHER BENEFITS OF USING A CPA

Your CPA will work with you to determine more than what practice expenses you can deduct. Depending on the needs of your practice, your accountant can also support your practice with the following items:

1. Ensure you are meeting your federal and state tax obligations on the income from your practice properly and in a timely manner
2. Set up practice safeguards to minimize the potential for employee theft
3. Advise you in service-line additions or eliminations
4. Work with you to find appropriate financing
5. Advise you regarding capital purchases for your practice

Many of these mental health practice-management tools are discussed in more detail in Zimmerman and Libby (2015).

## USING YOUR ACCOUNTANT AS A RESOURCE

Your accountant may not have the answers to all your questions, but most CPAs have developed a professional referral network to provide clients with quick access to the professionals they may need to handle a practice question or situation, such as labor attorneys, pension administrators, tax attorneys, investment advisors, and insurance professionals. Therefore, when you have a question or issue in your practice, in many cases your CPA should be your first phone call. If your CPA doesn't know the answer, he or she can direct you to a professional who does.

Your accountant is an essential resource for running the business side of your practice. As you attend to your clinical excellence, you should also attend to the health of your practice—you, your family, and your practice deserve it.

# REFERENCE

Zimmerman, J., & Libby, D. (2015). *Financial management for your mental health practice: Key concepts made simple.* Camp Hill, PA: TPI Press.

# CHAPTER 17

# THE ROLE OF THE ATTORNEY IN A PRIVATE PRACTICE

*A. Steven Frankel*

This chapter discusses the roles that attorneys play in the lives of mental health practitioners. I begin with a list of the types of services that practitioners need and the ways attorneys can be helpful in addressing those needs. I then turn to the issue of how to locate and engage attorneys with relevant skillsets.

## WHY WOULD I NEED AN ATTORNEY?

Mental health practitioners, like it or not, have many clear and relevant needs for legal counsel, at all stages of practice. Many practitioners have found out the hard way that legal advice and counsel can be critical for practice development, management, and termination, as well as to assist with the many "bumps in the road" that affect practitioners over the course of their work.

### PRE-INDEPENDENT PRACTICE NEEDS

Many practitioners begin their careers working as employees of more senior colleagues before attaining independent licensure themselves. During such stages of professional life, attorneys can and should play a helpful role in reviewing contractual agreements (employment contracts), payment plans, supervisory arrangements, record creation and maintenance (ensuring that records and their storage and possible destruction are consistent with state and federal law), and conflict resolution or employment termination. Such employees are often covered by workers' compensation programs, and records of supervised professional experience are maintained by the employer. As "W-2 employees," taxes are withheld from their paychecks. For all of these interests, attorneys who combine business and healthcare subspecialties are needed, both for employers and employees. They can draft needed contracts with appropriate provisions, especially ensuring against vulnerability to allegations of "fee-splitting," which has historically been viewed as an unethical way to pay for referrals.

## WORKING AS A SUPERVISED AND LICENSED COLLEAGUE

Professionals who are licensed and looking toward starting a practice career sometimes begin as independently licensed, yet supervised professionals. Such arrangements often reflect that the supervisor is helping the employee learn skills and treatment approaches that are new to the employee. This status is regarded as a "W-2 employee" rather than an independent contractor, and the considerations that lie in the business–professional interface are much the same as with pre-licensed professionals, cited above. In addition, for licensed professionals who work as W-2 employees, or even independent contractors, contracts should be carefully scrutinized by relevant attorneys to make sure that a W-2 employee is properly treated as such and an independent contractor is properly treated as such. Another of the particular issues of concern are contracts that have "non-compete" agreements, which prevent the employee from terminating a position and then setting up a practice that is geographically close to his or her former position or that in any way "invites" clients seen at the prior place of employment to see the clinician in the new practices. Such agreements are increasingly considered "void" and are highly problematic. However, they are enforceable in some jurisdictions, so it is important to carefully understand what such an agreement means from a business perspective, as well as what it means clinically for your clients.

## WORKING AS AN UNSUPERVISED AND INDEPENDENTLY LICENSED COLLEAGUE

A licensed and unsupervised employee is considered to be an "independent contractor" by the Internal Revenue Service. No taxes are withheld from payments and no supervision can be required (although consultation may be a standard part of the work agreement). Attorneys are needed to review the contracts and to look carefully for "non-compete" agreements.

## ESTABLISHING AN INDEPENDENT PRACTICE

Independent practitioners will need attorneys to review office lease agreements; contracts for the hiring, retention, promotion and termination of any staff members who may manage the office; and policies for record management and retention. Such contracts need to be consistent with state and federal law, fair and appropriate for their purposes, and written clearly and understandably for all parties involved. Further, consultation with an attorney is recommended regarding the various forms of insurance that practitioners should consider obtaining, including malpractice, office premises liability, and protection from unanticipated terminations of practice due to death or disability.

Practitioners who wish to add colleagues to their practices need to consider how to recruit, evaluate, employ and manage, and, if needed, terminate such colleagues. It is especially important to have an attorney with a combination of business and healthcare specialties to provide consultation for these purposes, particularly regarding resolution of conflicts, determination of who has what kind of control over client care, and billing and payment issues.

Further, legal consultation can be helpful when considering policies regarding client payment problems, such as how much of a balance buildup can be tolerated before taking action of one sort (e.g., collections agencies) or another (e.g., termination/referral), and other office policies, such as missed sessions, tardy arrivals for sessions, noise in the waiting room (clinicians need to ensure that soundproofing and/or "white noise" generators are available to keep clients' voices from being overheard, which would be viewed as a confidentiality breach), and access to records.

Attorneys who are healthcare law specialists can be helpful in reviewing and advising on plans for advertising and marketing practices (e.g., the content of advertisements is often limited and controlled by state law, and a licensing board can close the practice of a practitioner who violates such statutes and codes).

A related issue concerns the interest of practitioners to establish specialty standing in their fields of expertise and to use such specialty standing for marketing purposes. Appropriately trained attorneys are aware of the meaning of various ways that professionals may describe their specialties, and their consultation can be protective of practitioners.

Finally, practitioners may wish to establish multiple offices, to rent office space to other professionals, and so forth. Legal consultation as to those contractual relationships is both helpful and necessary. Insurance companies will need to know of multiple office locations, and the practitioner who is providing office space to colleagues will need to decide on charges for office renters and the services provided to them (e.g., marketing, billing/collections, record maintenance and storage, among others). Lease agreements must be written to address potential difficulties and to protect the practitioner's legal interest, should they arise. Contracts must also be written so they are consistent with state and local laws.

## DEALING WITH TROUBLES

It is crucial to involve an attorney as early as possible if you are facing various problems, any of which can mushroom into career-threatening circumstances. A healthcare attorney must be consulted in situations such as the following.

It is not unusual, particularly in mental health practice, for clients to become upset and angry with their treating practitioners. Coping with client dissatisfactions, threats, and angry actions is a domain that calls on the expertise of healthcare attorneys. Similarly, working with clients who become involved in litigation in their personal lives often involves demands that practitioners supply professional records and testimony, both at deposition and at the trial or hearing. Attorneys play vital roles in the preparation and representation of practitioners in such situations (e.g., advising clinicians not to change or modify any of their records, as well as how to respond to subpoenas and court orders). Whenever a client threatens you, you must notify your malpractice insurance carrier immediately, as the company's rules say that if you don't notify them as soon as you are aware of a threat, the company may choose not to cover your representation.

Complaints may be filed and become pursued by licensing boards for the life of a practitioner's license (in all states except California, which has a statute of limitations, as of this writing). Licensing board actions are far more psychologically stressful (shameful) and damaging to practitioners than lawsuits, as lawsuits (e.g., malpractice suits), painful as they are, are about dollars, while board actions are about identities and the ability to continue to practice. To fully grasp the intensity of this distinction, consider scenarios such as this: Someone who meets you asks what you do for a living. How often do you say "I practice . . ." (and then name your profession) versus "I'm a (professional)-ist?" The former is what you do, while the latter is "who you are."

Further, unlike lawsuits for money damages, licensing board actions remain in public view, on the websites of licensing agencies and often in professional society journals. Shame is perhaps one of the (if not THE) most noxious emotions known to us, and licensing board actions result in shamed states, with long-term negative consequences. Finally, while a lawsuit for financial damages does not require that a practitioner cease practice, a licensing board action may result in practice termination.

As a result of the impact that licensing board actions have upon practitioners, practitioners must retain attorneys who specialize in "administrative law," which is the type of law that licensing boards function under (as opposed to criminal law or civil law) and that is relevant to board actions. "Civil" attorneys, who may specialize in contract law, trusts and wills, employment law, and so forth, are not the types of attorneys who are best retained to represent practitioners who are contacted by their licensing boards as a result of a client complaint. Administrative attorneys can advise on how to prepare a response to a licensing board complaint and what types of responses to board inquiries can make situations worse (e.g., "This is a borderline client who is acting out their disorder on me" is NOT going to be helpful). They can cross-examine board experts to support their clients. Their knowledge of how administrative actions progress allows them to work toward resolution of board actions without resorting to hearings and so forth. Self-representation, in this specialized area of law, is more than risky.

There are some notable aspects of mental health practice that are associated with criminal complaints. Sexual encounters with clients and insurance fraud stand out at the top of this list, but there have been cases of "insider trading" (a practitioner learns of a stock opportunity from a client's personal life and attempts to purchase stock, based on that information) and breaches of confidentiality. Such criminal complaints can, and do, result in criminal indictments, prosecutions, and jail terms for practitioners.

For criminal complaints, criminal lawyers are required to provide representation. These lawyers understand that aspect of the legal world in ways that those not experienced with criminal law may never understand (just as civil lawyers, who deal with contract disputes and the like, may never understand administrative law—the law of licensing boards).

For these reasons, and especially given the consequences of a criminal action against a professional, practitioners facing criminal charges must retain a criminal lawyer. Criminal lawyers know what explanations are effective with judges and which ones are not, and particular information about a professional's history that may or may not be helpful to admit into evidence, as well as what elements of agreements may reduce the impact of court orders.

The insurance industry and the ways it acts upon its interests is one of the consequences of mental health professionals' insistence on calling themselves "healthcare providers." (The other consequence is regulation by licensing boards.) Changes in *Health Insurance Portability and Accountability Act (HIPAA)* procedures, business associate contracts with companies that maintain/manage records, post-payment audits by agents who contract with insurance companies to conduct audits of client records and billing procedures as well as policies regarding confidentiality, periodic reviews of client status, and the like, are all events that cause distress among professionals (as well as causing disruptions in payment, including demands for repayment of fees adjudged to be improper, pursuant to audit). Healthcare attorneys can be invaluable resources when such events take place, especially those who are trained, competent, and up to date on developments in the insurance industry.

When a practitioner decides to retire from practice and to sell the practice or refer the clients to other practitioners, or, due to death or disability, must suddenly cease practice altogether, attorneys who are trained and competent in the domain of practice transition are exceedingly helpful. As an example, in years past, practitioners could not ethically sell a practice because it was considered to involve the sale of the clients themselves, which is considered unethical. That has changed in recent years, and attorneys with specialty expertise in such practice sales and terminations can assist and preside over practice transitions, making the process tolerable to practitioners, their families, their colleagues (who otherwise might have to step in and "clean up" a practice when the practitioner can no longer practice), and their clients. For these interests, the estate-planning attorney who has drawn up a will or trust for the practitioner needs to be consulted as well. The same is true for the preparation of "professional wills."

# HOW DO I FIND AN ATTORNEY?

The information above provides an overview of the areas of legal specialty that are relevant to mental health practice: (1) business attorneys (e.g., contracts, leases), (2) employment attorneys (e.g., hiring, termination, benefits, W-2 vs. independent contractors), (3) business attorneys who specialize in marketing and advertising and who also have licensing board expertise, such that they know what kinds of marketing content is acceptable to licensing boards, (4) administrative attorneys who specialize in healthcare and mental health licensing board actions, (5) criminal lawyers who deal with criminal complaints against practitioners, (6) civil attorneys (including malpractice attorneys) who deal with actions against practitioners where money damages are claimed, and (7) practice sales attorneys, who should be conferring with the practitioners' estate-planning (trusts and wills) attorney.

How can practitioners locate these types of attorneys?

Word of mouth is the first method. For practitioners who have contacts with colleagues in the communities in which they practice, such colleagues may be the best referral sources when seeking an attorney. If the colleagues have practiced for some years, the odds are that they will have had contact with attorneys and may have solid recommendations based on personal experiences.

Advertisements in your professional society newsletters, magazines, and journals provide information about attorneys who specialize in your areas of practice. Such attorneys often provide administrative law consultation (re: licensing boards), practice building (e.g., hiring/retention of staff and colleagues), practice management (e.g., recordkeeping, storage, and retention), and marketing (e.g., ads in newsletters, newspapers, referral contacts).

Often, state professional societies are quite aware of attorneys in their jurisdictions who have been representing their members. One strategy that has been found to be highly effective is to call the professional societies for all of the mental health professions, tell them that you are a professional who is planning to move to their jurisdiction, and ask if they can give you names of attorneys you might contact to set up and develop your practice. If any attorney's name is given by more than one professional society, that person should be a good choice to contact for your needs.

Especially when searching for an administrative attorney, your licensing board staff are quite aware of the attorneys who have their respect, and they are often willing to make such recommendations to callers. When dealing with threats of licensing board actions, malpractice suits, and the like, a major source of referrals is your malpractice insurance company. In fact, while most mental health malpractice insurance companies will require you to use one of their "panel providers" (you've heard of "managed care," and this is "managed law") for malpractice actions, they often will allow you to use whomever you wish for administrative law actions. In any case, their panel attorneys are more than familiar with—they are experts in—malpractice and administrative actions. As "panel providers" for your malpractice company, they are quite aware of how the company works, what kinds of costs will be honored, and so forth.

It is a good idea to meet face to face with any attorney you are thinking of retaining. As with mental health treatment, the relationship between the provider and the client is an important ingredient in success and client satisfaction. Interviewing several attorneys may be costly, but if comfort and confidence in the relationship is important, those costs are worthwhile. Most of these costs will be covered by malpractice insurance, but contact your malpractice insurance company to learn its positions for coverage of such initial interviews.

Some practitioners make frequent enough contact with their attorneys that they maintain a "retainer agreement" (which typically results in rapid access to the attorney and, for most attorneys, reduced fees). Some attorneys require clients to pay a low monthly payment, regardless of whether services are used, in order to have such an agreement. Other practitioners choose to "pay as you go" for legal services.

## WHAT IF I DON'T THINK MY ATTORNEY IS WORKING WELL WITH ME?

You can discharge an attorney at any time during his or her representation of you. As with the mental health professions, law is a profession in which the professional–client relationship is highly important and personal. Terminating with an attorney or getting a consultation from an alternative attorney in order to make a decision about continuing to work with an attorney is not at all unusual.

## CONCLUDING THOUGHTS

This chapter has reviewed the various roles and interfaces between mental health practitioners and attorneys at law. We have seen that concerns regarding practice creation, development, enhancement and growth, and termination all properly involve attorneys, as do problems that arise over the course of practice, such as conflicts with clients, allegations of malpractice, and civil, criminal, and administrative actions.

We also reviewed the most effective ways to find and establish relationships with attorneys, including word of mouth, advertising in newsletters and journals, malpractice insurance companies, state and regional professional societies, and licensing boards.

# CHAPTER 18

# FINANCIAL PLANNING FOR THE PRIVATE PRACTITIONER

*Mary Gresham*

H ow did you feel when you read the title of this chapter? How you feel about money and money management in your life can help you to determine whether you want a simple, easy-to-follow guide or a complex, sophisticated, professionally informed set of documents that make up a comprehensive financial plan. Be honest with yourself about your level of motivation and your interest in planning your financial future; it is the first step toward knowing how to proceed. Your financial plan has to work for you and can vary from a simple one-page guide with "rules of thumb" to multiple binders full of graphs, pie charts, projections, assumptions, actionable items, goals, and potential barriers to success. Recent research has shown that general rules of thumb for decision making can be more effective for some people than traditional financial education (Binswanger & Carmen, 2012).

In financial planning, as with many important endeavors, getting started may be the most challenging aspect. As a mental health professional, you can understand and empathize with clients who are reluctant to engage in a process that is unknown and anxiety arousing. Not knowing how to start, whom to trust, and which of the bewildering array of choices to pursue can be just as paralyzing to you as it is to potential clients seeking mental health services. In addition, you may feel resistant to an honest examination of your finances, procrastinating and delaying gathering and integrating the information that is necessary to see the bigger picture. A recent study by Britt, Klontz, Tibbetts, and Leitz (2015) suggests that mental health professionals may be "money avoidant" (p. 20). These authors found that compared to other occupations, mental health professionals were at greater financial risk in terms of carrying credit card debt, setting money aside for emergencies, having a spending plan, and having adequate investment strategies.

# WHAT IS A FINANCIAL PLAN?

A financial plan incorporates activities in a number of spheres. The author has developed a model that includes examining and understanding money from the following four perspectives: Rational/Mathematical, Values/Spiritual, Emotional/Symbolic, and Process approaches to money management.

1. Rational/Mathematical: This is the traditional knowledge-based approach to money management based on the assumption that humans are rational and act in their own economic best interest with enough information. Financial literacy and education are part of this perspective.
2. Values/Spiritual: This aspect is comprised of your personal and spiritual values about money. Your values guide you to articulate the deeper purpose of money in your life.
3. Emotional/Symbolic: Symbolic and emotional aspects of money that are unique to you, plus common irrational money behaviors described in the behavioral finance literature are included in this category. Developing your awareness and consciousness of childhood experiences, family messages, feelings, needs, and personal money dynamics contributes to creating a healthy relationship with your money.
4. Process: How do you operate in relationship to money? Being able to stand back, observe, and describe your processes with money is a valuable skill. Developing new processes can make significant differences in your ability to implement your financial plan.

Incorporating all of these elements into your financial plan will allow you to start where you find the most interest and energy. Many mental health professionals might find the most engagement by beginning with understanding the emotional factors that affect their money decisions, including family history, money memories, money trauma, the symbolic importance of money, and cultural factors and feelings about money. The emotional and irrational side of money can derail the best-developed plans. Understanding and being aware of your potential impediments in this regard can keep you from getting frustrated when you have trouble implementing or persisting with your plan. From there, exploring your values and what is important to you can give meaning and purpose to the goals you set and increase your motivation to work toward them. Setting up processes that work for you is also essential in designing and carrying out an effective financial plan. This includes deciding with whom you will discuss your finances, how openly you will communicate, how you will track your money, and what kinds of automatic or manual systems you will use. Designing and observing your financial processes is a key element in your success. Being a mental health practitioner can provide you with a head start in knowing how to step out of the immediate situation and observe your own behaviors and money processes.

For many people, financial literacy is the least interesting and engaging piece of the puzzle. If you like mathematics and spreadsheets and enjoy reading about investing, you can study and use knowledge of economic and financial concepts to effectively manage your financial resources.

Although research shows that higher financial literacy is correlated with higher levels of wealth, the research does not indicate the direction of the relationship. We know that higher levels of financial literacy are associated with being male, being older, being more highly educated, living in an urban area, and being in an ethnic majority. Research studies have also affirmed the positive relationship between sophisticated financial knowledge, mathematical abilities, retirement planning, and wealth. One of the few studies using random assignment for treatment and control groups found that after completing workplace financial educational classes, participants significantly increased their retirement contributions (Lusardi & Mitchell, 2014). Unfortunately, the increase in financial well-being due solely to an increase in financial knowledge for self-employed professionals (e.g., those in private practice) is unknown and has yet to be researched. For most adults, learning financial concepts works best when you break topics down into smaller chunks and apply them to your immediate situation.

It is never too early and never too late to develop a plan. Getting interested in and engaged with your money can start for many reasons, from crisis to deliberate self-care. It is best to begin a financial plan while in graduate study so that you can make good decisions about your level of student loan debt, repayment plans, and expected earnings in a realistic way. On the other hand, many professionals do not get truly motivated to generate or follow a plan until their 50s when they are faced with a retirement shortfall. Planning that begins in later stages may mean that your options to decrease your commitment to work are limited. If it is important to you to have the choice to decrease your work in your 60s, even if you suspect that you will not actually do it, then planning at earlier stages will be required.

## WHO WILL HELP YOU WITH YOUR PLAN?

There is a confusing array of professionals who offer financial planning services. They may be called by any of a number of professional titles, such as financial planner, financial advisor, financial consultant, life planner, investment advisor, investment manager, personal financial specialist, wealth consultant, and wealth manager.

Financial planning is a relatively new profession, having started in the 1970s. Standards for practice were implemented in 1985. Until 2007, a Certified Financial Planner™ was not required to have a college degree but it is now a requirement, along with passing a test requiring knowledge in eight subject areas: ethical conduct, general principles, educational planning, risk management, investing, tax, retirement planning, and estate planning. The fiduciary standard, which should be familiar to mental health practitioners because we are also fiduciaries, requires that the client's best interests are the primary consideration. The CFP® mark indicates that the planner is required to operate as a fiduciary but only when providing planning services. Many stockbrokers are also CFPs, but if they are not engaged in a financial planning process with you, they are not required to put your interests ahead of theirs. In the financial services world, only CFPs and Registered Investment Advisors (RIAs) must put your interests first. The federal Securities and Exchange Commission regulates these two groups. Stockbrokers and other financial services professionals are only required to use a standard of general "suitability" for someone in your particular situation (e.g., your age, your income, your level of assets). They are regulated by the Financial Industry Regulation Authority (FINRA).

At the moment, there is heated debate in the federal government as to whether all professionals who advise about retirement accounts should be held to the higher fiduciary standard since the consequences of retirement account failure can be dire. The Department of Labor's new rule is that retirement advisers must put the client's interests first, while the financial services industry lobbyists are insisting that making all the fees visible will discourage lower-net-worth investors from getting good financial advice and trying to do it themselves. How this issue will be resolved is unknown at this point. Although the rule has been passed, there is a move in Congress to pass legislation to rescind it. Most consumers seem unaware of the current conflict, and there has been little interest from the general public directed to politicians. If consumers truly understood how often they are mistreated in retirement accounts, there would be a general outcry from the public.

To increase the confusion about financial planning, even CFPs and RIAs can have dual standards. For example, a CFP who works in a large brokerage firm may have a fiduciary standard when advising you about your comprehensive financial plan but only a suitability standard when actually setting up an investment account for you. The same can be true for a Registered Investment Advisor. This creates confusion for financial services consumers, who often do not know enough or feel comfortable enough to ask about whose interests come first when advisers are making recommendations. When working with financial services professionals, have them clarify this issue for you. Do not be shy about asking if they will sign an agreement that commits them to the fiduciary standard as they guide you, advise you, and manage your account.

Adherence to fiduciary standards is met when advisors disclose conflicts of interests, primarily related to fees, commissions, and restrictions about the products they are allowed to offer. Disclosure can be made in a variety of ways, both written and oral. In general, written disclosures are often ineffective as they can be written in obtuse, legalistic jargon. Research shows that oral disclosure can also be ineffective as consumers may be (a) reluctant to choose the product that either the advisor cannot sell or earns their advisor the least commission and (b) concerned about the impact of that choice on their relationship with the advisor (Sah, Lowenstein, & Cain, 2013). Mental health professionals, who may be averse to being seen as promoting their own interests, could be reluctant to openly and assertively advocate for their own financial well-being in these situations. Self-advocacy probably would result in choosing the product that earns the adviser the least commission or declining the product offered.

The choices in financial planning come down to five options: do-it-yourself, an hourly fee-only planner, a flat fee-only planner, a fee-only planner who takes a percentage of the assets under his or her management (AUM), or a fee-based adviser who is paid through a combination of fees, commissions, and incentives. There are advantages and disadvantages to all of these options. Do-it-yourself, the first option, is the least expensive, but it requires significant motivation and excellent financial literacy skills to plan and manage your money. If you are mathematical, fascinated by reading about finances, and self-disciplined, this can be a great option since no one cares about your financial well-being as much as you do. If you do not fit these characteristics, if you need accountability to implement financial decisions, if you lack financial literacy, or if you do not have the time to do this, it is best to hire a professional.

The least expensive professional planning option is to hire a planner by the hour. The Garrett Planning Network (www.garrettplanningnetwork.com) is a national network of CFPs who agree to charge clients by the hour for financial planning. Cheryl Garrett designed this network 15 years ago to give middle-class clients access to fiduciary services at a reasonable cost. The planners who belong to this network pay a fee to be listed and set their own hourly fees. Some financial planners do not want to manage money and prefer to do client sessions, teaching and helping clients to design and implement a plan. This is a cost-effective and reasonable option for an initial plan, yearly portfolio reviews, and retirement calculations. If you have the ability to take good advice and implement it on your own, this may be your preferred route. The National Association of Personal Fee-Only Advisors (NAPFA) also maintains a directory that can be found at www.feeonlynetwork.com. This list mixes both advisers who charge by the hour and those who charge for assets under management. The flat fee for CFPs is a new model that is gaining popularity with financial planners. Some of the innovators in this model charge a flat fee upfront and then a subscription-type monthly fee for continued advice. LearnVest is a website oriented toward young female consumers that offers flat-fee financial planning under this model for a reasonable fee. There are also a number of younger advisors who offer flat-fee and/or subscription models, and they can be found at the XY Planning Network website.

The AUM model has been the most popular model in the fiduciary advising profession. Both CFPs and RIAs have used this model extensively. The downside for consumers has been the cost and the minimum account requirements for the best advisers; many require investing accounts of $500,000 to $1 million. Their charges vary, but a common fee is 1% of the assets they hold, invest, and manage. Planning services are included in this fee. If you can meet the minimums and you want access to high-level expertise and alternative investments, this may be right for you. The services provided can be extensive and can include family meetings, creative estate planning, philanthropy plans, accounting work, and coaching you through major life transitions. Your net worth needs to be large enough that you do not mind paying the "fees on top of the fees." This means that not only are you paying the investment fee charges for the funds you are in, but you are also paying an additional 1% on top of that. Many of these advisers have access to wholesale and institutional funds that retail investors cannot access, and this may be a good option if you are affluent and want this level of service.

The final option for your planning needs is to use what is called a fee-based adviser. This is an adviser who may be a CFP, will write your plan, and is paid by the commission charges on the products you buy. Many CFPs now work for large brokers (like MorganStanley) and are excellent planners. However, they can only sell you the products that are available at their place of employment, and the charges and fees you pay are often hidden. This is one of the confusing cases I mentioned where the plan is "fiduciary" but the investing is "suitability." If you have few assets and are just starting out, you may need to start with this model if you cannot afford the hourly charge or flat-fee model and have no interest in the do-it-yourself model. Be particularly careful of financial advisers who work for large insurance companies; they may be CFPs and write you a beautiful plan, but they often want to sell you insurance products as investments. Many consumers believe that they are getting "free" financial planning in this model, but the costs of financial planning are buried in the product commissions and fees.

# WHAT SHOULD MY PLAN COVER?

A comprehensive financial plan is helpful because it involves gathering data about where you are today, where you want to go in the future, and how you will implement the plan. Periodic updating and monitoring of your progress is essential in meeting your goals. Being mental health practitioners who work with clients on a variety of goals, we know the importance of measuring, counting, and tracking over time.

Your comprehensive financial plan needs to incorporate the following topics:

1. Cash flow analysis (income/spending) and net worth
2. Debt management
3. Risk management (insurance)
4. Employee benefits
5. Investment planning
6. Tax planning
7. Retirement planning
8. Estate planning

# CASH FLOW AND NET WORTH

For the eighth year in a row, the American Psychological Association (2014) has noted money as the top stressor in their "Stress in America" series of surveys. Money and financial stressors are especially relevant when starting out as a self-employed professional, when changing your business model, or when going through a downturn in your practice. We hope that, long before you enter full-time practice, you will have examined your monthly cash flow needs and will have calculated what you will need to earn to meet your basic costs. Early-career professionals may have student loan obligations or other debts related to graduate study and getting started. If you are fearful of looking at your net worth (assets vs. liabilities), knowing that you will be in the red, you will be missing out on the motivation that comes with watching the red line inch down while the black line inches up. You also may be reluctant to analyze your cash flow in terms of your inflow and your spending, mistakenly equating this process with the dreaded word "budget." Professionals who are later in their careers are often so busy and so focused on earning money that they may not look at how they are spending it.

The word "budget" is not unlike the word "diet" in that for many people, it is associated with deprivation and not being able to follow through with intentions. A better label might be "values-based spending plan," which refers to looking at both your earning and spending and noticing what meets your truest needs and values. Are you spending your time and money in ways that enhance your well-being? Recall that the basic process of behavior change begins with the process of counting and self-monitoring. Once you begin to track and notice your monthly spending, it becomes easy to notice where you have and have not obtained true value. The biggest surprise most people have when they begin this process is how easy it becomes to identify expenditures that are not as important to them and don't resonate with their highest values. There are numerous apps and software programs (e.g., Mint, Quicken) to track personal cash flow, but they only work when you take the time to sit down and reflect on the patterns you see.

It is especially important to do this when you use "electronic" money, such as credit and debit cards. Research shows that consumers will pay up to 30% more for the same items when using electronic money versus using cash or checks. To counteract how easy it is to forget what you have spent via credit card, take time to sit down and reflect on the expenditures that have brought you the most value for your money. Using values-based spending processes is particularly important in helping you manage your money when your cash flows are less predictable, as is the case when you are self-employed. As an example, it may be important to you to have yearly vacations in which you can rest, relax, and renew the energy you have for your work. This will require you to put away more money for that expenditure in months when your income is high in lieu of celebrating a good month with expensive dinners out. The months in which your revenues are lower may necessitate spending most of your income on overhead, fixed expenses, and high-priority items such as taxes and retirement.

## DEBT MANAGEMENT

Although some practitioners may take a business loan to begin a practice, many prefer to "boot-strap" their practices. This might mean subletting and keeping overhead low as you build a case-load. Beginning with a good business plan will help you make this decision. The largest concern for most beginning practitioners is managing student loan and credit card debts accrued from graduate study. Student loan debt can create stress for many years and can even follow practitioners into retirement. The rule of thumb is to borrow no more than 30% of the average starting salary for someone in your profession. By the time you read this, you may have already accrued student loans above this line. Remember that student loan debt can no longer be discharged by a bankruptcy, so getting good financial guidance during graduate study is essential. Also remember that the interest on student loans is tax-deductible.

Federal student loans and private student loans have different payback options. We hope you will not have much in the way of private loans. Research the refinancing possibilities. If you are able to buy a house and can borrow additional money through a mortgage or home equity loan to pay off your private loans, this can be well worth doing for a number of reasons. Private student loans cannot be refinanced and interest rates can go up at any time. These loans lack basic consumer protections and can easily be declared to be in default. If you have a co-signer on your private student loan, the entire loan can be called due if your co-signer dies or declares bankruptcy, even if you have not missed a payment. Your options for federal student loan forgiveness may be limited if you have missed payments or have a poor credit rating. Parts of your loans can be forgiven if you sign up for federal loan repayment programs. However, one late payment can reset the clock on your 10- or 25-year repayment program. If you have the flexibility to work full time in an underserved area, you can speed up the process of repayment. Research into all of the possible programs offered, including whether to consolidate your loans, is a good use of your time.

# RISK MANAGEMENT

The first step in your risk management plan is to have six to 12 months of living expenses in a liquid emergency savings account. This money is your safety net when you have unexpected expenses and income fluctuations. Putting your savings on an automated program so that you contribute money each month automatically will make this process go more smoothly. Purchasing insurance is a necessity. You probably have a good level of knowledge about malpractice, health, auto, and homeowner or rental insurance. Periodically, you will need to shop those policies around to see if you can get a better rate. Companies predict consumer inertia while raising rates, so shopping around every two or three years can save you many dollars. When you have enough savings, raising your deductibles is a good way to save on your premiums.

As an independent practitioner, it is also important to have disability insurance. Many practitioners do not realize that during their working years they are statistically more likely to become disabled than to die. Consumers seem to link disability with accidents, but the greater risk is a long-term or chronic illness. The risk of disability can vary from 15% to 30% depending on your age, gender, and occupation (U.S. Department of Labor, 2012). The majority of U.S. workers could not pay their bills if their income loss due to an illness were to last beyond 90 days. Disability insurance is needed to cover your overhead expenses and loss of income when you are unable to work. Your policy's premiums will be determined by how long the waiting period is before your benefit begins, how long your benefit lasts, and whether you chose to insure being able to perform your own occupation versus doing any kind of work. Beyond losing your income, you will also no longer be able to make retirement contributions and you will need to cover increased medical costs. All of these factors add up to make disability insurance an important consideration. The Consumer Federation states that disability insurance is the only kind of insurance policy that tends to be undersold. For further discussion about disability insurance and other types of insurance important to the independent practitioner, see Chapter 4: Insurance Needs of the Private Practitioner.

Buying low-cost term life insurance if you have dependents is also an essential feature of your financial plan. At some time during your career, you may find someone who wants to sell you a whole life or universal life policy or an annuity as an investment. In general, the fees, commissions, and surrender costs associated with these policies do work in your favor not. Whatever you do, do not make the common mistake of purchasing one of these "investment" policies and placing it in a retirement account or buying it in lieu of investing in the market for retirement. Many of these policies are 80 to 100 pages long and so complex that consumers do not understand what they are buying. The highest rate of consumer complaints for financial products is found for insurance products. Variable annuities and index-based annuities are insurance products whose payouts vary with the returns of the stock market and are often marketed as investing products with no risk. Variable annuities are generally oversold to unsuspecting consumers and are costly to financial well-being. In contrast, a fixed immediate annuity guarantees a certain monthly payment for life when you put in a lump sum of cash. Although fixed annuities are also expensive, they can be appropriate for certain situations, such as wanting to guarantee a lifetime income for an older retiree or a younger disabled person.

If you are approaching your 60s you will also need to decide whether to purchase long-term care insurance. The longevity revolution means that many of us will live into our 90s and will need home healthcare, assisted living, or nursing home care at the end of our lives. Whether to buy long-term care coverage is a complicated question. Many of the companies that originally sold these policies will no longer underwrite them or have had breathtaking premium increases due to the difficulties in estimating the true costs of this kind of care. Your decision needs to factor in your ability to make continued premium payments, your marital and parental status, your longevity estimates, and your supported living preferences.

## INVESTING

Where you will invest is an important decision. You have a number of options. One is to invest with a traditional stockbroker in what is called a "broker-dealer" setting. Many people choose this because they do not want to do it themselves, the account minimums are low, and most people prefer not to see how much they are paying. Use the Broker Check on the FINRA website before you use a stockbroker to see if your broker has any disclosures on record. About 7% of brokers have misconduct records, and research finds that they continue to work in the industry after being disciplined (Egan, Matvos, & Seru, 2016). The same research also notes the importance of corporate culture for misconduct and finds that firms can be ranked by the amount of misconduct tolerated. An alternative to a broker-dealer in a large firm is an RIA. RIAs are held to a higher standard, the standard of best interest of the client. They are regulated by the federal Securities and Exchange Commission, and most charge a fee based on a percentage of AUM for their investing work. You can check the regulatory history of a firm or an individual RIA at http://www.adviserinfo.sec.gov. It pays to take the extra time to check out the person who is going to guide and manage your investments. Not surprisingly, the highest rate of adviser misconduct is found in areas with higher rates of wealth, the elderly, and uneducated consumers.

Although some people make investing complicated, the best returns are generally made with low-cost funds that follow an index (Fama & French, 2010). This is called passive index investing, and it is not that difficult. As students of statistics, we know that regression to the mean is the rule, so deciding to match the mean at a low cost is a good strategy. Buying index funds over different asset classes (domestic, international, bond, small companies, large companies) is how you can manage risk. If you rebalance your portfolio once per year, you will generally do better than those who trade more often. Rebalancing means that you look at the original asset allocations you chose and bring your portfolio back into line with those. It also means that you may want to change your allocations because your life has changed (i.e., you want more risk or less risk). If the market was very good for large U.S. companies and that part of your portfolio did well, you will need to sell off some of that and invest in the sectors that did not perform as well, such as the international sector of your portfolio. Asset rebalancing is necessary to keep your assets diversified and manage risk in the markets. One way to remember to do this is to rebalance every year on your birthday. You can do it yourself by opening an account with a discount online broker such as TD Ameritrade or Charles Schwab and purchasing and selling directly.

Index funds are available in two primary formats. One is a traditional mutual fund, which is a basket of stocks owned by a fund and is priced every day at the end of the day to determine its value. You must buy and sell these mutual funds at the market price when they are valued daily. An additional option is called an exchange traded fund (ETF), which is an index fund that trades like a stock and changes value every few seconds in real time. You can enter orders for these funds to buy and sell at prices you determine in advance, called limit orders.

There is now a hybrid option called a "robo-advisor." These companies offer online accounts that automatically give you low-cost index funds over different asset classes and rebalance for you. They will do this for a low fee, much lower than you would pay a traditional adviser but not as cost-effective as doing it yourself. Betterment and Wealthfront are currently well-regarded robo-advisors. Many millennials prefer to interact with technology and do not want a traditional personal adviser relationship. Be realistic about your level of interest, your need for a face-to-face adviser, and your comfort. Research shows that investors who purchase through financial advisers generally earn lower returns, but they also feel less anxiety and more confidence about meeting their goals (Burke, Hung, Clift, Garber, & Yoong, 2015). A new option is being offered by Vanguard called Personal Advisor Services. For an account minimum of $50,000 you can get investing guidance from a pool of financial advisers who will then implement your plan for you using low-cost index mutual funds. Vanguard has traditionally been a provider of low-cost index funds, and this new service has become popular with consumers.

Be sure to maximize your retirement account funding before you fund a non-retirement investing account. Index investing is a classic, timeless, low-risk method to invest the money you need for retirement. Investing can also be an interesting and fascinating personal hobby that you may wish to explore. If you wish to take more risk by investing in individual stocks or alternative instruments, do this in non-retirement accounts. Be sure that you are comfortable with the higher level of risk for the assets in those accounts. Unlike retirement accounts, losses in your "experimental" accounts can be taken against your taxes or against other capital gains you may have.

## TAXES

Just as many of us may not realize that our biggest financial asset is our career, we may also not realize that our biggest liability will be taxes. Full-time self-employment can be stressful in April if you have not planned well in the prior year. Underestimating and underpaying your taxes over the prior year can leave you with a large tax bill and penalties. You may need to consult with your certified public accountant to estimate your quarterly tax liability or your payroll taxes. In addition, your retirement account has to be funded by the April 15 deadline or you can lose a valuable tax deduction.

Knowing which expenses are deductible can save you a lot of money over your career. A good accountant can also save you money, but it is even better if you add your knowledge as well. This author still winces thinking of her lost deductions for investment management fees, a question never asked by a variety of accountants but one that will never be missed again! This is an area well worth studying and reading about since taxes will be the largest expense over your lifetime and tax laws change frequently. Your news sources will have articles and reports when new laws are passed. The resources at the end of this chapter can help you stay up to date. If you are a parent with children to educate, you may wish to put money away for future educational expenses. Coverdell and 529 accounts are tax-advantaged educational accounts with differing rules. A Coverdell account can cover educational expenses for private schooling from kindergarten through high school, and you may wish to fund both types of accounts if you are planning to send your children to private school.

# RETIREMENT PLANNING

Take a picture of yourself. Now put that picture into any software program that will age your photo. This is the "elder you." Research shows that people who can visualize and relate to themselves as elders will save more for retirement (Hershfield et al., 2011). Putting your retirement savings on autopilot and automatically deducting it from your checking account is an important step. In general, the Boston College Center for Retirement Research rule-of-thumb estimate is that saving 15% to 20% of your earnings will be adequate to fund your retirement, given a robust set of assumptions. As you get closer to retirement, you may want to have a CFP run a more sophisticated statistical calculation about the probabilities of your money lasting a certain number of years.

The amount of money you will need to save for retirement is determined by the lifestyle you wish to live in your retirement years. You will need to estimate your yearly budget in retirement and add in your estimated healthcare expenses as you decide how long and how much to work. Also, be aware that recent research (Dorman, Mulholland, Bi, & Evensky, 2016) shows that free online calculators for retirement planning give erroneous answers 70% of the time and tell you it is safe to retire when it is not. The most accurate calculators use a large number of variables and give you the probabilities of outlasting your money instead of saying "yes" or "no" to retirement. This is such an important decision that it pays to use a professional to run the calculation on more sophisticated software than you have available. The majority of independent practitioners are fortunate in that many of us are able to work part time for years past a traditional retirement age. This is called "bridge employment," and it is correlated with feeling happier as we move into the retirement phase of life. The financial and mental health benefits of delaying full retirement and gradually easing into stopping working are well documented.

The primary source of your retirement funds will need to come from your retirement investing account. Few of us will have pension income unless prior to independent practice you worked for a government agency or university system and then went into full-time practice. Your accountant can let you know how much you can contribute each year to your retirement accounts. Depending on your income and business structure, you can use a variety of retirement accounts: SEP-IRA, Simple IRA, Keogh, Solo 401K, and additionally either a traditional or Roth IRA. Your tax adviser can help you decide how to best structure your accounts. The money you contribute to the first four plans is tax deductible, as is the traditional IRA.

A Roth IRA can only be funded with after-tax dollars but can be very advantageous in retirement since your withdrawals after age 59.5 can be taken flexibly and tax-free. Once you hit a certain income level, you can no longer contribute to a Roth, so this is a good account to open and fund when you are young. A Roth must be funded with earned money, so starting a Roth account is one way you can give your child a head start. Earnings from jobs in the teen years (including working in your office) can be matched by a parent. As long as the money has been in there for at least five years, up to $10,000 can be taken out, penalty and tax free, to purchase a first home. In addition, unlike the other retirement accounts mentioned above, you are not required to begin taking payments at age 70.5, and your Roth IRA can be passed through your estate to your heirs. Some financial experts believe that the Roth IRA is too beneficial for consumers and at some point in time the government may decide to eliminate it. If this is your belief as well, you may want to open and start one so that you can be grandfathered in.

Recently the Department of Labor has passed new rules governing retirement accounts. All advisers who give guidance and help with investing on retirement accounts must now be held to a higher standard of doing what is in your best interest and they must fully disclose all of the fees and commissions involved. Traditional brokers have insisted this rule will make financial advice unaffordable for the ordinary worker, but the U.S. Consumer Financial Protection Bureau (2015) disagrees with that point of view. Most brokers are already adjusting and are prepared for the implementation of the new rule in 2017.

Many Americans mistakenly expect that Social Security will be their major source of funds in retirement. However, the Social Security system was not set up to operate as a pension system. It is best viewed as longevity insurance. This means that the system was designed to ensure that citizens did not outlive their money and would have a safety net against abject poverty if they had a long life. You cannot outlive your Social Security benefit as it has a lifetime guarantee. Given how long we are currently living, this can be quite reassuring.

Currently your benefit is calculated using your average wage based on the highest 35 years of earnings. You must work and pay into the system at least 10 years to be eligible for your own Social Security benefits. If you are married and your spouse has not worked enough to qualify for a benefit, he or she will be eligible for a spousal benefit, which is computed as half of your benefit when you claim Social Security. Following a divorce, a spouse is eligible to claim on the former spouse's earnings record if they were married for at least 10 years and are not currently married. Widows and widowers are also eligible for benefits calculated on their spousal earnings. Whether to claim on your own benefits or your spouse's is a calculation that Social Security will help you make so that you can receive the highest benefit for which you are eligible.

Social Security claiming strategies are somewhat of a moving target as the rules often change. Currently it is best if you do all you can to wait until at least your full retirement age (either 66 or 67, depending on the year you were born). If you can delay until age 70 you will receive an 8% increase each year you delay. Claiming at age 62 will permanently reduce your benefit and will also subject you to the earnings test. This means that if you earn over $15,000 in a year from ages 62 to 66, your benefit will be reduced. Although some people may find that they need to have that early income, the permanent reduction and the earnings test are costly.

One way to decide when to claim your Social Security benefits is to look at your life expectancy. For most us the "break-even" point for choosing to claim at age 70 instead of age 66 is to live until age 82 or longer. That may sound like a long time, but the average life expectancy is currently higher than age 82 for both men and women who make it to age 65.

A primary concern of those who have retired is outliving their money. Although financial planners can disagree on this, a general principle of safe money withdrawal is between 3% and 4% of your assets yearly. We are the only developed country where retirement planning is related to guessing how long we will live and in which there is no guaranteed pension system for all citizens.

# ESTATES

More than half of Americans have no will or estate plan. As you are now a small business owner, you have obligations that must be met if something happens to you. A very important but often disregarded aspect of estate planning is naming the powers of attorney—in other words, the people who can have access to your money and who can make decisions about your medical treatment if you are incapacitated. It is essential to have these powers in place even if you do not have many assets. Many young, single professionals do not realize how important it is for them to have these documents in place. Older professionals often have assets and family obligations and are likely to have completed an estate plan, but it is easy to forget to update your estate plan. In your personal plan or in another document, be sure you address the business you own and what you want to have done with the assets and liabilities of the business.

At the current time in the United States an individual can leave up to $5 million in assets without triggering estate taxes. Even though the tax exemptions are high, many chose to use a trust in their estate plan due to privacy concerns. When a will is sent through probate, it generates a public record. Using a trust vehicle can keep the details of your estate private. Many people forget to have an open and honest discussion with family members prior to drawing up a will. Be sure that your family knows what your intentions are and has had some input into your estate plan. This will reduce the amount of conflict generated between your heirs and will alert them to what is coming. The persons you have named as executors or powers of attorney will have a difficult time if they do not want the role and if the other heirs are opposed to them. "Open" estate planning is recommended for families since your heirs will need to know how much will be available for your healthcare when inevitable role reversals begin to occur. Be sure that you have your financial information organized and documents stored in an accessible place to make it easier on your powers of attorney. The book *The Other Talk* mentioned at the end of this chapter gives guidelines for families about having these hard conversations and preparing your heirs for your disability and dying.

# CONCLUSION

There are many advantages to the independent practitioner to gathering, consolidating, and integrating the financial information contained in a financial plan. Spending time on this endeavor will pay off in terms of accomplishing your financial goals, knowing where you stand, and increasing your sense of efficacy about finances. Studies of the Big Five personality traits (Duckworth, Weir, Tsukayama, & Kwok, 2012) show that over a lifetime, conscientious adults earn and save more money, as well as having higher subjective well-being. Conscientious adults are found to act in accordance with long-term goals, make careful decisions, complete tasks, and act responsibly. As such, paying careful, close attention to your finances as you go along can have a significant positive impact on your experience of financial health as you practice your profession and move into the retirement phase of life.

# REFERENCES

American Psychological Association. (2014). *Stress in America: Our health at risk.* Retrieved from http://www.apa.org/news/press/releases/stress/2014/stress-report.pdf.

Binswanger, J., & Carmen, K. (2012). How real people make long-term decisions: The case of retirement preparation. *Journal of Economic Behavior & Organization, 81*(1), 39–60.

Britt, S. L., Klontz, B., Tibbetts, R., & Leitz, L. (2015). The financial health of mental health professionals. *Journal of Financial Therapy, 6*(1), 17–32.

Burke, J., Hung, A., Clift, J., Garber, S., & Yoong, J. (2015). Impacts of conflict of interest in the financial services industry. Retrieved from http://www.rand.org/pubs/working_papers/WR1076.html.

Dorman, T., Mulholland, B., Bi, Q., & Evensky, H. (2016). The efficacy of publicly-available retirement planning tools. Retrieved from SSRN: http://ssrn.com/abstract=2732927 or http://dx.doi.org/10.2139/ssrn.2732927.

Duckworth, A. L., Weir, D., Tsukayama, E., & Kwok, D. (2012). Who does well in life? Conscientious adults excel in both objective and subjective success. *Frontiers in Personality Science and Individual Differences, 3*(356), 1–8.

Egan, M., Matvos, G., & Seru, A. (2016). The market for financial adviser misconduct. Retrieved from SSRN: http://ssrn.com/abstract=2739170

Fama, E., & French, K. (2010). Luck versus skill in the cross section of mutual fund returns. *Journal of Finance, 65*(5), 1915–1947.

Hershfield, H., Goldstein, D., Sharpe, W., Fox, J., Yeykelis, L., Carstensen, L., & Bailenson, J. (2011). Increasing savings behavior through age-progressed renderings of the future self. *Journal of Marketing Research, 48*, 23–37.

Lusardi, A., & Mitchell, O. (2014). The economic importance of financial literacy: Theory and evidence. *Journal of Economic Literature, 52*(11), 5–44.

Sah, S., Loewenstein, G., & Cain, D. (2013). The burden of disclosure: Increased compliance with distrusted advice. *Journal of Personality and Social Psychology, 104*(2), 289–304.

U.S. Consumer Financial Protection Bureau. (January 2015). *Financial well-being: The goal of financial education.* Washington, DC: U.S. Government Printing Office. Retrieved from http://files.consumerfinance.gov/f/201501_cfpb_report_financial-well-being.pdf.

U.S. Department of Labor. (2012). *Managing disability risks in an environment of individual responsibility.* Washington, DC. Retrieved from http://www.dol.gov/ebsa/publications/2012ACreport2.html.

# SUGGESTED READING AND WEBSITES RELATED TO FINANCIAL PLANNING

## BOOKS

Belsky, G., & Gilovich, T. (1999). *Why smart people make big money mistakes.* New York: Simon and Schuster.

This book is easy to understand and explains the basic concepts of behavioral finance and how we intuitively make bad decisions about money. If you keep selling your good investments and hold on to your weak ones, this book will tell you why.

Bennetts, L. (2007). *The feminine mistake.* Hyperion: New York.

Women often cut back on their careers without considering the financial consequences to them in terms of retirement funding, career interruptions, and marital risk. Read this book before you make irreversible career decisions.

Kahneman, D. (2011). *Thinking, Fast and Slow*. New York: Farrar, Straus, and Giroux.

This book explains the principles of behavioral economics and the science of decision-making in easily understood terms. He explains how errors in judgment and flawed thinking impact the decisions we make.

Klontz, B., Kahler, R. & Klontz, T. (2008). *Facilitating financial health*. Cincinnati: National Underwriters.

A great resource to understand how money operates in both our exterior and interior lives.

Klontz, B., & Klontz, T. (2009). *Mind over money*. New York: Broadway Books.

Applies the theory of scripting to our money lives. Good to understand the impact of family history.

Madanes, C. (1994). *The secret meaning of money*. San Francisco: Jossey-Bass.

A family therapist talks about money in the family life cycle. Good for systems theory.

Olen, H., & Pollack, H. (2016). *The index card: Why personal finance does not have to be complicated*. New York: Penguin.

Quick, easy to read and understand with lots of good information.

Prosch, T. (2013). *The other talk: A guide to talking with your adult children about the rest of your life*. New York: McGraw-Hill.

How to have the hard talks with your parents and children about the inevitable consequences of aging: death, disability, and money transactions.

Quinn, J. B. (2009). *Making the most of your money now*. New York: Simon & Schuster.

A good basic personal finance book by a well-respected writer.

Quinn, J.B. (2016). *How to make your money last*. New York: Simon & Schuster.

A good book focused on retirement and financial issues.

Zweig, J. (2007). *Your money and your brain*. New York: Simon & Schuster.

Neuroeconomics shows us how our brain responds to money experiences. If you like neuroscience, you will love this.

## MAGAZINES

*Money* magazine is a good resource to get you interested in your finances. The information on mutual funds and changes in mutual fund managers can be helpful, as is the information on fund expenses and fees. Stock information is not especially great.

*Better Investing* magazine is helpful if you are interested in starting an investment club. They offer good software and classes to analyze stocks for growth investing. They also feature a stock of the month and show you how to analyze for fundamentals.

*Journal of Financial Planning* is the monthly journal put out by the Financial Planning Association. If you are deeply interested in finance, this will be a good addition to your library. Articles are cutting edge and at the professional level.

*Journal of Financial Therapy* is the journal of the Financial Therapy Association. This is a good journal with some articles by academics from the programs at Kansas State, Texas Tech, University of Georgia, and University of Missouri. This is a good basic publication for psychotherapists interested in money issues.

## WEBSITES

www.clark.com: Clark Howard is a consumer advocate with lots of great information on money issues. Search here for the latest information on student loan repayment, credit scores, budget travel, credit unions, frauds, insurance information, and a wealth of other consumer-friendly topics.

www.kitces.com: Michael Kitces is the writer and speaker featured at most financial planning conferences. His website offers a paid membership to planners but you can sign up for his blog "Nerd's Eye View." His blog articles are for finance nerds everywhere and are free to your inbox with features such as suggested Weekend Reading.

www.kotlikoff.net: Dr. Kotlikoff is a Boston University professor of economics and knows more about Social Security than Social Security does. This site mentions his books and products but also has his academic papers.

www.LearnVest.com: A good website for beginning to learn about personal finance. You can also hire a financial planner for a $300 fee plus $20 per month. They will follow up and have you do steps as you are able. Recently this site was purchased by an insurance company and it's unclear how that will affect it.

http://www.nytimes.com/pages/your-money/index.html: Well-written columns and excellent source of information.

# CHAPTER 19

# MENTORSHIP IN THE LIFE AND WORK OF THE PRIVATE PRACTITIONER

*W. Brad Johnson*

Few relationships are as professionally important and personally meaningful as the mentoring relationship (mentorship). Mentoring is defined as a personal and reciprocal relationship in which a more experienced (often, but not necessarily, older) professional acts as a guide, role model, teacher, and sponsor of a less experienced (usually, but not necessarily, younger) professional (Johnson, 2015). An effective mentor provides the mentee with knowledge, advice, counsel, challenge, and support in the mentee's pursuit of becoming a successful member of a particular profession, each of which can be vital for achieving a successful and rewarding career in private practice. Mentoring is likely to be remarkably helpful, if not imperative, across the entire arc of a private practitioner's career. Early in one's career, it is often useful to be a mentee in at least one key mentorship with a more seasoned and successful practitioner. In truth, nurturing an entire network of helpful developmental relationships can be useful for the early-career practitioner. As one's career unfolds, it is quite natural to engage in more peer-oriented and collegial mentorships while also transitioning to the role of mentor for more junior private practitioners.

In this brief chapter, I will describe the unique qualities of mentorships and how to think about mentoring vis-à-vis other kinds of professional or developmental relationships. I will then discuss the seasons of mentorship in the life and career of the private practitioner. Beginning with the early-career phase, in which a practitioner is likely to benefit primarily as a mentee, continuing through midcareer, where peer relational mentorships are more prevalent and career enhancing, and concluding with the more seasoned or mature phase of one's career, when serving as a mentor while continuing to enjoy a rich network of collegial connections is important, I will describe the unique manifestations of mentorship at each phase of the practitioner's career.

# THE NATURE OF MENTORSHIP

In comparison to other common developmental relationships during one's training and career (e.g., academic advising, clinical supervision, consultation), mentoring relationships tend to be defined by several key elements or qualities (Johnson, 2014, 2015):

- *Mentorships are enduring personal relationships*: In comparison to teaching, supervision, or problem-focused consultation or coaching, mentorships tend to become more bonded and persistent. At times, they continue in perpetuity.
- *Mentorships are reciprocal relationships*: If you are receiving or providing clinical supervision, then you understand that such formalized training relationships tend to be more hierarchical and transactional, at least at the outset. For instance, the trainee pays tuition and the training supervisor delivers competent supervision, the academic advisor delivers advice and guidance about completing an academic degree, or a professor delivers a course in the required curriculum. But mentorships are characterized by increasing reciprocity and mutuality over time. Some of your best assigned training relationships are likely to evolve into mentorships.
- *Mentors provide mentees with direct career assistance*: Terrific mentors become committed to helping their mentees succeed in the profession and in their unique career trajectories. To that end, mentors often engage in coaching, teaching, sponsoring, challenging, and even protecting mentees when this is appropriate. For instance, if a mentee is the focus of harassment or unfair treatment within a training program, a mentor might step forward, raise concerns, and support a mentee in formulating an assertive response.
- *Mentors provide mentees with social and emotional support*: Mentors are empathic and acutely aware of the stressors and emotional challenges that accompany entrance into the mental health profession and private practice specifically. Therefore, they are likely to provide their mentees with deliberate affirmation, encouragement, counsel, and friendship. In survey research with mentees in a variety of fields, they consistently describe the critical importance of *both* career and psychosocial support from mentors (e.g., Allen, Finkelstein, & Poteet, 2009; Kram, 1985).
- *Mentors serve as intentional role models*: Although any teacher, supervisor, or colleague might serve as a role model for a junior private practitioner, genuine mentors are distinctively deliberate and intentional about modeling and demonstrating the attitudes, skills, and values of ethical and professional private practitioners.
- *Mentoring often results in a transformation of the mentee's professional identity*: When a mentee is well mentored by a more senior practitioner, an interesting thing happens: He or she experiences a shift in sense-of-self or self-identity within the profession. Mentees are more likely to see themselves as competent professionals. Having been encouraged and endorsed by a caring and committed mentor, they are more likely than unmentored colleagues to shed their anxieties and embrace an identity as a competent practitioner in their discipline (Palmer, Hunt, Neal, & Wuetherick, 2015).

- *Mentorships offer a "safe" space for self-exploration*: As rapport, trust, and a strong working alliance develop between a mentor and mentee, the mentorship often comes to serve as safe relationship wherein the mentee might explore and discuss concerns about self, career, and work–family issues. The mentee's career dreams and aspirations can be disclosed and then affirmed by the mentor as the pair collaborate to help the mentee chart his or her life course.

Any positive developmental relationship between a graduate student or early-career practitioner and a more seasoned professor, clinical supervisor, or colleague has the potential to evolve into a mentorship. Mentorships tend to be defined less in terms of formal role assignments and more in terms of the character and quality of the relationship and the specific functions provided by the mentor (Johnson, 2015). It is important for both early-career practitioners and those who are more seasoned and established in their careers to be realistic about the fact that not every graduate school advisor or practicum/internship/pre-licensure supervisor will become an important career mentor. Depending upon variables such as frequency of interaction, shared interests, personality "fit," and commitment on the part of both parties, some formally assigned training relationships remain somewhat transactional while others continue to deepen, develop, and ultimately become transformational in the life and identity of the junior member of the dyad. Evidence shows that both parties can increase the likelihood that a reciprocal and transformative relationship will develop, primarily by demonstrating interest and commitment to the relationship through deliberate interaction. Often, early-career mentorships persist in perpetuity; the relationship is such that even after the active phase of the relationship wanes, both parties are inclined to "check in" with the other from time to time as the mentorship takes on more of the elements of a seasoned friendship.

# THE EARLY-CAREER PRIVATE PRACTITIONER

If you are a graduate student, an intern, or an early-career practitioner, there are myriad reasons for you to deliberately seek strong mentoring relationships with more seasoned professionals in your field, ideally practitioners who have successfully established careers in private practice, perhaps work in your specific area of clinical interest, and demonstrate the clinical competence and ethical professionalism you hope to emulate. The research evidence shows that well-mentored junior mental health professionals simply do better in their careers than those who have not participated in ongoing effective mentoring relationships (Johnson, 2015). Here are some of the evidence-supported benefits of mentoring in higher education and practitioner training:

- *Academic and clinical performance*: During graduate school and clinical training, mentored practitioners are more likely to perform well, and finish their programs on time. Well-mentored trainees enjoy the advocacy of a well-placed training practitioner and are therefore held in higher regard within the training program.

- *Professional skill development*: As an aspiring private practitioner, you are more likely to "learn the ropes" of your mental health discipline and the nuances of successful private practice. Not only do mentees develop greater clinical mastery, but the mentoring relationship itself imparts a *relational cache* or set of relational skills and attitudes that are transportable to subsequent relationships. Being well mentored is likely to make you a better clinician, not to mention a better mentor yourself.

- *Networking*: Well-mentored trainees and early-career professionals are significantly more likely to report being "tied in" or connected to important colleagues, referral sources, and systems within the field that can make all the difference in getting a successful launch into private practice. Outstanding mentors tend to introduce their mentees to key powerbrokers, such that mentees—in contrast to those who are not mentored—enjoy a considerable boost in their social capital in professional circles.

- *Initial employment*: Evidence from a wide range of fields reveals that if you enjoy at least one excellent mentorship during your graduate school or clinical training years, you are more likely to have success landing a first job or launching a first practice. Networking, referrals, and stellar letters of recommendation, courtesy of your mentor, significantly increase your chances of landing on your feet in a first practice.

- *Professional confidence and identity development*: Research shows a strong positive relationship between the amount of early career mentoring one receives and mentee self-perceptions of capability and success. If your mentor is particularly good at providing copious doses of acceptance, confirmation, admiration, and emotional support, your sense of self-efficacy as a practitioner is likely to be irrevocably bolstered. Strong mentorship for the budding private practitioner can result in a positive *possible-self*, an image of what one can become in both life and in one's career in private practice (Packard, 2003).

- *Income and career eminence*: It is certainly good to be more competent and more confident in your early years in practice, but it is equally likely that if you are well mentored, you will earn more money and more rapid promotions (e.g., in a group practice or other organization) than unmentored colleagues. It appears that some combination of mentor-initiated networking, promotion, and opportunity simply results in higher rates of compensation in many fields.

So, how might you go about seeking and securing mentoring relationships during your early years in the field? In order to secure the high-quality mentoring relationships likely to boost your career in private practice, you should endeavor to master several attitudes and competencies of successful mentees (Johnson, 2015; Searby, 2014). Here are a few of the elements to developing an effective mentee mindset. Once you identify prospective mentors, consider implementing these strategies:

- *Be proactive*: Take the initiative and seek your mentor out. Evidence from social psychology reveals that *mere exposure* (more frequent interaction) leads to more mutual liking and fondness and, ultimately, commitment on the part of a mentor. So, arrange appointments and ask for some time or advice. By all means, make yourself visible!

- *Keep commitments and strive for excellence*: Here is a time-tested truth when it comes to the habits of mentors: We are drawn to trainees and junior colleagues who demonstrate self-motivation, reliability, dependability, and the consistent pursuit of excellent work. Consciously or not, all of us tend to be drawn to rising stars. This is especially important if you hope to join a mentor's private practice group at some point. Demonstrate from the start that you would make a desirable colleague.
- *Demonstrate openness and responsiveness to feedback*: Accept both praise and criticism with openness and try not to respond defensively when a mentor takes a risk and provides you with correction. Challenge, coaching, and correction are key elements of effective mentorship. These behaviors suggest caring and commitment on the part of your mentor. Consider them a gift. Later, provide your mentor with evidence that you have put such feedback into practice.
- *Be mindful of your mentor's goals*: Here is another truth: Some of the best career mentors are busy professionals. The best mentorships are two-way reciprocal relationships. Whenever possible, try to collaborate with a mentor on a project or initiative—perhaps linked to his or her private practice—that will benefit your mentor while simultaneously affording you more valuable time and interaction with your mentor.
- *Accept increasing responsibility and autonomy*: As a mentorship becomes less formal, less hierarchical, and more mutual, collegial, and transformational to your identity as an early-career practitioner, it will be both natural and desirable for you to take on greater independence and responsibility in your work. As you seek your mentor's guidance in setting up or joining a private practice, you will need to become steadily more autonomous both clinically and administratively.
- *Maintain a sense of humor*: All of us are drawn to colleagues who are kind, competent, and fun to be around. Be sure to prevent your own early-career anxieties and frustrations from causing you to lose perspective and become unreasonably needy. Laugh at yourself often, admit your imperfections, and work against taking yourself too seriously.

Here is a final comment on early-career use of mentoring relationships: Rather than rely on a single "guru" mentor to meet all your needs (this is rarely possible), deliberately construct a rich and diverse constellation or network of helpful developmental relationships. Although it is true that most of us benefit significantly from a primary graduate training and/or early-career mentorship, prevailing research evidence on mentoring shows that the most successful mentees rely on multiple people for developmental support (Johnson, 2014).

Think of your *mentoring constellation* as the set of relationships you have with key people in your training and early career who take an active interest in you. They will also take action to advance your career in various ways by promoting your personal and professional development. Because no single mentor can possibly meet all your developmental needs, it is important to customize a network of career helpers and supportive colleagues. Each of these constellation members is apt to bring different perspectives, skills, experiences, and connections to the task of encouraging and supporting you. Your own constellation might include one or two particularly helpful and invested professors, or one or two clinical supervisors with whom you developed an exceptionally strong rapport and with whom you have committed to remaining engaged and connected.

Your constellation might also include one or two private practitioners who you have come to know in the course of your training, continuing education workshops, or ongoing consultation or supervisory relationships. Once again, being proactive when it comes to finding a practicing mentor or two is essential. Consider becoming involved in your local professional association, attend professional conferences, and take the initiative to introduce yourself to speakers, request an opportunity to meet with them over lunch or coffee, and show that you are highly invested in learning as much as you can from them. Additionally, many private practitioners are highly engaged in ongoing peer support groups; many of these discover that members of their support group become crucial members of their own mentoring constellations (Johnson, Barnett, Elman, Forrest, & Kaslow, 2013). Finally, don't forget other trainees and early-career peers with whom you have developed strong collegial bonds. Often, one or two graduate school colleagues continue to play an active role in supporting and encouraging you in your professional work. Together, this network of cheerleaders, confidants, and career supporters will help to open doors, create opportunities, and continually refine your fledgling competence in the field.

# THE EARLY- TO MIDCAREER PRIVATE PRACTITIONER

As a new practitioner makes the transition from trainee and fledgling professional to established early-career practitioner, traditional mentorship—denoted by a clearly identified mentor and mentee—often becomes steadily less salient in his or her day-to-day career experience. Although early-career mentors may continue to play a role in the practitioner's life, the transition from early- to midcareer practitioner is often defined more by salient peer mentors and robust constellations of colleagues (Johnson et al., 2013). *Peer mentorships* are less focused on career formation and more generally on emotional support, personal feedback, friendship, and competence maintenance and enhancement. In your life as an early-career private practitioner, it is important for you to form a rich variety of lateral relationships with coworkers, professional friends, and organizational colleagues that afford you the opportunity to continue developing your professional competence while enjoying strong personal support. As you become ensconced in the day-to-day demands of growing and managing a private practice, you must engage in close, collegial relationships with selected peers who provide strong support and a nonjudgmental sounding board for processing professional dilemmas, personal struggles, and career transitions.

Strong peer mentorships are often more informal, collaborative, and egalitarian than more traditional mentoring relationships. Early- to midcareer developmental relationships are often characterized as *relational mentorships*. Here are some of the most notable qualities of these peer mentorships (Johnson et al., 2013):

- *Fundamentally reciprocal*: Strong peer mentorships involve the capacity for mutual influence, growth, and learning. In many ways, these are mutual or co-mentoring relationships that are often rooted in reciprocal assistance, mutual understanding, and shared interests.

- *Fluid expertise and complementarity*: As you wade into your career, it is often a delight to discover close colleagues with whom you can easily and naturally switch between learner and expert roles. Finding peers with knowledge, skills, and abilities that complement your own areas of competence can help to offset your own areas of relative weakness. Developing relational mentorships with several diverse and committed peers is likely to make any single practitioner stronger and more competent. Even if you share core values with these colleagues, your varying skills and competencies will allow you to address each other's developmental needs.
- *Communal norms and willingness to be vulnerable*: Competence constellations and peer mentorships will require you to practice revealing perceived shortcomings and developmental needs as a mental health practitioner and as a practice manager. Within the trusting space of a relational mentorship, it will be encouraging to have these relative shortcomings and weaknesses recognized, honored, and then addressed in a nonjudgmental and supportive way (McManus & Russell, 2007). It will behoove you to seek peer mentors who are humble and equally vulnerable. Recognize that such shared authenticity will serve as a source of wisdom, empathy, and compassion as you move forward in a mutually supportive relationship.
- *A wider range of intended relational outcomes*: Whereas more traditional early-career mentorships focus more specifically on outcomes such as academic success, career advancement, and landing key early jobs, relational peer mentorships are a bit broader in their intended outcomes. Although such lateral mentorships certainly bolster success in private practice and other career markers of achievement, they may also stimulate a stronger sense of professional identity, enhanced clinical competencies, more effective work–family balance, stronger financial management skills, and even resilience in the face of personal or medical challenges.
- *A holistic approach*: Terrific relational peers, key elements of your competence constellation (Johnson et al., 2013) are quite likely to recognize the interaction between the work and nonwork domains of life. These colleagues can influence the quality of your life generally, not just your success in private practice. Rather than a more traditional mentor whom you might most often approach with specific questions or concerns, a relational peer be just as attuned to ensuring your work–recreation balance, compassion, and self-care.

As you might surmise from these central elements of relational mentorship, excellent peer mentor candidates often show evidence of several key characteristics or relational competencies. As you enter private practice and carve out a professional life in the field, it will be wise for you to seek a network of key colleagues with some of these traits and competencies. Outstanding peer mentors are often authentic, self-aware, empathically other-oriented, willing to be vulnerable, nondefensive regarding their own weaknesses, good models of life balance and self-care, and collegially assertive when necessary. They easily transition from teacher to learner in the context of a collegial friendship.

# THE MID- TO LATE-CAREER PRIVATE PRACTITIONER: BECOMING A MENTOR

At some point along your career path in private practice, you might notice a transition in the role you tend to take vis-à-vis other practitioners. You may discover that you are more often serving in the role of mentor to practitioners-in-training or early-career practitioners. You are becoming a mentor. For some, this shift might be incremental and gradual; you find that over a period of years, you are accumulating more relationships with junior professionals who seem to regard you as a salient career champion and role model. For others, the transition to mentor might feel more like a sudden sea change in your professional self-perception; you may be invited to teach a graduate course, supervise a practicum student, or participate in a formally assigned mentor–mentee relationship through a local or national professional association (and you might just be startled when asked to serve as a mentor when you'd never considered yourself in that light before!).

As a successful practitioner, busy with all the demands of running a practice, you might ask, *Why in the world would I want to mentor someone?* After all, the hours you devote to shepherding junior members of the profession are often not billable, and the time spent pulling up and pushing forward a mentee means time not spent on other pursuits. But there is ample empirical evidence that professionals who mentor others often and well are prone to reap a number of key benefits and delightful personal outcomes (Johnson, 2015). Here are some of the most consistent benefits reported by professionals in a range of fields who mentor others:

- *Personal satisfaction*: Time and time again, surveys of mentors reveal that a deep sense of personal pleasure and satisfaction from seeing mentees develop and succeed is a key intrinsic benefit to mentoring often and well. Simply put, you are likely to find some genuine joy in helping a neophyte trainee or practitioner evolve into a confident and competent colleague.
- *Personal meaning*: Mentoring is often especially fulfilling in the middle to later phases of your career. By transmitting your skills and wisdom to the next generation, mentorship can represent a powerful act of generativity at midlife and midcareer. Through a rich series of mentorships, you can extend your contribution to society and the profession; your legacy may be powerfully immortalized in your work with both clients and junior members of your profession.
- *Creative synergy and professional rejuvenation*: Talented, creative, and energized mentees sometimes lead to a renaissance of sorts in the lives of private practitioners whose day-to-day clinical practices have become somewhat stale or redundant. Many mentors who guide early-career professionals fresh from graduate training report a delightful sense of creative synergy and a rejuvenation in their interest and excitement about clinical work and innovations in treatment.
- *Networking*: If you are a prolific and effective mentor, it is nearly certain that you will naturally build a much wider network of good colleagues. Sometimes, former mentees

create new opportunities and helpful referrals for their mentor. When it comes to mentorship, the old saying *what goes around comes around* appears to be true.

- *Motivation to remain current*: A mentor often feels an urge to reengage with the professional literature and become updated in his or her specialty areas. The desire to be on the cutting edge in your discipline when guiding a new professional can help prevent obsolescence and stagnation.

- *Friendship and support*: Don't be surprised if some of the trainees and early-career practitioners you mentor end up becoming solid colleagues and even close friends. This is particularly likely to be the case as a strong mentorship evolves, becoming more collegial, mutual, and friendly over time. Former mentees are often loyal colleagues.

As you move into the role of mentor and begin combining care and guidance of junior professionals in your repertoire of work-related activities, it will be useful to avail yourself of further continuing education in the area of mentorship. Rarely are the competencies associated with mentorship addressed in any formal way during graduate education, yet there are a number of functional competencies associated with excellent mentorship (Allen et al., 2009; Johnson, 2015). Here are some of the more salient competencies for consideration:

- *Accessibility and engagement*: Outstanding mentors make time and create space for mentees. Especially early in a mentorship, when a prospective mentee might most feel like an imposter and is least likely to "intrude" upon or "bother" a busy and established practitioner, the mentor must reach out, take initiative to start conversations, and as the relationship evolves, schedule routine conversations or perhaps meetings over coffee. Such initiative, availability, and accessibility on the part of a seasoned professional will be deeply heartening and professionally encouraging to a mentee.

- *Encouragement and support*: Survey after survey reveals that mentees deeply appreciate strong emotional support on the part of a mentor. Encouraging mentors highlight a mentee's talents and potential for success in the profession. Their stalwart encouragement emboldens a fledgling professional and helps him or her persist.

- *Intentional modeling*: Effective mentors realize that mentees will carefully observe them as role models for the profession. To that end they are deliberate about modeling professional and ethical practice, and they encourage mentees to ask questions about private practice and, within the boundaries of client confidentiality, to directly observe them performing important tasks as a professional (e.g., creating practice infrastructure, interacting with insurers, and consulting with colleagues).

- *Sponsorship*: At times it will be especially important to deliberately sponsor a mentee for membership in an association, licensure to practice, or entry into an established practice. Terrific mentors are not only supportive and encouraging, but they also help open doors. Sometimes, simply serving as a reference or talking with colleagues about your positive impression of a mentee can work wonders in terms of how the mentee is perceived and received in the community.

- *Delivering the "inside scoop"*: At times, informing a new professional about the political lay-of-the-land can be an invaluable mentor function. Specifically, good mentors are careful to help mentees avoid political landmines with established practitioners, understand the nuances of practice within a community of providers, and understand who their natural allies (and perhaps also the few toxic personalities) might be. Without resorting to needless gossip, a wise mentor will steer his or her mentee clear of trouble professionally, ethically, and collegially.

## CONCLUDING THOUGHTS

Mentoring relationships can be both career-essential and personally delightful connections in the life and work of the private practitioner. Across the arc of your career, mentorships are likely to play a key role in developing competence, solidifying a sense of professional identity, and imbuing your later career with a sense of meaning. Early in your career, it is important to deliberately and assertively construct a constellation of diverse mentors who can teach you about private practice, tie you in to important networks, open doors, and refine your competence in the field. At midcareer, many of these salient mentorships will have evolved into close collegial friendships, to which a practitioner will want to add strong peer support networks and consultation groups. As you enter the middle to later seasons of your career, it is often a delightful experience to intentionally contribute to the fledgling careers of junior members of the profession by accepting the mantle of mentor and passing along the gifts of time and wisdom that your own mentors so generously offered years earlier.

## REFERENCES

Allen, T. D., Finkelstein, L. M., & Poteet, M. L. (2009). *Designing workplace mentoring programs: An evidence-based approach*. New York: Wiley-Blackwell.

Johnson, W. B. (2014). Mentoring in psychology education and training: A mentoring relationship continuum model. In W. B. Johnson & N. J. Kaslow (Eds.), *The Oxford handbook of education and training in professional psychology* (pp. 272–290). New York: Oxford University Press.

Johnson, W. B. (2015). *On being a mentor: A guide for higher education faculty* (2nd ed.). New York: Routledge.

Johnson, W. B., Barnett, J. E., Elman, N. S., Forrest, L., & Kaslow, N. J. (2013). The competence constellation model: A communitarian approach to support professional competence. *Professional Psychology: Research and Practice, 44*, 343–354.

Kram, K. E. (1985). *Mentoring at work: Developmental relationships in organizational life*. Glenview, IL: Scott Foresman.

McManus, S. E., & Russell, J. E. A. (2007). Peer mentoring relationships. In B. R. Ragins & K. E. Kram (Eds.), *The handbook of mentoring at work: Theory, research, and practice* (pp. 273–297). Thousand Oaks, CA: Sage.

Packard, B. W. L. (2003). Student training promotes mentoring awareness and action. *The Career Development Quarterly, 51*, 335–345.

Palmer, R. J., Hunt, A. N., Neal, M., & Wuetherick, B. (2015). Mentoring, undergraduate research, and identity development: A conceptual review and research agenda. *Mentoring and Tutoring: Partnership in Learning, 23*, 411–426.

Searby, L. J. (2014). The protégé mentoring mindset: A framework for consideration. *International Journal of Mentoring and Coaching in Education, 3*, 255–276.

# THE BUSINESS OF PRACTICE

CHAPTER 20

# FEES AND FINANCIAL ARRANGEMENTS IN PRIVATE PRACTICE

*Jeffrey E. Barnett*

Mental health clinicians in private practice go through many years of education and training to develop their expertise so that they may fulfill their goal of providing high-quality clinical services to individuals in need. While many private practitioners enter the mental health field with the goal of assisting others as helping professionals, they may often overlook or be unprepared for some of the business aspects of being a private practitioner. In fact, many graduate schools do not prepare their students in the business aspects of private practice. Thus, while many private practitioners possess outstanding clinical skills, they may not be prepared to address the financial aspects of running a private practice.

As with any other business, the business owner must charge fees for the services provided. This must be done so that the private practitioner can stay in business. There are bills to be paid for rent, utilities, furniture, computers, office supplies, insurance, staff salaries, continuing education and license renewal, and many others, not the least of which is the private practitioner's salary. We must pay for our living expenses, save for retirement and (we hope) for vacations, and, for many, pay back student loans. Thus, we must charge a fee for the professional services we provide.

## GETTING COMFORTABLE WITH MONEY

We each bring to our professional roles our personal and family histories regarding money. In some practitioners' families money was spoken about openly; in others it may have been a taboo topic. For some, money was plentiful and used without guilt, while in others financial hardship may have created complex emotional reactions to the role of money in one's life. Haber, Rodino, and Lipner

(2001) recommend that practitioners reflect on the meaning of money in their lives growing up (and at present), such as autonomy and independence versus dependence on others as well as issues of power and control. Money issues may also stimulate feelings of anxiety, fear, insecurity, or other emotional responses that may impact both how we view money and how we address it in our private practices. Addressing and resolving such underlying conflicts about money can free up the private practitioner to comfortably charge fees commensurate with the value of the professional services provided and enable us to effectively assist clients with unresolved conflicts and issues they may be experiencing regarding money in their lives.

As Barnett and Walfish (2012) emphasize, "Fees are a part of psychotherapy in private practice, and clinicians must become as comfortable discussing this issue as any other personal material that may be relevant to treatment" (p. 35). Thus, we first must become aware of and come to terms with the meaning of money for ourselves personally as well as in regard to our roles as helping professionals. It may feel, both to ourselves and to clients, that we are charging a fee to participate in a caring relationship. While on the one hand we are businesspersons who are providing a professional service that clients value and thus pay a fee to receive, on the other hand this business aspect of the relationship may stimulate great ambivalence for the practitioner if these issues are not examined, worked through, and resolved. Charging a fee for creating an intimate relationship based on trust and on the client's needs and best interests, in which we are caring, compassionate, and warm, may stimulate feelings of guilt, shame, embarrassment, and even greed on the part of clinicians who have not resolved these money issues for themselves (Herron & Rouslin Welt, 1992).

Most mental health practitioners understand that they are in business and therefore must charge fees for the services they provide. But unless we come to terms with issues relevant to money, we may seek to avoid these issues. This is a situation that is likely to be unhealthy for ourselves as well as for our clients. Some practitioners may seek to avoid addressing money issues with clients and instead have their office staff members address the fees and financial arrangements. Yet, modeling avoidance behaviors, having unresolved conflicts, and experiencing discomfort when openly discussing the nature of the treatment relationship are all patterns that we hope practitioners will agree are not in their own and their clients' best interests.

Each private practitioner must effectively integrate the role of being an entrepreneur seeking to establish and maintain a successful business with the role of being a caring and compassionate clinician who develops meaningful therapeutic relationships with clients and who uses his or her clinical skills to assist clients to achieve their treatment goals. This integrated approach to our professional roles and responsibilities contrasts significantly with what Haber, Rodino, and Lipner (2001) describe as "the one-dimensional caring myth" (p. 26) that often develops as a result of our graduate education and training, where little attention tends to be paid to the business aspects of our professional roles. There the focus tends to be primarily on the development of our clinical skills and our professional identity as caring and compassionate clinicians who are engaged in helping relationships. We must see how these two roles are compatible with each other and in fact must coexist comfortably for us if we are to be successful private practitioners.

Similarly, resolving money issues is crucial for being able to charge fees commensurate with the value of the professional services we provide to clients (dare I say "customers"). Thus, for many this may relate to issues of self-esteem, self-worth, and valuing the assistance we provide to clients in our professional roles. Clients, like all consumers, pay for goods and services in their daily lives based on their needs, desires, and preferences. While of course consumers tend to look for a good value for the money they spend, we too must value the services we provide. This then enables us to be comfortable setting, charging, and collecting fees for the professional services we render. As highly educated, competent, and skilled professionals we must have a realistic appraisal of the great value of the services we offer to the public and be comfortable with our integrated role as businesspersons and mental health clinicians.

# FEE SETTING

Keeping in mind the value of the professional services we offer, each private practitioner must set the fees for each type of service offered. We may charge different fees for individual and group counseling and psychotherapy sessions, psychological and neuropsychological testing, consultation and clinical supervision, forensic evaluations and expert witness testimony, providing continuing education workshops, and any other services we may provide.

## ETHICAL CONSIDERATIONS IN FEE SETTING

The ethics codes of the mental health professions provide some useful guidance relevant to fee setting. For psychologists, the American Psychological Association (APA)'s Ethical Principles of Psychologists and Code of Conduct (2010) states in Standard 3.08, Exploitative Relationships, that psychologists should not exploit clients, including with regard to fee practices. The National Association of Social Workers (NASW)'s Code of Ethics states in Standard 1.06, Conflicts of Interest, that "Social workers should not take unfair advantage of any professional relationship or exploit others to further their personal, religious, political, or business interests" (2008, para. 28). Further, in Standard 1.13, Payment for Services, social workers are advised that "When setting fees, social workers should ensure that the fees are fair, reasonable, and commensurate with the services performed. Consideration should be given to clients' ability to pay" (para. 35).

The American Counseling Association (ACA)'s Code of Ethics (2014) provides similar guidance in requiring counselors to consider clients' financial status and locality when establishing fees (Standard A.10.c., Establishing Fees). Further, consistent with the values of the mental health professions, this standard requires that "If a counselor's usual fees create undue hardship for the client, the counselor may adjust fees, when legally permissible, or assist the client in locating comparable, affordable services" (p. 6). This ethics code also makes clear that counselors must not exploit any individuals with whom they are engaged in a professional relationship (Standard C.6.d., Exploitation of Others).

The American Association for Marriage and Family Therapy (AAMFT)'s Code of Ethics (2015) contains similarly worded standards prohibiting inappropriate conflicts of interest and exploitation of clients. It also requires in Standard 3.2, Knowledge of Regulatory Standards, that marriage and family therapists must be knowledgeable of and act in accordance with relevant laws and regulations in their professional roles, including their setting of fees and related financial arrangements. Further, Standard 4.8, Payment for Supervision, requires that marriage and family therapists "shall not enter into financial arrangements with supervisees through deceptive or exploitative practices, nor shall marriage and family therapists providing clinical supervision exert undue influence over supervisees when establishing supervision fees" (Standard IV, Responsibility to Students and Supervisees).

Thus, significant themes from the ethics codes of the mental health professions include that mental health practitioners should do the following:

- Ensure that fee practices are not exploitative of clients and are consistent with the values of one's profession.
- Consider the prospective client's ability to pay and the locality where one is practicing when setting fees.
- Ensure that all fee practices are consistent with relevant laws and regulations in the jurisdiction where one is practicing.

## PRACTICAL CONSIDERATIONS IN FEE SETTING

Knowing how much to charge for the various services mental health practitioners provide can be a challenging and vexing issue. In addition to the need to value the services we provide, practitioners will want to consider a broad array of factors when considering appropriate fees to charge.

The first is the nature of the services to be provided. Mental health practitioners may provide a wide range of professional services. Some vary by the amount of time involved and others by the nature of the professional service, to include the amount of expertise required or risk involved (e.g., forensic services). Practitioners often charge a higher fee when specialized training or experience is involved. While it is possible to establish a successful practice not participating in managed care or accepting insurance, offering a fee-for-service practice in which professional services are not reimbursed by managed care and insurance can help the practitioner to collect higher fees because he or she does not need to offer steep contracted discounts to the insurance company and can actually receive full payment for the services he or she provides. Many of the niche areas of practice described in the second section of this book provide an excellent overview of such practice opportunities.

The practitioner's expertise and professional reputation will also affect the fees he or she can charge. It seems reasonable to expect that recent graduates starting out in practice will charge less for their professional services than experienced practitioners. However, the number of years you have been in practice is not the key issue here; rather, your professional reputation as a clinician who offers high-quality services will directly impact the fees you can charge. Thus, offering excellent services, providing a high level of customer service, and effectively marketing your practice to develop your professional reputation are all of great importance. Possessing specialty training and being able to offer specialized services that are valued by consumers will also impact the fees you can charge.

It is important to consider the local economy and potential clientele in the community where you offer professional services. The fees charged in a private practice in a rural community might be significantly different than in an affluent suburb or upper-class section of a city. If you live and practice in a community where a large percentage of the residents are employed by a local business and that business closes, the impact on the local economy can be tremendous. Those offering professional services geared toward affluent individuals, such as executive coaching, corporate consultation, and the like, may be able to charge higher fees than those providing counseling and psychotherapy in a low- to moderate-income community. But, as Walfish and Barnett (2009) state: "Clinicians should charge fees that the market will bear. To charge less does not make good business sense. To charge more does not make good business sense" (p. 119). Charging less than the reasonable fees that the local market will bear undervalues the professional services you are providing and may even communicate this to potential consumers. To charge more than the market will bear may lead to many unfilled hours in your daily schedule and may convey a certain arrogance and being out of touch with the economic realities of the local community.

## DECIDING ON THE FEES YOU CHARGE

The following discussion assumes that you are not a participating provider with an insurance carrier or a managed care company. Clinicians who contract with these entities must adhere to a set fee schedule that both the clinician and client agree to. Even when considering the factors described above, private practitioners may struggle with knowing the "right" fees to charge. There are several strategies that can provide some context for making these decisions.

First, you can research salary data in your profession. Many professional associations conduct periodic salary surveys that include data on fees charged by private practitioners. Subscribers to the newsletter *Psychotherapy Finances* (available at http://www.psyfin.com/) have access to their annual survey of fees charged by practitioners in the different mental health professions.

Another strategy for learning about prevailing fees charged by mental health professionals in your local area is to ask colleagues what they charge for various services. Taking colleagues out to lunch to learn about their practices and the local community can provide an excellent opportunity for obtaining this information. While it may feel uncomfortable to ask colleagues about the fees they charge due to our own ambivalence about money and the common taboo about discussing money in our society, this information is actually readily available to members of the public and not a closely guarded secret.

To find out the fees charged by mental health professionals in your community, it is easy to find a listing of these practitioners and to contact their office, asking what their fee is for an initial evaluation session, for ongoing psychotherapy sessions, for psychological testing, or for any other professional service of interest to you. It is common for practices to receive such inquiries, since cost is one of the factors many consumers consider when deciding which mental health professional they will make an initial appointment with. In addition, many clinicians list their fees on their websites.

Another strategy is to select what you think is a reasonable fee to charge. Then, when a potential client contacts you and asks your fees, you share this information. If the client accepts this, then you have an indication that this may be a reasonable fee in your community. Of course, this one individual may not be representative of the entire community, but it's a start. Then for the next person who contacts you and asks your fee, increase the amount you charge, perhaps by $10, and see how he or she responds. Over a fairly short period of time you can learn what most individuals in your community will be comfortable paying for your services. This is an actual test of learning what the market will bear.

An alternative approach is to figure out your expenses and what you want or need your net income to be. Factoring in the number of hours you are willing and able to work each week, you can determine how much you need to charge per hour. Of course, the outcome of this computation must be realistic, and if the fee you are considering charging is significantly greater than what you think the market will bear, you can choose to work more hours per week so you still achieve the desired net income—or you can see if you can live with a lower net income.

While each of these strategies may be helpful, no one strategy is best for all private practitioners. We each must make our own decisions about this. But it is important to keep the following factors in mind when setting fees:

- The economic circumstances and prevailing fees in the local community.
- The amount of experience and expertise you possess.
- Any specialized training, certifications, or credentials you may have.
- The nature of the services you provide and if they are unique or specialized.
- The level of competition in the local community for the services you provide.

## DISCUSSING AND AGREEING ON FEES WITH CLIENTS

The mental health professions' ethics codes, and relevant licensing law and regulations, make it clear that fees and financial arrangements must be openly discussed and agreed upon at the outset of the professional relationship. This includes fees for the initial session and subsequent sessions (the former often higher than the latter), report-writing fees, and a late cancellation and no-show policy where fees will be incurred. This means that these issues will be included as part of the informed consent process with every client. For psychologists, the APA Ethics Code (APA, 2010) states in Standard 6.04, Fees and Financial Arrangements, that psychologists should reach an agreement with the recipients of their professional services on fees charged and payment arrangements "as early as is feasible" in the professional relationship (p. 9). Similarly, Standard 10.01, Informed Consent to Therapy, list fees and financial arrangements as required components of each client's informed consent agreement, and Standard 3.10, Informed Consent, requires that "written and oral consent, permission, and assent be appropriately documented" (p. 6).

Similarly, the ACA Code of Ethics (2014) requires in Standard A.2., Informed Consent in the Counseling Relationship, that "counselors inform clients about fees and billing arrangements, including procedures for nonpayment of fees" (p. 4) through the informed consent process. The NASW Code of Ethics (2008) requires in Standard 1.03, Informed Consent, that social workers include specific information on "relevant costs" in the informed consent process with every client (para. 23).

In addition to similar wording in its standard on informed consent, the AAMFT Code of Ethics (2015) provides detailed requirements in Standard 8.2, Disclosure of Financial Policies, stating that marriage and family therapists must disclose "all financial arrangements and fees related to professional services, including charges for canceled or missed appointments" prior to offering treatment or supervision services (Standard VIII, Financial Arrangements).

To meet these requirements, private practitioners must ensure that fees and applicable financial arrangements and obligations be discussed openly and fully as part of the informed consent process. This includes all likely fees, billing processes, and payment options. This process should occur verbally, with the practitioner making an active effort to ensure the client understands all that is included in this agreement. Additionally, each client should be provided with a written informed consent agreement that may be reviewed and referred back to over time. In addition to the myriad other elements of a comprehensive informed consent agreement, issues relevant to fees and financial arrangements must always be included in this process.

In addition to the above, private practitioners should inquire about and consider each client's likely ability to afford the professional services being offered. Thus, both the services being proposed and their likely cost should be included in this open discussion during the informed consent process. It would not be appropriate to plan long-term treatment for a client who can only afford six or eight sessions. Similarly, individuals seeking an evaluation may not have a realistic expectation of the time and cost involved. Such individuals will likely be surprised when receiving the bill for services rendered. The ethics codes of the mental health professions each address this issue, requiring that the practitioner, during the informed consent process, mention any financial limitations that may be likely to impact the client's ability to participate in treatment.

Informed consent is an ongoing process, not a one-time event, so it needs to be updated whenever substantive changes to the agreed-upon treatment plan are being contemplated. This enables clients to decide if the proposed changes to treatment are acceptable to them. It also enables clients to consider their finances, and if they can afford to participate in the proposed modifications to the treatment plan. For example, a practitioner may determine that an individual psychotherapy client would also benefit from group therapy, or that it would be beneficial to refer a client for a neuropsychological evaluation. While these services may be entirely appropriate clinically and in the client's best interest, they may fall outside of the client's financial resources.

When discussing fees and financial arrangements with clients, private practitioners should do the following:

- Include an open discussion of all likely fees and relevant financial arrangements, including billing and payment requirements, in each client's informed consent process and actively ensure the client understands them.
- Ensure that in addition to this discussion, the client is provided with details of all fees and financial arrangement requirements in a written document such as a financial agreement that is signed by both the practitioner and client.
- Consider each client's financial status and ability to afford the professional services being offered in this process.

- Update the informed consent/financial agreement whenever substantive changes to the professional services being offered are proposed. Ensure that clients understand the clinical and financial implications of these changes for them.

# RAISING FEES

For a variety of reasons, private practitioners may at times choose to raise the fees they charge. The expenses associated with running a private practice increase over time. We all experience increases in rent, utilities, staff salaries, insurance, and the like. Additionally, as our experience and expertise increase we may decide that we deserve to charge and collect higher fees; few practitioners will want to earn the same amount after 10 or 15 years in practice as they earned when they first went into practice. Thus, like all businesses, it is very common to raise the fees charged over time. Also, as Barnett, Zimmerman, and Walfish (2008) point out, in contrast with salaried employees who undergo annual performance reviews and whose employer increases their salary periodically, private practitioners must give themselves a raise if they expect to receive one.

As has been mentioned, fees must be addressed in the informed consent agreement. The periodic raising of fees should be addressed in this manner as well. This may be accomplished by including a statement of one's policy on periodic fee increases in the initial informed consent agreement. Mention can be made that the fee for each service provided increases by 10% on January 1 each year for clients who begin in treatment more than six months before that date. For clients who enter treatment less than six months before that date, the fee will increase by that amount the following January 1. While clients receiving brief or time-limited services may not be concerned about such fee increases, longer-term clients will find this to be important information that can impact their treatment planning; indeed, they may choose to work with another clinician who promises not to raise his or her fees.

An alternative approach is not to address potential fee increases in your initial informed consent agreement, but to address the issue on a case-by-case basis with clients when this becomes relevant. Thus, for longer-term clients you will likely want to increase fees over time, but, in keeping with the relevant standards from the mental health professions' ethics codes, you must provide clients with sufficient notice of any planned fee increases so that they will have ample time to make alternative arrangements should the fee increase prove to be outside their financial resources. By providing sufficient time clients may have the opportunity to work toward a timely termination of treatment or referrals may be made to less costly treatment providers if the client needs ongoing treatment.

No clear rule exists for how much notice to give clients about a pending fee increase, but the ethics codes make it clear that sufficient notice must be provided. For example, the AAMFT Code of Ethics (2015) includes in Standard 8.2, Disclosure of Financial Policies, that "Once services have begun, therapists provide reasonable notice of any changes in fees or other charges" (Standard VIII, Financial Arrangements). Similarly, the APA Ethics Code (2010) makes it clear that "Psychologists do not misrepresent their fees" (p. 9). Thus, it would be inappropriate to charge one fee initially and then, once the client becomes engaged in the treatment process and perhaps dependent on the clinician, to inform the client that the fee has now been increased. This would likely be seen as exploitative behavior on the private practitioner's part (Barnett, Zimmerman, & Walfish, 2014). If the clinician is not sure how and when a fee increase will occur, the informed consent agreement can include a statement that fees are subject to increase over time and any increase will be discussed in advance. This gives the client notice that the initial fee is not necessarily going to be in force for the duration of treatment.

## COLLECTING FEES

Processes and procedures for the collection of fees should also be addressed in the informed consent/financial agreement. If you are a participating provider with the client's insurance carrier, then a discussion should take place regarding filing of the insurance, and whether payments are needed for deductibles not met or required co-pays. It should be made clear if payment is due at the beginning or end of each treatment session or if the client will be billed and when payment is then due, such as within 30 days of the date of the billing. It also should be made clear if payment is accepted by cash, check, or credit card. All possible fees should be disclosed at the outset, to include any fees charged for cancelled or missed appointments. Representative of the mental health professions' ethics codes, the NASW Code of Ethics (2008) requires in Standard 3.05, Billing, that "social workers engage in billing practices that are accurate and honest, never misrepresenting fees, services provided, or responsibility for payment" (para. 54).

While it is certainly preferred that clients pay for services rendered in a timely manner, at times clients may forget their checkbook, miss an appointment, or cancel an appointment at the last minute. It is recommended that the financial agreement include the practitioner's policy on missed appointments and cancellations. Thus, if the full fee is charged for all missed appointments and appointments cancelled with less than 24 hours' notice, the client should be informed of this from the outset. While every practitioner has the right to enforce such a policy, since our time is valuable, caution is recommended in implementing this policy. It is recommended that if a client misses an appointment or cancels less than 24 hours before the appointment, the practitioner discuss this with the client and find out why it occurred. If the client was in the emergency room with a gravely ill child, it would be inappropriate to implement this policy. Doing so in such a circumstance could result in the client discontinuing treatment and thus could prove to be a rather shortsighted action on the practitioner's part. Even if a client reports having forgotten the appointment, apologizes for the oversight, and even offers to pay the full fee, it may be the most prudent course of action to thank the client, say you will not charge the fee this time, but that you will if this occurs again in the future. Such an action may prove to be an excellent clinical and business decision. It is also important to make sure that if you are providing services to the client via a managed care contract, you carefully read the contract to see if you are indeed allowed to charge fees for services that are not covered (e.g., late cancellations, missed appointments, psychological testing time the company deems not medically necessary).

# WHEN CLIENTS FAIL TO PAY

Sometimes clients fail to pay fees owed for professional services rendered. How such circumstances may be addressed should be clearly articulated in the informed consent/financial agreement. While this may include the use of collection agencies or possibly even suing for fees owed in small claims court, a preventive approach is recommended.

Clients are likely to view the use of a collection agency or small claims court as a rather antagonistic action on the part of the private practitioner. While we may be acting within our legal right to take this action (and our ethical right as long as adequate notice is provided before taking this action), if doing so results in the client filing a licensing board complaint or malpractice suit, it may cost much more to defend ourselves (in both time and money) than to write off the fee owed.

A preventive approach to this issue would involve including in the informed consent/financial agreement the maximum outstanding balance for fees owed at any one time in order for treatment to continue without interruption. For example, the private practitioner may only allow an outstanding balance equal to the charges for three sessions. When clients fail to pay for a session, they should be reminded of this policy that they agreed to at the beginning of treatment. If the client does not pay this bill and the outstanding balance increases further, the client should again be reminded of the policy, to include what will happen if the balance equals the fees charged for three sessions. In such situations no further treatment should be provided until the client pays the outstanding balance. Of course, clients should not be abandoned, so referrals to no-cost or low-cost providers may be made if the client is in imminent need of ongoing treatment.

If a collection agency or small claims court is to be considered an option for collecting fees owed, this should be clearly articulated in the informed consent/financial agreement. Consistent with the requirements of the other mental health professions ethics codes, the AAMFT Code of Ethics (2015) makes this clear in Standard 8.2, Disclosure of Financial Policies, which requires marriage and family therapists to address in the informed consent process "the use of collection agencies or legal measures for nonpayment; and (c) the procedure for obtaining payment from the client, to the extent allowed by law" (Standard VIII, Financial Arrangements). Further, when such actions are being contemplated, the private practitioner should inform the client of the possibility of such actions and offer the client the opportunity to make payment within a reasonable period of time to avoid these actions being taken. Also, be sure that attempts at collection, even before contacting a collection agency, are done consistent with state law and do not violate Health Insurance Portability and Accountability Act (HIPAA) standards.

Barnett and Walfish (2012) have also suggested obtaining a "credit card guaranty" from the client as part of the initial informed consent process. With such a document, the client provides his or her credit card information, and if fees are not paid in an agreed-upon amount of time, the client's account is charged. While this is not a "foolproof" method (e.g., cards reach their expiration date or accounts can reach their credit limit or be canceled by the client), it is an effective procedure for improving collections.

# ADDRESSING CLIENTS' FINANCIAL HARDSHIP

While some clients may avoid paying fees owed even when they are able to do so financially, at times the underlying issue may be a financial hardship experienced by the client. Clients may lose their job and their health insurance, they may experience unexpected expenses in their lives such as medical expenses for a family member, or they may experience a change in their financial situation for a wide range of reasons. It is hoped that clients will openly discuss such situations with us so that alternative arrangements that are in their best interests may be considered.

One option for assisting clients who are experiencing financial hardship is to offer a reduced fee, either for a specified time period or for as long as they are unable to pay the full fee. An example would be a client who recently lost her job but who is actively interviewing for new positions. Offering a reduced fee until she obtains new employment will demonstrate a significant commitment to the client and to your ongoing work together. The amount of the reduced fee will need to be negotiated through open discussion to ensure that it is fair to both client and practitioner.

For private practitioners who may consider offering clients in financial need a reduced fee, a written policy should be created and followed. In the informed consent process it should be stated that clients should let you know if they experience financial difficulties that may make continuing in treatment not possible. Then, if informed of this by a client, the written policy can be shared with the client and applied in a consistent manner. Typically, these sliding fee scale policies list what the fee will be for a client with a certain level of income, but this may become rather complex since income is not the only factor that may impact a client's ability to afford ongoing treatment; for instance, the number of dependent family members, current expenses, and other factors may all be relevant. Thus, some private practitioners may simply choose to discuss the situation openly with their client and then together reach an agreement on a fee with which that both parties are comfortable.

## PRO BONO SERVICES

The ethics codes of the mental health professions also address the need at times to offer pro bono, or free, mental health treatment services. Doing so is considered an obligation that is consistent with the values of our professions. Of course, as businesspersons it is not realistic to offer free services to a large number of clients on an ongoing basis, but offering this in a limited manner to clients in financial need who would not otherwise be able to receive the services you offer is consistent with the highest ideals of our professions. For example, the ACA Code of Ethics (2014) states in Standard C.6.e., Contributing to the Public Good (Pro Bono Publico), "Counselors make a reasonable effort to provide services to the public for which there is little or no financial return (e.g., speaking to groups, sharing professional information, offering reduced fees)" (p. 10).

Barter is the exchange or goods or services by the client for professional services offered by the private practitioner. Barter may at times be an alternative for clients who do not have the financial means to pay for the mental health services they require. This may occur during the course of treatment for a client whose financial situation changes or it may be the sole means that the client seeks to use to pay for treatment services. In some settings such as rural communities, barter may be consistent with prevailing community standards. Private practitioners with practices in these communities should be familiar with the use of barter and consider their comfort with accepting it.

The ethics codes of the mental health professions make it clear that barter should be used only if "it is not clinically contraindicated" and "the resulting arrangement is not exploitative" (APA, 2010, p. 9). Further, in Standard A.10.e., Bartering, the ACA Code of Ethics (2014) requires that barter be used only if the client requests it "and if such arrangements are an accepted practice among professionals in the community" (p. 6). The ACA Code of Ethics also requires counselors to consider relevant cultural implications of any use of barter.

When engaging in barter with clients, it is recommended that goods be used over services because the value of the goods may be easier to determine than would be the case with services. Additionally, having clients provide services for us may create conflict-of-interest situations (e.g., painting your home, having their band play at your son's wedding) and inappropriate multiple relationships. The NASW Code of Ethics (2008) addresses the clinician's responsibilities in these situations in stating that barter should be engaged in only when it is "considered to be essential for the provision of services, negotiated without coercion" and that social workers "assume the full burden of demonstrating that this arrangement will not be detrimental to the client or the professional relationship" (para. 33).

# OTHER FEE ISSUES

It is important that private practitioners be aware of all ethics code standards, laws, and regulations relevant to fees and financial arrangements with clients. While there may at times be conflicts between what is allowed under the law and what ethics codes require, when this occurs it is recommended that we choose the course of action that is most protective of our clients' rights and best interest.

An example is the practice of charging or accepting fees for making a referral. The ethics codes of the mental health professions require that fees be charged and accepted only for the provision of actual professional services. As an example, the AAMFT Code of Ethics states in Standard 8.1, Financial Integrity, "Marriage and family therapists do not offer or accept kickbacks, rebates, bonuses, or other remuneration for referrals. Fee-for-service arrangements are not prohibited" (Standard VIII, Financial Arrangements). Such arrangements, often referred to as "fee-splitting," are viewed as unethical by each of the mental health professions' ethics codes. Yet in some states (e.g., Maryland) mental health professionals are legally authorized to accept fees for making referrals if they first disclose this fact to clients. While doing so may seem helpful, it does not remove the potential for conflicts of interest and making referrals to obtain the fee rather than making referrals based solely on the client's best interest. So, while it is allowed under this law, engaging in this practice is not consistent with ethics code standards and does not appear to be in clients' best interests, so it should be avoided.

Due to their wide and varied skillsets mental health practitioners in private practice do not have to earn income solely by providing assessment and psychotherapy and other clinical services. In addition to these traditional services clinicians may also provide supervision and consultation to other clinicians, conduct workshops for both the public and other mental health professionals, and provide organizational consulting to both for-profit and nonprofit organizations, to name a few. As there is no set standard fee for providing these services, it can be challenging to know how much to charge.

If you possess a special or unique skill area, clinicians who want to learn more about your practice area may seek you out for supervision and consultation. Chapter 35: Ethics Issues Regarding Supervision and Consultation in Private Practice presents the difference between consultation and supervision. In the former the consultee is seeking information or skill development but there is no clinical responsibility for the client assumed by the consultant. In the latter, the supervisor assumes responsibility for the clinical work of the supervisee. Typically, consultees are licensed health professionals who are seeking to expand their expertise into new areas. Supervisees typically are unlicensed trainees who require clinical supervision to become licensed to practice independently.

In terms of setting fees for these two activities, several possible considerations are as follows: (a) Should this fee be similar to or different from my psychotherapy fees? (b) Does this specialized knowledge allow me to consider charging more than I would if I were spending the same hour with a client? (c) In the case of supervision, does the fact that I am taking a risk by assuming responsibility for the clinical work of someone else justify charging a higher fee than I would for a psychotherapy hour? (d) How long will the consultation or supervision relationship last? Will this be just a few hours of skill building or will it be a year or more of weekly meetings while the supervisee accumulates hours for licensure? There is no right or wrong answer, but these are just a few things to consider when deciding what to charge for these services.

Providing community presentations on mental health issues can be great fun for the private practitioner, can serve as an effective marketing activity, and can be a source of revenue that does not involve direct client care. Chapter 29: How to Promote Your Practice Through Community Presentations raises the question of "How much should I charge for community presentations?" The chapter's authors present a thoughtful discussion about the variables to consider, such as the experience level of the presenter, whether the group provides the potential for a large number of referrals to be directed to your practice if they like the presentation, and how much the clinician values his or her time. These are clearly important considerations; others to include as part of the equation include how much time it will take to prepare the presentation and how much time being at the presentation (including travel and speaking with participants afterwards) will mean that you are not spending time at your office seeing clients and generating fees for these clinical sessions. This last issue is quite important for the private practitioner making a community presentation when compared to someone working in an agency or university making the same presentation. These latter individuals are on salary and will be paid whether they are in their office working or out in the community making a presentation. In contrast, private practitioners are in a "service business" and, since they do not have a set salary, receive compensation only when they are engaging in revenue-generating activities.

If the private practitioner has developed a unique skillset, may have obtained some notoriety by publishing a book or article, or has developed a reputation as a great presenter, doing paid workshops may also be a possible revenue stream. There are continuing education companies that specialize in providing workshops on mental health topics (see www.pesi.com and www.cross-countryeducation.com as examples). I am aware of one psychologist who spends three weeks each month in his office conducting assessment and psychotherapy and the other week "on the road" doing workshops for one these companies. Other paid workshops may be presented at state and local professional associations. Once again, the private practitioner has to decide how much to charge to do these presentations. Considerations include how much preparation time is involved, whether this is a one-time workshop or will be replicated in other venues (in which case little or no new preparation time is involved for these subsequent presentations), how much travel time is involved, and, once again, how much lost revenue will be incurred by not being in the office seeing clients.

In setting fees for workshops or community presentations, the previous adage of charging what the market will bear also comes into play. How much is too much to ask for? You never know until you ask. A colleague was asked to do a workshop that required him to travel to an area of the country during the winter where it would be cold. He really didn't want to face the cold, but he wanted to develop a relationship with the sponsor of the workshop, so he asked for double his normal fee. The sponsor agreed to pay this higher fee. The colleague then felt much better about braving the conditions.

Mental health professionals have skillsets that can be helpful in improving the functioning of an organization. How do you determine how much to charge for such consultation? Should you charge your normal hourly clinical fee or should it be higher since the consultation may take you out of your office? Will the consultation be disruptive to your office practice (e.g., having to conduct a threat assessment at a moment's notice or a critical incident debriefing following a significant event), and if so should you charge a premium because you will have to cancel clinical office hours to be at the site? Do you charge a nonprofit institution the same fees as a Fortune 500 company or a small family-owned business?

Again, there are no right or wrong answers to these questions. The important issue is to take into consideration the variables discussed above and decide on an amount that is appropriate and reasonable to you. Almost certainly there are situations where "you could have made more," but you should instead focus on whether you set your fees in a reasoned and intentional manner and whether you felt comfortable with the amount when you negotiated the fee.

# CONCLUSION

While businesses must charge and collect fees if they are to survive and thrive, practitioners must follow ethics standards to ensure that clients are not exploited and that their best interests are considered. Important issues to address include the following:

1. Openly discuss fees and financial policies as part of the initial informed consent agreement and then again whenever changes to the services being offered are being contemplated.
2. Provide clients with sufficient notice before fees are increased, and maintain and follow written policies on fee increases and reductions.
3. Maintain and follow policies for how unpaid fees will be addressed.
4. At times, fees may be reduced or clients may be treated pro bono, but again, consistently follow written policies.
5. Barter may be used under some circumstances, but make sure it is done in a manner consistent with the client's best interests, ensuring that no exploitation occurs.

Attention to these issues as detailed in this chapter and as addressed in the ethics codes of the mental health professions will assist private practitioners to be successful in the business of practice while meeting clients' needs in the best manner possible.

# REFERENCES

American Association for Marriage and Family Therapy. (2015). Code of Ethics. Retrieved from http://aamft.org/iMIS15/AAMFT/Content/Legal_Ethics/Code_of_Ethics.aspx.

American Counseling Association. (2014). ACA Code of Ethics. Retrieved from https://www.counseling.org/knowledge-center/ethics.

American Psychological Association. (2010). Ethical principles of psychologists and code of conduct. Retrieved from http://www.apa.org/ethics.

Barnett, J. E., & Walfish, S. (2012). Billing and collecting for your mental health practice: Effective strategies and ethical practice. Washington, DC: American Psychological Association.

Barnett, J. E., Zimmerman, J., & Walfish, S. (2014). The ethics of private practice: A practical guide for mental health clinicians. New York: Oxford University Press.

Haber, S., Rodino, E., & Lipner, I. (2001). Saying good-bye to managed care: Building your independent psychotherapy practice. New York: Springer.

Herron, W. G., & Rouslin Welt, S. (1992). Money matters: The fee in psychotherapy and psychoanalysis. New York: The Guilford Press.

National Association of Social Workers. (2008). Code of ethics. Retrieved from https://www.socialworkers.org/pubs/code/default.asp.

Walfish, S., & Barnett, J. E. (2009). Financial success in mental health practice: Essential tools and strategies for practitioners. Washington, DC: American Psychological Association.

CHAPTER 21

# EFFECTIVE BILLING
# AND COLLECTING

*Thomas M. Kozak and Andrea Kozak Miller*

Mental health professionals provide important and much-needed services that have a tremendous impact on many individuals' lives. While most mental health professionals acknowledge a strong desire to assist those in need, in order to remain financially viable we must charge fees for the services we provide. While private practitioners may at times admirably provide their services pro bono so that those with limited financial resources may have access to these much-needed services, the private practice of mental health care has to run as a business.

Even in a setting as basic as a community mental health center, which can be funded by charitable organizations, it becomes quickly evident there are utilities to pay, salaries for staff members, costs of office supplies, and rent payments. The combination of endowment income and revenue generated by the center itself allows the center to operate. It is sometimes striking to see the number of practitioners who attempt to run a private practice only to fail because they cannot grasp the financial nature of running a business. Such clinicians often retreat back to employment with various agencies or other large organized healthcare settings, where the financial and business aspects of practice are managed by someone else and their earlier desires to be "their own person" and to function without a large bureaucracy end up shifting to a setting more in line with their needs.

## PROFESSIONAL CODES OF ETHICS
## AND BILLING

The professional associations of each of the mental health professions have adopted a code of ethics to set standards for the appropriate conduct of their members (e.g., American Association for Marriage and Family Therapy, 2012; American Counseling Association, 2014; American Psychological Association, 2010; National Association of Social Workers, 2008). These codes of ethics provide guidance and enforceable standards that apply to each aspect of members' professional activities, including their business activities. Ethical standards for the billing of professional services are specifically addressed in each of these codes of ethics. For example, consistent with the other mental health professions' codes of ethics, the AAMFT Code of Ethics (2012) requires in Principle VII, Financial Arrangements, that marriage and family therapists "make financial arrangements with clients, third-party payers, and supervisees that are reasonably understandable and conform to accepted professional practice" (p. 4). This standard goes on to state that at the outset of the professional relationship marriage and family therapists should disclose to clients and reach agreements on:

> all financial arrangements and fees related to professional services, including charges
> for canceled or missed appointments; (b) the use of collection agencies or legal mea-
> sures for nonpayment; and (c) the procedure for obtaining payment from the client,
> to the extent allowed by law, if payment is denied by the third-party payor. Once ser-
> vices have begun, therapists provide reasonable notice of any changes in fees or other
> charges. (p. 4)

The members of each professional association are obligated to meet or exceed the expectations for ethical conduct set in these codes of ethics. Also, each jurisdiction has licensing laws and accompanying regulations that regulate the practice of each profession in these jurisdictions. All licensed mental health professionals are required to follow the standards in these laws and regulations.

At times, there may be inconsistencies between a professional code of ethics and the relevant laws and regulations. In general, when such conflicts exist you should choose the course of action that is most protective of clients' rights and welfare. However, such inconsistencies can at times be confusing, so consultation with experienced colleagues, legal counsel, professional resources from one's professional association, and your licensing board may be helpful. All communications with the licensing board should be in writing to minimize any potential confusion or misunderstandings, and to provide a record of any recommendations or guidance received. When questions exist, such consultations should be sought before engaging in the practice in question.

# TYPES OF BILLING

Each practitioner should be familiar with the wide range of billing options and practices that exist. How you bill for the professional services you provide can vary based on factors such as if your practice is fee-for-service, if you accept insurance, or if you are either an in-network or out-of-network provider for a managed care organization (MCO). Each situation brings with it practical, ethical, and legal issues that you must deal with.

## FEE-FOR-SERVICE, NO INSURANCE

Before insurance coverage was available for mental health services, practitioners provided professional services on a fee-for-service basis. Today, some clinicians maintain this arrangement, whether they be psychoanalysts, forensic clinicians, various consultants, or those who practice in areas where clients are willing to pay out of pocket. Some clients who have health insurance may choose to pay out of pocket due to privacy concerns.

Depending on the arrangements made between practitioner and client through the informed consent agreement, clients may pay the fee owed at each session or they may be billed periodically, such as once each month. Methods of payment are also addressed in the informed consent agreement. These may include payment by credit card, check, or cash. Some practitioners will have their clients provide them with credit card information at the outset so that the practitioner can automatically bill the client for each professional service as it is provided.

## INDEMNITY INSURANCE

One of the first forms of insured mental health coverage occurred via indemnity plans. While they are becoming less common, these insurance policies paid fees at the "usual and customary" rate (UCR). Either the clinician was paid directly by the insurer or the client was expected to pay the bill and submit to the insurance company a receipt for services, which the company would reimburse. These plans may also have a specified co-payment and deductible that the insured is responsible for paying. Indemnity plans paid anywhere from 100% to as low as 50% of the allowable UCR. Typically no preauthorization was required from the insurance company for outpatient professional services. The services provided would be covered within the limits stipulated in the contract.

## THE "USUAL AND CUSTOMARY" RATE

There can be some confusion about this term in billing. Many clinicians think of the UCR as the rate a clinician charges for his or her services, like a price list. It is a fixed number, set by the clinician, that applies to all clients and all insurance plans. For example, if you bill $150 for an initial evaluation (Procedure Code 90791), that rate remains constant for all patients, whether they are private pay, indemnity, preferred provider organization (PPO), health maintenance organization (HMO), or Medicare/Medicaid.

Another definition of UCR comes from some insurance companies who compile statistics for our service charges, obtain an average for them in a particular region of the country, and set that average as what they refer to as the UCR. The very construct of UCR, however, is challenged by pure statistics. When clinicians become empaneled by an MCO, the fee agreement designates rates that are nearly always lower than the UCR, whether it is a clinician's billing rate or the insurance UCR set by regional averaging. If we were to statistically account for these variations, the rate of reimbursement would be significantly lower than either notion of the UCR.

The UCR then becomes an artificial construct set by either the clinician or the insurance company that is met only on occasion. So much for usual or customary, at least in the literal sense! Nevertheless, setting a UCR for clinicians is not only acceptable but routine and harkens back to the day when practitioners did have a set fee and adhered to it. The MCOs touted, to subscriber groups, that they were able to lower rates and produce costs savings by demonstrating the "bargain" rates for services they were able to achieve. (As a brief aside, the MCOs indicated to the clinicians that the tradeoff for these lowered fees was a flow of referrals that did not require advertising or marketing costs.)

## MANAGED CARE FEE AGREEMENTS

In mentioning managed care, we should briefly review the fee payment structure in this model. Typically an MCO solicits practitioners in a locale to join its panel of providers. The MCO will spell out various particulars for its insurance plan and offer a fee schedule that one can be fairly certain is below the UCR for that locale. The MCO will limit the number of providers to ensure those empaneled will receive a number of referrals.

Originally the MCOs restricted the number of sessions allowed or established treatment guidelines suggesting that various psychological problems could be solved within these shorter protocols. By so doing they hoped to keep insurance costs limited. In turn, they were able to offer insurance benefits at a more affordable rate to a greater population. Subsequently, legislation was passed allowing the client to go to "any willing provider" and essentially spelling the end of restrictions on the total number of sessions allowed (by having mental health coverage match regular medical coverage). This had a large impact on that original plan. The Paul Wellstone and Pete Domenici Mental Health Parity and Addiction Equality Act of 2008 (CMS.gov, 2015) also mandated that insurers spend 80% of premiums collected on actual care or refund money to the subscribers. In this way the bill sought to ensure the MCOs were not restricting care so as to maximize profits.

Managed care coverage is now ubiquitous, and while it is not as restrictive as originally formulated, some controversial issues remain. Many MCOs promote brief treatment and group treatment approaches in an apparent effort to reduce costs. Mental health professionals who are considering participating in managed care should be sure they are comfortable with this model and competent in providing these services before agreeing to participate.

### CAN I WRITE OFF THE DIFFERENCE AS A LOSS?

This question arises from time to time and can often be confusing. Even though we use our own consistent UCR (price list), managed care contracts specify the amount they will pay and what the co-pay and deductible should be, along with an understanding that neither the insurance company nor the subscriber is responsible for the difference. For example, if you bill $120 for Procedure Code 90837 but the agreed-upon rate is $85, the insurance company will pay $65 and expect the client to pay his or her $20 co-pay for the $85 total. What happens to the $35 difference? You have agreed to this discounted fee by signing a contract with the MCO and cannot write it off as a loss. Remember, contractually you expected to receive not $120 but rather $85 and were only using your UCR for your baseline.

## A VARIATION IN THIS SITUATION

If a client intended to pay the full fee as part of a private-pay arrangement and fails to pay, can you write that money off? The first answer would be, "no." Some might argue that the office overhead, expenses incurred trying to collect your fees, and lost wages (after all, we only have so many hours we can fill) should be deductible. This might be an interesting argument to pose to your accountant and the Internal Revenue Service, as it does have a somewhat plausible rationale. It will most likely fall under the "cost of doing business." Check first!

## BILLING FOR PSYCHOLOGICAL TESTING

Psychological testing has unfortunately suffered a difficult fate under the MCOs. What was once a fairly routine procedure now requires preauthorization in many cases. The psychologist is required to provide a rationale for the testing, designate the number of hours (read, procedure code hours) needed for the testing, and obtain authorization for a specific number of hours of testing. Any additional time that must be spent in the psychological testing, whether because the testing takes longer than anticipated or extra time is needed for the scoring, interpretation, or report writing, will in all likelihood not be covered by the MCO. Again, only the amount of time preauthorized will be paid, and only at the contracted rate.

## OUT-OF-NETWORK BENEFITS

PPO plans, unlike most HMO plans, are more open to out-of-network providers. This means that even if you are not part of the PPO panel, you may see clients insured by these plans. Either you will issue a bill to the subscriber, who pays you first and subsequently submits that bill to the insurance company for reimbursement, or the client pays the co-pay and deductible only and you are paid the remainder by the PPO company. Co-pays and deductibles are usually higher for these clients, but total reimbursement to the practitioner often exceeds the amount the clinician would have received if he or she were an in-network provider. The disincentive to the client, via higher out-of-pocket expenses, often keeps him or her seeing in-network providers rather than exercise freedom of choice. Other clients willingly accept the additional expense so they may be treated by the clinician of their choice.

# ELECTRONIC BILLING

Various forms of electronic billing programs are available, from commercially available billing software that clinics may use for online billing to remote outside billing services that are given demographic information about the client, procedure codes used, and fees charged and then perform that billing service for the clinician for an agreed-upon fee or percentage of the collections. More recently, insurers have initiated their own online billing service from which clinicians (or their administrative staff) can bill. These are free of charge and seem to work well; however, each insurer uses its own format. And although there are some similarities, the clinician's billing staff is forced to shift from one program to another depending on the insurer. We hope these will be homologated someday, but for now these programs at least save postage and are offered at no cost. If possible, it may be wise to keep your billing in house as potential errors are easier to correct using your own staff rather than someone unknown at a remote site.

## MEDICAL HOMES OR PATIENT-CENTERED MEDICAL HOMES

A current proposal discussed in the health service industry is the medical home or patient-centered medical home. This plan holds that better services and lowered costs can be achieved by a "one-stop-shopping" setting in which virtually all health services, including mental health, could be provided by one entity/organization, at essentially one location. That entity would then receive insurance company funds, most likely in capitated form, to provide those services. This plan, while touted as somewhat revolutionary, is much like the previous HMO model of service. It can offer creative solutions in care and can lower costs, but unfortunately there are some risks. What it may mean for mental health providers is giving up private practice settings and embedding themselves in a "medical home." Historically this did not always work well with HMOs as mental health contracts at first were carved out to existing freestanding clinics and eventually morphed into essentially "any-willing-provider arrangements."

It will be interesting to see how this new model develops, especially as it relates to mental health matters, as issues of privacy may impact clients accustomed to traditional medical care settings. Mental health providers may inevitably be resistant to surrender their independence, and clients' concerns for privacy may become a factor. However, the ever-increasing insurance costs to consumers and the overhead associated with providing services in multiple venues rather than under one roof are obvious areas of concern, and any schema addressing a reduction in insurance/medical costs should find favor. With that in mind, the next section, which covers capitated services, will be of interest to those who intend to pursue working with the "medical homes" concept. Keep in mind that this form of reimbursement has been implemented for many years in various healthcare settings and with varying results.

## THE CAPITATED SYSTEM

A capitated system of reimbursement for medical or mental health services can take several forms. The most common example is the HMO. For the purposes of this chapter we shall discuss the mental health portion solely. In this setting, a mental health clinic, either "standalone" or embedded in a larger medical system, is responsible for providing all the mental health care for a particular population. This population would be subscribers to a particular insurance plan. Rather than providing fee-for-service, the clinic receives a lump-sum payment at the beginning of each month. Those funds are to be used to provide all mental health services for those subscribers.

## HOW IT WORKS

Actuarial tables can predict both the likelihood and frequency of visits any one population might seek. Ordinarily we think in monthly increments, with a check arriving (or direct deposit) at the start of a month. Clinic staffing typically includes a psychiatrist, PhD/PsyD-level psychologist, a clinical social worker, and other master's-level therapists such as licensed professional counselors, licensed marriage and family therapists, and other professionals who provide substance abuse counseling. As subscribers from the insurance plan call the office, an intake administrator takes demographic data and is trained to refer those potential clients to the most appropriate clinician based on the client's stated treatment needs.

Naturally there will be some crossover as several of the clinicians can provide similar services. There should be some attempt to maximize "goodness of fit." Payments to those clinicians can be made either in salary form or based on an internal fee-for-service. The overall benefit to the clinic (or large practice) is that there is no billing to perform, only the collection of co-pays and/or deductibles from the clients. The clinic then renders an "encounter count" to the insurance company that lists only each client's identifying data, diagnosis, and procedure code for the date of service.

## WHAT THIS ACTUALLY MEANS

Let's say the clinic has been assigned a population of 10,000 subscribers and the capitated rate is set at $5 per person. This means the clinic receives a payment of $50,000 at the beginning of each month. If no one seeks service that month, the clinic keeps the entire amount. If everyone in the subscriber population seeks services, the clinic is overwhelmed and could end up in the red. In reality, neither of these happens; hence, the actuarial data that predict the likelihood of a request for services are very important if one is negotiating such a contract. Requests for services ebb and flow depending on time of year, school-related issues, or the particular subscriber group's demographics. It is important to take these factors into consideration over the course of a year and adjust cash flow accordingly. Full-time clinicians, employed by the clinic, see the clients in a timely manner.

## ADVANTAGES, DILEMMAS, AND CREATIVITY
## IN THE CAPITATED SYSTEM

The first advantage to this system is that no one has to bill for services. Other than the collection of co-pays/deductibles, the money routinely arrives each month, a salary is paid to the staff, and one can concentrate on providing services rather than worrying about fee collection. This system also saves considerable sums because staff members do not have to verify benefits, as they are provided each month by the insurer. Other than the previously mentioned "encounter count," nothing has to go out to the insurer in hopes of obtaining reimbursement.

Second, there is no need to contact the insurer to obtain preauthorization for services. All of that is handled internally by the clinic itself. Clinics also save considerable administrative time by not wrangling with insurance companies to determine why a bill was not paid.

There is also an opportunity for creativity. Rather than being hospitalized, clients who are in a crisis situation can be seen several times per week until the crisis has abated. Hospital care is expensive and could easily break the clinic's budget if not allocated judiciously. Also, how wise is it to have a client receive inpatient treatment when more intensive outpatient work will suffice? In a fee-for-service setting such creativity could be met by various types of resistance from the insurance company, enough so that hospitalization is the easier route to pursue (although not a very cost-effective option). Clinics (and large practices with such an arrangement) are also free to design and implement their own internal treatment plans that may include group therapy, art therapy, psychological testing, or didactic seminars that address various mental health problems in an effective but less costly form than traditional services. Marital therapy or marriage counseling, which is often a controversial issue in terms of whether it should be considered a covered benefit, disappears when the clinic provides didactic or group work that accommodates the anxiety, depression, or acting-out by either partner and its effect on the children, and the dynamics inherent in marital/family problems. In the past, these various symptoms often presented as individual conditions while the cause, rooted in family/couple dynamics, went unaddressed.

## DILEMMAS WITHIN THE CAPITATED SYSTEM

Because we are all human, complete with foibles, we must approach capitation in a serious manner. There can be an unconscious, if not conscious, push to limit services to maximize profit. These settings can then become even more restrictive than other managed care settings (where restrictions on services are a common complaint). The focus should be on providing needed services, although, as we stated, clinics and practices have the ability to do so in creative ways and focus more on prevention than is typically possible in traditional managed care. This can promote health and wellness while reducing costs to the clinic or practice.

Hiring well-qualified staff goes a long way because managers can rely on their judgment rather than attempting to control, oversee, or limit the care they provide. Clinics using a capitated system are also responsible for performing internal quality assurance reviews where patterns of care, utilization, and other issues can be addressed and improved upon, if needed.

# VARIATION OF PAYMENTS FOR OTHER CAPITATED SYSTEMS

While they were more common in the past, there may remain some employee assistance programs (EAPs) that operate using a variation of the capitated system. These plans offer the clinician a set fee for up to, for instance, five EAP sessions. At the completion of these sessions, the client must be referred to another provider on the client's insurance plan. Should it become evident, during initial sessions, that the client's problems are not likely to be solved within five visits, the clinician can discontinue the EAP visits early and refer the client to another provider on the client's insurance plan who can offer more extended sessions. Self-referral would not be permitted due to the obvious conflict of interest. The total fee allowed in this situation does not lend itself to using all visits available, as the average session rate would fall below the cost of doing business. However, just as capitated systems rely on actuarial data, this plan is predicated on the likelihood that the average number of sessions used for all cases will fall below the maximum.

## DOWNSIDES TO THE SYSTEM

It takes real integrity to resist finding methods to reduce care and hold on to capitated funds. HMOs were criticized in the past for restricting care and offering subpar services. Furthermore, there is hardly such a thing as a "nonparticipating provider." If you are not an internal part of the system, you cannot bill the insurance plan or the clinic receiving capitated funds. Clients' freedom of choice of provider no longer exists, and in only rare cases and under special circumstances do these organizations authorize care by an outside provider. In more recent years, some HMOs have added other providers to their networks, but at rates of reimbursement significantly lower than regular PPO reimbursements. The inherent problem with such a loosely knit structure is that the original benefits of the HMO model are lost, and this newer version resembles fee-for-service but at a very reduced rate of compensation.

Because of the reputation, deserved and sometimes not, HMOs have not fulfilled the potential they offered to bring to the marketplace. As mentioned, the possibility of moving mental health funding to a medical home or patient-centered medical home revisits the original HMO model. This plan holds all of the promise of the original HMOs along with their inherent problems. And while there has been some talk that this is a revolutionary model, the overall structure resembles the original HMO model. It remains to be seen whether this newer structure for care will improve the current situation. On the other hand, the ever-increasing costs of medical and mental health care have to be addressed in some fashion that offers effective care with premiums the average consumer can afford.

In one HMO clinic that one of the writers was privy to (Kozak), the vice-president of finance for the HMO asked the director, "How do you make any money? Your outpatient utilization is so high!" And it was true that this clinic used up a very significant amount of its allocated funds for outpatient psychotherapy, assessments, or medication checks, the highest for all participating clinics. The director pointed out, however, that their hospitalization rates were the lowest of all the participating clinics. By keeping clients out of the hospital, by offering multiple visits during the same week, he was able to avoid an otherwise preventable hospital stay and save funds to offer the needed services in a cost-effective manner.

# THE PROBLEM OF GREED IN BILLING
# UNDER CAPITATED SYSTEMS

Practitioners often complain when insurance companies lower their rates of reimbursement for mental health benefits. They are equally upset when rates do not keep up with inflation or the general increases in the cost of doing business. When the shoe is on the other foot, however, practitioners must not end up being guilty of the same practices. Receiving a large lump sum check at the beginning of each month certainly has its influences, conscious or otherwise. It takes real integrity for the clinician to deliver the contracted service and not imagine the money is somehow destined for him or her.

The two most common problems in this area are as follows:

1. Inflating the value (in other words, the salaries) of administrative leaders in the clinic. Clinics have often failed as a result of such policies where clinic leaders lose sight of the main ingredient they offer, namely the provision of care. Obsessive data collection, policy writing, or unnecessary oversight of staff results in funds being spent for something other than actual service. Such limitations in service often has subscriber groups shopping for other insurance plans—and there goes your contract.

2. Low-ball bidding, when a clinic or direct healthcare provider group bids for and accepts a capitated contract at rates that are below typical actuarial data predicted for those services. The clinic, in that situation, is then compelled to restrict the services it provides to keep its expenses within that budget. The ethical problem becomes one of promising important services the clinic cannot afford to provide. The fraudulent element occurs when the clinic knows full well the impending problem but nevertheless proceeds. One such mental health contract was so far below usual that the operating director quickly had his group acquired by another so as to bury his actions. He died not long after that transaction and was not brought to answer for his actions. At the invitation of a state attorney general's Department of Insurance, one of this chapter's writers (Kozak) was asked to help identify patterns of billing and utilization data that could help the office identify these types of poorly conceived contracts.

## MEDICARE/MEDICAID

While both of these health insurance plans are funded by tax dollars, they are not always entirely administered by governmental agencies. Recently some Medicare plans have become administered by traditional insurance plans. When this occurs, the rules that govern the benefits for those insurance companies are very closely aligned with the general policies of the new plan. It is not unusual to have Medicare recipients be solicited by major insurers. When this happens, the subscriber falls under the administrative policies of the new plan.

The degree to which Medicare/Medicaid influences the administration of these new plans may be subject to prior agreements made between the government and those plans. Participating providers, however, may expect to find that these new plans will mostly be indistinguishable from regular ones. Medicaid plans appear to be more creative in that they can be administered by a state governmental agency or carved out to separate organizations that may or may not be part of a major insurance plan. And although the plan may be administered much like major insurers would, practitioners should expect to see lower fee schedules.

Medicare has one complicating factor that many practitioners have difficulty grasping, that being the "opt-out" feature. Unlike other insurance companies where "nonparticipating" means you never signed up as a provider, or you resigned from the insurance panel after having been participating, with Medicare you must find your region (state or conglomeration of states) to pursue the opt-out feature. Typically you will sign a form that specifies your intention to opt out of Medicare and specify a starting date. You must then prepare a statement that both you and any potential Medicare client sign that spells out special conditions that apply. Certain conditions will not allow a strict opt-out and permit you to collect fees. For instance, you are required to make a referral to a Medicare-participating provider in an emergency case. The important feature here is that you cannot simply refuse to take Medicare unless you perform the opt-out protocol and receive a letter from Medicare indicating they have accepted this. This sounds unusual—hence the typical confusion in this matter—but to further complicate things, the various states or regions may have variations to their rules. It is best to contact your state/regional entity for clarification and instruction.

Billing for Medicare services takes on another twist, as fees often change more frequently than for regular insurers. Furthermore, the Medicare Physician Fee Schedule is determined not like fees set by the major insurers but rather by a complicated method. A Resource-Based Relative Value Scale yields a Relative Value Unit (RVU) that then determines the value of each procedure code. This fee is set by the federal Centers for Medicare and Medicaid Services (CMS) and varies as units for medical services are periodically recalculated. To the practitioner, the resulting fees often appear to take on random amounts for standard services. For instance, if your UCR fee for a 60-minute psychotherapy session (Procedure Code 90837) is $120, you may receive a payment of $109.27. As the CMS changes the RVU, that same procedure may allow $104.38 at a later point. That payment plus co-pay (customarily 20%) becomes your collectable fee and you professionally discount the remainder.

## NEGOTIATING WITH INSURANCE COMPANIES

A little-known fact is that practitioners receive different fees from the same insurer for various locales around the country; this may even occur within various metropolitan areas. Furthermore, there have been successful cases of petitioning the insurer for higher fees. It is striking that with the increased demands insurers place on our practices, they do not take into consideration the resultant increase in cost. Higher malpractice limits, 24-hour answering services, dedicated fax lines, the employment of administrative staff, the capability for computerized billing, and the expectation that office space will not only be compliant with the Americans with Disabilities Act but also easily accessible all add up to increased costs. Additionally, many states have increased the number of continuing education hours ("professional development" in some states) required for licensure renewal. Treatment for children and adolescents also requires administrative staff to monitor those children in the waiting room should the clinician visit with the parents privately for part of that hour.

# ERRORS IN BILLING

To err is human, and so it also goes with billing. Both insurers and clinicians can make mistakes. Unfortunately we don't have evidence to fall back on, but it might be interesting to see on whose side of the balance sheet mental health service billing errors fall, practitioner or insurer. That aside, there will be errors from both sides that require follow-up. (Note that this also creates another layer of administrative time/cost to the delivery of service.)

In this regard there are some pretty good rules to follow:

1. When you obtain verification of benefits for a client, get it in writing, as it is available online from the insurer. If you verify benefits with a representative, get his or her name. A badge number or employee identification number that would be helpful. If the representative gives you a first name only, ask for a last-name initial and ask if he or she is the only "Felecia R." in the department. Establishing a "therapeutic alliance," so to speak, with this person goes a long way down the road when correcting errors.

2. If you make an error, own up as quickly as you discover it. Often this becomes evident when you receive a payment that is more than what you billed. In one such error, a billing clerk entered the number 10, which was the code for location of service, into the column for number of units of service. The clinician then received a check for 10 times the actual service. In another case, where billing for members of a group clinic occurs, a billing clerk registered the proper procedure code, date, identifying data, and charges, except she forgot to change the name of the clinician for whom she had just finished billing and ended up billing under the wrong clinician's name. The tricky part to these errors is that the clinician will be asked to cash the check and the insurer will issue a letter asking for a refund for the incorrect payment or amount. It is important to document when and with whom you had this exchange, and it may be wise to inform the client lest he or she become concerned when he or she receives the explanation of benefits. The clinician's first impulse is to return the check, but for accounting purposes insurers will tell you it is easier for the insurer to follow the above-mentioned procedure.

3. When insurers make errors they may not be as gracious as clinicians in admitting an error. Be sure to have your facts straight. Errors include quoting wrong benefits (e.g., stating there is a deductible when there is not, or it has been met), misquoting the co-pay, or forgetting to inform you the client's benefits had terminated two months ago.

4. Errors also occur when an unmet deductible *has* been met during the interim between the initial benefit quote and your actual billing. When this occurs you will have to refund

the overcharge to the client or use it as a credit for future sessions (by mutual agreement with the patient). A word of advice here: Don't take the client's word that the deductible has been met from the cost of a recent procedure that easily outstrips the deductible amount. There is no telling when the other provider will bill for that procedure, and in the meantime your check will demonstrate that the deductible has not yet been met, so the fee paid to you is reduced by that amount Err on the side of the deductible not having been met for safety's sake. You can always refund the money should the opposite be true.

5. Establish a good working alliance with your client in regard to fees. Explaining that insurance companies sometimes make errors and indicating you will work with them to rectify those errors goes a long way in preventing patients from thinking someone is shortchanging them.

# THE USE OF A SLIDING FEE SCALE

Mental health professionals are typically encouraged to offer pro bono services such as helping in crises, giving lectures for groups, and volunteering in certain situations. In some circles, it is rumored that taking managed care fees *is* pro bono work. Humor aside, the question of sliding fee scales does arise. The following guidelines may represent a thoughtful consideration in this matter:

1. Sliding fee scales should be specified rather than arbitrary. Ordinarily the prime reason for offering a reduced fee is a client's financial hardship that would otherwise preclude his or her ability to receive needed services. In those cases, client income levels, adjusted for various factors (such as family size), could be written as a scale that is applied to fees as an established policy.

2. Remember, in your business you must maintain a significant income level. A failed practice due to insufficient capital helps no one in the end. Use of a sliding fee scale should be infrequent rather than common.

3. You cannot waive designated co-pays for insurance companies. These co-pays are intended as disincentives to use benefits or, put in a positive fashion, are designed to remind the patient that he or she has an investment in the treatment. When both the clinician and client have a contract with the insurance company, they must both fulfill their contractual obligations, and collecting co-pays is often specified in the contract with the insurer.

4. Community mental health centers are often available and referrals can be made for those unable to afford psychotherapy with you. These centers, as previously indicated, receive funds from endowments, charitable organizations, and the small fees their clientele can afford.

# THE USE OF COLLECTION AGENCIES

The short answer for this topic is to "just say no," but that isn't the only answer. Like any business where services sometimes go unpaid, there has to be some method to collect delinquent funds. When it comes to collecting fees, prevention is the best strategy. The first and best method in mental health care is to establish and maintain a good therapeutic alliance with clients so delinquent fees can be addressed as a therapeutic issue. Discuss fees and financial arrangements in the informed consent process and raise these issues with clients as needed over time. Include in the informed consent agreement a policy on a maximum outstanding balance allowed (e.g., the equivalent of the fees charged for three or four sessions). Never allow fees owed to accrue beyond that amount because as the balance due grows, it may become increasingly difficult to collect.

While we have the legal right to use a collection agency or file charges against a client in small claims court, such actions can be seen as antagonistic or threatening by clients and former clients. Individuals who had previously been satisfied with the treatment provided may now be very displeased and, in response to our collection efforts, file an ethics complaint or a licensing board complaint. And even in the case of frivolous complaints, we must respond, something that can be time consuming and costly in terms of time away from our practice and fees for an attorney to represent us at a licensing board hearing. Regardless of our view of the client's motivations or the legitimacy of his or her complaint, knowing that the licensure board will investigate it and take the matter very seriously, we must respond in kind. Failure to do so may result in an adverse action by the licensing board that could include fines, license suspension, or license revocation. Thus, a focus on prevention and avoidance of the use of collection agencies and small claims court is recommended.

# CONCLUDING THOUGHTS

Billing and fee collection are important issues, and every mental health clinician should give them careful attention. We must be able to collect the fees owed us so that we can pay our bills, salaries, and so on and our practice can stay in business. At the same time, our billing and collection practices must be done in accordance with our profession's code of ethics. We must continually strive to strike a balance between being a successful businessperson who is fairly compensated for the professional services we provide and ensuring that our clients receive needed services and that our fee and billing practices do not take advantage of them or violate the basic principles of our code of ethics.

# REFERENCES

American Association for Marriage and Family Therapy. (2012). *AAMFT code of ethics*. Retrieved from http://www.aamft.org/imis15/content/legal_ethics/code_of_ethics.aspx.

American Counseling Association. (2014). *ACA code of ethics*. Retrieved from http://www.counseling.org/Resources/aca-code-of-ethics.pdf.

American Psychological Association. (2010). *Ethical principles of psychologists and code of conduct*. Retrieved from http://www.apa.org/ethics/code/index.aspx.

CMS.gov. (2015). *Paul Wellstone and Pete Domenici Mental Health Parity and Addiction Equality Act of 2008*. Retrieved from https://www.cms.gov/CCIIO/Programs-and-Initiatives/Other-Insurance-Protections/mhpaea_factsheet.html.

National Association of Social Workers. (2008). *Code of ethics of the National Association of Social Workers*. Retrieved from http://www.socialworkers.org/pubs/code/code.asp

# CHAPTER 22

# THE BASICS OF MANAGED CARE AND ITS IMPACT ON PRIVATE PRACTICE

*Gordon I. Herz*

The earliest approach to group healthcare purchasing and delivery in the United States is reported to have occurred in 1928 in Elk City, Oklahoma, created by a physician named Michael Shadid (Potter, 2010). Dr. Shadid established a "cooperative" in which farmers and their families paid a monthly fee to obtain care at his clinic, also supporting his effort to develop a hospital and encourage medical specialists to come to this rural area. Within five years, it is reported that there were 600 subscribing families, along with several recruited medical specialists. Similar prepaid group plans were subsequently established in other locations, the names of which will sound familiar (e.g., Group Health, Kaiser), reaching increasingly larger numbers of enrollees.

In a theme that will seem very familiar and current, in 1973 the federal Health Maintenance Organization (HMO) Act attempted to "restrain the growth of health care costs and also to preempt efforts by congressional Democrats to enact a universal health care plan" (National Council on Disability, 2016, para. 4). The law included $375 million in "seed money" to establish HMO companies, overrode state laws that restricted prepaid plans, and required employers with 25 or more employees to provide an HMO option if workers were covered under employer-based health plans. "For profit" corporations that would focus on cost containment were born into a previously relatively nonprofit industry.

Two other noteworthy events occurred that continue to reverberate throughout healthcare in ways that directly impact mental health professionals. In the context of efforts to encourage the development of health insurance companies toward the end of World War II, the McCarran-Ferguson Act of 1945 was passed to specifically exempt insurance companies from federal antitrust scrutiny—which health professionals do not enjoy (Anderson, 1983). And, in *Goldfarb v. Virginia*

*State Bar* (1975), the "learned professions" were determined to have no antitrust exemption under the Sherman Antitrust Act of 1890. Even seemingly "independent" health professionals could be found liable if acting in an anticompetitive way, such as by restraining others' trade or promoting monopoly-like control in markets. This definitely extends to acting together to influence reimbursement.

These events created structural tensions between for-profit health insurers and health professionals that continue to this day, most directly in a "managed care" environment. The Patient Protection and Affordable Care Act of 2009 (ACA) and other reforms, such as federal mental health parity (Wellstone-Domenici Mental Health Parity and Addiction Equity Act, 2008), may have leveled the field to some extent.

# UNDERSTANDING MANAGED CARE

The definition of managed care depends to a great degree on one's perspective in relation to its pluses and minuses. Beyond the clinician/insurer/patient arrangement, with the intermediary functions by the insurance company, other companies evolved primarily to manage benefits, performing such activities as vetting, credentialing, and contracting with providers; determining "medical necessity"; paying, denying, or "repricing" claims (according the individual enrollee's policy); and monitoring clinician and patient adherence to policy requirements and, ostensibly, the "quality" of care. Generically, the companies are "managed care organizations" (MCOs) and, when focused on mental/behavioral health more specifically, "managed behavioral health organizations" (MBHOs). These are also known as "carve-outs," as they focus specifically on administering mental health benefits, carving out these particular benefits from each individual's overall healthcare insurance benefits. Over the years, mental/behavioral health benefits have been much more tightly controlled and managed than general medical health benefits, particularly with downward pressures on reimbursement and utilization (Herz, 2009).

Perhaps a most straightforward dictionary definition of managed care is apt, with a minimum of bias: a system of providing healthcare (as by a health maintenance organization [HMO] or a preferred provider organization [PPO]) that is designed to control costs through managed programs in which the physician accepts constraints on the amount charged for medical care and the patient is limited in the choice of a physician (Merriam-Webster, 2016). Insurance companies, of course, would emphasize patient choice and access to vetted and highly qualified professionals. Patient advocacy and professional groups would tend to emphasize limitations in access and intrusions into the doctor–patient relationship that could compromise treatment choices and privacy.

The U.S. National Library of Medicine articulated that managed care plans are:

> a type of health insurance. They have contracts with health care providers and medical facilities to provide care for members at reduced costs. These providers make up the plan's network. How much of your care the plan will pay depends on the network's rules. (U.S. National Library of Medicine, 2016, para. 1)

Three types of plans are identified: HMOs, PPOs, and point of service (POS). Each of these pays for varying levels of in-network versus out-of-network care. Plans with greater restrictions typically cost the purchaser less. Medicare has a "managed care" option called Medicare Advantage, described on its website as a type of Medicare health plan offered by a private company to provide hospital and doctors' services, including HMO, PPO, fee-for-service, and other structures, typically with prescription drug coverage (Medicare.gov, 2016).

The basic formula is an arrangement between three parties: patients (and often the employers who purchase policies for their employees) who purchase the coverage and receive healthcare; healthcare practitioners, who provide the services; and the insurance company, which contracts with healthcare practitioners to provide services to the patients to whom they sell coverage. The insurance company is an intermediary between patient and professional. The intermediary "services" are where the insurance company stands to profit, provided it can keep the costs of the professionals' services below amounts paid in by the patient/purchaser.

Those intermediary functions are where the crux of the tensions lie: decisions by you, the mental health professional, in relation to the extent you participate in such systems; decisions by patients related to the costs of purchasing the coverage in this manner (and whether there are any other options, such as patients purchasing services directly from professionals); and the restrictiveness versus flexibility of the plan in paying for the care patients desire. The insurer, of course, needs to maintain low enough costs to be profitable, while keeping the contracted professionals and purchasing patients happy. It is strongly in the interests of the insurance company to closely manage costs—to "manage care." The inherent conflicts of interest may be self-evident. Note the difference between this model and the first group care purchasing "Shadid" model, which was a more direct patient–professional dyad.

# PROS AND CONS FOR THE PRACTITIONER TO CONSIDER IN DECISIONS ABOUT PARTICIPATING

A managed care company may seek to contract with you as a provider, or you may seek to contract with a company to provide services. Advantages to the MCO or MBHO of seeking providers may include being able to expand the number of policy purchasers ("lives covered") to whom coverage can be sold, being able to better serve their current and expanding number of members, and being able to hold themselves out as engaging many well-qualified, vetted professionals. Advantages to the professional to contracting with an MCO could include expanding the number of patients who might be referred, seeking contract conditions that are favorable in terms of MCO expectations and reimbursement, and being able to hold oneself out to the public as having been vetted and qualified by companies that manage care for many people in one's community. Potential disadvantages for MCOs to increasing the number of providers include the costs of vetting and maintaining contracts with providers and accepting providers who may not follow contract requirements such as ongoing education, timeliness of access by referred patients, or recordkeeping, or who end up providing services "excessively" (e.g., more than typical as determined by the MCO for patient conditions or according to professional standards, thereby increasing costs to the company).

## THE CREDENTIALING PROCESS

Once a decision has been made to offer or seek a contract (become "empaneled") with the company, the professional will need to complete a credentialing process. Applications may be extensive, and the length of time needed to complete the process will vary from 30 to 45 days up to six months or longer. Fundamentally, professionals need to establish that they have appropriate education and training (degree), that they are licensed in their jurisdiction (typically at an independent level or with the level of supervision required by the license and professional services), that they have malpractice coverage at levels that are often specified by the MCO, and that they have had no prior "adverse events" (not meaning untoward patient outcomes but more typically defined as findings by an adjudicating body of improper practice) in terms of providing services. Advanced credentials such as board certification, or specialty services perhaps particularly desired by an MCO in a locale, may be to the applicant's advantage when seeking credentialing on an MCO's panel of approved providers.

Clinicians should be aware that not every MCO will be seeking, or accept, everyone who applies. Not infrequently panels will be "closed" to new applicants—potentially signaling that the MCO is attempting to minimize the disadvantages noted above or has sufficient numbers of providers to serve their subscribers. Many states now have "any willing provider" laws that require companies to accept every qualified applicant (National Conference of State Legislatures, 2014). These laws will interact with the requirements of ACA, which includes provision for "nondiscrimination in healthcare" (Section 2706), meaning that groups of licensed or certified providers (such as a particular profession) may not be discriminated against by insurance companies, although it does not mandate contracting with every willing provider. Meeting credentialing requirements does not guarantee that an applicant will be accepted, even if participation on a particular panel would be desired by the professional.

Similarly, by no means does an offer to apply mean that the professional has to accept or pursue this. Contracts "offered" tend to favor the MCO, which will say it is doing this for the advantage of its subscribers, and contract terms tend to be relatively fixed. But the professional has the choice to accept or reject contract "offers" and indeed should review the terms carefully and thoroughly. Some providers (e.g., Holstein, 2007) have been successful in negotiating modified terms, including reimbursement amounts.

## ISSUES RELATED TO CONTRACT REVIEW AND NEGOTIATION

Unless this is an area in which you have legal expertise—and even then the maxim about a person acting as his or her own attorney should be kept in mind—it is strongly recommended that mental health professionals have all contracts reviewed by an attorney specializing in this area of health-care law. The investment in this consultation will be well worth the possibility of preventing future problems. At the very least, a knowledgeable attorney will be able to advise the clinician whether the contract is relatively standard or has unusual requirements. Contracts will specify many expectations and aspects of the relationship between clinician and MCO, such as the length of time the professional will have obligations to the company and to their covered/referred patients (even, for example, after the contract ends, a "wind-down period"), how to ensure renewal of a contract, how to end the contact if it is no longer desired, how soon covered patients must be seen after referral (perhaps even the number of openings that should be made available for covered patients), recordkeeping and documentation requirements, collection and reporting of "quality" and outcomes measures, and allowed access for review of documentation by the company (perhaps even the potential for company representatives to visit the office/clinic setting). The clinician will certainly want to know all of these details before entering into a contract to ensure that the contract is acceptable and is not violated, intentionally or inadvertently.

On a contractual basis, MCOs likely will establish requirements for clinicians to submit treatment plans to be approved prior to initiating services that would be reimbursed (prior authorization). There likely will also be requirements to produce written progress updates—or participate in telephone reviews by case managers—during the course of treatment (concurrent reviews). Case reviewers/managers will have different levels and quality of mental health expertise, and this can at times be a frustrating process for the licensed professional who is fully focused on ethical and competent practice.

Typically the treatment record can be reviewed by the MCO during treatment as well as after treatment has ended, again for the company to determine whether services were "medically necessary" and documented according to agreed-on requirements. In the worst-case scenario for a clinician, services could retroactively be deemed to have not been "necessary" or correctly documented, and amounts reimbursed could be recouped (known as a "clawback"). Companies are now required to have processes in place for both internal and external reviews of "medical necessity" decisions, but recoupment (or withholding and application of payment to what would be approved reimbursement on new or other cases) could occur while such reviews are in progress and prior to a determination in response to an appeal. The contract will specify review and appeal procedures.

"Medical necessity" is a term that has had a quite fluid definition over the years and has been used at times by MCOs to deny coverage for treatment that professionals believe to be fully warranted based on case needs and professional standards, including egregious examples in mental health (e.g., NY Attorney General, 2014). A useful, consumer-oriented definition of medical necessity is,

> ...standards used by health plans to decide whether treatments or health care supplies recommended by your mental health provider are reasonable, necessary and appropriate. If the health plan decides the treatment meets these standards then the requested care is considered medically necessary. (National Alliance on Mental Illness [NAMI], 2016, para. 4)

Widely agreed-on standards of what is "necessary" tend to be less well established in mental/behavioral health services than in other areas of healthcare. This allows for "judgment calls" by both MCOs—which by definition emphasize minimizing their costs—and clinicians, who, even in the context of maintaining professional and fiduciary responsibilities to patients, may at times err in the direction of increased frequency or intensity of services (longer sessions, individual plus group sessions, testing when not indicated). It is strongly recommended that when becoming credentialed and before entering a contract, clinicians should ensure that "medical necessity" policies and procedures are in writing, transparent, and plain for the MCO, patient, and clinician to see. If these are not documented, circumstances may well be interpreted after the fact (e.g., after treatment has begun, is in progress, or has ended), and probably not to the advantage of the patient and clinician. For example, insurance companies may not consider marital or couples therapy to be "medically necessary," rather requiring a diagnosis of an individual. Similarly, "uncomplicated grief," premarital counseling, or client concerns about work-related issues may not meet medical necessity criteria. Health insurers typically do not consider assessment for academic needs such in learning disability to be sufficient for coverage, with the rationale that these are for academic and not health purposes. Unless specifically disallowed by the contract, such evaluations could be provided and directly billed to the client. Similar circumstances occur when assessments are for court and medicolegal purposes. Forensic assessments are almost never covered under a health insurance policy, as these are not deemed to be health-related activities, and services and costs may be arranged directly with clients. At a bare minimum, written medical necessity policies should specify which diagnoses are covered (or excluded); any limits on treatment frequency or levels of care (such as office, hospitalization, or specialty facility coverage); any special requirements for pre- or reauthorization of treatment for particular conditions or treatment types; and any limitations on treatment approaches allowed or disallowed. In the current context of the ACA (Healthcare.gov, 2016) and mental health parity, limitations and exclusions that are substantially different from those applied to medical care may be increasingly difficult to justify by MCOs, though clinician and patient appeals and enforcement will remain challenging.

## REIMBURSEMENT

One of the potential advantages of contracting with an MCO is the possibility of estimating numbers of referrals. One way to understand this is to ask the MCO how many policyholders ("covered lives") they have in the ZIP code or region where the clinician practices. Unless the clinician has particular expertise for which people will travel, one of the top considerations for those seeking care is convenience of location. Beware of MCOs that respond they "do not know" or are unwilling to provide the information. While watching their own corporate health, any sound MCO most definitely will know how many subscribers it has, and where they live. Most online searches for "find a therapist who specializes in X" will also include a component of the search "within Y miles of" an address or ZIP code. Indeed, the clinician will want to reasonably understand in advance the company's expectations for the numbers of subscribers the company will want to be seen, to ensure the clinician can meet those expectations.

Another advantage of contracting with an MCO is the ability to know in advance the reimbursement amount for specific services. Clinicians should not accept a contract without reviewing the current, to-be-agreed-on fee schedule. Avoid companies that will not provide this early during the process of deciding whether to apply to become empaneled. The clinician should determine whether the reimbursement offered meets the clinician's needs by performing all appropriate calculations. Practice cost factors could include major overhead expenses such as rent, employee salaries, purchased services such as billing and bookkeeping, and other costs, including projected likely future cost increases. MCO reimbursement is likely to show no or at best very minimal increases over time, probably not keeping pace with inflation. In terms of potential income implied by a contract, variables to consider could include such factors as the number of clients likely to be referred who are covered by the particular MCO and the number of appointments expected by contract to be made available for that population in relation to other referral source expectations, relationships, and reimbursement. Clinicians may have experiences at both extremes: too many clients referred for the clinician to reasonably provide care or that reduce access by other referral sources, to no clients referred at all covered by a particular payer. Remember, the MCO is in the position of keeping its enrollees satisfied by being able to readily receive services, and keeping the clinician panel happy with a predictable referral flow, while at the same time limiting its costs. Do not sign a contract without ensuring the attached fee schedule is the same as the one reviewed during the credentialing process, including all the same potential covered services.

As has been mentioned, some clinicians have successfully negotiated higher reimbursement rates for some services than the contract fee schedule in particular circumstances (Holstein, 2007). Such possibilities exist, for example, when a clinician has particular expertise sought by an MCO in a local area; when the company has insufficient numbers of clinicians in an region to serve its subscribers; when the clinician has an extended, favorable working relationship with an MCO (consider such at contract renewal); or when the clinician can demonstrate a particularly strong record of success with the MCO's referrals. Known local reimbursement rates, particularly those provided by other similar MCOs, are potentially very useful information for the clinician to have in such negotiations, to the extent these are known. Such numbers may be difficult to obtain, particularly as clinicians must be careful about openly sharing rates (remember the earlier mention of "anticompetitive" activity). Additionally, MCOs typically require clinicians to keep fee schedules confidential. Thus, even if a clinician holds contracts with several companies, it may not be possible to directly use such fee schedules in negotiations. Thankfully, data about national and regional charges and reimbursement are becoming more transparent and available in this era of big data, from public sources such as http://fairhealthconsumer.org/, or for purchase, such as http://pmiconline.stores.yahoo.net/mefe201.html.

# ANTICIPATING AND PREVENTING COMMON CHALLENGES

Assuming a successful credentialing and contracting process, ideally the clinician would begin to see clients covered by the MCO, provide and document services, successfully respond to prior and concurrent reviews, submit charges, and receive reimbursement in a timely manner. Yet, in each of these areas a number of common challenges may occur.

Suppose the clinician has a limited number of openings in the schedule in the near future. More new referrals are received than can reasonably be served. The clinician is well aware of the reimbursement amounts for clients referred, either covered by third-party payers or MCOs with which the clinician may hold contracts, or the full fee. Would it be proper to limit scheduling newly referred clients whose coverage is known to be less than others, or compared to those who might pay the full rate out of pocket?

First, recall that an MCO contract may well specify requirements for the timeliness with which covered individuals must be scheduled once a referral is received. This must be taken into account in accommodating new appointments, or there is the risk of violating a contract provision. All it would take would be for one or a few prospective patients calling a number of clinicians only to find they cannot actually make an appointment to complain to the MCO or possibly to the human resources department of the employer through whom their coverage was purchased, to raise awareness of specific clinician scheduling responses and availability. Worse, though the practice is rarer these days, MBHOs have in the past employed a "secret shopper" approach precisely to determine clinician/practice scheduling responses, with representatives posing as potential clients seeking services (http://www.socialworkers.org/pubs/news/2001/06/shopper.htm). From a business perspective, it may be a "good problem" to have an overflow number of referrals. But the clinician must know and honor the contractual timeliness and other availability requirements for scheduling, regardless of anticipated relative reimbursement.

A proactive solution would be to have a policy written in advance that specifies timeliness of scheduling, perhaps even the number or percentage of openings available to those with different resources, for example, including being seen on a pro bono basis, those with public insurance such as Medicaid, other third-party insurance, or out-of-pocket purchasers of service. This "payer mix" may reasonably be determined in advance, based entirely or in part on business factors, as long as this takes into account the requirements of existing contracts and is applied objectively to all new referrals.

What if a client is covered by one of the MCOs to which the clinician is contracted but says he or she cannot afford the required co-payment or co-insurance? ("Co-payment" is a set amount to be paid, such as $10 per visit. "Co-insurance" is a percentage of the amount the insurance company would reimburse, such as 20%.) May the clinician forego, or "write off," the co-payment/co-insurance amount?

Check the contract. In most cases, MCOs will not want clinicians to routinely waive co-payments or co-insurance. Insurance companies, and in some cases laws and regulations, might consider routine waivers to be "unfair" or even illegal "inducements." For example, if potential patients hear that you usually do not require co-payments, they might be more likely to seek you out rather than other clinicians. This potentially is an unfair practice that, from the MCO's perspective, could lead to patients using your services more than they might others, or more than necessary. Routine waivers of co-payments are flatly prohibited under Medicare (though "hardship" exceptions are possible periodically, based on objective criteria determined in advance and applied to all payers).

If allowed by the contract, then the clinician has the option to waive amounts for which patients are responsible. This still leaves the potential for intentional or unintentional bias about when and to whom to offer this "discount." In either event, a proactive approach again would be advisable.

For example, clinicians would do well to establish a policy, in advance and in writing, that could be part of a more complete informed consent and/or treatment agreement process. A policy that establishes how decisions are made about when patient amounts might be waived—with objective criteria such as defining financial need—would fully inform clients and allow the policy to be applied fairly and consistently.

What about "balance billing"? This would occur when the clinician's charge for a service is more than the amount reimbursed by the insurance company. May the clinician bill that difference directly to the patient? Again, this likely is specified in the contract. Some payers allow this, but many will not. This is another good example of the importance of understanding a contract in detail. A similar situation may occur if a clinician provides a service that is not covered under the policy, or for "no show" appointments. Is it possible for the clinician to directly bill the patient for these? In many cases, if a service is not covered under the insurance policy, clinicians may be allowed based on contract terms to make arrangements for service provision and billing directly with the patient. The potential to charge for missed appointments likely also will be specified in a contract.

# ETHICAL ISSUES AND DILEMMAS IN MANAGED CARE

Potential conflicts of interest and other dilemmas are inherent in the three-party arrangement between patient, insurance company (MCO, MBHO), and clinician. By contract, clinicians will be required to perform certain activities on behalf of the insurer. Patients, as purchasers of insurance policies, will be required to adhere to the terms of their policy. Clinicians will have responsibilities for clients based on licensure and other legal requirements as well as ethical standards. As businesspersons, professionals will certainly be mindful of the financial health of their practices, even extending to the implications of reimbursement in a particular case. These multiple roles and responsibilities are likely to conflict in a number of ways in this context.

For example, a clinician may diagnose a particular problem that, it turns out, is not reimbursable under a client's policy. There may be a temptation to "find" other diagnoses that are covered, though these otherwise would not be the focus of recommended assessment or treatment. It would be frankly improper to provide an unsupportable diagnosis, even though this might seem to be in the best interest of the client, who would have the cost of care covered, and also potentially to the benefit of the clinician, who might otherwise not be able to provide reimbursed services. (Recall, however, the prior discussion of the potential for direct-to-patient billing, if allowed by contract, for noncovered services or identified problems.) As language on the standard HCFA 1500 insurance form indicates, "Any person who knowingly files a statement of claim containing misrepresentation or any false, incomplete or misleading information may be guilty of a criminal act punishable under the law and may be subject to civil penalties." Federal laws would apply for insurance claims to federal programs, such as Medicare and its "managed care" version (Part C). All insurance companies would consider it potentially fraudulent to submit a claim with a diagnosis that did not exist. Most if not all health professional ethical standards would likely prohibit such a "false or deceptive statement" (e.g., section 5.01(a), American Psychological Association Ethical Principles and Code of Conduct, 2010).

Privacy and confidentiality are well-established foundations to successful mental health treatment, but in the managed care context, clinicians are required by contract to provide information, often in considerable detail, about clients' conditions, functioning, and progress in treatment. There is an inherent conflict in duties to clients, effective treatment, and contractual obligations to a third-party payer. In this instance, clinicians are reminded that clients, by virtue of their having purchased a health insurance policy, have already provided consent to the insurance company to obtain information from treating professionals in order to ensure the validity of claims. Of course, it may be argued that many consumers purchasing policies have not really provided fully informed consent about this possibility. The Health Insurance Portability and Accountability Act (HIPAA) also allows release of information for "treatment, payment and healthcare operations," which broadly would include claims submission and case reviews.

The proactive clinician will explain limits to confidentiality thoroughly to clients at the beginning of treatment, especially if claims will be submitted to an insurance company. Clinicians also would ideally review requests for release of records or clinical information when these occur, so that clients are involved in an ongoing way in the informed consent process. Client responses to release of information and the associated intrusion into the patient–clinician relationship may well become a focus of treatment at times. Other strategies in a managed care context have included having clients participate in live telephone case reviews, or reviewing and consenting to documentation provided. Additionally, using professionally driven documentation standards, for example by including only required elements in the formal record, reserving other information to "psychotherapy notes," as defined under HIPAA, has been recommended to minimize the extent of disclosures when these must occur (Herz, 2007).

One of the most vexing issues in working with managed care is when there is a difference of opinion between a case reviewer and the treating clinician about what is indicated—for example, the number or frequency of visits, continuing or ending treatment, whether or not testing might be necessary, or even the types of treatment approaches. Several considerations are worth bearing in mind. First, if clinicians are aware that such reviews and efforts to limit care seem to be occurring more intensively for mental health treatment than for reviews of medical care, there may be a pattern that violates federal requirements for equal treatment of medical and mental health benefits. In such cases, providing information to professional and other advocacy organizations—of course, with due consideration for patient confidentiality—may prove helpful to identify and intervene in potentially biased administration of benefits. For example, the American Psychiatric Association (2016) identifies how to report potential parity violations, and the American Psychological Association Practice Organization actively seeks reports of potential violations of the federal mental health parity law (http://www.apapracticecentral.org/update/2014/04-10/parity.aspx).

Second, clinicians will need to use their complete set of social skills, persuasive abilities, and knowledge base when interacting with reviewers. It may be natural to assume a defensive, adversarial approach when one's professional judgment and integrity seem to be questioned. Such a response is likely to work to the clinician's detriment, however, and potentially to the detriment of the client for whom the clinician is advocating services. Objective behavioral terms that will describe expected outcomes and potential improvements in a client's functioning—or prevention of a worsening condition potentially requiring more intensive (expensive) levels of service such as hospitalization—and reasonable timeframes are also advised in such interactions. Being able to refer to "evidence-based" reasons for recommended treatment may also be helpful.

Third, clinicians and patients certainly could pursue both internal and external review processes, to have other reviewers make a determination based on the facts. Finally, if reimbursement for care is denied either at the outset or during the course of treatment, this potentially places the clinician in the position of forgoing payment for services deemed by the clinician to be necessary, or having clients pay for services they thought would be covered. Clinicians should remember that initiating or continuing treatment certainly remains an option to be decided between clinician and patient. If an insurance company determines services not to be necessary, fundamentally this is a coverage and payment determination, not a decision about whether treatment is actually indicated, based on the clinician judgment in collaboration with the patient. A decision to move ahead with services, though not paid for by the insurer, is still available for the clinician and client. A payer's determination not to cover services may actually empower the clinician–client dyad to pursue their decisions. Ultimately, clinicians should not let insurance coverage and reimbursement decisions supersede their clinical judgment about clients' treatment needs. We should never abandon clients in need of treatment and can consider other payment alternatives, referrals to less costly treatment options, or continuing to provide needed treatment while adverse utilization review decisions are being appealed (see *Wickline v. State*, 1986).

# THE FUTURE OF MANAGED CARE

Micromanaging patient–clinician interactions adds costs for MCOs. Prior authorization, concurrent and post-treatment reviews, and similar activities are time consuming, labor intensive, and expensive. These may not save costs for the MCO by detecting or inhibiting "unnecessary" services. Up to now, common MCO strategies to maximize their own cost–benefit equation in such activities have included focusing greater attention on higher-cost services (such as hospitalization over outpatient visits), reducing or even eliminating the need for prior authorization, or allowing up to an established number of treatment visits before requiring review and reauthorization (Papatola & Lustig, 2015).

But healthcare delivery and payment systems are undergoing tremendous changes at this time, in the wake of the ACA, mental health parity, and other influences. Mental health and substance use disorder services are one of 10 categories of essential health benefits that health plans must now cover under the ACA (Healthcare.gov, 2016), including psychotherapy and inpatient treatment. Policies must cover preexisting conditions, and yearly or lifetime dollar limits are not allowed for mental health coverage. Coverage must also provide parity between mental health and medical/ surgical benefit limits, including financial limits such as deductibles, co-payments, co-insurance, and out-of-pocket costs, treatment limits such as number of days or visits covered, or "care management" such as prior authorization. The potential for MCOs to save costs by micromanaging these factors would appear to have become more limited, at least in relation to the management of other health conditions. On a broader level, the ACA requires (individual and small-group) insurance plans to spend to spend at least 80% of the premiums received for medical benefits (85% for large-group plans) or reimburse policy purchasers their share of premiums overpaid. In terminology that reflects the insurance industry's views of these amounts to be paid in healthcare benefits, this is called the "medical loss ratio" (MLR) (Congressional Research Service, 2014). Thus, there are a number of recent changes that would seem to limit costs savings by micromanagement of benefits.

How will companies limit expenses (maximize profits), and what are the implications for private practice? First, healthcare payment models are undergoing dramatic restructuring. Payers are identifying ways to shift "risk" (i.e., benefit payouts) to professionals. For example, groups of professionals might be paid an overall amount to provide services to an agreed-on number of patients over the course of a year. This may sound familiar to some as a previously much-reviled system known as "capitation," "based on a payment per person, rather than a payment per service provided" (see Capitation, American Medical Association), although attempts to build in important differences are now occurring. Should the clinicians sustain more costs when providing care than the total paid, clinicians would incur the losses.

Why would clinicians agree to this? Because the "carrots" on the other end of this arrangement could include bonus payments if costs of services are less than the total amount allocated. Insurance companies could provide incentive payments to clinician groups for cost containment, or for meeting other benchmarks such as collecting and reporting "quality" and outcomes data, and meeting health outcomes. Perhaps a group of clinicians might be expert and efficient at treating particular populations or conditions and able to closely estimate and contain its own costs. Such a clinician group might be able to estimate a total payment for the costs of care to which it could agree and work toward additional quality or other incentive payments for the total population. Such pay-for-performance or value-based care models are in full swing in accountable care organizations (ACOs) within Medicare as well as in the commercial insurance industry. At the end of January 2016, 838 ACOs were in operation, approximately 57% in Medicare and 43% in private insurance, in all states, an increase of about 13% from 2015, with about 28 million lives covered (Health Affairs, 2016). In March 2016, the U.S. Health and Human Services Department announced that fully 30% of $380 billion in projected Medicare payments were tied to "alternative payment models that reward the quality of care over quantity of services provided to beneficiaries" (HHS.gov, 2016, para. 1). Another estimate found that "90% of payers and 81% of providers are already using some mix of value-based reimbursement (VBR) combined with fee-for-service (FFS). . . . Providers using mixed models expect FFS to decrease from about 56% today to 34% five years from now" (McKesson Corporation, 2014, p. 5).

The implication for those in private practice is that mental health professionals should certainly take such systems into account for possible participation, referral, clinical activity, and payment resources. Given the recent and likely future growth, it may become nearly impossible to ignore such systems, particularly since 90% of U.S. citizens are now covered by insurance. Mental health professionals—even on an independent practice basis—certainly could join such organizations to provide clinical services, to serve in management, and to participate in other activities such as outcomes measurement and research. Such systems are actively collecting and reporting health outcomes data as well as fiscal outcomes, costs, and cost savings. Early results are mixed about which models might prove to fail or be most effective in improving patient experiences, population health, and reduced costs—the "triple aim" now being pursued amidst healthcare reforms (Institute for Healthcare Improvement, 2014). Note the key difference between the "triple aim"—with concurrent emphasis on quality for patients and improved health outcomes—and the prior single-minded focus on cost savings by managed care. It remains to be seen whether such systems will actually improve healthcare and maintain a focus on quality, without reverting to fixation on cost savings. But managed care likely will evolve away from the traditional methods of direct oversight of fee-for-service payment and activities to managing alternative payment models and measures of effectiveness and of value. Private practitioners likely will have to evolve in their understanding and work with such systems.

A further important change occurring in the context of healthcare system reform is the renewed interest in, and opportunities for, varieties of clinical/business entities owned and operated by health professionals, or other forms of integration among healthcare practitioners. These include "independent practice associations" and "member services organizations," or other arrangements such as co-location. Entities and arrangements such as these must certainly take into account state laws related to the corporate practice of medicine as well as federal requirements, including antitrust considerations, when independent practitioners coordinate services. Again, this is an area in which it would be essential to purchase expert legal consultation. But in the context of ACA and the increased emphasis on integrated and coordinated care, independent practitioners may have greater latitude than allowed by prior interpretations and enforcement of antitrust limitations. With proper clinical and financial integration, independently practicing mental health professionals may find much greater opportunities in the future to work together and with others toward common goals of improving care, saving costs, and increasing reimbursement than previously available. A number of such organizations are in operation around the country (e.g., Northwest Behavioral Health IPA, http://www.nwbhipa.org/; Rhode Island Primary Care Behavioral Health Network, http://www.ripcpc.com/about/behavioral-health-network). Indeed, mental health professionals could create, own, and operate systems of service delivery and reimbursement, for example by managing a local network of clinicians. Professionals could also create organizations that provide specialty care such as assessment, emergency care, and aftercare, or provide care more broadly, including efforts to contain costs and measure quality of services and outcomes.

Given that insurance companies will of course continue to manage costs, it is likely there will be increasing efforts for them to pursue contracts with larger groups of mental health professionals, rather than with many individuals. Independent practitioners will not be immune to contracting and service delivery issues, reimbursement negotiation challenges, and increasing practice costs that have contributed to the decrease from 57% of physicians in independent practice in 2000 to an estimated 33% by the end of 2016 (Accenture Consulting, 2015). There are likely to be ongoing clinical delivery, care integration, and cost-savings pressures for private practitioners. Solo and small-group independent practitioners may well find it necessary to form larger groups in the future. But such changes also potentially provide great opportunities to improve the care provided, to demonstrate one is doing so, and to increase leverage when negotiating reimbursement for one's value to systems of care. How to implement these changes in the context of independent practice will be the challenge of the future.

# REFERENCES

Accenture Consulting. (2015). The (independent) doctor will NOT see you now. Retrieved from https://www.accenture.com/us-en/insight-clinical-care-independent-doctor-will-not-see-you-now.

American Medical Association. (n.d.) Capitation. Retrieved from http://www.ama-assn.org/ama/pub/advocacy/state-advocacy-arc/state-advocacy-campaigns/private-payer-reform/state-based-payment-reform/evaluating-payment-options/capitation.page.

American Psychiatric Association. (2016). Mental health parity. Retrieved from https://www.psychiatry.org/psychiatrists/practice/parity.

Anderson, A. M. (1983). Insurance and antitrust law: The McCarran-Ferguson Act and Beyond. *William & Mary Law Review, 25*(1), Article 3. Retrieved from http://scholarship.law.wm.edu/cgi/viewcontent.cgi?article=2189&context=wmlr.

APAPracticeCentral.org. (2014). Retrieved from http://www.apapracticecentral.org/update/2014/04-10/parity.aspx.

Congressional Research Service Reports, Miscellaneous Topics. (2014). Retrieved from https://www.fas.org/sgp/crs/misc/.

FH Consumer Cost Lookup. (n.d.). Retrieved from http://fairhealthconsumer.org/.

*Goldfarb v. Virginia State Bar,* 421 U.S. 773 (1975).

Health Affairs.org. (2016). Accountable care organizations in 2016: Private and public-sector growth and dispersion. Retrieved from http://healthaffairs.org/blog/2016/04/21/accountable-care-organizations-in-2016-private-and-public-sector-growth-and-dispersion/.

Healthcare.gov. (2016). Essential health benefits—HealthCare.gov Glossary. Retrieved from https://www.healthcare.gov/glossary/essential-health-benefits/.

Healthcare.gov. (2016). Patient Protection and Affordable Care Act. Retrieved from https://www.healthcare.gov/glossary/patient-protection-and-affordable-care-act/.

Herz, G. (2007). To preserve, protect and defend (and simplify) documentation of psychotherapy. *Independent Practitioner, 27*(3), 136–139.

Herz, G. (2009). Reimbursement for psychologists' services: Trends, impact on access to psychologists, and solutions. Retrieved from http://www.drherz.us/blog42/ReimbursementAccessSolutions.pdf.

HHS.gov. (2016). HHS reaches goal of tying 30 percent of Medicare payments to quality ahead of schedule. Retrieved from http://www.hhs.gov/about/news/2016/03/03/hhs-reaches-goal-tying-30-percent-medicare-payments-quality-ahead-schedule.html.

Holstein, R. (2007). Make them (managed care) an offer they won't refuse: How to negotiate a raise. *Independent Practitioner, 27*(1), 23–24.

Paul Wellstone and Pete Domenici Mental Health Parity and Addiction Equity Act of 2008. H.R. 6983-110th Congress. Retrieved from https://www.federalregister.gov/articles/2013/11/13/2013-27086/final-rules-under-the-paul-wellstone-and-pete-domenici-mental-health-parity-and-addiction-equity-act.

Institute for Healthcare Improvement. (2014). A primer on defining the triple aim. Retrieved from http://www.ihi.org/communities/blogs/_layouts/ihi/community/blog/itemview.aspx?List=81ca4a47-4ccd-4e9e-89d9-14d88ec59e8d&ID=63.

McKesson Corporation. (2014). The state of value-based reimbursement and the transition from volume to value in 2014. Retrieved from http://mhsinfo.mckesson.com/rs/mckessonhealthsolutions/images/MHS-2014-Signature-Research-White-Paper.pdf.

Medicare.gov. (n.d.). Medicare Advantage Plans. (n.d.). Retrieved from https://www.medicare.gov/sign-up-change-plans/medicare-health-plans/medicare-advantage-plans/medicare-advantage-plans.html

Merriam-Webster. (2016). Definition of managed care. Retrieved from http://www.merriam-webster.com/dictionary/managed care

National Alliance on Mental Illness. (2016). What to do if you're denied care by your insurance. Retrieved from https://www.nami.org/Find-Support/Living-with-a-Mental-Health-Condition/Understanding-Health-Insurance/What-to-Do-If-You-re-Denied-Care-By-Your-Insurance.

National Conference of State Legislatures. (2014). Any willing or authorized providers. Retrieved from http://www.ncsl.org/research/health/any-willing-or-authorized-providers.aspx.

National Council on Disability. (2016). Appendix B. A brief history of managed care. Retrieved from https://www.ncd.gov/publications/2013/20130315/20130513_AppendixB.

New York Attorney General. (2014). A.G. Schneiderman announces settlement with health insurer that wrongly denied mental health benefits to thousands of New Yorkers. Retrieved from http://www.ag.ny.gov/press-release/ag-schneiderman-announces-settlement-health-insurer-wrongly-denied-mental-health.

Papatola, K. J., & Lustig, S. L. (2015). Managing managed care's outpatient review process: Insights and recommendations from peer reviewers at a health services company. *Professional Psychology: Research and Practice, 46*(3), 161–167.

Potter, W. (2010). *Deadly spin: An insurance company insider speaks out on how corporate PR is killing health care and deceiving Americans.* New York: Bloomsbury Press.

Socialworkers.org. (2001). "Secret shopper" to go. Retrieved from http://www.socialworkers.org/pubs/news/2001/06/shopper.htm.

U.S. National Library of Medicine. MedlinePlus. (2016). Managed care. Retrieved from https://www.nlm.nih.gov/medlineplus/managedcare.html.

*Wickline v. State.* Cal. Ct. App., 192 Cal. App. 3d 1630, 239 Cal. Rptr. 810 (1986).

# CHAPTER 23

# OPPORTUNITIES AND CHALLENGES OF MEDICARE

*Amy S. Rosett*

Medicare is the federal health insurance program for people aged 65 and older, and those with permanent disabilities, end-stage renal disease, or amyotrophic lateral sclerosis (ALS). Although it is widely used, it is poorly understood by beneficiaries, healthcare providers, and the general public. Since Medicare is a federal program, there are federal laws and regulations involved that are different than the rules of private health insurance. Periodically there are news stories about doctors leaving the program and disgruntled patients (Beck, 2013), and yet there are studies showing that (1) many providers continue to take Medicare patients (Boccuit, Fields, Casillas, & Hamel, 2015; Lieberman, 2013; Shartzer, Zuckerman, McDowell, & Kronick, 2013; Wasik, 2013) and (2) patients are highly satisfied with their Medicare insurance (Davis, Stremikis, Doty, & Zezza, 2012; Goforth, 2015). Finally, the program is often caught up in partisan politics; some legislators claim it cannot be sustained and should be dismantled whereas others want it to be expanded and available for all.

The number of Americans with Medicare coverage has been increasing steadily, especially as those in the "baby boomer" generation have been turning 65. Specifically, according to www.cms.gov, when Medicare reached its 50th anniversary in July 2015, over 55 million people were enrolled in Medicare. Furthermore, this number had increased by 3 million since 2012. Of historical interest, Medicare was started under President Lyndon Johnson's leadership as part of his social reforms. It was passed by Congress as Title XVIII of the Social Security Act, The Health Insurance for the Aged and Disabled Act, guaranteeing health insurance to those over 65 regardless of medical history or income.

An important issue for mental health professionals is whether the profession is ready to meet the growing needs of older adults. The Center for Workforce Studies of the American Psychological Association (APA), in its 2015 Survey of Psychology Health Service Providers (Stamm et al., 2016), found that 37% of licensed psychologists frequently or very frequently provided care to adults age 65 to 79 and an additional 25% did so occasionally. When asked about providing care to adults age 80 and older, only 9% reported doing so frequently or very frequently and an additional 17% did so occasionally. These data are consistent with the observations of many clinical geropsychologists that there is a growing need, and thus increasing work opportunities, for professionals with this interest and expertise.

Nearly all clinical geropsychologists and other health professionals who specialize in working with older adults are Medicare providers. The field has a number of subspecialties, including neuropsychological assessment, capacity evaluations, widowhood and grief, caregiver issues (including caregiving of others and the need for caregiving), promoting healthy aging, adjustment to changes in health and/or lifestyle, and diversity issues as related to older adults. For clinicians who have an interest in working in long-term care settings, such as skilled nursing and assisted living facilities, almost all the residents are Medicare beneficiaries. Several online resources provide more information about geropsychology, including www.gerocentral.org and www.pltcweb.org.

Colleagues sometimes state that they wouldn't want to be a Medicare provider because they don't want to work with "old people with dementia." This is a misguided assumption about working with these beneficiaries. People over the age of 65, and especially those in the first decade or so, often present with issues and lead lives that one would think of as being "middle-aged" rather than "elderly." There are many factors that contribute to this observation: People take better care of themselves and their health, and our culture today accepts that older people are working and living more actively. Frequent issues raised in psychotherapy by these "young older adults" include workplace stresses, even if it is ambivalence about retirement; parenting, even if it is about raising their grandchildren; concern about their parents who are still living in their late 80s and 90s; and wanting to reduce depression, anxiety, and a wide range of stresses.

Some psychotherapists recognize the importance of becoming a Medicare provider because they want to continue the clinical work with their current clients who are turning 65 years old. As described later, they could still opt out of Medicare and sign a contract to work together and be paid a private fee directly from the client. However, most Medicare beneficiaries want to use their health insurance rather than pay out of pocket. This is especially true if they had been submitting superbills to their previous health insurance company for partial reimbursement of their psychotherapy.

Since Medicare also covers people with a permanent disability of any age, providers do not necessarily work with older adults. Often, clients with disabilities have chronic medical needs and will benefit from treatment by health-oriented clinicians. With the current emphasis and growing opportunities within integrative care, psychotherapists interested in working in medical settings will very likely meet clients who have Medicare as their insurance. Medicare beneficiaries are likely to be seen by other specialties such as neuropsychologists and rehabilitation psychologists and social workers. Even children and adolescents with chronic illnesses and on the autism spectrum might qualify for Medicare.

Overall, there are many people with a great number of mental health needs for evaluation and treatment who seek the services of Medicare providers. Furthermore, physicians who appreciate the value of psychological and neuropsychological evaluations and treatment are often looking for psychologists and clinical social workers who are Medicare providers. If mental health providers network with physicians and other professionals who work with Medicare beneficiaries, it can be a relatively smooth process to build and sustain a private practice. Incidentally, at present licensed marriage and family therapists and licensed professional counselors cannot be Medicare providers.

Federal law requires that all physicians and other healthcare professionals who provide services to Medicare beneficiaries either enroll in Medicare or formally opt out of the program. Those who decide to opt out must still follow specific guidelines, including having clients sign a contract that neither they nor the healthcare provider will bill Medicare for the services. This law is one that many psychologists and clinical social workers are not aware of or ignore. It is an important decision to either enroll in or opt out of Medicare as a provider. One intention of this chapter is to offer a basic understanding of the program so that readers will be able to make an informed decision, taking into account their clinical interests and work experiences. Thus, this chapter will explain how the program is structured and both the opportunities and challenges of being a Medicare provider.

Although the information here has been researched to ensure it is current and accurate, aspects of Medicare change over time. Also, despite the fact that Medicare is a federal program, aspects of the program vary by state. Periodically the information provided by Medicare has a disclaimer that it is not a legal document and is subject to change. The same is true for this chapter. Although the basic structure of Medicare has been consistent over many years, it is likely that the laws and regulations regarding it may change, so readers should seek updated information.

## STRUCTURE OF MEDICARE

Medicare is the federal health insurance program for people who are 65 and older, people of any age with permanent disabilities (defined as being on Social Security disability for at least 24 months), and people with end-stage renal disease or ALS. It is administered by the Centers for Medicare and Medicaid (CMS). CMS contracts with insurance companies, referred to as Medicare Administrative Contractors (MACs), to provide most services, including processing claims, enrolling healthcare providers, handling claims appeals, answering beneficiary and provider inquiries, and detecting fraud and abuse. As defined in the Social Security Act, CMS has both national coverage determinations (NCDs) and local coverage determinations (LCDs). Most mental health services fall under LCD, which means that each MAC can determine whether a particular service is covered. The MAC for a particular location can be found on cms.gov or www.gerocentral.org. Incidentally, Medicare uses so many acronyms that one can search "Acronyms" on www.cms.gov to view pages of them arranged alphabetically.

Medicare coverage is separated as follows: Part A—Hospital Insurance, Part B—Medical Insurance, Part C—Advantage plans, and Part D—Prescription plans. The services provided by psychologists and social workers fall under Part B as "fee-for-service." In the past few years, CMS documentation often refers to the coverage provided under Parts A and B as "traditional" and/or "original" Medicare. These terms are used to distinguish this coverage from "Advantage" plans. Medicare Advantage (MA) plans are offered by private insurance companies to cover the benefits of Parts A and B. More information about the MA plans will be given later in this chapter.

Psychologists and social workers are required to "accept assignment" for all Medicare services. This means that they agree that the Medicare-allowed charge is the full payment for any service. The reimbursement for each service is determined by a complex formula that considers technical skills, risks and costs to the provider, and geographical region. The amount allowed can be found on the website of the MAC, under Medicare Physician Fee Schedules (MPFS). According to the website of Noridian, one of the MACs, over 7,400 unique services are covered in this schedule; the services reimbursable to psychologists and social workers are listed by the CPT code. Also on the Noridian website, below the MPFS is a tab labeled "Allowed Amount Reductions." The reimbursement reductions pertinent to mental health services will be explained in the "Challenges" section.

Beginning in 2014, Medicare pays 80% of the total allowed charge; this percentage increased gradually from 50% over the previous four years. By increasing to this level, there is no longer a disparity between mental health and non–mental health services. Who pays the remaining 20%, which is referred to as the co-insurance or co-pay? Technically it is the client's responsibility, so most clients also purchase a supplemental insurance plan. Although this is a dated term, sometimes clients refer to these plans as "Medi-gap" plans since they cover the gap between what Medicare reimburses and what is owed to the provider.

Numerous insurance companies offer Medicare Supplemental plans. A provider does not have to be "in-network" with the company in order to get paid the full amount due. For nearly all states, the plans, which are identified by a letter, vary in terms of coverage and benefits; the website www.cms.gov has a helpful tutorial that details this information. For practical purposes as a provider, it is helpful to know that if a client's supplemental insurance falls under "Plan F" (which is not always marked on the supplemental insurance card), then the annual deductible for Medicare Part B services will be covered.

In 2016 the annual deductible rose to $166 after being $147 for several years. Although these deductible amounts are significantly lower than those for most private insurance companies, Medicare beneficiaries usually do not expect to have to pay anything to their healthcare providers. Nonetheless, it is both allowed and appropriate to be paid directly by the client if the allowed amount is not fully covered by CMS or a supplemental plan. In addition to having an annual deductible, beneficiaries pay a monthly premium for Medicare Part B, which is usually deducted from a person's monthly Social Security benefits. Knowing such facts is important for both providers and clients: Providers should know what they are expected to be paid, but also it is reassuring to the beneficiaries that providers understand how Medicare works.

To provide guidance to Medicare beneficiaries, it is helpful to build a good working relationship with a reputable insurance agent who has specialized knowledge about the Medicare plans and regulations. There are numerous plans with slight differences in coverage. Also, there are only specific times in the year when Medicare patients can purchase and change their plans. Under specific conditions, if a person delays enrolling in Medicare, there will be additional costs.

If a client has not purchased a supplemental plan or the supplemental plan does not cover 100% of the co-pay, the client is expected to pay the amount due. This is how Medicare defines the term "balance billing." Within the field of psychotherapy, the term "balance billing" sometimes is referred to as billing the difference between the amount paid by insurance and the psychotherapist's full fee. However, this is not allowed within Medicare since psychologists and social workers cannot collect any fees beyond the allowed amount.

In the past few years some insurance companies have offered "high-deductible supplement" plans with much lower monthly costs. As the name implies, clients have to pay the 20% co-pay until they reach a specific out-of-pocket expense and then the plan begins to pay. This plan might make sense for someone with limited financial resources and excellent health who might not incur many medical costs. Another possibility is that a past and/or current employer may provide Medicare supplemental insurance as an employee benefit. However, these plans may not cover the full 20% of the co-pay.

At least one major private insurance company offers a supplement plan that is marked both "PPO" and "Exclusive Provider Organization" on the front of the card. Although stating "PPO" (preferred provider organization) would lead many to assume that it would cover any Medicare provider, the term "Exclusive Provider Organization" means that it is actually similar to a health maintenance organization (HMO) and covers the co-pay only if the clinician is also an in-network provider with the company. Sneaky, yes; allowed, apparently. It seems that such obfuscating rules occur more when working with private insurance; in general, Medicare rules and fees are more transparent.

Issues of insurance coverage, Medicare or otherwise, should be discussed openly, preferably during the initial phone contact or certainly during the first session. Most psychotherapists state their fees in their forms to consent for treatment. Striking through the full fee and writing something like "Will accept Medicare and Supplement (or co-pay of $XX) as full fee" with your initials can be a reassurance for the client and a protection for the provider.

Medicare does have one exception to this rule: The client is not responsible for the 20% co-pay if there is severe financial need, which includes having Medicaid. These clients are commonly referred to as "Medi-Medi." They are also referred to as "dual eligible" since they qualify for both federal government programs. Specific rules prohibit Medicare providers from "balance billing" Medi-Medi clients.

Medicaid is administered by the states and there are wide differences in how plans are structured. Therefore, whether or not a Medicaid program will cover the 20% co-payment for a Medi-Medi beneficiary varies among the states. Even within one state, whether the co-payment is covered might depend on other factors. Thus, providers should consult their state's Medicaid program to clarify if there will be any coverage. If the Medicaid program does not cover the co-payment, the provider will still be paid the 80% of the allowed amount by Medicare.

CMS has recently started the Medicare-Medicaid Coordination Office in order to improve the services available to dual-eligible clients throughout the country. The goal is to provide coordinated medical, behavioral health, long-term institutional, and home- and community-based services. For example, in California there is now a voluntary program called Cal MediConnect, which is part of the Coordinated Care Initiative. Some Medi-Medi beneficiaries are placed in managed care health plans, which are expected to offer more comprehensive and accessible services. However, these clients might not be able to continue treatment with their Medicare providers, including psychotherapists, if they are not in-network with the managed care plan. The program does allow them to disenroll and continue to have both traditional Medicare and Medicaid. Both options have benefits and limitations, so each client will have to decide based on his or her individual needs.

A nonpartisan, nonprofit organization, Center for Medicare Advocacy, Inc., offers more detailed information regarding coverage, rights of beneficiaries, costs, and legal matters. Started by one attorney in 1986, it is now staffed by attorneys, advocates, nurses, and technical experts. The group's website, www.medicareadvocacy.org, is an excellent resource for both Medicare beneficiaries and healthcare providers.

# BEING A MEDICARE PROVIDER

Psychologists and social workers who decide to become Medicare providers will be in demand, especially as the number of beneficiaries increases. The regulations, expectations, reimbursements, and limitations for providers are available. Unfortunately, many times they are described using terms and acronyms that can make them seem more complicated than they actually are. This section of the chapter will demystify the process by offering straightforward explanations and practical guidance about working within the Medicare system.

### ENROLLING

Medicare has slightly different rules for psychologists and social workers with regard to providing mental health services; these are outlined in a booklet titled "CMS Mental Health Services" that can be accessed on www.cms.gov. One advantage of Medicare, as opposed to many private insurance companies, is that it will accept any willing psychologist or social worker who meets the educational and licensing criteria as described in the booklet. Providers can apply right after they are licensed; in contrast, some private insurance companies allow applicants to apply to be in-network providers only after have been licensed for two years.

Becoming a Medicare provider begins with enrollment. The regulations about enrolling or opting out are found at www.cms.gov. The links to the provider enrollment form and the opt-out affidavit are on the websites of each MAC. Providers can enroll either through the Internet-based Provider Enrollment, Chain and Ownership System (PECOS) or by downloading the form called CMS-855I, completing it, and mailing it in with the supporting documents. The faster PECOS system allows providers to enroll, make any changes, view their enrollment information on file, or check on the status of an application via the Internet. For more information, search PECOS on www.cms.gov to access "The Basics of Internet-Based Provider Enrollment, Chain and Ownership System (PECOS) for Physicians and Non-Physician Practitioners."

Medicare providers sometimes complain about delays in being accepted in the program. However, in nearly every situation the reason is that the person made at least one error when completing the application. Therefore, regardless of how the application is submitted, the provider should fill in every question while talking on the telephone with a customer representative from the enrollment department of his or her MAC. This will increase the likelihood that the application will be processed efficiently. Overall, the CMS application form might seem long, but actually many of the pages are not relevant to psychologists or social workers.

Prior to applying, it is important to have the following: (1) an office address, which cannot be a post office box and should not be your home address since it will be listed on the website for the public, listed on www.Medicare.gov; (2) a copy of Internal Revenue Service documentation proving you have a tax identification number (TIN); (3) a National Provider Identifier (NPI) number; (4) a bank account for your business for the electronic transfer of funds (ETF), and this information will be in the Electronic Funds Transfer Authorization Agreement (CMS-588 form); and (5) a copy of your doctoral diploma for psychologists or master's diploma for licensed clinical social workers. There is a question on the application about the provider's specialty; licensed psychologists should mark only "Psychologist, clinical" and not "Psychologist billing independently," even though both categories might seem accurate.

Medicare regulations authorize clinical psychologists to (a) provide "physician" services consistent with their state laws; (b) have employees provide services to their Medicare clients under "Incident to" rules, described later in this chapter; (3) provide professional services without physician supervision, involvement, or oversight; and (d) perform and supervise psychological and neuropsychological testing without a physician's order. In contrast, independently practicing psychologists have more limited benefits. For example, any testing must be ordered by a physician or clinical psychologist, they cannot supervise testing done by others, and their work within facilities is more restricted. Also, independent psychologists are not listed as providers on the website used by the general public to find providers, which can be a good source for referrals.

Also, it is highly recommended to use a billing service, the Medicare portal, or a billing clearinghouse. Any of these services allow providers to submit their billing electronically; the advantages of doing this are discussed later in this chapter. Providers will need information about the selected billing service for the application. This can be added at a later date if you are unsure about using such a service.

The effective date of filing an enrollment application is the date the MAC receives all the information for verification. Once approved, a Provider Transaction Access Number (PTAN) will be assigned. This might happen before the application process is completed. Once the PTAN is received, the provider should confirm with his or her MAC the date he or she can begin to work with Medicare clients and the date when billing can be submitted.

## PROVIDING SERVICES

Medicare requires that all services meet "medical necessity." Throughout CMS documentation, this is described as items and services that are reasonable and necessary for the diagnosis or treatment of an illness or injury. Psychological assessments and interventions are covered services. In fact, Medicare recognizes the importance of services to maintain progress and to prevent decompensating, such as avoiding a psychiatric hospitalization. There are no restrictions on a psychotherapist's orientation or specific interventions. Mental health services do not need to be preauthorized, are not limited to a specific number of sessions, and are not routinely reviewed by CMS. Covered services include individual, family, and group psychotherapy, as well as hypnotherapy, biofeedback therapy, and psychoanalysis. Incidentally, family therapy, which includes couples therapy, is allowed when the primary purpose is treatment of the client's condition, while marriage counseling is not covered.

Health and Behavior (H&B) interventions have been allowed by CMS since 2002. The treatment focuses on the psychological factors that influence or interfere with physical health problems. The goal of the treatment is to improve the client's health and well-being, with the focus on the biopsychosocial factors of a physical illness. H&B interventions often involve collaboration with the primary care physician and thus might be particularly appropriate when working in an integrative healthcare setting. Likewise, since Medicare clients often have significant medical problems, due to age or being on permanent disability, allowing H&B services expands the range of services mental health providers can provide. A clinical example of when H&B interventions might be appropriate would be a referral from an endocrinologist of a diabetic patient who refuses to comply with dietary restrictions. In psychotherapy the provider could address any underlying psychological factors as well as needed behavioral changes.

Medicare also covers psychological, neurobehavioral, and neuropsychological assessments. Dr. Antonio Puente, a highly respected neuropsychologist and the American Psychological Association's 2017 president, has extensive information, including approximately 50 slides on the Medicare requirements for assessments; his website is www.psychologycoding.com.

Medicare specifies that there should be a "reasonable expectation of improvement." Thus, the provider should consider and document if the client can benefit from services during the initial evaluation. This issue should be periodically addressed in the session notes, especially if the patient has any cognitive impairment.

Medicare often denies psychotherapy services for clients diagnosed with dementia, while allowing neuropsychological assessments and psychiatric medication evaluations. However, if a person presents with symptoms of early dementia, the psychotherapy usually focuses on problems associated with the cognitive decline, such as an adjustment disorder, anxiety, or depression. Thus, the provider should diagnose and bill accordingly. Frankly, psychotherapy is not going to "treat" the dementia per se. Both legally and ethically, the client should be able to benefit from services, so psychotherapy should be discontinued if the dementia progresses to a level that this standard cannot be met.

Telepsychology, defined as the use of communication technologies to provide psychological services, is allowed by Medicare but only under specific conditions, and this may limit its usefulness. It is restricted to rural communities. The client must go to an "originating site" and not stay at home for the session. The sites must be approved by CMS; examples include doctors' offices, community clinics, and hospitals. The provider must use an interactive audio and video telecommunications system that provides real-time communication. Medicare does not reimburse for sessions via telephone.

Medicare does have some specific different rules for psychologists and social workers; these are described in detail on www.cms.gov in the booklet titled "CMS Mental Health Services." Although psychologists work independently, CMS expects them to consult with each client's primary care physician about the psychological services being provided and to do so only with the consent of the client. The chart should include the date the client did or did not give consent, as well as the date the consultation occurred. If the consultation does not happen, the psychologist should still record the date and how the physician was notified. This communication attempt is not required when the client's primary care physician made the referral. This rule might be considered a safeguard to ensure that the client's care is coordinated and/or an implicit presumption that the physician is treated with greater regard in the healthcare system. Similar rules are not described for social workers.

## DOCUMENTATION

Every billed service must have documentation that can stand on its own to meet the criteria of medical necessity. Therefore, the documentation for any service should include (a) an evaluation of symptoms necessitating the service, (b) an appropriate diagnosis, and (c) a treatment plan that addresses the therapeutic modalities and interventions the provider intends to use in order to meet the goals of the treatment. It is also important that the diagnosis and CPT procedures on the billing claim be consistent with what is documented in the client's chart.

When conducting the evaluation, the provider might find that the client does not meet the criteria for services or cannot benefit from psychotherapy. This should be documented in the initial evaluation and no additional services would be provided under Medicare. Nonetheless, if the provider is to be reimbursed for the evaluation, there would need to be a diagnosis rather than a Z code. Z codes are conditions that are not mental disorders and yet might be a focus in the evaluation and treatment because they contribute to a person's functioning; two examples include "parent–child relational problems" and "acculturation problems." For each situation the provider would have to decide if ethically there is an appropriate diagnosis in order to be reimbursed.

Since the CPT codes 90832, 90834, and 90837 for individual psychotherapy services are based on the number of minutes of "face-to-face" time spent with the patient, Medicare expects that the provider will record the time spent with the client. The provider should write down the exact start and stop times to fulfill this requirement. Incidentally, these codes correspond to 16 to 37 minutes, 38 to 52 minutes, and greater than 53 minutes, respectively.

If CMS audits a session note, one focus will be if the recorded time matches the CPT code used on the billing claim form. If the session is billed at a greater time than the time recorded, it is referred to as "Upcoding." "Downcoding" occurs if a session is billed as shorter that what is documented in the record. CMS also refers to "Miscoding" services when no time is documented. If this happens, the session is reimbursed at the lowest possible time period, namely 90832. Miscoding of individual psychotherapy services also occurs when the notes indicate that the actual services were not individual psychotherapy but instead a different type of service, such as an assessment or group psychotherapy.

Each psychotherapy session and the corresponding note must demonstrate medical necessity by documenting current symptoms observed and/or reported by the client, including quotes when appropriate. There is no required format for charting. However, notes that are strictly narrative might omit necessary criteria, which can be problematic if audited. To meet the requirements of Medicare, it is important to include the following: face-to-face time of the session, modality, frequency, results of clinical tests, functional status, medication monitoring, a diagnosis, symptoms, treatment goals, interventions, and progress to date. Many clinicians also include the client's responses to the interventions, progress to date, prognosis, and plan for ongoing treatment, which can be as simple as referring to the next scheduled appointment. The documentation should show continuity from one session to the next.

## BILLING AND REIMBURSEMENT

Medicare reimbursement fees might be considered moderate to many professionals. Of course this depends on factors such as their years in practice, geographical location, and demands for their services. Nonetheless, Medicare reimbursement rates are almost always better than or equal to most private insurance in-network fees.

Medicare strongly encourages providers to submit billing electronically. Services are billed using the HCFA 1500 claim form. Claims will be accepted up to one year after the date of service, but providers are encouraged to bill much sooner. Should there be any problems with the coverage of either Medicare or the supplemental plan, this will be discovered only when the claim is processed. Providers should use a billing clearinghouse, Medicare's portal system, or a professional biller. When bills are submitted electronically, Medicare will reimburse the 80% of the allowed fee via electronic funds transfer within 15 days, as is required by federal law.

Providers may submit paper claims if there are fewer than 10 full-time employees who are Medicare providers in their practice. However, there are several disadvantages to using paper claims: (a) the information has to be entered each time, (b) there is no check for errors prior to submitting the claim form, and (c) the claim will take approximately 30 days to be reimbursed. Apparently, Medicare has started to scan all non-electronic claims and then they are processed by a computer. If the form is not legible enough for this system, the claim may be returned and the reimbursement will be delayed.

As of October 2007, providers may charge a Medicare client directly for missed appointments. It is important to explain this in advance, such as when reviewing the informed consent policy, commonly during the first session. Medicare does not make any payments for missed appointments, and thus neither the provider nor beneficiaries can submit billing for missed appointments to Medicare.

## OPTING OUT OF MEDICARE

A psychologist or social worker might decide not to enroll in Medicare and prefer to opt out. This is done by submitting an affidavit form, which is located on the MAC's website; providers can find the list of the MAC websites by searching on www.cms.gov or www.gerocentral.org. A private contract must be signed between the professional and the beneficiary that explicitly states that neither one can submit billing to or receive payment from Medicare; instead, the beneficiary pays the clinician out of pocket. The exact wording and requirements for the private contract can also be found on the MAC's website. In 2015 there were several changes in the law related to Medicare, including that a provider now needs to opt out only once, rather than every two years. However, the contract with the beneficiary still must be signed every two years. A provider who decides to enroll in Medicare after opting out should contact his or her MAC for the exact rules for and time periods when this can happen.

Mental health professionals often ask how Medicare knows if they enrolled or opted out. Consider a psychologist or social worker who does not want to accept Medicare reimbursement and also does not know that he or she should opt out. The provider has not had his or her clients who are Medicare beneficiaries sign the private contact that specifies that they will not bill Medicare directly. Uninformed, the client, or someone on the client's behalf, might decide to submit his or her billing to Medicare for reimbursement. The CMS computer system will recognize that a provider has neither enrolled nor opted out of the program. The provider would likely receive a letter instructing him or her to reimburse the client all the fees collected or threatening him or her with large fines if he or she fails to enroll or opt out. These letters seem to vary depending on the MAC and the LCD policy.

# CHALLENGES

Medicare can seem like a daunting, highly regulated insurance system, especially when a clinician does not understand how it works. However, guided by the belief that "knowledge is power," understanding the potential challenges can help the provider be prepared for them. By including this section, it is expected that potential providers can make a more informed decision about enrolling in or opting out of the program.

## POLITICS

Since Medicare is a federal program, it involves politics. In Congress one party generally favors traditional Medicare and the other generally favors Medicare Advantage plans. The Center for Medicare Advocacy, www.medicareadvocacy.org, provides excellent information about this issue. According to its website, there is a concern that Congress may address proposals to shift Medicare to a voucher system to purchase private insurance and other proposed changes to traditional Medicare. Some providers appreciate certain advantages of being a Medicare provider rather than being an in-network provider for a private insurance company, such as the transparency of rules and fees. Thus, there is concern that traditional Medicare might be replaced with vouchers for private insurance companies.

As of April 1, 2013, CMS began paying 2% less than the MPFS due to the federal requirement under sequestration, as approved by Congress. This reduction applies only to the 80% of the total allowable fee. Three years later, sequestration is still in effect "until further notice." This is an example of how a political decision can be discouraging to Medicare providers.

For nearly two decades, reductions in the reimbursement rates to Medicare providers were often threatened as the result of a flawed plan to control spending on physician services, known as the Sustainable Growth Rate (SGR), which was part of the Balanced Budget Act of 1997. It was informally called the "Doc Fix" because if triggered, it could have required a significant cut to the reimbursements to providers. Some years the reduction was projected to be over 25%. Although widely recognized as problematic, including by both Democrats and Republicans in both the

House of Representatives and the Senate, for many years there were only temporary stopgap measures passed. Often these measures were part of other political bills that passed just days before, and even occasionally after, the SGR cuts were scheduled to occur. This created a stressful situation, discouraging some psychologists and social workers from enrolling as Medicare providers.

The Medicare Access and CHIP Reauthorization Act of 2015 (MARCA), which was signed into law in April 2015 with overwhelming support in both the Senate and the House of Representatives, included a permanent repeal of the SGR. MARCA stabilized the current reimbursement rates, although it permitted only slight increases between 2015 and 2019. It also included a new system of reimbursing providers with both incentives and reductions for quality performance.

The new plan, called the Merit-Based Incentive Payment System (MIPS), will incorporate (1) the Physician Quality Reporting System (PQRS), which will be outlined below, (2) a Value-Based Payment Modifier, and (3) a system for incentivizing the use of certified electronic health records. At the time of writing this chapter, details of the MIPS system are open for public comment. Therefore, the exact details are unclear; as they develop, the information will be available on www.cms.gov.

In general, it is important to recognize that Medicare will be shifting toward increasing the exchanging of client information among providers. Psychologists and social workers might find some of these expectations contrary to the ways in which clients' confidentiality and privacy are protected. After such programs are more clearly defined, each individual provider will have to decide if he or she will participate.

## QUALITY PAYMENT PROGRAMS

In the past few years, if you asked any provider about the greatest challenge of working within Medicare, it is very likely that the response will be "PQRS." The PQRS applies to nearly all providers, whether they are physicians or eligible providers, including psychologists and social workers. Overall, Medicare is moving away from paying providers a fee just based on time spent with clients. The goal is to focus on quality by having providers perform brief assessments relevant to their specialization.

One hears about primary care physicians having very brief appointments, such as annual examinations lasting under 15 minutes. The concern is that such brief visits might miss important health concerns and risks. By encouraging providers to assess their clients more thoroughly, Medicare is moving toward increased accountability of providers. Thus PQRS attempts to monitor if providers are doing their due diligence. As psychologists and social workers, we spend much more time with our clients than most other providers and ideally ask about a number of psychological and health-related issues. Therefore, using these measures may not seem necessary. However, Medicare doesn't distinguish between specialties with regard to the overall structure of the system, so this includes following the same regulation for all Medicare providers.

PQRS started with only "incentive payments" (awarding bonuses) for satisfactory participation. Beginning in 2013 "payment adjustments" (imposing penalties) for the failure to successfully report on PQRS measures was added. Starting in 2015, there were only penalties and no longer bonuses. The penalty is a reduction of 2% of all MPFS allowed charges for the calendar year two years after the year the provider did not participate in PQRS. Thus, if a provider who did not report PQRS measures in 2014 had a 2% reduction in all reimbursements in 2016, regardless of participation in 2015 and/or 2016.

One of the biggest challenges with PQRS is that the instructions for participation are detailed and poorly explained in any CMS documentation reviewed to date. CMS contacted providers at the end of 2015, informing them that they will receive the 2% cut because they had not participated in 2013. However, there was not a concerted effort to inform them of this in 2012 or even in early 2013 so that they could learn what to do in order to avoid this cut. Many providers report being frustrated and dismayed by the lack of communication and education about PQRS. Often they just assume that it is "only 2%" so they don't bother to participate.

Furthermore, the required number of measures to be submitted increased dramatically. In 2013 the minimum amount to avoid the penalty cut was completing only one measure on at least one client, although providers still had to understand PQRS in order to fulfill this requirement. In 2014 the minimum level of participation increased to reporting on three measures for at least 50% of "applicable" patients seen during the calendar year. Then in 2015 (and for 2016), the number of measures tripled to nine measures. In addition, many providers complained that participation is difficult and time-consuming. Although it does take time to learn how to comply with the requirements, actually doing the measures with clients can take just a few minutes, and all but one of the measures for psychologists and social workers are administered only once a year. Nonetheless, unless the provider learns the details of PQRS from someone with a strong knowledge of the system, it is extremely difficult to comply and thus a great challenge for Medicare providers.

In the spring of 2016 CMS announced that as part of the transition to the new quality payment program, MIPS, the current PQRS program will end that calendar year. Even though physicians are expected to start using MIPS in 2017, psychologists and social workers, as well as certain other non-physician providers, do not have to begin until 2019. Therefore, they will not be required to report on any quality measures in 2017 and 2018 and will not have MIPS adjustments applied to their Medicare payments until 2021.

Although aspects of the MIPS program have not been finalized at the time of writing this chapter, there are some important aspects that are known, according to a document under "Quality Payment Program" on www.cms.gov. First, the number of measures that providers will have to report on will be six, rather than the nine required by PQRS. Second, there will be both positive and negative payment adjustments. Finally, these adjustments, which are listed as "maximum negative adjustments" that have corresponding positive adjustments, are significantly greater than with PQRS: In 2019 it will be 4%, in 2020 it will be 5%, in 2021 it will be 7%, and in 2022 and after it will be 9%. There are other details involved that seem confusing and might be changed. Nonetheless, it is evident that the MIPS program will lead to larger reimbursement changes than the 2% cut with PQRS. Thus it will be important for psychologists and social workers to learn about the program. It is hoped they will be able to benefit from the positive payment adjustments. Incidentally, as with PQRS, there will still be a two-year gap, so participating in MIPS in 2019 means that the reimbursement will be adjusted in 2021.

## POOR COMMUNICATION

CMS provides several avenues to learn the rules and expectations of Medicare, and a number of topics can be found on www.cms.gov and the website of the provider's MAC. However, even though Medicare regulations are readily available, they can be difficult to comprehend. Although the MACs often have customer service representatives available to answer questions, often they are just reading and trying to explain the same regulations from the same sources. Although representatives can explain a Medicare regulation, often they cannot explain the subtleties of a situation, especially if it involves clinical intervention or judgment.

An excellent example of this is the issue of whether psychological assistants can work with Medicare clients in an outpatient setting. Medicare has specific rules for "incident to" services, and psychologists (but not social workers) are allowed to have an employee provide them in certain settings. These services are defined as "an integral, although incidental" part of professional services. Per the CMS website, the regulations include that the psychologist "personally performed an initial service and remains actively involved in the ongoing course of treatment" and "must provide direct supervision, that is, you must be present in the office suite to render assistance, if necessary" and that there be "a valid employment arrangement" between the psychologist and the psychological assistant. Furthermore, the services are "commonly rendered without charge (included in your physician's bills)," and then CMS details how to bill for "incident to" services, implying that there *can* be charges for these services. Incidentally, one rule that is clear is that "incident to" services cannot take place in a skilled nursing facility.

Given these regulations, psychologists quite familiar with Medicare can disagree about whether psychological assistants can conduct individual psychotherapy sessions. Can they lead psychotherapy group sessions? Is it different if the group sessions involve using mindfulness relaxation as opposed to a process-oriented group? There are no clear answers to these questions. Furthermore, this is an issue that might fall under LCD, so one MAC might consider the role of a psychological assistant differently than another MAC. This is one of the challenges of Medicare: Even though there might be precise wording, certain clinical issues are still ambiguous.

## AUDITS

There seem to be "urban legends" about Medicare audits and how to avoid them, short of not being a Medicare provider at all. Furthermore, tales about audits seem to vary by location, indicating that MACs deal with them differently. Also, they seem to vary by specific time periods. For example, in the greater Los Angeles area, many psychologists report getting audited at the same time in the mid-1990s, but that has not happened since that time. As with any health insurance, Medicare can review a provider's documentation to ensure that proper payment was made only for medically necessary services. However, these audits are rarely reported. Meanwhile, the best way to handle such an audit is to have thorough documentation of clinically appropriate services, as discussed earlier in this chapter.

In 2005 Medicare began the Recovery Audit Program in select locations using data based on a program called Comprehensive Error Rate Testing. In 2010, the Recovery Audits expanded nationally, performed by four companies that each have a distinct region of the United States. The goal of this program is to identify and correct both overpayments and underpayments for Part A and B services. Overall, a vast majority of the overpayments were found within Part A hospital services. Details of these programs, including the exact amounts of money involved by state, settings, and specific concerns, are readily available on www.cmg.gov.

In addition, Medicare is making a concerted effort to find and punish those who engage in fraud and abuse. Various Medicare-related websites for both providers and beneficiaries offer information about reporting possible abuse and fraud. Recently there seem to be more stories about such illegal actions, whether they are committed by large hospitals, skilled nursing facilities, small companies, or individual providers. Often the media reports stories of fraud in the millions of dollars. Frankly, exposing and punishing those who take advantage of the Medicare system makes it a better, more cost-effective program for everyone.

## MEDICARE ADVANTAGE

As mentioned earlier in this chapter, Medicare's Part C is hospital and medical insurance provided by private insurance companies called Medicare Advantage (MA) plans. Some MA plans are structured like a PPO plan; others are like HMOs. Although all MA plans must offer the same coverage as traditional Medicare, they vary greatly in terms of additional benefits and costs. Some of them include medication coverage, eliminating a beneficiary's need to purchase a separate Part D plan. In addition, the MA plan might add benefits that are not included in most traditional Medicare plans, such as dental and vision coverage and gym memberships.

However, the MA plans that are HMOs generally limit coverage to in-network providers, which might restrict a patient's access to services. The MA plans structured like a PPO usually allow clients to select any Medicare providers. However, a Medicare provider may not want to work with a PPO-style MA plan since the plan does not always have to pay the provider the allowed amount set by CMS. Furthermore, the MA plan might pay a smaller percentage of the fee to the provider and the client may be required to pay a greater percentage of the fee. Also, similar to private insurance rules for in-network providers, the MA plan may have its own rules for paperwork by the provider, such as requiring preauthorization for treatment, which is not necessary with traditional Medicare.

Sometimes even clients do not know whether they have an MA plan, especially since they still might have their original Medicare card. One way a provider can check is by looking on the back of the additional insurance card. If there is a statement such as "Providers should submit claims to XYZ insurance company directly and not bill Medicare," it is nearly certain that it is a MA plan. It is then best to call the insurance company directly to clarify the coverage, any co-payments due by the beneficiary, and any other expectations. Some providers are comfortable taking MA plans, especially if they are also providers for the particular insurance company. Others prefer not to because of the additional co-payments and/or other requirements of the company. Providers should consider such factors to decide whether to accept MA plans and from which insurance companies.

This leads to the final challenge and current controversial issue: The American Psychological Association is lobbying to have psychologists included in the CMS definition of "physician." Currently psychologists are the only doctoral-level healthcare providers who are considered "non-physician practitioners." In addition to physicians, the current CMS definition includes dentists, podiatrists, optometrists, and chiropractors. If the definition is changed, psychologists will be able to reimbursed for additional services and might earn greater bonus payments. However, they will likely be required to participate in certain value-based programs or be subject to greater pay reductions. Some people believe that it is only fair that doctoral-level professionals should be recognized for their extensive training and large role as providing a significant number of the mental health services to Medicare beneficiaries. Others are leery of the new and possible future regulations as there is a shift toward reimbursement based on performance and would rather observe the changes to other professions first. Since legislation has already been introduced in Congress about this issue, it is likely a matter of when, rather than if, the change occurs.

# CONCLUDING THOUGHTS

By being a Medicare provider, psychologists and social workers have the opportunity to work with diverse patients in a wide range of settings. In particular, providers who have an interest in clinical geropsychology would want to consider enrolling in Medicare. Overall, many Medicare psychologists and social workers seem to appreciate certain advantages: (1) there is a growing demand for their services, (2) Medicare will accept providers once they are licensed, (3) Medicare does not mandate preauthorization or other requirements that many private insurance companies have for their in-network providers, (4) the reimbursement is often equal to or better than that of private insurance companies, and (5) providers are paid in a timely manner.

Nonetheless, Medicare has rules, restrictions, and expectations that can be challenging. The shifting focus to pay-for-performance means that in the future providers may have to comply with additional requirements or face a reduction in reimbursement. Regardless of whether providers enroll in or opt out of Medicare, doing one or the other is required under federal law. It is hoped that the information provided in this chapter allows readers to make an informed decision in line with their clinical experiences and interests.

# REFERENCES

Beck, M. (2013, July 29). More doctors steer clear of Medicare. *Wall Street Journal*, p. 1.

Boccuti, C., Fields, C., Casillas, G., & Hamel, L. (2015, October 30). Primary care physicians accepting Medicare: A snapshot. Kaiser Family Foundation. Retrieved from http://kft.org/medicare/issue-brief/primary-care-physicians-accepting-medicare-a-snapshot/.

Davis, K., Stremikis, K., Doty, M., & Zezza, M. (2012, July 18). Medicare beneficiaries less likely to experience cost- and access-related problems than adults with private coverage. *Health Affairs Web First*. Retrieved from http://content.healthaffairs.org/content/early/2012/07/16/hlthaff.2011.1357.full?keytype=ref&siteid=healthaff&ijkey=8fHO335aIFad.

Goforth, A. (2015, March 31). High satisfaction with Medicare. Retrieved from http://www.benefitspro.com/2015/03/31/high-satisfaction-with-medicare.

Lieberman, T. (2013, August 12). Medicare uncovered: How many doctors still take Medicare? *Columbia Journalism Review*. Retrieved from http://www.cjr.org/the_second_opinion/how_many_doctors_still_take_medicare.php.

Shartzer, A., Zuckerman, R., McDowell, A., & Kronick, R. (2013, August). Access to physicians' services for Medicare beneficiaries. Office of the Assistant Secretary for Planning and Evaluation, Healthand Human Services. Retrieved from https://aspe.hhs.gov/basic-report/access-physicians-services-medicare-beneficiaries.

Stamm, K., Hamp, A., Karel, M., Moye, J., Qualls, S., Segal, D., ... Lin, L. (2016, January). How many psychologists provide care to older adults? *Monitor on Psychology, 47*(1), 17.

Wasik, J. (2013, September 4). Are doctors really ditching Medicare? *Fiscal Times*. Retrieved from http://www.thefiscaltimes.com/Columns/2013/09/04/Are-Doctors-Really-Ditching-Medicare.

# CHAPTER 24

# OPTIMIZING CUSTOMER SERVICE IN PRIVATE PRACTICE

*Tiffany A. Garner and Jeffrey E. Barnett*

Mental health professionals in private practice are in business. Accordingly, we must run our businesses effectively to stay in business and achieve the goal of having a successful practice that allows us to provide needed services to clients and to be financially rewarding to ourselves. In addition to the basic requirement of providing high-quality assessment, treatment, and consultative services, we must ensure a steady stream of clients in order to maintain a viable private practice.

It is thus extremely important to effectively market your practice. A lack of attention to marketing efforts can result in a decrease in referrals and a negative impact on your finances and livelihood. Detailed information on how to effectively market your private practice may be found in Chapter 26: The Basics of Marketing Applied to Private Practice. Two essential aspects of marketing are client reports back to referral partners, such as primary care physicians and schools, and client reports and recommendations made to family members and friends (word-of-mouth referrals).

## A FOCUS ON CUSTOMER SERVICE

While excellence in clinical skills is essential and has a direct impact on treatment success and thus client satisfaction, a focus on customer service is essential as well for developing and maintaining the robust stream of referrals that is so important for financial success in private practice. Consumers of mental health services have a wide range of options: They may seek the assistance of psychologists, social workers, professional counselors, marriage and family therapists, psychiatrists, psychiatric nurses, rehabilitation counselors, coaches, and even members of the clergy, among others. Depending on where you practice, it can be a crowded practice landscape indeed. With advances in telemental health the landscape can be even more crowded, as the client does not need to see a professional located in their local community. This environment pits clinicians against each other to compete for each prospective client's business.

A focus on customer service (yes, from a business perspective clients are the customers, and we want them to purchase the services we offer) is an important way to separate yourself from the multitude of businesses with whom you are competing. As Walfish and Barnett (2009) state: "There is no shortage of clinically skilled mental health professionals capable of doing excellent work. Those clinicians with the best customer-service practices will likely be the most successful in private practice" (p. 30). Thus, how we treat prospective clients, and the total experience they have when interacting with us and with our practices, can significantly impact how they view our practices, whether they choose to enter into treatment with us, and if and how they will communicate about it with others.

It is well accepted and supported by research from various service industries that product performance and satisfaction leads to repeat purchases. In the service industry, however, assessing performance, value, and quality can present the consumer with inherent challenges.

Consumers of health care services typically do not have the education or training to assess the technical quality of the care they receive. Therefore they rely more on nontechnical factors such as the client–practitioner relationship. In addition, Bowers, Swan, and Koehler (1994) discovered that healthcare consumers assess quality by the attributes associated with the delivery of care. Specifically, in a study of hospital patients designed to assess perceptions of quality, attributes like empathy, reliability, responsiveness, caring, and communication were found to be associated with increased perception of quality (Bowers, Swan, & Koehler, 1994). Thus, dimensions related not to the technical competency of the provider but rather to how the service was delivered rose to the top as predictors of the perceived quality of the service.

Relationship-based services are often difficult to evaluate prior to purchasing or experiencing the service; some are difficult to evaluate even after they have been performed (Berry, 1995). Additionally, the personal and unique nature of the service provided by a psychotherapist lends itself to a unique set of considerations for the potential consumer. Conducting psychotherapy is both science and art. While managed care has driven evidence-based treatment and the associated body of literature measuring efficacy, the art of mental health treatment lies in less tangible treatment factors like empathy, warmth, and the relationship between the provider and the client.

But how does one measure factors like empathy and rapport? Internal factors like empathy and caring are regularly expected of mental health practitioners. Responsiveness, communication, and reliability, however, are external factors that contribute to the day-to-day experience of what it's like to work with a particular provider and thus have the potential to increase a client's perception of provider quality. Perceived healthcare service quality can determine a provider's success or failure as the relationship between service quality and profit is related to client satisfaction (Choi, Cho, Lee, Lee, & Kim, 2004).

# FACTORS IMPACTING THE CLIENT EXPERIENCE

Customer service extends to every aspect of the client experience. This may include how responsive you are to emails or telephone calls in between treatment appointments, how your office is set up (e.g., comfortable furniture; free coffee, tea, juice, and water; magazines to read in the waiting room; age-appropriate toys for children to play with in the waiting room), and how you handle billing practices (e.g., not billing for brief telephone calls and emails in between treatment sessions; not using collection agencies or going to small claims court over unpaid bills; allowing clients the option to pay by credit card; assisting clients with filing insurance forms).

Fisher (2009) has stressed the importance of providing appropriate training and oversight to all staff members we employ. This should include a focus on customer service. The customer experience may begin with the initial telephone call to your practice. How the telephone is answered and how friendly and helpful the staff person is can set the tone for how the potential client views your practice and even if he or she will follow through with scheduling and keeping an initial appointment. If you do not employ any staff members and use a voicemail system, how quickly you respond to messages can have a significant impact on the potential client's perception of you and your practice.

One of us (JEB) has experienced a range of reactions from potential clients in response to when voicemail messages were responded to and phone calls returned. Some reactions included: "Wow, I just left that message. It's great to hear back from you so quickly" and "Oh, sorry, I already heard back from another practitioner and scheduled an appointment with her." Thus, reserving time in your schedule throughout the day to check for voice messages and to return telephone calls (and emails) can be an essential customer service action that may have a significant impact on the success of your private practice. This can easily be done by allowing a bit more time between appointments rather than seeing clients back to back. It can also change the pace of your day and how rushed you seem to your clients, thereby changing their experience as well.

If you employ office staff such as a receptionist or secretary, a billing service, or others, each of these individuals represents you and your practice to your clients and to potential referral partners. Even if you provide the most effective treatments and clients benefit greatly from the services you provide, one interaction with a rude or impersonal staff member can have a devastating effect on the client's view of you and your practice. Well-trained staff members help clients to feel welcomed to the practice and to be comfortable in the waiting room. They help to create a pleasant environment that can make a significant difference to how clients experience your practice.

Consider the potential cost of the loss of even one client to you and your practice. If a client is paying $150 per session and might be in treatment with you for 20 sessions, this equates to $3,000 of business. Thus, the loss of even one client is costly to you. The loss of multiple clients can be devastating to the viability of your private practice. Additionally, unsatisfied clients are twice as likely as satisfied clients to share their experience with 10 or more people (Chase & Dasu, 2001). With the rapid transfer of information among friends and friends of friends through social media, the potential impact of a client's negative experiences increases exponentially (Needham, 2012).

# CUSTOMER SERVICE AND REFERRAL PARTNERS

Good customer service also includes responsiveness to referral sources, or what Kase (2011) refers to as "referral partners." The term referral partner implies that the relationship between providers and their referring persons, institutions, or companies is bidirectional, meaning that the provision of service is beneficial to both. It is a given that the private practitioner *needs* referrals. Referral partners also *need* to identify skilled and trusted referral sources in order to meet the needs of their clients, patients, employees, and students.

When running your practice you cannot underestimate the value of cultivating a relationship with other providers who refer and have the potential to refer clients to you. In addition, this can go a long way to delight your clients, as consumer surveys have shown that healthcare consumers want more communication and coordination between their providers (Needham, 2012). Gitell (2002) has used the term "relational coordination" to refer to the process of mutually reinforcing interactions between service providers for the purpose of integrating care-related tasks. Research has also shown that relational coordination between service providers is associated with increased client satisfaction and the intent to recommend the providers to others, over and above the effects of the client–provider relationship (Gitell, 2002).

The relationship with a referral partner begins with the most basic element—letting that person know that you are willing and available to accept his or her referrals. This involves introducing yourself and educating your referral partner about the nature of your practice and your specialty, competency, and training. Referral partners are likely to want to know some of the basics about your practice such as your location, fees, hours, whether or not you take insurance, and your basic approach to treatment and assessment.

In addition, referral partners are often looking to connect with practitioners who share their values and views on providing care. They are trying to determine if you will do a good job, provide a valuable service, and ultimately help a client get better. Therefore, it is wise to get to know your referral partners and seek out common ground with respect to discussing mutual affiliations with institutions, organizations, schools, and other referral partners already familiar to them in the community.

Once you have entered into a relationship with a referral partner, it is in your best interest to tend to that relationship and treat the referral partner as an ally in growing your business, remembering that you are often working with the referral partner's customers (clients and patients) as well. Your work certainly can impact the referral partner's practice. One way to grow that interdependent relationship is to cultivate a sense of trust.

Gounaris (2005) asserts that the degree of trust that develops between two businesses (or in this case business practitioners) is a fundamental relationship building block and a critical element of economic exchange. In fact, Berry (1995) states that trust is perhaps the single most powerful relationship marketing tool available to a particular company. And the more one business practitioner (i.e., referral partner) trusts the other, the higher the perceived value of the relationship (Walter, Holzle, & Ritter, 2002), and thus the greater the likelihood that the relationship will continue. Gain the trust of a healthy referral partner and your practice can grow by leaps and bounds.

So what does it take to develop that trust? After all, for a strong relationship to exist, it must be mutually beneficial (Czepiel, 1990). Therefore, if trust can be understood as reassurance that a relationship is collaborative and will result in positive outcomes that meet the needs of both parties involved in the relationship, then we can see how important it can be to tailor our practices to meet the needs of the referral partner. Referral partners want to be able to rely on the fact that you will be available to take referrals, be responsive, take the time to coordinate care, and provide a quality healing service to clients, each of which is of value to the referral partner. They also want to know that you will not take cases that are better suited to be treated elsewhere.

Other customer service practices that have the potential to delight referral partners include how long it takes to schedule the initial appointment, your availability for scheduling emergency appointments right away, your willingness to be flexible with your schedule to make it easier for clients to meet with you (e.g., early hours before they go to work and evening or weekend appointments that do not conflict with clients' work or school obligations), and, with clients' consent, providing referral partners with timely, concise, and helpful reports and feedback on your work with the clients they refer to you.

Considering that trust is not inherent but something that develops over time as a result of personal experiences, it can be critical to identify the needs of a particular referral partner. For example, if you are seeking referrals from a particular physician, it is helpful to know his or her preference for coordinating care. Does he or she prefer telephone calls? Confidential email? Clinical notes? Written communication via letter? One particular referral partner of one of us (TAG) prefers a text message to schedule a telephone call.

One of us (JEB) had a pediatrician whose office was on the way to his practice. He regularly stopped by in person to give her the reports he had completed on evaluations of children she had referred, and to briefly provide her with feedback on the client and his recommendations for assisting the client. While this pediatrician regularly stated that there was no need to come in person to deliver the reports and discuss the cases with her, she nonetheless continued making numerous referrals to his practice. She also recommended his practice to several of her colleagues, resulting in even more referrals to him.

It can also be helpful to discuss with your referral partners what their needs and expectations are for what happens after the referral is made. For example, what are your responsibilities and actions taken if you do not accept a particular referral sent to you? There is value in educating your referral partner about your areas of expertise. By taking steps to provide good customer service even to clients not appropriate for your practice by providing additional referrals, you have another opportunity to "delight" your referral partner by demonstrating your commitment to fully care for the clients sent to you. This of course presumes that the particular referral partner does not want to make the referral himself or herself—hence the importance of being clear about the referral partner's expectations in advance.

For example, one of us (TAG) seized the opportunity to deepen the trust of a new referral partner, a pediatrician new to a familiar practice, by circling back to the physician to share with her the steps taken after a parent called her practice. After speaking with the parent of an elementary-age child, it became clear that the child required a specific type of reevaluation for a condition typically diagnosed and treated by a speech/language pathologist. Instead of simply telling the parent she did not provide that type of assessment, and educating the referral partner about the diagnoses conferred by psychologists and how they differ from speech/language pathologists, TAG referred the parent to a high-quality speech/language practice. She then contacted the pediatrician to explain the nature of the specific need and her ability to refer the family to another practice for treatment, highlighting her willingness to take the time to speak to parents about their children's needs and the best way to meet those needs. She also offered to consult on any clients prior to the referral if ever the pediatrician was unsure about next steps. These types of relationship-building steps can go a long way to cultivate trust, deepen the relationship, and show commitment to working collaboratively with a referral partner. They also demonstrate to your referral partners the type of customer service you provide, the care you take with potential clients, and the value you have to offer them and their patients. TAG has since received numerous assessment referrals from this pediatrician, most of which WERE appropriate!

# CUSTOMER SERVICE AND CUSTOMER DELIGHT

Customer (client) experiences and perceptions of our practices can have a significant impact on our financial success in private practice. Ralston (2003) highlighted findings that positive customer service experiences can have a great impact on customer loyalty, significantly impacting client retention, return for future services, referral of family members and friends, and positive reports back to referral partners. Berman (2005) added to the concept of customer service in speaking of the goal of customer delight. Customer delight goes beyond providing the client with a positive or good experience, and goes beyond the client's expectations for the experience he or she has with your practice. Customer delight involves exceeding the client's expectations, something that results in a very strong and positive emotional response on the client's part (often thought of as a "Wow!"). Those who experience customer delight can become what Finlay (1999) describes as apostles for your practice—individuals who actively sing the praises of your practice to all who will listen. These apostles can be some of your most valuable assets for successfully developing and growing your practice, generating countless new referrals for you.

We hope you can see how important good customer service is to running a successful private practice. Failure to give adequate attention to these issues can have a devastating effect on your practice, regardless of how competent a clinician you are and how effective your treatments are.

Developing a customer service plan should be seen as being as important as developing a business plan for your practice. A customer service plan is generally an outline of the internal operations that will be used by a given business to improve customer service (Wehmeyer, Auchter, & Hirshon, 1996). It examines customer perceptions and expectations and acts as a guide in the process of bringing customer service activities in line with customers' needs (Ingram, 2016). While there is no one correct way to go about creating such a plan, business owner and writer David

Ingram suggests the following five-step process to help you develop an effective, useful, and comprehensive plan to inform your business practices:

Step 1: Interview customers to understand their experience, expectations, and unmet needs.

Step 2: Visualize customers interacting with you and your staff. Consider writing a "process narrative" describing the average customer experience.

Step 3: List the most important customer service factors discovered through customer interviews and rate your performance in each area. Use this to identify areas in need of improvement.

Step 4: Generate a list of strategies to bring your practices in line with customer expectations.

Step 5: Implement your chosen strategy. Follow up with customers to measure the outcome.

Consider the time, expense, and energy put into developing and implementing a comprehensive customer service plan as an investment in the ongoing success of your practice. Don't view it as something extra that takes time away from providing clinical services. Rather, it is the force that actually enables you to provide clinical services (and thus generate income).

## CUSTOMER SERVICE ESSENTIALS

What are some of the ways that you promote a positive customer service experience for all those who come in contact with your practice? This can include the ease of use of your website and how easy it is to schedule an initial appointment; ease of understanding forms and billing procedures; interpersonal contacts by you and your staff with potential clients current, clients, and referral partners; how your office is set up and the amenities you offer; responsiveness to clients and referral partners; and so much more. How can you enhance customer service in each of these areas? Are there any additional or special things you can do that will enhance customer service? Examples may include reminder telephone calls, emails, or text messages the day before each appointment; providing clients with completed insurance forms for them to sign and then submit; and providing clients with needed letters to employers or schools at no additional charge. Also consider employing regular quality control checks in order to identify gaps in delivering good customer service. Ways to do so include asking clients for feedback about your website, ease of scheduling, billing practices, call wait times, experiences with front office staff, and perceived availability and responsiveness.

It may also be worthwhile to take the time to track the source of your referrals and the pace of your referrals over time. This allows you to quantify the value of a given referral partner (whether it's a physician or a former client) and take note of whether referrals from that partner are increasing or decreasing. An increase may inform your current practices by reinforcing healthy customer service practices and allow you to deepen the relationship with your referral partner by discussing the increase in referrals and asking what has contributed to him or her giving out your name more often. In contrast, noticing a decrease in the rate of referrals from a particular referral partner allows you to gather data in order to determine the reason for the decrease and troubleshoot any misperceptions, negative feedback, or other insults to your reputation or relationship with the referral source. Tracking decreases in referrals from a particular partner also helps you decide where to dedicate your resources when considering marketing, outreach, and other activities related to tending to your referral relationships.

Keep in mind the ultimate goal of customer delight and its resultant positive impact on your private practice over time. Good customer service, along with clinical excellence, adds to the development of your brand. Consider how you want to be known in your local community. Being known as a competent, friendly, and helpful practitioner who always goes the extra mile for her or his clients is a great reputation to have. The influence of this reputation on consumers and referral partners can be profound.

Below are examples of customer service activities reported by several colleagues who share how they approach customer service in their private practices.

## PROVIDING REFERRALS

Several colleagues take time to assist potential clients whose needs they are not able to meet for one reason or another (e.g., goodness of fit, availability, or insurance constraints) with finding an alternative provider by providing names and contact information of a few colleagues. After all, we are in the helping profession. While there is no guideline as to how many alternative referrals one should provide, clients often appreciate being given two or three names. Clients are often grateful that someone has taken the time to guide them through what can be an overwhelming and anxiety-producing process of reaching out for help. Going the extra mile to help potential clients builds your brand and can generate customer delight, which in turn builds trust, loyalty, and even commitment. It has been the experience of one of us (TAG) that this sense of commitment has even resulted in a parent calling back and reporting that after contacting the other providers she was referred to, she preferred to wait for an opening with TAG as she felt most confident that she would be responsive and understand her child's needs. Another colleague has reported that providing referrals has resulted in those families giving her name out to other potential clients.

## INCREASING COMMUNICATION

Communicating with clients is a given. How you communicate and the timeliness of your communications can enhance the overall client experience and also build trust, loyalty, commitment, and delight. One of our colleagues who manages not only her own caseload but that of the overall practice, which employs several other practitioners, makes a point of returning each and every call that comes in to the general practice within one to two days. She has experienced an all-too-familiar response that she is the only one of several (up to four or five) providers who returned the call.

Existing clients will generally expect regular communication about potential scheduling conflicts, advance notice of vacations, periods of provider unavailability, and changes in billing policies and fees. Another way to delight clients is by setting and managing expectations in a way that allows you to regularly exceed that expectation. Going beyond expectations may involve returning phone calls and emails the same day (despite a voicemail or autoreply that states all communications are returned within 24 to 48 hours), offering evening and weekend sessions, and responding to clinical issues between regularly scheduled sessions. Another practice that is becoming increasingly popular is the use of scheduling software that allows for email and text message appointment reminders. To that end, several of our colleagues also communicate with their clients about scheduling appointments or scheduling longer phone calls via text message.

For those who provide assessment services, timeliness can also provide an opportunity for increasing perceived value and bolstering customer delight. Communicating about the status of the scoring process, communication with schools, and the receipt of completed rating forms increases collaboration with families and schools, thus positioning the assessor as a member of the larger "team" dedicated to optimizing the child's academic success. One of our colleagues with a robust assessment practice has committed to adhering to proposed timelines with regard to completing reports and scheduling feedback sessions. If for any reason she anticipates a delay and cannot meet expectations, she communicates with families in advance rather than waiting for them to contact her. This can preempt dissatisfaction by keeping a client informed.

## FORMAT OF THE INITIAL CALL

Many agree that the initial call to you or your practice is the most important point of contact in the initial therapeutic relationship. How that call is managed and structured can determine whether the client schedules the appointment, keeps the appointment, speaks positively about you to your referral partner, and begins the relationship feeling positively about the prospect of getting better or learning more about himself or herself or his or her child. Even something as simple as the client's response to the initial call can lead to word-of-mouth referrals.

It has been the experience of one of us (JEB) that some providers approach these calls from a cost/benefit perspective, quickly comparing the cost of their time being on the phone with a potential client with the potential financial benefit of investing time in an initial call. This has never been more apparent than one provider's response to the initial call, which was to put off discussing the presenting concern and discuss only her limited availability and if the caller could fill her one or two midday openings. Perhaps needless to say, this did not result in the caller scheduling with this provider, as she was only one of three referrals. Instead, an appointment was scheduled with a provider who took the time to hear the presenting concern, offer a caring response, and only then discuss scheduling.

Given the importance of the initial call, it may be in your best interest to take the time to develop an agenda for the initial call and explain the expectations to your callers at the point of first contact. For example, you might thank the caller for the call, tell him or her that in the initial call you usually like to spend a few minutes discussing the reason for seeking services, how he or she was referred to you, and his or her history of prior mental health treatment, but then move on to discussing availability as this may contribute to goodness of fit. By taking charge of the call it likely decreases the caller's anxiety, models effective communication, and allows the caller and you, the provider, to clarify expectations and desired outcomes. But to do all this, you must first include in your daily schedule enough time to return telephone calls and to spend sufficient time with each individual to provide this type of positive customer service experience.

Providers often appreciate being informed about the progress of their patients. There are a myriad of ways in which this can be done. One practice of a colleague is simply to send a follow-up letter letting the provider know that the patient he or she referred has been scheduled for treatment. Another colleague communicates via email but then suggests finding a time to discuss more complex issues, should they present, in a regular weekly or biweekly phone call with the referral partner. One of us (TAG) goes beyond simply sending the assessment report to the referring pediatrician and writes a cover letter summarizing the clinical impressions, highlighting pertinent diagnoses, and summarizing the plan of action agreed upon with the family at the feedback session. The other of us (JEB) regularly asks new referral partners what type of communication they prefer regarding the patients they refer (e.g., brief regular communications by telephone or letters sent periodically) and then provides each referral partner with the type and frequency of communication preferred. One of our colleagues was told by a referring physician that he only wanted a checklist form to be filled out because he could get the gist of the recommendations more quickly that way than with a letter or a call; another physician told our colleague that he would abhor such abbreviated communication. Clearly, attending to the referral partner's expectations is central to building the relationship.

Practices that further support referral partner communication, trust, and perception of value include thanking your referral partner on a regular basis, communicating important changes in your practice, and even offering to provide education to them or their patients via talks, paying for and hosting brown-bag lunch programs, or conducting other psychoeducational activities that benefit providers, staff members, and patients.

## SUMMARY AND RECOMMENDATIONS

As you can now see, having a customer service plan in place is critical for the success of any private practice. While this does not necessarily mean that you need a written document detailing all your regular business practices, it is worthwhile to spend time considering how you'd like your practice to be perceived by others and what steps you can take to create and maintain that perception over time. Whether scheduling breaks in a busy day to respond to client communications, training front office staff to respond with care and empathy, and offering various creature comforts in your waiting room, there exists a wide range of things you can do to enhance your clients' experience and generate "delight" that they chose you as their practitioner. Add to the mix positive regular communication to referral sources in a manner that is convenient for their business practices, and you have yourself a recipe for delighting your referral partners as well.

Clients regularly communicate experiences (positive and negative) with their friends, family, and referral partners. Exceeding client expectations further enhances your brand value and increases the likelihood of your financial success. There is no shortage of ideas on how to achieve this goal. The next time you are at a conference, seminar, or networking event, take some time to talk to your colleagues about their regular business practices. What do they offer in their waiting rooms? How do they train their staff? What things do their clients report appreciating that make doing business with them more pleasant? And the next time you have a positive experience with a retailer or service provider, take note of what generated your own "delight" and consider how you can incorporate those factors into your own business practices. Be creative. There is no one formula for good customer service, but one thing is certain: Exceeding expectations generates trust, loyalty, and value, and these in turn lead to financial gain.

# REFERENCES

Berman, B. (2005). How to delight your customers. *California Management Review, 48,* 129–151.

Berry, L. L. (1995). Relationship marketing of services: Growing interest, emerging perspective. *Journal of the Academy of Marketing Science, 23*(4), 236–245.

Bowers, M. R., Swan, J. E., & Koehler, W. F. (1994). What attributes determine quality and satisfaction with health care delivery? *Health Care Management Review, 19*(4), 49–55.

Chase, R. B., & Dasu, S. (2001). Want to perfect your company's service? Use behavioral science. *Harvard Business Review, 79*(6), 78–84.

Choi, K.-S., Cho, W.-H., Lee, S., Lee, H., & Kim, C. (2004). The relationships among quality, value, satisfaction and behavioral intention in health care provider choice: A South Korean study. *Journal of Business Research, 57*(8), 913–921.

Czepiel, J. A. (1990). Services encounters and service relationships: Implications for research. *Journal of Business Research, 20,* 13–21.

Finlay, S. (1999, June). Survey returns to dealership roots. J.D. Power and Associates customer service index. Editorial. *Ward's Dealer Business,* 33.

Fisher, M. A. (2009). Ethics-based training for nonclinical staff in mental health settings. *Professional Psychology: Research and Practice, 40*(5), 459–466.

Gitell, J. H. (2002). Relationships between service providers and their impact on customers. *Journal of Service Research, 4*(4), 299–311.

Gounaris, S. P. (2005) Trust and commitment influences on customer retention: Insights from business-to-business services. *Journal of Business Research, 58,* 126–140.

Ingram, D. (2016). How to create a customer service plan. Retrieved from http://smallbusiness.chron.com/create-customer-service-plan-2047.html.

Kase, L. (2011). *Clients, clients, and more clients: Create an endless stream of new business with the power of psychology.* New York: McGraw Hill.

Needham, B. N. (2012, July/August). The truth about patient experience: What we can learn from other industries, and how the three Ps can improve health outcomes, strengthen brands, and delight customers. *Journal of Healthcare Management, 57*(4), 256–263.

Ralston, R. (2003). The effects of customer service, branding, and price on the perceived value of local telephone service. *Journal of Business Research, 56,* 201–213.

Walfish, S., & Barnett, J. E. (2009). *Financial success in mental health practice: Essential tools and strategies for practitioners.* Washington, DC: American Psychological Association.

Walter, A., Holzle, K., & Ritter, T. (September, 2002). Relationship functions and customer trust as value creators in relationships: A conceptual model and empirical findings for the creation of customer value. Proceedings of the 18th IMP Conference, Dijon, France.

Wehmeyer, S., Auchter, D., & Hirshon, A. (1996). Saying what we will do, and doing what we will say: Implementing a customer service plan. *Journal of Academic Librarianship, 22*(3), 173–180.

# GROWING A PRACTICE

# CHAPTER 25

# ISSUES IN DEVELOPING AND JOINING A GROUP PRACTICE

*Edward A. Wise*

A recent American Psychological Association Practice Organization survey (APAPO, 2014) found that only 15.5% of surveyed members (*n* = 2,546) counted an independent group practice as their primary work setting. However, the same poll found that nearly 30% of respondents anticipated becoming involved in a multidisciplinary system of care in the next three to five years. The latter finding appears to signal that some type of affiliation with larger entities, including group practice variations, is likely to double in the near future. In the current healthcare climate, there are a number of reasons you might consider such affiliations with larger systems of care. However, larger systems of care tend to favor doing business with other larger entities, whether these are payers, accountable care organizations (ACOs), integrated medical practices, or large medical practices.

In the current zeitgeist, as larger systems of medical care emerge, they will likely seek behavioral health entities capable of meeting their demand for mental health services (e.g., Agency for Health Care Research and Quality [AHRQ], n.d.; Substance Abuse and Mental Health Services Administration [SAMHSA], 2014). It is more practical and efficient for these systems of care to do business with other larger practices that serve similar populations, including those that provide services across the lifespan (e.g., child, adolescent, adult, and geriatric) and those with specialty lines of service that are frequently seen in those larger practices or systems of care (e.g., mood disorders, substance use, posttraumatic stress disorder), instead of referring to multiple independent providers for each individual patient. Whether an individual behavioral health provider joins or forms a larger behavioral health specialty group, or enters an existing medical group, there are an infinite number of complex issues to be considered, which include many personal, professional, and business decisions. The aim of this chapter is to introduce you to some of these more common and experience-near or micro-issues that you may encounter if you are considering joining or creating a group practice.

There are many personal, professional, and business benefits associated with a group practice. At the same time, there are a host of personal, professional, and business arguments against forming a group practice. A related overarching issue is whether to join an established group practice or start a new group practice. This may become particularly salient when considering your professional development and goals. Joining an established practice means entering an existing culture, with formal and informal norms, whereas starting your own group practice provides greater latitude for defining those norms. While there is certainly overlap between personal, professional, and business goals, if these goals do not align with a group practice model, and the goals of the colleagues you may be joining, it is likely that the liabilities of joining a group will outweigh the benefits.

A guiding personal framework requires you to identify and prioritize your personal, professional, and business goals in the context of the group practice model you are considering. A frequent example of goal misalignment involves joining a group practice primarily for referrals and camaraderie. While some groups may share these goals, others may not. Consider, for example, the case in which an existing practice of psychotherapists are busy, but each clinician has his or her own cross-referral networks and schedules his or her in-office time with back-to-back clients. If you are looking for professional contact and cross-referrals, you are not likely to be satisfied in this type of group setting. Alternatively, consider the situation where a group comprises a number of practitioners, each of whom maintains a part-time practice (less than 32 billable hours per week). This might be referred to as a "lifestyle" practice in that it allows the clinicians to be involved in the profession while maintaining a lifestyle that is not solely dependent on the practice. Such a group might also value the extra-professional social contact with colleagues. If you are a full-time practitioner who is solely dependent on practice-related income, joining this group for camaraderie might well meet your social needs, but you would also find that you are working harder than others in the group. Whether or not such a dynamic creates a problem depends on the individuals involved, but it is not hard to see that this could result in a less-than-optimal fit in the long run.

The following sections will address business, personal, and professional goals in more detail. Use the identified areas as a starting point to consider your own relative value framework, which can then serve as guide to assessing the goodness-of-fit with potential groups.

## BUSINESS GOALS

One goal for joining or forming a group practice could to be to improve the market position of your business. In this case, some benefits of a group practice that may interest you could be related to providing a more diverse array of services (e.g., individual, group, and couples therapy; psychological, educational, and neuropsychological evaluations); delivering services to more diverse populations (e.g., child, adolescent, adults, and geriatrics); providing specialty services (e.g., substance abuse, posttraumatic stress disorder, medical consultations, forensic evaluations); working in a multidisciplinary or interprofessional context (e.g., social workers, licensed professional counselors, psychiatrists, primary care physicians); or providing or developing services in multiple locations. The business opportunities for group practices are as varied as the clinicians who come together to create market share.

# PERSONAL GOALS

Personal reasons to consider a group practice could be related to a desire to pace the transition into full-time private practice, a preference for socialization over isolation, wanting to leave the business of practice issues to others (e.g., managing, hiring, and firing employees; dealing with collections, contracts, external vendors), and maintaining a practice that affords you the opportunity to only see clients and leave the daily operational practice management issues to others. In contrast to starting a new group practice, an established group practice is more likely to satisfy these types of preferences. For example, in a recent survey of psychologists who reported their work status as either full-time or part-time, 74% were full-time and 26% were part-time (American Psychological Association, 2015). Many part-time psychotherapists in independent practice rent space and possibly administrative services from an existing practice and are only peripherally involved in the administrative tasks of running a practice. While some of these benefits could be realized by renting space from a solo practitioner, renting space from a group practice may also result in cross-referrals and increased opportunities for socialization with other practitioners, in addition to the other personal advantages mentioned above. However, there are also personal advantages to renting space from an individual provider. Perhaps a "smaller is better" philosophy is a personal value of yours; you may want more of a "hands on" experience to learn more about how a practice works; or you may be transitioning into or out of a practice or handing your practice off to a colleague. Although the focus of this chapter is on issues in developing a group practice, it is important to recognize that some personal goals may align better with a smaller or solo practice.

# PROFESSIONAL GOALS

Similarly, some professional benefits of group affiliation could include collegiality, working with more or less experienced colleagues, having access to an interdisciplinary setting, cross-referrals, being a part of something larger than a solo or smaller practice, managing a business, or creating and leading an organization to a larger vision. Affiliating with senior colleagues can be especially helpful for early-career professionals, who can learn from the clinical and professional experience of their more senior group members. This may take the form of formal or informal supervision, learning about the day-to day operations of clinical practice (e.g., scheduling, notes, being on call), gaining an introduction to other professionals, learning about managed care utilization review, handling crisis situations, and the like. An interprofessional group may afford interaction across disciplines and learning about the perspectives of other mental health providers, developing strategies for collaborative care, and expanding networking opportunities into professional networks beyond that of one's own training.

Being able to give and receive referrals within a group is important but often misunderstood. Too often it is assumed that simply joining an existing group will result in a windfall of referrals, when in fact providers, particularly in established groups, tend to already have a network of professionals they give and receive referrals to and from. Hence, it is necessary to understand the incentives to send referrals to a new member who has yet to prove that he or she can bring business that can be shared with the group. From this perspective, it is helpful to have or develop a specialty area that complements those of the other members of the group practice. For example, a psychotherapist with expertise in couples and/or family therapy could provide an additional dimension to a practice that primarily provides individual psychotherapy. A forensic psychologist who specializes in custody evaluations could be a welcome addition to a group serving families and couples. Specialty areas that could be particularly helpful to groups serving medical populations might include psychotherapists who specialize in the treatment of eating disorders, pain management, or neuropsychology. These complementary areas of expertise will help group members recognize the unique value and talents of other members and contribute to a culture of referrals within the practice.

## EXTERNAL PROFESSIONAL CONSULTANTS

When considering joining or creating a group practice, a cadre of professional consultants is necessary. Many of the issues that consultants could provide assistance with (e.g., legal, accounting, and financial planning) are addressed more extensively throughout this volume, but a few should at least be mentioned in the context of a group practice. The expertise of an attorney specializing in healthcare will be necessary to identify potential legal issues related to the structure of the behavioral health group and risk management issues related to this entity. An employment or labor attorney may be of assistance in addressing personnel issues. An experienced tax attorney or accountant will be required to assist in evaluating the financial statements of the practice and the financial health of the business. An experienced healthcare accountant can be invaluable in identifying business opportunities, problems, and solutions. Financial experts, including accountants, can provide direction on ways to best finance your practice; handle income tax–related issues, including maximizing business deductions; develop retirement benefit plans; and conduct tax-related financial planning. A personal relationship with a banker can be helpful in securing loans, lines of credit, and access to related financial services. An insurance agent can be of assistance in identifying the types of insurance you may or may not need. In addition to malpractice insurance for the group and each individual, business insurance and workers' compensation insurance may be required in your state. Individual umbrella insurance, income protection, disability, and other coverage should also be explored. Ideally, some of these financial experts will collaborate on behalf of your interests. For example, in addition to taking care of your tax returns, your accountant may be able to refer you to a banker to obtain a line of credit, or an insurer who can provide a portfolio of liability coverage options. Hence, it is very important that your financial "quarterback" be someone whom you trust and who can introduce you to a network of related experts.

If possible, contacting other mental health professionals who are involved in group practices similar to the one you are contemplating and who are willing to share their experiences can also be beneficial, if not a necessity. These could include both colleagues or practice consultants who can bring a wealth of experience that may allow them to foresee issues, conflicts, and opportunities that may not otherwise become clear until significant financial and emotional investments have been made.

# GROUP STRUCTURE

How will the clinicians be organized and reimbursed? How will the practice make its business decisions? What will be the culture of the group? Are the clinicians in the group hired employees, independent contractors, members, officers, or some combination therein? Who owns the group? Group ownership will be determined by the type of legal entity formed. Should you form a group without walls, sole proprietorship, partnership, corporation, S corporation, or other type of entity?

There are a variety of group practice arrangements, and while there is some flexibility in finding a model that might work for you, there are a number of issues that should be considered. As has been advised in this book, an accounting and legal team should be consulted to develop a model that works for you. While it is beyond the scope of this chapter to provide a detailed review of the pros and cons of each of these entities, each legal structure has various tax and legal implications related to liability. Only a rough overview of these considerations is provided here, and the interested reader may also consult the U.S. Small Business Association (https://www.sba.gov/category/navigation-structure/starting-managing-business/starting-business/choose-your-business-stru).

A *group without walls* is technically not a group but a loose affiliation of providers for the purposes of networking and cross-referrals. They have no legal tax status or ability to enter into enforceable agreements as a single entity.

A *sole proprietorship* consists of a single owner who owns an independent practice. This is the most common type of private practice entity among psychologists (54%; APAPO, 2014). The individual practitioner bears all responsibility for all clinical and operational aspects of the practice.

You might ask, "How could an individual be considered a group practice?" A sole proprietor could technically create a *limited liability company* (LLC). Through the LLC he or she would hire all clinical and business associates and would retain or delegate all decision-making authority. The single-member LLC is the most efficient decision-making arrangement, but it is also one where the individual bears responsibility for the entire operation. However, an LLC could also be formed with multiple owners or as a professional corporation, with the some of the tax and liability risks and benefits being assumed by the entity.

A *corporation* is owned by shareholders, and shares may be sold and bought from existing or new members. Like an LLC, it affords the group practice some personal liability protection from business debts and claims in the event of a lawsuit; however, revenues may be taxed twice, once as profits and again as distributions to shareholders (Nolo, n.d.).

In their most basic form, *general partnerships* typically refer to co-ownership in which all partners share personal liability for obligations and debt, as well as decision-making authority. This would be a structure to consider when the equality of all members is important, because all partners typically have an equal say in all management decisions and share equally in costs, profits, and liability. However, in addition to liability for their own actions, equal partners are also liable for the actions of each other. For example, an unlimited partnership would expose members to full personal liability for another partner's acts of negligence as well as debts and contracts entered into on behalf of the partnership.

In contrast, *limited partnerships* typically have a general partner, who is responsible for managing the operations of the partnership and who is ultimately responsible for any personal liabilities, while the liability of the limited partners is capped based on their equity stake in the partnership.

An *S corporation* is a special type of corporation created to avoid double taxation. Unlike a corporation, there may be some limits for financial liability. Owners of an S corporation are liable for the company's debts and obligations based on their proportionate ownership in the practice. It is also possible to form a group practice with equal partners, employees, independent contractors, or some combination therein.

One related potential legal barrier to be considered in developing the structure for your group practice is related to forming interprofessional or multidisciplinary group practices that include physicians. The Corporate Practice of Medicine Doctrine varies from state to state but is essentially designed to prohibit a corporation from owning a physician's practice due to concerns that such ownership could undermine the physician's exercise of independent medical judgment (e.g., Silverman, 2015). In states where this doctrine is enforced, you cannot create a practice corporation with a physician partner.

Within the legal structure of a group, there are also a number of potential operational structures that distinguish common group models. For example, a variety of governing structures may operate within the legal structure of a group. Some groups may share responsibility for all operations-related actions, other groups may be governed by a board, some boards may rotate members, other groups have a designated individual (member) or even a sole proprietor who essentially "owns" the group and all staff are employees. Operational structures also vary; the least structured organization might be referred to as a "co-op" model, in which the group members benefit by proportionately sharing all overhead expenses, but they maintain individual practice autonomy and retain all individually generated revenue. A similar type of group could also be organized by retaining a management services organization, either internally or externally, to be responsible for all administrative and possibly marketing operations. At the other end of the spectrum are groups that function in a more integrated fashion, using common policies and procedures and sharing decision making and strategic planning. While the legal structure of a group defines how the entity will conduct external business, the governing and administrative structures determine how the group will manage operational issues on a day-to-day basis.

# GROUP PRACTICE STAFFING AND MANAGEMENT

As a group practice grows, it will need someone to manage daily operations. Depending on the size of the group, this could be a committee, a member manager, or an office manager. This would include renting office space and negotiating with landlords; hiring and firing employees; writing job descriptions, policies, and procedures; scheduling; billing; arranging for external subcontracting of services (e.g., answering service, telephone, computer and network support); and purchasing (e.g., routine office supplies, computers, fax machines, printers, network devices). If your group hires a receptionist and billing clerk, for example, a decision will need to be made about who will supervise those positions. Is it more economical for the group to hire an office manager, who will oversee other daily operations, or should owners who are also clinicians (owner/clinician) give up billable time to supervise these employees? An office manager, biller, and front desk receptionist are likely the minimum personnel needed to staff a group practice.

Many group practices continue to employ the same office staff they had in their solo or smaller practices. This may work for a while, but as your group grows, the demands for experience in finance, human resources, billing, supervision, and related matters often exceed the experience these employees were exposed to in an individual or solo practice. For example, an office manager with a business degree or corporate healthcare experience will likely be far more knowledgeable than a solo practice manager about writing and enforcing employment-related standards; providing financial checks and balances between multiple cost centers and throughout the practice; ensuring staff are cross-trained; developing policies and procedures for all daily operations, human relations, regulatory and compliance management; and supervision of payroll, accounting, and the like.

Similarly, someone who manages the front desk in a solo or small practice answering two or three telephone lines for several psychotherapists, while multitasking with billing, copying, filing, and other related tasks, would likely feel overwhelmed handling 12 or more telephone lines. Scheduling for psychiatrists is significantly different than scheduling for psychotherapy appointments, in that psychiatrists may see at least four established patients an hour and one or two new patients an hour, in addition to managing numerous pharmacy and patient calls related to medications. While offering psychiatric services will likely increase the demand for other services offered by the group, having psychiatrists as part of your group will increase the volume of calls (including those to pharmacies), front desk demands, and other consumables. A receptionist from a smaller, individual therapy office who is accustomed to scheduling patients for 45- or 50-minute individual sessions will likely require additional training to manage the scheduling of psychiatric patients.

Similarly, attempting to promote a receptionist or biller from a smaller office to a supervisory position is a frequently attempted but complicated endeavor. As is the case with front desk personnel, billers are neither trained nor experienced in running business organizations. Billing supervisors, on the other hand, can be invaluable, particularly if they have corporate health billing supervisory and management experience. Not only do they have specific experience in supervising receivables and personnel, but they have been exposed to the corporate world of regulatory compliance and the need to establish sound business policies and procedures, and they understand the financial implications of improper or poor billing practices.

A group will ultimately need someone to oversee its business and financial health. As stated above, this could be by committee, member manager, or office manager, in consultation with accounting services. This person or committee would need authority to enter into, or decline, binding business agreements, such as hiring accounting and business consultants, joining managed care plans, engaging in rate negotiations, and authorizing memorandums of understanding. At some point a decision will need to be made about how much of these administrative tasks should be assumed by the owner/clinician(s), which would take time away from the provision of direct (billable) services. Similarly, complicated committee structures often move too slowly to capitalize on fluid business opportunities, and invested group members want input into these decisions. Committee approval of daily operations is typically ill advised, as these decisions often need to be made rapidly. Committees could assist on more complex tasks, such as hiring and firing employees and larger-scale financial initiatives.

# BUSINESS AND STRATEGIC PLANS

In addition to assessing your personal, professional, and business goals that will shape your mission statement, you should also take stock of your group's business plan to execute that mission. The vision and mission of the group should be spelled out in concrete terms in a business plan. A vision statement describes the group's aspirational, long-term goals, describing how it will help others, the value of your services, and your plan to achieve those goals. A mission statement is a guiding document that succinctly articulates the purpose of the group, what the group does, who its clients are, how it provides services, and the value created by the group and its services (worksheets and examples may be found at "How to Establish Your Business's Vision, Mission, and Values" [n.d.]). The group's vision and mission statements will help clarify the values and goals that will be accomplished through its business plan.

The Small Business Administration provides a free template for developing a business plan (https://www.sba.gov/tools/business-plan/1. A sound business plan should provide you with a road map of your vision, mission, goals, market opportunities, competition, executables to deliver on goals, revenue stream, costs, timelines, and feasibility. The business plan for your group should include a description of all services, particularly those that differentiate your group from competitors, and the niche that your group will fill or serve in the local market. The market analysis section of your business plan should include a review of your target market, current market share, pricing, competition, barriers to entry, and projected growth or penetration into that market. The organizational structure of your group and management team, and their needed qualifications, will further define how your group is positioned to meet its goals. The financial section of the business plan should address historical market share and revenue, projected growth, assumptions underlying forecasts, the financial health of your group, and anticipated financial needs. If you are joining an existing group, a review of the business plan may help you determine the degree of fit between your goals and those of the group.

An important part of the business plan is the unique business position of the group. What makes your group different? Why is your group going to succeed? What is its value proposition? According to Skok (2013), a relatively simple model of a value proposition addresses these questions by providing a brief explanation of the benefit of your services from the consumer's point of view and in a way that differentiates your service from competitors. For example, "We use group therapy to help individuals find and adopt more effective ways to get their needs met in relationships and improve their satisfaction in life" could serve as a quick "elevator speech" and value proposition statement.

The business of a group practice based on couples therapy, divorce recovery, and custody evaluations might have a unique value proposition to referral sources such as attorneys and clergy, and this practice could also be uniquely positioned for a self-pay market. On the other hand, a practice geared toward presurgical evaluations, pain management, and smoking cessation might be uniquely positioned to partner with patient-centered medical homes (PCMHs) or ACOs. The latter group could be of added value to medical referral sources as well as third-party payers. Such value could improve the likelihood of negotiating insurance rates. It is important that group members all benefit from their affiliation with each other and consider each another a "good professional match" that is complementary. A well-done business plan will also be important to have if you apply for a business loan or line of credit.

Whether evaluating an existing or startup group, a companion document to the business plan should include an analysis of the group's Strengths, Weaknesses, Opportunities, and Threats (SWOT), which can guide your strategic plan. While most people engage in an informal SWOT analysis when considering a group formation, formalizing the exercise can be helpful in analyzing internal and external factors that may contribute to the growth, decay, or demise of a group practice. The analysis should be periodically repeated as both internal and external circumstances change. Internal factors are related to the strengths and weaknesses of your individual or group practice, while external factors include opportunities and threats to the execution of your business plan. For example, strengths might be related to the provision of child, adolescent, and adult individual, couples, and family therapy; central location; and multiple providers. Weaknesses could include the lack of a prescriber, only one location, and lack of specialty services. Opportunities could consist of recruiting a prescriber, expanding locations, and securing specialty evaluation services. Threats might be the expansion of a hospital system into the outpatient behavioral health service line, the presence of a competing group practice with multiple locations, and the existence of a psychiatric group practice with plans to expand. A SWOT analysis can be helpful in examining the relative position of the group in the local market and clarifying strategic growth opportunities for the group.

# FINANCIAL CONSIDERATIONS FOR BUYING INTO A GROUP PRACTICE

Whether you are part of a group practice or are considering joining an existing group, assessing the financial stability of the group is an important business decision. The level of ownership you are pursuing will influence the extent to which you will be allowed access to financial data. Employees and contractors, for example, will likely not be provided access to financials, whereas partners buying into a group practice should expect to see (and have their advisors review) what they are buying and how their shares are valued. Indirect indicators of the financial position of the group are related to issues such as the number of hours of direct service provided, trends in referral volume, diversity of referral sources, and history of and plans for practice growth.

You should expect to sign a nondisclosure agreement before reviewing any proprietary or financial data. Financial statements should be audited by an external accounting firm and should be reviewed by your accountant. These will likely cover a period of three to five years. It is important to examine monthly, quarterly, and annual cash flow to track income and expenses, particularly related to unusual or one-time expenses, recurring charges, depreciation of assets, and related financial information. Financial statements should clarify outstanding liabilities that may or may not be of value to the practice. Operating costs provide information about expenses but may also shed some light on the style of the practice (e.g., how often capital improvements are made in the way of office furniture, computers, or artwork; whether equipment is leased or owned; advertising costs).

Understanding the practice's collection procedures, percentage of allowed charges collected, average number of days to collection, and percentage of receivables over 90 days can provide important information about the management of money and cash flow within the practice. Revenues may be categorized by service lines and/or provider, which can inform you about the primary financial engines of the practice. If they are not, consider an analysis of services, referral sources, and payers for a clearer understanding of the economics of the practice. Determining the profit margin over the past few years will help assess the health of the practice. In conjunction with a business plan and SWOT analysis, you may be able to make some reasonable estimates about the future profitability of the group.

# BUSINESS OPPORTUNITIES FOR GROUP ENTITIES

Some business benefits of group practice might include service diversification, sharing administrative and personnel costs by eliminating redundant personnel, using the volume of the practice and diversity of providers in contract negotiations, contracting for services with other larger entities for volume, positioning a larger entity to take advantage of particular market dynamics, and single-signature contracts (where one individual has the authority to execute a contract on behalf of the group). Service diversification in a multispecialty group, for example, could include a practice comprising people who provide individual psychotherapy to children, adolescents, and adults, a couple and family therapist, a substance abuse counselor, a forensic psychologist specializing in custody evaluations, and a psychiatrist. While few practices are "one-stop shops," fulfilling a variety of needs helps to position the group practice in a number of ways. In addition to allowing for complementary cross-referrals, offering multiple service lines increases visibility to the general public, specific local referral sources (e.g., attorneys, physicians, clergy), and payers.

Depending on the group formation, having a single tax identification number for the group practice may allow for a single-signature rate and terms of service contracting with some payers, assuming the providers within the group are individually credentialed within the network. Other payers may reclassify the group as a clinic to achieve single-signature contracting status. Depending on the size and composition of the group, many payers are willing to entertain group negotiation of rates because they are able to contract with numerous providers on a single signature. The more demand there is for specialized services and the greater the volume of services you provide for a given payer, the more likely you will be able to negotiate favorable professional fees for your group. Similarly, the more volume your group is able to manage, the better positioned your group is to be viewed as a viable partner by other larger entities in your community. Insurers will also consider "geo-access," the accessibility of similar services in your geographical area, during rate negotiations. This can benefit a large group in a relatively remote area, specialty service groups, and groups willing to partner with insurers in meeting their particular clinical needs. For example, in order to maintain accreditation by the National Council for Quality Assurance (2009), insurers and managed care organizations are measured on post-hospital seven-day and 30-day ambulatory follow-up appointments for all psychiatric inpatient admissions. These measures are designed to prevent unnecessary hospital readmissions. Group practices are typically better able to schedule these ambulatory follow-up appointments and could partner with managed care organizations and local hospitals to capture this segment of the market.

Collaboration between behavioral health and medical practices has been facilitated by ACOs and initiatives related to PCMHs (e.g., AHRQ, n.d.; Meyers et al., 2010). In fact, in order to achieve accreditation as a PCMH, the National Council for Quality Assurance requires "agreements with behavioral health providers to enhance access, communication and coordination" (SAMHSA, 2014, p. 4). Group practices, particularly those with providers trained in healthcare settings, are uniquely positioned to collaborate with these larger medical entities. Thus, healthcare psychologists, neuropsychologists, psychiatrists, psychiatric nurse practitioners, prescribing psychologists (in states where this is allowed), social workers, and counselors who have expertise in treating comorbid medical conditions may find opportunities for their groups to collaborate with ACOs and PCMHs. In fact, there will also likely be opportunities for preferred provider status for groups prepared to collaborate with medical colleagues. Such affiliations, in turn, could lead to preferred provider status with medical colleagues and potentially increased payer visibility. That is, as PCMHs and ACOs develop contracts with payers, they will increasingly need behavioral health provider affiliations. An example of positioning a larger group practice to take advantage of market dynamics could involve a PCMH endorsing a practice group as a collaborator to a payer it is partnering with, thereby giving the payer an incentive to also collaborate with the behavioral health provider group. There are additional formal affiliations that could be developed between groups that are beyond the scope of this chapter (e.g., independent practice associations, integrated care models).

# GROUP DEVELOPMENT

Established solo practitioners often decide to come together to form a group to build something larger than their independent practices. Although this can be a complicated endeavor, it offers numerous benefits. For example, if each member has a successful independent practice, the logic often leads to the conclusion that such a group will be even more successful. While such synergy may indeed accrue, this strategy can often require sophisticated conflict management skills. Conflict management is important in all groups, but when attempting to meld successful independent providers into a unit with shared values, visions, and strategies, complementary perspectives can often become competing interests. Personal, professional, and business reasons for joining a group practice can also collide between members.

Groups can be expected to pass through developmental phases. Bonebright (2010) described and reviewed the past 40 years of research on Tuckman's (1965) work on group development as providing a "baseline of agreement on terms and ideas" (p. 118) pertinent to understanding evolving groups and reported that it was one of the most frequently used models for understanding team development. Tuckman originally (1965) reviewed and synthesized 55 articles on the developmental phases of small groups. These developmental phases were conceptualized as forming, storming, norming, performing, and adjourning. Forming refers to the initial tasks of working through the initial uncertainties, establishing trust, testing limits, and clarifying the roles and objectives of the group and its members. Storming refers to a period of conflict as group members vie for leadership roles, resist group influence, and work to resolve differences related to tasks, roles, and goals. In the norming phase, Tuckman describes a period of relative calm brought about by the resolution of conflict and the acceptance of tasks, roles, and goals. In the norming phase, accepted standards, cohesiveness, and roles are adopted that allow for the constructive expression of differences and the development of cooperative efforts to achieve shared goals. The performance phase is characterized by the resolution of structural issues, allowing the group to achieve functional roles and task performance. Conflict is resolved through group discussion that is focused on tasks and goals. Adjourning was added as a fifth phase by Tuckman and Jensen (1977) during a follow-up review of the literature. Adjourning refers to the natural life cycle or death of the group, characterized by a sense of loss and mourning. Some members will leave the group and in other cases the group itself will cease to exist.

All groups will experience conflicts and should be prepared to manage competing interests and personality styles. The group structure can be helpful in minimizing these, but conflict is an inevitable part of coexistence. While assertiveness is necessary, picking your battles and knowing what is important to your colleagues may also be valuable. It is therefore of considerable importance that group members not only respect one another but like one another and seek harmony. It is an old adage that business partnerships are like marriages, and along these lines, the predictors of marital dissolutions also have some relevance to group practices. Gottman and Silver (2015) have repeatedly shown that criticism, defensiveness, contempt, and stonewalling predict divorce between couples, and it stands to reason that these behaviors would also bode poorly for a group's survival. Alternatively, the behaviors Gottman and Silver cite as contributing to a lasting marriage likely lead to group survival: Know what is important to your partners; nurture fondness and admiration by reminding yourself of your partner's positive contributions; turn toward each other in conflict, not away, by seeking common ground; solve problems that are solvable, often by compromise; overcome gridlock by accepting your partner's dreams; and create shared meaning as well a sense of shared purpose.

Surviving conflicts and crises provides a sense of continuity and security to the group. As you can see, there is an interweaving of values that will contribute to a decision to join or create a group practice. As such, innumerable value conflicts within and between group members may also arise. However, appreciation for the other group members' expertise, both clinical and business, can result in the successful integration and continued development of a multispecialty group.

## SUMMARY

This chapter presents an broad overview of the issues likely to be encountered in the development of a group practice. The unique melding of business, personal, and professional goals will influence the move toward a group practice. Professional consultants will likely be necessary to assist you in the assessment, formation, and execution of formal agreements, labor contracts, finances, insurance policies, external contracts, and the type of legal entity best suited for your purposes. As your group practice grows, issues related to staffing and management will become more important and will require a delicate realignment of resources. A business plan will not only assist you in your initial appraisal of the health of the group but should be an ongoing process that is revisited periodically to review the strengths and weaknesses of the group, while developing a vision based on future opportunities. Professional groups may be expected to go through developmental phases, and conflict management skills will be necessary for the resolution of these processes and the continued growth of the group.

# REFERENCES

Agency for Healthcare Research and Quality (AHRQ). (n.d.). Defining the PCMH. Retrieved from http://pcmh.ahrq.gov/page/defining-pcmh.

American Psychological Association Center for Workforce Studies. (2015, February). 2014 APA member profiles. Washington, DC: Author. Retrieved from http://www.apa.org/workforce/publications/14-member/index.aspx?tab=1.

American Psychological Association Practice Organization. (2014, Spring/Summer). Highlights from the November 2013 survey of APA Practice Organization members. *Good Practice*, 16–17. Washington, DC: APAPO.

Bonebright, D. A. (2010). 40 years of storming: A historical review of Tuckman's model of small group development. *Human Resource Development International, 13*(1), 111–120.

Gottman, J. M., & Silver, N. (2015). *The seven principles for making marriage work: A practical guide.* New York: Harmony.

*How to Establish Your Business's Vision, Mission, and Values* - dummies. (n.d.). Retrieved November 14, 2016, from http://www.dummies.com/business/start-a-business/business-plans/how-to-establish-your-businesss-vision-mission-and-values/

Meyers, D., Peikes, D., Genevro, J., Peterson, G., Taylor, E. F., Lake, T., . . . Grumbach, K. (2010). The roles of patient-centered medical homes and accountable care organizations in coordinating patient care. AHRQ Publication No. 11–M005–EF. Rockville, MD: Agency for Healthcare Research and Quality.

National Committee for Quality Assurance (NCQA). (2009). *Follow-up after hospitalization for mental illness*. Retrieved from https://www.google.com/url?q=http://www.ncqa.org/ReportCards/HealthPlans/StateofHealthCareQuality/2014TableofContents/Followup.aspx&sa=U&ved=0CAYQFjABahUKEwie7MnT4J7HAhXMiQ0KHf7uBiY&client=internal-uds-cse&usg=AFQjCNFe4s58SLe54pWp40Lswwn0x8E9yA.

Nolo. (n.d.). Professional corporations. Retrieved from http://www.nolo.com/legal-encyclopedia/professional-corporations-29024.html.

Skok, M. (2013, July 14). Four steps to building a compelling value proposition. *Forbes*. Retrieved from http://www.forbes.com/sites/michaelskok/2013/06/14/4-steps-to-building-a-compelling-value-proposition/.

Silverman, S. I. (2015). In an era of healthcare delivery reforms, the corporate practice of medicine is a matter that requires vigilance. *Health Law & Policy, Brief, 9*(1), 1–23.

Substance Abuse and Mental Health Services Administration (SAMHSA). (2014). Advancing behavioral health integration within NCQA-recognized patient-centered medical homes. Retrieved from http://www.integration.samhsa.gov/resource/advancing-behavioral-health-integration-within-ncqa-recognized-patient-centered-medical-homes.

Tuckman, B. W. (1965). Developmental sequence in small groups. *Psychological Bulletin, 63*(6), 384–399.

Tuckman, B. W., & Jensen, M. A. C. (1977). Stages of small group development revisited. *Group and Organizational Studies, 2,* 419–427.

U.S. Small Business Administration. (n.d.). Build your business plan. Retrieved from https://www.sba.gov/writing-business-plan.

U.S. Small Business Administration. (n.d.). Choosing your business structure. Retrieved from https://www.sba.gov/category/navigation-structure/starting-managing-business/starting-business/choose-your-business-stru.

# CHAPTER 26

# THE BASICS OF MARKETING APPLIED TO PRIVATE PRACTICE

*Pauline Wallin*

Marketing is not something that gets most clinicians excited. But these days, when people have ready access to a multitude of resources to help them with their problems, effective marketing is essential in order to attract clients. No longer can you rely on the popular mantra, "If you build it, they will come." In order to be successful, you must not only build the infrastructure of your practice but must also earn trust and respect within your community and differentiate yourself from the competition.

Marketing need not be drudgery. In fact, once you start seeing results, you will likely get more and more comfortable with it. As your practice fills with the types of clients you most enjoy working with, you may even start looking forward to your next marketing campaign.

It is likely that marketing is one of the most misunderstood aspects of running a business. Unlike billing and recordkeeping, there are few rules, aside from following the standards of professional ethics codes, and results are harder to measure precisely. Many clinicians feel uncomfortable promoting themselves, and may question whether it is even ethical to do so.

## MISCONCEPTIONS ABOUT MARKETING

Until the landmark 1977 U.S. Supreme Court decision *Bates v. State Bar of Arizona*, professionals in private practice (including attorneys, physicians, mental health professionals, and others) were legally prohibited from advertising or marketing their services. After the court ruled that such bans violated free speech, it took several years before professional associations and licensing boards defined guidelines and parameters for marketing. It has taken even longer for mental health professionals to shake the assumption that any type of self-promotion is undignified or crass. This may be due to the fact that business skills have not been taught in most advanced-degree programs in mental health, leaving graduates confused about the ethics, the cost, and the goals of marketing. Misconceptions include the following:

1. Marketing is unprofessional. FACT: Some types of marketing do come across as pushy or devious, but there are many other options that will enhance your professional image.
2. Marketing is too self-serving and will turn people off. FACT: If done correctly, marketing does not focus on you, but addresses the needs of people who might need your help. When they read or hear something from you that is relevant to their own lives, they will be more apt to welcome additional information, rather than to be annoyed by your marketing messages.
3. Marketing is unethical. FACT: None of the ethics codes of psychologists, social workers, counselors, or marriage and family therapists state that marketing is unethical. The ethics codes do speak to issues such as protecting clients' privacy and not misrepresenting your competence. However, it is quite easy to market yourself within these parameters. Thus, not only is marketing ethical for mental health professionals, but I view it as our *ethical duty*. The public is already confused about how mental health treatment works and what type of psychotherapist to choose. If you do not market yourself effectively, people may not know about you and may instead turn to unlicensed and untrained self-proclaimed "therapists" who are ineffective—or, even worse, who could cause harm.
4. Marketing requires a big budget. FACT: You do not have to spend a lot of money to market yourself. There are plenty of free and low-cost options.
5. Marketing takes too much time. FACT: Marketing does require investment of your time, especially at the beginning of a marketing campaign. Once you get rolling, though, the time required will diminish. Keep in mind that marketing is an ongoing process. Your goals and strategies may change, but to stay ahead of the curve you will need to build marketing activities into your work schedule.
6. Only extroverts can succeed at marketing. FACT: Some marketing strategies, such as attending networking events, are easier for extroverts. But as a mental health clinician you can focus on public education and selective individual contacts, which are well within the comfort zone of introverts.

So let's get started!

## WHAT IS MARKETING?

The American Marketing Association's website defines marketing as "the activity, set of institutions, and processes for creating, communicating, delivering, and exchanging offerings that have value for customers, clients, partners, and society at large" (para. 1). Essentially, this means locating people who are likely to need and want your services and products, finding out what is important to them, and demonstrating to them that you can provide the services they need and want.

Marketing is different from advertising. While advertising focuses on promoting products or services (which will be described briefly toward the end of this chapter), marketing centers on creating and cultivating relationships with potential clients and referral sources, and communicating your value to them. In fact, you may already be marketing and not realize it. Every time you write a follow-up note to a physician who referred a patient, or you give a free talk to a community group, you are cultivating relationships and communicating how you can help people—in other words, marketing.

# HOW TO BEGIN MARKETING YOUR PRACTICE

The first step is defining whom you want to reach through your marketing messages. To begin doing so, answer these three questions:

1. *What types of people do I want to work with, and what sorts of problems can I help them with?* This is your target market of potential clients.
2. *Who has access to these people? Who is in a position to recommend me to others?* These are your referral sources, another target market.
3. *Where will I find both of the above, in the physical world and online?* Knowing where and how potential clients and referral sources spend their time and money will provide parameters for setting efficient marketing strategies.

Here is an example of how to apply the three questions above to your marketing plan. Suppose you enjoy working with couples. Is there a specific demographic or ethnic group that you are effective with (e.g., interfaith couples, late-life marriages, lesbian or gay couples)? What sorts of problems do you want to assist them with? Have you been successful in helping people with addiction, infertility, or other specific issues? Or do you have a special interest in addressing a particular situational problem, such as divorce or serious childhood illness? Having a firm idea of whom you want to help and what you want to help them with will serve as a basis for deciding on marketing tools and strategies that address the needs of your target audiences.

Next, where will you find the types of people that you enjoy working with, both in the community and online? Will you find them at church? At the soccer field? What types of clubs and organizations might attract such people? What keywords might they be typing into search engines when looking for help with their problems?

Who has access to these people and can refer those who need your help? For couples, the logical choice might be other mental health professionals who do not work with couples, as well as clergy, attorneys, and physicians. But also consider support groups such as Parents Without Partners, as well as real estate agents, hairdressers, bartenders, and others who regularly hear complaints about spouses. Referral sources are easy to find. You know where they work and you can find out which associations and organizations they belong to.

# COMMUNICATE YOUR VALUE TO YOUR
# TARGET AUDIENCES

Your training, your credentials, and your professional license all provide evidence that you are competent to help people with a variety of mental health issues—but this is true for most licensed clinicians. To stand out from your competition, you must communicate that you offer specific value to potential clients and referral sources.

"Value" is a subjective term that implies some benefit to the recipient, and it means different things to different people. What is of value to one person may be of little importance to another. For example, suppose you have experience in working with autistic children. That would be a big plus in attracting families with autistic kids to your practice, but it would not likely be important to college students with test anxiety. However, other aspects of your experience (perhaps having worked in a college counseling center) might be a determining factor in their choosing you to help them.

Once you have identified potential clients and referral sources and where to reach them, think about how you can demonstrate your value to them:

- Look for opportunities to give talks and presentations on relevant topics of interest.
- Write articles and tips sheets addressing the types of problems that your target audience typically experiences. Post them online and/or deliver them in person to your referral sources.
- Tailor the content of your website and of your online social networking to the people you want to help and the problems you want to help with.

## WHAT NOT TO DO

Do not try to appeal to everyone. The wider the audience you try to reach, the more general and diluted your messages will be, such that there will be little to differentiate you from other mental health professionals. On the other hand, if you focus your marketing to specific groups of people, you are more likely to be perceived as an "expert" for those people.

For example, suppose you want to create a fact sheet on coping with stress. If you try to appeal to everyone, your fact sheet will read like a page from a textbook—accurate, but not very inspiring. Suppose further that you enjoy working with autistic children and their families. Therefore, write your fact sheet to include common stresses that such families experience. This fact sheet will appeal specifically to your intended audience, with examples that they can relate to. Additionally, by focusing other marketing activities to this target audience, you will develop a reputation or "branding" as the go-to expert who can help them. Other mental health professionals in town may be equally competent to help families of autistic kids, but your name will probably come to mind first when one of these families needs help.

# MARKETING ACTIVITIES

A major goal of marketing is to gain name recognition and to build your brand as a trusted expert. Of course, this takes time, but it will take less time if people hear your name repeatedly, and if they see or hear frequent examples of your expertise. I am not suggesting that you bombard your target audiences with never-ending reminders. Rather, you can use a variety of approaches that are viewed as helpful rather than intrusive. Here are some examples.

## MARKETING VIA PUBLIC EDUCATION

Public education provides useful information to people, often at a time when they are receptive to it or when they are looking for it. Through public education you can demonstrate your expertise without coming across as pushy or as self-promotional. Consider doing some of the following public education activities:

- Give talks to local community groups.
- Write articles of interest to your target audience.
- Create handouts and tips sheets.
- Get quoted in mainstream TV, radio, and print news.
- Curate relevant mental health news and other content on social media.
- Volunteer in organizations that can use your mental health expertise.

While addressing your audience in person, via media, or in your writing, you will be forming a connection with them and solidifying your brand. As they learn more from you, and as they find the learning helpful, they will pay attention to what else you have to offer. At some point they may need your professional help and will then seek you out, or they may recommend you to others.

In other words, when you provide value to the members of your target audience, they will be more inclined to purchase your services, but only when *they* are ready, not when you want them to be ready. That is why marketing needs to be an ongoing, multifaceted process. You never know when someone will be ready to take action. But when they are, you want your name to be the one they think of first.

## MARKETING VIA YOUR WEBSITE

If you do not yet have a website, it is quite simple to set one up within a couple of hours, using website templates. However, if you are not ready to tackle the technical groundwork, hire someone to set up the site for you. From there you can add and change content using the built-in word-processing module.

People may land on your website for various reasons. Some may do an online search of your name on Google after hearing about you from someone else, or after reading something you have written. Others may search online for a psychotherapist in their local area. Still others may type a question into a search engine and find a link to your website within the search results.

When they land on your website, they will not spend more than a few seconds there unless they see something of interest or relevance to them. Your credentials, experience, and treatment approach are important, but that is not the first thing that a potential client would be interested in knowing. Initially, people want to know whether you can help them with their problem, and whether they might like you. Only then would they be interested in where you were trained and in your philosophy of treatment.

Here are hypothetical examples of home page excerpts from two psychotherapists' websites, paraphrased from a compilation of actual websites. If you were a prospective client, which of the two would make you feel more welcome and curious to know more?

a. *Welcome to Dr. Smith's website. Dr. Smith has been practicing for over 20 years. She specializes in cognitive-behavioral therapy (CBT), neurofeedback, mindfulness and schema therapy. She was trained at the University of Pittsburgh, where she also taught courses in abnormal behavior and biofeedback. Her publications include "A double-blind study of neurofeedback for treatment of trauma recovery" published in the Journal of Adjunct Psychological Methods, and a book, Panic is Uncomfortable, But It Won't Kill You. Her treatment approach is practical and science-based. Click this link to read more about Dr. Smith.*

b. *Has it been a while since you felt happy in your relationship? Have you tried communicating without success? People do change over time, but our fundamental needs remain the same. I have helped hundreds of couple re-discover the joy that brought them together in the first place. Most of my clients experience improvement in their communication within eight sessions or fewer. Before you call it quits, consider relationship counseling to get you back on track. Click here to learn more about working with me.*

Notice that in the first example above, the entire segment is about the psychotherapist. Dr. Smith certainly has impressive credentials, but by leading with a summary of her qualifications, she misses an opportunity to form a personal connection with visitors to her website. In contrast, the second example draws the visitor in from the beginning by asking a question, and again by giving the person a reason to consider getting help.

When setting up or redesigning your website, think of it as a storefront on a busy street. As people stop to look, what can you have in your window that would encourage them to pause and come in and browse? That will vary, depending on your target audience. However, all websites should be uncluttered, should be easy to read on all screen sizes, and should have clear navigation tabs indicating what is inside. Color is important, as it communicates values and emotions. Images (including your photo) are also important, both to break up blocks of text for easier reading, and because they, too, have emotional appeal.

The content of your website will include your address, phone number, and other details of your practice. But as noted above, it should focus primarily on the needs and interests of the members of your target audience. Once they have decided that you *can* help them, they next need to decide why they should choose you over another clinician. At this point they may be interested in your credentials and where you trained. They may also be interested in your exact location, your fees, whether you accept their insurance, whether you have evening appointments, and other details. This type of information need not be on the first page, but it should be quickly accessible via the navigation tabs.

If you do have something unique to offer, this should go on the first page—for example, Sunday office hours, free babysitting, free parking, home visits, free initial consultation, or fluency in a foreign language. Depending on the needs and preferences of your web visitors who are ready to get help, they may make the decision to work with you based on one or more such conveniences.

## MARKETING VIA A BLOG

While the content of your website does not change very often, a blog (truncated from the term "web log") is a series of articles and postings in chronological order, with the most recent at the top. Blog posts are a great way to be found via search engines. Every post—even if it's just a couple of paragraphs—is considered a separate page in Google's index, and gets its own line in search results. If you write one blog post per week, after 20 weeks you will have 20 separate hits on your name in Google search results just from your blog posts alone. If others quote your post on their blogs, you will see additional hits in the search results.

Needless to say, I urge every clinician to have a blog—even if you do not have a website—because blogging can help you quickly establish an authoritative online presence. It is easy to set up a blog for free at blogger.com (owned by Google) or at wordpress.com. Sign up for an account; choose your blog title; select your template; start typing; save and publish. Your blog post will show up on the search engines within seconds.

If you already have a website that was built or updated in the last five years, you can probably add a blog to your site with a few clicks. Check with your web host or web designer for how to do so.

Once your blog is set up, post regularly on the topic(s) that you want to be known for. Not only will this help boost your search engine rankings, but also when people visit your blog they will see a recent date and relevant content in your last post—which communicates an active online presence on your part. In addition, encourage interaction from visitors by inviting them to post comments. Make sure you set the comments to be moderated and approved by you, so as to prevent postings by spammers. Do respond to comments when appropriate, but avoid giving specific clinical advice. In fact, it would be advisable to have a disclaimer on your blog (and on other writing for the public) that the content is for educational purposes only, and not intended as professional advice.

## MARKETING VIA SOCIAL MEDIA

According to Pew Research (n.d.), a 2015 study found that social media engagement among the public has continued to grow over the past four years, with Facebook showing the least growth (perhaps because it had already experienced its growth spurts and had stabilized). The majority of people who are active on social media use their mobile devices, which makes it easy for them to check their accounts frequently. Thus, you have the opportunity to be on their radar at various times during the day. By posting links to high-quality information and by engaging in social media discussions, you can become recognized as a trusted source in your field.

There are hundreds of social media platforms. However, for marketing purposes you just need to be active on those that are most popular among your target audiences.

LinkedIn is useful for connecting with other professionals and with the business community. Fill out your profile as completely as possible so that you can be found by someone who is searching for a professional with your credentials, experience, or interests. Next, explore some groups to join. At the time of this writing, groups are accessed via the "Interests" tab at the LinkedIn website. To get the most out of LinkedIn, participate in group discussions so that your name becomes familiar.

Twitter (n.d.) has 320 million active users. It is most popular among people under age 50, but it is also widely used by journalists, who may look for story leads and/or post links to what they have written. As with LinkedIn and other social media accounts, you should include lots of detail in your Twitter account profile so that people can learn more about you.

For marketing purposes, use Twitter to post links to interesting content online, especially content that reflects the areas for which you want to be known. Thus, for example, if you want to develop a reputation as an expert on relationships, you would post links to press releases or news articles describing current research on the topic. You might also post links to noteworthy blog posts or other online resources that can help people in their relationships. In addition to posting tweets yourself, follow other experts and journalists, and re-tweet their postings. Since some of these influential people have opted to receive notifications when their tweets are re-tweeted, they may start paying attention to your tweets and follow you on Twitter.

Pinterest, a visual bookmarking site, is used primarily by millennial females. If that is one of your target audiences, then you should consider developing a presence there. Compared to Instagram, which is strictly photos, Pinterest "pins" do connect with your website.

YouTube is a versatile marketing tool. You can create a video greeting and embed it on your website. You can also make short videos to share tips or to do a demonstration such as deep breathing. For more ideas, check out the videos of other mental health clinicians at youtube.com.

Blogtalkradio is great for creating audio, either by yourself or by interviewing another expert. It works via telephone, and you can invite your audience to call in as they would to a radio talk show. The call is recorded, and after you are done it is automatically stored in your account for on-demand listening. It is also indexed by Google.

You may have noticed that I have not mentioned Facebook as a marketing tool. Facebook is used by some clinicians as a substitute for a website. It is easy to use and there are no hosting fees or other costs. You can circumvent potential ethics issues, such as friend requests from clients, by setting up a Facebook business page, which allows only "likes," not friend requests, and which does not give access to your private Facebook profile account. However, you have to abide by Facebook's rules and you have no control over the way your content is presented. Furthermore, Facebook has sometimes arbitrarily and abruptly shut down people's pages without notice. There is an appeal process, but in the meantime, the page is offline for days or weeks.

One of the benefits of social media marketing is that individual readers and visitors have the option to forward your messages or links to their social networks, thus extending your reach exponentially. They will be more likely to do so if your content is relevant, novel, and interesting to them. An analysis by Dan Zarrella (2013) of millions of tweets and re-tweets found that the most frequently re-tweeted word was "you." He also found that writing about oneself correlated with lower follower counts and fewer re-tweets. Zarrella emphasizes: "The bio is the only place you should be talking about yourself."

## MARKETING OFFLINE

While marketing online gives you wide exposure to an international audience, it is unlikely that anyone will make an appointment with you based on your Twitter feed. Your best sources of referrals are current and past clients, and other professionals and business owners in your community. If clients are pleased with your service (not just the professional aspect, but also customer service details like a clean, comfortable office and prompt attention to administrative requests) they are likely to recommend you to others. It may take a while to build a clientele through word-of-mouth referrals, as people are not always ready to take the big step at the time they hear about you. Some may wait months or years. One of my clients contacted me almost 20 years after she had heard me speak at a community event.

Other professionals who work with the types of people that you want to help are great referral sources. However, many of them may already have trusted clinicians to whom they refer clients. Thus, it might be better to focus first on those who are new to practice or new to the community, because they are less likely to have established referral patterns. As you build relationships with these referral sources, consider making them referral *partners* to whom you will refer your clients.

When marketing to potential referral partners, you need to do more than simply send a letter or drop off a stack of business cards. As with any marketing activity, the relationship is key. Look for opportunities to get personal introductions from mutual acquaintances. Ask for a five-minute appointment to visit them at their office. When you do meet them face to face, show interest in them before describing what you do. When describing your practice, emphasize how you can be of help to their clients, patients, students, or other people they serve.

Stay in touch with referral sources. Send them articles they might be interested in reading. If they are mentioned favorably in the local news, send them an email or a card acknowledging the mention. For clients who are referred to you by another professional, get their permission to co-ordinate care (when appropriate) with the referral source. When you have a client to refer out, ask the person's permission to briefly discuss his or her case with the other professional.

## SHOW UP!

Actor and film director Woody Allen once said that 80% of success in life is showing up. To become better known in your community, be visible. Get involved in nonprofessional activities, such as at your house of worship, with your kids' school or sports teams, with service clubs such as Kiwanis or Rotary, or in tennis or golf leagues. Serve on community boards and volunteer for organizations that can use your expertise. Such activities are less intimidating than attending networking cocktail hours, and they are more productive, too. Through repeated contact with the same groups of people you will develop an informal network of friends and acquaintances, each one a potential client or referral source.

## MARKETING VIA PRESENTATIONS AND NEWS MEDIA COMMENTARY

Giving talks to community groups and to professional groups provides an opportunity for you to demonstrate your expertise. If your presentations are interesting and helpful to your audiences, a few of those people will likely contact you for an appointment, or recommend you to someone they know.

Speaking opportunities are plentiful. Service clubs like Kiwanis and Rotary meet weekly, and they are always looking for speakers. Local organizations, such as support groups, bar associations, hospital staff, and other professional groups, also welcome speakers on topics of interest to their members. Meetup groups, organized through social media apps such as meetup.com, are becoming more popular. Most meetup groups are informal and focus on a specific hobby or activity—biking, cooking, pets, retirement, ethnic culture, and the like. Not all schedule speakers on a regular basis, but if you can address a common problem or challenge faced by their members, they may be open to having you come to do a brief presentation.

Whenever you give a talk, distribute a handout summarizing your key points. On the handout include your contact information, your website, and/or your Twitter handle. Some people will keep your handout (maybe even post it on the fridge), and perhaps contact you in the future or recommend you to others.

You probably will not get paid for your presentations, and your audiences may not be large. However, each person has made time to come to hear you speak, and each person is a potential client or referral source. Furthermore, the fact that you are being hosted by a given organization is an implied endorsement of your expertise—something that will enhance your overall professional credibility and reputation.

To boost your authoritative status even more, look for opportunities to be interviewed or quoted by news media. When you appear on TV or radio, or when you are quoted in newspapers or magazines, these are tantamount to being endorsed by the media as a knowledgeable expert.

Reporters routinely interview professionals who can provide helpful information related to current topics of general interest. For example, if a pedophile was recently arrested in your community, it is quite likely that many parents are concerned for the safety of their own children. This would be an ideal time to contact the news director at your local TV or radio station and offer to give a few tips to parents on how to help keep their kids safe, without overreacting in panic. If interested, the news station will send a reporter to your office to record an interview with you. If you do a good job, you will be called frequently to offer commentary on mental health issues, which will enhance your professional status in the community.

Given the ease of finding information online, people no longer need your business card for your contact information. However, business cards have other uses. For example, on the back of your card you can write a bit of information that you would like to share with someone, such as your private cellphone number. The person receiving this information will be more likely to keep your card, and to be reminded of you when looking at the information on the back.

You can have different business cards for different purposes. Besides your contact information, include a few words that describe your expertise vis-à-vis the interests of the recipient. Thus, a card you give to cardiologists might say "stress management." A card you give to divorce attorneys might say "psychological evaluations for child custody." A card you give to the program chair of a professional organization might list the topics you can speak about in a keynote address. The possibilities are endless. Just be sure that you are professionally qualified for any specialty that you list on a business card.

To encourage word-of-mouth referrals from current clients, place a stack of business cards in your waiting room, with a sign next to them that says, "Take one." Those two words will increase the likelihood that people will take a card—and maybe pass it on to a friend or family member.

# WHAT ABOUT ADVERTISING?

While marketing focuses on growing your reputation and on building relationships with potential clients and referral partners, advertising is a direct offer of service. Years ago, it was expensive to advertise. A small ad in the Yellow Pages could lock you in to paying hundreds of dollars per month for an entire year. TV and radio advertising was way beyond the budget of most mental health professionals. Now you have many free and low-cost options to advertise your practice, most of them online, where people generally go for new information these days.

First, sign up for a free account at "Google My Business," which adds you to the Google map that appears at the top of local search results. For example, if you are a marriage counselor in Cleveland, and someone in Cleveland runs a Google search for "marriage counselor," your office address will be included as one of the virtual pushpins on the map. You do not need to have a website to be included in Google My Business, but if you do have a website, your listing can link to it.

Psychotherapist directories, including PsychologyToday.com and GoodTherapy.org, charge a monthly fee, which can be offset by income you receive from clients who found you through your directory listing. These sites also have good search engine optimization, such that people who do not know about psychotherapist directories will still be able to find you through a Google search. If their keywords match what you are offering, their search results will include links to your listing at PsychologyToday or at GoodTherapy.

The number of referrals you will get from psychotherapist directory listings depends on many factors, including the description in your profile and whether it appeals to people who need your services. As described earlier in the section on websites, write directly to the person who is reading the description of your practice.

### OFFLINE ADVERTISING

Offline advertising can be a good investment if your ad is likely to be seen by the people you want to reach. For example, if your target audience includes teens and their families, you might place an ad in the school musical program brochure. Parents tend to read these from cover to cover and to take them home. If and when they need mental health help, they may recall that they saw your ad, and then contact you.

The Yellow Pages phone books are still around, but unless you have a large number of clients who found you this way (you can find out by asking them), I do not recommend advertising in the Yellow Pages. Not only do you have to commit yourself to a full year of monthly payments, but you are also stuck with the ad for the full year; you cannot change it.

# REFINE YOUR MARKETING AND ADVERTISING FOR BETTER RESULTS

The success of your outreach is not always immediately evident. It is quite common, for instance, to see a delay between talking to a family physician about how you can help her patients and booking a client referred by her. Over a period of time, however, if you ask new clients how they found you, you will see patterns emerging.

Use a spreadsheet to track how clients heard about you, as well as how much income you received from each. After a year or so you will probably notice that some sources yield more referrals and/or greater income than others. This will help inform your decision about where to focus your marketing efforts going forward.

For example, assume that 25% of your clients were referred by Dr. Smith, but most of them were covered by the insurance plan that pays you the least. Would you want more referrals from Dr. Smith? Or might it be a better use of your marketing efforts to focus more on Dr. Jones, who sent you only 5% of your clients, but they all paid your full fee out of pocket?

Similarly, if you received many inquiries from your PsychologyToday listing but very few actual clients, you will then need to decide whether it pays to continue with this directory. At the very least, if you have recouped the annual cost (about $360), then you might decide to leave the listing in place for the time being. But check your stats periodically and be ready to change the content of your listing or discontinue it altogether if it costs more than you earn from it.

For the individual professionals who send you many referrals, it's a nice gesture (not to mention a powerful reinforcer) to show your appreciation by bringing in lunch for their staff or sending boxes of treats. Many mental health professionals do this around the holidays, but it is appropriate at any time. In fact, your treats may have greater impact in the middle of the year, when they are not overshadowed by other people's holiday gifts.

# FIND WHAT WORKS AND KEEP DOING IT

You need not do all the above marketing activities. Start with one or two that you feel most comfortable with and that address the needs of your target audiences. If you get a positive response, continue.

If you get no response after a few weeks or months, this may mean your target audiences are not noticing, or that your message is not resonating with them. The most common error made by mental health professionals in their writing and speaking is being too complex. It may help to narrow the scope of your messages and to simplify the language.

As with any new endeavor, marketing has a learning curve. Assume that your first efforts will be your worst, so do not aim for perfection. Marketing is an ongoing process that will change and evolve, depending on your goals and on the opportunities available to you. The more experience you get with marketing, the easier it will be to determine the strategies that work best for you.

# FINAL WORDS

Marketing encompasses skills that you already have—writing, speaking, being helpful, and understanding other people's perspectives. Your greatest challenge may be not so much in knowing *what* to do, nor in *how* to do it, but rather in overcoming the resistance of procrastination.

The longer you put off getting started, the more daunting a task seems. Fortunately, as you have experienced countless times, once you do take action, your anxiety usually dissipates quickly, and you feel newly empowered.

Ethical marketing has few downsides and many upsides—building a reputation and brand, making new friends and contacts, and finding new opportunities, to name a few. In the current competitive environment, such advantages are essential to business success.

Think of marketing as an investment in your business and in your career, where you invest on a regular basis through some of the marketing activities described in this chapter. You won't see results right away, but over time, consistent, targeted marketing will help you build a solid practice, filled with the types of clients you most enjoy working with.

# REFERENCES

American Marketing Association. (n.d.). Retrieved from www.ama.org/AboutAMA/Pages/Definition-of-Marketing.aspx.

Pew Research. (n.d.). Retrieved from http://www.pewinternet.org/2015/10/08/social-networking-usage-2005-2015/.

Twitter. (n.d.). Retrieved from https://about.twitter.com/company.

Zarrella, D. (2013) *The science of marketing: When to tweet, what to post, how to blog, and other proven strategies.* Hoboken, NJ: Wiley.

## CHAPTER 27

# THE USE OF THE MEDIA IN MARKETING A PRIVATE PRACTICE

*Nancy A. McGarrah*

The first question mental health professionals in private practice may ask when thinking about this topic is this: "Why should I get involved in media work, and how would this enhance my marketing efforts?" There are many reasons for using media, including helping to educate the general public as well as for marketing your practice. Working with the media provides clinicians the opportunity to help the general public better understand mental health issues. Reporters will often want assistance from clinicians in explaining mental health issues in terms that are user-friendly to the public. For example, topics can include how divorce impacts children, methods to reduce trauma after a school shooting, and more typical concerns such as how to get children ready to go back to school after a break or vacation. Participating in interviews with members of the media can result in providing this information to the public and, if done well, can enhance both the image of the mental health professions and your own practice (McGarrah, Brownawell, & Hill, 2013). Participating in a radio, television, or print media interview can enable you to reach a vast audience, much larger than can be done in most traditional ways. You can be recognized in your community as an expert in the topic, as well as gain wider recognition if the interview is broadcast nationally. Individuals will often call for appointments after seeing a particular interview. Some of these interviews have been seen locally, while others have been seen in far regions of the globe, as news networks frequently distribute stories about mental health to other news outlets.

There are many reasons why mental health professionals would participate in media work, including marketing clinical services for independent practice, overcoming public speaking anxiety and improving public speaking skills, becoming the "face" of their profession in their region, using media to present their own services and programs, gaining exposure and credibility indirectly through media exposure, promoting responsible mental health reporting, and publicizing important research and making it easily understandable to the public. Many enjoy doing something different from the typical work activities of mental health practitioners. Others also comment that they find these experiences to be both fun and professionally rewarding (Kanaris, 2006; Martin, 2005).

## ARE YOU AN EXPERT?

In terms of considering a media request, it is important to realize what the definition of an expert in a particular area may be to the reporter. For example, one of my areas of expertise lies in the area of children, families, and forensic issues related to families. I have been asked to comment on a variety of topics, and for some of these I would not consider myself an expert. For example, I have been interviewed regarding mind–body health, swearing habits among children, girls dating older boys, economic stress on families, and maternity leave and new mothers' stress. Although all of these topics are somehow related to my expertise, I have to determine if I am able to add something valuable to the interview. Doing research ahead of time will often define whether this topic is the right one for you to respond to, or whether you should refer the reporter to someone who is more knowledgeable. For example, I was asked to do an interview regarding fetal alcohol syndrome and referred the reporter to the center in my city that has the most expertise in this area. On another occasion, I was asked to comment on the effect of violent comic books on children. Since I had never seen a violent comic book, I asked the reporter to bring one to the interview. I explained that although I did not know of any research in this area specifically, I would be able to comment on the research about the effects of violence on children. This is the type of broad discussion the reporter wanted for the story.

## PROS AND CONS OF MEDIA WORK

There are pros and cons of participating in a media interview. Working with the media can include a wide range of activities, such as a one-time interview, a regular interview on a television or radio program, or an interview for a news magazine or other type of publication. Making time for the interview will disrupt your usual work schedule. Often there is a time crunch for the reporter and you will have to respond quickly to the request for an interview. Even though pressed for time, you must prepare carefully and do your due diligence regarding the ethical aspects. There are many ethical issues when doing any media work, and these will be described in further detail later in this chapter.

## HOW TO GET STARTED

The most important place to begin in doing media work is making contacts and building relationships with different reporters. This most often happens when your name is given to a reporter because of your expertise in a particular area. These referrals can come from different sources, but frequently they can be generated from your state or national professional associations. In my experience, requests have generally come through my state association, where I have gone through media trainings and have become a member of the Public Education Committee's Speakers Bureau. When a call (or more commonly an email) comes in to the state association main office from a reporter, the staff knows who on the Speakers Bureau may have the best knowledge of that subject area. Several clinicians will usually then be emailed or called to see who is available and interested. Once a practitioner has been interviewed several times by a particular reporter, that reporter will have developed a relationship with that person and will call again when other interviews concerning mental health issues arise.

After a particular local or national crisis, such as a school shooting or natural disaster, there are many requests for mental health professionals to provide interviews. This is a time when a practitioner who may not otherwise do media work may be brought into the media field to help explain the best way the public can deal with these issues. It is an excellent time to work with the media to help the public find available resources and to explain coping mechanisms after a trauma. The American Psychological Association (APA) produces tips for answering media inquiries following a large crisis or tragedy. The APA Help Center has resources such as "Managing Your Distress in the Aftermath of a School Shooting" and "Helping Your Children Manage Distress in the Aftermath of a Shooting" (apa.org/helpcenter). Other professional organizations have similar help centers (aamft.org, counseling.org, and socialworkers.org/pressroom/features/genfactSheets.asp).

It is also possible to pitch your own ideas for interviews to different media outlets. Reporters often have asked in our media trainings to provide them with ideas for stories. On a slow news day, reporters need to have interesting human-interest stories that can be inserted into programming. Clinicians can frequently pitch stories related to current events in the neighborhood or in their community, public education initiatives through your state or national association, and new research in a particular area. When pitching your own story to a media outlet, the time crunch is usually not as significant, since this would be a story that the media can use whenever appropriate and is not usually time sensitive.

## PREPARING FOR AND PROVIDING EFFECTIVE INTERVIEWS

When practitioners want to promote their practices through media work, obtaining effective training in interviewing is imperative. This training is frequently available from state and national associations, as well as from other organizations. The APA Office of Public Communications has a training presentation that is available at www.apa.org/about/division/officers/dialogue/2011/03/dlc-media-interview-tips.pdf. It is helpful to have mock interviews with a reporter that can be videotaped and then reviewed. When I organize media trainings, reporters are invited to conduct interviews with mental health professionals and to then critique them. Those new to media work should also consider consulting with colleagues who have significant media experience. Their knowledge base will be helpful in learning the best way to approach an interview. The public relations office of your national professional association can be of use in giving specific information about an interview on a particular topic, as well as giving advice for the best way to approach the interview. Resources from the APA can be found at www.apa.org/pubs/authors/media/index.aspx. The National Association of Social Workers has media toolkits available (socialworkers.org), the Association of Marriage and Family Therapists has media assistance (aamft.org), and the American Counseling Association provides media information (counseling.org).

Once you have agreed to give an interview to a reporter (or write an article for a publication), the preparation and research stage begins. The topic may not be one that you know much about, but some quick research will usually give a good basis of understanding. It is also a good idea to ask the reporter to provide any research articles or other information on which he or she is basing the interview. In the initial conversation or email with the reporter, ask what specific questions the reporter would like answered during the interview. Reporters typically want some general information that is understandable without professional terminology. Reporters want an approachable spokesperson who can relate to the general public rather than provide an academic discussion of detailed scientific explanations in technical terms.

If you are asked to appear on a television interview, familiarize yourself with the style of the show. Many "talk shows" have a specific angle, and knowing this information in advance is important. This can prevent the feeling of "being ambushed."

When speaking with the reporter about the upcoming interview, discuss whether this will be a live or recorded media event, as well as what the time commitments are for the interview. Setting up for a media interview can take up to an hour for the reporter and cameraperson. When I do interviews in my office, I will try to have them set up in one room while I do work in another room. I also ask how long the actual interview process will take, so I will know how much of my professional time to block out for the interview. The reporter and cameraperson will then have to take down the set, which can take 15 to 30 minutes. It is helpful to ask the reporter in advance if there will be any editing ability on the clinician's part after the interview is recorded. Of course, if the interview is live, that will not be a factor. In my experience, I have never been able to edit a recorded interview. However, I have at times been able to see a written interview before press to see if edits are needed.

In terms of the actual interview, professionalism is extremely important. Most interviews either occur in a newsroom studio or in the practitioner's office. The clinician will learn in media training what to wear for an interview, because certain types of clothing (such as patterned, black, red, beige, or white clothing) do not translate well to a media presentation. When starting the interview, be sure to identify yourself with your professional title and/or credentials and areas of specialization, and state your full name. An example would be, "My name is Mr. John Jones, a Licensed Clinical Social Worker, who directs the Huntsville Family Services Center, specializing in the assessment and treatment of emotional and behavioral difficulties in children and adolescents." During the interview, realize that nothing is "off the record," even if it appears otherwise. Thinking in advance about the three most important points that need to be included in the interview makes the material easier to transmit. Using transitional bridges, such as "the most important point is . . ." can bring the subject matter back to the significant issues. Pausing before answering each question allows for editing by the media (and for you to think about your response a bit before speaking). If asked a question outside your expertise, it is appropriate to say you don't know the answer, or you can't comment on that question. The interviewer may pressure you to make statements that cannot be supported, but you must be careful to only comment accurately and only on topics that are in your areas of expertise. Your job is not to please the interviewer, but to give only information that is within your knowledge and expertise. At the end of the interview, give the reporter your business card. Reporters want a clinician who can calmly and expertly discuss the specialty topic. Clinicians are representing their profession as well as marketing themselves.

## THE FINAL PRODUCT

Once the interview is completed, ask the reporter when the story will air (or be printed). That way, you can record the interview and carefully observe your performance. It is important to learn from any mistakes you make in interviews. One of the most common problems in interviews is the tendency to hesitate, say "um," or otherwise disrupt the flow of conversation. Another problem is speaking in sentence fragments. All sentences in the interview should be a complete thought, so that when the reporter edits the interview, the message is still clear. If you can review the finished product before publication or airing, the reporter may be able to correct any problems in the interview. It is helpful to keep a list of all media interviews, including each reporter's name, contact information, and affiliation. This list of media contacts will be useful when pitching stories in the future.

## ETHICAL ISSUES IN TRADITIONAL MEDIA WORK

There are numerous ethical pitfalls to be aware of and avoid when doing media work, and these need to be carefully considered before agreeing to provide any interview. Preparing for these challenges and pitfalls should be part of every mental health practitioner's media training. Reporters frequently ask clinicians if one of their clients could be interviewed to make the story more engaging. Think carefully before agreeing to this, realizing the imbalance of power in the relationship. Always consider the ethics issue of exploitation if a client is asked to participate in any media work. A client who is asked by his or her psychotherapist to participate may feel pressured to do this to please the therapist. I personally have never agreed to have a client interviewed for a story. I had an experience when I did an interview about divorce without referring to any particular families. However, when the story aired, it was imbedded in a story about a particular evaluation that had been completed. The family involved in the evaluation had actually contacted the media and given them my name, but I was not told this by the reporter. Once it aired, viewers might have thought I was specifically referring to the case the reporter was using as the centerpiece of the story. I wrote a letter to the media representative explaining my concerns and displeasure. However, the story had already aired, and there was nothing the outlet did to correct it. Needless to say, I never agreed to work with that reporter again.

Concerns have recently been raised about the appropriateness of clinicians being involved in "reality" television. These programs usually show very limited and edited outtakes from psychotherapy sessions. The network has told clinicians who have considered participating in a program such as this that they would have no control over what is taped and what is aired. This raises many ethical concerns, including limits of confidentiality and misuse of the clinician's work. Clinicians must insist that clients be given the proper informed consent, as well as help them understand possible adverse consequences for them should they decide to participate.

When doing an interview, reporters will sometimes ask if they can record you doing regular work around the office (referred to by reporters as "B roll" material). When the segment airs on television, you or the reporter are heard discussing the topic, while you are seen sitting at your desk, talking on the telephone, or doing other tasks. It is helpful to discuss with the reporter what kinds of things are going to be discussed during this background information section. It is very important to review the recorded interview so you can make sure the reporter's comments during this background section are stating accurately what was said during the interview. Reaching an agreement with the reporter about this prior to the interview is important, since trying to address this after the fact is ineffective.

Consider which areas of expertise you are comfortable discussing. Professional codes of ethics (e.g., APA Standard 9.01, Bases for Assessments; American Counseling Association [ACA] Standard E.5.d, Refraining from Diagnosis; National Association of Social Workers [NASW] Standard 4.06, Misrepresentation; and American Association for Marriage and Family Therapists [AAMFT] Standard 3.11, Public Statements) state that clinicians should only offer opinions on information and techniques sufficient to substantiate their findings and provide opinions of the psychological characteristics of individuals only after they have conducted an examination of the individuals adequate to support their statements or conclusions. Therefore, clinicians must stay within the bounds of their data and their knowledge. For example, they cannot make definitive statements regarding any person in the public eye if they have not interviewed or assessed that person. It is helpful to use certain statements when asked about a particular person, such as, "I can't speak about that particular issue or person, but what we know generally about this kind of situation is . . ." There is what is called the "Goldwater Rule," which concerns making public diagnoses of public figures. This rule is named the Goldwater Rule because of the 1964 Goldwater–Johnson election when psychiatrists who had not evaluated him responded to questions about Mr. Goldwater, and the bulk of their responses (which were described in psychiatric terminology) were unfair and derogatory. Goldwater later sued and won a substantial settlement.

Occasionally a reporter will have heard about a clinician's case, such as something that was in the news or for which there is public record such as a trial transcript. A reporter may ask about this particular case in the course of a more general interview. At this point, you must say that you cannot say anything beyond what is in the public record and you cannot comment on individual clients without their specific permission to do so.

All mental health professional associations have ethics standards that are applicable to media work (AAMFT Code of Ethics, 2015; ACA Code of Ethics, 2014; APA Ethics Code, 2010, and NASW Code of Ethics, 2008). The first relevant ethics standard is informed consent. All ethics codes have sections regarding the requirement to ensure clear and understandable informed consent for clients (APA Ethics Code Standard 4.02, Discussing the Limits of Confidentiality; NASW

Code of Ethics Standard 1.03, Informed Consent; ACA Code of Ethics Standard A.2, Informed Consent in the Counseling Relationship; and AAMFT Code of Ethics Standards 1.2, Informed Consent, and 1.8, Client Autonomy in Decision Making). This is especially important if clients are asked to take part in any media interview. Closely related is the ethics issue of maintaining client's confidentiality (APA Ethics Code Standard 4.01, Maintaining Confidentiality; NASW Code of Ethics Standard 2.02, Confidentiality; ACA Code of Ethics Standard B.1.c, Respect for Confidentiality; and AAMFT Code of Ethics Standards 2.1, Disclosing Limits of Confidentiality, and 2.4, Confidentiality in Non-Clinical Activities). Because of the special relationship that occurs in psychotherapy, the mental health practitioner must safeguard the client's confidentiality and make sure the informed consent is thoroughly understood before considering including clients in media work.

Boundaries of competence (APA Code of Ethics Standard 2.01, Boundaries of Competence; NASW Code of Ethics Standards 1.04, Competence, and 4.01, Competence; ACA Code of Ethics Standard C.2.a, Boundaries of Competence; and AAMFT Code of Ethics Standard 3.1, Maintenance of Competency) are critical ethical considerations, especially when clinicians are pushed to comment on topics beyond their expertise. Some ethics codes have sections particularly aimed at media work. See, for example, APA Ethics Code Standards 1.01, Misuse of Psychologists' Work, and 5.04, Media Presentations; NASW Code of Ethics Standard 4.06, Misrepresentation; ACA Code of Ethics Standard C.6.c, Media Presentations; and AAMFT Code of Ethics Standard 3.11, Public Statements. One key issue mentioned in these standards is the accurate representation of your professional credentials, as well as making sure that your statements are based on your training and experience and the professional literature. Another important issue is the need to be clear that no professional relationship is implied in the public statement. If you become aware of misrepresentations of your statements, you must take steps to correct these.

In using media as a marketing strategy, you are donating your time in exchange for various benefits, including recognition as a local or national expert. It is important to differentiate legitimate media work from advertisements for the psychotherapist. Some "news stories," upon closer examination, appear to be actual ads for clinicians or testimonials by their clients. This is not the same as traditional media exposure, and it must be identified as an advertisement. Ethics codes require an advertisement to be identified as such. Mental health professionals may not pay for participating in a media interview.

In summary, when working with the media, many ethical quandaries may arise. You may need to consult with an ethics committee or an experienced colleague when ethics issues and concerns arise.

## CONCLUDING THOUGHTS

Working with the media can be an excellent experience for you as a mental health professional and can definitely expand your ability to market your practice. Even when you are asked to speak about someone in the news, you can agree to talk to the media as long as it is clear that comments are based solely on what you have seen or heard in the news and that there is no clinician–client relationship. Educating the public about relevant issues within your clinical expertise can be a valuable public service. Be sure to stick with the information you know through your experience, practice, and other knowledge base and do not get pulled away from this basis for comments. Your message should be simple and succinct, and doing your homework ahead of time will provide clarity about what you want to impart to the audience. Your information should be accurate and you should avoid jargon and complex concepts. All ethics obligations, particularly those discussed in this chapter, must be considered.

Working with the media can be daunting and even frightening, but it can also be a wonderful experience professionally (McGarrah, Martin, Alvord, & Haldeman, 2009). For more information regarding media work, consult with a "media mentor" (a colleague with experience in working with the media) and/or someone in the media psychology division or section of your local or national professional association.

# REFERENCES

American Association for Marriage and Family Therapists. (2015). Code of ethics. Retrieved from http://www.aamft.org/iMIS15/AAMFT/Content/Legal_Ethics/Code_of_Ethics.aspx.

American Counseling Association. (2014). Code of ethics. Retrieved from https://www.counseling.org/resources/aca-code-of-ethics.pdf.

American Psychological Association. (2010). Ethical principles of psychologists and code of conduct. Retrieved from www.apa.org/ethics/code/principles.pdf.

Kanaris, P. (2006). Public education outreach and the use of the media: A springboard to making psychology a household word. *Professional Psychology: Research and Practice, 37,* 460–466.

Martin, J. (2005). *Going public with your private practice: Using public education materials to enhance your practice.* Washington, DC: American Psychological Association Division 42.

McGarrah, N., Brownawell, A., & Hill, A. (2013, August). *Effective and ethical strategies for collaborating with media.* Paper presented at the Annual Convention of the American Psychological Association, Honolulu, HI.

McGarrah, N., Martin, J., Alvord, M., & Haldeman, D. (2009). In the public eye: The ethical practice of media psychology. *Professional Psychology: Research and Practice, 40,* 172–180.

National Association of Social Workers. (2008). NASW Code of Ethics. Retrieved from http://www.social-workers.org/pubs/code/code.asp.

# CHAPTER 28

# THE USE OF SOCIAL MEDIA IN MARKETING A PRACTICE

*Heather Wittenberg*

Social media can be a powerful practice-marketing tool for private practitioners. Learning the basics of social media allows you to communicate with a wide audience in order to promote your practice. Depending on your technical savvy, these feats can be accomplished at low cost, or even for free. A social media platform is now seen as replacing the use of brochures, pamphlets, or business cards in the promotion of a private practice, and has the potential to reach a much larger audience more efficiently.

## USES AND BENEFITS OF SOCIAL MEDIA MARKETING

Marketing a practice involves communicating with intended clients and referral sources about the services you offer, developing a positive professional reputation as an expert, and networking with referral sources. Clinicians opening up a new practice, or expanding their practices, can use social media to connect with local colleagues, schools, and agencies to spread the word about their services and build their referral base. A positive reputation as an expert can be built by posting useful information online. Connections with colleagues can be developed and strengthened, even over long distances.

Clinicians often provide public health education as part of their marketing plans. These educational programs usually focus on the practitioner's specialty and provide an important community service. Harnessing the power of social media allows the educational program to reach a far greater audience and to provide important, life-enhancing, or even life-saving information directly to the public. This might be something as simple as a series of blog posts with questions and answers on stress management, common parenting challenges, or relationships, or as broad as a long-term public education campaign on addiction, suicide prevention, or disaster response. In the past, this could be accomplished only by the rare few who were approached by media outlets for interviews. Now, it is available to nearly everyone.

Connecting with colleagues (and potential referral or employment prospects) from around the world is another marketing benefit of social media. You can now search for—and connect with—clinicians and researchers from all levels of academia, treatment centers, hospitals, and clinics from every continent. General social media sites such as Twitter, Facebook, and LinkedIn can be used for this purpose. Your LinkedIn profile is searchable and can serve as an online curriculum vitae. In fact, more and more institutions and agencies now use applicants' LinkedIn profiles in their review of credentials (Schawbel, 2012). Posting your profile on LinkedIn allows you to search for and connect with other professionals for information on clinical specialties, job searches, or media connections. I have initiated connections with highly respected clinicians and academicians worldwide solely via their social media profiles, developing relationships that resulted in further explanation of research findings, a mutual exchange of book-review blurb writing, referrals for clients moving to their area, and employment contacts.

Cultivating an interesting network on social media sites can generate opportunities to further build your profile as a media expert as well. An example illustrates the power of social media to build your contacts, experience, and platform within a couple of hours, and for no cost. I connected with several media producers on LinkedIn who listed topics in my area of practice as one of their main topics of interest. Several months later, one of the producers working for the British Broadcasting Corporation (BBC) contacted me. He needed an expert to comment on a radio segment about raising young children, which is my clinical specialty. The show was to be aired live in only 90 minutes—a common scenario in media requests. Fortunately, arrangements could be made to call in to the show in time. In the meantime, both the producer and I tweeted to our followers about the upcoming show. Followers re-tweeted it and spread the word, increasing the listenership for the segment. After the show, the BBC sent me a digital file of the segment, which I used as an example of my media work in other social media profiles.

Social media is also used by academics and thus can represent an excellent potential bridge between academics and clinicians. You can use it to build a referral base from within an academic center and can make direct contact with those conducting research of clinical interest.

More specialized science-specific social media sites such as ResearchGate and Academia. edu are developing rapidly and already have millions of scientists connecting from around the world. These sites are highly active and tend to have an informal format, which includes networking and collaborating with colleagues, sharing and discussing research results (both published and unpublished), and creating profiles that allow others to view your interests and accomplishments or to get in touch (Noorden, 2014). In this way, social media outreach to scientists can be used to gain a closer connection to current research in your clinical area, and build a referral base as well.

# SOCIAL MEDIA—WHAT IS IT, AND WHO IS USING IT?

The potential uses of social media for mental health practitioners are expanding rapidly. Nonclinical uses include the promotion of health behaviors and other public health goals, engaging with the public to answer general questions related to mental health, developing your professional network, engaging in professional education, promoting a program or organization, learning about clinical and scientific news and discoveries, coordinating and assisting with disaster-response efforts, and impacting public policy discussions and decisions (Ventola, 2014). Other uses, such as communicating with clients and discussing case material (even if disguised), are more complex and are ethically and clinically fraught.

Concerns about confidentiality, multiple relationships, and clinician privacy have long limited practitioners from jumping in to the sea of social media. Taking a "wait and see" attitude made sense in the early days of social networking, but things have changed so rapidly that such an approach must be reevaluated. Overall, 89% of Americans aged 18 to 29 use social networking sites, as do 82% of 30- to 49-year-olds. Most Americans use social media and are accustomed to finding information about most areas of their lives online. This will increase further over time (Perrin, 2015b).

Social media use drops to 65% of those aged 50 to 64 (Perrin, 2015a). This highlights the generational issues at play. The younger one is, the more likely one is to use social media. Over time, more and more clients, potential clients, and professional connections will expect to find online profiles of clinicians, as well as ways to interact online. The mental health professions' younger clinicians and trainees are also "digital natives," those who have been born into the world of social media; for them this is a natural way to communicate and to seek and share information (Prensky, 2001). They come to clinical training expecting to use social media in their practices, as they do in their personal lives. This means that an ever-increasing number of younger trainees are coming to training with the expectation of integrating these platforms into their practices (American Psychological Association, 2014). As mental health practitioners are increasingly expected to use and understand social media, they are also expected to be able to supervise and train students in its effective and ethical uses. Representative of the mental health professions' codes of ethics, the American Counseling Association (ACA)'s Code of Ethics (2014) states, "Counselors who engage in the use of distance counseling, technology, and/or social media develop knowledge and skills regarding related technical, ethical, and legal considerations (e.g., special certifications, additional course work)" (p. 17).

# AREAS OF CAUTION AND CONCERN

Social media certainly has its benefits, and ignoring social media has pitfalls for mental health practitioners. More and more clients (and potential clients) look up their healthcare providers online, as do potential employers, program or agency partners, and media contacts. Gone are the days when prospective clients looked for clinicians in their local telephone directory. The growing expectation that professionals of all kinds will maintain an online presence means that the lack of one is now considered unusual in many communities and specialties. In an age when use of social media is now the norm, it's natural for many to question why a mental health practitioner might not have an online presence. Clients, potential clients, employers, students, and trainees may wonder if you are no longer in practice or even if you have something to hide by remaining "un-findable" (Schawbel, 2012); at a minimum, this would have a negative impact on your stream of referrals.

Ignoring social media also prevents you from effectively monitoring what others post—whether accurately or inaccurately, positively or negatively—about your practice. On their websites, agencies may post or change information about past or present clinicians without alerting the clinicians to this fact. Recently, I conducted an online search for a previous supervisor in order to renew the contact. I found and watched a YouTube video of her providing a clinical training at an agency. When I reestablished contact, I told her how interesting the training was and she was shocked to hear that it was available online—and it had been there for over four years! She had prepared the talk for the agency's advanced clinicians only, not for a general audience, yet the agency posted it publicly on YouTube without her knowledge or permission. Only this serendipitous episode allowed her to contact the agency and ask that the video be removed from YouTube. Regularly reviewing your own presence on social media sites can help prevent similar incidents. Managing your online presence in this way is an important aspect of ongoing marketing efforts.

The presence of online reviews of clinicians' services is another reason for you to use social media. Many healthcare and general review sites such as Yelp now allow users to post online reviews about clinicians without notifying you of the review. These online review sites do not vet the accuracy of the clinician review. Inaccurate or negative reviews about your practice can have a deleterious impact on your marketing efforts. The only way you can influence the type and quality of information posted about you online is to be aware of and develop your own social media presence, and to review this online presence on a regular basis. This increases the chances that content generated and approved by you will appear more prominently in searches, allows you to respond to (or at least know about) negative reviews, and decreases the chances of unpleasant online surprises. Staying current with social media trends—and being comfortable navigating these sites—allows you to monitor (and respond to, if appropriate) the information posted about you by others.

The powerful impact of social media in the delivery of psychological information to benefit public health, to develop professional networks, and to further private practitioners' careers is well worth the effort needed to develop an effective and ethical social media presence. Learning and implementing practical strategies for accomplishing these benefits is the next step. The following sections will cover the manner in which practitioners can, and should, use social media—both effectively and ethically. "How-to" tips will also be provided.

## GETTING STARTED IN CREATING AN EFFECTIVE SOCIAL MEDIA IDENTITY

Creating an effective social media presence ideally starts in training. Clinical supervisors and instructors need to be able not only to use social media, but to understand it well enough to teach its effective and ethical use. Consistent with the guidance provided by the other mental health professions' supervisory requirements, the American Psychological Association (APA, 2014) states that:

> Supervisors ensure that policies and procedures are in place for ethical practice of telepsychology, social media, and digital communications between any combination of client/patient, supervisee, and supervisor . . . Supervisors model ethical practice, ethical decision-making, and professionalism, and engage in thoughtful dialogues with supervisees regarding use of social networking . . . (pp. 15–16)

Development of the clinician's online profile starts during training. As Voshel and Wesala (2015) state:

> It is critically important that students actively participate in the formation of their online persona and that they not be passive about the development of their online identity; such as photos, blogs, Twitter, and any other information that may represent them online. Everyone must set his or her identity with a purpose, and once established, must consistently in an ongoing fashion monitor, cultivate, and evaluate that online identity in order to stay appropriately relevant in the ever evolving social media landscape. (p. 69)

Once you decide to venture online, you must present a coherent professional identity that matches your practice and helps you meet your goals. Developing a professional identity via an online profile, or persona, is the first step in communicating your skills and goals to the online public. This can be accomplished by deciding on the most salient details of your practice, expertise, skills, accomplishments, and goals. Why do clients like and trust you? What makes your practice unique? These details should be reduced and refined to a few key sentences that communicate the most important points, in layperson's language. The wording should be simple, compelling, and genuine.

An online professional identity might also be called your "brand." Clinical training usually does not include business development courses, and mental health professionals are less likely to be comfortable with anything that appears to be "self-promotion." However, there are important marketing lessons to be learned in how to best communicate your unique professional identity. These are essential for success in independent practice. Creating several versions of your professional identity in varying lengths is useful. This writing process is often lengthy and benefits from multiple drafts, outside review, and fearless requests for feedback.

A good learning exercise is condensing this message into smaller and smaller lengths. Try creating several versions of your professional biography: for example, a 500-word blog post, a 200-word LinkedIn post, a single paragraph for Facebook, and the smallest "micro-blog" length, the 140-character tweet. A one- or two-sentence version can also be used as your "tagline," a simple, clever slogan for identifying your practice identity. Psychologist, professor, and writer Dan Gilbert, PhD, asks in his tagline, "How is the world *in here* different than the world *out there*?" Jessica Zucker, PhD, uses this blurb on her Twitter profile, "Psychologist + writer specializing in women's reproductive + maternal mental health. Creator of pregnancy loss card line + #IHadaMiscarriage campaign."

Psychologist and digital practice expert Keely Kolmes, PsyD, uses this tagline, "Psychologist. Speaker. Consultant. Writer. Researcher. Innovator." I have used "What's going on inside that cute little head?" as a tagline for my infant development expertise. These can all be shared in various times and places online to maximize the reach of your message, and to share your brand with as many individuals as is possible.

As a basic, "entry-level" social media activity, some clinicians use a static app that simply presents their professional profile and also allows users to post comments or questions if desired. As of this writing (mid-2016), LinkedIn is the simplest, most widely used social networking tool for presenting a professional profile online. A LinkedIn profile is static, free, and available regardless of whether content is posted in addition to the clinician's profile. It prevents the need for sending CVs by mail or email and is easily accessed by potential employers, clients, or media contacts seeking someone with particular expertise. Here are some additional tips for creating a professional online profile:

**Photo**—Include a professional, high-resolution photograph of yourself. Have several versions available (format, such as PDF or GIF, and resolution size) for different platforms.

**Consistency in name**—Be consistent in the name you use in online profiles, as well as your business name and the name used for any publications. This ensures that search features will find all of your content.

**Separate the personal**—Create separate *personal* profiles (and carefully examine and select privacy settings) to discuss *personal* interests online. Establish *professional* pages and profiles to market your practice and interact with others *professionally*. This is to ensure that your personal and professional contacts and communications are not intermixed. This is an important boundary protection in the digital age.

**Stay focused**—In creating content, stay focused on your main professional identity points. Do not stray into unrelated topics or "hot issues" (such as politics) in the creation of professional content, unless these issues are key points in your professional identity.

**Experiment**—Social media platforms are simply tools. Pick the tool that is most comfortable for you after a period of experimentation. What matters is the message. Platforms are all somewhat similar, and once one is mastered, others will be much easier to learn. Selecting one, two, or three platforms is a reasonable goal.

**Be friendly**—Once your profile is established, respond to relevant inquiries, and start conversations with interesting professionals. After all, this is "social" media.

**Be generous**—Share interesting research and news in your areas of expertise, and answer questions (as long as they apply to general psychological knowledge and are not directly clinical).

**Reach out**—Search for those agencies, institutions, clinicians, or researchers whose work is of interest to you. Comment on their posts and start a conversation within an area of your expertise. Think of how these contacts might be developed in the pursuit of your professional goals. Set a goal for reaching out to a handful of new contacts as often as is reasonable for you—every day, week, or month. Don't be discouraged if not every attempt at contact is reciprocated.

**Call in the professionals**—Having professional social media help can be worthwhile, since new social media platforms, resources, and privacy settings are continually developed. While you do not need to stay on top of every possible social media app, it is helpful to have an expert available who can advise on which platforms are most worthwhile to learn and use in order to reach your professional goals. This enables you to focus on social media content (articles, tweets, news, videos, and other media to post) instead of learning the whole universe of social networking tools. Further, apps such as Facebook have settings that allow practitioners to post a professional "page" rather than the better-understood personal profile.

Understanding the privacy and other settings required to comfortably navigate between your "page" and your "profile" can be a barrier for some. Expert help is essential if you are not comfortable navigating this type of technology. Social media consulting is now widely available and can be obtained by various means. Try asking colleagues who are more established in social media; they may have referrals. Most local community colleges now offer social media courses as well. You can enroll in these courses or retain their instructors for professional services. Make sure, though, that the consulting expert is comfortable and experienced with the unique ethical requirements of mental health professionals. You need to oversee your social media interaction and should not completely "hand it over" to an outside expert. In this way, you can ensure the accuracy and ethics of the communication.

## BEYOND THE PROFILE: CREATING CONTENT THAT REACHES YOUR AUDIENCE

The next level of social media activity includes posting information (or "content") to the application, along with your profile. On blogs, this is done by writing an article and simply posting it via the blog's software. Readers can respond by commenting and/or sharing, if desired. Unless your blog is already well read, though, it is useful to publicize the blog or article on other social media sites. Content can also be posted directly to LinkedIn and other sites. Sharing others' interesting content on your own profile feed is a way of spreading interesting information to your followers. Sharing others' content often triggers them to share your content in return. This builds the interest, "views," and "reach" of your content. It also builds "followers," which further extends your influence in the online community.

Sharing content online can be done on one, two, or more social media sites. There is no ideal number of sites or apps for mental health practitioners. This is an individual decision based on your interest, time available, and comfort with using social media. Many clinicians will be happiest using just the simplest apps, such as LinkedIn, for posting professional profile information. This is sufficient to meet the basic need to have your professional information online. Others will enjoy venturing out into blogging or micro-blogging platforms such as Facebook or Twitter, posting mental health content to supplement a basic LinkedIn profile, or even creating short-form videos to upload to YouTube. The most enthusiastic practitioners will develop multiple, connected social media profiles to amplify their social media presence, with a fairly complex content-posting calendar that helps guide the process over time. "Social Media Dashboard" apps such as Hootsuite, Buffer, or Social Oomph help manage and streamline that level of social media activity. Most of these apps have a free level of use, as well as paid levels; free levels are sufficient for most professionals.

# COMMUNICATING AND NAVIGATING IN SOCIAL MEDIA

Communicating via social media is best done through a style of writing that is different than the style used in most scientific and healthcare professions. Social media platforms demand messages in concise, bite-sized "nuggets" in order to maintain the interest of the reader and to match the quick communication culture of social media platforms. These tools benefit users who communicate using as few words (or characters) as possible. Holding the interest of viewers accustomed to short, abbreviated (but meaningful) messages is an important skill to develop. Mental health professionals accustomed to conveying complex ideas, advice, and scientific findings via long-form books, articles, and journals can view this process as learning the new culture—and language—of social networking communication. Like learning any new language or culture, training and practice are necessary to become fluent and culturally competent. Social media platforms have their own norms and culture, and the more you understand and follow these, the more impact your messages will have.

Finding professionals or topics of interest is another important use made possible by learning several social media shortcuts. Search-and-sort features allow you to quickly find what you are seeking. Using "@mentions" allows readers to direct a public comment directly to the attention of the person or account they want to reach. Write the post and include the name of the account you wish to contact with an "@" sign attached to the account name. As an example, to send a tweet directly to the APA Help Center's Twitter account, write @APAHelpCenter in the tweet. The tweet would then show up in the APA Help Center's feed for the staff's notice and response. Hashtags are another important convention to learn. These are identified by the use of the number (or pound) sign in front of a keyword, phrase, or topic (with no spaces in between the hashtag and words) to easily direct readers to a complete and current list of the conversations they seek about the topic. Examples of mental health–related hashtags include #depression, #therapyworks, #suicideprevention, and #parenting, as well as more time-limited (but "viral" or highly used) topics such as #ICD10 or #ThisPsychMajor. This allows clinicians to participate in real time in ongoing and contemporary discussions of interest in the field.

Use of social media for marketing your practice can be thought of as a professional adventure. Social media use presents a tremendous opportunity to "get the word out" about important psychological issues and to promote your practice. The privilege of this opportunity comes with tremendous responsibility. Clinicians must ensure that their social media communications not only are factually accurate but are also communicated in a way that is helpful to the public, safeguards clients' privacy, and is mindful of potential boundary complications. All of this must be considered before you press "tweet," "post," or "publish" on your social media platform.

# THE INTEGRATION OF ETHICS INTO SOCIAL MEDIA USE

Engaging in social media has its benefits, but those benefits require considerable investment in time and training to prevent potential pitfalls. Potential issues of confidentiality, multiple roles, and clinician privacy are present and must be handled skillfully. Prospective or current clients may attempt to make contact with you on a social media site. Confidential client information might be breached if you attempt to illustrate a diagnostic dilemma online. When ethical violations occur on social media, there is no "delete" button, due to the group communication aspect of social media. To safeguard against these risks, specific, knowledgeable, and ongoing training, as well as the opportunity to consult with knowledgeable colleagues when needed, is required.

Several ethical issues commonly present themselves while using social media, and you should plan for all of them in case they occur. Many of these issues arise from the fact that you can no longer hold on to a reasonable hope that details about your personal life, including your home address and names of family members, will remain private. Previous boundaries expected and practiced by psychotherapists regarding their privacy and anonymity no longer exist when anyone can look up your home address on a county website or find your personal or professional blog online. We are much more likely to "run into" a client online when we use social media. This naturally increases the opportunities for common ethical challenges, such as multiple roles or the crossing of boundaries, to occur.

While we cannot cover all of these ethical dilemmas here for space reasons, it may help to know the most common ones. Clients—past, current, or future—may seek to "follow," "friend," or otherwise engage you via social media, both on your professional site and your personal site. Clients' "likes" or comments may show up on your professional or personal blog, sometimes with personal or clinical information. A client might offer to post a testimonial about your skills. Clients may ask you to view and interact with their online postings. In some cases, this engagement may be ethical; in others, it may not. These and other common ethical dilemmas must be anticipated, and prevention and management must be handled on an ongoing basis.

Fortunately, each mental health profession's code of ethics, and the training mental health clinicians receive in navigating ethical dilemmas, can be directly applied to social media use. Social media is simply the next level in communication, and the field has more than adequate resources to guide us, if we continually integrate our practice of ethics along with our social media engagement.

In practice, it is important to have a set of policies and procedures about your professional social media use. Policies about whether and to what extent you might engage with clients in social media should be thought through and presented to clients at the outset of treatment, using guides provided by the field. A commonly cited and widely used example is Keely Kolmes's Social Media Policy, which is available at http://drkkolmes.com/social-media-policy/ and can easily be downloaded and modified for your own use. You should understand the privacy settings on social media platforms—and challenges and threats to client privacy despite them—and discuss them with all new and existing clients. These privacy settings evolve over time and need to be monitored regularly for updates.

The separation of personal and professional profiles is another essential step in setting boundaries that are clear to anyone who might wish to contact you. Your office policies should cover how you will—and will not—engage with clients online; you should present and discuss these issues as part of informed consent. In this way, we can decrease the likelihood that clients will feel hurt or rejected when their personal "friend" request is not accepted. Avoid "venting" your frustrations— or successes—about cases on your profiles (even if those comments are completely stripped of identifying information), as others may see those comments and wonder about your ability to maintain confidentiality. It's also important to note that "following" or "liking" a page (or tweet, or comment) is a statement of interaction and might be seen as revealing an individual's status as a client, depending on the specifics of the situation.

Online reviews of your practice (on platforms such as Yelp) are important to find—and address—as soon as possible. Even positive reviews must be responded to with care and attention to the ethical issues involved. If inaccurate or negative information is posted about your practice on social media, there is a way to ethically handle the situation without violating ethics standards. You might reply to a negative comment with this kind of language: "I am glad to have found your comment here. I am legally and ethically bound to protect client confidentiality, so I cannot comment as to whether this comment does—or does not—come from a current or past client. However, I would like to take this opportunity to explain the way I conduct my clinical practice, and my office policies and procedures. I do my utmost to stay up to date in my area of practice, and I always give my clients the opportunity to discuss their concerns directly with me. My office policies include . . . If anyone has a concern, I can be reached at my practice at (888) 555-1212. Thank you again for your comment."

When you are faced with any ethical dilemma, use an ethical decision-making model to clarify the situation and to help determine the most appropriate steps to take to resolve it (Pope & Vasquez, 2010). You could consult with recognized social media ethics experts such as Keely Kolmes, Psy.D., who has published numerous articles and provides training and continuing education on the subject. She offers guidance to common dilemmas such as how to respond to client reviews in online review sites, managing Facebook "friend" requests from clients, and more on her website, Dr.KKolmes.com. Ofer Zur, Ph.D., offers resources, training, and consulting on all areas of digital and social media use by mental health clinicians at ZurInstitute.com. Roy Huggins, LPC, NCC, offers extensive social media resources for mental health professionals at PersonCenteredTech.com. Of course the APA's Ethical principles and code of conduct should be reviewed frequently as well (American Psychological Association, 2010).

# CONCLUDING THOUGHTS

Clinicians have understandable concerns about the potential pitfalls of engaging in social media technologies. Mastering new technologies is complicated, and training in these new media lags behind our clinical training. Potential ethical dilemmas are a cause for serious concern as well.

However, the opportunities afforded by the new social media platforms are truly spectacular. The ability to reach large groups with public health information—important psychological information that may potentially improve the lives of many—is now in our hands. This largely free platform offers the chance to promote our practices and other important programs, meet and network with important colleagues, and learn about new scientific and clinical findings.

Learning new technologies, mastering strategies for managing them in clinical practice, and having clear structures and guidelines for handling ethical dilemmas offers the opportunity to reach out to the whole world with the important services and information that our field and our practices have to offer. In fact, mental health professionals have unique advantages in our ability to understand and use communication technologies, for the benefit of humanity. Good clinicians are experts in communication, and social media is just another form of communication, albeit the most technologically advanced form available today. In that sense, social media is a powerful fit for marketing your clinical practice.

# REFERENCES

American Counseling Association. (2014). 2014 ACA code of ethics. Retrieved from https://www.counseling.org/resources/aca-code-of-ethics.pdf.

American Psychological Association. (2010). Ethical principles of psychologists and code of conduct. Retrieved from www.apa.org/ethics/code/principles.pdf.

American Psychological Association. (2014). Guidelines for clinical supervision in health service psychology. Retrieved from http://apa.org/about/policy/guidelines-supervision.pdf.

Noorden, R. V. (2014). Online collaboration: Scientists and the social network. Retrieved from http://www.nature.com/news/online-collaboration-scientists-and-the-social-network-1.15711#/profiles.

Perrin, A. (2015a). Social networking fact sheet. Pew Research Center. Retrieved from http://www.pewinternet.org/fact-sheets/social-networking-fact-sheet/.

Perrin, A. (2015b). Social networking usage: 2005–2015. Pew Research Center. Retrieved from http://www.pewinternet.org/2015/10/08/social-networking-usage-2005-2015/.

Pope, K., & Vasquez, M. (2010). *Ethics in psychotherapy and counseling: A practical guide* (4th ed.). Hoboken, NJ: John Wiley & Sons, Inc.

Prensky, M. (2001). Digital natives: Digital immigrants. *On the Horizon, 9*(5), 1–6.

Schawbel, D. (2012). How recruiters use social networks to make hiring decisions now. Retrieved from http://business.time.com/2012/07/09/how-recruiters-use-social-networks-to-make-hiring-decisions-now/.

Ventola, C. L. (2014). Social media and health care professionals: Benefits, risks, and best practices. *Pharmacy and Therapeutics*, *39*(7), 491–520. Retrieved from http://www.ncbi.nlm.nih.gov/pmc/articles/PMC4103576/.

Voshel, E. H., & Wesala, A. (2015). Social media & social work ethics: Determining best practices in an ambiguous reality. *Journal of Social Work Values and Ethics*, *12*(1). Retrieved from http://jswve.org/download/spring_2015,_vol._12,_no._1/articles/67-JSWVE-12-1-Social%20Media%20and%20Ethics-Best%20Practices.pdf.

**CHAPTER 29**

# HOW TO PROMOTE YOUR PRACTICE THROUGH COMMUNITY PRESENTATIONS

*Eileen Kennedy-Moore and Elaine Ducharme*

s psychotherapists, we know things that matter in people's lives. We're experts on feelings, behaviors, and relationships. We understand life challenges and transitions. We've had extensive training in helping people cope with difficult circumstances. People need to learn what we know. We're also very good at connecting. We know how to share information clearly and to show that we care. We're good at empathizing, understanding different perspectives, and guiding people toward making positive changes. We are expert communicators.

This combination of deep knowledge and communication skills means that we have the potential to be excellent speakers. Offering community presentations is a way to educate people about important psychological issues and mental health, but it can also be a very effective way to promote your practice. It provides potential clients and referral partners a chance to get to see you as a valuable resource in your community and also get to know you as a person. Because they've spent time with you, audience members are likely to think of you when they or someone they know needs a psychotherapist.

In this chapter, we'll take you through the nuts and bolts of how to promote your practice by offering relevant and engaging community presentations. We'll highlight answers to the main questions clinicians ask about giving community presentations.

## HOW DO I PICK A TOPIC?

Unless you've been assigned a topic by a group that has invited you to speak, the first step in planning a community presentation is to decide what you'd like to talk about with your audience.

One approach is to ask yourself, "Who is my ideal client?" or "What types of clients do I really want to see?" Also consider this: "What pressing concerns or problems does my ideal client have?" Clarifying the types of clients you enjoying working with will help you identify the types of topics you'd like to offer. Drawing from your empathy and clinical experience, develop three possible topics that you think would be so useful to your ideal client that he or she will be eager to get a babysitter, skip doing the dishes, or cancel other plans in order to attend your presentation. Write a one-paragraph description of each topic, spelling out the benefits for attendees. Developing more than one topic will give you several options to propose to event organizers.

If you have a specialty area that you want to promote, select topics related to that area. If you are relatively new to the community or an early-career clinician, you may want to talk with key community figures to see what community needs might still be unmet. For example, you might ask the organizer of the event what topics are especially important to his or her group. On the other hand, don't feel you have to speak about topics that no one else has covered. There's always a need for good general mental health information and practical help for common mental health problems. Evergreen topics such as "Parenting Your Challenging Toddler" or "Thriving with ADHD" have broad appeal. Things that you might consider basic or obvious could be new and essential information for people who don't know a lot about mental health issues. Community members can also benefit from hearing different perspectives on the same general topic. For example, the topic "Key Ingredients in a Happy Marriage" would be presented differently by a clinicians specializing in sex therapy, divorce mediation, or mindfulness meditation.

Another approach to picking a topic is to focus on timely issues. It is easy to find out what kinds of events are celebrated each month by checking online lists of holidays. Events such as National Depression Screening Day, Mental Health Awareness Day, and Teen Dating Violence Awareness Month could provide timely inspiration. You could also present more general seasonal topics, such as "Preventing Homework Hassles" at the start of a new school year or "Dealing with Holiday Stress" in December. Topics related to relationships, communication, and jump starting your sex life are especially relevant around Valentine's Day. News events could also be a source of inspiration. However, try to choose topics that you can present more than once, or at least reuse with minimal modifications, so you're not starting from scratch with every presentation. Preparation time can be significant the first time that you develop a talk. General topics are more reusable than highly specific ones.

If you are invited to speak, ask the organizer about the challenges facing audience members. Understanding the community can help you tailor your presentation to make it relevant for your audience. This may be especially important if the audience is from a different ethnic or religious background than your own. Don't be shy about asking, "What is essential for me to understand about your community?" That is a sign of respect and will also help you design the presentation to meet the needs of the audience at hand.

## WHERE SHOULD I SPEAK?

To find potential speaking venues, start by looking in the events section of your local newspaper. This will help you identify organizations that offer speakers. You may even want to attend some of these events to get a sense of how they are run and what you and the audience admire in other speakers' presentations. Religious groups, clubs, senior centers, civic or professional organizations, parent–teacher associations, volunteer groups: Pretty much any group with regular meetings and a couple of dozen members or more will be interested in at least an occasional guest speaker. Schools often look for programs to help their teachers work more effectively. Some groups offer a regular speaker series. Large companies often have health and wellness programs as well. Bookstores and libraries also frequently host speakers. To promote your practice, ask yourself, "Where do my ideal clients—or people who can refer my ideal clients to me—tend to gather?" and "What can I do to contribute to that group's mission?"

Once you've identified some possible venues, check the newspaper or the organization's website to find contact information. If you're not sure whom to contact, call a general number and ask who is in charge of arranging speakers. Speaking to the event organizer by phone makes a personal connection right away and helps you tailor your program to the particular group. Explain who you are and what you can offer. Ask about their needs. You can follow up by emailing descriptions of your topics and your expertise. Keep in mind that some groups plan their speaking schedule in the spring or summer for the following year.

This type of "cold calling" can be effective in getting speaking engagements, but a far more effective method is becoming actively involved in your community. If people know you and have seen you putting in effort on behalf of your community, they're more open to having you present. Consider joining the local Chamber of Commerce, volunteering on the board of a local charity or mental health association, or running for a position on a school board. Participating in community health fairs is also a great way to connect with key community members. All of these roles allow you to become known within the community, to influence the conversation in your community, and to represent the mental health field in a positive way.

## HOW MUCH SHOULD I CHARGE?

Beginning speakers are often encouraged to speak for free, and that's certainly a way to gain experience. If the presentation is for a large audience, a prime referral source, or a group you care deeply about, it may make sense to speak for free even after you've gained experience. For instance, if you're a clinician who works with children, giving a regular series of free talks to the parents of patients in a pediatric practice on mental health–related topics (especially parenting or child development) could result in a steady source of new clients and thus would be well worth the "investment."

On the other hand, your time is valuable, and many presentations won't lead instantly to new clients. Charging twice your regular client rate per hour of presentation time is reasonable and quite "doable" for all but the smallest organizations. If the audience is not huge, and you don't have any special connection to the group, you should probably charge them for your presentation.

In general, you want to charge enough that you don't feel resentful of the time and effort it will take to prepare and give the presentation. Have that number in mind before you speak to event organizers. Also, keep in mind that it's easier to give a presentation that you've already written than to create one from scratch, so try to guide event organizers to choose one of your existing presentations, perhaps tweaked slightly to match the organization's focus.

When you're discussing fees, try to get the event organizer to say a number first. Ask "What have you paid speakers in the past?" One of us once received triple her usual speaking rate by remembering to ask that question and then responding to the higher amount by saying, "Yes, that rate would work for me."

If the organizer gives a lower number than you were expecting, ask, "Is there another organization you can partner with to meet my usual fee?" This is a win for everyone: The organizations get to pay less and you get a better fee, bigger audience, and wider marketing reach.

## HOW DO I BUILD CREDIBILITY AS A SPEAKER?

Speaking can be lucrative; private schools and business venues pay thousands of dollars for some speakers. However, to get these higher-paying engagements, you will need to build up your credibility. Having written a book helps, but having proof that you do a good job as a speaker helps even more.

At the end of every speaking event, consider having participants complete a feedback form asking: (1) What did you like best about this presentation? (2) Do you have any suggestions for improving this presentation? (3) What other groups do you know that might like to hear this speaker? (4) What other topics would be of interest to you? These questions will help you refine your presentation and collect audience reaction quotes you can use for marketing. Also, after every presentation, ask the organizer for two or three sentences recommending you as a speaker. Put these recommendations on your website.

The best way to promote yourself as a speaker is to have a short video of you "in action." When you're ready, consider hiring a wedding videographer to record one or more of your presentations. The organization hosting your presentation will sometimes want to record you, but these tend to be lower-quality recordings. Use imovie or other software to splice funny, poignant, or intriguing moments into a three- to five-minute speaker demo video that you can put on your website. Be sure that your clip looks professional. Just because we can do the recordings ourselves doesn't mean we should.

## HOW DO I MAKE MY PRESENTATION INTERESTING?

Making your presentation interesting starts with the physical setup. It is a good idea to visit the room ahead of time, if possible, to see the size and layout. If chairs and tables can be moved, ask for a setup that will work with your presentation. Tables with four or five chairs on one side may work well, especially if you will have small-group discussions. Theater seating and one big circle are other options for chair arrangements. If the audience will be small, be careful not to have too many seats out, because audience members tend to hide in the back. You can also ask people in the back rows to move forward before you begin.

If you're using PowerPoint, think about where you want the screen or seating to be, so everyone can see, and so you don't have to leap over cords to move around the room. If it's a daytime talk, you should have curtains or blinds on the windows to help your slides be more visible. And please do not turn your back on the audience and read them the slides!

Make sure you have the audiovisual equipment you will need and ask for a knowledgeable tech person to be there, at least at the beginning, to help if there are technical difficulties. If you're using PowerPoint, have your presentation on your laptop, on a flash drive, and online as backup. Try to get a clip-on or handheld microphone so you aren't tethered behind a podium. Use a handheld remote device to move the slides so you can move around and not have to go back to the laptop each time. Be sure to have the right adapter and connecting cords. These strategies will help your presentation go smoothly and make you seem more accessible to participants. Always arrive 45 minutes early so you can check the setup and test the equipment to be sure everything is working smoothly.

Beyond creating an inviting physical setup, the key ways to engage your audience are through stories, metaphors/images, and engaging activities.

## STORIES

Before you begin to create your presentation, ask yourself, "What stories can I tell about my topic?" Build your presentation around those stories. Starting with the stories, rather than the information you want to cover, will keep you focused on the most engaging material. The most effective stories describe small moments that illustrate a big truth. Stories about struggles followed by triumph over adversity can be inspiring.

Obviously, for ethical reasons, you don't want to tell stories about specific clients that would make those clients identifiable, but there are many other options. You could tell:

- *Humanizing stories about your own experiences.* The stories should be entertaining and highly relatable anecdotes about your foibles or challenges, rather than self-promotional "I'm so perfect" examples. For instance, telling an audience of parents about your own frustrations tackling fourth-grade math homework, or how your teenager asked you what you think of her being sexually active while you were in the middle of rush hour traffic, shows that you really have "been there." Your goal is to connect with your audience members and establish that you understand what they're going through.
- *Stories about common problems.* For instance, you could say, "Here's a situation I hear about a lot in my practice."
- *Stories about a specific client that illustrate a universal reaction.* Give no identifying information and only mention situational circumstances that apply to large numbers of people and are directly relevant to the topic. For example, you could say, "I once worked with a divorced mom who was anxious about starting to date. She told me the hardest part

was . . ." That could be anyone! You should not say, "I'm currently working with a divorced mom of twin ten-year-old boys who is a real estate lawyer and whose ex-husband owns his own computer repair business." Although this example doesn't mention a name, it gives far too many clues about the identity of the client.

- *Vignettes that you make up*. Creating a fictional vignette, one to three paragraphs in length, involving dialog or illustrating thought processes can be an engaging way to illustrate your points. Tell your audience, "I want to read you a vignette that's based on a composite of people I've known," then emphasize the universality by asking, "Raise your hand if you know someone like the person in this story" or "Raise your hand if you can relate to the person in this story."

## METAPHORS/IMAGES

Just like in psychotherapy, metaphors in a presentation can be a powerful way to communicate key ideas. Not every presentation has to have a central metaphor, but if you can provide one that creates a vivid image in participants' minds, this will be engaging and memorable. For example, a metaphor of a swan looking serene above the water and paddling like mad below the surface vividly represents the experience of stress or anxiety. It's easy to imagine, and it communicates an emotional "truth" that will resonate with many people.

If you use PowerPoint, you can include meaningful images to enhance audience engagement. Don't settle for generic clip art. If an image doesn't make your point more vivid, it's not worth including. Also, don't just grab any images you find online, because you need to respect copyright laws. Hunt for images that are labeled "Creative commons, commercial use allowed" on Google, Flickr, Morguefile, or other online sources.

## ENGAGING ACTIVITIES

Remember that professor you had who droned on and on and on? Don't be that person! Incorporating activities that allow audience members to interact breaks up the content and gets them actively involved. The longer your presentation is, the more important it is for you to incorporate activities for participants. Half-day or full-day workshops should be built mostly around participant activities.

Don't ask your audience members to do anything embarrassing! Also, don't require people to share very personal information. People have different comfort levels with public disclosure, so you need to accommodate those who are very private.

All activities should make audience members feel smart and capable. This is extremely important! No one likes to be embarrassed or have their weaknesses exposed, so design your activities with this in mind.

A simple way to get audience engagement is through a questionnaire-style handout. You can ask participants to indicate how relevant a particular issue you discussed is to them and which of the strategies you mentioned they would like to try. Emphasize that the handout is for their eyes only, so they don't feel shy about answering. After each main section of your presentation, ask participants to use the handout to reflect, and then take questions that emerge from this reflection. Giving people the chance to ask questions at the main transition points of the presentation gets audiences more engaged than saving all questions until the end. It makes it easier for people to remember what they want to know and allows participation to build. Think carefully about how and when you provide handouts. Questionnaire-style handouts or very simple outlines without too many words can help engage participants follow the structure of the talk and provide room for notes. Handouts with dense paragraphs or extensive lists of resources should be given out only at the end of your presentation, because you don't want people distracted and reading them during your talk.

Another easy way to engage audience members is to get their reactions to vignettes you make up. You could ask questions such as, "What is it that this child hasn't learned yet?," "How do you think her husband felt when she said that?," or "What do you predict will happen next in this situation?" The eyes point outward, so it's easier to see someone else's blind spots than our own. Try not to call on them (remember some people embarrass easily or are private individuals), but rather solicit audience participation.

Depending on your topic and timeframe, it may make sense to have audience members work in pairs or small groups. For instance, you could have them brainstorm how to respond to different scenarios, choose which response would work best in various situations, arrange things in some kind of order, or sort items into different categories. After the small-group work, you can give people the option of sharing their thoughts or reactions with the larger group.

Experiential activities that allow people to practice whatever skill you're teaching can be useful, as long as they are not embarrassing. Be careful about suggesting role-play activities, because most adults are reluctant to act things out, especially if they don't know the other participants well.

Telling jokes is a risky way to try to engage your audience. Some people are great comics; most are not. If you tell a joke, one-third of the audience will get it, one-third won't think it is funny, and one-third won't get it. Trying something that is only going to connect with one-third of the audience is not a great idea.

## WHAT IS THE MOST COMMON MISTAKE SPEAKERS MAKE?

The most common mistake speakers make is trying to include too much information. It's better to cover one idea clearly than to overwhelm people with too much information.

Plan on one main topic and three subtopics or sections. More than that tends to be unwieldy for the audience. If you use PowerPoint, limit yourself to only one to seven words per slide. Audiences don't want to know everything that you know about a topic; they want to walk away with a few useful ideas. And again, please do not turn your back on your audience and read them what is on the slides! Maintaining eye contact with your audience is important to develop a connection with them.

# HOW DO I GET OVER MY FEAR OF PUBLIC SPEAKING?

Offering community presentations is an excellent way to share important mental health information and to promote your practice. However, a lot of psychotherapists are reluctant to do them because they feel anxious about public speaking. In fact, some clinicians insist they would rather be in the coffin than have to speak at a funeral!

Preparation and practice are essential to help ease jitters. Yes, you really do need to practice your presentation aloud a few times! This will enable you to iron out rough spots, make adjustments, and become more comfortable with what you want to say so that your presentation flows smoothly. Practicing aloud also helps you judge timing, so you can tell if you have too much or too little material. The more you practice, the less you will need notes and the more you can focus on connecting with your audience. Starting by presenting to smaller audiences about topics with which you're very familiar can help build up your confidence.

The way you think about the task of presenting also affects how you feel about it. Telling yourself, "I have to be great or else I'll be publicly humiliated!" creates tremendous pressure and anxiety! On the other hand, thinking of the presentation as sharing information rather than performing can help you move past public speaking fears. Audience members are on your side. They want to learn from you. They're interested in what you know and how you can help them. They're not looking for a perfect performance or eloquent prose. They want to see that you understand them and care about their concerns. Long after they've forgotten the content of your presentation, they'll remember how they felt being in a room with you. This is what will influence people most in making a decision to seek out or recommend your services. So, talk with genuineness and compassion about topics that matter. You're good at that. It's what you do every day in your practice.

Be sure to send audience members home with something that has your name and contact information on it—a handout, business card, squish ball, or magnet—because now that they know you, some people in that audience are likely to want to come see you in your practice.

# SUGGESTED READINGS

Allen, R. H. (2002). *Impact teaching: Ideas and strategies for teachers to maximize student learning.* Boston: Allyn & Bacon.

Calamaras, M. R., Anderson, P. L., Tannenbaum, L., & Zimand, E. l. (2014). Public speaking anxiety. In L. Grossman & S. Walfish (Eds.), *Translating psychological research into practice* (pp. 253–258). New York: Springer.

Clifft, M. A. (1986). Writing about psychiatric patients: Guidelines for disguising case material. *Bulletin of the Menninger Clinic, 50,* 511–524.

Sieck, B. C. (2012). Obtaining clinical writing informed consent versus using client disguise and recommendations for practice. *Psychotherapy, 49,* 3–11.

# COLLABORATION

# CHAPTER 30

# COLLABORATING WITH HEALTHCARE PROFESSIONALS

*Steven M. Tovian*

Throughout the history of mental health professions, the phrase *collaboration with other healthcare professionals* most often translated into relations with *psychiatry*. As early as 1991, Wright and Friedman urged professional psychologists, for example, to follow the scientist-practitioner model to preserve and maintain an identity in healthcare settings and strive to develop adequate standards of training and maintain core curriculums pertinent to training, accreditation, and credentialing for psychologists working in healthcare settings. The authors believed this would be crucial for quality assurance and would serve as the means to differentiate mental health professionals from other professionals in healthcare settings. Wright and Friedman also urged psychology and other mental health professions to improve their relationship with numerous specialties in medicine and nursing, abandon the traditional links to psychiatry, focus on developing a relationship with primary care medicine, and continue to work in health promotion and disease prevention. They discussed the need for psychologists and other mental health professionals to expand their roles and scopes of practice within healthcare settings, and predicted that major changes would occur in the following decades in medical economics.

Consistent with Wright and Friedman's (1991) admonitions and predictions, research demonstrates how psychological and behavioral principles can be applied to the broadest range of medical problems as well as collaborative endeavors between psychology, for example, and various specialties in primary and tertiary care medicine that have contributed to improving health outcomes and reducing mortality. The mental health professions (psychology, social work, counseling, and marriage and family therapy) have successfully responded to the challenge of disease prevention by extending beyond traditional practice to new domains in the delivery of healthcare. In addition to the disease categories in which clinicians have been involved, mental health professionals have become involved in different stages of the prevention and progression of illnesses and diseases and have taken on the numerous and diverse roles in healthcare. Similarly, accumulating data demonstrate that providing mental health services to the medically ill can reliably offset medical costs (for further reviews, see Johnson, Perry, & Rozensky, 2002, as well as Rozensky, Tovian, & Goodheart, 2016). It is clear that psychology, for example, can be viewed, at a minimum, as a physical *and* mental health profession.

Mental health professionals are no longer outsiders in healthcare settings and should strive to be well-recognized members of modern-day healthcare alliances. Professional psychology's theme of science and service, for example, and the "politics of competence" (Tovian, Rozensky, & Sweet, 2003) now support our profession's rightful place in healthcare settings and healthcare in general. The scientist-practitioner model has resulted in both the advancement of knowledge in medical settings and the expansion of practice in such specialties as clinical psychology, clinical health psychology, clinical neuropsychology, and rehabilitation psychology (Tovian, 2006).

The biopsychosocial paradigm has also enabled mental health professionals, physicians, and other healthcare professionals to conceptualize problems in an integrative manner, enhancing dialog and encouraging successful collaboration in primary healthcare settings (Gatchel & Oordt, 2003) and in tertiary healthcare settings (Belar & Deardorff, 2009). This paradigm serves as a conceptual framework assisting the mental health professional and physician in understanding illness and disease processes and the experience of the patient in a more integrative and comprehensive manner, thereby enhancing patient care, promoting the efficient use of resources, and removing barriers to access to care. Therefore, mental health professionals working in healthcare settings can no longer assume that a linear relationship exists between biology and behavior or culture and behavior. A patient who has diabetes, for example, must be evaluated not only in terms of blood sugar levels, but also in terms of personal and interpersonal stress as well as attitudes and behaviors toward compliance with diet and treatment regimens. In the same way, a patient who enters a mental health setting complaining of lethargy and fatigue needs to be evaluated for hypothyroidism as well as for depression or stress.

This chapter will summarize several aspects of collaboration with healthcare professionals in healthcare settings that have supported and will continue to support this professional advancement in independent practice. Several best practices in integration or in collaboration with primary healthcare and tertiary healthcare (i.e., board-certified medical specialties) will be described. The terms *integration* and *collaboration* will be used interchangeably. The term *healthcare professionals* refers to physicians, nurses, nurse practitioners, physician assistants, physical therapists, occupational therapists, speech and language therapists, dentists, dietitians, and all other professionals who provide care for patients in healthcare settings (e.g., ambulatory, inpatient, rehabilitation centers, academic healthcare settings, patient-centered medical homes). Because physicians and, to some extent, nurses and nurse practitioners often remain "gatekeepers" and the primary care providers in our current healthcare systems, these professionals will be important professionals for collaboration discussed in this chapter. However, much of the content of this chapter can be generalized to other healthcare professionals as well.

This chapter will also address strategies needed to collaborate with healthcare professionals to ensure effectiveness. The contents of this chapter may be very familiar to readers who spend the majority of their professional endeavors working in a hospital or ambulatory health sciences center. However, the material may be new or need of review for those who are in independent practice in the community and may wish to increase their collaboration with healthcare professionals.

# INCREASING REFERRALS FROM OTHER HEALTHCARE PROFESSIONALS

In the current marketplace in healthcare settings, good clinical skills and solid credentials are necessary, but not sufficient, to create and maintain successful referral patterns with healthcare professionals. Mental health professionals must also be competent in their professional relationships and activities. For example, many have seen primary care (i.e., medical specialties involving family medicine, internal medicine, pediatrics) for psychologists as a relatively new endeavor, even though psychologists have functioned as de facto primary care providers for a sizable part of our history (Tovian, 2014). Clearly mental health professionals have been involved in medical care for many years even while many practitioners are seeking to expand their practices into this realm today. Belar et al. (2001) offer those practitioners a model of self-study that can be used "to assess their readiness to provide services to patients with physical health problems" (p. 136). Over the past two decades, mental health professions have made significant research and clinical contributions to the assessment and treatment of an expanding array of diseases across numerous biopsychosocial dimensions. The application of behavioral principles to the broadest range of medical problems and collaborative endeavors between mental health professionals and various specialties in medicine have contributed to improving health outcomes and reducing mortality. Continued documentation and growing recognition show that providing mental health services to medically ill patients can reliably offset medical costs. Understanding and practicing this "politics of competence" (Tovian, Rozensky, & Sweet, 2003) can also be instrumental in sustaining or helping to grow a substantial practice presence in healthcare systems.

Belar and Deardorff (2009) and Rozensky (2009) have outlined initial considerations necessary for practice in healthcare settings; they include ensuring ethical and competent expansion of practice, understanding the Health Insurance Portability and Accountability Act (HIPAA) and the management of protected health information, recordkeeping and hospital practice, interdisciplinary communication, credentialing and privileging for healthcare setting practice, competence to practice, thorough understanding of the healthcare setting organization and bylaws, and affiliations with appropriate professional groups.

Obtaining staff privileging and professional appointments in healthcare systems, for example, is important in obtaining patient referrals. Robinson and Baker (2006) offer important considerations for obtaining medical staff privileging professional appointments in healthcare systems. The authors recommend learning and understanding the culture and rules of the healthcare setting. If you are practicing outside the healthcare setting, you may wish to apply for staff privileges to a given healthcare setting. Clinicians are not allowed to see patients in a hospital setting for assessment or psychotherapy until they have received such privileges. Applying for privileges is essentially a credentials review. In deciding to obtain privileges, become familiar with programs and services already established within the existing Psychology Department or Psychology Division. Obtain medical staff privileges via the existing Psychology Department or Division, or Division of Social Work, for example, and not through separate individual medical departments that may reflect your practice niche. As a means to market yourself, make yourself known by attending medical staff meetings and join medical center committees relevant to both your expertise (e.g., pain management committee) and those relevant to the visibility and advancement of the field of mental health (e.g., promotions and tenure committees, ethics committees, quality assurance committees). If no separate mental health profession department or division exists at any given medical center, the bylaws at such a medical center or hospital may allow for "Allied Health" designation for staff privileges.

# MARKETING STRATEGIES

Marketing your professional services involves communicating and building relationships with potential clients and referral sources. It requires a basic understanding of the approaches that generally produce positive results and those that do not. See Chapter 26 in this *Handbook* for more information about marketing issues in independent practice. In addition, Tovian (2014) offers some practical considerations about marketing for healthcare professionals that are summarized as steps to consider and steps to avoid (Box 30.1).

Steps to consider include the following:

1. Getting your marketing materials (e.g., business cards, websites, brochures) in front of perspective referral sources and, literally, in their hands
2. Marketing services in terms that potential clients, patients, and referral sources can understand
3. Being succinct in explaining the value of the services you offer
4. Focusing on the benefits of the services you provide
5. Identifying your unique professional strengths and expertise
6. Building relationships with all other healthcare professionals who interact with patients in your target market
7. Observing how mental health professionals in other markets and healthcare settings, even competitors, market similar services
8. Measuring the effectiveness of your marketing efforts and tracking your results by talking to referral sources.

Steps to avoid include:

1. Basing your marketing efforts on untested assumptions
2. Becoming an "expert" in marketing in falsely believing that you can readily know all there is to know about marketing success
3. Not being available to referral partners
4. Stopping your marketing efforts
5. Shortchanging marketing efforts in your budget as an individual practitioner

## BOX 30.1. MARKETING CONSIDERATIONS IN HEALTHCARE SETTINGS

Attempt to . . .

- Place marketing materials in front of or in the grasp of potential referral sources.
- Market services using terms that potential clients and referral sources understand.
- Be brief and succinct in explaining the values of the services you provide.
- Focus on the benefits of the services your offer.
- Identify your or your group's unique professional strengths and expertise.
- Build relationships with all health professionals who interact with patients in the target market.
- Observe and learn how clinical health psychologists in other markets and medical settings market their services.
- Measure the effectiveness of your marketing efforts.

Avoid . . .

- Basing your marketing efforts on untested assumptions
- Becoming irrelevant to ongoing referral sources
- Assuming "expert" status in marketing
- Stopping your marketing efforts
- Excluding marketing costs from your or your program's budget
- Offering services that referral sources and patients do not value

Adapted from Tovian, S. M. (2014). Marketing health psychology. In C. M. Hunter, C.L. Hunter, & R. Kessler (Eds.), *Handbook of clinical psychology in medical settings: Evidence-based assessment and intervention* (pp. 151–168). New York: Springer.

Healthcare systems and hospitals often have public relations departments that market the mission and dimensions of the system to potential healthcare clients. Use such marketing or public relations departments in larger healthcare settings to know your client base and target base. Be familiar with and knowledgeable about the environment in the healthcare setting, the surrounding communities served, as well as reimbursement and important professional trends. Identify professional competencies that will become increasingly important and develop these skills. Marketing is an ongoing investment in your practice that requires constant review over time by you as an individual practitioner. Remember, patients and referral sources will not use irrelevant services even if they are well marketed.

# PROFESSIONAL IMAGE IN MARKETING

Patients and other referral sources decide to obtain or purchase a particular service that will meet their needs and standards of quality. Like a "brand," a strong professional image for your practice communicates a promise of quality, value, and reliability. Your professional image can set you and your program apart from competitors by making patients and referral sources aware of you and your program's unique strengths so you and your services are seen as the preferred choice. Like a brand, professional image reflects the way others think and feel about your practice and services.

Branding has both physical and psychological dimensions that relate to defining a professional image. Physical elements include distinctive graphic elements often seen in promotional materials such as brochures and websites. Consider working with a design or marketing consultant to create a look and feel that is best suited to your practice within a healthcare setting and patients in the community. Psychologically, your professional image as a mental health professional affects the way others perceive your practice, the value of the services you provide, and the type of patients who use your services. These factors can influence whether or not you receive referrals in a healthcare setting.

Purposefully define your image as a mental health professional by using statements that serve as an anchor for your promotional materials. An effective statement should reflect your mission and values, leverage your strengths, and address the needs of your target market. The main purpose of a professional image is to communicate the way in which your practice and program is unique. Claiming that your services as a mental health professional are "high quality" is simply not enough to set you apart. Instead, choose an aspect of your practice that differs from competitors, that cannot be easily duplicated, and that patients and healthcare professionals can value.

For example, if you provide family therapy for cancer patients and have well-established relationships with oncologists, emphasize your ability to work collaboratively with the entire oncology treatment team to help families through the process. Don't convey the message that you can be everything to everybody; rather, emphasize what you do best and deliver it consistently. Support service delivery, if necessary, with evidence of training, supervision, and professional experience. The professional image conveys your strengths and provides prospective referral sources and patients with a better understanding of the circumstances in which your services are appropriate and desirable.

Once you have defined your professional image and considered how to differentiate your services, the next step involves creating a communication plan. Identify each of your target audiences (e.g., patients, referral sources like physicians, colleagues, payers), the communication vehicles you have that reach each audience, and the purpose of each communication. Consider how to communicate your professional image in a way that tailors the message to each audience and purpose while maintaining a consistent message. Repeat the same, simple, and focused message year to year in all promotional materials. The effects of marketing are cumulative, so consistency is crucial. Box 30.2 summarizes some key factors involved in developing a professional image.

Tovian (2014) summarizes additional key points for marketing a practice or program. These points, which may be adapted for any healthcare organization or system, may involve the following:

**BOX 30.2.** KEY FACTORS IN DEVELOPING A PROFESSIONAL IMAGE IN HEALTHCARE SETTINGS

- Define your professional image.
- Distinguish how your services are unique.
- Communicate consistently over time and in your various communication venues.
- Evaluate, revise, and monitor results and efforts by asking these questions:
  - How do people perceive your practice or program in healthcare settings?
  - How aware of your practice are healthcare professionals, patients, and referral sources?
  - How well do others understand the ways you differentiate your practice?
  - Are the aspects that set you or your services apart valuable to patients and referral sources?
  - How visible is your practice in the healthcare organization or community?
  - Are competitors duplicating the unique characteristics of your professional image?

Adapted from Tovian, S. M. (2014). Marketing health psychology. In C. M. Hunter, C.L. Hunter, & R. Kessler (Eds.), *Handbook of clinical psychology in medical settings: Evidence-based assessment and intervention* (pp. 151–168). New York: Springer.

Develop quality materials to support your outreach efforts to potential referral sources (e.g., business cards, websites, brochures, letters of introduction).

Actively establish relationships with other healthcare professionals (e.g., spend time in a physician's outpatient office consulting with staff and patients; accompany physicians and residents during inpatient rounds; give grand-rounds presentations to medical departments; join medical center committees; give talks in the community and to medical self-help organizations; contribute regularly to local newspaper columns on health issues and to medical center publications typically produced by the medical center's public relations department).

Build and track your referral networks (e.g., build databases to track your referral sources and patterns as well as patient demographics; write thank-you notes to referral sources; refer to other healthcare professionals as appropriate as they may refer to you; maintain timely contacts with your referral sources and professional network).

Distinguish yourself by emphasizing what makes you a uniquely qualified healthcare professional (e.g., emphasize those areas of expertise based on training, continuing education, research, and clinical experience to referral sources; assess customer satisfaction and outcomes through validated questionnaires; obtain board certification, for example, if you are a psychologist).

# NATURE OF REFERRALS

In ambulatory settings, mental health services are often geographically separated from medical-surgical services, even in large healthcare systems. This can be a barrier to integrated care and can hinder patient follow-through with referrals as well as interprofessional collaboration in practice. Mental health professionals in primary care specialties may provide services where they can practice onsite, often in joint sessions with physicians and nurses. Such a practice location model is deemed crucial when dealing with difficult-to-refer patients such as those with a somatization disorder, for example, and serves to establish a close working relationship with referral sources.

Gatchel and Oordt (2003) describe five levels of practice location based on how closely the mental health professional's practice is to the primary care physician and nurse. They range from collaboration from a distance (which is typical of most independent practitioners in separate offices from the referring physician); to collaboration onsite, with regular meetings to discuss referrals or problem areas; to collaboration in joint sessions with the physicians as needed. The decision by the mental health professional to remain onsite in the physician's office depends upon many factors, including the physician's permission and practice style, patient permission and confidentiality, financial considerations, and scheduling, to name a few.

Mental health professionals working in primary care settings have found substantial success with onsite collaborative practice models (Tovian, 2014). In a modification of onsite collaboration in tertiary care, this author has "scrubbed" and observed surgeries as a member of a cardiac transplantation team and a bariatric surgery team. The experience allowed this author to enhance his relationship with the team members and to better understand what both the medical staff and patients experience in cardiac transplantation and gastrointestinal bypass surgeries.

# INTERDISCIPLINARY COLLABORATION

The development of collaborative practice in healthcare settings with physicians, nurses, and other allied health professionals requires patience, perseverance, and good marketing skills. Use those marketing strategies that emphasize your expertise and ask about the needs of physicians and their staff as means to ensure practice growth. Essentially, along with patients, healthcare professionals should be viewed as the primary customers of your services (Gatchel & Oordt, 2003). First decide on the specific services you are competent, trained, and skilled to offer, and then identify the key personnel in healthcare practices and medical departments you will need to contact.

You can also develop methods to educate and inform healthcare professionals about the profession, your competencies, and the need for and value of the services you offer. Again, you should apply for professional staff privileges at the healthcare setting and volunteer to give lectures and grand-rounds presentations to relevant medical departments consistent with your training, experience, and expertise (Tovian, 2006). You can also volunteer to provide smaller office seminars, perhaps at lunch (sometimes referred to as "Lunch and Learns"), on salient issues that affect physicians' and nurses' practices (e.g., management of the high-utilizing, somaticizing patient in a primary care practice).

Consider the advantages and disadvantages of spending time with physicians and nurses in their offices and seeing patients there. As discussed previously, mental health professionals in primary care have demonstrated the value in not waiting for patients to come to their offices but seeing patients in the physician's suite. Also consider the advantages and disadvantages of participating in managed healthcare panels and insurance plans. Primary care physicians often serve as "gatekeepers" for such plans, and collaborative work can be facilitated when the psychologist is a member of the same panel as the referring physician.

## DEVELOPING THE RELATIONSHIP

Successful collaborative relationships between healthcare professionals such as physicians and mental health professionals depend on the very interpersonal skills that we use with patients to facilitate psychotherapy. Good, inclusive communication is a crucial element of coordinated care. Clarify what information the physician or nurse expects you to provide about the patient, and in turn specify what information you will need from the physician and/or nurse. You should have an empathetic understanding of the physician's or nurse's worldview and how the physician or other healthcare professional may approach patient care differently than psychologists. Have tolerance for your position on a healthcare team that is often hierarchical, usually being led by physicians.

Avoid overidentifying with the profession of medicine or nursing or undermining a preexisting treatment plan. This can be an issue with regard to psychotropic medication in primary care, for example. For example, if you are skeptical about the efficacy and use of psychotropic medication in a specific case, be careful not to undermine the patient's motivation to follow through with the medication. In such a situation, a discussion with the primary care physician is warranted. Avoid triangulation with the patient if you disagree with the physician or nurse on the treatment plan (Tovian, 2014). Never compete for who cares more about the patient. Collaboration is the key and will benefit both the healthcare professionals and the patient.

You will also want to develop good working relationships with the physician's staff, which can include nurses, nurse practitioners, physician's assistants, rotating residents (if the physician is on staff at an academic health center), practice managers, secretaries, and even office billing and coding clerks.

## DIFFERING STYLES OF HEALTHCARE PROFESSIONALS

Primary care physicians and nurses attempt to meet the broad healthcare needs of their patients, whereas specialty tertiary care physicians and nurses provide in-depth care for selected patients who meet certain medical criteria. Make an effort to understand the culture of the organization where physicians and nurses may practice (e.g., large medical group practices, "boutique" independent medical practices) as well as the techniques and procedures necessary to function in a specialty.

## BOX 30.3. PARAMETERS FOR POSSIBLE REFERRALS FOR PSYCHOLOGICAL INTERVENTION IN HEALTHCARE SETTINGS

- The patient's emotional and behavioral responses interfere with his or her ability to seek appropriate treatment or to cooperate with the necessary procedures involved in the healthcare plan (i.e., compliance and adherence).
- The patient's emotional response causes greater distress than the disease/illness itself or increases disease/illness-related impairment.
- The patient's emotional response interferes with his or her activities of daily living and quality of life (e.g., decrease usual sources of gratification) at home, work, or school.
- The patient's emotional response results in severe personality or behavioral disorganization and is so severe and inappropriate that it results in the misinterpretation and distortion of environmental events.
- The patient has a history of psychological disorders, substance abuse, or suicide attempts.
- The patient has limited social support.

Adapted from Belar, C.D. & Deardorff, W.W. (2009). *Clinical health psychology in medical settings: A practitioner's guidebook* (Second Edition). Washington, DC: American Psychological Association.

Ask frequent referral partners whether they prefer written or telephone feedback about their referrals. Educate the physician about referral criteria in a manner that is clear and relevant for assessment and possible intervention. Parameters for referrals from healthcare professionals often include psychological and behavioral responses to disease and treatment interventions as well as the somatic effects of psychological distress (Belar & Deardorff, 2009). Some parameters for referrals for psychological assessment and intervention are summarized in Box 30.3. You may need to expand your expertise via additional training or supervision to meet the patient needs of a particular healthcare professional or group practice. If you are in primary care, you should also have established relationships with physicians in tertiary specialties to facilitate possible referrals of patients (Tovian, 2006) in an effort to best serve patient needs.

## COMMUNICATION PARAMETERS

Be precise in your verbal and written communications with healthcare professionals. Physicians, like most healthcare professionals, are often pressed for time. Consider a 30- to 45-second window of opportunity to make a verbally salient point about a patient. Written consultation reports should be brief, concise, and void of lengthy narratives. Reports should also offer specific and practical recommendations that are relevant to the patient's presenting problem(s) and should specify plans for follow-up. Use terms that are easily understood in verbal and written communications. This may also imply distancing yourself from mental health terminology and jargon; for example, not all healthcare professionals will understand the term "borderline personality." If possible, try to schedule regular times to meet with referring healthcare professionals and their staff to discuss referrals. These meetings are also excellent opportunities for you to make presentations about psychological issues in patient care.

Finally, you must protect patient confidentiality. Other healthcare professionals are often not accustomed to the different confidentiality obligations imposed on psychologists by laws and ethical standards. Address all necessary privacy concerns with patients before releasing confidential patient information or discussing this information with the collaborating physician, for example. In an effort to provide integrative outpatient care, appropriate documentation and recommendations need to be in the chart without revealing unnecessary sensitive information (Belar & Deardorff, 2009). Recommendations for effective communications with physicians are summarized in Box 30.4.

# NECESSARY SKILLS

Mental health professionals who are integrated into healthcare settings need specific skills to adapt to that setting and optimize success (Box 30.5).

Avoid the lengthy assessment measures typically used initially in mental health settings. Instead, use brief assessment measures (see Belar & Deardorff, 2009) targeted to biopsychosocial domains with norms from medical patient populations. Use broad, closed-ended questions to cover general areas such as anxiety and depression in initial assessments. You can make referrals for more in-depth, detailed assessments, such as neuropsychological assessment, later or as part of your long-term recommendations.

Traditional 50-minute psychotherapy sessions may not be relevant or even possible in ambulatory medical settings. The recent CPT codes for health psychology assessment and interventions with medical diagnosis are coded in 15-minute intervals or "units" (Tovian, 2006). In ambulatory healthcare settings, consultations, assessments, and interventions do not always "fit" into 50-minute segments as with traditional psychotherapy. When engaging in consultation with medical patients, expect periodic cancellations because of illness or treatment side effects (e.g., an oncology patient cancels an appointment secondary to a low platelet count from chemotherapy.) In addition, depending on the goals of treatment, psychotherapy may be short term and resumed at a later time depending on the course of the illness and the patient's or the family's biopsychosocial needs.

You will often have to make conclusions and recommendations based on limited and diverse sets of data from several biopsychosocial domains. Avoid making unsupported conclusions or treating all patients the same without regard to individual differences (e.g., not all diabetic patients are alike). Be knowledgeable about the best indicators, key factors, risk factors, and predictors for a particular disorder or problem area. Be prepared to expand your clinical services to different settings (e.g., inpatient milieu when following an ill patient) and to different targets (e.g., the patient and the family). Also be prepared to provide educational, didactic services to patients, families, and staff. Do not neglect opportunities to influence public policy and participate in the political process on behalf of patients, medical conditions, and our profession.

Understand models for attitude and behavior change and motivational interviewing (Tovian, 2006) that often appeal to the behavioral, action-oriented results favored by healthcare professionals. Within primary care, for example, problems involving weight control, substance abuse, exercise, smoking cessation, and adherence to medical regimens are often amenable to these approaches to behavior and attitude change (Gatchel & Oordt, 2003). Working in a primary or tertiary healthcare setting requires knowledge of medical terminology, a basic understanding of common diseases and their treatments, and a familiarity with the medications used in that setting. Establishing a well-selected reference library is essential for maintaining this knowledge. This library should include medical dictionaries, texts, medication handbooks, and access to reliable Internet sites.

Those in psychology, social work, professional counseling, and marriage and family therapy should seek to earn credentials at the highest level of their respective profession in order to increase public confidence in their work. If you are a psychologist, for example, board certification, as administered by the American Board of Professional Psychology, is intended to the serve the public and the profession by recognizing education, training, experience, and competence in specialty areas of psychology. Belar and Jeffrey (1995) have proposed that board certification be the standard for psychologists as it is in the medical and nursing professions. Physicians and nurses, for example, readily identify with the need and importance of "board certification."

# ETHICS CONSIDERATIONS

Practice in healthcare settings is accompanied by unique ethical challenges. Mental health professionals should always be well versed in professional ethical standards irrespective of their particular practice setting. Maintaining competence may be the most challenging aspect of practice in healthcare settings, especially for mental health professionals who have practiced in more traditional mental health areas and wish to expand their services to healthcare settings. With the pressure on practitioners to expand their scope of practice to remain financially viable, there is risk that insufficiently trained mental health professionals could provide substandard care to patients, would be unable to work well with physicians, and thus would damage the credibility of their profession (Papas, Belar, & Rozensky, 2004).

When you are working with healthcare professionals, for example, be very cautious about avoiding practicing medicine without a license (Belar & Deardorff, 2009). Do not offer opinions on issues of diagnosis and treatment within the biomedical sphere and violate boundaries of competence, training, and licensure. In fact, when treating patients with medical disorders and writing their reports, always indicate in the report that the medical diagnosis was made by the physician (e.g., "migraine headaches per A. B. Cee, MD"). This will avoid any confusion about who made the medical diagnosis.

Mental health professionals are often asked by both primary and tertiary physicians and nurses in ambulatory healthcare settings about psychopharmacological issues. Unless you are both privileged (i.e., trained and licensed to prescribe psychotropic medications) and practicing in those states and defense department areas that allow prescription privileges for psychologists, you should respond with a caveat about the limits of your practice regarding these specific medications. Completing level II psychopharmacological training from the American Psychological Association or a designated training institution will prepare a psychologist, for example, for collaborative practice and knowledgeable discussion of medication issues.

## FUTURE DIRECTIONS

Mental health professionals currently in independent practice must learn to apply standard business principles to their practices and programs without sacrificing their clinical and ethical integrity. Responses to the multiple and complex problems inherent in our nation's healthcare delivery system will have a direct impact on the future independent practice of professional psychology. The marketplace will reshape healthcare delivery systems and challenge healthcare professionals to provide high-quality services at a competitive costs. Mental health professionals must consider how their practices will fare in this new healthcare environment. The independent practice of mental health in the future will most likely be larger in group size, more efficient, more business-oriented while still quality conscious, better connected to primary and tertiary healthcare systems, and more vertically and horizontally integrated into healthcare.

## CONCLUSION

What are the three most important aspects of developing a collaborative relationship with healthcare professionals? "Build the relationship, build the relationship, and build the relationship." Very few professionals have more knowledge about relationship enhancement than mental health professionals. With changes in the healthcare system and increases in scientific knowledge base, our respective mental health professions can anticipate expansion of psychological practice across the spectrum of health problems. Collaboration with healthcare professionals offers many challenges and opportunities for mental health professionals who remain faithful to a scientist-practitioner model. Healthcare professionals need us, we need healthcare professionals, and patients need us both (adapted from McDaniel, 1995).

## REFERENCES

Belar, C. D., Brown, R. A., Hersch, L. E., Hornyak, L. M., Rozensky, R.H., Sheridan, E. P., . . . Reed, G. W. (2001). Self-assessment in clinical health psychology: A model for ethical expansion of practice. *Professional Psychology: Research and Practice, 32*, 135–141.

Belar, C. D., & Deardorff, W. W. (2009). *Clinical health psychology in medical settings: A practical guidebook* (Second Edition). Washington, DC: American Psychological Association.

Belar, C. D., & Jeffrey, T. B. (1995). Board certification in health psychology. *Journal of Clinical Psychology, 2,* 129–132.

Gatchel, R. J., & Oordt, M. S. (2003). *Clinical health psychology and primary care: Practical advice and clinical guidance for successful collaboration.* Washington, DC: American Psychological Association.

Johnson, S. B., Perry, N., & Rozensky, R. H. (Eds) (2002). *Handbook of clinical health psychology, Volume 1: Medical disorders and behavioral applications.* Washington, DC: American Psychological Association.

McDaniel, S. (1995). Collaboration between psychologists and family physicians: Implementing the biopsychosocial model. *Professional Psychology: Research and Practice, 26,* 117–122.

Papas, R. K., Belar, C. D., & Rozensky, R. H. (2004). The practice of clinical health psychology: Professional issues. In T. J. Boll, R. G. Frank, A. Baum, & J. Wallander (Eds.). *Handbook of clinical health psychology (Vol. 3): Models and perspectives in health psychology* (pp. 293–319). Washington, DC: American Psychological Association.

Robinson, J. D., & Baker, J. (2006). Psychological consultation and services in a general medical hospital. *Professional Psychology: Research and Practice, 37*(3), 264–267.

Rozensky, R. H. (2009). Clinical psychology in medical settings: Celebrating our past, enjoying the present, and building our future. *Journal of Clinical Psychology in Medical Settings, 13,* 343–352.

Rozensky, R. H., Tovian, S. M., & Goodheart, C. D. (2016). Health problems. In J. C. Norcross, G. R. Vandenbos, D. K. Freedheim, & N. Pole (Eds.). *APA handbook of clinical psychology (volume V): Psychopathology and health* (pp. 423–446). Washington, DC: American Psychological Association.

Tovian, S. M. (2006). Interdisciplinary collaboration in outpatient practice. *Professional Psychology: Research and Practice, 37*(3), 268–272.

Tovian, S. M. (2014). Marketing. In C. M. Hunter, C. L. Hunter, & R. Kessler (Eds.). *Handbook of clinical psychology in medical settings: Evidence-based assessment and intervention* (pp. 151–168). New York: Springer.

Tovian, S. M., Rozensky, R. H., & Sweet, J. J. (2003). A decade of clinical psychology in medical settings: The short longer view. *Journal of Clinical Psychology in Medical Settings, 10,* 1–8.

Wright, L., & Friedman, A. G. (1991). Challenges of the future: Psychologists in medical settings. In J. J. Sweet, R. H. Rozensky, & S. M. Tovian (Eds.). *Handbook of clinical psychology in medical settings* (pp. 603–614). New York: Plenum.

# CHAPTER 31

# COLLABORATING WITH LEGAL PROFESSIONALS

*Eric G. Mart*

The Specialty Guidelines for Forensic Psychology of the American Psychological Association define forensic psychology as

> professional practice by any psychologist working within any sub-discipline of psychology (e.g., clinical, developmental, social, cognitive) when applying the scientific, technical, or specialized knowledge of psychology to the law to assist in addressing legal, contractual and administrative matters. (American Psychological Association, 2013, p. 7)

Clinicians working in this specialty area provide evaluations, consultation, and expert testimony to assist courts and other deliberative bodies in coming to informed conclusion in areas that include criminal and civil capacities, child custody, personal injury, and need for guardianship. This is a rapidly expanding area of mental health practice that offers many opportunities for clinicians. Working in this role frequently involves providing services to lawyers and the courts.

## IS FORENSIC MENTAL HEALTH PRACTICE RIGHT FOR YOU?

Before exploring the nuts and bolts of how mental health professionals can assist attorneys and the courts, there are a several issues that anyone contemplating expanding his or her practice into forensic work should consider. The first of these is whether you are well suited for this type of work. Although the skillsets of clinical practice and forensic work overlap a great deal, they are not identical. Others have written about the important differences in the two roles; probably the best article on the subject is "Irreconcilable conflict between therapeutic and forensic roles" by

Greenberg and Shuman (1997). The authors point out a number of important differences between the therapeutic and forensic roles, including who you are working for (lawyer vs. client), the purpose of your work (assisting the court vs. helping your client with his or her distress), and a number of others that make it clear that it is not advisable to mix the two roles. But there are other important differences.

One of the most important differences is that in most cases, forensic mental health professionals have to go into court and testify. Many excellent clinicians either do not wish to do this or lack the skills to do it well. This is understandable, since many people find public speaking, particularly in an adversarial environment, extremely stressful, while others simply prefer to remain in the clinical/therapeutic role. When you testify, you have to present information to the judge or jury in a way that is clear, concise, and understandable by non–mental health professionals. When I train students to testify, I describe my general approach to testifying to jurors as follows. I pretend that I am speaking to my Uncle Harry, who never went to college but is an intelligent man who opened a plumbing supply store and who now makes a great deal of money with his chain of stores across the state. If Uncle Harry does not understand what I am getting at, I am probably using too much jargon or just not being clear. People considering forensic work probably have some idea of how well they speak in public, and if this is something that you really do not want to do, you should focus on another niche practice area.

Another difference between clinical and forensic work is that forensic mental health practice imposes an increased need for the practitioner to be familiar with the professional literature. It is important for forensic practitioners to update their knowledge of the field on an ongoing basis, and they need to be experts on everything about which they testify. This is not to say that clinicians do not need to be aware of what is going on in their areas of practice, but forensic psychology is a rapidly developing specialty: New tests are developed, courts come out with new rulings, and the terrain changes all the time. Additionally, opposing counsel will likely research your methodology and the strengths and weaknesses of any instruments you employ in your evaluation, and in some cases will hire forensic consultants to assist in their cross-examination. If you are not willing to put in the extra time to go to conferences and keep up with the literature, forensic work is probably not for you.

One of the reasons staying current is important is related to another aspect of forensic work that might make some mental health professionals avoid this area of practice. This is the adversarial nature of the American justice system. In my experience, clinicians, in general, place a high value on consensus and collegiality and it is unusual for a case conference to become heated or nasty. In contrast, one of the basic premises of our legal system is that the truth will emerge through vigorous and sometimes contentious debate. What this means in practice is that if you step into a court to testify, there is going to be a well-trained lawyer on the other side of the case whose job it is to challenge all aspects of your testimony, including your training, experience, and any apparent deficiencies in your assessment. This lawyer will attack your credentials, training, assessment techniques, and anything else he or she can think of to undermine your testimony. As a forensic professional, you have to expect that some lawyers will take your words out of context, misstate your testimony, and otherwise attempt to put words in your mouth. In some cases, they will crowd you in the witness box, raise their voice, or shake their finger in your face. Generally, the presiding judge will not let this get too out of hand, but it does happen. If you do not think that you could handle this well or just want to avoid the experience, then you should probably not testify. On the other hand, it is possible to learn to deal with these issues when they come up without losing your composure or being bothered by its occurrence. Stanley Brodsky (2004, 2013) has written a number of excellent books on how to deal with these ploys when testifying, and I recommend them highly.

## GETTING PREPARED

It is beyond the scope of this chapter to provide a detailed guide about how mental health professionals can gain the expertise necessary to practice in the forensic arena. Additionally, forensic practice is a bit different from clinical practice in that many of the individuals involved in this specialty did not set out to do this kind of work when they started their career. In recent years, a number of clinical/forensic psychology programs have sprung up, but in the past, such programs did not exist. There are also a number of MSW and licensed clinical mental health counselor programs that have forensic concentrations, but this has also been a recent development.

Generally, people move into forensic work as an extension of their particular areas of clinical expertise. For example, mental health professionals who work with children often find that the skills they have developed provide a good starting point for learning how to do child custody evaluations. In the same way, mental health practitioners who provide treatment in correctional facilities may segue into assessing criminal competencies. But it is important to remember that no matter how solid your clinical skills are, it takes a good deal of preparation to begin a forensic practice in any part of the field. One of the best ways to prepare is to find an internship or postgraduate fellowship with a forensic focus. These types of programs provide training and supervision and generally have a didactic component as well. However, this is not mandatory; many prominent forensic practitioners moved into forensics after completing training in other areas of practice, and returning to school or completing another fellowship is simply not practical. In such cases, a combination of finding a mentor, engaging in group supervision, and attending continuing education is another effective way to develop necessary skills.

If you decide to develop a forensic practice and did not complete this kind of formal postgraduate training, there are other ways of gaining expertise in forensic work. In my experience, mental health professionals who wish to gain expertise do so through a combination of supervised experience, workshops, conferences, and self-study. While all of these are important, I think that having an experienced mentor looking over your shoulder and providing advice is essential when you start doing the work. It is important to remember that in forensic practice, the stakes can be high for the individual being assessed, and your work will be heavily scrutinized. Under those circumstances, it is extremely important that you are aware of and follow best practices for assessment, report writing, and testimony. Careless or less-than-thorough work and lack of knowledge about the ethics standards governing this area of practice is one of the easiest ways I know to be reported to a professional board of conduct. Be sure you know what you are doing before you take on your first case independently, and remember that you are probably not the best judge of how ready you are. Input from a mentor regarding your readiness is indispensable in making sure you are properly prepared.

# HOW TO START A FORENSIC MENTAL HEALTH PRACTICE

One of the biggest problems faced by forensic professionals wishing to enter the private sector is marketing their new practice. Forensic work differs from other areas of mental health practice in that the market is composed almost exclusively of attorneys. While there are other sources of referrals (e.g., agencies working with the developmentally disabled, risk assessments for schools, fitness-for-duty evaluations for public safety agencies), the great majority of referrals will involve court-related issues. Areas of practice including criminal and civil competencies, mental state at time of offense, child custody, parenting, personal injury, and sentencing all take place within the context of our adversarial legal system, and it is attorneys and sometimes judges who will be looking for mental health experts to assist their clients and educate courts and juries. Consequently, it is necessary to develop a referral base in the legal community.

However, before getting into the specifics of practice development and marketing, it is important to address an attitudinal issue experienced by many mental health professionals. I have noticed that as a group, we are extremely reluctant to consider what we do from a business standpoint. This has improved in recent years, as graduate schools have begun offering advice about practice management, but there is still a great deal of discomfort about the whole idea of making money in mental health. I recall giving a workshop on marketing for mental health professionals in which I quoted my father (who was a successful restaurateur in Cleveland, Ohio) and an excellent small business owner. He had told me that if I planned to go into private practice I would be first, and foremost, a businessman. Several attendees told me that if they thought that was true, they would get into another line of work. So why this discomfort with the business of mental health practice? I have several thoughts:

1. People in mental health professions see themselves as empathic, insightful helpers of people with problems. In many instances a personal need to help others was the initial motivation for getting into this field. Thinking about making a profit from helping others this seems contradictory in this context. Walfish and Barnett's (2009) first "Principle of Private Practice Success" is that clinicians have to resolve the conflict between altruism and being a small business owner.

2. Although I understand that this has changed somewhat in recent years, in the past there was no discussion of the business of mental health in graduate programs. The entire time I was in graduate school, neither I nor any of my classmates ever raised his or her hand and asked the professor, "Hey, just out of curiosity, how much can you make at this gig?" Granted, back in the 1980s and 1990s getting through graduate school and into any of the professions was usually a guarantee of a reasonably comfortable lifestyle, and most people picked up what they needed to know about running their practices as they went

along. But for the most part, most mental health professionals simply have not thought much about the business aspects of their profession and enter the marketplace woefully ignorant of both opportunities and pitfalls.

3. Finally, while I am a bit reluctant to bring this up, it has been my experience that there is a problem with a subtle form of arrogance in the mental health professions. This arrogance takes the form of many of us (and I am not immune) thinking that what we do is somehow more important than what people do in more "mundane" jobs, and that worrying about profit margins is somehow beneath us. I think that it is important to remember that we are professionals providing a service and in that sense are no better and no worse than plumbers or mechanics; a little humility never hurts.

Clearly, the fact that forensic practitioners are engaged in running a business does not mean that the business aspects of practice have to be their sole focus. Providing the court with specialized information is an important role that must be taken seriously. Forensic mental health professionals have tremendous informal authority and influence over the lives of the people they assess or treat, and I do not believe that the potential impact your opinions can have on the lives of others should ever be forgotten. There is also the necessity of performing this role in a knowledgeable, conscientious, and ethical manner, and this requires ongoing study and feedback from fellow professionals. But none of this can happen if you cannot keep the doors of your business open. Consequently, if you are contemplating expanding into forensic work and you have an issue about this part of the job, it is important to resolve it before taking the next step.

# MARKETING YOUR PRACTICE

So, having gotten the "money hang-up" out of the way, the next matter to be addressed is marketing your skills. Forensic referrals come from many sources, and your market will depend on your specific areas of forensic practice. In my own practice, referrals come to me in a variety of ways:

1. Public and private schools refer students for violence risk assessments, generally after some aggressive action or threat. I also occasionally receive referrals for fitness-for-duty evaluations for teachers. While these types of assessments may not appear to be forensic, if the examinee appeals what he or she sees as an adverse outcome, the case could end up before a deliberative board and testimony could be required.

2. Agencies that provide services for individuals with developmental disabilities often refer their clients for assessments involving problematic sexual behavior, aggression, or legal problems.

3. Police and fire departments and certain governmental agencies such as the Federal Aviation Administration refer prospective employees for mental health screening and fitness-for-duty evaluations after critical incidents. These may also end up in front of an arbitration board or in civil court.

4. There are companies that employ forensic professionals to review files and in some cases perform independent examinations related to insurance claims that have mental health components.

However, the bulk of my forensic referrals come from attorneys, and I think that is the most important place to focus attention. How can mental health professionals market effectively to legal professionals? There are a number of methods that can be used, and some are better than others:

1. Print advertising: One method of marketing that is frequently used is putting advertisements in local legal journals. In my discussions with other forensic mental health professionals, this method of marketing seems to be of limited utility. I suspect this occurs for two reasons. The first is that when mental health professionals advertise, they do not effectively differentiate themselves and they give the reader no reason to pick them for a referral over some other similarly qualified mental health professional. The second reason is that attorneys like to see how a potential expert communicates with others to get a sense of how effective he or she would be communicating with a judge or jury.

2. Websites and blogs: Increasing numbers of forensic mental health professionals have websites, and this is a relatively inexpensive way to provide attorneys looking for an expert with contact information and a description of the professional's practice. Having some content that attorneys will find helpful will increase the number of hits. A good example of this kind of content is the blog that Karen Franklin, PhD, has created that provides information about recent forensic research and related issues (http://forensic-psychologist.blogspot.com; Franklin, 2016). It provides a great deal of useful information and demonstrates that Dr. Franklin is quite knowledgeable and on top of emerging forensic issues, but it is not overtly self-promoting. Having this kind of content not only increases traffic to a website but will help to bring up your name closer to the top of a Google search. One caveat is that if you are not very good at putting together websites, you should probably obtain professional design assistance; you do not want your website to look amateurish.

3. Writing articles is an excellent way to bring yourself to the attention of your referral base. Every state has a bar association that usually has a journal. In some states it can be difficult to get into the main bar journal, either because they are looking for very-high-level articles from attorneys or because they have planned out their publications for the next two years. In most larger states and some that are smaller, bar associations are broken up into practice sections similar to the American Psychological Association divisions. These can include subgroups that focus on criminal law, child custody, elder law, and a host of other areas of practice. Often these bar sections have their own newsletters or magazines, and it is much easier to place an article in one of these than in the main association journal. Additionally, there are legal associations separate from the main bar association. For example, in New Hampshire, where my practice is located, the New Hampshire Association for Justice is made up of trial lawyers, and they are willing to accept articles that are informal. Articles should be related to some aspect of your forensic practice. For example, if your practice includes child custody work, you may discover

that there has been a recent change in your state's laws regarding parent relocation after divorce. An article reviewing the literature on the effects of parental relocation on children would be informative to lawyers doing custody work. It would also bring to their attention that you are knowledgeable about this area.

4. The very best way to market yourself to attorneys is to provide presentations on subjects related to your practice. There are usually many opportunities to do this. Generally, bar sections meet on a monthly basis and they often have guest speakers at their meetings. Providing some type of presentation or training works well as a marketing tool for a number of reasons. Attorneys want to know that the experts they work with are knowledgeable about their subject. More importantly, attorneys want to see how potential experts present themselves in public as a way of gauging how they might testify in court. When I am consulted about marketing issues I urge forensic mental health professionals to speak to any group of lawyers who are potential referral sources, regardless of how small the group, and not to worry about being given any type of honorarium. I personally have never given such a talk that did not result in a number of referrals, and many of my friends or colleagues tell me that they have the same experience.

One additional consideration in marketing a forensic practice is whether to work in a variety of court-related areas or to specialize. For example, should you limit your practice to child custody work and parenting assessments, or should you also perform assessments of competence to stand trial and legal insanity? I think the choice has to do with temperament, confidence, and the nature of your market. For example, I engage in a wide variety of activities, but that is partly because I started in forensic work in New Hampshire, which is a relatively small market. It simply was not possible to have a practice solely limited to child custody evaluations or to exclusively criminal forensic work because there was not a high enough volume of any one type of case. Other forensic practitioners I know have become highly specialized and perform only one or two types of activities for the court. Individuals who take this route sometimes become nationally known experts and can charge much higher fees than generalists. It is probably a better idea to specialize if you can, but in a small market you do not want to spend too much time waiting for the phone to ring with a referral. Depending on where in the country you reside, one strategy is to become licensed in another nearby state, which will increase your potential referral base. Once you have a reasonable case flow, you can decide which areas of forensic practice are most interesting to you and then focus your marketing on those areas and become more specialized.

# AREAS FOR COLLABORATION

When most mental health professionals think about collaboration with attorneys, they generally view themselves in the role of expert witness providing testimony in a specific case. I have found this is generally where the bulk of forensic mental health work occurs. In criminal cases, counsel retains mental health experts for the defendant or by the prosecution and in some cases directly by the court. In civil matters, the mental health expert is retained either by counsel for the plaintiff or for the defendant. Expert witnesses differ from witnesses of fact (sometimes referred to as lay witnesses) in a number of important ways. If I were to witness a motor vehicle accident while walking down the street, I could be called to provide testimony. However, since I have not been trained as a forensic expert on motor vehicle accidents, I would be called as a fact witness. I would be allowed to provide testimony about what I observed and heard but would not be allowed to provide opinions about whether someone was driving too fast for conditions or other technical matters. An expert witness is someone who, because of his or her education, training, and experience, is able to provide the court with information that the average person would not be expected to know. An example of this would be an opinion that someone the expert evaluated suffers from a particular psychiatric condition. In court, the attorney who retained the expert services questions the expert regarding his or her qualifications. Opposing counsel may also ask questions designed to expose any weaknesses in the expert's training or knowledge. The court will then make a decision as to whether to qualify the mental health professional as an expert or not.

There are different types of testimony that a mental health expert can provide. One common role for mental health experts is to perform some type of assessment on an individual or individuals involved in the case and provide testimony regarding his or her conclusions based on that assessment. This is the case when mental health professionals provide testimony on a variety of topics. A partial list of these potential topics includes the following:

1. Assessments of criminal competencies, including competency to stand trial, competency to represent oneself at trial, and competency to enter a plea
2. Civil competencies, including capacity to make a will, manage one's affairs including financial and healthcare matters, guardianship, and conservatorship
3. Child custody assessment, parental fitness, forensic interviews of children in cases of suspected abuse
4. Risk assessments and sentencing evaluations
5. Civil personal injury evaluations (e.g., motor vehicle accidents, sexual harassment, intentional infliction of emotional distress) (Kane & Dvoskin, 2011)

Clearly, in order to provide this type of testimony, the expert performing the assessment must have specialized knowledge about the issue being evaluated. He or she must also must use tests and techniques that are appropriate for the specific purpose for which they are being employed, as well as a firm grasp of each test's psychometric properties. The mental health professional serving as an expert must also be knowledgeable about the ethics standards that apply to performing such assessments and providing testimony. The Ethical Principles of Psychologists and Code of Conduct of the American Psychological Association specifically state that "When assuming forensic roles, psychologists are or become reasonably familiar with the judicial or administrative rules governing their roles" (2010, p. 5). Finally, there is a requirement that experts have an understanding of the applicable legal standards of the jurisdiction in which the assessment is performed. Mental health experts sometimes neglect this last requirement.

As an example, early in my career I was asked to perform a competency-to-stand-trial evaluation in a county in which I had not often worked. After my services were retained, I received a call from the clerk of courts asking if I understood the legal standards associated with competency to stand trial. I assured her that I did. The next day I received a call from the judge who was presiding over the case, and he asked me the same question. I explained that it was my understanding that to be considered competent, the defendant had to be able to consult with his attorney with a reasonable degree of rational understanding and had to have a general grasp of the proceedings. The judge sounded relieved and told me that the last few experts who had testified in his court had not understood the standard or even known one existed and had testified that the defendants were competent to do such things as prepare food and pick out their own clothing. If you are testifying as a mental health expert, you have to know what the court is asking you to do.

There are other types of testimony that mental health experts can provide to the court, and not all of them involve doing an assessment of a particular individual. In some cases, experts provide the judge or jury with information about a specific topic that may be important to understanding certain aspects of the case as a whole. This is sometimes referred to as dissertational testimony. For example, an expert working for opposing counsel may diagnose a plaintiff who has experienced a mild traumatic brain injury (mTBI) with persistent postconcussion syndrome, with symptoms that have continued for over a year. The defendant's attorney may ask a properly qualified expert to testify about why the diagnosis of persistent postconcussion syndrome is highly controversial and generally unsupported in the recent research and literature. The expert may go on to explain that people who experience mTBI nearly always recover from the direct effects within a month, and that the symptoms of the syndrome are nonspecific, are common in the general population, and are seldom seen outside of the context of litigation. In this type of testimony, the expert has not examined the defendant and is not offering any diagnosis; the testimony is used by the defendant's attorney to undermine the opposing expert's conclusions in general terms.

Mental health experts may also review cases in which other mental health professionals have completed evaluations, usually for the purpose of highlighting problems with the other expert's assessment, report, or testimony. Following the review, if the mental health expert determines that, in his or her opinion, everything was done in an ethical and professional manner, he or she probably will not be asked to testify. On the other hand he or she may conclude that there are problems; best practices may not have been followed, conclusions may not be consistent with the data, or tests may have been misinterpreted. In this case, the mental health professional may be asked to testify about these deficiencies. As with dissertation testimony, the expert would refrain from providing opinions specifically about the evaluee since it is generally unethical to testify about specific characteristics of someone you have not evaluated yourself.

## ADDITIONAL FORENSIC ROLES

Although most of what forensic professionals do involves assessment and testimony, there are other roles they can and do fill. One of these is the role of consultant. There are cases in which an attorney needs specific information to assist in his or her case but does not want the mental health professional to testify; in some cases, opposing counsel does not even know the consulting expert is involved in the case. There are a number of important differences between the role of consultant and that of evaluator. One of these is that consultation generally involves record review and discussions with the retaining attorney rather than direct contact with criminal defendants or civil litigants. For example, a forensic mental health consultant may be asked to review a psychological evaluation performed by another expert and comment on topics such as the strengths and weaknesses of the methodology of the assessment. He or she might also be asked to help craft questions for the attorney to use when cross-examining the expert. Another role might be to educate an attorney on a particular area of forensic mental health practice, particularly in a rapidly developing area of practice such as forensic neuropsychology or child custody. One of the only books on this subject is Stanley Brodsky's *Principles and Practice of Trial Consultation* (2009), and it is an excellent resource for mental health professionals who wish to develop a consulting practice.

One consultation role I have served in has been helping to prepare other mental health professionals to testify in court. This usually occurs when a psychotherapist with little or no experience testifying is brought into a case, often involuntarily. For example, a psychotherapist may be working with a child with anxiety problems on an ongoing basis. In the course of his or her work, the parents of the child may begin divorce proceedings. Despite not having contemplated ever having to go to court as part of working with the child, one or both of the child's parents may request or demand that the psychotherapist testify about what the child has said about the parents in treatment sessions. In many cases of this sort, the psychotherapist is not only inexperienced but also terrified about appearing in court and being cross-examined. It is easy for those of us who make a living providing testimony in court to forget that public speaking is the most common phobia in the general population, and speaking in court is doubly frightening. In these kinds of cases, I have worked almost psychotherapeutically with clinicians to help them understand what to do when called to the stand, how to answer questions effectively, and how to deal with hostile cross-examination. This generally lowers their anxiety level enough that they can provide effective testimony.

## MULTIDISCIPLINARY FORENSICS

For the most part, the field of forensic mental health is dominated by psychiatrists and psychologists. I do not believe that there are any statistics available about the number of licensed social workers or mental health counselors who are involved in forensic activities, but it has been my experience that they are few and far between. Anecdotally, I have been involved in forensic practice since 1988 and I have seldom encountered a non-psychiatrist or psychologist in the role of an expert in a legal proceeding. One exception to this occurs in special education due process hearings, in which master's-level certified school psychologists testify as experts. However, even in these situations, the school psychologist is generally drawn into the proceeding because he or she performed a routine psychoeducational evaluation; there was no intention of becoming involved in a quasi-judicial matter at the time that the assessment was performed.

However, there is no good reason that professionals from other mental health professions cannot perform forensic work. While the ability to administer and interpret psychological tests is an expertise of psychologists, psychiatrists perform forensic assessments and frequently administer no testing at all. Social workers, mental health counselors, and school psychologists have the skills to assess and diagnose and are generally allowed to do so within the scope of their licensure. Many types of forensic assessments require no testing. For example, assessments of testamentary capacity (whether an individual understood what he or she was doing when he or she made a will) often occur after the person making the will has passed away. In those types of situations, what is needed to perform the assessment is an understanding of the legal definition of testamentary capacity and the ability to review and understand medical and legal documents and to gather information from collateral sources. The expert in a case involving wills would also need to be able to write an effective report and testify convincingly. None of this involves the administration of psychometric tests. There are other areas of practice in which this is also the case. Some examples include the following:

1. Parenting and bonding assessments
2. Cases involving ethics and standards of care
3. Educational due-process cases
4. Guardianship
5. Jury selection
6. Forensic interviewing in cases of suspected child abuse

This is not an exhaustive list, and in all these cases the mental health professional could provide testimony regarding his or her own assessment, testimony on a specific topic to help the judge or jury understand that issue, reviews of other's assessments, and attorney consultation. I think there is room in the realm of forensic practice for mental health professionals from a variety of professions, and doing so in your own practice has the potential to be stimulating, challenging, and potentially lucrative.

# REFERENCES

American Psychological Association. (2010). American Psychological Association ethical principles of psychologists and code of conduct. Retrieved from http://www.apa.org/ethics/code/index.aspx

American Psychological Association. (2013). Specialty guidelines for forensic psychology. *American Psychologist, 68*(1), 7–19.

Brodsky, S. (2004) *Coping with cross-examination and other pathways to effective testimony* (First Edition). Washington, DC: American Psychological Association.

Brodsky, S. (2009). *Principles and practice of trial consultation.* New York: Guilford Press.

Brodsky, S. (2013) *Testifying in court: Guidelines and maxims for the expert witness* (Second Edition). Washington, DC: American Psychological Association.

Franklin, K. (2016). In the News by Karen Franklin PhD: "Help! I Am Being Held Hostage in a Reality Show!" Retrieved from http://forensicpsychologist.blogspot.com/2016/01/help-i-am-being-held-hostage-in-reality.html.

Greenberg, S., & Shuman, D. (1997). Irreconcilable conflict between therapeutic and forensic roles. *Professional Psychology: Research and Practice, 28*, 50–57.

Kane, A. W., & Dvoskin, J. A. (2011). *Evaluation for personal injury claims.* New York: Oxford University Press.

Walfish, S., & Barnett, J. (2009). *Financial success in mental health practice: Essential tools and strategies for practitioners.* Washington, DC: American Psychological Association.

# CHAPTER 32

# COLLABORATING WITH THE EDUCATIONAL COMMUNITY

*Stephanie T. Mihalas and Lev Gottlieb*

Private practitioners have an array of opportunities available to them to collaborate and interact with the educational community. We define the educational community here as any practitioner or organization that supports the continued learning and education of the individual client (e.g., parents, teachers, administrators, tutors, developmental therapists, special education advocates). We focus primarily on roles of a psychologist and neuropsychologist interfacing with the school system, though being involved in the educational community is not limited to psychologists (Laundy, 2015). We chose a four-stage problem-solving model (Castillo, Cohen, & Curtis, 2007) as a framework to highlight how clinical work in private practice may be aligned with the embedded structure that many educators use in public schools. Integrating the perspectives and strengths of various disciplines, all bound by a common goal of promoting well-being for a client in the educational arena, facilitates a holistic approach. We include a case vignette to provide a concrete example of how this model applies, and the conceptual challenges that may be faced.

## KEY POINTS FOR A COLLABORATIVE PROCESS

We will start by describing the following factors that are important to consider as an outside consultant in private practice.

There are many ways to network within the educational community before direct collaboration occurs. We recommend the following:

1. Develop a list of neighboring schools, their culture, and educational philosophy so you are prepared to understand the overarching mission.
2. Contact school psychologists or administrators to find out whether there are needs that have not been met within their system that you could provide.
3. Tour schools and meet the key stakeholders who make referrals; consider offering an in-service related to your specialty so the staff learns about you, your work, and your paradigm.
4. Send out flyers or emails about your service specialty and your vision of educational collaboration.
5. Write blogs or tweets on social media that speak to educational issues, and share them with the educational community.

## BUILDING RAPPORT

Rapport with schools is based upon trust, mutual understanding of common goals, and a shared agreement that the client's best interest is forefront in the consultation process. Depending on who initiates contact with the mental health provider for consultation-liaison service in the school domain, the client can vary. Clients can include individual children, families, school administrators, teachers, and other support personnel. At the inception of treatment and/or consultation, informed consent must be obtained to identify who the client is, who holds rights to the file, and how confidentiality is maintained within the working relationship.

Building rapport should be considered a strategic and time-focused engagement whereby relationships, if possible, are built prior to entering a school. We recommend meeting with staff, administrators, and other personnel through pre-service lectures, onsite professional training, and/or scheduled introductory meetings. By maintaining a presence at a school, you can glean important information about the school's hierarchy, culture, and climate. As such, when the time arises for collaborative consultation about a student, you will be better able to understand how to navigate within a particular school.

Relationships may be enhanced and maintained by ensuring transparency of communication and identifying who ultimately the clinician is responsible to for deliverables. Even if the client is the family, the school may feel ownership or feel privy to the tangible strategies and outcomes of the assessment and/or therapeutic process. However, families may not want to provide full disclosure, which places the clinician in a bind in terms of collaboration and communication. Relationships are sometimes strained if, from the get go, a clinician does not state openly the holder of privacy and degree of disclosure that is authorized. That being said, including the school throughout the process and gathering information helps to align the parties. The way in which you communicate and collaborate from the start sets the tone throughout the treatment.

## KEY STAKEHOLDERS

Schools, like other organizations, are political arenas that require an understanding of who maintains the power and ability to make and implement decisions, both explicitly and implicitly. Key stakeholders are important to know in order to forge relationships and understand how they use their power and authority to manage decision making for children and school personnel. This varies from school to school. Furthermore, recognizing key stakeholders' preferences (e.g., curriculum-based measurement vs. psychoeducational battery) will afford a more successful collaboration.

## ROLES AND RESPONSIBILITIES

The questions of who, what, when, and where are critical to address during a collaborative problem-solving process as educators are frequently overburdened with multiple roles (e.g., lunch duty, supervision after school) and therefore, despite good intentions, assessment and/or intervention may not be achieved as planned. Thus, at each interdisciplinary meeting, explicit expectations should be clarified and any barriers to execution should be identified. Documentation of roles and responsibilities in the meeting notes is likewise important to maintain accountability for all team members.

## AVAILABLE RESOURCES

Districts and schools can vary in the availability of resources, including finances, personnel, and equipment. While the child's needs rather than available resources should dictate provision of services, in reality, institutional constraints may place a family and school in a quandary regarding service provision. Understanding the available resources before getting started allows the practitioner to connect an assessment to realistic setting-specific interventions and/or consider alternative educational placements.

That being said, understanding available resources is a challenging endeavor. This can be achieved formally by reviewing statistics for schools (e.g., progress toward meeting annual yearly goals and minimum donation expectations) or informally by gaining insights while networking with the broader educational community via an information interview on the number of special education support personnel and staffing constraints across schools.

## FORUM FOR COMMUNICATION

Communication may take many forms during collaborative consultation, including parent to teacher, teacher to practitioner, and so on. Regardless of the reason for communication or the manner in which information is disseminated, all parties involved in the student's care must be involved so that members of the team maintain an active role. Communication may transpire via scheduled phone check-ins on progress, email updates including data collection, or through collaboration at Student Study Team Meetings, 504 Plan Meetings or Individualized Educational

Plan meetings. Additionally, for members to feel comfortable expressing dissenting opinions, establishing a set of common values for the interdisciplinary process is recommended prior to on-going team engagement. Core values may include topics of team process, vision for growth for the student, and/or general educational aspirations.

# THE COLLABORATIVE PROBLEM-SOLVING MODEL

The collaborative problem-solving model we are discussing in this chapter has four stages: Problem Identification, Problem Analysis, Plan Implementation, and Plan Evaluation. For each stage we will provide an overview, school involvement, and application to a case. We will first discuss general variables that impact each stage and then will offer specific applications to our case vignette so the reader can visualize the complexities when working within a school system.

The approaches taken by the two authors of this chapter will be compared and contrasted. Stephanie Mihalas, PhD, NCSP, ABPP is a licensed psychologist and nationally certified school psychologist in private practice in Los Angeles, as well as an Assistant Clinical Professor at the David Geffen School of Medicine at UCLA. Mihalas is also a Board Certified Psychologist in the sub-specialty of School Psychology. She primarily works with children and families with comor-bid psychiatric and neurodevelopmental differences as well as children who have experienced complex trauma and bullying. While maintaining a full-time practice, she mentors and supervises students, consults with professionals and organizations, and is actively involved with Psychologists in Independent Practice, a division of the American Psychological Association. Lev Gottlieb, PhD, is a neuropsychologist in private practice in Los Angeles, as well as a Clinical Instructor at the David Geffen School of Medicine at UCLA. He assesses youth with neurodevelopmental differ-ences and/or acquired brain injuries, and coordinates their care. He also disseminates research to clinicians, educators, and parents via writing and speaking.

While it is understandable that clients would discuss slightly different concerns with the two of us based on our disciplines, we have found it interesting that the referral concerns were often quite different (sometimes even for the same client). For example, LG's clients typically express referral concerns related to memory, learning, or task performance, whereas SM's clients relay con-cerns pertinent to behavior, emotion, or affect regulation. We have come to appreciate that how the referral concern is presented may narrowly shape the course of action a clinician follows, yet with input collected from educators, a wider lens may be used for case conceptualization through treatment.

# CASE VIGNETTE

Susan[1] is a nine-year-old Caucasian girl who is enrolled in the third grade at a public school. Susan was referred to a private-practice clinician by her family physician for primary concerns related to daydreaming in class, disobedience at home, and difficulty sustaining meaningful friendships. The parents reported that Susan is a "good student" and receives Bs, but she appears "agitated" in the mornings at home or whenever school is discussed.

# PROBLEM IDENTIFICATION

The problem identification stage involves addressing the nature of the referral and the situational variants involved, as well as understanding what the client envisions for the goals of assessment and treatment. Routes toward making referrals to families and the types of referrals made depend upon whether you are working with a private versus a public school. Generally speaking, educators notice a deviation from the norm in terms of academic performance or behavior, which is discussed in a parent–teacher conference or on a report card. When progress continues to decline or is halted, schools will hold a team meeting (public school) or an upper-level administrator will make formal recommendations to parents (private school) for outside services. Information is co-constructed; rather than the clinician serving in a solely expert role, information is gleaned from the educational community (pending consent), the identified student, and the family to build a narrative of the presenting concerns.

To frame the referral concern, history is obtained in the following domains: family, birth/developmental, medical/psychiatric, psychosocial, trauma, and educational. Working in concert with other educational providers can help you avoid the common pitfalls of problem identification, including vague definitions of referral concerns or excluding persons who may provide unique information.

## SCHOOL REFLECTION ON PROBLEM IDENTIFICATION

Obtaining prior records naturally opens a discussion about collaboration with the broader educational community by conveying that it is essential to collect data from numerous sources. Authorization for release and exchange of information may be initiated by the clinician and/or educational community at the request of the legal guardian. Often both parties will want to maintain their own release to meet specific ethical and legal guidelines, and for documentation and recordkeeping. The parenting dynamic dictates who is required to sign the release. We recommend that if parents are in a contentious relationship, both parents should be made privy to information sharing and a release should be signed by both parties. Further, if the parents are divorced, the custodial paperwork should be reviewed to determine who may grant authority for medical and psychological care. Finally, if the identified client is over 12 years of age (in California; note that state laws vary), he or she should also be included in the release of information process through active consent.

We also encourage open dialog through interviews with educators and clinicians. If the family is not open to this idea, we make a note of the resistance for future reference and exploration, noting that the closed relationship with the school system may indicate a larger systemic issue impacting learning or emotional stress for the child and family. Generally, we begin to see very early on in the intake process a bidirectional relationship between the school environment and the behavioral and emotional concerns at home.

## APPLICATION OF PROBLEM IDENTIFICATION

We use a "funnel-down" approach during our interviews with everyone who is part of the system. Both general and specific questions are important to the problem identification phase. Here are some questions that we asked in Susan's case:

1. What are the concerns, and how might assessment and intervention be helpful?
2. How is Susan currently functioning with regards to academics, emotion-behavior, and socialization, and has a trend been evident over time (i.e., is it the same, improving, or worsening)?
3. What are the expectations for Susan held by the family and educational community? If Susan has not met them, what steps have been taken to address functioning, and with what outcome?
4. What is the preference and status of collaboration between Susan's family and the educational community?

Based on the answers obtained in problem identification, we developed hypotheses in various domains for Susan. Hypothesis testing in the clinical rather than the statistical sense takes on a functional approach whereby the clinician explores various reasons for behavior. This is completed by functional eco-behavioral assessments, narrative observations, teacher reports via interview or survey instruments, psychometric testing (e.g., of cognition and academics), and direct testing of discrete skills (e.g., taking turns, how to start a conversation).

SM tests specific hypotheses, as her treatment approach is practical and attempts to target specific symptomatology. Given Susan's primary referral concerns, below are possible reasons for her behavior that, if confirmed, could lead to direct intervention:

*Academic*: The instructional third-grade curriculum is more difficult than previous years, revealing specific areas of academic weakness for Susan. Alternatively, the curriculum might be too easy for her, or her attentional capacity interferes with her ability to focus on the curriculum.

*Individual Within Family System*: Susan may be experiencing family conflict at home that is manifesting in mood/anxiety symptoms that are limiting her socialization at school. Other family system issues that could be impacting the referral concern include parental time spent on academics and an increase in parental stress.

*Social*: Susan may be experiencing bullying by her peers at school, which would negatively impact the social, emotional, and academic domains. Alternatively, her interests may be different from her peers, or she is isolating rather than trying to engage in social relationships.

In contrast, LG develops hypotheses in a broader manner, taking a bottom-up approach to encompass all possibilities and honing in on what can be distilled from the data. Given Susan's primary referral concerns, below are possible explanations for her difficulties that neuropsychological testing can confirm or deny in order to develop a coordinated plan:

*Individual*: Susan has an attentional, anxiety, mood, learning and/or language disorder. Or, Susan does not have a diagnosable disorder but some features of these conditions that interact together, and/or a unique learning style.

*Contextual*: Susan has no problematic processing characteristics; rather, something about the expectations for her age, school culture, and/or family constellation is not a good fit currently.

*Combination*: Individual and contextual; that is, a combination of individual and contextual factors interact to explain Susan's presenting concerns.

# PROBLEM ANALYSIS

The cornerstone of problem analysis is collaboration among individuals within the client's system. Assessments are conducted across multiple environments, domains, and times to inform intervention development. This critical period calls upon the consultative relationships that have been built previously. If you have a reputation for providing excellent service and "being a team player" with your educational constituents, the likelihood of obtaining data with integrity is increased.

## SCHOOL REFLECTION ON PROBLEM ANALYSIS

The hypotheses in question are discussed during team meetings, and the type of data collection methodology or assessment procedures are outlined. All parties agree to a timeframe and how data will be submitted. The importance of contextualizing the assessment cannot be overstated, in that the problem analysis must be connected to and inform everyday functioning at home, in the community, and at school. When school concerns are identified, problem analysis transpires on an ongoing basis via phone or password-protected emails, and/or in-person meetings for training and standardization.

## APPLICATION OF PROBLEM ANALYSIS

Hypotheses developed from problem identification are outlined below and showcase how school personnel may be included in the treatment process to inform ongoing assessment (if needed) and. intervention development. Of note, problem identification and problem analysis are recursive and iterative processes, so there is some overlap in procedures administered across stages. That is, the stages fluidly inform one another and can be revisited as needed. Sometimes when the assessment results are provided or the intervention recommendations are made to the school, the parties feel like the answer has been provided and the route has been paved. However, we argue that without constant reevaluation and inquiry, the student's progress will be halted rather than observed and measured.

Hypothesis testing by SM is targeted to determine the discrepancy between the environmental expectations and Susan's present performance:

*Academic data plan:* A special education resource specialist will complete a curriculum-based assessment in all subjects with Susan. Testing will occur on different times and days, and results will be sent to SM. SM will interview Susan with a semistructured interview related to her perception of academics and self-efficacy. SM will conduct classroom observation of Susan's behavior compared to peers using the Behavior Observation of Students in Schools (BOSS; Shapiro, 2011). The interview and the observational data will be discussed with the classroom teacher to ascertain the representativeness of the data.

*Individual Within Family System data plan:* Susan's teacher will complete the Children's Depression Inventory and the Depression and Anxiety in Youth Scale (DAYS; Newcomer, Barenbaum, & Bryant, 1994) at multiple points to assess for mood and anxiety symptoms. The teacher will also complete the Social Skills Rating System (SSRS; Gresham & Elliott, 1990). SM will interview the teacher about Susan's peer relationships. SM will complete a recess, lunch, and/or playground observation to assess Susan's interactions with peers, with consultation from teacher. The Parent Stress Index Short Form (PSI-SF; Abidin, 1995) will be provided to Susan's parents to ascertain dyadic functioning in the home.

*Social data plan:* The school psychologist will interview recess/lunch personnel and students to develop a peer social network map. SM will interview the school psychologist to determine bullying culture on campus and whether Susan and/or her peer network have been involved in office referrals related to bullying. Given the importance of self-perception as it relates to the social milieu, Susan will complete the My Life in School Checklist (Arora & Thompson, 1999) and the California Bullying Peer Victimization Scale (CBVS; Felix, Sharkey, Green, Furlong, & Tanigawa, 2011).

A broad-based approach to neuropsychological assessment dictates that all domains of functioning are explored without too much influence of prior hypotheses. This means that while LG often has an a priori idea of the primary reasons for problematic presentation, he is open to the data dictating alternatives. For example, with Susan there appears to be an attention deficit identified during problem identification (i.e., the "daydreaming"); however, data may reveal that language deficits actually preclude her from attending to language-based instruction, and/or that preoccupying anxiety drives the inattention. Hypothesis testing by LG includes gathering a developmental history, collecting standardized ratings of functioning, making contextual observations, and conducting psychometric and/or projective testing. All domains of functioning are assessed with a relatively fixed battery, and then specific areas of concern are flexibly explored further, with an eye toward both the psychometrics (i.e., the data) and the process (i.e., how the client approaches tasks). Considering problem analysis as it applies to Susan and the potential hypotheses, attention, anxiety, mood, learning, and language will be specifically explored in greater depth.

First, LG will gather a developmental history and complete a record review of symptoms across settings since early childhood, extending from the history gathered in problem identification. LG will examine specifically for patterns of challenges with attention, anxiety, mood, learning, and/or language. Second, LG will collect standardized ratings from Susan, her parents, and educators. Forms may be broad-based (e.g., Behavior Assessment System for Children-3 [BASC-3]; Kamphaus & Reynolds, 2015) and/or more specific to the concerns (e.g., Conners Rating Scales-3rd Edition [Conners-3]; Conners, 2008). Next, LG will make contextual narrative observations of the referral concerns across settings. Finally, LG will conduct psychometric testing to explore areas of challenge, comparing Susan's performance to both the general population and her own performance across tests. In addition to overarching measures (e.g., Wechsler Intelligence Scale for Children-V [WISC-V]; Wechsler, 2014), specific tests will focus upon attention and executive functioning (e.g., A Developmental NEuroPSYchological Assessment-II [NEPSY-II]; Korkman, Kirk, & Kemp, 2007), anxiety or mood (e.g., Rotter Incomplete Sentence Blank [RSIBS]; Rotter, Lah, & Rafferty, 1992), learning and memory for rote versus contextual and verbal versus visual materials (e.g., California Verbal Learning Test-Children's Version [CVLT-C]; Delis, Kramer, Kaplan, & Ober, 1994; Rey Complex Figure Test [RCFT]; Meyers & Meyers, 1995), rote, speeded, and conceptual academics (e.g., Woodcock-Johnson Tests of Achievement-IV [WJ-IV]; Schrank, Mather, & McGrew, 2014), and receptive, expressive, and social language (e.g., Clinical Evaluation of Language Fundamentals-5 [CELF-5]; Wiig, Semel, & Secord, 2013). The entirety of data will be analyzed within a developmental context of expectations for Susan's age, school, and family.

# PLAN IMPLEMENTATION

Plan implementation involves selecting and clarifying interventions, monitoring progress, and planning interventions across settings. After data collection, results are analyzed and integrated to develop an accessible compendium (SM) or a neuropsychological report (LG). LG then coordinates care, whereas SM (in conjunction with other providers) implements interventions. Coordinating care means "quarterbacking" the intervention plan across providers without providing treatment directly. In essence, LG serves as an intermediary and consultant to all the team members so they have a common understanding of how to orient treatment for the family. Once the team has been established, LG is no longer an active part of the process. A rationale is provided for treatment recommendations to the interdisciplinary team, which includes the family, in order to motivate and facilitate treatment plan integrity and accountability. Furthermore, the importance of data collection is discussed to obtain quantifiable information on progress (or lack thereof) among parties, and methods for collection are agreed upon. Data collection may differ for each party (e.g., surveys, frequency counts) based on time, accessibility, and background experience in data collection.

## SCHOOL REFLECTION ON PLAN IMPLEMENTATION

The way in which the plan is implemented within public schools depends upon how the presenting problem directly impacts access to academic and social curriculum, school-based funding, and available resources/staffing on site. Once resolved, the challenges of this phase when working within schools are at least threefold: (1) stray from the original intended intervention because of varying beliefs or expertise; (2) motivation to continue once some positive change has been observed; and (3) completion of ongoing data collection because of time constraints.

To circumvent some of these challenges, private practitioners are advised to do the following:

1. Visit the classroom to observe the intervention and provide feedback on the integrity of the intervention. Inform the educational party that you are planning to do this, and link the rationale in support of the educator and student.
2. Frequently and honestly acknowledge the educator's efforts and offer support, as needed.
3. Follow up with the people who are collecting data with graphs or other visuals to highlight behavior change, if any.

The point is to circle back with meaningful information regarding progress monitoring so that educators are not merely "reporting" to the clinician. Educators are an important part of the assessment team and should be treated as such. Again, the educational collaborative model should consist of a flow of information back and forth, rather than being unidirectional.

## APPLICATION OF PLAN IMPLEMENTATION

Confirmation of numerous hypotheses was intentionally chosen so the reader could see different plans that result from a problem-solving model. General recommendations (SM) are given below to highlight the importance of institutional barriers and their impact on the type and intensity of an intervention. Specific recommendations (LG) also follow to provide a tangible example of what might be reflected in a neuropsychological report for Susan.

### INTERVENTION PLANS AND RECOMMENDATIONS DRIVEN BY HYPOTHESIS TESTING

#### Academic Intervention Plan/Recommendations

Frequently, advocacy is required when students' academic functioning is compromised but has not been acknowledged by the public school system. Consultation with parents may include a request for a Student Study Team meeting or Section 504 Plan, or an assessment for an Individualized Education Plan (IEP) for further instructional remediation. Private practitioners may be involved in informing parents about special education law and rights; however, if legal support is required, a referral to a special education attorney is warranted. Further, clinicians may provide feedback and commentary on assessments that are completed by the school to support parental understanding. Finally, clinicians may attend meetings to advocate on behalf of the youth to obtain services and render an expert opinion.

Depending on the nature of the skill deficit, families may also be referred to an in-house resource specialist or community learning specialist with expertise in the psychology of education and academic remediation. The resource specialist in schools is an important player to collaborate with when academic deficits are identified. The resource specialist will be able to consult with the teacher on educational strategies as well as provide group intervention. Outside learning specialists frequently work with psychologists and schools to provide guidance on a student's stress levels and ability to perform at grade level by providing recommendations that may be used in the classroom, as well as guide schools regarding educational accommodations.

## Individual Within Family System Intervention Plan/Recommendations

Depending on the transparency a family desires with the school, home–school logs serve as tools for parents and teachers to communicate on a daily basis about a child. Parents may be able to report to the teacher events that arose at home that can impact a student's school performance. Likewise, teachers might report to parents about school happenings to encourage parental understanding of what the student may exhibit emotionally or behaviorally at home.

When an IEP is developed, students could receive psychological services in the school system either via individual or group psychotherapy. Consultation with the school psychologist also may be productive to determine if the school has an organized social skills group on campus that uses programs like the Prepare Curriculum (Goldstein, 1988). Such school-based groups provide meaningful and realistic interactions for the client. Typically, this provider and the private practitioner collaborate, especially when there are major events that will affect treatment in either environment. This wraparound model frequently provides the enhanced support that students need when they are experiencing psychological distress by providing multiple support personnel who are focused on different but overlapping goals.

If groups will not be provided at school, outside clinicians might recommend that teachers support social skill development through natural activities on campus (e.g., line leader, class homework collector, and mentoring of younger students) where the client can receive positive reinforcement. Additionally, antecedent management (e.g., environmental manipulation of variables that promote success before a problematic behavior occurs) may be appropriate for educational professionals, such as establishing routines or specific rules and procedures, or using prompting and modeling to facilitate social skill development. Again, in working with the psychologist, teachers can make fairly minor changes that will have a major impact on the student.

## Social Support Intervention Plan/Recommendations

Bullying is for the most part a systemic issue in schools. When one child reports bullying, often there is a pervasive concern impacting not only the client but also other peers, the client's parents, and even school staff. Recommendations and intervention planning for bullying behavior on school grounds can be categorized into three domains: individual, parent, and school.

The etiology of the bully–victim paradigm needs to be ascertained before an individual intervention is implemented. Individualized approaches may include assertiveness training, social skills training, and/or enhancement of self-esteem. A key feature is providing psychoeducation to the school about the student's needs and why the accommodations could have a positive impact on the client and the entire educational forum (both for teachers and other peers).

Parents frequently request information on their role as an advocate for their child when bullying is reported. Providing parents insight into how to discuss and document the nature of the problem with the school is critical. Second, guiding parents to state legislation related to the scope of due diligence in schools provides justification to parents for requests of enhanced supervision. Finally, it is important to coach parents on how to speak to their children about the incidents in a manner that does not compound hysteria.

Private clinicians may speak to the school about general teaching approaches and how they promote or deflate bullying (e.g., modeling prosocial behavior and respect for diversity and differences; positive behavior support). Private clinicians might also speak with administrators about school policies and procedures specific to bullying (e.g., annual training, procedure manual for bullying, incident reporting system). If the school does not address bullying in a systematic way, there is an opportunity for organizational consulting and in-service training for outside providers with this expertise, as an adjunct to clinical practice.

These plans were general in nature so the reader may understand the multitude of variables involved in hypothesis testing and the possible avenues to explore for children in school. Next we will list specific recommendations by LG to provide a tangible example of what might be reflected in a neuropsychological report for Susan.

## INTERVENTION PLANS AND RECOMMENDATIONS DRIVEN BY NEUROPSYCHOLOGICAL TESTING

Susan has a language disorder that is impeding her progress at school (i.e., specifically in reading-writing) and is generating angst, confusion, and conflict across settings. Recommendations may encompass additional assessment (e.g., by language and learning specialists), treatment/remediation, accommodations, educational programming (e.g., via an IEP), and general considerations. This plan focuses upon treatment and accommodations.

Treatment recommendations are prioritized by importance given Susan's current stage of development and functioning. Note, however, that these interventions should work synergistically, in that a substantial amount of Susan's emotionality stems from her language and learning deficits, and her language and learning capacity are diminished when dysregulated.

Three primary treatments are offered for Susan:

1.  Begin language therapy for weaknesses in expression and verbal working memory. Exercises that may be helpful for expression include "mapping" words by category,

subcategory, similarities/differences or other associations, as well as practicing scripts that allow for more fluent expression. Build Susan's verbal working memory through practice of practical tasks, such as following multistep directions, listening while taking notes, and proofreading with several ideas in mind. Teach her strategies that functionally improve expression and verbal working memory in everyday life. Some cultivation of organizational learning strategies (e.g., paired-associate, chunking, chaining, semantic networks, graphic organizers) would also be beneficial given Susan's tendency to take a serial or haphazard approach to her learning when overwhelmed.

2. Start psychotherapy support for emotional regulation. Nonverbally model and teach coping skills for Susan to self-monitor and regulate, drawing upon cognitive-behavioral therapy and mindfulness techniques. Also foster Susan's verbal expression of emotions but do not expect Susan to communicate that effectively verbally, especially when upset.

3. Initiate learning specialist direct instruction in phonics and orthography to address Susan's underlying reading-spelling weaknesses. Multicomponent programs are most effective. These programs provide direct, multisensory instruction in decoding coupled with explicit strategy training on identifying and retrieving words (or word segments) and their meaning, with integration of cognitive-behavioral techniques to optimize motivation and self-esteem.

For accommodations, Susan's language disorder substantially limits her ability to address academics and activities of daily life. This is in concordance with the major life activities defined in Section 504. The following accommodations will allow Susan to access her environment and will ensure a valid assessment of her skills and ability:

1. Tap Susan's nonverbal strengths by teaching visually and kinesthetically whenever possible, and by pairing verbal with visual material. Verbal instruction should be delivered in short chunks (i.e., to accommodate Susan's learning profile and limited verbal working memory).

2. Provide Susan visual outlines for multistep activities and/or discreetly check in with her to make sure she remembers the steps (i.e., to accommodate Susan's limited verbal working memory).

3. Encourage active participation from Susan and speaking in full, grammatically correct sentences while also allowing for alternative means of communication (e.g., shorter phrases, nonverbal gestures). Avert withdrawal due to limited expressive language, both in class and on the playground.

4. Assess Susan's learning via recognition more than recall formats (i.e., because she knows much more than she can demonstrate via spontaneous retrieval and expression), and provide cues and scripts for writing (i.e., to accommodate limited retrieval of language).

5. If Susan's reading-spelling cannot be fully remediated, provide audible presentation for academic text, allow use of spell check, and grant Susan 50% extra time for assignments, tests, and exams that require reading.

# PLAN EVALUATION

Plan evaluation examines the effectiveness of the treatment plan and determines whether the goals have been met. Plan evaluation may reevaluate problem analysis if goals are not attained within the expected time. Decisions on generalization and fading of the treatment protocol are the final steps of this phase, pending improvement. Plan evaluation may take the form of readministering initial survey instruments and/or reviewing the data for a stable change in the target behavior. The team may have dissenting opinions on the need for further treatment and/or how and when to end the protocol during this phase.

## SCHOOL REFLECTION ON PLAN EVALUATION

Unless a client has a documented deficit on record through a Section 504 or IEP, this stage might not be formalized. Frequently, when clients partially meet their goals, the incentive to maintain the protocol or collect data wanes because of the following: (1) initial excitement that the client has progressed; (2) time constraints that limit data collection and ongoing discussion of the client; and/or (3) the needs of other students supersede the client's needs because of the presumed improvement. Unfortunately, the overarching sentiment often results in premature termination of a treatment protocol and/or a lack of insight into why a child regresses to baseline functioning. This sentiment should be addressed, and if dissenting opinions remain, educational advocacy, consideration of private services, and review and presentation of the data may be helpful.

Moreover, it is important to consider that serving as an offsite consultant to schools presents challenges different than those experienced by school-based clinicians. The degree of case management to stay apprised of a client's progress, with possibly multiple-school based informants, can become overwhelming when carrying a large caseload of clients requiring collaboration, ongoing communication, and data collection. Furthermore, when a client ceases to make progress, families frequently attribute challenges to the school (rather than other variables like the treatment program, client and family motivation, therapist fit), which creates further tension in this phase. As such, plan evaluation sometimes takes the form of multiple meetings with different subsets of the interdisciplinary team prior to meeting as a whole.

## APPLICATION OF PLAN EVALUATION

Plan evaluation may vary depending upon the data and process outcomes from plan implementation, as well as the parties and resources involved.

## PLAN EVALUATION (SM)

Plan evaluation begins with a review of the treatment plan and the progress made, which is conducted on a monthly basis with Susan's family. The review includes degree of goal attainment, which is ascertained from qualitative and quantitative information provided by the family and the educational community, as well as direct feedback from SM. This is also an opportunity to process the collaborative relationship more directly so that the practitioner, Susan's family, and educators can openly share concerns that may come to light through the review of progress. Often, a family may become uneasy about continuing services; this can be expressed by the following cues: commentary about client progress and concern over the impact of continued treatment; frequent missed sessions, with little to no information provided to the clinician for the absences; and/or diminished interest in ongoing data collection or the therapeutic relationship.

Given standard therapeutic issues like transference and interference of defense, frequent plan evaluation promotes communication in a structured way if either therapist or client develops conscious or unconscious barriers during the treatment phase. Once the family has had the privacy within the office setting to share and discuss progress, the school is then contacted. The same process ensues with the school in terms of each member sharing his or her impressions (and data) of progress and any concerns that may be impeding the student's progress.

## PLAN EVALUATION (LG)

Neuropsychological assessment as a billable service does not entail plan evaluation because the assessment process naturally ends once recommendations are made, and there is no ongoing treatment relationship with Susan and other parties. However, neuropsychologists in private practice may structure their services to maintain some ongoing consultation with the client and educational community so they can field questions as they arise given the assessment. There are also opportunities to monitor progress by reassessing targeted areas and/or doing a more complete reassessment years later at major life transitions and/or following a change in mental status.

# FINAL THOUGHTS

## GROWING OPPORTUNITIES FOR PRIVATE PRACTITIONERS IN SCHOOLS

Over the past several years, we have engaged in discussions about the nuances and complexities of working with children who present with psychological symptoms related to (1) the emerging pressures of private school and college applications; (2) peer-to-peer academic competition; and (3) media portrayals that focus on academic rigor and excellence rather than personal well-being. These pressures necessitate extra support for the individual, family, and organization. There are myriad opportunities for private practitioners, including applied research, organizational change projects, teacher in-services, consultation to administration for threat assessments and crisis management, and/or consultation focused on larger systemic school concerns such as teacher turnover and satisfaction.

Global, national, state, local, and school-specific trends directly impact the roles and responsibilities of private practitioners working in school systems. To enable success and promote a cross-discipline understanding, clinicians may consider the following questions facing the educational community:

1. What global issues impact educational decision making (e.g., social media, globalization, outsourcing of jobs)?
2. What national issues impact educational decision making (e.g., Response to Intervention vs. IEP implementation, Common Core, transgender student equality)?
3. What state issues impact educational decision making (e.g., special education eligibility criteria, intersection of state with federal funding mechanisms, privacy laws)?
4. What local issues impact educational decision making (e.g., socioeconomic strata, taxation, funding sources)?
5. What school issues impact educational decision making (e.g., changes in administration, alternations in curriculum, school climate)?

## CONCLUSION

By defining and understanding the roles that educators may play, we can lay the foundation for an active partnership whereby clients maintain the ability and autonomy to make decisions in their own care. Private practitioners should aim to support families holistically by acknowledging the importance of the educational community within the ecological context. By doing so, practitioners can help clients consider the clinical gestalt as well as identify the systems of care that may improve outcomes during the assessment and treatment process. The role of private practitioners in the educational community is to serve all parties in a collaborative way by providing education, enhancing communication, and promoting well-being.

## NOTE

1. Case vignette does not represent an actual client but is indicative of a typical pediatric case.

## REFERENCES

Abidin, R. R. (1995). *Parenting Stress Index, Third Edition: Professional Manual*. Odessa, FL: Psychological Assessment Resources, Inc.

Arora, C. M. J., & Thompson, D. A. (1999). My Life in School Checklist. In S. Sharp (Ed.), *Bullying behaviour in schools: Psychology in education portfolio* (pp. 7–10). Windsor, UK: NFER Nelson.

Castillo, J. M., Cohen, R. M., & Curtis, M. J. (2007, June). A problem solving/response to intervention model as systems-level change. *Communique, 35*(8), 34, 36, 38–40.

Conners, K. (2008). *Conners Rating Scales, Third Edition.* North Tonawanda, NY: Multi-Health Systems, Inc.

Delis, D. C., Kramer, J. H., Kaplan, E., & Ober, B. A. (1994). *California Verbal Learning Test-Children's Version (CVLT-C).* San Antonio, TX: Psychological Corporation.

Felix, E. D., Sharkey, J. D., Green, J. G., Furlong, M. J., & Tanigawa, D. (2011). Getting precise and pragmatic about the assessment of bullying: The development of the California Bullying Victimization Scale. *Aggressive Behavior, 37,* 234–247.

Goldstein, A. P. (1988). *The Prepare Curriculum: Teaching prosocial competencies.* Champaign, IL: Research Press.

Gresham, F. M., & Elliott, S. N. (1990). *Social Skills Rating System.* Circle Pines, MN: American Guidance Service.

Kamphaus, R. W., & Reynolds, C. R. (2015). *Behavior Assessment System for Children, Third Edition.* Bloomington, MN: NCS Pearson, Inc.

Korkman, M., Kirk, U., & Kemp, S. L. (2007). *NEPSY II. Clinical and interpretative manual.* San Antonio, TX: Psychological Corporation.

Laundy, K. (2015). *Building school-based collaborative mental health teams.* Camp Hill, PA: TPI Press.

Meyers, J. E., & Meyers, K. R. (1995). *Rey complex figure test and recognition trial: Professional manual.* Odessa, FL: Psychological Assessment Resources.

Newcomer, P. L., Barenbaum, E. M., & Bryant, B. R. (1994). *Depression and Anxiety in Youth Scale.* Austin, TX: PRO-ED.

Rotter, J. B., Lah, M. I., & Rafferty, J. E. (1992). *Rotter Incomplete Sentences Blank.* San Antonio, TX: Harcourt Brace.

Schrank, F. A., Mather, N., & McGrew, K. S. (2014). *Woodcock-Johnson IV Tests of Achievement.* Rolling Meadows, IL: Riverside.

Shapiro, E. (2011). *Behavior observation of students in schools.* New York: Guilford Press.

Wechsler, D. (2014). *Wechsler Intelligence Scale for Children, Fifth Edition.* Bloomington, MN: NCS Pearson, Inc.

Wiig, E. H., Semel, E. M., & Secord, W. (2013). *Clinical evaluation of language fundamentals, Fifth Edition.* Bloomington, MN: NCS Pearson, Inc.

# CHAPTER 33

# CONSULTING PSYCHOLOGY IN THE BUSINESS WORLD

*Shirley A. Maides-Keane and Bernard J. Liebowitz*

In the 1950s at the Menninger Foundation, clinical psychologist Harry Levinson (Levinson, 1956; Levinson & Menninger, 1954) established consultation services to industry. He pioneered the application of psychoanalytic concepts to industry and was first to note the major impact that psychological factors, like emotional stress, had on work performance. Subsequently, businesses consulted psychologists to address employee performance issues including intelligence, motivation, job fit, and job satisfaction. This focus on the individual employee arose from Levinson's early work that ultimately led to innovations like employee assistance programs and the widespread use of executive coaching.

Over subsequent decades Levinson and others (e.g., Diamond, 2003) turned to integration of psychoanalytic concepts and systems theory to address broader organizational issues. Consequently, both the scope of consulting psychologists' work and how businesses characterize their concerns have changed over the past 60 years and continue to evolve. While the focus on individual psychologically related concerns continues, consulting psychologists are engaging in areas that consider more systemic issues such as organizational redesign and strategic planning. Most of these areas tap psychotherapeutic skills (e.g., assessment, coaching, counseling, systems theory) but the work is quite different from the traditional practice of psychotherapy. Working with any business, from large corporations to family businesses or small entrepreneurial enterprises, requires the consultant to assume a different role and have a solid understanding of how businesses function. In business consulting, the client is the organization, not the individual employees. Since the organization is a system, any work is conducted within that systemic context. Even when the focus is on the individual, the organization's dynamics are still involved.

Professionals currently gain an understanding of business, and their roles as consultants, through either further formal degree training (e.g., a master's of business administration degree), working in a consulting firm or corporate setting, or taking specialty training through organizations such as the Society for Consulting Psychology (APA Division 13; www.societyofconsultingpsy-chology.org/students) or the Worldwide Association of Business Coaches (www.wabccoaches.com). There are some new consulting psychology doctoral programs, and there is a group within APA, Division 13, working on establishing competencies for the practice of consulting psychology. Whatever training a professional receives, it is best augmented by receiving mentoring from a seasoned consultant. Since much has been written about the training and experience required to transition from clinical psychology or psychotherapeutic practice into consulting psychology (Liebowitz & Blattner, 2015), this chapter will not dwell on that topic. Instead, we present an overview of the many types of consulting engagements psychologists perform within many business sectors.

We are clinical psychologists who have made the transition to consulting and continue to practice in that arena. Consulting engagements are categorized by their focus on the individual or on the organization. These categories are convenient classifications for purposes of presentation, but in reality they overlap: An assignment in one area can lead to one in the other area, and they may be inseparable in their impact. Our intent is to highlight the demands of training and experience that each area of consulting makes on the individual considering a transition into business consulting.

## COACHING

One area that gained considerable attention in the 1990s, and continues to evolve, is that of business coaching, most commonly referred to as executive coaching. In the 1990s an executive coach might be engaged to help a talented manager prevent derailing his or her career. These derailment projects involved assessing the manager's ability for, and/or interest in, his or her career path, interpersonal skills, and personality/interpersonal issues (e.g., overly domineering, anger management, sexual harassment). After an assessment process, the coach would collaborate with the individual to devise a developmental plan with specific behavioral benchmarks for improvement and would embark on coaching the manager to successfully complete the plan. Coaching for leadership development has evolved in the 21st century, and rarely do businesses contract for derailment prevention anymore. Instead, consulting psychologists are asked to coach for performance improvement, even though much of the actual coaching is similar to derailment prevention. Unlike psychotherapy, coaching involves a developmental plan that is agreed upon by both the individual and his or her supervisor. Behavioral benchmarks are addressed in the plan.

A hallmark of executive coaching is the feedback coaches provide the individual. Imparting feedback is perhaps the most important component of coaching: It may well be the only time an individual hears how others perceive him or her to be. We as individuals only know how we *think* we come across to others, and we can easily convert this assumption into fact, as most of us are subject to self-assessment bias. But to actually know how others perceive our intentions and behaviors. we must ask them. What can transpire is either a new vantage point from which an individual can view his or her behavior and its impact on others, or an outright rejection of this information. In either case the feedback offers the consulting psychologist a firm basis on which to provide coaching.

This information is frequently gathered using 360-degree instruments in which the coaching candidate's supervisor, colleagues, and direct reports (hence, the 360-degree appellation) offer information confidentially about his or her behavior and style. Other sources of information (e.g., standardized personality assessments) are also used to help the candidate understand personality traits that relate to his or her behavior. This information supports the developmental plan and provides specific content for the behavioral benchmarks.

How this information is conveyed to the individual depends almost entirely on the ability, sensitivity, and training of the consulting psychologist. In fact, virtually all of the services consulting psychologists offer the business community depend on an array of skills that include active listening, diagnostic acumen, ability to communicate information effectively, understanding how to assist people to enhance their self-esteem, and ability to facilitate behavioral change. Indeed, such skillsets are the major reason that a consulting psychologist is invited to offer consulting services that perhaps another consultant (without psychotherapy/counseling skills) might also provide.

In business success breeds success, and consulting psychologists with the optimal skillset can be highly effective and successful. When a derailment project produces outstanding results for the organization, it positions the consulting psychologist as a resource for other projects. In the largest organizations a consulting psychologist may begin working at the midlevel management level and, through successful coaching projects, move on to working at higher levels with broader organizational objectives. An example of a derailment prevention project follows.

> An operations manager for a Fortune 100 manufacturing company had difficulty with his staff's performance. He was constantly disappointed by the poor performance of his employees and felt little support from senior management to help with his departmental performance issues. However, the 360-degree feedback from this organization placed the blame for his department's poor performance squarely on his shoulders, with everyone agreeing that he had an "anger management" problem. Through the coaching process this manager took responsibility for his anger and stopped blaming his subordinates for his own lack of communication skills. Within a six-month coaching process his behavior changed dramatically. He let go of unrealistic expectations for himself, his subordinates, and his superiors. He learned to accept his own limitations, and the limitations of his staff, so that he could engineer a departmental turnaround. As a result of coaching, this manager learned to be more understanding of his own needs and less judgmental of himself and others. He transformed from an angry, unpleasant boss into a delightful, caring, charming leader whose department began to lead the company in productivity per employee.

Recognition of the organization as a system implies that coaching has to take into account the organizational context. The individual being coached may not be appropriate for the position in question. He or she may be too direct for the supervisor to contend with. Work expectations and goals may not have been clearly defined earlier, and therefore differences of opinion emerged on all fronts. An employee may feel that his or her work is being undermined by company policies and believe his or her concerns are given little attention. In each of these instances (and more) the consulting psychologist as coach has to ascertain how to proceed in assessing the situation: Is the individual right for the position but requires coaching, or is the individual better suited for a different position? A frequent observation is how an individual characterized as a bad fit in one division of the company becomes a star in another.

There are many additional business contexts for which executive coaching is considered. For example, individuals on their way up the corporate ladder need to become more strategic in how they think and plan. They have to become more aware of the needs, concerns, and plans of other corporate entities and how these issues impact their areas of responsibilities. Often coaching involves teaching interpersonal/management skills to technical professionals (e.g., accountants, computer experts) who have been promoted to a management position. All of these considerations require them to expand their cognitive horizon, an area (decision making) in which psychotherapists are well trained.

Executive coaching can play an important role in a corporate turnaround. When a division of a large corporation is performing poorly, coaching key leaders can be critical to make the transition from losing money to profitability. Here is another example:

> An extremely talented, Ivy League–educated, senior vice-president of a Fortune 50 major financial services corporation began receiving coaching at a critical time for the organization. Because he was in charge of the division publicly known as the loss leader of the corporation and was facing extreme people issues and midcareer burnout, the coaching process for this candidate had to be multifaceted. From the 360-degree data many specific burnout issues became clear to him and formed the basis of the developmental plan. As the candidate assessed options for career advancement in the organization, it appeared initially that institutional barriers would impede the developmental process. During the coaching process he began to believe that leaving the corporation (and a positive 15-year corporate track record) was the only option to overcome burnout and pursue a satisfactory career path, but the coaching process provided a new direction. By clarifying goals and developing action plans, the candidate gained a considerable understanding of his personal assets and leadership style. With such knowledge, he made some significant behavioral changes in working with peers, superiors, and staff. Much to his surprise, everyone noticed and responded positively. The new leadership style was openly praised and rewarded with substantial promotions and salary increases as the division turned around and became profitable. It was a win–win for the candidate and the organization.

More generally, these examples point to a meaningful role consulting psychologists can, and do, play—that of being a trusted advisor to senior-level executives and chief executive officers (CEOs). This role can be challenging and demanding in that it places the psychologist close to the prime decision-making center of a firm. It calls upon the full depth of consulting psychologists' training, experience, and self-awareness to be effective. Even though the examples given above are from large corporations, the coaching process is similar in all types and sizes of organizations. Most smaller organizations take their lead from the "big guys" and their business concerns closely parallel those of larger organizations. We have worked with organizations of all sizes, including firms with as few as 10 employees.

# ROLE CONSIDERATIONS

Even though consulting psychologists use skills they acquired in their clinical training, consulting in the business world differs significantly from practicing as a psychotherapist. In clinical practice the psychotherapist usually has a distant, more professional relationship with referral sources. These referral sources do not participate in clinical treatment. Distinct professional boundaries are critical for ethical clinical practice. In business not only are others in the organization informed about a coaching candidate's developmental plan but often they are actively engaged in that plan. The consulting psychologist's relationship to the organization and coaching candidates is on more of a peer-to-peer level and there is more social engagement than would ever be advisable in clinical practice. Not only are breakfasts and lunch meetings standard in business consulting, but the coaching work is done on a more public level at the client's convenience. When there are personal issues underlying the coaching process, the psychologist works with the candidate to craft a way to communicate about those issues that protects the individual's dignity. Such organizational communication issues are virtually nonexistent in clinical practice.

Another major difference in consulting to business is the level of interaction. Regardless of differences in theoretical orientation, clinical practice is highly personal and in depth. Business consulting may involve personal issues, but only to the extent that they relate to business concerns. As a result, the psychologist-consultant must refer candidates who might need psychotherapy in order to successfully complete their developmental plan. It is not wise for a consultant to treat psychotherapeutic issues alongside a coaching engagement. This referral process protects the developmental work and the employee's deeply personal issues. It is always the best ethical practice to refer clinical issues that arise in consulting work. That is not to say that personality issues are removed from coaching; it is just to note that more clinical issues need to be addressed in a psychotherapeutic context. Often when progress is made in psychotherapy, the coaching candidate can make even more significant developmental progress. Again, as a coach/consultant the psychotherapist has a distinct advantage knowing what can be addressed in a clinical context and what can be accomplished in the coaching process.

Particularly in family business consulting, personal issues are best referred. Boundaries between family and business concerns often blur and the consultant needs to facilitate healthy boundaries between family/personal issues and business concerns. Often in family businesses, substance abuse and mental health issues come into play and need to be addressed separately from the business concerns. For example, a family member who has a major substance abuse issue can be coached on the anger management issues that are impacting the business but would also receive treatment for the substance abuse and related personal issues separately from the coaching. Again, the decisions about what can be coached and what needs to be addressed in a psychotherapeutic context are best understood by a coach/consultant with a background in psychotherapeutic treatment.

# EXECUTIVE SELECTION

A major service consulting psychologists are trained to provide is individual assessment using data obtained through interviews and tests (e.g., objective personality inventories like the CPI or 16PF and projective tests like Sentence Completions and the Thematic Apperception Test) or assessments designed for specific issues such as aggressiveness, 360-degree feedback, and so forth. Graduate psychological training often includes extensive exposure to test development and usage. These assessments have been, and continue to be, oriented to deciphering emotional and mental health issues. Since the early 1940s testing has expanded its reach to include assessment of individuals for employment, including new hires, leadership and management abilities, and succession, among other purposes. Many businesses develop competency models and tools specific to the organization. They are based on data gathered within the organization and relate to the specific needs of the organization.

To augment the individual assessment, consulting psychologists are frequently asked to determine the "fit" between the candidate and the culture of the organization. Because of their training in psychological assessment, they may be asked to help determine those traits and characteristics that a candidate position might require in a particular situation ("fit"), or what abilities the company might need that it is not fully aware of needing. They may well offer advice regarding how to expedite the succession process, as well as the "onboarding" of personnel. (Onboarding is a popular business term that refers to the process of integrating new upper-level employees [e.g., a new CEO from the outside] into an organization.) These and many more services may land on the doorsteps of consulting psychologists because of their training in the use and development of tests and assessments.

## TRAINING AND ADVISING

Frequently, consulting psychologists are called upon to offer training to employees, staff, and executives in diverse areas, such as leadership, motivation (e.g., how to best motivate others), conflict resolution, teaching managers how to coach, how to develop teams, emotional intelligence, stress management, work–life balance, and how to raise morale, among many other subjects.

How well planned these programs are can have a direct and positive influence on the organization. Unfortunately, in the absence of planning their impact can be less than neutral. We underline this element because in many instances in our experience a program on a particular subject (e.g., how to reduce conflict) is introduced in response to an apparent problem in dramatic fashion to demonstrate how serious management is treating it, while the actual causes and circumstances of the situation are being disregarded. By "planning," then, we are suggesting that the impetus for any such program be taken into account in considering how best to present it.

There is a large training and development industry that provides all types of programs to businesses. Some consulting psychologists offer specific training programs, and others form strategic partnerships with companies to offer psychologically based programs for management training. We have consulted for and delivered programs to Fortune 50 companies and large professional organizations. These organizations vary considerably in their understanding of psychological factors, and the training programs are usually tailored to meet the specific needs of the organization. For example:

> A major international luxury brand in the hospitality sector was interested in having its leadership team trained in emotional intelligence and mindfulness as a way to help them

lead, and direct, selection and promotion of top-quality customer service managers. This expensive brand required superior customer service in order to grow and thrive. At the time of training the brand was expanding into new markets that required considerable cross-cultural understanding in order to meet their customer service mandate. The leaders of the brand, as well as a leader from the overall corporation, participated in a series of small-group workshops that taught the concepts and provided some experiential exercises as well. While the focus was on particular concepts, the overall workshops were a forum for leadership development within that industry. Coaching in that context was executed in the small-group format where the goal was to increase the leaders' emotional intelligence and to help them develop a mindfulness practice that would be useful in their work.

Business and professional organizations often sponsor workshops on stress management. Psychologists have an opportunity to conduct these workshops in a sophisticated way that can be highly regarded. We have presented workshops for large Chambers of Commerce, bar associations, trade associations, and associations of financial professionals. While such projects may seem a stretch for the practicing clinician, they simply evolve from relationships that the professional develops and maintains over time. As people become familiar with the types of work that a consultant does, opportunities present themselves. Often pro bono presentations can lead to paid work. Workshops are an area where professionals have an opportunity to educate larger numbers of people in business.

# ORGANIZATIONAL CONSULTING

Executive selection and executive coaching are both one step removed from the clinical activities regularly associated with psychotherapists. Being familiar with business issues and conversant with business concerns are basic prerequisites for the practice of consulting psychology. Understanding how to translate assessment and interview findings into useful recommendations for the business community is an art that psychotherapists should easily be able to learn.

However, when the focus extends beyond the individual to the organization—that is, to the wide swath of internal groups from two-person networks all the way to the entire organization— the clinician has to step back and reflect on what additional knowledge and training is required. Liebowitz and Blattner (2015) have outlined many of the obstacles facing novice psychologist-consultants, including new areas of learning that have to be mastered, a new self-awareness that needs to be developed vis-à-vis a focus on the organization and its dynamics, as well as learning to reframe much of their thinking that was useful in the clinical situation but is distracting in the consulting arena.

A first principle in addressing organizations is that because they are complex systems, their parts are best understood as interacting with each other in some way such that a single part is affected by the other parts. A system is a collection of parts that interact with each other to function as a whole. When applied to organizations, this way of thinking suggests that to understand how something goes wrong, how a problem develops and how to correct it, requires understanding of the context—that is, the other parts of the system.

# CONFLICT SITUATIONS AND TEAM BUILDING

To illustrate the system aspects of conflict in which consulting psychologists are asked to intervene, consider the example of an employee team that is at odds with each other. A personality issue between, and among, the warring parties might be seen as causing the uproar; an honest difference of opinion or understanding might be at the root of it; or some key players may have received disturbing news about salary raises (or lack thereof). In examining the conflict from a systems point of view (i.e., the context), it may well be that the senior executive has not laid out a clear set of goals and objectives for the team to follow; consequently, each team member has his or her own version of what is the goal.

Let us assume that the conflict is indeed a personality issue. The consultant may ask why the leader has not brought the combatants together to resolve the issue. One of us witnessed a chronic personality clash between two employees being maintained by a supervisor who insisted he didn't want to take sides and, therefore, chose not to intervene. The solution to the conflict was coaching the supervisor to be more assertive in leading his direct reports. In doing so the morale of his team improved significantly—the team in general had been negatively affected by the leader's passivity in many different situations.

Conflict resolution is one aspect of team building in which psychologists are asked to consult. Another is the situation where a team is not working together well—where coordination, support, and assistance among members is missing. There are many different techniques (e.g., simulations, tasks that require participants to share information to succeed as a group) that can prove helpful. Again, looking at the context may increase the understanding of why the group was allowed to continue as a group of unrelated individuals. In one situation these conditions persisted because the senior manager wanted to have all information passed directly to, and through, him rather than among the team members, thereby placing all control of the process in his hands. The team lacked any support for working together as a team.

Among the many types of team performance issues that are critical are relationships at the top of the organization. In that context, CEOs may require coaching around their relationship with their boards of directors. It is not uncommon that disagreements between CEOs and their boards become public and detrimental to the organization. An executive coach can be helpful in defusing such situations. An example:

> The CEO of a major sports organization had major conflicts with the board of directors, and had a board with intense conflicts among its members. Historically a charismatic leader, the CEO started to work with a coach, trying to figure out what had gone wrong in a leadership style that had been extremely effective for decades. The CEO was only a year away from retirement and was concerned not only with legacy issues but also with the future of the organization in light of the unresolved conflicts. Through the coaching process the CEO gained a radically different perspective on both the conflicts with a particular individual on the board of directors and conflicts between other board members. Armed with the new perspective, the CEO was able to institute several key organizational changes that facilitated a reemergence of past leadership success and resulted in a highly successful

succession planning process during his final year as CEO. Those accomplishments allowed the organization to reconnect with its primary mission. At the completion of his tenure as CEO, this talented leader retired to a seat on the board of directors and became a popular mentor for future leaders in the organization.

# SUCCESSION ISSUES

Consulting psychologists are often called upon to assist in succession of leaders in both family and nonfamily organizations. On the surface this would seem easy to accomplish: "Promote the best candidate." There are at least two difficulties standing in the way, both related to the theme presented earlier (the systems principle). One problem is determining not only those character traits that would presumably define the "best candidate," but also how these traits "fit" with those needed for the organization to continue to grow and thrive. The other difficulty is how to address the feelings and concerns of the surrounding management team. Contextual appreciation of both difficulties is important for the consulting psychologist to consider.

Drawing a list of desirable traits can be achieved through candidate interviews, tests and assessments, and 360-degree instruments, as discussed earlier. But what does the organization need in the way of leadership talent? Is it to be found inside or outside the firm? Considering the overall organizational context, how does the consulting psychologist determine what the organization truly needs in the way of leadership talent to sustain its growth and development?

Asking management, senior employees, and board members provides one source of information. Another is to ask the organization's suppliers, vendors, and bankers their opinions on what the firm might need. The results of organizational surveys (see below) can yield important information about action steps the organization needs to take. Matching for "fit" is a significant responsibility of the consulting psychologist.

The opinion of people who formerly were peers of, as well as senior to, the successor is another element that has to be taken into account. No doubt others had been vying for the role of successor but were not selected. Their support will prove vital to the successor. How those previously senior to the successor (either in the management hierarchy or on the board) respond to the successor is equally as important. Thus, for example, those from "the old guard" may continue to see the successor in his or her former role and status, not in the one for which he or she has been selected, or a director may feel slighted that his or her choice was not selected and prove resistant to being supportive. The range of reactions to a successor's promotion is more diverse than those presented here. How these reactions are responded to can be crucial to the success of the successor's reign.

Succession in the family business brings with it the same considerations as in other businesses in addition to several unique to the family business. Family business consulting is an area where coach/consultants with a family therapy background have a distinct advantage in being able to sort out and separate family dynamics from business issues.

While the common notion of a family business is a "Mom and Pop shop," there are many large organizations that are family businesses (Nordstrom and Marriott are notable examples). The family and business issues can be complex, and coach/consultants who work with family businesses often play a much bigger role in the organization than in other organizations. Conflicts in family businesses often play out both personally and professionally, influencing the organization more dramatically than in other businesses.

Often in a family business the entrepreneurial father who has built the business may be reluctant to begin the process of stepping down or naming a successor(s). The consulting psychologist can assist the father in learning to accept the need for change. Siblings in the business may be rivals for leadership, and evaluating who might be the best candidate for succession can call for the consulting psychologist's recommendation. Further, there are often situations where the entrepreneur's offspring are not equipped to lead the business. In these situations the consulting psychologist might help keep the business in the family by choosing a capable nonfamily member to assume leadership, or to sell the business, among many other decisions. If there is a potential leader among the siblings, the parents may be reluctant to name that person for fear of alienating the other siblings. Again, the consulting psychologist is well equipped to deal with these and related succession issues.

Once a successor has been named, there is a process of training and developing that individual. The consultant can be a valuable coach for that person, assisting him or her in the training and development process by developing a comprehensive plan with clear behavioral benchmarks. Other siblings may need assistance assuming their appropriate roles in the organization as well. Throughout these processes there may be a need for further conflict resolution and team building. In fact, the consulting psychologist may teach conflict resolution skills to team members during the business reorganization.

# ORGANIZATIONAL ANALYSIS

Although we have touched on organizational concerns, there are broader issues that span the entire spectrum of the organizational landscape and influence it more rapidly and intensely. To address these issues the consulting psychologist needs even more specialized training and experience than we have identified thus far. Some of these issues are listed in order of the increasingly advanced experience and training required to conduct such projects.

## ATTITUDE SURVEYS

Organizations that are targeting concerns about employee morale or culture change may engage a consulting psychologist. These, and related topics, require an understanding of the status quo—namely, what is the morale of employees and what is the culture that needs to be changed? Attitude surveys address these questions by directly asking employees their opinion about organizational morale and culture. There are many standardized assessments available that can be used, but quite often specific issues in morale and culture are targeted and unique questionnaires are designed for the particular setting in response.

Translating these findings into actionable activities can be the responsibility of the consulting psychologist. Categorizing the responses by department or division may add meaning to the results in that it clarifies how widespread or localized a sentiment may be. Deciding what to do about the results can frequently require the consultant's expertise—for example, in developing a program to change attitudes and/or culture.

## DECIPHERING WORK PROCESS DIFFICULTIES

Attitude surveys are designed primarily to elicit employee opinions about culture and morale, as discussed above. However, they also can function as aids to more intensive employee interview procedures and work process observations. In that context the survey elicits information about impediments to workflow such as duplication of effort, inefficient handling of product, incorrect ordering of needed material, lack of information needed by a work team, and the like. Though a consulting psychologist most likely would not know what new or different machinery is needed for a particular work process, he or she could learn (through interviews and observations) that a particular work process needs to be performed faster. Then the consulting psychologist could recommend that measures be taken to implement the appropriate changes.

## ORGANIZATIONAL DESIGN

A frequently overlooked contributor to a business's success is the structural flow of the organization—in other words, how a product/service is produced and turned into a useful and saleable offering. Organizational design centers on the customer's needs and how each department, and division of an organization, ensures that those needs remain a primary business objective.

How customer information flows through an organization forms one of the major bases of design. Another critical factor in design is how the various departments and divisions are aligned so that profitability is maintained while the customer's needs are met. An example will illustrate the importance of organizational design for the success of a company.

> The production arm of a firm providing financial information to three types of customers (banks, Fortune 1000 companies, and government agencies) selected the products that the business produced on behalf of its customers. It did so without any input from its salesforce. The company was rapidly losing its position in the marketplace. A consumer-based analysis discovered that what the firm offered its customers was not what customers wanted or needed. To correct the situation, three teams were formed, each dedicated to one of the three customer types. Each team was cross-functional—that is, it consisted of a member from sales, sales support, production, and finance. This redesign facilitated input from each department: Sales provided the necessary customer input about its needs, sales support customized products for each customer type, production provided input about its execution requirements, and finance ensured a profitable outcome. Thus, the organizational structure became more effective, efficient, and profitable.

## MERGERS AND ACQUISITIONS

Most mergers and acquisitions depend more on financial considerations than otherwise. What frequently tends to predominate is what the ideal merged company will look like, given the characteristics (e.g., customers, products, services, talent, personnel) of the two firms. What is often overlooked is that these readily observable features are only part of the story; there are also many assumptions that are hidden and presupposed, and they may be considered irrelevant. Not surprisingly, those assumptions may drive the success or failure of the merger. Eliciting such assumptions is a service that consulting psychologists can render. There are many different ways to do so.

A technique that one of us has developed is to have the management team of each firm separately design the merged company of the future (including financial issues, personnel, workflow, and the like) and then come together to compare their pictures. It is utterly amazing to witness how differently each firm pictures the future, and how the features of each picture can easily conflict. The consulting psychologist is well trained to engage in this type of activity because he or she is trained to deal with unspoken assumptions and presuppositions and can prove to be an invaluable resource.

## DOWNSIZING

Organizational downsizing can be a depressing, volatile, and unpleasant situation. The consulting psychologist may be asked to perform several services, including aiding the deployment of a policy or procedure for the process and/or helping with the emotional reactions of employees who will be let go, those who have already been let go, and those who remain in the firm. Given the delicacy of the situation, and its legal ramifications, the psychologist must have some training for, and prior experience with, organizational downsizing.

# ADDITIONAL TYPES OF BUSINESS CONSULTING

There are clinical and counseling psychologists, as well as other clinicians, who work in market research and advertising. These professionals are involved in both quantitative (big data) studies and qualitative (focus groups) research for marketing and advertising. In the 1980s there were many advertising and marketing campaigns based on "psychographic" data that were derived from segmentation studies (formal cluster analysis) designed to identify the personality types of different market segments. Once the "psychographics" were identified, marketing and advertising campaigns were crafted to appeal to specific consumer segments. Since that time psychologists have continued to be involved in market analysis by running focus groups and/or analyzing large databases to help businesses understand their consumer markets.

While demographic information is routinely used in market analysis, the larger organizations that spend substantial sums of money on launching new products need to be more sophisticated in their understanding of the consumer. Not only do they need to know the size and demographic features of a potential market, but they also need to understand how consumers think and behave in order to make decisions about how to bring a product to market. Psychologists who work in this segment of business often belong to the American Marketing Association (www.ama.org). AMA has local chapters that offer networking events and job listings. Academics who teach consumer psychology belong to APA Division 23, the Society of Consumer Psychology (http://www.myscp.org/).

Market research and advertising brings the consulting psychologist into the management circle that deals with organizational strategy. Frequently the consulting psychologist becomes a business advisor and mentor, and as such, is invited to offer his or her opinion or advice about critical strategic business issues. In this way, consulting psychologists can become involved in strategic planning (after receiving the necessary training). While many businesses aspire to do strategic planning, everyday concerns often take priority over longer-range planning. Strategic planning is performed in many different ways. There are models based on social psychology group process, and there are purely empirical forecasting models. One way that falls in the consulting psychology arena is scenario planning, in which a management team is divided into subgroups, each dealing with different versions of the future. One group may deal with "the future being the same as now, only better," another addresses the future as a "dog eat dog environment," and a third might view the future as "totally different from today." The members of each group do extensive research in their particular version of the future. Then each group delineates what has to happen in the business environment for the future to unfold that way and what the company needs to do to eventually succeed in each scenario. Pooling the insight from all of these scenarios allows the firm to decide how it might best meet the future no matter how the future unfolds.

## SUMMARY AND CONCLUSIONS

We have presented an overview of consulting psychology in the business world, drawing on our own experiences over the past 35 to 40 years. We hope we have conveyed the importance of further training and experience to transition into consulting psychology while shedding light on the variety of potential business consulting engagements. Again, there is training available from the Society of Consulting Psychology (www.societyofconsultingpsychology.org/students) and the Worldwide Association of Business Coaches (www.wabccoaches.com) and many other reputable training programs. The Society of Consulting Psychology is a good resource for finding other training programs and they are open to non–American Psychological Association members.

# REFERENCES

Diamond, M. A. (2003). Organizational immersion and diagnosis: The work of Harry Levinson. *Organizational & Social Dynamics, 3*(1), 1–18.

Levinson, H. (1956). Employee counseling in industry. *Bulletin of the Menninger Clinic, XX*(2), 76–84.

Levinson, H., & Menninger, W. C. (1954). Industrial mental health: Some observations and trends. *Menninger Quarterly, VIII*(4), 1–31.

Liebowitz, B., & Blattner, J. (2015). On becoming a consultant: The transition for a clinical psychologist, *Consulting Psychology Journal: Practice and Research, 67*(2), 144–161.

# ETHICS AND LEGAL ISSUES

# CHAPTER 34

# COMMON ETHICAL TRANSGRESSIONS BY PRIVATE PRACTITIONERS

*Gerald P. Koocher and Rachael L. Suffrin*

M ost ethical transgressions do not arise from intentional malevolent acts. More typically, such wrongdoing flows from cutting corners, lack of awareness, or lapses in judgment (Koocher & Keith-Spiegel, 2016). Even though many clinicians may lack awareness or rationalize committing ethical transgressions, these can have a significant negative impact on clients. The most common ethical transgressions committed by mental health practitioners in private practice often result from a degree of professional isolation, particularly in the case of clinicians in solo practice or those working in small groups. Without deliberate efforts to keep up with both clinical and business trends and associated technologies related to our practice, we may unknowingly run the risk of falling below the expected standards of care. Without regular clinical peer interactions, we may become insulated from questions that we ought to ask ourselves about clinical challenges. Without a critical mass of colleagues or resources, we may lack the ability to invest in, or supervise support staff and technology in the way that is necessary to uphold high professional standards. This chapter discusses these hazards under the main topical headings of (1) maintaining competence, (2) the business of practice, and (3) professional isolation and role slippage.

## MAINTAINING COMPETENCE

Maintaining one's professional practice skills in the face of research findings, new assessment tools, and the evolution of care settings presents a challenge for all practitioners. Using the analogy of radioactive decay, one psychologist estimated the half-life of the knowledge acquired by earning a doctoral degree in psychology at about 10 to 12 years (Dubin, 1972). Current perceived half-lives as assessed in Delphi polls of experts have varied from a high of 18.4 years (for psychoanalysis) to a low of 7.6 years (for clinical health psychology), with an overall durability of knowledge estimate across all specialties of 8.7 years (Neimeyer, Taylor, Rozensky, & Cox, 2014). This means that after a decade or so, half of what we learned in graduate school will become outdated.

Because professional practice in mental health often cuts across the worlds of behavioral science, medicine, and law, the complexity of keeping up to date becomes compounded. As science advances, technology evolves, regulatory legislation changes, and new case law rulings appear. The pressure for us to keep up builds constantly. In some fields, one must not only keep pace with the march of new knowledge, but actually strive to stay several steps ahead. Even if we agree on a decade-long half-life for mental health practice, how can one retain any modicum of professional competence over a career that spans more than a few decades?

A variety of strategies have emerged in an effort to ensure that professionals strive to maintain competence. These include mandated continuing education, recertification requirements, and professional development models. Most states now require practitioners to complete certain amounts and types of continuing education coursework to maintain a professional license, but some states do not. No states and few certifying bodies have yet deemed it appropriate to require formal reexamination or recertification of license or diploma holders. Even those that have done so allow extensive latitude for delay using grandparent clauses to exempt senior practitioners and use unvalidated processes, claiming these somehow link to actual clinical competence. For example, the American Board of Professional Psychology has launched a recertification process under the rubric "maintenance of competence", describing the procedure on its website as "involving a process of self-examination and documentation of one's continuing professional development." This would involve reporting professional activities such as attending meetings, maintaining organization memberships, publishing, or other such activities with no clear validation that such activities enhance competence in providing clinical services.

Part of the difficulty in implementing any plans to monitor practitioner competence over time originates with a definitional problem. What constitutes a meritorious step toward maintaining one's competence? Is attending a workshop commensurate with teaching one? Is reading (or writing) an article for a refereed journal a sign of continuing competence? Will taking or retaking a multiple-choice examination such as a licensure examination prove clinical competence?

Before we can address a means of maintaining professional capabilities, we must arrive at criteria that are linked to continuing competence. Professional skills, appropriately executed on a daily basis, will certainly enhance competence. However, experience alone does not immunize one against errors. It seems unlikely that a comprehensive solution to the problem of maintaining competence over time will be found in the near term. The most appropriate course of action for a mental health professional would involve striving for a constant awareness of one's limitations, recognizing that these can increase over time after formal training has ended, and seeking constructive remedies by both formal and informal means to keep one's skills current (e.g., attending conferences and workshops, keeping up to date with recently published peer-reviewed articles in the field, frequently consulting with colleagues or peers in case discussion groups, using trainees and externs for their potentially up-to-date knowledge of changes in the field). We discuss two strategies related to evidence-based and cultural examples next because these areas represent constantly evolving skill maintenance challenges.

## EVIDENCE-BASED PRACTICE AND CULTURAL COMPETENCE

All practitioners have an ethical obligation to ensure that their clinical decisions are informed by and reflect best practices. The responsibility for searching for and appraising available evidence also rests with the clinician, as does the need to obtain incremental education and training in newer well-validated techniques. These obligations existed before evidence-based practice became a buzzword, and they are important factors in clinical decision making, whether or not any particular evidence-based practice is offered to any given client. The ethical dangers of *not* attending to evidence are just as significant as the ethical issues attending to its application.

Implementing evidence-based treatments requires us to take account of the unique circumstances and characteristics of each client. This will include understanding the client's values, expectations, and willingness to follow treatment protocols, as well as recognizing the limitations of published research. Much of the extant research related to evidence-based psychotherapy excludes or overlooks issues of client diversity. Self-aware clinicians will consider how their own values and assumptions may impact their view and interpretation of the client, and will work to ensure they do not impose their own values on the client. This includes recognizing the wide range of clients and looking beyond gender, race, ethnicity, and religion to consider socioeconomic status, immigrant or refugee status, sexual orientation, other such factors, as well as the role of intersecting identities (Norcross, Hogan, Koocher, & Maggio, 2017).

Navigating the resulting complex decision-making matrix will prove particularly challenging for those in independent practice, who must know enough to recognize what they do not know (Koocher & Keith-Spiegel, 2016). Obtaining consultation or additional education and training when necessary to keep up to date on the best evidence and its implementation can prove more challenging in small practices without a breadth of clinicians or educational resources. In addition, because of the half-life of knowledge issues described earlier, clinicians should periodically check for updated treatment manuals and newly available treatments. Knowing when to refer, when to reach out for peer supervision, or how to become sufficiently self-aware poses greater challenges in private practice than when working in larger systems. Recognizing when one lacks the training, background, or competence to handle a case with the best evidence-based approach or cultural competence presents a constant challenge.

# BUSINESS OF PRACTICE

## RESOURCES AND CRITICAL MASS

Private practitioners who work solo or in small groups may encounter resource challenges as they strive to manage costs associated with quality service delivery. Such costs typically include office space, equipment, and ancillary services such as supplies, test materials or scoring, and billing. Professional services related to covering clients' medication needs (e.g., hiring or formally contracting for preferred access with a consulting prescriber) or legal advice can also come into play (e.g., for contract review, corporate/partnership documents, or employment agreements). The cost of such support or ancillary services will vary in a scalable manner. In larger practices the need for some ancillary services will increase, but the cost as a percentage of revenue will be lower. Small practice units will not require as many ancillary services, but the smaller the practice, the greater the relative percentage of revenue that must go to pay such expenses. This simple set of economic and service burdens can create a temptation to cut corners in ways that create risk, such as letting insurance policies lapse, not arranging coverage for vacations, mass photocopying of copyright-protected test protocol blanks, or not purchasing the latest editions of assessment tools.

Some solo practitioners find a way to reduce some of these costs by practicing in proximity with other individual practices. This could involve sharing office space, testing equipment, or even support services. However, before engaging in such sharing arrangements, practitioners should consult carefully with a personal attorney and their professional liability insurance carrier. In addition, listing the names of all practitioners at the door of a six-office suite with a common waiting room could give the impression of a group practice rather than a cluster of individual practices sharing resources. Litigation against one person in the shared space could lead to some liability for the others, depending on the circumstances. Thinking this through in advance and putting clients on notice about the relevant distinctions can prevent problems. The practitioners in the shared space may also need to formulate clear written agreements among themselves regarding rules for the use of their shared environs.

When forming actual group practices in which practitioners work together as a business unit, clear understanding of the policies will also become critical. This will include any corporate or partnership agreements, as well as operational policies for dealing with clients. One should consider the details of a future professional divorce at the time one joins a practice and clarify among all concerned how this would work. This would include discussion of records or computerized data access, financial terms, and the rights of clients to choose their provider (i.e., the client's right to continue treatment with a clinician who departs from a group practice). Discussing such breakup policies at the time a practice forms or when a new member joins can preclude later anger, misunderstandings, and emotional distress for all concerned.

## TECHNOLOGICAL CHALLENGES

Rapid changes in the ways we store, retrieve, and transmit data, including sensitive clinical and financial material, raise many new types of confidentiality concerns. Vast amounts of information can now be stored in small easily transported electronic, magnetic, or optical devices that can often be misused, stolen, or misplaced. Use of the Internet for communications provides great convenience as well as considerable unresolved confusion and controversy related to the rights and obligations of users. Mental health professionals making use of new technology must remain thoughtful and cautious about the hazards to confidentiality that result.

Clinicians are responsible for potential confidentiality breaches committed by students working in their practice, technicians, support staff, and other employees they supervise. This includes potential problems associated with those who use their own laptop, tablet, or handheld devices with client records or communications. Practices with multiple staff members who do not use secure or encrypted communications can create additional ethical risks. Clinics, hospitals, and large service delivery units typically have policies and systems in use that address these issues, but small or solo practices may not deploy adequate protections. While Health Insurance Portability and Accountability Act (HIPAA) requirements and penalties are scalable (e.g., the larger the practice, the greater the fines that may be imposed), such precautions remain important in any practice, regardless of size.

Another significant ethical issue for practices that do a lot of assessment work involves the larger test publishers (e.g., Pearson), who no longer sell "local" individual network computer scoring devices. Many publishers have moved to "cloud-based" global computer scoring on their own remote servers. This trend has triggered significant concerns about client confidentiality. For example, the newest BASC-3 and Woodcock Johnson Tests of Achievement all use only online scoring. Practitioners must take precautions to encode data properly to ensure that identifiable client data do not upload. A broader question involves what use test publishers will make of the large bodies of data that come into their possession and remain identifiable by practitioner, if not by client.

Violations of HIPAA regulations and related state laws require preventive steps and notification to clients if breaches occur. From the standpoint of private practitioners the potential fines associated with a violation are lower than for large entities, but the same is true of resources. Technological consultation and planning for handling any breach should become part of every clinician's personal disaster plan. For example, most clinicians will understand the need to thoroughly erase a computer hard drive before disposing of the equipment, but they may not be aware that many office copying machines also have such storage capability that must be attended to when selling or upgrading such equipment.

## REMOTE INTERACTION WITH CLIENTS AND SOCIAL MEDIA

The rapid growth in remote telecommunications and social media has created a broad array of personal communications and business transactions that occur in cyberspace. Such practice does not represent an ethical transgression, but the potential pitfalls pose significant risk. We cover them here because we believe these risks will prove to be greater hazards for private practitioners than for well-funded institutional or government agency practices. Clinicians will need to make careful decisions about how they use the options from the perspective of practical business use and client welfare. What contracts or agreements for providing distance services will we make with our clients? What competencies and standards of care will apply when offering services remotely? What new factors will constrain confidentiality protections and retention of any recorded or captured transmissions? Who will control the practice of telepractice (i.e., the regulation of practice and data access across jurisdictions)?

When we agree to work with clients via telehealth, the nature and terms of how we relate will change. We will need to reach accords on new contracts or agreements regarding the nature of the services we offer and manner of providing them. For example, we will have to obtain and document clients' informed consent to communicate with them electronically. Such consent will doubtless require many changes, such as requiring us to establish reasonable security and encryption precautions and to provide precise instructions regarding the nature of the services, access, and emergency coverage.

Consider these issues:

- Will we contract to provide services remotely only with existing psychotherapy clients, or will we readily accept new referrals of people we have never met for any or all of our professional services?
- What standards of care and liability obligations will apply?
- How long will it take to obtain regulatory clearance for inter-jurisdictional telepractice?
- Will we agree to conduct all assessment, consultation, or therapy relationships entirely via telepractice or only a limited range of services?
- Will we promise real-time electronic access to the primary or a backup clinician 24/7/ 365?
- How will recordkeeping change given the ease with which both practitioners and clients can capture, store, and alter such communications?
- Will fees and reimbursement policies differ from office-based services?
- Will we offer emergency coverage? If so, what backup must we organize for clients who live hundreds or thousands of miles away?

Consider carefully which services and types of communication you want to provide electronically (e.g., appointment scheduling, impromptu requests, clinical updates, emergency messages, or actual clinical service delivery). Discuss with clients in advance those topics that you are willing to discuss via electronic messaging, as well as the potential benefits, risks, and limitations involved with such communication (e.g., potential access by others to unencrypted email, text, and voice messages). Emphasize the limitations and constraints on access to you via such modalities. In most cases, you will want to advise clients to go to the nearest emergency department rather than rely on electronic communication in a true mental health emergency.

We recommend the following:

- Obtain and document (via a personally or electronically signed document) clients' informed consent to communicate with them in this manner.
- Establish HIPAA-compliant security and encryption precautions prior to using electronic means for mental health communications with patients.
- Monitor any online scheduling software or access by others to your account carefully to ensure preservation of patient confidentiality.
- Check your electronic message accounts frequently and securely.
- Print or otherwise preserve all electronic message exchanges with patients, and keep them with patients' treatment records.
- Make sure that any information posted on a practice website is up to date and accurate.

## PUBLIC IMAGE MANAGEMENT

Private practitioners must typically devote more time and effort to marketing and cultivation of referral sources than institutions or government-based service agencies. In that context, managing one's public image poses special challenges that can lead to ethical transgressions. We offer these comments as preventive guidance.

Consider how you will respond if an angry client posts comments critical of you on a public website. You may be unable to get bad reviews removed, but you can manage your own public information and should reply to any media criticism in a professional manner. For example, you could post a public response explaining why you cannot respond directly to bad reviews (because of confidentiality obligations). In addition, nothing in our ethical codes precludes us from asking colleagues who think well of our work to post positive reviews. Keep everything in perspective: A single bad review may not mean much, and venting in public can leave a bad impression and lead to an ethical complaint if a client feels harmed. If the same individuals keep posting negative material and become harassing or defamatory, consult an attorney.

Your own web-based advertising should be truthful and factual, containing information the potential consumer will find helpful. For example, list earned degrees, certifications and licensures, and affiliations accurately, avoiding misleading content. Take care to honor all commitments in advertising for the life of the announcement. Do not use exaggeration, superficiality, and sensationalism in any media forum. Do not solicit testimonials from current clients; in fact, give careful consideration before using them at all. Avoid making public statements purporting to speak for your entire profession. Do not make public comments on the emotional or psychological status of public figures; consider the 2016 election season, or the bad behavior of a popular celebrity as examples. Journalists may well reach out to clinicians in the community for comment, and doing so may seem like a good way to call attention to your practice. Unfortunately, such commentaries pose a significant risk of offering an assessment or analysis without adequate data or possibly leading to accusations of defamation.

## RECORDKEEPING AND RECORD SHARING

Recordkeeping can pose challenges for private practitioners for reasons described previously, particularly when the practitioner must manage all of his or her records alone or must train and supervise one or more employees to do so. Learn about the laws and regulations that govern confidentiality and privilege in the jurisdiction where you practice. Keep adequate clinical records and retain them in a manner that conforms to good practice and the law. Inform clients about the limits of confidentiality as early as possible in the professional relationship, and document this notification in writing. Remind clients of the limitations as appropriate. Make sure that your clients understand the nature and security of your recordkeeping system, including which other practitioners or employees may have access to their records.

Some general policies can help to keep a practice on track with respect to record releases:

- Do not release information about clients without an appropriate release or court order.
- When releasing records, require an appropriate authorization form and keep a copy.

- Obtaining consent from a client does not simply mean getting the client's signature. Consent is a process during which the practitioner should alert the client to the consequences of release and even discuss limiting the scope of the release, if warranted.
- Guard against electronic routing failures (such as accidentally speed dialing the wrong number) when sending faxes or using other electronic means.

Under HIPAA regulations (45 C.F.R. §164.508) each consent or release form must at minimum contain:

- A meaningful description of the information to be disclosed
- The name or specific identification of the person(s) authorized to disclose the information
- The name or specific identification of the person(s) or class of persons authorized to receive the information
- A description of the purpose or requested use of the information
- An expiration date or event related to the purpose of the disclosure
- The signature of the authorizing person and date of signing

If the signer is acting on behalf of another, their relationship should be indicated. Certain required statements must also appear on the release form to notify the signer that:

- The signer has a right to revoke the authorization in writing, any exceptions, and the procedure to follow.
- The care provider may not require the release as a condition of treatment, payment, or eligibility for benefits.
- Once released, the information could potentially be redisclosed by the recipient and thus no longer be protected.

Also, consider your clients' best interests and foreseeable adverse events, taking care to avoid them by considering the recipient's need to know and any vulnerabilities of the client. As noted above, this could include consultation with the client to limit the scope of the release to the minimum information needed to comply with the intended purpose of the release, so long as professional integrity remains intact.

When dealing with child and family contexts, practitioners should keep in mind the hazards that can accompany disclosure of sensitive information. For example, adolescents who discuss episodic alcohol use or consensual sexual activity with peers may wish such information kept confidential from their parents. Parents in conflicted families may ultimately seek divorce and fight over record access (or even authorization for treatment). Planning for these contingencies in advance and addressing them in the HIPAA forms provided and discussed at the start of client relationships through the informed consent process will help to avoid problems later.

Have a plan in place to cull obsolete materials from files and dispose of records properly when allowed to do so by the relevant laws or regulations in your jurisdiction. For example, obsolete materials may include psychotherapy notes kept separately from the clinical record or very old test protocols. States typically require that practitioners keep records for five to seven years following the last face-to-face clinical contact. In the case of children this may extend to at least a year beyond the age when the former child attains majority status. The ability to scan and store records digitally without space constraints may tempt some practitioners to keep records indefinitely. However, doing so increases the mass of records that one must protect from security breaches or that must be managed when a practice closes.

Good records management includes having a plan for what will happen if you become incapacitated. None of us wants to contemplate our own potential disability or death, but such considerations become very important for private practitioners. Unlike institutional practices that maintain client and clinical record databases, solo practitioners have no built-in backup for records management. Forming an agreement with one or more colleagues to provide such coverage and creating a professional will that designates a means of managing the closure of your practice in the event of unanticipated death constitute an important ethical need that is too often overlooked.

Understand the technology you use to manage sensitive data in your practice well enough to preserve confidentiality in storage, transportation, and transmission of records. In an assessment practice this will require making decisions about which and how many physical protocols to maintain (as opposed to reports and data summary sheets).

## BILLING

Private practice has become progressively less lucrative over the past few decades. In the late 1970s, a time when practitioners billed for psychotherapeutic services without managed care restrictions, a 50-minute "hour" of psychotherapy in the Boston area fetched about $60. The realities of independent practice are far less alluring today. The $60 rate that seemed impressive in 1978 would translate to approximately $217.32 in 2015 dollars when corrected for inflation. Conversely, the typical reimbursement rate for a 45- to 50-minute "hour" of psychotherapy paid by Blue Cross Blue Shield of Massachusetts in 2014 (approximately $100 for a doctoral-level psychotherapist and $75 for a master's-level therapist) translates to a 1978 value of just under $28 and $21, respectively.

One result of the declining profit margin available to clinicians in private practice may result in offering less pro bono service and needing to monitor competitive pricing closely. From an ethical perspective, this set of circumstances underscores the importance of communicating clearly with patients about the cost of services, what types of insurance are accepted, and what services third-party payers may not cover. In addition, practitioners will want to keep up to date on resources in the community for those in need of services for which they must pay out of pocket.

The vicissitudes of dealing with managed care plans and competition across a wide range of provider professions (e.g., gaining access to provider panels, incremental documentation of service needs, requests for additional sessions, reduced payments) have also made the small-business management of an independent practice far more demanding. Many third-party payers will no longer easily reimburse for services they might have covered a few decades ago (e.g., neuropsychological assessment for learning difficulties).

Here are some suggestions for billing practices:

- Inform clients about fees (and the potential of future fee increases), billing, collection practices, and other financial contingencies as a routine part of initiating the professional relationship, ideally in written form. Repeat this information later in the relationship as necessary.
- Carefully consider the client's overall ability to afford services early in the relationship and help the client to make a plan for obtaining services that will be both clinically appropriate and financially feasible. Encouraging clients to incur significant debt is not psychotherapeutic. In that regard, psychotherapists should be aware of less costly referral options in the community.
- Consider routinely performing some services on a sliding scale, for little or no fee, or as a pro bono service.
- Pay careful attention to all contractual obligations, understand them, and abide by them. Do not sign contracts with stipulations that might subsequently place you in ethical jeopardy (e.g., "hold harmless" clauses written to protect the insurer, not the practitioner).
- In dealing with third-party payers and managed care organizations, adhere to the same standards of competence, professionalism, and integrity as in other contexts. Be sensitive to the potential ethical problems inherent in such service delivery systems in which profitmaking strategies may trump client welfare.
- In all debt-collection situations, know the laws that apply in your jurisdiction and make every effort to behave in a cautious, businesslike fashion. Avoid using your special position or information gained through your professional role to collect debts from clients. Take responsibility for any collection agencies you hire.
- If you choose to engage in any bartering arrangements, follow policies that comply with tax laws and do not take advantage of clients (Zur, 2003).
- Avoid relationships involving kickbacks, fee splitting, or payment of commissions for client referrals. These may be illegal and unethical. While paying for actual services rendered or for productivity is perfectly appropriate, paying a fee simply in exchange for a referral is not.
- Do not manipulate billing policies or codes to mislead third-party payers (e.g., waiving co-payments, treating a couple or family while using billing codes that apply to individuals in order to increase coverage).
- Do not allow any misrepresentation of financial transactions effected in your name by an employee or agent you have designated (including billing and collection agents). Choose your employees and representatives with care and supervise them closely.
- Third-party payers may pressure you to meet their needs in ways that do not necessarily hold the rights of individual clients paramount. In such instances, ethical clinicians will act in the best interests of their clients.

# PROFESSIONAL ISOLATION
# AND ROLE SLIPPAGE

In many ways, individual and small-group independent practices have become more taxing than the work of mental health professionals at larger agencies, clinics, or hospitals. True, the independent practitioner is his or her own boss, but that must be balanced with overhead costs, employee relations (e.g., with a receptionist, answering service), backup coverage, billing, advertising, and a host of other mundane, but necessary, business-related tasks. In addition, a kind of professional loneliness can afflict the independent practitioner, especially one who is isolated in a small office with no easy access to colleagues (Barnett, Zimmerman, & Walfish, 2014).

The greatest problem in the ethical sense is probably related to the fact that the independent practitioner must be both a professional and a skilled business manager to survive, roles that are not always congruent. As an independent practitioner, you are in charge of planning and successfully managing the practice, all documentation and recordkeeping, dealing with third parties, protecting confidentiality, managing practice finances, staff training (if you have any staff), office/employment policies, advertising and marketing, and someday the closing of a private practice in full compliance with record maintenance laws (Bradley, Hendricks, & Kabell, 2012). In addition, not having peer collaborators may lead to less social comparison of a professional nature and a resulting failure to always think carefully about the manner in which one practices or manages cases.

Psychotherapists must prepare to evaluate each client and recognize that they may not be the best fit for a particular client. We must remain aware of our own limitations and stand ready to make appropriate referrals or seek consultation as needed (Barnett, Zimmerman & Walfish, 2014; Walfish & Zimmerman, 2013). Give consideration to the types of presenting problems that you may not have the clinical, emotional, or other personal resources and skills to adequately treat.

## SUPERVISING EMPLOYEES, ASSOCIATES, AND TRAINEES IN INDEPENDENT PRACTICES

Large solo or group practices may have an administrative assistant or other employees who require careful supervision. In smaller practices such administrative staff generally do not have the luxury of paid vacations or sick days and are far more susceptible to the mundane case management headaches of working with emotionally troubled people (e.g., the client who does not pay bills or often fails to keep scheduled appointments). Managing administrative personnel issues can be a significant complication in these contexts.

Clinicians have a responsibility to adequately train and oversee the employees who work in their practice and any clinicians-in-training they agree to supervise (Fisher, 2009). Training supervision will typically require that the licensed person remain onsite when the trainee is with clients in the event that urgent consultation becomes necessary. Setting up a general policy and procedure manual for employees and supervisees can serve as an important risk-management tool. Even when employees or associates can work independently, the supervising clinician should routinely check their work, particularly in matters related to recordkeeping and billing. Having a set of formal procedures in place to track actual hours will also prove important if the employee or trainee hopes to use the hours for qualification when seeking an internship, postdoctoral fellowship, or licensing.

## ROLE SLIPPAGE

Boundary crossings or multiple-role problems, including sexual and nonsexual role violations, cut across all professional settings and relationships. These are among the most common problems that lead to complaints against mental health professionals. Some of these problems do seem more likely to occur in solo practice situations, where the lack of regular peer interaction and monitoring can lead to judgment errors due to professional isolation (Koocher & Keith-Spiegel, 2016).

Attention to self-care will serve as one of the best risk-management strategies to prevent ethically compromising role slippage (Knapp et al., 2013). We have not focused significant space on these matters because no hard data clearly link either solo or independent group practice to boundary crossings or increased likelihood of ethical complaints. We do know, however, that practitioners in the midst of life crises, those affected by substance abuse, and those with significant emotional problems have an increased risk of transgressions (Knapp et al., 2013; Koocher & Keith-Spiegel, 2016). When one is not in regular contact with caring colleagues, when one does not have ready access to consultation, and when the temptation to take a wrong turn is not inhibited by the proximity of observant professional colleagues, slippage is more likely. Conflicts of interest may go unnoticed, become rationalized, or simply get disregarded. By making a consistent effort to remain professionally engaged and by taking care of oneself, the potential for ethical compromise will decrease.

# IN CONCLUSION

Can you guess the current most common cause of disciplinary action by licensing boards against psychologists? In states with mandatory continuing education statutes, the most common basis of disciplinary action is failure to produce evidence of such compliance when audited. The second most common involves multiple-role violations. The third most common involves practicing beyond one's areas of competence (including practicing while impaired). The competence issue often comes up in the context of custody evaluations or assessment issues related to forensic or disability cases. Fourth in frequency of complaints are alleged breaches of confidentiality. Finally, financial disputes weigh in as the fifth most common cause, but conflicts over fees can trigger complaints in the other categories.

Because most state psychological associations have ceased adjudicating complaints and because the American Psychological Association's Ethics Committee will typically defer acting on any cases simultaneously before the courts or licensing boards, the vast majority of complaints are heard by licensing boards, with a smaller number heading to court. The largest group of all (apart from continuing education violations) comprises the multiple-role cases, and that group far outnumbers all other categories combined. The reason for this probably relates to the seriousness of the damage caused. When considering civil lawsuits, as opposed to licensing board actions, multiple-role conflicts are the most frequent triggers, but close behind in seriousness are damages related to homicidal or suicidal clients. These latter categories are low in incidence but can cause significant damage.

As noted earlier, these common transgressions may not be overrepresented among practitioners in independent practice. However, focusing on maintaining one's own professional competence, creating and maintaining good records, communicating effectively with clients, promoting strong client confidentiality, managing one's own business operations well, taking care of oneself, and avoiding role slippage will all go a long way toward minimizing the likelihood of ethical or licensing board complaints.

# REFERENCES AND RESOURCES

American Board of Professional Psychology. (n.d.). Maintenance of certification information. Retrieved from http://www.abpp.org/i4a/pages/index.cfm?pageid=3892.

American Psychological Association. (2007). *Record keeping guidelines.* Washington, DC: American Psychological Association. Retrieved from http://www.apa.org/practice/guidelines/record-keeping.aspx?_ga=1.213332561.451432513.1419208517.

Barnett, J. E., Zimmerman, J., & Walfish, S. (2014). *The ethics of private practice: A practical guide for mental health clinicians.* New York: Oxford University Press.

Bradley, L. J., Hendricks, B., & Kabell, D. R. (2012). The professional will: An ethical responsibility. *The Family Journal, 2,* 309–314. doi:http://dx.doi.org/10.1177/1066480712449601.

Dubin, S. S. (1972). Obsolescence or lifelong education: A choice for the professional. *American Psychologist, 27,* 486–498.

Fisher, M. A. (2009). Ethics-based training for nonclinical staff in mental health settings. *Professional Psychology: Research and Practice, 40*(5), 459–466. http://dx.doi.org/10.1037/a0016642

Johnson, W. B., & Koocher, G. P. (Eds.). (2011). *Ethical conundrums, quandaries and predicaments in mental health practice: A casebook from the files of experts.* New York: Oxford University Press.

Knapp, S., Younggren, J. N., VandeCreek, L., Harris, E., & Martin, J. (2013). *Assessing and managing risk in psychological practice: An individualized approach.* Bethesda, MD: The Trust.

Koocher, G. P., & Keith-Spiegel, P. C. (2016). *Ethics in psychology and the mental health professions: Standards and cases* (4th ed.). New York: Oxford University Press.

Koocher, G. P., Norcross, J. C., & Greene, B. (Eds.). (2013). *Psychologists' desk reference* (3rd ed.). New York: Oxford University Press.

Luepker, E. T. (2012). *Record keeping in psychotherapy and counseling* (2nd ed.). New York: Routledge.

Neimeyer, G. J., Taylor, J. M., Rozensky, R. H., & Cox, D. R. (2014). The diminishing durability of knowledge in professional psychology: A second look at specializations. *Professional Psychology, 45*, 92–98. doi:10.1037/a0036176.

Norcross, J. C., Hogan, T., Koocher, G. P., & Maggio, L. A. (2017). *Clinician's guide to evidence-based practices: Mental health and the addiction* (2nd ed.). New York: Oxford University Press.

Walfish, S., & Zimmerman, J. (2013). Making good referrals. In G. P. Koocher, J. C. Norcross, & B. A. Greene (Eds.). *Psychologists' desk reference* (3rd ed., pp. 649–653). New York: Oxford University Press.

Zur, O. (2003). Bartering in psychotherapy and counseling: Complexities, case studies and guidelines. Retrieved from http://www.drozur.com/bartertherapy.html.

CHAPTER 35

# ETHICS ISSUES REGARDING SUPERVISION AND CONSULTATION IN PRIVATE PRACTICE

*Rodney K. Goodyear, Carol A. Falender, and Tony Rousmaniere*

Supervision and consultation are activities that provide mental health professionals in private practice with support, challenge, reality checks, varied perspectives, and reduced isolation, a known occupational hazard (American Psychological Association [APA], 2015a). As is true of any psychological activity or intervention, though, supervision and consultation present particular ethical demands and challenges. Even though many of these have been considered in both the conceptual (Barnett & Molzon, 2014; Corey, Corey, Corey, & Callanan, 2015; Goodyear & Rodolfa, 2012; Koocher, Falender, & Shafranske, 2004) and empirical (Ladany, Lehrman-Waterman, Molinaro, & Wolgast, 1999) literature, the more specific ethical issues that arise as a function of supervising and consulting in particular work settings have been largely ignored. This chapter addresses that gap, focusing on the ethical practice of supervision and the related function of consultation in private practice.

It is important to begin this chapter by differentiating supervision and consultation, especially as clinicians often incorrectly use these terms interchangeably (Knapp, Younggren, VandeCreek, Harris, & Martin, 2013). The *Guidelines for Clinical Supervision of Health Service Psychologists* (APA, 2014, 2015), define supervision as

> a distinct professional practice employing a collaborative relationship that has both facilitative and evaluative components, that extends over time, which has the goals of enhancing the professional competence and science-informed practice of the supervisee, monitoring the quality of services provided, protecting the public, and providing a gatekeeping function for entry into the profession. (APA, 2014, p. 5)

Consultation is defined as a process that involves

> a broad helping approach in which qualified psychological consultants help consultees (1) resolve work-related issues pertaining to individuals, clients, or programs that they are responsible for, (2) become active agents in achieving solutions to problems, or (3) strengthen consultees' work-related competencies to address similar issues in the future. (Wallace & Hall, 1996, p. 10)

Although consultation and supervision practice share a number of similarities, consultants do not have the liability or the evaluative, monitoring, and gatekeeping responsibilities of supervisors. Additionally, consultees are not required to accept and implement the consultative input. These responsibilities are not present, for example, when clinicians engage in what often is called peer supervision, which actually may be more accurately labeled as consultation, or when they consult with other licensed professionals who are learning some specialized techniques or models. In general, consultation occurs between two licensed professionals whereas supervision occurs with trainees (though there may be instances in which trainees seek consultation from someone who will have evaluative responsibilities for them).

Supervisors' foremost ethical responsibility is to protect the clients their supervisees treat. They also bear both direct and vicarious liability for their supervisees' work. Direct liability arises from negligent supervision that results in client harm; in vicarious liability, the supervisor can be held liable for the supervisee's actions even if she or he had no knowledge of them (see Disney & Stephens, 1994). This client-care responsibility comes with the associated responsibility to evaluate the supervisee's suitability for the profession, a responsibility often termed "gatekeeping." The evaluative role and the fact that the supervisee is working under the license of the supervisor give the supervisor power in the relationship. So if the supervisor tells the supervisee to assess for suicidality, for example, the supervisee *must* do so: It is an imperative. But if their roles were those of consultant and consultee rather than of supervisor and supervisee, the consultant's suggestion would be advisory rather than prescriptive, as the individual seeking consultation is responsible for treatment choices.

In short, supervision and consultation both can provide a safe, collaborative, reflective space that affords perspective, an opportunity to reflect and see the clinical issues through another person's viewpoint, and a chance to hone professional skills. But supervision carries added responsibilities and particular ethical considerations that affect not only practice but also the nature of the relationship (i.e., it is hierarchical in terms of power, whereas consultation is not). For example, the absence of evaluative and gatekeeping responsibilities makes multiple relationships a less prominent concern in consultation than in supervision—though a significant exception is that of intimate relationships between consultant and consultee, which would bias the consultation.

This chapter is organized into four sections. The first addresses general considerations. The next sections consider ethics issues related to competence, to multiple relationships, and to Internet-delivered supervision and consultation. We conclude with a section that illustrates some common ethical dilemmas or challenges along with the supervision or consultation best practices for each situation.

# GENERAL CONSIDERATIONS

A supervisor must adhere to the regulations for supervision of the state or province. In California, for example, a psychologist in private practice with a psychological assistant must complete a supervision agreement, develop a supervision plan that includes a plan for socialization into the profession, and obtain approval from the Board of Psychology before one hour of supervised experience or client contact may begin. In addition, the primary supervisor must be a licensed psychologist (Board of Psychology, 2015). These regulations vary by both jurisdiction and profession (e.g., social work, psychology, counseling, and marriage and family therapy all have different regulations), so it is important to be aware of the rules that apply in your locale, profession under supervision, and situation.

These regulatory matters correspond to supervisors' ethical responsibilities, particularly for the structure that is afforded by a supervision agreement or contract. The Supervision *Guidelines* (APA, 2015b), the supervision guidelines of the Association of State and Provincial Psychology Boards (ASPPB, 2015b), *Best Practice Standards in Social Work Supervision* (National Association of Social Workers [NASW], 2013), and counseling best practices (Borders et al., 2014) outline the parameters of a supervision contract, which include the context, structure, method, roles, and expectations of supervisor and supervisee, limits of confidentiality of supervisee disclosures, and legal and ethical parameters. In consultation, an agreement is also indicated (Thomas, 2010). Included in the agreement or contract is delineation of what the consultant has agreed to do and whether the consultation will be educational or case specific. The difference between supervision and consultation should be clear, indicating that the consultee holds responsibility for the case and decisions made. In contrast, the supervisee is working under the license of the supervisor and is responsible for ensuring that the supervisor is informed of all aspects of client care and emergent issues.

The supervision contract (see, e.g., APA, 2010, 3.10; NASW, 2013) is a form of informed consent for supervisees or consultees. There also are informed consent requirements for clients of supervisees and consultees. In the case of supervision, all clients need to understand and consent to the trainee being under supervision of someone who will have total access to records, session information including any recordings, and charting or records. In the case of consultation, the clients also should be made aware of anyone else who will have access to information and, if recordings or other forms of direct observation are used, should give consent to their use in the consultation.

Finally, there are two supervision-specific ethical issues: gatekeeping responsibilities and honesty in reporting hours of supervised experience.

## GATEKEEPING

Gatekeeping is a supervisor's responsibility (American Association for Marriage and Family Therapy [AAMFT], 2015; American Counseling Association [ACA], 2014; APA, 2015b; NASW, 2008) and is essential to protecting the public. In fulfilling that responsibility, supervisors must provide informed consent to the students about the for completion of a degree, clarity of expectations, clarity about competencies and ethical standards, and accurate feedback on all of these (Elpers & FitzGerald, 2013). However, because of their discomfort with the gatekeeper role, some supervisors will play the "hot potato game" (Johnson et al., 2008)—that is, they pass a marginally competent supervisee on to the next supervisor, whom they assume will close the gate to the profession if necessary. But supervisees in private practice settings typically have completed their graduate programs and so are sufficiently advanced that their supervisors often will be the last to sign off on hours for their licensure. The trainee will have no more supervisors: When the supervisor asserts that the supervisee has performed satisfactorily in meeting the requirement for hours, the supervisee becomes eligible for licensure as an independent professional and therefore responsible for unmonitored care of clients.

## HONESTY IN REPORTING HOURS OF SUPERVISED WORK

Virtually all (92.5%) respondents to the Pope, Tabachnick, and Keith-Spiegel (1987) survey considered it to be "unquestionably unethical" to attest to hours of psychology practice that supervisees did not actually provide. Such behavior also could result in sanctions for the supervisor. Significantly, the annual data that the ASPPB collect routinely show supervision-related infractions to be among the top 10 reasons for disciplinary sanctions nationally (e.g., ASPPB, 2015a), and supervision-related infractions are prominent among the disciplinary sanctions given to social workers as well (Strom-Gottfried, 2000).

# COMPETENCE

The codes of ethics of the AAMFT, ACA, APA, and NASW emphasize the importance of being competent in the professional services being provided. For example, the APA's Code of Ethics (2010, 2.01) stipulates that "psychologists provide services, teach . . . in areas only within the boundaries of their competence, based on their education, training, supervised experience, consultation, study, or professional experience." The NASW Code of Ethics (2008, 3.01) states, "Social workers who provide supervision or consultation should have the necessary knowledge and skill to supervise or consult appropriately and should do so only within their areas of knowledge and competence." Thus, both supervision and consultation require mental health professionals rendering service to self-assess their competence and ensure that they only practice within those boundaries.

Competence includes knowledge and skills that require specific training to attain. Those who provide supervision and consultation must be competent in both the particular professional service for which the person is supervising or consulting *and* in the practice of supervision or consultation (APA, 2015). The ACA Code of Ethics (2014, F.2.a) states, "Prior to offering supervision services, counselors are trained in supervision methods and techniques. Counselors who offer supervision services regularly pursue continuing education activities, including both counseling and supervision topics and skills." The NASW Code of Ethics (2008, 3.01a) states, "Social workers who provide supervision or consultation should have the necessary knowledge and skill to supervise or consult appropriately and should do so only within their areas of knowledge and competence." This means that the private practice supervisor or consultant should have had formal training to be a supervisor or should be working to develop that competence (e.g., by seeking consultation on the supervision she or he is providing) or, in the case of consultation, should have clarity about the ethical parameters and knowledge, skills, and attitudes regarding the subjects of consultation (Fouad et al., 2009).

Supervisors and consultants also should have emotional competence, which concerns awareness of personal problems that may interfere with their (or their supervisees' or consultees') adequate performance of work-related duties (APA, 2010, 2.06[b]). Self-assessment and self-care are important aspects of this competence. Barnett, Baker, Elman, and Schoener (2007) asserted, in fact, that engaging in the habits of self-care that facilitate well-being is an ethical imperative as it affects the psychotherapist's emotional well-being, which is essential to effective client care. A corollary is that clinicians should model these practices and help their supervisees and consultees to develop self-care habits.

Multicultural competence (see Inman & Ladany, 2014) requires that the supervisor or consultant be able to respond effectively to the multiple diversity identities (e.g., race, age, gender, gender identity, ethnicity, culture, national origin, religion, sexual orientation, disability, language, and socioeconomic status—and intersections of these) that clients, supervisees, consultees, and supervisors present (APA, 2010, 2.01[b]). It concerns (a) competence in working with supervisees and consultees with respect to these diversity dimensions and (b) competence in helping those supervisees and consultees develop their own diversity-related competence. For example, the NASW Code of Ethics (2008, 3.01b) states, "Social workers who provide supervision or consultation are responsible for setting clear, appropriate, and culturally sensitive boundaries." The ACA Code of Ethics (2008, F.2.b) states, "Counseling supervisors are aware of and address the role of multiculturalism/diversity in the supervisory relationship." Multicultural competence includes not only knowledge of differences but also self-awareness of one's multiple identities and worldview and how privilege and oppression may affect interactions (see Bernard & Goodyear, 2014). The importance of multiculturally sensitive practice is such that consultants and supervisors should be prepared to address these issues in every session, as appropriate.

Supervisors should be proactive regarding ethical considerations related to competence factors in delegating work to others. In particular, they should do the following:

> (1) not delegate work to persons (i.e. to supervisees) who have a multiple relationship with those being served and that would likely lead to exploitation or loss of objectivity, and (2) authorize only those responsibilities that such persons can be expected to perform competently on the basis of their education, training, or experience, either independently or with the level of supervision being provided. (APA, 2010, 2.05)

Similarly, the AAMFT ethical standards (2015, 4.4) stipulate that "Marriage and family therapists do not permit students or supervisees to perform or to hold themselves out as competent to perform professional services beyond their training, level of experience, competence."

# MULTIPLE RELATIONSHIPS

The codes of ethics of the AAMFT (2015), ACA (2014), APA (2010), and NASW (2008) all limit multiple relationships (also called dual relationships) that may be harmful to supervisees, as well as conflicts of interest within supervisory relationships. For example, the AAMFT Code of Ethics states that

> Marriage and family therapists are aware of their influential positions with respect to supervisees, and they avoid exploiting the trust and dependency of such persons. Supervisors, therefore, make every effort to avoid conditions and multiple relationships with supervisees that could impair professional judgment or increase the risk of exploitation. Examples of such relationships include, but are not limited to, business or close personal relationships with supervisees or the supervisee's immediate family. When the risk of impairment or exploitation exists due to conditions or multiple roles, supervisors document the appropriate precautions taken. (AAMFT, 2015, 4.6)

The APA Code of Ethics states that the supervisor or consultant will

> refrain from taking on a professional role when personal, scientific, professional, legal, financial, or other interests or relationships could reasonably be expected to (1) impair their objectivity, competence or effectiveness in performing their functions as psychologists or (2) expose the person or organization with whom the professional relationship exists to harm or exploitation. (APA, 2010, 3.06)

Although this section will focus on supervision, we want to acknowledge that multiple relationships can present ethical challenges in consultation as well. Earlier in this chapter, we noted, for example, the loss of objectivity that occurs when the consultee is someone with whom one has an intimate relationship. Knapp et al. (2013) addressed this issue when they observed that individuals may consult with friends or spouses, but those individuals may be reluctant or hesitant to be critical and thus are of no consultative value; they state that "arm's length consultants are often best" (p. 197).

Multiple relationships exist when two people enact more than one set of roles with one another. This becomes ethically problematic when one party in that relationship is put at risk by virtue of those multiple roles. As a result, some multiple relationships are proscribed, with sexual relationships with either clients or those you are supervising being a case in point (AAMFT, 2015, 4.3; ACA, 2014, F.3.c; APA, 2010, 7.07). Moreover, because of the evaluative relationship, for a supervisor to make any sexual overture constitutes sexual harassment, which is both unethical and illegal (see Friedlander & Dubovi, 2015). Explicit overtures are one form of sexual harassment; other forms include telling dirty jokes, making sexualized comments, and using the power of the position in an intimidating and unwelcome fashion.

But not all multiple relationships are unethical or exploitative, and navigating the distinctions among them can be challenging. In fact, when clinicians are asked to describe ethics-related critical incidents they have encountered, multiple relationship–related incidents are the second most frequently reported incidents (after confidentiality-related incidents; Pettifor & Sawchuk, 2006). When dual or multiple relationships are unavoidable, the NASW code (2008, 1.06[c]) states that "social workers should take steps to protect clients and are responsible for setting clear, appropriate, and culturally sensitive boundaries."

Whereas psychotherapists and clients usually have no face-to-face interaction between sessions, supervisors and supervisees typically encounter each other throughout the workday. Moreover, supervisees in a private practice setting typically already will have earned a terminal degree and be very close to being licensed and, therefore, are in that way almost the supervisor's peer. These factors make supervision role boundaries more permeable than is the case in psychotherapy.

It is useful, therefore, to consider Gottlieb, Robinson, and Younggren's (2007) distinction between boundary *crossings* and boundary *violations* in supervision. The former are situations in which "a professional deviates from the strictest professional role but is not unethical per se" (p. 241) whereas the latter situations "reflect exploitation of the supervisee, a supervisor's loss of objectivity, disruption of the supervisory relationship, or the reasonable foreseeability of harm" (p. 241). Boundary crossings in supervision are not necessarily bad; in fact, Kozlowski, Pruitt, DeWalt, and Knox (2014) found supervisees to report positive effects such as enhanced quality of the supervisory relationship. Their respondents gave examples of boundary crossings they had encountered, including

> [the] supervisor discussed his own reaction to difficult clients. Supervisees also . . . reported socializing with supervisors, such as going to lunch with a supervisor . . . visiting a supervisor's home . . . receiving a gift from a supervisor, and . . . [having] received extra supervision (e.g. while sharing car rides on the way to co-lead a group). (p. 116)

Burian and Slimp (2000) offered a useful decision tree for supervisors to determine whether a particular multiple relationship is likely to move into the boundary violation range. It includes considering the extent to which the relationship will benefit the supervisee versus the supervisor, the impact of the possibly perceived preferential behavior toward one supervisee over others, and the setting in which the relationship occurs (e.g., work vs. social).

Several types of multiple relationships in a private practice setting warrant particular attention. One derives from the financial aspects of private practice. Most supervisors recognize that taking payment directly from supervisees (whom they will need to evaluate) constitutes a proscribed multiple relationship. But what of a private practice setting in which the supervisor will receive some portion of the income the supervisee generates? This raises a possible conflict of interest for the supervisor who needs to ensure that his or her objectivity in evaluating the supervisee is not compromised by the income that supervisee generates. And, of course, the supervisor in this case must work in compliance with the relevant regulations in his or her state or province. Supervisors must also ensure that they do not refer clients to the supervisee with the goal of "filling their schedule" (which results in more income being generated for the supervisor) but rather always prioritize client welfare and the developmental needs of the supervisee (AAMFT, 2015; ACA, 2014; APA, 2010; NASW, 2008).

A multiple relationship challenge also can emerge from helping supervisees to manage countertransference. In so doing, the supervisee's personal issues that underlie that countertransference can become the focus of attention, evoking what Frawley-O'Dea and Sarnat (2001) termed the "teach/treat issue." The same is true when working with supervisees who may experience vicarious traumatization as a result of their empathic engagement with traumatized clients and their graphic descriptions of trauma. A supervisory responsibility is to assist the supervisee to manage his or her responses, attending to a continuum of over-involvement to avoidance, and ensuring client and supervisee safety. However, psychotherapy is distinct from supervision and psychotherapy must not be provided by supervisors, as this would constitute a harmful dual relationship, which is prohibited by the AAMFT (2015), ACA (2014), APA (2010), and NASW (2008). If supervisors expect personal experience to be a part of supervision, they should inform the supervisee of that from the onset of supervision (APA, 2010, 7.04).

Earlier, we addressed the prohibition against entering into a sexual relationship with a supervisee. Supervisors should also refrain from supervising someone with whom they have a preexisting committed relationship or a familial relationship. For example, a father should not provide supervision to his son or daughter upon joining his practice. Similarly, a wife should not provide supervision to her husband who has newly entered the field. This will affect both supervision processes (e.g., what the supervisee is comfortable revealing about feelings and reactions toward clients) and the objectivity needed for the supervisor to exercise evaluative and gatekeeping responsibilities to the profession and the public. Although most states have regulations that preclude this type of supervisory multiple relationship, it is useful to be mindful of the ethical issues as well.

Finally, supervision is a teaching relationship, so it is important that the supervisor help supervisees recognize and manage the multiple relationships that can occur in their work with clients. This can be especially important for those who practice in a small town or when the supervisee and his or her clients belong to a particular community (e.g., religion, racial/ethnic group; Schank & Skovholt, 2006). Another seemingly mundane but important dual relationship occurs when seeking consultation from friends in the profession who will likely not be able to maintain sufficient objectivity.

# TECHNOLOGY-DELIVERED SUPERVISION AND CONSULTATION

The ethical demand for competence also includes competence in technologies used for supervision and consultation (see APA, 2013, 2015; Fouad et al., 2009). The ACA Code of Ethics (2014, F.2.c) states, "When using technology in supervision, counselor supervisors are competent in the use of those technologies." While some technologies are simple to use (e.g., the telephone or video camera), emerging technologies (e.g., the Internet, videoconference) can be complicated to master. Furthermore, defining and assessing competence can be thorny because technologies change and emerge frequently. This is especially important with respect to Internet-related competencies. Private practice clinicians also may use the Internet for peer consultations (individually or in groups), workshops, and webinars, and many use the Internet for communication or scheduling. This section will review the most important ethical issues in this area, emphasizing security and technological competence.

The same security and confidentiality challenges from online psychotherapy apply to supervision and consultation, but this medium also poses additional challenges in providing supervision. For example, if a client or trainee has an emergency, the supervisor may have to step in with knowledge of local resources and laws (e.g., Kanz, 2001). Also, if a supervisee is found not to be competent, the supervisor might have to step in and provide direct services to the client from a distance, over the Internet. For these reasons, it is recommended that supervisors and consultants providing services online become competent in telehealth best practices (e.g., Mallen, Vogel, & Rochlen, 2005).

The growth in the literature concerning online supervision and consultation has matched the growth of its practice. This prompted a joint task group of APA, ASPPB, and the APA Insurance Trust to develop the "Guidelines for the Practice of Telepsychology" (APA/ASPPB/APAIT Joint Task Force, 2013), which includes some attention to online supervision and consultation. Likewise, the ACA Code of Ethics (2014) includes a section (H) on "Distance Counseling, Technology, and Social Media," and the AAMFT Code of Ethics (2015) includes a section (6) on "Technology-Assisted Professional Services." More recently, Renfro-Michel, Rousmaniere, and Spinella (2015) reviewed 33 empirical studies on online supervision and consultation. The highlights of this literature will be discussed below.

## TECHNOLOGY ISSUES

Supervisors should develop clear procedures for technology use, including how and where they will store, backup, and delete data; security procedures; and methods to use in case of technological failure (e.g., Kanz, 2001). Supervisors should pay particular attention to the use of mobile devices, social software, and cloud computing, as these technologies pose greater risk to violations of client confidentiality (Devereaux & Gottlieb, 2012; Rousmaniere, 2014). Supervisors should use software that is compliant with the Health Information Portability and Accountability Act (HIPAA).

## SUPERVISION PROCESS ISSUES

It is particularly important for supervisors working online to have clearly defined procedures for client emergencies, for supervisees judged to not be competent, or for situations in which supervision must be terminated (e.g., Panos et al., 2002). Local backup supervisors should be identified in case of a client emergency, when supervisees need assistance when the supervisor cannot be reached, or when a matter arises that is beyond the supervisor's competency, such as local customs, laws, or regulations (e.g., Abbass et al., 2011). Supervisors should clarify which technologies should be used for contacting the supervisor in an emergency (e.g., phone, text, IM, or email) and how long supervisees should expect to wait for responses to non-emergency questions (Barnett, 2011; Kanz, 2001). This may be especially necessary when working with younger supervisees, who may be familiar with using text messaging as a primary method of communication and expect to receive instant responses to texts throughout the day (Rousmaniere, 2014). Supervisors should also clarify the confidentiality and privacy limits for various methods of electronic communications and should emphasize the importance of not using social media (e.g., Facebook, Twitter) to share confidential information (see below). We know of no products that automatically protect confidentiality; each must be set to do so or used in a way to achieve that goal.

A concern frequently raised about online supervision is the risk of harm to the supervisory working alliance due to limitations on subtle nonverbal communication when using videoconference, email, and text-chat (e.g., Sørlie, Gammon, Bergvik, & Sexton, 1999; Vaccaro & Lambie, 2007). However, empirical studies and anecdotal reports to date have found no difference between the modalities in the quality of the supervisory working alliance (Renfro-Michele et al., 2015). Nevertheless, supervisors using online supervision should remain alert for potential negative effects on the supervisory working alliance and should emphasize a collaborative approach to supervision within the hierarchy (Rousmaniere, 2014).

Panos et al. (2002) discussed the cultural challenges that may be posed by online supervision, when the supervisor may be geographically distant from the supervisee and client. Powell (2011), who provided supervision online to supervisees in Turkey, Singapore, Vietnam, and China and throughout the United States, recommended that supervisors stay alert for cultural cues or miscommunications. Panos et al. (2002) proposed the "triad model" where supervisees have two supervisors or consultants, one onsite who is well versed in local culture and one online.

## SECURITY, CONFIDENTIALITY, AND PRIVACY

We close this section with four best-practice recommendations for using technology for consultation and supervision:

1. Extra care should be exercised with supervision or consultation across state lines, as laws and regulations vary in many jurisdictions. See DeAngelis (2012) for more information.

2. Email listservs should be considered semipublic forums, even if they are closed or invite-only. If listservs are used for consultation, clinicians should use extra caution to remove all identifying client information and phrase emails in respectful language, with the understanding that clients may read them. There have been instances in which listserv postings are referred to in legal proceedings, so it should be assumed that a listserv is not a confidential forum.

3. Social media (e.g., Facebook, Twitter) should not be used for consultation and supervision, even when set to "private."

4. Identifying client information (e.g., notes, session videos) should always be stored encrypted and password-protected. When transporting clinical information, use self-encrypting drives. HIPAA-compliant software should be used for any communication (e.g., videoconference) of confidential information.

# BEST PRACTICES FOR COMMON DILEMMAS AND CHALLENGING SITUATIONS

Some ethical issues occur frequently in supervision and consultation (Fly, van Bark, Weinman, Kitchener, & Lang, 1997; Worthington, Tan, & Poulin, 2002). We describe nine of those here, responding to each with suggested best practices by the supervisor or consultant:

1. **Professional boundaries, including sexual and nonsexual boundaries.** *Situation:* The supervisee has invited her depressed client who seems lonely to have dinner on Saturday. *Best-practice considerations:* Supervisors use a supervision contract that provides clarity about client relationships and the priority of considering the impact on the client as opposed to the supervisee's intent (Knapp, 2013). Supervisors also address supervisee responses to clients and risk factors regarding boundaries (Bernard & Goodyear, 2014). Multiple relationships and sexual and romantic relationships are prohibited (ACA, 2013, A.5.a; APA, 2010, 3.05). Immediate and preemptive supervisor action is required to address this situation.

2. **Integrity and truthful self-representation.** *Situation:* You overhear your supervisee introducing himself as "Dr." although he is a predoctoral intern and has not earned his doctoral degree. *Best-practice considerations:* This behavior demonstrates lack of integrity and misrepresentation of level of competence (APA, 2010, Principle C and 2.01) as well as misrepresentation of professional identification (AAMFT, 2015, 9.4) and professional disclosure (ACA, 2014, F.5.c.). Immediate and preemptive supervisor action is required to address this.

3. **Failure to disclose clinical data or information that the supervisor views as essential.** *Situation:* The supervisee does not disclose a multiple relationship with a client (a cousin) or an error that she has made in the therapy. *Best-practice considerations:* Supervisors should clearly identify ethical standards for the profession and the learning value of errors (describing an error a supervisor made in clinical work and its value as a clinical teaching moment). At issue are integrity (integrity in relationship, fidelity and responsibility, and multiple relationships; APA, 2010, Principles B and C, 3.05; AAMFT, 2015, 1.3). When supervisors learn of such nondisclosures they should obtain sufficient information from the supervisee to determine the appropriate clinical decisions to be made and also explore factors that contributed to the nondisclosure. To the extent that the nondisclosures are related to the supervisory alliance, those need to be addressed.

4. **Failure to disclose countertransference or reactivity.** *Situation:* The supervisee does not disclose his intense emotional response to the client who reminds him of his parent. *Best-practice considerations:* Responsiveness to countertransference is an important supervision task, and a supervisee's failure to disclose results in inadequate supervision and potential harm to the client. Under Standard 7.04, Student Disclosure of Personal Information, of the APA Ethics Code (APA, 2010), the supervisor is required to inform the supervisee of the value of such disclosures before the

initiation of supervision and then, if such a nondisclosure is identified, to address it and the reasons that this information was withheld.

5. **Failure to disclose disagreement or perceived conflict with the supervisor or consultant.** *Situation:* The supervisee disagrees with a supervisory directive but does not express or otherwise address that disagreement. The result is a weakened alliance with the supervisor and greater withholding of information during sessions. *Best-practice considerations:* Relationship strains or conflict are normal in supervision but become problematic when they are unacknowledged or unresolved (Nelson, 2008). The supervision relationship suffers, with the potential both to disrupt supervisee learning and to put clients at risk (i.e., when the supervisee fails to disclose treatment-related information). Supervisors therefore should at the outset of their work with the supervisee or consultee invite open discussion of disagreements or conflict. They should also be diligent in obtaining the supervisee's or consultee's input on how well they are working together, and should respond nondefensively to supervisees' or consultees' reports of perceived conflict.

6. **Supervisees' misunderstandings about supervisor–supervisee confidentiality.** *Situation:* The supervisee disclosed to the supervisor he was getting a divorce, believing that the disclosure was confidential. He was incensed when he learned the supervisor had revealed this information to the training team during discussions of the supervisee's sudden competence decline. *Best-practice considerations:* Supervisees may believe that all personal disclosures to the supervisor are confidential, when in fact the supervisor's highest duty is protection of the client (AAMFT, 2015, 3.7; APA, 2014). The supervision contract should clarify limits of supervisor–supervisee confidentiality. This includes the supervisor's obligations to report the supervisee's progress in developing competence and any factors affecting that development to other members of the training team as well as educational institutions, licensure boards, and administrators.

7. **Supervisee responding to clients on the basis of stereotypes concerning race, gender, sexual orientation, or other characteristics.** *Situation:* In listening to recordings of therapy sessions, the supervisor notices a pattern of the supervisee making comments to female clients that reflected stereotypical beliefs about women's abilities, traits, or preferences (see Owen, Tao, & Rodolfa, 2010). *Best-practice considerations:* The supervisor is responsible to ensure both professionalism and multicultural competence for all diversity identities and to directly address the bias implicit in these microaggressions toward women (ACA, 2014, B.1.a). This requires both that supervisors model professionalism and multicultural competence and that they help supervisees recognize and address stereotypes that affect the quality of treatment they offer.

8. **Maintaining appropriate supervisor–supervisee boundaries: the case of social media.** *Situation:* Dr. Navarro, a regular user of Facebook, is notified by an email from Facebook of "several people you may know" with links next to each person that enable the recipient to click to "add a friend." One of the people on that list is her supervisee. *Best-practice considerations:* Because of the power differential, it is incumbent on supervisors to engage in reflective self-assessment, to ensure compliance with ethical standards, and

to be aware of guidelines for supervisor competence. The supervisor, for example, should never invite a supervisee to be a Facebook friend or send a friend request to a supervisee (see Birky & Collins, 2011, for a more complete discussion).

9. **Consultee's failure to obtain fully informed consent.** *Situation:* Your consultee, a licensed marriage and family therapist, discloses readily identifiable, personal, and confidential information about the client. You discover that the client has not been informed that the consultee is seeking your consultation and certainly has not given consent to reveal this type of information. *Best-practice considerations:* Informed consent is an essential component of consultation (AAFMT, 2015, 2.7). Consultants should ensure that it has occurred.

# CONCLUSION

Mental health professionals in private practice often will engage in the practice of consultation and supervision, which can be personally edifying to them and can provide an important service to the profession. For those who do, we recommend being conscientious about the difference between consultation and supervision and addressing the ethical issues pertaining to competence, multiple relationships, gatekeeping responsibilities, and technology. Knowledge of the ethics codes of the various professions under consultation or supervision, skills for ethical problem solving, and attitudes of openness and respectful process are all essential.

# REFERENCES

Abbass, A., Arthey, S., Elliott, J., Fedak, T., Nowoweiski, D., Markovski, J., & Nowoweiski, S. (2011). Web conference supervision for advanced psychotherapy training: A practical guide. *Psychotherapy, 48*, 109–119. doi:10.1037/a0022427

American Association for Marriage and Family Therapy. (2015). *Code of ethics.* Alexandria, VA: American Association for Marriage and Family Therapy.

American Counseling Association. (2014). *The 2014 ACA code of ethics.* Alexandria, VA: American Counseling Association.

American Psychological Association. (2010). Ethical principles of psychologists and code of conduct (2002, amended June 1, 2010). Retrieved from http://www.apa.org/ethics/code/index.aspx.

American Psychological Association. (2014) Guidelines for clinical supervision for health service psychologists. Retrieved from http://www.apa.org/about/policy/guidelines-supervision.pdf.

American Psychological Association. (2015a). Board of Professional Affairs advisory committee on colleague assistance. Professional health and well-being for psychologists. Retrieved from http://www.apapractice-central.org/ce/self-care/well-being.aspx.

American Psychological Association. (2015b). Guidelines for clinical supervision in health service psychology. *American Psychologist, 70*(1), 33–46. doi:10.1037/a0038112

American Psychological Association. (2015c). 2014: APA member profiles. Center for Workforce Studies, American Psychological Association. Retrieved from http://www.apa.org/workforce/publications/14-member/index.aspx?tab=2.

APA/ASPPB/APAIT Joint Task Force. (2013). Guidelines for the practice of telepsychology. Retrieved from http://www.asppb.net/?page=Telepsych.

Association of State and Provincial Psychology Boards. (2015a). ASPPB disciplinary data study. Retrieved from http://c.ymcdn.com/sites/www.asppb.net/resource/resmgr/DDS/DDS_Historical_Report_2014.pdf.

Association of State and Provincial Psychology Boards. (2015b). Supervision guidelines for education and training leading to licensure as a health service provider. Retrieved from http://c.ymcdn.com/sites/www.asppb.net/resource/resmgr/Guidelines/Final_Supervision_Guidelines.pdf?hhSearchTerms=%22supervision+and+guidelines%22.

Barnett, J. E. (2011). Utilizing technological innovations to enhance psychotherapy supervision, training, and outcomes. *Psychotherapy, 48*, 103–108. doi:10.1037/a0023381

Barnett, J. E., Baker, E. K., Elman, N. S., & Schoener, G. R. (2007). In pursuit of wellness: The self-care imperative. *Professional Psychology: Research and Practice, 38*(6), 603–612.

Barnett, J. E., & Molzon, C. H. (2014). Clinical supervision of psychotherapy: Essential ethics issues for supervisors and supervisees. *Journal of Clinical Psychology, 70*(11), 1051–61. doi:10.1002/jclp.22126

Belar, C. D., Brown, R. A., Hersch, L. E., Hornyak, L. M., Rozensky, R. H., Sheridan, E. P., . . . Reed, G. W. (2001). Self-assessment in clinical health psychology: A model for ethical expansion of practice. *Professional Psychology: Research and Practice, 32*, 135–141. doi:10.1037/0735-7028.32.2.135

Bernard, J. M., & Goodyear, R. K. (2014). *Fundamentals of clinical supervision* (5th ed.). Boston: Pearson.

Birky, I., & Collins, W. (2011). Facebook: Maintaining ethical practice in the cyberspace age. *Journal of College Student Psychotherapy, 25*(3), 193–203.

Board of Psychology, State of California. (2015). Supervision agreement. http://www.psychology.ca.gov/forms_pubs/sup_agreement.pdf

Borders, L. D., Glosoff, H. L., Welfare, L. E., Hays, D. G., DeKruyf, L., Fernando, D. M., & Page, B. (2014) Best practices in clinical supervision: Evolution of a counseling specialty. *The Clinical Supervisor, 33*(1), 26–44. doi:10.1080/07325223.2014.905225

Burian, B. K., & Slimp, A. O. C. (2000). Social dual-role relationships during internship: A decision-making model. *Professional Psychology: Research and Practice, 31*(3), 332–338. doi:10.1037//OT35-7028.31.3.332

Corey, G., Corey, M. S., Corey, C., & Callanan, P. (2015). *Issues and ethics in the helping professions* (9th ed.). Pacific Grove, CA: Brooks Cole.

DeAngelis, T. (2012). Practicing distance therapy, legally and ethically. *Monitor on Psychology, 43*, 52–53.

Devereaux, R. L., & Gottlieb, M. C. (2012). Record keeping in the cloud: Ethical considerations. *Professional Psychology: Research and Practice, 43*, 627–632. doi:10.1037/a0028268

Dolan, P., Edlin, R., Tsuchiya, A., & Wailoo, A. (2007). It ain't what you do, it's the way that you do it: Characteristics of procedural justice and their importance in social decision-making. *Journal of Economic Behavior and Organization, 64*(1), 157–170. doi:10.1016/j.jebo.2006.07.004

Elpers, K., & FitzGerald, E. A. (2013). Issues and challenges in gatekeeping: A framework for implementation. *Social Work Education, 32*(3), 286–300. doi:10.1080/02615479.2012.665867

Falender, C. A., & Shafranske, E. P. (2004). *Clinical supervision: A competency-based approach*. Washington, DC: American Psychological Association.

Fly, B. J., van Bark, W. P., Weinman, L., Kitchener, K. S., & Lang, P. R. (1997). Ethical transgressions of psychology graduate students: Critical incidents with implications for training. *Professional Psychology: Research and Practice, 28*(5), 492–495. doi:http://dx.doi.org/10.1037/0735-7028.28.5.492

Fouad, N. A., Grus, C. L., Hatcher, R. L., Kaslow, N. J., Hutchings, P. S., Madson, M. B., . . . Crossman, R. E. (2009). Competency benchmarks: A model for understanding and measuring competence in professional psychology across training levels. *Training and Education in Professional Psychology, 3*(4, Suppl), S5–S26. doi:10.1037/a0015832

Frawley-O'Dea, M. G., & Sarnat, J. E. (2001). *The supervisory relationship: A contemporary psychodynamic approach*. New York: Guilford Press.

Friedlander, M. L., & Dubovi, A. (2015, November). Sexual harassment in supervision. Retrieved from www.societyforpsychotherapy.org/sexual-harassment-in-supervision.

Goodyear, R. K., & Rodolfa, E. (2012). Negotiating the complex ethical terrain of clinical supervision. In S. J. Knapp, S. J., M. C. Gottlieb, M. M. Handelsman, & L. D. VandeCreek (Eds.), *APA handbook of ethics in psychology, Vol. 2: Practice, teaching, and research* (pp. 261–276). Washington, DC: American Psychological Association.

Gottlieb, M. C., Robinson, K., & Younggren, J. N. (2007). Multiple relations in supervision: Guidance for administrators, supervisors, and students. *Professional Psychology: Research and Practice, 38*, 241–247. doi:10.1037/0735-7028.38.3.241

Inman, A. G., & Ladany, N. (2014). Multicultural competencies in psychotherapy supervision. In F. T. L. Leong, L. Comas-Díaz, G. C. Nagayama Hall, V. C. McLoyd, & J. E. Trimble (Eds.), *APA handbook of multicultural psychology, Vol. 2: Applications and training* (pp. 643–658). Washington, DC: American Psychological Association.

Johnson, W. B., Elman, N. S., Forrest, L., Robiner, W. N., Rodolfa, E., & Schaffer, J. B. (2008). Addressing professional competence problems in trainees: Some ethical considerations. *Professional Psychology: Research and Practice, 39*(6), 589–599.

Kanz, J. E. (2001). Clinical-supervision.com: Issues in the provision of online supervision. *Professional Psychology: Research and Practice, 32*, 415–420. doi:10.1037/0735-7028.32.4.415

Knapp, S., Younggren, J. N., VandeCreek, L, Harris, E., & Martin, J. N. (2013). *Assessing and managing risk in psychological practice: An individualized approach* (2nd ed.). Rockville, MD: The Trust.

Koocher, G. P., Shafranske, E. P., & Falender, C. A. (2008). Addressing ethical and legal issues in clinical supervision. In C. A. Falender & E. P. Shafranske (Eds.), *Casebook for clinical supervision: A competency-based approach* (pp. 159–180). Washington, DC: American Psychological Association.

Kozlowski, J. M., Pruitt, N. T., DeWalt, T. A., & Knox, S. (2014). Can boundary crossings in clinical supervision be beneficial? *Counselling Psychology Quarterly, 27*(2), 109–126.

Ladany, N., Lehrman-Waterman, D., Molinaro, M., & Wolgast, B. (1999). Psychotherapy supervisor ethical practices adherence to guidelines, the supervisory working alliance, and supervisee satisfaction. *The Counseling Psychologist, 27*(3), 443–475.

Mallen, M. J., Vogel, D. L., & Rochlen, A. B. (2005). The practical aspects of online counseling: Ethics, training, technology, and competency. *Counseling Psychologist, 33*, 776–818. doi:10.1177/0011000005278625.2005

National Association of Social Workers. (2008). *Code of ethics.* Washington, DC: National Association of Social Workers.

National Association of Social Workers. (2013). Best practice standards in social work supervision. Retrieved from http://www.naswdc.org/practice/naswstandards/supervisionstandards2013.pdf.

Nelson, M. L. (2008, September). Conflict in supervision: Avoidable or useful? Retrieved from http://societyforpsychotherapy.org/conflict-in-supervision-avoidable-or-useful.

Owen, J., Tao, K., & Rodolfa, E. (2010). Microaggressions and women in short-term psychotherapy: Initial evidence. *The Counseling Psychologist, 38*, 923–946.

Panos, P. T., Panos, A., Cox, S. E., Roby, J. L., & Matheson, K. W. (2002). Ethical issues concerning the use of videoconferencing to supervise international social work field practicum students. *Journal of Social Work Education, 38*, 421–437. doi:10.1177/0020872805057095

Pettifor, J., McCarron, M. C. E., Schoepp, G., Stark, C., & Stewart, D. (2011). Ethical supervision in teaching, research, practice, and administration. *Canadian Psychology/Psychologie Canadienne, 52*, 198–205. doi:10.1037/a0024549

Pettifor, J. L., & Sawchuk, T. R. (2006). Psychologists' perceptions of ethically troubling incidents across international borders. *International Journal of Psychology, 41*(3), 216–225. doi:10.1080/00207590500343505

Pope, K. S., Tabachnick, B. G., & Keith-Spiegel, P. (1987). Ethics of practice: The beliefs and behaviors of psychologists as therapists. *American Psychologist, 42*(11), 993–1006.

Powell, D. (2011). Cyber supervision: Welcome to the 21st century. *Counselor, 1*, 12–14.

Renfro-Michel, E., Rousmaniere, T. G., & Spinella, L. (2015). Technological innovations in counselor supervision: promises and challenges. In T. G. Rousmaniere & E. Renfro-Michele (Eds.), *Using technology for clinical supervision: A practical handbook* (pp. 3–18). Alexandria, VA: American Counseling Association Press.

Rousmaniere, T. G. (2014). Using technology to enhance clinical supervision and training. In E. E. Watkins & D. Milne (Eds.), *International handbook of clinical supervision* (pp. 204–237). New York: Wiley Publishers.

Schank, J. A., & Skovholt, T. M. (2006). *Ethical practice in small communities: Challenges and rewards for psychologists*. Washington, DC: American Psychological Association.

Shaw, H. E., & Shaw, S. F. (2006). Critical ethical issues in online counseling: Assessing current practices with an ethical intent checklist. *Journal of Counseling & Development, 84*, 41–53. doi:10.1002/j.1556-6678.2006.tb00378.x

Smith, D. (2003). 10 ways practitioners can avoid frequent ethical pitfalls. *Monitor on Psychology, 34*(1), 50. Retrieved from http://www.apa.org/monitor/jan03/10ways.aspx33.

Sørlie, T., Gammon, D., Bergvik, S., & Sexton, H. (1999). Psychotherapy supervision face-to-face and by videoconferencing: A comparative study. *British Journal of Psychotherapy, 15*, 452–462. doi:10.1111/j.1752-0118.1999.tb00475.x

Strom-Gottfried, K. (2000). Ensuring ethical practice: An examination of NASW code violations, 1986–97. *Social Work, 45*, 251–261.

Thomas, J. T. (2010). *The ethical practice of supervision and consultation*. Washington, DC: American Psychological Association.

Vaccaro, N., & Lambie, G. W. (2007). Computer-based counselor-in-training supervision: Ethical and practical implications for counselor educators and supervisors. *Counselor Education & Supervision, 47*, 46–57. doi:10.1002/j.1556-6978.2007.tb00037.x

Vasquez, M. J. (2005). Independent practice settings and the multicultural guidelines. In M. G. Constantine & D. W. Sue (Eds.), *Strategies for building multicultural competence in mental health and educational settings* (pp. 91–108). New York: John Wiley & Sons.

Wallace, W. A., & Hall, D. L. (1996). *Psychological consultation: Perspectives and applications*. Pacific Grove, CA: Brooks/Cole.

Worthington, R., Tan, J., & Poulin, K. (2002). Ethically questionable behaviors among supervisees: An exploratory investigation. *Ethics and Behavior, 12*, 323–351.

# CHAPTER 36

# MALPRACTICE ISSUES FOR THE PRIVATE PRACTITIONER

*David L. Shapiro and Jeffrey N. Younggren*

hen we present workshops on professional liability, negligence, and risk management, a frequent question is "How do I keep from getting sued?" The most appropriate response in this age is "You can't." However, there is a vast difference between being sued and losing a lawsuit. There are several basic principles of risk management that, if carefully followed, can considerably reduce your risk of losing a lawsuit.

The mental health professions, over the past 20 years, have embraced a changed perspective on professional risk and risk management. At the time that the American Psychological Association Insurance Trust (APAIT) started its risk management programs, few clinicians thought in these terms. Litigation risks were low and many licensing boards exercised limited oversight over the conduct of those whom they licensed. This, however, has changed as a result of a variety of factors, including the growth of managed care, the more aggressive stance of many licensing boards, changes in the scope of professional identity, and increased attention to issues of medical malpractice. Some will argue that because the rate of successful malpractice suits is quite low, the concern about being sued is poorly placed and a waste of energy. However, the reality is that successfully defending yourself against even a frivolous complaint can be stressful, expensive, and time-consuming. The purpose of this chapter is to review the area of malpractice in the mental health fields and to offer ways to reduce the likelihood that legal action will be taken against a clinician or, if it is taken, will be successful.

Professional malpractice is called a "tort," a civil as opposed to a criminal wrong. In criminal cases, it is the government that brings charges against someone who allegedly has committed a crime. In civil cases, these actions are taken by one person or a group of individuals who allege that another individual or group of individuals have in some way harmed him, her, or them through their conduct. Malpractice is a special category of civil wrong, or tort, where the alleged negligent party is a professional and the issue focuses on professional misconduct. In these types of cases

·there exists what is called a "standard of care" for that profession, and the plaintiff (the person filing the suit) needs to prove in court that the professional (the defendant) deviated from the standard of care, and as a result of that deviation the plaintiff, or the plaintiff's legal representative, suffered some harm or injury. There is, however, more to these types of cases than this simple summary. To win this type of legal action the plaintiff must prove four things, often referred to as the "four D's of malpractice." The plaintiff in a malpractice action must prove that the professional had a duty to the person injured, that he or she breached or deviated from that duty, which in turn caused damages, and the damages were directly due to the deviation. Thus, the four D's are duty, deviation from the standard of practice, that directly causes damages. This may sound deceptively simple, but in fact each of the elements is quite complex.

For instance, in healthcare, a duty exists only when there is a professional relationship that creates a duty of care. As often as the concept of professional relationship is discussed, there is not a good, agreed-upon definition of exactly what it means or when such a relationship is established. Usually it refers to the time when the mental health professional agrees to treat someone. However, this raises lots of unanswered questions: Does a duty exist when the appointment is set up, or when the patient or client actually appears? Does it start when clients speak with administrative staff, or when they leave a message on a voice mail system? What about someone who talks to a suicidal person on a crisis hotline; is that a professional relationship? A number of cases have focused on whether or not the client perceives it as a professional relationship even though the practitioner never agreed to see the individual in psychotherapy. What complicates the "professional relationship issue" even more is the fact that, for the most part, only the person having a professional relationship with the health care provider, or the personal representative of that person, has the legal grounds to initiate a lawsuit. If the client is deceased, the executor/personal representative of the estate can file suit.

A duty of care might even extend to another professional who is actually a "collateral contact" in a matter of some sort. For example, this could include someone brought into a case to assist with the treatment. Does this "collateral" individual have a professional relationship and therefore a duty of care? The answer to this is "Yes." In the 1994 case of *Ramona v. Isabella et al.* the court found that this collateral duty did exist.

In 1989, Holly Ramona began seeing a marriage, family, and child counselor, Marche Isabella, in Irvine, California. Holly had an eating disorder and was told that 80% of persons with eating disorders had been sexually abused. When she started psychotherapy, she did not claim she had been sexually abused. After months of meetings with Isabella, often three or four times a week, Holly had a flashback of sexual abuse. In an effort at clarification, Holly was administered the drug sodium amytal by Richard Rose, MD, a collateral to her treatment, and was told that it would help her find the truth of whether she had been abused, even though there is no scientific evidence to support the claim. While under the influence of the drug, Holly recounted multiple episodes of abuse, although her descriptions were sketchy. As a consequence of the allegations of sexual abuse, Mr. Ramona (her father) lost his job as a senior administrator with a wine company. He subsequently sued Marche Isabella and others in a third-party action, including Dr. Rose, since he had participated in a psychotherapy session where Holly confronted her father with her recovered memories of abuse. The jury decided on a 10–2 vote that Marche Isabella, Dr. Richard Rose, chief of psychiatry at Western Medical Center in Anaheim, and the hospital were negligent in their treatment of Holly and that they owed a duty to Mr. Ramona. It awarded her father $500,000 in damages.

To further broaden the definition of duty, we have a limited number of cases in which the psychotherapist has been found to have an obligation to third parties to protect them from harm. Only when the clinician is regarded as having a "special relationship" with the patient (namely the ability to control his or her behavior) is the possible duty to protect third parties important. In the famous 1976 case *Tarasoff v. Regents of the University of California* the California Supreme Court ruled that when a psychotherapist's client makes a credible threat of harm to an identifiable third party the psychotherapist must take "reasonable steps to protect the intended victim against the harm" (17 Cal.3d at 350). According to the Court, "The protective privilege ends where the public peril begins" (at 425). Many critics of this ruling (e.g., Bersoff, 2012) argue that the extension of a "special relationship" to outpatient psychotherapy does not make any sense since we cannot control the behavior of someone whom we may see once weekly. In addition, the requirement frequently removes the psychotherapist as a threat-reduction agent from the picture because of the frequent dramatic and negative impact of such a report. Even in the landmark *Tarasoff* case Tarasoff's murderer never returned to psychotherapy after the report had been made. One can only speculate whether the murder could have been prevented if the murderer remained in treatment. Regardless, this landmark case clearly created a duty of care to people outside of the treatment setting.

# DUTY

Clearly, the creation of a duty is a complex dynamic and the degree of duty may differ depending on the nature of the relationship. Furthermore, these duties vary widely across jurisdictions, with some states describing the duty as mandatory, others as discretionary, others having no duty, and others referring to case law rather than statute. For instance, does a clinician providing a time-limited behavioral treatment for a specific phobia not have the same duty as a clinician providing long-term intensive psychodynamically oriented psychotherapy? It would appear that this is an important issue, but it generally is not addressed in the courts except on a case-by-case basis by the court.

The standard of care under which mental health professionals are supposed to operate is also far simpler in its definition than in actual practice. It essentially is defined as the level of care of the average or relatively prudent professional, or sometimes as the level of skill and care possessed by other members of the profession in the same or similar circumstances. How does one define this level of skill and care? Certainly, practicing in accord with the Code of Ethics (Ethical Principles of Psychologists and Code of Conduct, APA, 2010) and related Specialty Guidelines (Specialty Guidelines for Forensic Psychology, APA, 2012) for various disciplines such as forensic psychology, neuropsychology, and custody evaluations is necessary but not sufficient. It must also include an incorporation of the use of the best-validated assessment instruments, and the level of contemporary knowledge in a particular field. One of the problems here is that different groups will define the current state of knowledge differently depending on their theoretical orientation. Therefore, a behavior therapist would not be called upon to judge the appropriateness or adequacy of a psychodynamic treatment approach. Various schools of thought are acknowledged, and even those that constitute a "respectable minority" are acknowledged to have their own standards. But how do we define respectable minority? Generally, if there is peer-reviewed literature supporting a particular approach, it can be called a "respectable minority," but even some approaches that have no scientific basis (such as Thought Field Therapy or crystal therapy) have their adherents who publish papers in their own journals. Should these groups be given "respectable minority" status?

Another problem with defining the standard of care is found in the concept of "under the same or similar circumstances." A number of years ago, the standard of care was described in terms of a "locality rule," so that depending on the locale the standard of care would be different (e.g., a metropolitan as opposed to a rural area). This has given way to more of a national notion, where, because of the profusion of continuing education, the Internet, and other media sources, even people in rural areas are expected to have the same basic knowledge as people in cities, recognizing, of course, that resources may not be as available in a rural as in an urban area and, consequently, all things are still not equal.

## DEVIATION FROM DUTY

The second "D" is dereliction of duty, sometimes also called deviation from the standard of care. In this, the mental health professional must fail to exercise the reasonable and ordinary skill and care possessed by other practitioners in the same field. Here there must be evidence of reliance on customary practice. In addition, this deviation can be an act either of omission or commission; that is, the practitioner failed to do something that an average skilled practitioner would do under the same circumstance, or did something that the average practitioner would not have done. Since there is so much disagreement about what constitutes "customary practice," this element is often left up to the "battle of the experts" in court, with one side contending that there was a deviation from the standard of care and another saying that there was not. In theory, a mental health professional who can demonstrate adherence to the standard of care should be found not negligent, even if the outcome is poor. However, according to Stromberg (1988) this is often not the case: When a particularly tragic outcome occurs, juries may want to blame someone and hold someone responsible, and they may find the psychotherapist negligent even if he or she has adhered to the standard of care.

An excellent example of this is found in the 1983 case *Davis v. Lhim*. In this case, a young man, while high on hallucinogenic drugs, had stated to a staff member in a hospital emergency department that sometimes he wants to kill his mother when she will not give him money for drugs. As soon as the drug was out of his system he went into full remission, had appropriate visits with his mother, and in fact was placed on convalescent leave a few months later. Approximately 18 months later, he decompensated and was pointing a shotgun at the "voices" that were tormenting him. His mother tried to take the gun away, but it discharged accidentally, killing her. Another family member sued the hospital and the doctor in charge (Dr. Lhim) and retained the services of a psychiatrist who testified that the one isolated comment in the emergency department 18 months earlier should have alerted the staff to the inappropriate nature of their decision to place him on convalescent leave. The jury found in favor of the plaintiff despite the fact that the testimony of the plaintiff's expert had no correspondence to the limited ability we have to predict violent behavior, especially 18 months into the future. This case and others like it highlight the need for clinicians to develop well-defined standards of care for work in different specialty areas. Some have contended that developing these standards of care will make it easier for an aggressive attorney to "strangle us" with our own standards. However, as illustrated by this case, when there are no well-defined standards of care, the expert witnesses make them up, and unless the triers of fact are knowledgeable or sophisticated, they may accept as plausible the fact that a prediction of future violent behavior can be based on one statement 18 months earlier.

## DAMAGES

The third "D" is damages—that is, there must be a measurable damage sustained by the plaintiff secondary to the violation of the standard of practice. These often are defined in two ways: economic (cost of healthcare, loss of earnings, and loss of earning potential) and noneconomic. In the former case, the plaintiff will bring into court an expert statistician or actuary who will predict into the future the plaintiff's wage-earning capacity given the harm or injury sustained, as opposed to the plaintiff's wage-earning capacity had he or she not been injured. Noneconomic damages often include physical and mental pain and suffering, loss of ability to enjoy life (sometimes called hedonic damages), and loss of function caused by the defendant's negligence. There has been a great deal of controversy surrounding these noneconomic damages regarding the amount of money awarded for vague complaints of pain and suffering. As a result, some states, as part of what has been called "tort reform," have artificially capped noneconomic damages at a certain dollar amount.

What we have been describing is called compensatory damages, or compensation for some loss. In some cases, though it is rare in negligence, there may also be an award of punitive or exemplary damages, which is an award given over and above the compensatory award in order to punish the defendant or make an example of him or her. These are usually found only where the behavior is extremely deviant from any accepted standard of care, such as having sexual relationships with a client.

## DIRECT CAUSE

The final element that the plaintiff must demonstrate is that the deviation from the standard of care was the direct cause of the damage, sometimes called the proximate cause. Absent the deviation from the standard of care the harm or injury would not have occurred. This is sometimes called a "but for" test. It does not necessarily mean that the dereliction is the sole cause of the injury, but that it is a substantial factor in the causation process. The damage must also be one that is reasonably foreseeable by the defendant, and not caused by an intervening event that breaks the chain of causation.

On occasion, the defendant will argue that there is contributory negligence, that the plaintiff himself or herself contributed to the unfortunate outcome by failure, for instance, to follow the treatment plan. In most states, if this contribution of the client is accepted, the jury will subtract out the portion of the damages contributed by the plaintiff from the total damage; this is sometimes called comparative negligence. In a few states, if any contributory negligence is found the case essentially is wiped out and the plaintiff cannot recoup any damages.

The level of proof required in these cases in order to sustain a claim is called the "preponderance of evidence." This essentially means "slightly more certain than not." In other words, each of the four elements described here must be proven by the plaintiff by a preponderance of the evidence.

The suit must also be filed within the statute of limitations for a particular jurisdiction (usually two or three years) after the plaintiff has been injured. In certain cases, where the plaintiff's condition prevents him or her from realizing that he or she has been injured, the statute of limitations starts when he or she becomes aware of the harm or injury.

# OTHER TYPES OF TORT ACTIONS

What we have been describing up to this point are the criteria for most of the forms of malpractice claims that are found; these are called "negligent torts." Negligence is essentially some harm or injury that comes about as a result of the practitioner doing something that an average or relatively prudent practitioner would not have done, or failing to do something that an average or relatively prudent practitioner would have done, given the same or similar circumstances. There are, however, two other kinds of malpractice actions, though admittedly they are rare when it comes to mental health professionals.

## INTENTIONAL TORTS

In an intentional tort, the wrong is knowingly and purposefully done. This does not mean that the practitioner actually intended to harm the patient, but rather that he or she knew or should have known that the action or conduct could cause harm. The most frequent example of an intentional tort is one filed as a result of a psychotherapist being involved in sexual relations with a client. Interestingly, not all intentional acts are excluded from coverage by malpractice carriers. While criminal acts, a type of intentional act, are excluded, other types of intentional acts, like giving a gun back to a suicidal client, are covered. In general, professional conduct is usually not covered by insurance for fraudulent, criminal, malicious, or materially dishonest acts or materially dishonest omissions, nor is it covered for conduct expected or intended to cause physical injury or property damage (The Trust, 2013). It would be wise for clinicians to check with their respective insurance carrier for policy exclusions, since all policies differ.

## RECKLESS TORT

Another form of tort action comes from what is called reckless conduct, which is regarded as the conscious disregard of a known risk. *West's Encyclopedia of American Law*, second edition (2008) (The Gale Group), notes that "To be reckless, conduct must demonstrate indifference to consequences under circumstances involving peril to the life or safety of others." The two important elements here are that the risk must be known at the time that the service is being rendered, and that there was a deliberate action to minimize or deny the risk. A good example is that there were several claims of reckless behavior against medical professionals during the 1960s by attorneys representing patients who had been given, during the 1950s, large doses of psychotropic medications and had later developed symptoms of tardive dyskinesia. The cases were summarily dismissed because at the time the medication was being prescribed, in the 1950s, tardive dyskinesia was not a known risk. Subsequent psychopharmacological research demonstrated a link between some antipsychotic medications and tardive dyskinesia, and subsequent cases filed in the 1980s resulted in successful pursuit of these tort claims.

### WHAT IS CONSCIOUS DISREGARD?

The second element that creates professional liability difficulties is called "conscious disregard." However, risk from conscious disregard is mitigated when a psychotherapist demonstrates that there has been a carefully crafted informed consent document, talking about the risk and benefits of the treatment, discussed with the client, understood by that individual, and voluntarily agreed to by the client. With such a signed document in the records, the psychotherapist cannot be said to have consciously disregarded the risks associated with that procedure.

# FREQUENT AREAS OF MALPRACTICE LITIGATION

It is difficult to get an accurate picture of which areas of practice are at higher risk of malpractice claims than are others. This is because professional conduct that is described in one way in a particular set of cases is described differently in others. For example, claims of "loss from evaluation" (e.g., losing a job due to an unfavorable psychological evaluation) may in other statistics be broken down into "fitness for duty," child custody, or some other type of claim. What follows will be a more generic discussion of major areas of malpractice risk.

### NEGLIGENT DIAGNOSIS

Negligent diagnosis is not merely a misdiagnosis; anyone can miss a diagnosis. In fact, several well-trained professionals may see the same patient as suffering from different disorders. Negligent diagnosis is something different: It refers to failure to make a proper diagnosis because one has not followed accepted standards in doing the evaluation. For instance, let us consider the case of a psychologist who is examining a client who says he is grieving the loss of his wife. He is depressed and is also complaining of severe headaches. The psychologist concludes that the headaches are due to unresolved grief and never performs a neuropsychological screening or refers the patient to a medical professional for follow-up. The patient later dies from a brain tumor that was not diagnosed because of the failure to do a complete evaluation. This would arguably be an example of diagnostic negligence.

In another case, on which one of us (DS) consulted, a woman presented to a psychologist with complaints of depression, nausea, and loss of appetite. She asked whether she should have an examination by her primary care physician, and the psychologist told her it was not necessary because the nausea and loss of appetite were symptoms related to depression. He commenced a treatment program of cognitive-behavioral therapy, which she attended for about three months. Then she missed several sessions, and when he called to find out why she had been missing sessions, her husband told him she had been admitted to the hospital and soon thereafter died. The diagnosis related to the cause of death was Hodgkin disease. The psychologist was sued for negligent diagnosis because he had failed to refer the patient to a medical doctor who could have evaluated her and properly diagnosed the illness.

Another area of diagnostic negligence occurs when psychologists fail to use psychological tests in the manner they should be according to the professional manual, interpret the testing in ways inconsistent with interpretive guidelines, or use the tests on groups on whom the tests have not been validated, all of which lead to inaccurate conclusions about the person being assessed.

## CASE 1

A psychologist was screening a young man who wanted to undergo gender reassignment surgery. The clinic that performed the surgery needed to have a psychological assessment before clearing a candidate for surgery to rule out the presence of any serious mental illness. The psychologist conducted a clinical interview and administered the Rorschach test; however, having been trained a number of years ago, he did not do a formal scoring of the test and his report indicated that there was no evidence of a psychosis, and the young man was cleared psychologically for surgery. As he was being prepped for surgery, the young man panicked, ran out of the clinic, and returned home. He later sued the psychologist, alleging that he had coerced the patient into the surgery. While there was no evidence of this coercion, the fact that the psychologist had failed to formally score the test according to current standards of practice made his whole practice seem suspect. In fact, when the testing was formally scored, it did reveal many evidences of psychotic thinking, further exposing the psychologist to claims of misdiagnosis.

## CASE 2

A psychologist had developed a reputation for "rescuing abused children" by testifying, based on an MMPI-2 profile, that the father was a pedophile. He claimed in sworn testimony that he reached this determination by using "the only known psychological test for lying"; therefore, if the person's score was elevated on this scale, it meant that he was lying when he said he did not molest his child. The scale in question was the L scale on the MMPI-2. People familiar with the MMPI and MMPI-2 know that this scale is not a measure of lying but rather a measure of extreme social desirability: The person denies, in a naïve way, such items as ever laughing at a dirty joke. This was a flagrant misuse of the scoring rules for the test, basically making up an interpretation that does not appear in the professional manual or in any literature about the test. This conduct could easily raise claims of misdiagnosis.

## NEGLIGENT RELEASE

Negligent release deals primarily with cases where a patient is prematurely discharged from a hospital before an adequate treatment program has been completed or when the patient needs continued care. Frequently these types of decisions are based on economic grounds and not on successful completion of treatment. In some cases the insurance coverage has run out and the hospital covers itself by saying the patient has received maximum hospital benefits. While economics is a reality in the healthcare world, and healthcare decisions frequently involve issues of cost, decisions made solely on economic grounds and contrary to the needs of a patient are arguably acts of professional negligence. Consider the following case.

A man was admitted to a private psychiatric hospital after having assaulted his wife on several occasions. After she told him to leave and told him she was planning to file for divorce, he made a serious suicide attempt. The initial authorization for hospitalization by the insurance company was for two weeks, though it clearly stated that if, at the end of that period, he remained a danger to himself or others, the hospital could request an extension. During this period of time he received individual and group psychotherapy and was placed on antidepressant medication. There was no evidence from a subsequent review of the record that a formal risk assessment for violence to others or danger to self was ever completed. When the two weeks ended he was discharged, with the hospital not requesting additional hospitalization or considering transferring him to another facility for continued treatment. After discharge, the client stalked his wife, followed her automobile, forced her off the side of a mountain road, and subsequently was arrested for attempted murder. When his wife recovered from her injuries, she successfully sued the hospital for negligent release.

## SUICIDE

The fact that a client commits suicide does not, in and of itself, lead to a conclusion that the psychotherapist was negligent. Rather, negligence is determined only if the suicide was reasonably foreseeable and if the psychotherapist failed to act to reduce that risk in some way. How does one determine reasonable foreseeability? There needs to be a formal assessment of the person's potential for suicide; it really does not matter which one is used (and there are many) but rather that it is a well-validated assessment, and that the practitioner carefully explores all of the parameters listed on the instrument. One particularly important matter is to look carefully at patients' history, not only of actual suicide attempts but of what is sometimes referred to as passive suicide, such as driving erratically, or driving under the influence of drugs or alcohol, or provoking police into shooting them (sometimes called "suicide by cop"). History is always important because the best predictor of future behavior is past behavior, and a history of past suicide attempts is a serious risk factor that must be assessed (Joiner, 2011). At high risk for missing this important dimension are psychotherapists who are unfamiliar with the assessment of suicidal risk and who fail to conduct themselves in a fashion consistent with prevailing professional standards for dealing with a suicidal client. For example, especially at risk for a malpractice suit are those clinicians who contend that history is irrelevant, that they only deal with the here and now, and that they are only concerned with the ongoing interaction between themselves and the client.

Of course, merely asking clients in a cursory manner whether they are planning to hurt themselves is inadequate, and any adequate assessment must include evaluating whether a suicidal patient has a suicidal plan and intent. Finally, some psychotherapists like to take comfort in what they call a "do no harm" contract, which they get the client to sign. Legally, these are not worth the paper they are written on, for, in the case of a suicide, questions will be asked about how the psychotherapist evaluated the competence of the client to sign the contract, whether in fact it was truly voluntary on the part of the client, and finally whether sufficient information was given to the client regarding the nature of the procedure, the role of the examiner or therapist, and the applicable limits of confidentiality, in order that the client could make an autonomous decision whether or not to participate. There is also no information in the relevant literature that these contracts have any efficacy in reducing suicidal behavior.

## SEXUAL MISCONDUCT

While, as we have noted before, this is most often regarded as an intentional tort, and therefore not covered by most malpractice carriers, a few points about sexual misconduct with clients are worth making. First, even though sexual contact with a client is clearly unethical, it does not necessarily mean that it will yield a finding of liability against the psychotherapist. Consider the case of Douglas Carmichael, a well-known psychotherapist in the Washington, DC area during the 1970s. Dr. Carmichael was treating a woman with whom he later commenced a sexual relationship, and eventually married. Subsequently, marital problems developed, and Mrs. Carmichael not only filed for divorce but also sued Dr. Carmichael for psychological damages caused by his having had an affair with her while she was his client (*Carmichael v. Carmichael*). She contended that her psychological distress was proximately caused by the affair. Dr. Carmichael's defense was that his wife had had serious psychological problems beforehand (given that was why he started seeing her in psychotherapy) and that, as a matter of law, her psychological damages could not be related exclusively to the sexual misconduct. The jury found in favor of Dr. Carmichael, deciding that while what he did was unethical, it could not be considered malpractice because the wife's psychological damages could not be attributed exclusively to the unethical behavior.

Prior to the 1992 APA Ethics Code, there was no consideration in the code of sexual relations with former clients; it was merely assumed that a therapeutic relationship existed in perpetuity. Several psychotherapists in fact sued their state boards for revoking their licenses after they had sexual relationships with former clients. The boards contended that the therapeutic relationship existed forever, but these clinicians contended that this was merely an interpretation, that it was good public policy, rather than actually being a part of the ethics code or law. The courts agreed, stating that the public policy argument was legally insufficient, and ordered that the boards reinstate the licenses of these psychotherapists. In response, several of the states then added the concept of the therapeutic relationship existing in perpetuity to their licensing law, raising a slew of new problems to include legal rights to consortium.

In 1992 APA took the formal position that no sexual relationships could be entered into with clients or former clients for at least two years after termination (though there was no empirical research that substantiated the two-year rule). In addition, the psychotherapist had to bear the burden of proving that there was absolutely no evidence of exploitation and no evidence that the psychotherapy was terminated in order to pursue a sexual relationship. Of course, it could be argued that this really is a prohibition without it being called a prohibition, because a former client could well say that she was exploited, and it would be difficult, in the face of this, for the psychotherapist to prove that there was no exploitation. Jokingly, this has led to some attorneys stating that sex with former clients is fine as long as everything works out and everybody stays happy. However, if the relationship falls apart, any defense of the previous sexual behavior being acceptable professionally becomes problematic.

## INJURIES DUE TO NONTRADITIONAL PSYCHOTHERAPIES

This area is not one where there are many cases, but when they do occur, they are somewhat dramatic, frequently attract attention, and deserve some discussion here. In these cases, the assertion is that the psychotherapist embarked on a new, innovative, or untested therapy, and as a result, the client suffered harm. The landmark case here is *Hammer v. Rosen*. Dr. John Rosen was a very charismatic psychiatrist/psychoanalyst who contended that he had developed what he called "direct analytic therapy" in which he would talk directly to the unconscious of psychotic patients by interpreting symbolic, very primitive material. Rosen's theory was that after establishing trust at a very primitive level, the psychotherapist could gradually draw the patient out of his or her psychosis and more into reality. There was, of course, not a shred of research evidence to support this hypothesis. Hammer was a patient of Dr. Rosen's whom Dr. Rosen beat on several occasions during her treatment. Hammer signed discharge papers and then sued Dr. Rosen. Dr. Rosen tried unsuccessfully to demonstrate to the judge that within the framework of direct analytic therapy, it was acceptable to beat a patient.

In another case, Betty Grove Eisner was a psychologist who graduated from a prominent academic institution who developed her own technique called "blasting." "Blasting" was a technique in which a client was encouraged to release hostility by yelling while muffled by a washcloth. In 1976, one of Eisner's clients died following mineral bath treatment and blasting therapy. A wrongful death investigation ensued, as well an ethics investigation by the APA. The Psychology Examining Committee of the California Board of Medical Quality Assurance revoked Eisner's license to practice in 1978 (http://socialarchive.iath.virginia.edu/ark:/99166/w6qr7snm). Clearly "blasting" was seen as negligent on Dr. Eisner's part.

Less dramatic but equally problematic issues arose over such fringe therapies as Rolfing (intense physical massage), Primal Scream Therapy, Thought Field Therapy, crystal therapy, and nude hot tub marathons. While the best advice is to avoid these unusual therapies, if one chooses to use them or anything close to them, it is important to make sure there is a complete and comprehensive informed consent to the treatment, detailing all the risks and benefits. Also, psychotherapists should keep in mind that a client can consent to an illegal act.

## FAILURE TO OBTAIN INFORMED CONSENT

While informed consent has been briefly discussed already, it is worth more comment because, despite many books and articles being written about it, it is still an area that practitioners fail to completely understand. On the one hand they fail to do it at all, or, on the other hand, they have a legal document so complex that most clients would not be able to understand it. Models of excellent informed consent documents are available from The Trust (http://www.trustinsurance.com/resources/download-documents), as well as monographs that place informed consent in the forefront of basic principles of risk management (the others being documentation and consultation).

Basically, an informed consent document should deal with the parameters of the intervention (psychotherapy or assessment), limits of confidentiality, issues of referral and consultation, and, if there are specific mandatory reporting requirements established through state and federal law, the inclusion of these. If there are other needs, such as periodic reports to a judge or to school districts, for example, these must be included as well. One area that psychotherapists often forget is the need to spell out alternative forms of treatment so the client can make an autonomous choice of approaches. An excellent illustration of this was the 1985 case *Osheroff v. Chestnut Lodge Hospital*. Dr. Osheroff voluntarily admitted himself to Chestnut Lodge Hospital, a very well-known prestigious, private psychoanalytically oriented hospital in a suburb of Washington, DC for the treatment of depression. Dr. Osheroff was told that the mode of treatment would be intensive psychodynamically oriented therapy but was apparently not told that the hospital did not believe in or use medication, or that if he just wanted relief of his depressive symptoms, he could seek a practitioner outside the hospital who would prescribe such medication. After months of treatment Dr. Osheroff signed himself out of the hospital and eventually contacted a psychiatrist, who prescribed medication for him. His depression was relieved within three weeks. He then sued Chestnut Lodge for failure to provide him with this necessary adjunctive treatment. The hospital argued, in its defense, that as a hospital policy, they did not prescribe medication. The court found in favor of Dr. Osheroff, noting that the hospital should have informed the patient of alternative forms of treatment that were available. It is important to note that the fact that medication was seen as a mainstream intervention among psychiatrists, contrary to the policy of Chestnut Lodge, also drove the allegations of negligence. Some psychologists have misinterpreted this case as the court telling psychologists that they must use medication. That is not the importance of the case; rather, it centers around the issue of informed consent and the failure to tell the client about alternative forms of treatment that may be available.

# BREACH OF CONFIDENTIALITY

While confidentiality issues frequently are involved in malpractice cases, various laws create certain exceptions to confidentiality that make this topic in mental health practice confusing and difficult to navigate. Exceptions to confidentiality are many and include, but are not limited to, mandatory reporting of suspected child abuse and neglect, situations involving the need for involuntary commitment, in certain states the duty to protect third parties, when clients put their mental state at issue in litigation, and, in a few states, a criminal defense exception. Problems occur, however, when clinicians do not understand or misinterpret the law; given that few clinicians are also attorneys, this is fairly common and understandable. This makes legal and/or ethical consultation extremely important when one is contemplating violating confidentiality, and practitioners must be familiar with legal mandates that require violating a client's confidence. What is important to remember is that in the case of mandated reporting, good faith reports are immune from civil litigation, truly a safe harbor for worried professionals.

So, what should a practitioner consider when confronted with a mandated report or a potential violation of client confidentiality? Under most circumstances, clinical judgment must be the primary factor, avoiding the need for "knee jerk" responses. Some would argue that mandatory reporting of child abuse trumps this clinical discretion, but even then we must use some clinical judgment in reaching an opinion as to whether there is reasonable suspicion of abuse. When the situation and the law permits, careful consideration of the issues at hand, along with documentation of those considerations and consultation, is a great defense against an allegation of violating confidentiality. Of course, some clinicians argue that even though laws mandate such reporting, the reporting will have a negative impact on the therapeutic relationship, and for that reason they are reluctant to report. Of course, as in any situation where there are conflicting ethical and legal demands, well-documented consultation with colleagues is essential. While failure to report is not a malpractice issue, it is a crime, if it is proven to be "willful" failure to report. Consider the following case.

Mrs. H had been in treatment with Dr. A for some period of time. She frequently displayed a rather volatile temper in psychotherapy sessions, making a variety of verbal threats, which Dr. A, in his own assessment, merely took as "blowing off steam." She had never acted on any of the threats; thus, his clinical judgment was that she would not act out on them in the future. On one occasion, Mrs. H stated that she was being harassed at work, and if the harassment did not stop, she intended to "blow up the whole factory." Dr. A had no documentation of any reason that this occasion seemed any different from those in the past, but on this occasion he chose to breach confidentiality and notified the factory that Mrs. H was planning to blow up the factory, indicating that state law mandated that he do so. In fact, at the time, there was no law in that state mandating a duty to warn and Dr. A was confused about his exact duty. The supervisors at the factory subsequently terminated Mrs. H's employment. She filed suit against Dr. A for breach of confidentiality and won the lawsuit. The central point here, apart from the fact that the law did not require this type of warning, was that Dr. A mistakenly believed that he had to abandon his clinical judgment and make this report. This case example is a good illustration of the fact that even in cases where there is a duty to warn, the law does not require that clinicians abandon their judgment. There was in fact no compelling reason for the breach of confidentiality.

## ABANDONMENT

There are ethical standards that prohibit abandoning clients and a requirement that usually termination be done thoughtfully and responsibly, making referrals as appropriate and carefully documenting the reasons for termination. While there is much worry about abandonment leading to civil action, in fact there is not a single case of a successful abandonment case being brought against a mental health practitioner in the United States (Younggren & Gottlieb, 2008). That said, clinicians would be well advised to make sure that they use good risk management when considering terminating clients against their will. First, psychologists should familiarize themselves with Standard 10.10 of the Ethics Code (and social workers 1.16 of the National Association of Social Workers Ethics Code; marriage and family therapists 1.11 of the American Association for Marriage and Family Therapy Ethics Code, and counselors A.11 of the American Counseling Association Ethics Code). Interestingly, these codes allow for the termination of clients under a variety of reasons, including misconduct on the part of clients themselves. For example, in the well-known 1990 case *Ensworth v. Mullvain*, Heather Ensworth was a psychologist treating Cynthia Mullvain. Mullvain began to engage in a series of boundary violations, including stalking and threatening Dr. Ensworth. Dr. Ensworth subsequently terminated her. This resulted in a civil action taken by Mullvain that wound its way up to the appellate court for a variety of reasons. The appellate court, however, upheld Dr. Ensworth's conduct, which included getting a restraining order against Mullvain, because Mullvain had engaged in conduct that was threatening and arguably a violation of Dr. Ensworth's rights.

## DUTY TO WARN/PROTECT THIRD PARTIES

As mentioned previously, this is a broad area that is highly misunderstood. Some research by a doctoral student (Leedy, 1989) revealed the somewhat amazing finding that many licensed psychologists (93%) did not even understand the duty to warn/protect laws in their own states. A subsequent similar study (Pabian et al., 2009) revealed that the percentage of licensed psychologists who did not understand the law had dropped to about 76%, but that is still a high number. What is vital here is that licensed clinicians must be familiar with the statutes of their own state and just their own state. Since these laws differ from state to state, one must be careful not to get them mixed up and apply the law of one jurisdiction to another. For example, while in California after *Ewing v. Goldstein* (2004) psychologists arguably have a duty to warn based on hearsay, such a provision does not apply in Texas, where the duty is unclear.

As noted earlier, despite a popular misperception that this type of litigation is widespread, in fact such cases are relatively rare. Of course, the impetus for the duty to protect and/or warn came from the 1974 ruling in *Tarasoff* that when a psychotherapist reasonably believes that a client poses a threat of bodily harm to an identifiable third party, the psychotherapist has to take reasonable steps to warn the intended victim about such violence. In the original case the psychologist did notify the authorities of the threat and they did evaluate Prosenjit Poddar, who later murdered Tatiana Tarasoff. What is important to note here is that there has to be a "reasonable belief" that the threat will be carried out. This reasonable belief, of course, must be based on clinical judgment based on an assessment that meets current standards of care for risk assessment. Once again, the clinical judgment is central; it should not be, as noted before, a knee-jerk response to a seemingly threatening statement; some degree of assessment based on clinical judgment must be included. In fact, *Tarasoff* even notes that clinicians are not expected to do anything different than they normally do, assessing the situation carefully and choosing an appropriate course of action, based on the assessment. In fact, if the assessment leads to a specific intervention, and it turns out the psychotherapist was wrong, that does not mean that the clinician was negligent. The case noted that proof aided by hindsight that the clinician judged wrongly is insufficient to establish negligence; there must have been a deviation from the standard of care in the assessment or in the implementation of a treatment plan that logically derives from that assessment.

In fact, this case, which was in fact the second *Tarasoff* case, broadened the earlier cause for action, which was called a "duty to warn," to a "duty to protect" third parties. In so doing, the court acknowledged that there could be many interventions in addition to warning; while the court did not specifically comment on these alternatives, many have written about alternatives, such as placing the client on medication, changing medication, increasing the number of psychotherapy hours, giving the client your cellphone number, voluntary or involuntary hospitalization, and, as a last resort, notifying the intended victim or the police. It is interesting that while several dozen duty-to-protect cases have been reported in the case law, many of them reflect a flexibility, recognizing the need for clinical discretion, questioning the ability of psychotherapists to accurately predict future violence, and also questioning the ability of psychotherapists to control the behavior of their clients.

While these cases have been reported, in fact, in actual practice, the law favors overprotection; it leans in the direction of encouraging false positives in order to protect the intended victim. In other words, if clinical judgment turns out to be wrong, the law does not want to hear from the practitioner who bases her or his lack of warning or protection on such beliefs. We need to find a "happy medium" between warning all of the time and "dying with our clinical judgment on." Equally important is to know the law in your own jurisdiction. Currently, 22 states have mandatory duty-to-warn statutes, while 19 jurisdictions have a permissive "may warn" statute that also gives clinicians other options based on their clinical judgment. Four states have no statutory duty to warn but have imposed it through case law. Six jurisdictions have not clarified the law, either through statute or case law, and three jurisdictions either limit the duty or foreclose it (Werth et al., 2009).

## DEFENSES IN MALPRACTICE ACTIONS

There are several defenses of malpractice allegations that need to be discussed, but the overriding principle is the same as we have discussed before: Do good clinical work, document it well, seek consultation from trusted colleagues, and make sure that there is a clear, well-crafted informed consent to whatever the intervention one proposes to use. This is simply good risk management (Knapp, Younggren, VandeCreek, Harris, & Martin, 2013).

With the above in mind, anyone who is concerned about being the subject of a malpractice claim must consider various defenses. Here the elements of malpractice law provide some guidance and the worried professional must answer the following: First, is there a professional relationship? With the exception of the situations noted above (when the client is a minor or mentally incompetent, when the client is deceased, or when there is a situation in which, due to a "special relationship," there is an obligation to protect third parties) usually only the person who has the professional relationship with the practitioner has legal standing to file a malpractice complaint. Make sure that the boundaries of a professional relationship are well documented, and if you have referred the client to another professional, make sure that is documented as well. If there is a gap in time between the initial contact and the setting up of an appointment, make sure that there is a mutual understanding whether or not the patient/client can contact you or a colleague in case of an emergency.

Second, if there is a professional relationship, what is the standard of care that characterizes that relationship? What do the Code of Ethics and other relevant professional standards and guidelines tell us about what the proper procedures are in a given area? What does the recent research and professional literature tell us about the "state of the art" in a given specialty? Make sure that your assessment or treatment protocol conforms to these suggestions. If there are differences from standard practice in the way you approach a particular intervention, make sure to document the reasons you are departing from these accepted practices. Be mindful of the concept "under the same or similar circumstances"; if there are geographic location or other factors that prevent you from doing what is necessary, document that as well.

Third, if you deviate from the accepted standard of care, ask yourself whether it is just a difference of opinion or a difference in professional judgment. If so, document the reasons for the different opinion or approach. You need to demonstrate that you are aware of the "standard of care" and that what you are doing that may appear to be different is a carefully thought-out alternative.

Fourth, if is there a harm or injury to the client or former client (though this may be more of a legal determination) be prepared to consult with an attorney about these issues. Remember, harm is a required component of a civil suit, since without it the civil arena is not the forum for the resolution of the matter.

Proximate cause and direct causation are complicated legal concepts. They require us to look at the contributions of our professional approach and the relevant past history and behavior that might be expected of a client with a particular diagnosis. We need to examine each of these areas in an objective manner. If there is a harm or injury alleged, is there anything in the treatment approach that might have led to or exacerbated injuries? Was there similar behavior (e.g., suicide attempts) in the past, and if so, did your treatment plan address it?

This leads to an important final consideration, what is called "contributory negligence." The law recognizes that if the client has "contributed" to the unfortunate outcome in some way, usually by failing to follow the treatment plan, he or she has "contributed" to the outcome. In most states, however, the damages are "apportioned," with the judge or jury determining what percentage of the damage can be attributed to a client's noncompliance with the treatment plan and what percentage can be attributed to negligence on the part of the psychotherapist. There is then a subtraction of that part contributed by the client from the total in determining the final amount of damages. This issue makes it critical for psychotherapists to document not only progress in treatment but also every instance in which the client has failed to comply with the treatment program. Therefore, if a psychotherapist refers the client for a medication evaluation and the person does not go, or does go but fails to take the medication, that needs to be carefully documented.

## SOME CLOSING WORDS OF ADVICE

In addition, be aware of state rules and regulations, professional ethics codes and standards, and any updates to these documents. There are certain situations and/or clients that pose a higher risk of malpractice suits; be aware of these and take extra precautions to manage them. Be aware, for instance, that child custody evaluations lead to a disproportionately high number of complaints, as do complaints from individuals with borderline personality pathology.

Practitioners should develop and nurture good relationships with clients and their families; all too often, in the details of malpractice suits, there will be mention by the client or their family of the cold or distant attitude on the part of the practitioner. If a client hurts or kills himself or herself, you should offer support to the grieving family; if a defendant has an unfortunate outcome in court, be receptive to communications from the family.

In addition, we need to re-emphasize the importance of well-documented records. These need to be contemporaneous with the contact with the client. Do not under any circumstances attempt to alter a record after the fact; no matter how well documented the rest of the record is, altering the record will cast a "web of suspicion" over the remainder of the record, if it is examined in a particular case. When there are such allegations of negligence, the entire record may come under scrutiny. The Health Insurance Portability and Accountability Act (HIPAA), of course, makes provisions for the maintenance of a separate set of private notes that it calls "psychotherapy" notes. However, not even these records are immune from legal discovery when professional negligence is alleged.

Finally, and most importantly, if you are sued, contact your malpractice insurance carrier and retain the services of a competent attorney who has experience in dealing with mental health torts. Sometimes the insurance carrier will refer you to an attorney, and on other occasions you may try to retain an attorney on your own, and make sure they are acceptable to the company. Do not under any circumstance attempt to resolve a case yourself, and do not interact with the complaining party without the approval of legal counsel. What is good here is that usually your malpractice carrier will provide such an attorney to you at no cost and, until you are competently represented in the matter, you should do nothing.

In summary, the best defense against malpractice is to do careful, well-documented clinical work, along with careful consideration of informed consent and consultation with colleagues, and practice with warmth, genuineness, and empathy.

## REFERENCES

American Psychological Association. (2010). Ethical principles of psychologists and code of conduct. Retrieved from http://www.apa.org/ethics/code/index.aspx

American Psychological Association. (2013). Specialty guidelines for forensic psychology, *American Psychologist, 68*(1), 7–19. doi:10.1037/a0029889

Bersoff, D. (2012). *Tarasoff*: An Example of Bad Law. Paper presented at the Division 42 Forensic Conference, May 2012, Miami, Florida.

*Carmichael v. Carmichael*, 597A.2d 1326 (1991).

*Davis v. Lhim*, 422 NW 2d. 688, Mich Ct.App. 1983.

*Ensworth v. Mullvain*, No. B043890, Second Dist., Div. Three, Oct. 24, 1990.

*Ewing v. Goldstein*, 15 Cal. Rptr. 3d 864, 867 (Ct. App. 2004).

*Hammer v. Rosen*, 7 App. Div. 2d 216, 181 N.Y.S.2d 805 (1959), modified, 7 N.Y.2d 376, 165 N.E.2d 756

Joiner, T. (2011). *Myths about suicide* (reprint ed.). Cambridge, MA: Harvard University Press.

Knapp, S., Younggren, J., VandeCreek, L., Harris, E., & Martin, J. (2013). *Assessing and managing risk in psychological practice: An individualized approach* (2nd ed.). Rockville, MD: The Trust.

Leedy, S.(1989). Clinician's knowledge of the duty to warn, unpublished dissertation.

*Osheroff v. Chestnut Lodge, Inc.*, 62 Md. App. 519 (1985).

Pabian et al. (2009). Psychologists' knowledge of their states' laws pertaining to Tarasoff –situations. *Professional Psychology: Research and Practice, 40*, 8–14.

*Ramona v. Isabella, et al.*, Superior Court of California, County of Napa, Case No. C61898, 1994.

Stromberg, C. (1988). *The psychologist's legal handbook*. Washington, DC: National Register of Health Service Providers in Psychology.

*Tarasoff v. Regents of the University of California*, 551 P.2d 334 (1976).

The Trust, Psychologists Professional Liability Policy, ACE. (2007). http://www.trustinsurance.com/resources/download-documents.

Werth, J. T., Welfel, E. R., & Benjamin, G. A. (2009). The Duty to Protect: Ethical, Legal, and Professional Considerations for Mental Health Professionals Washington, DC: American Psychological Association, ISBN 978-1-4338-0412-0. $69.95 doi: 10.1037/a0017409

West's Encyclopedia of American Law, 2nd ed. (2008).

Younggren, J., & Gottlieb, M. C. (2008). Termination and abandonment: History, risk, and risk management. *Professional Psychology: Research and Practice, 39*, 498–504.

# CHAPTER 37

# HIPAA 101 FOR THE PRIVATE PRACTITIONER

*Lorna Hecker*

Mental health practitioners are typically well versed in client confidentiality but are often less familiar with electronic security of client information. Clients, however, are rightfully concerned about the security of their treatment information. Both identity theft and medical identity theft have increased in recent years (Federal Trade Commission [FTC], 2007). Identity theft occurs when personal data such as Social Security numbers and bank or credit card numbers are lost or stolen and used for economic gain (U.S. Department of Justice, 2015). Medical identity theft occurs when health insurance information is used to procure medical and/or mental health services, potentially leaving a victim with someone else's treatment bills as well as treatment records with someone else's health information, diagnosis, and treatment. Identity and health insurance information may also be used to obtain government benefits and housing (FTC, 2007). Additionally, loss of private client information can have a negative impact on the relationship between the client and practitioner.

In response to these concerns, the Health Insurance Portability and Accountability Act of 1996 (HIPAA) was enacted. HIPAA helps to ensure each practitioner's commitment to client privacy by outlining specific safeguards to secure oral, written, and electronic health data. Most mental health practitioners who are covered entities under HIPAA will typically find that their state confidentiality laws are stricter than HIPAA and should be followed when that is the case. "Stricter" means that the law gives clients greater privacy rights or rights to access their protected health information (PHI). HIPAA also has stringent security regulations about digital data that must be followed; state law may or may not address this issue.

This chapter summarizes some of the more salient aspects of HIPAA compliance of which practitioners should be aware. Issues related to HIPAA privacy and security regulations will be discussed, along with additional regulations that have increased clients' privacy rights, increased fines and penalties for noncompliance, and established rules for notification of clients if their health data are considered breached. Because of the depth of HIPAA regulations, aiding the reader with full compliance efforts is well beyond the scope of this chapter. However, additional resources are provided at the end of the chapter for readers who want to learn more about HIPAA requirements and how to comply with them. Further, this chapter should not be used as a substitute for legal and risk management advice.

## HISTORY AND PURPOSES OF HIPAA

HIPAA has two general purposes: to guarantee that an individual can maintain health insurance between jobs (i.e., portability) and to ensure the privacy of client health information (i.e., accountability). It was under Title II of HIPAA, Administrative Simplification, that the privacy and security regulations were established. The *privacy rule* requires safeguards to protect individually identifiable client health information, termed *protected health information* (PHI). PHI is "any health information that can be used to identify a patient which relates to physical or mental health, relating to a past, present, or future condition, and includes both living and deceased patients" (45 CFR §160.103, 1996). HIPAA gives clients certain rights and establishes limits on the uses and disclosures of PHI. The *security rule* protects an individual's electronic PHI (ePHI). In 2009, the Health Information Technology for Economic and Clinical Health Act (HITECH) was enacted, which increased restrictions of disclosure of PHI, increased clients' rights over their PHI, and increased fines and penalties for HIPAA violations. HITECH also brought resources to the U.S. Department of Health and Human Services (HHS) to enable it to conduct increased compliance audits of healthcare practitioners and facilities.

HIPAA regulations are set by HHS with enforcement through the Office for Civil Rights (OCR). There are over 2,000 pages of HIPAA and HITECH regulations; suffice it to say that practitioners who believe that a Notice of Privacy Practices and "HIPAA compliant" software fulfill their HIPAA requirements are misinformed.

## CONSEQUENCES OF BREACH OF PHI

There is no such thing as "HIPAA compliant," as many vendors promise. Instead, a practitioner needs to manage ongoing compliance with the HIPAA regulations consistently over time. Civil monetary penalties for noncompliance range from $100 to $1.5 million (per violation). Ignoring the regulations is considered willful neglect, which increases the fines and penalties. Criminal monetary penalties can range from $50,000 to $250,000, when health information is wrongfully disclosed under false pretenses and with malicious intent. Criminal penalties can also include a sentence of between one and 10 years in prison.

A *breach* is an impermissible acquisition, use, access, and/or disclosure of PHI that compromises the security of PHI. The most common reason for a breach of PHI is theft of unencrypted portable computing devices such as laptops, tablets, and smartphones (Ponemon, 2014). However, hacking and other unauthorized online access to PHI are responsible for the largest data breaches; the largest to date occurred when Anthem Blue Cross Blue Shield suffered a breach of over 80 million records (Redspin, 2015). Mental health professionals suffer breaches as well:

- A nonprofit community mental health center in Indiana lost the health data of 45,000 clients after several laptops were stolen from its offices (Databreaches.net, 2015).
- A psychology service provider in South Carolina had a laptop stolen that included both psychological records and child custody evaluations (Health Privacy Project, 2003).
- A community mental health service in Alaska failed to patch its data systems, ran outdated software, and had a breach of 2,743 records (HHS, n.d., a).

Fines can be severe:

- A health plan returned multiple photocopiers to a leasing agent without erasing the data on the hard drives and was fined $1,215,780 (HHS, n.d., b).
- An employee at a government agency in Alaska had a USB drive stolen from a vehicle, and the agency, after failing to take corrective action, was subsequently fined $1.7 million (HHS, n.d., c).

Penalties have included prison time. A physician in Los Angeles was fired and yet read records of several high-profile celebrities and his supervisor. He was sentenced to four months in prison and fined $2,000 (Dimick, 2010).

Affected individuals must be notified of each breach without unreasonable delay and no later than 60 days following the discovery of the breach. Breaches of less than 500 records must be reported to HHS within 60 calendar days of the end of the calendar year in which the breach was discovered; individuals are notified without unreasonable delay if it is determined their PHI is at risk. Breaches of 500 records or more must also be reported to media serving the state or jurisdiction without unreasonable delay, and no later than 60 days following the discovery of the breach. Breaches of 500 records or more are posted on the HHS website, colloquially known as the "Wall of Shame." HIPAA does not provide for a private cause of action for violations, though state attorney generals can bring suit for violations. Additionally, mental health practitioners may be subject to state consumer protection laws, state breach statutes, and/or accrediting body sanctions.

HIPAA is becoming the standard of care for the healthcare professions (Hecker & Edwards, 2014) and lawsuits have started using HIPAA as the standard of care for privacy and security of client/patient information. An example related to mental health is the 2006 case of *Acosta v. Byrum* in North Carolina, when psychiatric and other medical records were improperly accessed and released during a custody case. It seems clear that not only is HIPAA compliance a law, but it also outlines ethical obligations and defines solid risk management practices.

# COVERED ENTITIES AND BUSINESS ASSOCIATES

If a practitioner furnishes, bills, or receives payment for healthcare in the normal course of business, and any transactions are sent in electronic form, the practice is considered a covered entity under HIPAA (this does not include faxing). Covered entities must be compliant with both the HIPAA privacy and security regulations. If an entity or organization creates, receives, maintains, or transmits PHI on behalf of that entity it is considered a business associate; business associates are required to be compliant with only the security regulations. Examples of business associates include billing services, attorneys, accountants, claims processors, and so on. When entities do not directly handle PHI, they are not considered a business associate. For example, landlords and janitorial services do not handle PHI and would not fall under the business associate designation. Any PHI that these individuals would see would be limited to what is considered "incidental use," which is not considered a violation of the regulations.

Covered entities are responsible for obtaining satisfactory assurances from a business associate that it too is meeting the requirements of HIPAA (a subcontractor of a business associate is also required to be compliant). Covered entities are required to have a privacy official in place. The privacy official oversees compliance with the privacy regulations and handles client privacy complaints. In a solo mental health practice, the clinician also may function in that role and needs to document the steps taken to ensure compliance. Business associates are not required to have a privacy official.

Covered entities must have business associate agreements in place with their business associates; the content of the contracts is specified within the regulation Examples of business associate agreements can be found at www.hhs.gov. The contracts aid the covered entity in obtaining satisfactory assurances that the business associate will appropriately safeguard PHI. Covered entities are liable for breaches by their business associates. Business associates who use subcontractors (a person or entity to whom a business associate delegates a function, activity, or service) must also have written contracts in place to ensure compliance by the subcontractor. Business associates are responsible for breaches by their subcontractors.

# NOTICE OF PRIVACY PRACTICES

Nearly everyone is familiar with the Notice of Privacy Practices (NPP) required by HIPAA. Covered entities must provide the NPP or make it available to clients who ask for it. The NPP educates clients about how their PHI will be used and disclosed. With some state exceptions, PHI may be released without an authorization for treatment, payment, and healthcare operations. Commonly, mental health practitioners use a "boilerplate" NPP and fail to integrate state law. Typically, mental health state laws are stricter than HIPAA; there is nothing that precludes practitioners from integrating stricter state law into their NPP. Many state laws, however, do allow release for treatment, payment, and healthcare operations; in these cases state law and the privacy rule coincide. All states and HIPAA allow release of some information during an emergency or life-threatening event.

Nuances of the NPP are not always recognized. For example, not every practitioner stays abreast of the regulation and knows when the NPP needs to be revised and redistributed. At the time of this writing, the latest iteration of the NPP was 2013, but many practitioners have NPPs reflecting the earlier compliance date of 2009 (HHS provides listservs on both privacy and security regulations). Clients should be asked to sign an acknowledgment that they received an NPP; some practitioners put this "acknowledge" statement in their informed consent. If a client refuses to sign the acknowledgment, practitioners may not refuse to see the client solely for this reason (the laws apply whether or not the client acknowledges them). The NPP must be written in "plain English." Additionally, the NPP must be prominently posted in a practice and must be available on a practice's website. Examples of NPPs are available at www.hhs.gov, but applicable state law must be integrated into the document.

# PSYCHOTHERAPY NOTES

HIPAA provides federally established protection for psychotherapy notes. However, while practitioners gather much information about clients, only a small portion of that information is federally protected. Psychotherapy notes are considered deserving of special protection; they are defined as follows:

> notes recorded (in any medium) by a health care provider who is a mental health professional documenting or analyzing the contents of conversation during a private counseling session or a group, joint, or family counseling session and that are separated from the rest of the individual's medical record. (CFR §164.501)

They are to be kept separate from the medical (i.e., case) record and cannot be used to substantiate billing.

## DEFINING PSYCHOTHERAPY NOTES

Psychotherapy notes include the practitioner's impression of the client, include details of the psychotherapy session inappropriate for the medical record, are solely for the use of the practitioner (e.g., for planning future sessions), and are kept separate to limit access (including in electronic records). They must be kept in a separate location from the medical record in order for them to qualify for special protection under HIPAA regulations, with access only by the practitioner or possibly a supervisor, depending on the practice. Psychotherapy notes are not offered heightened protection in the following two situations: (1) if a client requests a release of psychotherapy notes to another party, the psychotherapy notes are not afforded special protection under HIPAA regulations once they are released, and (2) testing does not qualify for heightened protections. If a practice is part of an integrated health network and session notes are routinely shared with others in the network, they are not considered "psychotherapy notes"; they must be maintained and used only for the originator of the notes, with few exceptions.

## LIMITATIONS ON RELEASE
## OF PSYCHOTHERAPY NOTES

Clients may request access to their psychotherapy notes, but the notes do not need to be shared with clients unless required by state law. The decision to deny the psychotherapy notes is not appealable. HHS does not require psychotherapy notes be kept, but if done so clients must sign an authorization for their release. Information that does not fall under the heading of psychotherapy notes, and thus is not afforded a higher level of protection under the privacy rule, includes the following:

- Summary information, such as the current state of the client
- Summary of the theme of the psychotherapy session
- Medications prescribed and side effects
- Current state of the client
- Treatment plan, symptoms, and progress
- Diagnoses and prognosis
- Counseling session start and stop times
- Modalities and frequencies of treatment furnished
- Results of clinical tests
- Any other information necessary for treatment or payment.

Practitioners may recognize these exceptions to compose what is commonly referred to as "progress notes," while the HIPAA term "psychotherapy notes" is most closely akin to "process notes."

A third-party payer may have access to this general treatment information but is not privy to the more private psychotherapy notes of the provider. The privacy rule does not mandate that psychotherapy notes be kept. This means that any information besides psychotherapy notes may be disclosed without a signed authorization from the client; clients acknowledge this fact in the NPP. Psychotherapy notes are the only (mental health) information that requires an authorization for release according to HIPAA. There is no requirement in the HIPAA regulations that practitioners keep psychotherapy notes, though state laws may differ, and all state laws relevant to the release of records should be followed.

# PERSONAL REPRESENTATIVES

Individuals and their personal representatives may access their medical records (excluding psychotherapy notes). Personal representatives are those persons legally authorized to act on behalf of the client regarding health information. Unless there are more stringent state laws that limit access, parents or legal guardians do have access to the treatment records of minors (excluding psychotherapy notes) under HIPAA regulations. All practitioners should be familiar with local statutes (or seek competent legal and risk management input) when it comes to minors (and also the deceased) so that confidential information is not inadvertently released.

# AUTHORIZATIONS

There are specific elements that must be included in an authorization to release psychotherapy notes. Authorizations need to include the following:

- Specific description of health information to be disclosed
- Name of the person or organization authorized to release the information
- Name of the person authorized to receive the information
- Description of each purpose of the requested disclosure
- Expiration date or event
- Signature of the client or legal representative
- Statement that the client has the right to revoke the authorization, in writing,
- Statement that the client's treatment or payment may not be conditioned on his or her permission to release private information
- Statement of the potential for redisclosure of the information by the recipient

The form must be written in plain language.

State law may require additional elements in an authorization, such as requiring original signatures on documentation. Authorizations are prohibited if the expiration date has passed, the form has not been filled out correctly, it has been revoked, or the practitioner knows the form is false.

# STATE LAW AND HIPAA

HIPAA provides a floor of privacy protection but defers to state law that is more protective of clients' privacy. This means that a state law that provides more privacy protections for a client, or a law that gives the client greater access to her or his PHI, preempts HIPAA (with few legal exceptions). For example, state law may give clients access to their psychotherapy notes; this would preempt HIPAA and allow clients to have access to their notes.

# USE AND DISCLOSURE OF PHI IN MENTAL HEALTH PRACTICE

Under HIPAA, there is a regulatory difference between use and disclosure of PHI. *Use* includes the sharing, application, utilization, examination, or analysis of PHI within a covered entity or business associate. *Disclosure* refers to the release, transfer, provision of, access to, or divulging PHI in any other manner to any outside entity. The privacy regulations detail both uses and disclosures of PHI.

Practitioners may use and disclose PHI to other providers involved in a client's care without an authorization when it is for treatment, payment, and healthcare operations, but not about the specific content of their psychotherapy notes (unless the practitioner has the client's written authorization). This means that as a covered entity summary information, including the current state of the client, treatment plan, symptoms, progress, diagnoses, and so forth, can be shared with others involved in a client's treatment, payment, and healthcare operations (e.g., credentialing audits). While HIPAA allows sharing of patient information (not including psychotherapy notes), state law may be more prohibitive about sharing PHI, though many state have statutes that allow client information to be shared for these purposes (Hecker, 2016).

## MINIMUM NECESSARY STANDARD

Generally, any disclosure of information that is not for treatment, payment, or healthcare operations requires an authorization. When sharing information pursuant to an authorization, the information shared must be the minimum necessary to accomplish the intended purpose unless the disclosure is to the individual himself or herself, pursuant to a client's authorization, to another treatment provider, to HHS during an investigation, or other legally sanctioned disclosures. The minimum necessary standard specifies that PHI should not be used or disclosed when it is not necessary to satisfy a particular purpose or carry out a function. The minimum necessary standard also applies to sharing of information within an organization. For example, receptionists should not have access to a client's entire record; presumably they need only enough information to facilitate scheduling and similar transactions.

## WHEN PSYCHOTHERAPY NOTES MAY BE DISCLOSED WITHOUT AN AUTHORIZATION

There are a few exceptions whereby psychotherapy notes can be disclosed without authorization under the regulations. These include the following:

- For your own training or supervision
- For defense in legal proceedings brought by the individual
- For HHS to investigate or determine the covered entity's compliance with the privacy rules
- To avert a serious and imminent threat to public health or safety (e.g., abuse reporting, "duty to warn," "duty to protect")
- To a health oversight agency for lawful oversight of the originator of the psychotherapy notes
- For the lawful activities of a coroner or medical examiner or as required by law

Practitioners must manage different types of disclosures of PHI, some governed by HIPAA, some by state law, and some by a professional's code of ethics. Practitioners typically obtain a "release of Information" to disclose PHI to others outside the treatment team; state law often governs this practice. Under HIPAA regulations, a signed authorization for release of information is not needed to divulge psychotherapy information for purposes of treatment, payment, and health-care operations. This is considered "use" of PHI; clients are informed of this potential use in the NPP with the exception of psychotherapy notes, for which a HIPAA-compliant authorization is needed. Practitioners are required to give clients a NPP and attempt to obtain their signature acknowledging receipt of the notice. HIPAA does not prevent a practitioner from establishing a policy on disclosures that would otherwise be allowed under HIPAA regulations. More stringent state law or references to professional codes of ethics that give greater privacy protection or rights can and should be included in the NPP.

## ACCOUNTING OF DISCLOSURES

Clients may request an accounting of disclosures, which gives them a record of unauthorized disclosures of their PHI covering the prior six years to the date of the request. Unauthorized disclosures are disclosures made for reasons other than treatment, payment, and healthcare operations or regulatory mandated disclosures. These include disclosures about reports of abuse, neglect, or domestic violence, health oversight activities (e.g., Medicaid/Medicare audits), judicial or administrative proceedings (e.g., subpoenas, court orders), law enforcement disclosures, and disclosures required or permitted by law (e.g., workers' compensation), as well as other types of disclosures typically less applicable to mental health practitioners. Accounting of disclosures excludes treatment, payment, and healthcare operations information, as well as information released to the individual or his or her personal representative for healthcare or payment for healthcare, or information that is pursuant to a signed authorization, among others. An organization's information technology professionals can aid in setting up an accounting of disclosures for electronic records; a paper logging of disclosures suffices for paper records. In the future, HHS intends to include treatment, payment, and healthcare operations information in the accounting of disclosures in electronic health records. This will be referred to as an "access report" and excludes paper records (HIPAA Privacy Rule Accounting of Disclosures, 2011). At the time of this writing, it has not yet been implemented.

# SECURITY SAFEGUARDS

The privacy rule covers written or oral PHI; the security rule covers ePHI. The security rule aids in safeguarding the confidentiality, integrity, and availability of ePHI. Under the security rule, there are three types of safeguards to PHI: administrative, physical, and technical. These regulations may be accessed at www.hhs.gov. There are 54 safeguards and implementation specifications. Some are "required," and some are "addressable." "Addressable" means that a covered entity or business associate may take into consideration its size, capabilities, and the costs of the security measures. Smaller practices are not required to implement the same security measures as larger entities if the cost is prohibitive. If a practice decides not to institute an "addressable" implementation specification, the reason for not implementing the specification must be documented and kept on file for use if HHS conducts an audit of the practice or facility.

## ADMINISTRATIVE SAFEGUARDS

Administrative safeguards are administrative actions, policies, and procedures protecting PHI. These include issues such as a security management process, workforce security, information access management, and security incident procedures, among others. Each covered entity and business associate must assign a security official to oversee compliance with the security regulations. A practitioner's security official may be the same person as the privacy official, but this need not be the case. A sanction policy must be in place that details consequences if workforce members violate the privacy and security regulations. The "workforce" includes all persons who conduct work for a covered entity and is under the direct control of the covered entity, typically including management, employees, volunteers, and trainees. Regular security training for all members of the workforce is a requirement under the regulations.

## PHYSICAL SAFEGUARDS

Physical safeguards are the physical measures, policies, and procedures put in place to protect ePHI from natural and environmental hazards and unauthorized intrusion. These include facility access controls, a facility security plan, access control and validation procedures, device and media controls, and data backup and storage, among others. Contingency plans must be in place to safeguard PHI in the event of an environmental threat, such as a flood or fire, or human threat, such as vandalism.

## TECHNICAL SAFEGUARDS

Technical safeguards are policies and procedures to control access to ePHI. These include unique user identification, emergency access procedures, automatic logoff on computing devices, and encryption and decryption. Encryption is one of the most cost-effective ways to protect ePHI. Further, if a portable device is lost or stolen that is encrypted, it qualifies for a "safe harbor exemption," which means that the breach does not need to be reported to the client or HHS.

## POLICIES AND PROCEDURES

Policies and procedures on the security standards are required and must be available to the pertinent workforce members, with updates as needed when there are specific changes to a practice such as relocation or changes in specific procedures. While HIPAA regulations do not address social media platforms, due to the risk of breach from this type of media, practitioners are strongly encouraged to include policies regarding the use of social media for the workforce, with sanctions clearly stated.

## DOCUMENTATION

Documentation of HIPAA compliance efforts must be stored for six years (or longer, depending upon state statute). For example, when HIPAA training occurs, sign-in sheets and training materials must be kept for this six-year period. It is helpful if all privacy and security documents note an enactment and/or revision date to aid in compliance efforts, as well as audits (Hecker, 2016).

# SECURITY RISK ASSESSMENT

A large part of safeguarding PHI is the security risk assessment, which is the foundation of all HIPAA compliance efforts. In this process a covered entity must evaluate all potential threats to PHI and ePHI (in the administrative, physical, and technical areas), determine the likelihood and impact of the threats, and then prioritize the threats from high to low. The HIPAA risk management implementation specification requires covered entities and business associates to implement security measures sufficient to reduce risks and vulnerabilities to a "reasonable and appropriate" level (HHS, 2007).

A covered entity will then evaluate existing mitigation strategies for effectiveness. When the evaluation finds that current strategies and developing strategies are lacking, a remediation plan is put in place to help prevent, correct, and contain security risks. For example, upon doing the security risk assessment, despite a policy and procedure of encrypting stored data, a practice finds that not all of its laptop computers are encrypted. Because loss or theft of laptops is one of the most common ways ePHI is breached, this would be deemed a high threat to ePHI. A risk remediation strategy would be to have each computer encrypted. This strategy has the added advantage of encrypted data falling under the HIPAA "safe harbor" exemption, where loss of encrypted ePHI does not need to be reported to the individuals (i.e., clients) or HHS. Monitoring and documentation are crucial to the process of risk assessment and remediation.

The security rule is based on fundamental concepts of flexibility, scalability, and technological neutrality; thus, no specific types of technologies are recommended by HHS. Additionally, covered entities can scale compliance efforts to fit their practice and budget, remembering that required standards and specifications must be instituted and addressable specifications must be addressed. If addressable specifications are not met, a covered entity or business associate must document its reason for not implementing the specification. HHS understands that covered entities or business associates will suffer breaches; however, HHS expects that risk management strategies will be in place to reduce the risk of breach, and that the risk action plan will be instituted upon discovery of a breach. Best practice is to complete a security risk assessment once a year, or whenever the infrastructure or operations change in one's practice. Risk analysis must be completed each time there is a breach of PHI or ePHI.

# BREACH NOTIFICATION RULES

In 2009, HITECH brought clarification regarding breach with the breach notification rule. Covered entities and business associates must provide notification to the client and HHS if a breach is discovered. Discovery occurs on the day the breach is discovered, or when a covered entity or business associate reasonably should have known about the breach. A breach must be assumed unless there is a low probability, assessed in a risk analysis of the incident, that PHI has been compromised. The risk analysis examines the following:

1. The nature and extent of the PHI involved
2. To whom the disclosure was made or who impermissibly accessed the PHI
3. Whether the PHI was actually acquired or viewed
4. The extent to which the risk has been mitigated

If it is determined that PHI is compromised, the breach notification rule (Breach Notification for Unsecured Protected Health Information, 2009) is triggered.

There are three exceptions to the breach notification rule. The first exception is when there is acquisition, access, or use of protected health information that was made in good faith and within the scope of the provider's authority and does not result in further use or disclosure—for example, if a provider inadvertently looks at the wrong patient's chart but does not further use or disclose the information in the chart. The second exception is where there is inadvertent disclosure by a person who is authorized to access the protected health information at the same covered entity or business associate, and the information is not further used or disclosed. An example of this is when an email is sent to the wrong colleague, and the email is subsequently returned or destroyed. The third exception is when the covered entity or business associate makes a disclosure with the good faith belief that the unauthorized recipient would not reasonably be able to retain the protected health information. For example, no breach notification is required if a practitioner mistakenly hands health information to the wrong patient but immediately retrieves the information before the recipient has a chance to read or retain it.

Providers will also regularly have "incidental disclosures," which is when client information is disclosed where care is delivered or coordinated. Common examples include names being called in a waiting room, other clients seeing a client's name on a sign-in sheet, or janitors or cleaning services that may inadvertently see protected health information. These are not considered breaches *if* providers have reasonable safeguards in place and implemented the minimum necessary standard. Additionally, as previously stated, protected health information that is breached but that is encrypted falls under the "safe harbor" exemption and does not need to be reported to HHS.

## SUMMARY

HIPAA compliance is quickly becoming the standard of care for privacy and security of client confidential information (Hecker & Edwards, 2014), spurred in part by identity theft and medical identity theft, but also is beginning to be established through legal cases. Title II of the HIPAA regulations, administrative safeguards, applies to practitioners who are covered entities or business associates. The privacy rule outlines requirements for protection of written or oral PHI; the security rule outlines requirements for protection of ePHI. Security rules include administrative, physical, and technical safeguards. HITECH brought further requirements, increasing fines and penalties for noncompliance with the regulations and increasing clients' privacy rights. In addition, the Breach Notification Rule of 2009 outlined specific requirements entities must complete if PHI is breached.

Clients receive heightened federal protection of psychotherapy notes, but what is included in the definition of psychotherapy notes is narrowly defined. If state laws are stricter (i.e., giving clients more privacy rights or increased access to their records), state law is to be followed (with some federal preemptions). Practitioners should heed the call of increased privacy and security protections to ensure client trust, as well as to avoid the penalties that willful neglect of the regulations can bring.

Sources of help that can aid practitioners in compliance efforts include the following:

- HHS website, helpline, and email
  - HHS HIPAA information: http://www.hhs.gov/ocr/hipaa
  - HHS phone: 866-627-7748
  - HHS email: Askhipaa@cms.hhs.gov
- HHS Privacy and Security Listserv Information
  - www.hhs.gov/ocr/privacy/hipaa/understanding/coveredentities/listserv.html
- HHS Security Risk Assessment Tool
  - www.HealthIT.gov/security-risk-assessment
- HIPAA Collaborative of Wisconsin (HIPAA COW)
  - www.hipaacow.org
- HIPAA Demystified
  - www.logerpress.com
- American Health Information Management Association
  - www.ahima.org
- Carosh Compliance Solutions (with links to state mental health statutes)
  - www.carosh.com

- National Institute for Standards and Technology: Guide to Storage Encryption Technologies for End User Devices
  - www.csrc.nist.gov/publications/nistpubs/800-111/SP800-111.pdf

# REFERENCES

*Acosta v. Byrum*, 180 N.C. App. 562, 638 S.E.2d 246 (North Carolina, 2006).

Breach Notification for Unsecured Protected Health Information, 45 CFR §164 and §61. (2009). Retrieved from http://www.hhs.gov/ocr/privacy/hipaa/administrative/Breach%20Notification%20Rule/index.html

Databreaches.net (Feb. 9, 2015). Aspire Indiana notifies over 45,000 employees and clients after burglars nab office laptops [Blog post]. Retrieved from http://www.databreaches.net/aspire-indiana-notifies-over-45000-employees-and-clients-after-burglars-nab-office-laptops/

Department of Justice (2015). Identity theft. Retrieved from https://www.justice.gov/criminal-fraud/identity-theft/identity-theft-and-identity-fraud

Dimick, C. (2010, April 29). Californian sentenced to prison for HIPAA violation. *Journal of the American Health Information Management Association.* [Blog post]. Retrieved from http://journal.ahima.org/2010/04/29/californian-sentenced-to-prison-for-hipaa-violation/

Federal Trade Commission (2007). *2006 Identity theft survey report: Prepared for the Commission by Synovate.* Retrieved from https://www.ftc.gov/reports/federal-trade-commission-2006-identity-theft-survey-report-prepared-commission-synovate

Health Information Technology for Economic and Clinical Health Act of 2009, Title XII of Division A and Title IV of Division B of the American Recovery and Reinvestment Act of 2009 (ARRA), Pub. L. No. 111-5. Retrieved from http://www.hhs.gov/ocr/privacy/hipaa/understanding/coveredentities/hitechact.pdf

Health Insurance Portability and Accountability Act of 1996. 1996 Pub. L. No. 104-191, 104th Congress. Retrieved from http://www.hhs.gov/ocr/privacy/hipaa/administrative/statute/hipaastatutepdf.pdf.

Health Privacy Project. (2003). *Medical privacy stories.* Retrieved from http://patientprivacyrights.org/wp-content/uploads/2013/08/True_Stories1.pdf.

Hecker, L. (2016). *HIPAA demystified: HIPAA compliance for mental health professionals.* Crown Point, IN: Loger Press.

Hecker, L. L., & Edwards, A. A. (2014). The Impact of HIPAA and HITECH: New standards for confidentiality, security, and documentation for marriage and family therapists. *American Journal of Family Therapy,* 42(2), 95–113. doi:10.1080/01926187.2013.792711

HIPAA Privacy Rule Accounting of Disclosures under the Health Information Technology for Economic and Clinical Health Act, 2011, 75 Fed Reg. (May 31, 2011) (to be codified at 45 CFR pt. 164).

HIPAA, Public Law 104-191, 45 CFR §160.103

Ponemon Institute. (2014). Fourth annual benchmark study on patient privacy and data security. Retrieved from http://www.ponemon.org/blog/fifth-annual-benchmark-study-on-patient-privacy-and-data-security

Redspin. (2015). Breach report 2014: Protected Health Information (PHI). Retrieved from https://www.redspin.com/resources/whitepapers-datasheets/request-2014-breach-report-protected-health-information-phi-redspin.php

U.S. Dept. of Health & Human Services. (n.d., a.). HIPAA settlement underscores the vulnerability of unpatched and unsupported software. Retrieved from http://www.gov/ocr/privacy/hipaa/enforcement/examples/acmhs/index.html

U.S. Dept. of Health & Human Services. (n.d., b.). HHS settles with health plan in photocopier breach case. Retrieved from http://www.hhs.gov/ocr/privacy/hipaa/enforcement/examples/affinity-agreement.html

U.S. Dept. of Health & Human Services. (n.d., c.). Alaska DHSS settles HIPAA security case for $1,700,000. Retrieved from http://www.hhs.gov/ocr/privacy/hipaa/enforcement/examples/alaska-agreement.html

U.S. Dept. of Health & Human Services. (2007). HIPAA security series, security 101 for covered entities, 2 (paper 1). Retrieved from http://www.hhs.gov/sites/default/files/ocr/privacy/hipaa/administrative/securityrule/security101.pdf

# CHAPTER 38

# ETHICAL AND LEGAL ASPECTS OF THE PRACTICE OF TELETHERAPY

*Sara Smucker Barnwell and Linda F. Campbell*

The provision of psychological services, mental health services, and general health services through telecommunication technologies is known by several names: telepsychology, telemental health, telehealth, telecounseling, telemedicine, and teletherapy, to name a few of the most common. Any and all communication using an electronic medium is teletherapy, ranging from the telephone to synchronous international videoconferencing and the many options along the continuum. This chapter is written for independent mental health clinicians who primarily conduct psychotherapy and counseling and, as such, the term *teletherapy* is adopted. Teletherapy is not a specialty; it is not a separate practice enacted by certain clinicians. Practice through telecommunications technology is an aspect of every clinician's professional work. Mental health professionals make decisions about the degree to which they will adopt electronic communication as a vehicle for their practice. Given some degree of participation, however, all clinicians will need to become familiar with the fundamental aspects of teletherapy.

The mental health professions share the core ethical standards of competence, informed consent, confidentiality, and standards of care. The ethical practice of teletherapy can be conceptualized as the extension of those fundamental standards from in-person practice to electronic practice. That is, teletherapy focuses on those activities beyond in-person practice that are critical to ethical practice in an electronic environment.

The modes of telecommunications and specifically teletherapy range in complexity. Solo and group clinicians may have access, most certainly, to a smartphone and to email, texting, and the Internet. More tech-savvy clinicians are employing blogs, websites, and social media in their work. Teletherapy is a relatively new means of delivering clinical services that many clinicians will integrate into their professional work. The purpose of this chapter is to introduce the reader to the scope and continuum of telecommunication and to inform the reader of the ethical and legal implications of teletherapy practice and the standards of care for this practice.

# DOCUMENTATION FOR TELETHERAPY IN A PRIVATE PRACTICE SETTING

Generally, technology creates new points of clinical contact with clients (e.g., videoconferencing, email, text, telephone). In most cases, the provision of teletherapy services does not necessitate the addition of new documentation but rather requires that documentation standards for clinical practice expand their scope to address issues specific to technology use. Clinicians could think about documentation in terms of external and internal use. External documentation primarily includes informed consent as the contract between the clinician and the client, the Notice of Privacy Practices (NPP), billing notice, and other information given to the client upon service agreement. Internal documentation (i.e., recordkeeping) includes clinical intake, case notes, psychotherapy notes, and decision-making notations that would support justification for decisions made regarding electronic versus in-person services. External and internal documents are maintained for in-person services also; however, the expansion of services to accommodate teletherapy should particularly be noted.

# INFORMED CONSENT

Under professional codes of ethics, clinicians seek to obtain and document informed consent when providing clinical services (American Psychological Association [APA], Standard 3.10, Informed Consent [2010]; American Medical Association, Standard 8.08, Informed Consent [2001]; American Telemedicine Association, Practice Guidelines for Videoconferencing Based Telemental Health [2009]). Informed consent documents are formulated to apprise clients of the risks and benefits of receiving care. When providing teletherapy services, clinicians develop informed consent documentation that "offers a complete and clear description of the [telehealth] services they provide" (APA, 2013, p. 1063).

Informed consent documentation can help clients understand the technology that the clinician will use to deliver care, including its risks (e.g., confidentiality, privacy, data security) and benefits (e.g., care access), and offer insight into any practices or policies that the clinician develops to govern technology use (e.g., not connecting with clients on social media). Specifically, clinicians who use videoconferencing or other electronic means of conducting psychotherapy will want to address their use of these technologies and the inherent risks and benefits in their informed consent documents. Thus, a client entering into videoconferencing psychotherapy understands why this service is being selected over traditional in-person care and comprehends the advantages and disadvantages of receiving care remotely. Clinicians would be wise to develop a template that includes standard elements of the teletherapy component of the informed consent, which would include (a) screening for appropriateness, (b) emergency procedures, (c) procedures for interrupted service, (d) means of communication and timeline for response, (e) assessment for culture and language on relationship to technology (e.g., cultural attitudes toward technology; opportunity to use translation services through technology), (f) clarification regarding storage and disposal of electronic clinical material, (g) means of verifying conditions of remote environment, (h) notice of risks to confidentiality, and (i) statement of billing policies.

Similarly, technology use in practice may impact how clinicians elect to convey standard documentation to remote psychotherapy clients during the informed consent process. Clinicians who maintain a website for clients may wish to display their NPP on their website, just as they might in their waiting room. A clinician may allow new clients to download new client paperwork directly from their website, or even email documentation to them. This accommodation is particularly salient to clients who will receive teletherapy services and may not have the opportunity to complete necessary documentation in the clinician's office. The APA's telepsychology guidelines (2013) and other guidance developed for telemental health recommend an in-person session in which the clinical intake would take place and an initial assessment would be made regarding the appropriateness of the client for teletherapy. An in-person intake also importantly facilitates a diagnostic impression, which (a) is a factor in variables that are difficult to ascertain remotely (e.g., gait, olfactory cues, more subtle physical cues), and (b) offers the opportunity to discuss the modality and review research regarding the appropriateness of teletherapy before engaging in remote care for the presenting case.

Informed consent is the contract clinicians develop in full disclosure of their services, the risks/ benefits of services, the range of potential effects on clients, and procedures and practices that protect clients. Informed consent is a process, not a document to be signed and stored. The essence of the informed consent should be regularly revisited and discussed with the clients. Informed consent, although meant to protect clients and provide transparency in delivery of services, also protects clinicians. The informed consent documentation is evidence for standard-of-care practices that will support the clinician's decisions in times of legal or jurisdictional challenge.

# RECORDKEEPING

Technology has fundamentally altered the manner in which clinicians maintain their records, as well as generate new types of protected health information. The APA's Record Keeping Guidelines (APA, 2007) advise that "[e]lectronic records, like paper records, should be created and maintained in a way that is designed to protect their security, integrity, confidentiality, and appropriate access, as well as their compliance with applicable legal and ethical requirements" (p. 999). The Record Keeping Guidelines advise clinicians to conduct a detailed analysis of their own practices and use of electronic media to maintain records in accordance with the Health Insurance Portability and Accountability Act (HIPAA) security rule. As telecommunications technologies become ingrained into recordkeeping practices, clinicians entrust the safekeeping of electronic protected health information (ePHI) to business associates. Conducting an analysis of recordkeeping practices can feel daunting. In addition, the use of technology introduces new types of information (e.g., client emails) or storage mechanisms (e.g., a media storage device) that may be considered part of the medical record itself.

Some clinicians elect to maintain their electronic records on locally stored media. Clinicians who maintain their electronic records are advised to conduct a thoughtful audit of their practices to ensure information security. Maintaining robust passwords on all electronic files, backing up records, limiting record access through the use of distinct computer profiles, and storing physical electronics (e.g., computers, storage media) that contain records in a secure manner help to ensure record safety.

Increasing numbers of clinicians elect to maintain records through electronic health records (EHRs). Federal programs seek to promote meaningful use of EHRs among medical providers (see the Medicare and Medicaid EHR incentive programs). Many clinicians find that a locally stored or web-based EHR use improves care quality, provider convenience, and practice efficiency (U.S. Department of Health and Human Services [HHS], 2015). Yet selecting a new EHR or reviewing the risks and benefits of an existing selection stretches many clinicians outside their scope of usual practice and comfort. An EHR that is compatible with ethical practice offers features aligned with the concerns of clinicians who comply with HIPAA:

1. It includes mechanisms to control and monitor record access (e.g., usernames and robust passwords) to safeguard against unauthorized access.
2. It encrypts all information stored (e.g., the "scrambling" of data that requires a complex key to decrypt it).
3. It provides an "audit trail" that records who has accessed and/or changed information within the EHR.
4. It notifies the clinician of any security breech (HHS, 2015).

Clinicians may wish to ensure that their EHR also maintains secure backups of records, consistent with APA Record Keeping Guidelines. Record backups may be stored at a separate site from records to ensure protection from record destruction (e.g., fire, damage). Clinicians should also seek a Business Associate Agreement (BAA) that indicates that the company offering the EHR recognizes appropriate handling or ePHI in accordance with HIPAA standards (HHS, 2015).

Anecdotally, many clinicians report preferring EHRs that facilitate secure use of other types of technologies. Increasing numbers of EHRs offer integrated, encrypted email portals, messaging services, or even videoconferencing. Thus, clinicians auditing their use of EHR may wish to consider these features, not as a requirement but as a convenience.

Outside of the EHR, other types of information delivered through technology may become a part of the client record. There are 18 types of ePHI, including client names, addresses, email addresses, photographic images, and others. Consider an email that a client sends through an encrypted email program external to the EHR or a USB storage device that contains backups of client records. If relevant clinical information is included and/or the information includes one of the 18 types of ePHI, the email or storage device may become part of the record itself. Thus, as part of a thoughtful audit of practices, the clinician may consider the types of technology used in client care, the administrative safeguards (e.g., security policies, staff training) in place to govern the technologies, physical safeguards for equipment and records, organizational standards (e.g., who can access the information within an organization, requirement of BAA from technology vendors), and the policies and procedures of the technology vendors (HHS, 2015).

Clinicians will want to seek a BAA in which the company offering the EHR recognizes appropriate handling or ePHI in accordance with HIPAA standards (HHS, 2015). A BAA is a signed document that indicates that the vendor recognizes appropriate handling or ePHI in accordance with HIPAA standards (HHS, 2015) to users. The BAA ensures that the company offering the product is aware of HIPAA requirements and recognizes its duty to the clinician, a covered entity, to maintain HIPAA standards. A company offering a BAA will typically also offer other features, including information encryption, mechanisms to ensure security/authorized access, the ability to audit who has accessed the product, and other features to help establish privacy, confidentiality, and information security. Clinicians engaged in teletherapy select products with the ability to limit unauthorized access to ePHI, the ability to audit activity/use of the product, policies that protect unauthorized alteration or destruction of information, and technical security measures that protect information when it is transmitted (e.g., encryption; HHS, 2015). Examples of business associates include third-party administrators, accounting firms, attorneys, consultants, medical transcriptionists, and pharmacy benefits managers. A full explanation of the business associate requirements related to HIPAA can be located at http://www.hhs.gov/hipaa/for-professionals/privacy/guidance/business-associates.

In documenting teletherapy sessions, clinicians should plan to include additional documentation in their recordkeeping. As noted elsewhere in this chapter, documenting the emergency plan for remote care ensures easy access to time-sensitive information when it is needed. In addition, the clinician should document the reasons that the client was deemed appropriate for teletherapy, as well as why teletherapy services are offered instead of in-person care.

Clinicians delivering teletherapy should also note details often taken for granted in in-person care (e.g., client and practice location). Teletherapy clinicians will include notation in each psychotherapy note that indicates the clinician location, the client location, the client's confirmation that he or she is alone in the space and cannot be overheard, a brief review of the emergency plan, and the offer to answer any questions related to the technology used. A brief note template that addresses each of these considerations may both reduce the time required for documentation and provide a useful checklist for issues to revisit at the commencement of each psychotherapy session conducted over videoconferencing or by other technological means. During initial visits, clinicians may wish to include additional documentation of the informed consent process, the manner in which they explained the technology being used, the thorough review of the emergency plan, the discussion of technology risks and benefits, and any client questions.

In some instances, technology use creates entirely new considerations in clinical practice and requires new types of documentation to address its use. For example, clinicians expert in videoconferencing advise the creation of an emergency plan (see APA, 2013; American Telemedicine Association, 2009). Creating an emergency plan template (e.g., where the client is located during care, contact information for this location, local emergency services) demonstrates an understanding of the unique demands of delivering remote care and an investment in client safety.

Because the practice of teletherapy is a relatively nascent modality, perhaps under greater scrutiny and with less codified regulatory guidance than traditional in-person care (DeMers, 2011), clinicians may elect to document their decision-making processes related to technology use for their own internal reference and risk management processes. Clinicians faced with negotiating challenges related to decision making (e.g., a board complaint, a lawsuit) may be grateful for documented evidence of their thoughtful and ethically oriented processes. Seasoned videoconferencing clinicians often advise the development of a standard assessment for telehealth appropriateness (Shore et al., 2011) or, more informally, a form that documents the clinician's own standards regarding which clients are appropriate for telehealth (e.g., client stability, availability of in-person care, clinical symptoms) and a note in the client's chart addressing his or her appropriateness for telehealth (Smucker Barnwell, 2014). These factors are considered client variables that are important in any treatment decision, but when applied to teletherapy, they have an expanded meaning, such as language, culture, the technology competence of the client, and risk level.

# HIPAA 101 FOR THE PRIVATE PRACTITIONER

HIPAA addresses several themes, including the creation of national standards for electronic healthcare transactions. Perhaps of greatest relevance to teletherapy are HIPAA's privacy and security rules.

The privacy rule applies to covered entities (i.e., health care clinicians and other healthcare workers who must comply with HIPAA) who conduct electronic transactions subject to the standards established by HHS. This includes most psychotherapists. The privacy rule requires covered entities to protect health records and other identifiable client information by implementing privacy protections and by setting limits and conditions on the disclosure of PHI. ePHI refers to any PHI that is addressed by HIPAA security regulations and is produced, saved, transferred, or received in an electronic form. This includes information such as client name, address, email address, IP address, full photographic images, and others (HHS, 2015). Thus the HIPAA privacy rule directs clinicians engaged in teletherapy to protect ePHI, just as all covered entities are directed to guard PHI against inappropriate disclosure.

The HIPAA Security Standards for the Protection of Electronic Protected Health Information (known informally as the security rule) establish a national set of security standards for protecting ePHI. The security rule operationalizes how covered entities must protect ePHI. It aims to protect ePHI while allowing psychotherapists and other covered entities the flexibility to adopt technologies that will improve client care. It offers guidance on physical, administrative, and technical safeguards that clinicians may take to protect ePHI (HHS, 2015). Psychotherapists interested in engaging in teletherapy may review these suggestions to ensure that their practices comply with HIPAA and protect ePHI. These standards can be located at http://www.hhs.gov/hipaa/for-professionals/security/laws-regulations.

# COMMON ETHICAL TRANSGRESSIONS BY PRIVATE PRACTITIONERS

Well-intentioned private practice clinicians can accidentally commit ethical transgressions when practicing outside their usual scope. Whereas technology pushes many clinicians outside of their usual area of comfort, it is worthwhile to consider those areas where many clinicians have unknowingly acted unethically. As discussed above, pursuing competence in the technologies used in psychotherapy and maintaining the mission of public protection safeguard against large-scale ethical concerns (e.g., using a technology inappropriately, offering inappropriate care to clients for financial gain). However, most clinicians take seriously their ethical charge of safeguarding the welfare of clients and clinicians. For these clinicians, the more nuanced pitfalls pose a more serious threat.

When providing remote psychotherapy, the question "where is the office" is salient. Videoconferencing and other technologies allow the client and clinician mobility but require thoughtfulness regarding where care occurs. Gone are the days when an answered telephone informed the caller that the other person was at home. Substantiating that the client is located in a private space appropriate for care and relevant to the established emergency plan is critical at the onset of a psychotherapy session. Without this information, the clinician could accidentally provide care without an appropriate emergency plan and in an environment where the session is overheard or even over jurisdictional boundaries. The control of the remote location becomes very important in any evaluation made through telecommunication.

The practice of teletherapy across jurisdictional lines has increased significantly through companies that provide e-therapy with variously credentialed clinicians. Further, some clinicians are providing teletherapy without verifying the rules and laws in their own state or the state in which the client is located. Interjurisdictional practice is addressed later in this chapter.

The clinician must consider where and when it is appropriate to interact with clients. Mobile technology may make it possible for a clinician to speak with clients in a diversity of settings (e.g., in their home, in their car, in the grocery store), but that does not necessarily mean that this is consistent with good care. Maintaining firm boundaries between personal and professional technology use assists clinicians in maintaining ethical boundaries in psychotherapy as well. Consider a clinician who uses professional videoconferencing software with friends as well as clients and risks personal callers interrupting or, worse, entering into an unsecured client session. Or, consider a clinician who emails with clients on an account that he shares with his spouse. Or perhaps most notably, consider a clinician who accepts social media contact requests from clients. In each of these cases, the blurred boundaries between personal and professional technology use could readily lend themselves to ethical violations related to client privacy and confidentiality, information security, and dual roles.

Clinicians need to think about setting limits on their availability and including such a statement in the informed consent. Acceptance of emails late at night or on weekends implies 24/7 services and can be considered a vulnerability in sound risk management.

Treatments that demonstrate evidence-based validity in person may not yet have substantiation in telecommunicated psychotherapy. This fact does not need to deter use but should be noted for monitoring and evaluation of effectiveness. Similarly, some forms of assessment have been converted or adapted for electronic use and some have not. Clinicians should be aware of the application of norms for tests that are commonly administered in person and have not been validated for electronic use.

Teletherapy practice must meet all of the standards of in-person practice. Electronic communication does not mean a diluting of standards of care. For example, informed consent should be a fluid document that is continually revisited because the electronic environment can change in ways that a physical environment would not. Availability and the securing of emergency services are also fluid in ways that in-person service is not.

Clinicians need to apprise clients of the fact that the risks of a breach in confidentiality are significantly greater by teletherapy. These risks can be diminished by security safeguards but cannot be eliminated. Clinicians need to consider use of technology products designed for healthcare. Encrypted email and text software, HIPAA-compatible file transfer programs, and other technologies mindful of the legal and ethical requirements related to healthcare can assist the provider in ethical technology use. Clinicians should be aware of HIPAA regulations regarding electronic records and accordingly should make deliberate decisions about what clinical information is stored as clinical records, the length of time records are maintained, and how such records will be disposed of.Clinicians must educate clients regarding their role in proactively protecting their own privacy and confidentiality. Clinicians should help clients be sound partners in ethical technology use. They should advise their clients to password-protect email accounts they use to communicate with the clinician, attend teletherapy sessions only from private locations, and be thoughtful about how technology use impacts their privacy. Whereas many clients have more casual attitudes toward technology use than clinicians concerned with HIPAA, the conversation may highlight important differences in attitudes about technology, privacy, and even psychotherapy.

# SELECTING TECHNOLOGIES: LEGAL AND ETHICAL CONSIDERATIONS

Selecting which technology product to use in the delivery of teletherapy services pushes many clinicians outside of their usual scope of competence. Clinicians are rarely formally trained in technology, and the number of choices may feel overwhelming. Many professional authorities (e.g., professional organizations, associations) are understandably reluctant to recommend or even opine on product options because the technology marketplace changes so quickly. Clinicians are tasked with selecting products that are well designed to meet their clinical needs as well as the security demands of a HIPAA-covered entity. As a result, clinicians may feel immobilized by the enormity of the task and may even elect to avoid offering a valuable technology-enabled service.

Selecting a product designed for healthcare may alleviate many of the clinician's concerns. A technology product (e.g., videoconferencing, email, text service) designed for and marketed to healthcare clinicians will offer features unavailable in the more commonly used and often free products designed for the general public. Most notably, clinicians may wish to select a product that addresses concerns related to HIPAA and offers a BAA.

Clinicians must consider whether the product will work well for their practice. Is it easy for both clinicians and clients to use? Consider viewing a product demonstration and trying the product before purchasing it. Does the vendor offer sound technical support? Before making a purchase, clinicians may wish to call the customer support line to assess the timeliness of the response, the expertise of the staff, and the quality of customer service. Is the product affordable, and is the vendor willing to negotiate pricing? Finally, the clinician should research the vendor's reputation online. How long has the company been in business? Are there any complaints registered against it with online quality watchdogs (e.g., Better Business Bureau)? Have a significant number of prior users left unfavorable reviews online? By reviewing these more practical considerations, clinicians will be more likely to identify a product that is well aligned with their information security needs but also easy to use, well established, and affordable.

# SUPERVISION AND CONSULTATION IN TELETHERAPY PRACTICE

Providing remote supervision and consultation via videoconferencing or other technology creates the opportunity to transmit needed expertise that would otherwise be unavailable due to multiple access barriers. A specialist consultant may provide valuable insights to a client via videoconferencing; a trainee working in the field may receive time-sensitive supervision from a clinician at another location. Just as in psychotherapy, the introduction of telecommunications technology to the established practice of supervision and consultation introduces questions regarding how to maximize convenience without sacrificing ethical practice.

Professional guidelines addressing the provision of supervision and consultation via telecommunications technologies suggest that the clinician "make reasonable efforts to be proficient in the professional services being offered, the telecommunication modality via which the services are being offered to the supervisee/consultee, and the technology medium being used to provide the supervision or consultation" (APA, 2013, p. 794). Thus, it is important to find a supervisor or consultant well matched not only in terms of subject matter expertise, but also in the technology that will be employed to conduct supervision and consultation. Videoconferencing-based supervision that includes client PHI must attend to the same information security concerns as teletherapy. Thus, supervisors and consultants using technology to deliver services should select products specifically designed for healthcare, even though they may not use the technology to interact directly with clients.

In addition, since the development of basic professional competencies for supervisees is often conducted in person, clinicians conducting remote supervision via videoconferencing or other technologies must ensure that adequate in-person supervision time is included so that the supervisees can attain the required competencies or supervised experiences (APA, 2013). In-person time is recommended for the initial stage of supervision in that supervisors need only to assess the technological and clinical competency of the supervisees and establish basic competence in its use.

Supervision for training and consultation with another licensed professional are distinctly different activities in person and through technology. Supervision carries the legal and ethical responsibility for the supervisee who is practicing under an extension of the licensed clinician. The supervisor may include in a contract or informed consent document the conditions of supervision, the protocols, the procedures, and the variables of supervision introduced by telecommunications. The supervisor will want to determine the following:

1. Is the supervisee technologically competent?
2. Have decisions been made about appropriateness of clients for supervisees?
3. How will interruptions be handled?
4. Are all parties located in the same jurisdiction?
5. Have the conditions of supervision been explained to the clients?

Providing a consultation service rather than supervision involves some of the same obligations for transparency, conditions of practice, and standards of care; however, licensed peer clinicians carry the responsibility for their own legal and ethical professional behavior.

# IMPLEMENTING A RISK/BENEFIT ASSESSMENT

Development of a risk/benefit plan that includes technology of choice, emergency services, the remote environment, and client variables is an important standard of care. Creating a practice environment with physical, administrative, and technical safeguards conducive to psychotherapy represents an investment that will pay dividends to the clinician—that is, protections that will minimize risks introduced by technology and risks based on client variables. Clinicians must consider what types of technology they use in client care, the administrative safeguards (e.g., security policies, staff training) in place to govern the technologies, physical safeguards for equipment and records, organizational standards (e.g., who can access the information within an organization, requirement of BAA from technology vendors), and an understanding of the policies and procedures of the technology vendors (HHS, 2015).

Establishing a secure physical space in which teletherapy cannot be overheard is especially relevant for clinicians considering delivering care from home. Clinicians must also physically secure technology equipment that might contain ePHI (e.g., computers, mobile devices, mobile storage) when not in use, as the equipment may become part of the record itself.

Remote emergency management emerges as a chief concern for many clinicians interested in delivering teletherapy. Despite research that suggests that delivering care in clinically unsupervised settings does not increase risk to clients and that emergency planning addresses client needs (see Luxton, Sirotin, & Mishkind, 2010), many clinicians cite this concern as the reason to avoid offering teletherapy services. Indeed, the delivery of remote clinical services diminishes the clinician's ability to respond directly to emergencies (e.g., administering cardiopulmonary resuscitation). However, thoughtful advance screenings of client appropriateness for a service, a thoughtful plan for remote services, and a thorough response to emergencies may ensure that a remote care clinician is well prepared for such an event.

Assessing telehealth appropriateness, discussed above, is an ongoing endeavor. Establishing which clients will be seen remotely will significantly impact the probability of the need to manage emergencies remotely. For example, the clinician who elects to offer remote services to new clients and/or clients with a known history of recent clinical instability is at a higher risk to be called upon to manage a remote emergency compared to the clinician who elects to offer teletherapy services only to established clients with a stable history of no emergency needs. Of course, there are no guarantees; a client's telehealth appropriateness at the commencement of services is no guarantee that he or she will remain a good fit for telehealth services. Emergency management planning is critical for all clinicians and clients. As noted above, creating an individualized emergency plan for each remote client will ensure a plan of action tailored to the client's needs. Still, clinicians delivering teletherapy services should examine their own willingness and comfort with managing remote emergencies and should establish inclusion/exclusion criteria for telehealth accordingly.

In the event of an emergency, clinicians must respond quickly and thoroughly. Consider a clinician serving a client over videoconferencing. In the case of a medical emergency, the clinician would use a readily available emergency plan to contact emergency services local to the client. If the client provided contact information and/or release of information for a supportive person located nearby, the clinician might also elect to contact this individual for supplemental help (e.g., opening the door for emergency services, if the client is incapacitated). The clinician would endeavor to remain on the videoconferencing call with the client until emergency services arrive, and would seek to provide information to emergency responders as needed. As in in-person care, the clinician should document the adverse event thoroughly and follow up with the client after the event. An assessment of whether videoconferencing psychotherapy remains the safest and most appropriate modality for this client would be merited.

An assessment plan becomes a document that stands in evidence of the clinician's intent to meet standards of care and provides a means by which the clinician engages in ongoing evaluation of all aspects of his or her telepractice. Some client risk factors (e.g., prior hospitalization, current and recent mental status, diagnostic classification, family or social support, self-regulation capability, prior suicide attempts and ideation, remote environment) and the legal/regulatory statutes in both jurisdictions would be considered in making decisions about conducting teletherapy and in documenting one's reasoning and decision factors. The adoption of a risk/benefit assessment plan is valuable to clinicians in opting for teletherapy or in-person services.

# SOCIAL MEDIA: THE BOUNDARIES OF PROFESSIONAL AND PERSONAL USE

Adolescents and young adults communicate through social media as naturally and spontaneously as middle-aged and older individuals picked up the phone as an integral part of their adolescence and young adult socialization. Understanding and managing the ethical implications of social media is one of the greatest challenges of engagement in teletherapy. Separation of personal and professional communication has not been a need or a skill for many individuals who are vulnerable to violations of confidentiality, competence, standards of care, and other ethical concepts. Clinicians who learned ethical concepts of boundaries, multiple relationships, and confidentiality prior to engagement in social media may be able to make judgments about professional communication more easily than those who have not had to make such discernment.

Posting photos, sending tweets, and posting information to online social media forums are examples of information exchange that cannot be controlled or monitored for access, storage, or disposal. Clinicians are often faced with requests from clients to participate in online communication. Just as clinicians are responsible for ensuring the technical competence of clients in use of teletherapy, so are they responsible for clients' understanding of the consequences of transmitting clinical information through social media. Factors clinicians may want to keep in mind include the following:

There is no guarantee of confidentiality through social media, regardless of advertised firewalls or other security measures.

Accessing information about clients online presents ethical dilemmas of confidentiality and a risk of perceived deception.

Clinicians should be prepared for clients to search for information about them online, so they should be cognizant of what information is publicly available about them through social media.

Decisions about social media engagement should be made before beginning teletherapy services.

Social media policy should be included in the informed consent agreement with each client.

# INTERJURISDICTIONAL AND INTRAJURISDICTIONAL PRACTICE

Interjurisdictional teletherapy occurs when the clinician and the client are in different states or jurisdictions. Intrajurisdictional teletherapy occurs when the clinician and the client are in the same state or jurisdiction. Currently, there are no reciprocity agreements among states that would allow ongoing interjurisdictional practice, so a clinician who wants to provide services to a resident of another state would have to acquire a license from that other state. There are initiatives afoot that would result in compacts of agreement among the member states that would allow practice with a license in only one of the member states. Many clinicians want to practice in another state temporarily because their client has gone on vacation or lives elsewhere part of the year; conversely, clinicians may want to continue providing services while they themselves are on vacation or out of state for some time. Uninterrupted in-person psychotherapy is a common reason for interest in teletherapy.

Approximately 48 of the 50 states have some allowance for temporary practice, most either 20 or 30 days per year. Clinicians who are interested in following a client out of state for a given period of time may contact the licensing board of that state or may go online to the licensing board and notify them that the clinician is going to be providing teletherapy to an ongoing client who is temporarily in that remote state. The clinician should review the licensing rules and regulations of that state before beginning services.

Many clinicians do not realize that some jurisdictions allow teletherapy to be practiced in their home state if the client is also in that state. The licensing rules and regulation of that state should be reviewed; however, many states are still silent on teletherapy. If the state is silent, then the licensing board should be contacted to determine the allowance for telepractice.

# OPPORTUNITIES AND ETHICAL PRACTICE

Teletherapy expands opportunities to grow one's practice while also overcoming client care access barriers (e.g., distance from care, medical issues that prohibit travel). The provision of remote clinical services helps clinicians build robust practices and matches clients with high-quality specialist care aligned with their needs regardless of otherwise insurmountable obstacles to receiving care. Technology use may expand the convenience and efficiency of a clinician's existing practice, saving valuable time and costs. Simultaneously, teletherapy carries with it the requirement to revisit and maintain ethical standards for public protection and competence.

Consider the opportunities that videoconferencing offers to a clinician establishing a practice. Offering videoconferencing services could potentially expand one's client base, resulting in a more financially prosperous business. Still, the clinician must first address a myriad of questions:

Does the clinician possess the training necessary to competently deliver videoconferencing services and a videoconferencing program that is compatible with HIPAA requirements?

How will the clinician identify clients, confirm client identity, assess telehealth appropriateness, and capture informed consent?

What will the clinician do if technology problems interrupt the teletherapy session?

Does the clinician understand that his or her license extends only to care within his or her own practice jurisdiction?

Alternatively, consider a clinician who wishes to email homework forms to clients following a videoconferencing session:

Does the clinician possess an encrypted email program and maintain robust passwords on email?

Does the client understand that even encrypted email possesses information security risks?

Are these risks well detailed in informed consent documentation?

Does the clinician explain to clients how their behavior can impact their privacy and confidentiality (e.g., maintaining passwords on their email accounts; not forwarding medical information over email to others)?

These caveats are not intended to discourage technology adoption; indeed, ethical adoption has never been more important. As technology becomes more democratized and integrated into daily life, it is critical to delineate how professional technology use differs from personal use and how ethical practice differs from everyday convenience. The thoughtful provision of teletherapy services promises to benefit client and clinician, as it protects the public from diminished standards of care and sets important precedents for future generations of clinicians.

# REFERENCES

American Medical Association. (2001). Code of medical ethics. Retrieved from www.ama-assn.org/go/codeofmedicalethics.

American Psychological Association. (2007). Record keeping guidelines. *American Psychologist, 62,* 9, 993–1004. doi:10.1037/0003-066X.62.9.993

American Psychological Association. (2010). Ethical principles of psychologists and code of conduct. Retrieved from http://apa.org/ethics/code/index.aspx.

American Psychological Association. (2013). Guidelines for the practice of telepsychology. Retrieved from http://www.apa.org/practice/guidelines/telepsychology.aspx.

American Telemedicine Association. (2009). Practice guidelines for videoconferencing based telemental health. Retrieved from http://www.americantelemed.org/docs/default-source/standards/practice-guidelines-for-videoconferencing-based-telemental-health.pdf?sfvrsn=6.

DeMers, S. (2011, August). TelePsychology practice within a regulatory minefield: Outdated, inconsistent and inadequate rules across states & provinces. In M. Maheu (Chair), Telehealth and telepsychology licensure: Barriers and possible solutions as psychology adopts the psychotechnologies. Symposium conducted at the American Psychological Association Annual Convention, Washington, DC.

Luxton, D. D., Sirotin, A. P., & Mishkind, M. C. (2010, July/August). Safety of telemental healthcare delivered to clinically unsupervised settings: A systematic review. *Telemedicine and e-Health, 16*(6), 705–711. doi:10.1089/tmj.2009.0179.

Shore, P., Goranson, A., Ward, M. F., & Lu, M. W. (2014). Meeting veterans where they're @: AVA homebased telemental health (HBTMH) pilot program. *International Journal of Psychiatry in Medicine, 48*(1), 5–17.

Smucker Barnwell, S. V. (2014, April). Technology in clinical practice. Presentation at the Washington State Psychological Association Annual Conference, Seattle, WA.

U.S. Department of Health and Human Services. (2015). Health information privacy. Retrieved from http://www.hhs.gov/hipaa/index.html.

# CHAPTER 39

# DEALING WITH THIRD PARTIES

## Legal and Ethical Considerations

*Joe Scroppo*

Confidentiality and privilege are foundational elements of psychotherapy. Confidentiality refers to the psychotherapist's fiduciary duty to maintain the secrecy of a client's communications—clients need and expect that their psychotherapist will keep secrets and will not disclose any information to third parties. Clients also benefit from the legal "privilege" that attaches to their communications to their psychotherapists—"privilege" is a legal doctrine that prevents the use of the client's communications to a psychotherapist as evidence in a legal proceeding. For the purposes of this chapter, a third party is defined as any person or entity that is outside of the professional relationship between the psychotherapist and the psychotherapist's client; a third party is, by definition, not a recipient of the psychotherapist's services.

Despite the strong ethical, regulatory, and legal boundaries that shield the psychotherapist–client relationship from third-party intrusion, when psychotherapists deliver services to clients, they can often expect to deal with third parties. The confidential and usually privileged relationship between a psychotherapist and a client can be penetrated by various entities, in various ways, and for various purposes.

Usually, a psychotherapist can easily differentiate between a client and a third party. There are situations, however, where another entity hires or directs a mental health professional to deliver services to a recipient. In such cases, the hiring or directing entity may actually be the client (i.e., not a third party), or that entity is at least professionally involved in the relationship between the psychotherapist and the service recipient. The following are examples of such cases:

- An attorney hires a mental health professional to conduct an evaluation of the attorney's client with regard to a potential or actual legal matter.
- An employer hires a mental health professional to conduct a fitness-for-duty evaluation of one of its employees.

- A court appoints a mental health professional to conduct a child custody evaluation regarding a set of parents and their children.

These situations are highly complex and require that the mental health professional has specialized training and expertise in dealing with them. As a start, mental health professionals dealing with such a situation would be wise to follow the ethical requirements articulated in the relevant standards in their profession's code of ethics. Representative of these codes of ethical standards, the American Psychological Association's 2010 Code of Ethics states in Standard 3.07, Third Party Requests for Services:

> When psychologists agree to provide services to a person or entity at the request of a third party, psychologists attempt to clarify at the outset of the service the nature of the relationship with all individuals or organizations involved. This clarification includes the role of the psychologist (e.g., psychotherapist, consultant, diagnostician, or expert witness), an identification of who is the client, the probable uses of the services provided or the information obtained, and the fact that there may be limits to confidentiality. (p. 6)

The focus of this chapter, however, is not on cases where there is a third-party request for a mental health professional's services. Rather, this chapter focuses on the situation where a third party seeks to penetrate the boundaries of, or is invited into, a pending, ongoing, or already-concluded psychotherapist–client professional relationship.

Third-party entities can include the following:

The client's family members or friends
The client's current or potential future employer
Insurance companies (health, disability, life)
Government agencies (e.g., Social Security)
Law enforcement entities
Courts or administrative bodies
Attorneys representing the client or a third party
Other mental health professionals

The ways in which a third party can attempt to penetrate the boundaries of a psychotherapist–client relationship are relatively limited:

The psychotherapist has an affirmative mandate to disclose information to a third party without the client's authorization (e.g., danger to self or others, child abuse, elder abuse).
The client or the client's legal guardian can authorize disclosure of treatment information to a third party.
An attorney may attempt to subpoena treatment information.
A court may order disclosure of treatment information.

A legal mechanism may remove, by operation of law, the confidentiality and privilege that normally attaches to treatment information and thus give a third party access to the treatment record.

Third parties may attempt to penetrate the boundaries of the psychotherapist–client relationship for several reasons:

To obtain information about the client

To obtain information about the psychotherapist's conduct (i.e., a licensing board or an insurance company auditor)

To exert some influence or control over the client, the clinician, or the psychotherapy (e.g., a family member or spouse of a client seeking to influence the course of the psychotherapy)

# GUIDING PRINCIPLES IN DEALING WITH THIRD PARTIES

The basic principles of responding to attempted third-party penetration of or involvement with the client–psychotherapist relationship are essentially the same across all situations.

A psychotherapist has a legal and ethical duty to avoid disclosure to others of the client's communications, or even of the very existence of the psychotherapy relationship, to a third party, unless the client or guardian authorizes the disclosure, or a specific legal authority permits or mandates that disclosure. At the inception of the psychotherapist–client relationship, the psychotherapist informs the client about the circumstances that would permit or require the psychotherapist to disclose information to a third party.

If a third party attempts to penetrate the boundaries of the psychotherapy relationship, the psychotherapist informs the client and seeks the client's input about how to respond to that attempted penetration. In response to a request or demand to disclose treatment information to a third party, the psychotherapist considers how that disclosure might impact the client and the psychotherapy, and, whenever possible, discusses with the client the potential effects of the disclosure on the client and the psychotherapy.

A psychotherapist can disclose treatment information to others with the client's or the client's legal guardian's authorization to do so, but the psychotherapist takes additional steps before acting on the client's authorization. Prior to disclosing any confidential information, the psychotherapist informs the client about the general nature of the information that would be disclosed in response to the request or demand (including the presence of any particularly sensitive information), so that the client can make an informed decision about whether to authorize, or continue to authorize, the disclosure; and, in the case of a mandated disclosure, so that the client can make an informed decision about whether to try to block that disclosure. The psychotherapist may also want to encourage the client to consult with the client's attorney about the making of the disclosure. In the absence of a client's or a client's legal guardian's authorization, the psychotherapist requires the third party to demonstrate the existence of an adequate legal authority that mandates the psychotherapist to disclose the requested information without the client's authorization.

A psychotherapist, whenever possible, attempts to keep the amount of information disclosed to the third party to the minimum amount necessary to achieve the purpose of the disclosure. The psychotherapist, for example, might offer to provide a brief treatment summary to the third party in lieu of the entire treatment record. A psychotherapist avoids giving opinions to third parties about the client or the psychotherapy that exceed what a psychotherapist can reasonably have an opinion about, or that would put the psychotherapist into an impermissible dual role with the client. For example, the psychotherapist would refrain from offering opinions about who should have custody of a child or about what was the cause of a client's injuries.

Once there has been a disclosure to a third party, a psychotherapist monitors the consequences of that disclosure on the ongoing psychotherapist–client relationship.

A psychotherapist who adheres to these procedures whenever there is an attempt to penetrate the boundaries of the psychotherapist–client relationship will minimize the risk of an adverse outcome for the psychotherapist and the client. Nevertheless, whenever the psychotherapist is unsure about how to proceed or is faced with a truly novel situation, he or she should seek consultation from knowledgeable colleagues or from an attorney.

# WHEN THE PSYCHOTHERAPIST IS MANDATED TO PROACTIVELY DISCLOSE INFORMATION TO A THIRD PARTY WITHOUT THE CLIENT'S AUTHORIZATION

State laws almost universally mandate that, under certain circumstances, a psychotherapist must proactively disclose to a specified third party certain information contained in a client's communications to the psychotherapist. The following are the most common circumstances where this affirmative duty to disclose client information arises:

   Mandated reporting of suspected child abuse to a state or county agency
   Mandated reporting of suspected elder/dependent person abuse to a state or county agency
   Mandated reporting to a state agency of a healthcare professional who is impaired and
      endangering clients, or who is engaging in unprofessional conduct

Generally, the psychotherapist's failure to make a report when such a report is mandated under these laws will expose him or her to civil and sometimes criminal sanctions.

The psychotherapist must be familiar with the particular mandated reporting duties in his or her jurisdiction. Information about these mandates can be obtained through the therapist's state licensing board or state professional association. The specific elements of these mandates can vary greatly across jurisdictions. With regard to child abuse reporting, for example, some states limit the mandate to make a report to situations where the alleged perpetrator of the child maltreatment is a caretaker of or lives in the home with the alleged child victim, whereas other states do not impose such limitations. Moreover, the psychotherapist is ethically required to notify the client about these mandated reporting duties at the outset of the psychotherapy.

Although not a mandated reporting duty in the same sense as the previously specified reporting duties, most states have a statutory or common-law provision that permits psychotherapists to breach client confidentiality in order to protect a third party from a current client who communicates to the psychotherapist the intent to inflict serious and imminent physical harm upon that third party (i.e., *Tarasoff*-type laws). Where such laws exist, they generally do not impose a criminal or civil sanction on a psychotherapist who fails to take steps to protect the endangered third party; instead, these laws usually simply permit the psychotherapist to breach client confidentiality (i.e., they provide an explicit exception to the psychotherapist's regulation-imposed confidentiality duty), or they simply provide the psychotherapist with immunity from civil or criminal sanctions when the psychotherapist breaches client confidentiality under these circumstances. Nevertheless, these laws tend to implicitly establish the prevailing standard of professional practice, and psychotherapists who fail to take steps to protect a third party when such is permitted (or, in very rare instances, required) run the risk of a successful lawsuit against them by the harmed third party or face the potential of some other adverse action. Consequently, as with explicit mandated reporting duties, psychotherapists should be aware of the "duty to protect" laws in their jurisdiction and should notify the client in advance that they may have to act accordingly if the requisite circumstances arise in the client's case.

# WHEN DISCLOSURE OF TREATMENT INFORMATION TO THIRD PARTIES WILL BE BASED ON THE CLIENT'S AUTHORIZATION

In some situations a client may choose to authorize disclosure of information to third parties. One common example of this is when a client wants to use a third party to pay for the psychotherapist's services, which usually takes the form of using his or her health insurance plan. Typically, the client, in applying for coverage under a health insurance plan, and in agreeing to the submission of claims to the insurer, has contractually agreed to the disclosure of some and possibly all treatment information to the health insurer for payment and other healthcare operations purposes.

Applying the recommendations above, the psychotherapist would clarify with the client, at the beginning of the treatment relationship, that, by using healthcare insurance, the client has authorized some disclosure to the insurance company. The psychotherapist would be aware of any contractual obligations (e.g., being a contracted provider for the client's insurance plan) and of the state and federal rules and laws that govern what and how much treatment information the insurance company is entitled to receive for payment and auditing purposes. State laws vary as to what limitations they impose on a third-party insurer's access to treatment information— some jurisdictions impose relatively strict limits, some do not. Health Insurance Portability and Accountability Act (HIPAA) regulations also impose limits on the nature and extent of what the third-party insurer is entitled to receive, most notably in the form of the "Minimum Necessary Rule," which mandates that healthcare providers limit the extent of the disclosure to only the amount necessary to fulfill a health insurance company's legitimate request (see 45 CFR 164.502(b) and 45 CFR 164.514(d)). The essential point is that the psychotherapist should know and understand these contractual and legal limitations on disclosures of treatment information to third-party payers and would inform the client at the outset of the psychotherapy about them.

Continuing to apply the guidelines, the psychotherapist would notify the client when the insurance company actually does request disclosure of any treatment information that exceeds what is typically requested (i.e., more than just a treatment plan or basic claims-related information). Under certain circumstances (e.g., the client is using out-of-network benefits), the client may be able to prevent or limit such disclosures by ceasing to use the insurance plan. In any event, the psychotherapist would actively seek to limit the disclosure to the third-party payer to the minimum necessary to fulfill the purpose of the request, and the psychotherapist would cite the ethical and regulatory standards (e.g., the ethics code of his or her professional association, the HIPAA Minimum Necessary Rule, and/or state law) to the insurance company in an effort to obtain a more narrowly tailored disclosure request from the company. Finally, in advance of taking action, the psychotherapist should discuss with the client what impact the release may have on the ongoing therapeutic relationship as well as what provisions need to be in place if there is no insurance reimbursement.

The following are examples of other situations where the psychotherapist may encounter a client who is considering authorizing, wants to authorize, or is being encouraged by a third party to authorize disclosure of treatment information to a third party. Although these situations vary in some respects, the psychotherapist would generally apply the same principles.

## CASE 1

A minor client's parents want specific information about the client's communications reported to them after each session, including information about the minor's sexual behavior and substance use.

Although the minor's parent/guardian is often legally empowered to access the minor's treatment record without the minor's consent, the psychotherapist would, at the outset of the psychotherapy, explain that confidentiality is important to the success of the psychotherapy and seek to come an agreement, preferably in writing, with the minor and the parent/guardian about what treatment information will and will not be shared with the parent/guardian. The psychotherapist would limit disclosures to the amount that respects the parent/guardian's legitimate interest in the psychotherapy but also protects the minor's confidentiality. The psychotherapist would regularly monitor the effectiveness of this arrangement and seek to modify it as necessary. Because parental legal right of access to a minor patient's treatment information is a highly jurisdiction-specific matter, especially when parents are divorced, psychotherapists should consult with knowledgeable colleagues or with an attorney when faced with complex scenarios of this type.

## CASE 2

An adult client's parents are paying for the client's psychotherapy and inquire about what is occurring in the psychotherapy because they perceive that they are entitled to updates about its progress and want to make sure that their concerns about the client are being addressed.

The psychotherapist considers how the requested disclosure might affect the client and the psychotherapy, and discusses with the client the potential effects of the disclosure. The psychotherapist would seek to minimize the disclosure to the amount necessary to achieve its purpose without compromising the client's confidentiality and by trying to limit any counter-therapeutic third-party penetration into the psychotherapy.

## CASE 3

A client has applied for a job with a governmental national defense agency, and the agency has contacted the psychotherapist and wants the client's records and an opinion as to whether the client's psychological condition is inconsistent with the client handling sensitive information.

The psychotherapist would discuss with the client the general contents of the record, or perhaps suggest that the client review the record in its entirety prior to the client authorizing the disclosure to the agency. The psychotherapist would explain to the client that he or she cannot provide an opinion about the client's fitness for the position, because the client was not evaluated for that purpose. The psychotherapist might also offer to provide a treatment summary to the agency in lieu of the complete record. Finally, the psychotherapist would monitor how this attempted or actual disclosure might affect the continuing psychotherapist–client relationship.

# WHEN DISCLOSURE OF TREATMENT INFORMATION TO THIRD PARTIES IS BASED ON A SUBPOENA ISSUED TO THE PSYCHOTHERAPIST

A subpoena, which is an attorney's formal demand for a client's treatment records or for the psychotherapist's testimony about the client's evaluation and/or treatment, generally does not, by itself, overcome the confidentiality and privilege that protects a client's treatment information from disclosure. In most jurisdictions, in order for the psychotherapist to provide the subpoenaed information, the client must simultaneously authorize the disclosure of the information requested by the subpoena, or the court must issue an order directing release of the treatment information. The rules regarding a psychotherapist's compliance with subpoenas, however, vary by jurisdiction, and psychotherapists should be familiar with those local rules when deciding how to respond when a subpoena for mental health records is received. Generally, the psychotherapist would be wise to consult with an attorney if he or she has any uncertainty about how to respond to a subpoena.

Following the guidelines above, the psychotherapist would notify the current or past client about the receipt of the subpoena and the nature and extent of the information demanded by the subpoena, would remind the client about the contents of the sought information (especially any particularly sensitive information), and would ascertain whether the client wishes to authorize the disclosure of the subpoenaed information. The psychotherapist may also encourage the client to consult with an attorney regarding whether to authorize the disclosure.

If the client decides to authorize the disclosure, the psychotherapist would have the client execute a HIPAA-compliant authorization form that contains the necessary elements (e.g., to whom the release is to be made, what is to be released) and proceed to release the requested information. Both before and after the release, the psychotherapist would explore with the client the potential impact that the disclosure might have on the psychotherapy. For example, if the client is authorizing disclosure of treatment information in furtherance of the client's lawsuit against another entity, the psychotherapist may want to explore how the disclosure (and potential future disclosures) may inhibit the client from speaking freely in the psychotherapy. The psychotherapist may also want to explore the client's perhaps inaccurate expectations regarding the psychotherapist's participation or involvement in the client's lawsuit.

If the client decides that he or she does not want to authorize disclosure, or the psychotherapist cannot locate the client, the psychotherapist would respond to the subpoena with a letter to the subpoenaing attorney that states, in essence, that the psychotherapist can neither confirm nor deny the existence of a professional relationship with the person at issue, but that, if such a relationship existed, the therapist could not disclose any confidential and/or privileged information about that relationship without a client's authorization, a court order, or some other legal authority that mandates the disclosure. This letter puts the ball in the subpoenaing attorney's court to produce an adequate legal authority to compel disclosure of the sought-after information. The psychotherapist would consult a local attorney and/or his or her professional liability insurance carrier should the matter persist or if he or she is unsure about the legal authority the subpoenaing attorney subsequently cites as mandating compliance with the subpoena.

# WHEN DISCLOSURE OF TREATMENT INFORMATION TO A THIRD PARTY IS MANDATED BY A COURT ORDER OR OTHER COMPULSORY LEGAL MECHANISM

In contrast to a subpoena, a court order, which is an order issued and signed by a judge and directed at the psychotherapist, does not require the client's authorization in order for the psychotherapist to comply with the order. Failure to comply with a court order usually constitutes "contempt of court" and can result in fines and/or imprisonment for noncompliance. Sometimes it is difficult to tell the difference between a subpoena and a court order; moreover, administrative bodies (e.g., workers' compensation boards, administrative law judges) are often empowered to issue administrative orders. Whether these administrative orders are binding on the psychotherapist depends on often-arcane state laws and regulations and varies across jurisdictions. Consequently, the psychotherapist who has any uncertainty about the issue should seek advice from a local attorney or consult his or her professional liability insurance carrier.

Upon receipt of a valid court order, the psychotherapist must comply, but would, if possible, still notify the client of the receipt of the court order, inform him or her about the nature and extent of the information demanded by the order, remind the client about the contents of the sought-after information (especially any particularly sensitive information), and encourage the client to consult with an attorney if he or she wishes to attempt to challenge the court order before the information is actually released.

In addition to court orders, there often exist certain legal mechanisms that automatically remove the confidentiality and/or privilege that protect records from disclosure to third parties. Some of these mechanisms, for example, relate to treatment information sought by a child protective agency in furtherance of the agency's investigation and prosecution of a child maltreatment matter. When a psychotherapist practices in a jurisdiction whose law provides for the automatic waiver of the confidentiality/privilege of a client's treatment records under such circumstances, he or she can be compelled to disclose the requested information without the client's authorization.

A second example of such a legal mechanism often found in many jurisdictions is the coroner/medical examiner exception, which allows a medical examiner to obtain a deceased client's treatment records, without the authorization of the client's next of kin or personal representative, so that the medical examiner can determine the deceased client's cause of death.

A third commonly found such mechanism is the automatic waiver of confidentiality/privilege when there is a demand for treatment information in the context of an involuntary civil commitment proceeding to establish the need for, or to maintain, a client's psychiatric hospitalization.

The existence and specific nature of these automatic legal waivers of client confidentiality/privilege vary significantly from jurisdiction to jurisdiction—some have them, some do not. Consequently, a psychotherapist cannot assume that a demand made by one of these, usually governmental, entities automatically authorizes disclosure of confidential/privileged treatment information. Thus, whenever a psychotherapist receives a demand from a governmental agency that purports to have the inherent authority to obtain disclosure of confidential/privileged treatment information without the client's authorization, he or she would respectfully request that the entity making the demand produce, in written form, the specific legal authority that would justify the disclosure without client authorization. If the psychotherapist has any uncertainty about the validity of the authority the governmental agency produces in response, he or she should consult a local attorney or his or her professional liability insurance carrier for assistance. If it turns out that the psychotherapist must comply with such a demand, he or she should attempt, whenever possible, to inform the client about the demand and the need for the psychotherapist to comply with it.

# CLIENT/PSYCHOTHERAPIST INVITATION OF THIRD PARTIES INTO THE PSYCHOTHERAPY

Sometimes the client or the psychotherapist may want to invite a third party into the session. For example, a client in individual psychotherapy may feel that bringing a third party into a session would help to resolve a problem concerning the client and the third party (e.g., the client's family member). In such situations, the psychotherapist must carefully evaluate whether the clinical benefits of including the third party in the session outweigh the risks. These risks include the possibility that the third party

- Will gain information about the client that the client would not want him or her to have, or that would not be in the client's best interest
- May misunderstand his or her role in the psychotherapy and mistakenly believe that the psychotherapist is now in a psychotherapist–client relationship with him or her
- May disclose information that may trigger a psychotherapist's duty to intervene (e.g., by revealing the existence of serious and imminent homicidal or suicidal intent; by disclosing information that triggers the psychotherapist's child abuse reporting duties)

To minimize these risks, the psychotherapist must understand the role of the third party in the client's psychotherapy, which includes understanding whether the third party is becoming a client in the psychotherapy or is a collateral whose presence simply serves to advance the client's own psychotherapy. If the psychotherapist is confused or unsure about the third party's status, it is almost certain the client and the third party will be similarly confused or unsure, which greatly increases the risk of a negative outcome for all involved.

The psychotherapist should then do the following:

- Carefully assess and discuss with the client what the client expects to achieve by bringing the third party into one or more sessions with the client, and whether these expectations are likely to be realized by doing so.
- Explicitly discuss what information the psychotherapist may and may not disclose to the third party during the joint sessions.
- Document the client–psychotherapist discussion on the issue, as well as the client's agreement to the terms of the third party's involvement.
- Consider setting a time period for the duration of these joint sessions, at which time the client and the psychotherapist would decide whether to continue such sessions.

In addition, the psychotherapist must carefully inform third parties about their status in the psychotherapy. Typically, third parties would be collateral informants and not clients of the psychotherapist, although this may not be obvious to the third party. Consequently, the psychotherapist would use a written "collateral informed consent form" with third parties; the form would notify third parties that they are not clients of the psychotherapist, that the third party's communications in the psychotherapy session will be noted in the client's chart but will not be available to the third party, and that the third party is not owed a duty of confidentiality or privilege in the event that the client authorizes disclosure of the treatment record or the psychotherapist is forced to disclose the treatment record to others. Finally, the collateral participant would be informed that, despite his or her non-client status, the psychotherapist is still required to make child abuse, duty to protect, and other mandatory disclosures if the collateral informant discloses information that triggers these mandated reporting duties.

There may be circumstances where a psychotherapist believes that a third party's involvement in the psychotherapist–client relationship would indeed further the goals of the psychotherapy. For example, when dealing with a potentially suicidal client, the psychotherapist may decide that involving a particular family member could reduce the client's suicide risk, because the family member may be able to monitor the client between sessions, may provide increased support to the client, and may be more readily available to openly discuss the client's suicidality once disclosure of such has occurred in the joint psychotherapy session. Although in this case it is the psychotherapist that is inviting the participation of a third party in the treatment, he or she would still follow the same principles outlined above regarding the presence of a third party in a treatment session.

Sometimes the client's attorney or employer or a court-appointed evaluator will contact the psychotherapist and ask him or her to discuss the client or the client's treatment (i.e., rather than simply requesting copies of the client's treatment record). The psychotherapist, of course, cannot disclose any information to these entities without the client's authorization. But often the client will grant such authorization because the client believes it is in his or her best interest to do so, or because the client is being pressured to authorize such disclosure. In such a situation, the psychotherapist would follow the guidelines articulated in this chapter. However, a psychotherapist who believes that such a discussion would be unhelpful to the psychotherapy or would create risks for the psychotherapist is not obligated to engage in such a discussion with any third party. He or she can instead simply provide the treatment record or offer a written treatment summary. Doing so allows the psychotherapist to avoid making inadvertent or erroneous statements during a spontaneous and unstructured conversation with the requesting party.

The problems that can arise when the psychotherapist engages in an informal discussion with such a third party include the following:

The third party may inadvertently misinterpret or, in extreme circumstances, deliberately distort the psychotherapist's oral statements, in furtherance of the third party's own interests.

The psychotherapist may, in the spontaneity of an oral discussion, omit relevant information or make accidental misstatements that will negatively affect the client and/or the psychotherapist.

The psychotherapist, in a genuine but misguided effort to be helpful to the client and the third party, may violate the ethical and regulatory rules that are intended to keep a psychotherapist from straying into an impermissible dual role or exceeding the psychotherapist's level of competence with regard to giving an opinion about a particular issue.

For example, the client's attorney may press the psychotherapist to offer the opinion that a motor vehicle accident, rather than a preexisting psychological condition, is the cause of the client's current distress—an opinion that the attorney will then use to support the client's lawsuit against the other driver. Or, a forensic child custody evaluator may contact the psychotherapist and seek to elicit opinions that exceed the psychotherapist's treating role—asking, for example, whether the client is a fit parent, when the psychotherapist has had no opportunity to evaluate the client's parenting ability. Providing such opinions, especially in the context of an ongoing legal, administrative, or employment matter (where the client faces a potentially serious outcome), can place the psychotherapist at significant risk from regulatory authorities, from other involved mental health professionals, and from the client.

When asked to orally discuss a client's case with a third party, the psychotherapist must proceed cautiously. Rather than engaging in such a discussion, the psychotherapist might ask the third party to submit a set of written questions for him or her to consider. The psychotherapist would then review the written questions, determine if he or she can properly answer some or any of them, and then compose responses in an unpressured and thoughtful manner that minimizes the risk to the psychotherapist (e.g., the risk of making inadvertently erroneous or misleading statements or of being misquoted), the client, and the psychotherapy. It can often be helpful for the psychotherapist to review his or her proposed responses with the client. Alternatively, the psychotherapist might offer to provide a brief treatment summary in lieu of an oral discussion with the third party. In constructing such a summary, the psychotherapist would provide an accurate summary that is limited to the facts of the psychotherapy and that does not express opinions or give information that would exceed the treating (i.e., nonevaluative) role. Finally, the psychotherapist might simply decline the request for an oral discussion and indicate that the third party's recourse is to seek copies of the client's treatment records or possibly to submit written questions to which the psychotherapist can provide written responses.

In choosing how to proceed in these circumstances, the psychotherapist should discuss the matter with the client and document in the client's chart the reasons for choosing a particular course of action. The psychotherapist can also seek input (without releasing protected information about the client) from his or her malpractice carrier and well-respected colleagues, being sure to document these discussions in the client's file.

## CONCLUSION

A psychotherapist must be aware of the local laws and regulations that govern the disclosure of treatment information to a third party and must notify the client in advance about the circumstances that permit or mandate such disclosure. A psychotherapist should always consider the effect that the disclosure of treatment information may have on the client and the psychotherapy and should seek, whenever possible, to protect that information while realizing there are circumstances where the disclosure of treatment information to, or the involvement of, a third party may be beneficial for the client and/or the psychotherapy. A psychotherapist should use a thorough informed consent process and should carefully document all actions taken in regard to third-party interactions with the psychotherapist–client dyad.

# RESOURCES

American Psychological Association. (2010). Ethical principles of psychologists and code of conduct. Retrieved from http://www.apa.org/ethics/code/index.aspx.

American Psychological Association Practice Organization. (2012). How to handle subpoenas and depositions. Retrieved from http://www.apapracticecentral.org/good-practice/secure/2012-winter.pdf.

Fisher, M. (2012). Confidentiality and record keeping. In S. Knapp (ed.), *APA handbook of ethics in psychology: Vol. 1. Moral foundations and common themes* (pp. 333–375). Washington, DC: American Psychological Association.

Knapp, S., Younggren, J., VandeCreek, L., Harris, E., & Martin, J. (2013). *Assessing and managing risk in psychological practice: An individualized approach* (2nd Ed.). Rockville, MD: The Trust.

Mental Health Professionals' Duty to Warn. (2015, September 28). Retrieved from http://www.ncsl.org/research/health/mental-health-professionals-duty-to-warn.aspx.

State Statutes Search. (n.d.). Retrieved from https://www.childwelfare.gov/topics/systemwide/laws-policies/state/.

U.S. Department of Health and Human Services. (2003, April 4). Health information privacy: Minimum necessary requirement. Retrieved from http://www.hhs.gov/ocr/privacy/hipaa/understanding/coveredentities/minimumnecessary.html.

# CHAPTER 40

# MANAGING HIGH-RISK SUICIDAL CLIENTS IN PRIVATE PRACTICE

*Jeffrey C. Sung and David A. Jobes*

Managing clients at high risk of suicide in private practice requires clinical skills related to managing the risk and providing effective suicide-specific treatment within a framework of care. Evidence-based treatments for suicide risk have been described with some treatments offering guidance on providing effective care (Jobes, 2016; Weinberg et al., 2010; Wenzel, Brown, & Beck, 2009). Structured protocols for assessing and managing suicide risk in an outpatient setting are also available (Columbia-Suicide Severity Rating Scale [C-SSRS]; Linehan et al., 2012). The focus of this chapter is therefore less on specific treatment models for suicide risk and more on conceptualizing clinical work with high-risk clients (management vs. treatment) and the practice management implications for private practitioners. We will begin by reviewing key elements of suicide risk assessment and evidence-based care for suicide risk and follow with a discussion of practice management issues and two common clinical problems with high-risk clients.

## SCREENING FOR SUICIDE RISK

Essentially all clients seen in a behavioral health setting are at some elevated risk of suicide. Suicide risk—as the life-or-death issue in behavioral health—will require more assessment if identified. We therefore recommend that psychotherapists screen all clients for suicide risk early in every initial assessment. We would compare screening for suicide risk to wearing a seatbelt while driving.

While any given car trip is unlikely to result in an accident, routine seatbelt use helps protect the driver and passengers from rare but potentially fatal outcomes. The psychotherapist should screen for suicide risk by summarizing the client's situational and symptomatic risk factors for suicide and using these to create a context for asking directly about lower levels of suicidal ideation (passive wishes to be dead, wanting to sleep and not wake up). For example, one might ask: "You've talked about how painful this divorce has been. Has it ever reached the point where you wished you were dead?"

Clinicians who use a written intake questionnaire may include screening questions about suicide risk. For example, questions based on the PHQ-9 (Kroenke, Spitzer, & Williams, 2010) and C-SSRS might include the following:

- PHQ-9: "Have you had thoughts that you would be better off dead or of hurting yourself in some way?"
- C-SSRS: "Have you wished you were dead or wished you could go to sleep and not wake up?"

# EPIDEMIOLOGIC VERSUS THERAPEUTIC ASSESSMENT

A client who affirms suicide risk factors and ideation at the screening level will require a more in-depth suicide risk assessment. We recommend that the clinician use a therapeutic assessment style that seeks to build an emotional connection with the suicidal client, who is typically feeling deeply disconnected and demoralized. Therapeutic assessment leads with open-ended questions that encourage a narrative response from the client. For example, following the Aeschi approach of narrative interviewing (Michel & Valach, 2011), cognitive therapy for suicide prevention (Wenzel et al., 2009) recommends beginning the assessment with an instruction for the client to tell as complete a story as possible regarding the suicidal crisis: "Please tell me the story of what brought you to the point of considering suicide." Common themes that may emerge from this narrative include unbearable loneliness, feeling like a burden to others, and hopelessness about the future (Joiner, 2005). Another narrative interviewing approach, the Collaborative Assessment and Management of Suicidality (Jobes, 2012, 2016), encourages the psychotherapist to sit next to the client physically while the client completes the Suicide Status Form, which elucidates essential aspects of the experience of being suicidal (emotional pain, stress, pressure, agitation, hopelessness, self-hate, reasons for living and reasons for dying). With each of these two models of therapeutic assessment, the clinician's explicit goal is to empathically understand the client's painful emotional experience of suicidality.

After thoroughly understanding the client's subjective experience, the psychotherapist may then continue with an epidemiologic assessment that reviews essential risk factors for suicide, including suicide attempt history and current suicidal ideation, intent, planning, and access to lethal means.

# MANAGEMENT VERSUS TREATMENT

When suicide risk has been identified, the psychotherapist is responsible for developing a management plan to mitigate imminent risk. Keeping the client alive with suicide risk management strategies is always the first priority in care. Beyond an initial management plan, the psychotherapist may negotiate with the client to develop a treatment plan for ongoing care to resolve suicide risk. Management refers to short-term and intermediate-term strategies to mitigate suicide risk; suicide risk management strategies should include the following:

- Fostering connectedness (Luxton et al., 2012): Scheduling regular follow-up, expressing care and concern, engaging in between-session contacts, contacting and coordinating treatment with family members, troubleshooting treatment nonadherence, obtaining contact information for emergency contacts:
  "I'm glad you're here; let's team up to work through this and schedule appointments as needed."
  "Is there a way we can build some more support for you by talking to your (family member)?"
- Treatment of comorbid psychiatric conditions (Fawcett, 2009; Rutz et al., 1989): Initiating or referring for medication treatment of depression, anxiety, insomnia, substance use, and so forth:
  "I am concerned about your level of depression and would like to arrange an appointment for you with a psychiatrist."
  "Can we make an appointment for you to see your primary care doctor? I am thinking that she can talk to you about options for medication to help with sleep."
- Reducing access to lethal means (Yip et al., 2012): Counseling on access to lethal means, involving family members in confirming removal of lethal means:
  "I'm concerned about you and want to make sure you stay alive to see things get better. We know that reducing access to lethal methods of suicide is one of the most effective ways of preventing suicide. Can we talk about finding a way to remove . . . or find a safer way to store . . . while we work together on helping you feel better?"
- Brief interventions such as "safety planning" (Fleischmann et al., 2008; Stanley & Brown, 2012): Collaborative generation of a safety/crisis plan, providing emergency contact numbers, counseling the client and family members on warning signs of suicide:
  "I'd like to suggest that we make a crisis plan to help you get through those dark moments when you might start to think about suicide. We'll start by figuring out how you know a crisis might be developing and then work on finding coping strategies you can use."

Suicide risk management targets risk factors that are extrinsic or related to suicide risk and is optimally, but not necessarily, a collaborative process. For example, if a client who is judged to be at imminent risk of suicide does not or cannot participate in collaborative management of risk, the psychotherapist may be obligated to initiate involuntary psychiatric hospitalization. Alternatively, a psychotherapist may call a client's prescriber to discuss a plan for restricting the number of pills dispensed to reduce access to lethal means. These two examples of management strategies seek to reduce risk without necessarily engaging the client's participation in a collaborative process of co-managing risk.

Treatment of suicide risk refers to a collaborative process of identifying and resolving emotional and psychological factors that are thought to be intrinsic to suicide risk. While management of suicide risk is *optimally* collaborative, treatment of suicide risk is *necessarily* collaborative. That is, the psychotherapist and client agree upon a contract for treatment that defines the roles and responsibilities for each person with a shared goal of resolving suicide risk. To summarize:

Management
- **Collaboration:** Optimal when collaborative
- **Goal:** Reduction of risk
- **Target:** External factors that relate to suicide risk
- **Summary:** Doing what it takes to keep the client alive

Treatment
- **Collaboration:** Necessarily collaborative
- **Goal:** Resolution of risk
- **Target:** Internal factors that are intrinsic to suicide risk
- **Summary:** Working together to resolve the problems that are causing the client to consider suicide

# NEGOTIATING THE FRAME OF TREATMENT

Because ongoing management of suicide risk by the psychotherapist does not necessarily reduce suicide risk over time, the task in management mode is to shift into treatment mode such that the client will grow in his or her own capacity to self-manage risk over time (Ellis, 2004). Making this shift from management to treatment requires a strong therapeutic alliance whereby the clinician and client join together with a shared goal of resolving suicide risk. For example:

> Dr. A has been seeing Ms. B in weekly psychotherapy. Ms. B has expressed varying levels of suicidal ideation and intent while becoming increasingly depressed and dysphoric. Ms. B rejects all of Dr. A's recommendations for coping with suicidal thoughts, stating, "I've tried all that, and it doesn't work." At the end of her Friday appointment, Ms. B states, "I can say that I won't do it tonight or this weekend." Dr. A schedules an additional appointment on Monday morning and presses Ms. B until she agrees to a phone call over the weekend. Dr. A advises Ms. B that if she does not answer the phone, Dr. A will be calling 911. In this example, Dr. A is in management mode, using connectedness to manage suicide risk without the client's participation in learning to self-manage risk.

Building a treatment alliance with a suicidal client requires the psychotherapist to empathize with the client's desire to escape hopelessness and pain through suicide while presenting treatment as a compelling alternative to reducing emotional pain. When conducting clinical work, we assume that every suicidal client who presents for care is ambivalent about suicide. That is, a part of the client wishes to live, and a part of the client wishes to die. If the client were not ambivalent, he or she would have already died by suicide rather than presenting for care. Even a client who reports no hope for the future, by virtue of arriving for the appointment, demonstrates an objective manifestation of hope. The clinician's task is to join with the part of the client that wants to live and externalize the suicidal process such that the psychotherapist and client form an alliance together to understand and manage suicide risk. For example:

> **Dr. A:** "I want you to feel better, and I'm worried we might be getting into a pattern that keeps things where they are."
> **Ms. B:** "What do you mean?"
> **Dr. A:** "When we schedule extra appointments and phone calls, I think about how that might leave you feeling more helpless and hopeless that you could ever find ways to cope on your own."
> **Ms. B:** "I've always been helpless and hopeless. Nothing helps when I feel this way."
> **Dr. A:** "Maybe that's a place for us to start. Can we look at how you got to feeling so helpless and hopeless? You've survived this long, which means you're a resilient, even strong, person. I think we'll be able to find the person who's still strong and knows how to survive."
> **Ms. B:** "I know I'm a strong person."
> **Dr. A:** "Let's build on that strength to find a way through the helplessness and hopelessness."

A client who expresses willingness to consider treatment may be engaged in a process to negotiate an initial period of time during which suicide can be relinquished as an option while treatment to resolve suicide risk proceeds. Articulating a reasonable discrete period of time *to delay suicide while treatment proceeds* is central to obtaining a commitment to potentially life-saving treatment. We recommend an initial period of one to three months for the psychotherapist and client to commit to a shared treatment effort, and the clinician should define a set of conditions for management of suicide risk that must be in place for treatment to proceed in good faith. For example, the CAMS framework defines a stabilization plan consisting of reducing access to lethal means; an agreed-upon plan to manage any suicidal crisis, including emergency contacts to co-manage crises should that be necessary; an effort to reduce social isolation; and a plan to anticipate any potential barriers to care (Jobes, 2016).

The psychotherapist should decide, sometimes with the assistance of a consultant, on a minimum level of meaningful, good-faith engagement from the client that represents willingness to collaborate in a process to resolve suicide risk. A client who will not or cannot agree to a minimum set of conditions to manage suicide risk while treatment proceeds is not a candidate for collaborative outpatient treatment and may require a higher level of care or alternative treatment setting. For example, a client who refuses to dispose of a lethal stockpile of medications, refuses to allow a family member to hold the medications, refuses to place the medications in a sealed box during the course of treatment, and refuses to allow contact with the physician prescribing the medication does not demonstrate a level of meaningful engagement that suggests the potential for collaborative therapeutic work. A client who insists on absolute privacy in treatment such that the psychotherapist has no access to potentially supportive family members for collateral history or care coordination may also not be ready to participate in treatment. In these settings we recommend that the psychotherapist designate a time-limited period to explore the meaning of the client's conditions for treatment with a goal of resolving the impasse or ending the treatment relationship in a responsible manner. During this period of negotiating a treatment contract, the psychotherapist should continuously assess for the need for psychiatric hospitalization, use suicide risk management strategies as appropriate, and document that the focus of care is to determine whether a collaborative treatment relationship can proceed.

Outcomes of the process of negotiating a treatment contract include the following:

- Mutual agreement on a framework for crisis management and ongoing care that allows collaborative treatment to proceed
- Suicide risk management (rather than collaborative treatment) until a crisis resolves
- Referral for emergency evaluation or psychiatric hospitalization if the client is judged to be at near-term risk of suicide or if ongoing management is failing to resolve a crisis
- Referral to other providers with lower requirements for the client to engage in collaborative treatment, such as primary care or case management

For clients who will not or cannot consent to a minimum set of suicide risk management strategies, the psychotherapist may need to end the course of care. A principled decision to end treatment is distinct from clinical abandonment (i.e., abrupt and inappropriate unilateral termination) in that the psychotherapist does the following (Jobes, 2011, 2016):

- Transparently works in the best interests of the client
- Is clear about the necessary elements of the treatment and why they are necessary
- Makes reasonable effort to make referrals to bridge the client to other indicated care
- Seeks professional consultation
- Documents the decision-making process in relation to the client's best interests

The distinction here is between "I refuse to treat you" (abandonment) and "I am not able to provide safe treatment for you without the necessary conditions that we have discussed" (a clear professional recommendation for suicide-safe care that is in the client's best interests) (Jobes, 2011). The decision to end the relationship is based on the principles that a psychotherapist is not under obligation to provide a treatment that is not judged to be safe and that a client with risk factors for suicide who is not judged to be at short-term, immediate risk of suicide may make an informed decision to refuse treatment. For example:

Client: "So you're saying you can't help me."
Clinician: "I can tell that you are suffering and that you want to feel better. The path that I know out of that suffering is by taking steps to make sure we can work together safely."

**Client:** "I don't think you really understand me. Those rules are for you, not me. Why do you need my husband's phone number, and why do I need to fill out a piece of paper?"

**Clinician:** "I could not possibly understand all of what you're going through. From what I know about working under these circumstances, our best chance of keeping you alive and getting you feeling better includes the parts of crisis plan we discussed. Is there another emergency contact we can use? Is there anything we can list on a safety plan?"

**Client:** "This isn't working. It's obvious you can't help me. I think we're done here."

**Clinician:** "I hope you'll think about what we talked about. Please, when you're ready, I am here for us to talk again. I'd like to give you some referrals and some crisis contacts."

**Client:** "I don't need those." [*Walks out*]

**Documentation:** The client was counseled regarding suicide risk management strategies for safe ongoing treatment, including the need for a regular appointment schedule, removal of lethal means, emergency contacts, and a safety plan. The client declined participation in these risk management strategies and refused referrals and crisis contacts. This client has a history of chronic suicidality and does not present with warning signs to suggest near-term risk of suicidal behavior. Also, this client does not appear impulsive with regard to suicidal behavior and reported a history of denying suicidality convincingly during emergency evaluations. Referral for emergency evaluation or psychiatric hospitalization appears likely to be ineffective under these circumstances with an added risk of further alienating the client from treatment. The client was offered follow-up to discuss a plan for collaborative treatment should she elect to pursue this.

# TREATMENT OF SUICIDE RISK

Treatment of suicide risk seeks to resolve risk by targeting emotional and psychological factors that are deemed to be intrinsic to the suicidal process. Many clients experience life circumstances such as mental illness, physical illness, losses, family conflict, unemployment, and social isolation. These life circumstances that predispose or relate to suicide risk may be conceptualized as *indirect drivers of suicide* (Jobes, Jobes et al., 2016). In response to these indirect drivers, subsets of clients have particular emotional experiences and psychological interpretations of these stressors that cause them to develop suicidal ideation or behavior. These emotional and psychological factors that are deemed to be intrinsic to the suicidal process and that distinguish between nonsuicidal and suicidal clients may be conceptualized as *direct drivers of suicide*. That is, if a client becomes suicidal in response to life stress, the client may have direct drivers of suicide that have caused him or her to become acutely suicidal (see also Tucker et al., 2015, for more on drivers). For example:

> A 56-year-old man has been living alone in an apartment during adversarial divorce proceedings. During a telephone call from his lawyer, he is told that he has temporarily lost custody of his children. Indirect drivers: family conflict, social isolation, interpersonal crisis.

**Suicidal**: Upon hearing this news, he becomes enraged and ruminates on his loneliness, isolation, and feelings of worthlessness while thinking, "It's over. There's nothing left for me now." After becoming intoxicated on alcohol, he shoots himself, leaving no suicide note. Direct drivers of suicide: thwarted belongingness, perceived burdensomeness, hopelessness, selective attention, attentional fixation (Joiner, 2005; Wenzel et al., 2009).

**Nonsuicidal**: Upon hearing this news, he becomes depressed and thinks over "all the mistakes I've made in my life." After isolating himself for the afternoon, he thinks, "beating myself up isn't going to change anything. I need to get out of my head." He makes a series of phone calls to friends, some of whom he has not seen in years, until he finds someone to meet him for dinner.

Psychotherapies that have been shown to be effective for suicide risk have different conceptualizations regarding drivers of suicide risk, and each treatment offers interventions to resolve these issues. Regardless of the theoretical understanding of suicide, each of these treatments engages the client in a pretreatment process of informed consent to agree upon a framework of suicide risk management strategies that will keep the client alive and protect the treatment relationship while ongoing psychotherapy proceeds. In a suicide-specific treatment, the priority is not necessarily on actual resolution of the client's overarching life problems per se (indirect drivers) but rather on resolution of the emotional and psychological experience of suicidogenic problems (direct drivers) that compel the client to consider suicide. For example:

- Mindfulness to resolve attentional fixation: "Maybe I'll always think about suicide when something bad happens. The difference now is that I know I don't have to dwell or act on it."
- Emotion regulation to resolve pain and hopelessness: "Even though it still hits me, I know that the pain of my husband's death won't last forever."
- Cognitive restructuring to resolve hopelessness and no reasons for living: "I don't know the reason this is happening to me, but there's got to be a reason. I just haven't found it yet."
- Pros and cons to address attentional fixation and access to lethal means: "I see your point. It's probably not good for me to have all of those pills right there, all the time, where I can get them when I'm in that zone. If I really wanted to kill myself I could get more later."
- Behavioral experiment to resolve hopelessness regarding thwarted belongingness and burdensomeness: "That was a wakeup call to realize how many people actually care about me. To be honest, I don't think I ever really knew that."
- Interpretation to facilitate identification with a lost object: "I kept thinking I wanted to join my mother in death by killing myself. Now I have other ways to keep her memory alive. I know she's still with me."
- Interpretation to clarify internal object relations: "I still hate that part of myself, but I don't have to actually kill all of myself to deal with these feelings."

After resolving the direct drivers of suicide with a course of care that includes a relapse prevention plan, the psychotherapist and client may reassess the treatment goals and decide to continue in treatment to address other issues, coordinate a referral, or end treatment altogether.

# MALPRACTICE LIABILITY
# AND DOCUMENTATION

The higher risk of adverse outcomes with clients at high risk of suicide generally exposes a psychotherapist to greater malpractice liability. Adverse outcomes may relate to suicide attempts, suicide death, or unauthorized disclosures of confidential information. As described above, clinical care of suicidal clients requires an assessment of suicide risk, a suicide-specific plan to manage that risk, and follow-through with the treatment plan. Appropriate clinical care and contemporaneous documentation that encompasses these elements of care are the primary means of mitigating malpractice liability. Documentation demonstrates the psychotherapist's knowledge of the level of risk, steps to mitigate the risk, and a rationale for the decision making in selecting the treatment interventions. Complete and thorough documentation may include five elements:

1. **Database**: Relevant risk factors, protective factors, and warning signs
2. **Risk stratification**: A clinical judgment regarding the overall level of risk. Many risk stratification schemes exist to guide decision making in regard to a treatment setting and treatment interventions. The risk stratification scheme used by the National Suicide Prevention Lifeline takes into account elements of suicidal desire, suicidal intent, suicidal capability, and buffers against suicide (Joiner et al., 2007). Risk stratification is not meant to predict suicide but rather to suggest a setting for care (inpatient vs. outpatient) and a level of intervention (frequency of sessions and range of interventions).
3. **Interventions for suicide**: Suicide risk management and treatment strategies that were implemented to mitigate risk
4. **Justification of the level of care**: A rationale for why the psychotherapist selected the level of care (inpatient or outpatient) and specific interventions to mitigate the client's level of risk. In the event of a suicide attempt or death, the psychotherapist's work will be judged against the retrospective finding that a higher level of care may have been warranted. Given the *impossibility of predicting suicide death* (American Psychological Association, 2003), a psychotherapist's work can only be evaluated according to whether the clinical judgment met the standard of care in *reasonable assessment and management of the foreseeable level of suicide risk* (Bryan & Rudd, 2006). Because the presence of an adverse outcome will suggest that a higher level of care was warranted, documentation of an outpatient plan should include a justification of the level of care that explains why higher-level, more restrictive (i.e., emergency or inpatient) options were considered and rejected in favor of lower-level, less restrictive (i.e., outpatient) options. Reasons to continue seeing a high-risk client as an outpatient include the following:
   - Higher levels of intervention appear likely to be detrimental to the client's clinical status.
   - Higher levels of intervention appear likely to be detrimental to the treatment.
   - Higher levels of intervention appear likely to be ineffective in reducing risk.
   - Current suicidal threats or behavior are judged to be a behavioral operant; that is, suicide risk appears closely connected with environmental responses, and higher

levels of response (referral for emergency evaluation or psychiatric hospitalization) appear likely to reinforce suicidal behavior and increase suicide risk over time.

5. **Consultants**: Noting within the medical record that colleagues were consulted to develop the plan is critical to decreasing liability.

For a client with a level of risk sufficient to warrant a full suicide risk assessment, we recommend documenting the assessment with these five elements at least once at baseline, with updated documentation when clinically relevant changes that influence the level of risk occur (e.g., impending crisis, end of a relationship, loss of employment, relapse on substances).

## DOCUMENTATION: CASE 1

53-year-old woman seen in weekly psychotherapy

**Risk factors:** Female in mid-life, family history of suicide, major depression, alcohol use, social isolation, sleep disturbance, hopelessness, active suicidal ideation with thoughts of overdosing. No previous attempts, current suicidal intent, or planning. No firearms in the home.

**Protective factors:** Engaged in treatment, fear of the act of suicide, responsibility to family members, use of coping skills (work)

**Overall risk of suicide:** Based on the presence of suicidal desire (suicidal ideation, hopelessness), some elements of suicidal intent (active suicidal ideation with known method), some elements of suicidal capability (family history of suicide, alcohol use), and some protective factors, overall level of risk is judged to be high.

**Interventions for suicide:**

- **Connectedness:** Plan to schedule for weekly psychotherapy and to coordinate treatment with client's mother
- **Depression treatment:** Client has been referred for medication evaluation for depression and insomnia with her primary care physician. Client was engaged in a plan to remove all alcohol from the home with confirmation from her mother when this has been done.
- **Reducing access to lethal means:** Client confirms that she has no firearms or stockpiled medication in the home. Plan to discuss care with her physician to limit access to potentially dangerous prescription medication.
- **Safety planning:** Client participated in generating a safety plan to manage suicidal crisis. The safety plan was signed by the client and a copy of the plan was placed in the chart.
- **Treatment:** Ongoing psychotherapy using cognitive-behavioral therapy is focused on addressing social isolation and hopelessness as factors that appear most closely connected with suicide risk.

**Justification for level of care:** While this client presents with a high level of suicide risk, she has continued to work and values this as a means of coping and a reason for living. Referring for emergency services or inpatient hospitalization would likely disrupt her ability to work, increase feelings of hopelessness and purposelessness, and risk unemployment—all of which would likely increase the risk of suicide. Furthermore, an outpatient suicide risk management plan that includes initial twice-weekly contact, coordination with a family member, medication treatment of depression, removal of alcohol, limiting access to prescription medications, and a detailed safety plan is in place.

**Consultants:** Case was discussed with Dr. A to review the plan for session frequency, care coordination with family, removal of alcohol, managing prescription medications, and safety planning.

## DOCUMENTATION: CASE 2

28-year-old man seen in weekly psychotherapy

**Risk factors:** Male, Caucasian, depression, borderline personality disorder, previous suicide attempts, family conflict, social isolation, current suicidal ideation with thoughts of jumping from a height. No current subjective suicidal intent or planning. No substance use.

**Protective factors:** Engaged in treatment, responsibility to family members

**Overall risk of suicide:** Based on the presence of suicidal desire, some level of suicidal intent (suicidal ideation with known method), clear suicidal capability (multiple previous attempts), and some protective factors, overall long-term risk is judged to be high. Current acute risk is judged to be moderate to high.

**Interventions for suicide:**

- **Connectedness:** Weekly psychotherapy, in-session practice calling the National Suicide Prevention Lifeline
- **Depression treatment:** Ongoing medication management of depression
- **Reducing access to lethal means:** Client confirms no firearms or stockpiled medications. Client was counseled regarding a plan to stay indoors and avoid heights when in a suicidal crisis.
- **Safety planning:** A detailed safety plan was developed with a copy signed by the client and placed in the chart.
- **Treatment:** Ongoing psychotherapy using skills training and cognitive-behavioral therapy is focused on emotion dysregulation and hopelessness over chaotic interpersonal relationships as factors most closely connected with suicide risk.

**Justification for level of care:** This client has a history of previous psychiatric hospitalizations that have not decreased suicide risk over time. Hospitalization in this case appears to be of limited value in mitigating risk, and the client has demonstrated a capacity to deny suicidality in a convincing manner during mental health evaluations. Outpatient treatment appears more likely to resolve suicide risk over time, and referring for psychiatric hospitalization will likely destroy the treatment relationship and thereby increase suicide risk.

**Consultants:** Case was discussed with Dr. A to review the plan for session frequency, treatment of depression, managing access to lethal means, safety plan, and focus of ongoing psychotherapy.

# PRACTICE MANAGEMENT IN WORKING WITH SUICIDAL CLIENTS

Issues of liability, reimbursement, and practice structure may affect a private practitioner's ability to manage high-risk clients. Psychotherapists in private practice are typically reimbursed only for in-session work and often work relatively independently. This contrasts with a high-risk client's clinical needs, which may require the psychotherapist to have additional training, out-of-session availability, and care coordination with colleagues. While some clients will not require this level of care, most treatments that have been shown to be effective for suicide risk include some of these elements. Therefore, psychotherapists in private practice will need to review their personal limits around tolerating higher liability, expending financial resources for additional training and consultation, as well as engaging in nonreimbursed clinical work such as after-hours crisis management and care coordination. A psychotherapist who cannot provide the level of care indicated for a high-risk client's clinical needs may need to refer the client for hospitalization or an alternative treatment setting. Examples include the following:

- **Malpractice liability:** Three months after the suicide death of a client, a psychotherapist receives an angry letter from the client's mother criticizing her work, requesting the medical records, and refusing to pay the outstanding balance. While no litigation ensues, the psychotherapist becomes depressed and preoccupied with malpractice liability. She then screens every new client for suicidal ideation or previous suicide attempts and develops a practice of referring any potentially suicidal clients to other psychotherapists.
- **Additional training:** A psychotherapist has been seeing a 45-year-old woman with chronic suicidality. To increase his clinical skills consistent with prevailing reasonable practice standards for the treatment of chronically suicidal clients, the clinician attends a two-day weekend seminar to learn dialectical behavior therapy skills (Linehan, 1993) to apply in the client's treatment.
- **Out-of-session crisis management:** A psychotherapist has been seeing a 20-year-old woman who has developed progressive paranoid ideation. The client calls the psychotherapist over the weekend reporting that the government has been controlling her computer and that she plans to kill herself before they come to take her into custody. The psychotherapist calls 911 from a different phone and spends the next three hours coordinating an emergency response with the client's mother, the police, an emergency department physician, and a social worker.
- **Out-of-session care coordination:** A 47-year-old woman with severe depression states during her appointment, "I can understand why some people end it." While the client denies actual suicidal thoughts, the psychotherapist is aware that she has potentially lethal sleep medications at home. The client agrees to a plan for her husband to dispense her medications temporarily, and the psychotherapist spends time on the phone in the evening with the client's husband coordinating this plan.
- **Consultation:** A clinician has been seeing a 32-year-old man for weekly psychotherapy without clear therapeutic benefit. The psychotherapist begins to dread seeing the

client and frequently jumps when her phone rings with the thought that the call will provide news that the client has died by suicide. After months of progressive anxiety, the psychotherapist begins weekly consultation with a former supervisor to discuss the client and countertransference.

- **Financial constraints:** A 58-year-old woman has returned to psychotherapy following a suicide attempt where she overdosed on pills while intoxicated on alcohol. Despite having excellent medical insurance, she incurred an enormous medical bill and cannot simultaneously make payments on her bill and private pay psychotherapy. Given the recent crisis, the psychotherapist agrees to provide continued treatment at a significantly reduced rate.

# HOSPITALIZATION AND DISCLOSURE OF INFORMATION

High-risk clients may require high-level suicide risk management strategies such as psychiatric hospitalization or engaging friends or family members in treatment against the client's wishes. These risk management strategies often strain the therapeutic alliance and require the clinician to balance ethical principles of beneficence and respect for autonomy. Here we outline therapeutic principles and a framework for decision making when the clinician is faced with escalating suicide risk that has not responded to ongoing treatment.

## INPATIENT HOSPITALIZATION

Psychiatric hospitalization represents the highest-order risk management intervention for a suicidal client. A psychiatric facility provides immediate 24-hour oversight and support, ready access to medication treatment for psychiatric symptoms, and an environment with reduced access to substances and lethal means. Psychiatric hospitalization should be considered for any client judged to be at near-term risk of suicide, and documentation should note the factors that resulted in a decision to pursue or reject this option. We recommend pursuing hospitalization if three conditions are met:

- The client is judged to be at high near-term acute risk of suicide.
- An outpatient plan is not feasible or in the best interest of the client.
- No foreseeable events in the near future will resolve the immediate crisis.

Because ethical treatment will require a psychotherapist to intervene if this is judged to be necessary to keep the client alive, as part of their informed consent discussions clinicians will need to clarify with clients their *duty* to make efforts to protect clients against suicide and the grounds under which they will initiate involuntary hospitalization for any acutely suicidal patient. Psychotherapists can emphasize that while ethics standards and the law require them to retain hospitalization as a treatment option, the priority in treatment will always be to work together to develop less-restrictive management strategies that will facilitate safe outpatient care.

## HIGH RISK OF SUICIDE

Because risk factors alone or in combination have never been shown to predict suicide, the estimation of suicide risk will always be an informed clinical judgment (APA, 2003). Review of healthcare records suggests that only a minority of suicide decedents endorsed suicidal ideation during an assessment prior to suicide death (Busch & Fawcett, 2003), and a client consumed by the suicidal process may view the psychotherapist as an adversary (Resnick, 2002). In practice this means that the psychotherapist's subjective, "gut feeling" of elevated risk will often occur while the client is denying suicidal ideation, denying subjective suicidal intent, and providing reassurance that he or she is "not suicidal." The psychotherapist should review the objective, behavioral indicators of suicidal intent (e.g., recent self-interrupted attempt, preparatory behavior, substance use, domestic violence) and warning signs of suicide (e.g., withdrawal, hopelessness, anger, agitation). If the psychotherapist highlights the discrepancy between the objective markers of intent and the verbal denial of suicidal ideation, some clients may subsequently acknowledge the presence of suicidal ideation (Rudd, 2008). Even if the client persists in denying suicidal ideation or subjective intent, objective indicators of intent, if present, should be given more weight than the client's verbal report. A similar situation arises with suicide-related dreams, artwork, mental images, or hallucinations that occur while a client is denying subjective suicidal ideation or intent. In effect, the client is showing rather than telling the psychotherapist that he or she is seriously considering suicide.

## AN OUTPATIENT PLAN IS NOT FEASIBLE

The inability to follow through with an outpatient plan may result from outright rejection of the plan or low participation due to a compromised decision-making capacity or an escalation of the suicidal process. For example, a client may simply refuse to relinquish a firearm in the home or allow a family member to participate in treatment planning. Alternatively, a depressed client may become symptomatic to the point of being unable to participate in implementing a safety plan. Other clients may agree to parts of a comprehensive management plan while rejecting others. The psychotherapist should establish clearly, often with the help of a consultant, a minimum "bottom line" level of meaningful engagement in care that is judged to be safe for outpatient management of the level of risk. Clients at high risk of suicide with only partial participation or an unconvincing verbal endorsement of plans to follow through with an outpatient plan may need a higher level of care for stabilization to help save their life.

## NO FORESEEABLE FUTURE EVENTS TO RESOLVE
## THE IMMEDIATE CRISIS

Given the shifting nature of suicide risk, internal or external circumstances can rapidly influence a client's acute risk of suicide. For example, a client who expresses suicidal ideation while intoxicated on alcohol may stabilize after sobering up. Alternatively, suicide risk for a client who has been home alone may decrease when family members return from a trip. In considering hospitalization, the psychotherapist should judge whether future events might reduce a client's risk such that an outpatient plan may be implemented. For example:

Ms. C, a 60-year-old, unmarried woman, came to treatment for lifelong depression and social isolation. A crisis in Ms. C's life had developed when her employer "replaced me with someone younger." When Ms. C arrived 30 minutes late for an appointment following a two-week absence, she appeared disheveled and seemed emotionally distant while discussing who would care for her cat "if I weren't around anymore." On direct questioning, Ms. C denied suicidal ideation or intent and assured the psychotherapist that "I'm not suicidal." Ms. C refused to allow the psychotherapist to contact a friend "because she's busy with her family, and I don't want to bother her." The psychotherapist openly expressed concern for Ms. C and highlighted the missed appointments, decline in self-care, indirect reference to death, and feeling of burdensomeness as worrisome indicators of a suicidal process. Ms. C then reported having received an eviction notice after failing to pay her rent for two months. She reported spending her days alone in her apartment while ambivalently considering hanging herself "to finally have some peace." Ms. C passively agreed to the psychotherapist's suggestions for addressing the eviction and finding more support during the week while reiterating, "It's fine. I'll be fine. I'll just see you next week."

In the setting of multiple objective markers of suicidal intent and low participation in collaborative treatment planning, the psychotherapist, lacking a reliable plan for social support, timely medication treatment of depression, reducing access to lethal means, or safety planning, called 911 from her office with the client present to initiate an emergency evaluation for hospitalization. The psychotherapist explained the rationale for the call, emphasized that the hospitalization was intended for short-term stabilization, and emphasized to the client they would continue their work in psychotherapy after she was discharged.

**Documentation:** This client presents with suicide risk factors of depressive disorder, social isolation, currently depressed mood, anhedonia, feelings of burdensomeness, active suicidal ideation with thoughts of hanging herself, and suicide preparation. Outpatient care has not been successful in managing risk, given low session attendance, persistence of depression, social isolation, and no supports to assist with outpatient safety planning. High acute risk of suicide was managed by facilitating emergency evaluation for psychiatric hospitalization.

## DISCLOSURE OF INFORMATION: BREAKING CONFIDENTIALITY

The confidential nature of mental health work ensures that clients have a safe setting to discuss emotionally difficult topics. For clients at acute risk for suicide, confidentiality must be weighed against the benefits of involving friends, family members, or other clinicians to provide additional support. High-risk clients may insist that their treatment occur in isolation from other supports for any number of reasons, such as fear of losing control over the decision to live or die, concerns about burdening others, or shame about their circumstances. If the client refuses to involve others who could be supportive with his or her care, the psychotherapist should explore the meaning of the client's refusal in an effort to resolve the impasse. In an emergency, a psychotherapist deciding whether to break confidentiality in order to enlist support from friends or family members should consider whether "confidentiality" that is meant to facilitate safe treatment has evolved into "keeping secrets" in a manner that perpetuates a suicidal process. We recommend that the psychotherapist break confidentiality to involve other parties in a high-risk client's care if the following conditions are met (PRMS, 2015):

- The client is at high near-term risk of suicide.
- Family members are likely unaware of the risk.
- Family members are likely to have an ability to intervene in a therapeutic manner.

For example:

> Mr. D is a 58-year-old man who has been seeing Ms. E for weekly psychotherapy through an employee assistance program. Mr. D has become increasingly depressed and anxious as he nears the end of a probationary period at work. At his current appointment, he recounts how he has failed his family and how money from his life insurance policy would "provide for them when I'm gone." He reports having driven to a bridge "to see what it would look like." Ms. E, noting the expressions of burdensomeness and preparatory behavior, validates his level of desperation and states that she would like to call his wife to gain her support in helping him through what appears to be a suicidal crisis. Mr. D pleads with Ms. E not to call his wife, stating that "I've already put her through enough." When the discussion fails to progress, Ms. E states that, "I know we disagree about whether to call your wife. I would not do this unless I believed it would protect your safety. I want your wife to have the chance to know how you are feeling and a choice about what to do."

> **Documentation:** This client presents with suicidal ideation with thoughts of jumping from a bridge, feelings of burdensomeness, and recent preparatory behavior in the setting of a crisis related to employment. Acute risk of suicide is judged to be high. This client's wife is likely unaware of the risk and is likely able to intervene in a manner to reduce risk. Breaking confidentiality to coordinate crisis management with this client's wife is judged to be necessary to facilitate immediate safety.

# CONCLUSION

Clinical work with high-risk clients offers psychotherapists the opportunity to help clients navigate and overcome a life-and-death struggle. Engaging in this work requires knowledge and skills related to suicide risk assessment, management, and treatment. The rewards of this challenging work must be balanced against the risk of malpractice liability and the need for additional resources. In work with high-risk clients, clinical problems related to engaging emergency services and breaking confidentiality benefit from having a set of principles to guide decision making. We thus believe that the prepared private practitioner can play a key role in clinically saving lives.

# REFERENCES

American Psychiatric Association. (2003). Practice guideline for the assessment and treatment of patients with suicidal behaviors.

Bryan, C. J., & Rudd, M. D. (2006). Advances in the assessment of suicide risk. *Journal of Clinical Psychology, 62*, 185–200.

Busch, K. A., & Fawcett, J. (2003). Clinical correlates of inpatient suicide. *Journal of Clinical Psychiatry, 64*(1), 14–19.

Columbia-Suicide Severity Rating Scale (C-SSRS). Available from http://cssrs.columbia.edu.

Ellis, T. E. (2004). Collaboration and a self-help orientation in therapy with suicidal clients. *Journal of Contemporary Psychotherapy, 34*, 41–57.

Fawcett, J. (2009). Severe anxiety and agitation as treatment modifiable risk factors for suicide. In D. Wasserman & C. Wasserman (Eds.), *Oxford textbook of suicidology and suicide prevention: A global perspective* (pp. 407–411). New York: Oxford University Press.

Fleischmann, A., Bertolote, J. M., Wasserman, D., De Leo, D., Bolhari, J., Botega, N. J., De Silva, D., . . . Thanh, H. T. T. (2008). Effectiveness of brief intervention and contact for suicide attempters: A randomized controlled trial in five countries. *Bulletin of the World Health Organization, 86*, 703–709.

Jobes, D. A. (2016). *Managing suicidal risk: A collaborative approach (2nd edition).* New York: Guilford Press.

Jobes, D. A. (2011). Suicidal blackmail: Ethical and risk management issues in contemporary clinical care. In W. B. Johnson & G. P. Koocher (Eds.), *Casebook on ethically challenging work settings in mental health and the behavioral sciences.* New York: Oxford University Press.

Jobes, D. A. (2012). The collaborative assessment and management of suicidality (CAMS): An evolving evidence-based clinical approach to suicidal risk. *Suicide and Life-Threatening Behavior, 42*, 640–653.

Jobes, D. A., Comtois, K. A., Brenner, L. A., Gutierrez, P. M., & O'Connor, S. S. (2016). Lessons learned from clinical trials of the Collaborative Assessment and Management of Suicidality (CAMS). In R. C. O'Connor & J. Pirkis (Eds.), *International handbook of suicide prevention: Research, policy, & practice* (2nd ed., pp. 431–449). West Sussex, UK: Wiley-Blackwell.

Joiner, T. E. (2005). *Why people die by suicide.* Cambridge, MA: Harvard University Press.

Joiner, T., Kalafat, J., Draper, J., Stokes, H., Knudson, M., Berman, A. L., & McKeon, R. (2007). Establishing standards for the assessment of suicide risk among callers to the National Suicide Prevention Lifeline. *Suicide and Life-Threatening Behavior, 37*, 353–365.

Kroenke, K., Spitzer, R.L., & Williams, J.B.W. (2010). The PHQ-9: Validity of a brief depression severity measure. *Journal of General Internal Medicine, 16*, 606–613.

Linehan, M. M. (1993). *Cognitive-behavioral treatment of borderline personality disorder.* New York: Guilford Press.

Linehan, M. M., Comtois, K. A., & Ward-Ciesielski, E. F. (2012). Assessing and managing risk with suicidal individuals. *Cognitive and Behavioral Practice, 19*, 218–232.

Luxton, D. D., June, J. D., & Comtois, K. A. (2012). Can postdischarge follow-up contacts prevent suicide and suicidal behavior?: A review of the evidence. *Crisis, 34*, 32–41.

Michel, K., & Valach, L. (2011). The narrative interview with the suicidal patient. In K. Michel & D. A. Jobes (Eds.), *Building a therapeutic alliance with the suicidal patient* (pp. 63–80). Washington, DC: American Psychological Association.

Professional Risk Management Services (PRMS), Inc. (2015). Lessons to be learned: A review of post-suicide lawsuits. *Rx for Risk, 23*(1), 1–6.

Resnick, P. J. (2002). Recognizing that the suicidal patient views you as an "adversary." *Current Psychiatry, 1,* 8.

Rudd, M. D. (2008). Suicide warning signs in clinical practice. *Current Psychiatry Reports, 10,* 87–90.

Rutz, W., Wålinder, J., Eberhard, G., Holmberg, G., von Knorring, A.L., von Knorring, L., Wistedt, B., & Åberg-Wistedt, A. (1989). An educational program on depressive disorders for general practitioners on Gotland: Background and evaluation. *Acta Psychiatrica Scandinavica, 79,* 19–26.

Stanley, B., & Brown, G. K. (2012). Safety Planning Intervention: A brief intervention to mitigate suicide risk. *Cognitive and Behavioral Practice, 19,* 256–264.

Tucker, R. P., Crowley, K. J., Davidson, C. L., & Gutierrez, P. M. (2015). Risk factors, warning signs, and drivers of suicide: What are they, how do they differ, and why does it matter? *Suicide and Life-Threatening Behavior, 45*(6), 679–689.

Weinberg, I., Ronningstam, E., Goldblatt, M. J., Schechter, M., Wheelis, J., & Maltsberger, J. T. (2010). Strategies in treatment of suicidality: Identification of common and treatment-specific interventions in empirically supported treatment manuals. *Journal of Clinical Psychiatry, 71,* 699–706.

Wenzel, A., Brown, G. K., & Beck, A. T. (2009). *Cognitive therapy for suicidal patients.* Washington, DC: American Psychological Association.

Yip, P. S. F., Yousuf, S, Chang, S., Wu, K. C., & Chen, Y. (2012). Means restriction for suicide prevention. *Lancet, 379,* 2393–2399.

# CHAPTER 41

# ISSUES IN PLANNED AND UNPLANNED DISRUPTIONS IN CLINICAL PRACTICE

*A. Steven Frankel*

Sadly, one of the topics rarely taught in graduate training programs concerns the need to prepare for interruptions of practice, especially unanticipated interruptions, due to a practitioner's death or disability. While practitioners do consider and implement arrangements for planned interruptions, such as vacations, the birth of children, trips to professional conferences, weekend coverage for their practices, and the like, the most overwhelming and most ignored problems occur when unplanned (and often unforeseen) disruptions take place.

Consider Martha's story. I had been a lawyer for only about a year when she called me. She was crying, distressed, frightened, and angry. Her husband of well over 30 years, a psychologist, had passed away unexpectedly. He was in his early 60s and had no immediate plans to retire, as he loved his work. Martha told me, between tearful outbursts, that a colleague of her husband suggested she contact me because I was both a psychologist and an attorney. She said, in the midst of her grief, that she had begun receiving calls from various creditors, including her husband's office landlord and—the most distressing to her—many of her husband's clients.

The landlord said she needed to pay another month's rent or he would put her husband's office furnishings—including his patients' records—out in the street. Further, while in the midst of their own grief over losing their treating clinician, her husband's clients began to contact her (the Internet makes it quite easy to find anyone), wanting their records. Some were involved in litigation; others needed records to support claims for insurance reimbursement for payments to her husband, while still others needed records to document disabilities. She wanted to help them, but she was in "overwhelm" status and didn't know how to cope with the demands that found their way to her door. She said that, in addition to her grief, she was aware of feeling enraged at her husband for leaving her with these burdens—and then terrible guilt about feeling so angry.

She asked me whether she was allowed to look at his records, to talk to his clients, and to give them their records. Would something bad (translation: "legal") happen if she did get his records, find the clients, and hand them over? Was she exposing herself to any sort of legal consequences for that? If so, then what might she do to deal with the (unpredicted) demands on her? At that time in my life (as I was an early-career attorney at the time), I had no idea what to tell her. Now, I would know.

John's story is similar with one legal distinction: He and Barbara, a mental health clinician, had been life partners for 15 years but were not married. Barbara had been in practice for about 20 years when she was suddenly struck and killed by a drunk driver as she was crossing a street. In the state in which they lived, John had no idea whether he had legal standing to act as if he had been her husband. He knew where her office was and a little about how it was laid out but had never visited her there, did not know what furniture or furnishings she had, and knew little of the people she served or her recordkeeping responsibilities. He received the same kind of contacts and requests as Martha but decided he didn't need to do much except to pay people to take everything out of the office, shred all the records, and auction off everything else. One of Barbara's close friends, also a mental health clinician, called to support him at the time of Barbara's death and tried to help him understand that the people she served and cared for needed their records and that bills had to be paid, lest there be actions against Barbara's estate (her will left everything to him) that might impact him.

Who knew about "professional wills" at that time in history? Even though all of the mental health societies have ethics codes requiring us to prepare for disruptions in practice due to unanticipated death or disability, how many come out of denial and do it? How many colleagues put in about 80 hours of work to "clean up" a colleague's practice?

At present, relevant guidance is found in the codes of ethics of each of the mental health professions (American Association for Marriage & Family Therapy, 2015; American Counseling Association, 2015; American Psychological Association [APA], 2010; National Association of Social Workers, 2008). As an example, the APA Code of Ethics (2010) states, in Standard 3.12, Interruption of Psychological Services:

> Unless otherwise covered by contract, psychologists make reasonable efforts to plan for facilitating services in the event that psychological services are interrupted by factors such as the psychologist's illness, death, unavailability, relocation or retirement or by the client's/patient's relocation or financial limitations. (p. 7)

Additionally, Standard 6.02, Record Keeping and Fees, states: "Psychologists make plans in advance to facilitate the appropriate transfer and to protect the confidentiality of records and data in the event of psychologists' withdrawal from positions or practice" (p. 9).

However, and despite the fact that these standards are legally and professionally enforceable, the overwhelming majority of clinicians do not make such preparations (Alban & Frankel, 2010). Rather, their families, helpful colleagues, and clients are burdened with these responsibilities while managing intense grief and loss. And, when those who try to assist with the closure of a practice are not themselves professionally trained, client records may be mishandled, with confidentiality breaches and legal actions by clients whose records have been misplaced, lost, or destroyed. In the legal world, the failure of clinicians to ensure that client records are available when the practitioner leaves practice (for any reason) is considered "abandonment," and 14 states specifically authorize legal actions against the estate of the professional for abandonment, while the remaining states expose the estate of the professional to investigations/actions pursuant to the Health Insurance Portability and Accountability Act (HIPAA) (Frankel & Alban, 2010).

Given that the "baby boomer" generation is aging, there is great concern that over the coming years there will be a significant number of colleagues whose practices will require transition services. Of course, there are cases where younger practitioners also face such circumstances, as they may experience periods of illness, accidents, and premature death. But the period of time from 2016 to 2030 is particularly critical, in that it is within this period of time that the baby boomer generation is likely to be retiring or succumbing to death or disability.

There are three fundamental reasons why clinicians fail to prepare for interruptions/terminations of practice: lack of training, denial, and the effort and expense involved (Frankel, 2013).

Graduate training has not been known to cover practice terminations (Frankel, 2015). Training programs tend to focus on the acquisition of assessment and treatment skills and practice development, but not practice closure. Students are not taught that one of the measures of a successful professional life is the way it ends, as much as the way it begins and develops over time. Further, and given that the 2002 version of the APA Code of Ethical Conduct was the first rendition of the psychology code that includes concerns about practice disruptions, denial—a phenomenon well known to clinicians—makes it easier to focus on practice development and management than on practice termination. Clinicians have been known to say "What do I care? I won't be there" and "I'll have to deal with this someday, but not now" when asked about such preparations. Finally, those who do put some thought into solving the problem soon learn how much time and effort it takes to address it.

# THE DYADIC MODEL

The initial model developed to cope with the problem was a "dyadic" one ("I'll do it for you if you do it for me"). However, those who decide to use the dyadic model begin to see how difficult it is to use when they examine the list of responsibilities that await them. Pope and Vasquez (2005) have presented a list of preparations that clinicians should make for unanticipated disruptions of practice. Their "to-do" list offers dramatic evidence why this type of planning has not been actively pursued by colleagues. Box 41.1 lists what Pope and Vasquez state should be addressed in a "professional will."

Thus, finding a colleague who is willing and able to assume ongoing responsibility for the management of practice transitions is not easy. This is especially true given that the two colleagues must maintain such a mutual arrangement for many years, an agreement that can be disrupted by one colleague relocating, retiring, and so forth. Given the length of time that a practitioner is actively engaged in practice, this dyadic agreement may not be a viable option. And, since it is

## BOX 41.1. ITEMS TO ADDRESS IN A "PROFESSIONAL WILL"

1. The person you designate to assume primary responsibility:

   Who would respond effectively in the event that you suddenly die or are incapacitated? Who can make necessary arrangements in a time of great stress; take care of matters sensitively, efficiently, and effectively; and make sure nothing important is overlooked? Who is the best person to talk to many, if not all, of your clients? A good professional will clearly designates a qualified person to serve as the executor of the will and explicitly authorizes that individual to carry out the tasks that the will specifies.

2. The people serving as backups:

   Life tends to be full of surprises and sometimes hesitates to cooperate with our plans. At the time he or she needs to step in and take charge, the person you designated to assume primary responsibility may be overseas at a conference or on vacation, attending to a family emergency, seriously ill, or otherwise unavailable. It's important to have a second and third designee, each ready to step in if necessary.

3. Coordinated planning:

   Coordinated planning can make for a more useful professional will and make it easier for the executor to carry it out. You can meet with your primary designee and both backups to outline what you want done, what needs to be done, and what information the designee will need. One person may think of something that the others have overlooked, and what the clinician may think "goes without saying" ("You all know that bookshelf where I keep my appointment book, don't you?") may need clarification for the will's executor.

4. Your office, its keys, and its security:

   In addition to providing your office address, it's helpful to be as specific as possible about where each key to your office can be found. For example, "There are four copies of the key to my office. One is on the key ring I always carry with me. It is the key with the blue plastic on it. My partner, whose contact information is _____, also has a key to the office. My secretary, whose contact information is _____, has a key. The building manager, who can be contacted in an emergency at _____, has a key."

5. Your schedule:

   Where is your schedule kept? In a daily planner you keep with you, in an appointment book at the office, on your computer, or in a personal digital assistant (PDA)? Once the record of your scheduled appointments has been located, is additional information needed to access it? For example, if you keep your schedule on your computer, what passwords are used to log on and access the schedule? Where on the drive is the schedule kept? What are the names of the relevant files? Is there a backup somewhere if the copy on your computer has become corrupted of if the computer itself is unavailable (e.g., destroyed in an office fire or earthquake or stolen)?

6. Avenues of communication from clients and colleagues:

   Do clients and colleagues contact you through an answering machine, e-mail, or other method? Clearly describe each one and how the person implementing your professional will can access the messages. What is the code used to retrieve messages from your answering machine? What are the names of any relevant e-mail accounts, along with the user name, password, server address for receiving and sending mail (POP and SMTP) [encryption codes], and so on?

7. Client record and contact information:

   Depending on the method of notification you choose, the person implementing your professional will may need to initiate contact with your clients. He or she may also need to return calls from clients whose message lacks a return number. A professional will needs to include clear instructions about how to locate and access client records and contact information. The ability to locate treatment records promptly may become exceptionally important because the sudden death of a psychotherapist may trigger a crisis for some clients.

8. Further client record and contact information:

   The professional will should also designate whether the person implementing the will or someone else will maintain the psychotherapist's client records. This information can be announced in the local newspapers or filed with the state licensing board and state professional association.

9. Client notification:

Psychotherapists may choose one or more methods to notify clients of their death. They can choose to have their executor call each client, place a notice in the local newspaper, change the outgoing message on the answering machine to include the announcement or ask clients to call the clinician implementing the deceased therapist's professional will, or by letter. It is worth spending some time considering the potential impact of each method in terms of the Golden Rule and how each of the current and former clients might respond.

10. Colleague notification:

Which colleagues should be notified immediately? Are you a member of a group practice or do you share a suite of offices with someone? Are there clinicians who provide consultation or supervision to you on a regular basis, or are there clinicians who receive those services from you? Do you co-lead a therapy group or family sessions with anyone? Are there conferences or workshops that you present on a regular basis?

11. Attorney for professional issues:

It's useful to provide contact information for an attorney whom the clinician has consulted for practice issues.

12. Billing records, procedures and instructions:

The person whom the professional will designates to take charge will need to know where the billing records are, how to access them (e.g., if they are maintained by computer software), who prepares and processes the bills (e.g., a billing service, accountant, or office clerical worker), and how pending charges are to be handled.

13. Expenses:

How have the clinician preparing the professional will and the person designated to serve as professional executor decided that the executor will be compensated? Perhaps the easiest arrangement is at the executor's customary hourly rate, but other approaches can be used (e.g., a flat fee, a token payment, the executor declining any compensation for rendering this service to a friend, or a contribution to a charity chosen by the executor). A professional will needs to include clear instructions about how all business-related expenses are to be paid.

14. Your personal will:

   To avoid unintended problems and conflicts, it's helpful to review both your professional will and your personal will side by side to ensure they are consistent. If a personal will, for example, directs all its assets to be disbursed in a certain way but makes no mention of the funds to be used to pay the executor of your professional will, problems can arise. It is useful if each will makes explicit reference to the other.

15. Legal review:

   A review of the professional will by an attorney skilled and experienced in mental health law can prevent numerous problems. The executor of the professional will can consult with the attorney should any legal quandaries arise in the days, weeks, and months after the clinician's death. The attorney can also advise on whether, in light of state legislation and case law, the professional will is best authenticated simply by the signatures of disinterested witnesses, the seal of a notary, or other means.

15. Copies of the professional will:

   Copies of your professional will can be given to those designated as potential executors and to your attorney. Some clinicians may consider making special arrangements to ensure the executors' access to such information as their passwords for retrieving e-mail and answering machine messages is granted only after their death. This avoids having this confidential information distributed to others in multiple copies of the will.

16. Review and update:

   People, practices, times, and situations change. A professional will that is perfectly suited to us when we draw it up may have out-of-date contact information and aspects that don't fit us well at all just a year or two later. It's helpful to review a professional will on a regular basis—say, once per year, and make an immediate update whenever there is a significant change in circumstances. (pp. 58–63) unlikely that both colleagues will confront disruptions/terminations of practice at the exact same moment, the most difficult aspect of the dyadic model is that one of the colleagues will have to engage another colleague in the process at some time, and perhaps even a third time.

# AN ALTERNATIVE MODEL: THE TEAM APPROACH

Steiner (2010) has developed a model that addresses these problems in a more workable way. Her model involves the formation of a group of colleagues who divide the duties and responsibilities among group members so that none of them carry the full burden. Steiner's model includes a group leader and describes how the responsibilities might be split up. Of note is that the group members' practices are all managed by the group, such that the group members work to solve the same problems for all of its members. Since the professional community has not embraced the dyadic model due to the overwhelming number of required activities, the group approach may have greater appeal. Ironically enough, however, the group approach also has a major weakness: group process.

In this model the colleagues form a group and divide the work among them, and the intent of the group is to remain intact for a significant time (measured not just in years, but in decades) so that the group members, their families, and their clients will all benefit from the group's work. However, as time passes, members may relocate or change their practice styles and locations, and will confront their anticipated and unanticipated practice disruptions and terminations. There may be some conflict between group members, and some may wish to leave the group altogether due to personal changes, problems with cooperation, and so forth. Such problems are especially difficult for practitioners in small communities, as there is difficulty finding new colleagues to re-place those who joined the group at its inception. Thus, while the group model may seem much more practical than the dyadic model, it may not solve the problem for all professionals.

At the time of this writing, there are no known data on how often these two models are chosen by clinicians. Informal data I have gathered at educational presentations are consistent with the view that no more than three out of 100 conference attendees have engaged with a colleague, and that even fewer colleagues employ the group model. The amount of work involved and the need for stability of the relationships between participating colleagues are viewed as obstacles in either of these two models. Even though model "professional wills" are available for purchase on the Internet, the tasks involved in closing or transitioning a clinical practice go beyond what such purchased wills cover.

# ENTER THE "INSURANCE" INDUSTRY

Many practitioners may not know whether their professional liability ("malpractice insurance") companies offer coverage for what the insurance industry terms "abandonment." Historically, the professional community uses the word "abandonment" to describe the discontinuation of mental health services to a client that is sudden and potentially damaging. The insurance industry is aware that, when a professional terminates practice, it is expected (indeed, required) that clients have access to their records, and that failure to do so is associated with what the insurance world terms "risk." Many insurance policies have provisions to cover the costs associated with (and prevention of) abandonment. Those that do contain such provisions offer sums of financial reimbursement to their insureds in the event that they have not prepared for unanticipated disruptions or terminations of practice. For example, when a professional's practice is terminated due to death or disability, and he or she has not made needed preparations for such events, a proportion of the costs of addressing the problems would be covered by the professional liability policy.

For example, when either of the two professionals described earlier in this chapter experienced the unanticipated termination of practice, their survivor could have been able to hire someone to clean up the office, post the notices, contact the clients, and so forth, and would have had access to insurance funds for those purposes. However, the amounts of such funds from professional liability companies do not come close to the actual amounts that would be needed under these circumstances. For example, let's say that a colleague wants to be helpful by contacting clients upon the passing of their professional. If there have been no releases signed by the clients that allow for the helpful colleague to look at the client records, then the helpful colleague (or the family of the deceased professional) would have to retain a probate attorney to obtain a court order that allows the helpful colleague to examine the files and contact the clients. The costs for such enterprises may be in the $10,000 range, and this is more than insurance companies would cover (in fact, I have seen insurance policies that offer approximately $2,000 for such coverage).

# A THIRD APPROACH: THE "QUASI-INSURANCE" MODEL

From the time that I began to receive the distressing phone calls described above, I became increasingly concerned about the fact that neither the dyadic model nor the group model described above had taken hold, despite the fact that our colleagues are aging, passing away, and becoming disabled, leaving their families, clients, and colleagues who want to be helpful with no idea of what they will encounter when they begin to close a colleague's practice. This lack of professional response not only endangers all of those involved but will also increase in urgency over the coming years.

Even though all of the national professional societies for mental health professionals have made such preparations into enforceable ethical standards, and some states (e.g., Oregon) have even enacted statutes/laws that require practitioners to do the needed preparation, through my teaching efforts I learned that hardly any of our colleagues are responding. I came to the conclusion that, rather than legislative and ethics-based "threats," colleagues need support to address these issues. Thus was formed Practice-Legacy Programs, a quasi-insurance model approach that provides not only emergency intervention when a colleague's practice is interrupted but also a subscription service that creates the necessary components of a transition plan, including advising all clients to whom they will be referred if their treating clinician leaves practice, providing the releases for having records sent to the subsequent treater, contact information for the clients, instructions for the staff who implement the plan, and related actions.[1] The subscription agreement between the company and the clinician involves a free evaluation of a potential subscriber's practice, the use of a HIPAA-compliant web program that contains releases for both the Practice Legacy staff and the planned subsequent clinician to have access to client contact information, as well as that contact information itself. Thus, at the time of the practice transition, all clients are contacted, apprised of the situation, and referred to a planned subsequent clinician. Client reports to date suggest a positive feeling of being "taken care of" by such planning. The subscriber agreement also provides for planned disposition of office furniture/furnishings, coordination with office landlords regarding rental contracts and payments, accounts receivable/payable, and data storage and accessibility plans. Thus, clients and families of subscribers are offered competent support at a time when distress and grieving are powerful forces.

In emergency situations in which a clinician who has not contracted for practice transition services can no longer provide services, Practice Legacy offers the services that will be needed during the practice transition, which is likely to require a local court appearance to secure a court order that allows the company's representatives to enter the office, review the records, contact clients/ family, and proceed with the practice transition. The company has already supported the transitions of both subscriber and emergency situations.

In the future, other such companies may emerge, and they will be welcomed, as it is increasingly clear that the "normalization" of the needed services must occur for practice transitions to be effective for all involved. In sum, this is a problem whose time has come.

## SUMMARY AND CONCLUSIONS

Even though legal and ethical principles require clinicians to prepare for unanticipated terminations of practice due to death or disability, few clinicians have developed such plans, putting family members, clients, and colleagues at risk for significant distress at times of crisis. The significant responsibilities associated with such practice transitions suggests that neither the dyadic model (pairs of colleagues) nor the group model has been well received or widely adopted by clinicians, with the result that unplanned transitions are characterized by chaos and disruption in the lives of families, clients, and colleagues. Thus, a "quasi-insurance" model has been developed to assist clinicians by providing the structure and planning needed to arrange for practice transitions at times of crisis. This approach lets clients know how transitions will be managed, whom their subsequent treating clinicians will be, and how their records will be transferred. It provides protection for the families of clinicians, because their grief will not be disrupted by distressed clients and office landlords. It also eases the burden for helpful colleagues, who otherwise may find themselves facing significant demands on their time, concerns about the propriety of their reviewing client records, and the challenges of finding referrals to subsequent treating clinicians.

# NOTE

1. I created Practice-Legacy Programs, LLC (www.practice-legacy.com) and am its chief executive officer. I thus stand to benefit from funds generated by the company, and it is ethically important that I disclose this fact. At the time of the writing of this chapter, there are no other companies that provide the services provided by Practice-Legacy Programs.

# REFERENCES

Alban, A., & Frankel, A. S. (2010). "Professional Wills": The ethics requirement you haven't met. *California Psychologist, 43*(1), 25–26.

American Association for Marriage and Family Therapy. (2015). Code of ethics. Retrieved from https://www.aamft.org/iMIS15/AAMFT/Content/legal_ethics/code_of_ethics.aspx.

American Counseling Association. (2015). ACA code of ethics. Retrieved from http://www.counseling.org/Resources/aca-code-of-ethics.pdf

American Psychological Association. (2010). Ethical principles of psychologists and code of conduct. Retrieved from http://www.apa.org/ethics/code/index.aspx.

Frankel, A. S. (2013). Denial is great, but our patients, families and colleagues need our attention. *Newsletter of the Life Member Division*, American Psychiatric Association. Reprinted in *California Psychiatrist*, (2014), *29*(1), 4–5.

Frankel, A. S. (2015, May). Beyond the professional will: Three things they never taught us in graduate school. Presentation to the Care Committee of the San Francisco Psychological Association.

Frankel, A. S., & Alban, A. (2010). Professional wills: Protecting patients, family members and colleagues. *California Psychiatrist, 25*(3), 4–6.

National Association of Social Workers. (2008). Code of ethics. Retrieved from http://www.socialworkers.org/pubs/code/code.asp?print=1&.

Pope, K., & Vasquez, M, (2005). *How to survive and thrive as a therapist: Information, ideas and resources for psychologists in practice*. Washington, DC: American Psychological Association.

Steiner, A. (2010). The therapist's professional will: If not now, when? Retrieved from www.sfrankelgroup.com.

# CHAPTER 42

# CONSIDERATIONS IN CLOSING A PRIVATE PRACTICE

*Janet T. Thomas and Steven Walfish*

Much has been written on what it takes to establish and manage a successful, ethical private psychotherapy practice (Barnett, Zimmerman, & Walfish, 2014; Stout & Grand, 2004; Walfish & Barnett, 2009). Closing a practice has received less attention, but it is no less important (Ballard, 2005). Like launching a private practice, closing one requires that, when possible, clinicians carefully think through and develop a plan taking into account client needs, legal and ethical requirements, and the need for emotional preparation (Thomas, 2015). Clearly, closing a practice is not an event, but a process.[1]

Mental health professionals of many stripes engage in private practice as permitted in their jurisdictions. Marriage and family therapists, clinical social workers, counselors, and psychologists are such examples. Most private practices offer psychotherapy, but others may provide mental health evaluation or neuropsychological assessment. Although ethics codes and regulations vary according to the type of service provided, profession, and jurisdiction, some challenges associated with closing a practice pertain to all private practitioners.

Not all services offered by licensed mental health practitioners are considered "mental health" per se. For example, private practitioners may offer forensic evaluation, neuropsychological or academic assessment, or organizational consultation. Although the focus here is on the closing of mental health practices, many of the issues involved are similar for those providing non-mental health services, and much of what follows is applicable to these types of practice as well.

This chapter focuses primarily on the process of a planned practice closure. Chapter 41 in this *Handbook* provides further discussion of unplanned closures.

# REASONS FOR CLOSING OR LEAVING A PRACTICE

Mental health practitioners in private practice must consider how they will close the doors when the time comes. Unless a practice is sold and therefore not closed, this phase of a private practitioner's career must be anticipated and planned for in advance.

Ideally, the closing of a solo practice is the result of a deliberate decision on the part of the clinician. A planned retirement, probably the most common such circumstance, allows for thoughtful preparation and adequate time to implement the plan with due consideration for all concerned (McGurk & Advisory Committee on Colleague Assistance, 2005). The expiration of practice licenses, professional liability insurance, and office leases are factors to consider in determining the timing of the closing. The type of practice and commensurate needs of clients must be taken into account so that plans for concluding treatment or facilitating transitions to other providers are effective.

Retirement is not the only circumstance resulting in practice closure. When continuing a practice becomes financially untenable, alternatives must be considered. The costs associated with independent practice can be significant. Clearly, clinicians must generate a certain amount of income to offset basic expenses and generate a profit in order to earn a living. Not all private practitioners are financially successful. Private practitioners are also vulnerable to changes in the insurance industry, local economy, social policy, and referral partners. Such changes can certainly impact individual practices, but they could necessitate the closing of an entire group practice as well. When they occur, a prosperous practice can be turned into one that is no longer financially viable. Consider the following example:

> A particular practice was established when the clinicians secured a contract with an insurance company. According to the agreement, all of their subscribers would be referred to this practice. This reliable referral stream continued for 3 years, and the practice was extraordinarily successful. Then one day, the practitioners received a certified letter from the insurance carrier indicating that the arrangement was going to terminate in 30 days. The practice had to close its doors 2 months later.

When a practice ceases to be profitable, clinicians may seek employment before closing in order to maintain a source of income during the search for a new position. Major geographic relocations and career changes are other situations that will necessitate the closing of a practice.

The decision to discontinue a practice may be due to acute or exacerbated health problems or sudden death, resulting in a precipitous closure that allows for minimal or no advance notice to clients. In such circumstances, clinicians may not be capable of closing the practice themselves, necessitating closure management by designated colleagues. Also rare are situations in which a practice must be closed in the wake of license suspension or revocation by a licensing board. Practitioners in such circumstances may or may not be given time or permission to manage the closing themselves.

# PREPARATION FOR A PLANNED PRACTICE CLOSING

A planned departure allows clinicians to prepare a deliberate and thoughtful plan for closing their practices. Once the decision to close a clinical practice is made, the process often begins with setting an end date and working backwards to determine the timing of the many steps required. This process focuses on notifying current and former clients, ensuring continuity of care for clients, arranging for appropriate storage of records, and making decisions about liability insurance.

## NOTIFICATION OF CURRENT, FORMER, AND PROSPECTIVE CLIENTS

Notification of current clients is one of the first considerations. The amount of notice given will depend upon factors such as the circumstance precipitating the closing. In planning a departure, the psychotherapist may establish a timeline taking into account the type of treatment he or she provides and the needs of particular clients. That timeline commonly ranges from 6 weeks to 6 months but may be protracted with longer-term clients such as those seen in psychoanalytic practice. Similarly, how far back a psychotherapist decides to go in notifying former clients will vary. With these factors in mind, the clinician determines a date after which no new psychotherapy referrals will be accepted. If the clinician performs evaluation services that are time-limited (e.g., psychoeducational or presurgical assessments, eligibility evaluations for vocational rehabilitation services), the work may continue until the practice actually closes.

Current clients are typically informed in person, during a regular psychotherapy session. Presenting this information at the beginning of a session allows time for the client to begin processing the news. Often it takes time for a client to absorb this new reality, so a reminder that there will be opportunity to talk during subsequent appointments may be helpful. Admittedly, raising this issue at the beginning of the session may preempt the client's agenda for the day. That risk must be weighed against the alternatives of interrupting the client's process midway through the session or dropping the news as the session ends, thus allowing no time for processing his or her initial response. Clients may well be able to shift back to their original agenda following some discussion of the import of the news of their psychotherapist's departure, particularly if given plenty of notice. Nevertheless, the difficulty of such conversations, for both clients and the psychotherapists, should not be underestimated.

Following the oral disclosure with a written version of the announcement is critical. The psychotherapist may personally hand a letter to the client on the day of the oral notice or during a subsequent session, deliver it electronically, or send it by regular mail. Alerting clients that such a letter is forthcoming allows them to prepare for receiving it. Clients are likely to find it difficult to remember the specifics of the psychotherapist's plans, so sending a letter serves to reiterate the announcement. The letter should include information about referral alternatives, instructions for requesting records, and other logistical details that would be difficult for a client to fully comprehend while absorbing the more significant news of the therapist's departure. Further, from a risk management perspective, written notification provides documentation verifying that clients have been adequately informed about the termination, offered referral alternatives, and given instructions for accessing and transferring their clinical records.

A similar notification letter is useful for informing former clients of a closing practice. The type of practice will determine how far back the psychotherapist decides to go in selecting those to be apprised. Lower-volume practices (such as a psychoanalytic practice) allow for the review and consideration of individual cases in deciding which former clients to notify. With particular individuals, such as long-term clients seen intermittently but not currently, the clinician may wish to inform them by phone before sending them the notice. Offering the option of scheduling an appointment to discuss the termination may also be helpful.

In summary, the announcement to current or former clients should include a brief explanation about the practice closure, the practitioner's feelings about his or her work and decision (e.g., "I have enjoyed my work, and I'm looking forward to opportunities to engage in other activities"), referral options, and instructions for accessing clinical records. Most such letters conclude with a statement of well wishes for the recipient. A more personal, handwritten addendum might also be included when appropriate. The clinician should retain copies in the client record of all such correspondence.

Some types of practices do not require the same kind of notification. A planned closing of a forensic or assessment practice, for example, requires the clinician simply to stop accepting new cases, notify referral sources, and complete any open cases. Reports are commonly provided at the conclusion of such cases. Thus, the need for future access to records is negligible, but there will be situations in which clients lose their reports and will request that another one be sent. In any case, information about how to obtain records must be made available.

The clinician who is closing a practice also must inform prospective clients and others attempting to contact him or her. Such public notification will include a modification of the clinician's online presence. Ongoing advertising accounts must be closed and professional websites modified to include notification that the practice is closing. Eventually, the site will be shut down.

Any electronic systems used to communicate with consumers must include notification of the closing (e.g., email and voicemail), with a clear statement that the practitioner will not be monitoring or responding to these communications. Instructions for requesting records and a generic referral (e.g., a local crisis program or mental health center) should be included.

## OTHER NOTIFICATIONS

Running a psychotherapy business also requires clinicians to interface with many other entities, all of which must be apprised of a practice closing. Some of the simpler notifications include contracted service providers such as for office cleaning and billing services, and property owners in the case of an office rental. The duration of office leases and notice required before moving out must also be considered. The disposition of office furniture, decor, and equipment, including test materials, also must be considered. A letter or email, in addition to a website announcement, serves to inform colleagues and other referral partners. Discontinuation of professional memberships and journal subscriptions is optional and not urgent, but the clinician may wish to consider such expenses in determining a closing date.

Decisions about resigning from insurance provider panels, retiring a practice license, deactivating a National Provider Identification number, and discontinuing professional liability insurance must take into account the likelihood that additional work may be required following the official practice closure. Insurance billing and communication with other professionals to facilitate coordination of care or follow-up conversations with clients regarding referrals are two examples. Procedures and timelines for resigning from insurance panels vary and are detailed in each contract. Careful attention to these requirements will obviate unintentional violations of contract provisions.

## CONTINUITY OF CARE AND REFERRALS

Before giving notice to clients, the clinician must think through all the issues related to closing the practice. For example, he or she must identify colleagues who will accept referrals. In some cases, preparing a list of referral alternatives, including information about at least one clinic that will accept clients and match them with appropriate psychotherapists, may be wise, given that none of the alternatives provided may suit a particular individual. It could also be noted that health insurance companies can direct subscribers to in-network providers. Finally, free or low-cost alternatives should be included for clients with limited financial means.

## CLINICAL RECORDS

Clients will want to know what will happen to their clinical records and how those records can be accessed should they want to obtain copies or have them sent to another provider. Thus, psychotherapists must establish a procedure for clients and other professionals to request clinical records. Some will decide to manage records themselves, assuming their health and lifestyle allow them to do so. In selecting this option, however, clinicians must allow clients to contact them, and doing so may create complications.

Simply responding to a written request (one that includes all the components necessary to authorize the release of information) and sending records likely will not result in boundary confusion, but a telephone conversation could make a clear termination problematic. Such interaction may encourage the perception of continuing treatment, and therefore, it carries the potential to complicate a former client's attachment and engagement in a subsequent psychotherapeutic relationship. Further, the clinician risks the possibility that such direct communication will permit a subtle or blatant request for therapeutic help (e.g., a suicide threat). When psychotherapists are no longer licensed or covered by malpractice insurance, such communication may be interpreted as unauthorized, uninsured practice. Similarly, offering professional advice or making additional referral recommendations may create legal liability for clinicians, underscoring the rationale for providing referral alternatives in a termination letter.

Perhaps more problematic is the risk that the psychotherapist's effort to avoid engaging in dialog about clinical issues will result in a more social conversation. Particularly after some period during which the psychotherapist has been regularly apprised of developments in a client's circumstances and relationships, the temptation to inquire about how things are going may be difficult to resist. Doing so, however, may inadvertently leave the client confused about the nature of the relationship and plant seeds of hope for some kind of social relationship in the future.

One strategy for avoiding such confusion is for the clinician to avoid making inquiries about the progress of a former client's life and to discourage such disclosures by the client. As it represents a marked departure from earlier patterns of interaction, doing so may feel uncomfortable and foreign. The psychotherapist's own curiosity, as well as his or her instinctive inclination to convey interest, caring, and empathy, may present a significant challenge to limiting a conversation to arrangements for providing clinical records. From the perspective of the former client, interaction devoid of the familiar therapeutic interest may be hurtful and distressing. The risk of undoing therapeutic gain and internalized learning must be considered.

Of course, a relatively innocuous interaction with a former client, even when it includes a cordial exchange of superficial social information, also carries the potential of a neutral or positive experience for both parties. And for many clients, this is the most likely outcome. For clients whose treatment has been characterized by complex transference reactions, boundary challenges, and significant difficulties associated with termination, however, such posttreatment interactions are fraught with complications. Lacking the continuing treatment in which to process negative responses, the risk of harm is substantial. Thus, psychotherapists must consider these factors and be mindful of the risks associated with fielding requests for records by telephone. Clarifying that all record requests must be made in writing and that they will be responded to only in writing will obviate difficulties. It should also be stated that requests for any other communications will not be answered.

An alternative to responding to requests for closed records personally is to identify a practicing colleague who agrees to maintain the closing clinician's electronic or paper records or to serve as a conduit for requests. Either of these arrangements provides a buffer between former clients and psychotherapists, diminishing the risk of confusion about the termination. In the latter arrangement, the identified colleague might receive a request for records and forward it to the clinician, who would fulfill it. This plan preserves client privacy, requires less work on the part of the colleague, and is therefore less expensive.

The disadvantage to any arrangement in which the closing psychotherapist maintains client records is that he or she must then monitor a mailbox, email account, or other channel of communication with former clients. This may not be difficult or problematic for some. But should the psychotherapist be traveling or otherwise engaged in activities not conducive to monitoring the channel, responding in a timely manner may be impossible, and the system may become onerous. Anecdotal reports from retired psychologists suggest, however, that most requests for records come in the weeks preceding or immediately following the departure. Requests in the post-retirement months and years are rare, but they do occur.

Monitoring requests for records, even with the buffer of a colleague mediating such requests, may be impractical, undesirable, or even impossible. Thus, another alternative is for the clinician to enlist one or more colleagues to manage requests and to appropriately dispose of records following the required time period in that particular jurisdiction. Agreeing to manage a colleague's records entails significant responsibility in addition to the time and labor necessary to do so. Therefore, an agreement about financial compensation should be arranged.

## DISCONTINUATION OF LIABILITY INSURANCE

Cancellation or nonrenewal of professional liability insurance entails careful consideration. Whether the clinician has a claims-made or occurrence policy will determine the need for purchasing additional coverage at the time of closing.

Claims-made insurance provides coverage limited to liability for claims that arise from incidents or events that occur and are reported to the insurance company while the policy is in force (www.thedoctors.com/Glossary/index.htm). In other words, the policy must be in effect at two points in time in order for it to provide coverage: when the incident cited in the lawsuit occurs and when the complaint/lawsuit is formally filed. Upon discontinuation of the policy, the clinician who has a claims-made policy can generally purchase additional protection (commonly referred to as "a tail") to cover claims regarding events transpiring during the term of the original policy but resulting in complaints after termination of the policy.

An arguably simpler type of professional liability policy is occurrence. This type of insurance covers the clinician for any incident occurring when the policy is (or was) in force, regardless of when that incident is reported or becomes a claim. For further discussion regarding liability insurance, see Chapter 4 in this *Handbook*.

# ETHICAL RESPONSIBILITIES

The clinical and ethical responsibilities of mental health professionals in regard to their clients continue through the process of terminating therapeutic relationships and closing a practice. Licensing board regulations and ethics codes promulgated by mental health professional associations clarify these responsibilities. Such organizations typically require members to provide pre-termination counseling and to offer referral alternatives when possible and appropriate (American Association for Marriage and Family Therapy [AAMFT], 2015; American Counseling Association [ACA], 2014; American Psychological Association [APA], 2010; National Association of Social Workers [NASW], 2008). Further, APA Ethical Standard 6.02, Maintenance, Dissemination, and Disposal of Confidential Records of Professional and Scientific Work, requires that clients be informed about plans for maintenance, storage, and access to records, and the NASW (2008) mandates that social workers promptly notify clients and arrange for their continuing care. Similarly, the AAMFT Ethics Code describes what members must do to prepare for practice changes:

In preparation for moving a practice, closing a practice, or death, marriage and family therapists arrange for the storage, transfer, or disposal of client records in conformance with applicable laws and in ways that maintain confidentiality and safeguard the welfare of clients. (p. 2)

Standards related to confidentiality, informed consent, and record maintenance also have implications for the termination process. Communicating with future treatment providers promotes the continuity of care and facilitates referrals, but this must be done with authorization from clients (AAMFT, 2015; ACA, 2014; APA, 2010; NASW, 2008). If a psychotherapist plans to discontinue a practice in the foreseeable future, new clients must be informed at the outset and so are allowed to consider whether they want to participate in treatment with this limitation. Professional ethics codes also address members' responsibilities regarding the maintenance of clinical records. Further, regulations regarding record retention and notification of the public vary by jurisdiction. Therefore, clinicians must review all applicable rules and laws.

Another ethical responsibility of mental health clinicians involves planning for unanticipated absences from practice. For example, Ethical Standard, 3.12, Interruption of Psychological Services, requires psychologists to "plan for facilitating services in the event that psychological services are interrupted" (APA, 2010, p. 7). Like psychologists, social workers must "make reasonable efforts to ensure continuity of services in the event that services are interrupted by factors such as unavailability, relocation, illness, disability or death" (NASW, 2008, p. 10).

These standards are also applicable at the time of a practice closing. The APA Record Keeping Guidelines (2014) recommends that psychologists maintain records for 7 years beyond the last contact with the client or, in the case of minor clients, 3 years after the individual reaches the age of majority. Additionally, state licensing board regulations may stipulate how long records must be maintained. Thus, whoever is designated to manage the clinician's records must be aware of the applicable regulations and agree to follow them. Even when a clinician closing a practice elects to manage the clinical records, he or she should identify an alternate custodian of those records and provide that custodian with the information necessary to assuming that responsibility should the clinician no longer be able to do so.

# CLINICAL CHALLENGES

Most of the time, clients' issues are clearly delineated from those of their psychotherapists. The occasions upon which they converge typically occur one client at a time. In the case of closing a practice, however, a major event in the psychotherapist's life overlaps with an important development in the lives of each of the clients, engendering the possibility that the psychotherapist will experience a desire to self-disclose in unprecedented ways. Here the confluence of clinical and ethical responsibilities becomes apparent as clinicians attempt to manage their countertransference, maintain appropriate boundaries, and remain cognizant of each individual's history and therapeutic needs.

Leaving a practice under almost any set of circumstances will precipitate a range of feelings in the clinician who is orchestrating the closing. He or she may feel guilty about causing distress in clients by initiating an untimely termination of their treatment. Sadness about saying goodbye to clients and the concomitant grief in leaving a significant phase of life are to be expected.

Clients certainly are impacted by a psychotherapist's announcement of impending departure. The memory of earlier experiences of abandonment, disappointment, grief, and loss may be triggered, engendering the potential for an enhanced or even unprecedented transference response. Clearly, potential exists for the depth of the clinical work to be amplified at this time.

This increased intensity is likely to require heightened effort on the part of the psychotherapist closing the practice. He or she may experience discomfort in the face of a client's expression of anger, feeling of abandonment, or, conversely, strong feelings of affection and gratitude. This may be particularly challenging for those whose theoretical orientations do not focus on the interpersonal relationship between psychotherapist and client. In fact, the clinician may be quite unaccustomed to managing such emotional intensity.

Complicating these challenges may be feelings of great excitement, anticipation, and even relief on the part of the clinician closing a practice. A muted self-disclosure to clients may be helpful in facilitating the termination (e.g., "I'm looking forward to opportunities not available when I am working"). The client, however, may experience a psychotherapist's expression of unmitigated exhilaration as insensitive and injurious. A cautious approach to self-disclosure is advisable.

When the closing of a clinical practice is precipitated by an unwelcome circumstance, such as a serious mental or physical illness, cognitive impairment, or license restriction, the psychotherapist is challenged to sequester his or her own response so as to attend to the response of the clients. Some determination of the psychotherapist's ability to manage these clinical challenges must be made, and if the welfare of clients cannot be ensured, another professional should be appointed to manage notification of closure.

The therapeutic frame establishes the professional and ethical boundaries of psychotherapy and contributes to the creation of the safe therapeutic environment (Langs, 1979). Breaking that therapeutic frame at any point during treatment may compromise client welfare. Doing so during the termination process introduces the risk of undoing previous therapeutic gains with no opportunity for subsequent repair, at least in the context of that therapeutic relationship.

Perhaps the best inoculation strategies for minimizing the risk of compromise to psychotherapist objectivity are self-care and collegial support. Having resources in place to help clinicians manage their own response is critical. The support of family and friends—along with consultation with knowledgeable colleagues—is imperative. Having one's own psychotherapist may also be helpful during this time.

When a clinician retires or leaves employment at a clinic or other similar organizational setting, a celebratory event commonly marks the occasion. When a solo practice is closed, there is no built-in ritual to commemorate this important event, yet the longing for closure is predictable and justified. Planning a function to memorialize the occasion with colleagues and friends diminishes the likelihood that the psychotherapist will turn to clients to meet that need.

# SELLING A PRACTICE

Many clinicians dream about building a successful practice and then one day selling it as a way to help finance a retirement. Although it is possible to sell a practice, it rarely happens. The process is quite complex, takes a great deal of planning, and is complicated by the ethical duties owed to clients. However, it can and has been done.

## PLANNING

Ideally, mental health professionals will design their practices from the beginning with the idea that the business will someday be sold. For example, a clinician has operated a successful solo practice for 25 years and then decides to retire in 6 months. The seller's ability to make the practice attractive to a buyer may depend upon the groundwork laid during those 25 years. A potential practice buyer will inevitably ask, "Why should I purchase this practice when I might be able to create my own successful practice in a year?" The practice owner must make a compelling case as to why the purchase would be advantageous to the buyer. For example, sellers might point out how their professional reputations and highly developed referral relationships could help buyers to build their practices much more quickly than could be accomplished independently.

Walfish and Barnett (2009) present an interview with Henry Harlow, who discussed the selling of mental health practices. Harlow makes the distinction between a "personality-based practice" and a "systems-based practice." A personality-based practice focuses on the individual skills and referral relationships that the practitioner has developed over the course of the practice. Conversely, a systems-based practice focuses on a structure that is *not* solely dependent upon the personality, charisma, or goodwill of any individual. In other words, sellers may facilitate the transition, but the practice is viable and profitable regardless of their ongoing participation.

A personality-based practice is more difficult to sell because the primary assets are the individual practitioner and the goodwill that he or she has cultivated in the community over time. Even if the individual has developed a full practice and has developed excellent relationships with referral partners, there is no guarantee that current or former clients will seek out the new practice owner for services. This may especially be the case in urban or suburban areas where there may be a large number of mental health practitioners who can also provide high-quality services to clients of the referral partner.

However, personality-based practices have a higher likelihood of being sold if there is a thoughtful plan for the buyer to assume ownership over time (e.g., one to two years). Weitz and Samuels (1990) have described such a transition in which Samuels joined Weitz's practice over the course of 2 years. During this time, Weitz introduced Samuels to his referral partners and helped him to build his practice. These deliberate efforts to identify Samuels with the practice resulted in a smooth transition when Weitz retired. The practice carried on as before, but with Samuels as the new owner. As mentioned above, such a transition period requires significant planning and efforts to overcome the nature of the practice being personality-based.

A systems-based practice may be more attractive to a buyer. The idea is that the practice has value as an entity beyond the goodwill and expertise of the owner who is selling it. The following are examples of systems-based value:

- Clinicians in the practice contribute to overhead and to the growth of the practice, and will be staying under the new ownership.
- Contracts are established with companies to provide their employee assistance programs, and the agreements will transfer to the new owner.
- Contracts are in place for clinicians in the practice to provide services in other settings (e.g., schools, medical clinics, nursing homes), and the contracts will transfer to the new owner.
- The building is owned by the seller and is included in the sale. This feature is particularly attractive if all the offices are rented and tenants include a variety of professions who will continue to occupy the space.

Although the seller may have been the person to develop these relationships and contracts, if he or she will continue to work in the practice for a time, then this will be of significant value to a potential buyer. As is the case in the sale of a personality-based practice, some transition time will allow for the introduction of the new owner to the community and referral partners. However, the duration of the transition and overlap may be shorter in the case of a systems-based practice.

## ETHICAL ISSUES IN SELLING A PRACTICE

Selling a mental health practice is not like selling a hardware store or a restaurant. Mental health professionals have clinical and ethical responsibilities to consumers of their services. Clients are encouraged to vest confidence, trust, and good faith in their psychotherapists, who assume a concomitant obligation to act for the sole benefit of those clients' interests. This obligation is reflected in the ethics codes of all major mental health organizations (e.g., AAMFT, 2015; ACA, 2014; APA, 2010; NASW, 2008).

In the APA's Ethics Code, Principle A: Beneficence and Nonmaleficence states that "Psychologists strive to benefit those with whom they work and take care to do no harm" (2010, p. 3). Further emphasizing this responsibility, Principle B: Fidelity and Responsibility clarifies that "Psychologists establish relationships of trust with those with whom they work" (2010, p. 3). Similarly, Ethical Standard 1.01 of the NASW's Ethics Code states that "Social workers' primary responsibility is to promote the well-being of clients. . . . clients' interests are primary" (p. 8). Marriage and family therapists are specifically instructed not to "use their professional relationships with clients to further their own interests" (AAMFT, 2015, p. 1). Organizations representing professional counselors incorporate similar recommendations and admonitions in their ethics codes (ACA, 2014).

Clearly, the fundamental principle undergirding the ethics of all mental health professions is that the best interests of consumers must be considered foremost in the minds of clinicians as they make any decisions about their practices. Therefore, when these professionals consider selling their practices, they must maintain their fiduciary responsibility to their clients and act consistently with the ethics codes described above.

Although mental health practitioners can sell their practices, they cannot "sell their clients." First, the best interests of the clients must be considered when responsibility for their care is being transferred to another clinician. It may be advantageous to clients to continue with the new practice owner if they have been introduced and feel comfortable with him or her, and the problems they are working on in psychotherapy fall into the area of expertise of the new owner. However, when the expertise needed by a particular client falls outside of the competencies of the new owner, the client must be referred to someone who could better meet his or her clinical needs. This caveat should be clearly articulated in the contract between buyer and seller.

Walfish and Zimmerman (2013) have noted that each referral decision must be made with the best interests of the client as paramount. The benefits of the clinicians involved in the sale and purchase of the practice must be secondary. The key, as it relates to the ethics codes noted above, is to make sure the decision is not exploitive of the client.

Second, clients maintain their rights to confidentiality, and the right of access to private information is not automatically conferred on the new owner. Written authorization from current clients must be obtained before their records are shared with a new owner (Koocher, 2003).

Decisions about the management of former clients' records maintained by the seller are more complex. The current practice owner may have alerted clients at the outset that one or more mental health professionals will be custodians of their clinical records in the event that the clinician sells the practice, becomes incapacitated, or is otherwise unable to continue to maintain the records. If clients have consented to this arrangement in advance, no further action will be needed when a practice is sold. However, in most cases, the seller will need to take additional steps to ensure clients' privacy rights. Regulations detailed in the Health Insurance Portability and Accountability Act (HIPAA) must be considered. Specifically, the new owner must sign a Business Associate Agreement. Such an agreement ensures that any business associate of a "covered entity" (i.e., a clinician accountable to HIPAA) will protect personal health information in accordance with HIPAA guidelines.

Other relevant rules and laws vary by jurisdiction and should be carefully reviewed as decisions about the sale of a practice are made. For example, some states require clinicians to post a notice announcing the closing of the practice and specifying the way clients can access their records. In any case, the sale of a practice must reflect attention not only to its ethical dimensions, but to the legal issues as well. Consultation with an attorney is imperative.

# CONCLUDING THOUGHTS

Closing a private practice brings with it many emotional and practical challenges. Consultation with colleagues throughout the process is essential. Review of relevant professional literature will provide further guidance. Many authors offer additional suggestions for managing the practical and emotional aspects of closing a practice, particularly in the case of retirement (e.g., Blakelee, 2014; Heller, 2007; Holloway, 2003; Thomas, 2015; Zuckerman, 2008). The NASW Center for

Workforce Studies (2012) has provided a helpful checklist for private practitioners to consider when closing their practices. Despite the many demands attendant upon mental health professionals at this juncture, taking advantage of the resources available will facilitate the process and ease their transitions into the next phase of their lives.

## NOTE

1. Steve Walfish and I spent many months working on this chapter together. We talked at length about our practices and about how best to close them when the time came.

    Like most clinicians in independent practice, we both envisioned a scenario in which we would choose the ideal time to leave our practices. We would plan carefully and provide clients, colleagues, and referral sources with plenty of notice. We imagined making thoughtful referrals, facilitating clients' transitions, and gently easing out of practice at a comfortable pace. How very sad that Steve never had that opportunity.

    Steve and I were scheduled to have dinner near his office in Atlanta to finalize our work on this chapter. He cancelled, saying that he was not feeling well. I texted him a photo, and he responded characteristically with what would be his last communication with me. He said, "Smile."

Janet T. Thomas, PsyD

## REFERENCES

American Association for Marriage and Family Therapy. (2015). Code of ethics. Retrieved from http://aamft.org/iMIS15/AAMFT/Content/Legal_Ethics/Code_of_Ethics.aspx.

American Counseling Association. (2014). Code of ethics. Retrieved from http://www.counseling.org/Resources/aca-code-of-ethics.pdf.

American Psychological Association. (2010). Ethical principles of psychologists and code of conduct. Retrieved from http://www.apa.org/ethics/code/index.aspx.

American Psychological Association. (2014). Record keeping guidelines. Retrieved from http://www.apa.org/practice/guidelines/record-keeping.pdf.

Ballard, D. (2005). Planning ahead to close or sell your practice. In J. E. Barnett & M. Gallardo (Eds.), *Handbook for success in independent practice* (pp. 165–172). Phoenix, AZ: Psychologists in Independent Practice.

Barnett, J. E., Zimmerman, J., & Walfish, S. (2014). *The ethics of private practice: A practical guide for mental health clinicians.* New York: Oxford University Press.

Blakelee, M. K. (2014, July/August). Retiring ethically. *National Psychologist*, 23. Retrieved from http://nationalpsychologist.com/2014/07/retiring-as-a-psychologist-ethically/102590.html.

Heller, K. M. (2007, Winter). Closing the door for the last time: The process of retiring from private practice. *Independent Practitioner*, 26–31.

Holloway, J. D. (2003). Shutting down a practice: Psychologist face legal, ethical and emotional issues when they close their practice doors. *Monitor on Psychology*, 34, 32.

Koocher, G. (2003). Ethical and legal issues in professional practice transitions. *Professional Psychology: Research and Practice*, 34, 383–387.

Langs, R. (1979). *The therapeutic environment.* Northvale, NJ: Jason Aronson.

McGurk, W. S., & Advisory Committee on Colleague Assistance. (2005). Retirement: Making a successful transition. *Practice Central.* Retrieved from http://www.apapracticecentral.org/ce/self-care/retirement.aspx

NASW Center for Workforce Studies. (2012). *Retiring? Tips for closing your private practice.* Washington, DC: National Association of Social Workers.

National Association of Social Workers. (2008). Code of ethics. Retrieved from http://www.socialworkers.org/pubs/code/code.asp?print=1&.

Stout, C., & Grand, L. (2004). *Getting started in private practice.* New York: Wiley.

Thomas, J. T. (2015). Closing an independent practice: Practical, ethical, and clinical dimensions. *National Psychologist, 24,* 16.

Walfish, S., & Barnett, J. E. (2009). *Financial success in mental health practice: Essential tools and strategies for practitioners.* Washington, DC: American Psychological Association.

Walfish, S. & Zimmerman, J. (2013). Making good referrals. In G. P. Koocher, J. C. Norcross, & B. A. Greene (Eds.). *Psychologists' desk reference* (3rd ed., pp. 649–653). New York: Oxford University Press.

Weitz, R. D., & Samuels, R. M. (1990). The sale and purchase of a private health-service-provider psychology practice. In. E. Margeanau (Ed.), *The encyclopedic handbook of private practice* (pp. 384–390). New York: Gardner Press.

Zuckerman, E. L. (2008). *The paper office* (4th ed.). New York: Guilford Press.

# SPECIAL ISSUES

# CHAPTER 43

# THE PRIVATE PRACTITIONER AND FAMILY ISSUES

*Lauren Behrman*

This chapter is born through my own life experience of blending private practice and motherhood over three decades, in addition to listening to the voices of women practitioners all over the country who have shared their concerns and questions with me on a "Moms in Practice" virtual support group for the past four years. The group addresses issues arising from all aspects of the intersection of practice and motherhood from contemplating practice, motherhood, pregnancy, practice with babies, up through all of the stages of childhood development. Women practitioners have brought questions and concerns about all aspects of the worlds of practice and parenthood and related unique topics, including special needs children, adopting babies and older children, acquiring children in new relationships, their children's illnesses, emergencies and sick days, their miscarriages, divorces, and college searches as these intertwine with and impact their practice. This chapter explores the reciprocal impacts of practice on parenthood and parenthood on practice. To gain a perspective of the experiences of fathers in private practice, I interviewed a small sample of "Dads in Practice," both married dads and divorced dads with shared parenting time.[1]

## ONE MOM'S STORY

It was 1999 and I was sitting on the floor in my home office working with Sandy, a feisty four-year-old girl with gleaming deep brown eyes. We were "playing" with my dollhouse, and she was weaving an intricate family drama with my Playmobil dolls, playing out her struggles and worries in her story. On the other side of the double doors, my three children, aged two, four, and six were home from school, and even though they knew to be quiet when mommy was working, I could imagine the sound of their voices. They were playing and doing homework with their nanny, and I began to question myself: "Here I am, sitting on the floor and giving my undivided attention to other people's children, while my own children are with a nanny inches from where I sit. What is wrong with this picture?" It was at that moment that I realized that the practice model that had worked for me for the past 14 years was no longer viable, and I needed to shift my practice paradigm.

I had been in practice for close to nine years prior to becoming a mother and had a well-established referral base in two different locations. At the time I became a mother, over 80% of my practice time was being spent conducting psychological evaluations and psychotherapy of preschool and school-aged children, as well as parent guidance sessions for their parents. Much of my work took place from 3 p.m. to 8 or 9 p.m. That model worked for the years before my three children were born, as well as during the time they were infants and preschoolers. By closing my two outside office locations and working solely out of a home office, I was able to tailor my hours to be most available to my children before they entered elementary school. I was home with my children much of the day to take them to Mommy and Me, Gymboree, Musical Munchkins, the playground, play dates, and their doctor's appointments, and was then able to work in the afternoons while my children napped and after they went to bed. With some childcare in the late afternoons, I could take time off for dinner and then see a few clients after the children were asleep. However, once they entered elementary school, the landscape completely changed.

When my oldest son went to elementary school and was out of the home from 8 a.m. to 4 p.m., I was seeing the bulk of my clients during afternoons and evenings and often missed my children's bedtime routine and did not see my children until the next morning. On days when I had early morning patients after working late the prior evening, I might not see my children for close to 48 hours; it felt as if I had been in another city, even though my office was in my home. I realized that if I didn't change things quickly, I was about to miss a great deal of my children's childhood.

## MY SOLUTION

The writing was on the wall; the hours I had carved out for my practice were no longer feasible with school-aged children. The practice population I had focused on was primarily available during the hours I needed to be available for my children, and I quickly needed to find clients who could be seen primarily during daytime hours. With that intention, I went to an annual convention of the American Psychological Association, "shopping" for ideas for a practice niche that would interest me, would match my skillset, and would primarily be limited to the hours that my children were in school. I attended seminars on anger management groups for children, couple therapy, psychotherapy with women undergoing infertility treatment, and co-parent counseling for divorced parents, to name a few. By the end of the convention, I came away with many ideas for shifting my practice focus and population so that the majority of my work could be carried out during daytime hours.

After much thought, I decided that the co-parent counseling niche would best meet my skillset, areas of interest, and hours that I wanted to devote to practice. Co-parent counseling was more of a time-limited intervention, meetings could be scheduled less frequently than psychotherapy, and it was often court-ordered, which compelled clients to engage in the intervention. As a result, my clients were more willing to come in to see me during the daytime. Over time, what began as a niche practice in co-parent counseling blossomed into a full-spectrum divorce-services niche that included mediation, parent coordination, and collaborative divorce roles as a child specialist and neutral process facilitator. This supplemented my psychotherapy practice and expanded my network of referral partners.

Not only had I shifted my practice into a specialty niche that was free of insurance and managed care, I had also found an area of practice that was protective of children and families, which meshed with my core values. Additionally, when I had a predominately child psychotherapy practice, I was isolated in my home office seeing clients much of the workday. In my new practice niche, I began to work in conjunction with attorneys, judges, financial professionals, and other mental health professionals and found myself in a stimulating and supportive professional community. Some of the collegiality I had always treasured during training, or when working on a team in a professional setting, was now part of my everyday work experience. Becoming part of multiple interdisciplinary organizations focusing on this area of practice, I found myself in leadership roles, founding local chapters of national organizations, writing, speaking, teaching, and participating in a supportive peer supervision group, rich in resources for parenting coordinators that has been going strong for over 10 years. All of these additional professional activities were growth-producing and enlivening for me.

## LESSONS LEARNED IN THE TRENCHES

Looking back at my own professional journey, I wish I had recognized that I was a small business owner early on in my career and that I had focused on mastering the business skills that I needed to make that part of the practice more efficient and less stressful. Somehow, flying by the seat of my pants, I always figured out how to make it work.

As a mom and independent practitioner, it's important to recognize that as your children grow and develop, their needs change as well, and your way of working in private practice needs to change too. For example, infants and preschool children have more fluid schedules, and parents have more choice about when to enroll them in structured programs and what kinds of schedules to set up (e.g., three-day preschool, half or full days, mornings or afternoons, no preschool, full daycare). Once children enter elementary school, their schedule becomes more fixed and determined by their school districts and governmental requirements. Children also begin to engage in more afterschool activities, sports teams, and so forth. The needs of elementary school children are different than those of children in middle school, high school, and college. A proactive approach is needed that considers how the needs of your developing/growing family will impact your private practice and how you schedule clients, the types of work you accept, and the possible need to do different kinds of work or see different types of clients at different phases of your family's life cycle. While I was able to shift my work as my family evolved and grew, I did not approach it with the consciousness that would have allowed me to strategize, anticipate, and plan for the shifts that my practice would require as my children grew. I have recognized this only in retrospective.

# AN OPPORTUNITY TO PAY IT FORWARD

One of my greatest professional pleasures is "paying it forward," sharing experiences, resources, frustrations, and satisfactions with moms in practice from around the country once a month in an open conference call I facilitate through The Practice Institute (TPI). Women who are considering becoming parents and those who are at all stages of parenthood and practice have joined together and brought their questions and concerns to our conference call. Pregnant first-time mothers-to-be, mothers of teens, adoptive moms, stepmoms, gay moms, moms of special needs children, and moms of college-age and adult children all have been represented on our calls. The calls are a mixture of practice consultation and support and are open to TPI members as well as the general public.

These calls are announced in weekly email announcements by TPI, and any practitioners can add themselves to the distribution list. You can also check TPI's website (thepracticeinstitute. com) for upcoming events and sign up for the event right on the website. On any given call, there may be anywhere from one to 15 participants, and each call addresses different topics based on the needs of the women who are attending.

# FINDING BALANCE: A UNIVERSAL CONCERN

The most common concern among these mothers in independent practice has to do with finding balance; that is, being able to juggle the demands of motherhood with being a clinician and small business owner. These concerns are also common to single fathers in practice and dads shouldering equal parenting responsibilities with their partners. Research has found levels of professional autonomy and flexibility of hours to be the highest-rated satisfaction variables with this choice of a career path (Walfish & O'Donnell, 2008). Independent practice lends itself perfectly to blending with parenthood at all stages of life. The flip side is that there is a huge occupational hazard—the risk of burning yourself out by taking care of dependent children and needy clients while not taking adequate care of yourself. Additionally, at some stages of our lives, we may also be taking care of members of our extended families as well. It is critical to attend to self-care and to consciously and intentionally set up your practice so that there is a balance between practice and your own life. The flexibility and autonomy of independent practice allow you to choose one or more niche populations that will be available when you want to work and during the times that work best for the needs of your family. It is the intentionality and planning that are so important. Rather than letting the practice take over your life and seep into all available moments, planning the hours you want to work, and then matching your interests and skills with a population available during those times, will allow you to work smarter and not shortchange either your family or your practice.

You can approach your practice with either a model of scarcity or one of abundance. The scarcity model calls for you to work every possible moment and take every client who calls because you are fearful that the well will dry out and if you don't take this new client there will never be another one. The model of abundance calls for intentional planning of what is optimal and feasible for you. Intentionally focus on what hours you want to fill, and then work to fill those times while maintaining the balance and boundaries that are necessary so that your practice and personal life can coexist. There is an additional benefit of creating strong referral partnerships by referring clients to colleagues who are available during the hours you have chosen not to work. These cross-referrals breed goodwill and build your referral network, offering the opportunity to "cross-refer" and keep you on the "top of mind" in your referral partners' stable of resources. There are so many different options available for niche practices that can suit a practitioner's availability and interests; it is important to find the one or two that work well for you.

As the owner of your independent practice, it is also possible to shift and change as your family's needs evolve through the developmental stages. Anticipating those transitions and actively researching your options in advance can help create a smooth flow, integrating the needs of yourself and your family with a manageable practice that allows you to find that optimal work/life balance and avoid burnout.

## CAN WOMEN HAVE IT ALL?

In an article in *Atlantic Monthly*, Anne-Marie Slaughter (2012) writes about her experience combining work in a high-profile government position as the former State Department Undersecretary while at the same time parenting young children. "Can women have it all?" she asks. In this article she explores the problems and challenges faced by professional women and posits that women "tell themselves stories and lies" about their ability to "have it all"—healthy marriages, exciting careers, and thriving children. She states:

> Here I step on to treacherous ground mined with stereotypes. From years of conversations and observations, however, I've come to believe that men and women respond quite differently when problems at home force them to recognize that their absence is hurting a child, or at least that their presence would likely help. I do not believe fathers love their children any less than mothers do, but men do seem more likely to choose their job at a cost to their family, while women seem more likely to choose their family at a cost to their job. (p. 92)

She goes on to say:

> Many factors determine this choice, of course. Men are still socialized to believe that their primary family obligation is to be the breadwinner; women, to believe that their primary family obligation is to be the caregiver. But it may be more than that. When I described the choice between my children and my job to Senator Jeanne Shaheen, she said exactly what I felt: "There's really no choice." She wasn't referring to social expectations, but to a maternal imperative felt so deeply that the "choice" is reflexive. (p. 92)

I believe these concepts extend to the experience of fathers in practice, and that the stereotypes she alludes to in her article are applicable to my male colleagues, modified by cultural, sociological, and generational factors.

# EXPERIENCES OF FATHERS IN PRACTICE

My conversations with Dads in Practice confirmed my hypothesis that the experiences of fathers in practice depend highly on the degree to which these fathers envisioned themselves as primary caregivers, and the ways in which they had set up childrearing responsibilities with their partners. For many dads, being in practice was comparable to any other full-time career, perhaps with the added benefit of greater flexibility in scheduling to allow for attending children's school events and activities.

In my dialogs with male colleagues who are fathers in practice, many of the themes were consistent with the ideas Slaughter posited. One independent practitioner father stated: "Men's lives don't change so much when children are born; women's lives do . . . caring for children falls more on women's shoulders . . . in dual-income families, mothers still do more childcare and housework" (S. Demby, personal communication, April 22, 2016). This practitioner and father imagines that there is some gender difference, saying "as a group, mothers tend to feel more preoccupied about the time work takes them away from their children than fathers." Dr. Demby went on to state that there is a cultural shift under way in certain segments of the population in which "Gender roles and norms are becoming more fluid and changing . . . some subgroup of parents where fathers are as involved in child care as mothers. I see fathers walking around my neighborhood with baby carriers on their chests—it's a different generation" (S. Demby, personal communication, April 22, 2016).

In speaking with male colleagues, I did have a dialog with two fathers who have taken more of a shared caretaking role in their children's lives and have found that they were able to have the flexibility to do this as a result of being in independent practice. One of the major concerns for independent practitioner fathers was the stability and predictability of their income. While women practitioners have certainly expressed concerns about the predictability of their income in practice, the emphasis is not the same as the men's in families where women are contributing a second income.

One model discussed consisted of maintaining a full- or part-time institutional position for a steady paycheck and benefits while gradually building up a private practice. For this father, it was only after his children went to college that he embarked on a full-time independent practice. He now finds himself working longer hours in his practice, including evenings and weekends, and believes he would not have had as much quality time with his children had he been in independent practice during their younger years. In their family, his wife was working part time and was more available to the children (S. Demby, personal communication, April 22, 2016).

Concerns about income stability for practitioners solely in private practice were echoed by a father of young children currently in full-time private practice. This man and his wife chose to partner equally in the care of their children, each taking shifts of childrearing time and working time. This father feels he is one of the few practitioner fathers he knows who is solely in private practice, with most preferring to have some stable source of income: "Most take on gainful employment and their private practice is moonlighting on the side" (D. Sonotore, personal communication, February 15, 2016). He believes that most practitioners who embark on independent practice are often not the main breadwinners in the family and have a partner who is working full time or has some other source of income and can operate at a loss for a few years until the practice gets off the ground. For him, the stress of income instability is palpable on a daily basis, and he wishes that he had become more established in his practice before he became a father (D. Sonotore, personal communication, February 15, 2016).

Another dad in full-time private practice, who is divorced with residential parenting time with his son 50% of the time, remarked that he had to design his life around parenting his son. He saw his practice as what made it possible to be present for his son after school on days when his son was with him, and he never scheduled work on those days. Like myself, he too found a practice niche that allowed him to manage his hours to allow for optimal time parenting his son. He realized that he often needed to sacrifice his work for the needs of his son, such as by cancelling his clients on days that his son was ill and could not go to school. He found that the flexibility offered by being in practice made it possible to experience parenting in the full way that he wished.

Looking back, this practitioner saw that he succumbed to stress and anxiety at times as the demands of being a parent, attending to his practice, and producing income as a single father were intense. He did not prioritize self-care and found himself not as relaxed and accepting in his parenting as he would have wished to be. He reflects on his experience as a father and private practitioner, stating, "Private practice offers autonomy, and along with that comes some financial unpredictability. One needs to be one's own boss when asking for so much time off—you're the only one that would give it to yourself" (D. Sonotore, personal communication, February 15, 2016).

# OPPORTUNITIES VERSUS CHALLENGES FOR PARENTS

Practitioners with family obligations must weigh their options prior to embarking on a private practice. It is always prudent to look at the cost/benefit analysis to determine whether the benefits of making this choice outweigh the potential costs or risks. This is an important decision that needs to be carefully thought out.

### BENEFITS

When I look back upon my 31 years of practice, I have no regrets about my career choice. Having been in practice while raising a family has afforded me a significant degree of independence and empowerment in being able to develop new interests and opportunities, pursue a variety of other professional activities, sustain a healthy work environment, and earn a good income. One of the great benefits has been the freedom from worry about "job security." Throughout these years of practice in the busy times and the quiet times, I have always known that my "job" is secure. Whenever there was a downturn in referrals and the practice was quieter than I would have liked, I always knew that I could develop other practice areas and populations, invest time in developing professional relationships, learn new skills, and pursue other professional activities such as writing, leadership, speaking presentations, committee work, and networking, for example.

I began to welcome the periods of relative quiet and felt secure in knowing that the work was cyclical and that the practice would rebuild. At one time, when the practice was in a longer-than-typical lull, I reinvigorated it by "borrowing" a colleague's office in a new location and using this opportunity to reconnect with all my old colleagues, mentors, and peers. Within a few months, the referrals began to flow into both locations and the practice had rebooted. When I became a mother, I was heartened by the flexibility of scheduling and the ability to adjust my schedule (sometimes at the last minute) when necessary. With a full-time at-home office, I was able to fit in rescheduled clients very early in the morning or late at night, or even on a weekend if necessary, with little disruption to my family.

Throughout the course of my career, my private practice took many different forms and was able to shift and change to sync up with the changing needs of my growing family. I was able to target a population that was available during the hours that worked best for my family and to build a practice that allowed me to work when my children were in school and spend quality time with my children when they were home. In addition, I was able to work around their class trips, special events, recitals, and parents' meetings by being able to anticipate these events and adjust my schedule accordingly. By having the freedom to try new ways of working, including carving out the time for continuing education training and mentoring, the practice remained fresh, stimulating, and suited to my professional needs, the needs of my family, and the needs of my clients.

## CHALLENGES

Some of the greatest advantages of being in private practice for working moms and dads with shared parenting responsibilities are also some of its greatest challenges. Independent practitioners must keep the referral pipeline strong and open. That might translate into carving out time to focus on networking and other marketing activities. Maintaining strong personal and professional relationships is particularly important for sustaining a strong network of referral partners. It is wise to make the time to follow up with referral partners and to demonstrate excellent customer service, both to clients and professional colleagues who refer. For parents in practice, this additional time invested in practice building and maintenance activities takes away from time spent with children and family.

## ANXIETY OVER FINANCIAL UNCERTAINTY

This is a particular challenge for solo independent practitioners, especially single moms and dads and those parents who are sole or primary providers in their families. In speaking to both moms and dads in practice, the uncertainty of income was a primary concern. Many men I have spoken with chose not to be in full-time independent practice when their children were young and sometimes held a part- or full-time job in an institution in addition to a small private practice "on the side" so they could maintain a consistent and predictable income. In these cases, these men saw themselves as primary providers, and their wives were either stay-at-home moms or worked more of a part-time schedule and took on more responsibility for childrearing.

## CAREGIVER BURNOUT

Being in independent practice can be emotionally challenging when you are dealing with a heavy caseload of clients in crisis, clients with traumatic histories, and those in high conflict. You are a caregiver at home as well as at work. You also are exposed to the second-degree stress that arises from recurrent exposure to clients' trauma; this can activate your "fight, flight, or freeze response" while you must remain in an empathic stance (Izzo & Karpel-Miller, 2010).

# IMPACT OF BEING PARENTS ON OUR WORK WITH PARENTS

I began working with children and families early in my practice, long before becoming a mother myself. For years, my education in child development and the psychotherapeutic and assessment techniques I applied to working with that population were sufficient to work effectively with children and their parents. However, once I became a parent and experienced the intensity of emotions, the exhaustion, the devotion, and the ways my own vulnerabilities were tapped, and my resilience and strengths were tested in relationships with children at all developmental stages, I recognized the element that had been missing in my earlier understanding of what it means to be a parent. I joked that I wanted to write apology letters to all the parents I had ever worked with before I became a mother. As one colleague states:

> When our clients talk to us about their parenting experience, our experience with our children informs our work. We have deeper understanding of what it means to have children. The tension and the gifts . . . we know firsthand what it means to have all kinds of stressors in your life . . . loving your kids and having to balance all kinds of things. ( J. Steiger, personal communication, March 12, 2016)

Since we are psychotherapists, have studied child development, and see every day the importance of good parenting and the impact of bad parenting, there is an additional layer of challenge for parents who are also practicing in the mental health field. We are painfully aware of child development and the impact of stressors on our children. We are also more aware of the complexity involved in raising children. Our own experiences of being parents help us to be much more realistic about the challenges of parenting, and as a result we can be much more empathic to what our clients are experiencing with their children.

In our offices, we often hear husbands who make the statement:

> "I'm the one with all the pressure; you're home all day, how hard can it be?" Do these fathers understand the emotional agility required when raising children, how one has to expand their capacity? There are no conquests in childrearing and the work and responsibility increase exponentially with more than one child. (J. Steiger, personal communication, March 12, 2016)

As parents in independent practice, we "develop an empathy for the experience of parenthood, and approach parents who have made many errors with a lot of good intentions with the empathy necessary to break the pattern, break the cycle" (J. Steiger, personal communication, March 12, 2016).

## CONCLUDING THOUGHTS

Mary Matalin, who spent two years as an assistant to President George Bush and the counselor to Vice President Dick Cheney before stepping down to spend more time with her daughters, wrote: "Having control over your schedule is the only way that women who want to have a career and a family can make it work" (as cited in Slaughter, 2012, p. 87). This is what we can access as a parent in practice: If we intentionally and purposefully build it, we can have a great deal of control over our schedule, and in this way, we can make having a meaningful career and a family work without shortchanging either our children or our practices.

By choosing independent practice and setting up our work with intention, we not only have the best opportunity to participate both in family and professional life, but we also have control over our work hours, the type of work we do, the amount of work, and the culture of our work environments. We also have control over our choices of when and how to diversify and reinvigorate our practices, and what kind of outside professional communities and activities we wish to engage in. As primary caretakers of young children, we are able to shift our work hours and foci as our children grow and their developmental needs change. To me, independent practice has been the key to being present for my children through all their stages of development, while simultaneously experiencing a rewarding professional life.

## NOTE

1. With gratitude to my colleagues Steven Demby, PhD, David Sonotore, CSW, and Jeffrey Steiger, CSW.

# REFERENCES

Izzo, E., & Karpel-Miller, V. C. (2010). *Second-hand shock: Surviving & overcoming vicarious trauma.* Scottsdale, AZ: High Conflict Institute Press.

Slaughter, A-M. (July/August, 2012). Why women still can't have it all. *Atlantic Monthly,* 85–101.

Walfish, S., & O'Donnell, P. (2008). Satisfaction and stresses in private practice. *Independent Practitioner, 28,* 135–138.

# CHAPTER 44

# SUSTAINING SELF-CARE AND THRIVING AS A PRIVATE PRACTITIONER

*Patricia A. Rupert and Ellen K. Baker*

When we began our careers in the 1970s—Ellen to become a full-time private practitioner and Pat an academic with a part-time practice—little attention was given to self-care. It was not discussed during our graduate education and there were few, if any, writings or resources available to assist practicing professionals. As we have journeyed down our career paths, however, we have each become committed to its importance. For Ellen, this commitment came early in her career as she came face to face with the reality that in order to sustain caring for others, we need to care for ourselves. That new-found awareness led to her involvement in the then-nascent movement of psychologists beginning to speak and write about psychotherapist self-care, and to 30-plus years of writing, consulting, and leading experiential workshops on psychotherapist well-being. For Pat, the commitment came somewhat later as her research on ethics issues evolved to study burnout and psychotherapist well-being and her data led her to the recognition that work-life balance and self-care behaviors were essential to our well-being and professional functioning.

Over the past several decades, we have both been heartened by the growing recognition and discussion within psychology and other mental health professions of the ethical imperative and importance of psychotherapist self-care. Manifestations of progress include the evolving critical mass of available resources in several areas: psychotherapist self-care literature that is increasingly informed by research; educational programs for professionals; and professional association recognition and support. In the *Encyclopedic Handbook of Private Practice* (Margeneau, 1990), in contrast to the current publication, there was no mention of self-care. Now a wide range of books on the topic is available, including more recently one specifically for graduate students (Carter & Barnett, 2014). In addition, a growing number of graduate school curricula now include modules on self-care, research labs study self-care, and a host of continuing education modules address the ethical imperative and practice of self-care for practitioners. With financial backing, programmatic support, and leadership of major professional associations, we have every expectation that self-care resources available to mental health professionals will continue to increase.

In writing this chapter, we have drawn upon our experiences as well as the growing literature to offer a discussion of self-care that we hope will be particularly relevant for private practitioners. Our primary goals are to offer a perspective on the role of self-care in our personal and professional lives; to present a framework for thinking about self-care; and to provide some specific ideas and suggestions for integrating self-care into our lives as private practitioners. Toward this end, we begin with a brief discussion of the challenges of private practice and then discuss issues related to making a commitment to self-care, developing a self-care plan, and sustaining self-care.

# RECOGNIZING THE CHALLENGES (AND REWARDS) OF PRIVATE PRACTICE

*You are nearing the end of a long day—back-to-back psychotherapy clients with only a couple of short breaks. For the most part, the day has gone well. Your clients seem to be making progress; even that typically resistant client was beginning to explore some important issues today, and your suicidal client seemed to be more emotionally stable and hopeful. Your last client has just left and the office is quiet. You are feeling ready to relax and unwind, but the day is not quite over yet. There is paperwork—the progress notes for the final clients of the day and the managed care appeal that is due at the end of the week really should be completed before you leave for the day. Oh, and there is a message on your answering machine from the client who needs to talk to you as soon as possible.*

This might be a typical day for a private practitioner. It is certainly not a bad day. At the end of a day like this, there are many reasons to feel satisfied. But there are also reasons to feel tired, perhaps even emotionally drained and exhausted. As mental health professionals, the work we do is challenging. In fact, much has been written about the demands of psychotherapeutic work and the stresses of the current healthcare environment. While these demands and stresses may vary depending on the specifics of an individual's practice and his or her personal circumstances, they affect us all to some degree at various points in our professional lives. Some are inherent in the nature of psychotherapeutic work, many relate to institutional or contextual requirements, and others involve pressures we put on ourselves. Recognizing these demands and stresses represents an important step in developing effective professional self-care strategies.

By its very nature, psychotherapeutic work poses unique challenges (Norcross & Guy, 2007). The process of listening attentively and responding empathically to the problems of others can be emotionally and even physically draining. Some clients may be particularly demanding of our time and resources. For example, clients may be suicidal, may threaten harm to others, or may be severely disturbed. In fact, research has consistently found that having to deal with these types of negative client behaviors is linked to higher levels of burnout (Rupert, Miller, & Dorociak, 2015). Because the confidential nature of our work requires that it be carried out in private, psychotherapists are also emotionally and physically isolated during much of their workday. We sit in sessions alone and uninterrupted with clients, focusing on their concerns and problems. We leave these sessions unable to talk about what we have heard or done with family or friends. This isolation may be especially challenging for private practitioners without colleagues close by or structured opportunities to discuss their feelings and work-related concerns. For those individuals, the office may indeed be quiet once that last client leaves.

Recordkeeping, paperwork, and the requirements of third-party payers add significant burdens to our daily work lives. Although private practitioners may be less likely to have to deal with some types of bureaucratic paperwork than their colleagues in institutional settings, many face unique challenges associated with establishing recordkeeping systems and managing the business aspects of a practice. And, in the current healthcare environment, we have to deal with new regulations and requirements, increased demands to justify our work, and external constraints that may limit our ability to provide optimal services. For those in private practice, these changes may translate into more work for less money and create increased financial pressures. Interestingly, research suggests that these types of administrative business demands may be even more stressful than the demands our clients place on us. For example, burnout research has found that although the number of hours spent doing psychotherapy does not predict burnout, the time spent doing administrative paperwork is linked to higher levels of burnout (Rupert et al., 2015). Further, the most highly ranked sources of stress for private practitioners tend to be those associated with aspects of the current healthcare environment: external constraints on services, managed care paperwork and reimbursement rates, and excessive paperwork (Rupert & Baird, 2004).

Perhaps equally troubling are the pressures we put on ourselves. Although these may vary depending on each person's background, experience, and personality, we all share a vulnerability to certain internally generated pressures. Our desire to help brings with it a sense of responsibility for the lives of others and may lead us to become overly concerned and perhaps overly involved with our clients. Navigating the fine line between helpful caring and overinvolvement is critical, as the latter is linked to increased risk for burnout (e.g., Rupert et al., 2015).

In a parallel way, as the "experts," we may also feel pressure to have all the answers, to be strong, and to be in control of both our professional and personal lives. Consequently, it may be difficult to show weakness or to turn to someone else for help: What will colleagues, friends, and family think? These internally generated pressures may be especially salient for private practitioners, who are less likely to have ready access to informal support from colleagues.

And, of course, we all have lives outside of work—family, friends, and responsibilities that compete for our time, energy, and emotional resources. In fact, the very personal nature of our work presents some special issues when it comes to balancing work and life demands. After a long day listening to the problems of others, it may not be easy to offer a sympathetic ear to a child, spouse, or friend who wants to vent about a tough day. After a chaotic morning at home or an argument with a spouse, it can be tough to concentrate on that client who seems to ramble on and on. The boundary between our professional and personal selves can be blurry, and demands or pressures from one area of life can easily spill over into the other area. When work and family lives conflict, research indicates that the risk for burnout increases (e.g., Rupert et al., 2015). Thus, we face a diversity of externally and internally generated challenges at work and at home that tax our resources on an ongoing basis, that can lead to stress and distress, and that can ultimately impact our personal and professional functioning in negative ways.

The good news, however, is that there is another side to this story. Private practice has many rewards associated with helping others, and private practitioners have some autonomy to take initiative, to set work hours, to make choices about work activities, and to make decisions about the services they provide. This type of autonomy, or ability to control—to some degree—important aspects of work life, is a resource that is consistently associated with lower levels of burnout across a wide range of occupations (Rupert et al., 2015). If exercised thoughtfully, autonomy provides opportunities to structure our professional lives so that we may meet challenges without allowing them to overwhelm or deplete our resources, and most importantly, so that we may thrive in both our professional and personal lives. The process of doing this, however, requires attention to our own needs and well-being. In essence, it requires that we be attuned to and care for ourselves as persons and as professionals.

# MAKING A COMMITMENT TO SELF-CARE

*So you are finally at the end of that long day—all the paperwork is done, you have returned the phone call from your client, and you are ready to go home. You have a busy day planned for tomorrow. In fact, tomorrow is going to be a little more hectic than you had expected. In addition to your typical schedule, you have an initial session with a new client whom you agreed to see at the request of a colleague. You also just squeezed in an extra appointment with a client who called today. It would be so nice to just go home and relax, but there is an article you should read, some work around the house, and some family obligations that demand your attention. As all these thoughts are running through your head, you recall the article on self-care that you read a couple of weeks ago. The authors presented a good case for self-care as an ethical imperative and offered some good tips. It made a lot of sense. You've been feeling a little stressed lately and maybe you should follow their advice—you could go to the fitness club tonight and work out, call a friend and go out for dinner, or watch a movie. No, you really don't feel like doing anything; besides, it's getting late and you don't have the time. It would better if you just get a bit more work done tonight. You promise yourself that you WILL make time to think about this matter of self-care some other time.*

Perhaps some of the above may strike a chord. With the increased professional recognition of the importance of self-care, most of us have done some reading on the subject, talked to colleagues about it, or perhaps even completed a continuing education workshop on self-care. But it's also the case that we all face challenges in practicing self-care. We have many responsibilities, personally and professionally, and limited time. We may find it hard to say "no" to clients, colleagues, friends, and family. Some of us may have learned, and feel, that it is selfish or self-indulgent to take time for ourselves. Sometimes self-care may feel like a burden—one more thing we "should" do! And even with the best of intentions, it's easy to get caught up in the responsibilities of our hectic lives and forget about ourselves. In fact, as mental health professionals, we are trained to do this—to focus on others, not ourselves. Some of us were pulled toward the field out of a deeply engrained familiarity with attuning and tending to others—caring for others first is a natural, almost automatic response. For a range of reasons, caring for ourselves can easily be or become a low priority. Effective self-care, to be realized and sustained, requires a conscious and ongoing commitment.

It may help to remind ourselves that, for mental health professionals, self-care is a professional ethical responsibility (e.g., Barnett, Baker, Elman, & Schoener, 2007; Norcross & Guy, 2007; Wise, Hersch, & Gibson, 2012). The American Psychological Association's Ethics Code (2010) states that "psychologists strive to be aware of the possible effect of their own physical and mental health on the ability to help those with whom they work" (p. 3) and directs psychologists to be aware of personal problems and take action to prevent them from interfering with work performance (Standard 2.06). Some codes are even more direct in mandating self-care. For example, the Canadian Code of Ethics for Psychologists (2000) specifically directs psychologists to "engage in self-care activities that help to avoid conditions (e.g., burnout, addictions) that could result in impaired judgment and interfere with their ability to benefit and not harm others" (p. 17). From a professional standpoint, then, self-care is not ultimately about us; it is about our clients and our capacity to serve them well. In order to care for others, we need to care for ourselves.

Inherent in this professional self-care directive is the view that self-care is a proactive, prevention-oriented process. It is not just for times when we are feeling stressed and it is not just for when we are feeling vulnerable, in distress, or having problems. To varying degrees, all private practitioners—as professionals and human beings—face the demands highlighted in the preceding section. As a result, self-care is a valuable personal resource for all. In fact, self-care might be conceptualized as a *foundational* resource in that it has the potential to influence many other personal resources that are critical for our work—e.g., energy, efficiency, mental sharpness and judgment, concentration, and enthusiasm.

What does self-care involve? The literature to date refers to "caring for ourselves" across various spheres of our lives—physical, psychological, emotional, spiritual, social, intellectual, and recreational. Self-care is thus multidimensional and within each dimension, there are many ways in which we can care for ourselves. No one activity or practice works for everyone. To quote Norcross and Guy (2007), "Different folks need different self-care strokes" (p. 60). Each person must find what works for him or her, and finding what works often involves trial and error. Further, what works may vary over time as our practices change, our personal lives change, and we change across our professional lifespan. Thus, self-care requires an ongoing, conscious commitment to paying attention to—and responding to—our personal and professional needs.

## DEVELOPING A SELF-CARE PLAN

Developing a plan may sound a bit formal—a little too serious perhaps for some. But that is exactly the point: Self-care *is* to be taken seriously, and thinking in terms of a plan prompts us to take a step back, look at our professional and personal lives, and consciously ask ourselves: How well am I taking care of myself? How might I more effectively integrate self-care into my daily life? It also prompts us to take action, to identify something that we can try that is different, and to approach self-care in an organized, intentional fashion. Developing a plan engages us in a proactive process with self-care in the forefront as a central, rather than peripheral, focus in our lives.

But where to start? With the emerging self-care literature, there is certainly no shortage of excellent ideas. We can find principles to follow (e.g., recognizing the hazards of psychotherapeutic work), areas to focus on (e.g., physical, emotional, spiritual, social, recreational), and specific things to do (e.g., create variety during the workday) (e.g., Advisory Committee on Colleague Assistance [ACCA], 2010; Baker, 2003; Norcross & Guy, 2007; Wise et al., 2012). Across this literature, several underlying themes emerge: the importance of developing self-awareness, maintaining balance, and building connections. These themes represent critical goals of self-care and provide an organizing framework for thinking about self-care. Thus, in developing a self-care plan, we can begin by thinking about where we stand and what we might do in each of the important areas of awareness, balance, and connections.

## AWARENESS

Not only is self-awareness a consistent theme in the self-care literature (e.g., Baker, 2003; Norcross & Guy, 2007), but research indicates that psychologists endorse maintaining self-awareness and self-monitoring as very important to their functioning (e.g., Rupert & Kent, 2007). Put simply, self-awareness is the key to self-care. Practicing effective self-care requires that we know ourselves; that we be attuned to our evolving needs, both physical and emotional; that we understand the demands of our work as well as our unique vulnerabilities and strengths; and that we be sensitive to our feelings, to our reactions to our clients, and to our stress levels on an ongoing basis. Cultivating this awareness is a process that requires open, honest self-reflection. In this regard, a logical starting place in developing a self-care plan is an assessment of our current self-care attitudes and behaviors, as well as a close look at our needs and opportunities in this area. In essence, we should begin with an assessment of our stresses, vulnerabilities, and resources. These initial assessments provide a basic self-understanding for moving forward to think specifically about self-care strategies. But it is also important that we continue to pay attention to these areas and "tune in" to our inner life. Cultivating awareness is thus a multifaceted process involving ongoing assessment across many areas of our lives.

## ASSESSING SELF-CARE ATTITUDES AND BEHAVIORS

Given that we are always evolving as persons and professionals, periodically reviewing our self-care attitudes and behaviors is important. Questions we might ask ourselves, across all phases of our professional lifespan, include:

How important is self-care to me?
What do I currently do to take care of myself as a psychotherapist?
What has been most helpful for me in terms of self-care? What has been least helpful?
What is my greatest challenge/ barrier to practicing self-care?

## ASSESSING STRESSES, VULNERABILITIES, AND RESOURCES

The importance of recognizing the demands and stresses of psychological work is emphasized in various ways throughout the self-care literature (e.g., ACCA, 2010; Norcross & Guy, 2007). In fact, many books or articles on self-care begin, as we do, with a discussion and review of research on the many stresses associated with our work, particularly with the practice of psychotherapy. Recognizing these potential stresses allows us to plan and be prepared to deal with them.

While there are certainly challenges that all private practitioners face, we should not assume that these are identical for all. Private practitioners differ professionally and personally in many ways that have implications for self-care needs. Some face special challenges because of their work settings; for example, practitioners in rural settings have a smaller professional network and may be expected to handle a wider range of cases. Some may find certain demands uniquely challenging due to personal vulnerabilities or life circumstances. Thus, truly recognizing the hazards of our work requires a personal assessment of our own unique circumstances and characteristics.

Planning for self-care also involves assessing strengths and resources that can help us meet demands and enhance our functioning. Awareness of demands and stresses in our lives helps us clarify our self-care needs. Awareness of our strengths and resources is critical when considering options, or opportunities, for caring for ourselves. In assessing needs and opportunities, some questions we might ask ourselves are:

What aspects of my current work are most challenging?

Am I currently seeing any clients who are especially challenging or difficult for me (e.g., who are threatening to me, who may pose a danger to themselves or others, who are dealing with trauma or abuse, who leave me feeling emotionally drained or exhausted, who stretch me to the limits of my tolerance or expertise)?

What personal vulnerabilities do I bring to my work?

What pressures am I putting on myself, as a professional and as a person?

What personal and professional strengths can I draw upon in dealing with demands and stresses?

## "TUNING IN" TO OUR FEELINGS, OUR REACTIONS TO CLIENTS, OUR WORK, OURSELVES

Life is not static. Work life changes as clients begin and end their therapy; we change as we gain experience and enter new phases of our lives; our professional and personal worlds are continually evolving. Thus, while assessment of our current attitudes, behaviors, and needs provides necessary information for planning self-care strategies, it is only the beginning. Cultivating self-awareness—becoming attuned to our thoughts, our emotions, and our visceral experience, is a lifelong process. As many of us can attest, it is one that benefits from practice and also from benign self-observation—that is, "tuning in" and paying attention to our inner life in a nonjudgmental fashion. Just as with our clients, more is revealed when we proceed with care and genuine interest in deeper understanding. Likewise, the more that we can consciously process our feelings, concerns, and vulnerabilities on an ongoing basis, the more possible it is to respond constructively and to seek out helpful resources, both internal and/or external, and (importantly) the more possible it is to reduce the risk of unwittingly acting out unprocessed and thereby unmanaged feelings and needs in ways that could be potentially harmful to us and our clients.

As we think about cultivating this dynamic, ongoing self-awareness, we might ask ourselves:

How attuned am I to my inner life?
Do I take sufficient time to reflect on my reactions to clients, my feelings, and needs?
Would I benefit from doing more or from seeking help in doing this?

## BALANCE

Life is a balancing act. It includes balancing responsibilities at home and at work, juggling demands throughout the workday, keeping our thoughts and feelings in perspective. When aspects of our lives are in balance (or at least close to it), we have a sense of stability that helps us function well across all life domains. When things get out of balance, however, we feel a sense of unease or distress and our functioning in one or more areas of our lives may suffer. Not surprisingly, balance has been described as a "driving force" behind a healthy self-care regime (ACCA, 2010), and self-care recommendations often relate to balance across and within critical life domains. With balance as an organizing theme, we find it helpful to think about self-care strategies that are directed toward balance in three areas—balance between work and life outside work, balance within our work lives, and balance within our personal or inner life.

## STRIVING FOR WORK-LIFE BALANCE: BUILDING A LIFE OUTSIDE WORK

Research has consistently found that psychologists identify maintaining a balance between professional and personal lives as important to their functioning (e.g., Rupert & Kent, 2007). Self-care recommendations for maintaining this balance focus largely on building a life outside work that is, as much as possible, free of intrusions from work life.

"Leaving it at the office" is, in fact, the central theme of Norcross and Guy's (2007) book on psychotherapist self-care. This is not, however, always easy to do. It can be hard to say no to individuals who seek our help. And in the current electronic age with cellphones and ready access to email, work can frequently impinge on our private lives. Thus, minimizing spillover of work life into our personal time requires a conscious effort to clarify and set boundaries for our clients and ourselves. Emergencies do occur and at times intrusions may be unavoidable, but as much as possible, we all need to protect some personal time.

"Leaving it at the office" means more than just setting aside and protecting time; we must also be aware of other, more subtle ways that our work can interfere with our personal lives. After an emotionally demanding day, we may come home exhausted and preoccupied with the events of the day. We may find it hard to listen to the concerns of family or friends or even engage in a relaxing, fun activity. Genuinely "leaving it at the office" requires managing the internal, emotional demands of our work and minimizing spillover of negative thoughts and affect so that we can relax and fully engage in "life outside work."

The lives we build outside of work will vary greatly depending on our age, family circumstances, home responsibilities, and personal interests. For those with families and children, life outside work may be filled with another set of tasks and responsibilities; others may have more unstructured time. While we all have very different personal situations, we can nonetheless strive to set aside some time outside of work to engage in activities that we enjoy. This may range from spending time with family and friends, participating in a hobby or sport, or just spending some quiet time alone, activities that bring us pleasure, take our minds off work, and help to reenergize us!

As we think about striving for work-life balance, some questions we might ask ourselves are:

How well do I balance my professional and personal/family lives?
How does my work life spill over into my personal/family life in both negative and
    positive ways?
How does my personal/family life spill over into my work life in both negative and
    positive ways?
What activities do I find most relaxing and refreshing in my personal life?

## STRIVING FOR BALANCE DURING
## THE WORKDAY: STRUCTURING ONE'S DAY

Psychological work is challenging, and research tells us that certain aspects of our work (e.g., paperwork and negative client behaviors; Rupert et al., 2015) may be particularly exhausting. We also all have our own unique strengths and weaknesses, likes and dislikes, and so forth. While we certainly cannot build a career and structure workdays that avoid all stressful or unpleasant activities, private practitioners have some autonomy to make choices and structure their workdays. Self-care involves making conscious, constructive choices. It is easy to fall into a pattern of accepting all referrals, filling up those appointment slots, and then "powering" through the day, seeing client after client. But it is also to possible to plan a workday that is more balanced, includes some variety, and provides time to replenish resources.

One commonly recommended, straightforward self-care strategy is to build in breaks between clients (e.g., Norcross & Guy, 2007). For some, particularly solo practitioners, physical isolation is an issue, so taking a short walk down the hall or outside the building, saying hi to a colleague, may provide a welcome break. Other strategies involve more planning, such as scheduling specific workday activities to avoid being overloaded on any given day with clients or tasks that are difficult or stressful. These may include some rewarding or enjoyable activities in each day. One may also add some variety in the form of different professional activities (e.g., supervision, consultation, teaching or conducting workshops) to the workweek. Sometimes saying no may be a healthy self-care choice. For example, if you find it stressful to work with aggressive or potentially dangerous clients and/or your physical space is not well suited to ensure a safe environment, it may be best to refer such clients to colleagues. Although concerns about disappointing referral sources or about financial pressures may make it difficult to say no, accepting all referrals can be counterproductive.

On a broader level, the ACCA's Tips for Self-Care (2010) include "assess and readjust your caseload" (para. 5). We suggest that such an assessment might be expanded to overall workload, with goals of avoiding overcommitment, minimizing involvement with clients or professional activities that are a source of stress or frustration, maximizing involvement with clients and professional activities that are rewarding, and planning "balanced" workdays. In this regard, some questions we might ask ourselves are:

How do I feel about my overall workload?

Are there days or times when I feel overwhelmed and exhausted by my work?

What aspects of my practice (activities and types of clients) do I find most rewarding?

What aspects of my practice (activities and types of clients) do I find least rewarding?

Are there ways that I can balance my workload and workday to spend more time doing what I really like—what I feel good about?

## STRIVING FOR INNER BALANCE: TENDING TO PHYSICAL, PSYCHOLOGICAL, AND EMOTIONAL NEEDS

Taking care of ourselves physically—eating well, getting enough sleep, and exercising, is basic to our ability to maintain an inner equilibrium and to function well in both our professional and personal lives (e.g., ACCA, 2010; Baker, 2003; Norcross & Guy, 2007). At the same time, given that we are the "instruments" of our work, it is imperative that we also care for ourselves psychologically and emotionally. In this regard, we have talked about the value of "tuning into" our feelings, reactions, and needs. Awareness of our inner life, however, is only the first step; it is necessary but not sufficient for achieving the inner balance. We must also develop ways of meeting our emotional needs, of keeping our feelings and reactions in perspective and using them constructively, and of managing our stress. Not easy tasks!

The self-care literature offers many suggestions and, although we each must find what works best for us, there are some general strategies that seem fundamental for inner balance. First, practicing self-compassion (Baker, 2003; Wise et al., 2012) plays a key role. This suggests an accepting, empathic approach to ourselves that is free from the pressures and self-criticism that can get in the way of honest self-examination and positive growth. As human beings, we all have strengths and vulnerabilities, positive qualities and imperfections. Accepting and valuing ourselves lays a foundation for achieving inner balance.

In addition, developing personal, internally focused strategies for regulating our thoughts and feelings is important (e.g., Baker, 2003; Norcross & Guy, 2007; Rupert et al., 2015; Wise et al., 2012). These may be purely cognitive strategies such as taking time to reflect on rewarding or satisfying experiences and trying not to take the ups and downs of work too personally. They may also involve more active strategies such as journaling, relaxation exercises, mindfulness meditation, or pursuits aimed at cultivating a sense of spirituality. These internally focused strategies serve to help us avoid becoming preoccupied with negative thoughts, encourage us to see the "big picture" and keep life in perspective, and help us maintain a sense of inner calm. There are also times, however, when inner balance may be fostered by more externally focused strategies, by reaching out to others, such as to share frustrations with trusted colleagues or friends, to seek consultation or guidance, or to engage in psychotherapy (e.g., ACCA, 2010; Baker, 2003; Norcross & Guy, 2007).

As the demands and stresses of our professional and personal lives evolve and change over time, maintaining a sense of inner balance may involve a range of self-care activities and strategies. In planning for these strategies, some questions we might ask ourselves are:

What pressures do I put on myself? How do these pressures affect me?
How do I see myself in terms of practicing self-compassion? How could I do better?
What helps me keep things in perspective? What helps me feel relaxed?
What would I like to do better regarding my physical self-care? My emotional or spiritual self-care?

## CONNECTIONS

Relationships play a central role in self-care. They help us meet human needs and bring balance to our lives in many ways. As we have already discussed, spending time with family and friends is critical for work-life balance; a brief chat with a colleague can brighten a workday; and reaching out to others for support or advice can help us keep an inner balance. Relationships with friends, family, colleagues, and the professional community provide support and nurturance in ways that our relationships with our clients cannot and should not (e.g., Guy, 2000; Norcross & Guy, 2007). Developing these important relationships involves building and maintaining connections with others across many areas of our lives.

## BUILDING CONNECTIONS WITH FAMILY AND FRIENDS

Family and friends not only fill a personal need for relationships, but research suggests they also help our functioning at work. Psychologists consistently endorse spending time with a spouse/partner/family or with friends as highly important for their professional functioning (e.g., Rupert & Kent, 2007), and family support has been linked to less emotional exhaustion at work (e.g., Rupert et al., 2015). But building connections involves more than just having contact with family or friends. In his book *The Personal Life of the Psychotherapist*, Guy (1987) discusses the need for an "intimate" other; a trusting, caring relationship that offers comfort, a sense of safety, and the opportunity to share feelings and vulnerabilities openly. Without this type of relationship in our personal lives, we run the risk of seeking to fulfill our human need for intimacy with clients, an action that violates our ethics code and, in the worst-case scenario, harms the individuals we seek to help.

For many reasons, building relationships that include a network of family and friends outside of work is important for our personal and professional well-being. Of course, not all these relationships will be close, intimate ones, nor should they be. But we should strive to ensure that our need for intimacy is met through this network; this requires giving time and attention to nurturing our relationships and to strengthening and deepening connections with those we value. In this regard, some questions we might ask ourselves are:

Who are the persons whose company I most enjoy outside of work?

What has facilitated the growth and deepening of these relationships over the years?

How satisfied am I with what I am giving and receiving in my relationships with family, friends, and significant others?

How would I like to change, or grow, in these relationships?

## BUILDING CONNECTIONS WITH COLLEAGUES

While some colleagues may become part of our friendship network, research suggests that colleagues play a special role at work. Psychologists often endorse case consultation and colleague support as important to their functioning (e.g., Rupert & Kent, 2007), and workplace support has been linked to a greater sense of personal accomplishment at work (e.g., Rupert et al. 2015). Colleagues play a role in our professional lives that family and friends cannot. Given the confidential nature of our work, we are limited in our ability to share work experiences, seek advice, or talk through problems with family or friends. Family and friends may also find it difficult to appreciate and truly understand the nature of our work. Even if we have family members who are also mental health professionals, talking about work at home can make it more challenging to leave work stress at the office and build a healthy work-life balance. Thus, finding colleagues with whom we feel safe, whose views we value, and whose company we enjoy is important. Under times of particular stress, a trusted colleague may be an invaluable resource for seeking help with an especially complicated, disturbing clinical situation and sorting through a range of thoughts and feelings.

Private practitioners are less likely than their agency peers to have ready access to colleagues and consultation or supervision opportunities. There is a risk of becoming isolated! We need to reach out to, make contact with, and nurture relationships with colleagues. The self-care literature also underscores the value and benefits of peer consultation and/or formal supervision (e.g., ACCA, 2010; Baker, 2003; Barnett et al., 2007; Norcross & Guy, 2007). Private practitioners may need to make a special effort to make sure these opportunities are available and to take advantage of them. In this regard, some questions to ask ourselves are:

Who is in my "close" circle of peers?

Who are the colleagues I would be most comfortable turning to for consultation or advice about a clinical issue or problem?

Who would I turn to for help with a significant personal problem?

## BUILDING CONNECTIONS WITH A PROFESSIONAL COMMUNITY

Research indicates that psychologists consistently endorse maintaining a sense of professional identity/values as important for their functioning (e.g., Rupert & Kent, 2007). Although research doesn't address specific ways of doing this, professional identity is certainly enhanced by involvement in an organized professional community—one's state and national professional associations or other organizations representing professional specialty areas and interests. In fact, active involvement in some type of professional association, including attending meetings and conferences and taking advantage of seminars and structured learning opportunities, serves many valuable self-care functions. It reinforces our professional identify and values, it contributes to our professional growth, it helps us avoid professional isolation, and it provides opportunities for developing and expanding our network of professional colleagues. In thinking about connecting to a professional community, we might ask ourselves:

> What am I currently doing at a professional level?
> How could I meet my professional self-care needs through participating in the larger professional community?
> What types of involvement at what level (local, regional, national) might be most interesting and beneficial to me?

## SUSTAINING A SELF-CARE PLAN

*So you have thought more about self-care, assessed how things were going for you, and actually made some changes. You shuffled some things around in your schedule to give yourself a few more breaks and even out your days a bit; you scheduled a weekly lunch with a colleague down the hall; you started going to the gym twice a week; and you have been working on relaxing and finding ways to take your mind off work outside the office. It seemed to make a difference; over the past month, you have noticed that you felt more on "top of things," a little more energetic, a little less tense. But last week was tough; that new client proved to be more challenging than you expected; one of your longstanding clients had a crisis and you had to cancel lunch with your colleague to squeeze in an extra appointment; a family emergency required your attention; you were just too exhausted to make it to the gym . . .*

Do we need to continue? Probably not; we think the message is clear. We have many people and demands competing for our time and that is not going to change just because we decide to pay more attention to self-care. So at this point, let's return to the section on "Making a Commitment to Self-Care" and, with compassion and understanding, gently remind ourselves of two points. First, self-care requires a conscious and ongoing commitment. Without our considered attention, it can easily become a low priority, sometimes before we realize it. Second, self-care is an ongoing process, a practice that, by necessity, changes and evolves as our personal and professional lives change and evolve. There may be times when life gets in the way of our ideal self-care plan and we have to try a little harder to find at least some time for ourselves, even if it is just a few minutes each day to take a short walk, to relax, to clear our minds. There may be times when a new self-care opportunity emerges, such as a new supervision group or a chance to learn a new hobby, and we will want to find a way to take advantage of it. Here is where self-awareness is important; being attuned to our feelings and needs allows us to make adjustments with conscious reflection. It is vital that we pay attention to what is working, try new things when appropriate or necessary, and, hopefully, maintain a sense of equilibrium in our professional and personal lives.

Even with a good proactive self-care plan, there may be trouble spots, times when we are thrown off balance. For example, a client triggers personal issues; a clinical experience is upsetting and challenges our sense of competence; problems at home begin to affect our energy, attention, and concentration at work. Being self-aware and attuned to our feelings can help us identify these trouble spots early and take action before they become highly problematic—that is, before they lead to personal distress that might impair our functioning. At these times, self-care becomes a top priority, and increased self-care efforts might involve taking a break, adjusting workload, and focusing more attention on our own needs. These efforts may be facilitated by consulting with a colleague, seeking supervision, or perhaps seeking personal psychotherapy. While it may not always be easy to reach out for help, it can be easier if we have trusted colleagues to turn to and if we have connections in place. Thus, sustaining a good proactive self-care plan serves us well in times of trouble; it makes it more likely that we possess the self-awareness to identify potential trouble spots plus the supports available to manage them effectively. In sustaining a commitment to self-care, we are building resources, both internal and external, that we can draw upon to benefit ourselves and our clients throughout our professional careers.

How well am I taking care of myself? Asking ourselves this question on a regular basis will help keep self-care in the forefront of our minds. It will prompt us to pay attention to our inner life, to review our self-care behaviors in light of our evolving needs, and to think again about where we stand relevant to central goals of self-care—cultivating awareness, achieving balance, and maintaining connections.

# REFERENCES

Advisory Committee on Colleague Assistance. (2010). *Tips for self-care*. Retrieved from http://www.apapracticecentral.org/ce/self-care/acca-promoting.aspx.

American Psychological Association. (2010). Ethical principles of psychologists and code of conduct. Retrieved from http://www.apa.org/ethics/code/index.aspx.

Baker, E. K. (2003). *Caring for ourselves: The therapist's guide to personal and professional well-being*. Washington, DC: American Psychological Association.

Barnett, J. E., Baker, E. K., Elman, N. S., & Schoener, G. R. (2007). In pursuit of wellness: The self-care imperative. *Professional Psychology: Research and Practice, 38,* 603–612.

Canadian Psychological Association. (2000). *Canadian code of ethics for psychologists* (3rd ed.). Retrieved from http://www.cpa.ca/docs/File/Ethics/cpa_code_2000_eng_jp_jan2014.pdf.

Carter, L. A., & Barnett, J. E. (2014). *Self-care for clinicians in training*. New York: Oxford University Press.

Guy, J. D. (1987). *The personal life of the psychotherapist*. New York: John Wiley & Sons.

Margeneau, E. (1990). *The encyclopedic handbook of private practice*. New York: Gardner Press.

Norcross, J. C., & Guy, J. D. (2007). *Leaving it at the office: A guide to psychotherapist self-care.* New York: Guilford Press.

Rupert, P. A., & Baird, K. A. (2004). Managed care and the independent practice of psychology. *Professional Psychology: Research and Practice, 35,* 185–193.

Rupert, P. A., & Kent, J. S. (2007). Gender and work setting differences in career-sustaining behaviors and burnout among professional psychologists. *Professional Psychology: Research and Practice, 38,* 88–96.

Rupert, P. A., Miller, A. O., & Dorociak, K. E. (2015). Preventing burnout: What does the research tell us? *Professional Psychology: Research and Practice, 46,* 168–174.

Wise, E. H., Hersh, M. A., & Gibson, C. L. (2012). Ethics, self-care and well-being for psychologists: Re-envisioning the stress-distress continuum. *Professional Psychology: Research and Practice, 43,* 487–494.

# CHAPTER 45

# STALKING AND ONLINE HARASSMENT OF THE PRIVATE PRACTITIONER

*Aaron J. Kivisto and Hannah M. Paul*

In 1991, Dr. Kent Shinbach, a psychiatrist in private practice on Manhattan's Upper East Side, began treating David Tarloff, a patient with paranoid schizophrenia who had not previously been diagnosed with or received treatment for a psychotic disorder. Dr. Shinbach hospitalized Mr. Tarloff and the two went their separate ways for nearly two decades. But while the patient had been long gone from Dr. Shinbach's calendar, he never left the recesses of his patient's mind. To the contrary, the patient apparently carried the memory of his encounter with this private practitioner with him and 17 years later, in the context of a psychotic decompensation, he came to develop the delusional belief that his own mother would die unless he killed Dr. Shinbach. On February 12, 2008, this patient entered Dr. Shinbach's office building with a suitcase full of knives, a rubber mallet, rope, duct tape, and adult diapers for his mother, delusionally planning to rob Dr. Shinbach of $50,000, break his mother out of a nursing home that he perceived to be abusive, and flee to Hawaii with her. Tragically, the patient encountered Dr. Kathryn Faughey, a psychologist who shared office space with Dr. Shinbach, and instead stabbed her to death. Dr. Shinbach, hearing the commotion, was seriously injured in his attempt to stop the attack perpetrated by his former patient, who had evidently maintained a dangerous fantasied relationship with his former psychiatrist for nearly two decades after their professional relationship had ended.

While the case of David Tarloff provides a tragic, high-profile, and fortunately rare example of the dangers that can arise for private practitioners working with severely mentally ill individuals, managing patients' potentially dangerous fantasies and enactments is essential for all clinicians. In this chapter, we will (1) provide an overview of the literature on the experiences of mental health professionals confronted by patients who engage in stalking, threatening, and harassing behavior (STHB); (2) examine the characteristics of patients who engage in STHB and their motivations for doing so; (3) consider three conceptual models that have been advanced for clinicians dealing with patients engaging in STHB; (4) review the limited empirical data regarding the effectiveness of different risk management responses; (5) examine differences in STHB victimization and risk management responses among mental health professionals in private practice compared to other settings using data from a survey of American Board of Professional Psychology (ABPP) diplomates; and (6) conclude with STHB risk management recommendations tailored for private practitioners.

## MENTAL HEALTH PROFESSIONALS' EXPERIENCES WITH STHB

In the words of television host Dennis Wholey, "expecting the world to treat you fairly because you're a nice person is like expecting a bull not to attack you because you're a vegetarian." For few professions is this advice more salient than for mental health professionals, whose commitment to helping alleviate others' emotional suffering often entails intensive, emotionally evocative work with individuals who might be uniquely prone to dangerous transferential reactions. Consistent with this, surveys of mental health professionals (Ashmore, Jones, Jackson, & Smoyak, 2006; Purcell, Powell, & Mullen, 2005) consistently suggest that a sizable majority will be confronted by a client who engages in STHB at some point in their career. For instance, in a recent survey of ABPP diplomates practicing in a wide range of settings, we found that nearly three in four (71%) psychologists had been harassed by a patient at some point in their careers, more than one in five (21%) had been threatened, and about one in seven (14%) had been stalked (Kivisto, Berman, Watson, Gruber, & Paul, 2015). This is highly consistent with the extant literature, which converges to indicate that clinicians practicing in a range of settings, with differing professional backgrounds and across a range of clinical experience and expertise, are more likely than not to be confronted at some point in their careers by a client engaging in STHB. Further, whereas large-scale surveys such as the National Violence Against Women Survey (Tjaden & Thoennes, 1998) have found that women are approximately four times more likely than men to be the victims of stalking in the general population, surveys with mental health professionals have typically found few if any gender differences in stalking victimization (Purcell et al., 2005). In short, there is little evidence that patients discriminate in whom they target for STHB, so all clinicians should be prepared to manage these challenging situations.

While concerning in its own right, such findings take on added meaning in the context of clinicians' perceived readiness for handling these situations. In the survey of ABPP diplomates noted above, for example, which was ostensibly limited to a sample with a demonstrably high level of professional skill, fully 60% of respondents who had been a victim of STHB reported feeling unprepared for dealing with their experience. In extreme cases, such as that of David Tarloff described above, the outcomes can be tragic. Fortunately, while not unheard of, fatal attacks on mental health professionals appear to be quite rare. Similarly, survey data suggest that nonfatal physical assaults against mental health clinicians are also quite uncommon in most contexts (Kivisto et al., 2015; Purcell et al., 2005), although the prevalence of physical assaults has been shown to be significantly higher in certain forensic settings (Leavitt, Presskreischer, Maykuth, & Grisso, 2006).

However, simply because physical violence is relatively rare, even in the context of STHB directed toward clinicians, it would be premature to conclude that STHB therefore does not often result in serious adverse consequences for unprepared clinicians. To the contrary, a considerable body of research shows that STHB in the absence of violence can have pervasive consequences for victims' emotional and physical functioning. Importantly, STHB does not necessarily require face-to-face contact to meet legal criteria for stalking, and clients engaging in repeated harassing phone calls, vitriolic emails, and harassment through various forms of social media, among other forms of online harassment, are indeed engaging in STHB. Among stalking victims in general, research has shown that approximately one in three women and one in five men seek psychological treatment as a result of their experience (Tjaden & Thoennes, 1998). Physical symptoms among victims of stalking are not uncommon and include gastrointestinal disruptions, headaches, fatigue, and weight fluctuations (Mullen, Pathé, & Purcell, 2000). In Purcell and colleagues' (2005) survey of 830 Australian psychologists, 19.5% ($n = 162$) met criteria for lifetime stalking victimization, defined as 10 or more intrusions over a period of two weeks or longer that resulted in fear. Of those who had been stalked, 19% reported missing work as a result of the stress created by the clients' STHB, 10% decreased their social outings to prevent additional harassment, 36% increased their home security, 21% changed their home telephone number, 6% relocated their professional practice, and 4% went to the extreme of changing their home address. Although the risk of violence posed by clients who engage in STHB should be carefully evaluated and managed, these findings indicate that violence is but one of many adverse outcomes for clinicians resulting from STHB. The importance of understanding and managing STHB, although typically underemphasized in mental health clinicians' training programs, emerges quite clearly from findings such as these.

## WHO ENGAGES IN STHB AND WHY

Those who receive professional services from mental health professionals, whether for evaluation or treatment, frequently possess some combination of characteristics that, under certain circumstances, can increase their likelihood of stalking. Pathological attachment systems, persecutory object relations, engrained patterns of mistrust, unmodulated dependency needs, obsessional tendencies, and mismanaged transference/countertransference paradigms are but several of the likely contributing factors driving the heightened rates of stalking directed toward clinicians. While still in its infancy, empirical research has recently begun to examine the characteristics of those who engage in STHB toward mental health professionals and their motivations for doing so.

Research efforts examining the characteristics of stalkers, in the general population as well as those who specifically stalk mental health professionals, have tended to emphasize three features: the stalker's motivation, the relationship between stalker and target, and the personality characteristics of the stalker. Distinguishing different motivations for stalking, in combination with differentiating the nature of the pre-stalking relationship between stalker and target, has proven particularly useful for categorizing subtypes of stalkers. For example, in their influential five-part typology of stalkers, Mullen, Pathé, Purcell, and Stuart (1999) used stalkers' motivation as a central discriminating feature, while stalker–target relationship status further differentiated different types of perpetrators. Within their framework, *rejected* stalkers were those who were estranged most typically from an intimate partner but sometimes from relatives, friends, or coworkers and whose motivation for pursuing their target included a mixture of a desire to reconcile and a desire for revenge. The *intimacy-seeking* stalkers, in contrast, were motivated primarily by a desire to establish an intimate relationship with the target. Erotomania was commonly observed among intimacy-seeking stalkers, and psychotic diagnoses were common. *Incompetent* stalkers were similar to the intimacy-seeking group in that they were primarily motivated by a desire for closeness with the target, although they were distinguished by a lack of cognitive and social skills and the fact that they did not exhibit the erotomanic delusions common to intimacy seekers. The *resentful* stalkers, in contrast, were motivated primarily by a desire to frighten their victims. The targets of resentful stalkers appeared about equally likely to be a specific person with whom the stalker had a particular grievance than to be an apparently random person who became ensnared in the stalker's obsessional fantasy by sheer misfortune. Finally, *predatory* stalkers were motivated by a desire to carry out a sexual assault. Their stalking behavior served as preparation for the attack.

The value of any typology derives from its clinical utility. Perhaps the most valuable contribution of Mullen and colleagues' (1999) typology of stalkers has been its contribution to risk assessment in stalking situations, as different types of stalkers appear to present distinct levels of violence risk and to require different risk management responses. In their seminal study, for instance, these authors found that rejected and predatory stalkers assaulted their targets at rates of approximately 50%—prevalence rates twice as high as were seen among resentful, intimacy-seeking, and incompetent stalkers (Mullen et al., 1999). These findings, as well as others that followed, also served to highlight the importance of the nature of the relationship between stalker and target. In contrast to common misconceptions of stalking, which tend to view stalking primarily as a crime involving a male stalker pursuing a female stranger, research suggests that the most common stalking scenarios involve former intimate partners. More importantly, and again in contrast to common misconceptions, stalking situations involving former intimate partners have consistently been found to present the highest risk of violence. In other words, although there certainly exist some stranger stalkers who fit common stereotypes, such perpetrators are both few in number and low in risk relative to the scorned lovers who initiate campaigns of obsessional harassment after a breakup. Driving this point home, Mullen and colleagues' (1999) research found that intimacy-seeking stalkers—a group primarily composed of former intimate partners—perpetrated violence more often than not and at rates matched only by predatory stalkers, a group defined primarily by the fact that they were planning for a sexual assault.

Pathé and Meloy (2013) suggested that two primary motives appear to characterize those who stalk mental health professionals—anger/resentment and infatuation. Among psychologists who endorsed having been stalked in Kivisto and colleagues' (2015) survey of ABPP diplomates, 45% perceived their client to have been primarily motivated by resentment and 23% were perceived to be motivated by infatuation. These distinct motivations for stalking were associated with varying outcomes, such that those whose stalking was motivated by infatuation persisted for significantly longer (31 weeks vs. 152 weeks). Although clients who were motivated by resentment were more likely to threaten the psychologist over the course of the stalking episode, they were no more likely than those motivated by infatuation to physically attack their target. Although rates of physical assault were low in Kivisto and colleagues' (2015) survey (2.5%), Purcell and associates' survey of Australian psychologists found that 9% of psychologists who had been stalked had been attacked. Although most assaults did not result in injury, there were several exceptions: Three reported having been strangled, there were several abrasions and bruises reported, and one psychologist suffered a broken wrist. Overall, however, rates of violence toward clinicians who are stalked appear to be significantly lower than *any* of the subtypes of stalkers identified by Mullen and coworkers (1999).

Although stalkers and general offender populations tend to exhibit similar rates of psychopathology, stalkers are more likely to have personality disorders in general but less likely to have antisocial or psychopathic personalities (Storey, Hart, Meloy, & Reavis, 2009). Kivisto and colleagues' (2015) survey of psychologists' experiences with STHB was the first to obtain psychometric data on the personality characteristics of the perpetrator using a clinician-rated personality measure and found that fully 60.7% of STHB perpetrators met criteria for at least one personality disorder. Further, this research converged with previous work to suggest that the personality pathology among those who stalk mental health professionals tends to be reflected primarily within cluster B, which includes personality pathologies characterized by dramatic and dysregulated interpersonal relationships. This is perhaps unsurprising given that stalking might be conceptualized as a compulsive enactment of a pathologically preoccupied, as opposed to dismissive, attachment system.

## CONCEPTUAL MODELS OF STHB RISK MANAGEMENT

Two sets of general guidelines have been offered for helping mental health professionals manage risk with patients who stalk them. In the seminal set of recommendations for psychotherapists confronted with such patients, Meloy (1997) offered 10 guidelines: "a team approach, personal responsibility for safety, documentation and recording, no initiated contact, protection orders, law enforcement and prosecution, treatment if indicated, segregation and incarceration, periodic violence risk assessment, and the importance of dramatic moments" (p. 174)—which Meloy defined as events in stalking cases "which humiliate or shame the perpetrator, stoke his fury, and increase his risk of violence" (p. 183). Clinicians are well advised to appreciate the limited role of traditional psychotherapeutic efforts with most patients who have initiated a pattern of stalking. In contrast, the "team approach" advocated by Meloy is designed, in part, to interrupt the obsessional transference that the patient develops within the therapeutic dyad by injecting others into the relational matrix. For instance, in certain situations it is preferred that administrative staff members as opposed to the psychotherapist handle communication with the client. Clinicians adopting such an approach are reminded to be mindful of the power of intermittent reinforcement and, once the decision is made for the psychotherapist to sever contact with the patient, they must be resolute in maintaining a zero-contact policy. In addition to the role of administrative staff within Meloy's "team approach," he recommends that psychotherapists establish a coordinated risk management network of colleagues, public law enforcement, and private security professionals.

Recently, Carr, Goranson, and Drummond (2014) introduced a "dual pathway, three-tiered" management model for those who stalk mental health professionals. Drawing on the public health principles of primary, secondary, and tertiary prevention (i.e., the three tiers), they distinguish the risk management responsibilities of the clinician from those of the organizational system in which the clinician practices (i.e., the two pathways). Although the secondary and tertiary risk management strategies overlap considerably with Meloy's (1997) guidelines—emphasizing risk management strategies, such as ongoing consultation, maintaining detailed documentation of stalking incidents, clear limit setting, ongoing risk assessment, and the inclusion of others within the system, whether with or without the clinician, to help mitigate risk—Carr and colleagues' (2014) model is particularly noteworthy for its overarching emphasis on primary prevention. Recommendations for the clinician seeking to be proactive rather than merely reactive include seeking training on stalking risk management, maintaining awareness of client behaviors and personal reactions, and maintaining a working knowledge of "where, to whom, and how to ask for assistance" from colleagues, administrators, law enforcement, and legal professionals (p. 14). The systems in which clinicians work can further mitigate risk by providing education, supporting collegial relationships that foster open consultation, maintaining organizational relationships with law enforcement and threat assessment professionals, and helping providers anonymize themselves online. Combined with survey data consistently showing that clinicians feel unprepared for responding to patients who engage in STHB (Kivisto et al., 2015; Purcell et al., 2005), better primary prevention appears essential.

# EMPIRICAL FOUNDATIONS OF STHB RISK MANAGEMENT RESPONSES

To date, only two studies have examined clinicians' perceptions of the effectiveness of different risk management responses to clients engaging in STHB. In the first, Sandberg, McNiel, and Binder (2002) surveyed 62 clinical staff in a university-based inpatient psychiatry unit regarding their experiences with STHB. Of the 33 (53%) who had experienced some type of STHB, 17 agreed to participate in a follow-up interview in which they described the various strategies they used when confronted by these challenging patients and how effective they perceived each strategy to be. Sandberg and associates (2002) identified 15 risk management responses (Table 45.1). Each of the risk management responses described was perceived by clinicians to have "made things better" more often than not, but some responses appeared to carry a higher risk of adverse consequences. For example, directly confronting the patient, which emerged as the third most common response, was rated as making the situation better 56% of the time and making it worse 17% of the time. By contrast, the risk management responses most consistent with Meloy's (1997) team approach, such as notifying colleagues, supervisors, administrative staff, police, and security, all tended to be consistently perceived as making the situation better. Notably, however, the resources available to the private practitioner—and particularly the ready access to an onsite risk management team—likely differ considerably from the academic medical center in which Sandberg and colleagues'

**TABLE 45.1: STHB Risk Management Strategies Identified by Previous Researchers**

| Sandberg et al. (2002) | Purcell et al. (2005) |
|---|---|
| • Notified coworkers (informally) | Clinical Risk Management Responses |
| • Notified attending physician, clinical director, team leader, or supervisor | • Confront client directly |
| • Patient directly confronted about his or her behavior and told to stop | • Refer client elsewhere for services |
| • Contact with patient actively avoided or discouraged | • Have client hospitalized |
| • Situation discussed during formal staff meeting | • Have client arrested |
| • Notified front desk/reception | • Obtain restraining order against client |
| • Patient prohibited from entering the building or being on campus | Changes to Personal/Professional Life |
| • Notified police | • Increase workplace security |
| • Notified security | • Increase home security |
| • Patient referred elsewhere for treatment | • Change home telephone number |
| • Consultation sought from an expert | • Change work telephone number |
| • Patient hospitalized | • Change work address/relocate |
| • Patient escorted out of the building | • Change home address |
| • Patient arrested or taken into legal custody | • Reduce social outings |
| • Restraining order obtained against patient | Assistance Sought From |
|  | • Family or friends |
|  | • Work colleagues/superiors |
|  | • Police |
|  | • Lawyer |
|  | • Psychotherapist |
|  | • Professional indemnity provider |

(2002) findings emerged. As such, it is likely that modifications would be necessary for the private practitioner to fully utilize these findings.

We recently examined the perceived effectiveness of Purcell and colleagues' (2005) risk management responses,[1] as seen in Table 45.1, in a national sample of board-certified psychologists practicing in diverse settings (Kivisto et al., 2015). Overall, our findings corroborated the need for enhanced emphasis on primary prevention—as evidenced by the fact that 60.2% of respondents indicated that they did not feel prepared to deal with STHB when they were confronted by it. Further, results of our survey provided evidence that certain widely used and perhaps intuitive clinical responses to STHB can be quite problematic. For example, directly confronting the client, referring him or her elsewhere for services, or having the patient hospitalized was each perceived as making the situation worse by a substantial minority of targeted psychologists. By contrast, nearly all of the responses consistent with the team approach were perceived as helpful, including consultation with colleagues, police, attorneys, and professional liability insurance providers (e.g., all clinicians covered by The Trust liability insurance have free, confidential access to clinical and legal risk management consultation with an attorney-psychologist).

Synthesizing relevant aspects of previous guidelines, Kivisto and colleagues (2015) recommended a progressive seven-step risk management sequence for clinicians to consider when confronted by a client engaging in STHB:

1. Proactive risk management planning
2. Ongoing assessment of risk and protective factors

3. Consultation
4. A crisis therapy approach with enhanced structure to minimize the intensity of transferential reactions
5. Triangulation of third parties into the clinical dyad (i.e., implementing a team approach)
6. Discontinuing all contact with the patient
7. Criminal justice intervention

# EMPIRICAL DATA ON STALKING EXPERIENCES AND RISK MANAGEMENT IN PRIVATE PRACTICE

Although different practice settings likely influence the nature of clinicians' experiences of STHB, as well as the potential risk management responses available to them, no research to date has examined differences in stalking victimization and risk management strategies between private practitioners versus others. Using data from our survey of 157 ABPP diplomates (Kivisto et al., 2015), we conducted several exploratory analyses based on a sample of 103 clinicians for whom we had valid data on their practice setting in an attempt to shed some light on the potentially unique challenges faced by private practitioners. Strikingly, although clinicians practicing in different settings were equally likely to experience some form of STHB, including more mundane forms of harassment, our data revealed significant differences in stalking victimization between private practitioners and others: Private practitioners were more than twice as likely to be the victims of stalking (31.1% vs. 13.8%).[2] Although our data cannot address why this difference might have emerged, it points clearly to the increased importance of primary prevention efforts for clinicians working in private practice. Further, although clinicians in private practice were no more likely to be physically attacked, our data indicate that private practitioners who experienced STHB were more likely to miss work as a result of their experience. Because missing work is more directly tied to adverse financial implications for the private practitioner, these findings indicate likely financial consequences in addition to the well-documented emotional and physical impacts of stalking victimization for clinicians in private practice.

As seen in Table 45.2, there were few differences in the risk management responses used by private practitioners versus clinicians in other settings responding to various forms of STHB. The differences that did emerge, however, seem to point to limited resources available to clinicians in private practice and the consequent need to find alternative strategies to manage risk. In light of the importance of a team approach and ongoing consultation, the finding that private practitioners were significantly less likely to seek assistance from colleagues or superiors—presumably due to fewer colleagues or superiors in their work environment—highlights a particular concern for the private practitioner confronted by STHB. That is, given the relative isolation that private practitioners can experience, it is essential to proactively navigate this hazard to ensure adequate support when the need arises. Several additional findings point to the strategies private practitioners might use to compensate for this relative isolation. For instance, they were significantly more likely

| | Prevalence | | |
| --- | --- | --- | --- |
| | Private Practitioners ($N = 45$) | Other Practitioners ($N = 58$) | $\chi^2$ |
| Stalking prevalence | 14 (31.1%) | 8 (13.8%) | 4.52* |
| **Risk management responses to STHB** | | | |
| *Clinical risk management responses* | | | |
| Confront client directly | 23 (51.1%) | 34 (58.6%) | 0.58 |
| Refer client elsewhere for services | 14 (31.1%) | 23 (39.7%) | 0.80 |
| Have client hospitalized | 8 (17.8%) | 4 (6.9%) | 2.81+ |
| Have client arrested | 3 (6.7%) | 2 (3.4%) | 0.57 |
| Obtain restraining order against client | 5 (11.1%) | 2 (3.4%) | 2.35 |
| *Changes to personal/professional life* | | | |
| Increase workplace security | 10 (22.2%) | 23 (39.7%) | 3.54+ |
| Increase home security | 8 (17.8%) | 10 (17.2%) | 0.01 |
| Change home telephone number | 1 (2.2%) | 3 (5.2%) | 0.59 |
| Change work telephone number | 0 (0.0%) | 1 (1.7%) | 0.78 |
| Change work address/relocate | 0 (0.0%) | 1 (1.7%) | 0.77 |
| Change home address | 0 (0.0%) | 0 (0.0%) | — |
| Reduce social outings | 2 (4.4%) | 2 (3.4%) | 0.80 |
| *Assistance sought from* | | | |
| Family or friends | 15 (33.3%) | 20 (34.5%) | 0.02 |
| Work colleagues/superiors | 29 (64.4%) | 47 (81.0%) | 4.30* |
| Police | 11 (24.4%) | 12 (20.7%) | 0.17 |
| Lawyer | 17 (37.8%) | 11 (19.0%) | 4.52* |
| Psychotherapist | 6 (13.3%) | 4 (6.9%) | 1.13 |
| Professional indemnity provider | 13 (28.9%) | 6 (10.3%) | 6.40* |

\* $p < .05$; + $p < .10$

to consult with lawyers as well as their professional indemnity providers, and there was a trend approaching significance suggesting that they were more likely to hospitalize patients in response to STHB. Hospitalization might reflect an additional strategy for recruiting other professionals to assist in the risk management of STHB.

# RECOMMENDATIONS FOR RISK MANAGEMENT OF STHB IN PRIVATE PRACTICE

Private practitioners in particular need to be prepared for patients who wage campaigns of frightening harassment. Due to the narrow circumstances under which mental health professionals can disclose confidential information regarding potentially dangerous patients, psychologists victimized by STHB can find themselves in the unique predicament of protecting the confidentiality of patients who are causing them to fear for their lives. Therefore, it is important that practitioners become familiar with the legal standards governing confidentiality in their jurisdiction and with extant guidelines for managing risk in these situations, such as those offered by Meloy (1997), Carr and colleagues (2014), and Kivisto and associates (2015). However, none of these guidelines were offered with the unique needs of private practitioners in mind.

Therefore, in addition to these existing guidelines, the private practitioner would be well served by placing a premium on primary prevention, and in particular on having contacts prepared (and ideally collaborative relationships established) to respond flexibly when the need arises. Among these contacts should be mental health professionals well versed in violence risk assessment and management, contacts within local law enforcement agencies, case managers and hospital admissions staff, clinical and legal risk management consultants available through many professional liability carriers, and a personal attorney versed in local laws and regulations.

In smaller practices, and particularly solo practices, clinicians should be mindful of the absence of an organizational risk management pathway as advocated by Carr and colleagues. Private practitioners should bear in mind such fundamental differences in the organizational structure between many small private practices and, for example, the academic medical centers from which some of the data on the risk management of STHB has been derived, and compensate for it by organizing a coherent network of professionals. For example, a number of private practitioners may form a risk management consultation group that can be used when a member is being stalked or at risk of being stalked. The need for a team approach presents a pragmatic hurdle for many in private practice but, with proper preparation, need not result in these clinicians feeling unprotected and unprepared for managing these challenging patients. In addition, primary prevention efforts aimed at enhancing physical workplace security are essential (e.g., having office space secured with appropriate locks and buzzer systems and having cameras in common areas that the practitioner can monitor).

# CONCLUSION

Most mental health professionals will encounter, at some point in their career, a patient who engages in STHB. Private practitioners appear to be at a particularly high risk for being stalked, with nearly one in three meeting a conservative definition of stalking victimization. The significance of private practitioners' heightened risk for stalking victimization is amplified by the lack of access to resources that are essential to safely managing risk in these situations compared to clinicians practicing in other contexts—namely, a team of professionals who can interrupt the patient's fixation and provide logistical and emotional support to the targeted clinician. The importance of proactive planning for managing clients who engage in STHB, important for clinicians in all settings, is essential in private practice. Because when mental health professionals find themselves in the position of Shakespeare's Merchant of Venice, whose client demands a pound of his flesh as part of doing business with him, the proverbial ounce of prevention is essential to exacting one's needed pound of cure.

## NOTES

1. Purcell and colleagues (2002) developed an expanded list of risk management responses that is likely more relevant to clinicians practicing in diverse settings, including private practices. Unlike Sandberg and associates (2002), however, Purcell and colleagues did not evaluate the perceived effectiveness of these risk management responses.
2. Consistent with Purcell and coworkers' (2005) conservative definition, stalking was defined as 10 or more intrusions over a period of two weeks or longer that resulted in fear.

## REFERENCES

Ashmore, R. R., Jones, J. J., Jackson, A. A., & Smoyak, S. S. (2006). A survey of mental health nurses' experiences of stalking. *Journal of Psychiatric and Mental Health Nursing, 13*, 562–569.

Carr, M. L., Goranson, A. C., & Drummond, D. J. (2014). Stalking of the mental health professional: Reducing and managing stalking behavior by patients. *Journal of Threat Assessment and Management, 1*, 4–22.

Kivisto, A. J., Berman, A., Watson, M., Gruber, D., & Paul, H. (2015). North American psychologists' experiences of stalking, threatening, and harassing behavior: A survey of ABPP diplomates. *Professional Psychology: Research and Practice, 46*, 277–286.

Leavitt, N., Presskreischer, H., Maykuth, P. L., & Grisso, T. (2006). Aggression toward forensic evaluators: A statewide survey. *Journal of the American Academy of Psychiatry and the Law, 34*, 231–239.

Meloy, J. R. (1997). The clinical risk management of stalking. *American Journal of Psychotherapy, 51*, 174–184.

Mullen, P. E., Pathé, M., & Purcell, R. (2000). *Stalkers and their victims*. Cambridge, MA: Cambridge University Press.

Mullen, P. E., Pathé, M., Purcell, R., & Stuart, G. (1999). Study of stalkers. *American Journal of Psychiatry, 156*, 1244–1249.

Pathé, M., & Meloy, J. R. (2013). Stalking by patients—psychiatrists' tales of anger, lust and ignorance. *Journal of the American Academy of Psychiatry and the Law, 41*, 200–205.

Purcell, R., Powell, M. B., & Mullen, P. E. (2005). Clients who stalk psychologists: Prevalence, methods, and motives. *Professional Psychology: Research and Practice, 36*, 537–543.

Sandberg, D., McNiel, D., & Binder, R. (2002). Stalking, threatening, and harassing behavior by psychiatric patients toward clinicians. *Journal of the American Academy of Psychiatry and the Law, 30*, 221–229.

Storey, J. E., Hart, S. D., Meloy, J. R., & Reavis, J. A. (2009). Psychopathy and stalking. *Law and Human Behavior, 33*, 237–246.

Tjaden, P., & Thoennes, N. (1998). *Stalking in America: Findings from the National Violence Against Women Survey* (NJ Report No. 169592). Washington, DC: U.S. Department of Justice.

# CHAPTER 46

# CONTINUING EDUCATION AND LIFELONG LEARNING STRATEGIES

*Jennifer M. Taylor and Greg J. Neimeyer*

The purpose of this chapter is to facilitate effective lifelong learning and continuing professional competence. The chapter discusses lifelong learning generally, as well as the issues at stake with continuing education (CE), the multiple functions it is designed to fill, and challenges faced by the current mechanisms designed to fulfill these functions and objectives. But most importantly, it supports the thoughtful utilization and orchestration of these mechanisms in support of maximizing the utility of CE in the maintenance of professional competence. By reviewing the issues, outlining the purposes, discussing the outcomes, and anticipating the rapidly developing trends in the field, we hope this chapter will contribute to a "road map" that will help support more effective lifelong learning and continuing professional development.

## LIFELONG LEARNING AND CONTINUING EDUCATION

If professional competence can be viewed as the "destination" for psychologists in their professional endeavors, it is fair to say that it is an ever-elusive one. The increasing rapidity with which new knowledge is generated (Neimeyer, Taylor, Rozensky, & Cox, 2014), the ongoing forces of specialization within the allied fields of mental health, (Rozensky & Kaslow, 2012), the radical reconfiguration of the healthcare system (Neimeyer, Taylor, & Rozensky, 2012), and the continuing pressures of accountability all converge to assure the practitioner that professional competence is better characterized as an ongoing quest than a final destination. Fortunately, psychotherapists have a wide range of alternative routes to take in pursuit of this goal, and those routes collectively form what can be referred to as professional "lifelong learning." Efforts to conceptualize these different routes to professional growth and development have identified at least four distinctive roadways that are nonetheless neither mutually exclusive nor exhaustive. The signposts that mark these routes have been designated formal, informal, incidental, and nonformal routes to learning.

*Formal learning* occurs when the learner is in a structured educational setting with predetermined learning objectives under the guidance or direction of a designated instructor, organization, or agency. Formal learning is supervised or closely observed, and includes some measure or assessment of the amount and type of learning that occurs during the educational experience. Formal learning takes place in a recognized institutional or organizational context that is accountable for the quality of the experience and that provides mechanisms for feedback and consequent improvement of the educational experience. For example, a graduate course or a formal CE program would be a type of formal learning.

A second avenue consists of *informal learning* (Lichtenberg & Goodyear, 2012; Neimeyer, Taylor, & Cox, 2012; Neimeyer, Taylor, Wear, & Linder-Crow, 2012). Informal learning is defined as self-directed learning that is not supervised, nor is it assessed. In informal learning there is no organizational or institutional context that is accountable for the quality of the programming. As is the case with formal learning, however, the practitioner is nonetheless placed in the express role of a learner. Examples of informal learning might include reading journal articles or relevant books, or attending conferences or listening to professional CDs.

*Incidental learning*, on the other hand, is learning that occurs as a consequence of engaging in professional activities, as a byproduct of another professional activity. The main purpose of incidental learning is not learning per se, so the professional is not placed in the role of a "student." In fact, he or she may actually be placed in the role of being an expert but may still learn a great deal from the experience. Serving on professional boards, reviewing manuscripts, teaching classes, and presenting professional workshops, for example, all reflect the practitioner's engagement in learning, but the express purpose of the activities is not knowledge or skill acquisition. Unlike formal CE, these learning activities are not supervised or assessed. Instead, they represent the vast realm of learning that is best characterized as "profiting from professional experience," which is consistent with Skovholt and Starkey's (2010) reminder that most psychotherapists find their clients and their clinical experience to be their single greatest source of learning.

The fourth and final route to learning we will discuss is *nonformal learning*. Nonformal learning occurs when the professional is placed in the role of a student or a learner, but unlike formal learning, it occurs outside of a recognized or accredited institutional or organizational context. It is both organized and structured (unlike informal learning), and its intent is expressly educational (unlike incidental learning). However, the "learner" is not accountable to an institution or professional organization. Examples of nonformal learning might include attending professional conferences or grand rounds and participating in a university colloquium. Nonformal learning is in many ways like formal learning but without the organizational structure, accountability, assessment, or feedback associated with formal types of learning.

Of course, these four types of learning are neither mutually exclusive nor exhaustive of all the potential sources of learning that can contribute directly to professional competence and clinical outcomes. Skovholt and Starkey (2010) have noted the significant role that personal experiences, such as loss, grief, and recovery, can play in relation to our ability to empathize effectively with the suffering that can be addressed in clinical and counseling contexts. "In order to be most effective with clients," Skovholt and Starkey note, "therapists need to realize and accept their own humanness" (p. 129), a reminder that critical sources of learning have to do with the potent forces of personal maturation that owe allegiance to life experience and pay dividends in the form of developing personal "wisdom." A colorful reminder of the potency of this personal maturation comes from Mark Twain's characterization of his leave-taking as a young adolescent from what he described as his "stupid, no-nothing father," only to return home several years later, astonished to find over the course of that time "how much the old man had learned" in the meantime!

Recognizing that ongoing professional development and competence derive from multiple, intertwined sources, this chapter will emphasize those more formal mechanisms of learning that are expressly designed to support the ongoing professional development of practitioners underneath the broader category of lifelong learning that encompasses them. These are the express mechanisms of ongoing professional development and CE.

# UNDERSTANDING CE

During their years of training, budding mental health professionals spend some years under the watchful eye of their instructors, supervisors, and mentors in carefully orchestrated and evaluated sequences of coursework, practica, internships, and supervised research. Upon graduation, however, they are sent into a world of independent practice armed only with professional and ethical mandates to maintain their currency and their competence, where for the next few decades they confront a loosely federated (Neimeyer, Taylor, & Cox, 2012), and widely variable (Adams & Sharkin, 2012), set of activities that fall under the umbrella of CE activities. Most states mandate CE for license renewal in the allied mental health professions, though some do not (unlike medicine or nursing, where it would be unheard of not to have mandated CE). But what qualifies for CE is a variegated assortment of professional activities lacking in both conceptual coherence and empirical warrant (Neimeyer, Taylor, & Cox, 2012). Reading books and articles, listening to CDs, teaching (or taking) classes, completing workshops, sitting on professional boards, writing papers, consulting with colleagues, conducting client assessments, presenting papers or workshops, and completing formal CE courses all count as creditable CE activities, though different states (and different professions) vary widely in how many CE credits are required for license renewal, as well as which particular activities "count" for CE activity. In short, like snowflakes or fingerprints, no two states are alike in their requirements, despite strong consumer preference for a single national set of requirements (Fagan, Liss, Ax, Resnick, & Moody, 2007).

The mandate for practicing professionals is to somehow fashion this patchwork of creditable activities into a meaningful fabric that covers the idiosyncratic needs of the particular practitioner according to his or her interests and experience, workplace needs and demands, and ongoing developing competencies across the course of the ever-changing professional lifespan. Unlike the carefully monitored, supervised, and assessed learning sequences in their graduate training program, once they have graduated mental health professionals are left to their own devices to figure out how best to address their needs in cycles of self-constructed learning euphemistically referred to as "autodidactic" learning (Candy, 1991).

For many professionals, this process is a disorienting, frustrating, and sometimes anxiety-producing endeavor in which they must end up in the right place (i.e., with the right number of CE credits) at the right time (i.e., the time of license renewal) without having a particularly clear road map regarding where they are or which direction they should be headed. It's a little like Lewis Carroll's *Alice's Adventures in Wonderland*, when Alice falls through the magical mirror into the discombobulating world of Wonderland and finds herself disoriented, anxious, and a bit desperate. She sees the Cheshire Cat sitting in the bough of a tree and, in an effort to get her bearings, she asks him to "Tell me please, which way I ought to go from here," to which he replies, "Well, that depends a good deal on where you want to get to."

The world of CE is much like this. It places an ongoing demand on the practicing professional to stay current, but without much guidance about how best to accomplish this task. And make no mistake about it, the task IS an important one, not only because most practitioners are under ethical mandates to do so, but also because of the demands that attend the increasingly rapid proliferation of new knowledge, and the attendant diminishing durability of the knowledge that is acquired. The literature on the "half-life" of professional knowledge in psychology is particularly revealing in this regard.

Dubin (1972) introduced the concept of the "half-life" of knowledge in the field of psychology 45 years ago. Borrowing the concept from the field of physics, he defined the concept as the time it would take, in the absence of any new learning, to become roughly half as knowledgeable or competent, as a function of the passing of time and the generation of new knowledge. Dubin's original estimate for the half-life of knowledge in the field of psychology, for example, was about a dozen years.

Two recent Delphi studies have examined the current half-life of knowledge in professional psychology and reported some sobering findings. Although the half-life of knowledge varied widely across different areas of specialization, many areas were estimated to have a half-life of as little as five or six years. Areas such as psychopharmacology, forensic psychology, clinical health psychology, and clinical neuropsychology showed particularly short half-lives, leading the researchers to conclude that many practitioners' knowledge bases may begin becoming obsolete, perhaps disconcertingly so, only a few years after the completion of their graduate training programs, while they are still early-career professionals (Neimeyer, Taylor, & Rozensky, 2012; Neimeyer, Taylor, Wear, & Linder-Crow, 2012; Neimeyer et al., 2014). And, as Rodolfa, Schaffer, and Webb (2010) have noted, mandated continuing education is the only licensing mechanism in place to contend against the ever-greater pressures of knowledge obsolescence and to help ensure ongoing professional competence and protect consumer welfare.

# PURPOSES OF CE

CE is designed to fulfill a range of functions, which are neither mutually exclusive nor exhaustive. In other words, they are interrelated objectives that nonetheless do not fully exhaust the value of

CE, which extends as well to such factors as the intrinsic value of learning, the confidence associated with remaining current, and the ever-enlarging understanding of human behavior and the causes and consequences of mental health issues or psychological disorders.

# FUNCTIONS OF CE

## CE AS A MEANS TO REMAIN CURRENT IN AREAS OF INTEREST AND NEED

Most definitions of continuing education allude to its role in helping practitioners remain current, maintaining familiarity with advances in the field, and continuing to update their knowledge and skills in areas of interest based on advances in contemporary understandings and practices within the profession. Developing literatures suggest that this is an intrinsic, driving factor behind the selection of particular CE activities for many practitioners. Neimeyer, Taylor, and Philip (2010) found, for example, that the two most common reasons for selecting a particular CE program to complete were its topical interest to the practitioner, followed by the need to remain updated in that particular topic. Although professional networking, burnout prevention, and marketing of services were all secondary considerations in the selection of particular CE activities to complete, the overall covariation of CE topic to workplace setting clearly supports the fact that the selection of CE programs is generally a rational, not a random, process (Neimeyer et al., 2009, 2010), with workplace needs and professional interests figuring highly in the reasons behind the choice of particular CE activities to complete.

## CE AS A MEANS TO ENHANCE CLINICAL OUTCOMES

A second purpose of CE is to increase the effectiveness of mental health services. Although this is a widely cited objective of CE, the effectiveness of CE in generating more favorable outcomes has operated more as an assumption than as a demonstration within the field. As Bloom (2005) as noted, when it comes to demonstrating the effects of CE, the weakest forms of assessment have been the most common forms, while progressively more rigorous assessments, like knowledge gains and skills assessments, have been progressively less frequent.

The most common form of assessment of CE, for example, has been simple satisfaction ratings, and numerous studies have noted that as many as 83% of mental health professionals view their CE experiences as good to excellent (Fagan et al., 2007; Neimeyer et al., 2009, 2010; Sharkin & Plageman, 2003). Further, nearly 95% of psychologists have reported that they learned either a moderate amount, quite a bit, or a great deal throughout their previous year's CE experiences, with a substantial majority indicating that these experiences frequently translated into their practices (Neimeyer, Taylor, & Philip, 2010).

But direct evidence of improved outcomes, or even changes in practitioner competence or behavior, is far harder to come across. The closest approximation to these data would be correlational studies examining the relationship between CE participation and a range of professional perceptions and accomplishments. Taylor, Neimeyer, Zemansky, and Rothke (2012), for example, demonstrated that higher levels of CE participation were related to higher levels of perceived professional competence, greater involvement in the professional community, and higher numbers of professional accomplishments and recognitions.

Not all continuing professional development activities appear to operate similarly, however. In a recent study of over 1,600 psychologists, researchers found that self-directed learning, peer consultation, and formal CE courses were perceived as strongly impacting professional competence, while other activities, such as serving on professional boards, taking or teaching courses, or administering client assessments, were perceived as contributing very little to enhanced professional competence (Neimeyer, Taylor, & Cox, 2012). These findings underscore the likelihood that different kinds of CE activities may contribute differently to the objectives of CE, calling attention to the importance of the judicious selection of CE activities according to the intended purpose(s) associated with participation in them.

## CE AS A MEANS TO SUPPORT ETHICAL PRACTICE

In addition to promoting more effective clinical outcomes, CE is also designed to facilitate and ensure more ethical practice and, in so doing, to protect the public. In fact, the area of ethics is the single most stipulated content area mandated for completion (Adams & Sharkin, 2012), based on the assumption that CE will improve ethical behavior. The evidence in favor of this assumption is best characterized, however, as provisional and mixed. Some large-scale research has found that most practitioners at least *perceive* their ethics training as improving their ethical practice (Neimeyer et al., 2009). But other researchers have found only minimal support for the influence of such courses on increased understanding of ethical issues (Welfel & Lipsitz, 1983). Vasquez (1988) notes that ethics courses may not focus enough on specific ethical concerns and thus may not be as useful or as meaningful as intended. Moreover, the largest study to date concerning the impact of ethics CE mandates on ethical infractions and disciplinary actions did not find any association between them (Neimeyer, Taylor, & Orwig, 2013). In this study, the researchers accessed the entire disciplinary database of the Association of State and Provincial Psychology Boards and examined the base rates of states with, and without, CE mandates to complete courses on ethics prior to license renewal. Results revealed no relationship between disciplinary actions and ethics mandates, leaving questions about the actual impact of those mandates on ethical behavior. Other research has noted that the imposition of disciplinary sanctions themselves may register little demonstrable impact on reducing future ethical violations (Layman & McNamara, 1997).

## CE AS A MEANS TO FACILITATE COLLEGIAL INTERACTION

In addition to the functions of CE in relation to remaining current, improving outcomes, and maintaining ethical practice, a fourth rationale for CE is as a means of promoting professional interaction and consultation. A number of studies in other professions, for example, have linked membership in professional associations with lower rates of disciplinary actions. One study among orthopedic surgeons found that professional association members had a lower frequency of malpractice complaints than nonmembers (Kilmo, Daum, Brinker, McGruire, & Elliott, 2000). Knapp and VandeCreek (2012) generalized this finding to the field of professional psychology. Using archival data from licensing board adjudications and membership lists of the Pennsylvania Psychological Association over a 14-year period, they found that the likelihood of being disciplined by the state board was higher for psychologists who were not members of their state association than for those who were members. The nature of the causal relationship remains unclear, but it may be that the interaction, consultation, and education that occur as part of the association's activities facilitate more ethical behavior. This finding is broadly consistent with related work showing that participation in a wide variety of forms of collegial interaction (publications, service on professional committees, completion of formal and informal CE) is associated with higher levels of professional competence and recognition (Taylor, Neimeyer, Zemansky, & Rothke, 2012).

# FROM PURPOSE TO PRACTICE: MAKING CE WORK FOR YOU

CE comes in many different forms and formats and is designed to fulfill many different functions, so it follows that not all forms will fulfill each of the functions equally. Some activities are probably better suited than others to fulfill specific objectives, and this likelihood has been supported in a series of studies in the field of psychology. In a study of 1,606 licensed psychologists, Neimeyer, Taylor, and Cox (2012) examined the perceived contribution of 10 different types of continuing professional development activities (e.g., presenting a workshop, sitting on a professional board, teaching a class, completing formal CE, self-directed reading, consulting with colleagues) in relation to three of the primary objectives of CE: to maintain competence, to improve clinical outcomes, and to protect the public. Overall, self-directed learning, peer consultation, and formal CE were regarded as the most significant contributors to ongoing professional competence, for example, while publishing papers, teaching classes, and completing a graduate class were all viewed as making progressively smaller contributions to ongoing professional competence. These findings suggest that not all continuing professional development activities contribute equally, or are perceived as contributing equally, to the stipulated objectives of CE.

Building upon this work, Taylor and Neimeyer (2015) surveyed public opinion regarding the extent to which various professional development activities fulfilled the stipulated objectives of CE, and again found that different activities were viewed as contributing differentially to the objectives of CE. Conducting client assessments and peer consultation, for example, were both viewed as being more highly related to protecting the public than to improving clinical outcomes, again highlighting the likelihood that different types of CE activity may differentially satisfy the objectives of CE.

The selection of particular CE activities, therefore, needs to be informed by the objectives that they are designed to fulfill, as well as a range of other factors. While formal forms of continuing education and certification (e.g., board certification by the American Board of Professional Psychology) may be more strongly related to public perceptions of competence (Taylor & Neimeyer, 2015), other forms of informal learning (e.g., self-directed study) or incidental learning (e.g., publishing, serving on professional boards) may nonetheless contribute importantly to maintaining or developing new competencies, even though they may register relatively little impact on other objectives, such as improving clinical outcomes.

As practitioners make reasoned decisions about how best to select their CE experiences, it may be helpful to consider a range of contemporary developments within the field. Those developments include emerging consensus regarding five key areas: (1) the importance of self-assessment, (2) attention to best practices, (3) the expanding models of CE, (4) considering the relationship between personal and professional development, and (5) monitoring emerging markets. A set of reflexive questions related to each of these five areas is included as an appendix to this chapter to help readers select and use CE programs and trainings to promote ongoing professional competence.

## SELF-ASSESSMENT

One of the most important skills mental health providers must develop in order to maximize the value of CE concerns the concept of self-reflection and self-evaluation. Creating a "culture of competence" (Hatcher et al., 2013) requires a culture of self-assessment. Accurate self-assessment is an important precursor to effective self-directed learning and lifelong maintenance of competence (Candy, 1991; Morris, 2012). Davis and colleagues (2006) performed a systematic literature review of 725 articles on physician self-assessment accuracy. They then examined the 17 most relevant studies and those that had the strongest empirical rigor. Over half of the comparisons that were made between self-assessment and objective assessment demonstrated little, no, or inverse relationships between self-assessments and objective assessments. More troubling still, those who performed the poorest, as measured by objective assessments, had some of the most inaccurate self-assessments, reflecting the concept of "unconscious incompetence"—in other words, professionals who were the least competent were the least able to recognize, and correct, their deficiencies and areas in need of remediation.

Parker, Alford, and Passmore (2004) discovered similar findings, noting that medical residents who scored in the lowest quartile of a family practice knowledge-based examination assessed their learning needs least accurately. Dunning, Heath, and Suls (2004) noted that incompetent individuals have "deficits [that] cause them to make errors and also prevent them from gaining insight into their errors" (p. 73). In concluding their review, Dunning and colleagues (2004) noted that, "When one looks at the accuracy of self-assessment in the workplace, from the office cubicle to the executive boardroom, one sees that people tend to hold overly inflated self-views that are modestly related to actual performance" (p. 90).

But several activities can increase the accuracy of self-assessments; overt review is a case in point. For example, research suggests that when medical residents watch videotapes of their performance, their self-assessment accuracy is significantly enhanced (Lane & Gottlieb, 2004). Their accuracy is strengthened still more when they watch the tapes with a faculty member. When students rate their own performance and then meet with a faculty member who conducts a separate assessment of their competence, their skill appraisal becomes more accurate still (Cochran & Spears, 1980).

Benchmarking, which involves comparing one's own performance to the performance of others, can also increase the accuracy of self-assessment (Martin, Regehr, Hodges, & McNaugton, 1998). Researchers invited family practice residents to conduct mock interviews with a mother suspected of physically abusing her child. The residents were then asked to rate their performance. Next, residents watched their videotaped interview, in addition to watching four benchmark interviews with varying competence levels. After watching the benchmark interviews, the relationship between the residents' self-ratings and the independent ratings of the supervisor was significantly stronger.

Peer assessment can also be a useful tool to enhance the accuracy of self-assessment (Falchikov & Goldfinch, 2000; Topping, 1998). In fact, in Ontario, Canada, psychologists develop their own tailored Self-Assessment Guide and Professional Development Plan as a key component of the Quality Assurance Program of the College of Psychologists of Ontario (Morris, 2012). Through a series of questions, psychologists critically examine their strengths, growth areas, and gaps in their learning. After conducting the self-assessment, they develop their own personal plan to remediate areas of weakness and enhance their overall professional competence, sharing their plans with a colleague who reviews it and provides input.

Creating a community around self-assessment can generate a range of benefits. On the one hand, clinicians can solicit the ideas and input of colleagues into the plans; on the other, having such a community can enhance accountability in relation to carrying out the plans and evaluating the extent to which they have been implemented during the licensing cycle prior to renewal. Critically engaging in self-reflection serves multiple functions. Self-assessment provides an opportunity for practitioners to consolidate their learning and to evaluate their CE needs for the future.

## BEST PRACTICES

The allied fields of mental health are just now turning to identifying best practices in CE. Much of what is known about best practices can be gleaned from the literatures in the broader fields of health, particularly within medicine. Unlike the behavioral health fields, medicine has a longstanding history of controlled research concerning the impact of different instructional methods on the outcomes associated with CE, as well as longitudinal and meta-analytic studies based on decades of research.

The gist of this work suggests that we may not be maximizing the effectiveness of training and education efforts in the field of CE. Didactic presentations predominate in the CE field, eclipsing all other instructional methods many times over, even though research has demonstrated that these methods generate substantial "forgetting curves" and are poorly designed to enhance critical thinking on the one hand and clinical application on the other. Interactive programs are better suited to translation into practice, particularly when accompanied by feedback and serial rehearsal (Dunning et al., 2004; Institute of Medicine, 2010; Wise et al., 2010). As Shern (2010) notes, didactic programs are the equivalent of a "spray and pray" technique where the instructor "sprays" information out across the participants and "prays" that some of it sticks. This is consistent with the Institute of Medicine's (2010) conclusion that

> health professionals often need multiple learning opportunities and multiple methods of education, such as practicing self-reflection in the workplace, reading journal articles that report new clinical evidence, and participating in formal CE lectures if they are to most effectively change their performance and, in turn, improve patient outcomes. (p. 47)

Research points to the importance of practice demonstrations, role plays, and multimodal learning opportunities for learners. After an extensive review of a 20-year period of controlled research on the effectiveness of CE in the medical field, Bloom (2005) concluded that interactive methods were the most effective at improving physician care and the outcomes of patients, whereas didactic programs had "little or no beneficial effect in changing physicians' practice" (p. 380; see also Institute of Medicine, 2010). Davis, Thomson, Oxman, and Hayes (1995) further noted that interactive techniques, simulations, and online learning experiences tend to be most effective when they are combined with learning across several occasions or through a variety of different instructional formats to reinforce learning and facilitate translation into practice. Interactive workshops that combine demonstration, discussion, practice opportunities, and direct feedback tend to enhance the satisfaction and outcomes associated with CE training experiences (see Institute of Medicine, 2010; O'Brien et al., 2001).

## EXPANDING CE ACTIVITIES

A third trend in CE involves efforts to expand the modes of CE delivery and the "creditable" activities that "count" toward CE. The Association of State and Provincial Psychology Board's Task Force for the Maintenance of Competence and Licensure (MOCAL), for example, has recently advocated for widening the scope of continuing professional development to include activities beyond formal CE per se. This recommendation would credential a wide variety of informal (e.g., self-study), nonformal (e.g., attending job talks), and incidental (e.g., sitting on professional boards) forms of learning, as well as those more formal educational experiences that place participants in the role of a learner and require that they evaluate both the nature of their training experience and their own learning.

The broadening of CE to include this wider range of creditable activities balances appeal against peril. Several of the activities offer the strong appeal associated with adding "real world" learning, but weighing against this advantage is the disadvantage that these experiences are neither regulated nor evaluated. Moreover, in a national study of more than 1,600 psychologists, researchers discovered that, using the MOCAL proposal, most practitioners would first count all of the creditable activities in their day-to-day professional lives rather than participating in new activities to support lifelong learning and ongoing professional competence (Neimeyer, Taylor, & Cox, 2012). This raised the disconcerting possibility that the net effect of the proposed MOCAL system would be to substantially *reduce* both the range of learning activities and the time spent in them if the system were to be adopted by the state licensing boards.

An alternative model is emerging from the professional development literatures in the teaching profession. This model is based on the concept of "micro-credentialing." The purpose of micro-credentialing is to make professional development more personalized, engaging, and relevant. Micro-credentials often take the form of earning "badges" that reflect the development of mini-competencies, providing a vehicle for shifting away from the credit-hour–based requirements that dominate professional development in many areas of CE. This is an appealing concept within a field like the behavioral health field that has struggled to rigorously evaluate and demonstrate the effects of its CE efforts on actual practice and relevant service delivery outcomes. Teachers in North Carolina's Surry County school system recently completed a micro-credentialing pilot. Teachers can now access an online platform and participate in a number of "quests" (self-guided modules, often with a gamelike component) that terminate with a micro-credential in areas such as problem solving and classroom management, which certify their competency in performing the basic tasks associated with the stipulated domain. Micro-credentialing represents an alternative model for facilitating and documenting relevant skills acquisition, and for that reason coheres well with the broader competency movement in the field of professional psychology and other allied mental health professions.

## PERSONAL AND PROFESSIONAL SELF-CARE

The relationship between aspects of personal well-being and professional functioning has been the subject of ongoing attention. The literature on personal impairment stands testament to the importance of self-care as a buffer against professional dysfunction, for example (Baker, 2003; O'Connor, 2001). Beyond the realm of impairment per se, aspects of personal maturation and adjustment have figured prominently in the conceptualization of professional development. Skovholt and Starkey (2010), for example, have drawn attention to what they call the "three legs of the practitioner's learning stool," noting that personal maturation, scholarly development, and ongoing clinical experience all play important roles in developing professional competence (p. 125). As a result, drawing a distinction between personal experiences and professional capabilities may be a false one given the interdependence between the two.

Recent evidence seems to support this notion. In a study of licensed practitioners, for example, Taylor, Neimeyer, and Wear (2012) noted the measures of perceived professional competence were inversely related to levels of stress and positively associated with overall life satisfaction, adjustment, and self-care. Findings such as this suggest the potential value of CE programs that attend to aspects of personal well-being as a prospective mechanism for enhancing professional functioning and competence (Wise, 2010). Express attention to facilitating self-care and reducing stress, for example, could register measureable impacts on clinical efficacy and outcomes.

## EMERGING DEMANDS FOR TRAINING AND EDUCATION

The allied fields of behavioral health are experiencing quantum challenges and demands, both from outside the field and from within it. As Neimeyer, Taylor, and Rozensky (2012) have noted, there is a diminishing durability of knowledge in the field of mental health, precisely because there are now so many rapid advances all across the landscape of professional practice. While the overall durability of knowledge may average as long as six or seven years, rapid advances in a number of areas make it important to pursue more frequent refresher courses in areas of specialization that may have half-lives of professional knowledge as short as two or three years.

Beyond those familiar domains of practice, however, rapid advances are occurring in areas outside of traditional clinical practice that nonetheless require sustained efforts to keep pace in order to maintain competencies at contemporary levels. The rapid rise in problematic Internet use, for example, challenges practitioners to keep pace with technology trends that provide distinctive clinical challenges. With Internet gaming having been added to the "Conditions for Further Study" in the American Psychiatric Association's Diagnostic and Statistical Manual of Mental Disorders, fifth edition (DSM-5), and gambling disorder (online and onsite) already having received official recognition, the area of problematic Internet use is a rapidly developing one, both in terms of its conceptualization (Grant, Potenza, Weinstein, & Gorelick, 2010) and its therapeutic interventions (e.g., Internet boot camps).

The same can be said in relation to the larger area of behavioral addictions (Rosenberg & Curtis Feder, 2014). Now that the first of these behavioral addictions has been officially recognized in the DSM-5 (i.e., gambling disorder) under the category of "Substance-Related and Other Addictive Disorders," we can expect a rapid rise in the literatures surrounding the conceptualization and treatment of other impulsive and compulsive disorders (e.g., sexual addiction, food addiction, compulsive buying, exercise addiction).

Perhaps no single change is likely to rival the field's move toward integrated care, however, which creates a critical need for considerable training and education. While each allied health field has its own traditions, there are also important points of convergence within the interprofessional workforce that constitute the world of integrated care. The distinctive skillsets within integrated care contexts place a substantial demand on the allied health professions to update their skills in critical areas such as understanding the concept of the medical home, knowing how to best work within medical teams, the effective and ethical use of electronic health records, understanding integrated care management, and many more. To date courses in integrated care for behavioral health professionals are offered online through the University of Massachusetts, the University of Michigan, and Cherokee Integrated Care Training Academy, though the demand for training is likely to eclipse the availability of the training resources in this area for the foreseeable future.

# CONCLUSION

The field of CE and lifelong learning in the allied behavioral health field is changing rapidly and is confronting a range of challenges owing to its rapid developments and the objectives it is designed to satisfy. The purpose of this chapter has been to facilitate effective lifelong learning and continuing professional competence. The chapter outlined a range of issues at stake within the field of CE and lifelong learning, the multiple functions CE is designed to fill, and challenges faced by the current mechanisms designed to fulfill these functions and objectives. But most importantly, our purpose has been to encourage the thoughtful utilization and orchestration of these mechanisms to maximize the utility of CE in the maintenance of professional competence. The reflexive questions in the chapter appendix are designed to support that goal. By reviewing the issues, outlining the purposes, discussing the outcomes, and anticipating the rapidly developing trends in the field, we hope this chapter will contribute to a "road map" that will support more effective lifelong learning and continuing professional development.

# APPENDIX

# REFLEXIVE QUESTIONS IN SUPPORT OF CONTINUING PROFESSIONAL DEVELOPMENT

## SELF-ASSESSMENT

1. What are my areas of greatest interest and need?
2. How do my I view my skills in targeted areas of interest or need compared to those of my colleagues? What would they say about my areas of strength or weakness?
3. What could I use as benchmarks to evaluate myself and determine where I stand in relation to my areas of greatest professional interest and/or need?

## BEST PRACTICES

1. How do I learn best?
2. What instructional modalities do I value most and which best support my comprehension, retention, and utilization of the material I learn?
3. What can I do to enhance the translation of my new learning into my clinical practice?

## EXPANDING CE ACTIVITIES

1. Where and how am I learning the most in my professional life right now?
2. List the professional activities you regularly engage in, and rate each of them on a 10-point scale in relation to how much you learn from them.
3. If I were going to be more self-conscious or deliberate about becoming involved in professional activities that would enhance my learning, what could I do?

## PERSONAL AND PROFESSIONAL

1. If I were to think of my levels of "state" and "trait" stress (i.e., acute and chronic), using a 10-point scale, how might I rate them?
2. When I am particularly stressed, how can I tell the effect that it has on my therapy or clinical work? In what way(s) does it affect what I do and how I do it?
3. What do I use/do to take care of myself? What helps me let go of stress and what can I do more of?

## EMERGING TRENDS

1. What areas of my practice are changing most rapidly?
2. What trends in education, technology, or training do I see developing that could be helpful to me in my professional development and learning?
3. If I were to envision myself developing greater competency or proficiency in any areas over the next year or two, what might those areas be? What kinds of things could I be doing now to ensure that outcome at that time?

# REFERENCES

Adams, A., & Sharkin, B. S. (2012). Should continuing education be mandatory for re-licensure? Arguments for and against. In G. J. Neimeyer & J. M. Taylor (Eds.), *Continuing professional development and lifelong learning: Issues, impacts, and outcomes* (pp. 161–182). Hauppauge, NY: Nova Science Publishers.

Baker, E. K. (2003). *Caring for ourselves: A therapist's guide to personal and professional well-being.* Washington, DC: American Psychological Association.

Bloom, B. S. (2005). Effects of continuing medical education on improving physician clinical care and patient health. *International Journal of Technology Assessment in Health Care, 21,* 380–385.

Candy, P. C. (1991). *Self-direction for life-long learning: A comprehensive guide to theory and practice.* San Francisco: Jossey-Bass.

Cochran, S. B., & Spears, M. (1980). Student self-assessment and instructors' rating: A comparison. *Journal of the American Dietetic Association, 76,* 253–257.

Davis, D. A., Mazmanian, P. E., Fordis, M., Van Harrison, R., Thorpe, K. E., & Perrier, L. (2006). Accuracy of physician self-assessment compared with observed measures of competence: A systematic review. *Journal of the American Medical Association, 296,* 1094–1102.

Davis, D. A., Thomson, M. A., Oxman, A. D., & Hayes, R. B (1995). Changing physician performance: A systematic review of the effect of continuing medical education strategies. *Journal of the American Medical Association, 274,* 700–705.

Dubin, S. S. (1972). Obsolescence or lifelong learning: A choice for the professional. *American Psychologist, 27,* 486–498.

Dunning, D., Heath, C., & Suls, J. (2004). Flawed self-assessment: Implications for health, education, and the workplace. *Psychological Science in the Public Interest, 5,* 69–106.

Fagan, T. J., Liss, M., Ax, R. K., Resnick, R. J., & Moody, S. (2007). Professional education and training: How satisfied are we? An exploratory study. *Training and Education in Professional Psychology, 1,* 13–25.

Falchikov, N., & Goldfinch, J. (2000). Student peer assessment in higher education: A meta-analysis comparing peer and teacher marks. *Review of Educational Research, 70,* 287–322.

Grant, J. E., Potenza, M. N., Weinstein, A., & Gorelick, D. A. (2010). Introduction to behavioral addictions. *American Journal of Drug and Alcohol Abuse, 36,* 233–241.

Hatcher, R. L., Fouad, N. A., Grus, C. L., Campbell, L. F., McCutcheon, S. R., & Leahy, K. L. (2013). Competency benchmarks: Practical steps toward a culture of competence. *Training and Education in Professional Psychology, 7,* 84–91.

Institute on Medicine. (2010). *Redesigning continuing education in the health professions.* Washington, DC: National Academies Press.

Kilmo, G., Daum, W., Brinker, M., McGruire, E., & Elliott, M. (2000). Orthopedic medical malpractice: An attorney's perspective. *American Journal of Orthopedics, 29,* 93–97.

Knapp, S., & VandeCreek, L. (2012) Disciplinary actions by a state board of psychology: Do gender and association membership matter? An update. In G. J. Neimeyer & J. M. Taylor (Eds.), *Continuing professional development and life-long learning: Issues, impacts and outcomes* (pp. 155–158). Hauppauge, NY: Nova Science Publishers.

Lane, J. L., & Gottlieb, R. P. (2004). Improving the interviewing and self-assessment skills of medical students: Is it time to readopt videotaping as an educational tool? *Ambulatory Pediatrics, 4,* 244–248.

Layman, M. J., & McNamara, J. R. (1997). Remediation for ethics violations: Focus on psychotherapists' sexual contact with clients. *Professional Psychology: Research and Practice, 28,* 281–292.

Lichtenberg, J. W., & Goodyear, R. K. (2012). Informal learning, incidental learning, and deliberate continuing education: Preparing psychologists to be effective lifelong learners. In G. J. Neimeyer & J. M. Taylor (Eds.), *Continuing professional development and life-long learning: Issues, impacts and outcomes* (pp. 71–80). Hauppauge, NY: Nova Science Publishers.

Martin, D., Regehr, G., Hodges, B., & McNaugton, N. (1998). Using videotaped benchmarks to improve the self-assessment ability of family practice residents. *Academic Medicine, 73,* 1201–1206.

Morris, R. (2012). Self-assessment guide and professional development plan: Facilitating individualized continuing professional development. In G. J. Neimeyer & J. M. Taylor (Eds.), *Continuing professional development and lifelong learning: Issues, impacts and outcomes* (pp. 103–130). Hauppauge, NY: Nova Science Publishers.

Neimeyer, G. J., Taylor, J. M., & Cox, D. R. (2012). On hope and possibility: Does continuing professional development contribute to ongoing professional competence? *Professional Psychology: Research and Practice, 43,* 476–486.

Neimeyer, G. J., Taylor, J. M., & Orwig, J. P. (2013). Do continuing education mandates matter? An exploratory study of the relationship between CE regulations and disciplinary actions. *Professional Psychology: Research and Practice, 44,* 99–104.

Neimeyer, G. J., Taylor, J. M., & Philip, D. (2009). Continuing education in psychology: Patterns of participation and perceived outcomes among mandated and nonmandated psychologists. *Professional Psychology: Research and Practice, 41,* 435–441.

Neimeyer, G. J., Taylor, J. M., & Rozensky, R. (2012). The diminishing durability of knowledge in professional psychology: A Delphi poll of specialties and proficiencies. *Professional Psychology: Research and Practice, 43,* 364–371.

Neimeyer, G. J., Taylor, J. M., Rozensky, R., & Cox, D. (2014). The diminishing durability of knowledge in professional psychology: A second look at specializations. *Professional Psychology: Research and Practice, 45,* 92–98.

Neimeyer, G. J., Taylor, J. M., Wear, D., & Linder-Crow, J. (2012). Anticipating the future of CE in psychology: A Delphi poll. In G. J. Neimeyer & J. M. Taylor (Eds.), *Continuing professional development and life-long learning: Issues, impacts and outcomes* (pp. 377–394). Hauppauge, NY: Nova Science Publishers.

O'Brien, M. A., Freemantle, N., Oxman, A. D., Wolf, F., Davis, D. A., & Herrin, J. (2001). Continuing education meetings and workshops: Effects on professional practice and health care outcomes. *Cochrane Database System Reviews, 2,* CD003030.

O'Connor, M. F. (2001). On the etiology and effective management of professional distress and impairment among psychologists. *Professional Psychology: Research and Practice, 32,* 345–350.

Parker, R. W., Alford, C., & Passmore, C. (2004). Can family medicine residents predict their performance on the in-training examination? *Family Medicine, 36,* 705–709.

Rodolfa, E., Schaffer, J. B., & Webb, C. (2010). Continuing education: The path to life-long competence? *Professional Psychology: Research and Practice, 41,* 295–297.

Rosenberg, K. P., & Curtis Feder, L. (Eds) (2014). *Behavioral addictions: Criteria, evidence and treatment.* New York: Academic Press.

Rozensky, R. H., & Kaslow, N. J. (2012). Specialization and lifelong learning. In G. J. Neimeyer & J. M. Taylor (Eds.), *Continuing professional development and life-long learning: Issues, impacts and outcomes* (pp. 345–358). Hauppauge, NY: Nova Science Publishers.

Sharkin, B. S., & Plageman, P. M. (2003). What do psychologists think about mandatory continuing education? A survey of Pennsylvania psychologists. *Professional Psychology: Research and Practice, 34,* 318–323.

Shern, D. (2010, February). *Health care reform, chronic disease and the emerging role for psychologists.* Presentation to the Council of Charis of Training Councils Joint conference of Training Councils in Psychology: Assuring Competence in the Next Generation of Psychologists, Orlando, FL.

Skovholt, T. M., & Starkey, M. T. (2010). The three legs of the practitioner's learning stool: Practice, research/theory, and personal life. *Journal of Contemporary Psychotherapy, 40,* 125–130.

Taylor, J. M., & Neimeyer, G. J. (2015). Public perceptions of psychologists' professional development activities: The good, the bad, and the ugly. *Professional Psychology: Research and Practice, 46,* 140–146.

Taylor, J. M., Neimeyer, G. J., & Wear, D. (2012). Professional competency and personal experience: An exploratory study. In G. J. Neimeyer & J. M. Taylor (Eds.), *Continuing professional development and life-long learning: Issues, impacts and outcomes* (pp. 249–261). Hauppauge, NY: Nova Science Publishers.

Taylor, J. M., Neimeyer, G. J., Zemansky, M., & Rothke, S. (2012). Exploring the relationship between life-long learning, continuing education, and professional competencies. In G. J. Neimeyer & J. M. Taylor (Eds.), *Continuing professional development and life-long learning: Issues, impacts and outcomes* (pp. 81–97). Hauppauge, NY: Nova Science Publishers.

Topping, K. (1998). Peer assessment between students in colleges and universities. *Review of Educational Research, 68,* 249–276.

Vasquez, M. J. T. (1988). Counselor-client sexual contact: Implications for ethics training. *Journal of Counseling and Development, 67,* 238–241.

Welfel, E. R., & Lipsitz, N. E. (1983). Moral reasoning of counselors: Its relationship to level of training and counseling experience. *Counseling and Values, 27,* 194–203.

Wise, E. H. (2010). Maintaining and enhancing competence in professional psychology: Obsolescence, life-long learning, and continuing education. *Professional Psychology: Research and Practice, 41,* 289–292.

Wise, E. H., Sturm, C. A., Nutt, R. L., Rodolfa, E., Schaffer, J. B., & Webb, C. (2010). Life-long learning for psychologists: Current status and a vision for the future. *Professional Psychology: Research and Practice, 41,* 288–297.

# CHAPTER 47

# HOW SOCIAL POLICY IMPACTS PRIVATE PRACTICE

*Catherine Gaines Ling, Sarah Huffman, and Patrick H. DeLeon*

S ocial policy is a tool in a behavioral health practitioner's cache. Social policy shapes all aspects of care through legislation, regulation, payment, delivery systems, and interdisciplinary collaboration. Behavioral health providers of all backgrounds need to be aware of and shape policy because they are subject to the boundaries imposed by those policies. Concurrent with mental health–specific policy is the concept of parity, which refers to comparability between behavioral health policy components and those of physical health providers. By examining each of the aspects of policy along with the implications of parity, behavioral health providers can examine current forces shaping their practice (who they can see; when, where, and how they can see their clients; and what the mechanisms for payment are) and work for changes to improve practice in the future.

## BACKGROUND

One resource for quality practice is social policy, which has been described as a legislated or organizational formalized structure to ensure goals that benefit society (Midgley & Livermore, 2009). This structure can involve communication, services, infrastructure, and resource allocation. In developed nations, these policies are often codified through legislation and regulation at local, regional, and federal levels.

Practitioners should care about and participate in the formulation of social policy because that policy will ultimately determine the opportunity, scope, and fiscal viability of their practice. Social policy can act as a promoter, inhibitor, or neutral influencer of practice. Policy is derived from perceived needs at either a grassroots or population level. In the United States, social policy regarding healthcare includes several facets: legislation (historical and contemporary), regulations, payers, delivery systems, and interdisciplinary collaboration. While not an exhaustive list, these particular facets are critical to informing clinical practice. We will discuss and give examples of each of these facets.

# LEGISLATION

Many practitioners are simply unaware of the evolutionary legislative history of their current practice, although they spend many years learning their specialty's specific skills and theoretical rationales. Previous generations of non-physician providers have endured at times titanic political struggles to expand professional "scopes of practice" and to obtain insurance reimbursement for clinical services. Within the mental health professions, it is surprisingly rare for training institutions to provide the social/political context for clinical practice in which their graduates will function for the rest of their careers. The societal good of quality psychological and behavioral health care—not to mention preventive care—has clearly not been a sufficient reason to expect that they will be covered by third-party payers. This is true even if considerable objective evidence exists that in the long term these interventions will be highly cost-effective and meaningful. Only within the relatively recent past have mental health providers begun to consider themselves as "healthcare" professionals. Also, only within the same contemporary timeframe have there been serious discussions by national health policy experts regarding the appropriateness of integrating mental health care into organized systems of care, particularly on an interdisciplinary basis.

Of particular historical interest, Adelphi University and its postdoctoral program in psychotherapy were actually sued, in the early 1950s, by the Nassau County Neuropsychiatric Society for allegedly practicing medicine and founding an institution for medical training without licensure solely because the program was teaching psychologists to do psychotherapy. In 1977, future American Psychological Association (APA) President Robert Resnick became one of the leading psychologists in the landmark "Virginia Blues" case, in which the U.S. Supreme Court ultimately upheld psychology's autonomous status and further ruled that psychology and psychiatry were indeed competitors. In 1977, Missouri became the 50th state in the nation, along with the District of Columbia, to credential and regulate the practice of psychology. It was also during that era that many health providers, including psychologists, nurses, and mental health counselors, began their systematic quest to become legislatively recognized as autonomous providers under a wide range of federal reimbursement programs, including the Department of Defense CHAMPUS program, the Federal Employees' Health Benefit Program, Medicare, and Medicaid, as well as to be authorized to serve as expert witnesses before the federal judiciary. For all of these disciplines, it has been a long and arduous journey that continues today, in the face of constant opposition from organized medicine. Advances in access to care can be made by working to the full extent of one's training and building on the successes of other professions. For psychology, perhaps the next frontier will be obtaining prescriptive authority similar to that already possessed by nursing in all jurisdictions, under varying conditions.

During the tenures of Presidents George W. Bush and Barack Obama one of the most significant societal changes impacting our nation's healthcare system has been the unprecedented advances occurring in the communications and technology fields, and particularly their increasing use by the federal government (especially by the Departments of Veterans Affairs and Defense). In highlighting the successes of Veterans Affairs, President Bush opined on April 27, 2004, that

> [t]he way I like to kind of try to describe health care is, on the research side, we're the best. We're coming up with more innovative ways to save lives and to treat patients. Except when you think about the provider's side, we're kind of still in the buggy era. . . . And the health care industry is missing an opportunity. . . . It's like IT, information technology, hasn't shown up in health care yet. But it has in one place, in one department . . . and that's the Veterans Department. . . . By introducing information technology, health care will be better, the cost will go down, the quality will go up, and there's no telling whether other benefits will inure to our society.

In response to the changing healthcare environment, the various healthcare professions have recently begun to seriously explore under what conditions they would recommend modifying their current licensure act to meet contemporary society's needs and resources. At the APA's 2015 annual convention in Toronto, the Council of Representatives voted to endorse, in principle, the Association of State and Provincial Psychology Boards (ASPPB) Psychology Interjurisdictional Compact (PSYPACT), which was developed by the Joint Task Force for the Development of Telepsychology Guidelines, comprising representatives from the APA, ASPPB, and the APA Insurance Trust to facilitate telehealth and temporary face-to-face practice of psychology across jurisdictional boundaries.

Steve DeMers, ASPPB's chief executive officer, and Martha Storie, ASPPB's president, envision that the PSYPACT will promote further cooperation and standardization of requirements among psychology licensing boards and consequently will serve to protect consumers of psychological services. An interstate compact is an agreement between states to enact legislation and enter into a contract for a specific, limited purpose or to address a particular policy issue. They are unique in their duality as statute and contract. ASPPB will be working with the Council of State Governments to create a resource kit to serve as an informational document in support of this development. The compact will standardize practices that are currently jurisdiction-specific, such as how many days of face-to-face practice are permitted in a state where the psychologist does not hold a license, and credentialing and authorization to practice telepsychology from an identified "home" state with a client in a state that has joined the compact. The PSYPACT would need to be adopted by state legislatures; the compact would establish further rules and regulations regarding interjurisdictional practice. The American Mental Health Counselors Association has advocated for similar standardization and clarification of licensure, training, and payer recognition of mental health counselors in all 50 states (Colangelo, 2009).

Policy advances at the federal level are often followed by the private sector, and an increasing number of state legislatures have recently begun requiring insurance companies to pay for telehealth (i.e., telepsychology) services. In 2015, more than 200 telehealth bills were introduced in state legislatures. As of 2016, 29 states and the District of Columbia had enacted parity laws that require insurers to reimburse telehealth providers exactly as they would for an in-person visit.

Historically, it has been the responsibility of the various states to determine the conditions under which healthcare providers may practice (including what their educational requirements will be and which services can be provided) within their geographic boundaries. This has, not surprisingly, resulted in a variety of restrictions on non-physician providers (for political reasons), notwithstanding the lack of any supporting objective evidence. Accordingly, with the advent of increasingly sophisticated technology and the excellent quality of care being demonstrated in the federal system, societal pressure has been steadily building to make legislative adjustments that would allow the expansion of necessary clinical expertise across historical geographic boundaries. Interestingly, back in 1998, the Pew Health Professions Commission had raised the underlying issue of whether the nation was ready to enact national health professions licensure laws (O'Neil, 1998).

The compact approach in psychology is developing and is conceptually very similar to that being proposed by professional nursing (adopted by 25 states) and organized medicine (currently 11 states, with more expected over the next year); physical therapy and emergency medical technicians are also exploring this approach. ASPPB had received a grant from the Health Resources and Services Administration (HRSA) to facilitate its efforts to address licensure mobility, with telepsychology representing one aspect of this larger vision. Change always takes considerable time, and as the various health professions experiment with their implementation and political details, modifications will undoubtedly evolve.

# REGULATIONS

Practice regulation is statutorily defined by state legislatures with oversight provided by practice boards. Practice boards determine scope of practice, specific rules and regulations, and licensure requirements, so the membership of these boards is critical. The agendas of the individuals or organizations represented on these boards can have far-reaching impact on clinical practice. As mentioned earlier, compact agreements are working to create consistency, reciprocity, and geographic parity of scope and quality of care. However, while such reciprocity is defined nationally, it is interpreted locally. One example within social work is that the number of internship/supervised hours needed for licensure varies state by state, and those hours are not necessarily recognized or transferable by or between states. In another example, Maryland is a compact state for nursing. This means that Maryland recognizes registered nurse (RN) licensure from other compact states. However, an RN who moves to Maryland from a compact state and wishes to practice in Maryland will need to obtain Maryland licensure as an RN and not simply renew his or her RN license from the compact state. Knowing who controls the legislative process that sets criteria for and scope of practice is critical, as well as who has routine oversight and regulation of the legislated practice.

Along similar lines, mental health professionals of all backgrounds are subject to regulatory control at the state level (Colangelo, 2009). Additionally, organizations like the National Association of State Mental Health Program Directors (2014) seek parity of recognition, oversight, and payment between mental health and other health providers.

As parity of payment and access are critical subjects for groups lobbying on behalf of mental health providers, it is logical to view other non-physician provider groups' reports and advocacy as a societal and policy "canary in the coalmine" to indicate policy trends. For example, the importance of identifying and monitoring regulation of practice can be seen through Federal Trade Commission's report on competition and regulation (Gillman & Koslov, 2014). This report (the focus was on advanced practice registered nurses, but the statement has implications for behavioral health providers) states that regulation of scope of practice should be set to provide healthcare consumers with the best and safest care. However, regulations that limit or set up barriers to practice that are not based in evidence can create harm and potential healthcare disparities for the very people the legislation is intended to protect. One provider group's fears and agenda are not evidence sufficient to limit the practice parameters of another group. The Federal Trade Commission approaches regulation of practice from a marketplace perspective wherein a larger spectrum of qualified providers creates a competitive arena in which patients and communities benefit from choice. Regulation is then a point within social policy where the regional need for healthcare services, legislated scope, and credentialing and broader national forces meet to create practice.

## PAYERS

Another facet of social policy involves those who pay for healthcare resources. President Obama's landmark Patient Protection and Affordable Care Act (ACA) envisions the development of unified *systems* of coordinated care (e.g., accountable care organizations and patient-centered medical homes) that would provide comprehensive care, including mental health care, for all their enrollees. Those administering the implementation of ACA envision an era of hospitals and other larger health organizations "buying up" smaller private practices to create accountable care organizations. For some, this will be reminiscent of the health maintenance organizations of President Richard Nixon's era and the managed care focus of President Bill Clinton's administration. Capitalizing on the advances in communications technology, electronic health records would ensure that clinicians have ready access to all aspects of their patients' health records. Mental health services would be fully integrated into primary care and would no longer be viewed as a "standalone specialty." Further, the ACA provides significant resources for interdisciplinary training efforts, with additional financial support for research targeting modifications in the federal reimbursement system (i.e., Medicaid and Medicaid) that will be necessary to provide coverage for this care, including faculty supervision of trainees. Historically, Medicaid has been the single largest payer for mental health services. The ACA has also created stipulations for the need for adequate coverage; specifics are determined by the states and the various managed care plans.

Those with a broader public health perspective can appreciate that the ACA's emphasis upon interdisciplinary (or interprofessional) collaboration was not developed in a policy vacuum but instead is based on changing societal dynamics and considerable thoughtful deliberation among national health policy experts, such as those within the Institute of Medicine (recently renamed the National Academy of Medicine). In 2015, the Institute of Medicine released its report on inter-professional education, noting that

> [i]nnovators at that time [2002] stressed the importance of "patient-centered care," while today they think of patients as partners in health promotion and health care delivery. Patients are integral members of the health care team, not solely patients to be treated, and the team is recognized as comprising a variety of health professionals. This changed thinking is the culmination of many social, economic, and technological factors that are transforming the world and forcing the fields of both health care and education to rethink long-established organizational models. (p. xv)

Also,

> Widespread adoption of a model of inter-professional education across the learning continuum is urgently needed. An ideal model would retain the tenets of professional identity formation while providing robust opportunities for inter-professional education and collaborative care. Such a model also would differentiate between learning outcomes per se and the individual, population, and system outcomes that provide the ultimate rationale for ongoing investment in health professions education (Institute of Medicine, 2015, pp. xv–xvi)

To a very real extent, this evolution toward direct involvement by patients in shaping their own individual healthcare undoubtedly reflects the increasing educational level of the nation's population (i.e., "educated consumers").

That need for interprofessional preparation and the expectation that mental health will be an integral part of the care team raises again the need for parity in patient access as well as reimbursement. Mental health agencies and programs can draw from the experiences of clinical pharmacy, which has been in the forefront of this movement. The efforts of the School of Pharmacy at North Dakota State University are a prime example:

> With more than 80 telepharmacy sites in the state, it is one of the largest (if not the largest) telepharmacy networks in the U.S., if not the world. Thirty-six of North Dakota's 53 counties are designated by Health and Human Services as "frontier counties" which is defined as less than six people per square mile. So we are very rural and have a very large geographic area that is considered "medically underserved" with many people having problems accessing even basic health care. Telepharmacy has worked very well for us. It has established or restored access to pharmacists and pharmacy services in areas of the state that had no services or had lost their services. The North Dakota Board of Pharmacy established rules for telepharmacy practice that are now the standard of practice in delivering pharmacy services to remote rural communities. Our research has demonstrated that the quality of services being delivered through telepharmacy vs traditional pharmacy services is the same including medication error rates. All telepharmacy sites are receiving standard reimbursement for pharmacy services from third party payers and federal programs and all sites are still up

and operational, not one has been lost, so our model has demonstrated that it is economically viable and sustainable. Telepharmacy has increased the profit margins of pharmacists practicing in rural locations thus keeping our rural pharmacy businesses strong. We have developed our telepharmacy services in both community and hospital settings. We have developed a mobile wireless telepharmacy unit (R2D2 robot) for critical access hospitals that can provide 24-hour access to a pharmacist to any location in the hospital (emergency room, nursing station, patient bedside, pharmacy). (Dean Charles Peterson, personal communication, November 2015)

Mental health clinicians of all disciplines, particularly those in rural America, will soon be faced with the challenge of being responsive to the changing expectations (i.e., demands) of increasingly educated consumers/patients who have experienced the willingness on the part of other healthcare providers to be responsive to their individual circumstances. Effective clinicians of the 21st century will have to be demonstrably aware of the evolving practice patterns of the entire healthcare system, not just their own professional specialty.

# DELIVERY SYSTEM

Attempts to meet growing consumer, economic, and political demands for healthcare must include building more efficient combinations of healthcare providers and healthcare delivery models. For example, access to basic healthcare for most underserved and vulnerable groups falls under the HRSA, an agency of the U.S. Department of Health and Human Services. The ACA endorses key expansion of components of the HRSA-supported safety-net clinics for these underserved groups. The Health Center Program, the National Health Service Corps, and other forms of health workforce programs are key components of how the ACA is shaping delivery models to meet increasing demands on an already burgeoning healthcare system. These changes are significant, as the introduction of the ACA potentially adds about 3 million newly insured patients representing impoverished populations, underserved minorities, residents of rural areas, and populations with language barriers (HRSA, 2015). While these changes will bring about an increased demand for primary care providers and delivery systems, there is estimated to be a shortage of primary care physicians of over 7,550 by 2025 (Auerbach et al., 2013). This lack of access to primary care is also associated with over 9 million costly non-urgent visits to emergency departments in the United States every year (Auerbach et al., 2013).

The implications for mental health providers are just as startling. ACA mandates adequacy of care, and Massachusetts Commonwealth Care is an example of how this is interpreted by states (Miller, Gordon, & Blover, 2014). Adequacy of behavioral health care consists of a choice of at least two providers who are within 60 minutes or 60 miles, among other provisions. These provisions do not create additional providers but do fund access, leading to a need to find new models to do more with less.

Healthcare policy change through the ACA has kick-started innovative changes to healthcare delivery models and opened windows for alternate provider types such as nurse practitioners and physician assistants. This is a particularly salient point for mental health providers as it signals an expansion of the healthcare team beyond a physician-driven and fee-for-service model. A major concern influencing some change has been the overreliance on costlier, less efficient specialty care services to the detriment of primary care delivery models (Naylor, 2006). Nurse practitioners, practicing independently or with physicians in primary care, are uniquely prepared to offer alternate healthcare delivery models, especially in community settings less favored by traditional medical practices (U.S. Government and Accountability Office, 2008). Use of these diverse provider mixes and alternate models of healthcare delivery has the potential to improve access to primary care, decrease costs, and change healthcare patterns in the United States (U.S. Government and Accountability Office, 2008).

Capitalizing on the availability of a diversity of potential healthcare delivery models, the ACA explicitly included nurse practitioners as providers in multiple sections. These changes implemented by the ACA have great potential to influence the delivery of healthcare, especially in underserved areas. These ACA programs specific to nurse practitioners include a test program for a payment incentive and service delivery model that uses physician- and nurse practitioner-directed home-based primary care (Section 1866D), a 10% Medicare bonus payment for primary care providers in underserved locations (Section 5501), and funds to support nurse-managed clinics (Section 5208). Mental health providers would do well to monitor these non-physician–driven models as the models will be able to provide a basis for parity and a practice template.

As defined by the ACA, a nurse-managed health clinic is "a nurse practice arrangement, managed by advanced practice nurses, that provides primary care or wellness services to underserved or vulnerable populations and that is associated with a school, college, university or department of nursing, federally qualified health center, or independent health or social services agency" (42 U.S.C. § 330A–1, 2010). These nurse-managed clinics, also referred to as nurse-managed health centers, provide primary care, management of chronic diseases, family and reproductive health, disease prevention, and health promotion to vulnerable populations in multiple venues in underserved areas. These clinics also contain multidisciplinary members such as psychologists, community outreach workers, consulting physicians, and researchers and also are linked with local universities to fill an additional role in training future health professionals.

The National Nursing Centers Consortium is a nonprofit organization that supports over 250 successful nurse-managed health centers. Over 2.5 million patients from vulnerable urban and rural neighborhoods are served by these centers. Services are based on community needs and are accessed through close cooperation with community members and outreach workers.

Another alternative model of delivering primary healthcare is a walk-in clinic run by nurses. These clinics, which have been implemented in some areas, can decrease costs for patients and healthcare systems while expanding access to quality care. These clinics also reduce the burden placed on emergency departments in terms of both volume and patient safety. A study in California found that emergency department crowding was associated with significant increases in mortality, length of stay, and cost, supporting the need to divert these non-urgent visits to a more appropriate level of care (Sun et al., 2013). From an economic perspective, a nurse-run walk-in clinic in Rhode Island treated non-urgent medical issues with an average return on investment of over $2 for every $1 spent. When preventive services were included in the equation, the return increased to $34 for every $1 invested, as compared to using emergency departments for these non-urgent services (Bicki et al., 2013).

As the ACA is implemented, millions of patients will enter the healthcare system, increasing the demand on already stressed delivery models. Evolving healthcare delivery models must provide vital, expeditious, and cost-effective care while addressing the shortage of primary care physicians. Healthcare centers recognize the need to provide comprehensive care tailored to unique patient population needs and the need to decrease expensive and inappropriate levels of care. Healthcare systems with the appropriate mixture of providers and the utilization of alternate delivery models, such as nurse-run clinics, offer a mechanism for reducing burdens on healthcare resources while meeting patient care needs.

# INTERPROFESSIONAL PRACTICE

All Western healthcare fields are exhibiting shifts toward complexity and systems interconnectedness. The past 30 years have seen the rise of the field of psychoneuroimmunology, advances in therapies for psychiatric trauma, and a veritable explosion of psychotropic medications. With the variety of these clinical tools comes a variety of clinicians with expertise to wield them and a marketplace and legislative dictate to use them comprehensively. Just as ACA is expanding and redefining care delivery systems, it is also giving providers the opportunities to redefine clinical practice. That redefinition begins with training.

As a result of the visionary efforts of Don Peterson and Nick Cummings, psychology's professional school movement began in the late 1960s. By 2016, there were 379 APA-accredited graduate programs (clinical, counseling, school, and combined), more than 70 of which would be considered professional programs (most granting the PsyD degree). These programs now graduate the majority of the nation's psychology practitioners. Under the newly adopted APA accreditation standards, they will soon be called "programs in health service psychology." Only recently, however, has there been any concerted effort to foster a culture of interdisciplinary collaboration within psychology's training initiatives. One notable exception is the efforts of Gill Newman at the Wright Institute, which emphasizes training within its local community health center network—a national program established by President Lyndon Johnson as a component of his Great Society legacy. We would suggest that most clinicians, even those being trained today, have not been exposed to the language, culture, and expertise of other mental health disciplines, particularly during their formative years. Nevertheless, as a direct result of federal legislation, we expect that this landscape will dramatically change over the next five to 10 years.

Partnerships are now not looking for transmission between specialty silos of care but are expanding beyond geographic and historical boundaries into more complex and comprehensive structures. Embedded and co-located mental and physical health services, pharmacy as a part of primary care visits, email correspondence, and electronic transmission of real-time data are all part of current practice, as previous discussions of telepsychology and telepharmacy have emphasized. A solo provider will have an increasingly difficult if not impossible task given the emphasis by the healthcare system, payers, and the government on quality, comprehensive care. For example, if it is to survive, a solo or specialty niche practice must draw patients from a source and account for a continuum of care from chronic to acute and along the lifespan. These niche practices may also benefit from individuals who want to create their own path forward and are willing to pay out of pocket for all services. Each visit must reflect current standards of care, must be clearly documented, and must be accurately coded and submitted for reimbursement.

## SUMMARY

Social policy, the political aspect of healthcare, includes legislation (historical and contemporary), regulations, payers, delivery systems, and interdisciplinary collaboration. Each of these informs the others and derives priorities from population, institutional, historical, or economic influences. While not an exhaustive list, these particular aspects are critical to shaping clinical practice. Mental health providers have unprecedented opportunities for regulatory and reimbursement parity with physical health professionals and would do well to learn from them. During this tumultuous time, mental health providers must always keep in mind that clinical practitioners either can help shape policy or must be content to be shaped by others.

## REFERENCES

Auerbach, D. I., Chen, P. G., Friedberg, M. W., Reid, R., Lau, C., Buerhaus, P. I., & Mehrotra, A. (2013). Nurse-managed health centers and patient-centered medical homes could mitigate expected primary care physician shortage. *Health Affairs, 32*(11), 1933–1941. doi:10.1377/hlthaff.2013.0596.

Bicki, A., Silva, A., Joseph, V., Handoko, R., Rico, S.-v., Burns, J., . . . Groot, A. S. (2013). A nurse-run walk-in clinic: Cost-effective alternative to non-urgent emergency department use by the uninsured. *Journal of Community Health, 38*(6), 1042–1049. doi:10.1007/s10900-013-9712-y.

Bush, G. W. (2004, April 27). Remarks in a discussion on the benefits of health care information technology in Baltimore, Maryland. *Weekly Compilation of Presidential Documents, 40*(18), 697–702.

Colangelo, J. J. (2009). The American Mental Health Counselors Association: Reflection on 30 historic years. *Journal of Counseling & Development, 87*(2), 234–240. http://doi.org/10.1002/j.1556-6678.2009.tb00572.x

Gillman, D., & Koslov, T. (2014). *Policy perspectives: Competition and the regulation of advanced practice nurses.* Washington, DC: Federal Trade Commission.

HRSA. (2015). Shortage designation: Health professional shortage areas and medically underserved areas and populations. Retrieved from http://www.hrsa.gov/shortage/.

Institute of Medicine. (2015). *Measuring the impact of interprofessional education on collaborative practice and patient outcomes.* Washington, DC: National Academies Press.

Midgley, J., & Livermore, M. (Eds.). (2009). *The handbook of social policy* (2nd ed.). Thousand Oaks, CA: Sage Publications, Inc.

Miller, J., Gordon, S., & Blover, R. (2014). *Striking a balance: Mental health provider network adequacy under health care reform* (ACA Implementation No. 7). Alexandria, VA: National Association of State Mental Health Program Directors.

National Association of State Mental Health Program Directors. (2014). *Parity implementation: A state best practices guide* (No. 6b). Alexandria, VA: National Association of State Mental Health Program Directors.

Naylor, M. (2006) Transitional care: A critical dimension of home healthcare quality agenda. *Journal for Healthcare Quality, National Association for Healthcare Quality, 28*(1), 20–28.

O'Neil, E. H., & the Pew Health Professions Commission. (December, 1998). *Recreating health professional practice for a new century: The fourth report of the Pew Health Professions Commission.* San Francisco: Pew Health Professions Commission.

Patient Protection and Affordable Care Act (ACA). [P.L. 111-148]. (HR 3590). (March 23, 2010).

Sun, B. C., Hsia, R. Y., Weiss, R. E., Zingmond, D., Liang, L.-J., Han, W., . . . Asch, S. M. (2013). Effect of emergency department crowding on outcomes of admitted patients. *Annals of Emergency Medicine, 61*(6), 605–611. doi:10.1016/j.annemergmed.2012.10.026.

U.S. Government and Accountability Office. (2008). *Primary care professionals: Recent supply trends, projections, and valuation of services.* Report #GAO-08-472T. Retrieved from http:/www.gao.gov/new.items/d08472t.pdf.

# SECTION 2

## NICHE CHAPTERS

# ASSESSMENT AND EVALUATION SERVICES

# CHAPTER 48

# CHILD CUSTODY EVALUATIONS

*Allison B. Hill*

I completed a joint JD/PhD program at Villanova University and Drexel University, with the hope of having a private forensic practice. My graduate training was in Philadelphia, Pennsylvania, and for personal reasons I found myself moving to Atlanta, Georgia, for internship and postdoctoral residency. I completed my internship at Emory School of Medicine/Grady Health Center. Although my graduate training and internship had a great deal of training in criminal forensic settings, I had not had a great deal of training in civil forensic settings, or child custody, which was an area of interest of mine. Given that, I wanted to ensure my postdoctoral residency had some child custody training. I decided to do two postdoctoral residencies, one at Emory and another with a private practice group that had a specialty in child custody evaluations.

Following my postdoctoral year, the practice I had been working with had an extra office available to rent and offered it to me. I decided to rent the office and open a full-time private practice. At the time I started renting office space, there were six other professionals in the office space—five with PhDs in clinical psychology, one with a JD and an LCSW. Many of the other professionals were involved in working with families in transition—child custody evaluations, parental fitness evaluations, parent coordination, co-parent counseling, and psychotherapy with adults and children in families going through a divorce. In the beginning, the office I was renting was available only for three days a week. As my practice grew and I needed more time in the office, I rented temporarily at a second location. When the initial location had availability five days a week, I moved my practice to one location permanently and have remained there ever since in Atlanta.

## THE NICHE PRACTICE ACTIVITY

There have been many changes to divorce rules and precedents, and this has led to the increased involvement by mental health professionals in child custody disputes to evaluate parenting strengths and weaknesses of the parties involved in the custody disputes. Often termed child custody evaluations, these typically involve evaluations of the parents and children. These evaluations require a tremendous amount of commitment and effort and are more time-consuming than typical evaluations—even other forensic evaluations.

Child custody evaluations are almost always court-ordered and are comprehensive. The most commonly used procedures include parent interviews, interviews with the children, psychological testing of the parents and children, parent–child observations, interviewing of significant others and collateral contacts, document review (e.g., police and medical records), and report writing. Some evaluators use home visits to assess parent–child interaction. Some evaluators conduct an initial conjoint session with both parents.

Child custody evaluations must include assessments of the following: (1) each parent and significant others, (2) personal histories of each parent, (3) parenting skills, (4) each parent's ability to meet the child's needs, and (5) the stability of the living situation provided by each parent. At times, such assessment involves the use of psychological testing; the tests used vary. Bow (2006) surveyed mental health professionals who conduct child custody evaluations regarding the assessment techniques they most frequently use and found that the test most frequently used for adults in child custody evaluations is the Minnesota Multiphasic Personality Inventory-2 (MMPI-2). Use of the Millon Multiaxial Personality Inventory-III is more mixed, but it is also widely used. The Rorschach Projective Method is consistently used by some evaluators and is the most popular projective technique. Parenting inventories (e.g., Parent-Child Relationship Inventory and Parenting Stress Index) were also often used in these evaluations, and at times parent rating scales were used (e.g., the Child Behavior Checklist and Conner's Parent Rating Scale). Bow (2006) emphasized that although testing is not required in a custody evaluation, it is an important way to generate and test hypotheses in these evaluations and to ensure the evaluator is not falling prey to bias.

Child custody evaluators must have a good awareness of forensic versus psychotherapeutic roles, and these roles should not be mixed. The primary difference involves expectations of confidentiality. There is no expectation of confidentiality in the relationship when the psychologist is acting in a forensic role; this differs from the expectation of confidentiality in a therapeutic context and the more traditional therapeutic privilege. This distinction should be made clear to clients during the informed consent procedure. Additional differences include "the amount of scrutiny applied to the data, the degree of structure and control in an evaluation, the goal of the relationship, the cognitive set (supportive/empathetic v. objective/investigative), and whom the evaluator is serving (patient v. court/litigant)" (Bow & Martindale, 2009, p. 129).

Child custody evaluators must also be aware of many areas of mental health—most importantly family dynamics and child development. There is a particular need for evaluators to be aware of domestic violence, child abuse and neglect, and safety issues in high-conflict divorce cases (Bow, 2006). Some evaluations involve special allegations and concerns such as sexual abuse, substance abuse, child development, alienation, and serious mental health problems.

Most evaluators offer explicit recommendations about custody and visitation at the end of their evaluations. This issue remains hotly debated (Tippins & Wittmann, 2005). Psychologists disagree as to whether they should testify about the ultimate question or issue before the presiding judge (e.g., who should have custody of the child) as that is ultimately up to the discretion of the fact finder—the court. In my jurisdiction, many of the judges request that psychologists do offer a recommendation on custody. At times, additional supplementary interventions and recommendations are offered as well—for example, individual psychotherapy, family therapy, child psychotherapy, or co-parenting counseling.

Finally, the child custody report is one of the most important aspects of this practice. Some evaluators, myself included, use a classic report format. The reports are comprehensive and use multiple sources of data to support conclusions and recommendations. As you do in the initial meetings with the clients during the informed consent process, in the report it is important to document a statement of understanding, which informs the participants of the limits of confidentiality. It is important also to include a clinical description of the parents, including their mental status at the time of the evaluation; to provide a child history, including any special or developmental considerations; and to include information about the parent–child observation, specifically noting any observed factors that may impact each parent's parenting ability.

# DEVELOPING AN INTEREST AND TRAINING IN THIS NICHE ACTIVITY

There are different paths to doing this type of work. Many evaluators I have spoken with began doing child custody work as an extension of a previous forensic practice. Other evaluators received a referral for an evaluation and began to look into this area to see if it might be of interest to them. Practitioners with an interest in children and families may also find themselves involved with families in transition or going through a divorce in a different context (e.g., therapy), which may also lead them to consider beginning to conduct child custody evaluations. An interest in children and families is certainly an asset to this type of practice.

The referral source for these evaluations is most likely to be judges and attorneys, so it is important to get to know the judges and attorneys in your area. For networking, it is important to get involved in the state bar association, particularly the family law section. As you grow your practice, it is important to network at continuing education seminars and workshops and local state bar events; you could volunteer to speak at state bar events about topics that attorneys are less familiar with, such as child development and child interviewing. It is important to have a good understanding of the needs and desires of the legal profession in this area. Evaluators also need to be aware of their state statutes and administrative codes regarding family law and child custody (Bow, 2006).

Although it is important for graduate studies training to provide strong clinical foundational training, the majority of child custody evaluators have not received specific training in graduate school or internship/postdoctoral training in the area of child custody. Therefore, it is important to seek additional training via seminars, workshops, books, journal articles, and supervision/consultation.

Several professional organizations have developed child custody guidelines and parameters that provide direction for child custody evaluators. Among others, these include the American Psychological Association's *Ethical Principles of Psychologists and Code of Conduct* (2003) and *Guidelines for Child Custody Evaluations in Divorce Proceedings* (2010), and the Association of Family and Conciliation Courts' *Model Standards of Practice for Child Custody Evaluation* (2006). It is important to be familiar with, and follow the dictates of, these guidelines and parameters.

Some states (California) have instituted mandatory training for child custody evaluators, but that is not the case where I practice in Georgia. However, I had direct supervision on each of my cases during my first year and continue to meet with a consultation group monthly to ask questions regarding ongoing evaluations. I would encourage anyone performing child custody evaluations to have a good, collaborative consultation group with whom to discuss latest research findings and current cases.

## JOYS AND CHALLENGES RELATED TO THIS NICHE ACTIVITY

As with many areas of niche practice, there are joys and challenges related to the practice of child custody evaluation. One of the joys is knowing that you are assisting a family during a time of tremendous need. Often, the litigants are highly stressed and overwhelmed, and you have the ability to provide insight to the court on a family system and how it functioned before and during the litigation, and make a recommendation of what will be best for the family after the litigation. Child custody evaluators have a professional duty and ethical obligation to the court and the families they serve and must take this responsibility seriously. These evaluations require a tremendous amount of commitment and effort because of the amount of information that must be considered, reviewed, and presented to the court.

In terms of challenges, child custody cases are litigious and adversarial in nature. Many parties are not happy with the outcome of the child custody evaluation. Given that, child custody evaluations are high risk for evaluators—there is often a threat of malpractice suits and board and ethics complaints, and the evaluations themselves are highly complex. Most child custody evaluators should anticipate an eventual and inevitable complaint (Bow & Martindale, 2009). The high number of board and ethics complaints and malpractice suits makes it important to consistently and frequently examine your practices and procedures. Given this, in addition to ensuring you receive appropriate training and comply with guidelines and standards, as mentioned above, it is important to have other professionals with whom you may collaborate.

## BUSINESS ASPECTS OF THIS NICHE ACTIVITY

The business aspect of child custody evaluations is challenging. Many referrals come from legal professionals—judges and attorneys. Studies have found that attorneys rate the following characteristics of an expert as very important: an unbiased approach, experience in conducting child custody evaluations, communication skills, professional presentation, competence and fairness, good credentials, licensed/board certified, good witness, timely, cooperative, and flexible (Bow & Quinnell, 2002; LaFortune, 1997). Custody evaluators must maintain a neutral, unbiased role in the work being performed as that is clearly a characteristic that is valued and will likely lead to more referrals.

These evaluations are not covered by insurance, so parties must always privately pay. Although I take an initial retainer, the costs of the evaluation tend to accrue over time. I request a replenishment of funds at various times, but there is generally a balance due when I finish my report. I do not release my report until my fees have been paid in full. This is particularly important because, as mentioned above, often at least one party is not happy with your recommendation and the outcome of the evaluation. This information should also be included in the informed consent agreement clients sign at the start of the evaluation.

Given the litigious nature of this work, it is important to check with your malpractice insurance carrier to ensure you are covered for work done in this area, have good malpractice insurance, maintain detailed and thorough paperwork, and document all interviews and communications. Most evaluations are done via court order, which should outline the referral questions, the procedures to be used, who is responsible for fees, and how those fees are to be paid. It is important to take a retainer for 10 to 15 hours per party of work up front and request for replenishments as needed.

It is important to keep track of your billing. Send billing statements regularly and ensure that the documentation of your billing is up to date and professional. As noted above, insurance does not cover these types of evaluations, and this is an important point to highlight to the participants, who tend to become increasingly frustrated by the costs of the evaluation as the process progresses. In my practice, I accept cash, check, or credit card.

# DEVELOPING THIS NICHE ACTIVITY INTO A PRACTICE STRATEGY

Developing adequate expertise in these evaluations can be overwhelming as they involve many areas of psychology—child and adolescent development and psychopathology, adult adjustment and psychopathology, family systems, impact of and adjustment to divorce, and post-divorce planning (Bow & Martindale, 2009).

It is important to establish your method, your testing battery, and a rationale for each testing measure you will use. As noted earlier, I encourage you to find a mentor or consultation group to meet with regularly. To stay up to date on current trends, best practices, and literature, attend conferences, seminars, and workshops in the area of child custody and read relevant articles, journals, and books. Finally, continue to get training on other supplemental but important areas involved in this work, to include domestic violence, child abuse, substance use, and parental alienation.

Keep child custody work as a portion of your practice while providing other services, even other services involving families in transition or going through divorce, such as psychotherapy, psychological testing, parent coordination, co-parent counseling, and reunification therapy. It can be difficult to devote an entire practice to child custody work, given the intensity and demanding nature of the work. Having a well-rounded practice will allow you to draw from relevant clinical experiences when evaluating a family system; however, make sure you do not engage in dual roles within one particular family. When approached for work with a given family, clarify your role at the outset and do not change roles. If you perform a child custody evaluation for a family, you may not subsequently engage in therapeutic or consultation services for that family.

# FOR MORE INFORMATION

There are many resources available to those interested in child custody work. I would recommend joining the Association of Family and Conciliation Courts. The journals I would recommend include *Family Court Review, Behavioral Sciences and the Law, Journal of Child Custody*, and *Journal of Forensic Psychology Practice*. Some excellent books are listed below.

# RESOURCES AND REFERENCES

Bow, J. N. (2006). Review of empirical research on child custody practice. *Journal of Child Custody, 3*, 23–50.

Bow, J. N., & Martindale, D. A. (2009). Developing and managing a child custody practice. *Journal of Forensic Psychology Practice, 9*, 127–137.

Bow, J. N., & Quinnell, F. A. (2002). A critical review of child custody evaluation reports. *Family Court Review, 40*, 164–176.

Drozd, L., Saini, M., & Olesen, N. (2016). *Parenting plan evaluations* (2nd ed.). New York: Oxford University Press.

Gould, J. (1998). *Conducting scientifically crafted child custody evaluations.* Thousand Oaks, CA: Sage Publications.

Gould, J. W., & Martindale, D. A. (2007). *The art and science of child custody evaluations.* New York: Guilford Press.

Johnston, J. R., Roseby, V., & Kuehnle, K. (2009). *In the name of the child: A developmental approach to understanding and helping children of conflicted and violent divorce.* New York: Springer.

Kelly, J. (1994). The determination of child custody. In *The future of children: Children & divorce.* Los Altos, CA: The David and Lucille Packard Foundation.

LaFortune, K. A. (1997). An investigation of mental health and legal professionals' activities, beliefs, and experiences in domestic courts: An interdisciplinary survey. Unpublished doctoral dissertation. University of Tulsa, OK.

Otto, R., & Collins, R. (1995). Use of the MMPI-2/MMPI-A in child custody evaluations. In Y. Ben-Porath, J. Graham, G. Hall, R. Hirschman, & M. Zaragoza (Eds.), *Forensic applications of the MMPI-2* (pp. 222–252). Thousand Oaks, CA: Sage Publications.

Schutz, B. M., Dixon, E. B., Lindenberger, J. C., & Ruther, N. J. (1989). *Solomon's sword: A practical guide to conducting child custody evaluations.* San Francisco, CA: Jossey-Bass.

Stahl, P. (1994). *Conducting child custody evaluations.* Thousand Oaks, CA: Sage Publications.

Stahl, P. (1999). *Complex issues in child custody evaluations.* Thousand Oaks, CA: Sage Publications.

Tippins, T. M., & Wittmann, J. P. (2005). Empirical and ethical problems with custody recommendations: A call for clinical humility and judicial vigilance. *Family Court Review, 43*, 193–222.

# CHAPTER 49

# PERSONAL INJURY EVALUATIONS

*William E. Foote*

I have been in private practice as a forensic psychologist in Albuquerque, New Mexico, since the late 1970s. Early in my practice, I felt obliged to take many kinds of cases, but, over time, my practice narrowed to several areas, including conducting evaluations of plaintiffs in personal injury (PI) cases. These evaluations now occupy about half of my practice, although they account for a larger proportion of my income, as fees are less limited in the tort arena than in criminal and other cases. It is also the case that fees for forensic work are significantly higher than those for psychotherapy, without the additional paperwork and headaches associated with obtaining payment from insurance companies and government payers.

For almost my entire career I have had an office in a suite that I have shared with other psychologists. I like the camaraderie as well as sharing office and administrative expenses with others. I have preferred office contexts in which other forensic psychologists are practicing because of the opportunity for "curbside consults," which allows for getting quick feedback on the sometimes perplexing practice of forensic psychology. My office has two comfortable chairs that I use for the interview portion of the evaluation, and a large table that I use for some testing and for consultations with lawyers and the occasional deposition. I take notes on my laptop, and I am usually able to keep up with any but the most manic evaluee.

## THE NICHE PRACTICE ACTIVITY

PI evaluations usually occur in the context of tort law. This is a part of civil law that allows for disputes between individuals to be settled through a legal process. In PI cases, the plaintiff (the person alleging that he or she was injured or harmed) is suing the defendant (or tortfeasor, in traditional language), who the plaintiff alleges is legally responsible for the harm or injury to the plaintiff. For the plaintiffs in tort cases to prevail they must prove four things: (1) the defendant owed a legal duty to the plaintiff; (2) the defendant breached that duty (by doing something that should not have been done, or failing to do something that should have been done); (3) that breach caused harm to the plaintiff; and (4) that harm produced compensable damages.

The psychologist's role in PI cases is usually to provide evidence on the last two issues. Psychological evaluation can help the finder of fact (jury and/or judge) to determine whether the actions or inaction of the defendant caused the alleged harms to the plaintiff. In some cases, these harms have no legal remedy. In others, the psychologist may assist the court by providing a prognosis and a course of treatment or other interventions that may assist the plaintiff to recover from the harms caused by the defendant.

## DEVELOPING AN INTEREST AND TRAINING IN THIS NICHE ACTIVITY

I came to forensic psychology early in my training. My first clinical assistantship was a position at the New Mexico State Penitentiary in Santa Fe (about 60 miles from Albuquerque). That was an eye-opener if there ever was one, but I had good supervision and learned how to use psychological testing and write a coherent evaluation report. My other graduate school experiences included a year on the rehabilitation ward of a local hospital, which was my introduction to the psychological consequences of physical injuries. I was lucky enough to get one of the few (at that time) forensic psychology internships, at Atascadero State Hospital in California. I had excellent supervision and learned even more about the use of testing and the art of preparing a good report. After that I was hired by the New Mexico State Department of Vocational Rehabilitation and worked there during my postdoctoral supervision years. Once I was licensed, the agency allowed me to cut to half-time work for about six months while I was building my practice with the assistance of a senior psychologist who mentored me into the private practice of forensic psychology. I shared offices with him for about 10 years while my practice grew.

My first referral on a PI case came shortly after I started my practice, when a plaintiff's lawyer asked me to evaluate a young man who had suffered serious spinal cord injuries as a result of an auto accident. The lawyer who hired me in the case knew that I was a "baby psychologist" and helped me understand enough of the law to be able to work on his case. I was interested in learning more, so I read up on the personal injury case law in New Mexico and was able to use that information to write reports that met the legal requirements.

About that same time (the early 1980s) I focused on getting board certified in forensic psychology, which was (believe it or not) a new practice specialty at that time. I was certified by the American Board of Forensic Psychology in 1984. The learning process involved in preparing and submitting the work sample and passing the examination for the diplomate was very helpful in providing me not only with information about working in PI cases, but also with a broad base of understanding about the law and legal processes, which I have been able to use ever since.

# JOYS AND CHALLENGES RELATED TO THIS NICHE ACTIVITY

I have done thousands of PI evaluations over my long career. I have found a number of challenges in doing this work, including dealing with feigning and exaggeration, untangling complex issues of causation, time pressures, and the emotional toll of working with trauma.

Everyone who comes into the forensic psychologist's office wants a specific outcome, and in PI cases, that outcome is almost always a sizable financial award from the defendant. This provides substantial motivation for making up symptoms, exaggerating real problems, or attributing to the tortfeasor damages that were caused by something or someone else. This makes the PI evaluator's first job sorting out the real from the fabricated. That is why good training in the use of psychological assessment is critical. Without the use of testing, along with effective and comprehensive record review, good interviewing technique, and good skills at questioning collateral sources, you will be left with the plaintiff's account, which may be inaccurate. This skill is just as important for the psychologist working for the plaintiff's counsel as for the defense; both need to know if the presentation of the plaintiff is genuine and if the claimed damages are real and what caused them. I have attempted to maintain a practice in which I work for both civil defense and plaintiff's lawyers, and I have been largely successful. In fact, the most gratifying referrals have come from, for example, a defense lawyer who had recently cross-examined me in a case in which I had been hired by a plaintiff.

Everyone entering a forensic psychologist's office also has a history. A disproportionate number of those coming for PI evaluations suffered prior trauma in the form of child physical or sexual abuse or neglect. This provides a difficult but doable task for the PI evaluator. The job is to sort out the preexisting symptoms and problems from those caused by the event(s) that prompted the PI lawsuit. Again, testing, record review, and good interviewing are the tools to bring to bear in this task.

Using these tools sometimes takes extensive professional time. Depending on whether the PI case has been filed in state or federal court, the rules of civil procedure may have a timetable that places pressure on the psychologist to produce a report in a couple of weeks. This pressure is part of the job, but in some cases it creates problems. For example, in federal cases, the plaintiff must generally produce expert reports first. In some cases, this production happens early in the discovery process, before other relevant evidence, including depositions of the principals, can be produced. This means that the PI expert may have to ask to amend a report based upon data that only becomes available later.

It also means that the PI expert may have to deal with a lot of emotional challenges in a short time. One of the joys of working in PI cases is the brief but very intense work done with a plaintiff. After completing a good forensic evaluation with a plaintiff, the forensic psychologist knows that person better than almost anyone. In some cases, the plaintiff may reveal secrets that he or she has never told anyone else. I have specialized in working with plaintiffs who claim to have been sexually abused by teachers or clergy, and I have conducted hundreds of those evaluations. This work involved me asking very detailed questions about the abuse experiences of each plaintiff, which meant that I was vicariously exposed to each plaintiff's trauma.

Over the years, that vicarious traumatization took its toll, and I no longer accept those cases. The point is not to stay away from traumatic cases, but to take care of yourself when you do. One way to mitigate the emotional cost of this work is to try to have a mix of different kinds of cases so as to reduce the impact of carrying too many of these cases at one time. Talking with another professional is also part of the self-care regime, and getting support from significant others can really help.

If you are able to manage these stresses, you can enjoy the rewards inherent in this work, including learning about new aspects of psychology research, working with people who are not necessarily seeking treatment, being able to tell the story of people who often cannot speak effectively for themselves, and functioning as a "teacher" in the system.

Personal injuries come in many forms, ranging from near-miss auto accidents to rape and mutilation. Some of these events are relatively rare, and so even a mental health professional with an extensive forensic or psychotherapy career may not have ever seen one of these. I recall an instance early in my career when I was asked in two separate cases to evaluate men who had lost functioning in one eye. This forced me get the literature on the emotional consequences of losing an eye. I was surprised to find a reasonable literature on the topic and used it as a basis not only for areas to be explored in the evaluation process, but also for aspects of my report and testimony. The evaluation of trauma is a field that is constantly growing, with a complex and extensive literature. Keeping up with that science and relating that science to the impact of trauma on more or less normal people is part of the PI evaluator's job.

Forensic psychologists conducting evaluations with criminal defendants generally deal with people who are at the severe end of mental illness and personality disorder continua. Some of these people (at least the things they have done) are very unpleasant. Not so with PI plaintiffs: Most of these folks were plucked out of their relatively normal life by an accident or other trauma. Many, before they were injured, have had mostly normal histories and are doing their best to cope with the emotional and physical consequences of the events related to the tort. This can be refreshing and renew your optimism about humankind.

It also requires the PI evaluator to learn and tell all sorts of life stories. In some cases, PI plaintiffs cannot explain exactly what has happened to them. Even for those with no communication impairments, the job of telling how a traumatic event has affected their lives may be beyond a layperson's ability. It is an expert's job to put into terms that a jury and judge can understand the complexity of posttraumatic stress disorder and comorbid disorders and the course that these problems take—and you are the expert. This is an art, but one that can be mastered and is very satisfying.

The art of telling this story means that the PI evaluator is also asked to teach the lawyers, judges, and juries about emotional reactions to traumatic events. This brings to bear skills common to good teachers—simplifying complex information, providing a cognitive framework to understand emotional reactions, and summarizing extensive research. When the mental health professional leaves the courtroom, if the job has been done well, everyone there knows more about the psychology of personal injuries, and how that psychology played out in the plaintiff's life. That takes expertise.

# BUSINESS ASPECTS OF THIS NICHE ACTIVITY

### REFERRALS

Forensic psychology is all about one's expertise—that is, the expert is hired because he or she knows more when it comes to this type of situation than the average psychologist. This means that potential customers (read lawyers or judges) have to know how much you know in order to see you as a potential witness. Lawyers learn about experts mostly by word of mouth. With social media and the Internet, that word of mouth is often quick and widespread. Most of my new referrals come from lawyers who have heard about me from other lawyers, have read about me on a lawyer listserv, or have seen my name mentioned in a case that went up for appeal or was otherwise published in legal literature. I cultivate my referral sources and often will ask a new referral from what source my name was obtained. That will give me an opportunity to personally thank the referring legal professional. I also will often call a lawyer after I testify to determine if there are things that I could improve in my preparation or court testimony.

Another small point—be nice to paralegals and secretaries. Not only do they make sure you can contact the lawyer when you really need to, they will sometimes chat up your name when a case comes into the office. That free marketing may pay off in your financial bottom line.

### FINANCES

Your professional expertise, as applied in forensic work in PI cases, may pay off. Fees in forensic cases generally, and in PI cases particularly, are higher than those in psychotherapy practice. As ethical standards require, it is a good idea to get the financial aspects of the case clarified during the first conversation with a potential retaining attorney. I usually require a deposit that is roughly equal to my fees for the time preparing for and conducting the evaluation.

I have learned through hard experience to keep up with the bills as they accrue. Do not put yourself in the position of waiting until the case is done in order to collect fees. Some less-than-ethical lawyers will essentially allow you to fund their case, and then, if the plaintiff fails to prevail, not pay your fees from the nonexistent payout from the defendant. A well-written contract can reduce the chances of such problems. Such financial preparation is a commonly overlooked but essential part of your practice.

# FOR MORE INFORMATION

Overall, working in PI cases takes preparation and, in the early phases of this work, some supervision and training. I recommend the workshops provided by the American Board of Forensic Psychology (http://aafp.abfp.com/continuing_education_programs.asp) and American

Psychological Association Division 42 (Private Practice) (http://division42.org/) and Division 41 (Psychology and Law) (http://www.apadivisions.org/division-41/education/index.aspx) to help you develop and sharpen your skills. The Division 41 website is also a useful source of information about training in forensic psychology, offering listings of graduate programs, internships, and postdoctoral training.

Several journals provide useful information about forensic practice. These include the Division 41 journal *Law and Human Behavior*. Although the focus of this journal is generally social psychology, eyewitness identification, and jury research, it occasionally has articles on ethical issues and malingering that are helpful. *Professional Psychology Research and Practice* is also a fine resource for forensic practitioners, as is the journal *Personal Injury and the Law*, which focuses specifically on the topic.

Also, I would recommend several references. Joel Dvoskin and Andy Kane wrote an excellent volume on PI for the "Oxford Best Practices" series (Kane & Dvoskin, 2011). With Craig LaRue, I wrote a chapter that covers both the law and provides a model for conducting PI evaluations (Foote & LaRue, 2013).

# REFERENCES

Foote, W. E., & LaRue, C. R. (2013). Psychological damages in personal injury cases. In R. Otto & I. B. Weiner (Eds.), *Comprehensive handbook of forensic psychology, Volume 11: Forensic psychology* (2nd ed.). New York: John Wiley & Sons, Ltd.

Kane, A. W., & Dvoskin, J. A. (2011). *Evaluation for personal injury claims*. New York: Oxford University Press.

# CHAPTER 50

# PRESURGICAL BARIATRIC EVALUATIONS

*Caroljean Bongo*

I am a licensed psychologist who practices in Cheyenne, Wyoming. In 2005 I began working at the University of Wyoming Counseling Center in Laramie, where I completed my postdoctoral residency. I began my full-time private practice in June 2007 and completed my first bariatric evaluation in November 2007.

I work out of two locations in Cheyenne. My main office is located in a building where I lease a suite for my private practice. There are other counselors and helping professionals in the building. My main office is where I provide individual counseling to adults and also complete some bariatric psychological evaluations. My second practice location is housed in the conference room of the bariatric clinic where I consult. There I lease the conference room one day each week and complete the evaluations for that clinic.

## THE NICHE PRACTICE ACTIVITY

The American Society of Metabolic and Bariatric Surgery (ASMBS: https://asmbs.org/) recommends that individuals complete a psychological evaluation prior to having bariatric/weight loss surgery (Roux-en-Y gastric bypass, vertical sleeve gastrectomy, gastric banding). My responsibility is to perform these evaluations for individuals in Wyoming who are having surgery in Cheyenne and surrounding states such as Colorado and Nebraska. Patients from these states come to my office to complete their evaluation. These evaluations account for approximately 20% of my practice. During the other 80% of my time, I provide individual counseling services to adults. The number of evaluations I complete monthly varies, depending on the volume of referrals from the weight loss surgery programs. This is the only type of psychological evaluation that I provide, and I prefer to do just the one type of evaluation. I started with this type of evaluation as an early-career psychologist, and now, eight years later, I feel very competent in this area. From November 2007 to April 2016 I have completed over 1,100 bariatric psychological evaluations.

## DEVELOPING AN INTEREST AND TRAINING IN THIS NICHE ACTIVITY

I became interested in doing pre–bariatric surgery psychological evaluations while in graduate school. I was fortunate to have completed my graduate program psychotherapy practicum hours at an eating disorder treatment facility that provided outpatient and intensive outpatient (IOP) services. As I neared the end of my practicum year, the practice was approached by a local bariatric surgeon who was looking for a clinician to provide presurgical evaluation services, as well as a presurgical IOP for his bariatric patients. I was honored to be asked to remain on staff to assist in developing a presurgical bariatric IOP. Over the next year, we implemented this IOP, and I was also involved in co-facilitating some of the weekly group sessions. This was a rich experience that provided me with first-hand psychotherapeutic involvement with the bariatric population.

During my American Psychological Association–accredited PsyD graduate program, I learned a great deal about conducting psychological evaluations and writing evaluation reports, but no specific training was provided in completing bariatric psychological evaluations. I did not participate in any formal postgraduate training in completing these types of evaluations. While my graduate studies provided the necessary foundational training, the majority of my training has mainly come from my own efforts in studying the current literature and the ASMBS guidelines. Additional training came from consultation with bariatric psychologist mentors, by attending annual ASMBS meetings, and through the day-to-day work experience completing these evaluations.

## JOYS AND CHALLENGES RELATED TO THIS NICHE ACTIVITY

Completing bariatric psychological evaluations can be rewarding and somewhat enjoyable, as well as challenging. I believe that providing these evaluations plays an important role in preparing surgical candidates for weight loss surgery, and screening out or delaying individuals who for some reason are not psychosocially suitable for surgery. It is not only an evaluation but also a consultation during which I provide information about postsurgical adjustment and weight loss. I often challenge the candidates to consider the ways in which their actions are going to support or detract from their postsurgical outcome and sustained weight loss. We also discuss the ways in which they may cope with stress and difficult emotions, and I encourage them to consider healthier coping alternatives. Many people initially dread coming to their appointments with me (fearing that I may delay or deny them the surgery), only to complete the evaluation and say that it was a pleasant or positive experience for them. Many express gratitude for the information I provided and the ways in which I challenged them to think about how their life is going to be (or needs to be) different after surgery. I believe this work is important, and I take great pride in doing it to the best of my ability.

Life as a solo practitioner can be lonely. My work with the bariatric teams with whom I consult has provided me with beneficial professional interaction. Specifically, the Cheyenne bariatric clinic considers me as one of the key people on their team. By completing the evaluations at the bariatric surgery program office, I am involved in their day-to-day operation. As an example, patients will often meet with the bariatric nurse practitioner, the registered dietitian, and myself in one day. Being onsite allows for immediate consultation and collaboration with other team members, as well as allowing the patient to have a more cohesive experience.

In addition to being professionally rewarding, completing these evaluations has given me the opportunity to get to know and understand many candidates on a deeper level. If I dare to generalize, the bariatric candidates have been mostly pleasant to work with on a professional basis. Some of the more challenging aspects of completing these evaluations include the times in which I provide candidates with presurgical requirements to complete before they will be deemed "psychosocially suitable" for weight loss surgery. While this is uncomfortable at times, it is necessary, and in the candidates' best interest. Their responses to my presurgical requirements have included anger, rage, tears, arguments, feigned agreement, as well as genuine agreement and gratitude for the presurgical requirements and guidance. Examples of such requirements may include attending bariatric support group meetings; reducing disordered eating behaviors such as bingeing, grazing, emotional eating, and meal skipping; and receiving individual counseling. Additionally, I may require that they undergo a psychotropic medication evaluation by a medical professional with advanced training in prescribing psychotropic medications. If they smoke, they are required to be nicotine free for 60 days, and if they have a history of or current alcohol abuse, one year of sobriety will also be required. I rarely deem a person entirely unsuitable for weight loss surgery; what is more common is a delay until certain contraindicating issues are significantly improved or resolved.

When a candidate is currently in psychotherapy and/or is taking psychotropic medication, I request specific information from the respective providers, which is another challenging aspect of this work. Sometimes I receive a prompt response, but often I have to send second requests and even ask for the candidate's assistance in getting the provider to respond to my requests. Waiting for this information can delay my completion of their report and can contribute to a delay in the scheduling of their surgery. My reason for requesting information from the candidate's mental health providers and prescribers is that I believe they often know the candidate much better than I, and they may have some insight or specific recommendations that would be in their client's/patient's best interest.

My inquiry of the candidate's providers follows the suggestions provided by the ASMBS's "Suggestions for the Pre-Surgical Psychological Assessment of Bariatric Surgery Candidates." I ask the prescribing clinicians about the medications prescribed; the duration of the patient's emotional stability; any specific concerns or recommendations; whether they believe the patient needs mental health counseling before or after surgery; and whether they have discussed a postsurgical plan for monitoring malabsorption of psychotropic medications and mood symptoms. I ask the psychotherapists some of the same questions I ask the prescribing clinicians, and whether their client has any impulse control issues and compulsions; what coping skills and psychological resources are in place and the client's ability to manage stressors; if they have any reservations about the client pursuing weight loss surgery; and the frequency of sessions recommended after surgery.

Generally, most evaluation reports can be written from start to finish within two hours. However, if the candidate has a complex history and clinical presentation, if I need to review extensive collateral data, and if there are numerous presurgical requirements that need explanation, these reports can take as long as three to five hours to write. I may not be reimbursed for the additional time, depending on the circumstances and/or the insurance company.

Reimbursement is another challenging aspect of completing bariatric evaluations. Prior to meeting with bariatric surgery candidates, my billing company contacts the respective insurance companies to verify benefits and, if necessary, obtains preauthorization for my services. These efforts are in part to help avoid surprise denials, unexpected expenses, upset candidates, and an unpaid provider. While I try to collect co-payments and deductibles at the time of service, it does not always happen. Unfortunately, it is not uncommon for individuals to not pay their balance due, after they have had surgery. In trying to avoid nonpayment or sending accounts to collections, I request that all individuals provide a guarantee of payment at the time of service. However, not everyone has the means or the willingness to provide their credit/debit card information as a guarantee of payment.

Because my appointments at the Cheyenne bariatric clinic are at their facility and are often coordinated with the patient's appointments with other providers, my appointments are scheduled by their staff. Currently, I set aside time for two evaluations per week onsite at the Cheyenne bariatric clinic. Depending on the flow of business and the efficiency of their staff, the actual number of evaluations completed weekly varies. This often means that the time set aside for bariatric evaluations goes unfilled, and therefore is time unpaid. I have come to accept this as a normal part of business. I do my best to keep a positive outlook and use any open time to collaborate with the team and to work on writing reports.

# BUSINESS ASPECTS OF THIS NICHE ACTIVITY

The business aspect of bariatric evaluations is complex and challenging. Referrals for bariatric evaluations are generated from bariatric surgery programs. Most of my referrals come from the Cheyenne bariatric clinic, some come from programs in Fort Collins and Denver, Colorado, and Scottsbluff, Nebraska. Prior to meeting with candidates, their insurance information is obtained, their benefits are confirmed, and pre-authorizations are requested, if necessary. Next, my documents are sent to patients so they can complete them before the appointment. These documents include my patient registration form, Notice of Privacy Practices, Professional Disclosure Statement and Informed Consent, an authorization to release information to the referral source, a financial agreement, a guarantee of payment form, and a questionnaire. When patients arrive at the office, I obtain copies of their insurance cards and identification and try to collect any co-pays and deductibles that are due. If it has not already been discussed, a plan for payment is arranged and expectations are made clear. I charge for a clinical interview (CPT 90791) and the appropriate number of psychological testing (CPT 96101) units provided.

Various fee arrangements are possible for bariatric evaluations. When insurance companies are being billed, my billing company submits the claim, which is then processed. Billing statements are sent out by my billing company for any balance due. For those who wish to take advantage of a discount for payment at the time of service and not bill their insurance, a significant discount of 44% is offered. I accept payment in the form of cash, a local check, credit or debit cards, and electronic checks. I also offer the option of online payment through my payment portal, where patients can submit payment with a credit or debit card, health savings account debit card, or electronic check. I also can arrange payment plans for larger balances due.

# DEVELOPING THIS NICHE ACTIVITY INTO A PRACTICE STRATEGY

I have several suggestions for other mental health providers who are interested in competently providing bariatric psychological evaluations. Most importantly, become familiar with the ASMBS's "Suggestions for the Pre-Surgical Psychological Assessment of Bariatric Surgery Candidates" (https://asmbs.org/resources/pre-surgical-psychological-assessment). This document helped me create an assessment battery that I use to obtain the information necessary in completing a thorough evaluation.

To competently provide bariatric psychological evaluations, clinicians should have knowledge and training in psychological testing and diagnostic interviewing. They should be skilled at report writing and competent in administering the tests they decide to include in their evaluation battery. Competence with a personality assessment instrument, such as the Personality Assessment Inventory (PAI: Morey, 1991), which I use, or the Minnesota Multiphasic Personality Inventory-2 (MMPI-2: Butcher et al., 1989), is important because a personality inventory is integral to a thorough battery. For more challenging cases, the ability to consult with other bariatric psychologists has been helpful in reviewing cases and arriving at a sound list of presurgical requirements that will potentially support the candidate's long-term success. The ability to collaborate, and having close working relationships with my bariatric evaluation referral sources, has allowed for teamwork to help the candidate prepare for surgery and to have the best possible outcome. Also, it is important for the psychologist to understand what a candidate needs to do post-surgically to lose weight and maintain weight loss. I found that my willingness to be guided and mentored by another bariatric evaluation professional was immensely helpful in my professional development. Thus, I believe that specific training and education are essential before a psychologist begins providing bariatric psychological evaluation services.

If you have not already determined your potential referral sources, I recommend that you introduce yourself to any or all bariatric surgical centers within a 100-mile radius (more or less, depending on the locations of the bariatric facilities). You should market yourself outside of your local area, as some patients will travel outside of their hometowns for weight loss surgery. If your practice can absorb a larger volume, you might consider offering services onsite at the bariatric facilities to enhance patient convenience.

My introduction to the Cheyenne bariatric program began when I attended an informational seminar presented by one of their bariatric surgeons. After his presentation, I introduced myself, shared my business card, and expressed an interest in helping their practice in any way that I could. The surgeon was receptive to my introduction and told me that they had a psychologist doing their evaluations, but he thought my services could be used in their support groups. As it turned out, their psychologist began to be less available to their practice and their referrals, and I was there to fill the gap. Clinicians interested in doing bariatric evaluations should find a way to meet some of the key people in the programs with which they would like to develop a referral relationship. My attendance at this informational seminar was vital in beginning my work in this area. In speaking with potential referral sources, think about ways in which you will provide what other professionals may not. I suggest attending multidisciplinary meetings, facilitating bariatric support groups, and being as available and helpful as reasonably possible. Also, if it fits into your scope of practice, offer to be a psychotherapeutic resource for their patients before and after surgery.

Many mental health professionals offer bariatric evaluation services. If this is an area that interests you, I encourage you to learn as much as possible and provide the best service you can; this will set you apart from others who do not. This is a competitive area, but if you are good at what you do, your referral sources will notice and value what you do, and you will continue to receive referrals.

## FOR MORE INFORMATION

To learn more about completing bariatric psychological evaluations, I recommend joining the ASMBS and attending the annual meeting of Obesity Week (http://www.obesity.org/meetings/obesity-week, a combined effort of ASMBS and the Obesity Society http://www.obesity.org). During Obesity Week, two or three days of meetings are offered specifically for the behavioral health providers and allied health professionals. Thus far I have attended six such annual meetings and have found them valuable for obtaining knowledge of best practices, learning about current research literature, and professional networking. My attendance at these meetings most definitely sets me apart from the other psychologists who complete evaluations for my referral sources.

As a member of ASMBS, I also subscribe to their professional journal, *Surgery for Obesity and Related Diseases*, which contains a fair amount of valuable information and research for allied health and behavioral health professionals. Many of articles are presented and discussed by the authors and researchers at Obesity Week.

I have found three books to be particularly helpful in this niche area. Mitchell and de Zwaan's 2005 guide was informative to my early practice in this area; also helpful was their 2012 volume. The 2014 textbook edited by Still, Sarwer, and Blankenship is an excellent compendium in the area of bariatric psychology.

# REFERENCES AND RESOURCES

Butcher, J. N., Dahlstrom, W. G., Graham, J. R., Tellegan, A., & Kaemmer, B. (1989). *The Minnesota Multiphasic Personality Inventory-2 (MMPI-2): Manual for administration and scoring.* Minneapolis: University of Minnesota Press.

Mitchell, J. E., & de Zwaan, M. (Eds.). (2005). *Bariatric surgery: A guide for mental health professionals.* New York: Taylor and Francis Group, LLC.

Mitchell, J. E. & de Zwaan, M. (Eds.). (2012). *Psychosocial assessment and treatment of bariatric surgery patients.* New York: Taylor and Francis Group, LLC.

Morey, L. C. (1991). *Personality Assessment Inventory professional manual.* Odessa, FL: Psychological Assessment Resources.

Still, C., Sarwer, D. B., & Blankenship, J. (Eds.). (2014). *The ASMBS textbook of bariatric surgery, Volume 2: Integrated health.* New York: Springer Science+Business Media.

# CHAPTER 51

# EVALUATIONS FOR TESTING ACCOMMODATIONS FOR ADOLESCENTS AND ADULTS WITH SPECIFIC LEARNING DISORDERS OR ATTENTION-DEFICIT/HYPERACTIVITY DISORDER

*Robert L. Mapou*

I am a board-certified clinical neuropsychologist and licensed psychologist practicing in Maryland, just outside of Washington, DC. I am part of a large group practice that specializes in neuropsychological evaluations of individuals with developmental disorders across the lifespan. Most of our clients are refereed for evaluation of specific learning disorders (SLDs), attention-deficit/hyperactivity disorder (ADHD), or autism spectrum disorders (ASDs). Most of our clinicians have training in neuropsychology. Several are trained in clinical or school psychology but have an understanding of the neuropsychological basis of SLDs, ADHD, and ASDs. The focus of this chapter will be on SLDs and ADHD, rather than disabilities more broadly, as this has been the bulk of my niche practice.

## THE NICHE PRACTICE ACTIVITY

I was asked to join this group in 1993 because of my expertise in adult neuropsychology. Following passage of the Americans with Disabilities Act (ADA) in 1990, the practice, which at that time consisted of only two psychologists, was seeing an increased number of adults seeking assessment for SLDs and ADHD. Some were already in the workforce but had struggled over the years and were interested in understanding the cause of the struggles. Parents sometimes sought assessment after their children had been seen in our practice, and they recognized similar problems in themselves. Others were young adults in college, graduate school, law school, or medical school who needed an updated assessment to document their need for accommodations in school or on standardized tests (e.g., LSAT, MCAT, GMAT, GRE, professional licensing and board examinations).

Shortly after starting, I immersed myself in the research literature on adults so that my evaluations would be evidence-based. Fortuitously, two edited books were published (*A Comprehensive Guide to Assessment of Attention Deficit Disorder in Adults*, by Kathleen Nadeau, in 1995, and *Adults with Learning Disabilities; Theoretical and Practical Perspectives*, by Noel Gregg, Cheri Hoy, and Alice F. Gay, in 1996). I quickly learned that many evaluations used outmoded notions and definitions of SLDs and ADHD that were unrelated to what research told us about these disorders in adults. Over time, I compiled this research and, in 1995, began giving workshops, teaching others how to complete evidence-based assessments of SLDs and ADHD in adults.

A few years later, guidelines for documentation began to be developed. As colleges and testing organizations were inundated by accommodation requests, sometimes supported by no more than a doctor's note with a diagnosis and a request for accommodations, they realized that guidelines were necessary to standardize assessment. The first were established in 1997 by the Association for Higher Education and Disability (AHEAD) for SLDs, followed by guidelines from the Educational Testing Service (ETS) for SLDs (1998) and ADHD (1999). AHEAD ultimately withdrew their guidelines to focus instead on best practices. However, ETS continued to revise and add to their guidelines (i.e., psychiatric disabilities, physical disabilities, health-related disabilities; see www.ets.org/disabilities/evaluators/ for current guidelines). The ETS guidelines have been adopted in similar form by colleges, universities, and testing agencies across the country.

As my clinical work in this area grew, I extended my age range downward. Now, I see preadolescents and adolescents from age 11 and up, although the bulk of my practice focuses on college-bound high school students, college and postgraduate students, and adults. Approximately 50% of my practice involves individuals specifically seeking evaluations for accommodations, either for the first time or after having had them in the past. The rest of my practice focuses on complex differential diagnosis of individuals with a range of neurological, developmental, and psychiatric disorders. These individuals are seeking diagnosis and recommendations, but not always accommodations. I complete six comprehensive evaluations each month. This is the norm for our practice but is different from the workload of neuropsychologists working in medical settings, where many more but briefer evaluations in a week are typical.

## DEVELOPING AN INTEREST AND TRAINING IN THIS NICHE ACTIVITY

When I started graduate school in 1978, the first special education law, the Education for All Handicapped Children Act (PL 94-142), had just been put into place in 1975. Research on SLDs (mostly dyslexia and other reading disorders) and ADHD in children was in its infancy, although textbooks had been written (e.g., *Learning Disabilities and Brain Function*, by William Gaddes, in 1980). So, we had some rudimentary training in these disorders, including in my first psychological assessment course, which focused on intellectual and academic testing. My first neuropsychology mentor, David Freides, who taught this course, also was interested in developmental disorders and ultimately published a book on developmental neuropsychology. However, there was hardly any research on adults.

During my internship at the Boston VA Medical Center with Edith Kaplan, who was my second neuropsychology mentor, I was introduced to Norman Geschwind. He had developed a theory regarding the interaction of hemispheric dominance, handedness, and testosterone exposure in utero and the relationship of these factors to the development of dyslexia. His work and that of others in Boston taught me early the neuropsychological basis of SLDs and the importance of basing assessment on empirical knowledge. Clinically, Edith Kaplan taught her interns to look for hints of SLDs by inquiring about strengths, weaknesses, and interests outside of school. She emphasized the importance of understanding developmental disorders when examining older adults with new-onset neurological conditions.

During my internship (and even earlier, in graduate school), I began working with people who had suffered severe traumatic brain injuries and continued this work in my postdoctoral year and first job. However, in 1988, I returned to my home state of Maryland for a job on a new neuropsychiatric evaluation unit, where some of the patients were adolescents with SLDs and/or ADHD. I gave my first lecture on assessment of SLDs in 1989.

## JOYS AND CHALLENGES RELATED TO THIS NICHE ACTIVITY

Completing these evaluations is rewarding because I can help people move ahead and succeed in school and in their jobs. At the same time, I have found that the increased pressure on middle school, high school, and college students has caused students (and often parents) to seek accommodations or medication for ADHD to help them "get an edge." Although these students may have some areas of weakness, many are not disabled, based on the definition established by the 1990 Americans with Disabilities Act (ADA). It can be challenging to explain to parents (and students) that there is nothing wrong, that high school or college is always more challenging than earlier schooling, and that they have to work harder to achieve. This is especially the case when students have skills that are solidly average, and parents expect straight As. However, there is always room for improvement, and I always recommend interventions and compensatory strategies to make school easier, even when I also recommend accommodations.

Being part of a large group practice is also rewarding. My colleagues and I constantly talk to each other about our clients, especially when there is a challenge. We have monthly staff meetings and, because we are close to academic medical centers and research centers, we often have guests come and fill us in on the latest research and treatment on SLDs, ADHD, ASDs, and psychiatric disorders. We also spend time presenting and brainstorming cases, which helps all of us conceptualize cases and make more effective recommendations.

The reports that I write tend to be lengthy. I see reviewing the client's history and explaining the test results in the context of that history to be a key part of what I do; it is not simply about the test scores. My histories typically run three to five pages, and my recommendations run about the same. Most reports require six to eight hours of time for a first draft and run between 15 and 20 pages, including the test scores.

## BUSINESS ASPECTS OF THIS NICHE ACTIVITY

Referrals come from many places. Because our practice is now 30 years old and because the founder of the practice lectures frequently in the area, word-of-mouth referrals from past clients and from people who attend his lectures are common. I have also received referrals through clinicians who have attended my workshops throughout the country and/or have read my book and book chapters. Other referral partners include psychiatrists, psychotherapists, primary care physicians, school counselors and special education staff, college disability support services, and, on occasion, neurologists.

Unlike other parts of the country where psychologists must rely entirely on insurance for reimbursement, we are fortunate to be able to have a cash-based practice. Clients pay us for our services at the time of the first appointment, although we work out payment plans when necessary. Everyone also does at least one pro bono evaluation yearly. We will complete precertification for an added small fee and always provide a CMS-1500 form for clients to submit to their insurance company. In addition, our billing staff, based on many years of experience, can advise clients on whether or not they may get reimbursement from a particular insurance carrier. It is unfortunate that no insurance company will reimburse for an evaluation that is solely focused on an SLD as they claim the schools should be providing this service. However, most companies will reimburse for ADHD, ASDs, and psychiatric conditions. These are frequently considered in the differential diagnosis and can reasonably be used as rule-out diagnoses to support reimbursement. Also, some clients have documented neurological disorders (e.g., epilepsy, moderate to severe traumatic brain injury, concussion, genetic disorders) that have prompted the evaluation; as medical conditions, these are far more likely to lead to reimbursement.

## DEVELOPING THIS NICHE ACTIVITY INTO A PRACTICE STRATEGY

Psychologists who are interested in this area need to have a thorough knowledge of the research on SLDs and ADHD. This knowledge should be obtained through continuing professional education workshops, books, original research articles, and review articles. Supervision by a colleague is recommended as one begins this practice. It is essential to know which SLDs are evidence based, as only these should be diagnosed. For example, there is no such thing as a "learning disability affecting processing speed," which I have seen as a diagnosis in many reports. Slow processing speed can be associated with SLDs (e.g., dyslexia) or ADHD, but it does not define a disorder. Nonverbal learning disorders, despite popular use, have mixed research support, which is why the category was not included in the American Psychiatric Association's *Diagnostic and Statistical Manual of Mental Disorders*, fifth edition (DSM-5). However, the three SLDs in the DSM-5 (and their corresponding diagnoses in the ICD-10) were specifically designed based on extant research, with the best support established for dyslexia and other reading disorders.

Psychologists must also be familiar with special education law, which guides identification and services in kindergarten through high school (e.g., Individuals With Disabilities Education Act of 2004, in its most recent iteration), and disability law, which mandates access through accommodations to people with disabilities in all settings (e.g., ADA, ADA Amendments Act of 2008, Section 504 of the Rehabilitation Act of 1973). It is important to understand the significant differences between the two sets of laws, as the methods and standards for establishing a disability differ between the two. Although criteria for a disability can vary widely across school districts (e.g., discrepancy model, cutoff model, response-to-intervention model), the ADA and Section 504 establish a standard that a disability must impair a person's everyday functioning in comparison with most people. Psychologists must understand that when evaluating individuals in college, graduate school, or professional school, they will usually not be considered disabled by standardized testing agencies when all of their skills are in the average range, even if these skills are statistically discrepant from their intellectual abilities. Rather, they must show impairment in everyday life. It is also essential to understand that just having a diagnosis is not equivalent to having a disability.

Based on this knowledge, one can be fair to all students by not diagnosing a disability and not recommending accommodations when a person is not truly disabled, based on the legal definition. At the same time, one can be sure that high school or college students with a disability are not overlooked, because there was only a cursory review of their academic history. This is why I regularly request all academic records and earlier standardized test scores, to see exactly what the problems were during early schooling. By demonstrating, through objective records, that a person has always performed below the level of most people, it is easier to make the case for accommodations, even when the first evaluation is in high school or college.

Finally, clinicians must be familiar with documentation requirements of colleges, universities, and testing agencies. These can always be found on the school or organization's website. Requirements may differ, and it is important to review the guidelines when preparing a report. I learned this the hard way, as a report of mine was once rejected by a testing agency because the candidate had not been taking his medication for ADHD when I tested him. The organization required candidates to take medication that they used in school and would be using at the time of the standardized test so that the potential mitigating impact of the medication on cognitive and academic performance can be assessed. Sometimes, with medication, accommodations are not needed.

In summary, I have found this focus to be a rewarding career path. However, anyone wanting to do these evaluations must seek knowledge and training. Even with assessment experience, there are critical areas of knowledge that one must have and that I sometimes find lacking in the reports I review.

# FOR MORE INFORMATION

Although designed for schools rather than practitioners, the Manual for Accommodations (3rd ed.), from the Council of Chief State School Officers, can be helpful (www.cehd.umn.edu/ NCEO/OnlinePubs/ASESAccommodationsManual3rdEdition2011.pdf). Government websites can provide current information regarding special education law (e.g., IDEA: idea.ed.gov/ explore/home; Special Education: www2.ed.gov/about/offices/list/osers/osep/index.html) and disability law (e.g., ADA: www.ada.gov). However, the law is constantly being updated, and clinicians must stay current. The best example of this is the recent class action suit that ultimately involved the U.S. Department of Justice and the Law School Admissions Council. This led to a settlement and a consent decree in May 2014 and changes in the requirements for documentation (see www.dfeh.ca.gov/lsac.htm), recommendations from a Best Practices panel in January 2015 (see www.lsac.org/lsac-final-panel-report), and a document on testing accommodations from the Department of Justice in September 2015 (www.ada.gov/regs2014/testing_accommodations.pdf). Although websites of advocacy organizations (e.g., Learning Disabilities Association, ldaamerica.org/) or educational websites (e.g., LDOnline, www.ldonline.org) can provide useful information for clients, for clinicians doing these evaluations, it is best to go to original sources for information.

# RESOURCES

Barkley, R. A. (Ed.) (2014). *Attention-deficit/hyperactivity disorder: A handbook for diagnosis and treatment* (4th ed.). New York: Guilford Press.

Barkley, R. A., Murphy, K. R., & Fischer, M. (2008). *ADHD in adults: What the science says.* New York: Guilford.

Fletcher, J. M., Lyon, G. R., Fuchs, L. S., & Barnes, M. A. (2007). *Learning disabilities: From identification to intervention.* New York: Guilford Press.

Gordon, M., & Keiser, S. (1998). *Accommodations in higher education under the Americans with Disabilities Act: A no-nonsense guide for clinicians, educators, administrators, and lawyers.* New York: Guilford Press.

Gregg, N. (2009). *Adolescents and adults with learning disabilities and ADHD: Assessment and accommodation.* New York: Guilford Press.

Katz, L. J., Goldstein, G., & Beers, S. R. (2001). *Learning disabilities in older adolescents and adults.* New York: Kluwer Academic/Plenum Publishers.

Lovett, B. J., & Lewandowski, L. J. (2015). *Testing accommodations for students with disabilities: Research-based practice.* Washington, DC: American Psychological Association.

Mapou, R. L. (2009). *Adult learning disabilities and ADHD: Research-informed assessment.* New York: Oxford University Press.

Pennington, B. F. (2009). *Diagnosing learning disorders: A neuropsychological framework* (2nd ed.). New York: Guilford Press.

Wolf, L. E., Schreiber, H., & Wasserstein, J. (Eds.). (2008). *Adult learning disorders: Contemporary issues.* New York: Psychology Press.

## CHAPTER 52

# ASSESSMENT OF EGG
# AND SPERM DONORS

*Adam J. Rodríguez*

am a licensed clinical psychologist in private practice in Portland, Oregon where I treat adolescents and adults in individual, couple, and group psychotherapy. I work predominantly with a lesbian, gay, bisexual, transgender, intersex, questioning (LGBTIQ) population and with infertility. I have been practicing psychotherapy for nearly 10 years and was licensed in California in 2012 and Oregon in 2016. I treat a variety of conditions in my practice and also provide supervision and consultation. Additionally, I perform psychological evaluations for egg and sperm donor and gestational carrier candidates and/or the intended recipients/parents. On average, I perform eight to 10 of these evaluations per year.

## THE NICHE PRACTICE ACTIVITY

Assisted reproductive technologies (ARTs), subfertility (often called "infertility") treatments, and the field of reproductive endocrinology in general have made significant clinical advancements in recent years. A variety of factors have contributed to an increase in the number of individuals and couples using these services. The options are vast and often confusing and overwhelming. The subfertility process, including treatments, is physically and emotionally demanding. The experience has been described as similar to receiving a cancer diagnosis (Domar, Zuttermeister, & Friedman, 1993). Many of these individuals can benefit from receiving psychological services. In fact, stress reduction in and of itself has been cited as a major component of the success of fertility treatments (Harrison et al., 1984; Smeenk et al., 2004). In addition to psychotherapy, psychologists can play an important role in providing necessary evaluations for individuals who are using egg or sperm donors, as well as gestational carriers.

Some individuals and couples cannot conceive, even with the assistance of ARTs. Some choose to enlist the services of egg or sperm donors or gestational carriers or surrogates. Sperm donation is a fairly straightforward process involving the donor providing one or more sperm donations. It is not an invasive procedure. Oocyte (egg) donation is a more involved process and significantly more invasive. Being a gestational surrogate or carrier is an even greater commitment. Carriers are implanted with an embryo through in vitro fertilization that is composed of the intended parent's egg and sperm. Surrogates donate their own egg and then subsequently carry the child. Due to the invasiveness of these procedures, as well as their commitment and the emotional ramifications to the intended parents and child, many clinics and hospitals require a psychological evaluation of any individual who provides egg donation or becomes a gestational carrier or surrogate. Evaluations for sperm donors are rare but do occur. An evaluation of the intended parent(s) is also sometimes requested.

Individuals choose to donate or become a carrier or surrogate for various reasons, although the most frequent are altruism and financial gain. A number of physical and psychological risks exist for donors and carriers or surrogates. Psychological risks exist for intended parents and the resulting children. Most individuals who donate or become carriers or surrogates report satisfaction with the process (Kenny & McGowan, 2008; Klock, Braverman, & Rausch, 1998). There is evidence, however, that when the donor is unknown to the intended parents, those "with high levels of predonation financial motivation or ambivalence should be carefully screened and counseled before oocyte donation to ensure satisfactory psychological outcome" (Kenny & McGowan, 2008, p. 229). In these cases, I am evaluating to determine if excessive financial need may be influencing the decision, or if the donor's ambivalence is significant enough that she may regret her decision. Some ambivalence is expected and normal, but it should not be so strong that the individual is consistently wavering from one decision to the other. If the donor is primarily motivated by financial concern, the donation may be seen as coercive.

The psychological evaluation always involves an interview/assessment. It often, but not always, involves the administration, scoring, and interpretation of the Minnesota Multiphasic Personality Inventory (MMPI-2; Butcher et al., 2003). The psychological evaluation is intended to assess the candidate's motivation for serving as a donor or carrier/surrogate; understanding and appreciation of the psychological and emotional implications involved; understanding and appreciation of the time commitment and medical aspects of treatment involved; perspectives about the future child and oneself in relation to that child now and in the future; if the donor or carrier is previously known, considerations of the impact on the existing and future relationship; personal and familial mental health history, including any background of trauma or loss; current psychological and emotional stability; preparedness for various cycle outcomes; reliability and responsibility; and lifestyle factors. The evaluation also serves as an opportunity for education and discussion about relevant topics such as preferences regarding the nature, frequency, and parameters of contact with the parents or resulting offspring; number of embryos to be transferred and potential for multiple gestation; parameters for consideration of multifetal reduction; and decisions about remaining embryos.

## DEVELOPING AN INTEREST AND TRAINING IN THIS NICHE ACTIVITY

My education, training, and licensure as a psychologist has prepared and enabled me to perform these types of evaluations. A thorough knowledge and understanding of the field of subfertility and ART is also exceptionally important. Candidates should be aware that you have expertise in this area, which includes the physical and medical procedures and processes and the psychological/emotional ramifications of those processes. As stated above, the subfertility experience is immensely challenging for individuals. Possessing a strong familiarity with this field not only provides you with the ability to provide emotional support to candidates, but it also enables you to be able to perform competent evaluations.

This expertise can be acquired in a number of different ways. I have attended numerous conferences related to the field. I strongly encourage the establishment of a network of disparate clinicians and practitioners. At these conferences, as well as other training events like workshops and seminars, you will encounter acupuncturists, herbalists, nutritionists, functional medicine experts, chiropractors, nurses and nurse practitioners, physicians of various types, and others. It is important to build a relationship with these individuals as they have expertise in various areas of the field, all of which can be helpful to your own growth and knowledge. Additionally, there is a wealth of literature related to subfertility and infertility. It is important to be familiar with this literature, ranging from significant foundational articles that are older to more current studies and discussions.

## JOYS AND CHALLENGES RELATED TO THIS NICHE ACTIVITY

Although the process of subfertility treatments is arduous, when I perform these evaluations I am often encountering individuals during a hopeful and encouraging phase of their experience. Carriers, surrogates, and donors are generally excited to be able to support the individual(s) trying to have a child and feel good about the opportunity. There is often a warm and eager feeling among all those involved. It is a pleasure to be a part of this complicated process. Donors, carriers, surrogates, and prospective parents can be confused, however, about what is necessary from an evaluation.

The donation that a donor is making may have significant emotional and physical impacts in his or her life. During an assessment, I am looking for evidence that he or she is informed and aware of the implications of the donation. Does the donor appear likely to be able to endure any challenges—physical, psychological, or interpersonal—related to the process? I am further attempting to determine if the donor is approaching the opportunity with a clear mind, hope and excitement, and realistic expectations, as well as openness to other strategies should the donation be unsuccessful. Finally, I am looking for any other information that may provide me with reservations about the donor's suitability. These may include significant mental illness, significant substance abuse issues, or physical or medical hardships.

A challenge to be aware of is that donors, carriers, and intended parents may not reside in state. I am licensed only in California and Oregon. If you are providing services in another state or via telehealth, the issue of where the client resides is key, and you must be aware of that state's laws and limitations. Some states have guest licensure provisions for such practices, but these provisions have specified conditions. See your licensing board and consult with the American

Psychological Association (www.apa.org) for more information. The Association of State and Provincial Psychology Boards (www.asppb.net) can also provide support.

The number of individuals undergoing all forms of ART is increasing steadily. It can be a complicated process to perform the evaluations that assist individuals in egg/sperm donations and gestational surrogacy/carrying, but it is also a tremendously rewarding process. I play a small but important role in the process. The ultimate reward for parents is the birth of a child, often at the end of a very long and stressful journey. It is an awesome thing to be a part of the joy they experience.

# BUSINESS ASPECTS OF THIS NICHE ACTIVITY

One of my initial steps is to clarify what the evaluation must include (e.g., psychological interview only or interview and MMPI-2). This is always done through the intended parents, since they are the primary individuals coordinating the treatments. Unfortunately, there is often confusion on their part regarding the details of what the evaluation must cover. In some circumstances, the fertility specialists that the intended parents are working with articulate only that "an evaluation" is required, without stipulating what must be included in the evaluation. This can delay the process, although usually only minimally. This is resolved by the intended parents speaking with their fertility specialist. The determining factor leading to the decision to include an MMPI-2 or not appears to be individual to the clinic, hospital, or physician rather than the specific referral. My experience is that a particular organization has a standard that is maintained for all referrals.

The MMPI-2 is time intensive to administer, score, and interpret. I use Q Local for scoring, but it can also be used for interpretation (http://www.pearsonclinical.co.uk/Q-Local/Q-Local-Scoring-and-Software.aspx). This service can be used to administer the test on a computer, or you can have the client take the test on paper and then you can enter the results into the system. I have found it far more efficient to have clients take the test directly on the computer. Q Local charges an annual membership fee and a small fee for each test scored. Unless you have extensive experience scoring an MMPI-2, I strongly suggest using a service and not scoring it by hand. These services can also provide test interpretation for an additional fee. However, there are significant limitations to computer-generated interpretations. Should you use that service, those interpretations should be treated as broad hypotheses. It is up to you as the clinician to consider the entire clinical picture, including all data you have derived from the evaluation. To simply take the provided interpretations without question and without synthesizing it with other information is unethical and clinically unsound. With increased practice, though, comes expertise, speed, and efficiency.

The same may be said about the final report. The first few reports can be challenging to write. After completing perhaps the first dozen or so reports, I found that I can perform the interview and complete the MMPI-2 and report in a brief amount of time. Many reports use boilerplate language that minimizes the amount of writing I need to do. The reports are structured in the format of traditional psychological evaluations. They include the client's name and demographic information, along with the following sections: Reason for Referral, Tests Administered, Background Information, Behavioral Observations, Assessment Results, Diagnostic Information (usually completed as "not applicable"), and Conclusions. I choose "Conclusions" rather than "Recommendations," as is often seen in psychological reports, because it seems more appropriate. Reports are often two to three pages in length. If only an interview is required by the referral source, I can produce the completed report within 30 to 45 minutes, if not more quickly. Scoring and interpreting an MMPI-2 may require an additional 45 to 60 minutes, or more.

Fees are based upon my hourly rate of service. The following are the approximate number of hours that an evaluation would require, including in-person contact and report writing:

- Gestational carrier candidates—3 to 5 hours
- Donor candidates not previously known to recipients—2 to 3 hours
- Donor candidates previously known to recipients—1 to 2 hours

The number of hours required for an evaluation will vary based on a number of different variables relevant to the evaluation. The fees apply regardless of the recommendations of the psychological evaluation. Unfortunately, insurance cannot be used to pay for the psychological evaluation. Given the nature of the service, the evaluation is focused on the candidate's understanding of and suitability to fulfill a certain role rather than on diagnosing or treating a mental health condition. Insurance companies typically require a billing code that reflects the diagnosis or treatment of a mental health disorder to reimburse for services, which is not applicable in this case. The billing always goes to the intended parent. Cash or check can clearly work for payment; however, because you may not actually meet with the intended parent (e.g., when assessing a surrogate only), it is particularly effective to be able to accept an alternative form of payment, like credit cards.

It is important to disclose payment procedures and information from the outset so that all parties are very clear on how much will be charged and how. My initial paperwork includes an intake form for the donor or carrier, covering necessary medical and mental health information, not unlike what one would use for psychotherapy. Additionally, I have a consent form written specifically for a psychological evaluation. I also have a credit card authorization form for the payer, as well as a release of information form for the donor or carrier, which includes both the payment as well as the report.

# DEVELOPING THIS NICHE ACTIVITY INTO A PRACTICE STRATEGY

At this stage in my practice, referrals largely come on their own as a result of the network and reputation I have established. That referral network, however, took years to nurture and develop. This practice is relatively rare, which means that I am sometimes located by clients through an Internet search. Initially, my referrals came through a variety of sources. It is essential to build a broad network. This should include other psychologists and psychotherapists, particularly those who work with not only infertility specifically, but also with couples generally. My predoctoral internship at a local hospital had a women's mental health and wellness program that I participated in through classes and patient work. In addition, it is important to build relationships with obstetricians, gynecologists, urologists, and reproductive endocrinologists in your area, as well as with any area fertility clinics and hospitals. When I began this practice, I cold-called and then invited and treated to lunch as many obstetricians and reproductive endocrinologists in the area as I could. I also contacted acupuncturists because the area I live in has many acupuncturists who specialize in fertility. Contacting and meeting these practitioners provided an opportunity for me to introduce my services and discuss how we may be mutually beneficial to one another and, most importantly, to our shared clientele. Attending conferences, conventions, and workshops is also essential to building a broad network. Finally, advertising through related associations and joining relevant listservs increases your exposure to individuals in need of this service. These listservs are often available through hospitals or fertility organizations.

## FOR MORE INFORMATION

If you are interested in becoming involved in providing these evaluations, I encourage you first to be sure you feel comfortable performing brief evaluations and administering, scoring, and interpreting the MMPI-2. In addition, I strongly recommend that you begin to attend workshops, trainings, seminars, and conferences related to subfertility and treatments. I recommend the annual Integrative Fertility Symposium (https://ifsymposium.com/).

Explore becoming a member of any of the following organizations: RESOLVE: The National Infertility Association (http://www.resolve.org/), the American Society for Reproductive Medicine (https://www.asrm.org/splash/splash.aspx), the Society for Reproductive Technology (http://www.sart.org/), Childlessness Overcome Through Surrogacy (COTS; http://www.surrogacy.org.uk/), the National Infertility Network Exchange (NINE; http://www.nine-infertility.org/), and the Society for Reproductive Endocrinology and Infertility (SREI; http://www.socrei.org/). These organizations' websites provide an array of resources.

The *International Journal of Infertility and Fetal Medicine* (http://www.ijifm.com/) is well known, but there are other leading journals in the discipline, including *Journal of Women's Health* (http://www.liebertpub.com/jwh), *Journal of Psychosomatic Obstetrics & Gynecology* (http://www.tandfonline.com/loi/ipob20), *Human Reproduction* (http://humrep.oxfordjournals.org/), *British Journal of Medical Psychology*, and more.

Determine which clinics and hospitals in your area perform ART and connect with them. These organizations may keep a registry of individuals who provide psychological services. Further, they often offer workshops and trainings on a variety of related topics. Also familiarize yourself with the leading national clinics, including the Colorado Center for Reproductive Medicine in Englewood (https://www.ccrmivf.com/colorado/); the Center for Reproductive Medicine and Infertility at New York-Presbyterian Hospital/Weill-Cornell Medical Center (http://www.ivf.org/); University Fertility Consultants at Oregon Health & Science University in Portland (http://www.ohsu.edu/xd/health/services/women/services/fertility/index.cfm?ref=home); and the Infertility Center of St. Louis at St. Luke's Hospital in Missouri (http://www.infertile.com/).

# REFERENCES

Butcher, J. N., Graham, J. R., Ben-Porath, Y. S., Tellegen, A., & Dahlstrom, W. G. (2003). *MMPI-2. Minnesota Multiphasic Personality Inventory-2.* Minneapolis: University of Minnesota Press.

Domar, A. D., Zuttermeister, P. C., Friedman, R. (1993). The psychological impact of infertility: A comparison with patients with other medical conditions. *Journal of Psychosomatic Obstetrics & Gynecology, 14,* 45–52.

Harrison, R. F., O'Moore, R. R., & O'Moore, A. M. (1984). Stress and fertility: Some modalities of investigation and treatment in couples with unexplained infertility in Dublin. *International Journal of Infertility, 31*(2), 153–159.

Kenny, N. J., & McGowan, M. L. (2008). Looking back: Egg donors' retrospective evaluations of their motivations, expectations, and experiences during their first donation cycle. *Fertility and Sterility, 93*(2), 455–466. doi:10.1016/j.fertnstert.2008.09.081.

Klock, S. C., Braverman, A. M., & Rausch, D. T. (1998). Predicting anonymous egg donor satisfaction egg donor satisfaction: A preliminary study. *Journal of Women's Health, 7*(2), 229–237. doi:10.1089/jwh.1998.7.229.

Smeenk, J. M. J., Verhaak, C. M., Vingerhoets, A. J. J. M., Sweep, C.G.J., Merkus, J. M. W. M., Willemsen, S. J., . . . Braat, D. D. M. (2004). Stress and outcomes success in I.V.F.: The role of self-reports and endocrine variables. *Human Reproduction, 20*(4), 991–996.

# PSYCHOTHERAPY SERVICES

# CHAPTER 53

# COUNSELING WOMEN WITH BREAST CANCER

*Sandra Haber*

I am a psychologist in independent practice with a niche specialty of working with patients with breast cancer. My office is located in New York City, with a part-time home office in Brooklyn, New York.

## THE NICHE PRACTICE ACTIVITY

I have worked with breast cancer patients for almost 20 years and at any given time these patients make up about 20% to 25% of my practice. I work with cancer patients and their families during the entire cancer experience, including the diagnosis, treatment, and posttreatment phases. Examples of some issues that typically arise include medical decision making; managing the side effects of surgery, radiation, and chemotherapy; and dealing with changes in body image and level of functioning. In addition, there are usually anxieties about recurrence once treatment has ended that I address with clients.

## DEVELOPING AN INTEREST AND TRAINING IN THIS NICHE ACTIVITY

By 1980, my broad-based adult outpatient psychotherapy practice was thriving. I worked with the usual myriad issues including concerns of young adulthood, problems in marriage and partnerships, and parenting concerns. My patients were middle-class, well educated, and reasonably sophisticated about psychotherapy. I felt that I had good training, based in psychoanalytic psychotherapy, and was enjoying my career, my family, and my work in the governance of the American Psychological Association. Things were going along quite well.

In the mid-1980s one of my young adult patients, Mary (not her real name) presented me with a complex issue. She was a woman in her early 30s who was quite anxious—about her relationship with her mother, her female lover, and an earlier bout of breast cancer from which she was declared cured. Every now and then she worried that her cancer would recur. She worked for an oncologist and, although she did not particularly like him, he was reassuring to her about her cancer. She also felt that he would care for her if she had a recurrence.

After a few years of working together, mostly on interpersonal issues, Mary became ill. She was diagnosed with ovarian cancer. We were both surprised, not realizing at that time that breast cancer will often metastasize to the ovaries. Nowadays, with the awareness of BRCA 1 and BRCA 2 genes, there would be genetic testing for this young woman. At that time, my patient had no genetic testing. And nowadays, prophylactic options for mastectomy and oophorectomy are typically discussed. In those days, none of this was the norm.

While visiting Mary in the hospital, I remember thinking how ill prepared I was as a psychologist for working with breast cancer. My training had a heavy emphasis on unconscious processes, transference, countertransference, regression, and psychological defenses. I don't remember any discussion of the psychological issues of breast cancer or of serious illness in general. As I began to read, I learned that breast cancer is the most common cancer in women worldwide. In the United States, breast cancer will be diagnosed in one out of eight women (12%) over the course of their lifetime (men also get breast cancer and make up about 1% of the cases). Doing my research, I knew there was a hole in my training, but at that time few training programs or continuing education courses addressed this issue.

Soon after my patient died, my long-time friend, colleague, and neighbor was diagnosed with breast cancer. Dr. Michelle Siegel was in her late 30s at the time of diagnosis and pregnant with her second child. Michelle's breast cancer was aggressive. Her psychological anguish over her three-year-old son and unborn child were intense. I spent time with Michelle and we talked as friends, as young mothers, and as colleagues. We both believed that our training was seriously remiss and clinicians were simply not skilled in handling this frequently occurring issue. So together, with Michelle's story as the catalyst, we along with eight other psychologist colleagues and the support of the Division of Independent Practice of the American Psychological Association decided to write a treatment manual for psychologists working with patients who had breast cancer. *Breast Cancer: A Psychological Treatment Manual* was written and published by the Division of Independent Practice in 1992 under the auspices of President Richard Mikesell, PhD. It was republished by Springer Publishing Company in 1995.

For my own part, I contacted Memorial Sloan Kettering Cancer Center, a major institution in New York City, and told them about the project. With the imprimatur of the Division of Independent Practice, I was able to visit the hospital and interview several social workers who worked in the posttreatment center. They permitted me to observe their groups for patients with breast cancer. Additionally, I interviewed Cancer Care director Carolyn Messner and consulted with her staff on the psychological issues surrounding patients with breast cancer. I then did a series of informal interviews either in person or on the telephone with women who were currently being treated for breast cancer or who had had such treatment in the past. I educated myself on the medical issues by reading and through conversations with hospital social workers and nurses. I articulated the psychological issues after interviewing women who had breast cancer. I also spoke to several partners of these women to get an understanding of their concerns for themselves, their partner, and their children.

## JOYS AND CHALLENGES RELATED TO THIS NICHE ACTIVITY

Once I was "trained," I found working with patients with breast cancer to be incredibly meaningful. I felt that I now had the skills to help them navigate and cope with both the medical interventions and psychological sequelae. I was comfortable with the complexity of the illness. "Breast cancer," a simple diagnostic term, covers a multitude of different situations. Some breast cancer is early stage, some late stage, some metastatic. Many breast cancers will be curable but some will be fatal. Sometimes death is swift; sometimes it takes many years. Some breast cancers occur in very young women. My youngest so far has been 27 years of age. She recovered and went on to write a book about her experiences (Lucas, 2005). Indeed, the psychological factors are particularly challenging in that young cohort. Each step of the breast cancer process, from diagnosis to treatment to posttreatment, brings a new set of psychological challenges that I am honored to be part of.

I like helping women manage this complex illness and feel like I am both an anchor and navigator in the inevitable sea of chaos, confusion, and anxiety. I firmly believe that it is burdensome for patients to have to educate their psychotherapist on each medical intervention and medical decision. Unlike my earlier work, where all I could offer was support, I can now be helpful in a variety of ways: shaping appropriate medical questions, assisting in medical decision making (including lumpectomy vs. mastectomy, reconstruction choices, chemotherapy decisions, hormonal interventions), managing the side effects of chemotherapy through stress management techniques and hypnotic interventions, helping patients form a "buddy system" to manage both medical needs and family needs, addressing the concerns of partners and children, and assisting in the sometimes unexpectedly difficult posttreatment process.

The only aspect of this specialty niche that is difficult for me is that some of my patients will die from their disease. Those facing a premature death will need help saying goodbye to aging parents, young children, and a loving spouse. And it is difficult for me to say goodbye too.

## BUSINESS ASPECTS OF THIS NICHE ACTIVITY

In terms of the reality of a private practice, the business aspects of working with breast cancer vary according to how you choose to run your main practice. If you run an insurance-based practice, you will have an easier time procuring referrals from oncologists and breast surgeons who are on the same panels.

I run a fee-for-service practice. My referrals tend to be from other patients and psychologist colleagues. Patients with out-of-network benefits do get reimbursed for my services. The billing code you might consider is F43.23 (adjustment disorder with mixed anxiety and depressed mood), though a number of other diagnostic codes may apply.

If you would like to pursue this specialty niche, I would suggest that you interview women who have had breast cancer—young and old, recent disease and past disease, early stage and metastatic, lumpectomy and mastectomy, those who have had chemotherapy and who have not, and those with and without reconstruction. For each woman you speak with, ask her if she knows any other women who have had breast cancer and ask if she can get their permission for you to call.

You can easily create a talk or write an article on an aspect of breast cancer (e.g., young women with breast cancer, sex after breast cancer, body image and mastectomy). Such media pieces are usually welcome all year round but are highly relevant during the month of October, which is Breast Cancer Awareness Month. College campuses, churches, synagogues, PTA groups, and local newspapers are common venues.

Another strategy is to offer a one-session interactive workshop in the office of an oncologist or breast surgeon, using his or her waiting room after hours. If you accept insurance, the fee for this workshop can be billed to the patient. If you are private pay, you can charge each participant a modest fee (even $25 for a 15-person workshop yields $375). Or, you can consider a free workshop with the potential of future referrals. Your key referral source will usually be the office nurse, so it is wise to ask if he or she would like to sit in on the workshop. During my time at Adelphi University, I taught a graduate course in the psychology of breast cancer and ran several such workshops with my graduate students in nearby medical offices.

# FOR MORE INFORMATION

Haber (1995) wrote a brief manual on psychological interventions for patients with breast cancer. Holland and Rowland's handbook (1990) is the bible of psychooncology. The medical information is outdated, but the psychological issues and interventions remain unchanged. Link (2012) wrote a step-by-step guide to decision making for patients diagnosed with breast cancer. It is an excellent resource with a strong section on how to get second opinions, and it demystifies current medical interventions. Love's classic, easy-to-read book (2015) describes issues related to breast development and breast problems. It clearly explains breast cancer and the standard treatments and includes information on complementary and alternative treatments and issues of recurrence. Lucas (2005) wrote a first-person, often humorous account of a 27-year-old diagnosed with breast cancer.

Web information on breast cancer is easily accessible. Excellent resources include the National Cancer Institute (www.cancer.gov), Cancer Care (www.cancercare.org), and the Susan G. Komen Foundation (www.komen.org).

# REFERENCES

Haber, S. (Ed.) (1995). *Breast cancer: A psychological treatment manual*. New York: Springer.

Holland, J. C., & Rowland, J. H. (Eds.) (1990). *Handbook of psychooncology: Psychological care of the patient with cancer*. New York: Oxford University Press.

Link, J. (2012). *Breast cancer survival manual*. New York: Henry Holt and Co.

Love, S. (2015). *Dr. Susan Love's breast book*. New York: Addison-Wesley.

Lucas, G. (2005). *Why I wore lipstick to my mastectomy*. New York: St Martin's Griffin.

# CHAPTER 54

# TREATING ANXIETY DISORDERS

*Sally Winston and Steven Shearer*

We are co-directors and co-owners of the Anxiety and Stress Disorders Institute of Maryland (ASDI) in Towson, a suburb of Baltimore. ASDI is a group private practice that currently includes 20 part-time clinicians, two part-time office staff, two interns in training, and a volunteer exposure therapy aide. We began as an independent group practice in 1992.

## THE NICHE PRACTICE ACTIVITY

We specialize in the treatment of all of the anxiety disorders and obsessive-compulsive disorder (OCD). Although these make up the majority of our work, all of our clinicians have varied case-loads that include affective disorders and other co-occurring conditions. Our approach generally integrates aspects of behavioral, cognitive, Acceptance and Commitment Therapy (ACT), and mindfulness-based orientations. After all these years, we've seen so many cases that symptomatic presentations that are unusual for many general psychotherapists may be quite familiar to some in our niche practice.

## DEVELOPING AN INTEREST AND TRAINING IN THIS NICHE ACTIVITY

Our origins were at Sheppard-Pratt Hospital in Baltimore in 1978. Before the term "panic disorder" appeared in the diagnostic manual and long before "specialization" was an accepted practice in psychiatry or psychology, Dr. Douglas Hedlund, a service chief, approached the first author with an idea. He was being lobbied by a middle-aged woman named Zelda Milstein[1] with a unique mission. She had recovered on her own from years of being housebound with agoraphobia using a book called *Hope and Help for Your Nerves* by Claire Weekes. She had given up on many years of failed attempts at psychodynamically oriented psychotherapy, had found Dr. Weekes' books, and wanted to help others who were caught in the same spiral of panic attacks as she had been.

At the same time, Dr. Hedlund had met Dr. Arthur Hardy while on sabbatical. Dr. Hardy had founded an organization called TERRAP (an acronym for "territorial apprehension") after meeting Dr. Weekes. In TERRAP, people approached symptoms directly by facing their phobic situations in the company of a psychotherapist rather than sitting in offices looking for the origins and meanings of their fears. Suddenly, previously refractory cases of agoraphobia were responding to treatment.

In the next months, the first author, Ms. Milstein, and Dr. Hedlund studied this new approach and ended up visiting Dr. Diane Chambless and Dr. Alan Goldstein in Philadelphia, who were piloting a similar direct approach to phobias after publishing a groundbreaking article that reconceptualized agoraphobia as a complication of panic disorder rather than a simple phobia. We took clients into the subway system of Philadelphia to get them anxious deliberately and tried to teach them to think and breathe and react differently to the bodily sensations of panic that they were experiencing. In late December 1978, the Agoraphobia Clinic, housed in the outpatient department of Sheppard Pratt Hospital, was born. Eight agoraphobic women met with the first author and Ms. Milstein while their phobic companion husbands hung out with Ms. Milstein's husband in the hallway. We met once weekly to talk and once weekly to go "in vivo," to face their fears and to deliberately induce symptoms. We used Dr. Weekes' four steps: "FACE, ACCEPT, FLOAT, and LET TIME PASS."

Four decades before "third wave" cognitive-behavioral treatments such as ACT arrived on the scene, Dr. Weekes had developed an ACT-like approach that was effective for people who had struggled with anxiety symptoms for many years. As the evidence base and theories about anxiety disorders treatment have evolved since, we continue to marvel at her prescient thinking.

Within one year, we had two groups going, and within 10 years, we had a staff of 12 psychotherapists, multiple groups and individual therapies, and recovered clients who volunteered as "phobia aides," and we constituted more than a third of the outpatient department. During that time, we did a lot of free public education. We coordinated our public outreach with the national Phobia Society of America, the precursor of the Anxiety and Depression Association of America (ADAA), spearheaded by a small group of advocates and early researchers in the field. We made it onto the *Donahue Show, Dateline*, and local talk shows and even into *Cosmopolitan* magazine. Early on, clients were almost entirely self-referred, as they arrived holding an article from a magazine or newspaper, or saw a local or national TV show, or had attended our free public lecture series about the anxiety disorders. Many of the clients were already in other treatment and their doctors were highly skeptical of a psychotherapy they considered simultaneously dangerous and superficial.

There were no graduate training or specialized workshops to learn from, as we ourselves were the pioneers. The national network of clinicians and researchers at ADAA served as our source of creativity and inspiration, and we ourselves were the ones giving early workshops. Interaction with such original thinkers as Donald Klein, MD, Martin Seif, PhD, James Ballenger, MD, Reid Wilson, PhD, David Barlow, PhD, and Jerilyn Ross, MA, the inspirational first president of ADAA, kept us abreast of new developments in the field. It was exciting to be part of the beginning of a whole new field.

In 1992, when the hospital was undergoing financial stressors as it tried to adapt to the onslaught of managed care, a generous severance package was offered to professional staff. We (the co-authors) decided to separate ourselves from the hospital and begin our own private practice group. We met with our psychotherapists and virtually the entire staff decided to resign their hospital positions and embark on the journey together. The hospital administration offered us rental space on campus with a year's free lease. With the hospital's blessing, our clients all came with us. So we began with many advantages.

## JOYS AND CHALLENGES RELATED TO THIS NICHE ACTIVITY

It is gratifying to work with anxiety disorders and OCD because most sufferers improve significantly and are grateful for the change in their lives. Because anxiety disorders are stress-sensitive and recurrent, we sometimes see people periodically over many years and truly know them; because of the genetic component, we sometimes know families across generations. We have been proud to be part of the explosion in interest and useful knowledge about anxiety disorders and OCD over the past 30 years. And because we are specialists, we often see clients who gained little from traditional therapies and are seeking additional help. Our goals are often larger than simple symptom relief. They include a more profound change in the client's relationship with his or her own mind and body.

The challenges are few: the minority of sufferers who don't respond to our best efforts to provide evidence-informed treatment and the financial and insurance limitations that are familiar to all out-of-network clinicians. Providing behavioral exposures may require longer than usual sessions, odd hours of operation, more electronic communication, unusual arrangements, and extra planning time than the standard 45- or 50-minute in-office sessions. If someone needs to drive over the Bay Bridge repeatedly, that can be a whole day; if exposure to an evening theater event is needed, or a visit to an Alcoholics Anonymous group accompanied by a psychotherapist, logistics can get complicated. Scheduling may need to have more flexible time built in.

## BUSINESS ASPECTS OF THIS NICHE ACTIVITY

We remain in the same location on the Sheppard Pratt Hospital grounds to this day, renting 19 offices and a few hours of conference room meeting space. We had virtually no startup money so our business model was as low risk as we could make it, keeping overhead expenses low. We hired just two part-time employees (an office manager and someone to manage billing and client records), and that is all we have to this day. The original furnishings were slightly used and bought in bulk. Our brochure was a self-produced trifold. Our offices are comfortable but modest. The owners paid ASDI for their own office rent and we still do. As co-owners, we chose to keep each of our own solo practice's finances independent from ASDI to preserve our own autonomy and to preempt potential conflict about unequal financial contributions. ASDI is a management services entity that provides administrative support, screening and referrals, office space, and collegial support to our clinicians.

Many of the policies and practices of ASDI were grounded in our experience of being part of a larger bureaucratic system—in other words, we wanted to do things differently. All ASDI psychotherapists are independent contractors who receive a percentage of collected fees. Although this has been critical for minimizing financial risk, it can provoke scrutiny by the Internal Revenue Service (IRS), so we have carefully detailed the agreement in writing per IRS checklists defining the issue (see https://www.angelo.edu/services/sbdc/documents/library_resources/IRS%20 20%20Factor%20Test.pdf.) A caution to others who want to consider this mode of practice: beware of the IRS. We recently came through an extensive audit with flying colors, but only because we were meticulously careful to follow IRS guidelines as to what constitutes an employee and what is a true independent contractor. Probably the factor that helped the most was that most of our psychotherapists also work in other locations, as college faculty, in other agencies, or in their own private practice location. We provide space to work in and patients to see, but we do not pay for their malpractice insurance and we do not set their hours or have productivity requirements. Review the current guidelines very carefully or the IRS will call your contractors "employees" and your costs will be completely different, including the possibility that you will need to pay employment taxes that were not previously paid but now deemed due (IRS, n.d.).

The aspect of work that was most important to us as a group was *individual autonomy*. To that end, we have tried to make the experience of our psychotherapists highly autonomous. This means that we offer rather than assign cases. Hours are set by the psychotherapists themselves, with the only limitation being shared office space. Any psychotherapist can turn down any case for any reason, such as not having the perceived expertise, not wanting another difficult case, or not wanting to work another evening hour.

Psychotherapists can develop their own mini-specialties such as emetophobia or trichotillomania or blood-injury phobia. Psychotherapists can develop other modalities based on their own special interests (e.g., a Fear of Flying program; a Social Anxiety/Improv Group; mindfulness meditation classes; use of FreeSpira, a biofeedback system for treating panic-related chronic hyperventilation). Some cases are shared by, for example, a family therapist, an individual psychotherapist, and an intern doing home visits involving exposure therapy. Such teams are developed spontaneously according to the needs of individual cases. Teams can also be arranged in some circumstances to provide nearly daily, intensive outpatient work.

Another value at ASDI is to have as little bureaucratic demand as possible. This means one *voluntary* staff meeting per week with attendance encouraged by emphasizing collegial and educational aspects rather than ASDI housekeeping. In contrast to our background as hospital employees, ASDI has no committees, no taskforces, and no productivity reports, expectations, or deadlines. Documentation, other than that needed for billing and that required by law, is at the discretion of the psychotherapist and remains the psychotherapist's property. Group and individual case peer consultation is available as well for everyone. In addition to individual and group supervision, trainees are encouraged to sit in on intakes, exposure therapy outings, home visits, and groups run by more senior clinicians.

Professionals in the community refer to us because of our reputation and 35 years of experience. There is a large network of primary care physicians who know us. Sheppard Pratt sends us anyone who calls with anxiety or OCD. The emergency department in the community hospital next door sends us their panic attack patients. There is also by now a large network of local mental health professionals who have been trained by us in workshops, ongoing consultation groups, internships, and lectures.

More than half of our referrals are now self-referrals via the Internet. Our website (www.anxietyandstress.com), which portrays our range of expertise and years of experience, generates requests for help or appointments every day. Many of these are people who cannot afford to see us, but we reply and, if necessary, refer everyone who contacts us. All clients are screened in a 10- to 15-minute, free telephone screening by one of us co-directors, and we have developed a reputation for giving free brief consults to clinicians in the area. We believe that our unreimbursed time is a continuing investment in ASDI branding and reputation building. We no longer do any print, radio, or TV advertising as it is no longer worth the price. We are listed in professional directories such as the ADAA, the Association of Behavioral and Cognitive Therapies, the International OCD Foundation, *Psychology Today*, and the Maryland Psychological Association.

Once a client has been accepted for treatment, the screening co-director offers the case to one or more psychotherapists and the one who is "matched" calls the client personally to make a first appointment. There is no appointment secretary, as we want the whole process to be individualized for both client and clinician. We do have an answering service that takes calls and forwards them to us around the clock. In an old-fashioned twist, we two co-directors still carry a beeper and are on call for the whole group for emergencies.

Originally, we participated as "in-network providers" for selected third-party payers. But as diminishing reimbursement, collection problems, and demoralization seriously threatened ASDI's future, we gradually left all such contracts. Some of us still participate with Medicare; however, for our psychotherapists to be willing to accept poorly reimbursed Medicare referrals, ASDI takes only a token portion of the fee. For all other clients, we collect payment at the time of service. Patients pay by cash, check, or credit card since we have not yet moved to other payment strategies that are still evolving. We issue monthly, generated statements so that clients may seek reimbursement from their insurance companies. In keeping with the value of autonomy, we do not offer a practice-wide sliding scale. Rather, any psychotherapist is at liberty to reduce the fee of any client from our standard fees, based on his or her own clinical and financial judgment. Their percentage of that which is collected remains the same, so most psychotherapists have some pro bono or low-fee clients at their own discretion. Our trainees see low-fee or no-fee clients in exchange for their training.

Our business model has not created wealthy owners; rather, our profits essentially pay for our administrative hours at about the same rate as we would be paid for clinical hours. We deliberately chose this model rather than a high-volume contract-with-all-third-party-payers practice with clinicians as full-time employees. Although potentially more lucrative, we felt such a practice entailed more risk, given the whims of third-party payers, as well as much more aggravation. It also seemed the antithesis of our values emphasizing autonomy, individualized treatment, and quality of life. Admittedly, this model means that more than half of the people who contact us cannot afford our services, either out-of-network or out-of-pocket, which does not jibe with our social conscience. So we co-owners still participate with Medicare and provide occasional pro bono services. We supervise interns who provide low-fee services. Daily we help callers with referrals to in-network care.

In the years since 1992, we have grown and expanded. We are multidisciplinary, including psychologists, social workers, licensed professional counselors, pastoral counselors, nurse specialists, and a training director. Over the years we have attempted to have a psychiatrist on board, but the economics of this are prohibitive so we have a network of local private practitioners to whom we refer on a regular basis.

In summary, we believe that nurturing shared, specialized expertise among a group of like-minded clinicians, promoting the autonomy of those clinicians so that turnover is rare, and keeping our overhead low have been the primary reasons for ASDI's continuing success. Our local and national reputation as a specialty practice and our willingness to train and consult with local clinicians serve as low-key marketing that keeps the flow of referrals coming.

## DEVELOPING THIS NICHE ACTIVITY INTO A PRACTICE STRATEGY

The best place to learn about this kind of niche practice is to attend the national conferences of the ADAA and the International OCD Foundation (IOCDF) and spend a lot of time networking. These are smaller, more personal conferences than the annual meetings of the Association for Behavioral and Cognitive Therapies or the American Psychological Association. Both ADAA and IOCDF offer day-long workshops on special topics at their annual meetings, and IOCDF offers a three-day intensive training in OCD treatment. Individual or group supervision with a specialist in anxiety disorders and/or OCD can be arranged with our practice and is readily available in most other population centers.

Developing this niche also should include designing a comprehensive website with downloadable free information about anxiety disorders and OCD, with links to other notable websites, resources, and self-help literature. We have always maintained collegial rather than competitive relationships with other groups and professionals who specialize in the same field, maintaining cross-referrals and consultations and occasionally collaborations. This applies locally, regionally, and nationally. There are enough patients to go around. In addition, if there is someone with this specialty but who is also willing to be on insurance panels and be medical assistance providers, we maintain a steady flow of referrals to them of patients who cannot afford to see us.

## FOR MORE INFORMATION

We recommend that those interested in pursuing this niche practice read the books in the resources list. Useful websites include the Anxiety and Depression Association of America (http://www.adaa.org) and the International OCD Foundation (https://iocdf.org).

# NOTE

1. Zelda Milstein, who openly discussed her clinical history, was an inspiration to many in her 40 years working as Maryland's first paraprofessional exposure therapist. She was working until shortly before her death in 2015.

# REFERENCES AND RESOURCES

Carbonell, D. A. (2004). *Panic attacks workbook: A guided program for beating the panic trick*. Berkeley, CA: Ulysses Press.

Carbonell, D. A. (2016). *The worry trick: How your brain tricks you into expecting the worst and what you can do about it*. Oakland, CA: New Harbinger.

Grayson, J. (2014). *Freedom from obsessive compulsive disorder* (updated edition). New York: Berkley Books.

Internal Revenue Service. (n.d.). Independent contractor (self-employed) or employee? Retrieved from https://www.irs.gov/Businesses/Small-Businesses-&-Self-Employed/Independent-Contractor-Self-Employed-or-Employee.

Seif, M. N., & Winston, S. (2014). *What every therapist needs to know about anxiety disorders: Key concepts, insights, and interventions*. Abingdon, UK: Routledge.

Weekes, C. (1972). *Peace From Nervous Suffering*. New York, NY: Hawthorne Books.

Wilson, R. (2016). *Stopping the Noise in Your Head: The new way to overcome anxiety and worry*. Deerfield Beach, FL: Health Communications Inc.

# CHAPTER 55

# TREATING OBSESSIVE-COMPULSIVE AND RELATED DISORDERS

*Helen G. Jenne*

am a licensed psychologist who is board certified in clinical psychology. I have been in private practice for over 14 years. My practice is solo and is in the affluent Buckhead area of Atlanta, Georgia. I work approximately 40 hours per week and see approximately 25 to 30 patients per week.

## THE NICHE PRACTICE ACTIVITY

I have a niche private practice in the areas of obsessive-compulsive disorder (OCD) and related disorders as well as anxiety disorders. I spend approximately 98% of my time in my practice with patients with these disorders as primary disorders. Within the obsessive-compulsive and related disorders component of my practice, I predominantly see patients with OCD; however, I also see clients with trichotillomania, excoriation disorder, and body dysmorphic disorder. I have some patients with hoarding disorder as well. I also see patients with many types of anxiety disorders, including generalized anxiety disorder and panic disorder.

## DEVELOPING AN INTEREST AND TRAINING IN THIS NICHE ACTIVITY

My interest in these disorders began when I took a course in cognitive-behavioral therapy (CBT) in graduate school and was able to see the connection between a person's thoughts, mood, and behavior. I was taught the feedback loop of anxiety and the concepts of schedules of reinforcement. I also took an existential psychology course, an area that was already of interest for me prior to graduate school. I subsequently wrote my clinical dissertation based on extrapolating concepts from Martin Buber's work into the therapeutic relationship. Merging CBT and Buber's work has become a foundation for my work today. Buber focused on principles that involved aiding a person to be heard and to work toward his or her ultimate goals, and I have applied these concepts through the therapeutic relationship in my treatment work with patients. I knew that I wanted to pursue private practice prior to graduate school, so I was interested, early in graduate school, in the types of issues patients can struggle with that I might want to work with later in my career to help me inform the type of internship and postdoctoral experience I desired.

I had completed my dissertation when I left for my predoctoral internship year. I had been very focused on Buber's work at that time and wanted to balance that with more specific CBT training. I chose an American Psychological Association–accredited predoctoral internship that had a broad array of patient populations. The program director, who was involved in my supervision, identified as a cognitive-behavioral therapist and was working on several CBT-based projects. This internship allowed me to practice interweaving Buber's concepts regarding the therapeutic relationship and the structured evidence base CBT can provide.

I then chose a postdoctoral supervised work experience in a private practice setting such that I could further my development as a psychotherapist. I learned about the business side of being a mental health clinician in a private practice setting to help round out my desire to ultimately have my own practice. This supervisor helped me reinforce the concepts of both the therapeutic relationship and CBT with a variety of patient populations. I was exposed to many clinical issues and began realizing that I particularly enjoyed working with anxious clients and those who had obsessive-compulsive and related disorders.

After I had completed my postdoctoral year I opened a solo private practice. I started with a wide variety of patients who had clinical issues I had experience treating from my training years. I also concurrently worked at a residential treatment facility for two years, during which time I had a private practice. For board certification, I chose a case in my area of interest of combining the clinical issues as well as CBT and Buber's concepts. The preparation as well as process of this certification in clinical psychology sealed my desire to pursue a specialty in obsessive-compulsive and related disorders as well as anxiety disorders, and to deepen my knowledge and application of evidence-based treatments.

I started attending conferences through the International OCD Foundation (www.iocdf.org) and further researching obsessive-compulsive and related disorders. These activities enhanced my interest even further. These conference opportunities include patients, researchers, and mental health practitioners and have been powerful in providing me with up-to-date and relevant research, treatment, and experiences related to OCD. I was also able to pursue training in the model of Acceptance and Commitment Therapy (ACT) through the conferences and through other trainings; I use this as a treatment approach in my practice as well. These conferences enhance my network of like-minded psychotherapists around the world, which is crucial in this specialty as there are not enough mental health practitioners in the area to meet patient needs. Attending conferences can help reinforce your knowledge and broaden your connections beyond your office.

I decided to pursue further formal training within my area of interest through the International OCD Foundation, which offers a formal program to become certified in treating OCD through the Behavior Therapy Training Institute. This training enhanced the knowledge I had and offered many practical examples.

I also joined what was previously called the Trichotillomania Learning Center (now called the TLC Foundation for Body-Focused Repetitive Behaviors, www.bfrb.org) and completed its Virtual Professional Training Institute training program, a CBT-based program in body-focused repetitive behaviors. This program was helpful in teaching me about trichotillomania and excoriation disorder as well as other body-focused repetitive behaviors and the relevant treatments for these disorders.

I have been a member of a small group of several psychologists who specialize in treating the same population as I do, and this has been a wonderful group for consultation and learning. Further, I have done presentations at a variety of locations on areas and treatments in my niche, and these have been excellent experiences in educating others about the evidence-based treatments available.

# JOYS AND CHALLENGES RELATED TO THIS NICHE ACTIVITY

Having a niche area such as this has been an incredibly rewarding experience. I truly enjoy the process of treatment, from the beginning assessment to the psychoeducational component to the actual treatment. Being a direct part of the change process when I can do exposure/response prevention (ERP) treatment in session with patients who have OCD is rewarding. Exposure involves exposing a patient to thoughts, images, or stimuli that induce anxiety, and response prevention focuses on the elimination of compulsive responses. Patients learn to rate their anxiety levels and continue exposures with response prevention until their anxiety levels significantly reduce and they gain greater tolerability for anxiety. For treatment to be maximally effective for any of the disorders I specialize in treating, the patient needs to work on the concepts of treatment outside of session as homework between visits. This type of treatment for OCD can involve leaving the traditional therapy office setting to assist patients in carrying out their ERP treatment when necessary.

There can be difficulties for clients on issues with willingness, commitment, and follow-through with homework, as well as family members evidencing difficulty with treatment concepts. These issues can significantly interfere with treatment progress and thus the ultimate effectiveness of the treatment. The psychoeducational component of treatment is very helpful for teaching patients and their family members (if possible) about the treatment methods employed. It initiates the process of inducing hope that their situation can improve and that there are evidence-based treatments for their disorder. This requires a curiosity and openness as well as readiness to hear this kind of information, and if a patient is unable to do so, treatment can be compromised early on in the process as these issues need to be addressed.

Perhaps the largest issue I have seen in practice is lack of the patient following through with homework. I work to collaborate with patients on assigning homework so that they are as much a part of the process as I am to increase the chances of follow-through. At times, a plan is put in place for patients to check in with me in between sessions to promote homework compliance. The ERP process requires repetition in order for learning to occur and for the anxiety to decrease in intensity, frequency, and duration, so if clients do not obtain this repetition, the effectiveness of treatment is limited.

There are many obstacles that can interfere with homework completion, and these need to be addressed to maximize treatment effectiveness. I try to include the family members who are most involved with the patient's life from the outset of treatment to provide a "team" of support and so that I can try to redirect any collateral behavior that could be interfering with treatment. One of the largest issues with family members and OCD is that a they can unknowingly be reinforcing the patient's compulsions. This is addressed early in the psychoeducational phase of treatment as well as throughout treatment. A primary example of this is providing reassurance to an anxious patient who is compulsively seeking reassurance. Another is engaging in rituals for the patient. If the family member does not work on ceasing these behaviors at the right times in treatment, it could alter otherwise effective treatment.

# BUSINESS ASPECTS OF THIS NICHE ACTIVITY

In the past, I was in-network with several insurance panels, but I ultimately decided to no longer remain in-network and have transitioned into a 100% self-pay practice. I had a billing service for the time I was on insurance panels but I no longer require one as I bill at the time of service. One of the main reasons for altering my practice to be self-pay was that patients can need more and different arrangements for treatment than the traditional once-weekly psychotherapy session. At times patients need to meet more frequently than the traditional session frequency that insurance will reimburse. Preauthorizations from insurance companies may be required for providing these treatments. I have more time for patients when I spend less time with insurance companies and their requirements. Further, treatment also involves travel time outside of the office to provide ERP. I have found that having flexibility and addressing each patient's needs session by session works best for my patients.

# DEVELOPING THIS NICHE ACTIVITY INTO A PRACTICE STRATEGY

The International OCD Foundation as well as the TLC Foundation for Body-Focused Repetitive Behaviors are incredibly active with offering training opportunities, conferences, and community experiences that garner much attention. They have been a key aspect for developing the needed competence in my niche area. There is incredible community involvement in my niche area that has also generated many referrals.

My marketing is broad-based and includes schools, pediatricians, general practitioners, dermatologists, and other mental health professionals as well as psychiatrists. I have given talks to a mental health center and to other agencies in the community and have reached out to many doctors in the community to inform them of the type of work I do. I have served on ABPP committees for candidates undergoing examination, and this has connected me with a variety of psychologists who learn about my work. I have met many psychologists at the conferences I have attended as well as psychologists in the community who share my specialty, and these efforts have culminated in many client referrals. Patients also often refer others they know are suffering to me.

I keep in touch with referring doctors throughout treatment (with the patient's written authorization for consent), which provides collaboration on the patient's care and helps me maintain the relationships with my network of doctors. I also have a website that describes my specialty, and I have included that website in my profile of the organizations to which I belong. When patients are looking for a psychologist with my specialty, my website helps them learn about my work and provides my contact information.

## FOR MORE INFORMATION

The key books for me regarding the treatment of OCD are by Grayson (2003) and March and Mulle (1998). I would recommend the trainings that the International OCD Foundation, the TLC Foundation for Body-Focused Repetitive Behaviors, and the Anxiety and Depression Association of America provide. I also suggest you attend conferences offered by these organizations. The training provides the foundation, and the conferences allow you to network with like-minded clinicians who can possibly be a part of a consultation group, could serve as referral sources, and could become consultants and friends. I would have been limited in my niche area had I not pursued these avenues.

The websites for these organizations (www.iocdf.org, www.bfrb.org, and www.adaa.org) provide a wealth of information on the disorders I specialize in treating, and they also provide resources, from books to support groups to treatment information. I would recommend reading the books and articles that these organizations suggest because they focus on evidence-based treatments. Further, these organizations send out newsletters with helpful information regarding the disorders if you are a member.

I would also advise joining a strong consultation group that meets at least once per month to discuss all aspects of treating these disorders. There is great variability in cases and nuances of the treatments that are often very helpful to review with others.

# RESOURCES

Grayson, J. (2003). *Freedom from obsessive compulsive disorder: A personalized recovery program for living with uncertainty.* New York: Penguin Group.

March, J. S., & Mulle, K. (1998). *OCD in children and adolescents: A cognitive-behavioral treatment manual.* New York: Guilford Press.

# CHAPTER 56

# COGNITIVE-BEHAVIORAL THERAPY FOR HOARDING DISORDER

*Michael A. Tompkins*

I am a psychologist and co-director of the San Francisco Bay Area Center for Cognitive Therapy. This is a group practice in which we are sole proprietors of our practices and share overhead and the costs of other activities, such as supporting our website, conducting trainings, and marketing our services. I provide cognitive-behavioral therapy (CBT) and other evidence-based treatments for anxiety and mood disorders and for obsessive-compulsive spectrum disorders that include hoarding disorder (HD), obsessive-compulsive disorder (OCD), and body-focused repetitive behaviors such as trichotillomania.

## THE NICHE PRACTICE ACTIVITY

In my practice, I treat anxiety disorders and obsessive-compulsive spectrum disorders. HD is an obsessive-compulsive spectrum disorder. I treat perhaps eight to 10 clients per year who present for the treatment of HD; this number is small in part because so few individuals seek treatment for the condition. More often, I provide consultations to family members of loved ones who have HD. In addition, once or twice each year I offer a treatment group to individuals with HD and a support group for family members.

## DEVELOPING AN INTEREST AND TRAINING IN THIS NICHE ACTIVITY

Because I specialize in CBT for OCD, and because prior to 2014 what is now termed HD was subsumed under the diagnosis of OCD, I often evaluated individuals for the treatment of their OCD who reported hoarding behaviors. A subset of patients with hoarding behavior exhibited extreme hoarding symptoms such that their living environments were unsafe. This piqued my interest, and I searched for research articles on the topic, which at the time was known as compulsive hoarding. I soon discovered active research in this area that included a randomized controlled trial of CBT for compulsive hoarding. This treatment appeared to help individuals with hoarding behaviors (Steketee & Frost, 2013). I began to treat compulsive hoarding (now known as HD) in my practice. At that time, few clinicians understood the condition and fewer still were trained in the use of CBT. I attended several workshops by Drs. Randy Frost and Gail Steketee, recognized experts on the condition, and read all the relevant research on the topic that I could find. Because I had received extensive training in CBT during my doctoral and postdoctoral years, through internships, workshops, and ongoing supervision with experienced CBT practitioners, the transition to treating HD was not difficult for me.

## JOYS AND CHALLENGES RELATED TO THIS NICHE ACTIVITY

HD is a fascinating psychological problem, and few clinicians understand the condition or how to treat it effectively. For these reasons, I have focused on disseminating the treatment to other clinicians and give six to 12 trainings every year. In addition, I have broadened my practice to include consultation to family members with a loved one with HD. This interest in assisting family members of people with HD resulted in my writing two books on the topic (Tompkins & Hartl, 2009; Tompkins 2014a). Both books present a harm reduction approach, and this model has provided me with many opportunities to train a wide audience, clinicians and nonclinicians, throughout the United States and Canada.

In addition to providing a variety of professional opportunities, the topic of HD presents a host of clinical challenges. Even individuals who have sought professional help remain ambivalent about treatment and struggle to engage fully in certain aspects of the treatment. They also typically have a number of comorbid psychological conditions: For example, approximately 60% have a major depressive disorder and perhaps 25% have attention-deficit/hyperactivity disorder.

If you enjoy clinical challenges, HD is a great clinical problem to tackle. Every day I learn something new about both HD and CBT from my clients.

## BUSINESS ASPECTS OF THIS NICHE ACTIVITY

Many individuals with HD are older adults on fixed incomes and are accustomed to paying for health and mental health services through their health insurance or Medicare. For this reason, I recommend clinicians become members of insurance panels or Medicare providers. If you are open to broadening your interest to include group treatment, you can generate income by offering consultations to family members of people who hoard or to other professionals, such as professional organizers, who often work with people who hoard.

Another business challenge is securing payment for the clinical services you provide outside the office. To treat HD effectively, CBT includes a series of home visits to help clients apply the skills taught in the therapy to organizing and decluttering their home. Many insurance companies do not pay for any clinical services provided outside the office, so clients may have to pay for in-home visits out of pocket.

## DEVELOPING THIS NICHE ACTIVITY INTO A PRACTICE STRATEGY

Clinicians interested in the treatment of HD would be wise to think broadly about ways to help individuals. Because it is a low-insight condition, few individuals will seek treatment for the condition because they do not believe they have a problem. For that reason, I recommend clinicians broaden their expertise to include consultations to family members and to agencies that work with people who hoard, and to develop cost-sensitive ways to assist older adults with HD who have limited means, such as CBT groups for the condition (Muroff, Underwood, & Steketee, 2014). Furthermore, clinicians may wish to develop or participate on hoarding taskforces in their communities. These taskforces are multidisciplinary organizations that can have a variety of missions. Some provide resources and referrals to professionals working with people with HD. Some provide oversight on community responses to hoarding situations. Others work with communities to develop policies and guidelines to respond to hoarding situations. Hoarding taskforces are forming throughout the United States and are a valuable resource to communities looking for a coordinated and multidisciplinary response to this growing problem.

## FOR MORE INFORMATION

The Mental Health Association of San Francisco (www.mentalhealthsf.org) is a not-for-profit organization dedicated to the dissemination of information and resources to those with mental illnesses. It was the first organization to present an annual conference on the topic of hoarding in the early 1990s and since then has educated hundreds of clinicians, nonclinicians, and consumers about the condition and expanded its services to include treatment and support groups for people who hoard, a support group for family members with a loved one who hoards, peer-led decluttering assistance, referrals to clinicians and other professionals trained to assist people who hoard, and ongoing training to professionals through workshops and lectures.

The International Obsessive Compulsive Foundation (www.ocfoundation.org) is a not-for-profit organization dedicated to the dissemination of information and resources to those with obsessive-compulsive disorder. Because HD was initially thought to be a form of OCD, the foundation began to disseminate information on HD through its website and annual conference. Now, the foundation has devoted a section of its website to HD and includes information about the condition, referrals to therapists trained to treat the problem, and other resources of value to people who hoard. A few years ago, the foundation began to offer daylong workshops on CBT for HD to professionals and has now trained dozens of people in the treatment. I highly recommend that clinicians join this group take these workshops. The website lists clinicians who treat HD and specifically those who have received this specialized training.

# REFERENCES AND RESOURCES

Bratiotis, C., Schmalisch, C. S., & Steketee, G. (2011). *Hoarding handbook: A guide for human service professionals.* New York: Oxford University Press.

Frost, R. O., & Steketee, G. (Eds.). (2014). *The Oxford handbook on hoarding and acquiring.* New York: Oxford University Press.

Muroff, J., Underwood, P., & Steketee, G. (2014). *Group treatment for hoarding disorder.* New York: Oxford University Press.

Steketee, G., & Frost, R. O. (2013) *Treatment for hoarding disorder* (2nd ed.). New York: Oxford University Press.

Tolin, D., Frost, R. O., & Steketee, G. (2014). *Buried in treasures: Help for compulsive acquiring, saving, and hoarding* (2nd ed.). New York: Oxford University Press.

Tompkins, M. A. (2014a). *Clinician's guide to severe hoarding: A harm reduction approach.* New York: Springer Publications.

Tompkins, M. A. (2014b). Hoarding disorder: Clinician application. In L. Grossman & S. Walfish (Eds.), *Translating psychological research into practice* (pp. 204–207). New York: Springer Publishing.

Tompkins, M. A., & Hartl, T. L. (2009). *Digging out: Helping your loved one manage clutter, hoarding, and compulsive acquiring.* Oakland, CA: New Harbinger Publications.

# CHAPTER 57

# TREATING TRAUMA AND ABUSE

*Elaine Ducharme*

I am a licensed psychologist who has been in a solo private practice for nearly 30 years. The last 15 I have been located in Glastonbury, Connecticut. It has been and continues to be a wonderful ride. Sure, there have been a few ups and downs, but I feel very blessed to be able to do what I love and be my own boss.

## THE NICHE PRACTICE ACTIVITY

I have specialized in treating patients who have experienced trauma and abuse. My work has included both victims and perpetrators, as I feel that understanding both sides of the trauma is critical in maintaining professional objectivity. I also have found that most victims can have some perpetrator-type behaviors and many perpetrators have been victims of trauma and or abuse themselves. My nursing background has also helped me work with victims of medical trauma.

## DEVELOPING AN INTEREST AND TRAINING IN THIS NICHE ACTIVITY

Looking back, I realize my journey began during my first career as a nurse. I had received my bachelor's degree in nursing from Boston University. The program was very much oriented to understanding our own emotional needs as well as those of our clients. As a result, I found myself working on a pediatric unit, frustrated by the lack of mental health services. I managed to start a suicide sitter program so that we could have 1:1 coverage for suicidal children, bought sleeper chairs so parents could spend the night with their sick child, and gathered a team to set up a behavioral medicine unit. In the 1970s little was really being done in the field of trauma and abuse. I began asking questions about certain types of injuries, worked with children who had been sexually assaulted and impregnated, and realized that this was an area where I could possibly make a difference. I returned to graduate school for a master's degree in developmental psychology and continued on to earn my PhD in clinical psychology.

In graduate school, I think that somehow one of my supervisors sent me all the clients whom we so affectionately refer to as "borderlines." For whatever reason, I found working with these clients challenging, frustrating, but interesting work. So many of them, who were primarily women, had horrific experiences of physical and sexual trauma. For many, the trauma had begun in early childhood. For others, the traumatic events, such as rape or domestic violence, were relatively recent. My graduate program was psychoanalytically based. Although I am now a much more active psychodynamically oriented psychotherapist, and I often employ other techniques such as cognitive-behavioral therapy (CBT) or relapse prevention for treatment of specific issues, I believe that one must have a good psychodynamic background to work with clients who have experienced early childhood trauma. Early trauma clearly has an impact on future behaviors. To move forward in this area and help a client make significant and lasting changes, I feel that a clinician, at the very least, must consider the following in formulating a treatment approach:

An emphasis on the centrality of intrapsychic and unconscious conflicts, and their relation to development

Seeing defenses as developing in internal psychic structures in order to avoid unpleasant consequences of conflict

A belief that psychopathology develops especially from early childhood experiences

A view that internal representations of experiences are organized around interpersonal relations

A conviction that life issues and dynamics will reemerge in the context of the client–psychotherapist relationship as transference and countertransference

As I thought about my dissertation topic, a wonderful professor suggested the topic of the "God concept" of sexually abused women. I was working in a primarily Catholic community. I am Jewish and clearly not a theologian, but I found the topic fascinating. So many of my clients felt so guilty about what had happened to them that they had either lost their faith in God or perceived God as evil and wanting them to suffer. Either way, for many of them a spiritual and/or religious support was gone. It was exciting research and became the basis of my first book (Ducharme, 2000), which was about premature forgiveness of sexual abuse.

I began private practice in Palm Beach Gardens, Florida, with a wonderful business partner. I didn't really intend to focus on trauma; it just seemed to happen. I became the consulting psychologist for the sexual abuse section of the Center for Children in Crisis. This agency assessed and treated both physically and sexually abused children as well as sexually reactive youth. During my work there, the team realized there were few individuals trained to assess the adult sexual offenders. The research was slim, but I began reading everything I could find and attended numerous conferences to gain understanding of the offenders. This work was incredibly helpful. I learned to recognize that many victims behaved in aggressive ways, at times even victimizing others. Many perpetrators had experienced victimization themselves. I received a lot of experience testifying about my reports in court and became known as an expert in the areas of trauma and abuse.

After 15 years, my husband's job forced us to move up to Connecticut, but I have been extremely fortunate in reestablishing my practice. I am certain, however, that the reason is that I do have a specialty niche. I have maintained my license in Florida, which has made it easy to continue to work with clients via telecommunication, and I make periodic trips back to a warm climate.

## JOYS AND CHALLENGES RELATED TO THIS NICHE ACTIVITY

I know that many psychotherapists argue about whether we "re-parent" our clients, and in this particular niche there is a role of re-parenting. Helping women find a safe place to ask questions, not be judged, and try out new behaviors as they learn to trust themselves is incredibly satisfying. I feel fortunate that I had parents who provided me those opportunities, and I hope I share a bit of that with my clients.

There are the downsides as well. For example, the crises often happen at night or on weekends, so being able to tolerate and handle these situations while teaching clients about clear boundaries can be a challenge. Having a support consultation group can be extraordinary helpful when you are dealing with tough cases and can help protect you against liability. The work is also long-term. Progress can be slow but incredibly rewarding. Your own self-care and support system are critical for anyone doing this work. My family, vacations, and massages keep me sane (okay, and sometimes chocolate!).

I used to participate on insurance panels, but over the years I have moved to a fee-for-service practice. Many clients who have backgrounds with extreme trauma may have difficulty paying for services out of pocket. Sometimes I feel badly that I have to turn down clients who cannot afford my fee, so I try to see a couple of clients for a reduced rate. I don't see anyone in my office for free. Even if they pay $20, it helps them see our work as valuable. I collect fees at each session, take credit cards, and am more than willing to help clients complete forms to send to their insurance companies so they can receive out-of-network benefits.

## BUSINESS ASPECTS OF THIS NICHE ACTIVITY

I think it is really important for those of us in private practice to understand that we are running a business. We have to get over our fears of asking for payment. When I worked in Florida we had a secretary help us with insurance billing and other administrative work, but now I manage the business end myself. Even if you have help, you must keep an eye on your own finances. I have friends who have lost a lot of money because they left the finances completely up to someone else.

My practice has varied from about 60% to 80% trauma-based, when I factor in victims and perpetrators. However, to keep my own sanity, I have maintained a general practice assessing and working with children, teens, and adults. My pediatric and nursing background made developmental assessments of young children a comfortable part of my work. There is clearly a crossover between sexual trauma and eating disorders, so I have had to be sure I knew what I was doing with these challenging clients. I have also loved working with women in their 50s and older as they try to figure out what they want for themselves as they finish raising their children. And over the past six years, I have begun working in the area of "collaborative divorce," helping families achieve divorce with dignity. Having a team to work on managing the trauma of divorce has been emotionally and financially gratifying and lots of fun.

## DEVELOPING THIS NICHE ACTIVITY INTO A PRACTICE STRATEGY

My referrals have come from a variety of sources, including other clients, physicians, school counselors, attorneys, and sometimes the Connecticut Department of Children and Families. I have been the Public Education Coordinator for Connecticut through the American Psychological Association. As a result, I spend a lot of time speaking, writing, and doing guest appearances on radio and television, providing education on mental health issues. I write a weekly blog for a popular radio station, where I am also a monthly guest. The bottom line here, I believe, is that if you want to have a private practice, you can't just sit in your office. You need to be active in your community and let people know what you do.

## FOR MORE INFORMATION

For those who feel that working in this field might suit them, I would recommend a couple of books. Courtois's 2009 book is a great beginning. I would also recommend my own books (Ducharme 2000, 2015). Understanding issues related to domestic violence, eating disorders, and sexual offenders can help one feel more competent and be better prepared to recognize these issues and know when to refer to someone else. I recommend being a member of Division 56 (Trauma Psychology) in the American Psychological Association to stay current in the research and treatment issues and Division 42 (Psychologists in Independent Practice) for incredible support in the area of private practice. I also recommend joining the International Society for the Study of Trauma and Abuse. Books on the business of practice such as Walfish and Barnett (2009) are important for any of us working in niche practices.

David Hoffman produced a 2006 video entitled *Four Men Speak Out* that presents survivors of sexual abuse.

I have found that *The Psychotherapy Networker* is a journal that regularly has articles on trauma and abuse and also hosts webinars that are extremely helpful to those working in this field. To remain current in the research in this area, one should subscribe to the *Journal of Trauma and Dissociation* published by Taylor and Francis.

The bottom line here is that I have been blessed to find a niche that I enjoy, I believe I help make a difference, and I have been able to make a nice living. I can't ask for much more.

## REFERENCES AND RESOURCES

Courtois, C., and Ford, J. (2009). *Treating complex traumatic stress disorders*. New York: Guilford Press.

Ducharme, E. (2000). *Must I turn the other cheek?* West Palm Beach, FL: Denlan Productions.

Ducharme, E. (2015). *Assessment and treatment of dissociative identity disorder*. Camp Hill, PA: TPI Press.

Hunter, M. (1990). *The neglected victims of sexual abuse*. New York: Random House.

Walfish, S., and Barnett, J. E. (2009). *Financial success in mental health practice*. Washington, DC: American Psychological Association.

# CHAPTER 58

# INTENSIVE OUTPATIENT TREATMENT FOR EATING DISORDERS

*Linda Paulk Buchanan*

I am a licensed psychologist in Atlanta, Georgia, who began working with individuals with eating disorders 30 years ago. I received a master's degree from Georgia State University in 1983 and several years later returned to GSU to earn a doctoral degree. Twenty-two years ago, I developed the Atlanta Center for Eating Disorders (ACE), which offers an intensive outpatient program (IOP) for individuals with eating disorders. This private practice has now grown to three locations, one of which also offers a day treatment program for eating disorders that is accredited by the Commission on Accreditation of Rehabilitation Facilities.

## THE NICHE PRACTICE ACTIVITY

As the vast majority of people with eating disorders cannot recover with traditional outpatient psychotherapy, a multidisciplinary team approach is widely recognized as the best practice (Joy et al., 2003). After working for over 30 years with this population, I am convinced that the most effective approach is to gather a team of professionals who specialize with this population and who are willing to work together as a cohesive team. This team generally consists, at a minimum, of a psychotherapist, a physician, and a nutritionist. It is also my experience that although individual therapy is a necessary component of the treatment, group therapy is actually more powerful than individual therapy for this population.

Treatment, therefore, begins with a multilevel assessment process. We conduct a psychological assessment and a nutrition assessment and determine the patient's medical stability through consultation with internists, family practitioners, or pediatricians. As a result of this assessment, the need for treatment and the optimal level of care are determined. We offer several levels of care through our program. The IOP is the most often recommended and generally consists of nine to 20 hours of therapy per week, including individual, family, nutrition, and group counseling, and one meal group session per day. Day treatment or the partial hospital program (PHP) consists of 20 to 40 hours a week and includes all the above components with two meal group sessions a day. Finally, aftercare, which is basically the same level of care as traditional outpatient therapy, may be recommended for patients if they do not have active eating disorder symptoms, if the symptoms are very mild and do not reach diagnostic criteria, if the symptoms have begun within the previous two months, or as a stepdown from the more intensive levels of treatment. About 15% of the people we assess are determined to be medically unstable and are referred for residential or inpatient treatment.

The accepted treatment for eating disorders involves a multimodal approach (Halmi, 2005, Stein et al., 2012) consisting of multiple psychotherapy modalities: individual, family, nutrition, and group counseling and sessions with a psychiatrist. It's my experience that a combination of types of groups is most effective. We combine skills groups such as cognitive-behavioral, Acceptance and Commitment Therapy, motivational interviewing, and dialectical behavior experiential groups such as art, yoga, meal groups, and process-oriented groups into the treatment plan.

I spend about 20% of my time conducting initial psychological assessments and about 20% of my time leading therapy groups. At this point in my career, I no longer conduct individual sessions, as I have come to believe that group therapy is more powerful and, for me, more exciting work. However, we have a talented staff of individual therapists providing this component of treatment. The remainder of my time is devoted to training, supervision, writing, and administrative responsibilities.

## DEVELOPING AN INTEREST AND TRAINING IN THIS NICHE ACTIVITY

I developed my interest in this population quite by accident. In the early 1980s, when I was practicing as a master's-level therapist, I developed an interest in treating eating disorders. I was working with an individual with bulimia who was also attending a group at a hospital that had a unit for the treatment of eating disorders. In the late 1970s, when eating disorders first became a topic of interest, units for treating eating disorders in hospitals seemed to spring up everywhere. However, by the early 1980s many were beginning to close, probably in part due to overreach and in part due to insufficient understanding of the treatment needs of this population. Such was the case at the hospital where my client was receiving group therapy. As it closed, she told the members of the group that she had a psychotherapist who worked with eating disorders, and approximately six of these individuals called me for psychotherapy. I began to read everything I could find about eating disorders, and I thoroughly enjoyed working with these women. I had heard how difficult it was to treat people with eating disorders, so I thought that I must be very talented.

Then reality began to hit. I was too inexperienced to fully understand that the first women I had treated were in an aftercare group and had already received much therapy before contacting me. As I began working with women who had acute and more serious eating disorders, I decided I needed more training and returned to school for a PhD in psychology. I oriented my doctoral program to learning about eating disorders by using it as the topic whenever I had to write paper or do a project of any kind. As I continued working with people with eating disorders, I became frustrated because it seemed that most of these beautiful, loving, talented women needed more than I could offer them in an outpatient practice—but didn't need to be hospitalized. When I completed my doctoral training, I opened ACE to provide an IOP for this population. It has been my experience that about 80% of individuals with eating disorders will not recover with traditional psychotherapy alone but also do not need the disruption caused to their lives by inpatient and residential programs.

There is very little in the way of formalized training for this population. The International Eating Disorders Professionals Association provides education and high-level training standards as well as a certification process. The Association of Professionals Treating Eating Disorders is an affiliation of eating disorders specialists based in the San Francisco Bay Area. It provides support and training for clinicians and referrals and direct service for clients. And finally, the Eating Disorders Certificate program at Lewis & Clark University may be the only graduate program in the country devoted to the topic.

## JOYS AND CHALLENGES RELATED TO THIS NICHE ACTIVITY

Working with this population is extremely rewarding in that I am working with some of the most caring and talented people I will ever meet. These men and women tend to be more sensitive than the average population (physiological differences) and are, thus, more vulnerable to cultural and familial stressors, but they are also extremely loyal, perceptive, and hard-working. This creates in them much ambivalence about themselves and their place in the world, which, when resolved, produces some of the most dynamic people I have ever met. One of the most rewarding aspects of the group work is to see them support and help each other, what we call the power of the milieu. I see more love expressed in one day at work than I would guess most people see in a month in other types of occupations.

Eating disorders are the most fatal of all mental health disorders, including depression, yet they are so misunderstood (Bulik, 2014). Knowing that we are saving lives and helping to change public opinion is also rewarding beyond words.

Another joy is working together with a team who support each other in a common mission. There is much camaraderie among our team, and we are there to support each other when a patient is not responding to the therapy.

Clinically, the biggest challenge is dealing with what I term *pathological ambivalence*. I've written a book entitled *A Clinician's Guide to Dealing with Pathological Ambivalence* (publication in process) where I teach strategies for staying out of the inevitable power struggles that arise when these patients are attempting to recover. Another challenge is the possible medical problems that develop and the need at times to refer patients to medical facilities where their psychological needs may not be well cared for because their medical needs get more aggressive treatment. The other challenges center primarily around working with insurance companies and other administrative tasks involved such as scheduling, charting, and billing.

# BUSINESS ASPECTS OF THIS NICHE ACTIVITY

In most parts of the country, there are very few intensive outpatient programs for patients with eating disorders. It has generally been easy to get referrals to the program since for about 20 years we were the primary option for this level of care in the whole southeastern United States. Marketing directly to psychotherapists, schools, and pediatricians has been the most successful strategy. We also have developed strong relationships with many inpatient and residential programs throughout the area who refer to us for stepdown treatment. I have also developed a talk titled "Common Myths About Eating Disorders" that is on our website (www.eatingdisorders.cc), with the offer to provide speakers for interested groups. Recently, treatment options for eating disorders have been increasing, with a growing number of IOP, PHP, and residential programs being developed. However, outside of major cities there is still a dearth of options.

Approximately 70% of the income received is from third-party payers. About eight years ago ACE was awarded accreditation through the Commission on Accreditation of Rehabilitation Facilities (renewed every three years), which enabled us to contract with all the major insurance companies. This is a great benefit to our patients but requires much administration on our part related to the policies and procedures required and careful monitoring of utilization of services. We had assumed that becoming an in-network provider would result in less management by the insurance companies, but that has not turned out to be the case. Although it varies by company, we have to provide updates every few days to two weeks for continued treatment.

The remaining 30% of the income received is self-pay from noninsured patients, deductibles, or co-pays. We bill monthly for current fees. For patients who have very large deductibles (which seems to be rising), we offer payment plans.

# DEVELOPING THIS NICHE ACTIVITY INTO A PRACTICE STRATEGY

Readers who are interested in developing a practice focusing on the treatment of eating disorders should start by connecting with other professionals in their area who are also interested in this population. Putting together a team as described above, developing a peer consultation group, and developing several therapy groups is a great way to get started. Becoming active in national organizations such as International Association of Eating Disorder Professionals and the National Association of Anorexia Nervosa and other Related Disorders can be very helpful and can provide a network of local providers, certification options, and treatment resources. The next step would be to develop a website and begin marketing as described above. I would not recommend trying to treat this population in a solo practice unless you have other components and a team you can work with. As stated before, I became frustrated trying to treat these patients with individual psychotherapy alone as it seemed analogous to taking half an aspirin for a headache; we were going through the motions but it simply wasn't powerful enough to result in change.

## FOR MORE INFORMATION

These websites are useful: National Eating Disorders Association (www.nationaleatingdisorders. org), National Association for Anorexia and Related Disorders (www.anad.org), International Association of Eating Disorder Professionals (www.iaedp.com), and Academy for Eating Disorders (www.aedweb.org). I also recommend the *International Journal of Eating Disorders* and *Eating Disorders: The Journal of Treatment and Prevention* (www.onlinelibrary.wiley.com).

## REFERENCES AND RESOURCES

Buchanan, L. P. (in progress). *A clinician's guide to dealing with pathological ambivalence: How to be on your client's side without taking a side by utilizing ambivalence and side-stepping projections.*

Bulik, C. (2014) 9 eating disorders myths busted. Retrieved from http://www.nimh.nih.gov/news/science-news/2014/9-eating-disorders-myths-busted.shtml.

Halmi, K. A. (2005) The multimodal treatment of eating disorders. *World Psychiatry*, 4(2), 69–73.

Joy, E. A., Wilson, C., & Varechok, S. (2003). The multidisciplinary team approach to the outpatient treatment of disordered eating. *Current Sports Medical Report*, 2(6), 331–336.

Kaye, W. (2008), Neurobiology of anorexia and bulimia nervosa. *Physiology & Behavior*, 94(1), 121–135.

Stein, D., Hashomer, T., & Latzer, Y. (2012). *Treatment and recovery of eating disorders.* New York: Nova Science Publishers.

Yager, J., Devlin, M. J., Halmi, K. A., Herzog, D. B., Mitchell, J. E., Powes, P., & Zerbe, K. J. (2014). Practice guideline for the treatment of patients with eating disorders (3rd ed.). Retrieved from http://psychiatryonline.org/pb/assets/rax/sitewide/practice_guidelines.

# CHAPTER 59

# ASSESSMENT AND TREATMENT OF ATTENTION-DEFICIT/HYPERACTIVITY DISORDER

*Daniel Lennen*

am part of a multidisciplinary outpatient group practice in Portland, Oregon, and have been a licensed psychologist in Oregon since 2012.

## THE NICHE PRACTICE ACTIVITY

I am a co-founder, with Danell Bjornson, a psychiatric mental health nurse practitioner, of the Northwest ADHD Treatment Center, Inc. (NWADHD). NWADHD was founded to meet the ever-growing need in Portland, Oregon, to diagnose and treat attention-deficit/hyperactivity disorder (ADHD) in children and adults. At present there are no other practices like ours in our local market. NWADHD brings together psychological and psychiatric treatment of ADHD in one center that includes services that provide diagnosis and multiple modes of psychotherapeutic treatment, coupled with psychiatric care. Many clients arrive at intake believing that they have ADHD but actually have another psychiatric disorder. Due to misdiagnosis and the high comorbidity of other psychiatric disorders, NWADHD also treats depression, anxiety, and bipolar disorders that either co-occur or are the primary diagnosis for those being treated at our center. ADHD is the primary diagnosis for nearly 80% of our clients.

# DEVELOPING AN INTEREST AND TRAINING IN THIS NICHE ACTIVITY

I had several placements at university counseling centers and received training at Oregon Health and Science University's Child Development and Rehabilitation Center focusing on assessment in their neuropsychological and child development clinics. With this focus on neuropsychological assessment and treatment of ADHD in university counseling centers, I developed a strong interest in treating neurodevelopmental disorders such as ADHD. My postdoctoral residency focused on treating children and families with ADHD.

I was drawn to this population due to the common traits among this group. These clients are often creative and lively, have a high desire to achieve, and frequently live in the here and now. Parents are often confused about how ADHD affects their children and frequently implement overly harsh or punitive measures in an attempt to help their children. Frequently parents have traits of, or have been diagnosed with, ADHD, and their symptoms frequently interfere with their parenting skills.

Another advantage of working with this population is that I get more rapid feedback from clients about the effectiveness of treatment. As a psychologist, I am also able to incorporate the teacher–student role foundationally rooted in cognitive-behavioral therapy (CBT) focusing on skill building, educating, and identifying irrational thought patterns that sustain maladaptive habits and thinking that interfere with the client's functioning.

# JOYS AND CHALLENGES RELATED TO THIS NICHE ACTIVITY

I enjoy this practice for many reasons. These include the short feedback loops with clients that allow treatment gains to be measured within the first few sessions. Second, this population is often very amusing, lively, and creative. Our clinic has had many artists, musicians, writers, actors, and business owners in unique and creative businesses. Third, treatment of ADHD allows for the intersection of psychology, psychopharmacology, and neuropsychology. Finally, this population fits well with CBT practitioners, who tend to be directive, skill-oriented, and homework-focused.

Difficulties with this population include the high levels of substance abuse that frequently complicate the treatment. These clients have significant difficulty with their abstinence, primarily due to poor impulse control and the use of substances to manage comorbid symptoms (e.g., anxiety disorders). Screening individuals who are "drug seeking" to assess potential abuse of their medications is a top priority in working with this population. Adolescents and young adults exhibit higher substance abuse or wish to gain an academic or occupational advantage through medication management. As I noted above, parents often complicate treatment by using overly harsh strategies with their children, have similar symptoms to their children, and/or have difficulty identifying symptoms as a challenge because they were often much like their children when they were younger and do not want identify their own past challenges as problematic. Children often have many behavioral challenges, including school refusal, fighting with peers, stealing, and engaging in risky behaviors, that can be difficult to manage.

# BUSINESS ASPECTS OF THIS NICHE ACTIVITY

Early in the development of the company, we marketed to primary care clinics within the market to develop referral sources. Active marketing was done often in person by meeting with referral coordinators, case managers, psychologists who were part of a larger organization, and pharmaceutical representatives, who have wide access to many clinics. More passive marketing, such as mailers, newspaper ads, and sponsoring teams by advertising in their programs. did not seem to have much effect.

The use of technology is a core value of NWADHD. Our clinic uses an electronic health record system, tablet and computer-based assessment, and text/email reminders to our clients. Our clients are very familiar with technology and paper-free practice. They report that they value this feature of our practice. It also has significantly reduced the frequency of missed appointments. Clients connect with our clinic through a dedicated phone number to our intake coordinator, who screens potential clients and creates access to the online portal to our Electronic Health Record (EHR). Then, clients have access to our intake measures, office policies, and Release of Information forms (completion of these is mandatory to make an appointment). Having clients put effort into securing an appointment ensures that these measures are completed before the intake and that medical records have been requested, and it increases the likelihood that they will attend their first appointment. Most insurance companies give us access to member information online. Thus, our intake coordinator is able to check clients' insurance benefits before their appointment, allowing the clinic to verify benefits and determine any co-pays, co-insurance, or deductibles. Our clinic collects estimated payments at check-in and claims are sent primarily electronically through a third-party payment system. Finally, we are sent an explanation of benefits by the insurance company, and fees are billed directly to the client if money is due.

# DEVELOPING THIS NICHE ACTIVITY INTO A PRACTICE STRATEGY

We learned several lessons from developing a new clinic. We decided to accept commercial and public insurance as a convenience to our clients. The choice of which insurance companies to contract with was based first on their rates and second on how restrictive the insurance company would be with their benefits. Managing insurance companies and using correct billing practices are complex endeavors. First, hiring a credentialing specialist who can manage insurance credentialing and management of insurance contracting is a must. Second, learning how to navigate each insurance company to check benefits, dispute claims, and manage chargebacks is invaluable. Third, the practitioner must have a good understanding of Current Procedural Terminology (CPT) billing codes. This is crucial to avoid insurance fraud and ensure ethical billing practices.

Developing extraverted skills in building a practice is critical. Many of our referral partners came from directly contacting local agencies, building relationships with pharmaceutical representatives, attending pharmaceutical dinners to interact with local providers, and developing relationships in the community. Most large organizations are looking for reliable referral sources who provide good treatment to their patients and timely records for their review. As a practice rule, intake notes (with appropriate releases) are routinely sent to primary care physicians both to provide records and to market to providers who may not be aware of our clinic. Also, we go to conferences and are not shy about socializing with peers. Many research opportunities and business opportunities come from meeting professional peers.

Finding consultants for your business is important. We learned early that we could not run our business alone. Spending money on an employment lawyer, business lawyer, and certified public accountant is a must. I had the advantage of working in banking in undergraduate and graduate school to gain experience with business. This experience has been quite beneficial; however, NWADHD also subcontracts with a business consultant/mentor who has managed and consulted for many small-to-large businesses to help with growth, cash flow, lending, and negotiating contracts. As a new business, it is difficult to fit these expenses into the budget, but for long-term viability, practitioners will need to find mentors who know more about business to help them succeed. You will never lose out by paying for a well-qualified business mentor to help run your business. If you are able, manage your own books. This allows you to see how the business is performing, monitor accounts receivables, and make projections. You will likely sleep better at night if you have data about the health of your business.

Know the laws regarding businesses, employees, and taxation. You are bound by the employment and business laws of your state and the federal government. A new business cannot endure penalties for ignorance of the law. Also, one of your biggest business expenses (other than salaries) will be the taxes and insurance that you pay. These include federal tax, state/local tax, taxes on your assets (e.g., furniture, computers), workers' compensation insurance, liability insurance, and business insurance. Do not be afraid to pay for being well insured. With your liability insurance, make sure that you are also well insured for license protection. This allows for reimbursement of legal defense expenses from client complaints filed with the state licensing board. You are much more likely to need to defend against board complaints rather than clients suing the business.

Look into the possibility of hiring students and recent graduates to help manage the demand and increase revenue. Most large cities have training programs or recent graduates who are often looking for placements in the community. And please, offer to pay these students a small stipend. You will get highly qualified applicants and you get to have a one-year interview with potential employees. We are able to hire students because they qualify as "qualified mental health providers," who can bill at a reduced cash rate directly to clients or Medicaid. This requires that they are supervised both through their graduate program (usually two hours per week) and onsite in the clinic (one hour per week). Clients respond well to student providers, especially knowing that they are supervised by a psychologist who is reviewing their work. Also, another benefit of hiring students is that they offer the latest research and education to the clinic and provide a good source of revenue. You may need to be licensed as a "clinic" to gain the opportunity to hire students.

Lastly, writing employment policies that are both flexible and comprehensive is not a strength for many mental health practitioners. Early in our development, we wanted our policies to be flexible and spent little time formulating them. Partly, we were inexperienced at this, and also this task can be quite tedious. However, without policies, employees become quite confused and have little to reference to do their job. Just writing policies is not enough, however: You must formulate policies that will function for the business you will grow into, not just for the business that currently exists. If you plan to grow, these policies must function for a business with possibly 50 employees (which we are), not for the business that you begin with (we started with three employees). You might be able to get help from employment consultants (sometimes through your local Chamber of Commerce) in writing employee policies.

It would appear that there are many individuals who treat ADHD in the community, but surprisingly many psychologists, psychiatrists, and other mental health providers do not feel comfortable treating this disorder. A center model such as ours gives clients and other providers a central place to get services to treat this disorder. If interested in this population, I would encourage you to adopt a similar approach, continue to get good training in neurodevelopmental disorders, and provide excellent work to this exciting group.

## FOR MORE INFORMATION

Helpful professional organizations include the following: American Professional Society of ADHD and Related Disorders, a professional society for psychiatrists, psychologists, and physicians; Canadian ADHD Resource Alliance (www.caddra.ca); and Children and Adults with Attention-Deficit/Hyperactivity Disorder (www.chadd.org).

## RESOURCES

Barkley, R. A. (2010). *Taking charge of Adult ADHD.* New York: Guildford Press.

Barkley, R. A. (2013). *Taking charge of ADHD: The complete, authoritative guide for parents.* New York: Guildford Press.

Barkley, R. A. (2014). *Attention-deficit hyperactivity disorder: A handbook for diagnosis & treatment* (4th ed.). New York: Guildford Press.

Steele, D. A. (2012). *The million dollar private practice: Using your expertise to build a business that makes a difference.* Hoboken, NJ: Wiley.

# CHAPTER 60

# COUNSELING CLIENTS WITH ASPERGER'S

*Frank W. Gaskill*

I am a psychologist and co-founder of Southeast Psych. We are one of the largest group practices in the United States, with over 40 clinicians serving nearly every niche you could imagine. Our offices are located in Nashville, Tennessee; Charlotte, North Carolina; and New Zealand. We are a fee-for-service practice and strive to create a fun, unique environment, including life-size *Star Wars* characters as well as movie posters and videogame rooms. I have been practicing psychology for nearly 20 years, and my niche practice area is Asperger's,[1] autism, and parenting. I serve 25 clients (individually or family-based) for 45-minute sessions and also conduct five or six social skills groups per week with anywhere from eight to 14 children per group. The groups are divided into three age ranges: nine to 11, 12 to 14, and 15 to 18. During summer and winter breaks, I also offer social skills and gaming camps as well as social, coed teen nights. Most would consider this to be a burnout schedule; however, when I am not seeing clients, I feel bored and unproductive. My clients give me energy and inspiration.

## THE NICHE PRACTICE ACTIVITY

As a child psychologist, my bread and butter has always been helping parents manage defiant kids and improving parents' ability to be warm and authoritative. However, over the years the majority of my clients tended to live within the realm of the autism spectrum and, more specifically, Asperger's as defined by the American Psychiatric Association (APA)'s *Diagnostic and Statistical Manual of Mental Disorders,* fourth edition (DSM-IV; APA, 2000). At least 75% of my practice is focused on the autism spectrum through a variety of modalities, including client groups, parent support groups, individual/family sessions, camps, and social get-togethers.

# DEVELOPING AN INTEREST AND TRAINING IN THIS NICHE ACTIVITY

Autism captured my interest while I was in graduate school at the University of North Carolina—Chapel Hill. In the early 1990s, UNC was one of the major centers of the autism universe. I was exposed to many professors who specialized in early childhood development and who were also involved in mainstreaming autistic kids into regular classrooms. However, as Asperger's was introduced to the DSM-IV in the early 1990s, specific clinical training was nearly nonexistent for clinicians seeking to serve those with this differently wired mind. Most of my training occurred on the job and in reviewing the limited research articles that were available.

While understanding social skills training is crucial, the most valuable training experience I had was learning to speak the language of "Dungeons and Dragons," *Star Wars*, and "Super Mario Brothers." As I can speak their language, "Aspie" kids trust me, let down their guard, and allow me to teach them the social skills they need to thrive in society. Therefore, an important component of training is to understand "geek culture." The key to success in this niche is understanding and embracing the Aspie culture so clients feel validated, knowing someone genuinely understands and values them. I have found that providing an environment in which they are celebrated and included is more than 70% of the battle in improving the quality of their lives and building success. Working with Asperger's clients is not difficult if you are accepting and do your research into their culture. If you cannot appreciate their culture and understand them, this population is likely not for you.

# JOYS AND CHALLENGES RELATED TO THIS NICHE ACTIVITY

I consider my work as more of a mission of spreading the gospel that "Asperger's is Awesome!" and the world would be lost without this differently wired brain. I love the fact that most of my colleagues are unable to understand many of the conversations my Asperger's kids have with me about the intricacies of "Super Smash Brothers Brawl," the need for 20-sided dice, and why "Portal 2" and "Fallout 4" are amazing. If these pop-culture references do not interest you, working with Asperger's clients may not be your niche.

The primary joy for me is seeing a marginalized child or family feel embraced at Southeast Psych. My clients often tell me they have found their family and have never felt so proud of who they are. Many of my clients find their "Why" of life and come to a level of self-acceptance and discovery that they did not believe was possible. After reading my comic book about Asperger's entitled, "Max Gamer: I'm a Superhero," a client looked up and asked me if I followed him around each day. The story resonated so with him that he instantly felt supported. He was no longer alone.

While I love working with clients on the spectrum, there is a downside, and most of the time the downside is the father. The autism spectrum is genetic, and many times a dad sitting across from me is on the spectrum. Not only does he usually not know that he is on the spectrum, but his ability to be open-minded about this issue can be limited. I have had several dads immediately shut down and become unwilling to explore the possibility that their son or daughter could be on the spectrum. A parent's black-and-white thinking can make treatment difficult. A cornerstone of working with an Aspie client is self-awareness and self-acceptance. Without this understanding, little progress can be made. A truly rewarding experience is the dad who says, "Wow, I was a lot like him when I was a kid. Maybe I'm on the spectrum too." This therapeutic moment is exceptionally rewarding because as a dad is able to recognize his place on the spectrum, it often alleviates years of battles with his son or daughter. They now can relate to one another and recognize how they can work together.

One other downside to working with kids who are Asperger's is dealing with the *Diagnostic and Statistical Manual of Mental Disorders*, fifth edition (APA, 2013). The DSM-5 has made my clinical life frustrating and also added a session to most clients with whom I work. The most common question I get is, "But I didn't think Asperger's existed anymore?" This question leads me into an explanation that I have to give to the parents as well as my clients (child/teen) about the social engineering and politics behind the creation of autism spectrum disorder. While the enjoyment of sharing the complex neurodiversity of the spectrum allows me to discuss Einstein, Daryl Hannah, and Andy Warhol, the downside of explaining the politics of autism and all of the misunderstandings about the spectrum can be exceptionally frustrating. In addition, reeducating professionals and parents who buy into the stereotype of the Asperger's kid who does not want friends and who is introverted can be exhausting. Asperger's kids typically want to have friends but do not necessarily know how to go about finding and keeping friends. I would say the biggest downside to working with people on the spectrum is advocating for them in a world that does not understand or appreciate them.

# BUSINESS ASPECTS OF THIS NICHE ACTIVITY

I actually know little about insurance. My philosophy is that people will pay a great deal of money for elective surgery, attorneys, cars, and homes, so my assumption, correct or not, is that people will pay a reasonable fee to care for their children and family. My hope is more people will pay attention to the value of psychology in their lives and realize that the money spent in this arena is well spent and greatly improves the quality of their lives. To that end, my current rate is $250 for 45 minutes. I charge $75 per group per child, which includes help for the parents through a support group that occurs at the same time as the social skills group. My practice bills each individual at the time of service. In the case of groups, we charge for nine weeks of service at a time. I provide a reduced fee or a payment plan when needed. I do not work on insurance panels at all as time spent doing paperwork could be better spent sharing my passion for the spectrum.

# DEVELOPING THIS NICHE ACTIVITY
# INTO A PRACTICE STRATEGY

Upon entering private practice, I consistently ran into preteens who were bullied or excluded due to being perceived as "different." Social skills groups were commonly recommended, and as I first began to teach such groups, I noticed many of my clients had similar characteristics: a specialized and specific interest, poorly developed social skills, and above-average intelligence. In bringing children together with similar interests who had been excluded from the social mainstream, I found positive outcomes. When these "spectrum" children were in groups of like-minded kids, they no longer felt different or excluded, their anxiety was reduced, and their self-worth improved. In group therapy, these kids found their peers and social support. In experiencing a social connection and losing a sense of loneliness, my clients improved across a number of domains, including anxiety, depression, and defiance. The one thing all of these clients had in common was Asperger's.

For clinicians looking to build a niche practice for those on the spectrum, traditional insight-oriented psychotherapy is typically a waste of time for both the clinician and the client. Being behaviorally and cognitive-behaviorally skilled is typically the best background for a clinician in this area. Social activities that are "outside the box," consistently provided, have helped me build my practice more than anything. Development of this niche also means thinking outside the box. Have a board gaming tournament night at the office or even a videogame tournament with prizes has helped build a community of Aspie kids and families.

Word tends to spread quickly if you build a haven for these often bullied and neglected kids. As a practice-building resource, the following, in the form of a letter to families, is a suggested guide and resource for those considering building social skills groups within the community of Asperger's kids.

> The purpose of my social skills groups is to help all of my Aspies find friendship. Underlying all of our sessions is the theme of becoming connected beyond special interests and to find lifelong friends. The following gives you a general outline about each of our weeks together. Another psychologist will be facilitating the parent group and he/she can also facilitate communication between the parent and child groups.
>
> And as always, please try to set up get-togethers and play dates. Your kids need you to help them organize these get-togethers as such communication does not come naturally to them.
>
> **Each Week**
> 1. Share one high and one low of the week (15–20 minutes). Problem solve one "low."
> 2. Group lesson (20 minutes)
> 3. Fun activity or deeper conversation time.
>
> **Session 1: Psychoeducation**
> - Parents and kids get to know each other and exchange contact information.
> - What is Asperger's?

- Agenda and discussion of future groups and intro to parent facilitator
- What are specific goals and concerns for this group of parents?

### Session 2: Fight-or-Flight Night

- Introduction to the neurobiology of the fight, flight, or freeze response
- Creation of list of relaxation strategies that work best for each client
- Actual practice of relaxation training and discussion of situations where such strategies could be used best

### Session 3: Bully Night

- Introduction to bullying and the reasons behind such behavior
- Understanding power and control as well as how bullies identify their targets. We also discuss safe and unsafe locations in schools.
- Role-play is a big component of the session, and we practice responding to bullies and understanding when to seek help.

### Session 4: Goal Setting

- Many kids struggle with how to set goals and tend to struggle with knowing what goals are important and what goals are not. This session helps them understand how to target goals in an effective manner.
- In this session we imagine a future self and the steps needed to achieve that future. The steps often lead back to the basics, including cleaning rooms, finishing homework on time, and doing what they need to do before they do what they want to do.

### Session 5: Conversation Skills

- By this point in group, my clients are typically having their first play dates. This session is all about how to get to know another person. I call it becoming "a human detective."
- We role-play and practice open-ended questions versus closed-ended questions, working specifically on getting one another to talk about themselves as well as engaging in active listening.

### Session 6: Etiquette Night

- Etiquette night, otherwise known as pizza night, is one of my favorite evenings. This is the night in which I challenge kids to address their table manners.
- During the week prior we discuss food allergies as well as expectations for pizza night. While I do discuss manners and place settings, my emphasis is on chewing with their mouths closed, not talking with their mouths full, etc.
- During the night we play a good manners behavior game that makes manners fun. Group accountability is a big component of tonight's session.

### Session 7: Game Night

- Game night is exactly what it sounds like. Yes, videogames! The point of tonight is to further our connections, build friendship, and learn to deal with frustration while practicing strategies learned throughout our groups.

- The cornerstone of tonight's group is called "controllers down." Kids learn to tolerate frustration and set videogame controllers down when told to, without question or complaint.
- We discuss the role of videogames, frustration tolerance, and how to use gaming for good and friendship rather than an obsessive escape from reality or frustration.

### Session 8: Group Choice
- During group, themes often arise such as bullying issues, family problems, or worries about girls or friends at school. This session allows us to go deeper into one of the specific topics that is tailored to this group. We use active listening, open-ended questions, group problem solving, as well as learning to be a human detective and friend. This can be a very powerful group experience.

### Session 9: Wrap-up
- During our final session, we revisit our topics and provide words of encouragement and affirmation. We also revisit themes from our sessions together, and I emphasize how to maintain connection away from group and how to share our experiences together with family.

The resources that I list below will point you in the right direction, but the greatest guide on my journey of serving and celebrating kids on the spectrum has been getting involved in their lives. Knowing their stories and helping them feel valued is your best resource in being successful in this very specific niche.

# FOR MORE INFORMATION

The Internet is filled with incredible resources that are both professional and personal. As always, be wary about what you read, when it was published, and the credibility of the publisher. As mentioned earlier, I find some of the best information on Twitter from Aspie Nation itself.

The primary resources in terms of books I recommend for clinicians as well as families are Steve Silberman's incredible overview of all things spectrum in his book *NeuroTribes* (2015). I also strongly recommend *Asperger's in Pink*, which provides a great review of Aspergirls from the mom of an Aspie, Julie Clark (2010). For marriage and relationship perspectives, the only book I recommend is David Finch's *Journal of Best Practices* (2012). For kids, a therapist's best introduction to the spectrum is my comic book *Max Gamer*, as kids on the spectrum can easily relate to the story of Max and it begins excellent conversations.

In addition to books, the absolute best resource online is the Asperger/Autism Network (www. aane.org). Per their description, this group "works with individuals, families, and professionals to help people with Asperger Syndrome and similar autism spectrum profiles build meaningful, connected lives." I have found no other website that compares to their resources.

# NOTE

1. I don't see Asperger's as a syndrome or a disorder.

# REFERENCES AND RESOURCES

American Psychiatric Association. (2000). *Diagnostic and statistical manual of mental disorders* (4th ed., text rev.). Washington, DC: Author.

American Psychiatric Association. (2013). Diagnostic and statistical manual of mental disorders: DSM-5 (5th ed.) Washington, DC: Author.

Asperger & Autism Forum Community: Wrong Planet. (n.d.). http://wrongplanet.net/

Attwood, T. (2008). *The complete guide to Asperger's Syndrome*. London: Jessica Kingsley Publishers.

Clark, J. (2010). *Asperger's in pink: A mother and daughter guidebook for raising (or being!) a girl with Asperger's*. Arlington, TX: Future Horizons.

Finch, D. (2012). *The journal of best practices: A memoir of marriage, Asperger Syndrome, and one man's quest to be a better husband*. New York: Scribner.

Gaskill, F., & Kelly, R. (2010). *Max Gamer: I am a superhero*. Charlotte, NC: HeroHouse Publishing.

Ledgin, N. (2002). *Asperger's and self-esteem: Insight and hope through famous role models*. Arlington, TX: Future Horizons.

Silberman, S. (2015). *NeuroTribes: The legacy of autism and the future of neurodiversity*. New York: Penguin Random House.

# CHAPTER 61

# COUNSELING DEAF AND HARD-OF-HEARING CLIENTS

*Barrie Morganstein*

I am a licensed psychologist living and practicing in Charlotte, North Carolina. I work with clients of all ages by providing individual therapy, family therapy, and psychological assessment. I have been serving clients in private practice since early 2001, but have been working with the Deaf and Hard-of-Hearing (DHH) population for about 20 years.

## THE NICHE PRACTICE ACTIVITY

Given that there are so few clinicians with a DHH specialization, it has been important to be well versed in a variety of presenting issues and needs. I typically work with DHH clients in three major ways: individual and family therapy; psychological and neurodevelopmental evaluations; and consultation and outreach on behalf of DHH individuals.

The day-to-day work of psychotherapy with DHH individuals is similar to that with any of my hearing clientele; we generally work together in weekly or biweekly 50-minute appointments. However, because it is not uncommon for a DHH client to travel some distance to see me, I may see these clients for an extended session and/or work with them remotely by videoconferencing.

An interesting part of my practice has been conducting evaluations with individuals who are seeking cochlear implants. At the request of their implant team, I seek to identify their knowledge of the implantation and recovery process, the reasonableness of their expectations, their risk and protective factors (including family and social support), and the likelihood they will follow through with the recommended course of treatment.

One of my most pleasurable clinical activities is conducting psychological, psychoeducational, or neurodevelopmental evaluations with DHH individuals of all ages. While I am sometimes sought by DHH individuals or parents of DHH children, I have also contracted many times with school systems, governmental agencies like Vocational Rehabilitation, disability rights advocates, and attorneys. These contracted assessments typically include additional services like observations, interviews with collaterals, consultation with related professionals, and court testimony. Supporting and advocating for DHH individuals in this capacity has been exceptionally fulfilling and reinforces the importance of providing access to mental health services to all individuals in need.

Consultation and outreach have taken on many forms, including collaborating with other professionals treating DHH clients, participating in individual educational program (IEP) team meetings for DHH clients, presenting on topics relevant to DHH individuals (e.g., psychological assessment, social-emotional development), attending support groups for DHH individuals or parents of DHH children, and volunteering at local deaf-awareness events.

## DEVELOPING AN INTEREST AND TRAINING IN THIS NICHE ACTIVITY

Since college, my focus has been on working with DHH individuals of all ages. As part of my undergraduate work, students were required to research an area of clinical interest. At the time, I was thoroughly enjoying—and excelling in—learning American Sign Language (ASL). I had studied several languages over the years (French, Spanish, and Hebrew), but none of them was as pleasurable or as natural for me as ASL, and I soon immersed myself in learning about deafness from a clinical perspective. As I expanded my ASL skills and pursued my interest in deafness, I chose to study in the clinical psychology doctoral program at Gallaudet University in Washington, DC. It is the world's only liberal arts university for DHH individuals and provides exceptional graduate training to students who wish to work in the field of deafness.

Our coursework and clinical work emphasized a strong understanding of the audiological components of hearing loss, the cognitive and educational implications of hearing loss, the linguistic components of ASL, and the cultural impact of deafness. All of our coursework was conducted in ASL and our program required a high level of sign competency. Since my second year in graduate training, I have been providing clinical services to DHH individuals of all ages.

## JOYS AND CHALLENGES RELATED TO THIS NICHE ACTIVITY

I am one of only a few doctoral-level psychologists in North Carolina specializing in working with this population. Working with a small and specialized population like this is akin to being a mental health professional in a small town, where you may be called upon to provide clinical services to your barber, electrician, or councilperson. Because multiple relationships have the potential to bring harm to the client, clinicians are often dissuaded from entering this type of dynamic. However, the tenets of psychology ethics also emphasize the importance of ensuring that all individuals have equal access to the benefits of services. Treating a DHH individual whom you may know from the Deaf community can be ethically appropriate if you enter the relationship with great care and consideration. Potential harm can be minimized by establishing clear expectations from the outset, discussing confidentiality, and striving to ensure objectivity.

To appropriately treat members of the DHH community, a clinician needs to be able to match the wide range of communication needs of the DHH community. Not all DHH individuals are fluent in ASL or even use ASL. Some use a type of "pidgin" sign language (i.e., signing, but without ASL grammar) or an alternate form of signing; some are "auditory verbal" (i.e., use speech, residual hearing, or lip reading) and do not sign; some have minimal language skills altogether. I also work with some late-deafened clients who have lost their hearing but have not learned sign language, so we develop our own communication strategies, like gesturing and typing on the computer in a large font for them to read in real time (which serves as captioning). Training and experience, coupled with the openness for learning and the desire for new challenges, will be indispensable in matching the needs of DHH clients.

In working with DHH individuals, it is important to be knowledgeable about specific issues that are relevant to the DHH population but lack significance for hearing individuals. A few of those topics are (1) language acquisition and how communication mode (e.g., ASL, Signed English) may affect this, (2) the multitude of educational settings available to deaf children (e.g., deaf institutes, mainstreaming, self-contained classrooms) and how each impacts their access to learning, (3) how deafness and communication influence family and social relationships, (4) technology (e.g., hearing aids, cochlear implants, FM systems, videophones), (5) cultural aspects of deafness, (6) self-esteem and identity, and (7) legal and ethical implications of deafness.

While many clinicians have particular conditions in which they specialize (e.g., mood disorders, addiction), a clinician treating DHH clients should have a strong clinical foundation in a wide variety of issues. As you may be the only DHH expert for miles, you will want to be well versed in a range of concerns so you can best treat the majority of deaf individuals who walk through your door. Of course, it is impossible to be an expert at everything, and you will need to seek supports like continuing education and consultation with colleagues, but developing a broad clinical base is very important in working with this population.

Providing assessment services to DHH individuals does not stop at obtaining appropriate testing measures and learning sign language (or hiring an interpreter). Clinicians must also understand the limits of the tools they are using and must remember that the ability of those tools to accurately assess DHH clients depends on many factors, such as their hearing loss, preferred communication mode, language skills, and access to education and information. Clinicians must be able to use clear and concise communication that best matches the needs of the client and must ensure continued understanding both expressively and receptively. Most importantly, clinicians must provide accurate interpretations of the test results that take into account the many variables of DHH individuals. Reports must clearly describe the test findings to readers who are unfamiliar with deafness and its many implications for findings.

The tagline "Psychology for All" explains the mission for our private practice group. The goal of our practice is to promote access to mental health, be that in the form of psychotherapy, assessment, education (through media like presentations, webinars, books, podcasts, and blogs), support groups, and consultation. Working with and on behalf of DHH clients gives me the opportunity to provide psychology to individuals who may otherwise not be able to access it, and I find that exceptionally invigorating! Seeing a client for psychotherapy or administering a full neurodevelopmental evaluation to individuals who had previously been unable to obtain culturally appropriate services in their first language is both professionally and personally rewarding. Experiences like having a school system implement much-needed supports as a result of better understanding the needs of a deaf student or explaining to the court how a particular deaf defendant's lack of access to formal language for all of his childhood now prevents him from being able to assist in his defense are exceptionally fulfilling.

## BUSINESS ASPECTS OF THIS NICHE ACTIVITY

One of the benefits of having a narrow specialty is that there are rarely other clinicians with that same skillset. This not only helps in establishing a niche practice but is an advantage in negotiating with insurance companies for coverage and reimbursement. Like the other clinicians in my practice, I have avoided insurance panels because of the many restrictions and obligations. However, since most insurance panels do not include any providers who are fluent in ASL or who specialize in working with DHH individuals, companies are often willing to negotiate a "single case agreement" where they essentially consider me an in-network provider to their insured DHH client. This agreement then enables those clients to pay their same co-pay and receive the same coverage as they would with another clinician who is on their insurance panel. While this process often requires a bit more time and paperwork, the inconvenience has been relatively minimal and has been valuable in ensuring that I am able to provide care to my DHH clients.

When I first began working in private practice, the most common way to communicate with DHH individuals was by phone with a machine called a TTY (TeleTYpewriter), also called a TDD (Telecommunications Device for the Deaf); it looked like a small typewriter with a digital screen. You would dial a call or answer a call as usual, place the phone receiver into the device, and two TTYs would communicate with each other through various beeps, just as fax machines do; the beeps are then turned into words on the screen. If you didn't have a TTY, an operator with a TTY could be the intermediary between you and the deaf person with the TTY. Today, TTYs have been replaced by videophones where individuals communicate with each other through sign, very similar to using FaceTime or Skype. Again, if you don't have a videophone or know sign language, you may use an operator as the go-between. For quick conversations, email is often the most useful, but to conduct psychotherapy sessions remotely, a videophone would be essential.

At my office, clients pay and schedule future sessions with our receptionist. While most DHH individuals have spent all of their lives negotiating communication with hearing individuals and feel perfectly comfortable checking out alone, I make myself available to support any clients who prefer to have my assistance. At our first session I ask my DHH clients their preference; if they choose to have me accompany them, I will facilitate this transaction at the conclusion of each session. I also make sure to clarify for them the best ways for them to get in touch with members of my office staff should they have any questions outside of the office.

# DEVELOPING THIS NICHE ACTIVITY INTO A PRACTICE STRATEGY

Expertise in working with the DHH population is comparable to working with many other specialized populations with their own language and culture. Proficiency in ASL and extensive knowledge of deaf culture are exceptionally important for providing mental health services to DHH individuals. However, unique to the Deaf community is the audiological and linguistic component where DHH individuals have complex and varying degrees of hearing loss, use a wide array of communication methods (e.g., ASL, speech-reading), and may use different types of assistive technology (e.g., cochlear implants, hearing aids). Competence in working with this population will require extensive coursework and research in the field of psychology and deafness, consultation with professionals in the field, interactions with DHH individuals, and thorough understanding of the uniqueness of treating this population.

The American Psychological Association (APA) has been working to ensure that psychologists are aware of the specific implications for working with clients of various populations. In their Guidelines for Assessment of and Intervention with Persons with Disabilities (www.apa.org/pi/disability/resources/assessment-disabilities.aspx), the APA addresses some of the factors to consider when working with DHH clients, including specialized training, linguistic competency, assistive technology, and diversity within that particular population. APA's Guidelines on Multicultural Education, Training, Research, Practice and Organizational Change for Psychologists (www.apa.org/pi/oema/resources/policy/multicultural-guidelines.aspx) is also relevant in working with DHH individuals. The tenets of ethical standards of the social work, counseling, marriage and family therapy, and psychology professions have many commonalities; in her article, Gutman (2005) applied many of these professions' ethical principles to treating DHH clients.

Like most private practices, the best way to build a referral base is through networking. Actively collaborating with agencies and organizations related to deafness is highly recommended. Some of those are support groups for parents of DHH children, support groups for adults with hearing loss, state and local agencies that provide services and/or support to DHH individuals, local schools with hearing-impaired programs, medical professionals who specialize in treating individuals with hearing loss (e.g., audiologists, otolaryngologists), and professionals in any field who may serve as advocates or supports for DHH individuals (e.g., attorneys).

# FOR MORE INFORMATION

The *American Annals of the Deaf* (www.gupress.gallaudet.edu/annals), which has been in publication for over 150 years, focuses on the education of DHH children and addresses related issues like communication methods and language acquisition. The *Journal of Deaf Studies and Deaf Education* (www.jdsde.oxfordjournals.org) provides research related to cultural, developmental, educational, and linguistic issues of DHH individuals. The *Journal of American Deafness and Rehabilitation Association* (www.jadara.org) addresses issues of deafness in the fields of mental health, social services, rehabilitation, and related areas.

The National Association of the Deaf (www.nad.org) was designed to protect the "civil, human, and linguistic rights" of DHH individuals in the United States, predominantly through advocacy and education. The American Society of Deaf Children (www.deafchildren.org) is a national organization whose goal is to support deaf children and their families through a variety of means including education, advocacy, mentoring, and provision of resources. The American Deafness and Rehabilitation Association (www.adara.org) is a networking organization for professionals who provide services to DHH individuals.

## RESOURCES AND REFERENCES

Andrews, J., Leigh, I. W., & Weiner, M. T. (2003). *Deaf people: Evolving perspectives from psychology, education, and sociology.* Upper Saddle River, NJ: Pearson.

Glickman, N. S. (2009). *Cognitive-behavioral therapy for deaf and hearing persons with language and learning challenges.* New York: Routledge.

Glickman, N. S. (Ed.). (2013). *Deaf mental health care (counseling and psychotherapy).* New York: Routledge.

Gutman, V. (2005). Ethical reasoning and mental health services with deaf clients. *Journal of Deaf Studies and Deaf Education, 10*(2), 171–183.

Leigh, I. W. (Ed.). (1999). *Psychotherapy with deaf clients from diverse groups.* Washington, DC: Gallaudet University Press.

Leigh, I. W. (2009). *A lens on deaf identities (perspectives on deafness).* New York: Oxford University Press.

Miller, M. S., Thomas-Presswood, T. N., Metz, K., & Lukomski, J. (2016). *Psychological and psychoeducational assessment of deaf and hard of hearing children and adolescents.* Washington, DC: Gallaudet University Press.

Morere, D., & Allen T. (2013). *Assessing literacy in deaf individuals: Neurocognitive measurement and predictors.* New York: Springer.

National Association of the Deaf. (2015). *Legal rights: The guide for deaf and hard of hearing people* (6th ed.). Washington, DC: Gallaudet University Press.

Padden, C. A., & Humphries, T. L. (2006). *Inside deaf culture.* Cambridge, MA: Harvard University Press.

Parasnis, I. (1996). *Cultural and language diversity and the deaf experience.* New York: Cambridge University Press.

Vernon, M., & Andrews, J. F. (1989). *The psychology of deafness: Understanding deaf and hard-of-hearing people.* London, England: Longman Group United Kingdom.

# CHAPTER 62

# COUNSELING CLIENTS WITH BORDERLINE PERSONALITY DISORDER

*Lauren Moffitt Edwards and Noelle Santorelli*

We began our joint endeavor after first meeting during our postdoctoral fellowship year. We currently both have full-time fee-for-service private practices in Atlanta, Georgia, and founded a separate group therapy practice, Daily DBT, in 2014. Lauren started her individual practice in 2010 and primarily works with young adults, ranging in age from high school–aged adolescents through adults in their early 30s. Noelle began her practice in 2012 working primarily with adolescents through older adults as well as families.

## THE NICHE PRACTICE ACTIVITY

Daily DBT is a practice offering dialectical behavior therapy (DBT) skills groups to high-functioning individuals in the Atlanta area. The defining feature of both of our practices is working with patterns of dysregulation (emotional, behavioral, interpersonal, cognitive, and self) that often group together into the more pervasive problems known to most practitioners as Borderline Personality Disorder (BPD).

Many psychotherapists shudder at the thought of consistently working with BPD and many have horror stories from their token BPD training case. While our practices do include some of those special cases, more often we encounter a range of clients from within the BPD spectrum—for example, an anxiously attached college student struggling to develop healthy friendships and romantic relationships as well as a middle-aged adult, working part time due to interpersonal conflicts, who shows up to sessions one week with gifts and the next with disparaging comments about the psychotherapist and the lack of progress. Despite the clinical picture, a variety of clients do in fact meet full criteria for BPD, not simply those who are difficult to work with from the outset and regularly generate strong feelings in the psychotherapist.

Many of these clients have never had a suicidal thought or engage in self-harm, despite the popular conception of BPD clients. In our individual practices we see approximately 20 individual clients per week with 25% meeting full criteria for BPD and an additional 50% exhibiting strong BPD traits but not meeting full criteria for a BPD diagnosis. Many of our clients are unique in that they are typically of above-average intelligence and high on *apparent competence* (a DBT term meaning the ability to handle everyday life problems with skill but in an inconsistent and context- or mood-dependent manner).

We also have a variety of tasks involved in running our group business, Daily DBT. We currently offer nine DBT groups that meet weekly (six adult groups and three teen groups). We structure our groups to have two group leaders and a maximum of eight group members per group. Within these groups 50% to 75% of clients meet full criteria for BPD while others have lesser forms of dysregulation. We personally co-lead three of these groups while supervising other leaders, developing materials, and conducting a variety of workshops for parents, professionals, and community members.

One final piece of our niche includes providing supervision for much lower-functioning DBT groups as adjunct faculty for Emory University School of Medicine and providing continuing education training to various professional groups.

## DEVELOPING AN INTEREST AND TRAINING IN THIS NICHE ACTIVITY

Neither of us set out to hang a shingle on working with BPD (who would!?), but in retrospect we have been on this path from the outset of our careers. Even during our training experiences we both were drawn to complex cases, expressive clients, and intensity. We enjoyed the more concrete therapeutic techniques that involved developing specific skills and at the same time were excited and interested in long-term, attachment-based, and insight-oriented aspects of psychotherapy that required deep relationships with our clients. Lauren then became more specifically interested in working with BPD clients while she was working as the clinical and program coordinator for Emory University's Garrett Lee Smith Suicide Prevention Grant. Having a longstanding interest in childhood trauma naturally led Noelle to working with BPD individuals within a hospital system.

## JOYS AND CHALLENGES RELATED TO THIS NICHE ACTIVITY

We both appreciate the complexity and genuineness that BPD clients bring to sessions. The effectiveness of a two-pronged approach of stabilizing DBT skills and emotion-focused interpersonal psychotherapy is rewarding. Our clients often come into our practices desperate for change and feeling chaotic. We have the opportunity to experience relatively quick and satisfying change and then settle into doing deeper work for a much longer period of time.

Working with BPD clients is also rewarding from a business perspective. We are able to have clients use two services (group and individual therapy), we have a healthy stream of clients coming from colleagues who are anxious or less enthusiastic about working with dysregulation, and we have deep relationships with our clients, who then stay for longer courses of psychotherapy. Many clients benefit from multiple individual sessions a week, therefore reducing the need for many new referrals and allowing us to focus in depth on a smaller caseload. From a financial point of view, these are often clients who are willing to pay outside of managed care for our level of expertise, as they have often seen multiple providers previously who were unable to help. We have never participated in any insurance panels, which has not yet been a challenge.

Then there are the challenges . . . working with BPD clients means that many of the rewards can often also become challenges. For example, intensity of emotion can feel authentic and connecting when discussing painful traumas but can feel annoying or attacking when discussing rescheduling and other routine office policies. As another example, sensitivity can be engaging and allow for deeper insight when a relationship is off balance but can be excruciating when it's directed at some detail in the psychotherapist's physical space (e.g., the color of the sofa, the brightness of the lights, the room temperature). One particular area of difficulty with BPD clients is setting and maintaining boundaries. It's critical to be prepared to stick to what you believe are important clinical frameworks and then to tolerate the anxiety that comes when a client begins to push those. For example, neither of us is responsive to texts or emails that contain significant clinical information and are clear about the importance of discussing clinical information in session. We recommend that clinicians include their policies about these boundaries in their informed consent materials. This requires both having the conversation about a boundary that can feel overly harsh to a BPD client and then tolerating the anxiety of not responding when an email arrives that you know could leave the client in a painful space until your next appointment (obviously, this is hard when we both value compassion and responsiveness in our therapeutic relationships).

## BUSINESS ASPECTS OF THIS NICHE ACTIVITY

Referrals are generated mainly through our community of providers and former clients. This primarily includes referrals from other psychotherapists and psychiatrists. Many psychotherapists encounter clients in whom they recognize a personality disorder early on and believe that does not work with their expertise and therefore are looking to refer out. Other psychotherapists find themselves working with a client with BPD and recognize the need for an adjunctive service such as a DBT skills group or a short course of one-on-one skills training. This collaboration with other individual providers in particular expands our referral networks dramatically. It has afforded us the opportunity to have our therapeutic skills and personalities well known with the psychotherapists and psychiatrists of the 50+ individual clients currently enrolled in group services. Frequently, group members themselves recommend our services to others. In addition, the combination of doing individual therapy from various theoretical orientations, as well as offering the structured DBT component, allows us to converse fluently and form relationships with a broader network of community providers than we would have access to if we focused solely on one treatment modality to target BPD. Referrals are also generated through various other business activities, including providing supervision, offering continuing education workshops, and parent and community speaking engagements.

Given the boundary issues that arise with BPD clients, the billing and payment arrangements have to be clear from the outset. Specifically, when discussing services, potential individual clients are made aware of the base fee for individual sessions as well as crisis or coaching calls. This policy is also included in the information shared during the informed consent process. For clients who intend to use these latter services we require a credit card to be placed on file so that payment can still be taken at time of service. When discussing DBT skills group polices with potential clients, we make clear that group members pay for all group sessions within each module regardless of attendance. Therefore, for group services, cancellations, no shows, and so forth are still billed regardless of notification prior to the absence. For individual services a 24-hour cancellation policy is consistently enforced. From a business perspective we have learned that this policy dramatically reduces absences and allows for a consistent income. Unfortunately we did not come to this more streamlined billing process early in the growth of our practice. We adjusted our payment policy to prevent clients' emotional reactions from interfering with consistently obtaining funds (i.e., desire to overpay or underpay, refusal to pay for late cancellations, early terminations with an outstanding balance).

# DEVELOPING THIS NICHE ACTIVITY INTO A PRACTICE STRATEGY

For mental health providers who are interested in working with BPD clients, we have a variety of recommendations. First of all, we would encourage psychotherapists to seek training experiences that include longer-term insight- and emotion-focused therapies (e.g., attachment, interpersonal, psychodynamic), cognitive-behavioral therapies such as DBT, and process group experience that allow a psychotherapist to see interpersonal dynamics at work. We also recommend that psychotherapists develop a solid consultation and mentoring network that would allow for authentic discussion of transference and countertransference processes. This network should include other professionals who are committed to being available for consultation if and when risk issues or boundary issues arise outside of scheduled business hours. Being able to reach out to close colleagues at times that feel random and imposing can be critical to managing the emotions and practical problems that can arise when working with BPD clients.

A variety of group experiences can be useful for psychotherapists who are also interested in adding a DBT group component to their practice. Experiences with specific behavioral or DBT groups is an obvious requirement. Skills learned by observing or co-leading interpersonally oriented process groups can also be critical for recognition of the processes that are occurring in and impacting the group, regardless of whether or not it is an explicit component of the group. This in turn can lead to DBT groups that form well and work on multiple levels.

Positive self-care strategies are essential when working with BPD clients. Engaging in consistent and ongoing personal psychotherapy and/or supervision can be extremely helpful, especially in situations where a client triggers significant person-of-the-therapist issues. Our experience is that process-oriented supervision has been particularly supportive. To work in a personality disorder niche, psychotherapists need to develop the ability to be transparent, to consider criticism as it comes to you, to be mindful of personal reactions and where they are coming from, and to tolerate the anxiety of behaviors typically associated with BPD pathology (e.g., criticism, suicidal risk, triangulation, splitting, manipulation, pushing boundaries, refusing limits). Additional personal self-care strategies outside of the workplace also help sustain psychotherapists in this line of work. These can range from cooking, to meditating, exercising, vacationing, or simply eating and sleeping well on a regular basis.

While working with BPD surely is not for everyone, we have found this to be a stimulating, rewarding, and business-savvy niche. We would encourage psychotherapists to challenge themselves by working with increasingly dysregulated clients and start building a skillset that can sustain a rewarding life-long practice.

## FOR MORE INFORMATION

The following associations have useful websites:

Linehan Institute: Behavioral Tech (www.behavioraltech.org)
Linehan Institute (www.linehaninstitute.org)
American Association of Suicidology (www.suicidology.org)

Your local state psychological association can also be a good resource; see http://www.apa.org/about/apa/organizations/associations.aspx.

## RESOURCES

Germer, C., Siegel, R., & Fulton, P. (2013). *Mindfulness and psychotherapy* (2nd edition). New York: Guilford Press.
Johnson, S. M. (1994). *Character styles*. New York: W.W. Norton & Company.
Koerner, K. (2011). *Doing dialectical behavior therapy: A practical guide*. New York: Guilford Press.
Linehan, M. (1993). *Cognitive-behavioral treatment of borderline personality disorder*. New York: Guilford Press.
Linehan, M. (1993). *Skills training manual for treating borderline personality disorder*. New York: Guilford Press.
Linehan, M. (2014). *DBT skills training manual* (2nd ed.). New York: Guilford Press.
Miller, A. L., Rathus, J. H., & Linehan, M. (2007). *Dialectical behavior therapy with suicidal adolescents*. New York: Guilford Press.

Norcross, J. C., & Guy, J. D., Jr. (2007). *Leaving it at the office: A guide to psychotherapist self-care.* New York: Guilford Press.

Rathus, J., & Miller, A. (2014). *DBT skills manual for adolescents.* New York: Guilford Press.

Teyber, E. (2005). *Interpersonal process in therapy: An integrative model* (5th ed.). Belmont, CA: Thomson Brooks/Cole.

Wallin, D. J. (2007). *Attachment in psychotherapy.* New York: Guilford Press.

# CHAPTER 63

# PSYCHOTHERAPY WITH COLLEGE STUDENTS

*Rachel G. Smook*

I am a licensed psychologist in independent practice in Northborough, Massachusetts. I completed my doctoral education at the Massachusetts School of Professional Psychology, now William James College. Following an internship and postdoctoral fellowship at Harvard University, I took some time away from practice to care for my young children. During this time, I stayed connected to the field through speaking and writing engagements and through committee and leadership roles in several American Psychological Association Divisions. I began my private practice in 2007 and have been in Central Massachusetts ever since. Northborough is a small suburb about 40 miles west of Boston. My practice typically draws from five surrounding towns, five local colleges and universities, and the nearby University of Massachusetts Medical School.

## THE NICHE ACTIVITY

I have a niche practice providing psychotherapy services to college students and young adults. At any time, 30% to 50% of my practice is dedicated to the young adult population. I initially began working solely with college students within this niche, but as my practice has grown, I've expanded to include services to recent college graduates, graduate students, medical students, and young physicians in residency. I have worked consistently at marketing locally so that when there is a referral for someone in the 18-to-24-year-old age range, my name comes quickly to mind as a good resource.

## DEVELOPING AN INTEREST AND
## TRAINING IN THIS NICHE ACTIVITY

I fell into young adult mental health somewhat by accident. My early-career goals centered around child and family therapy, and so my first two practicum experiences focused on work with children and their parents. It was with some reluctance in my third clinical placement that I sought to train at a college counseling center. My aim was to correct for the fact that I had learned about working with children and with adults, but not with people who were developmentally on the bridge between the two. Secretly I was a little worried about it; it just was not my interest area. I expected to check off that box on my own internal human development roster and then return to my original plan. Instead I fell in love with working with this population. The work I did at the college counseling center felt stimulating and challenging, and I developed a tremendous fondness and respect for the work that young adults are doing as they come into their own. Although I did spend another year at a clinical placement that offered the chance to work with children as well as adults, I missed the college population and was very clear that I wanted to return to that setting for internship. I accepted an internship at the Bureau of Study Counsel at Harvard University. When Harvard also offered me a postdoctoral fellowship, I accepted with enthusiasm. My training at the Bureau of Study Counsel allowed for in-depth psychotherapy with both undergraduate and graduate students, extensive psychodiagnostic testing and consultation experience, group psychotherapy, and structured small-group supervision.

## JOYS AND CHALLENGES RELATED
## TO THIS NICHE ACTIVITY

Young adulthood is a wonderful time for psychotherapy. For most students, college offers the first extended chance to begin figuring out who they are and what matters most to them without being under the daily watch and influence of their parents. They are learning to manage their day-to-day experiences, desires, needs, and challenges. They are sorting through close friendships and romantic relationships and exploring their sexuality. They are handling crises as they arise without having a parent at the ready to help them. As college nears its end, they are making ongoing decisions about where and with whom they want to live, what and whether they wish to continue to study, and which kinds of employment opportunities they will pursue. They are dealing with the tremendous transition of not having an automatic next step for the first time in their lives. For most of them, the knowledge of what comes next has been automatic and quietly comforting: after first grade, they will go to second grade; after junior year, they will go on to senior year. Many of the students I see have viewed college the same way: after high school, they knew they would go to college. After college, though, what comes next is entirely up to them, and the process around preparing for that and navigating its challenges is a unique and important piece of developmental and therapeutic work.

I am nearly always impressed to watch them do this work and am grateful to have the chance to offer support. Eighteen years after I first trained in a college counseling center, I am still excited to get a new college student or young adult on my caseload, and I still feel challenged, interested, and fulfilled in that work.

The challenges of this niche area are often financial ones. Many of the students I see have no idea how payments work when they first come in, and they have never navigated asking questions of their own health insurance companies. Mine is a self-pay practice, and often for young adults, this means that their parents are paying for their treatments. This leads easily to an ethical gray area in which the person paying my fee is not automatically entitled to any information at all about what is taking place in psychotherapy, since most of my students are 18 years of age or older.

I have found that privacy is especially important to young adults regardless of the quality of their relationships with their parents. I broach the financial and ethical issues in a phone consult prior to the first appointment, and then again at the intake session. I have found accepting credit cards to be an important part of being paid for this population. Many of the students I work with have credit cards that are funded by their parents and I can charge them at the time of the session. I also have parents who choose to pay online through a secure link on my website, and other parents who prepay for a block of sessions (I keep those numbers small so that I am not faced with reimbursing a large amount of money if the patient doesn't stay in psychotherapy). I have found that most long-distance parents are extremely grateful to have someone helping to care for their adult child in distress, and I rarely run into payment issues. Occasionally I have parents who balk at the confidentiality constraints, but I have become fairly comfortable handling those concerns. Being direct with students about these issues when they first come in is a helpful and necessary part of the work. The same is true for talking about money when I have a young adult who needs to self-pay and cannot afford my full fee. The skills I have developed in those conversations are useful in the rest of my practice as well.

## BUSINESS ASPECTS OF THIS NICHE ACTIVITY

Local colleges and the local medical school have been important referral partners for me. I work to cultivate ongoing working relationships with local college counseling centers and am active with a referral network of colleagues in the area. Because I was starting my practice in an area in which I had no local professional connections, learning to market and network was critical in building a successful practice. I think of marketing as talking with people who need my help about why I love what I do and how that enthusiasm translates into making THEIR jobs easier. I find that professors, counseling center staff, and physicians are relieved to know where to send their students and residents when they are in distress, and that most people are open to sharing what their needs are from a mental health professional. When I can explain how my work fills those needs, I can likely solidify a lasting relationship with a good referral partner.

I began marketing by touting a strength area with college students that I had identified as lacking locally. My training at Harvard provided me a good bit of experience with eating disorders, and well-trained eating disorders clinicians are hard to find in my locale. Currently, I need only accept the occasional eating disorder referral, but in the beginning, it gave me an easy way to begin to market myself. Once I was taking good care of those clients, referrals for other presenting concerns started to come in fairly regularly.

It has also been valuable to get to know a good network of other clinicians practicing locally. My colleagues and I often refer to one another and share each other's names when we need to make a referral. I firmly believe that there is enough work to go around and have steered clear of "turf" issues in a way that has netted me a fairly steady stream of referrals from other clinicians.

Because I have a self-pay practice, as described above, it's also important for me to be seen as someone accessible and worth calling. If I cannot see a client for payment or insurance reasons, I will almost always help him or her find another qualified mental health professional. This approach results in referrals whether or not the referring party thinks the patient can self-pay. Enough of them can do so that it has been worth my while to stay off insurance panels, but colleagues can refer to me knowing that I will try to help connect the patient with someone good if I am unable to treat.

# DEVELOPING THIS NICHE ACTIVITY INTO A PRACTICE STRATEGY

Young adulthood comes with a very particular set of developmental challenges and an almost unlimited range of presenting concerns. I have treated clients with eating disorders, crisis pregnancies, relationship questions and concerns, friendship struggles, learning issues, time management difficulties, depression, anxiety, psychosis, social skills difficulties, grief and loss, difficulty with decision making, struggles around life transitions, sex and sexuality concerns, and many more presenting problems. Each of these is both enhanced and complicated by the developmental tasks of young adulthood. Expertise in any of them will result in a solid marketing strategy for clinicians wishing to develop a niche practice with college students and young adults. Openness to most or all of them will help ensure a busy, thriving practice once a good referral network is established.

I recommend contacting local college counseling centers and talking in person with the directors there. Offer trainings and in-service presentations for staff, consultation off campus, and assistance connecting students with good care in the event that they need to be seen off campus and you are not available. Look for local networking groups and get to know the other clinicians in your area. Find out what off-campus doctors the local colleges refer to and take those doctors out for coffee. Contact the training directors at local medical schools or graduate programs and talk in person; putting names with faces is always a helpful step in securing a good referral base.

The developmental requirements of the young adult life phase mean that there will always be students who need therapeutic support. If you are interested in developing a niche practice area in young adult mental health, it is also important to consider carefully where your office is located. Will it be accessible to students who do not have cars on campus? How far is it from where they have to be for class? In young adult mental health, it is also important to accept credit card payments, as these clients do not tend to carry cash and almost never write checks.

Psychotherapy with college students and young adults differs from psychotherapy at other ages primarily because of the developmental stages of the clients in this population. As with any niche, it is important to train adequately with the population you are serving. I gained a wealth of experience in three years of training on college campuses and highly recommend that setting as a training choice if you are interested in working with young adults. If you have not previously treated young adults, consider seeking supervision from someone who is well versed in the needs of that population as you begin to build this area of your practice. The national professional association of each of the mental health professions and many state professional associations hold conventions, conferences, and continuing education events related to psychotherapy with college students, and these are another excellent resource for continuing your education. There are continuing education courses related to college mental health available from the Association for the Advanced Training in the Behavioral Services (https://www.aatbs.com/). All are good resources for furthering your education with the young adult population.

If you enjoy psychotherapy with young adults, I encourage you to consider building it as a niche practice area. It is creative, varied, and rewarding work with an ongoing stream of clients in need.

## FOR MORE INFORMATION

The National Alliance on Mental Illness conducted a survey in 2012 about college student mental health that is worth reading if you are considering working with this population (https://www.nami.org/collegesurvey). It is quite a good resource because it illuminates the kinds of presenting issues that current college students are facing and identifies places where the colleges they attend may need your support as a practicing clinician.

Whether or not you plan to work with students with eating disorders, the "Learn" section of the National Eating Disorders Association's website (http://www.nationaleatingdisorders.org/learn) provides a wealth of information. I have not yet had a year in which I didn't see a student with eating concerns, regardless of whether those concerns were the presenting problem. It is prudent to be well educated about eating disorders if you are treating the young adult population.

The American College Counseling Association is a division of the American Counseling Association and focuses on clinicians who work with college students on campus. It hosts a conference relevant to college student mental health and produces the *Journal of College Counseling*, which addresses college mental health practice issues. It is available to members as well as non-members (http://www.collegecounseling.org).

The resources list includes a number of books about college student mental health counseling, incorporating everything from developmental insights to treatment planning to mindfulness-based strategies for working with young adults. *College Student Mental Health: Effective Services and Strategies Across Campus* by Sherry Benton and Stephen Benton (2006) and *College Student Mental Health Counseling: A Developmental Approach* by Suzanne Degges-White and Christine Borzumato-Gainey (2014) are accessible and relevant resources for the college population.

*Mindfulness and Acceptance for Counseling College Students: Theory and Practical Applications for Intervention, Prevention, and Outreach,* edited by Jacqueline Pistorello (2013), is also a highly regarded resource.

# REFERENCES AND RESOURCES

Benton, S. A., & Benton, S. L. (2006). *College student mental health: Effective services and strategies across campus.* Washington, DC: NASPA.

Degges-White, S., & Borzumato-Gainey, C. (2014). *College student mental health counseling: A developmental approach.* New York: Springer Publishing Company.

Pistorello, J. (2013). *Mindfulness and acceptance for counseling college students: Theory and practical applications for intervention, prevention, and outreach.* Oakland, CA: New Harbinger Publications.

# CHAPTER 64

# BEYOND LESBIAN AND GAY

A Private Practice for Bisexual, Transgender, Polyamorous, and Kinky Clients

*Geri D. Weitzman*

I am a licensed psychologist working in solo private practice near San Francisco. When I was first licensed in March 2002, I began working at a community mental health agency so that I had a stable income. I opened my private practice on the side beginning in July 2002, subletting three days a week at a colleague's office in San Francisco. By 2004, I could make my private practice my sole income source, and I rented my own office. In 2008 I moved in with my partner, his wife, and their three children (then ages 11 to 17), creating a polyamorous household, and I relocated my practice closer to our home.

## THE NICHE ACTIVITY

Today was a typical day at my office. My first client explored how to set boundaries at a sexuality workshop and grieved the ending of a relationship in which her partner had not respected their agreements around polyamory. My second client spoke of negotiations with his partner around their upcoming BDSM (bondage, domination, sadism, and masochism) skills demonstration at a kink event. My third client talked about coming out as transgender at her workplace. And so on . . .

A common thread among these sexuality and gender subculture clients is the need for a psychotherapist who is informed about their lifestyle and who is warmly accepting. Each of these subcultures also has unique themes to bring to psychotherapy. For polyamorous people, the element of negotiation is key, as there are many ways to have an open relationship. Themes include how often to see other partners, how to soothe one another through feelings of jealousy, how to maintain a sense of specialness as partners, whether it is okay to have dates with other partners in their home, and whom to come out to—boss, mother, kids?

People in kinky relationships also have negotiating and self-discovery to do. What activities are enjoyed—bondage, spanking, dominant-submissive role-playing? What safe words should be established for clear communication around desired intensity? How does one distinguish consensual BDSM from abuse? Where does one go to properly learn how to do rope bondage? Informed psychotherapists can help to normalize kink as something that approximately 2% of the general population engages in (Richters et al., 2008) and can provide local resources. They can help partners who are into kink to communicate their interests and boundaries and to dispel myths about how doms and subs "should" behave.

Bisexual individuals often feel caught between communities—they fear that they will be too outré for the straight mainstream but will not be accepted as "queer enough" by lesbians and gays. If there is a bisexual support or social group in town, it is often small. Myths and stereotypes abound, but there is also a sense of invisibility—if one walks down the street with one's same-sex partner one is seen as gay, and if one walks down the street with one's other-sex partner one is seen as straight. Psychotherapists can help their bisexual clients to identify books and support networks to help them feel a sense of belonging.

Transgender and genderqueer people seek psychotherapists who are familiar with the internal struggles of persons who are exploring their gender, as well as with the steps that a person takes to transition. Often there is sense of non-belonging, as their internal experience of their gender is not how society reflects their gender based on their appearance. There are wrenching decisions about coming out, amidst fears of rejection from loved ones, plus uncertainty about how to change their external appearance to truly reflect how they see themselves inside. The process is often long and painful, involving procedures like hormone injections, facial hair removal, and surgeries to remove breasts, transform genitals, or reshape the face. There are also logistical steps such as changing one's legal name and gender, learning how to apply makeup or re-pitch one's voice, and arranging for sensitivity training and single-use bathrooms at work. When one does not fully "pass" as one's gender of choice, there may be shame about one's appearance, embarrassment at being called by the wrong pronoun, or the fear of being attacked on the street. Psychotherapists who are gender-aware can help their clients explore their readiness for each of the steps that they will take, and learn about what support resources are out there.

# DEVELOPING AN INTEREST AND TRAINING IN THIS NICHE ACTIVITY

As a kinky, polyamorous, bisexual person myself, I came of age keenly aware of how few psychotherapy providers were aware of these populations' needs. Very few graduate training programs even mention these themes in their curricula. I gave my university's first trainings on working with bisexual and polyamorous clients while still a graduate student. The write-up of my talk, *What Psychology Professionals Should Know About Polyamory* (Weitzman, 1999), was the first article written about doing psychotherapy with polyamorous clients. It was informed from a combination of community immersion, political activism, group discussion, and life experience.

My training in how to work with transgender clients was more systematic. Not a member of the transgender communities myself, I represented myself as trans-friendly but not trans-aware at first. In the mid-2000s I attended the few workshops that were offered at that point, I followed postings on transgender email lists, and I sought consultation from a colleague about how to write letters allowing clients to receive hormones and surgeries. Eventually I felt informed enough to list transgender concerns among my specialties.

Not all of my clients are from sexuality and gender subcultures. Issues of work/life balance abound in the technological pressure cookers of the Silicon Valley, as well as typical concerns about anxiety, depression, and substance abuse. But I would say that over half of my clients fall into one or more of the categories of kinky, polyamorous, transgender, and/or bisexual, plus there are some who are lesbian and gay.

## JOYS AND CHALLENGES RELATED TO THIS NICHE ACTIVITY

I love this work because it is deeply satisfying to help people to express their gender and their sexuality and to feel pride in these aspects of themselves, and it feels good to help people to achieve the types of relationships that most fit their needs.

It can be a challenge to balance personal and professional needs in serving the subcultures of which I am a part. I have to keep appropriate professional boundaries in mind when attending gatherings that may be clothing-optional or sensually themed, or when speaking about my own experiences in support forums. I am often one of the few people wearing a bathing suit at clothing-optional poly pool parties, just in case a client arrives.

Another challenge is colleague prejudice. At a consultation group, if I speak about a client who is kinky, I run the risk of hearing derisive comments, which I then need to address. I have received negative attention from coworkers about the rainbow sticker on my door, and my choice of polyamory as a topic for Diversity Week. I have been blessed with many open-minded colleagues and the opportunity to practice in liberal cities, but there is always the fear of prejudice when one has a specialty that involves sexuality themes.

## BUSINESS ASPECTS OF THIS NICHE ACTIVITY

Many clients find me via directories that have been created specifically to help people to find therapists who are friendly to sexuality subcultures. The Kink Aware Professionals Directory (https://ncsfreedom.org/resources/kink-aware-professionals-directory/kap-directory-homepage.html), the Poly Friendly Professionals List (http://www.polyfriendly.org), the Bisexuality Aware

Professionals Directory (http://www.bizone.org/bap/), and "A List Of Therapists Experienced in the Treatment of Transgender Persons" (http://drbecky.com/therapists.html) are international resources. In the San Francisco Bay Area, there is also Gaylesta (http://gaylesta.org/locate-a-therapist) and Bay Area Open Minds (http://bayareaopenminds.org/about/members/). In my ads on these websites I note my specialties (both sexuality-related and psychologically related) as well as which types of insurance I accept. My work is frequently reimbursed by insurance companies. Commonly coded diagnoses include gender dysphoria, depression, anxiety, adjustment disorder, and partner relational concerns.

As psychotherapists we have an ethical commitment to working within our scope of practice, so the most important first step in developing this niche area into a practice strategy is to attain competence in it, via reading, supervision, workshop attendance, and community immersion. Once informed, it is most helpful to promote one's practice via the directories mentioned above, and via the LGBT-focused therapist directories in one's own region.

## FOR MORE INFORMATION

In closing, I would like to recommend some resources that can help psychotherapists to develop skills in working with these groups. Interested professionals can learn more by joining the American Association of Sexuality Counselors and Therapists (https://www.aasect.org/) or by attending classes at the Institute for the Advanced Study of Human Sexuality (http://www.humansexualityeducation.com/about-iashs.html). For those interested in community support around researching these topic areas, there is also the Community-Academic Consortium for Research on Alternative Sexualities (https://carasresearch.org/about-us).

For working with transgender clients, *Transgender Emergence* (Lev, 2013) is frequently recommended, and the American Psychological Association is releasing a new book titled *Affirmative Counseling and Psychological Practice with Transgender and Gender Nonconforming Clients* (Dickey & Singh, 2016). Another important book on transgender themes is *Trans Bodies, Trans Selves!* (Erickson-Schroth, 2014).

For working with polyamorous clients, I have written an article titled "Therapy with Clients who are Bisexual and Polyamorous" (Weitzman, 2006). "Making Friends with Jealousy: Therapy with Polyamorous Clients" (Easton, 2010) is an excellent article that addresses jealousy themes. Two recently acclaimed books are *More Than Two* (Veaux & Rickert, 2014) and *The Polyamorists Next Door: Inside Multiple-Partner Relationships and Families* (Sheff, 2013). The comprehensive website Alt.Polyamory (Polyamory.org) has a useful FAQ section about many polyamory themes.

For working with bisexual clients, Tucker (1995), Ka'ahamanu and Hutchins (1991), and Firestein (2007) have written excellent books.

And for kink, there is *Sexual Outsiders: Understanding BDSM Sexualities and Communities* (Ortmann & Sprott, 2012). Good articles include those by Kolmes (2015), Barker and colleagues (2007), and Kleinplatz and Moser (2004).

# RESOURCES AND REFERENCES

Barker, M., Iantaffi, A. & Gupta, C. (2007). Kinky clients, kinky counselling? The challenges and potentials of BDSM. In L. Moon (Ed.), *Feeling queer or queer feelings: Radical approaches to counselling sex, sexualities and genders.* (pp. 106–124). London, UK: Routledge.

Dickey, L. & Singh, A. (Eds.) (2016, in press). *Affirmative counseling and psychological practice with transgender and gender nonconforming clients.* Washington, DC: APA Books.

Easton, D. (2010). Making friends with jealousy: Therapy with polyamorous clients. In M. Barker & D. Langdridge (Eds.), *Understanding non-monogamies* (pp. 207–211). London, UK: Routledge.

Erickson-Schroth, L. (Ed.). (2014). *Trans bodies, trans selves: A resource for the transgender community.* New York: Oxford University Press.

Firestein, B. A. (2007). *Becoming visible: Counseling bisexuals across the lifespan.* New York: Columbia University Press.

Ka'ahumanu, L., & Hutchins, L. (1991). *Bi any other name: Bisexual people speak out.* Bronx, NY: Riverdale Avenue Books LLC.

Kleinplatz, P., & Moser, C. (2004). Toward clinical guidelines for working with BDSM clients. *Contemporary Sexuality, 38*(6), 1–4.

Kolmes, K. (2015). *An introduction to BDSM for psychotherapists.* Retrieved from http://societyforpsychotherapy.org/an-introduction-to-bdsm-for-psychotherapists/.

Lev, A. I. (2013). *Transgender emergence: Therapeutic guidelines for working with gender-variant people and their families.* New York: Routledge.

Ortmann, D. M., & Sprott, R. A. (2012). *Sexual outsiders: Understanding BDSM sexualities and communities.* Lanham, MD: Rowman & Littlefield Publishers.

Richters, J., De Visser, R. O., Rissel, C. E., Grulich, A. E., & Smith, A. (2008). Demographic and psychosocial features of participants in bondage and discipline, "sadomasochism" or dominance and submission (BDSM): Data from a national survey. *Journal of Sexual Medicine, 5*(7), 1660–1668.

Sheff, E. (2013). *The polyamorists next door: Inside multiple-partner relationships and families.* Lanham, MD: Rowman & Littlefield.

Tucker, N. S. (1995). *Bisexual politics: Theories, queries, and visions.* New York: Routledge.

Veaux, F., & Rickert, E. (2014). *More than two: A practical guide to ethical polyamory.* Portland, OR: Thorntree Press, LLC.

Weitzman, G. (1999). *What psychology professionals should know about polyamory.* Retrieved from http://www.polyamory.org/~joe/polypaper.htm

Weitzman, G. (2006). Therapy with clients who are bisexual and polyamorous. *Journal of Bisexuality, 6*(1-2), 137–164.

CHAPTER 65

# INTERRACIAL COUPLES THERAPY

*Kyle D. Killian*

I am a licensed couple and family therapist, and about a third of my private practice in Boston is interracial or intercultural couples, many of whom have multiracial children. I work in a suburb, and many referrals are by word of mouth, with none coming via advertisement. Frequently, professionals are not sure what to do with a multiracial family when they request services, and they quickly contact someone with experience with this population. I bill about half of interracial couples directly, and about half of the cases involve insurance.

## THE NICHE PRACTICE ACTIVITY

Many clinicians, and laypersons, would be surprised to know that among opposite-sex married couples, 1 in 10 (5.5 million) are interracial (U.S. Census, 2012) and 21% of same-sex couples are mixed race. These statistics represent a more than 28% increase in interracial couples since the turn of the century. Interracial couples, and multiracial families, are on the rise, adding to the increasing diversity of society and of our clinical practices.

A strengths-based, narrative approach to interracial couples can facilitate partners' conscious creation of a relationship identity that is enriched by cultural traditions, customs, and rituals from both families. Clinicians can assess whether each partner's racial and cultural identities are valued and are permitted expression and representation as they work together to forge new couple and family identities. In my clinical and research experience, when many interracial couples talk about their lives, they frequently stress that they are "ordinary" couples who, just like same-race couples, experience normative life cycle stages and transitions and struggle to make ends meet, to strike a balance between work and home life, to divide the labor, and to parent their children (Killian, 2013). However, an additional layer of complexity is often added to these normative stages and tasks in the case of intercultural, interfaith, and interracial couples.

Many couples may say that race becomes relevant only when they are reminded of it in public situations (Karis & Killian, 2008; Killian, 2002) through scowls, stares, rubbernecking, being ignored (e.g., poor service in restaurants), or being criticized as a "sell out" (Killian, 2013). Biracial children can experience questioning about their backgrounds and asked to make explicit their racial identity (e.g., "What are you?"). Some interracial couples, and multiracial families, are subjected to hostile prejudicial treatment that denies them a basic sense of security and even status as legitimate citizens in public spaces.

In embodying racial border crossings in public spaces, interracial couples sometimes have difficult choices to make. The wish to protect partners and children from attack is a powerful motivator in participants' attempts to render their interracial couplehood and multiracial family relations as totally *unremarkable* or even *invisible* (Killian, 2002). Some interracial couples may decentralize or deprioritize the significance of race by pointing to some other social location, or axis of power, such as religious affiliation, as a source of prejudice or negative attention (Killian, 2013). By making another axis of difference salient, couples can push discussions of difference along lines of race, gender, and class to the margins (Killian, 2013).

These approaches can be viewed as a protective response to negative cultural stereotypes that make racial border crossings *transgressive* (Killian, 2002). Interracial couple relationships exist within a social/historical context that pathologizes them as deviant, or as undermining the myth of white racial purity and superiority. The mass media (e.g., news magazines, tabloids, talk shows, the Internet) sensationalize interracial couples, and the research literature is replete with cautionary tales and bleak predictions regarding their chances of achieving stability and bliss. Thus, interracial couples may respond to this phenomenon by minimizing the presentation of differences both "out there" in public and "in here," within the relationship. Competing senses of how they see themselves as a couple, and how they perceive they are seen by the rest of the world, can develop in a form of *dyadic double consciousness* (Killian, 2013). This involves having their own sense of who they are and what their life is really about. Interracial couples can also be aware of the ways in which society at large articulates them and their lives through interactions with others (e.g., expressions of curiosity or disgust regarding interracial relationships) as well as their exposure to popular representations of couples like them. Depictions by various media, and academia as well, of interracial couples are frequently fraught with conflict, controversy, and innuendo, and various media rarely feature interracial couples whose relationship is stable and satisfactory to both partners. Thus, the way interracial couples present themselves to the public may be organized by their resistance to media portrayals. If one chooses to view couples' responses to stigmatization as *survival strategies*, one can suspend, at least temporarily, judgment regarding their "reasonableness," or how they may affect the couple's long-term health (Killian, 2013).

Regarding best clinical practices, there are at least three factors to assess when interracial couples come to your door: (1) the partners' levels of racial awareness and sensitivity, (2) how they negotiate or work through difference (fighting fair vs. conflict avoidance vs. destructive conflict), and (3) what their narrative is about race. Since race can be a button issue for many couples, walking straight up to them and pressing that button is not advisable. Another way to go is asking about how they have worked through differences between the two of them. Another is to ask, "What are the hot topics or button issues between the two of you?" Finally, if they appear willing or able to talk about it, you can say, "Tell me how race plays a role in how your relationship has developed." Clinicians can assess if there is any indication that a couple has thought about race before; a couple might provide a detailed, thoughtful narrative about the significance of race or otherwise indicate they have discussed it at some time in the past. One or both partners might engage in an explicit devaluing of blackness or an overvaluing of whiteness, and sometimes the source of devaluing or overvaluing may be surprising to you. Two instruments that assess the partners' cultural assumptions, values, and beliefs and the degree to which they value their partner's identities are the Cultural Assumptions and Beliefs Inventory and the Index of Cultural Inclusion (Killian, 2013). These easily administered and scored assessments are a great conversation starter in psychotherapy.

Relationships are "dependent on couples' ability to deal effectively with the tension inherent in maintaining both shared and separate identity" (Snyder, 1986, p. 250). Interracial couples negotiate partner differences in various ways; some resolve this tension by either jointly or individually divesting themselves of portions of their family histories and ethnic identities (Killian, 2013). Couples who decentralize race and color tend to establish a couple identity through relationship milestones and shared events. Navigating *around* difference, these couples deemphasize partner differences in two ways: (1) by "not seeing" race, class, and sometimes gender in their relationships and (2) by "starting from scratch," leaving behind their history, rituals, and traditions from the families of origin. Another way of handling the tension is to acknowledge different familial traditions and consciously and collaboratively re-envisioning their integration. Since each couple possesses its own interactional style, implicit rules, and identity, therapists should avoid making generalizations about interracial couples.

# DEVELOPING AN INTEREST AND TRAINING IN THIS NICHE ACTIVITY

I first became interested in this population when I married a woman from another country, and my white male best man from the United States, at a traditional wedding overseas, commented, "This is a cross-cultural situation, and many would say, you're entering into an *interracial* marriage." It struck me that sometimes, in public situations, persons had thought that we were not together ("Table for one?" questions at restaurants and so forth), and it clicked that we had been and would continue to be seen as exogamous or heterogamous, and embodying difference, by many people and in many situations. When I returned stateside for my doctoral training in marriage and family therapy at Syracuse University, a program that emphasized cultural diversity and self-of-the-therapist training, I noticed that little research had been conducted related to interracial couples, and even less literature was available regarding effective clinical interventions with this population. My dissertation project focused on interracial couples, and I continue to write articles, chapters, and books about best practices for assessment and intervention with couples whose partners come from divergent backgrounds.

## JOYS AND CHALLENGES RELATED TO THIS NICHE ACTIVITY

I enjoy working with intercultural and interracial couples because I have both personal and professional appreciations for the ongoing negotiations involved in forming a relationship identity that is inclusive of both partners' backgrounds. It is important to meet couples (and partners) where they are and not make assumptions about what "the issue" is before exploring their situation in therapy. The variety of presenting challenges with this population helps make clinical work with them so enjoyable.

The only challenge that I have experienced is one shared in work with all couples: divergent agendas on the part of the partners. If one partner has initiated therapy as a means of extricating himself or herself from the relationship and the other partner has "just received the memo" that something is amiss, it is a bit more difficult for the clinical work to reach a mutually satisfactory conclusion.

## BUSINESS ASPECTS OF THIS NICHE ACTIVITY

This is couples therapy, which may or may not involve a traditional or relational diagnosis. As psychotherapy, it may be reimbursed by insurance or be charged as an out-of-pocket service. Clients usually pay me at the time that I deliver the service. Payment covers the time we meet in session at the office, as well as time outside of sessions devoted to the case, such as writing emails to each partner, which serve as electronic versions of post-session narrative letters (White & Epston, 1991) to emphasize key elements of sessions and invite further exploration of themes. A challenging aspect of this niche practice involves managing partners' assumptions about core cultural values, racial identity, and expectations for how children will be raised. I obtain most of my referrals from local psychotherapists. A key method of marketing is attending events hosted by the state association for marriage and family therapy.

## DEVELOPING THIS NICHE ACTIVITY INTO A PRACTICE STRATEGY

Regarding training and continuing education in cultural competence, clinicians may subscribe to a universalist paradigm that "we are all humans," effectively relegating ethnic and racial differences to the margins in the therapeutic dialog. Pinderhughes (1989) asserts that a colorblind stance "protects those holding it from awareness of their ignorance of others and the necessity of exerting the energy and effort to understand and bridge the differences" (p. 44). Helping professionals who hold that "all people are alike" may experience discomfort when faced with racial and ethnic differences and may tend to deny the importance of difference as a way of distancing from their own negative reactions. Cultural competence starts with ourselves.

If you are thinking about adding this niche to their practice, I first suggest educating yourself about interracial and intercultural couples and multiracial families. Two books that provide an excellent overview and understanding of couples who negotiate differences in their backgrounds are Killian (2013) and Karis and Killian (2008). I would also suggest locating professionals in your community who practice in this area and meet with them over coffee to talk about how this niche is working in their practice. It is wise to assess through trainings your own level of cultural awareness and sensitivity before pursuing this particular niche. Psychotherapists seeking to develop this area of their practices can also present talks and workshops on the topic so that their knowledge base about this population becomes well established and circulates by word of mouth in the communities of which they are part.

## FOR MORE INFORMATION

The Interracial Family Circle (http://interracialfamilycircle.org/) provides opportunities for the education, support, and socialization of multiracial individuals, families, people involved in interracial relationships, and transracial adoptive families in the Washington, DC metropolitan area. Their email address is info@interracialfamilycircle.org. The MAVIN Foundation (www.mavinfoundation.org) is dedicated to building healthy communities that celebrate and empower mixed-heritage people and families. MOSAIC (http://www.mosaicbrighton.org.uk/) is a community organization of black, minority ethnic, and mixed-parentage families. The site http://multiracial.com/site/content/view/273/45/ lists multiracial organizations by state. Other useful websites are Metis Nation (http://www.metisnation.org/) and the Multiracial Activist (http://multiracial.com/site/).

## RESOURCES AND REFERENCES

Karis, T., & Killian, K. D. (Eds.). (2008). *Intercultural couples: Exploring diversity in intimate relationships.* New York: Routledge.

Killian, K. D. (2001). Reconstituting racial histories and identities: The narratives of interracial couples. *Journal of Marital and Family Therapy, 27,* 27–42.

Killian, K. D. (2002). Dominant and marginalized discourses in interracial couples' narratives: Implications for family therapists. *Family Process, 41,* 603–618.

Killian, K. D. (2012). Resisting and complying with homogamy: Interracial couples' narratives. *Counselling Psychology Quarterly, 25*(2), 125–135.

Killian, K. D. (2013). *Interracial couples, intimacy, and therapy: Crossing racial borders.* New York: Columbia University Press.

Pinderhughes, E. (1989). *Understanding race, ethnicity, and power*. New York: Free Press.

Seshadri, G., & Knudson-Martin, C. (2013). How couples manage interracial and intercultural differences: Implications for clinical practice. *Journal of Marital and Family Therapy*, 39(1), 43–58.

Snyder, S. (1986). *Love making: A symbolic interactionist approach to the experience of love among young adult couples*. Unpublished doctoral dissertation, Syracuse University, New York.

White, M., & Epston, D. (1991). *Narrative means to therapeutic ends*. New York: Norton.

U.S. Bureau of the Census. (2012). 2010 Census shows interracial and interethnic married couples grew by 28 percent over decade. Retrieved from https://www.census.gov/newsroom/releases/archives/2010_census/cb12-68.html.

# CHAPTER 66

# PSYCHOTHERAPY WITH INTERFAITH COUPLES

*Susan S. Needles*

I am a graduate of Smith College School for Social Work and am a licensed clinical social worker. For more than 20 years I worked therapeutically in mental health agencies, eventually developing a small private practice. I trained in an analytic institute and finished that course of study after four years.

## THE NICHE PRACTICE ACTIVITY

Interfaith couples counseling is a complex undertaking that involves two people falling in love who come from different worlds. They may be from the same country, or not. They may share a common language. They do not share the same religion. They do not share the same ethnicity. What they share are feelings of love and strong attachments for each other. But given their differences, it is within this multiplicity of universes that we must struggle to find a way to bridge the gaps for them to develop a lasting and trusting bond with each other.

I live and work in New York City. For many years I have had a part-time practice while I have had another job. My interfaith couples niche practice has been in my apartment across the street from Lincoln Center. This location is central for patients and large enough for me to have group meetings. I have sometimes been contacted by couples from distant cities. To work together we have used the telephone and Internet-based communications. If I were to work long term with one of these distant couples I would arrange to see them in person at some point during the treatment. It was not difficult to convince a couple to make a trip to New York City.

The history of my niche practice began when I was the director of a large mental health clinic in East Harlem, where there were many Spanish-speaking patients. I hired a psychologist from

Argentina to work with some of our monolingual population. He features in my finding my way to my niche practice of working with interfaith couples, predominately Christian and Jewish. I was unaware of the fact that he was at the time studying to be a rabbi. He was working with interfaith couples in his training (as a rabbi) and suggested that I could do this kind of work too (and, he thought, better than he could as I would be "more neutral").

He asked if I would be interested. I was very enthusiastic and said I would love to do the work. I had become fascinated by the topic of identity. I would listen to our patients in the waiting room have lively discussions (all in Spanish) about where they were from (many different countries in Latin America).

## DEVELOPING AN INTEREST AND TRAINING IN THIS NICHE ACTIVITY

The introduction made by Marcelo, the psychologist, was to the Union of Hebrew Congregations. That organization was for the most liberal arm of Judaism, Reform Judaism. They were developing a program of "outreach to interfaith couples" and I became the person who did the couple workshops for them. I had a brief training in the issues by a woman who was a cantor and herself a convert to Judaism. She had some knowledge of the issues and I was given some workbooks. I think more than anything, though, I learned from the couples themselves.

I ran groups for this organization for six or eight weeks and we had on average four or five couples participate. In addition, once the groups were over, couples sometimes sought me out for therapy—individual and/or couple therapy. I was paid my fee or I billed their insurance company when feasible. Most of the time this form of couple therapy is not reimbursable as neither person is being treated for a psychiatric disorder.

It is entirely possible to build this niche program through religious institutions—synagogues, churches, mosques. Couples themselves can lead you to their institutions. They are very eager to resolve their issues so they can move on with their lives. It might be necessary to involve the extended family. I have found with Indian families that even though they have the same religion, they may have different degrees of religiosity, which can cause a great deal of conflict.

## JOYS AND CHALLENGES RELATED TO THIS NICHE ACTIVITY

What is satisfying about this work is that you are working with people who are in love and eager to engage and work out their conflicts. On the other hand, when they can't, it is heartbreaking. The groups are very dynamic and each one is different. At the outset of a group, I would never know how it would develop—which members would aid the process of reconciliation and which ones would hinder it. That took a few sessions to realize, so there was some suspense. In a way, I began to understand that I needed to accept liking the riskiness of the process or the adventure of it. It can, however, be challenging to find the time to meet with eight or ten busy young people in a group for a period of many weeks.

## BUSINESS ASPECTS OF THIS NICHE PRACTICE

My interfaith couples practice occupied a small portion of my total practice; in its most active times it represented about 25%, with the remainder of my time spent providing general mental health treatment services to adults and children. When I did workshops I was paid a lump sum. These usually generated more work because some of those group members wanted to see me about other issues. They paid me out of pocket or their insurance was billed.

It could very well be in the future that this service will be marketed as a premarriage workshop through clergy. For example, Roman Catholics require the Pre-Cana. In fact, I have attested for those couples who had to go to Pre-Cana as this was considered equivalent. In this case fees are paid directly by the participating couples.

## DEVELOPING THE NICHE ACTIVITY INTO A PRACTICE STRATEGY

I believe there is a growing population for this kind of work and therefore a need for it. The population may have different names: Instead of Jewish/Christian it may be Muslim/Christian or Hindu/Christian.

As long as the population shifts and young people meet and fall in love, especially in urban centers, there will be a great need for them to find a way to understand each other. They will also require extra assistance in creating a way for their less open and more rigid extended families to accept their choices. Therapists who undertake this work must know a great deal about different cultures and how to tread carefully.

When I began my niche activity I contacted religious leaders and social institutions such as community centers to get my name out. I wrote a brochure that explained what I did. I volunteered to speak at community meetings. Once there was an Internet I developed a website. These are all ways to build your practice; as well as speaking at local professional organizations. Many social workers (themselves interfaith) have said they wanted to do this work when I presented my work. I replied that they should; it is amazing how folks want to do this but don't.

# FOR MORE INFORMATION

The following websites provide useful information: http://www.interfaithcommunity.org/#!resources/; http://the-family-school.org/ (Chicago area); and http://www.iffp.net/ (Washington, DC area).

# RESOURCES

Cotner, J. (2003). Wedding blessings: *Prayers and poems celebrating love, marriage and anniversaries.* New York: Broadway Books.

Gruzen, L. F. (1987). *Raising your Jewish/Christian child: How interfaith parents can give their children the best of both their heritages.* New York: New Market Press.

Mayer, E. (1985). *Love & tradition: Marriage between Jews and Christians.* New York: Springer.

McGoldrick, M., Giordano, J., & Garcia-Petro, N. (2005). *Ethnicity and family therapy.* New York: Guilford Press.

Miller, S. K. (2013). *Being both: Embracing two religions in one interfaith family.* Boston, MA: Beacon Press.

Petsonk, J., & Remsen, J. (1988). *The intermarriage handbook: A guide for Jews and Christians.* New York: William Morrow.

Rosenbaum, M. H., & Rosenbaum, S. N. (1994). *Celebrating our differences: Living two faiths in one marriage.* Shippensburg, PA: Ragged Edge Press.

# OTHER SERVICES

## CHAPTER 67

# DEVELOPING A SPORT PSYCHOLOGY PRACTICE

*Kate F. Hays*

I am licensed as a psychologist in Ontario, Canada, as well as in New Hampshire (currently on inactive status). Following traditional clinical psychology training, I engaged in institutional, group, and solo practice in New Hampshire. During much of that time, I developed expertise in working with people with eating disorders, adults with traumatic histories, consultation to systems and organizations (primarily schools), and program evaluation. Although I developed an interest and training in sport psychology while in New Hampshire, it wasn't until moving to Toronto in 1998 that I was able to establish a practice in which I am primarily known for my work in sport (and performance) psychology.

I became interested in sport psychology about 10 years after receiving my doctorate. This was unanticipated and inadvertent: I began running and, much to my surprise, fell in love with it. I was especially intrigued by the ways in which I thought "differently" during or shortly after running. This in turn led to learning everything that I could about the interaction of running—or exercise—and the mind. Learning about this constructive aspect of the mind–body relationship subsequently opened me up to the academic and practice field of sport psychology, working with athletes to assist them in optimal performance. Further, as an avocational musician, I became interested in exploring the elements of performance excellence that are generic to a variety of domains.

My practice, "The Performing Edge," is primarily geared toward work with athletes (and other performers) of all ages as well as varying levels of skill and accomplishment. In addition, I serve as a sport and clinical psychology consultant to a sports medicine clinic.

# THE NICHE PRACTICE ACTIVITY

At any one time, most of my clients are performers, typically athletes or performing artists (musicians, dancers, actors). Examples include a 10-year-old gymnast who has "forgotten" how to do one of her newer moves due to performance pressure; a high-performance athlete needing to make a certain qualifying time in order to enter an international competition; a professional musician preparing for an important audition; or a dancer coping with recovery from a potentially career-ending injury while dealing with eating and weight-related issues.

For a variety of reasons having to do with professional skills and preference, clientele, and convenience, I tend to work with clients in my downtown, easily accessible office or at the sports medicine clinic. At times it is important, useful, or preferable to work at the client's locale, whether with the client directly, a team, or team personnel.

# DEVELOPING AN INTEREST AND TRAINING IN THIS NICHE ACTIVITY

My own experience of stumbling into sport psychology is both dissimilar and similar to the experiences of many others. Most people who engage in sport psychology practice have had an interest in (competitive) sports over a period of time. On the other hand, many of those receiving primary training in a mental health field are not even aware that there is an academic field known as sport psychology. Undergraduate and graduate courses and degrees in sport psychology are typically housed within academic departments of health, physical education, or kinesiology (Burke, Sachs, & Schweighardt, 2011).

Applied sport psychology is a hybrid field, a combination of knowledge of sport sciences and counseling or psychotherapy. Competence in such practice involves knowledge of both counseling and aspects of sports. Among the latter, the most important for practitioners new to the field are aspects of motor learning, systemic issues, the culture of sport, and the particular concerns that people involved in sport performance deal with at a cognitive and emotional level.

In actuality, there are various routes to competent practice. Currently, ideal professional training would include some combination of graduate or postgraduate academic training in both sport psychology and the mental health field. Some graduate programs offer such combined training and opportunity for licensure (Burke et al., 2011). These are still few in number, however; most mental health practitioners develop expertise through postgraduate formal or informal training and mentored practice.

Mental health practitioners who like the idea of working with athletes and assume that their knowledge of mental skills can be applied to this population without any further training or supervised or mentored experience do themselves and the field a disservice. The hubris of appending the adjective "sport" to psychology misses the rich academic, research, and practice literature developed in an entire field of study; the practitioner may have little to go on other than his or her own experience, with its potential limitations of generalizability. One arrogant practitioner can damage future constructive connections for any number of athletes, organizations, and competent practitioners.

Recognition of competence by the Association for Applied Sport Psychology occurs as a result of a document review process including coursework and mentored practice (Association for Applied Sport Psychology, n.d.). In defining the practice of sport psychology as a subset of psychology practice more broadly, the American Psychological Association (APA) has developed a Proficiency in Sport Psychology (American Psychological Association, n.d.). Guidelines for practice in sport psychology are under development by the Society for Sport, Exercise and Performance, APA's Division 47.

## JOYS AND CHALLENGES RELATED TO THIS NICHE ACTIVITY

Practicing sport psychology is intriguing and satisfying for a number of reasons. Clients are typically interested in growth and change, they are goal-directed, and they are used to practicing particular skills in order to improve.

Potential clients are likely to search out such services. Whether for mental health issues or performance enhancement, media attention has increased the awareness of the general public to professional athletes' use of sport psychologists. This public awareness of sport psychology has served to destigmatize such services much faster and to a larger degree than other areas of mental health. For example, teenagers not infrequently encourage their parents to find a sport psychologist for them to work with (Hays & Lesyk, 2014). Further, nonathletes who are interested in performance improvement through mental skills may seek out sport psychologists. They have already made the conceptual leap regarding the potential transfer of knowledge to their particular domain of performance.

Another positive aspect of this niche practice is the impact on the self of the practitioner. Working with people who are physically active and take care of themselves, and assisting them concerning their well-being, can be a motivator or reinforcer for the practitioner's own self-care through appropriate physical activity, nutrition, recovery, and sleep.

Knowledge and skill in sport psychology can lead to additional areas of interest and expertise. For me, this involved developing knowledge about the mental benefits of physical activity. I was then able to assist my nonactive clients to develop exercise programs for themselves as a scientific, nonpharmacological method for decreasing depression or anxiety (Hays, 2015). As mentioned, I have developed expertise in working with other types of performers, based on my sport psychology knowledge but with application to their particular performance domain. At the same time, it has been especially important to remain mindful of the differences as well as the similarities between working with athletes and working with other performers (Hays, 2012; Murphy, 2012).

An additional area that has been both satisfying and complex has been the provision of counseling or psychotherapy to this population. On the one hand, it offers an opportunity to use the full range of one's skills. On the other, however, mental health practitioners need to be cognizant of the complexities regarding boundaries and confidentiality; multiple role relationships; determination of treatment focus; systemic issues; and third-party factors such as contractual obligations, adjunctive collaboration, expectations, and financial recompense (Herzog & Hays, 2012).

Even when practice is straightforward, focused only on performance enhancement, there can be challenges. Particular issues that need to be considered include the following:

- Boundary crossings (Gutheil & Gabbard, 1998) of various kinds may be more likely in this type of practice. For example, one may work outside of a traditional office setting; the professional relationship is more likely to include third parties (parents, coaches, teams) where norms around confidentiality are different and may need to be negotiated; appropriate clothing and attire for both the client and professional may be different than in a traditional clinical setting. Practitioners need to be aware of these potential hazards and have appropriate rationale, disclaimers, and consultative supports available (Stapleton, Hankes, Hays, & Parham, 2010).
- Location: For myself, practicing this niche in rural New Hampshire was financially unsustainable. In a large urban area with many people, universities, and sports teams, it is much more likely that such a practice can be successful.
- Interjurisdictional practice: At present, this is a complicated and unresolved issue. Sport psychology practice at times may involve traveling with a team or working with a client at a distance. Maintaining awareness of the current regulatory provisions for practitioners, and joining with other consultants who are working on appropriate interjurisdictional practice, is critical.
- Some practitioners not bound by the strictures of licensed practice may advertise and operate without some of the limits imposed by licensure. In the competitive market, it can be tempting (but unwise) to emulate some of their disregard for ethical practice.

# BUSINESS ASPECTS OF THIS NICHE ACTIVITY

Referrals for sport psychology services may come from a variety of sources. Referrals depend in part on one's wishes concerning the focus of practice. A web presence that includes information about one's practice and competence is essential. Referrals may come from physicians, coaches, colleagues, organizations or groups involved in a particular type of sport, word of mouth, or one's social media visibility. Contractual relationships with sports, medical, or educational organizations or institutions can be developed. These contracted relationships can offer predictable income. In the fickle world of sports and other performance, though, where "you're only as good as your last success," contracted services can also end quite abruptly.

Practice in sport psychology—that is, working with athletes regarding the mental aspects of competent performance—is not technically a healthcare activity; it is much more of an educational or consulting relationship. The good news is that the practitioner does not need to stick a diagnostic label of psychopathology on a client. A consulting or coaching model for fee-setting and payment is more appropriate in this regard.

Billing depends on who has hired the practitioner for what. It may be the athlete himself or herself, or a parent. It might be a professional organization, an institution such as a high school or university, or a sports team. Services may be billed on an hourly basis or may be arranged contractually, for a particular service.

# DEVELOPING THIS NICHE ACTIVITY INTO A PRACTICE STRATEGY

Graduate students have the greatest flexibility in learning or incorporating sport psychology coursework, practica, mentoring, supervision, theoretical or research papers, or even internship sites into their graduate training (Burke et al., 2011). For those who have completed a terminal degree in a mental health profession, new or other opportunities for learning will be most appropriate.

Understanding the gaps in one's knowledge is the first step toward developing competence. The certification criteria developed by the Association for Applied Sport Psychology (AASP) or APA's Proficiency in Sport Psychology can be used as a guide. Opportunities for knowledge development can include self-directed learning, online or traditional coursework, attendance at relevant conferences and workshops, and active mentoring (Fletcher & Maher, 2014).

Active engagement with sport psychology organizations is an important aspect for developing and maintaining one's knowledge and skills. Involvement with AASP or Division 47 is an excellent method for understanding the field, recognizing one's own learning needs and addressing them, becoming acculturated, developing connections with like-minded individuals and potential mentors, learning from the leaders in the field, becoming engaged in a fairly "young" niche practice, and helping to strengthen this field for the next generation.

# FOR MORE INFORMATION

Information concerning graduate programs in sport psychology (albeit primarily in sport sciences rather than psychology or another mental health field) is available through the *Directory of Graduate Programs in Applied Sport Psychology* (Burke et al., 2011). Updated every few years, this directory contains program descriptions, provides a current functional guide to the field, and offers detailed information regarding career options, licensure and certification, as well as relevant readings.

There are two relevant North American professional organizations in sport psychology. The first is the Society for Sport, Exercise and Performance Psychology, Division 47 of the American Psychological Association (www.apadivisions.org/division-47/index.aspx). Along with a newsletter, a journal, and presentations within the annual APA Convention, Division 47 is connected with the larger organization of psychologists through APA. The second is AASP (www.appliedsportpsych.org/). This freestanding organization includes sport scientists as well as psychologists, with a strong graduate student contingent as well. Membership includes a newsletter, a journal, and an annual conference focused exclusively in this field. Information found on the websites of each of these organizations is invaluable. Each organization also has an active and open email list (i.e., one need not be a member to be part of the email list).

Journals with a particular focus on practitioner issues in sport psychology are *The Sport Psychologist: Sport, Exercise, and Performance Psychology* (a member benefit of Division 47) and *Journal of Applied Sport Psychology* (a member benefit of AASP).

# RESOURCES AND REFERENCES

American Psychological Association. (n.d.). Sport psychology. http://apa.org/ed/graduate/specialize/sports.aspx

Andersen, M. B. (Ed.) (2000). *Doing sport psychology*. Champaign, IL: Human Kinetics.

Anderson, M. B., & Hanrahan, S. J. (Eds.). (2010). *Routledge handbook of applied sport psychology*. New York: Routledge.

Association for Applied Sport Psychology. (n.d.). Become a certified consultant. http://www.appliedsport-psych.org/certified-consultants/become-a-certified-consultant/

Burke, K. L., Sachs, M. L., & Schweighardt, S. L. (2011). *Directory of graduate programs in applied sport psychology* (10th ed.). Indianapolis, IN: Association for Applied Sport Psychology.

Etzel, E. F., & Watson, J. C. (Eds.). (2014). *Ethical issues in sport, exercise, and performance psychology*. Morgantown, WV: Fitness Information Technology.

Fletcher, D., & Maher, J. (2014). Professional competence in sport psychology: Clarifying some misunderstandings and making future progress. *Journal of Sport Psychology in Action, 5*, 170–185.

Gutheil, T. G., & Gabbard, G. O. (1998). Misuses and misunderstandings of boundary theory in clinical and regulatory settings. *American Journal of Psychiatry, 155*(3), 409–414.

Hays, K. F. (2012). The psychology of performance in sport and other domains. In S. M. Murphy (Ed.), *Oxford handbook of sport and performance psychology* (pp. 24–45). New York: Oxford.

Hays, K. F. (2015). Let's run with that: Exercise, depression, and anxiety. In M. B. Andersen & S. J. Hanrahan (Eds.), *Doing exercise psychology* (pp. 217–230). Champaign, IL: Human Kinetics.

Hays, K. F., & Lesyk, J. J. (2014). Incorporating sport and exercise psychology into clinical practice. In J. L. Van Raalte & B. W. Brewer (Eds.), *Exploring sport and exercise psychology* (3rd ed., pp. 485–504). Washington, DC: American Psychological Association.

Herzog, T., & Hays, K. F. (2012). Therapist or mental skills coach? How to decide. *The Sport Psychologist, 26*, 486–499.

Murphy, S. M. (Ed.). (1995). *Sport psychology interventions*. Champaign, IL: Human Kinetics.

Murphy, S. M. (Ed.). (2012). *Oxford handbook of sport and performance psychology*. New York: Oxford.

Stapleton, A. B., Hankes, D. M., Hays, K. F., & Parham, W. D. (2010). Ethical dilemmas in sport psychology: A dialogue on the unique aspects impacting practice. *Professional Psychology: Research and Practice, 41*, 143–152.

Van Raalte, J. L., & Brewer, B.W. (Eds.) (2014). *Exploring sport and exercise psychology* (3rd ed.). Washington, DC: American Psychological Association.

Weinberg, R. S., & Gould, D. (2010). *Foundations of sport and exercise psychology* (5th ed.). Champaign, IL: Human Kinetics.

Williams, J. M. & Krane, V. (Eds.). (2014). *Applied sport psychology: Personal growth to peak performance* (7th ed.). New York: McGraw-Hill Education.

# CHAPTER 68

# SOCIAL SKILLS (SOCIAL COMPETENCE) TRAINING FOR CHILDREN AND ADOLESCENTS

*Mary Karapetian Alvord and Lisa H. Berghorst*

M KA is a licensed psychologist who owns, directs, and practices at Alvord, Baker & Associates, LLC, located in Rockville and Silver Spring, Maryland, in the suburbs of Washington, DC. As an adjunct associate professor of psychiatry and behavioral sciences at the George Washington School of Medicine and Health Sciences, I also supervise second-year psychiatry fellows in cognitive-behavior therapy. After receiving my PhD in 1977, I worked for two years in a community mental health center prior to working for five years in a residential/day treatment center for youth. In 1983, I began a part-time solo practice (overlapped for a year with my other position and shared a small office space with my eventual business partner) while raising young children. Eight years later, my business partner and I moved to a larger building space, creating offices large enough to run groups for children and teens. Alvord, Baker & Associates incorporated in 1997 and grew to 20 psychologists and social workers by 2006, with two office locations to widen the geographic net and range of clientele. The original office is located in a building where we lease space, which has allowed for expansion over the years. Adding the second location 10 years ago was primarily driven by our long waitlist, especially for groups. I purchased a large space in a medical office building. All clinical offices are large enough to fit six children/teens to facilitate group therapy. This is key to running multiple groups simultaneously, especially on Saturday mornings. Alvord, Baker & Associates now comprises (1) a clinical practice that has a range of evidence-based services, (2) a research arm that collaborates with Catholic University to investigate the treatment effectiveness of our Resilience Builder Program (RBP) groups within both practice and school settings, and (3) a continuing education (CE) program that includes a cognitive-behavior therapy (CBT) training institute for children and adolescents, as well as general CE programs.

LHB is a licensed psychologist who practices at Alvord, Baker & Associates in the Rockville, Maryland, office. I received my PhD from Harvard University in 2012 and began working at the practice the same year. Dr. Alvord provides weekly supervision for all clinicians in the practice for the first two years, including individual supervision and peer consultation. I was particularly attracted to this practice due to its dedication to evidence-based treatments, the fact that the RBP group therapy was offered in addition to individual psychotherapy services, the practice's commitment to research related to evaluating the effectiveness of the RBP, and the practice's active participation in CE programming. I had previous experience running CBT- and dialectical behavior therapy (DBT)- based therapy groups during my practicum training and internship at McLean Hospital and valued the beneficial impact of group therapy for building social competence skills in youth. I also came from a strong research background, so it was important to me to continue in both clinical and research endeavors professionally. Alvord, Baker & Associates is a unique private practice in its synthesis of clinical work and research, and I have felt very lucky to be able to actively engage in both, including currently serving as our director of research.

# THE NICHE PRACTICE ACTIVITY

RBP (Alvord, Zucker, & Grados, 2011) is the group curriculum that we follow in the practice to build social competence and emotion regulation skills in children and adolescents (http://www.alvordbaker.com/groups/). We use the term "social competence" to encompass both the learning and the application of social skills. Thus, generalization of skills is emphasized. This is accomplished through free play/behavioral rehearsal during part of each group, weekly resilience builder assignments that are completed between sessions, a weekly success journal, and a field trip to practice skills in a public setting. Moreover, to encourage parents to be active partners in the generalization of skills, we provide weekly letters to parents, conduct mid-semester parent meetings, and ask parents to join the end of sessions approximately once per month. In addition, the groups also focus on building emotion regulation skills, which share a reciprocal relationship with social competence skills and are integral to successful interpersonal functioning. To this end, the RBP includes relevant group topics such as anxiety management and anger management (among others), and there is dedicated time at the end of each group to practice relaxation and self-regulation techniques (e.g., calm breathing, progressive muscle relaxation, visualization).

The RBP curriculum was developed by and for practicing clinicians rather than in a university clinic. Treatment goals are resilience-based and reflect the protective factors that have been found in the research literature to enhance resilience (Alvord & Grados, 2005). A CBT orientation guides the strategies employed. While evidence-based CBT skills provide the framework for the RBP, we are also in the process of empirically evaluating the effectiveness of the RBP. We have been collecting treatment outcome data in the practice since 2009, and in schools since 2015. Our research team is composed of four psychologists within our practice (all of whom also provide individual and group therapy), one master's-level research coordinator, one psychology professor at the Catholic University of America (CUA; we collaborate with his Child Cognition, Affect, and Behavior Laboratory and our research is overseen by the CUA Institutional Review Board), and several CUA undergraduate and graduate research assistants.

Our clinical practice runs approximately 30 weekly RBP groups per school "semester" for grades kindergarten through high school. During the summer, a shorter session is offered and we enroll approximately half the number of groups. Groups are provided in both office locations and run by the majority of the clinicians in the practice. Dr. Alvord personally runs five groups in the practice and one in a school during the academic year, and four groups in the summer. The other clinicians typically run two to five groups, predominantly in the practice, with four other clinicians also running groups in the schools. The demand for these groups is high, and we always have a lengthy waitlist. The fact that we offer evidence-based, structured groups with notable qualitative and quantitative positive outcomes has been one of the major driving forces of the practice expansion.

## DEVELOPING AN INTEREST AND TRAINING IN THIS NICHE ACTIVITY

While in graduate school, I (MKA) took a formal course in group psychotherapy, primarily focusing on Yalom process groups and skills-based behavioral groups. My doctoral dissertation focused on pro-social behaviors through modeling and imitation learning in preschool and kindergarten children. The dissertation study was conducted in small groups: experimental and control groups within several schools. The statistically significant changes that I witnessed as a result of the experimental intervention led to my further interest in group therapy as a means to teach and develop social competence. Social learning theory as an explanation of how we develop and enhance relationships intrigued me, and I was interested in helping children who had difficulty navigating peer interactions. We know from longitudinal studies that children with poor peer relationships and weak self-control do not fare well along multiple domains. During my internship and postdoctoral year, I had the opportunity to run groups in community mental health and school settings. After receiving my PhD, I sought CE training and was introduced to Sheldon Rose's group behavioral therapy books. However, I did not run groups for the first eight years of private practice, primarily due to a lack of sufficiently large physical space. Once we moved office locations, I was able to initiate a group program. In preparation for running groups, I developed a social competence group therapy program, which evolved—with input from many clinicians—into the RBP. The formal manual of the RBP was published by Research Press in 2011.

## JOYS AND CHALLENGES RELATED TO THIS NICHE ACTIVITY

I (MKA) am passionate about running social competence groups as I have seen the tremendous benefits and positive changes over time. The groups help children and teens feel validated and supported, which is key to gaining "buy-in" and embracing proactive change. Including parents in the process contributes to this change on a systemic level, which is rewarding. Given the well-known imbalance between need and services, providing therapy in a group setting enables the clinician to reach more children within the same timeframe. Moreover, every single group is unique, even if the agenda and skills topics are the same; diverse combinations of children bring different dynamics and interactions. I find that I am most excited about running groups because this variation keeps me interested, creative, and energized.

The logistics of forming and maintaining groups present the greatest challenge. It can be difficult to cluster together (for each of at times 30 weekly groups) five or six families of children who are a developmental and diagnostic fit and can attend group on the same day and time for at least 12 weeks. Thereafter, group absences and commitment are inherent hurdles. Over the years we have learned that children's sickness and activities can get in the way of full participation. We allow two absences per semester without charge to address this issue. Though we have a low dropout rate once groups commence, we have found that some families change their mind immediately before the group starts (e.g., an extracurricular activity unexpectedly conflicts with the timing of the group). It can be problematic if, for example, a group suddenly drops from four members to two members; it can squash that group altogether and the remaining members need to try to be integrated into other groups. To mitigate this problem, we ask for a deposit of a small activity fee and one session to be paid in advance.

Behavior management presents a second challenge to running our groups. Given that deficits in social and emotional functioning are common denominators in the children and adolescents who join groups, it is not surprising that some participants have particular difficulty navigating how to act in the group setting. During groups, we try to draw attention to the positive behaviors we want the kids to demonstrate, rather than attending to the negative behaviors. To this end, the children earn points for exhibiting positive, cooperative behaviors (which they can later exchange for small prizes) and this positive reinforcement usually helps shape the behaviors of all the kids in the group. However, sometimes there are one or two children in a group who have significant difficulty with talking or acting in inappropriate ways and require regular redirection, which can be disruptive to the entire group flow. It may be necessary for a child to step outside the group to talk one on one with the leader before reentering the group room, and individual meetings outside of group time are also sometimes warranted to address continued behavioral disruptions.

# BUSINESS ASPECTS OF THIS NICHE ACTIVITY

Our practice brand is built on evidence- and strength-based treatment. This positive frame parallels the resilient protective factors and has led to excellent success. Parents, school personnel, and local providers are drawn to the strength-based frame of the RBP and appreciate that we are collecting empirical data to measure effectiveness.

Group referrals come primarily from school counselors, pediatricians, psychiatrists, clinicians, and parents. We are careful to respect and support the therapeutic relationships that other providers have with mutual clients; we collaborate with all providers. All incoming calls from parents interested in groups are screened by an intake coordinator who conducts a brief phone interview to determine appropriateness of fit for group services. If the youth is not a good match, recommendations are made for other services (e.g., individual psychotherapy, testing, or services outside of our practice). If the youth would likely benefit from participation in our groups, then the RBP is explained, the family's preference for day/time/office location of groups is collected, and the youth is placed into a master group spreadsheet. Once enough potential members are clustered together by age/gender/day/time of group, their information is passed to a clinician, who then completes an intake session to confirm they are an appropriate match for group.

We are a fee-for-service practice and do not participate on any insurance panels. However, families can submit for reimbursement from their insurance companies. Unfortunately, although one hour of group costs half of what we charge for a 45-minute individual therapy session, insurance companies seem to reimburse at a lower rate for group therapy. We decided long ago not to charge for the entire 12 weeks of group up front in order to make it more affordable for families; instead, we ask for monthly payments via credit card, or weekly payments by check. From the client's perspective, group therapy is cost-effective.

# DEVELOPING THIS NICHE ACTIVITY INTO A PRACTICE STRATEGY

For other mental health providers interested in running social competence groups for children and adolescents, we have various suggestions with regard to ethical and logistical parameters. The International Association for Group Psychotherapy and Group Processes offers ethical guidelines specific to group practice (http://www.iagp.com/about/ethicalguidelines.htm). The American Psychological Association (APA)'s Division 49, Society of Group Psychology and Group Psychotherapy, promotes ethics of both clinical practice and academic/research activities in the field (http://www.apa.org/about/division/div49.aspx); national APA guidelines for training are currently being developed. While there are no standard treatment guidelines for providing group psychotherapy, the American Group Psychotherapy Association (AGPA; www.agpa.org) has clinical practice guidelines that aim to integrate research with ongoing clinical practice and encourage the use of assessment and outcome measures.

There are multiple factors to take into consideration from a logistical standpoint. To begin with, you need to determine the setting in which groups will take place (e.g., office, school, hospital) and be sure you have adequate private space. The latter will in part depend on the number of members in each group. We have found that keeping groups small is ideal both in terms of space needed and, more importantly, in terms of enabling each group member sufficient time to actively participate. The setting will also be a factor in the frequency and duration of each group (e.g., coordinating with academic schedule in school settings; feasibility of weekend groups in private practice setting). Regardless of group setting, for social competence groups kids must have the opportunity to practice skills in natural settings outside of group (e.g., field trip) to generalize behavior changes.

It is important to determine whether you want to have time-limited versus ongoing groups. From our experience, one advantage of time-limited groups is that parents may find it easier to commit to a specified number of group sessions at a time. Deciding which group curriculum (or combination of curricula) you are going to use will go hand in hand with meeting the needs of the target population (e.g., age, developmental level, gender, diagnoses). In our groups, members have mixed presentations of internalizing and externalizing challenges and diverse strengths. We have found this provides group leaders with opportunities to highlight different positive behaviors in each member; this promotes self-esteem and helps them learn from each other. Along these lines, behavior management focused on attending to and reinforcing positive behaviors, while drawing minimal attention to negative behaviors (i.e., differential reinforcement), has been integral to effectively running our groups. Prior to the start of groups, it is also important to identify recordkeeping methods (e.g., notes on each member to track attendance, completion of at-home assignments, behavior and participation in group) and outcome measures (e.g., Behavior Assessment System for Children [BASC-3]) to evaluate the progress of group members and overall program effectiveness. The extent of parent involvement will depend on the curriculum used, goals, setting, and their availability; we recommend trying to involve parents to the greatest extent possible via multiple modes of communication. Cost of groups and payment structure need to be established, taking into account factors addressed in the business section above. Group leaders should have appropriate training prior to running groups (e.g., didactic, observation, co-leading). We typically have one primary leader per group, with co-leaders (leaders in training and/or graduate students) in some groups. Privacy and confidentiality need to be addressed with group members and parents with regard to discussions and interactions within and outside the group setting.

Group providers can start small and stay small, or grow larger. I (MKA) started by running two groups 33 years ago, and it has taken many years to develop a large-scale program. We hope that the reader will be willing to face the challenges and share in the joys of running groups and changing kids' lives in positive ways!

# FOR MORE INFORMATION

Clinicians interested in providing group services would benefit from reviewing online and/or printed materials from APA Division 49, Society of Group Psychology and Group Psychotherapy, and AGPA (links provided above). APA and AGPA both offer journals, workshops, symposia, open sessions, and other learning opportunities at their annual conferences. Social workers can find helpful resources through the International Association for Social Work with Groups, Inc. (http://iaswg.org/), including standards, group work strategies, and peer-reviewed journal publications.

In the Washington, DC, metro area, Dr. Sylvia Stultz assembled a consortium of therapy groups approximately 20 years ago. Practices and organizations paid a fee to be listed in a booklet that was distributed to schools and practices throughout the Virginia/Maryland/DC region. Ten years ago, I (MKA) took over coordinating the community of group therapists, and today we advertise in local parent magazines and host a website (www.groups4kids.com) and listserv. The website is most helpful for the community to view available groups. The listserv is for providers and allows us to discuss openings in specific groups and to gain support on various clinical topics; we also have an informal annual gathering of group providers. This type of consortium can be replicated in other communities to facilitate awareness and utilization of group services.

There are numerous group curricula available on the market to help children build social skills. For example, in addition to RBP (2011), other programs include the Skillstreaming series (McGinnis, 2011) and some that focus on special populations (e.g., autism spectrum disorders) such as Unstuck and On Target! (Cannon, Kenworthy, Alexander, Werner, & Anthony, 2011).

## REFERENCES AND RESOURCES

Aduen, P. A., Rich, B. A., Sanchez, L., O'Brien, K., & Alvord, M. K. (2014). Resilience Builder Program therapy addresses core social deficits and emotion dysregulation in youth with high-functioning autism spectrum disorder. *Journal of Psychological Abnormalities in Children, 3*(2), 1–10.

Alvord, M.K. & Grados, J.J. (2005). Enhancing resilience in children: A proactive approach, *Professional Psychology: Research and Practice, 36,* 238–245.

Alvord, M. K., & Rich, B. A. (2012). Resilience Builder Program: Practice and research in a private clinical setting. *Independent Practitioner, 32,* 18–20.

Alvord, M. A, Rich, B. A., & Berghorst, L. (2014). Developing social competence through a resilience model. In S. Prince-Embury & D. H. Saklofske (Eds.), *Resilience interventions for youth in diverse populations* (pp. 329–351). New York: Springer Books.

Alvord, M. A., Rich, B. A., & Berghorst, L. (2016). Resilience interventions. In J. C. Norcross, G. R. VandenBos, & D. K. Freedheim (Eds.), *American Psychological Association handbook of clinical psychology* (pp. 505–519). Washington, DC: APA Books.

Alvord, M. K., Zucker, B., & Alvord, B. (2011). *Relaxation and self-regulation for children and teens: Mastering the mind-body connection* (audio CD and digital). Champaign, IL: Research Press.

Alvord, M. K., Zucker, B., & Alvord, B. (2013). *Relaxation and wellness techniques: Mastering the mind-body connection* (audio CD and digital). Champaign, IL: Research Press.

Alvord, M. K., Zucker, B., & Grados, J. J. (2011). *Resilience Builder Program for children and adolescents: Enhancing social competence and self-regulation—A cognitive-behavioral group approach.* Champaign, IL: Research Press.

Cannon, L., Kenworthy, L., Alexander, K., Werner, M., & Anthony, L. (2011). *Unstuck and on target! An executive function curriculum to improve flexibility for children with autism spectrum disorders* (research ed.). Baltimore, MD: Pail H. Brookes Publishing Co.

McGinnis, E. (2011). *Skillstreaming the elementary school child: A guide for teaching prosocial skills* (3rd ed.) Champaign, IL: Research Press.

Reynolds, C. R., & Kamphaus, R. W. (2015). *Behavior Assessment System for Children, Third Edition* (BASC-3). Pearson.

Rich, B. A., Hensler, M., Rosen, H. R., Watson, C., Schmidt, J., Sanchez, L. . . . Alvord, M. K. (2014). Attrition from therapy effectiveness research among youth in a clinical service setting. *Administration and Policy in Mental Health and Mental Health Services Research, 41*(3), 343–352.

Watson, C. C., Rich, B. A., Sanchez, L., O'Brien, K., & Alvord, M. K. (2014). Preliminary study of resilience-based group therapy for improving the functioning of anxious children. *Child and Youth Care Forum, 43,* 269–286.

CHAPTER 69

# BEHAVIORAL SLEEP MEDICINE

*Catherine C. Loomis*

I was licensed as a psychologist in 1996 and began working in traditional settings, first in outpatient clinics providing general psychotherapy and then in a residential program for eating disorders. In 2006, after taking time off to help my elderly parents, I started my postdoctoral education and subsequent practice in the specialty area of behavioral sleep medicine. In recent years, my sleep practice has involved three settings in the greater Milwaukee, Wisconsin, area: (1) my own independent practice co-located with a physician who is board certified in sleep medicine and otolaryngology within his ear, nose, and throat clinic, (2) a small psychology outpatient practice, and (3) a sleep center within a regional healthcare organization. In each of these settings, my practice is exclusively focused on sleep disorders.

## THE NICHE PRACTICE ACTIVITY

Behavioral sleep medicine is a fascinating area that involves "the study of behavioral, psychological, and physiological factors underlying normal and disordered sleep across the life span" and "the development and application of evidence-based behavioral and psychological approaches to the prevention and treatment of sleep disorders and co-existing conditions" (Society of Behavioral Sleep Medicine, n.d.). Most of my clients present with insomnia and receive a structured, manual-based treatment called Cognitive-Behavioral Therapy for Insomnia (CBT-I). The effectiveness of CBT-I has been well demonstrated over many high-quality randomized clinical trials and meta-analyses (Edinger, Wohlgemuth, Radtke, Marsh, & Quillian, 2001; Wu, Appleman, Salazar, & Ong, 2015). Its effectiveness has been shown with a number of populations, for example those with chronic pain and fibromyalgia, cancer survivors, and the elderly. A review of randomized controlled trials comparing CBT-I to sleep medication found evidence that CBT-I showed more lasting benefits (Mitchell, Gehrman, Perlis, & Umscheid, 2012). CBT-I is now considered a first-line treatment, and it is recommended by the National Institutes of Health and the American Academy of Sleep Medicine.

In addition to insomnia, I work with clients who have been diagnosed with sleep apnea and need assistance adjusting to the gold standard treatment, positive airway pressure (PAP). PAP therapy involves a device that delivers air through a tube and into a mask that the client wears over his or her nose and/or mouth. The pressure of the air is set at a level high enough for it to act as a "splint" to keep the client's airway open as he or she sleeps. Clients may have difficulty using this device for a number of reasons. They may not understand the significance of their diagnosis or otherwise lack motivation and a sense of self-efficacy to undertake the treatment. They could have comorbid insomnia or poor sleep hygiene. For some, claustrophobia is a significant barrier to use.

Treating these clients can involve motivational interviewing, improving sleep hygiene, providing education about the condition, or providing graduated exposure therapy for their claustrophobia. The work often involves encouraging clients to have persistence in engaging their equipment providers to troubleshoot difficulties with the mask and device. I sometimes step in to advocate if needed, often working closely with the respiratory therapists who specialize in these devices. I frequently obtain data, downloaded from their device, that contain information about adherence and other aspects of their PAP therapy. This feedback helps clients evaluate their progress and guides goal setting.

Behavioral sleep medicine also addresses circadian rhythm sleep–wake disorders. Often, clients struggle with shift work, but the most common problem I see is a delayed sleep phase. This is a condition where the client's natural circadian rhythm is shifted later so that he or she doesn't get sleepy until much later than what is normal in society, and then sleeps much later into the morning or afternoon. The delayed rhythm can be a diagnosable condition if it causes insomnia or excessive sleepiness, and distress or interference with daily functioning. Clients with this condition often feel isolated and misunderstood, as they are told by family members or friends simply to go to bed and wake up earlier. It is very rewarding to help them understand the biology of the condition and move toward acceptance. Additional treatment involves use of timed melatonin supplements, timed light therapy, and sometimes an intensive treatment called chronotherapy, which involves helping clients delay their circadian rhythm by going to bed successively later around the clock until they reach their desired wakeup time.

Given the many veterans and others with posttraumatic stress disorder (PTSD), behavioral treatment of chronic nightmares has great potential and is underused. Chronic nightmares often coexist with poor sleep habits, insomnia, and undiagnosed sleep apnea. Nightmares can improve with CBT-I; however, if they remain problematic, imagery rehearsal therapy is a treatment recommended by the American Academy of Sleep Medicine (Aurora et al., 2010). In this therapy, clients reconceptualize their nightmare as an ingrained habit that disrupts sleep instead of an intractable part of their PTSD. The treatment involves invoking imagery to create a different nightmare ending or outcome and then practicing imagining the new, more benign, dream (Krakow, 2002). Because few know that it is available, I do not receive many referrals for this treatment.

Finally, clinicians can play a significant role in helping clients with hypersomnia. They can aid in assessment, using their expertise to identify the impact of co-occurring psychiatric disorders. They can apply behavioral analysis to understand antecedents and consequences of sleepiness. They use activity scheduling, and they help clients to nap and exercise more strategically. Unhelpful thoughts and excessive attention toward sleepiness and fatigue can be targeted for change.

# DEVELOPING AN INTEREST AND TRAINING IN THIS NICHE ACTIVITY

At the time I became interested in sleep disorders in 2006, there was an abundance of advertisements touting the wonders of the newer sleep medications. Curious about the extent of the problem, I began to look at the literature and saw the strong research support behind the behavioral treatment of insomnia. Surely there were many who wanted an alternative to medications, and yet the treatment was mostly unrecognized and unavailable. At the same time, I was volunteering as a public education coordinator for my state psychological association and observed efforts to position psychologists as professionals who could integrate mind and body in healthcare. I envisioned a practice that would meet a very specific need that would give clients the opportunity to address mental health in a very different way but within healthcare settings that were familiar to them.

Because I envisioned a practice exclusive to sleep, I wanted to understand the broader field of sleep medicine first. I joined the American Academy of Sleep Medicine and attended the group's intensive continuing education course on sleep disorders. This involved three days of presentations, each one hour long, delivered by nationally known experts (http://www.aasmnet.org/upcomingcourses.aspx). The majority of attendees were sleep medicine physicians. Although the course was challenging, it was heartening to receive an enthusiastic response from physicians who needed the services I would provide.

I then took several more courses, such as the in-depth introductory course on cognitive-behavioral therapy for insomnia by Michael Perlis, PhD, who is now with the University of Pennsylvania. I attended a consensus conference on insomnia, where those in the field came to discuss and debate the future direction of the field. In 2007, I was chosen by the American Academy of Sleep Medicine to participate in the first behavioral sleep medicine "mini-fellowship." I was able to spend three weeks in Manhattan, shadowing at the Sleep Center of the New York-Presbyterian Hospital. It was unfunded but turned out to be a great opportunity and quite an adventure, and it was followed by funded attendance at the annual sleep convention. In 2010, I became certified in behavioral sleep medicine by the American Board of Sleep Medicine (http://absm.org/bsmcertification.aspx). This required independent study in the field, documentation of practice hours in behavioral medicine areas, and supervised hours in behavioral sleep medicine, which I obtained through phone consultation with an expert.

# JOYS AND CHALLENGES RELATED TO THIS NICHE ACTIVITY

Behavioral sleep medicine is a wonderful specialty area. Sleep medicine physicians say they often find it difficult to deliver behavioral interventions due to time constraints, and the clients can be challenging. They are happy to hear that a specialist is available. Clients often comment that this service was what they needed all along, but never knew it was an option. Treatment is specific, directive, and outcome-based, and there is more opportunity to see progress quickly, observed through both verbal report and sleep log data.

However, the advantages of the practice can also present some of the biggest challenges. Both the public and many professionals will not be familiar with the treatment, causing clients to be more hesitant to begin. A great deal of time is spent providing education about the services. I often need to address the common misperception that I am merely providing sleep hygiene tips that many clients have already followed without success. Due to the short-term nature of the treatment, there is frequent client turnover. This is a practice that takes some time to build, and therefore would be ideal for someone who is adding the area to an existing practice.

## BUSINESS ASPECTS OF THIS NICHE ACTIVITY

Most of my referrals come from sleep medicine physicians. I also receive more and more referrals from primary care physicians. Some have received letters from insurance companies discouraging them from routine prescription of sleeping pills. Fewer clients than I expected come self-referred. I have tried radio and community newspaper advertising with little success. Many still believe that insomnia is a condition that must be endured. Therefore, I have focused my marketing efforts on the healthcare community.

Physicians and clients alike wonder if their insurance will pay for the services. I explain that these services fall under routine outpatient mental health care. There can be glitches in billing, however, because some insurers view insomnia as a medical condition and do not accept the insomnia diagnosis. Some of the sleep disorders in the American Psychiatric Association's *Diagnostic and Statistical Manual of Mental Disorders* are not covered through the mental health component of an insurance plan. This has not posed too much difficulty, as usually other appropriate diagnoses can be applied. Because most referrals are physician-based, my practice is heavily dependent on insurance payments. I also accept Medicare and Medicaid.

## DEVELOPING THIS NICHE ACTIVITY INTO A PRACTICE STRATEGY

For those who wish to start their practice in this area, I would recommend first communicating with board-certified sleep medicine physicians in your area. I went to our local academic medical center and was able to attend their weekly sleep medicine case conferences, where I was able to get to know many sleep medicine physicians. You may also want to contact the primary care physicians you are working with to tell them about your new area of interest.

In speaking with others who have started practicing in this field within the context of an ongoing psychotherapy practice, I have noticed that one of the challenges for them is to adjust their style of engaging in psychotherapy. If your engagement with clients is less structured and directive, it is helpful to think about how to integrate a more directive approach with sleep clients. This involves knowing ahead of time what you plan to cover and setting the agenda with the client in the session. Before I started practicing in this area, I spent time planning a "script" for my sessions, thinking about how I could present certain subjects most effectively, and writing handouts to supplement what was being discussed.

The work also involves assessing whether detours from the agenda in the session are valuable or whether they could lead to a poorer outcome or a longer time to achieve sleep-related goals. Of course, clients who want better sleep can also present with factors such as depression, anxiety, and relationship conflict, and if you are expert at treating these in your practice, they can easily, and perhaps inadvertently, become a focus of treatment. When clients come to me for their sleep, I assess and acknowledge these other factors. If the client wants to address these issues first, or if I get a sense the work on sleep would not be effective without treating other conditions first, I refer the client to another provider. Otherwise, we proceed to work specifically on the client's sleep-related goals, and continue to monitor the other conditions.

Sleep disorders affect many aspects of our physiology and have a significant effect on mental health. Mental health clinicians have much to contribute to this critical and fascinating area, and additional practitioners are needed to make treatments more accessible for all.

## FOR MORE INFORMATION

There is a well-defined path toward competence in this field, and a variety of helpful resources are available. *Cognitive-Behavioral Treatment of Insomnia: A Session-by-Session Guide* by Perlis, Jungquist, Smith, and Posner (2005) has been most influential in guiding the insomnia treatment I provide. Another helpful book on insomnia is *Insomnia: A Clinical Guide to Assessment and Treatment* by Morin and Espie (2004). *Behavioral Treatments for Sleep Disorders: A Comprehensive Primer of Behavioral Sleep Medicine Treatment Protocols* by Perlis, Aloia, and Kuhn (2011) provides summaries of the interventions used in behavioral sleep medicine.

Those interested in behavioral sleep medicine may want to contact the Society of Behavioral Sleep Medicine (www.behavioralsleep.org), which publishes the journal *Behavioral Sleep Medicine*. The University of Pennsylvania is one of the academic institutions at the forefront of training in behavioral sleep medicine, and it has a helpful website that includes step-by-step recommendations for developing expertise in this area (www.med.upenn.edu/cbti/index.html). The American Academy of Sleep Medicine (www.aasmnet.org) is a useful resource for broader topics in sleep medicine and publishes two respected journals: *Journal of Clinical Sleep Medicine* and *Sleep*. State sleep societies often have excellent conferences. I was fortunate to have the time and opportunity to attend many in-person continuing education courses. Now there are many additional online training options. The Society of Behavioral Sleep Medicine can also provide lists of graduate programs, internships, and postdoctoral placements that include behavioral sleep medicine training.

Because the field is new, there are inevitable growing pains. The certification I received is currently unavailable at the time of this writing. However, in 2013, the American Psychological

Association recognized sleep psychology as an official specialty, and this may open up new opportunities for recognition.

## REFERENCES AND RESOURCES

Aurora, R. N., Zak, R. S., Auerbach, S. H., Casey, K. R., Chowdhuri, S., Karippot, A. . . . Morgenthaler, T. I. (2010). Best practice guide for the treatment of nightmare disorder in adults. *Journal of Clinical Sleep Medicine, 6*(4), 389–401.

Edinger, J. D., Wohlgemuth, W. K., Radtke, R. A., Marsh, G. R., & Quillian, R. E. (2001). Cognitive behavioral therapy for treatment of chronic primary insomnia: A randomized controlled trial. *Journal of the American Medical Association, 285*(14), 1856–1864.

Krakow, B. (2002). *Turning nightmares into dreams: Audio series and treatment workbook.* Albuquerque, NM: Author.

Mitchell, M. D., Gehrman, P., Perlis, M. L., & Umscheid, C. A. (2012). Comparative effectiveness of cognitive behavioral therapy for insomnia: A systematic review. *BMC Family Practice, 13*(40). Retrieved from http://bmcfampract.biomedcentral.com/articles/10.1186/1471-2296-13-40.

Morin, C. M., & Espie, C. A. (2004). *Insomnia: A clinical guide to assessment and treatment.* New York: Kluwer Academic/Plenum Publishers.

Perlis, M. L., Aloia, M., & Kuhn, B. (Eds.) (2011). *Behavioral treatments for sleep disorders: A comprehensive primer of behavioral sleep medicine treatment protocols.* London: Elsevier.

Perlis, M. L., Jungquist, C., Smith, M. T., & Posner, D. (2005). *Cognitive-behavioral treatment of insomnia: A session-by-session guide.* New York: Springer.

Society of Behavioral Sleep Medicine. (n.d.). About Society of Behavioral Sleep Medicine. Retrieved from http://www.behavioralsleep.org/About.aspx.

Wu, J. Q., Appleman, E. R., Salazar, R. D., & Ong, J. C. (2015). Cognitive-behavioral therapy for insomnia comorbid with psychiatric and medical conditions: A meta-analysis. *JAMA Internal Medicine, 175*(9), 1461–1472.

# CHAPTER 70

# COLLABORATIVE DIVORCE

*Lisa Gabardi*

I have been licensed and maintained a solo private practice in Beaverton, Oregon (a suburb of Portland) for the past 25 years. I began my solo practice one day per week while I worked full time at a community mental health center. After having children, I made the transition from working in community mental health to operating a solo private practice part time while raising my children. As my children got older, my solo practice grew to full time and I started thinking more about the business of private practice, my ideal clients, and developing a niche.

## THE NICHE PRACTICE ACTIVITY

In the past 15 years collaborative divorce grew in the Portland area as a divorce settlement option that focused on peaceful, alternative dispute-resolution techniques and a team approach to helping families. In my networking with local attorneys, I met an attorney who specifically practiced collaborative divorce. This was my first exposure to this field. I was excited by the potential for this new settlement option to support families in obtaining a peaceful divorce, being child-focused, and supporting an effective co-parenting relationship. The model fit well with my values and my experience base. I took the collaborative divorce training so that I could be a neutral mental health coach and I began seeing cases. Currently about 25% to 33% of my practice is collaborative divorce and other divorce-related services. I receive ongoing continuing education in such areas as parenting plans, conflict coaching, mediation, and collaborative divorce.

Collaborative divorce is a specific settlement option whereby the divorcing parties agree not to go to court or litigate. It is a voluntary process that uses alternative dispute-resolution techniques to come to settlement agreements while each party is represented by an attorney. This team approach has the benefit of being interdisciplinary in that a mental health coach, a child specialist, or a financial specialist may be added to the team to assist the parties in managing emotions, receiving education, and reaching agreements. It provides a supportive, nonadversarial option for divorcing.

The role of the mental health coach is unique; it is neither mediation nor psychotherapy or family therapy, but does involve skills similar to mediation, psychotherapy, and coaching. A single, neutral coach may be used as a process facilitator at meetings with clients and their attorneys or may be used to help both parties manage their emotions, manage conflict, and transition from being spouses to co-parents. When the process uses two mental health coaches, the parties have their own coach to support them and assist them with managing emotions, communication, and conflict/negotiation. A child specialist is another mental health professional available to the team. This role is to be the "voice of the child" as he or she assists parents in creating a child-centered parenting plan.

Clinical training in individual, couple, family, and child therapy and child development and specific knowledge of the divorce literature and effects of divorce on adults and children are necessary. Mediation and other alternative dispute-resolution training and conflict/negotiation training are useful. I received training in graduate school and completed an internship and residency in individual, couple, family, and child therapy, as well as training in addictions and abuse. I became familiar with the literature on divorce in graduate school and have continued educating myself.

## DEVELOPING AN INTEREST AND TRAINING IN THIS NICHE ACTIVITY

A convergence of events led me to expand the divorce services area of my practice. I was interested in the impact of divorce on families and wrote my graduate thesis and dissertation on the effects of divorce on young adults. In private practice, many of my clients struggled with relationship issues and relationship loss or divorce. Then, I experienced my own divorce, which gave me a whole different perspective and education about the divorce process. A few years later, as I was building my practice, a colleague suggested that I would be a good family mediator: I have good boundaries, can be direct if needed, and don't shy away from conflict. I completed a 40-hour mediation training, shadowed and received mentorship from a colleague, and started doing parenting plans for divorcing parents. I also began providing consultation to divorced parents wanting to build or improve their co-parenting relationship and communication. In 2011 I wrote a short book on the essentials for effective co-parenting entitled *The Quick Guide to Co-Parenting After Divorce: Three Steps to Your Children's Healthy Adjustment*. This book helped me develop credibility and recognition for expertise about divorce.

## JOYS AND CHALLENGES RELATED TO THIS NICHE ACTIVITY

I have found this niche practice to be fulfilling professionally and personally! As a divorced person, I understand personally as well as professionally what damage can be done to families through an adversarial divorce. I also know what healing and growth can come from peaceful alternatives and professional support for families. It is immensely gratifying to me to be a part of a peaceful alternative for families. It is professionally stimulating and satisfying to be part of a multidisciplinary team helping a family make a good transition, durable agreements, and a strong co-parenting foundation for their children's ongoing adjustment. On a practical level, I enjoy getting out of my office as a solo practitioner and engaging with other professionals; it is much less isolating than traditional private psychotherapy practice. I also enjoy the variety this niche brings to my professional life. Some of my day is spent doing psychotherapy with individuals or couples and some of my day is spent doing coaching or consultation on divorce cases. Sometimes I might meet with the team, while at other times I might meet with one or both of the divorcing parties. Sometimes I am drafting minutes of meetings or a parenting plan. On other occasions I am meeting at an attorney's office in the community.

For all of the jokes about attorneys and all the fear I hear many psychologists voice about having to interact with attorneys (often on the other end of a subpoena), I have to say that I really enjoy working with attorneys! Of course, in collaborative divorce, these are attorneys who also support the notion of a peaceful divorce and supporting families in nonadversarial ways. The attorneys working in collaborative divorce have been experienced, professional, highly interested and respectful of what mental health professionals can bring to the collaborative team, and caring about the families with whom they work. Also, they have been fun to get to know and bring to the table a different perspective and vibe than mental health professionals. I also like the opportunity to be part of an interdisciplinary team. In Portland, the collaborative divorce community has begun forming practice groups in the past five or so years. I recently joined a newly formed practice group. The goals of a practice group might include continuing education and case sharing, support, and finding ways to educate the community of lay people and professionals about collaborative divorce as an alternative settlement option to traditional two-attorney or mediation options. I enjoy the collegiality and camaraderie.

# BUSINESS ASPECTS OF THIS NICHE ACTIVITY

No discussion of this niche practice would be complete without discussing financial compensation. This is another great benefit of this niche! Collaborative divorce coaching is an out-of-pocket service not reimbursed by insurance. No diagnosis is made. The service is not psychotherapy; it is a coaching or consultation service and is paid directly by the clients to the professional. All members of the collaborative team can have their own fee structure for the service they provide. The mental health coach, the financial professional, and the attorney can charge their own fee for their time. My fee for this service is at or above my fee for psychotherapy. Clients pay me at the time that I deliver the service. I also get paid for time outside of sessions devoted to the case (reading and writing emails, writing meeting notes, consulting with professionals on the team, and writing parenting plans). In this way, the billing model is similar to attorneys in that time spent on the case is billed, prorated at the hourly rate. I find clients open to using mental health professionals on the team not only because of the value they add, but also because mental health professionals often charge lower fees than attorneys, so there is potential cost savings to clients if mental health professionals are conducting some of the divorce discussions that do not require legal knowledge.

The most challenging aspect of this niche practice involves the need and ability to manage high conflict and emotionality. Professionals are meeting clients under highly emotionally charged circumstances. Clients are not at their best and sometimes present in highly angry, blaming, defended states or in highly regressed, avoidant, passive ways. This may be due to longstanding personality patterns but is more commonly a function of the high stress of the divorce. The professional interested in this niche must have the ability to tolerate high levels of conflict and high emotionality, a centered and soothing temperament, and strong professional and personal boundaries to be effective. If you don't like dealing with conflict or strong personalities (including at times the attorneys'), this might not be a good fit for you.

I obtain most of my referrals from local attorneys and psychotherapists. A key method of marketing has been attending collaborative divorce events in the community. The events might be hosted by the state association or might be training events. Networking with attorneys as well as mental health professionals has been helpful. Many mental health professionals are not aware that collaborative divorce exists. They appreciate the information to give to their clients to support a nonadversarial option for divorcing. Child psychotherapists especially are interested in divorcing parents being able to have some assistance during their divorce process from a mental health professional who can help them make a transition to effective co-parenting. Mental health coaches and child specialists can help support parents in this process during and after the divorce. This allows the child psychotherapist to remain focused on the child and not drawn into the parents' divorce.

Collaborative cases can begin with an attorney who begins to put together a team and may recommend me as a coach to join the team. Clients also will contact me directly to initiate services for help separating or talking to their children about the divorce. This initial contact can be the beginning of a case. I present collaborative divorce to them as a settlement option, and if they choose this option as the best fit for their family, I will offer attorney referrals and we will begin to put a team together. Having a good website that educates potential clients about collaborative divorce as a settlement option, as well as providing other helpful information about divorce, is an effective marketing tool (www.gabardi.com). Being known, through networking and community talks, as an expert in divorce issues can be a way for clients to find you.

## DEVELOPING THIS NICHE ACTIVITY INTO A PRACTICE STRATEGY

If you are thinking about adding this niche to your practice, I would first suggest you educate yourself about collaborative divorce. I would also suggest you find mental health professionals and attorneys in your community who are practicing in this area and take them out for coffee or lunch and talk to them about how this niche is working in their practice and in your community. If you are serious about learning more, I recommend taking an introductory collaborative professionals training. Consider your own training background and what other training and reading you might need. Begin networking with professionals practicing in this area and attending local events for divorce professionals.

## FOR MORE INFORMATION

For ongoing education and training, I recommend joining the International Academy of Collaborative Professionals (https://www.collaborativepractice.com/) and your state or local collaborative association or practice group(s). I also recommend joining the Association of Family and Conciliation Courts (http://www.afccnet.org/) as well as your state's chapter of this national organization. Both of these groups publish excellent journals, *The Collaborative Review* and *Family Court Review*, offering research on collaborative divorce, alternative dispute resolution, and divorce and families. If your community is organizing a collaborative practice group, considering joining one.

I recommend reading the books by Mosten (2009), Tesler and Thompson (2007), and Webb and Ousky (2007). Other reading on conflict resolution and negotiation that is useful includes the books by Fisher, Ury, and Patton (2012) and Stone, Patton, and Heen (2010). Resources on effective co-parenting include my book (Gabardi, 2012), mentioned earlier; Thayer and Zimmerman (2001), a book co-authored by a co-editor of this *Handbook*; and Bonnell and Little (2014). An excellent overview of divorce and children is the book by Emery (2006).

## REFERENCES AND RESOURCES

Bonnell, K., & Little, K. (2014). *The co-parent's handbook: Raising well-adjusted, resilient and Resourceful Kids in a two-home family from little ones to young adults.* Create Space.

Cameron, N. (2015). *Collaborative practice: Deepening the dialogue.* Amazon Digital Services.

Emery, R. (2006). *The truth about children and divorce: Dealing with the emotions so you and your children can thrive.* New York: Plume.

Fisher, R., Ury, W., & Patton, B. (2012). *Getting to yes.* New York: Penguin Books.

Gabardi, L. (2012). *The quick guide to co-parenting after divorce: Three steps to your children's healthy adjustment.* Create Space.

Mosten, F. S. (2009). *Collaborative divorce handbook: Helping families without going to court.* San Francisco, CA: Jossey-Bass.

Stone, D., Patton, B., & Heen, S. (2010). *Difficult conversations: How to discuss what matters most.* New York: Viking Press.

Tesler, P., & Thompson, P. (2007). *Collaborative divorce: The revolutionary new way to restructure your family, resolve legal issues, and move on.* New York: William Morrow.

Thayer, E., & Zimmerman, J. (2001). *The co-parenting survival guide: Letting go of conflict after a difficult divorce.* Oakland, CA: New Harbinger.

Webb, S., & Ousky, R. (2007). *The collaborative way to divorce: The revolutionary method that results in less stress, lower costs, and happier kids.* New York: Plume.

# CHAPTER 71

# CO-PARENTING

*Annette Rotter*

I have been a practicing licensed clinical psychologist for the past 26 years. Currently, my solo practice is located in White Plains, New York, about 40 minutes north of New York City in Westchester County. For 10 years my clinical work included individual psychotherapy with adults and adolescents who had anxiety, depression, relationship issues, and parenting challenges. Client struggles relating to the painful impact of acrimonious divorce often found their way into my consultation room, but this was not a specialty area of mine.

## THE NICHE PRACTICE ACTIVITY

Co-parenting therapy focuses on providing parents with tools to diminish conflict and develop co-parenting skills before, during, and after divorce. The goal is to diminish the long-term negative effects of parental conflict on children's mental health, but parents themselves also benefit from reducing their stress during this difficult life transition. Unlike traditional couples therapy, co-parenting treatment entails skill building in the present and does not aim to explore the relationship history or the past. Nevertheless, this therapeutic model requires the use of clinical skills including empathy, active listening, reframing, and interpretation, all in the context of a strong therapeutic alliance in order to foster a collaborative partnership between parents despite their prior relationship difficulties. Co-parenting therapy often demands that the clinician engage clients with unique challenges. Psychiatric disorders, difficult personality dynamics, and conflict addiction are among the issues that co-parenting clinicians must manage in order to create an effective therapeutic alliance with both parents.

Co-parenting therapists teach clients how to uphold the central tenets of successful co-parenting: (1) a child benefits from the love of two parents; (2) a child needs to feel that both parents support these two attachments; and (3) all parents disagree sometimes, but their children need them to tolerate their differences and compromise because having two parents who get along is the critical ingredient for their child to thrive. These tenets are repeatedly woven into interventions as the therapist facilitates positive behaviors and limits hostile comments or behaviors by bringing parents back to the impact of continuing aggression on their child's healthy emotional development. Conducting a co-parenting treatment can be extremely challenging as the clinician attempts to engage both parents in a positive relationship in the midst of their longstanding and ongoing toxic relationship with each other. However, this work can be surprisingly successful even when encountering severely entrenched hostility.

Often during litigation, a parenting coordinator is assigned by the court to make decisions for high-conflict parents who have demonstrated they cannot make parenting decisions for their children. Alternatively, the work of co-parenting therapy is to teach parents strategies to make decisions for their children together even though they are divorced or divorcing rather than relying on a third party to make these key and personal parenting decisions. Ideally, parents learn the communication skills that allow them to communicate respectfully and come to reasonable decisions that reflect the needs of their children independently. In some cases, parents are able to learn co-parenting strategies in just a few sessions and learn to cooperate for the sake of the children's adjustment quite easily. In other cases, for parents who have their own mental health challenges or where conflict is more entrenched, longer-term ongoing support may be needed for the two to cooperate. Nevertheless, with the co-parenting treatment approach, they decide parenting issues on their own and out of court with the support of a co-parenting therapist. The advantages of parents staying out of court and learning skills to co-parent their families is something that co-parenting therapists can emphasize and communicate to all professionals working in the divorce field.

## DEVELOPING AN INTEREST AND TRAINING IN THIS NICHE ACTIVITY

In the late 1990s I learned about an extraordinary clinical approach to divorce that intrigued me. A colleague invited me to participate in a training taught by Jeff Zimmerman, PhD and Elizabeth Thayer, PhD who were co-founders of Parents Equally Allied to Co-Parent Effectively (PEACE), a program to help high-conflict parents during and after divorce. The training presented a clinical approach to teach parents how to work toward becoming partners in parenting their children and put the conflict that ended their marriage to the side. My work as a co-parenting therapist began in the early 2000s at a time when few clinicians were working with divorcing parents. As word spread of my work in this area among colleagues and clients, I received a variety of referrals, including couples who were beginning the divorce process, those who were stuck in protracted litigation, and those who were long divorced but still not able to cooperate effectively on behalf of their children. In general, about 15% of my private practice involves co-parenting therapy. The remainder of my clinical work includes marital therapy, parenting therapy, and family therapy as well as individual adult and adolescent therapy.

## JOYS AND CHALLENGES OF THIS NICHE ACTIVITY

One aspect of this work that I especially enjoy is the gratification of knowing that I have helped a divorcing family develop healthy and thoughtful strategies to weather this transition. In cases where parents prepare for their divorce together, they can communicate the news of the separation or divorce to children employing a unified and comforting message that emphasizes their commitment to work together despite the change in their marital status. This approach empathically addresses children's fears and anxieties about potential ongoing conflict and loss. Often I have helped parents develop a cooperative spirit that results in them choosing to reside in the same neighborhood and thereby ease the transition between the two homes for their children. The feedback from parents clearly corroborates the literature that parents who make the transition to divorce with less conflict, and who manage to provide coordinated, loving care for their children, have children who adjust well to this significant and potentially difficult change in their lives (Garrity & Baris, 1994; Rotter, 2016).

It is always moving for me to see parents who are struggling with feelings of loss and failure over the end of their marriage find pride and confidence in themselves as parents through the co-parenting counseling. Even if there has been ongoing hostility and aggravated conflict, it is possible to help parents break these negative patterns and learn new strategies to cooperate on behalf of their children. In these cases parents and children clearly report improved mental health as their lives settle down due to the success of this treatment intervention. I also enjoy the way that this concrete and behaviorally oriented treatment provides a welcome balance with my more psychodynamic, longer-term individual and marital cases. In addition, developing strong clinical skills with high-conflict couples has strengthened my capacity to engage in family and marital therapy and connect to all parties simultaneously and effectively.

Co-parenting therapy can be especially challenging and unpleasant when couples are involved in protracted litigation. In these cases, clients may become more demanding and difficult to engage in a genuine process. In addition, parents might choose to ask a therapist to testify in court about the case, which is clearly unproductive to the co-parenting therapy stance. I have made the decision to draw a line in my work. I advise parents directly about the negative impact of the adversarial litigation process on children and explain that I will only work with parents who commit to avoid litigating their divorce and agree to proceed in either mediation or with lawyers who agree to work toward an out-of-court settlement. Alternatively, clients can be asked to sign informed consents that they will not try to use their therapist or clinical records in any court proceedings. The idea is to empower parents to recognize that they are in the best position to determine the unique needs of their children and that working with a clinician who can guide them is preferable to engaging in an adversarial process where everyone loses, especially their children.

# BUSINESS ASPECTS OF THIS NICHE ACTIVITY

Generally, billing is handled as an out-of-pocket expense by parents, who often split the cost of sessions. Parents can be advised that although insurance may not reimburse them for couples work in all states, learning to cooperate in this therapy will address and help resolve current stresses and save them from far greater litigation expenses.

Co-parenting counseling referrals come from a number of sources. Many clinicians are not familiar with this kind of work and will be happy to make a referral when they are working with an individual who is getting divorced or hear of this kind of high-conflict case. In addition, clinicians will benefit from developing relationships with lawyers who handle divorce matters or represent minors. Guardians *ad litem* often need to make referrals as well in the hope of quieting down destructive conflict during litigation. Likewise, if lawyers are finding that their clients cannot agree about a parenting schedule or plan, they will make a referral to a co-parenting therapist to help resolve this matter so the rest of the case can move forward successfully.

# DEVELOPING THE NICHE ACTIVITY INTO A PRACTICE STRATEGY

Interestingly, although this field has been in existence for approximately 20 years, it is still in its infancy. Many clinicians who work with divorcing couples avoid working with both parties in the same room at the same time. Clinicians are also often not educated in specific strategies to help couples who divorce avoid the long-term damaging effects of litigation for children and the adults themselves. As a result, being trained in this area continues to be a marketable skill. It is clear that the need for this type of intervention is great and measurable improvements are apparent within a few sessions, but few clinicians are trained to practice as co-parenting therapists.

Specific training courses in co-parenting counseling are not widely available. It is wise to be on the lookout for isolated offerings or presentations on this topic through the Association of Family and Conciliation Courts or online. More generic mediation trainings do provide some background. Couples therapy training also helps clinicians develop the critical empathic tools to balance dual perspectives and keep both parties engaged in the process. In addition, clinical experience working with children is invaluable for clinicians to understand how to advise parents about the impact of divorce and the developmental needs of children of different ages. Most critical is identifying a mentor with experience in this specific field to provide ongoing consultation and training in navigating co-parenting therapy successfully and avoiding pitfalls.

Marketing this niche area can be accomplished in many different ways. Presenting at a professional meeting of clinicians who work with adults and/or children is likely to yield referrals as clinicians are eager for resources to help couples and families who are moving toward or are in the midst of a high-conflict divorce. Along those lines, presenting at a bar association meeting will provide the opportunity to educate lawyers who practice family law about this treatment strategy and encourage them to understand the value of making a referral for their clients.

## FOR MORE INFORMATION

The Association of Family and Conciliation Courts (http://afccnet.org) is the central national organization in this field. It offers a variety of helpful resources to clinicians, including conferences, trainings, and publications, in addition to providing opportunities to develop networking relationships. Getting involved in a local chapter is a great way to begin meeting all of the diverse professionals in this field and stay abreast of the latest developments. In addition, the American Psychological Association's Division 42, Psychologists in Independent Practice, occasionally offers worthwhile presentations on co-parenting.

The books by Garrity and Baris (1994) and Thayer and Zimmerman (2001) will provide invaluable background in this field. Rotter's article (2016) is a case study that illustrates specific effective techniques for co-parenting therapy and offers an inside view of the consultation room.

## REFERENCES AND RESOURCES

Blau, M. (1995). *Families apart: Ten keys to successful co-parenting*. New York: Berkley Publishing Group.

Garrity, C., & Baris, M., (1994). *Caught in the middle: Protecting the children of high-conflict divorce*. San Francisco: Jossey-Bass Publishers.

Ricci, I. (1980). *Mom's house, dad's house: Making shared custody work*. New York: Macmillan.

Rotter, A. (2016). A model for developing a co-parenting relationship after protracted litigation: The case of Antonia, a 14-year-old caught in the crossfire. *Journal of Clinical Psychology: In Session, 72*, 484–497. doi:10.1002/jclp22263

Thayer, E., & Zimmerman, J. (2001). *The co-parenting survival guide: Letting go of conflict after a difficult divorce*. Oakland, CA: New Harbinger Publications.

Wallerstein, J., & Blakeslee, S. (2003). *What about the kids? Raising your children before, during and after divorce*. New York: Hyperion.

Wallerstein, J., & Kelly, J. (1996). *Surviving the breakup*. New York: Basic Books.

Wallerstein, J., Lewis, J., & Blakeslee, S. (2000). *The unexpected legacy of divorce*. New York: Hyperion.

Zimmerman, J. (2015). Divorce and alternative dispute resolution: Expanding roles outside the courtroom and managed care. Retrieved from http://www.societyforpsychotherapy.org/divorce-and-alternative-dispute-resolution-expanding-roles-outside-the-courtroom-and-managed-care.

Zimmerman, J. (2015). Reflections on mental health professionals working with divorcing parents outside the courtroom. Retrieved from http://societyforpsychotherapy.org/reflections-on-mental-health-professionals-working-with-divorcing-parents-outside-the-courtroom.

# CHAPTER 72

# TREATING CHRONIC PHYSICAL ILLNESS

*Katherine S. Spencer*

I am an early-career clinical psychologist who specializes in providing therapeutic services for children, adolescents, adults, and families coping with severe and chronic medical conditions and associated emotional and behavioral problems. In early 2012, after completing my internship and fellowship at an academic medical center, I became a member of a group behavioral psychology practice in Atlanta, Georgia. The group is composed of 10 licensed psychologists, a licensed clinical social worker, an educational consultant, and a learning specialist. Psychologists in the group each have an area of specialty, and my experience in treating chronic physical illness was uniquely suited for expanding the group's services.

## THE NICHE PRACTICE ACTIVITY

Providing services as part of a group practice, outside of a medical center setting, was a new venture with which I had very little familiarity. My goal was to maintain my focus on providing psychological services to individuals with chronic illness, and to accomplish this goal I strategically marketed my practice to physicians in medical specialties, such as neurologists, anesthesiologists, and gastroenterologists. I also obtained credentialing at a large local children's hospital as an associated community psychologist. Credentialing at this hospital turned into an opportunity to provide occasional coverage for the attending psychologist in the pediatric cancer and blood disorders center (also called PRN coverage). This type of work offered regular interface with medical professionals, who often provided referrals to colleagues and patients. Additionally, I provided PRN pain psychology coverage at a local rehabilitation hospital for patients with brain and spinal cord injuries, which further expanded my network. Since September 2013, I have worked within this blended health psychology focused practice arrangement. I typically see clients two or three days a week at the group private practice and spend the other two or three days completing related administrative work or providing PRN psychology coverage at one of the above hospital settings.

Referrals for my practice in this specialty niche are generated from other psychologists with different areas of specialization, from local primary care and specialized physicians, and by word of mouth. Approximately 75% of my practice is devoted to working with children, adolescents, families, and some adults coping with chronic illness and/or injury (e.g., sleep disorders, chronic pain, concussion, gastrointestinal disorders, and neurological disorders). The other 25% of my practice is devoted to treating individuals with anxiety, depression, chronic stress, and often comorbid learning, social, or academic problems. In my practice, I use empirically supported behavioral and cognitive interventions. I also provide training in biofeedback, mindfulness, and relaxation as appropriate. My work in the group practice is a more traditional cognitive-behavioral therapy model, where I see clients for an average of 10 sessions. I do have some shorter- and longer-term clients. In the hospital setting, my work is based on a consultation-liaison model in which I am providing brief targeted interventions to address a specific concern as part of a specialized interdisciplinary medical team. For example, I may have a referral for pain interfering with physical therapy progress, anxiety interfering with tolerance of medical treatment, or premorbid mood disorder interfering with recovery from concussion. I find that this blend of group practice and hospital-based provision of psychological services offers me a well-balanced and fulfilling career.

## DEVELOPING AN INTEREST AND TRAINING IN THIS NICHE ACTIVITY

My journey to this specialty niche began during high school, when I volunteered in pediatric hospital settings and thrived in my interactions with the patients. As a psychology major in college, I remember my fascination with the complex interaction between physical health and psychological functioning. Then, I distinctly remember the first day of my graduate school assessment practicum in a hospital setting, when I was observing the behavior of a child with a severe brain injury. I knew that day that I wanted to work with individuals with medical issues. It was as if there was an innate drive for me to work in this specialty niche.

In my general clinical PsyD graduate program, I worked closely with two faculty supervisors with specialized training in pediatric settings. I also contributed to ongoing research studies involving pediatric populations. I sought externship opportunities in hospital settings, applied to American Psychological Association internships at pediatric hospitals, and completed my predoctoral internship and postdoctoral fellowship at a prestigious pediatric hospital known for exceptional training in pediatric psychology. To maintain proficiency in this niche, I continue to participate in education opportunities related to pediatric and health psychology, provide talks to other medical professionals, read peer-reviewed journals related to this specialty, and maintain credentials at local hospitals.

# JOYS AND CHALLENGES RELATED TO THIS NICHE ACTIVITY

There are many reasons I enjoy my role as a psychologist who specializes in treatment of individuals with chronic physical illness. Not only is there an extensive evidence base regarding the benefit of this type of work on health outcomes, but also I find this practice niche to be incredibly rewarding. For instance, I am grateful to have the opportunity to teach a child with a newly diagnosed life-threatening illness how to use guided imagery to improve tolerance of medical procedures and reduce anxiety. It is gratifying to provide psychological treatments that help clients cope with medical complications, improve adherence to prescribed medical treatments, reduce stress, or learn techniques to improve overall quality of life in spite of illness.

At the same time, this niche specialty offers challenges when working with clients experiencing severe physical and emotional suffering or nearing the end of their life due to a medical condition. It can also be frustrating working with parents of a child with chronic physical illness when family dynamics present as a barrier to the child's recovery from illness. I find ongoing case consultation with other psychologists and the client's other health providers particularly beneficial given the complexity of such cases. When working with healthcare teams in hospital settings, I find that interdisciplinary collaboration fuels comprehensive treatment that truly encompasses the biopsychosocial model. I believe this approach, which addresses the interplay between the biological, psychological, and social needs of patients, contributes to improved patient outcomes. This is in fact the essence of my job as a psychologist with a specialized niche in treating patients with chronic physical illness.

# BUSINESS ASPECTS OF THIS NICHE ACTIVITY

With respect to the financial aspects of practice management, I am not on any insurance plans in my group practice. Clients are self-pay at time of service, and many submit the bill to insurance for possible reimbursement. For clients with financial limitations, I offer sessions on a reduced-fee basis. Occasionally I treat adult clients with chronic health issues due to work-related injuries, and their bills are paid directly to my practice group by workers' compensation insurance. One of the challenges of practice management for me is billing for time spent consulting with a patient's primary treating physician, psychiatrist, other healthcare providers (e.g., physical therapist, acupuncturist), and schools when applicable. Interdisciplinary collaboration is a necessary aspect of health psychology, and while communication with other medical providers is not unique to this specialty niche, it is of the utmost importance in the treatment of individuals with chronic physical illness. Cohesion of the client's medical team improves client outcomes. Another challenge is billing for time spent completing administrative tasks such writing letters and notes, which can be particularly time-consuming. To manage challenges with billing for consultation or administrative work,

I inform my client that case consultation or additional paperwork (beyond usual documentation) that takes more than 15 minutes per session will be billed to the client. I also work closely with the other treatment providers to find the most efficient and effective mode of sharing pertinent information, which may be a brief after-hours phone message, scheduled calls, secure email, or faxing records. Despite my efforts to overcome these challenges, this remains a "growing edge" for my practice.

Within the hospital setting, I am a medical staff member who is paid per hour by the hospital for time spent seeing clients, conducting other practice-based activities such as writing notes and billing, and consulting with medical teams. With a client's physician, nurses, and other providers onsite, referrals and case collaboration occur mostly in person. This type of work can pose a challenge given the constantly changing, fast-paced environment and the need to adhere to all of the same documentation, billing, credentialing, and training expectations of the full-time psychology staff. Not all of the time spent completing necessary credentialing or training is paid, but my personal investment and interest in maintaining my position in a hospital setting greatly outweighs that loss.

In both my group practice and the hospital setting, I attempt to maintain brief notes. The exception is my initial consultation note, which incorporates a standard diagnostic assessment and detailed medical information, with a focus on health and behavioral interactions. In the hospital setting, there are often very specific report-writing guidelines and other considerations to keep in mind when writing notes, such as who has access to the mental health electronic health record.

## FOR MORE INFORMATION

For those who would like to develop this specialty area, I highly recommend joining the American Psychological Association's Society of Health Psychology (Division 38; http://www.health-psych.org/), Society of Pediatric Psychology (Division 54; http://www.societyofpediatricpsy-chology.org/), or the Society for Social Work Leadership in Healthcare (http://www.sswlhc.org/index.php). The American Association of Marriage and Family Therapy (www.aamft.org) is nonspecialized yet also offers information on medical family therapy practice as a specialty niche (http://www.aamft.org/imis15/documents/jasinglepagefinal.pdf). These societies offer extensive resources, peer-reviewed journals, annual meetings, community outreach, and much opportunity to grow and strengthen your skills in these areas. Membership in these health-focused psychological societies also provides networking connections to even more special interest groups, such as my interests in pediatric sleep disorders or pain disorders. Meetings such as the Pediatric Sleep Medicine Meeting (https://www.brown.edu/academics/medical/education/other-programs/continuing-medical-education/annual-conference) or the American Academy of Pain Management Meeting (http://www.aapainmanage.org/annual-clinical-meeting/) offer focused continuing education training in these areas, which can deepen your knowledge in this niche. There are specialized health and pediatric psychology graduate programs, internships, and fellowships. If you already have your license and are looking to expand your expertise in this area, supervision and case consultation from a mental healthcare provider in this specialty niche is highly advised.

There are a number of scholarly journals devoted to understanding the scientific relations among psychological factors, behavior, and physical health and illness, such as *Health and Social Work* (http://hsw.oxfordjournals.org/), *Journal of Pediatric Psychology* (http://jpepsy.oxfordjournals.org/), and *Health Psychology* (http://www.apa.org/pubs/journals/hea/). Book recommendations include Friedman (2011), Roberts and Steele (2009), and Allen and Spitzer (2006). These books cover the history of these areas of expertise, clinical research related to behavioral health, and specialized evidence-based treatments and provide guidelines regarding competencies for practicing in the areas of health and/or pediatric psychology.

## RESOURCES AND REFERENCES

Allen, K. M., & Spitzer, W. J. (2006). *Social work practice in healthcare: Advanced approaches and emerging trends.* Los Angeles, CA: Sage Publications.

Friedman, H. S. (Ed.). (2011). *The Oxford handbook of health psychology (Oxford Library of Psychology)* (1st ed.). New York: Oxford University Press.

Roberts, M. C., & Steele, R. G. (Ed.). (2009). *Handbook of pediatric psychology* (4th ed.). New York: Guilford Press.

# CHAPTER 73

# DATING SKILLS COACHING AND PSYCHOTHERAPY

*Jessica Engle*

I am a dating coach, drama therapist, and licensed marriage and family therapist located in the San Francisco Bay area of Northern California. I established my company, Bay Area Dating Coach, in 2010 to help singles acquire the dating skills needed to find love. While working as a dating coach, I interned at a private practice–style agency and specialized in the use of drama therapy to treat social anxiety and dating difficulties. I became a California-licensed marriage and family therapist in 2014. I've since expanded Bay Area Dating Coach to provide dating psychotherapy as well as coaching, and have brought on additional staff, including associate clinicians and coaches. All of my associates hold a master's degree in counseling psychology, and some are drama therapists and/or licensed marriage and family therapists. I look forward to expanding further by adding staff, locations, and additional services such as specialized groups, online courses, and offerings for LGBTQIA singles

## THE NICHE PRACTICE ACTIVITY

At Bay Area Dating Coach, we help singles develop the skills, knowledge, and confidence they need to find love, affection, and connection. We work with singles 18 years of age and older from a variety of backgrounds. Our individual and group coaching and psychotherapy focus on four key areas of healthy dating: strategy, skills, confidence, and "wisdom," or the ability to recognize and build secure attachments. We also provide "field coaching," wherein we offer feedback and support to clients in real-life social/dating settings. Our groups and workshops give singles a chance to learn skills and receive support and feedback from like-minded singles. Examples of past groups and workshops include "Overcoming Social and Dating Anxiety," "Five Simple Steps to Better Dates," and "Practice Dating."

At Bay Area Dating Coach, we find that offering both coaching and psychotherapy allows us to serve a wide range of clients and dating issues. Via coaching, we help clients who are mentally well and/or contemporaneously receiving psychotherapy take their love life to the next level. Many of these clients seek us out because they've found it difficult to obtain the specialized dating support they need from other providers. Coaching gives us the freedom to provide creative, out-of-the-box services such as field coaching and practice dates, as no regulatory body currently exists in the field of coaching. In the case of psychotherapy, we not only help clients define and pursue their dating goals but also provide mental health treatment for issues that may underlie their dating difficulties. Where coaching focuses on taking concrete steps toward an envisioned future, psychotherapy allows us to identify, explore, and heal difficult past experiences and psychological blocks.

Both coaching and psychotherapy carry positives and negatives. While coaching provides some with an opportunity to pursue personal growth in a society that stigmatizes psychotherapy, clients must pay for coaching sessions out of pocket. On the other hand, clients may receive reimbursement for psychotherapy via their health insurance; however, such coverage requires the client to receive a diagnosis, which can affect the client psychologically and have a negative impact on future opportunities, such as applications for insurance or national service positions.

As providers of both coaching and psychotherapy, we must constantly monitor our services to ensure we are providing ethical and legal treatment. Specifically, per our state and professional ethics codes, we must ensure clients receive the kind of service they expect and have agreed to. For example, if a client has signed on for coaching services, we are careful to focus on the client's present-day, concrete issues rather than delving into the psychological blocks underlying those issues. Or if a client is receiving long-term, depth psychotherapy, the psychotherapist will not offer services such as field coaching. We employ an extensive intake process to determine which services are most appropriate for a client, then continue to assess the appropriateness of services provided by monitoring the client's progress and responses to treatment. Should the client need a different or additional service, we discuss this with him or her, obtain consent, and make the appropriate referral or service adjustment, making sure to document and justify each action taken. While this process requires our vigilance, it allows us to serve a wide range of clients and issues by offering a variety of coaching and psychotherapy services.

## DEVELOPING AN INTEREST AND TRAINING IN THIS NICHE ACTIVITY

My labor of love began early: I grew up shy, sensitive, and a hopeless romantic. In high school, I blossomed socially and romantically, partially thanks to the confidence I gained through the performing arts. My love life served as a great experiment (though I didn't know it then) wherein I sometimes painfully, sometimes blissfully, gathered observations about the mysteries behind love, attraction, and lasting relationships. Fast-forward to graduate school at the California Institute of Integral Studies in San Francisco, where I studied counseling psychology with an emphasis in drama therapy: I woke one morning in a dreamy epiphany, seeing myself helping singles through role-playing and other drama therapy techniques.

Being in the tech startup capital of the world and having a number of male friends who, despite being quality gents, struggled with dating due to being "nerdy," I found myself especially interested in working with socially awkward heterosexual men. I shared my vision with my then boyfriend, a successful entrepreneur who himself had found improvisational theater pivotal in overcoming his own social and romantic blind spots, and I was lucky enough to build my coaching business under his tutelage.

I began training to work with singles in graduate school. Opting for an independent study project as one of my electives, I wrote a paper on heterosocial anxiety—"Drama Therapy for Girl-Shy Heterosexual Males Seeking Relationship." I became familiar with the existing data on and approaches to treating heterosocial anxiety in males and used this information to identify appropriate drama therapy approaches. Once I graduated and established Bay Area Dating Coach, I sought further trainings and resources on the topics of sexuality, gender, diversity, trauma, attachment, healthy relating, and social anxiety. As my original independent study revealed, there was little written from a clinical perspective about treating dating difficulties, so self-education and trainings on a variety of related topics were key. My previous work as a sex educator and theater activist proved helpful, as did ongoing postgraduate drama therapy trainings. I did not seek coaching certification or training, as I found the skills developed in my master's program to be sufficient. I have found that ongoing training is key not only for clinical integrity, but because the dating world and my business and client needs constantly evolve. For example, as I expanded my work to support women, LGBTQIA, differently abled, widowed, and elderly singles, I've sought resources focused on these populations and continued my training in anti-oppression, diversity-inclusive clinical care.

## JOYS AND CHALLENGES RELATED TO THIS NICHE ACTIVITY

I find working with singles highly satisfying. Many of my clients have gone from little or no dating experience to first kisses, lost virginities, committed relationships, and happy marriages. As such, I recommend working in this niche but would like to offer some disclaimers. Check in with yourself: How excited do you feel about helping clients find love? Just as singles must have hearts resilient enough to withstand the loneliness and rejection inherent in dating, you will need a well of passion from which to draw when your clients' frustration and learned helplessness begin to distort your clinical vision. In addition, keep in mind that dating/sexuality work invariably incites erotic (counter)transference. Be sure that you're willing and able to confront and explore these issues. With eroticized transference—that is, erotic transference that a client cannot address effectively in the therapeutic work—comes safety risks. I've received inappropriate and frightening romantic advances from clients, and in one (unusually extreme) case eventually had to obtain a restraining order. I've learned a great deal from these experiences and am now highly selective and safety-conscious in my practice as a result. Make sure you're well supported and respond immediately to any hints of erotic(ized) transference or safety risks. Also, keep in mind that when dealing with chronic relational issues, a large segment of those seeking services will struggle with severe trauma histories, personality disorders, and severe substance abuse. Establish self-care structures and practice boundaries to help prevent burnout. For example, due to our current capacity and scope of competence, we provide trauma treatment but refer out in the case of personality disorders or severe substance abuse.

## BUSINESS ASPECTS OF THIS NICHE ACTIVITY

While establishing Bay Area Dating Coach, I generated business largely through low-cost workshops. I advertised these workshops on Meetup.com and other local listservs and found that singles are eager to gather, as they tend to feel isolated and ostracized. In addition to workshops, I found it helpful to run ongoing groups and maintain a blog and newsletter, both of which can be accessed at bayareadatingcoach.com. As I've established myself, I've begun to receive referrals via word of mouth, Yelp.com, social media sites, clinician and power partner (i.e., those in allied fields such as matchmakers and online dating photographers) referrals, and web searches.

I have clients pay privately, as insurance plans typically do not cover coaching and they provide reimbursement for psychotherapy at rates that do not, in my mind, justify the resources and stress required to manage claims.

## DEVELOPING THIS NICHE ACTIVITY INTO A PRACTICE STRATEGY

If you're interested in developing a dating skills niche in your practice, I recommend familiarizing yourself with modern dating. Speak with as many singles as you can; get a sense of their difficulties. Use the newest, trending dating technologies. For example, online dating at the time of this writing generally includes two types of platforms: online, profile-driven sites such as OKCupid and Match.com, and mutual match apps such as Tinder and Bumble. Read all the books you can get your hands on (see bayareadatingcoach.com/resources for recommendations). While you engage in this self-education, notice which aspects of dating pique your interest. Dating skills, while seemingly a narrow niche, is actually a rather general term. I've had much more success running highly focused workshops, such as "Confidence in Dating," than offering general dating workshops. It may also be helpful to focus on a particular population—I've seen dating coaches who work only with divorced women at midlife, LGBTQIA singles, and other specific groups. I have had success targeting single heterosexual men, socially anxious singles, and women age 40 and older.

We give our clients a great gift when we as clinicians pursue self-actualization. Whether you develop a practice focused on dating skills or another niche, I wish you fulfillment. May you find and manifest your calling, not only for yourself but for the benefit of those you serve.

# FOR MORE INFORMATION

There are no foundational or classic resources in the field of dating skills therapy and coaching, so you'll need to tailor your education according to your needs and interests. It is vital to gain foundational knowledge in social skills, social anxiety, trauma, attachment, and the building blocks of healthy relationships. You may want to join a (dating) coaching organization for networking, referrals, and education (e.g., the International Coach Federation at https://www.coachfederation.org/join). I also strongly suggest getting some basic training in drama therapy so you can help your clients build skills through experiential techniques such as role-playing and improvisation. See the North American Drama Therapy Association (www.nadta.com) to learn more about drama therapy and find a trainer near you.

# REFERENCES AND RESOURCES

Antony, M. M., & Swinson, R. P. (2008). *The shyness and social anxiety workbook: Proven, step-by-step techniques for overcoming your fear.* Oakland, CA: New Harbinger.

Glover, R. A. (2003). *No more Mr. Nice Guy: A proven plan for getting what you want in love, sex, and life.* Philadelphia, PA: Running Press.

Gottman, J. D., & Declaire, J. (2002). *The relationship cure: A 5-step guide to strengthening your marriage, family, and friendships.* New York: Three Rivers Press.

Grover, R. L., Nangle, D. W., & Zeff, K. R. (2005). The measure of adolescent heterosocial competence: Development and initial validation. *Journal of Clinical Child and Adolescent Psychology*, 34(2), 282–291.

Levine, A., & Heller, R. S. F. (2010). *Attached: The new science of adult attachment and how it can help you find—and keep—love.* New York: Jeremy P. Tarcher/Penguin.

Matchmaking Institute. (n.d.). Matchmakers and Date Coaches Conference. Retrieved from https://matchmakinginstitute.com/conference/.

Relationship Coaching Institute. (n.d.). Become a dating coach. Retrieved from http://www.relationshipcoachinginstitute.com/become-a-dating-coach.

Zur Institute. (n.d.). Certificate program in coaching & psychotherapy. Retrieved from http://www.zurinstitute.com/certificateincoaching.html.

# INDEX

Page numbers followed by *f* and *t* refer to figures and tables, respectively.

techniques for, 636
assessment forms, 56–63
    academic needs, 270
    filling out during sessions, 50
    forensic, 270
    treatment plan, 63
Assessment for Signal Clients (ASC), 83–85, 85f
assisted reproductive technologies (ARTs), 660
Association for Applied Sport Psychology
    (AASP), 753
Association for Higher Education and Disability
    (AHEAD), 655
Association of Family and Conciliation Courts, 637,
    773, 778
Association of State and Provincial Psychology
    Boards (ASPPB), 621, 663
Association of State and Provincial Psychology
    Boar's Task Force for the Maintenance
    of Competence and Licensure
    (MOCAL), 611
assumptions, about Medicare, 281
*Atlantic Monthly,* 569
attention-deficit/hyperactivity disorder (ADHD),
    assessment and treatment of, 654, 701–5
    benefits and challenges of, 702–3
    business aspects of, 703
    developing an interest in, 702
    field overview, 701
    as practice strategy, 703–5
    technology in treating, 703
    training in, 702
attitude surveys, 421–22
attorney(s), 199–205
    administrative, 202, 203
    advertisements for, 204
    business, 203
    civil, 202, 203
    and client dissatisfaction, 201
    and client threats, 201
    collaborating with, 384–94
    and collaborative divorce, 771–72
    complaints, 202
    contractual agreements, 199
    credentialing process, 269
    dealing with issues, 201–3
    discharging your, 204–5
    employee payment problems, 201
    employment/labor, 203, 314
    and establishing independent practices, 200–201
    finding an, 203–4
    for group practices, 314
    healthcare, 201–3, 314
    meeting with, 204

    need for, 198–203
    payment plans, 199
    practice sales, 203
    and pre-independent practice needs, 199–200
    and professional wills, 542
    record creation, 199
    record maintenance, 199
    referrals from, 389
    retainer agreement, 204
    and retirement, 203
    state professional societies, 204
    supervisory arrangements, 199
    working as supervised/licensed colleague, 200
audience, for marketing, 329
audiovisual equipment, 362
audits
    collection procedure, 320
    fraud/abuse, 294
    group practices, 319
    under Medicare, 280–94
AUM model, 210
authorizations, HIPAA, 483
autism spectrum disorders (ASDs), 654
autodidactic learning, 605
automatic increases, in rents, 139–40
automobile expenses, 197
autonomy of group practices, 18

backups, in professional wills, 540
balance billing, 273, 283–84
Balanced Budget Act, 290
balance sheet
    bookkeeping and accounting, 183–84
    in financial plan, 131
bank borrowing
    costs, 197
    finances, 28
bankers (group practices), 314
bariatric/weight loss surgery, 647, 648
bartering, 246
*Bates v. State Bar of Arizona,* 325
Beck Depression Inventory, 78
behavioral health practices
    collaboration with, 321
    and continuing education, 613
*Behavioral Sciences and the Law* (journal), 640
behavioral sleep medicine, 763–68
    benefits and challenges of, 765–66
    business aspects of, 766
    developing an interest in, 765
    as a practice strategy, 766–67
    and PTSD, 764
*Behavioral Sleep Medicine* (journal), 767

interpersonal/management skills, 415
cognitive-behavioral therapy (CBT)
    for hoarding disorders, 687–90
    and social skill training for children and
      adolescents, 757
*Cognitive-Behavioral Treatment of Insomnia: A Session-
    by-Session Guide* (Perlis), 767
collaboration, 651
    with attorneys, 384–94
    available resources, 397
    with educational community, 395–410
    with forensic mental health practices, 384–94
    forum for communication, 397–98
    with healthcare professionals, 369–82
    key stakeholders in, 397
    with legal professionals, 384–94
    plan evaluation, 398
    plan implementation, 398
    problem analysis, 398
    problem identification, 398
    process of, 395
    roles and responsibilities in, 397
    skills for, 380
Collaboration Assessment and Management
    of Suicidality, 520
collaborative divorce, 769–73
    and attorneys, 771–72
    benefits and challenges of, 770–71
    business aspects of, 771–72
    developing an interest in, 770
    as a practice strategy, 772–73
collaborative problem-solving model, 398–409
    plan evaluation stage in, 408–9
    plan implementation stage in, 403–7
    problem analysis stage in, 401–3
    problem identification stage in, 399–401
*Collaborative Review, The,* 773
collateral contact (malpractice), 460
collateral informed consent form, 516
colleague notification, 542
collecting fees, 243
collection procedures, 320
*College Student Mental Health: Effective Services and
    Strategies Across Campus* (Benton), 729
*College Student Mental Health Counseling:
    A Developmental Approach*
    (Degges-White), 729
college students, psychotherapy with, 725–30
    benefits and challenges of, 726–27
    business aspects of, 727–28
    developing an interest in, 726
    as a practice strategy, 728–29
    training in, 726

color
    emotional response to, 146
    hue, 146
    light, 145
    monochromatic environments, 147
    in office design, 146–47
    and size of office space, 147
Colorado Center for Reproductive Medicine in
    Englewood, 665
commercial banks, 28–29
commercial finance companies, 30
Commission on Accreditation of Rehabilitation
    Facilities, 696
Common Area Maintenance (CAM) charges, 137
communication(s)
    and customer service, 304–5
    electronic, 434
    encrypted/secure, 433
    issues with, 293
    marketing, of value, 328
    by Medicare, 293
    multiple means of, 177
    parameters for healthcare professionals, 377
    programs, 177
    with social media, 353–54
    and staff management, 177–78, 178t
    symbolic, in office design, 154
    transparency of, with educational community, 396
    verbal, 378
communication parameters, 379
    assessment measures, 380
    credentials, 381
    for patient confidentiality, 379
community blessings, 115–16
community presentations, 358–65
    audiovisual equipment, 362
    charging for, 360–61
    credibility as speaker, 361
    developing interesting, 361–64
    engaging activities in, 363–64
    and experiential activities, 364
    fees for, 247–48
    group work, 364
    handouts in, 363–64
    length, 363
    marketing for, 358–65
    metaphors/images in, 363
    and overcoming fear of public speaking, 365
    personal stories in, 362–63
    physical setup, 361
    picking a topic, 358–59
    PowerPoint in, 362
    self-promotions, 361

cooperative healthcare, 265
Coordinated Care Initiative, 284
coordinated planning, in professional wills, 540
coordination of care, 306
co-parenting counseling, 774–78
    benefits and challenges of, 776
    business aspects of, 777
    as career focus, 566–67
    developing an interest in, 775–76
    as a practice strategy, 777–78
co-payments/co-insurance
    fees, 262
    managed care organizations (MCOs), 272
coroner/medical examiner exception, 514
Corporate Practice of Medicine Doctrine, 316
corporations (group practices), 315
COTS (Childlessness Overcome Through
    Surrogacy), 665
countertransference, 453–54
couples therapy, interracial. *See* interracial couples
    therapy
court orders, and disclosure, 513
Coverdell accounts, 215
covered entities, 487
CPAs. *See* certified public accountants
credentialing process
    for attorney(s), 269
    for managed care, 268
    nondiscrimination in, 268
credit cards, 30, 197
criminal competencies, 391
criminal complaints, 202–3
criminal lawyers, 202–3
criminal wrongs, 459–60
crowdfunding, 31–32
CST (Clinical Support Tool), 84
cultural challenges, 452
cultural competence, 431
culture of competence, 609
"curbside consults," 641
customary practice, 462
customer delight, 302–3
customer information, 422
customers. *See* clients
customer service, 297–307
    appointment scheduling, 301
    client satisfaction, 297–307
    and communication, 304–5
    coordination of care, 306
    and customer delight, 302–3
    education/training, 298
    email, 303
    essentials of, 303–6

factors impacting client experience, 299
    focus on, 297–98
    loss of clients, 299
    positive experience, 303
    providing referrals, 304
    recommendations for, 306–7
    and referral partners, 300–302
    telephone call format, 305
    telephone calls, 303
    text messages, 303
    timeliness, 305
    total experience, 298
    treatment success, 297–307
customer service plan, 302

daily structure
    breaks between clients, 584
    in self-care plan, 584–85
damages
    compensatory, 463
    economic, 463
    malpractice, 463
    noneconomic, 463
dashboards, 184–86
databases, and malpractice liability, 527
data storage, 432
dating skills coaching, 784–88
    benefits and challenges of, 786–87
    business aspects of, 787
    and dating apps, 787
    developing an interest in, 785–86
    as a practice strategy, 787
    training in, 785–86
*Davis v. Lhim*, 462
deaf and hard-of-hearing clients,
        counseling, 713–18
    benefits and challenges of, 714–16
    business aspects of, 716
    developing an interest in, 714
    as a practice strategy, 717
death of patient, 670
debt-collection, 438
debt financing. *See* loans (debt financing)
debt management, 212
decision making, independent
    for expense-sharing practices, 9
    for group practices, 8
    for private practice, 6
    for solo practices, 8
degree training, 412
delivery system, mental health care, 625–27
demo videos, self-promotion with, 361
derailment project, 414

ePHI (electronic protected health information), 494
equity ownership
    in expense-sharing practices, 10
    in group practices, 9, 20
    in private practice, 7
    in solo practices, 8
ERP (extended reporting period endorsement), 38
ERP (exposure/response prevention) treatment, 683
estates, in financial plan, 218
estate taxes, 218
ETF (exchange traded fund), 215
ethical issues, 429–41
    billing, 437–38
    boundaries of competence, 344
    business of practice, 431–38
    communicating with future treatment
        providers, 555
    competence, 381, 429–31, 446–47
    complaints, 638
    continuing education, 607
    diagnosis, 273
    difference of opinion, 274
    and electronic message accounts, 434
    in fee setting, 237–38
    gatekeeping, 445–46
    healthcare professionals, 381–82
    licensing, 381
    malpractice, 459–75
    managed care, 273–75, 274
    marketing, 337
    in media work, 342–43
    multiple relationships, 448–50
    negative impact on clients, 429
    privacy/confidentiality, 274
    professional isolation, 439–40
    public image management, 435
    recordkeeping and record sharing, 435–37
    referrals, 559
    regarding supervision and consultation, 443–55
    remote interaction with clients, 433–34
    responsibilities when closing the practice, 554–55
    role slippage, 440
    in selling a practice, 558
    and social media, 354–55
    supervision-specific, 445
    technology, 432–33, 450–52
    and teletherapy, 504–5
    treatment of suicidal clients, 531
    videoconferencing, 498
    violations on social media, 354
    website, 434
*Ethical Principles of Psychologists and Code of
    Conduct,* 637
ETS (Educational Testing Service), 655

evaluations
    Americans with Disabilities Act (ADA), 654
    assessment techniques, 636
    child custody, 635–40
    insurance, 639
    Medicare, 288
    personal injury, 641–46
    presurgical bariatric, 647–52
    testing accommodation evaluations, 654–59
evidence-based practice, 431
*Ewing v. Goldstein,* 472
exchange traded fund (ETF), 215
Exclusive Provider Options, 284
executive coaching, 413, 418
executive selection
    assessment, 416
    and consulting psychology, 416–17
    data obtained for, 416
    and organizational consulting, 418
executive summary (business plans), 118
expenses
    in professional wills, 542
    variations in, 25
expense-sharing practices
    administrative activities in, 9
    clinical/administrative management for, 9
    clinical support in, 10
    compensation in, 10
    independent decision making for, 9
    personnel issues in, 10
    referral/business development in, 9
    risk taking in, 9
    starting, 9–10
    startup investment for, 9
experiential activities, 364
experts, characteristics of, 638–39
exposure/response prevention (ERP) treatment, 683
extended reporting period endorsement (ERP), 38

Facebook
    marketing with, 331, 332
    for networking, 167
FaceTime, 716
familiarity (office design), 152
family businesses, 420
*Family Court Review,* 640, 773
family issues
    caregiver burnout, 573
    and changing priorities, 565–66
    co-parent counseling, 566
    for fathers, 570–71
    financial uncertainty, 572–73
    finding balance, 568–69
    flexibility of working hours, 566–68

money issues, 207, 236. *See also* finances
monochromatic environments (office design), 147
MOSAIC, 740
MPFS (Medicare Physicians Fee Schedules), 283
MSW programs, in forensic psychology, 386
multicultural competence, 447
multidisciplinary forensics, 393–95
multidisciplinary practices, 17
multi-owner practices, entity choices for, 195–96
multiple relationships
  boundary crossings, 449
  challenge of, 450
  ethical issues in, 448–50
  sexual harassment, 448
  sexual relationships, 450

Nadeau, Kathleen, 655
NAPFA (National Association of Personal Fee-Only
  Advisors), 210
Nassau County Neuropsychiatric Society, 620
NASW Code of Ethics
  bartering, 246
  collecting fees, 243
  and competence, 446
  destroying records, 76
  disclosing records, 74
  fees, 237
  maintaining records, 69
  storing records, 71
National Alliance on Mental Illness, 729
National Association for Anorexia Nervosa
  and other Related Disorders, 699, 700
National Association of Personal Fee-Only Advisors
  (NAPFA), 210
National Association of Social Work (NASW), 159.
  *See also* NASW Code of Ethics
National Association of State Mental Health
  Program Directions, 622
National Council for Quality Assurance, 320
national coverage determinations (NCDs), 282
National Eating Disorders Association, 700, 729
National Infertility Network Exchange (NINE), 665
National Nursing Centers Consortium, 626
National Provider Identifier (NPI), 286, 552
National Registry of Evidence-Based Programs
  and Practices, 90
National Violence Against Women Survey, 592
natural elements, in office design, 148
NCDs (national coverage determinations), 282
negligence
  diagnosis, 465–67
  release, 467
negligent torts, 464

negotiation
  with high-risk suicidal clients, 521–25
  and managed care, 271
  for office space, 138–40
*NeuroTribes,* 711
New York-Presbyterian Hospital, 665
niche activities
  anxiety disorders, treating, 674–79
  attention-deficit/hyperactivity disorder,
    assessment/treatment of, 701–5
  behavioral sleep medicine, 763–68
  child custody evaluations, 635–37
  chronic physical illness, treating, 779–80
  collaborative divorce, 769–73
  college students, psychotherapy with, 725–30
  co-parenting, 774–75
  counseling clients with Asperger's, 706
  counseling clients with borderline personality
    disorder, 719–20
  counseling deaf and hard of hearing clients, 713
  developing a sport psychology practice, 749–54
  eating disorders, outpatient training for,
    696–700
  egg and sperm donors, assessment of, 660–65
  hoarding disorder, cognitive-behavioral therapy
    for, 687–90
  interracial couples therapy, 736–41
  LGBTQIA, 731–35
  obsessive-compulsive disorder (OCD),
    treating, 681–85
  personal injury evaluations, 641–46
  presurgical bariatric evaluations, 647–52
  psychotherapy with interfaith couples, 742–45
  social skills training for children and
    adolescents, 756–62
  trauma and abuse, treating, 691–95
  women with breast cancer, counseling, 669–72
NINE (National Infertility Network
  Exchange), 665
non-compete agreements, 200
nondiscrimination, 268
noneconomic damages, 463
nonformal learning, 603
non-physician providers, 622
nontraditional psychotherapies, 469–70
Nordal, Katherine, 96
Northwest ADHD Treatment Center
  (NWADHD), 701
Notice of Privacy Practices (NPP), 480, 650
  boilerplate, 480
  and HIPAA, 480–81
  state law, 480
  teletherapy, 493

NPI (National Provider Identifier), 286, 552
nurse-managed clinics, 626
NWADHD (Northwest ADHD Treatment
    Center), 701

Obesity Society, 652
Obesity Week, 652
obsessive-compulsive disorder (OCD),
    treating, 681–85
  benefits and challenges of, 683–84
  business aspects of, 684
  field overview, 681
  as practice strategy, 684–85
  training for, 681–83
occurrence policy premiums
  claims-made vs., 39
  insurance, 37–38
OCR (Office for Civil Rights), 478
OFAID procedure, 59
office cleaning, 551
office design, 144–55
  acoustic aspects of, 149–50
  and conflicting needs, 144
  cost of, 196
  diversions, 148
  and emotion, 145
  environmental control, 151
  and environmental psychology, 144
  familiarity, 152
  form, 153
  furniture, 147, 150
  haptic aspects of, 150
  indoor climate, 150–51
  olfactory aspects of, 149
  personal space, 151–52
  prospect and refuge, 153
  research on, 154
  seating, 152–53
  and sensory experiences, 145
  spatial concerns in, 151–53
  and stress, 149
  symbolic communication, 154
  territoriality, 151
  visual aspects of, 145–49
Office for Civil Rights (OCR), 478
office managers, 173–74, 317
office sharing, 16
office space, 135–43
  acoustic aspects of, 149–50
  automatic increases, 139–40
  Common Area Maintenance (CAM) charges, 137
  comparing options for, 137

haptic aspects of, 150
indoor climate, 150–51
and integrated care considerations, 141
lease for, 138–39
leasing, 135–36
negotiating for, 138–40
olfactory aspects of, 149
preparing to look for, 136
purchasing, 141–43
real estate agents, 136–37
researching, 154
and sensory experiences, 145
spatial concerns in, 151–53
subletting, 140–41
taking time looking for, 139
using other advisors, 140
visiting potential, 136–37, 140
visual aspects of, 145–49
walking away from, 139
office staffing needs, 193
office supply cost, 196
older patients
  assumptions about, 281
  and Medicare, 280–95
online reviews, 349, 355
online risk management, 167–68
online scheduling, 434
oocyte donation, 661
operational plan
  business plans, 128–29
  client experience, 128
  legal environment, 129
  location, 129
  payments, 129
  staffing, 129
opt-out feature (billing), 260
OQ-45. See Outcome Questionnaire-45
Oregon Health & Science University, 665
organizational analysis
  attitude surveys, 421–22
  and consulting psychology, 421–23
  design, 422
  downsizing, 423
  mergers/acquisitions, 423
  work progress difficulties in, 422
organizational consulting
  addressing organizations in, 418
  and consulting psychology, 418
  elective selection in, 418
  executive coaching in, 418
organizational design, 422
organized context, 414
*Osheroff v. Chestnut Lodge Hospital,* 470